T3-BSF-165

THE GREAT
CONTEMPORARY
ISSUES

THE UNITED STATES AND THE WORLD ECONOMY: THE POSTWAR YEARS

THE GREAT CONTEMPORARY ISSUES

OTHER BOOKS IN THE SERIES

DRUGS
Introduction by J. Anthony Lukas

THE MASS MEDIA AND POLITICS
Introduction by Walter Cronkite

CHINA
O. Edmund Clubb, *Advisory Editor*

LABOR AND MANAGEMENT
Richard B. Morris, *Advisory Editor*

WOMEN: THEIR CHANGING ROLES
Elizabeth Janeway, *Advisory Editor*

BLACK AFRICA
Hollis R. Lynch, *Advisory Editor*

EDUCATION, U.S.A.
James Cass, *Advisory Editor*

VALUES AMERICANS LIVE BY
Garry Wills, *Advisory Editor*

CRIME AND JUSTICE
Ramsey Clark, *Advisory Editor*

POPULAR CULTURE
David Manning White, *Advisory Editor*

THE PRESIDENCY
George E. Reedy, *Advisory Editor*

FOOD AND POPULATION: THE WORLD IN CRISIS
Sen. George McGovern, *Advisory Editor*

1976 PUBLICATION

SCIENCE IN THE TWENTIETH CENTURY
Walter Sullivan, *Advisory Editor*

THE GREAT
CONTEMPORARY
ISSUES

THE UNITED STATES AND THE WORLD ECONOMY:

THE POSTWAR YEARS

The New York Times

ARNO PRESS

NEW YORK/1976

LEONARD SILK
Advisory Editor

Library of Congress Cataloging in Publication Data
Main entry under title:

The United States and the World Economy.

(The Great Contemporary Issues)
"Collection of pieces from the New York Times."
"A Hudson Group Book."
Bibliography: p. 353
Includes index.
1. United States — Economic conditions — 1945. 2. United States — Foreign economic relations — History. 3. United States — Economic policy — 1945. I. Silk, Leonard Solomon, 1918. II. New York Times. III. Series.
HC106.5.U48 330.9'73'09 75-24618
ISBN O-405-06671-6

Manufactured in the United States of America by Arno Press, Inc.

The editors express special thanks to The Associates Press, United Press International, and Reuters for permission to include in this series of books a number of dispatches originally distributed by those news services.

A HUDSON GROUP BOOK
Produced by Morningside Associates. Edited by Joanne Soderman

Contents

Publisher's Note About the Series

It would take even an accomplished speed-reader, moving at full throttle, some three and a half solid hours a day to work his way through all the news The New York Times prints. The sad irony, of course, is that even such indefatigable devotion to life's carnival would scarcely assure a decent understanding of what it was really all about. For even the most dutiful reader might easily overlook an occasional long-range trend of importance, or perhaps some of the fragile, elusive relationships between events that sometimes turn out to be more significant than the events themselves.

This is why "The Great Contemporary Issues" was created—to help make sense out of some of the major forces and counterforces at large in today's world. The philosophical conviction behind the series is a simple one: that the past not only can illuminate the present but must. ("Continuity with the past," declared Oliver Wendell Holmes, "is a necessity, not a duty.") Each book in the series, therefore has as its subject some central issue of our time that needs to be viewed in the context of its antecedents if it is to be fully understood. By showing, through a substantial selection of contemporary accounts from The New York Times, the evolution of a subject and its significance, each book in the series offers a perspective that is available in no other way. For while most books on contemporary affairs specialize, for excellent reasons, in predigested facts and neatly drawn conclusions, the books in this series allow the reader to draw his own conclusions on the basis of the facts as they appeared at virtually the moment of their occurrence. This is not to argue that there is no place for events recollected in tranquility; it is simply to say that when fresh, raw truths are allowed to speak for themselves, some quite distinct values often emerge.

For this reason, most of the articles in "The Great Contemporary Issues" are reprinted in their entirety, even in those cases where portions are not central to a given book's theme. Editing has been done only rarely, and in all such cases it is clearly indicated. (Such an excision occasionally occurs, for example, in the case of a Presidential State of the Union Message, where only brief portions are germane to a particular volume, and in the case of some names, where for legal reasons or reasons of taste it is preferable not to republish specific identifications.) Similarly, typographical errors, where they occur, have been allowed to stand as originally printed.

"The Great Contemporary Issues" inevitably encompasses a substantial amount of history. In order to explore their subjects fully, some of the books go back a century or more. Yet their fundamental theme is not the past but the present. In this series the past is of significance insofar as it suggests how we got where we are today. These books, therefore, do not always treat a subject in a purely chronological way. Rather, their material is arranged to point up trends and interrelationships that the editors believe are more illuminating than a chronological listing would be.

"The Great Contemporary Issues" series will ultimately constitute an encyclopedic library of today's major issues. Long before editorial work on the first volume had even begun, some fifty specific titles had already been either scheduled for definite publication or listed as candidates. Since then, events have prompted the inclusion of a number of additional titles, and the editors are, moreover, alert not only for new issues as they emerge but also for issues whose development may call for the publication of sequel volumes. We will, of course, also welcome readers' suggestions for future topics.

Introduction

The United States emerged from World War II as the strongest economy in the world. The mission it assumed was to lead its wartime allies and its former enemies, Germany and Japan, toward reconstruction and economic growth. This mission was considered crucial in its own right, following the massive destruction of the war and the tearing apart of the international economy, and as a means of ensuring that the weakened economies of Europe and Asia did not fall prey to communism.

For the United States to fulfil its chosen international economic and political mission, it was essential that prosperity be preserved at home. At the end of the war, memories of the Great Depression of the nineteen-thirties were vivid, and there were anxieties that, once the stimulus of war production was removed, the United States economy would lapse back into a state of chronic depression and unemployment.

Such worries proved unfounded — in good measure because, as George Soule makes clear in the first article in this collection of pieces from *The New York Times*, the United States had learned the major lesson of 1929: That Government cannot stand by in the face of economic disaster but must actively work for full employment. With the passage of the Employment Act of 1946, Congress made it a solemn responsibility of the United States Government "to promote maximum employment, production and purchasing power." Although it was not precisely clear how future governments would go about discharging that responsibility, the passage of that act did usher in a genuinely new economic policy for the United States. And the combination of government fiscal and monetary measures to halt recession and spur expansion, a modified capitalist system (a "mixed economy") whose institutions had been strengthened by New Deal reforms, and the forces set in motion by worldwide reconstruction and development produced a quarter-century of economic growth such as the world had never seen. American policies of opening the way toward relatively free movement of trade and investment helped to bind the world economy closer together.

Regional blocs emerged — most importantly, the European Common Market, which held forth hope of a new "Europe." The growth of the European community was a direct outgrowth of the Marshall Plan adopted by the United States as its basic policy instrument for rebuilding the international economy and shielding the democratic states from communist penetration or invasion. The Marshall Plan was the economic counterpart of the North Atlantic Treaty Organization and other international security arrangements.

In retrospect, it is easy to see that there was an excess of pride and a dangerous rigidity in the way the United States pursued its postwar mission. That reckless and rigidly ideological approach ultimately led to the tragedy in Vietnam, Cambodia and Laos — a tragedy that has not entirely played itself out.

Yet it should not be forgotten that, in the flush of victory over fascist enemies in World War II, when its strength was at a pinnacle, the United States rose to the opportunity to prove that a nation could behave generously, intelligently and creatively in the mutual interests of all nations within what was called, in a more confident day, "the free world." In my view, remembering the spirit of the time, there was a remarkable degree of idealism and verve that marked American international economic policy after World War II — a spirit that should not be underrated or denigrated; it will be needed again — from this country and others.

The world monetary system that emerged after World War II was based on an American design through which this country assumed both the burdens and powers of world leadership. That monetary system, which was christened "Bretton Woods" after the small New Hampshire town in which it was born in 1944, was founded on the strength of the American economy, with its "hard" dollar, convertible into gold, and its huge supply of international monetary reserves. Just after the war, United States gold reserves constituted more than 70 per cent of the reserves of all the developed regions, including Britain, Western Europe, Canada, Japan, Australia and South Africa. But as the nineteen-fifties and sixties wore on, the world monetary system gradually eroded as U.S. monetary reserves declined and the dollar, rigidly bound by fixed exchange rates to all other currencies (including those that chose to devalue against it), steadily weakened. The source of the trouble was the chronic deficit in the American balance of payments. Domestic inflation contributed to the weakening of the dollar. And the heavy outflow of funds for investment, foreign aid and military programs worsened the strain.

Political hegemony, whatever its benefits, comes at a heavy cost. Professor Fritz Machlup has observed that whenever a nation has the dominant economic role in an international coalition — as Britain did after the Napoleonic wars — it has invariably been forced in the end to suspend gold convertibility and devalue its currency. Britain finally did so after World War I — after first depressing its economy in the futile effort to maintain an overvalued pound. Similarly, the United States reached the end of the line that had begun with the Marshall Plan and the building of the North Atlantic Treaty Organization when the Vietnam war accelerated both domestic American inflation and dollar outflow in the late nineteen-sixties and early seventies.

The European nations, striving for greater independence, were no longer willing to accept American political and economic hegemony — or the continuing vast inflow of dollars that they saw as the root cause of their own inflation and as the means by which American business interests were taking over their own industries.

Thus the Bretton Woods monetary system — which permitted the United States to cover unlimited deficits with its own currency — was doomed. The final blow to the old monetary order came early in 1973. In January of 1973, what had begun as a barely noticed flow of funds from Italian lire to Swiss francs suddenly became a raging dollar crisis. Billions of dollars in the hands of speculators, Arab oil sheikhs, multinational corporations and some foreign central banks went pouring into West Germany. The German central bank paid out billions of marks to speculators in a vain effort to prevent the mark's exchange rate from rising — until fears of inflation and the folly of endlessly throwing good money after bad at last caused the German officials to yield. The mark was permitted to float upward, and the dollar floated down. All the world's currencies were, in effect, floating. Bretton Woods was dead.

It was a timely demise, for still greater economic blows lay ahead. In 1973 a severe world commodity inflation erupted. Bad growing weather for cereals, the failure of much of the Soviet wheat crop, the massive Soviet-American wheat deal and such mysterious factors as the disappearance of anchovies off the coast of Peru all fed that commodity inflation.

Yet the overall inflationary trend was no accident; virtually all nations were in a simultaneous boom, and world demand was outrunning supply. The public perception of rising prices was transformed, as finally happens when an inflation is severe enough, into a perception that paper money is losing its value and is not worth holding. So people rushed into gold and into commodities, causing their prices to soar. By October of 1973 world commodity prices had more than doubled from the start of the year. And then came the outbreak of war in the Middle East — and the Arab's launching of their oil weapon against the West.

The use of the oil weapon was at least in part a consequence of the unleashing of world commodity inflation. Soaring prices had given the oil-producing countries both the motivation and the opportunity to boost their own prices skyhigh. The rising costs of imports to the Arabs, Iranians and others, the rapidly growing demand for oil thanks to booming worldwide demand, the disappearance of American buffer stocks of oil — all these gave the member nations of the Organization of Petroleum Exporting Countries the golden chance for a killing.

They seized it. The Arab oil embargo, designed to induce the Western powers to force Israel to yield to Arab demands, cut the world oil supply at the critical moment, threw the Western alliance into disarray in a mad scramble for access to oil, and paved the way for the massive increase in oil prices, with non-Arab Iran leading the drive for higher prices. The price of Persian Gulf crude was roughly quadrupled from about $2.10 a barrel to $8 a barrel. That meant a $70 billion increase in revenues for the oil producers in a single year. And oil prices were to go higher still.

This oil coup — perhaps the greatest financial coup in history — gave an unprecedented shock to the world economy. It was, paradoxically, both inflationary and contractionary. The huge increase in oil prices and payments worsened inflation in the United States, Japan and Western Europe by increasing both living costs and costs of production. It put powerful pressures, both direct and indirect, on the industrial and developing countries to raise their export prices to cover their oil import bills. At the same time, the transfer of funds caused a wrench to consumption and investment. In 1974 the United States and other Western economies gradually slid into recession; in the fall of 1974 the fall became precipitate in the United States. It was the worst slump of the postwar period, and the oil-poor developing countries suffered worst of all.

Fears of a new depression were widespread. Yet it looked as though a disaster as serious as that of the nineteen-thirties would be averted. The timing of the move to floating exchange rates had fortunately enabled nations to avoid measures to block trade and investment as a means of trying to defend fixed exchange rates. The floating system proved to be an effective shock-absorber for the twin blows of rapid inflation (at widely different rates among different countries) and serious slumps in production and employment. Greater knowledge of how to use fiscal and monetary policies to counter recession and prevent a vicious deflationary spiral have helped to save the world economy from a tragedy as cataclysmic as that which followed the collapse of the postwar boom in 1929.

All the same, the post-World War II era is ending amidst heavy economic and financial storms. At this writing, the nations of both the developed and developing world have begun to struggle with the problem of creating a New International Economic Order; it is too early to know what that will be. But the stories in this volume chronicle an economic era that was rich in achievement, full of excitement, high in aspiration — but which ended in disillusionment. The "American Century" lasted only about one quarter of a century.

Leonard Silk
July 26, 1975

CHAPTER 1
Business Cycles

The floor of the New York Stock Exchange, one minute before closing on a day of heavy trading.
Courtesy The New York Times

Have We Learned the Lesson of 1929?

Yes, says an economist, because we have erected defenses against 1929's mistakes.

By GEORGE SOULE

DISINFLATION, recession—pick your own name for it—has been bringing not only lower prices, which are welcome, but unemployment, which is not. Few would greatly mind a little dip in the business cycle, but the slide downhill might go too fast or too far.

The last time a really bad smash occurred was in 1929. Every expert has his favorite theory about what brought it on, but almost all would agree on the main disturbances which characterized it. The most dramatic was the collapse of the stock market, in which more people lost more millions in a shorter time than ever before.

Other important events leading up to the tragedy were overbuilding of monumental skyscrapers and other commercial structures financed by easy bank credit, the tapering off of a housing boom which had reached its peak in 1926, overstimulation of the market for automobiles by installment loans, an anomalous "favorable balance of trade," which had been maintained by shaky foreign investments and was suddenly curtailed when these investments ceased; the distress of the farmers, who had been hard hit by the earlier post-war deflation and had few reserves with which to combat new misfortune. Some believe also that the gains resulting from extraordinary improvements in technology were channeled too largely to profits and not enough to consumers.

Whatever may have been the chain reaction leading to the 1929 explosion, the American people were so stunned by it that they could not get the economy going again for a long time. Unemployment spread, income shrank, and finally the wheels nearly stopped altogether when the banks had to be closed.

HAVE we learned our lesson? Is it likely that we shall let the same thing happen to us again? We do not yet understand how to eliminate all upward and downward swings of employment. Only a rash prophet would say that there never will be another serious depression. But we have made headway; if we diligently apply what is now known we can somewhat moderate the vagaries of the business curve. In particular we have erected defenses of some sort against every one of the major mistakes which are plainly visible in the years preceding and following 1929.

At present there is no danger of calamitous losses in the stock market. That is because there has been no appreciable boom; the "public" is not even in the market as it was twenty years earlier, in spite of the recent enormous increases in incomes, savings and business profits. Plain caution on the part of those who once burned their fingers, and the popular legend of what happened before, are in part the reason. That caution might in time wear away. But now there exists power on the part of the Federal Reserve authorities to limit credit for margin trading and so to prevent rapid pyramiding of speculative gains and a roaring bull market—gains which can disappear overnight when for any reason margin loans are called. The power has been effectively used during the recent inflation. If it had been in existence in the late Nineteen Twenties the market might have risen and fallen but it could not have behaved like a skyrocket.

Perhaps the strongest single support of the prosperity of the Nineteen Twenties was the boom in the building of houses. There had been a shortage after World War I as after this one. When the war ended, building costs were high and construction did not get a good start, but after prices settled down not only was the accumulated shortage made up but expansion continued until after the middle of the decade. Then the real estate market began to sag. Roosevelt's poorer "one-third of the nation" (it was probably nearer to two-thirds) could not afford new dwelling places at their prevailing cost. The resulting decline of residential construction, which made up at least half of all the building in the country, gradually pulled the piers from under the house of prosperity, while the wild speculative parties were going on in the upper stories from 1927 to 1929. Later, residential construction sank to 10 per cent of normal.

COULD this happen again? To meet the danger we have a device not tried during Coolidge prosperity or Hoover depression—public housing, which has proved that it can produce good units within the reach of lower-income families. In cities the estimated need is for a million or more dwelling units a year for the next ten years—a higher rate of building than any so far achieved. A coordinated effort by the industry to reduce costs and by public agencies to fill the housing gap at the lower end of the

GEORGE SOULE was an editor of The New Republic from 1924 to 1947. Among his many books is "An Introduction to Economic Science."

Werner in The Indianapolis Star

"Danger of applying the brakes too suddenly."

income scale could go far to prevent any serious unemployment crisis in the United States, and could do so without any great burden on the public treasury.

Industries making automobiles, furniture, radio and television, electrical appliances and other durable consumers' goods may temporarily sate the demand at the prices charged. The boom-bust cycle in these industries was exaggerated in the Nineteen Twenties by too rapid an expansion of installment credit on the way up, succeeded by attempts to collect the installments from a public loaded up with more debt than it could carry. Meanwhile, factories waited for new customers. Now we have Regulation W, adopted during the recent war by the Federal Reserve, limiting the use of installment credit at a time when demand exceeds supply. Its effect will be to postpone some sales to future years when there is more danger of unemployment.

No lesson of the Nineteen Twenties has been more thoroughly learned, and no more complete reversal of policy has taken place, than in the area of economic relations with other countries. During the first war we sold the Allies billions of dollars' worth of war materials on credit. This time we arranged the transfer by Lend-Lease, without building up any debt. Immediately after World War I we boosted our tariff, thus making it harder for them to pay, to say nothing of earning the dollars with which to buy our goods. Now we have the Reciprocal Trade Agreements Act, with its tariff reductions.

All during the Nineteen Twenties we deliberately sustained our surplus of exports by encouraging great private loans from Americans to foreign countries. Now we are granting Western Europe the dollars necessary to buy what it needs as a public policy rather than by private investment. The whole program is carefully designed to enable the recipients to produce and export more, so that before too long the grants may cease.

But suppose, in spite of everything we have done to prevent a slump, unemployment does grow enough to become serious. Must we wait helplessly as we did before, peering around every corner for the prosperity we were told was just there?

In 1929 we did not have unemployment compensation. Now any insured wage-earner who loses his job soon begins to draw benefits, which help his family to keep on paying the rent and buy food. Unemployment insurance cannot prevent depression, but it is a cushion to sustain consumer demand when need arises. It is like an elastic defense: reserves are thrown in to delay an enemy advance as soon as it begins to penetrate the front lines.

Consumers also have reserves of their own. Though some, like teachers, other public employes and those with fixed incomes, have suffered from high prices, consumers have gained as a whole. The average consumer, with purchasing power even at the high prices of 1948 almost 40 per cent greater than before the war started, has managed to save a good deal. Individuals had saved a net total of $129.6 billions from 1940 to 1945, and put by an additional $35.2 billion in 1946-48. Much of this is in cash, government securities or other assets which can be drawn upon quickly in case of need. No such savings were available in 1929.

The 1929 calamity descended upon farmers who had not fully recovered from the deflation of 1921, which began with a sharp fall of crop prices. These prices, which were cut in half within a few months, never before 1929 rose enough to bring farmers within reach of the prosperity enjoyed by city dwellers. Even worse, during the first World War boom many farmers had not only wasted their profits on purchase of additional land, but had borrowed on mortgage to do so. Farmers were in mortgage difficulties all through the decade.

Now the post-war decline of crop prices has been checked by Government supports. And the farmers also have large resources of their own. Between 1940 and 1948 they reduced their mortgage debt from $6.6 billion to $4.9 billion, increased their holdings of deposits and currency from $3.9 billion to $15.6 billion, bought $4.7 billion of United States Savings Bonds. They are prepared to withstand an economic siege, buying what they need and so keeping workers employed; they are prepared to pay their debts and so do their share in maintaining financial confidence. All this is the result of what farmers and Government learned from the former depression.

In the early Nineteen Thirties, as production and employment fell away, banks began to get into trouble. Loaded up with depreciated securities and mortgages, and with dwindling reserves, they were menaced by a rising tide of bank failures. Now the gold reserves are so ample that the banks could multiply the money in the hands of the public perhaps as much as twelve times without reaching the legal limit. The danger is, and will indefinitely remain, a surfeit of money rather than a famine. Even if a money crisis could arise, the existence of insurance for bank deposits would probably prevent runs like those which occurred in 1932. Depositors would not be so nervous about being able to withdraw cash, knowing that the privilege was guaranteed by a Federal agency. The danger is exceedingly remote, but the Federal Deposit Insurance Corporation is nevertheless one anti-depression weapon which did not exist until 1933.

Many believe that when a serious depression is in prospect the Government should step in to bolster employment by increasing its expenditures on public works, or reducing taxes, or both. There would now be no need, as there was in the middle years of the past decade, to look around for good ways for the Government to utilize any labor power unused by private industry. This would be true even if, by good fortune, we should be relieved of the necessity to rearm ourselves and Western Europe, and to invest in world recovery. Doles and leaf-raking would hardly be necessary, in view of the dozens of urgently required domestic programs which await action. Conservation of soil, forests and minerals, river valley developments, urban redevelopment, the building of schools and hospitals, repair and improvement of roads, extended medical service and the provision of additional trained teaching staffs for the oncoming younger generations, the development of atomic power —these and other programs ought to be undertaken promptly even if there were no unemployment throughout the nation.

Nor would there be the slightest difficulty in obtaining any needed tax reduction. Prices of fifty-two types of articles and services could be lowered by removing Federal excise taxes alone. Few people understand the extent to which their purchasing power is now diminished by these taxes. The list includes gasoline, oil, cigarettes, liquor, theatre admissions, automobiles, tires and parts, long-distance telephone calls, telegrams, electric energy, railroad tickets, mechanical refrigerators, radio sets, club dues, toilet preparations, furs, jewelry and many other things. To these are added state and local excise and sales taxes. What Representative or Senator would not welcome word from the White House that a tax cut was desirable in the general interest?

With more than a $40 billion margin theoretically available for tax reduction, the Federal Government could hand back to the public an amount of money sufficient to throw any conceivable recession back on its heels. This would be more than enough to compensate for a complete cessation of private investment—which in 1948 amounted to $38.8 billion. Even in 1932, at the lowest ebb in history of the American economy, private investment went on at a considerable magnitude.

The danger is, not that we do not possess ample anti-depression reserves, but that we might call out our heavy bombers unnecessarily. A budgetary deficit can be a powerful weapon, and it should be handled with care. If events should show that it was needed, however, we could call it into action without first suffering three years of disastrous unemployment and then debating acrimoniously whether anything at all should be done.

For, finally, Congress has enacted as a national policy the declaration that government should use its resources "to promote maximum employment, production and purchasing power." The detailed means to be utilized to this end are not, happily, specified in the Employment Act of 1946, but then, for the first time, the Government of the United States did formally avow the obligation to stabilize the economy at a high level. From this historic resolution it would be difficult to retreat, especially in the face of the pressures that a serious depression would activate.

Perhaps the most important of all the safeguards against depression is the mental preparation to tackle the problem. In 1929 the country was victimized by a fatuous optimism, the prevailing conviction was that we had achieved a self-balancing economy which never again could suffer a serious crisis. Now there is widespread recognition of the

need to think ahead and to be alive to any possible danger. The education of both the experts and the rank and file of citizens has made great advances. We have an unprecedented accumulation of pertinent economic statistics which are regularly put together and interpreted for the President, Congress and the public by a Council of Economic Advisers who have no other duties.

THE members of the Council, like other economists, are not infallible, and their advice, even if always correct, is not likely always to be taken. But it is an immense advance to focus attention on the current operation of our economy and to pose the issues. If we had had such an agency in 1929, together with the growth of information and analysis which has taken place since that date, the chances are that we should not have been overcome by so tragic a series of follies and misfortunes. The greatest lesson we have learned is to acknowledge the existence of the problem and to concentrate our attention on dealing with it.

May 8, 1949

TRUMAN TO STATE POLICY TOMORROW; ENDS CONTROL ON WAGES AND PRICES EXCEPT FOR RENTS, RICE AND SUGAR

LAW 'UNWORKABLE'

President Lays That to Congress—Cites Lack of Public Support

LABOR, INDUSTRY WARNED

Put on Their Own to Maintain Production With Shortages Ceasing—Rents May Rise

By JOSEPH A. LOFTUS
Special to THE NEW YORK TIMES.

WASHINGTON, Nov. 9—President Truman abandoned tonight all price, wage and salary controls, except the ceilings on rents, sugar and rice.

In one great swoop, the President virtually cut the American economy loose from the shaky moorings of a four-year-old stabilization program.

"In short the law of supply and demand operating in the marketplace will, from now on, serve the people better than would continued regulation of prices by the Government," he said.

Although rent controls were retained, even the landlords were permitted to infer that some relief might be given to them as Mr. Truman's statement said:

"It may be that some adjustment of rents will be required, but control of rents and control over evictions must be continued."

The future of the housing program remained uncertain in view of the lifting of restraints on the prices of materials and labor. But Wilson W. Wyatt, housing expediter, said that allocations and priorities would be continued for the present.

The President said that a new approach to housing problems would be necessary and asked Mr. Wyatt to report to him promptly on this.

The President stressed that his action on wages completely restored collective bargaining and that this "places squarely upon management and labor the responsibility for working out agreements for the adjustment of their differences without interruption of production."

It was said authoritatively that this did not necessarily imply that the Federal Coal Mines Administration immediately would turn over to the private owners of soft coal mines the demands of John L. Lewis for a new contract.

THE EXECUTIVE ORDER

An Executive Order accompanying the President's statement terminated all wage and salary controls under the Stabilization Act of 1942, including controls over decreases. It read as follows:

By virtue of the authority vested in me by the Constitution and statutes of the United States, and particularly by the Stabilization Act of 1942, as amended, and for the purpose of further effecting an orderly transition from war to a peace-time economy, it is hereby ordered as follows:

All controls heretofore in effect stabilizing wages and salaries pursuant to the provisions of the Stabilization Act of 1942, as amended, including any Executive Order or regulation issued thereunder, are hereby terminated; except that as to offenses committed, or rights or liabilities incurred, prior to the date hereof, the provisions of such Executive Orders and regulations shall be treated as still remaining in force for the purpose of sustaining any proper suit, action, or prosecution with respect to any such right, liability, or offense.

HARRY S. TRUMAN.
The White House,
November 9, 1946.

Situation Laid to Congress

President Truman acknowledged in his statement that price control had lost popular support. For this he blamed "the unworkable price-control law which the Congress gave us to administer."

The President also declared that the major problem which the Administration had faced was "the withholding of goods from the market."

"As price controls are dropped, one by one, many sellers naturally hold onto their goods in the hope that their turn will come next and that they can obtain a higher price," he explained.

Mr. Truman said there was no virtue in control for its own sake. Asserting that the country had reached the point where many shortages had disappeared, he added:

"The situation is far more favorable for the return to a free economy today than it was when the present badly weakened stabilization law was finally enacted by the Congress."

The President said he recognized that some shortages remained and that some prices would advance sharply. But he declared that the effect of consumer resistance to excessive prices had already been demonstrated and that if this resistance continued prices would come down.

In decontrolling wages and salaries, the President warned of "the illusion of prosperity" which might result from wage rates that are not justified by labor productivity and prices not justified by manufacturers' costs.

In the long run, he said, good wages, full employment and sound business profits must depend upon management and workers cooperating to produce the maximum volume of goods at the lowest possible price.

November 10, 1946

'Planless' Economy Here Outworks Ordered Rivals

American Crises Called Those of Abundance, Against Scarcities, Shortages Abroad

By RUSSELL PORTER

A great paradox seems to be developing in the post-war economic world. The "planless" economy of the United States, which was expected to collapse in a major depression—at least as predicted by advocates of planned economy—thereby endangering the stability of the rest of the world, is still going right ahead, overcoming its own obstacles one after another and shipping abroad goods for the United Nations Relief and Rehabilitation Administration and for private relief as it sent lend-lease during the war, while the planned economies of Europe and Asia, despite all the aid that we have given them, are running into one economic crisis after another.

The coal shortage in Great Britain, despite its possession of some of the world's finest coal deposits, has furnished the most dramatic news of the week, threatening British industry with paralysis and the population with freezing, but difficulties have been reported elsewhere also. There are wheat crises in parts of Soviet Russia, threatening starvation in a land of almost unlimited agricultural resources; there are inflationary crises in France and China, threatening poverty and misery.

In America the immediate reaction has been traditionally humanitarian, as shown by President Truman's offer to divert coal shipments to England. There has been little or no gloating or smugness by the believers in free enterprise. Whatever ill-natured comment has come from the extreme Right has been more than matched from the extreme Left, notably in demands of the Communist press that British Socialists abandon the attempt to make nationalization conform to democracy and adopt the coercive methods of communism.

There has been wide agreement

that Americans would be wise to study these foreign crises against the economic background of the countries in which they are taking place, with a view to learning whatever lessons may be applicable to our own economic future.

In this background two things seem particularly pertinent:

1. The crises of foreign countries under socialism and communism continue to be crises of scarcity, of shortages of food, clothing and shelter, the necessities of life, which grind down the people; whereas the crises of free enterprise in the United States have been crises of abundance.

2. Foreign countries in general have never known free enterprise in the American sense—that is, individual competition protected by anti-trust laws as well as private capitalism—but have allowed private capitalism to degenerate into private monopoly, which finally has become governmental monopoly in varying forms of socialism, communism or fascism. Russia went directly from the monopoly of feudalism into the monopoly of communism; Britain, by way of domestic monopolies and international cartels under private management into Socialist monopoly.

Some of the lessons which Americans seem to be drawing at least tentatively from world events today seem to be somewhat as follows:

1. Neither communism nor socialism can be depended upon to free the world automatically of militarism, imperialism or poverty, despite all the claims of propagandists and all the dreams of Utopians. In fact, these evils of monopoly capitalism seem to have been accentuated by government monopoly, with the rivalry of Communist Russia and Socialist Britain keeping the world an armed camp nearly two years after the end of the war in Europe. With all the sympathy in the world for the people of the war-devastated areas, it is recognized that their Governments still are keeping under arms men who might better be digging coal in Britain and growing wheat in Russia, and are forcing us to maintain a huge and costly military establishment.

2. Under any economic system, hard work and productivity remain the keys to individual and social well-being. Coal can not be dug with Socialistic tracts, nor wheat grown in communist manifestoes.

3. The opportunities and incentives of free enterprise have given the American economic system a dynamic quality which has stimulated production and an ever-rising standard of living over the years, and have enabled it to save the world with its industrial machine in time of war and to feed and clothe it during peacetime emergencies.

4. So far communism and socialism have proved themselves as economically static as monarchy or private monopoly. Instead of goods for the people, they seem to produce an over-abundance of sterile intellectualism or pseudo-intellectualism, just as monarchy produced a shallow aristocracy, and private monopoly, an idle rich.

5. The great enemy of the people is monopoly, either private or governmental, because it restricts production, raises prices, lowers real wages and the standard of living, and exploits workers and consumers in the interests of a privileged class. But government monopoly is the worst, because, backed by military power and secret police, it is the hardest to get rid of. Legislation and public opinion can curb business and union monopolies, but only a revolution can free a people from a government monopoly that wants to perpetuate itself in power.

In view of such considerations, plus the first-hand reports of conditions abroad brought home by several million GI travelers, the American people seem to have made up their mind that free enterprise has proved itself both as an essential element of democracy and also as an economic asset.

February 16, 1947

The Economic Test: Will We Act in Time?

An expert says we have the facts about present dangers, and we know what to do—if we will.

By LEON H. KEYSERLING

WASHINGTON.

UNTIL recently, rising prices caused a mounting fear of inflation and a growing sentiment for an affirmative program to combat it. Many felt that an uncurbed boom might lead quickly to a substantial recession in employment and business activity.

Today opinion has perceptibly changed. There are some who think that the peak of prices has been reached, although the odds are even that these people are in for a rude awakening. There are others who think that, let prices do what they may, the European Recovery Program and the new preparedness program will help to maintain such a high level of business activity for a few years that worry should be shelved and affirmative measures ignored.

It is, indeed, becoming more likely that high employment and production may continue for some time. But there is little novelty or surprise about a few years of prosperity after a great war; we have seen all this before. And nothing in the present boom has led reputable economists to claim that it will be of indefinite duration, or that it will not be succeeded by a depression if left to its own devices.

The main question is *when* a vigorous anti-depression program should be commenced. The tendency to postpone action until the eleventh hour of crisis disregards the supreme lesson of the last great depression—that it is easier to retain prosperity with mild measures than to regain a lost prosperity with heroic measures. Those in the area of economic policy who do not acknowledge this are as far behind the times as those physicians who remain unaware that the early detection and prevention of disease now weighs more heavily in the scales of the nation's health than surgery or the treatment of epidemics.

The most deep-rooted dogma of the totalitarians regarding democracy is that we remain passive until too late. Fortunately, in international affairs we are moving ahead. To deal more tardily with our domestic affairs would erect the hope of stable world relations upon a foundation as unstable as the traditional business cycle. Depression deferred is not disaster averted, and a setback some years from now would leave us relatively weaker in the face of economic reconstruction elsewhere in the world.

AGAINST this background we may better appraise the current economic situation and some of the reactions to it.

Looking at three significant periods—the last pre-war year (1939), the first post-war year (1946), and the present time—the index of wholesale prices has risen from 77 to 121 to 163, and the consumer price index has risen from 99 to 139 to 169. The annual rate of compensation to employes has risen from 48 billion dollars to 117 billion to 135 billion; proprietors' and rental income from 15 billion to 42 billion to 53 billion; and corporate profits and inventory valuation adjustment from 6 billion to 17 billion to 26 billion. The total value of national output has risen from 90 billion to 204 billion to 244 billion.

THESE advances in prices and in dollar incomes have been accompanied by large gains in employment, production and standards of living. Viewing the same three periods, civilian employment has risen from 46 million to 55 million to 58 million. The index of industrial production has risen from 109 to 170 to 191. Per capita income after taxes, which is one measurement of living standards, rose (in first half of 1947 dollars) from 838 dollars in 1939 to 1,251 dollars in 1946, and stands at 1,184 dollars according to the most recent figures.

Before discussing the seeds of depression in this "boom" it is noteworthy that those who reject an affirmative program because the depression seems not imminent are re-

THE TREND SINCE 1939 IN SIX IMPORTANT AREAS OF THE NATION'S ECONOMY

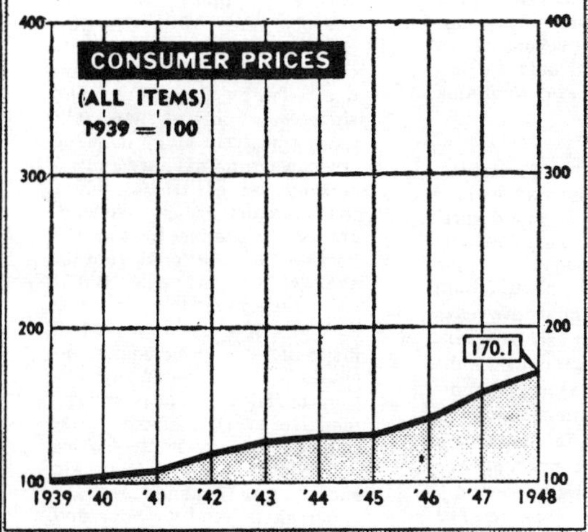

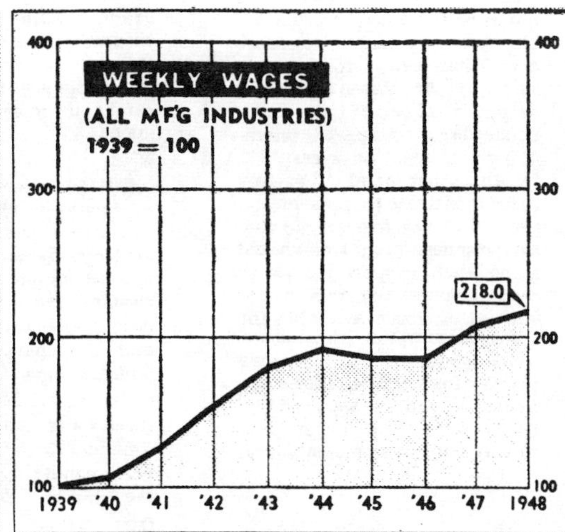

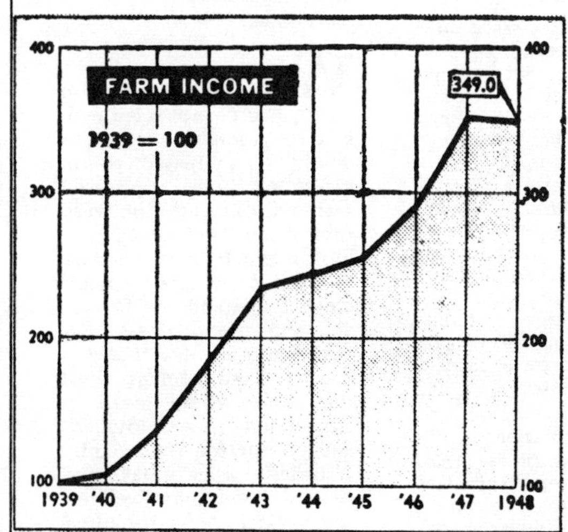

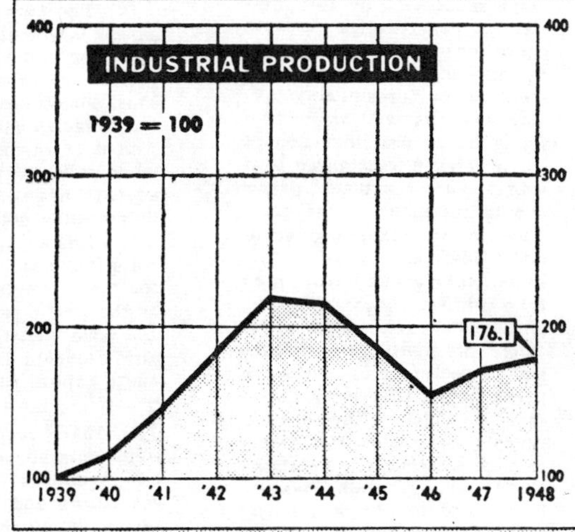

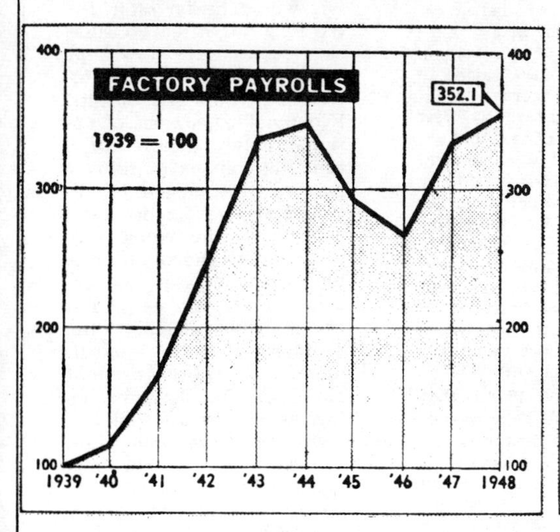

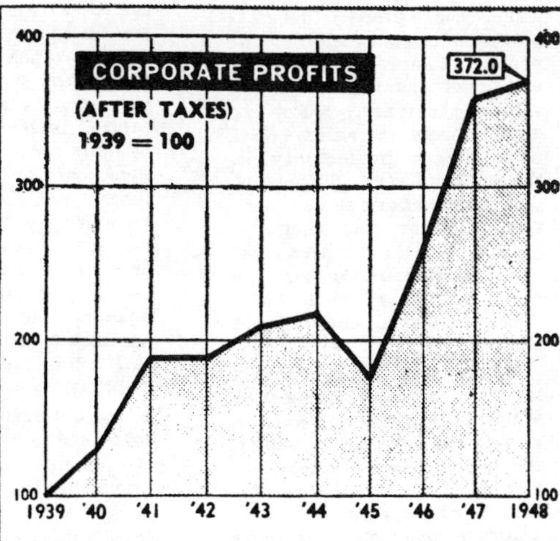

The figures for 1948 are estimates, based ih most cases on the first six months.

inforced by those who say that natural forces will rid it of these seeds before they sprout. It is stated that "inflation" will be followed by "stability" when "supply catches up" or when there is a "softening of demand." These predictions usually contemplate some "leveling off" or lowering not only of prices but *also* of employment, production and trade.

THIS kind of "leveling off," to be sure, may take place without an affirmative program. However, while price adjustments that promote full activity are desirable, price adjustments as the *counterpart* of rising unemployment and below-capacity operations would reflect neither stability nor safety. These would reflect rather a phase of the swing of the business cycle from ascent to plateau to descent; and although the plateau might last for a spell it would still be the connecting link. If the disease of instability has three discernible phases, and we are now in the first, now is the best time to act.

Occasionally this prospect of "leveling off" is dressed up in bright clothes. It is said that an economy running at four-fifths capacity could avoid the wide swings from full operations to 50 per cent operations. Even if this were true we must do better. With other nations using their resources to the hilt America cannot afford less efficiency because its endowments are greater, lest we be surpassed in the long run. Besides, all experience denies that an economic machine hitting on seven cylinders will run more smoothly than when hitting on all eight.

In the dynamics of national and world events the only meaningful stability is a steady rate of continuous growth. This means job opportunities that grow with a growing labor force, and maximum production that keeps pace with improved efficiency and new techniques. We may not succeed completely in this effort; but only by steering in this direction can we be reasonably secure.

SIMPLY stated, a stable rate of growth depends primarily upon a flow of national income so balanced that producers receive adequate funds and incentives for capital investment at a rate which assures maximum utilization of resources and skills, while consumers of final products earn enough to absorb the increasing output.

In this context of economic balance profits affect the amount of money available for business undertakings. Wages are the largest item in consumer incomes. Prices determine the real amount of goods that wages can buy and the real amount of capital equipment and expansion that business men can purchase with their profits. Recognizing this function of prices, wages and profits, one may dispose of some current fallacies which fan bitterness and partisanship where good-will and objectivity are vital for sound adjustments.

The first fallacy is that economic balance depends arbitrarily upon whether the price level is rising, falling or stable. The fairly stable price level for a few years before 1929 did not store up the conditions for permanent stability; the main debate is whether prices and profits too low for adequate investment, or prices too nigh and wages too low for adequate consumption, had more to do with the ensuing depression.

THE falling price level in the early Thirties was accompanied by a progressive worsening of the economic situation; the debated question is whether a more or less rapid reduction of wages in relation to prices would have checked the downward spiral sooner. The upswing of prices after 1932 was accompanied by improved economic conditions; the debated question is whether recovery would have been faster and more solid if the movement of wages relative to prices and profits had been slower or faster.

While all do not agree what the relationship among these three items should be, there is more general agreement that this relationship is more crucial to economic balance than the separate levels or trends. It follows that, in the current situation, economic balance cannot be achieved solely by voluntary agreements or laws which would hold prices, wages and profits where they are now or by a fiscal policy which would lower all three by contracting the monetary supply. Such blunderbuss methods, without more, might make the relationships worse instead of better.

THE second fallacy is the belief that economic balance depends upon the movement of prices, wages and profits at the same speed. Since 1939, for example, the consumer price index has increased by 71 per cent, and compensation to employes by 181 per cent.

Whether one believes that wages have increased too much or too little, it is palpable that they had to increase more than prices to help absorb an increased national output of about 171 per cent. Otherwise, widespread unemployment would have resulted. On the other hand, if at any time (contrary to present expectation) the foreign aid and preparedness programs should reach such proportions as to cause a downward trend in the amount of goods available for home consumption, the cost of living would have to rise more rapidly than wages unless affirmative policies were adopted to withhold a larger part of wages from immediate use.

THE recent General Motors wage settlement has two merits: it encourages smooth operations for two years, and by allowing for an improvement factor (presumably productivity) as well as cost of living in the determination of wage rates it recognizes that wages and consumer prices should not move at the same pace in an expanding economy. However, the G. M. formula, while an important step forward for these reasons, does not cover the whole range of considerations that should enter into a wage policy before it is applied lastingly or widely. The formula reveals no guides for determining whether the relationships among costs, wages, prices and profits within the industry and between it and other industries are workable. Further improvement in wage-price-profit policies, pointed toward better economic balance, will require additional criteria furnishing a broader perspective. For example, wage increases based upon higher productivity in the auto industry will not enable such workers to buy more food, clothing and shelter except at the expense of other consumers—unless the economy as a whole produces more food, clothing and shelter.

While some of the criteria for this broader perspective will require something akin to a national prosperity budget (to be described shortly), we already know enough to discern in the current economic situation some clear balances which call for an affirmative program *before* they upset us completely. These observations fall under five main points.

(1) *The foreign aid and new preparedness programs* mean that less goods will be available for domestic consumers than if these programs were not necessary. But these programs neither impair profit accumulations for healthy capital growth nor prevent price-wage policies that balance consumer incomes and available goods.

THE war period demonstrated this even when almost half of our total output was diverted from civilian use. Further, a total annual export surplus ranging from 5 to 10 billion dollars over the next few years and a preparedness program which as now formulated indicates total defense expenditures and commitments of around 15 billion dollars a year should not prevent our 244 billion dollar economy from providing even higher standards of living if its growth is maintained.

(2) *The business profit situation* is sometimes confused by indiscriminate charges that profits are beyond all reason. This sometimes results from the fallacies earlier discussed. And it is an incomplete story when dollar wages are adjusted to changes in the cost of living while dollar profits are not adjusted to the cost of doing business. There is need for more penetrating analysis of the profit picture. Yet the available facts do not reveal any imminent threat of inadequate capital funds.

IN 1947, corporations utilized unparalleled funds—26.7 billion dollars—for plant and equipment and working capital, including the replacement of inventories at high prices. This sum was provided by retained earnings after taxes and dividends of 10.1 billion dollars, which were raised to 14.4 billion by accrual of depreciation charges; by new capital issues of 4.1 billion; by long-term and short-term bank loans of 3 billion; and by funds from other sources amounting to 5.2 billion. Thus, even in a year of extraordinarily high demand for funds, the largest portion was supplied by internal financing in an amount almost equal to the 14.7 billion dollars spent for plant and equipment.

The outlook for 1948 is that corporations will have available for internal financing an amount at least equal to their likely investment in plant and equipment even if the current record level of investment is maintained. Dividends and other savings must also have outlets for investment, and there have been sizable tax reductions which will add to investment capital.

(3) *Trends in consumer income* show a greater potential danger. Although production and employment have risen sharply since 1946, the purchasing power of per capita consumer income after taxes has fallen by about 8 per cent since the middle of 1946. It is true that, through drawing down wartime savings and increased use of credit (which cannot go on forever), consumers are still able to buy the portion of national output available for their use. But if full employment is maintained and productivity improved, a large increase in consumer incomes will be needed in addition to high business investment to avert a sharp recession or depression in the Fifties unless still larger foreign aid and defense expenditures are undertaken. And we hope and expect that within a few years these expenditures will move sharply downward.

WHEN this situation arises, it does not seem realistic to anticipate that wages would be increased voluntarily or prices decreased systematically at the very time when the business outlook might be dampened by a decline in government-created demand for foreign aid and preparedness. Experience indicates that the delay of adjustment until that time would result in curtailment of employment and production followed by disorderly price breaks and general economic decline—the typical spiral of depression.

It would be far safer, for the long run, if real consumer incomes were now kept more nearly abreast of increases in domestic output. If compelling reasons of national policy require for a time that an extraordinary part of this output be diverted away from domestic consumers, the worst way to deal with the situation is by price increases that ration goods unfairly and enormously magnify the problem of future adjustment. A more prudent approach, for the time being, would be to follow a restrained price policy and to cut consumer spending rather than consumer income by voluntary savings and high taxes.

WE should then have a

better chance to maintain a full economy later on by enlarging consumer spending when more output becomes available for domestic use.

(4) *The plight of millions of families on fixed or low incomes* is more immediately unsettling. In desperation they have watched the cost of living index rise by 71 per cent since before the war, by 27 per cent since the middle of 1946, and by 8 per cent since the middle of last year. According to the most recent information (1946), almost 7 per cent of the four-person urban families in the country had annual incomes below $1,500, about 27 per cent fell below $2,500 and almost 39 per cent below $3,000. A recent Bureau of Labor Statistics study indicated that the annual cost of maintaining an acceptable family standard of living in typical cities was more than $2,700 in the middle of 1946 and more than $3,200 in the middle of 1947. The friction and turmoil created by this strain upon broad segments of the population translate themselves quickly into disturbances affecting the whole structure.

(5) *The uncertainty of the price-wage outlook* is the most serious present danger. The conscious decisions of business men and labor unions, far more than impersonal forces, now enter into the making of prices and wages. The maladjustments already created make it certain that neither side will accept the status quo. And with the cost of living now its peak and rising sharp- at its peak and rising sharply, according to the most al prices also at their peak, and with demand from many sources still expanding faster than production and now being increased, the current outlook in the absence of an affirmative economic policy is for additional wage increases, price increases, industrial disturbances and attendant maladjustments. These may not stop prosperity for a few years, but they may lead to an awful reckoning if we are lulled into unwatchful waiting.

THESE conditions define outlines of desirable action:

First, the social and economic tensions already created by recent price-wage changes, and likely to be exacerbated by coming events, call for a breathing spell. Hence President Truman's requests for consumer credit restrictions and powers of allocation and selective price and wage control. This would not be a permanent solution. But the calmness and discernment necessary for lasting solutions cannot be found when industry and labor are kept breathless in a mad chase to catch up tomorrow with the changes of today.

Second, this respite should be used at once to develop better criteria for price-wage-profit policies that promote stable growth based upon broad economic perspective rather than the prevailing fallacies already discussed, and effectuated by agreement rather than by the force of government or of blindly contending parties. This calls for the development of a national prosperity budget.

Such a budget would not be a "National Plan," it would not deal with all the minutiae of economic life and it would be forced upon no one. But it would focus national attention upon a few broad goals for maximum employment, production and purchasing power.

BY broad delineation of the capital needs for stable growth it would provide realistic standards for profit policy; by projecting the farm production needs for a wellfed people and a well-supplied industry it would shed light upon workable levels of farm prices and income; by striking a balance between resources to be consumed now and resources needed for further production it would provide a guide to wage policy. This would give management and labor a basis for improved relations by demonstrating their essential interdependence.

Third, better machinery is needed for the formulation and follow-through on such a national prosperity budget. In the work of the Council of Economic Advisers under the Employment Act of 1946, in the efforts of the Administration and the Congress to develop a long-range agricultural policy, and especially in the Economic Reports of President Truman, there have appeared the beginnings of this approach.

But further progress should depend increasingly upon voluntary organizations of business, labor, agriculture and consumers. Professor Slichter, recently in THE NEW YORK TIMES, set forth in excellent perspective the new tasks that industry and labor must assume in a highly integrated economy where the alternative to excessive government controls lies in the exercise of affirmative policy outside of government and not in helpless drift.

Fourth, those measures that are essentially within the governmental sphere, such as fiscal policy, regulation, social security, and various resource, construction and welfare activities, should be harmonized with a national prosperity budget and thus measured in terms of all their effects upon the economic life of the country. Whether these government programs are larger or smaller, they should certainly have this common frame of reference.

If we compute our total national income over the next decade on the basis of a steady but unspectacular rate of constant growth, and then compute it on the assumption of a boom-bust cycle, the ten-year *difference* comes to about 850 billion dollars.

THIS difference is far more than twice the cost to us of World War II. One-tenth of it would be sufficient to rebuild and modernize all the obsolescent and slum areas of all our cities. If even a sizable portion of it accrued to those in the lower ranges of the income structure, we could achieve satisfactory living standards throughout the country; and the balance would assure vast sums for capital improvements and for superior reward based upon ability and initiative. A moderate fraction would enable the financing of adequate programs of resource development, conservation, health, security and education without increased tax burdens. We could meet without strain any likely international commitments or requirements for national defense. The difference between prosperity and depression would mean the difference between safety and danger for our free institutions at home and our place in world affairs.

But there is grave likelihood that an affirmative economic policy will not be adopted. This is because the present prosperity, even if we call it inflation, is rather pleasant and assuring for so many people. Paradoxically, while a period of prosperity is the time when action to preserve that prosperity could be taken with relative ease and through moderate measures, it is also the time when psychologically we are least ready to act at all.

DEMOCRACY has repeatedly demonstrated its capacity to cope with crisis. We survived the depression and won the war, albeit at terrific cost. Today democracy is faced with a far more searching test: can democracy act *without* a crisis?

This, indeed, is the core problem of democracy in the twentieth century. For even as we by firmness in foreign policy avoid a clash of arms with totalitarian forces, there remains the ideological conflict competing for the minds of men and the decisions of whole peoples. The totalitarian system does not have purpose and unity only in times of crisis. It has these positive qualities at all times. Democracy, to thrive and triumph in this ideological conflict, cannot afford to have purpose and unity only on occasion. We must achieve a continuing purpose by inspiration rather than by arbitrary decree. We must achieve a continuing unity by glad consent rather than by suppression. We must conserve our institutions without standing still and we must preserve our liberties without becoming aimless.

Our present test is not what we would do in the event of depression but rather what uses we shall now make of prosperity, just as our real test is not what we would do in the event of war but rather how we shall preserve peace.

No opportunity so great ever confronted any people. The spirit in which we face this opportunity will set the pattern for the future of free people in this century.

June 13, 1948

PROSPERITY PROPS URGED BY COUNCIL

Truman Advisers List 7 Areas of Economy Where 'Wise Adjustments' Are Needed

RELIANCE ON CHANCE HIT

Board Puts Stress on Fiscal, Credit Policies, Controls and Plant Expansion

By H. WALTON CLOKE
Special to THE NEW YORK TIMES.

WASHINGTON, Jan. 7—President Truman's Council of Economic Advisers told him today that to fulfill 1949 goals for maximum employment, production and purchasing power it would be necessary to make certain "wise economic adjustments" in seven areas of the national economy.

The council, headed by Dr. Edwin G. Nourse, emphasized that the country's present tremendous prosperity was not maintained by chance, and that 1949 economic goals could not be achieved without careful consideration of the problems involved.

The recommendations were set forth in the council's annual Economic Report to the President, which he submitted to Congress together with his Economic Message. The latter was based, for the most part, on the council's suggestions and discussed in detail the economic background for the recommendations Mr. Truman made in his State of the Union message Wednesday.

The council proposed adjustments in the following areas: fiscal policy, credit policy, prices and wages, treatment of critical shortages and capacity expansion, selective controls, rent control and farm price supports.

Million More Workers Seen

The report stated that the labor force would be increased by nearly 1,000,000 in 1949. Employment last year ranged from 57,000,000 to nearly 62,000,000 civilian workers and averaged above 59,000,000. More than 1,000,000 were added to the labor force in 1948, while unemployment remained at the low level of about 2,000,000.

The civilian employment goal for 1949 should include provision of useful work opportunities for the net increase in the labor force, the council said, since "maximum employment means steady work at customary hours, not work sharing."

An increase in goods and services of 3 to 4 per cent, or $8,000,000,000 to $10,000,000,000 measured in 1948 prices, was recommended as "a reasonable objective" for this year. In 1948, production was reported, in the dollar value of goods and services turned out, at the record level of $252,700,000,000.

The council said that it was aware of the improvements in the country's industrial productivity, but it stressed that there would still be several bottlenecks where there were persistent shortages of capacity for producing electric power and critical materials, particularly certain metals.

"Industry and Government should press their efforts to overcome these shortages," the report asserted.

To achieve "maximum purchasing power," the council said that the income generated by productive effort should flow to groups and individuals throughout the economy in a manner that would provide adequate funds and incentives for maximum production in the factory and on the farm. This would also furnish buying power to consumers and business sufficient to take promptly off the market the goods available for their use.

Proper Balance Stressed

Prices and wages are considered the main channels through which buying power is distributed and as a result their movements and relationships decisively affect the outlook for stable prosperity. The council stressed that there was a need for a proper balance between the two as well as between total money purchasing power and the supply of goods "if inflation or deflation are to be avoided."

Mr. Truman supported the council's position in both respects in his message.

As for the seven areas of adjustment in the national economy, the council said that to maintain a sound fiscal policy tax measures should be devised to increase revenues by at least $4,000,000,000. It did not, however, recommend in specific language an excess profits tax.

"The range of prime considerations in matters of tax policy extends so far beyond purely economic analysis that ultimate decisions must be made within that wider prospective," the council stated, adding:

"In formulating a tax program for 1949, the following principles seem paramount: the additional tax measures should provide a budget surplus; and absorb some of the high current profits, while avoiding tax measures which would lead business firms to charge higher prices or impair their ability to maintain desirable rates of expansion."

The council suggested that any additional tax measures should guard against aggravating recessionary tendencies and provide sufficient fiscal flexibility to enable quick readjustments if such tendencies should become strong. It also urged that present inequities be reduced and enforcement of the tax collecting system strengthened.

Corporate Taxes Discussed

"With respect to taxes on corporate profits," the council said, "there are some arguments for an excess profits tax and others for an increase in the regular corporate tax rates.

"The excess profits tax has these advantages: It is sensitive to changes in business conditions, and therefore will rapidly reduce its demands on taxpayers in the event of a recession; it is difficult to shift to the consumer; it reduces incentive to increase prices; it may reduce the pressure for increases in wages of a kind that would be inflationary."

An increase in regular corporation rates has certain advantages, too, "provided the increase is moderate," the council added. "It has administrative simplicity; it avoids the high marginal rate that would exist in some concerns under an excess profits tax, and that might lead to a relaxation of marginal efficiency; and it avoids some of the inequities which might result under the excess profits tax.

"In any event, the non-economic elements involved in the choice between these two types of taxes, or in a combination of the two, make it clear that the decision should rest on the broadest grounds of policy."

The three-man council emphasized that under present conditions increases in taxes on personal incomes should be limited to the middle and upper brackets, primarily on the ground of equity.

The President accepted the council's suggestions on taxes for inclusion in his message, and added that he believed that "some additional excise taxes may be desirable, but some excise taxes, particularly on oleomargarine, should be repealed."

Flexible Credit Rules Urged

The council argued that the Government's credit policy should supplement the fiscal policy by exerting effective restraint on excessive credit expansion in an inflationary period and conversely of easing credit conditions in a deflationary period.

Critics of the Government's support policy for its bonds received little solace from the council. It said that the stability of the bond market had been a significant element in "the smooth post-war conversion."

"This stability," the council added, "has contributed to the underlying strength of the financial structure of the country. It would be a serious error to introduce new elements of uncertainty and possible financial disturbances which would follow a change of the policy with respect to the support of bond prices."

Critics of the Government's buying of bonds on the market to support the price of its securities assert that this policy is inflationary. They emphasize that insurance companies are selling large quantities of bonds and using the proceeds to expand credit.

A constructive approach to the credit problem would be to grant additional powers to the Federal Reserve Board to vary the level of reserve requirements of member banks, the council said. The board's ordinary power in this respect is limited to an increase of 2 percentage points against demand deposits for all member banks and two additional percentage points against such deposits for central reserve city banks.

The council proposed that any new authority should apply to all banks insured by the Federal Deposit Insurance Corporation, as well as members of the Federal Reserve System.

Under temporary authority granted by Congress last August and expiring next June 30, the board had power to raise reserves against demand deposits by 4 percentage points and against time deposits by 1½ points. Two percentage points against demand deposits and the 1½ points against time deposis have been applied.

The council also urged that the authority for the regulation of consumer installment credit, regulation W, which expires June 30 be extended, because abandonment of "this restraining influence at this time would be to increase our vulnerability to inflationary strain."

Mr. Truman adopted these suggestions with respect to credit and passed them on to Congress with a request for action.

Easing of Inflation Noted

The council said that since the end of the war, the country had been faced with an inflationary spiral of wages and prices from which "we are witnessing a welcome abatement" at the moment. It then added:

"Much as we may hope that the present relaxations of inflationary pressures will continue and spread to the rest of the economy, it would be foolhardy to count on it. This is no time to relax our vigilance against the dangers of a possible spurt in the inflationary spiral."

In his message to Congress, the President recommended that selective price control authority should promptly be made available to the Government as well as power to limit wage adjustments "which would force a break in a price ceiling."

Critical shortages of some materials and curtailed expansion present one of the most important problems confronting the country, the council asserted. Steel has presented the outstanding shortage problem since the end of the war, it said, "and would present grave danger in case of the need for a much enlarged defense program."

"It is, therefore, necessary to give special attention to policies which may be needed in these fields," the council added.

The President urged Congress to provide immediate laws to deal with the problem of capacity and supply. In his State of the Union Message he stated that if the Government found it necessary, it should authorize loans for the expansion of productive facilities and construct such facilities itself if private industry failed to do so.

Mr. Truman referred specifically to steel, and representatives of that industry argued that his proposal was a "definite step toward nationalization of the steel industry."

With respect to rent control, the council said that if it were extended for a year or two, "we might hope that return to free market conditions could be effected at a time when other items in the cost of living had eased." Removal of rent control would bear most heavily on families with fixed incomes, the report said, and would quite possibly stiffen demands for wage increases.

Mr. Truman also accepted this recommendation, and he told Congress:

"The present housing shortage makes it necessary to continue rent control for at least two years and to strengthen its enforcement. I recommend that this be done."

January 8, 1949

ECONOMIC ADVISERS URGE WIDER TAXES, FIXED MILITARY AIM

Action on Wage-Price Controls Demanded as 'Peril Is Great and Our Time Is Short'

NATION FOUND TO BE SOUND

Annual Report to the President Recommends 'Pay-as-Go'—Output Rise Held Possible

By AUSTIN STEVENS

Special to THE NEW YORK TIMES.

WASHINGTON, Dec. 30—President Truman's Council of Economic Advisers today pronounced the nation's economy essentially sound at a time when "our peril is great and time is short," but urged immediate action on wage and price controls, a broader tax program and fixing the size of military requirements.

Throughout their thirty-one-page fifth annual report, the Economic Advisers warned of the dangers of inflationary pressures. They recommended a balanced budget and a "pay-as-you-go" policy as the only equitable and realistic way to meet the high defense expenditures of the years ahead.

This report, although it is drawn in broad terms and is more a statement of the problems confronting the nation than a list of specific recommendations, nevertheless is considered a foretaste of the President's annual economic report to Congress early next month and of the Council's own interpretive economic review.

The annual report is also held to be an expression of Administration economic philosophy. Even though it is prepared by advisers and does not strictly bind the President, it is customarily drawn up under close White House scrutiny.

Ask "Common Dedication"

In posing the problems of the nation, the advisers rhetorically asked in their report if, in the present crisis, there will be a "scramble for self-protection" by business, farmers and labor or "common dedication to the protection of the United States?"

Placing at 8½ per cent the industrial output now devoted to the country's military and its support of friendly nations, the council declared:

"The concentration of our productive efforts upon defense objectives could rise far above this point, and we could still maintain a vigorous national economy capable of meeting additional demands upon it."

The council predicted that with a combination of growing labor force, longer work-week and the application of technology "it should be possible to increase the total of private and public output by about 25 per cent over the next five years."

No matter how extensive the restrictive measures on the economy—taxation, credit controls, supply allocations and wage and price controls—the Council observed, they will fall "far short of an opponent whose entire economic and political system is founded upon the most rigid control of every button and every grain turned out by every factory and farm."

Defense Estimate Criticized

The Council inferentially criticized the defense establishment for failing thus far to appraise accurately its own requirements. Not until the armed forces more clearly state their expected needs in terms of material, services and dollars, can other policies be fully formulated, the Council reported.

Budget experts of the Defense Department disclosed a few days ago that they would be unable to provide Congress next month with anything more than a "one line," or virtually lump sum estimate of funds needed in the fiscal year 1951-52 and that that figure would be highly tentative.

The Council, which is headed by Leon H. Keyserling, developed one theme throughout all sections of its report of the economic health of the nation. It was that despite the United States' industrial potential, its flexibility and determination of its people, the defense effort would be long-drawn out and would demand sacrifices.

The Council observed that "it is certainly not too much to ask that wage earners forego efforts to increase their living standards during a time when the economy simply cannot produce more civilian goods and also carry the heavy burden of rapid rearmament."

The Council urged a degree of flexibility in whatever wage and price controls should be imposed and declared that "the trend of wages available for spending after taxation and other restraints should be kept in line with trends in the availability of consumer goods."

The report declared that two courses were open in setting a wage control policy—one to hold wages approximately where they now are until consumer supplies can be expanded again or, working out wage increase formulas similar to those of peacetime and taking into account productivity and cost-of-living adjustments.

The latter approach, the Council said, would have the advantage of providing the wage earner with incentive, but could be dangerous if taxes were not increased sufficiently to keep the wage gains out of the spending stream.

The Economic Advisers hinted that a "general freeze" on prices and wages was a possibility as a start in setting final policy, but the council did not endorse that approach any more than it did the alternative course of starting with limited controls and broadening them gradually.

In stressing the importance of a pay-as-you-go tax policy the council noted the anti-inflationary effects of taxes and declared that the alternative method of borrowing "presents serious dangers of present or future inflation."

"Unless the borrowing is accompanied in the present by a decrease in spending (an increase in consumer saving) or by a reduction in business investment, the inflationary pressure of increases in Government expenditures will not be offset and immediate inflation will result," the council said, adding:

"The prospect that the defense effort will be prolonged makes it particularly important to cover the cost through taxes. Borrowing has its place in the financing of a short, intensive effort; but it is dangerous for a long-drawn-out effort."

The council also said, however, that defense spending might be too rapid to balance the budget in the current year because tax collections would lag behind the tax legislation. Another possibility is that were defense spending to become much greater, the increase in tax rates might result in a loss of incentive. Nevertheless, the economists said, "the pay-as-you-go principle should not be relinquished unless it should become absolutely hopeless to maintain it."

Rigidity Viewed Askance

For all its endorsement of controls, both direct and indirect, the Council warned against too great rigidity and commented that "in the worthy desire to be vigorous we should look where we are going. And we should not too rapidly sacrifice on the altar of automatic conformity the dynamic qualities which thus far have made our industrial system almost as productive as those of all the rest of the world."

Another suggestion was that the public be given "the fullest and most candid information" about the economic mobilization.

Other members of the council who, with Mr. Keyserling, prepared the report for the President were John D. Clark and Dr. Roy L. Blough.

December 31, 1950

PRICES AND WAGES FROZEN TO CURB INFLATION

PAY TALKS HALTED

Mine Increase of $1.60 a Day, Set for Feb. 1, Blocked by Order

RELIEF IN INEQUITIES

Stabilization Policy Due Next Week to Provide Wage Flexibility

By JOSEPH A. LOFTUS
Special to THE NEW YORK TIMES.

WASHINGTON, Jan. 26—The Government froze wages, salaries and other compensation of employes today for the second time in less than nine years. The rates of the freeze are those paid yesterday and those rates may not be increased without Government approval.

Temporarily the freeze is absolute, but the Wage Stabilization Board expects to have ready by Monday or Tuesday a policy whereby inequities of various kinds may be adjusted.

The effect of the order is to bring to a standstill hundreds of collective bargaining negotiations throughout the country. Even wage increases already negotiated but not in effect are blocked by the order. These include the $1.60-a-day increase won by more than 400,000 bituminous and anthracite mine workers. These increases were to go into effect Feb. 1.

Violations are punishable under the Defense Production Act, with penalties ranging up to a fine of $10,000 or a year's imprisonment, or both.

Basic Provision of Order

The basic provision of the order reads:

"No employer shall pay any employe and no employe shall receive 'wages, salaries and other compensation' at a rate in excess of the rate at which such employe was compensated on Jan. 25, 1951, without the prior approval or authority of the Wage Stabilization Board.

"New employes shall not be compensated at rates higher than those in effect on Jan. 25, 1951, for the jobs for which they are hired."

Eric Johnston, Economic Stabilization Administrator, authorized the wage freeze order despite the refusal of some members of the Wage Stabilization Board to sign it. Mr. Johnston did not appear at the news conference where the announcement was made. Cyrus S. Ching, chairman of the W. S. B., read the order, which, he said, had been handed to him a few minutes earlier.

The authority given to the board by the order is extraordinarily broad. It says:

"This regulation may be modified, amended or superseded by orders or regulations hereafter issued by the Wage Stabilization Board."

Mr. Ching told reporters:

"I just received this order. We have a responsibility to stabilize wages. We are quite conscious of the responsibility of stabilizing relationships and making a contribution to production. All those factors will be taken into consideration."

He said that he had a crew of experts at work tailoring formulas to fit the diverse problems resulting from the Government's inter-

Text of the White House Order

WASHINGTON, Jan. 26 (AP)—In connection with today's economic stabilization orders, the White House issued the following directive to the heads of all executive departments and agencies:

The White House
Washington
Jan. 26, 1951

TO THE HEADS OF EXECUTIVE DEPARTMENTS AND AGENCIES:

It is imperative that the economic stabilization orders issued today receive the fullest possible support by business and industry and by the people of the nation. The initial success of these orders in accomplishing their purposes for the good of all will require sacrifice and a high degree of self-restraint. The Federal Government must be prepared to do everything in its power to insure equitable and just administration of these orders and to obtain full compliance with them.

Until such time as the Economic Stabilization Agency can recruit and train the staff it will need, all departments and agencies should make whatever contribution they can to assure the success of our efforts to stabilize prices and wages.

Therefore, as President of the United States and pursuant to the authorities vested in me by the Constitution and statutes, I call upon each agency to make its resources in staff, and knowledge and experience available to the Economic Stabilization Administrator to the extent requested by the Director of the Office of Defense Mobilization.

Specifically, each agency shall provide such cooperation and assistance, consonant with law, as it can to meet the following needs:

1. Assignment of personnel in Washington, D. C., and in regional and field offices on a reimbursable loan basis for temporary periods as agreed upon in individual cases, including

[A]

Personnel qualified in investigation, intelligence and enforcement duties and functions, and the supervision and administration thereof.

[B]

Personnel qualified in the study and analysis of costs, prices, wages, working conditions and other economic and social data relating thereto.

2. Furnish any available reports, information or other data concerning costs of production, distribution and transportation, prices and price trends, profits, wages and wage trends.

3. Provide such other services, information and facilities as may be appropriate.

HARRY S. TRUMAN.

vention in free collective bargaining.

The formulas will permit wage increases in some circumstances. The law does not deal with wage controls in terms of a freeze or ceilings. It says that wages shall be "stabilized."

One part of the stabilization policy, for example, probably will cover cost-of-living increases, as the Little Steel formula did in World War II. It will take care of those workers whose wages or salaries have lagged.

There also will be provisions to correct "in-plant" inequities so that merit increases, length-of-service increases, promotions, reclassifications and so on may proceed normally. Inter-plant inequities and substandards also will be covered, it is expected, and perhaps some provision will be made for adjustments necessary to divert labor to the most essential defense plants.

Whether the stabilization policy will dispose of the "escalator" problem was not definite tonight. "Escalator" clauses in union contracts provide for automatic wage adjustments geared to the Federal Consumers Price Index. The major contracts containing escalator clauses, such as those in the automobile industry, do not provide for any further adjustments before March 1.

The order provides relief for employes who may be caught by unusually low wage rates for seasonal or other causes. It says that nothing shall be construed to require the stabilization of rates below those paid during the period from May 24, 1950, to June 24, 1950. That is the period immediately preceding the Korean fighting.

Some parts of the stabilization policy probably will be self-interpreting, but thousands of petitions for approval of adjustments probably will start pouring into the board. Regional boards of labor, industry and public members will be set up to interpret and apply the policy.

A large number of disputes is regarded as inevitable. How long the Federal Mediation and Conciliation Service will continue to handle labor-management disputes involving wage stabilization problems remains to be determined.

The Wage Stabilization Board is geared to act only on wage adjustments where there is agreement by the employer and employe.

January 27, 1951

WHITE HOUSE ENDS ALL WAGE CONTROL, MANY PRICE CURBS

Actions in Force Immediately —11,000 Petitions on Pay Enabled to Take Effect

MEATS, FURNITURE FREED

Ceilings Also Go Off Long List of Department Store Items —Reuther Hails Step

By JOSEPH A. LOFTUS

Special to THE NEW YORK TIMES.

WASHINGTON, Feb. 6—President Eisenhower suspended all Government controls on wages and salaries today and decontrolled a long list of consumer goods, including meat, furniture, clothing, nearly all the items normally sold in department stores and meals and drinks sold in restaurants and bars.

The actions were taken under Executive order and are effective immediately.

The order on wages means that employers and unions are back in the full collective bargaining business after two years of Federal restraint. Anything they agree on, they can put into effect, including retroactive payments. In the absence of an employe bargaining organization, the employer is free to make any adjustment by himself.

The impact of the President's action is a matter of conjecture. The wage and salary agencies had on their dockets at least 11,000 petitions for approval of higher pay or other benefits. Such increases may go into effect immediately, as far as the Federal Government is concerned.

Whether these increases would have a mild effect on other bargaining relationships or set off a new round of demands, no one could foretell. A great deal depends on what happens to prices.

Many Goods Affected

Many consumer goods now will be free to find their own price levels. These include children's wear, toys, yard goods, leather goods, small appliances, sporting items, towels and sheets, as well as the broader categories of meat, meals and furniture. Some prices had already been taken off the controls list temporarily, or "suspended"; today's decontrol order, covering many of these and other items, is a final action.

The President declared that supply and demand in the national economy were "approaching a practicable balance" and that "the earliest possible return to freedom of collective bargaining in the determination of wages will serve to strengthen the national economy and thereby the national security."

Labor leaders in general have felt the time had come to take off wage controls and have contended that wages had been more restricted than prices.

Walter P. Reuther, president of the Congress of Industrial Organizations, commented that he had told President Eisenhower today that the removal of pay controls was "a constructive step." He and David J. McDonald, president of the United Steelworkers of America, C. I. O., reported that they had had "a very pleasant conference" with the President.

Asked whether he thought the end of pay controls would touch off a fresh round of demands, Mr. Reuther said that that was a matter of interest for each individual union.

Some labor leaders thought there would be a period of unrest as unions sought to reopen their contracts—some contracts specifically provide for a reopening on the termination of wage controls. Still others provide for improvements of certain kinds immediately upon the end of controls. It has been illegal, however, for an employer to agree to set aside funds to pay out later what had previously been forbidden.

Permissive in Nature

One labor leader thought that some of the pending wage agreements had been made by employers in the hope that they would be disapproved in whole or in part, and that these employers now might try to hedge on their offers. Where this happens, it is considered a private dispute. The Executive Order does not compel anybody to live up to any agreement; it is permissive in nature.

There are some cases where the wage board already had disapproved part of a wage increase agreed to by an employer and a union. The union cannot, as a matter of legal right, claim the disapproved part now on the ground that wage controls have ended, unless the contract provides for the beginning of such payments automatically when controls end.

On the other hand, if the contract has a reopening clause, or if the employer is willing to reopen it, there is nothing to prevent a union demand, or union-management agreement, to pay now what had been illegal until today.

Charles C. Killingsworth, chairman of the Wage Stabilization Committee, said today that the automatic "clearance" of petitions for wage adjustments applied to all pending cases, including appeals from prior decisions at the national or regional level.

Wage controls have been administered by the committee since the industry members withdrew from the Wage Board several months ago in a protest. Harry S. Truman, then the President, had overridden the board in its modification of a soft-coal wage agreement.

The committee, consisting of the former public members of the board, is composed of Mr. Killingsworth, Herman Lasarus, the vice chairman; Harold L. Enarson and Meyer S. Ryder.

Mr. Killingsworth said the President's order today did not excuse past violations of wage regulations. More than 4,000 enforcement actions are pending.

"Generally, we will not initiate any new investigations unless flagrant instances of violations come to our attention," Mr. Killingsworth said.

In its two years of operation, the Wage Stabilization Board and its regional boards received about 134,000 cases for wage adjustments and pensions or profit-sharing. About 17 per cent of these were modified or denied. Some self-administering regulations permitted certain increases without review by the board. The agency also received about 33,000 health and welfare reports.

Mr. Killingsworth said that from January, 1951, when the wage controls were imposed under the Defense Production Act, until September, 1952, the straight-time average hourly earnings of factory workers had risen by an average of 0.4 per cent a month, compared with an average rise of 0.9 per cent a month in the latter half of 1950.

The liquidation of the wage control agency will proceed rapidly, and all but a few of its 1,700 employes will be off the payroll on March 5.

February 7, 1953

Eisenhower's Four Years

An Assessment of Republicans' Aims And Achievements in Economic Policy

By EDWIN L. DALE Jr.
Special to The New York Times.

WASHINGTON, July 23— When President Eisenhower led the first Republican Administration in twenty years to office in January, 1953, many Americans with long memories were plain scared—about their bread and butter.

Today, most are scared no longer, and they have more bread and butter.

That says a great deal, and symbolizes the single greatest triumph of the Eisenhower economic policy. But it by no means says that all the key aims of that policy were achieved.

In no area of the national life were those aims and goals more clearly and specifically stated in the pre-election period. They can be broken down into three main categories:

1. The national economy: Reasonably full employment without inflation. Use of the Government's powers to curb both boom and bust.
2. Fiscal management: An eventual balanced budget with lower spending and lower taxes. Tax policy to encourage investment by business as well as consumption by the people.
3. Economic "decision-making": Less in the hands of Government and more in the hands of private enterprise. No controls except where overridingly necessary. "Get the Government out of business."

It should be noted that as these goals were refined during the pre-election campaign and subsequently in budgets and Presidential economic reports, they emerged as a package considerably removed from the goals of orthodox pre-Eisenhower Republicanism. The Eisenhower performance must be tested not against Republican orthodoxy but against his own stated philosophy.

But before making that test, it is worth recalling that when the Eisenhower Administration came into office, it promptly frightened many by adopting the tightest credit squeeze since the Nineteen Twenties—one that also drove interest rates up to the highest level in three decades.

The Senate rang with dire warnings from rural Democrats that "hard money" was going to ruin the country once again under Republican leadership. And when a recession began in late 1953, it seemed that those warnings might prove correct.

The key point about the Administration's performance is not so much that the warnings, fortunately, proved mistaken. It is that those who had been frightened of a Republican Government—understandably — had been frightened needlessly. For in fact the men who have run United States economic policy under General Eisenhower are as different from the "Wall Street crowd" of the Nineteen Twenties as the President himself is different from, say, Warran G. Harding.

A quick glimpse at these five men forms a prelude to an assessment of just how well the Administration did what it set out to do.

They are:

George M. Humphrey, the Secretary of the Treasury. His instincts are the most "orthodox" conservative of the lot, but he has a flexible, non-doctrinaire mind. He knows how to listen.

Dr. Arthur F. Burns, the chairman of the Council of Economic Advisers. He is a quiet, pipe-smoking professor, and genuinely conservative, but emphatically "modern." He might be said to be equidistant in philosophy between his predecessor under the Democrats, Leon H. Keyserling, and the National Association of Manufacturers.

William McChesney Martin Jr., chairman of the Board of Governors of the Federal Reserve System. He is a Democrat who was kept in the job by President Eisenhower on Mr. Humphrey's recommendation. He is an intellectual who has spent his life in the world of finance, and also is non-doctrinaire, modern and conservative.

Gabriel Hauge, the President's special assistant for economic affairs. He is an economist and former magazine editor. His thinking runs strikingly parallel to that of Dr. Burns.

W. Randolph Burgess, the Under Secretary of the Treasury. He is Mr. Humphrey's financial man, who deals with managing the public debt and money problems. He is a monetary expert from way back, and he, too, has deeply conservative instincts but a flexible mind. Like the others, and unlike many in the Republican old guard, he does not find the modern age an intellectual and political affront.

What of Their Record?

What, then, of the record these men have forged? The record provides a wealth of evidence for testing performance against promise.

THE NATIONAL ECONOMY

Probably the most important economic decision of the Eisenhower Administration is one of the least known. It had major historical and practical significance. It was the decision in the fall of 1953 to incur deliberately a sizable deficit in the budget for the fiscal year beginning July 1, 1954, although a balance could have been achieved by preserving existing tax rates.

This was the situation:

The first sign of a recession, induced by excessive inventories and declining defense spending, had become apparent by about September, 1953, although employment then was still full. Meanwhile, two major Korean war taxes were due to expire the following Jan. 1: the excess profits tax (two billion dollars) and an emergency 10 per cent increase in income taxes (three billion dollars).

The Administration had made defense policy decisions that, with the end of the Korean war, guaranteed that Government spending would decline substantially in the next fiscal year. If those taxes could be retained, the budget could be balanced.

Deficit Policy Followed

But modern economic theory holds that if an economy is in recession, it is probably better to have the budget in deficit. This means that the Government is pumping more money into the economy than it is taking out.

The Republican managers decided to let the budget fall into a deficit because of the impending recession. Their decision was, of course, made easier by the legal situation—that is, with the taxes due to decline automatically. But not only did they let the $5,000,000,000 in taxes expire, they also approved further reductions of $2,400,000,000, in the teeth of the deficit.

This decision was one of the two major moves by the Government to cushion the recession. The other was a rapid and timely shift by the Federal Reserve System (acting independently of the Administration but, in this as most instances, with the Administration's warm blessing) from tight money to easy money.

The Administration itself insists that an equally important decision involved the refusal to rush headlong into vast public works schemes or to adopt even stronger deficit financing. This, it argues with conviction, preserved the all-essential confidence in the business community necessary to prevent the recession from snowballing.

Whichever was the more important, the results by any test were brilliant.

The decline phase of the recession lasted only six months, followed by about four months of leveling off. It proved to be possibly the mildest recession in United States business cycles, with peak unemployment of only 3,700,000 (compared with a peak of 4,700,000 in the almost forgotten 1949 recession under the Democrats). And the recession was followed by the greatest boom in history.

A Leopard Changes Spots

The actual budget deficit turned out to be $4,200,000,000. But the important point historically is that a Republican Administration was willing to accept such a deficit as sound economic policy in the circumstances. A rather frightening leopard had indeed changed its spots—or at least some of them.

The Administration's over-all economic policy, aside from the 1953-54 recession, has faced only two difficult periods:

1. The aforementioned "hard money" era in 1953 just before the recession.
2. The immediate present.

The "hard money" era is still being debated. The Administration, in agreement with the Federal Reserve, decided that inflation was a real threat in the first half of 1953. Money was kept tight by the Federal Reserve. The tightness was reinforced by certain Treasury financing decisions (particularly the famous Humphrey 3¼ per cent 30-year bond of April).

All the Administration economic leaders concede privately now that they let things get too tight for a while. Basically, they misjudged how much their onslaught in the credit field would frighten the money markets.

But they reversed the policy quickly when tightness reached the stage of near panic. They insist that the over-all approach was right for the time. They felt—and many outside observers agree—that the policy was simply a proper living up to their commitment to fight inflation by tough policy when necessary.

'Tough' Line Taken

In the present period the basic decision has been not to reduce taxes while the economy remains strong, despite a modest budget surplus and despite some signs of an impending decline. In this instance, the Federal Reserve has kept money even over the initial objections of Administration leaders. This has been done on the ground that inflation and excess are still the main threats to the economy. Here again, the Government as a whole has shown willingness to take the "tough" anti-inflation line, although both political and economic arguments could have been made for lower taxes and easier money.

Has the anti-inflation pledge been fulfilled? The only fair answer is that it has, with the important proviso that the postwar inflationary juggernaut had actually been pretty well halted in the last eighteen months of the Democratic Administration. The consumer price level is about to hit a record, but it is only 1 per cent above where it was at the beginning of 1953. This is negligible over three and one-half years.

In part this record has been achieved only because farm and food prices have declined while other prices were rising. The Republicans have still not proved that a modern economy can have both full employment and stable prices at once. But they can argue reasonably just the same that their over-all record on the national economy has lived up in all essential respects to their promises.

FISCAL MANAGEMENT

Here the record has not been what the Eisenhower "team" hoped for and expected when it took office. But the campaign will nonetheless find Republican orators claiming triumphs here too.

In the long run, the most significant result of the first Republican fiscal management in twenty years is the discovery, and indirect admission, that Government spending cannot be cut.

With the end of the Korean War and accompanying mobilization build-up, spending on national security did decline from an annual rate of $54,300,000,000 in the second quarter of 1953 to $40,600,000,000 by the end of 1954. There it leveled off. This decline was speeded to some extent by defense policy decisions of the Administration itself.

But that, in effect, is the sum total of Republican economy efforts. Over-all civilian spending is now at the highest level in history and can go nowhere but up. The big new highway program alone will increase spending by several billion a year.

What is more, the Pentagon is unanimous that defense spending also is heading higher next year—the only issue being how much higher. Foreign aid shows no sign of declining.

The Republicans did, of course, make a considerable number of tiny savings through "efficiency." They reduced Government personnel by some 300,000—most of this as a result of the dismantling of price and wage controls. But the crucial point is that these savings were swallowed up in a host of new programs and by the facts of Government life in the modern world.

The Budget Balanced

Already, the record of successive annual declines in spending, resulting from the reduction in national security spending, has been broken. The fiscal year just ended saw a spending total of $66,400,000,000, up slightly from the year before. The Administration pledged fervently to "economy in Government" did not even come close to its preelection target of a budget of $60,000,000,000 some time during the four years.

In the face of all the spending, however, the Administration did achieve its goal of a balanced budget in the year just ended. This was simply because the booming economy produced the greatest revenues in history. And tax rates, as pointed out earlier, were cut.

Besides the $5,000,000,000 in Korean war taxes, that expired, the Republican tax package has included three other items.

In 1954 excise taxes were reduced almost across the board, with a tax loss of $1,000,000,000. This reduction was pushed through Congress over initial Administration protests. Far more important, the same year saw enactment over strong Democratic opposition of the huge, complicated tax revision and reform bill, which carried estimated reductions of about $1,400,000,000.

A Clear-Cut Party Issue

By granting tax relief to stockholders and to business for depreciation, and by many other devices, this bill represented the major Republican effort to live up to the pledge to reform the tax system to stimulate the economy.

The bill and its basic philosophy are one of the few clear-cut party issues in the whole four years. They are still being debated. While it is impossible to say how much the tax revision bill was a factor, it is now a historic fact that investment in new plants and equipment by United States industry has reached a record level far above anything ever dreamed of by the Republican managers themselves.

Finally, there was the series of tax increases (almost never mentioned by the Republican orators) associated with the big highway bill. The main one is a penny increase in the Federal gasoline tax. Taken together, the increases come to just short of $1,000,000,000 a year.

Despite some relief for individuals and some for business under the Republicans, it is clear that taxes have not been cut nearly so much as the Eisenhower Administration hoped and expected when it took office. The basic reason was the Republican discovery that running a Government in the decade of the Nineteen Fifties is just plain expensive.

ECONOMIC DECISION-MAKING

Here again the record is decidedly mixed. Perhaps the measure of the Republican failure to live up to initial hopes is the comment of a Washington hotel man:

"It seems to me there are just as many business men coming to Washington to settle one thing or another as there were under the Democrats."

By far the most important single action in this area by the Administration was the decision as early as January, 1953, to end price and wage controls. It was a difficult decision, which proved to be the right one. Prices did not spurt upward (in part because the Administration worked to check them through its tight money policy). It ought to be said, however, that events were rushing in that direction anyway, and a Democratic Administration certainly could not have preserved controls until even the end of 1953.

Otherwise, there has been a paradox: the Administration genuinely believes that the Government ought to interfere less in individual sectors of the economy, but it keeps interfering. For example:

¶Under policies adopted virtually out of necessity, close to half of all farm exports are now made under Government programs or with a Government subsidy.

¶The Administration used the national strategic stockpile as a device for propping the price of lead and zinc, and for preserving **domestic producers of severe minor metals.**

¶The Administration has undertaken the most complex and expensive program of shipbuilding subsidies and devices in peacetime.

¶It has proposed completely new programs of Government intervention—such as aid to economically distressed areas and Government flood insurance.

Federal Activties Curbed

Perhaps most important of all, it has not abandoned a single one of the really important Government "interventions" that have grown up through the years. Despite all the haggling over the "philosophy" of the farm program, the crucial point is that precisely as many crops are dependent on the Government for price support as in 1952.

On the other side, besides the ending of direct price and wage controls, there has been a genuine effort to curb Government-owned commercial and industrial activities. In the Defense Department alone, more than 100 of these have been ended.

But the over-all task has proved troublesome; no more than a small fraction of the total of these enterprises (most of them extremely minor, anyway) has been discontinued.

The Administration has resisted new incursions of Government into one area or another affecting business; it can, if it wishes, say it has stopped the "drift to socialism" if there ever were such a drift. But on the whole, the basic role of the Government in the decisions business has to make—for better or for worse—is not much different from what it was when the Republicans took office.

SUMMARY

The Republican economic record as a whole is a sort of paradox: President Eisenhower's team proved to be "modern"—to the benefit of the economy generally. But their very modernity prevented them from doing some of the things they would have liked to do.

This paradox results as much from the pragmatism of the Eisenhower Republicans as from their intellectual theories. They found out what Government was like, and they decided to live with it. The result was an economy prosperous beyond all previous measures. But it was an economy otherwise not markedly different from the structure that a lot of Republicans had once thought was a Frankenstein monster. Big Government not only proved tough to cut down, but rather useful.

July 24, 1956

Lessons of the 1957-58 Recession

Some positive actions of government and some built-in correctives of laws and society helped to pull us out of the slump, but the biggest factor was plain good luck.

By EDWIN L. DALE Jr.

WASHINGTON.

AS this is written more than 4,000,000 Americans are still out of work and looking for jobs. And yet it can be stated confidently that the 1957-58 recession—the most severe since World War II—is over. That is, the economy has moved decisively upward from the low point reached about last April, is still moving upward and shows every sign of continuing to do so well into 1959.

This is an event of very great importance. A prolonged and severe economic slump in the United States would have had the worst possible effects at home and abroad. This is old stuff, of course, yet it is frequently forgotten. In the endless barrage of crises and bad news from around the globe, success stories tend to get lost. A post-mortem on the 1957-58 recession, therefore, clearly is in order.

There is a certain pattern about recessions. Something or other causes a slump in one or more major sectors of demand (this time it was defense orders, exports and business investment in plant and equipment). The change in dollar magnitude may be quite small at first, but it has the major effect of reducing the flow of orders to business and thus changing business sentiment. Business men, acting with ordinary prudence, suddenly stop building inventories and, instead, start living off the inventories they have. This shift quickly becomes the major cause, in dollar terms, of the decline in production and employment. The 1957-58 recession was no exception.

The threat, of course, is that the quick drop in production and thus in workers' incomes—though caused almost entirely by inventory change—will reduce consumer purchasing power and thus consumer buying. Then there would be a major additional downward force and a sort of cumulative downward spiral would be under way.

Obviously, however, inventory liquidation cannot continue forever, provided the total of final demand is maintained. Thus the anatomy of recovery is the anatomy of those forces and events that kept final demand high long enough for the "inventory cycle" to run its course and for normal growth factors in the economy to assert themselves again.

What bolstered final demand this time? The number of factors involved is surprisingly large, but since each played its part there is no escape from listing them. They group themselves naturally into three broad categories:

I. GOOD LUCK

THE first category has to be labeled simply that, for it consists of items that helped the economy out of the recession without having been adopted or planned for that purpose. Together, they were very important, indeed:

(1) *The sputniks.* One of the important contributing factors to the slump's beginning in 1957 was a drastic cutback in defense ordering that began about July of that year — a cutback ordered by Secretary of Defense Wilson in order to help the Government stay within its debt limit. Had defense spending continued at the pace reached in the spring of 1957, the debt limit would have been pierced, and the President was determined to avoid asking Congress for another increase.

Then, in October, came the first sputnik and an aroused reaction in the public. Before long, the old "ceiling" on total defense spending was lifted, then a big supplemental appropriation went up to Congress and, after about four months, the flow of defense orders increased sharply. In the first six months of 1958 these orders totaled $10.8 billion, compared to only $6 billion in the final six months of 1957.

The orders had gone down faster than actual spending, and they went up faster. But many economists believe that orders influence economic activity more than does actual spending. In any case, there is no doubt whatever that the big surge in defense ordering in the first half of this year was a major element in recovery.

(2) *The highway program.* This mammoth undertaking was gathering momentum when the recession struck. As we shall see, highways also come under the "management" side of recovery, but, in this case, they qualify more under the "luck" side. Spending in the first six months of 1958—almost all related to earlier actions taken before anybody had dreamed of the recession—was $2.2 billion, the highest six-month total ever.

(3) *Government benefit programs.* A handful of little-noticed actions by Congress in 1954, 1956 and 1957, taken for reasons wholly unrelated to the recession, proved a big help in bolstering the total of personal incomes, and thus of consumer spending.

AN increase of $170 million a year in veterans' disability benefits took effect in October, 1957. Changes in the Social Security Law made farmers eligible, and allowed women to collect benefits at the age of 62. And there was a new program of disability benefits under Social Security.

All of these hit the economy at just the right time — last winter. Leaving out entirely the regular rise in old-age benefits that occurs every year —to be touched upon later— they added about $1.2 billion to the annual rate of personal incomes in the first half of 1958.

(4) *The farm economy.* A number of elements worked toward a higher farm income, none of them associated with Government policy. Mainly because of long-run supply conditions with pre-recession

roots, there were excellent prices for livestock last fall and winter. A freeze brought a sharp rise in fruit and vegetable prices. Government programs, as we shall see, cushioned potential declines in prices of other items, with the result that the annual rate of farm income in the first half of 1958 was up by $2.3 billion over the same period of 1957.

(5) *The Federal pay rise.* Past inflation and a coming election made this piece of legislation inevitable this year. It pumped out about $350 million in lump-sum retroactive payments in July and added $1.5 billion to the annual rate of incomes of Federal civilian and military employes.

II. BUILT-IN STABILIZERS

THE second broad category of factors that bolstered demand consists of those changes in the economy—all tending to maintain incomes—that have been legislated into the economy in the past, or have been worked into it by changing ways of operation. There are four main items:

(1) *Income maintenance for workers.* This, of course, is the most familiar—unemployment compensation. It made up about one-third of the drop in wage income for those laid off, supplying $3 billion to the annual rate of incomes by the second quarter of 1958.

(2) *Income maintenance for farmers.* Farm price supports effectively insulate growers of several major crops from the effects of over-supply. They work all the time — in boom and in slump. They helped to keep up farm income in this recession.

(3) *Income maintenance for the aged.* Every week of every month, more people qualify for Social Security retirement benefits. Besides, in contrast to the days of the great depression, there are formal programs for relief, partly financed from Washington, for the needy aged who do not have Social Security or have so little they cannot get along. Old age checks of both kinds now go out every month at the annual rate of nearly $10 billion—the highest ever.

(4) *Income maintenance for stockholders.* This is something not generally realized. Corporations suffered the sharpest drop in profits in the postwar period during the 1957-58 recession, but they scarcely cut their dividends at all. This is the result of a number of factors, one of the most important of which is the modern 52 per cent corporate tax rate—which means that half of a loss in profits is absorbed by the Government. In any case, the dividend maintenance in this slump paralleled a similar occurrence in each of the two previous postwar recessions.

A few other built-in items in our modern society probably deserve a mention.

There are, of course, the purely financial reforms of the New Deal years — bank deposit insurance, control of stock market margins and mortgage insurance. No one heard anything about bank failures in this slump, but even if there had been some failures the sheer panic of the depression days would have been avoided because of deposit insurance.

Then there is the steady impact of a rising population on the spending of state and local governments for such things as schools, water and sewer systems. The rise in state and local spending has been going on for years at the rate of about $3 billion a year, and it continued during the recession. There is every reason to expect it to continue indefinitely.

Note probably should be taken, too, of our shifting labor force. This is a point not yet thoroughly analyzed. But it seems fairly clear that the large relative shift toward white collar jobs and away from blue collar jobs, together with a parallel shift out of farming and mining and manufacturing and into trade, government and services, has given a far higher proportion of our population than ever before a feeling of job security. Consumers all through the recession spent money about in line with their incomes, and showed no important signs of panic. One reason may well be that the great bulk of them never felt much fear that their jobs would disappear.

III. MANAGEMENT

THE last broad category of reasons for recovery is the only one that qualifies for the term "management" —things the Government did specifically to halt the slump. Despite a great deal of talk and an air of feverish activity, the catalogue of significant actions is modest. Of the five items that are worth listing, only two had a major effect on the recovery, the others being small, or having taken effect only after the economy was solidly on the upward path.

(1) *Easy money.* The Federal Reserve System switched dramatically last November from credit restraint to credit ease. It is obvious that easy money and low interest rates cannot generate recovery by themselves, but they are almost certainly a precondition for recovery. The nation's money supply did not contract in the recession, as it used to in old-fashioned slumps.

The sharp drop in interest rates made it far easier for state and local governments to float their bonds and finance their expanding activities, and their borrowing reached a record in the first half of this year. Easy money was also a major contributor to the change in the housing market, the next item on the list.

(2) *Housing.* This is one of the few activities that the Government can juggle quickly. The Administration and Congress together took a series of actions reducing down payments in connection with mortgages insured by the Government, reviving the moribund G. I. housing program and even providing $1 billion in mortgage money at subsidy rates through a special emergency program.

TOGETHER with the effect of easy money on the mortgage situation generally, these actions had a tremendous impact. Housing starts hit their low in February and then zoomed starting in May — in the face of a widespread belief that the market was pretty well saturated and that the recession was frightening potential buyers. There is no doubt whatever that the change in the housing market, in this recession as in the other two postwar recessions, contributed materially to recovery.

(3) *Highways.* As noted, this program was already rolling as a result of past actions. The big anti-recession program did, however, begin to have some effect on new contracts by, perhaps, June. The major effect, just the same, will be in 1959 and afterward.

(4) *Public works speed-up.* It is doubtful whether all the the actions taken and the flood of directives from the White House resulted in the addition of much more than $300,000,000 to total spending in the economy, and much of that is still to come.

(5) *Emergency unemployment compensation.* This was the legislation providing additional weeks of jobless pay for workers who had exhausted their benefits. It was undoubtedly warranted on humanitarian grounds alone, but Congress took so long passing it that by the time the first benefits were paid, in late June, recovery had already started. The program will, however, help to add steam as the recovery proceeds.

The fruit of most, though not all, of these items showed in a single, all-important statistic: personal incomes. While industrial production fell off 13 per cent from peak to trough, personal income fell off only 1.6 per cent. It was actually on the rise from

ON THE JOB—The American economy showed enormous resiliency in weathering the recession, but nothing has happened to rule out future slumps.

March onward, and by July had passed its former peak. This was the reason for the strength of personal consumption throughout the recession, and thus the explanation of why the vicious downward spiral never had a chance to take hold.

* * *

SO much for the anatomy of recovery. What has the 1957-58 recession taught us about the modern American economy?

Undoubtedly the most important lesson is also the most obvious: the modern economy is still very susceptible to the business cycle. Nothing has happened to rule out slumps. We shall undoubtedly have more of them from time to time.

THIS "fact of life" produces something of a split in the academic and political worlds. One school believes all slumps are a tragic waste and can be avoided by proper governmental measures — both improved built-in stabilizers and vigorous and massive action at the earliest stages of a downturn. Another, and almost certainly larger, school feels mild slumps are preferable to the probable results of the type of governmental action needed to prevent them altogether: namely, inflation far worse than we have had.

Whichever school one prefers, it seems likely that in practice the second school will prevail, and that we shall go on having slumps. They are probably inherent in our economic system.

Another lesson is that one of the new factors in the economy that was supposed to make us more slump-proof is clearly not as potent as some analysts had thought it. It concerns the key sector of business investment in plant and equipment.

The new factor, so the theory went, was that modern business men schedule their investment on a long-term basis and do not change their plans with the first sign of economic squalls. Well, perhaps some of them do. But enough do not, as evidenced in this recession, to make business investment almost as volatile a part of the economy as ever.

THE evidence comes from a comparison of reported investment plans, as surveyed by the Government, and actual spending. Total investment spending in the first and second quarter of 1958 was a whopping $5 billion, at annual rates, below the originally reported intentions last fall and winter. The conclusion is clear: a very large number of businesses took fright and halted their investment, thus making the slump worse.

The next lesson from the recession is equally disconcerting. It emerges from the rundown of factors that brought recovery—the tremendous role of luck. Next time, there might not be such a favorable combination of events. In the 1953-54 recession, incidentally, the most important single action helping to bring recovery was a $5 billion tax cut that took effect in January, 1954, under an automatic provision of existing law that had nothing to do with recession.

Finally, on the unhappy side, this recession strongly bolstered evidence from the 1953-54 slump that in the modern economy prices are strongly resistant to drops in demand. Price cuts, except in the case of sensitive raw commodities that operate on a fairly pure supply-and-demand basis, were few and far between. The consumer price index, influenced by "lagging" service prices and by special factors affecting food, actually rose.

The disquieting lesson is not so much this rise as the failure of prices in the industrial part of the economy to fall. What happened to prices, incidentally, also happened to wages, and this helped considerably in preserving a high level of personal incomes.

BUT there are also some rather more comforting conclusions to be drawn from this slump.

Again, the most important is perhaps the most obvious: the built-in stabilizers actually work. Mainly because of legislated changes, but partly because of new ways of operating in the modern economy, such as the shifting of the labor force, the economy clearly has strong resistance to recession. The stabilizers will surely work next time, too, though few economists believe they are enough to do the whole job of preventing severe trouble by themselves.

Furthermore, the 1957-58 recession should have put to rest for good the idea that "when America sneezes, Europe catches pneumonia." Europe's international balance of payments actually strengthened throughout the slump. The pound sterling has never been stronger since the end of World War II.

THIS slump showed, too, what a number of economists have been suspecting for quite some time—that automobiles are by no means decisive in the American economy. The myth of the importance of Detroit is an extremely hard one to shake, but the fact is that production of new cars makes up well under 5 per cent of our total economy. The figures put out by the industry to the effect that one out of seven workers makes his living directly or indirectly from the automobile are misleading in one sense because they include such people as gasoline station operators and repair men, whose business suffers not a jot by a slump in new car sales.

It is true, of course, that the bad reception of the 1958 model cars contributed to the slump (although the money that was not spent on cars was spent on other things, contributing to prosperity for other sectors of the economy, ranging from travel agencies to food processors). But the important thing is that a decisive recovery began and is continuing without any improvement at all in the auto sector.

The next lesson is a bit less clear-cut. But it seems safe to conclude that the "confidence" factor—as it affects the consumer—is working in the modern economy against slump and for recovery. This item probably should not be overrated. But because of a feeling of job security, or whatever, consumers as a whole kept right on spending all through the slump, despite all the talk about the enormous amount of "discretionary" spending that now exists in America. A University of Michigan survey concluded:

"While a larger proportion of American workers have been affected by this recession than at any time since World War II, the amazing thing is that a generally optimistic attitude continued to prevail, in spite of large economic losses."

Finally, there is the happy thought that the Government did not even try the most drastic weapon it has—a tax cut. Needless to say, the decision of the President and Treasury Secretary Anderson against using this weapon has been thoroughly vindicated by events. But if, next time, the luck factors should not be as favorable, the tax weapon would always be available. It can rapidly create a significantly large amount of demand, and there is good reason to hope—though still no proof—that it could do the job if a future slump became bad enough to require its use.

ADDING up these lessons from the 1957-58 recession, the observer is almost forced to the conclusion that the ever present threat of a cumulative decline—that is, a severe depression—has not yet been abolished from the system, and that good management as well as good luck is going to be required when the business cycle again starts on its ominous way. The American economy clearly has enormous strength and resiliency—a fact worthy of no small feeling of satisfaction. But this has not been the last time that it will suffer a severe stomach ache.

What Kind of Economy Is It?

The members of the President's Council of Economic Advisers talk about the state of the nation's economy and the Government's role in keeping that economy healthy.

The great influence of Government policy on the nation's economy—especially in the recent months of recession—has made the Council of Economic Advisers one of the key groups in Washington. Set up by the Full Employment Act in 1946, the three-man council is charged with advising the President on the health of the economy, recommending to him policies for economic growth and stability and evaluating the Federal Government's economic programs.

The present members are Chairman Walter W. Heller, 45, former chairman of the University of Minnesota's Economics Department; Kermit Gordon, 44, former Professor of Economics at Williams College; and James Tobin, 43, former Professor of Economics at Yale.

The ideas of the council members were probed during a morning's conversation in Washington with Harry Schwartz of The New York Times editorial board. The main points touched on in that conversation are reported herewith; the questions are those put by Mr. Schwartz.

KEY MEN—The Council of Economic Advisers keeps the President posted on the state of the economy and recommends policy. From the left are Kermit Gordon, Chairman Walter W. Heller and James Tobin.

WHAT KIND OF ECONOMY?

What kind of economy do we have? Is our economy a welfare state, free enterprise or a planned economy?

MR. HELLER: First of all, let us avoid labels. What one person means by a welfare state or planned economy may be very different from another person's meaning.

Clearly this Government has substantial planning and economic control powers. But for the most part it is rather indirect.

MR. TOBIN: There is a lot of private enterprise in the country and a smaller amount of public enterprise. It is a mixed economy in which decisions are made by a whole range of units, including different levels of government, different kinds of businesses and millions of ordinary families.

MR. HELLER: This mixture is the source both of our economy's strength and of its weaknesses. What we produce is decided by the meeting of supply and demand in the market place. The result is that we satisfy consumers' demands efficiently for the most part. The private economy works well here. But, on the other hand, the same mixed mechanism is subject to such occasional ills as excessive unemployment and inflation.

Government in our economy is primarily concerned with providing such services as defense, education, protection against fire and theft, and the like. These are of a different character from the goods and services the private economy produces for individual consumption. For example, the benefits of education flow in large part to the community as a whole in the form of a sound base for democratic government and a stronger economy. These are benefits we can't sell through the market place.

HOW MUCH PLANNING?

Granted we have a mixed economy, where is our economy likely to go in the future? President Kennedy recently said that the purpose of his Labor-Management Advisory Committee "is to give direction to the general movement of wages and prices so that the general welfare of this country can be served." Isn't this an approach to increased government planning?

MR. HELLER: I think this has to be looked at bearing two facts in mind. One is the problem we have of creeping inflation. The second is the limited power the Government has to enter bargaining over wages and prices, except where there is an element of conspiracy or monopoly.

What the President is saying is that he hopes

through the Labor-Management Advisory Committee to find a middle way in which both labor and management will exercise a certain amount of voluntary self-restraint in order to serve the interests of the people as a whole.

MR. GORDON: The President is being realistic. These days, the existence of powerful unions and large corporations introduces an element of discretion in the determination of prices and wages. The old idea of prices and wages being determined by impersonal forces in the market place often does not describe the realities. Moreover, the decisions made by large corporations and unions as regards prices and wages affect our competitive position in world markets where we have been having problems.

Is it realistic to expect that because a small group such as the Labor-Management Committee agrees that there should be, say, no more than a 3 per cent increase in wages in a given year unions and management will go along voluntarily?

MR. TOBIN: The labor-management group may strengthen the forces in the private economy making for wage and price stability. It may be able to provide guidelines or leadership which will be helpful without any powers of compulsion.

MR. GORDON: My belief is that we simply have to feel our way slowly and cautiously. The object is to generate in labor and management understanding of the important relationship between their decisions and broad national goals. I see no evidence that this is hopeless.

Do we have broad national goals? Are they implicit or explicit?

MR. GORDON: We have both explicit goals and implicit ones. The Full Employment Act, for example, represents a consensus on the importance of maintaining high employment. There is, I think, something close to national agreement on the desirability of more rapid growth in production than we have had recently. Implicit in the Employment Act, I think, is the goal of reasonable price stability.

MR. HELLER: To reach these goals in a market-oriented economy we have to show a capacity for creative experimentation. The labor-management group has one advantage worth noting at this time. It has begun work in a period when inflationary forces are weak, and this gives it a chance to make plans before inflationary pressures build up again.

The group involved is small, but it is certainly composed of very high-level people from business, labor and government. The President and the Administration have given it an importance far beyond anything of the sort ever known before. This gives me hope the experiment may be successful.

MR. GORDON: As for the desirability of extending direct price controls over more industries: at an earlier stage in my bureaucratic career I spent two highly educational years in the Office of Price Administration. Anybody who endured that ordeal came out of it, I think, with a deep-seated aversion to expansion of direct control over prices where there was any sensible way to avoid it and still achieve a relatively efficient performance.

But I want to be correctly understood. The market alone can't solve all problems, and sometimes it needs help.

It's as much of a mistake to be blind to particular limitations of the free market as it is to underestimate its great power for good.

PUBLIC SPENDING?

Professor Galbraith's book "The Affluent Society" paid a lot of attention to the need for changing the proportions in our society between private consumption of luxuries and public spending on things such as education. What do you think of this problem?

MR. TOBIN: I would say there is a good case for saying that we overemphasize private consumption as against certain items of public investment and consumption. I certainly would not say that there is no value to increased private consumption as well. There certainly is value to it, especially concentrated in the areas of poverty and need that still exist all through our society.

How can the proportions in our economy be changed? Do you levy higher taxes, or what?

MR. HELLER: We are fortunate to have a Federal tax system which probably generates all the revenue needed, and more in the long run, for the kind of public services that we are referring to. As our national production expands, Federal tax revenues grow more than proportionately, in part because of the increasingly high rates on higher individual incomes.

This raises an interesting long-run prospect if the cold war doesn't worsen. If our production increases, we can have the kind of improvements and expansion of our public services that make for efficient use of our resources, greater human well-being, and reduced poverty, and yet at the same time we can reduce taxes, if we so choose.

Federal Government spending in recent years has been a shrinking portion of our total national income. If our aim for the future were to keep the spending of all governmental units — Federal, State and local—at a constant proportion of rising national income, a cut in Federal taxes would have to be compensated in part by increased state and local taxes.

The point might be best made by noting that if our economy were operating at reasonably full employment today, our Federal budget would be running a surplus of about $10.000.000,000 a year.

MR. TOBIN: The problem of level of government is important. State and local governments are not as well provided with elastic sources of revenue as is the Federal Government. We need grants in aid from the Federal to the state governments because many of the services we want to improve in the area of public consumption—education, for instance—are responsibilities of state and local governments.

THE OLD COMPETITION?

Monopolistic practices by some businesses—price fixing for example—have been the subject of much publicity and Government attention recently. Can we hope to restore the kind of competitive economy Adam Smith wrote about almost two centuries ago?

MR. GORDON: My personal answer is, No. Any such hope is illusory.

I do think however that there are major areas of the economy which are now under close public regulation which should be re-examined to see if we can allow them to be governed to a greater extent by competitive forces. We ought to look at changes in technology and changes in demand to see if areas that needed public regulation in the past still need it today.

For example, I feel that technological changes in transportation have been of such a fundamental character that it is almost certain that a structure of regulation appropriate for the year 1920 is not appropriate for the year 1961.

What about those who argue that we can't really depend on the Anti-Trust Acts to produce real competition?

MR. GORDON: I think the anti-trust laws have had a far greater impact than such people realize. If anyone questions that, I suggest comparing the competitive tone of markets in this country with the tone of markets in Western Europe where there has been no anti-trust tradition.

MR. HELLER: In my work in Germany, I was struck by the existence of gentlemen's agreements in many industries where, apparently, competition is not supposed to get too rough. This, I think, is changing to some extent. The Europeans are showing more interest in the anti-trust approach.

MR. TOBIN: We should also encourage competition from imports. Free markets should extend across international boundaries. We have seen some recent examples of the healthy effect of import com-

petition on American business firms.

How do your remarks on the desirability of competition square with the Administration's farm policy, which seems to be a continuation of the long tradition of increasing Government economic planning in agriculture?

MR. GORDON: I'm not close enough to the details to want to pronounce on particular measures, but I do feel that agriculture is an area in which the free market does not work well. One reason is that productivity has been increasing so fast on our farms—far faster than have our markets for farm products.

Now, if the competitive market system worked ideally, there would be a steady flow of people and investment out of agriculture into other sectors of the economy where the productivity of these resources would be greater. In fact, there has been such a movement, but it hasn't worked fast enough to relieve the strain on the market.

When manufacturers of electrical equipment get together to fix prices and output, they are fined or jailed. But farmers are encouraged to get together and do what looks like much the same thing. Should there not be equality of treatment?

MR. GORDON: I think there is a big difference between the market for electrical equipment and the market for wheat.

MR. HELLER: Yes, but, even more, this isn't the conspiracy of farm groups to gouge the public which the question implies. Agricultural policy is set within the framework and under the eye of the Department of Agriculture and of the Government in general.

MR. TOBIN: Another reason the Government has to do something for the farmers is that we can't solve our farm-surplus problems by export even when our crops are competitive. Other countries also have farmers who exert political influence for protection, and often get it.

THE SOVIET CHALLENGE?

What about Premier Khrushchev's boast that he is going to outproduce us in the next decade?

MR. HELLER: We have done pretty well in the past, but our feeling is that we can do better in the future than we are doing right now.

We have to keep the economy more nearly at full employment and full production. The Kennedy Administration is dedicated to this goal. The President has said specifically that at least as an intermediate objective we want to get back to a 4 per cent level of unemployment as against our nearly 7 per cent rate now. This implies $50,000,000,000 more of output annually than our present level of about $500,000,000,000.

MR. TOBIN: I don't accept the idea that we need the same rate of growth as the Soviet Union. The struggle between the two worlds isn't going to be won in the statistical handbooks. Still, we have got to give a demonstration that a free society, a decentralized society, can do things which serve the national purpose, such as increasing its rate of growth. Also, I think we must accelerate the rates of growth of the under-developed countries even more.

MR. HELLER: In part the Soviet performance is a matter of an economy in an earlier stage of development than ours having a naturally faster rate of growth. But if the Soviet rate of production growth is, as the best data seem to suggest, about 6 or 7 per cent annually, clearly we can't be satisfied with 2½ or 3 per cent. Our immediate potential rate of growth is 3½ per cent, if we just take account of normal increases in the labor force and in productivity per worker. The President wants this country to realize its 3½ per cent potential, and then substantially improve on it.

We also have the problem of the division of this desired growth among different uses. The President's programs have already made clear that one of the most important uses of our economic growth must be more public investment in human beings—in education, training, health and the like. These improve human well-being at the same time that they sow the seeds of faster growth.

Is there any reasonable prospect that the Soviet economy will outproduce the United States economy in the next decade or two?

MR. HELLER: The Soviets can outproduce us in the next 25 years only if we fall miserably short of our potential and if they maintain their present high growth rate of 6 per cent per year. One of the major jobs facing the country today is to step up our present growth rate of 3½ per cent substantially. Many of this Administration's proposals—tax incentives, aid to education, resource development, stimulation of research—are designed to accomplish this end. Success in these efforts would mean that the Soviets would not catch up with us in this century.

* * *

MR. SCHWARTZ: Let me try to summarize. The key to many of our problems—agricultural, industrial, cold war, etc.—is the attainment of full employment, or something close to it, and a faster growth rate. You gentlemen think this can be done without substantial changes in basic American institutions. Outside of agriculture, you favor increased competition and more vigorous enforcement of the anti-trust laws.

MR. HELLER: That's a good summary. I would add that the Government has to make full and intelligent use of its indirect monetary and fiscal controls to keep the economy moving toward these goals of full employment and rapid growth.

July 23, 1961

PRESIDENT FINDS ECONOMY GAINING UNDER HIS POLICY; CALLS FOR FASTER GROWTH

Incentives to Business Among Proposals in Annual Report

By RICHARD E. MOONEY
Special to The New York Times.

WASHINGTON, Jan. 22 — President Kennedy reported confidently today that the economy was responding well to his Administration's efforts to foster its growth. He proposed new measures to prevent too fast or too slow a pace.

"The momentum in our economy has been restored," the President said. He added that the means to "sustain our prosperity and accelerate our growth" were within reach.

These means were detailed in his first annual Economic Report to Congress and a companion report by his three-man Council of Economic Advisers.

The bulk of the President's program consisted of the many measures he has initiated or proposed in his first year in office. These include enlarged Federal programs, tax incentives, direct aid for those who are "short-changed" even in good times, and money and credit conditions to stimulate investment.

Outlines His Program

He said that the long-term pace of economic growth could be lifted to 4½ per cent a year during the Nineteen Sixties.

His council indicated that it could be increased even more.

The growth rate has been 3½ per cent, on the average, since World War II—higher in the earlier years and lower more recently.

To guard against recessions, the President detailed the three proposals he had set forth in his State of the Union Message two weeks ago—Presidential authority to cut taxes, authority to increase spending for public works, and a strengthening of the unemployment insurance program.

He noted that the economy had spent seven out of the last fifteen years making up ground lost in the four postwar recessions, and that the rate of unemployment had been greater than 4 per cent in two months out of every three.

"We must do better in the Nineteen Sixties," he said.

To guard against inflation, the council laid down price and wage "guideposts" to restrain big companies and strong unions. The guideposts were not a specific formula applicable to all cases, but a statement of principles and conditions.

Inflation Danger Cited

The general principle is that wage and "fringe benefit" gains should be kept within the postwar average of gains in productivity—output per man per hour—for the whole private economy, and that industries with above-average productivity gains should cut prices. The postwar average has been 3 per cent.

"Our success in solving the international payments problem will depend to a major extent on our ability to avoid inflation," the council said.

One of the four chapters of the council's report was devoted to the payments problem alone. References to it were made throughout both reports.

The United States' balance of international payments—the relationship of money flowing into and out of the country—has shown large deficits for the last four years.

Dr. Walter W. Heller, the council's chairman, reported at a news conference that the 1961 deficit was $2,400,000,000—the net result of a sharp improvement at the start of the year and a worsening as the year progressed. The previous three years' deficits had been $3,500,000,000 and greater.

President Kennedy said he was "hopeful" that a reasonable balance could be restored within the next two years.

Third Message of Month

The Economic Report is the third of three—following the State of the Union and the Budget Message—that the President is required to submit to Congress each January.

In the Eisenhower years the Council's report and the President's were one, signed by the President. The filing of a separate report by President Kennedy's economists today permitted them to express their own ideas more freely than could be done in the name of the President.

The council presented 4.9 per cent as an attainable growth rate, but not a prediction. The President said 4½ per cent was "in the range of our capabilities." The two reports were substantially the same, however, differing mostly in the council's greater length, detail and philosophizing.

Reviewing 1961, the reports gave the Administration high marks.

"The task before us [last January] was to recover not from one recession but from two" because recovery from the 1958 recession had stopped before it was complete, the President said.

The gap between the nation's economic capacity and its lagging rate of activity has been narrowed by nearly one-half, he went on. Unemployment is down, prices have been stable, and "confidence in the dollar has been restored," he said.

On policy, the President cited his balanced budget for the fiscal year 1963, beginning July 1, as evidence that fiscal (tax and spending) policy "is assuming a large share of the burden of forestalling inflationary excesses of demand."

That was an indirect way of saying that monetary policy, exercised by the Federal Reserve system, need not be so "tight," or interest rates so high, as in the past.

The council said that the 1961 experience had demonstrated that the budget was "a flexible tool" that can be adjusted during the year, and that interest rates "do not have to rise sharply" in a business recovery.

In fact, the council said, 1961 "may have signaled the ending of the upward trend in rates from the low levels at which they were pegged" until 1951.

The President made only two specific proposals with regard to the Federal Reserve. He recommended that the seven governors of the system be paid more, and that the chairman serve a four-year term coinciding with the Presidential term, starting in 1965. Their terms now overlap each other by two years.

The two terms used to coincide but were thrown off by mid-term changes in the chairmanship. Mr. Kennedy said that William M. C. Martin Jr., the present chairman, agreed that the terms should match. Mr. Martin's term expires next year.

The salary and chairmanship proposals were based on last June's report of the Commission on Money and Credit—a privately financed group.

The President also suggested that Congress "examine carefully" the commission's proposals to remove the ceilings on the national debt and on Government bond interest rates, and the requirement that a certain amount of gold be kept in official reserve.

He also said he would set up three special groups in the Government to study the commission's ideas on the regulation of banks and similar institutions, Federal loan and guarantee programs, and corporate and other private retirement programs.

Looking ahead, the President said that "we face 1962 with optimism but not complacency." In the first half of the year, he said, "vigorous expansion in production and incomes" is expected. In the second half, "business investment in plant and equipment should pick up speed."

The council's report went into the prospects for 1963 and beyond. It indicated that the 4 per cent rate of unemployment predicted for mid-1963 meant an over-all $600,000,000,000 rate of activity then, and that the potential for 1970, was $825,000,000,000.

"Faster economic growth in the United States requires, above all, an expansion of demand, to take up existing slack and to match future increases in capacity," the council said.

'Concerted Effort

"A full employeemnt economy can achieve more rapid growth than an economy alternating between boom and recession. . . * * * But [stabilizing] is not enough. A sustained inprovement in the growth rate requires also a concerted effort, private and public, to speed the increase of potential output."

To increase potential capacity, the council discussed expanded education and health programs, elimination of racial discrimination, increased research and development, and greater investment in business plant and equipment, natural resources, and housing.

The President described his three anti-recession measures as "the greatest step forward in public policy for economic stability" since the Government—in the employment committed itself in the Employment Act of 1946 to promote "maximum employment, production and purchasing power."

It is generally agreed here, however that Congress will not enact the package this year.

The tax proposal would authorize the President, subject to Congressional veto within thirty days, to cut personal income rates by one-to-five points across-the-board. A five-point cut for six months would release $5,000,000,000 at today's levels of income.

The simple way for an individual to figure what his share would be is to calculate 5 per cent of his taxable income, and divide it in half because the cut would be for six months unless renewed.

The authority to step up public works spending would be tied to a formula based on unemployment trends. Unemployment would have to rise in three out of four (or four out of six) months, and would have to rise at least one percentage point in a four-month or six-month period.

Conditions would have fit the formula within four months of the start of each of the postwar recessions, the President said. Authority to start the actual spending would rest with the President. If there were false signals, such as a major strike, he could hold off.

The $2,000,000,000 would be divided this way: up to $750,000,000 for Federal projects already authorized, up to $750,000,000 for matching grants for existing or planned state and local projects, and up to $250,000,000 for loans to state and local governments that could not meet their matching shares. The remaining $250,000,000 could be used for any of those purposes.

The unemployment benefit strengthening—all proposed previously—would extend coverage to 3,000,000 more workers, make permanent the program of extra Federal benefits when recessions hit, require states to meet minimum standards for weekly payments, and increase the employers' tax that finances the program.

Advisers Offer an Outline Of Wage-Price Restraints

Economic Council Would Rule Out Raises Above Productivity and Govern Prices by Related Standard

Special to The New York Times.

WASHINGTON, Jan. 22—President Kennedy's economic advisers pleaded again today for a common front in the fight against inflation. They supported their appeal by laying down general guidelines for restraint on wages and prices.

The Council of Economic Advisers said that the rate of increase in wages in any industry should not exceed the trend in the rate of productivity for industry generally.

For example, if productivity in industry generally is found to be rising 3 per cent a year, the council indicated, an industry with a 6 per cent productivity rise still should limit wage rate increases to 3 per cent and cut prices, unless there were sound reasons to the contrary.

Since the end of World War II, productivity generally has risen at the rate of 3 per cent a year. For some industries it has risen more, for some less. If the 3 per cent rule were applied generally, the high productivity industries would still limit wage increases to 3 per cent.

As a general guide to price adjustments, the council said that price reductions were in order if an industry's rate of productivity exceeded the over-all rate, for this would mean declining labor costs in that industry. The guide would sanction an appropriate increase in price if the productivity rate of an industry failed to match a general rise in productivity.

There was no mention of wage reductions in the council's report.

The council emphasized that it was offering guides, not rules or mechanical formulas, and that the guides were general ones.

Even so, the report set out, in more detail perhaps than ever before in peacetime, what the Administration meant by a productivity guide in determining the size of wage increases.

President Eisenhower's Administration, and the Kennedy Administration until today, had urged productivity gains as the outer limits of wage gains. But they did not define clearly what was meant and did not recognize the many variables that enter into specific cases.

Productivity, as distinguished from production, means the rate of output rather than the volume of output. Generally this is measured on a man-per-hour basis.

This does not mean that the individual worker is the controlling factor in the rate of output. More and more, as mechanization progresses, the rate of output is determined by the employer's investment in capital machinery.

In the total private economy, the productivity trend has been on the rise since measurements began. However, the rate of rise has not been steady.

Thus, while productivity has risen at an average annual rate of 3 per cent since World War II, it has risen only 2.4 per cent since 1909 and only 2.6 per cent since 1954.

Members of the council, in a session with newsmen, indicated that the intermediate period, 1947-1960, was the logical base now for measuring productivity against wage-rate increases.

At the same time, the council's report recognized that the immediate future might bring substantially higher productivity rates. Historically, in the emerging from a recession, productivity rates, as well as production, move up faster than the long-term trend.

In writing about wage rates, the council made clear that it included fringe benefits, such as pensions, medical plans, and holidays. It spoke of wage rates, rather than wages, so there was no implication that workers should refrain from raising their wage income by working more hours or days.

The council, though aware of the impending wage negotiations in the steel industry and their pattern-setting possibilities, avoided mentioning any particular industry.

January 23, 1962

BUSINESS TAXES ARE CUT 1.5 BILLION BY TREASURY; DIVIDEND-LEVY PLAN FAILS

WRITE-OFFS SPED

Step on Depreciation Is Intended to Spur Economic Growth

By JOHN D. MORRIS
Special to The New York Times.

WASHINGTON, July 11 — The Kennedy Administration gave business a $1,500,000,000 tax cut today in the form of more liberal allowances for depreciation of machinery and equipment.

The Treasury issued new rules and guidelines that will enable business concerns and individual business men, including farmers and other self-employed persons, to deduct the cost of machinery and equipment from their taxable income more rapidly than most of them are now permitted to do.

The Treasury's action, culminating years of study that began during the Eisenhower Administration, was a long-awaited and welcome gesture to business.

It was designed to stimulate investment in modern and more efficient facilities, and thus increase the country's productivity, spur economic growth and employment and enable American producers to compete more effectively for world markets.

Statement by Kennedy

President Kennedy declared.

"By encouraging American business to replace its machinery more rapidly, we hope to make American products more cost-competitive, to step up our rate of recovery and growth and to provide expanded job opportunities for all American workers."

While the new depreciation procedures are aimed at achieving long-range goals, officials said they were likely to have an immediate impact on the lagging national economy.

Secretary of the Treasury Douglas Dillon declined to estimate the extent of the impact either immediately or over the long range.

However, he observed at a news conference that Roger M. Blough, board chairman of the United States Steel Corporation, had recently said that the steel industry would immediately invest the entire tax saving in new equipment.

This alone would amount to about $40,000,000 in the next twelve months, Mr. Dillon noted.

If the year's over-all tax savings of $1,500,000,000 were similarly invested, according to Administration economists, an increase of at least $3,750,000,000 in the gross national product would result, and employment would rise proportionately.

The gross national product is the dollar value of all goods and services produced in a year. The present rate is about $544,000,000,000.

Some economists believe the actual increase in the gross national product over the long run might range as high as

$15,000,000,000 a year under the new depreciation rules.

President Kennedy and Secretary Dillon issued statements in which they emphasized that the new depreciation procedures represented only half of a two-part plan.

The other part, a special tax credit on new outlays for machinery and equipment, is embodied in a tax revision bill passed by the House on March 29 and now before the Senate Finance Committee.

The committee approved the bill's tax-credit provisions today.

In his statement on the new depreciation procedures, President Kennedy quoted estimates by some business spokesmen that perhaps as much as four times the amount of tax savings would be invested in new machinery and equipment.

"In any event," the President said, "it is clear that at least an equal amount will go into new income-producing investment and eventually return to the Government in tax revenues most, if not all of the initial costs."

The President and other officials estimated that the new procedures would automatically permit "more rapid and more realistic depreciation" on 70 to 80 per cent of the machinery and equipment of business men and farmers.

No legislation is needed in the establishment of new guidelines for depreciation. Tax law gives business "reasonable" deductions for depreciation and the Treasury is empowered to determine what is reasonable.

The Treasury action represented the first time since 1942 that the tax depreciation system had been overhauled by administrative action. The last major changes were made by legislation in 1954. A law passed in that year allowed greater deductions in the first few years of the "useful life" of business facilities.

The useful life of such an asset is the number of years over which tax deductions for depreciation must be spread. Until today, the guidelines established in 1942 for determining the useful, or depreciable, lives of more than 5,000 separate items had been in effect without change except for a few additions and revisions last fall for the textile industry.

The items were listed in a green-covered Treasury pamphlet entitled Bulletin F. They ranged from mules, which were assigned useful lives of ten years, to blast furnaces, fifteen years, and warehouses, seventy-five years.

In today's action, the Treasury replaced Bulletin F with a maroon-covered pamphlet destined to be known by tax lawyers and accountants as "Revenue Procedure 62-21."

The new bulletin substitutes fewer than 100 categories of depreciable property for the old pamphlet's 5,000 items.

However, there are still a number of individual items, such as "horses, breeding or work, ten years" and "portable sawmills, six years."

The average depreciable life of manufacturing assets listed in the 1942 bulletin was about nineteen years. But many companies, by individual negotiations with the Internal Revenue Service, were permitted to use shorter lives. The actual average, according to Treasury estimates, is now about fifteen years.

The guidelines published today allow an average life of about twelve years, according to Under Secretary Henry H. Fowler.

All taxpayers, under the new rules, will be allowed to switch to depreciable lives as short as those specified by the new guidelines, and pay taxes on that basis, for at least three years without challenge by the Internal Revenue Service.

At the end of three years, the Internal Revenue Service will use an arithmetical formula to indicate whether the guidelines are suitable in individual cases. Known as the "reserve ratio" formula, it is designed to determine whether the depreciation deductions taken by a concern are consistent with its actual practice in retiring and replacing machinery and equipment.

If the ratio exceeds designated levels, the taxpayer will be subject to possible increases in the useful lives over which his tax deductions must be spread. However, the reserve ratio test will be used as a guide rather than a binding rule, the Treasury said. Individual taxpayers, officials explained, may be able to justify more advantageous treatment by presenting other pertinent facts and circumstances.

Some taxpayers already are taking deductions at a faster rate than the newly published guidelines suggest. They may continue to do so, the Treasury said.

Other taxpayers now within the guidelines may want to go beyond them and are free to do so, officials said, if the reserve ratio formula does not indicate that their new depreciation rates are too fast. In that event, other pertinent facts and circumstances will be weighed before a change is ordered.

The same considerations will prevail, the Treasury said, in cases where taxpayers are already taking deductions at a faster rate than the guidelines suggest and decide to move to an even faster basis.

Penalty taxes no longer will be imposed on those who claim depreciation deductions at a faster rate than the Internal Revenue Service determines to be justified. Instead, the service will merely adjust future deductions to compensate for any such miscalculations.

The procedures are effective tomorrow. That is, they may be applied to all tax returns due after last April 1 and returns returns for the calendar year 1962 as well as corporation returns for fiscal years starting after last April 1 and returns by nonincorporated businesses for fiscal years starting after last March 31.

Secretary Dillon said nearly all of the initial $1,500,000,000 in reduced taxes would be reflected in lower Treasury revenues in the present Federal fiscal year, which started July 1. This removed any remaining hope that the budget for the year would be balanced. President Kennedy projected a precarious surplus of $500,000,000 last January. The revenue loss from today's action alone will assure a deficit of at least $1,000,000,000.

Mr. Dillon declined to estimate the revenue effect in future years. He noted that increased depreciation allowances would exceed $1,500,000,000 a year if the desired increases in new outlays for machinery and equipment resulted. However, he said, the resulting rise in economic activity would yield greater total revenues and probably offset any long-run loss.

July 12, 1962

New Expense Cuts Abroad Will Be Made to Aid Dollar

Administration Plans Another Slash of Billion in 2 Years Starting July 1 —Defense Budget Mirrors Aim

By JACK RAYMOND
Special to The New York Times.

WASHINGTON, Dec. 25 — The Administration is planning to cut overseas dollar expenses $1,000,000,000 more in the next two fiscal years beginning July 1, 1963.

The plan is part of intensified efforts to reduce the aggravating deficit in that part of the balance of payments that the United States attributes to the cost of maintaining huge military forces overseas.

The balance of payments is based on this country's dollar income from overseas compared with dollar expenses abroad.

The Administration already had slashed some military expenditures overseas and expects that $1,000,000,000 in foreign exchange costs will have been saved in the two-year period ending next June 30.

With increasing stringent controls on military spending, abroad, the Administration has set a goal of saving $1,000,000,-more in the succeeding two fiscal years.

Thus, it is hoped, the defense deficity of $3,000,000,000 a year in the international balance of payments will be reduced to about $1,000,000,000 by July 1, 1965.

So determined is the Administration to cut overseas dollar expenses that for the first time the huge defense budget has been prepared with an eye to such expenses.

Assistant Secretary of Defense Charles J. Hitch, the Pentagon controller, disclosed the following to the Joint Congressional Economic Committee's subcommittee on international exchange and payments the other day: "The [military] service requests have been reviewed not only for their budgetary implications but also for their foreign exchange costs.

"Literally hundreds of individual decisions which Secretary [Robert S.] McNamara has made on the tentative 1964 military program have been made in full knowledge of their likely impact on the United States balance of payments."

In the months ahead, Mr. Hitch said, the Pentagon hopes to "refine and perfect" its techniques for studying the fine exchange implications of "every major program choice" that is made in the Department of Defense.

This country's basic balance of payments problem covers more than overseas military costs and is caused primarily by decreasing export trade. During the years 1958-1961, the deficit totaled more than $13,500,000,000.

Leaders note the Eisenhower and Kennedy Administrations have stressed that continued deficits would endanger the position of the dollar as the world's chief reserve currency.

Mr. Hitch pointed out that the problem was of special interest to defense planners "as continued large deficits would jeopardize our ability to maintain our overseas deployment and thereby threaten to undermine the entire mutual security structure of the free world."

Administration officials believe that the most promising method of reducing the military factor in the net adverse balance of payments is to encourage the Allies to buy military equipment from the United States.

In that connection they are specially pleased with the agreement of the West German Government to extend through the calendar year 1964 an agreement to buy arms in this country in an amount that would offset a dollar drain of $675,000,000 a year in that country. A recent Italian agreement to do the same for a total of $100,000,000 is also cited.

The Pentagon also says that appeals o military and civilian personnel abroad to cut dollar spending have resulted in a savings estimated at $50.000.000 for the fiscal year 1962 that ended last June 30.

Reductions in procurement contracts placed abroad have resulted in the diversion of $71,400,000 worth of business to United States producers, it was explained. The additional cost in dollars was about $10,400,000. Officials believed it was worth spending the extra money to avoid the negative effect on the balance of payments.

The Pentagon also explained that reductions in military assistance - offshore - procurement expenditures—that is, the buying of equipment in one country to help another—were made to the extent of about $25,000,000 in the fiscal year 1961.

Reviews of the need for certain overseas basis and for military construction to support the overseas forces has resulted in the announced intentions of closing 67 installations with ultimate foreign exchange saving of as much as $120,000,000 a year.

December 26, 1962

ECONOMIC SURGE IS TAX CUT'S AIM

Nation Is Now Embarking on a Historic Experiment

By EDWIN L. DALE Jr.
Special to The New York Times

WASHINGTON, Feb. 26 — A stroke of President Johnson's pen today started the nation on what is probably the most important innovation and experiment in its economic history.

With the enactment of the $11.5 billion tax cut, after 13 months of debate and doubt, the United States has been firmly set on the road of economics developed nearly 30 years ago by the British economist John Maynard Keynes.

The essence of this modern economics is a change in the way a nation views its budget and its taxes. Tax rates are not set solely so as to make Government receipts balance expenditures. Rather, the rates are based on the state of the general economy.

Hence, in the present situation, the United States for the first time is cutting taxes at a time when the budget is already in deficit—an historic change of course. The purpose is to speed economic expansion and thus sharply reduce unemployment.

Reduction Was Automatic

The only previous occasion that was remotely comparable occurred in 1954, when a tax cut took place before the budget was in surplus. But at that time Government expenditures, after the Korean war, were turning sharply down. In addition, most of the tax reduction was automatic because existing legislation set a term on Korean war taxes.

Despite the unusual nature of today's economic experiment, the debate over the tax cut eventually developed a surprising consensus in favor of the reduction. At the end, the great bulk of the business and banking community, the organized labor movement and virtually the entire economics profession supported the experiment.

In part, this support was achieved through the growing conviction that the budget could never be balanced until the nation's rate of economic growth speeded up and generated more receipts.

It was increasingly accepted that recent American budget deficits were the result, not the cause, of the state of the economy. Sluggish growth, and above all recession, produced deficit after deficit as receipts failed to rise enough to match spending.

It was also increasingly accepted that a major reason for the sluggish growth was the existing high rates of taxation.

There were other reasons why the experiment was agreed upon by Congress. One was a growing realization that recent budget deficits had not been inflationary, as prices remained stable by comparison with the period up to 1957.

Another was the Administration's decision to seek a tax cut with a relatively conservative mixture, with a good part of the reduction going to corporations and high-bracket taxpayers.

Under the experiment, a deficit is deliberately created with the aim of eliminating the deficit in a few years through surging receipts from a surging economy. This will be the first purposeful American deficit in peacetime, the others having come about almost inadvertently.

Britain and some other countries have long used such a policy, with considerable success. A British tax cut enacted almost a year ago, at a time of a large budget deficit, has already sharply reduced unemployment and speeded industrial expansion. Receipts have already begun to rise.

The innovation in the United States is due mainly to the initiative and philosophy of the three men who made up President Kennedy's original Council of Economic Advisers—Walter W. Heller, James W. Tobin and Kermit Gordon.

After examining the American economy, they concluded that a major stimulus to overall demand, and hence spending power, was necessary to cure chronic unemployment. With the aid of one of their consultants, Charles L. Schultze, they developed the concept of the "full employment surplus."

This showed that, at present tax rates, the American economy, if it were working with full employment, would generate a huge budget surplus. It was this theoretical surplus that reflected the true restraining effect of the Government's overall budget upon demand and activity in the economy.

Even though the budgets continually showed deficits, which are supposed to be stimulative, the mixture of tax rates and spending levels was actually restrictive. This, in the council's view, was a major reason why unemployment was high.

Hard to Sway Kennedy

The three advisers had considerable difficulty in swinging President Kennedy to their viewpoint and an even more difficult time persuading Secretary of the Treasury Douglas Dillon. Although the council would have liked to have seen a tax cut very early in the Kennedy Administration, the decision to seek one was not made until the beginning of 1963.

If the experiment works as expected, it is probable that future tax changes to influence economic activity may be less difficult to get through Congress.

In most European countries with parliamentary systems, tax rate changes, both up and down, can be decided upon by the Prime Minister and his Cabinet and quickly enacted into law by the parliamentary majority to meet changes in the state of the economy.

But in the United States, as the last year has shown, such flexibility is difficult if not impossible to attain. This has meant that the United States has had to use the other main weapon of economic policy, monetary policy, more than other nations.

February 27, 1964

Johnson Signs Bill To Fight Poverty; Pledges New Era

By MARJORIE HUNTER
Special to The New York Times

WASHINGTON, Aug. 20 — A smiling President Johnson signed today his $947.5 million antipoverty bill.

It was a perfect summer morning, and the President moved the ceremony to the broad steps overlooking the White House Rose Garden.

There, squinting into the bright sun, he promised that "a new day of opportunity is dawning" for the nation's poor.

"The days of the dole in our country are numbered," he said.

The program is designed to wage a nationwide attack on poverty and its causes. It has been estimated there are between 30 million and 35 million Americans living in poverty or on its fringes.

Republicans Are Absent

Administration leaders have said the antipoverty program will attempt to "break the cycle of poverty" and make "taxpayers out of taxeaters."

Federal funds would be used for a variety of programs, including job training and basic education for idle young men and women, part-time jobs for teen-agers and college students, community antipoverty projects, loans to low-income farmers and businessmen and a domestic peace corps.

In explaining the goals of the program, Mr. Johnson has frequently referred to the words of the late Philip Murray, president of the Congress of Industrial Organizations. In speech after speech, the President has said:

"A great labor leader, Phil Murray, once said that about all the worker hopes for is a school that his children can attend, a church where his family can worship, a roof over their heads, some food for their bodies, a picture on the wall and a rug on the floor, and some music in the house."

It was the first major legislative program to come exclusively from his Administration, and the President beamed happily on the almost exclusively Democratic gathering.

Republican leaders in Congress had been invited, but did not attend. Republicans had fought the bill almost every step of the way on the ground that it was a "hodgepodge" and an election-year bid for votes.

Within hours after the antipoverty bill became law, the President's billion-dollar Appalachia bill was cleared by the House Rules Committee.

The bill, calling for a five-year program of highway construction and other economic aid for the depressed Appalachia region, is closely allied to the antipoverty program.

House leaders said the Appalachia measure would be taken up when Congress reconvened after next week's Democratic National Convention. The Senate has not yet acted on the bill.

Although the focus of the signing ceremony was on poverty, there were political currents in the air, too.

Standing side by side, right behind the President, Attorney General Robert F. Kennedy and Mayor Wagner of New York talked softly.

Later, they declined to say if they had discussed Mr. Kennedy's expected Senatorial candidacy from New York.

Also right behind Mr. Johnson was Senator Hubert H. Humphrey, Democrat of Minnesota, who may be the President's choice for Vice President.

McCarthy Present, Too

Farther back in the crowd was the other half of what he politicians are calling the "Minnesota twins"—Senator Eugene J. McCarthy, another Vice Presidential possibility.

Each received a pen, a long handshake and a few private words from the President.

Mr. Johnson made no direct reference to the Republican opposition to his antipoverty program.

But in an obvious reply to Senator Barry Goldwater's charge that it was "an attempt to reap political rewards," the President said:

"This is not in any sense a cynical proposal to exploit the poor with a promise of a handout or a dole."

Aware that others, outside the Republican ranks, have misgivings over whether the program will succeed, Mr. Johnson praised those who helped draft the bill and push it through Congress.

"In the days and years to come," he promised, "those who have an opportunity to participate in this program will vindicate your thinking and vindicate your action."

Pointing out that the program will seek to train and educate idle youths, help communities erase the causes of poverty, and aid low-income farmers and businessmen, the President said:

"We are not content to accept the endless growth of relief rolls or welfare rolls. We want to offer the forgotten fifth of our people opportunity and not doles."

The program, he said, would help the poor to lift themselves out of "the ruts of poverty" and join the majority of Americans in sharing in prosperity.

United Press International Telephoto

CHAT IN THE GARDEN: Mayor Wagner and Attorney General Robert F. Kennedy yesterday in garden at White House. Both attended antipoverty bill-signing ceremony.

The first of the 72 pens used by the President to sign the bill went to Representative Adam Clayton Powell Jr., Democrat of Manhattan, who is chairman of the House Education and Labor Committee, which first handled the bill.

Mr. Powell accepted two pens —one for himself and one for Representative Phil M. Landrum, Democrat of Georgia, who guided the bill through the House.

Mr. Landrum flew to Georgia earlier in the morning to fill a "campaign commitment," according to his office.

The third pen went to Senator Pat McNamara, Democrat of Michigan, who was floor leader for the bill in the Senate. Another went to Sargent Shriver, who will direct the antipoverty program.

Adam Yarmolinsky, who helped draft the program but who was ruled out of administering it, also received a pen.

In exchange for their votes, North Carolina Representatives demanded and received Administration assurances that Mr. Yarmolinsky would not get an antipoverty post.

August 21, 1964

Anatomy of Expansion

Economists Are Divided on Reasons For Long Life of U.S. Business Boom

By M. J. ROSSANT

Economists are as impressed as everyone else with the strength and duration of the expansion in business activity which, after four full years, is still full of bounce. But they are divided about the reasons for its long life—and about the policies needed to keep it going.

The Administration's own economists do not seem bothered by doubts. They contend that the economy's upsurge is mainly due to their new fiscal policy, especially the big tax cuts enacted last year.

There is no denying that the tax cut has been effective. But economists argue that the reduction in taxes did not do it all, and some fear that fiscal policy will be asked to do too much in the future.

Disagreement among economists over the tax cut and its impact is evident in a compendium of 48 individual views issued by a subcommittee of the Joint Economic Committee of Congress. The economists were invited to discuss the major tax and spending problems of the next decade, but many devoted a large part of their responses to observations that definitive answers depend on a more exhaustive analysis of the expansion. Some probing, of course, is already being carried out. It shows that no single factor is responsible for the expansion's long life.

Most economists claimed monetary policy had played a major role, one that some authorities regard as even more important than fiscal policy. Despite a rise in short-term interest rates to defend the dollar, it is a matter of record that credit has been kept easier for a longer time during this expansion than in any previous upturn.

Government spending also has made a significant contribution. Economists point out that the rate of spending was stepped up during the early stages of the rise, then slowed down last year when the tax cut took effect.

These preliminary findings, made while the business expansion is still ticking, have been passed over lightly by Gardner Ackley, chairman of the President's Council of Economic Advisers. To hear him tell it, the tax cut is not only responsible for the present good showing of the economy, but was working its magic when it was just a gleam in Washington's eye.

The council's economic report notes that President Kennedy proposed reducing taxes in 1963 as far back as August, 1962. Although the tax cut did not take effect until last year, the council infers that expectations of its passage increased "confidence that prosperity would be maintained" and served to promote an acceleration of activity well before its approval.

In a speech last week, Mr. Ackley came dangerously close to the conclusion that fiscal policy can continue to work its wonders.

All it takes, he suggested, is "wise and timely adjustments in Federal expenditures and tax rates" to "keep our total production steadily expanding in line with our rapidly-growing capacity to produce, and to narrow gradually—and eventually to erase — the unnecessarily wide margin that still exists between our total production and our productive capacity."

But there is a danger that hasty analysis can lead to the wrong conclusions. Just a few years ago, the council itself made the mistake of leaping before it looked deeply enough.

Vigorous Strength

As its present report admits, early in 1962 "many observers, recognizing that there were special explanations for the weakness and brevity of the recovery of 1958-60, expected a return of the vigorous expansionary strength of 1954-57. In fact, conditions had changed."

What the report does not admit is that the most prominent of the "many observers" was the council, which had been convinced by its analysis of the previous recession that the economy in 1962 was ripe for a boom. When the boom failed to materialize, it proceeded to expound the theory that the economy was afflicted with permanent sluggishness that could be cured by tax reductions.

The Administration's policy-makers only switched to their present position that tax cuts can promote and sustain growth last year, when it became obvious that the expansion was anything but sluggish.

The statements made to the Joint Economic Committee indicated that other economists are more cautious. Most favor making more use of fiscal policy, agreeing that recent experience has shown that it can be made into a more flexible and responsive instrument than it has been.

But many still believe that it cannot substitute for monetary policy in either flexibility or responsiveness.

This disagreement suggests that it is far too early to conclude that the policy-makers have hit upon a sure way to maintain the growth. Indeed, many economists doubt that there could be a repeat performance of last year's massive tax cut.

They also question whether fiscal policy is the preferred remedy for dealing with unemployment or the balance of payments problem—two major economic issues that remain unresolved.

These speculations emphasize the importance of continuing the autopsy of the expansion.

The Administration has done a good job and has learned a good deal about the way the economy ticks. But the record makes plain that it does not know it all.

March 15, 1965

Reserve Board Chief Compares Boom Today With That of 20's

By DOUGLAS W. CRAY

William McChesney Martin, chairman of the Federal Reserve Board, said yesterday he saw a series of "disquieting similarities between our present prosperity and the fabulous twenties."

He was careful to note, however, some important "differences" between the present and the past. If the lessons of history are followed, he said, these differences reduce the likelihood of a depression like that of the 1930's.

His remarks, delivered at the Commencement Day luncheon of the Alumni Federation at Columbia University's Ferris Booth Hall, were followed by a sharp drop in the stock market, where the Dow Jones industrial average dropped 9.51 for the day to 908.53.

Recalling the period immediately preceding the depression, Mr. Martin observed:

"Then as now, many government officials, scholars and businessmen were convinced that a new economic era had opened, an era in which business fluctuations had become a thing of the past, in which poverty was about to be abolished, and in which perennial economic progress and expansion were assured."

The experience of the "Great Depression" has strengthened the resolve of all responsible leaders to avoid a repetition, the chairman said.

"But, while the spirit is willing, the flesh, in the form of concrete policies, has remained weak. With the best intentions, some experts seem resolved to ignore the lessons of the past," he added.

Mr. Martin, whose speeches are not cleared by the White House, did not elaborate on the "concrete policies" he believed remained "weak."

But the Federal Reserve Board, acting in its capacity as an independent agency, has recently been maintaining a higher monetary policy than some Administration policy makers would like to see. In this respect, Mr. Martin's talk was viewed as an independent statement of position as well as a personal and public evaluation of economic history.

Noting that the Great Depression stemmed from "maladjustments born of the boom of the twenties," Mr. Martin declared: "We must continuously be on the alert to prevent a recurrence of maladjustments —even at the risk of being falsely accused of failing to realize the benefits of unbounded expansion.

"Our common goals of maximum production, employment, and purchasing power can be realized only if we are willing and able to prevent orderly expansion from turning into disorderly boom."

Among the similarities between the twenties and the present noted by Mr. Martin were the following.

¶There had been almost uninterrupted progress for seven years and, "if we regard some relatively short though severe fluctuations, expansion had been underway for more than a generation."

¶Prosperity had been concentrated in the fully developed countries and, within them, in the industrialized sectors of the economy.

¶There was a large increase in private domestic debt; "in fact, the expansion in consumer debt arising out of both residential mortgages and installment purchases has recently been much faster than in the twenties."

¶The supply of money and bank credit and the turnover of demand deposits had been continuously growing; and "this time monetary expansion has been superimposed upon a dwindling gold reserve."

¶The Federal Reserve had been accused of lack of flexibility in its monetary policy, "of insufficient ease in times of economic weakness and of insufficient firmness in times of economic strength."

¶The payments position of the main reserve center—Britain then and the United States now—was "uneasy, to say the least; but again, our recent cumulative payments deficits have far exceeded Britain's deficits of the late twenties."

Offsetting Factors

Offsetting these and other "disquieting similarities," Mr. Martin capsuled some of the differences between the earlier period and the present. Among them were:

¶The distribution of our national income now shows less disparity than in the earlier period, "in particular personal incomes and especially wages and salaries have kept pace with corporate profits and this has reduced the danger of investment expanding in excess of consumption needs."

¶The increase in stock market credit now has been much smaller.

¶Instead of a gradual decline in wholesale prices and stability in consumer prices, "there has now been stability in wholesale prices though consumer prices have been creeping up."

Even in his list of differences however Mr. Martin was still guarded. He noted that the potentialities of monetary and fiscal policies today were, "we hope," better understood. But then he went on to warn:

"The rise in government expenditures even in times of advancing prosperity threatens to make it difficult to be still more expansionary should a serious decline in private business activity require it."

Gold Policy Weighed

Turning to international monetary policy and balance-of-payments considerations, Mr. Martin questioned the wisdom of such proposals as increasing the dollar price of gold, of returning to pure gold-standard principles or delegation of monetary policy to an international agency.

"We must," he said, "avoid any impairment of the value and status of the dollar, which today acts—just as sterling did until its devaluation in 1931—as a universal means of international payment between central banks as well as among individual merchants, bankers, and investors."

He warned that the initial success of President Johnson's balance - of - payments program must not "blind us against the need of permanent cure."

Insofar as possible conflict be tween domestic economic requirements and balance - of - payments restraints are concerned, Mr. Martin declared: "A stable dollar is indeed the keystone of international trade and finance; but it is also, in my judgment, the keystone of economic growth and prosperity at home."

June 2, 1965

PRESIDENT SEEKS $1.7 BILLION MORE FOR VIETNAM WAR

Request Sent to Congress —McNamara Supports It Before a Senate Panel

SITUATION IS REVIEWED

Secretary Says Position of Saigon Has Deteriorated —Cites Aid by North

By JACK RAYMOND
Special to The New York Times

WASHINGTON, Aug. 4 — President Johnson asked Congress today for $1.7 billion in extra defense appropriations to strengthen United States military power in the war in Vietnam.

In support of the President's request, Secretary of Defense Robert S. McNamara restated before a panel of Senators the Administration view that United States national security was at stake in the war.

He reported that the Communist Vietcong retained most of the initiative in the current ground fighting and that the full weight of the Communist attack had not yet been felt.

He reaffirmed President Johnson's plan to ask for supplementary defense funds in January to cover new costs of the commitment in Vietnam.

Increase in Strength

The Secretary did not, however, indicate the size of the planned January request. But he announced that a general increase of 340,000 men in the size of the armed forces was being planned that would bring the total up to 2,980,000.

The Army, which has been ordered to create a new division for a total of 17, will be increased by over 235,000, to 1,188,000; the Navy by 35,000, to 720,000; the Marine Corps by 30,000, to 223,000, and the Air Force by 40,000, to 849,000.

Mr. McNamara said also that the Administration planned to send reinforcements to Vietnam and to increase the size of the armed forces without recourse to mobilizing the Reserves and with only a limited extension of service tours in the Navy.

The Administration asked that Congress regard the request as an amendment to the appropriations bill for fiscal year 1966, which began July 1.

The Senate Appropriations Committee is now working on a $45.2 billion defense appropriations bill that has passed the House.

Today's appropriation request, which the President forecast in his news conference July 28, was contained in a two-paragraph note to the Appropriations Committees in Congress.

The President's request for $1.7 billion was somewhat larger than the $1.2 billion expected in Congress, but was well within the official forecast between $1 and $2 billion.

Mr. McNamara, testifying in behalf of the request, appeared at a closed session of the Senate Defense Appropriations Subcommittee, to which members of the Senate Armed Services Committee were invited.

The Secretary's opening statement was made public.

In it, he reviewed past United States policy under Presidents Eisenhower and Kennedy in support of the South Vietnamese Government against Communist insurgency as well as the conflict between the Soviet Union and Communist China over the efficacy of so-called "wars of national liberation."

A Communist success in Vietnam, he went on, would be taken as proof that Peking's position was correct and would invite similar aggression "in other parts of the world wherever the existing governments are weak and the social structures fragmented."

Mr. McNamara said it was "now clear" that Communist forces in South Vietnam had been increased in size and that they were embarked upon "an all-out attempt to bring down the government of South Vietnam."

"The entire economic and social structure is under attack," he went on. "Bridges, railroads and highways are being destroyed and interdicted, agricultural products are being barred from the cities. Electric power plants and communication lines are being sabotaged. Whole villages are being burned and their population driven away, increasing the refugee burden on the South Vietnamese government."

The Secretary said organized units of the North Vietnamese Army had been identified in South Vietnam. He estimated Vietcong hard-core strength at 70,000 men, including a recently reported increase in combat battalions.

He said the Vietcong also had 90,000 to 100,000 irregulars and 30,000 in political cadres.

At the same time, he said, the government in Saigon had found it "increasingly difficult to make a commensurate increase in the size of its own forces, which stand at about 545,000 men, including the regional and local defense forces but excluding the national police," he said.

Most important, he emphasized, the ratio of South Vietnamese to Vetcong strength has seriously declined in the last six or seven months from about 5 to 1 to about 3½ to 1.

United States aerial attacks in South Vietnam will be increased "many fold" by the end of the year, he said. Armed helicopter sorties will increase "dramatically" over the same period, he said, and extensive use will be made of heavy artillery, both land- and sea-based.

The South Vietnamese paramilitary forces would be used to deal with the "pacification" of areas cleared of organized Vietcong and North Vietnamese units, "a role more appropriate for them than for our forces," Mr. McNamara said.

August 5, 1965

Whither the Boom?

Economists Find Peacetime Advance Changing to War-Propelled Expansion

By M. J. ROSSANT

The expansion is changing its character. Economists attending the annual meetings of the American Economic Association suggest that the longest peacetime expansion in history has turned into a war-propelled b⸺m.

These economists expect that business activity will continue to climb throughout next year spurred by increased spending for the war in Vietnam. They do not know just how big the future military budget will be, but they assert that the Pentagon's present outlays are already acting as a stimulant—both on business and on business sentiment.

As they see it, this change in the character of the expansion will intensify in 1966 as military spending increases even more because of the escalation in Vietnam. But while some think that the economy can adjust itself to new conditions fairly easily, others predict considerable strain and dislocation unless the Johnson Administration reverses some of its economic policies.

The confusion about the potential impact of military spending stems from differences about the present state of business and the probable size of the budget. Some think that the economy is operating at close to the limits of its capacity and are afraid that the military increase will touch off demands for manpower and for output that will result in inflationary pressures and stresses.

Yet others stress that the economy has greatly expanded its productive capacity, which should enable it to take military escalation in stride. Those who hold this position say that inflation would be a danger only if the defense budget goes much higher than present estimates of $60-billion a year.

Few economists characterize the situation in terms of a strict "guns or butter" choice. They emphasize that the economy has been big enough and strong enough to provide both—up to a point.

In the first stage of the expansion, when the economy was slack, both military and civilian spending were increased. Later, most of its stimulation came from either tax reductions or increases in outlays for the civilian sector. Military spending was fairly steady until the Vietnam conflict accelerated last summer.

Now, military spending is rising fast. Economists think that there will be some increase in nondefense expenditures, but they look for the defense sector to provide most of the fuel for maintaining the momentum of the expansion.

The 'New Economics'

Some economists argue that the Vietnam build-up has kept the advance from slackening, as it showed signs of doing last summer.

But others, mostly partisans of the "new economics" favored by the Administration, say that rapid rise in military spending, although acting as a powerful stimulant, has forced the Administration to abandon other measures—tax reductions and additional welfare outlays—that could have given the expansion a new lease on life.

Orthodox economists take still another view. They fear that inflation was raising its head even before the shift in military spending. Now they say that an expansionary budget is too heady a tonic, making inflation a clear and present danger.

Those concerned about inflationary pressures recognize that military demands must be met. But most of them favor a reduction or holding down of civilian outlays and think that another round of credit tightening may soon be needed.

Followers of the "new economics," who make up a majority at the meetings, concede that inflation may be a danger. But they want to see increased civilian as well as military expenditures, arguing that neglecting welfare would make for a much more expensive program later. And many of them prefer tax increases to credit tightening if restraint is needed.

But even though there was general agreement that the economy is now war-oriented, there was little talk of imposing wartime controls. Some orthodox economists said they feared that controls might have to be relied on if the Administration failed to take appropriate restraining action. Those in the "new economics" school were confident that the Administration would act and that the changed situation would not require wage and price controls.

December 29, 1965

Martin Urges a Tax Rise In a Break With Johnson

By H. ERICH HEINEMANN

William McChesney Martin Jr., chairman of the quasi-independent Federal Reserve Board, said last night that a "simple, clean-cut, across-the-board increase in taxes," both corporate and personal, would be the "logical way" to deal with the inflationary problems posed by the Federal Government's present budget deficit.

Taxes should be increased, Mr. Martin said, despite the "political problems" that might be involved in so doing.

Mr. Martin, who has long been regarded as one of the nation's leading financial conservatives, thus appeared to challenge directly President Johnson's judgment that the case for a tax increase at the present time was not a compelling one.

This is the first time that a member of the "quadriad" that the President consults regularly on economic matters—Mr. Martin; Gardner Ackley, chairman of the Council of Economic Advisers; Henry H. Fowler, Secretary of the Treasury, and Charles L. Schultze, director of the Bureau of the Budget—has broken publicly with the Administration on the question of whether or not there should be a tax increase.

Mr. Martin also broke with the White House last December in voting to increase the Federal Reserve discount, or lending, rate to 4½ per cent from 4 per cent. This move has since been welcomed by most Administration spokesmen.

The White House had no comment last night when asked about Mr. Martin's latest remarks, which were made in an informal talk here.

Associated Press

FOR TAX INCREASE: William McChesney Martin Jr., chairman of Federal Reserve Board, called for rise to fight inflation.

It was not clear last night what, if any, effect Mr. Martin's speech would have on prices on the New York Stock Exchange, which have been declining this week, at least partly in reaction to comments by Mr. Ackley on Monday that the present level of corporate profits might be too high.

It was almost a year ago, on June 1, that Mr. Martin, in a speech at Columbia University, drew attention to what he called "disquieting similarities" between the then-current economic situation and that of 1929.

That speech was widely believed in Wall Street to have contributed to the sharpest break in common stock prices since the precipitous market decline of May and June in 1962.

The Federal Reserve chairman made his remarks last night in the course of an off-the-cuff address at the closing banquet of the Eighth International Savings Banks Congress at the Waldorf-Astoria Hotel here.

Mr. Martin's remarks appeared to broaden the debate over the Government's present economic policy.

Earlier this week, Walter W. Heller, who was chairman of the Council of Economic Advisers in both the Kennedy and Johnson Administrations, called for a temporary $5-billion tax increase and a temporary suspension of the 7 per cent tax credit accorded to business on new investment under present tax law.

Mr. Martin implied, though he did not say so directly, that if the Administration did not move to increase taxes, the Federal Reserve would be forced to act on its own to combat inflationary pressures.

If it did, it would presumably do so by further reducing the availability of credit in the economy, and thus further increasing the level of interest rates, which are already at the highest level since 1929.

"When there is no other weapon at hand," Mr. Martin said, "then there is a place for monetary policy."

But Mr. Martin, who was first appointed to the Reserve chairmanship by President Truman in 1951 and has served in the post longer than any other man, made it plain that he would prefer that monetary policy not have to bear the full burden of slowing the booming American economy.

"There is a limit to monetary policy as such," he said, adding that an indefinite escalation of interest rates could have undesirable effects on the economy.

Mr. Martin made clear his principal concern at the very opening of his remarks. He was glad, he said, to be with a group of savings bankers who were as "anxious" as he to prevent inflation.

Mr. Martin drew an analogy between the maximum safe speed on a highway and the maximum rate at which the economy could expand safely. He quoted a police officer as having told him that "107 out of 109 people were killed on highways going 10 miles over the speed limit."

"When I stop someone, it is to save his life, not to arrest him," Mr. Martin quoted the officer as having said.

There is room for debate, Mr. Martin conceded, on just what is the maximum safe speed for the economy. But with the economy "tilting along" with "easy money" and "deficit finance," he said, the time has come "to reverse gears."

Trend of 1950's Recalled

Mr. Martin expanded on his analysis by saying that there was "general agreement" that during the nineteen-fifties Government economic policy had relied "too much" on monetary restraint.

He thus implied that the Federal Reserve bore some measure of responsibility for the slow rate of economic growth that characterized that period.

However, Mr. Martin said, the tight-money policies of the nineteen-fifties had laid the foundation for the relative price stability that characterized the early nineteen-sixties. This price stability, he said, was a major ingredient in the high rate of economic growth since 1961.

But the Federal Reserve chairman emphasized that he thought the situation had changed by the end of 1965. By then he said the over-all economy was close to full employment, and in skilled labor there was "overemployment."

May 5, 1966

JOHNSON ACTS AGAINST INFLATION BY ASKING CONGRESS TO SUSPEND TAX CREDIT GRANTED TO BUSINESS

A 16-MONTH HALT

7% Deduction to Aid Buying of Equipment Would Be Stopped

By MAX FRANKEL
Special to The New York Times

WASHINGTON, Sept. 8—President Johnson moved against inflation and high interest rates today by asking Congress to suspend tax incentives for business investment in new equipment and construction for 16 months.

The President recommended a temporary suspension of the tax credits granted to business in recent years to stimulate economic growth.

He hopes thus to slow down the rate of corporate expansion, ease the demand for loans, bring down interest rates on those loans, halt the rise in the cost of living, regain the confidence of the financial community and restore calm in the stock market.

Carefully waiting until the New York stock market had closed at 3:30 P.M., Mr. Johnson called a news conference to unwrap his promised "program of action" to shift the economy into "lower gear."

Bonus For Deferment

He requested a suspension of the 7 per cent tax credit given to corporations for purchases of machinery and equipment and of the fast tax write-off, or accelerated depreciation, allowed on commercial and industrial building.

Instead of canceling these benefits, Mr. Johnson proposed their suspension from Sept. 1, 1966, until Jan. 1, 1968. This, he said, would in effect offer a bonus to all who are willing to defer major expansion.

A suspension, instead of repeal, will also win more votes for his program, Mr. Johnson suggested. The first reactions on Capitol Hill proved him right. Legislators welcomed the decision to act and indicated general support.

Representative Wilbur D. Mills, chairman of the House Ways and Means Committee, immediately introduced the Administration's bill. The Arkansas Democrat will begin hearing testimony on Monday.

The President promised Congress to do his part by reducing Federal expenditures on low priority items, which he did not identify. But he also implored the members not to cripple his Great Society programs, not to "make the poor carry the burden of fighting inflation."

Mr. Johnson estimated that he could make a reduction of about $3-billion in the $31-billion in new appropriations in that part of the budget not marked for defense or firmly committed by law. Most of these savings will be sought in appropriations that exceed the Administration's money requests from Congress, but some may also involve cuts in Mr. Johnson's original $112.8-billion budget.

Wherever possible, the President said, he will not spend money that he did not request. He called on Congress to restrain itself in the eight remaining appropriation bills before it and set targets for savings for his major agencies.

Earlier today, in signing a bill of appropriations for the Department of Agriculture, the President described himself as "deeply disturbed" by several of its provisions, especially the addition of $312.5-million above his requests. Instead of vetoing the bill, he said, he would simply not spend the money.

But Mr Johnson hoped that his action would not lead to destruction of the $1.75-billion poverty program, or the relatively modest but high-priority demonstration-cities plan.

As a further contribution, Mr.

Johnson promised to slow to a minimum the sale of Federal securities, which would compete in the financial market for long term capital and thus help to keep interest rates high.

The Treasury will explain its plan to move in and out of the market, as conditions permit, at a news conference Saturday.

President Johnson conceded that he was responding to the pressure of the financial community to ease the great pressure on money markets. He promised even further action if necessary.

In return, he asked the Federal Reserve Board and large commercial banks to recognize his determination to check inflation and to "seize the earliest opportunity" to lower interest rates and to allocate existing supplies of credit more fairly.

The Federal Reserve Board welcomed the news. The proposed measures should help, it said. It promised to remain alert to any easing of inflationary pressures so that its policies can be adjusted.

Extreme Moves Shunned

Though less extreme than the increases in personal and corporate income taxes recommended by many economists this year, Mr. Johnson's program was in keeping with their new economic theories. These call for governmental intervention in the economy to stimulate or retard spending so as to avoid great fluctuations between inflation and recession.

Further longer-range actions may be necessary, the President said, when he sees how much money Congress appropriates in the rest of this session and when the Defense Department determines how much it will need in supplementary appropriations for material and equipment in Vietnam.

The cost of the war, concern for the Administration's welfare legislation and the political consequences of any tampering with the economy in an election year have all been serious considerations in the debate here about what, if anything, the President should do about inflation.

The pressure to do something began to build up last spring, but Mr. Johnson hoped he could get through the year safely.

The economy boomed on, causing long delays and labor shortages in the machine industries, hurting trade balances because foreign orders could not be filled and squeezing out small businessmen and home builders in the competition for loans.

Many members of Congress and even former President Harry S. Truman joined the clamor for action, believing — like President Johnson himself — that high interest rates transfer money from the poor to the rich while they drive up the cost of living for middle-class families with fixed incomes.

Moreover, the stock market has declined almost without interruption since February, suggesting a diversion of investment capital to more lucrative opportunities and, perhaps, a fear of recession.

Rumors of a cancellation of the investment tax credit began to spread here last week. Some corporations tried to duck under the wire by placing new orders before Labor Day. Notable among this group was Trans World Airlines, which purchased $450-million in new planes.

But by backdating its proposed actions to Sept. 1, the Administration would nullify the benefits contemplated for orders placed during the last week.

The investment credit has been saving business about $2-billion a year in taxes, but officials say they cannot now estimate how much of this saving would be wiped out by the 16-month suspension.

The effect of the suspension of the fast tax write-off on construction is equally hard to measure, but estimates here run to a loss for business of several hundred millions of dollars.

Spending Curb Is Goal

The Government's main interest is not in raising new revenue, but in curbing private spending at a pace that the economy has not been able to manage without shortages of money, labor and goods.

The reverse was true when the investment credit was created in 1962. At that time, expansion and growth were unsatisfactory, causing relatively high unemployment. To stimulate activity, a new tax law allowed business to deduct from its tax bill 7 per cent of the cost of machinery and equipment usable for more than eight years.

The device worked extremely well, producing an unparalleled burst of plant expansion. For the last three years, this investment has been rising more than twice as fast as the gross national product, "too swiftly," in the President's words today.

A suspension of the 7 per cent credit the President said, will relieve pressures on the producers of machinery and on the financial markets. The result, the Administration hopes, will be stable prices both for machinery and loans.

"We should not continue to press on the accelerator," the President said. We should not now provide a bonus to do something that we do not want done now and will very much want and need to be done later on," Mr. Johnson said.

'Accelerated Depreciation'

The device known as "accelerated depreciation" has been in effect since 1954. Whereas under normal depreciation schedules, a business may deduct from its taxes a fixed amount of the cost of an investment over a number of years, the principle of acceleration permits the deduction of a much higher proportion of the cost in the early years after purchase or construction.

Mr. Johnson urged the suspension of the fast write-off for construction of commercial and industrial buildings. Under his plan, the write-off could not be used for any building started in the 16-month period.

Officials said the prohibition would continue for the life of the building, even after the suspension was lifted or the building sold.

The write-off, Mr. Johnson said, is contributing to the inflation of building costs and to the pressures on financial markets, which are reflected in high interest rates. Commercial and industrial construction has gone up 27 per cent in the last 12 months.

The President's 4,000-word message to Congress included two themes that he has recently sounded on the campaign trail.

One paid tribute to the nation's unmatched prosperity and expressed a preference for the problems of boom to the problems of the bust.

The second was a plea to business and labor to hold down prices and wages and otherwise to cooperate in the effort to stabilize the economy.

"We do not want to resort to controls," Mr. Johnson said. With the right action now, next year should bring new heights of prosperity, he added.

And if it works, his plan indicated, the Presidential election year of 1968 will even bring back the tax incentives that Mr. Johnson asked to have suspended today.

September 9, 1966

COST OF THE WAR CONTINUES TO RISE

Reaches 1.2-Billion a Month and Is Still Mounting

By EDWIN L. DALE Jr.

Special to The New York Times

WASHINGTON, Sept. 21 — The cost of the war in Vietnam has reached $1.2-billion a month and is still rising.

In addition, it was disclosed today that the adverse effect of the war on the United States balance of international payments had reached an annual rate of $800-million by the second quarter of this year.

The monthly budgetary cost of the war derived from expenditure figures made public by the Treasury is less than the $1.5-billion to $2-billion a month estimate widely used in Congress and in financial circles. But it is well above the costs assumed in the President's budget of last January.

The Treasury statement covered all budget expenditures for August. The $1.2-billion monthly cost of the war is the average increase in defense expenditures for June, July and August of this year over last year. In those three months last year, the war had not yet begun to affect defense expenditures.

Fluctuations Erased

The use of three months eliminates fluctuations that typically occur from one month to another. As it happens, however, August military outlays were the same as the average—$1.2-billion higher than a year earlier.

Government economic officials said this method of calculating the cost of the war — comparing defense outlays with year-ago levels — was the best available.

Starting with September, however, comparisons with a year ago will not be valid as a measure of the cost of the war because by September of last year defense outlays had already begun to rise.

The major military commitment to the war began with a Presidential announcement at the end of July last year.

The best estimate, though it is subject to change, is that monthly expenditures attributable to the war will reach a level of $1.7-billion to $1.8-billion by the middle of next year.

Defense expenditures in June, July and August totaled $15.913-billion compared with $12.054-billion in the same three months last year. This works out to an average monthly increase of $1.286-billion.

Pay Rise Reflected

However, a little less than $100-million a month of this

reflects a military pay increase, which is not attributable to the war. Thus the war "add-on" to defense outlays works out at about $1.2-billion a month. This "add-on" to normal defense outlays, which had been running $4-billion a month, represents the cost of the war.

This means an annual rate of war cost at present of $14.5-billion, just under 2 per cent of the gross national product, or total output of goods and services.

The annual rate of defense outlays is expected, under the best available estimates that are subject to change, to rise by $2-billion each quarter until mid-1967. This would bring the annual rate of the cost of the war to $20-billion by the second quarter of 1967.

President Johnson declined today at his news conference to give any details of current or future costs of the war. This has consistently been his position for months.

The figure on the balance of payments cost of the war came from the Council of Economic Advisers in its monthly publication, "Economic Indicators."

This showed that overseas military expenditures grew in the second quarter to an annual rate of $3.652-billion. This was $850-million higher than the same quarter of 1965, with almost the entire difference accounted for by expenditures in Southeast Asia.

The rate of military dollar outflow rose to $2.980-billion in the third quarter of last year, $3.084-billion in the fourth quarter and $3.416-billion in the first quarter of this year.

September 22, 1966

To Labor, Guideposts Are Straitjackets

By A. H. RASKIN

The fever chart of labor militancy is rising with the cost of food and everything else that goes into the family budget. The combination of higher prices, unprecedented corporate profits and acute shortages of skilled labor in many industrial centers has turned a year that Federal mediators felt sure was going to be a quiet period for them into one of rising strike turbulence. Next year threatens to be even more stormy, with major contracts expiring in trucking, autos, rubber, construction and other key industries.

The biggest immediate conflict involves General Electric and a coalition of 11 A.F.L.-C.I.O. unions, operating under the personal command of George Meany. A two-week truce obtained by President Johnson in the intefest of uninterrupted production of war plane engines and other defense equipment made by G.E. expires next weekend, and the chances for a settlement appear decidedly slim.

Installers at Western Electric have just voted to reject a 4.8 per cent settlement their union leaders hoped would set a pattern for all units of the huge Bell System. A flurry of quickie strikes in pivotal plants of the Big Three automobile companies has stirred new worry that members of Walter P. Reuter's United Auto Workers will express in wildcats their irritation at the industry's refusal to reopen its wage agreements a year early and give higher pay to 125,000 skilled workers. Unresolved local grievances add to inflation as a source of employe discontent.

Labor's frustration over wages has been slowly building up for five years—a period in which its political allies have controlled both the White House and Capitol Hill, yet union chiefs felt their rank-and-file was getting too small a slice of a richer economic pie.

Labor's Target

The specific target of labor's anger was the anti-inflation guideposts erected by the President's Council of Economic Advisers early in the Kennedy Administration. **These had the effect of fixing a de facto ceiling of 3.2 per cent on settlements the Administration could bless as consistent with the national interest. The absence of yardsticks of any kind for profits or executive salaries — both of which have skyrocketed all through the period—made the guideposts doubly galling for labor.**

The fact that prices crept up at an average level of only 1.3 per cent a year from 1960 to 1965 was all that kept the strike explosion from erupting much sooner. Since the start of this year prices have been going up at a rate of more than 3.5 per cent, enough to leave a net deficit in what a worker's wages will buy if his increases are kept in balance with the productivity yardstick. **The Administration is no longer making any serious effort to preserve that balance; its problem is what line it can fall back to without uncorking a wage-price spiral as costly as the one that shot holes in the value of the dollar just after World War II.**

Informally, the new holding position has been established at 5 per cent, the level that emerged from mediation under White House **auspices in last summer's strike of machinists against five large airlines. Fumbling,** rather than **design, accounted for that figure; but it has now become the threshhold of expectation for all other strong unions and the Administration cannot disown it.**

The real concern in Washington is that the lid will move even higher into the stratosphere. That explained the sharpness of the rebuke Gardner Ackley, the President's chief economic adviser, administered to American Airlines **last week after it avoided a strike by giving its mechanics as much in two years as the other airlines had given in three.** The same concern lay behind an Ackley speech cautioning unions not to feed the inflationary fires by insisting that higher wages offset all the rise in living costs.

That warning turned the spotlight on a crucial battlefield in the fight over new inflation curbs —labor's belief that a cost-of-living escalator should be incorporated into all new contracts to guard worker purchasing power. The Administration considers such escalators engines of inflation, not cures for it. The President himself said last summer that general adoption of automatic wage increases geared to higher prices would trap the nation "in an endless chain — a chain that would imprison the wage earner behind the bars of inflation."

But a modified escalator clause was part of the price of peace in the White House-sponsored settlement of the airline strike. A full-fledged escalator is a central union demand in the General Electric strike threat. And the A.F.L.-C.I.O. is pounding away at Federal statistics showing that the real spendable earnings of factory workers went down in the last 12 months, even though the money in the average pay envelope went up.

The dilemma for the White House is heightened by two contradictory pulls. One is the imminence of the elections in which the A.F.L.-C.I.O., after a bad case of the sulks last winter, is all-out in support of pro-Administration Congressional candidates. The other is the example being set by Britain's Labor Prime Minister, Harold Wilson, in his fight against inflation. He has not only frozen wages and prices; he has rolled them back.

There is no prospect that anyone in the Administration will propose anything that drastic, but some counterpart of the statutory wage-price controls that the United States had in the Korean war is not impossible early in 1967, especially if the pace of the fighting in Vietnam quickens.

October 9, 1966

Associated Press

The President signing the tax surcharge bill in White House Rose Garden With him are his wite and their grandson, Patrick Lyndon Nugent. Photo was released by White House.

Tax Bill Is Signed; Withholding to Rise By 10% in 2 Weeks

By EDWIN L. DALE Jr.
Special to The New York Times

WASHINGTON, June 28—President Johnson signed today the bill increasing taxes and reducing Government spending, saying its passage meant that "our democracy passed a critical test."

Withholding taxes for all but the lowest-income taxpayers will go up by 10 per cent in about two weeks.

The President also signed a bill making four national holidays fall on Mondays to provide long weekends. The new law applies only to Federal and District of Columbia employes.

Mr. Johnson, in a prepared statement, said the tax measure would cut the budget deficit by $20-billion in the 1969 fiscal year beginning Monday, which he called "the largest shift of the budget toward restraint in the past two decades."

It was "most unwise," he said, for Congress to impose a spending reduction of $6-billion and "shift to the President the responsibility for making reductions in programs which the Congress itself is unwilling to do."

He also said he thought Congress had acted "unwisely" in requiring a cutback in Federal Government employment to the level of two years ago.

But he signed the bill, the President said, because it was "so imperative to the economic health of the nation."

The income tax surcharge of 10 per cent, retroactive to April 1, will be in effect for three-quarters of 1968 and thus amounts to a tax increase of 7.5 per cent this year.

The tax is due to expire on July 1 of next year and thus would be effective for only half of 1969. One of the crucial early decisions of the new President will be whether to ask Congress to extend the tax.

Mr. Johnson repeated that the surcharge "will return to the Treasury about half the tax cuts I signed into law in 1964 and 1965." He also said "it honors the democratic principle that taxes should be based on ability to pay."

Apart from his complaint about the spending and personnel reductions, the President said the decision in Congress "should have come sooner and should never have been in doubt." He added: "This is not the last time that we will have to act in applying flexible and rational fiscal policies to keep our economy flourishing."

He said that in making the required spending cuts, beyond those Congress was able to accomplish, he would "do my best to fulfill our most urgent priorities and to continue the essential operations of Government."

So far the President's position has been that he would decide where to make cuts after Congress has made its reductions in the budget. Officials have let it be known that every effort would be made to find $3-billion of the $6-billion in defense expenditures not associated with the war in Vietnam.

Apart from the tax increase and expenditure reduction, the bill has other features. It would delay for a year a state-by-state freeze of the number of children on welfare rolls, would drastically reduce the use of tax-free industrial revenue bonds by local communities, would extend existing excise taxes on telephone service and automobiles, and would provide a further speedup in corporate tax collections.

June 29, 1968

NIXON SAYS WAR HURTS ECONOMY

Views Conflict as Widened by 'Stealth' Amid Promises of Both 'Guns and Butter'

By CLAYTON KNOWLES

Richard M. Nixon indicted the Johnson Administration yesterday for what he termed escalating the Vietnam war "by stealth" while encouraging Americans to believe they could "go on enjoying guns and butter."

In a major statement on the nation's economy, the Republican Presidential hopeful declared that the Administration had "failed the people abysmally as trustee of the economy and guardian of the dollar."

"The American people are not sick—they are massively frustrated," Mr. Nixon said. "They speak and no one heeds them. The leaders speak and no one takes their words at face value.

'A Mutual Withdrawal'

"What appears to be a collapse of the system is in fact a breakdown of the democratic dialogue, a mutual withdrawal of trust between the people and their leaders who have failed them."

Asserting that the nation was caught in an inflationary spiral that was driving up living costs, negating wage increases and reducing the yield from savings, Mr. Nixon declared:

"It illustrates the erosion of trust, the retreat from responsibility, the growth of a paralysis at the top of the Government."

The statement of the former Vice President was reviewed earlier in the week by his newly established Economic Advisory Committee, made up of 51 national leaders of industry, business and finance.

Titled "A New Direction for America's Economy," the 22-page statement dealt more with events of the last five years that have lead to the present situation than with solutions.

Mr. Nixon, however, did call, as a first task, for a "halt in" the inflationary trend in our fiscal and monetary policies, for a re-examination of "the whole sweep of America's foreign economic policies" and for the "desperately urgent modernization of urban America."

Asserting that the Administration got "its vision of the future from the rear-view mirror," he maintained that it "had tried to preserve existing arrangements [on foreign economic policy] simply because they do exist and without asking whether they fit dramatically changing realities."

"Ironically, the early postwar goal of creating a true international economic community," he said, "has receded as a result of these policies and we are in danger of slipping backward into narrowly nationalistic rivalry and competition."

'They Need Our Example'

And again, he said: "Our allies and trading partners no longer need our protection as much as they need our example."

Mr. Nixon was equally strong in dealing with urban renewal. He declared that too much of the wealth created in cities was being "pumped into the remote bureaucracies of Washington" and that the "small fraction that does return comes in the form of rigid programs which do not meet the real needs of the cities."

"The cities do not need larger Federal handouts," he said. "They need a larger and more equitable share of the wealth they produce. But before new economic resources are committed to the cities, they must receive an infusion of the nation's best intellectual resources, drawn not only from the Government and the academic community but also from the relatively untapped business and financial community."

Sound expansion of the economy, he predicted, could produce "a gross national product of a trillion dollars of stable purchasing power" and 82-million jobs—6 milion more than at present. The gross national product for 1967 was at the rate of $785.1-billion.

July 7, 1968

JOHNSON OFFERS PLANS TO CHECK INFLATION IN 1969

ASKS 'COOLING OFF'

But Economic Report Still Sees a 'Highly Prosperous Year'

By EDWIN L. DALE Jr.

Special to The New York Times

WASHINGTON, Jan. 16—President Johnson laid out before Congress today an economic strategy for 1969 involving both less boom and less inflation than last year — a strategy known to be endorsed in all its essentials by the incoming Nixon Administration.

Its main elements are a small surplus in the budget and a monetary policy by the Federal Reserve Board allowing money and credit to expand, but at a much lower rate than in the inflationary 1966-68 period.

Mr. Johnson, in his annual Economic Report to Congress, cautioned that restraint on expansion of the economy should not be pushed to the point of bringing on a recession. He said that his strategy involved a "cooling off of the economy and a waning of inflationary forces," but that it still foresaw "a highly prosperous year."

Nixon Team Agrees

His Council of Economic Advisers, in their companion and lengthier report, forecast that "the unemployment rate should remain below 4 per cent" of the labor force this year despite the slowdown. Inflation, according to the forecast, should drop from a rate of more than 4 per cent to "a little more than 3 per cent."

To some extent in public comments, and privately even more, the economic team of President-elect Richard M. Nixon has made plain its view that this basic policy is the right one.

Mr. Nixon has reserved the right to change a key element of it—extension of the 10 per cent income tax surcharge—but only if this can be done and still preserve a budget surplus, thanks perhaps to a sharper tapering off of the war in Vietnam than President Johnson projects.

The President essentially agreed with this reservation today.

"My proposal for a one-year extension preserves the option of the new administration and the Congress to eliminate the surcharge more rapidly if our quest for peace is successful in the near future," he said.

The monetary policy part of the strategy is not under the direct control of the President. But several members of the Federal Reserve Board have made clear their agreement with it—a slower rate of money and credit expansion without pushing restraint so far as to produce a credit "crunch." The policy appears to be already under way.

The Federal Reserve, using various devices, influences the amount of money that banks have available to lend and thus influences total borrowing and spending. Occasionally, as in 1966, it cuts such funds to a point where banks have to turn most borrowers away and interest rates soar. The aim is to avoid that this year, though still forcing some slowdown in bank lending.

The Economic Advisers' projection of the economy foresaw a "real" growth—after correcting for higher prices—of 3 per cent in the gross national product, compared with 5 per cent last year and in most other recent years. The projection was for a fairly marked slowdown in the first half of the year and then some pickup in the second half.

The report emphasized that some slowing of the boom had already begun. Real growth, it said, fell from a rate of 6½ per cent early in 1968 to 4 per cent by the final quarter.

"I look upon the steady and strong growth of employment and production as our greatest economic success," the President said. "In recent years, prosperity has become the normal state of the American economy. But it must not be taken for granted."

"No longer," the President went on, "do we fear that automation and technical progress will rob workers of jobs rather than help us to achieve greater abundance. No longer do we consider poverty and unemployment permanent landmarks on our economic scene."

A chapter in the report of the Council of Economic Advisers showed that prosperity, rather than special Government programs, had been by far the greatest factor in bringing some 12.5 million persons above the officially defined poverty line in the last five years. The poverty line, fixed annually by the Social Security Administration, is now $3,335 in annual income for a nonfarm family of four.

Mr. Johnson said the "challenge" to economic policy this year "is difficult indeed."

"Enough restraint must be provided to permit a cooling off of the economy and a waning of inflationary forces," he said. "But the restraint must also be tempered to insure continued economic growth. We must adopt a carefully balanced program that curbs inflation and preserves prosperity."

2 Kinds of Skeptics

Skeptics on this strategy are of opposite kinds—those who fear it will be tough enough to topple the economy into recession despite the Government's wishes, and a larger group that believes it is not tough enough to cope significantly with inflation.

The President gave his view in these terms, backed up later by the Council of Economic Advisers:

"Price stability could be restored unwisely by an overdose of fiscal and monetary restraint. This has been done before, and it would work again. But such a course would mean stumbling into recession and slack, losing precious billions of dollars of output, suffering rising unemployment, with growing distress and unrest. It would be a prescription for social disaster as well as for unconscionable waste."

But the President also rejected another course—"throw up our hands and allow the price-wage spiral to turn faster and faster."

"This counsel of despair," he said, "would eventually undermine our prosperity and our financial system—wrecking the strong international position of the dollar and imposing unjust burdens on millions of our citizens."

Council's Prediction

The council's forecast of the 1969 outlook had these main elements:

¶A rise in business investment of $7-billion to $8-billion.

¶Housing starts "somewhat below" the recent rate of 1.6 million a year, despite strong demand for housing.

¶Federal spending up $10-billion in the calendar year 1969, compared with $19-billion in 1968, with very little of the increase in defense.

¶A rise of another $10-billion in state and local government spending.

¶Consumer spending growing "rather slowly" in the first half and "more strongly" in the second half, with a growth for the year of about $35-billion.

¶Inventory growth showing slight decline from 1968.

The Economic Report confirmed, as the President disclosed to Congress in his State of the Union Message on Tuesday, that the nation's balance of international payments—all international transactions — moved into a surplus last year for the first time since 1957. The report forecast improvement next year in the trade balance—exports and imports—but suggested that inflows and outflows of dollars for investments of various kinds, known as the capital account, "may deteriorate."

January 17, 1969

PRICE RISE OF 4.7% IN YEAR IS BIGGEST SINCE KOREAN WAR

December Increase of 0.2%, Low for Recent Months, Puts Index at 123.7

EXPORT SURPLUS DROPS

It Stands at $726-Million—Interest on Treasury Notes Highest Since 1865

By EDWIN L. DALE Jr.

Special to The New York Times

WASHINGTON, Jan. 29 – The Nixon Administration found itself confronted today with Government reports showing the worst inflation since 1951, the lowest export surplus since the Depression and the highest interest rate on a Government security since the Civil War.

None of the reports were unexpected, and they showed little or no worsening of a well-known situation in the economy in the last month. But they illustrated why President Nixon in his news conference two days ago put economic problems among his most "urgent."

The Labor Department reported that the Consumer Price Index rose two-tenths of 1 per cent in December, less than in most recent months, bringing the increase from a year earlier to 4.7 per cent. The last time inflation was as large was 1951, the first full year of the Korean War, when consumer prices rose by 5.8 per cent.

U.S. DEPARTMENT OF LABOR
BUREAU OF LABOR STATISTICS
(1957-59 = 100)

UNITED STATES

	Index for Dec., 1968	Percentage Change From Nov., 1968	Percentage Change From Dec., 1967	Point Chg. From Nov. 1968
All items	123.7	+0.2	+4.7	+0.3
*Food	121.2	+0.6	+4.3	+0.7
†Housing	122.3	+0.5	+5.4	+0.6
‡App. & upkeep	124.3	+0.2	+6.4	+0.3
Transportation	120.2	—0.8	+2.0	—1.0
Health and rec.	132.8	+0.3	+4.9	+0.4
Medical care	149.1	+0.6	+6.2	+0.9
Personal care	123.4	+0.5	+5.3	+0.6
Reading & rec.	128.2	+0.2	+4.9	+0.2
Other goods, serv.	125.6	+0.2	+3.5	+0.2

NEW YORK

	Index for Dec., 1968	Percentage Change From Nov., 1968	Percentage Change From Dec., 1967	Point Chg. From Nov. 1968
All items	127.2	+0.2	+5.3	+0.3
*Food	122.3	+0.4	+4.9	+0.5
†Housing	126.4	+0.6	+5.9	+0.8
‡Apparel & upkeep	130.3	+0.2	+7.6	+0.3
Transportation	121.1	—0.9	+1.8	—1.1
Health and rec.	138.6	+0.1	+5.6	+0.1
Medical care	151.9	+0.1	+6.8	+0.2
Personal care	120.6	+0.3	+5.7	+0.4
Reading and rec.	138.7	+0.1	+4.0	+0.1
Other goods, serv	134.9	+0.1	+6.1	+0.1

*Includes restaurant meals.

†Includes hotel and motel rates, home purchase and other home-owner costs not shown separately.

‡Includes infants' wear, sewing materials, jewelry and apparel upkeep not shown separately.

time inflation was as large was 1951, the first full year of the Korean War, when consumer prices rose by 5.8 per cent.

The index last month was 123.7, compared with 100 in the base period 1957-59. Thus, it cost $12.37 to buy the same goods and services that cost $10 a decade ago.

6.42 Rate on Notes

There were these other developments today:

¶The Treasury announced it would have to pay 6.42 per cent interest to sell a 15-month note issue, the highest rate on one of its securities since 1865. This and a companion seven-year note bearing 6.29 per cent were offered to replace $5.4-billion of maturing issues with much lower interest rates.

¶The Commerce Department said the surplus of exports over imports fell to $726-million last year, the lowest since 1937, as exports continued to grow but imports soared. If about $2.5-billion of exports paid for by Government aid programs are left out, there was a trade deficit last year, in contrast with normally large surpluses.

However, the over-all balance of payments, reflecting all transactions with foreign countries, showed a small surplus last year, the first since 1957. This was because the flows of capital into and out of the country turned sharply in the United States' favor, more than offsetting the worsening in the export-import account.

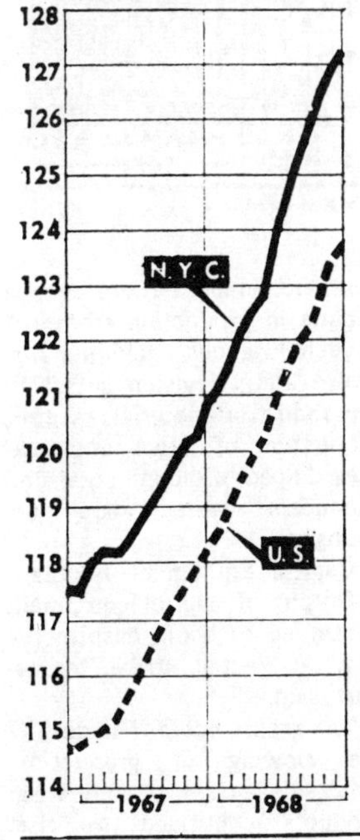

The New York Times Jan. 30, 1969

Today's report on prices said the increase in the consumer index was 4.7 per cent from December to December. Taking average prices in the year 1968 as a whole in comparison to 1967 as a whole, the rise was 4.2 per cent, also the largest since 1951.

The wholesale price increase, December to December, was less, at 2.8 per cent. But today's report contained an ominous note.

The index of wholesale prices for all "industrials" — leaving out farm and food products — rose three-tenths of 1 per cent in December and, on a preliminary basis, five-tenths of 1 per cent in January. This is regarded by many economists as perhaps the single most sensitive indicator of inflation.

The December Consumer Price Index of 123.7 compares with a November index of 123.4. The change amounted to a rise of two-tenths of 1 per cent, the smallest increase since September.

Compared with the previous December, those parts of the index showing the sharpest increases last year were medical care, mortgage interest rates, apparel, shoes, public transit and restaurant meals. These increases ranged between 6 and 7 per cent.

The food-at-home index rose somewhat less, by 4 per cent, but it was still more than in nearly all recent years.

Area Prices Up 0.2%

The smallest monthly increase in the New York area's Consumer Price Index in 11 months—two-tenths of 1 per cent—was recorded in December, Herbert Bienstock, regional director of the United States Bureau of Labor Statistics, announced yesterday.

The increase, the 20th consecutive monthly rise, advanced the index to 127.2.

While the November to December change was small, the total change for the year, 5.3 per cent, was substantially more than the 2.6 per cent change for 1967.

The biggest advances in the 12-month period were in mortgage interest, up 9 per cent; fresh fruits and vegetables, 8 per cent, and medical care, 7 per cent.

January 30, 1969

OUTPUT DECLINES, GIVING EVIDENCE OF ECONOMIC LAG

Industrial Production Fell 0.4% During October—Payments in Deficit

By EDWIN L. DALE Jr.

Special to The New York Times

WASHINGTON, Nov. 17—Industrial production declined in October for the third consecutive month, the Federal Reserve Board reported today.

The report supplied the most convincing evidence yet that the long-awaited slowing of the economy was under way, even though part of the October drop was related to strikes.

The output decline in October was four-tenths of one per cent, or 0.6 of a point on the index, which was larger than in the two previous months. The October production index was 173.3, with 1957-59 taken as 100, compared with 173.9 in September.

Confirmation Suggested

Although not all of the economic indicators for October are available, those published so far tend, on the whole, to confirm the picture painted by the production index. Retail sales continued sluggish; unemployment remained higher than in the earlier part of the year; hours of work declined, and personal income showed its second consecutive small growth after booming earlier.

Meanwhile, the Commerce Department reported that the United States balance of payments in the third quarter had shown large deficits on both bases of measurement — the familiar "liquidity" yardstick and the "official settlements" criterion.

Today's report from the Reserve Board attributed some of the October decline in production to the strike at the General Electric Company and to scattered strikes in the automobile industry. But it also said there was "a falling off in output of some other durable and nondurable goods."

Auto production, the report said, was at a rate of 8.4 million units, down 4 per cent

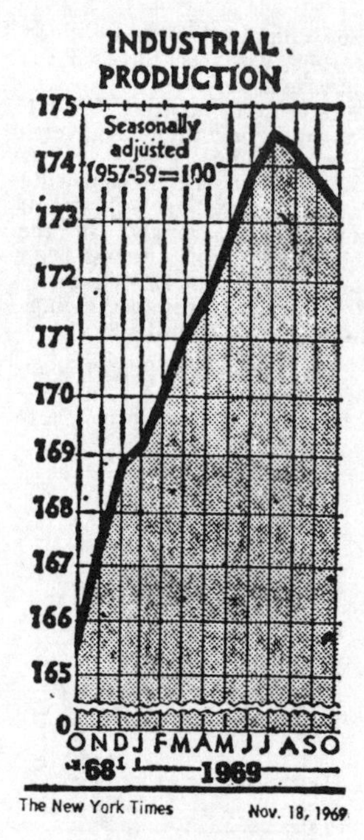

The New York Times Nov. 18, 1969

from September. There was a decline in production of "most household goods, including furniture and television sets." In the industrial-materials sector, production of paper and textiles dipped, although steel and chemicals" were "about unchanged."

Capital Equipment Booms

Output of capital equipment continued to boom despite the General Electric strike, the report said.

The report noted that despite the slowing of production, wholesale prices of industrial products continued to rise. The October increase of five-tenths of one per cent was unusually large and covered a wide variety of products.

Earlier this year industrial production, like many other indicators, was rising strongly despite the Government's policy of fiscal and monetary restraint. Thus, despite a decline of seven-tenths of one per cent in the Federal Reserve index since July, output in October was still 4.4 per cent above a year earlier.

If the decline continues long enough, one result could be a recession, as officially measured by the National Bureau of Economic Research. Normally, however, a recession is characterized by a decline in the "real" gross national product—the G.N.P. after correcting for higher prices—and that has not yet yappened.

The apparent aim of the Government's policy is to bring about a very slow growth in the G.N.P. in the first half of next year—perhaps at an annual rate of as little as one per cent—but not an actual decline. It is possible for the G.N.P. to rise as industrial production declines because the G.N.P. includes the base services sector of the economy, but in the postwar period there has been no prolonged decline in industrial production without a drop in the G.N.P. as well.

The main indicators yet to come for October are housing starts and new orders for durable goods. The latter was unusually strong in September, giving rise to doubts that the policy of restraint was working as well as hoped.

Reserve Restraint Seen

The Federal Reserve System has intensified its credit restraint since last June, the Federal Reserve Bank of St. Louis said yesterday. In its monthly publication, Monetary Trends, the bank said that from June through October, "the money stock and the demand deposit component of the money stock have been about unchanged."

By contrast, the bank said, "from last December to June these aggregates increased at about a 4 per cent annual rate, a moderation from the 7 per cent growth in 1967 and 1968."

The recent restrictive pattern of monetary policy, the St. Louis bank asserted, "can be attributed largely to slow growth of Federal Reserve credit during the same period."

Monetary Experts Differ

Many monetary analysts, including economists at the Federal Reserve in St. Louis, believe that the slower growth in the supply of money will result in a slowdown in the rate of over-all economic growth, lower demands for funds and, eventually, a reduction in the rate of inflation.

Pierre A. Rinfret, a private economic consultant, expressed a sharply different view at a luncheon meeting in Cleveland yesterday.

According to United Press International, Mr. Rinfret—who is chairman of Rinfret-Boston Associates—said that the nation would be lucky if it could hold inflation to 4½ or 5 per cent in 1970.

The economy will smash every record next year, Mr. Rinfret said, because in the first quarter "we will duplicate everything we did in 1964 to stimulate the economy." In 1964, there was a major cut in Federal income taxes, which in the view of many economists had the effect of stimulating business activity.

Mr. Rinfret also said that interest rates would continue to climb. He predicted that the prime rate—the minimum interest rate for loans to the best credit risks—would be between 9½ and 10 per cent by mid-1970, in contrast to its present level of 8½ per cent.

Higher capital spending, the proposed increase in Social Security benefits, reduction and then elimination of the 10 per cent Federal income-tax surcharge and higher take-home pay were cited by Mr. Rinfret as factors likely to push the economy ahead.

In a separate development, the New York Chamber of Commerce in a statement yesterday reiterated its view that fiscal and monetary restraints should "be vigilantly maintained until there is conclusive evidence that inflation—now at a pace of 6 per cent a year—has slowed appreciably and the tenacious and deeply imbedded inflationary psychology throughout the country is broken."

November 18, 1969

Marxist Saws Die Hard

Charge That 'Establishment' Battens On War Challenged by Vietnam Data

By LEONARD S. SILK

The old Marxist charge that capitalist economies depend on war to provide prosperity and full employment dies hard. Not only orthodox Communists but radicals of the New Left take it as axiomatic that what used to be known as "merchants of death" and is now called "the military-industrial complex" controls the nation's

Economic Analysis

basic foreign and domestic policies. The "complex" does this, according to the Marxist doctrine, not by conspiring against the economic interests of business and labor but by actually serving the interests of those who seek higher profits and wages through the expansion of the capitalist system.

A careful look at the economic impact of the Vietnam War upon the United States provides a challenge to this ancient Marxist thesis.

The escalation of the war in Vietnam came in 1965—not when the nation's economy was suffering from heavy unemployment, but when it was rapidly approaching full employment in the wake of the stimulation provided by the huge tax cut of 1964.

Keynesian Doctrine

In fact, whatever validity the Marxist charge might once have had in contending that only war could cure capitalist depressions was undermined by the modern Keynesian doctrine that tax cuts, spending on civilian programs, and easy money could generate full employment without resort to war.

Vietnam, coming on top of a fully employed economy, bred inflation, deprived the nation of resources needed for housing, education, and other social expenditures, and worsened the economic lot of most businessmen and workers.

If some groups got something extra out of the war, this only increased the net loss of the rest of the nation.

Professor Robert Eisner of Northwestern University has made some calculations to show just how costly the Vietnam war has been to the United States economy.

Measured in constant fiscal 1970 dollars, Vietnam has cost $113.4-billion in the last five years, according to the Federal budget.

But this figure does not represent the war's true "opportunity cost"—that is, the cost of shifting resources away from their normal and better-paid employment.

If the men conscripted to wage the war in Vietnam had been able to take civilian jobs, their earnings would have been $82.5-billion higher than it cost to pay them in uniform, according to Professor Eisner's estimates.

The casualties of Vietnam have been an incalculable human loss to their families and friends—but also a measurable economic loss to the nation.

As of May 16, 1970, there had been 50,067 American deaths in the Vietnam theater, 140,286 injuries requiring hospitalization, and 137,720 injuries not requiring hospitalization.

GI's with service-connected disabilities from Vietnam now total 145,008; their average disability rate is 35.5 per cent.

Professor Eisner estimated that the cost of the dead and wounded to the nation has been $23.1-billion.

He gets this figure by discounting to their present value some detailed estimates of the lost incomes these men would have earned, had they not been killed or seriously wounded.

Thus, the total cost of the war, according to Professor Eisner, has come to $219-billion in the past five years, as shown in the following table:

Total Cost of Vietnam
July 1965 to June 1970 Only

	Billions of Fiscal 1970 dollars
Budgeted Current Expenses	$113.4
Added Economic Cost of Conscription	82.5
Cost of the Dead	11.6
Cost of the Wounded	11.5
Total Costs	$219.0

Those dollar figures represent real resources taken from alternative uses that might have increased the welfare of the nation.

Some Government outlays represent transfers of income; military outlays eat up real goods and services.

Obviously, Professor Eisner's calculations leave out of account the economic impact of these expenditures on other countries.

Vietnam, for instance, has a raging inflation as well as vast destruction of resources.

But has all this outlay somehow increased corporate profits or industrial wages in the United States? The data provide a flat negative answer.

Corporate Profits Fell

From 1965 to the first quarter of 1970, corporate profits, adjusted for inflation, fell by 16.8 per cent; in 1961-65, the five years before the escalation of Vietnam, corporate profits rose by 61.2 per cent.

The value of corporate stocks has fallen by 36.5 per cent in the last five years — after climbing by 48.5 per cent in 1961-65, years of relative peace.

As for wages, the average worker with three dependents had experienced a gain of 11 per cent in his spendable income, adjusted for inflation, in the five years before 1965.

Workers' Income Off

But in the five years since the 1965 escalation in Vietnam, the average worker's spendable income has actually declined by about 2 per cent.

Since, with normal economic growth, the worker might have been 10 per cent or more ahead, Vietnam may be said to have set him back by 12 per cent or more.

Professor Eisner suggests that the economic drain of the war, in checking the growth of living standards, is a major underlying cause of the anger and resentment of blue-collar workers and "middle Americans" generally.

Other Losses of War

Yet the war does not always get the blame it deserves for this loss; workers, faced with cuts in defense spending, more clearly perceive the threat to their jobs than the damage to their real incomes via inflation, higher taxes, and lost output.

Wall Street, however, is more sophisticated. It has sold off on news of a widening war and bought on hopes for peace. The market's greatest recent decline came with the "incursion" of American troops into Cambodia.

If this be economic determinism, Marxists should make the most of it—but recognize that it is exactly the reverse of what their classic thesis asserts.

July 15, 1970

Nixon's Program—'I Am Now a Keynesian'

The nation last week received another large dose of bad economic news: Unemployment for December climbed to 6 per cent—the highest rate in nine years. . . . Long-term unemployment continued to climb. The number of persons out of work for at least 15 weeks passed the million mark—the highest level since 1964. . . . Layoffs, especially in key industries, continued to rise. The Chrysler Corporation announced that it planned to furlough 1,275 employes in an effort to bring "over-all production into line with the current market demand."

President Nixon, increasingly concerned about the downslide, outlined at a national television interview last week his Administration's scheme for reducing unemployment and curbing inflation before the 1972 election. This economic plan, Mr. Nixon disclosed, has two positive elements:

- An expansionary budget for fiscal 1972. In the President's words, "It will be a budget in deficit, as will be the budget in 1971. It will not be an inflationary budget because it will not exceed the full-employment revenues."
- An expansionary monetary policy. Mr. Nixon said enough money would be poured in "to fuel a growing economy." To be sure, monetary policy is primarily under control of the Federal Reserve System. But Mr. Nixon assured his viewers that, "according to Dr. Arthur Burns," the Fed's chairman, monetary policy would be "adequate to meet the needs of an expanding economy."

But there is a third major element in the President's plan—and this one is negative: Mr. Nixon let it be known that he has turned thumbs down, at least for the present, on a stronger "incomes policy" to restrain wages and prices while his budget and monetary policies are stimulating expansion. The President said he was rejecting not only wage and price controls—no surprise to anyone—but even wage and price guidelines or a wage-price board, as proposed by Dr. Burns. "I have considered all those options. I have decided that none of them at this time would work," said Mr. Nixon.

"And, consequently," he added, "I feel that the best course is to proceed, as I have suggested, with an expansionary budgetary policy, but one that will not exceed full-employment revenues."

The President's announcement of a budget for next year that would be in deficit but that, at the same time, would not be in full-employment deficit must have baffled millions of television viewers.

Simply stated, it meant that the budget would be calculated as if the nation were enjoying full employment, in which case tax revenues would of course be considerably higher than under today's high unemployment conditions. Thus, using this economist's device, the President could say on the one hand that his budget would *not* be in deficit—while granting that, without the "full-employment" concept, it actually *would* be in deficit.

If such considerations confused many viewers, Mr. Nixon's comment to one of his interviewers, Howard K. Smith, immediately after the broadcast must have staggered conservatives in the audience: "I am now a Keynesian in economics," said the President. John Maynard Keynes, the late British economist who advocated higher government spending and deficit financing as the cure for unemployment, is the patron saint of the New Economists of the Kennedy and Johnson Administrations. For Mr. Nixon, who had come to the White House lambasting the Democrats for deficit spending, this was, as Mr. Smith put it, "a little like a Christian crusader saying, 'All things considered, I think Mohammed was right.'"

New Economics

But faced with an economic slump, unemployment and big deficits in his own budget, Mr. Nixon has indeed accepted the fiscal doctrine of the New Economics.

Mr. Nixon has decided to go the spending route in order to stimulate the economy toward full employment (defined as 4 per cent unemployment). He told his television audience that he plans to ask for no increase in tax rates for next year—and no "tax reform," which has often been a euphemism for tax cutting, as it was in 1969. Actually, tax rates will be dropping again next year as a delayed effect of the Tax Reform Act of 1969.

Mr. Nixon's budget figures for fiscal 1972 will doubtless stay secret until the Budget Message itself is released. However, the President has already disclosed that his biggest recommended spending boosts will be for Federal revenue sharing with states and cities and for the Administration's Family Assistance Plan.

Total Government spending in fiscal 1972 will probably be budgeted for about $230-billion, about $18-billion higher than the current fiscal year. This is the program that Mr. Nixon's new Secretary of the Treasury, John B. Connally, former Democratic Governor of Texas, will have to sell to Congress.

How much of a deficit resulting from a shortfall of tax revenues will Mr. Connally have to disclose? Actually, the Treasury has considerable latitude in what level of tax revenues it can project; its tax estimate will depend on its forecast of real economic growth and inflation in the next fiscal year.

The educated guessing in Washington is that the Administration will assume real economic growth slightly in excess of 4 per cent and a rate of inflation of 3 per cent during fiscal 1972. On those assumptions, tax revenues (given slightly lower tax rates) should total about $220-billion — $10-billion higher than in the current fiscal year.

Thus, with tax receipts of $220-billion and projected expenditures of $230-billion, the actual budget deficit for fiscal 1972 should be about $10-billion.

What, then, will be its "full-employment" budget? If the economy were to run at full employment in fiscal 1972, with individuals and corporations making more money, tax revenues would probably run some $15-billion higher than with unemployment above 5 per cent. This would lift full-employment tax revenues to $235-billion—and yield a budget surplus of $5-billion. Mr. Nixon holds that, with a small full-employment surplus, his budget is not inflationary.

Biding His Time

The President did not venture into detail on what monetary policy he expected from Dr. Burns and the Federal Reserve. But Mr. Nixon's decision against the tougher incomes policy advocated by Dr. Burns may well mean that the Fed will follow a more cautious monetary policy than the White House economists want. However, it now appears that Mr. Nixon is prepared to bide his time and hope that unemployment and inflation will gradually wither away, as a result of a "good" year in 1971 and a "very good" year in 1972.

Is the Administration's forecast reasonable? At this point most private economists think it is on the optimistic side. Most private economists forecast that real economic growth next year will be only about 3 per cent (the Nixon figure presumably is more than 4 per cent) — not enough to make a real dent in the recent unemployment rate of 6 per cent. And most private economists would be surprised if the rate of inflation, which has been running close to 5 per cent, should average only 3 per cent in the coming year, the figure which Mr. Nixon's economists are hoping for. As for 1972, there is as yet no "standard forecast"; most economists' crystal balls go black after twelve months.

But what is clear is that Mr. Nixon is saving his real steam for the election year, 1972. His budget for the coming fiscal year—which looks only moderately expansionary—will carry him only to the threshold of the 1972 election contest, since the budget years end in midsummer. Hence, Mr. Nixon—convert to Keynesian economics though he may be—must still count on a far more expansionary monetary policy than yet seems in the cards, if the economy is to get close to full employment by then.

—LEONARD S. SILK

January 10, 1971

NIXON ORDERS 90-DAY WAGE-PRICE FREEZE, ASKS TAX CUTS, NEW JOBS IN BROAD PLAN

SPEAKS TO NATION

Urges Business Aid to Bolster Economy—Budget Slashed

By JAMES M. NAUGHTON
Special to The New York Times

WASHINGTON, Aug. 15 — President Nixon charted a new economic course tonight by ordering a 90-day freeze on wages and prices, requesting Federal tax cuts and making a broad range of domestic and international moves designed to strengthen the dollar.

In a 20-minute address, telecast and broadcast nationally, the President appealed to Americans to join him in creating new jobs, curtailing inflation and restoring confidence in the economy through "the most comprehensive new economic policy to be undertaken in this nation in four decades."

Some of the measures Mr. Nixon can impose temporarily himself and he asked for tolerance as he does. Others require Congressional approval and — although he proposed some policies that his critics on Capitol Hill have been urging upon him—will doubtless face long scrutiny before they take effect.

2 Tax Reductions

Mr. Nixon imposed a ceiling on all prices, rents, wages and salaries — and asked corporations to do the same voluntarily on stockholder dividends — under authority granted to him last year by Congress but ignored by the White House until tonight.

The President asked Congress to speed up by one year the additional $50 personal income tax exemption scheduled to go into effect on Jan. 1, 1973, and to repeal, retroactive to today, the 7 per cent excise tax on automobile purchases.

He also asked for legislative authority to grant corporations a 10 per cent tax credit for investing in new American-made machinery and equipment and pledged to introduce in Congress next January other tax proposals that would stimulate the economy.

Combined with new cuts in Federal spending, the measures announced by Mr. Nixon tonight represented a major shift in his Administration's policy on the economy.

Cuts Ruled Out Earlier

Only seven weeks ago, after an intensive Cabinet-level study of economic policy, the President announced that he would not seek any tax cuts this year and would hew to his existing economic "game plan," confident of success.

Eleven days ago, Mr. Nixon reasserted his opposition to a wage and price review board—a less stringent method of holding down prices and wages than the freeze he ordered—and said only that he was more receptive to considering some new approach to curtailing inflation.

The program issued tonight at the White House thus came with an unaccustomed suddenness, reflecting both domestic political pressures on the President to improve the economy before the 1972 elections and growing international concern over the stability of the dollar.

The changes represented an internal policy victory for Paul W. McCracken, chairman of the Council of Economic Advisers, and Arthur F. Burns, chairman of the Federal Reserve Board, both of whom had pushed over a number of months for a wage-price curtailment. It marked the first major defeat for George P. Schultz, Mr. Nixon's director of management and budget, who has vigorously opposed such an incomes policy.

The President adopted the new tactics following a week-end of meetings at the Presidential retreat at Camp David, Md. With him there were Dr. Burns, Mr. McCracken, Mr. Shultz and John B. Connally, the Secretary of the Treasury.

'Action o n3 Fronts'

"Prosperity without war requires action on three fronts," Mr. Nixon declared in explaining his new policies. "We must create more and better jobs; we must stop the rise in the cost of living; we must protect the dollar from the attacks of international money speculators.

"We are going to take that action—not timidly, not half-heartedly and not in piecemeal fashion," he said.

As a corollary to his tax cut proposals, the President announced that he would slash

United Press International
President Nixon after delivering televised address

Economic Advisers Who Met With Mr. Nixon

The New York Times

John B. Connally
Secretary of the Treasury

United Press International

Dr. Arthur F. Burns
Chairman of the Federal Reserve Board

The New York Times

Dr. Paul W. McCracken
Chairman of the Council of Economic Advisers

Associated Press

George P. Shultz
Director of Office of Management and Budget

$4.7-billion from the current Federal budget to produce stability as well as stimulation. The budget cutback would come from a 5 per cent reduction in the number of Federal employes, a 10 per cent cut in the level of foreign aid and through postponement of the effective dates of two costly domestic programs — Federal revenue sharing with states and localities and reform of the Federal welfare system.

Mr. Nixon's sudden adoption of a wage and price freeze represented his most drastic reversal of form. He established an eight-member Cost of Living Council to monitor a program under which management and labor must keep wages and prices at the same levels that existed in the 30 days prior to tonight.

Wage or price increases that had been scheduled to go into effect during the next 90 days, such as a 5 per cent raise for the nation's rail workers due to take effect on Oct. 1, must be postponed at least until the 90 days expire. But wage improvements that took effect before tonight, including the 50-cent-an-hour increase won by the steelworkers on Aug. 2, will not be affected.

The White House did not include interest rates in the freeze on the theory that they cannot properly be kept under a fixed ceiling. Although describing the freeze as "voluntary," officials noted there was a provision for court injunctions and fines as high as $5,000 for failure to adhere to the ceiling.

The freeze could be extended after 90 days if Mr. Nixon should decide it still is needed. This authority to impose a ceiling will expire on April 30.

Political pressures for some form of an incomes policy have been building for weeks. Public opinion polls have certified concern over unemployment and prices as the No. 1 domestic issue. Democratic Presidential hopefuls have singled out the economy as the primary area for criticizing Mr. Nixon.

At a White House briefing just before the President's address, Secretary Connally said that the changes had been "long in the making." But he conceded in response to questions that he had left last week on vacation without any expectation that Mr. Nixon would put the program into effect tonight.

Why Strategy Changed

In explaining why the White House had shifted its economic strategy since he expressed confidence on June 30 that "we're on the right path," Mr. Connally cited tonight an "unacceptable" level of unemployment—currently running at an annual rate of 5.8 per cent—as well as continued inflation, a deteriorating balance of trade and an "unsatisfactory" balance of payments in dealings abroad.

Congress, which is in recess until after the Labor Day weekend, must approve the President's request for new consumer tax breaks and investment credits.

The individual income tax exemption, currently $650 for each member of a family, is scheduled to rise to $700 next Jan. 1, and $750 a year later. Mr. Nixon asked that it go to $750 in one step next January.

"Every action I have taken tonight is designed to nurture and stimulate [the] competitive spirit, to help snap us out of the self-doubt, the self-disparagement that saps our energy and erodes our confidence in ourselves," the President said.

In calling for repeal of the tax on automobiles, the President said it would represent an average drop of about $200 in the price of a new car. "I shall insist that the American auto industry pass this tax reduction on to the nearly eight million customers who are buying automobiles this year," he emphasized, but did not say how he would keep that pledge.

The tax would continue to be collected until Congress acts to repeal it, with the provision for rebates later to customers who do not wait to purchase a car.

Mr. Nixon's political advisers have been hoping to cast him as the President of peace and prosperity in a bid for re-election next year.

With every speech in recent weeks emphasizing his initiatives toward global peace — his forthcoming journey to Peking, disengagement from Vietnam and negotiations on arms, the Middle East and Berlin with the Soviet Union — Mr. Nixon has faced a proliferation in Democratic statements criticizing him for permitting continued unemployment and inflation.

Possible 1972 Theme

Mr. Nixon's address tonight contained the kernels of what could become, if his policies have the desired impact, the prosperity rhetoric of 1972.

"Today we hear the echoes of those voices preaching a gospel of gloom and defeat," he said.

"As we move into a generation of peace, as we blaze the trail toward the new prosperity," he added, "I say to every American—let us raise our spirits, let us raise our sights, let all of us contribute all we can to this great and good country that has contributed so much to the progress of mankind."

The Cost of Living Council, which will recommend to Mr. Nixon some form of "second-stage" of wage and price stabilization to follow the 90-day freeze, will be chaired by Mr. Connally and will also have Mr. McCracken and Mr. Shultz on it.

The other members are:

Clifford M. Hardin, Secretary of Agriculture.

Maurice H. Stans, Secretary of Commerce.

James D. Hodgson, Secretary of Labor.

George A. Lincoln, director of the Office of Emergency Preparedness.

Virginia H. Knauer, assistant to the President for consumer affairs.

Dr. Burns will serve as an adviser to the council.

August 16, 1971

PRESIDENT SAYS STABILITY IS KEY TO ENDING CURBS

Report on Economy Asserts Wage-Price Controls Will Stay as Long as Needed

CUT IN JOBLESS SOUGHT

Advisory Council Forecasts Increase of $98-Billion in Nation's Output in 1972

By EDWIN L. DALE Jr.
Special to The New York Times

WASHINGTON, Jan. 27 — Price and wage controls will remain indefinitely until "reasonable price stability can be maintained without controls," President Nixon told Congress today.

"How long that will take," the President said, "no one can say."

The President made his statement in his Economic Report to Congress, which accompanies the Annual Report of the Council of Economic Advisers.

In their reports, Mr. Nixon and the council said essentially the same thing in different ways: that controls would be maintained until Americans stopped acting, through such things as labor contracts and business pricing policy, as if inflation was going to be permanent. Thus, in this view, the test of the end of controls will be the end of what is called "inflationary psychology."

Calls Jobs 'Great Problem'

Mr. Nixon, in his brief message, again emphasized that "the great problem" of the economy was to reduce unemployment from its current level of 6 per cent of the labor force. He said that he was "determined to reduce that number significantly in 1972."

In its relatively detailed forecast of the economy, the council put the probable growth of the gross national product this year at $98-billion, or 9.4 per cent, with unemployment declining to "the neighborhood" of 5 per cent by the end of the year. The gross national product is the dollar value of all goods and services produced in the country in a year.

The report said that this picture was "not one of takeoff into a cyclical boom."

Of the expected total growth, the council said that about 6 percentage points would be "real" and about 3¼ points would be a result of inflation. The inflation rate will decline as the year progresses, the council said.

For last year, 2.7 points of the growth in the gross product was considered "real" and 4.7 points was attributed to inflation.

The forecast emphasized a number of "uncertainties" and noted what it called the Administration's "readiness to take additional steps" if necessary to bring about the projected expansion in output and jobs.

However, the report said, "The possibility that, with the policy now in place, the economy will rise even more rapidly than we foresee today is a strong reason for not seeking to stimulate the economy more now."

In two important respects the forecast was relatively conservative. It projected no reduction in the recent unusually high rate of consumer saving, and thus did not rely upon a booming burst of consumer spending.

And, in the key case of business inventory accumulation, the report projected an increase from the unusually low level of 1971. But, again, the expected rise of $8-billion would not be of boomlike proportions.

The President, in his message, said that 1972 "begins on a note of much greater confidence than prevailed six or 12 months ago." He said, "Output is rising at a rate which will boost employment rapidly and eat into unemployment."

The issue of the duration of price and wage controls has aroused much speculation, some confusion, and some apparent differences in statements by various high officials. C. Jackson Grayson Jr., chairman of the Price Commission, at one point objected to statements by Herbert Stein, chairman of the Council of Economic Advisers, and George P. Shultz, director of the Office of Management and Budget, that seemed to imply an early end to controls.

The report by the council today did not settle the question, but it gave the clearest picture yet of the Administration's policy. Indefinite controls were not ruled out, though the clear aim was to end them eventually.

The following citations from the report give the essence of the policy:

¶"If excess demand is avoided, the control system can help to break the habitual or contractual repetition of large price and wage increases that keeps inflation going. It can generate the expectation of reasonable price stability that is essential to the achievement of reasonable price stability. And as that happens it will be possible to eliminate the controls. How soon that can be done will have to be determined in the light of experience."

¶"Speculation that the Administration will abandon the controls prematurely — out of fatigue, ideological aversion, or other causes — is groundless. Having embarked upon this course the Administration has no intention of departing from it in circumstances where it would risk either resumption

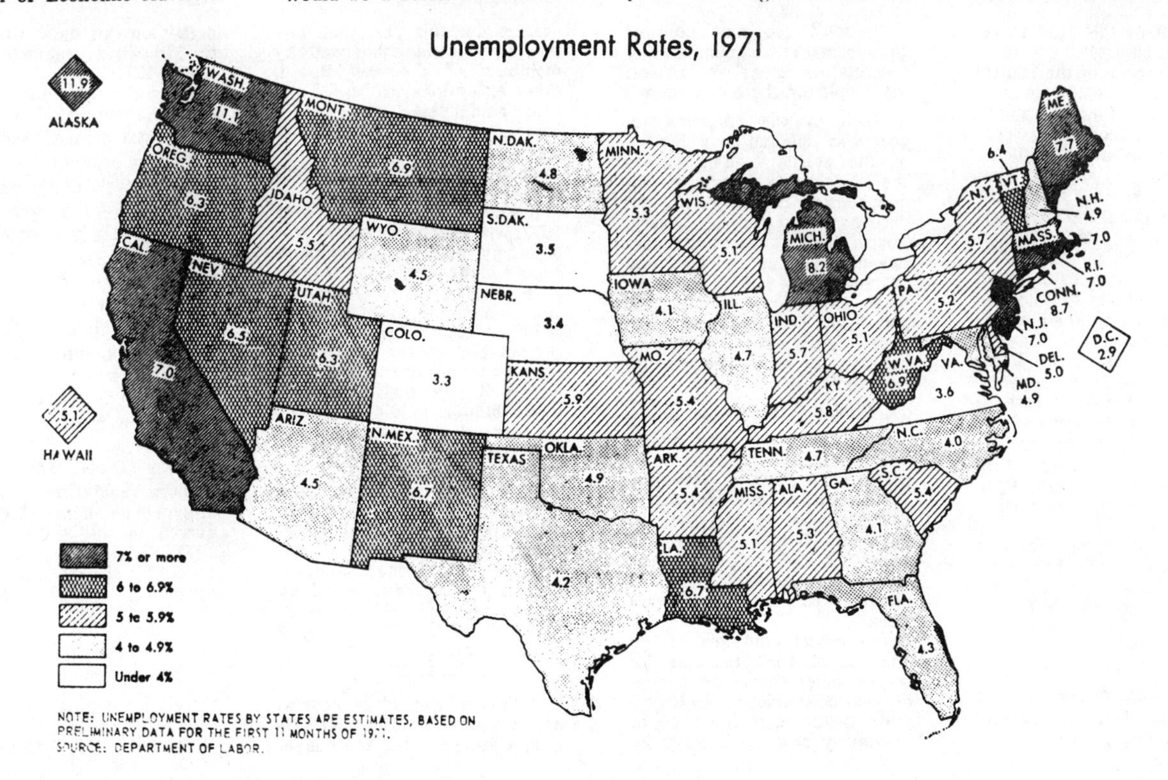

Interest Rates

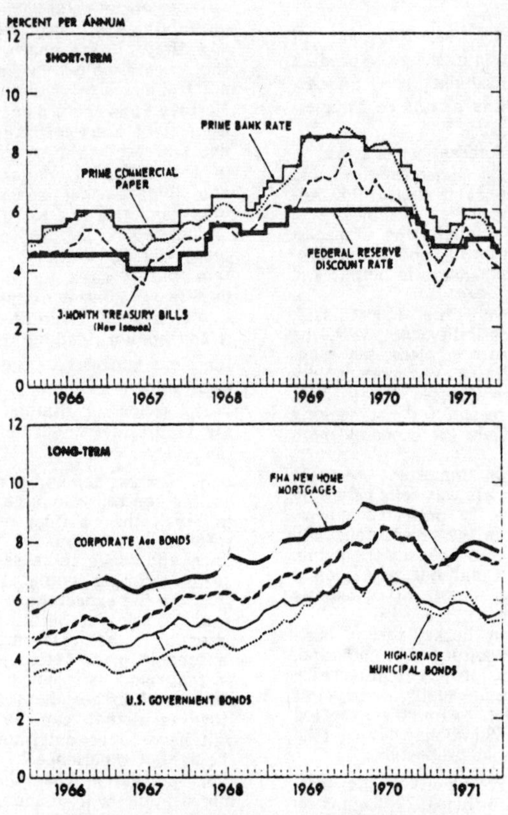

SOURCES: DEPARTMENT OF HOUSING AND URBAN DEVELOPMENT, TREASURY DEPARTMENT, BOARD OF GOVERNORS OF THE FEDERAL RESERVE SYSTEM, MOODY'S INVESTORS SERVICE, AND STANDARD & POOR'S CORPORATION.

Changes in Consumer Prices

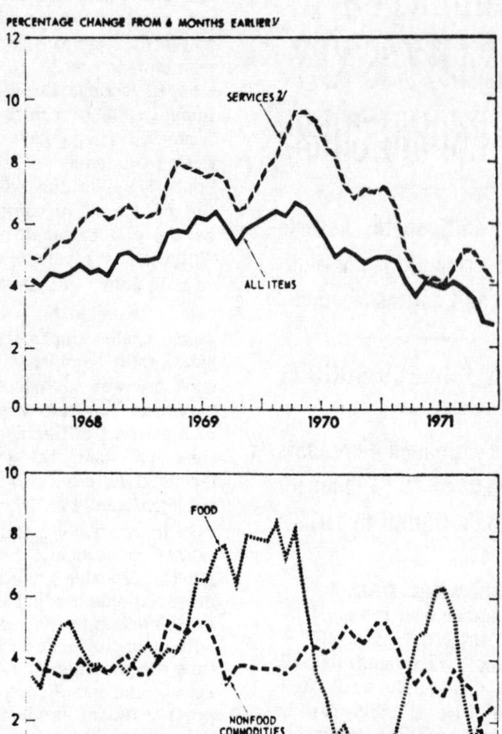

1/SEASONALLY ADJUSTED ANNUAL RATES.
2/CHANGES BASED ON UNADJUSTED INDEXES SINCE THESE PRICES HAVE LITTLE SEASONAL MOVEMENT.
SOURCE: DEPARTMENT OF LABOR.

of inflation or the need to reimpose the controls."

¶"The purpose of the control system is to give the country a period of enforced stability in which expectations, contracts and behavior will become adapted to the fact that rapid inflation is no longer the prospective condition of American life. When that happens, controls can be eliminated."

The report was cautious in forecasting success for the controls in achieving their objective of reducing the rate of inflation to from 2 to 3 per cent by the end of the year It emphasized that "there is little relevant experience" to go by in predicting the success of controls at a time when basic economic forces were also working toward less inflation.

But it said, "The character and operation of the price-wage control system give grounds for confidence."

Mr. Stein, the chairman of the council, was asked if "political" factors might not force an end to controls. He replied that he was "just an amateur" in politics, but added:

"I don't see any political gain from the abandonment of controls. As far as we can see, the people out there love them."

Much of the council's report was devoted to a history of the events leading up to the President's dramatic announcement last Aug. 15, imposing a wage-price freeze, suspending convertibility between the dollar and gold and proposing new tax cuts to stimulate the economy. The report contained the most complete account yet of the reasoning that lay behind the Administration's decisions.

Global Aspects Stressed

Great emphasis was placed on the international side of the problem. The report said that the need to act to improve the nation's balance of international payments finally "tipped the scales" in the long debate on price-wage policy and led directly to the wage-price freeze.

The report contained a full analysis of the prospects for wages under the second phase of the economic control program, including such aspects as previously negotiated wage increases due this year that may or may not be challenged by members of the Pay Board; other exceptions to the 5.5 per cent guidelines for wage increases; and movements of wage costs, such as a rise in overtime, that are not subject to control.

It said, "In the conditions of 1972, when labor shortages will be highly infrequent, we should expect many wage increases to be below the normally permissible amount." It concluded, "Our expectation is that the combination of the Pay Board rules and the natural forces at work will, after the initial post-freeze bubble, hold the rate of increase of compensation per hour close to 5.5 per cent."

The report asserted that the Federal budget would be "stimulative" this year. As usual, the council translated the budget into what is called the "national income accounts" basis, the form most often used by economists, and assessed it on the basis of the calendar year rather than the fiscal year, July 1 to June 30.

It found that total Federal expenditures would rise $29-billion this year and the budget deficit on this basis would rise to $36-billion, against $23-billion in 1971.

As to the companion weapon of Government policy to stimulate total demand and spending in the economy — the Federal Reserve's policy on money and credit — the report said:

"The steady, strong expansion we seek will require support from monetary policy. An abundant supply of money and other liquid assets, and favorable conditions in money markets, should encourage an expansion of outlays by consumers, businesses, and state and local governments.

"This process would involve a more rapid rise of currency and demand deposits than occurred in the second half of 1971. Steps have already been taken by the Federal Reserbe System to start this acceleration."

Burns Is Hopeful on Nation's Economy

By EDWIN L. DALE JR.
Special to The New York Times

WASHINGTON, Dec. 5—Dr. Arthur F. Burns, chairman of the Federal Reserve Board told Congress today that the renewed strength of the dollar in the world's foreign exchange markets has "served to bolster confidence in our nation's future at a time when we have been beseiged with all sorts of unhappy economic and political news."

In testimony before a subcommittee of the House banking committee, Dr. Burns did not try to paint a picture of general optimism about the economy. He called the problem created by the energy shortage "very difficult."

He stressed the "extraordinary" growth of about 47 per cent in United States exports this year and the "decisive turnaround" in the over-all United States balance of payments, concluding that "the dollar is again a strong currency" in the international sense.

Dr. Burns clarified somewhat, an immediate issue in international monetary matters — the question of whether foreign central banks should and would intervene in daily trading in foreign exchange markets in order to halt the recent rise of the dollar by selling dollars that they hold.

He said a "substantial reduction" of foreign-held dollars, to be achieved by such intervention, "is clearly desirable as a long-run objective." He added that he would "anticipate sales of dollars on an increased scale."

But he said he sensed a "general willingness, particularly now in light of the energy shortage, to test markets rather than to characterize this or that situation as an equilibrium exchange rate and try to peg it there." This implied that rates would not be fixed at the levels established last February at the time of the last formal devaluation of the dollar, or at any other specific level.

In his prepared statement and in answer to questions Dr. Burns made these other points:

¶The oil shortage, while "manageable" will cause "shifts in the structure of industry and have adverse effects on overall production and employment." This creates for Government economic policy "the extremely difficult task of contributing to the objective of regaining price stability, while at the same time minimizing the risks of any extensive weakening in economic activity." The problem now "is not a shortage of money."

¶It "may be feasible" to take action "over the coming months" to remove the controls on outflow of United States capital, such as the interest equalization tax on purchases of foreign securities, removal of these controls has "priority" over ending the ban on purchases of gold by United States citizens, though that ban would probably also be removed eventually.

¶Official sales of gold in the private market, now possible after the recent termination of a 1968 agreement barring such sales, "can be useful in preventing wide fluctuations in the gold market that at times generate instability in currency markets." But he gave no hint as to when there might be official sales of gold.

¶The "basic" United States balance of payments — for which figures are not yet available—showed "a large surplus" in the third quarter of this year.

¶Because of the "astronomic prices" for imported oil, total United States payments for oil imports next year will "probably exceed by a substantial margin the $8-billion paid in 1973" even if no Arab oil is imported.

¶Floating exchange rates have worked well in the recent period of stress, but "I remain skeptical of the long-run viability of a floating exchange rate regime."

¶"The protection that we have against large short-term movements of capital from one currency to another is very small at this time." Controls in other countries have failed when the movements become massive.

December 6, 1973

Facing the Crisis of Scarcity

By Leonard Silk

The economic crisis in which the United States and the other highly industrialized countries of the West now find themselves could not be more radically different from the Great Depression of the nineteen-thirties, which was a catastrophe of idle machines and men. The poet W. H. Auden warned of the waste and rot still to come:

Power stations locked, deserted,
since they drew the boiler fires;
Pylons fallen or subsiding, trailing
dead high-tension wires;
Head-gears gaunt on grass-grown pit-
banks, seems abandoned years ago;
Drop a stone and listen for its splash
in flood dark below.

The Great Depression, like other earlier crises of capitalism, was the result of a failure of governments to understand the necessity of creating enough monetary demand to call forth the goods that the men and machines of society were capable of making.

But the current crisis stems not from a deficiency of demand but of supply, the most dramatic manifestations of which have been shortages of food and soaring food prices, and shortages of oil and soaring energy prices.

There are also rumors and speculations of a host of other raw-material shortages to come: bauxite, copper, lead, zinc, manganese, magnesium, and even iron ore. Arable land is short, urban land is scarce. The world is caught in an onrush of inflation, the clearest evidence of an insufficiency of supply to meet persistently growing demands.

Is the age of plenty over so soon? Have we suddenly come up against the "limits to growth," as the Club of Rome report predicted we would by the middle of the next century? Has the monster lily pad been doubling and doubling even faster than expected and will it soon blot out the lake of life-supporting resources?

The immediate crisis does not resemble the doomsday that would result from an actual exhaustion of the world's resources.

Rather, the scarcities that have struck the industrial world and many of the developing countries as well are chiefly the result of the fierce pursuit of unenlightened self-interest by governments, businesses and individuals.

An upsurge of nationalism and resentment against the rich capitalist powers is a critical cause of the new crisis of scarcity. Colonialism has been suffering its death throes in India, Africa, Indochina, and now in the Middle East. The oil-producing nations are not only bent on acquiring wealth but on avenging old grievances.

And within the capitalist nations, it is the blind pursuit of self-interest that aggravates the crisis of scarcity. Britain starts the New Year with energy so short that all but the most essential services have been cut back.

to a three-day week; but the reason for the energy shortage is less the Arab oil embargo than the conflict between the Conservative Government and the British coal miners, trainmen and other workers, bitter over their low pay and smoldering with class hatred.

The energy shortage in the United States was fostered both by public demand and by hard industrial selling and lobbying. Immediately, the fuel shortage is being exacerbated by hoarding; the Government has sent out Internal Revenue Service agents to find out what "refiners, importers, wholesalers and end users" are stockpiling fuel in "excessive and unreasonable amounts."

Threats are voiced and fights break out in the long queues at filling stations. Some dealers gouge on price. Truckers block highways, demanding more fuel, faster speed limits. But some truckers can't decide whether they are involved in a big steal or a big social reform. One trucker tells Studs Terkel, writing in New Times:

"During the last thirty years we were taught in this industry that the only way to get ahead was to cheat and steal and cut corners. . . . Now we're having a re-evaluation of the way we treat each other. . . . The reforms we may see in our union may at the same time take place in the Government and in our social world. I think maybe the whole nation is beginning to see that the sharp operator isn't the one to look up to."

Could this crisis be a stroke of luck? Could it restore our sanity and sense of mutual interdependence—in the society and in the world—before it is too late? This crisis of scarcity isn't yet one of physical exhaustion of resources, though that could come, but of how we live and how we use what we have. It is confronting us with the necessity of rediscovering the nonmaterial aspects of life: thinking more, feeling more, knowing each other better, expressing our concerns for one another.

The crisis of the nineteen-seventies, radically different from the crisis of the nineteen-thirties, requires an even more basic change of social direction:

If we really want to live, we'd better start at once to try;
If we don't, it doesn't matter, but we'd better start to die.

January 3, 1974

APRIL 30 WINDUP OF MOST CONTROLS URGED BY SHULTZ

Exception Asked for Health Care and Oil Products—Stand-By Law Opposed

By EDWARD COWAN
Special to The New York Times

WASHINGTON, Feb. 6—The Nixon Administration recommended to Congress today that it let all wage-price controls expire on April 30 except for health care and petroleum products.

Secretary of the Treasury George P. Shultz said the Administration opposed even stand-by controls because they "can become an inflationary force in and of themselves." He explained that the expectation that they would be used could accelerate price and wage increases.

Some members of the Senate Banking subcommittee that heard Mr. Shultz and John T. Dunlop, director of the Cost of Living Council, thought stand-by authority should be extended beyond the scheduled expiration on April 30 of the Economic Stabilization Act, the enabling authority for controls.

To Seek Commitments

No Senator present, however, said that controls themselves should be kept in effect beyond April 30. Mr. Dunlop testified that in the 83 days until then he would seek price-restraint commitments from more industries in exchange for suspensions of controls.

The reluctance of some members of Congress in this election year to appear to be leaving consumers without a shield from an inflation that the Administration forecasts at 7 per cent was expressed by Senator J. Bennett Johnston Jr., Democrat of Louisiana, who is chairman of the Subcommittee on Production and Stabilization.

"I am searching for a middle ground," he said, "a meeting place for those who see total decontrol as a sublime but perilous experiment as well as those for whom controls are a nightmare of economic inefficiency and inequity."

Senator Johnston introduced yesterday a bill that he said would provide "orderly transition to selective controls."

Senator William Proxmire of

The New York Times

John T. Dunlop, right, head of Cost of Living Council, and George P. Shultz, Secretary of the Treasury, discussing end of most controls before Senate Banking Subcommittee.

Wisconsin, the ranking Democrat on the Banking Committee, backed the Administration, but for his own reasons.

"This wage-price act has to go," he said. "The working people of this country are really being hurt badly by this program. Wages are being held down. Prices are going through the roof."

The two Republicans at the hearing, Senators John G. Tower of Texas and Bill Brock of Tennessee, endorsed the Administration position.

Later, at a news conference, Mr. Dunlop echoed the view of many on Capitol Hill that the legislative situation was wide open.

"I haven't the slightest idea what Congress will do," he said.

Mr. Shultz explained that no action by Congress was necessary to keep crude oil and refinery products under price controls because the Emergency Petroleum Allocation Act signed in November does that until March 1, 1975.

The fact was thought to give the Administration a slight advantage in pressing Congress for a separate bill along the lines proposed today. Some observers expect the key issue will be whether President Nixon signs stand-by controls authority, as he did reluctantly in 1970, when he said he would not use it.

Arthur F. Burns, chairman of the Federal Reserve Board, generally supported the Administration proposal. As for credit policy, he acknowledged that the central bank was coming under "a great deal of pressure" to "step up the rate of growth of the money supply" and bring down interest rates to ward off an economic "recession." Dr. Burns used that term, then moments later changed his usage to "slowdown or recession."

"We will not open up the spigot and permit the money supply to increase rapidly," he said. To do so, he added, would make no significant dent in unemployment and would add to inflation.

The Banking Committee hearing room was packed to overflowing as Mr. Shultz, who is also chairman of the Cost of Living Council, Mr. Dunlop and James W. McLane, Mr. Dunlop's deputy, made their way to the witness table.

Business and labor lobbyists stood in the back row and waited in the corridor to learn what the Administration proposed to do about the price-wage controls program Mr. Nixon announced with startling suddenness two and a half years ago, on Aug. 15, 1971.

Mr. Dunlop submitted a loosely bound volume of 63 pages of testimony and 157 pages of graphs, charts and statistics, largely written by him. Running through it was his strongly held view that inflation over the years has been a many-faceted problem that must be examined afresh in each context and dealt with in highly specific, flexible ways.

Various studies have indicated that wage-price controls have moderated the rate of inflation by perhaps 1 or 2 per cent, he testfied.

Nevertheless, he said, the effectiveness of direct wage-price restraints is short-lived. "They tend to run down and wear out," he added.

Mr. Dunlop recommended that Congress enact legisaltion to keep health care under controls until enactment of national health insurance legislation. He said a great deal of the inflationary pressure in the health field resulted from the infusion of large sums of Federal money for Medicare and Medicaid in recent years.

Dr. James H. Sammons of Baytown, Tex., chairman of the board of trustees of the American Medical Association, recommended that all controls be allowed to lapse on April 30. He criticized controls on hospital fees as a "capricious and unwise" attempt "to restructure health care." He accused the Cost of Living Council of having "attempted to dictate medical practice patterns under the guise of price control."

The Administration asked that Congress extend the life of the council so that it could press for anti-inflationary government policies, especially in agriculture, monitor performance by industry and labor under stabilization commitments given in exchange for early release from controls, keep an eye on potentially inflationary problem spots in the economy, promote productivity and watch for developing shortages.

Mr. Dunlop said the council should have authority to compel individual companies, industries or unions to explain "price and wage decisions" at public hearings. Dr. Burns in a similar proposal would give a review board the power to delay increases pending the outcome of the hearing.

In response to a question, Secretary Shultz held out the possibility that "if they are way out of bounds for no good reason," the Administration could ask Congress to intervene.

February 7, 1974

Inadequate Stimulus

Ford's 'Quick Fix' Seen as Too Weak With Energy Plan Only Shuffling Funds

By LEONARD SILK
Special to The New York Times

WASHINGTON, Jan. 14 — President Ford's new economic and energy program is supposed to "turn America in a new direction." But is the $16-billion tax cut Mr. Ford is proposing strong enough to reverse the recession and reduce unemployment? And will his energy program, which calls for $30-billion in natural gas, give a new twist higher taxes on petroleum and to the inflationary spiral by increasing the cost of fuel paid by consumers, public utilities and industry generally?

Economic Analysis

While the $16-billion tax cut is designed to give a "quick fix" to the economy, its net stimulus appears inadequate.

Three-fourths of the tax cut $12-billion—will go to individuals in the form of cash rebates amounting to 12 per cent of their 1974 tax payments—upto a $1,000 maximum. That is a figure that would give a $1,000 rebate to taxpayers with incomes of $40,000 and higher.

A larger fraction of the proposed $12-billion cut would be spent immediately rather than saved if the tax cut were focused on the lower end of the income ladder. The across-the-board percentage increase, even with a $1,000 "top," creates a smaller bang for a buck.

If the aim of the President was to give a greater stimulus to "discretionary" spending on autos and other durable consumer goods, by giving more to middle- and upper-income taxpayers, that effect has been somewhat dissipated by cutting the rebates into two parts—the first half to be mailed in May (if Congress, dominated by liberal Democrats, acts by April 1) and the second-half by September.

The Democrats are not expected to feel that the size of the tax cut is too large, but they may well quarrel with its distribution and equity.

It will be difficult for many members of Congress representing working class constituencies to explain why they should go along with a proposal that would give $1,000 to a taxpayer with $40,000 income or more, but only about $50 to the head of a family of four with an income of $10,000, $12 to a family of four with an income of $5,000—and nothing at all to those with incomes too low for them to pay taxes.

This relates to the initial $16-billion in rebates on 1974 taxes.

The Democratic economic program, issued by a Congressional task force this week, calls for focusing tax relief on low- and middle-income families—by increasing the personal tax exemption, the standard deduction and minimum income allowance, by reducing the payroll-tax liabilities of the working poor, or by a system of individual tax credits. Such proposals, if enacted, might constitute permanent tax reductions rather than the one-shot rebates proposed by the President.

Conceivably, however, the Democrats may be willing to trade off their types of tax cuts for the sake of a quicker and seemingly simpler cut in order to get the economy moving.

The $4-billion in tax cuts that the President proposes to give to business by way of an increase in the investment tax credit from 7 per cent to 12 per cent appears unlikely to run into Democratic opposition. However, with business investment in new plant and equipment likely to decline all through 1975 because of the slump, excess industrial capacity and falling profits, it seems improbable that an increase in the investment tax credit would be strong enough this year to turn capital spending around.

Mr. Ford has said his "combined program adds up to $46-billion—$30-billion in returned energy tax revenue to compensate for higher fuel costs—and $16-billion in tax cuts to help provide more jobs." This $46-billion, however, does not represent the net fiscal impact of his program.

The $30-billion that he would allocate to the energy program represents no net stimulus to the economy; it is essentially a shuffling around of funds for the purpose of trying to curb oil and gas consumption and to induce producers and consumers to switch to other sources of energy.

Indeed, the energy program of the President might be a net drag on the economy, while at the same time giving it an inflationary push. In that respect it is not unlike the "stagflation" effect of the huge increase in oil prices put through in the last year by the Organization of Petroleum Exporting Countries.

The $3-increase in the import tax on each barrel of foreign crude oil, which the President asserts he has the emergency power to do himself, will raise its price to about $14 a barrel—assuming that OPEC does not raise the price still higher.

Domestic oil, if decontrolled, appears likely to rise to the same level. This could increase the present "blend" price of a barrel of oil from about $8 to $14—a jump that, even with "windfall" taxes on oil producers, would be felt by consumers directly in their gasoline prices and prices of home-heating oil and indirectly through the prices of virtually everything else.

Electricity, chemicals, food and all sorts of other manufactured goods in which petroleum is a significant input to production would rise. The cost of living index might go up a few percentage points as a result. This would feed into wages by way of escalator clauses and higher demands by labor.

How much this increase in oil and gas prices would curb fuel use remains to be seen, but economists generally believe the elasticity of demand for oil for industrial use is less than it is for gasoline. Mr. Ford, however, was apparently sensitive to the insistence of the auto industry that higher petroleum taxes not fall on gasoline alone.

The give-back of $30-billion in energy taxes might prove to be less than an equal offset to the contracting effects of those taxes on the economy, if the money is given back in the form Mr. Ford proposes. This would include payments and credits to individuals, businesses and state and local governments.

The corporate income tax, under this plan, would be cut from 48 per cent to 42 per cent, at a cost in tax revenues of about $6-billion. A comparable sum added to consumer spending might have a quicker and more stimulative impact on the economy. In effect, under Mr. Ford's plan, income would be transferred through excise taxes on oil from consumers to businesses.

As it is, President Ford is proposing to give individuals a $16.5-billion tax cut on 1975 income as their share of the redistribution of the $30-billion in higher oil and natural gas taxes. However, this is conditional on increasing fuel taxes by $30-billion.

Democrats and liberals may balk at an energy program based almost entirely on higher taxes and higher prices. Mr. Ford may have given the Democrats — still undecided about their own energy program—a big shove toward oil-import quotas, allocation and gasoline rationing as their preferred approach to cutting petroleun consumption.

Mr. Ford appears to have stressed the huge budget deficits he says are in prospect—"$30- to $50-billion this year and next"—as a means of curbing any tendency on the part of the Democrats to go beyond what he is offering either in tax cuts or in future spending programs. It is not easy to calculate the net size of the prospective deficits or their fiscal stimulus until his spending figures for fiscal 1976 are known.

However, his deficit figures appear to assume very little if any economic recovery this year and next—as indicated by the negligible gain in tax revenues that would apparently result from the program he is offering.

In fact, Mr. Ford warns Congress that he will not hesitate to veto any new spending programs it sends to him—and will even ask Congress to put a 5 per cent ceiling not only on Federal pay but even on Social Security escalation — which means that inflation this year will cut the pensions of old people, if Congress goes along with Mr. Ford.

If Congress does accept Mr. Ford's program lock, stock and barrel, the nation appears to be facing not only two years of a cumulative $80-billion budget deficit, but a very sluggish economy with unemployment this year likely to reach 8 per cent or higher.

January 15, 1975

The Budget Deficit: How Dangerous?

By RONALD A. KRIEGER

Just 200 years after Paul Revere galloped through the countryside to alert an imperiled populace, cries of alarm are again troubling the slumber of nervous Americans. This time around the shouts of danger warn not of Red-coats, but of red ink.

From Washington to Wall Street, latter-day midnight riders are attempting to awaken the nation to the threat of an impending credit crunch. Unless swift action is taken, they warn, the economy may be permanently crippled by the strain of financing the massive Federal deficits contemplated for fiscal 1975 and 1976.

Like Paul Revere, those sounding the current alarm are clearly raising a valid issue. But unlike the Massachusetts patriot their timing is open to serious question.

According to legend, Revere was able to synchronize the start of his ride with the appearance of a reliable "leading indicator" on the opposite shore. His present-day counterparts, however, have no lantern in the Old North Church to guide them.

In the view of some economists, it is possible that today's alarmists have sent their message as much as a year too early. If so, they may doom their cause since a premature alarm can fatally endanger credibility. If the worst does not happen, the counsel may be disregarded even when it does become timely.

Timing has thus become the key issue in the credit-crunch debate that has split economists and the financial community. The alarmists believe the danger is at hand and must be met without delay, while their calmer colleagues see no reason for quick action.

The ranks of those worrying most about budget deficits, although thin, include some vocal economists and Wall Street analysts, as well as an influential segment of the financial press and some middle and high Government officials. The recent nervous behavior of the credit markets indicates that many market participants find their case persuasive.

Their basic warning is that as the United States Treasury elbows its way into the capital markets to finance the Federal deficit, private borrowers will be crowded out. In the process, it is argued, interest rates will soar, private capital formation will decline, economic growth will be choked off and any recovery from the recession may well be aborted. Furthermore, the relative size and influence of the private sector will shrink as the Government grabs off a larger and larger share of the nation's stagnating output.

If this interpretation is correct, the only immediate solutions appear to be extreme on monetary expansion. Either the Government must curtail its deficit spending or the Federal Reserve must step in to finance much of the new debt with the printing press.

Neither of these alternatives holds much appeal for more moderate economists, who generally assert that the recession can be fought without re-inflating the economy. They believe there is plenty of room in the slack business situation for noninflationary financing of the deficit, at least through the end of 1975. And they do not see the Treasury displacing private borrowers from the capital markets until a broad economic recovery is well underway next year.

Therefore, moderates say, there is no reason to curtail deficit spending before it has been given a proper chance to stimulate the sluggish economy. In any event, the grim mood of Congress in the face of a rising unemployment rate seems to preclude a policy of fiscal restraint this year.

The greater fear of the middle-of-the-road group is that the Federal Reserve will knuckle under to the fears of a credit crunch despite the best intentions of Federal Reserve Chairman Arthur F. Burns. As it helps to finance the deficit by absorbing much of the new Treasury debt, it will pump reserves into the banking system at a rate guaranteed to rekindle double-digit inflation within a year or two.

The moderates believe the Reserve has plenty of room for a policy of vigorous monetary expansion without carrying it to an extreme. The money supply has grown only about 4 per cent in the past 12 months, and the monetary authorities could probably double that growth rate for a few months without overshooting a 6 to 7 per cent annual target.

It normally takes a year or two for changes in monetary growth rates to work themselves into the inflation rate, so there is not much chance of an inflationary explosion in the near future unless the Fed reacts to the most extreme fears of the alarmists and immediately monetizes the bulk of the new Government debt.

The policy disagreements of economists center, for the moment, on whether those fears are justified. Opposing viewpoints appear to arise in the main from conflicting interpretations over just what is happening today in the capital markets.

It is not hard to see why the markets are nervous over the red ink in the Federal budget. As the recession cuts into tax receipts and expands social spending, the projected deficit for the fiscal year that ends June 30 will probably come in some $10-billion above the $35-billion contemplated in President Ford's February budget message. For the fiscal year beginning July 1, the current median forecast is for a deficit around $80-billion.

The back-to-back deficits for fiscal 1975 and 1976 will thus require about $125-billion to be financed by Treasury borrowing in the two years. Even in inflated dollars the figure is staggering. By way of comparison, from 1965 through 1974 the total red ink generated by the deficit-ridden Federal budget was only about $100-billion, or $10-billion a year.

The Treasury plans to borrow more than $40-billion in the first half of 1975 and a similar amount in the second half, with further massive borrowing planned for 1976. In the process it is likely to absorb the major share of the funds supplied to the credit markets. This means, according to the alarmist interpretation, that it will draw off tens of billions of dollars that otherwise would have gone to corporate borrowers. In this view, some corporations have already been crowded out of the bond market by the Treasury. Those who fear that the credit crunch is already visible cite as evidence a number of corporate bond issues that have been postponed in recent weeks, including a $300-million debenture offering by Texaco, Inc.

"The crowding out is going on right now and has been for some time," says Norman B. Ture, a Washington-based economic consultant. "When you see company after company either withdrawing an offering or selling it at a deep discount, you know there is substantial displacement of private offerings by Treasury credit operations."

Such a displacement worries those who perceive it as constituting a threat to the capital formation that the private sector must generate to get the economy back on its long-term growth path. The sagging of bond prices in recent weeks has raised fears that many of the less creditworthy corporate borrowers will be pushed right out of the credit queue.

"For an objective indicator that crowding out is taking place, all you have to look at is what is happening to interest rates," says Mr. Ture. "They are on a continuous upturn, and I think the trend will probably accelerate."

Economists who minimize the threat of a credit crunch tend to interpret the evidence in a different way. There has to be a crowd before there can be any crowding out, they say. And even with the Treasury financing, the capital markets hardly resemble a mob scene.

Corporations borrowed heavily in the credit markets

in the first quarter of this year, and it is not surprising that some companies are now dropping out, according to critics of the crowding-out interpretation. They note that much of the borrowing early in the year represented refunding of short-term liabilities in the long-term market, in response to declining long-term rates. Even if some of it represented hedging against a projected credit crunch, their subsequent retreat in the face of rebounding long-term rates does not mean that a crunch has arrived.

Why, then, have some borrowers postponed their bond issues? According to this interpretation, it probably just reflects expectations of lower long-term rates in the near future.

"Texaco was not crowded out of the bond market," contends Roger Klein, director of economic research for the Securities Industry Association. "They just think long-term rates are too high relative to where they will be in the future. So for now they're borrowing short."

Mr. Klein, who monitors securities markets closely, expects little disruption to result from Treasury financing this year. He believes, in fact, that long-term rates will soon decline.

"There will be no interest-rate problem in 1975," says Mr. Klein. "Private demand for credit is weak and falling, and the government is just filling the vacuum."

Contrary to the crowding-out hypothesis, Mr. Klein regards the postponement of issues by corporations as positive proof that these institutions anticipate neither a credit crunch nor rising interest tates.

"If they really believed there were going to be double-digit rates, they wouldn't be postponing their issues," he says. "They would be buying their credit at the 'cheap' rates we have now before they get any higher."

If the moderates are right, the damage done by premature cries of alarm may be hard to repair. Most analysts agree that there will be an unmistakable credit crunch in 1976 as business loan demand picks up and the Treasury continues its large financing operations.

When that happens, voices of restraint will be desperately needed. They may, however, end up talking into ears of policy makers who will already be deafened by the premature cries of alarm.

Mr. Krieger is professor of economics at Goucher College.

April 13, 1975

Awaiting a Recovery

Prospects Are Linked to Inventories, Tax Cut's Impact and Pace of Inflation

By LEONARD SILK

Economic Analysis

Is the recession really bottoming out, as so many businessmen and economists assert? And, if it is, will the recovery be strong and sustained or weak and uncertain? As of the moment, real evidence of the beginning of an upturn is hard to find. On the contrary, last month's drop in new orders for durable goods—a decline of $1.3-billion, or 3.6 per cent—looked more like evidence of a continuing slump. That drop, in fact, more than wiped out the 2.7 per cent gain in February that Government economists had hailed as evidence that the slump was ending.

Consumers, still worrying about hanging onto their jobs as unemployment continues to rise toward 9 per cent, are not yet rushing out to buy expensive items, such as new homes or autos.

Elsewhere, the fall of Cambodia to the Communists and the imminent collapse of South Vietnam, after President Thieu's resignation and bitter denunciation of the United States as "untrustworthy," seem bound to darken the national mood.

Yet the case for a second-half recovery of the American economy is founded on more than wishful thinking.

The first major element is the likely turnaround in inventories. After climbing at an annual rate of $11-billion in the fourth quarter of 1974—a build-up that was involuntary — inventories were worked down by about $11-billion in the first quarter of this year.

That $22-billion net swing helped make the first-quarter drop in the gross national product the worst on record, 10.4 per cent at an annual rate, but is unlikely to be repeated. Though industries may go on paring inventories for another quarter or two, even a slower rate of decline and ultimately a leveling off of stocks will give the economy at least a moderate boost in the second half.

More Cash to Spend

The second major element is the impact of the tax cut. Individuals and corporations will have $23-billion more to spend—and even a small increase in the savings rate will not prevent a strong inflation of funds into the spending stream.

The third major factor pointing toward recovery is the slowing of inflation, which should help quicken consumer spending. In March consumer prices rose only 0.3 per cent, the smallest rise in 20 months.

But are these positive factors enough to do the job—or is the recovery likely to be dragged or even aborted by too restrictive a monetary policy?

There has never been a time when the Federal Reserve System has been subjected to such withering criticism from all sides — monetarist economists and Keynesians, businessmen and labor leaders, home builders, bankers, and members of Congress.

A leading monetarist, Prof. Karl Brunner of the University of Rochester, has denounced the Fed for contradicting its own instructions to the Open Market Committee and replacing net open-market purchases of about $5-billion in November-December, 1974, with net sales of about $1-billion in January-February this year. (Open-market purchases of securities increase the money supply, while sales contract it.)

The failure of the Fed to make the money supply grow at an adequate rate, said Professor Brunner, is "serious and regrettable. It prolongs and amplifies an already substantial economic downswing quite unnecessarily."

A leading Keynesian, Prof. James Tobin of Yale, takes much the same position. He contends that the Fed is "not pushing hard and could be pushing harder" without danger of rekindling inflation. With interest rates still high by historical standards, Professor Tobin denies that the economy is in a "liquidity trap." He says the banks will not, as some fear, sit on additional reserves, but will lend or invest them.

Burns's Viewpoint

But Arthur F. Burns, chairman of the Federal Reserve Board, insists that he has been doing quite enough to get monetary expansion rolling. He feels that his critics believe there is a more automatic relationship between Fed actions and the growth of the money supply — especially of M-1, which is demand deposits plus currency in circulation—than actually exists.

After growing at the slow rate of 4.15 per cent in 1974—and actually declining at an annual rate of 9 per cent during January, 1975, driving the monetarists up and over the wall—the money supply (M-1) suddenly spurted upward during the last two months at an annual rate of nearly 13 per cent.

It was as though the Fed had been pulling on a rubber band, with a heavy weight attached to the other end. Suddenly—as happens in mechanics—the rubber band overcame the resistance of the weight and it snapped ahead.

It seems unlikely that any such rapid rate of growth in the money supply will continue. On the contrary, that sudden burst of monetary expansion seems likely to cause the Fed to tighten up again. Indeed, **if the recent 13 per cent rate of increase were to continue for even a few weeks longer, the monetarists who have been denouncing the Fed for causing and prolonging the recession would attack it for regenerating inflation.**

But Dr. Burns has given no grounds for worry on that count; he has emerged (with Secretary of the Treasury William E. Simon as his principal supporter) as inflation fighter No. 1.

Some careful observers, including conservatives not given to ideological prescriptions on how to stabilize the economy, fear that Dr. Burns and Mr. Simon are upsetting the markets and burdening the recovery by excessive fears of inflation.

Matter of Timing

One such observer, normally a supporter of the Fed, is James J. O'Leary, vice chairman of the United States Trust Company, who is afraid that overly tight Fed policies and overly aalrmist Treasury pronouncements are checking the decline in short-term interest rates and pushing long-term rates higher at just the wrong time—while the economy is still deep in the recession and while inflation is coming down — and thereby jeopardizing the recovery.

"I am worried," says Mr. O'Leary, "about the recent flattening out of short-term rates and the upward bulge of corporate bond yields. The latter may be correcting itself, but I fear that there has been a rather profound change in capital market psychology, which will make it difficult to bring down long-term corporate bond yields very much from current levels."

The big factor in this changed psychology, as he sees it, has been "scare talk" about the **rise of the Federal deficit to the $80-billion to $100-billion level.**

Mr. O'Leary thinks the Fed has let the market become convinced that it has gone as far as it can in pushing down short-term rates. "From the standpoint of the business recovery," he says, "it seems to me that it would be very harmful if short rates bottomed out at current levels, and it would be especially hurtful if they proceeded to move upward."

A further climb in corporate bond yields could be particularly damaging to the recovery. With corporate profits likely to be down sharply this year, business hopes of raising capital for investment in plant and equipment would be hurt. And the hoped-for recovery in housing would also be dragged by a rise in long-term mortgage rates.

A strong anti-inflationist himself, Mr. O'Leary concludes, "Consistent with maintaining a proper balance between fighting inflation and fighting business recession, I think that the Federal Reserve can safely push further toward lower short-term rates and hopefully toward encouraging lower long-term rates."

Inflation Still High

The crucial issue facing both **the Fed and the Treasury is one of timing. Inflation is subsiding but is still uncomfortably high.**

The over-all price index used to deflate the gross national product came down from an annual rate of 14.4 per cent in the last quarter of 1974 to an 8 per cent rate in the first quarter of 1975. Wholesale prices have actually dropped, by more than 2 per cent since their November peak, and the inflation curve seems likely to slow further, even if recovery soon begins.

Unemployment is still growing, and a great deal of excess capacity hangs over many industries after the steep slump of 1974 and early 1975.

At the same time, interest rates are still high by comparison with the final phase of past recessions. The Treasury it is felt, could help in this area by avoiding new issues of long-term Government bonds that would overload the market and push up rates.

But in the final analysis a healthy and ongoing recovery — and a faster dip in unemployment than the Administration or most economists now expect — would require a stronger monetary push than yet appears to be in the cards.

April 23, 1975

GATT
LABRADOR SEA
NEWFOUNDLAND
ECUADOR
PERU
BRAZIL

CHAPTER 2
Foreign Trade

The General Agreement on Tariffs and Trade, a post-World War II effort toward a new economic order; establishes and administers codes for the orderly conduct of international trade.
Courtesy The New York Times

NORMAL TRADE LED BY EXPORTS HERE

More Than Two Decades of Records Reviewed In Light of Bretton Woods Ideas

LONG DEPRESSION PERIOD

Foreign Attitude Toward Our Policies—Changes Under State Department

By KENNETH AUSTIN

It is probable that many nations in both hemispheres will not look kindly on the Bretton Woods proposals, after approval by Congress, if this country does not also ratify the Government's program to strengthen and extend the Trade Agreement Act of 1934, it appears to those conversant with international economic relations in the 1920-to-1940 period.

To such observers, our willingness to broaden the policy of bilateral trade agreements and to enter into multi-lateral pacts not only is an essential base for the future functioning of the world bank and the monetary fund proposed at Bretton Woods, but also for all remaining facets of the international economic program, including measures dealing with distribution of farm products and raw materials for industry and the plan to establish a permanent international trade organization.

The Trade Agreement Act came into being soon after the regrettable failure of the World Monetary and Economic Conference of 1933. As with our decision not to join the League of Nations, it is futile to speculate on what the course of events might have been had we entered into close association with other nations under the League in 1920 and in the economic sphere in London in 1933.

Changes in Tariffs

Nonetheless, observers here and abroad believe that trade relations between this country and others became more tolerable when our State Department was enabled to negotiate trade agreements that abandoned the fixed and, in the opinion of many, excessive tariff walls set up in previous years.

Statistically, the over-all figures of exports and imports by the United States do not show any benefit to ourselves or others following adoption of the Act, although advantages may be traced in particular instances. On the contrary, there was worsening in the ratio of our imports to exports, but one must consider the results in the light of the almost utter chaos affecting foreign trade and the variety of restrictive and isolating devices adopted by many principal nations to keep out all but essential foreign goods and the growth of inter-governmental barter to replace vanishing trade.

For the six years from 1923 to 1928 inclusive our exports were $28,451,000,000 and our imports were $24,336,000,000, or 88.5 per cent. Without going into the shipments of gold and other elements of the balance of payments, should one consider this period quite as unfair as many have contended?

In the following six years from 1929 to 1934 inclusive, most of which were depression years all over the world, we exported $16,927,000,000 of goods and imported $13,978,000,000, or 82.5 per cent. It was only in this period, when our own deflationary trends had made it impossible for us to continue the heavy foreign loans made in the previous six years, that foreign experts almost unitedly began to attack our trade policies as the source of much of the world's economic troubles.

Statistics for Later Years

In the six years that followed 1935 to 1940 inclusive, our exports were $18,381,000,000, and our imports $14,458,000,000, or 78.7 per cent. Only in 1936 and 1937 were our imports better than 90 per cent of exports; one may attribute this to the first fruits of our new trade policy and the trend of ensuing years to the hurried rearming of Western European nations and, consequently, heavier purchases here. In 1936, on two-way transactions of only $4,879,000,000, our imports were 98.6 per cent of our exports; in 1937 the ratio was 92 per cent; in 1938 it was 63.4 per cent; in 1939 it was 72.9 per cent and in 1940 it was 65.3 per cent, with the trade volume built up to $6,647,000,000, the highest since 1930.

We have had more than a century of almost uninterrupted export balances, and since the end of the Civil War the trend has been sharply toward increasingly higher excess balances because of our protective tariff policies. Under these policies we have become the greatest producers in virtually every field of manufacture, with the highest wage scales and standards of living.

This assuredly is not a condition of which to complain, yet it is undeniably the cause of much of the resentment expressed against us abroad between the two World Wars. Administration experts are confident that we can, by free negotiation, maintain satisfactory standards of living, productiveness and employment here while encouraging improvement abroad; that, by increasing the size of the "pie," we can eat more heartily than by cutting a wider slice from a narrowing dish.

April 22, 1945

COMPROMISE TO PERMIT BRITAIN TO GET LOAN

In Return for Credits She Will Have To Surrender Her Trade Controls

By JOHN H. CRIDER

WASHINGTON, Sept. 29—The Anglo-American negotiations to find a solution to the British balance of payments problem, which is the main obstacle to early resumption of international trade, appeared definitely to have made progress in the little more than two weeks since the talks commenced. Early next week parallel negotiations on commercial policy will be started.

In essence the problem is an extremely simple one, but in detail extremely complicated, so that negotiations seem slow. It took Lord Keynes about five sessions with the top negotiators to lay the British factual case on the table. And then the American experts asked for and obtained additional data.

Thus far the negotiations, beyond exploring and agreeing upon the facts in the situation, have been a feeling-out process. After five meetings at which they heard Lord Keynes explain the case of our ally, the top negotiators adjourned and for the last week have been meeting informally in pairs here and there around the capital in the kind of talks at which a real meeting of minds can be attained. It can be stated emphatically that the whole procedure has started off in an atmosphere of mutual cordiality, with a desire on both sides to succeed.

The Basic Problem

The over-all problem, which can be stated simply, arises from the fact that Britain has so used up her overseas assets and her foreign exchange (foreign purchasing power) that she cannot operate during the next three years without a deficit of dollars (American purchasing power) of around $6,000,000,000. The problem is how to help her out.

That the United States should help the British in this critical situation is beyond question so far as the Administration is concerned. After all, the British are where they are because they gave up their export trade and depended on lend-lease throughout most of the war in order more completely to give their resources to conduct of the war.

Most of the American negotiators feel that we have as much to gain as the British, if not more, from the contemplated aid. These are the primary gains for the United States:

(1) British sterling area trade

NEGOTIATORS

Associated Press, Pix, Inc.

Lord Keynes and Assistant Secretary of State Clayton who are negotiating for a loan to Britain.

with the United States, now halted, for lack of dollars, could be resumed. In 1938 these countries bought from us around $300,000,000 worth in finished manufactures alone. Total United Kingdom imports from the United States, it is estimated, will double the pre-war level and approximate $1,000,000,000 in the first year of trade resumption. Britain has long been our best market. The figures do not include Canada, which is outside the sterling area.

Restrictions Removed

(2) Restrictions on the free movement of world commerce would be removed or minimized. Without American help, Great Britain would have to trade for some time within the sterling area, thus dividing the world into competitive trade blocs—a dollar and a sterling area—with inevitable economic warfare.

There would be other gains of less measurable character, such as the continuance of the good-will that has marked Anglo-American relationships during the whole war period.

The toughest aspect of the problem for the American negotiators is to find a means of granting the needed aid which will be acceptable to Congress and the American people. The officials in the executive departments who are conducting the negotiations know that they will have to "sell" whatever agreement they make to Congress. They are frankly fearful of the residue of isolationist sentiment in Congress, of the professional anti-Britishers and of those who are so concerned over the state of our own finances that they cannot see the benefits which would appear to accrue to the United States from the deal.

Use of Gold Reserve

That is one reason why a proposal, now under discussion, to grant the credit from the $20,000,000,000 gold reserve is attractive to some of the American negotiators. This would permit making the advance—it is conceded that it will have to be a loan—without borrowing the money internally, thus avoiding further swelling of the Federal debt.

The British appear to recognize that outright grants or continuance of lend-lease under any guise is out of the question. Thus the debate is on the interest rate and the term. The Americans generally agree that a very long term is desirable, under the circumstances, but will insist upon as much interest as they can get.

But one of the cries that the American conferees feel sure they will hear uttered most lustily from opponents in Congress is "empire preference." That is where the commercial policy aspects of the negotiations impinge upon the financial. For the Americans know full well that the credit advance will have to be conditioned upon agreement by the British to get rid of, if not eliminate, their Commonwealth preference system—largely a tariff arrangement—which serves to keep a large part of empire trade within a specific channel.

The consensus is that there will be an agreement and that there will be compromises on both sides. The British will have to surrender the bulk of their trade and exchange controls, and we will hand over some credits which, if all goes well, will come back with dividends.

September 30, 1945

CHURCHILL ASSAILS SOVIET POLICY

BRITON SPEAKS OUT

Calls for Association of U. S., British to Stem Russian Expansion

APPEASEMENT IS OPPOSED

'Iron Curtain' Dividing Europe Is Not What We Fought For, Churchill Says at Fulton, Mo.

By HAROLD B. HINTON
Special to THE NEW YORK TIMES.

FULTON, Mo., March 5—A fraternal association between the British Empire and the United States was advocated here today by Winston Churchill to stem "the expansive and proselytizing tendencies" of the Soviet Union.

Introduced by President Truman at Westminster College, Great Britain's wartime Prime Minister asserted that a mere balance of power in the world today would be too narrow a margin and would only offer "temptations to a trial of strength."

On the contrary, he added that the English-speaking peoples must maintain an overwhelming preponderance of power on their side until "the highroads of the future will be clear, not only for us but for all, not only for our time but for a century to come."

Says Curtain Divides Europe

Mr. Churchill painted a dark picture of post-war Europe, on which "an iron curtain has descended across the Continent" from Stettin in the Baltic to Trieste in the Adriatic.

Warsaw, Berlin, Prague, Vienna, Budapest, Belgrade, Sofia and Bucharest are all being subjected to increasing pressure and control from Moscow, he said, adding:

"This is certainly not the liberated Europe we fought to build up. Nor is it one which contains the essentials of permanent peace."

Even in front of the "iron curtain," he asserted, Italy was hampered in its efforts to return to a normal national existence by "Communist-trained Marshal Tito's claims to former Italian territory," and the re-establishment of a strong France was impeded by fifth columns working "in complete unity and absolute obedience to the directions they receive from the Communist center."

He strongly intimated a parallel between the present position of the Soviet Union with that of Germany in 1935, when, he said, "Germany might have been saved from the awful fate which has overtaken her and we might all have been spared the miseries Hitler let loose upon mankind without a single shot being fired."

But time is running short, he warned, if the world is not "to try to learn again, for a third time, in a school of war incomparably more rigorous than that from which we have just been released."

His words, he continued, were not offered in the belief that war with the Soviet Union was inevitable or imminent. He expressed the view that Russia does not desire war, but cautioned that Moscow does desire the fruits of war and the indefinite expansion of its power and policies.

Appeasement Is Opposed

The difficulties of the Western democracies, he said, will not be removed by closing their eyes to them, by waiting to see what happens, or by a policy of appeasement.

Expressing admiration and regard for Marshal Stalin, Mr Churchill asserted that the English-speaking peoples understood Russia's need to secure her western frontiers against renewed German aggression and welcomed Russia into her rightful place among the leading countries of the world.

From his experience with them, he said that he learned that Russians admired nothing so much as strength, and that they had no respect for military weakness.

Given an overwhelming show of strength on the side of upholding the principles of the United Nations Organization, Mr. Churchill asserted, the Soviet Union would be prepared to come to a settlement of outstanding differences with the Western world.

He suggested that the secret of the atomic bomb be kept in the hands of the United States, Great Britain and Canada, because "it would be imprudent and wrong" to confide it to the UNO, while that

DISTINGUISHED VISITORS AT WESTMINSTER COLLEGE

President Truman and Winston Churchill in the procession with Dr. Franc McCluer, head of the school at Fulton, Mo.

Associated Press Wirephoto

organization was "still in its infancy."

He said that no one in the world had slept less well because the atomic secret was in its present custody, but the people of the world would not rest so soundly if that secret were possessed by "some Communist or neo-Fascist State."

He also called for immediate establishment of a UNO air force, to be made up of a number of squadrons from member countries capable of supplying them. These squadrons would be trained and equipped at home, but would be stationed abroad. They would not be required to go into action against their own country, but would otherwise be at the orders of the UNO.

Although he expressed confidence in the ultimate ability of the UNO to preserve the peace of the world, Mr. Churchill said that it must become "a true temple of peace" and not "merely a cockpit in the Tower of Babel."

Comparing its inception with that of the League of Nations, he regretted that he could not "see or feel the same confidence or even the same hopes in the haggard world at this time."

The fraternal association he advocated between the British Empire and the United States would include interchange of officers and cadets among the military schools of the associates, similarity of weapons and training manuals, **common war plans, joint use of all naval and air bases and intimate relationships among high military advisers.**

With this potential strength behind them, he said, the English-speaking peoples could reach "now, in 1946, a good understanding on all points with Russia."

The special relationships of the type he urged, Mr. Churchill argued, would be fully consistent with loyalty to the UNO.

He recalled the special relations between the United States and Canada, the United States and the other American republics, and the twenty-year treaty between Great Britain and Russia (he interjected that "I agree with Mr. Bevin [British Foreign Minister] that it might well be a fifty-year treaty") as examples of international cooperation which serve to buttress, not undermine, the peace of the world.

The United States now stands at the pinnacle of world power, Mr. Churchill asserted, and shares with the other English-speaking peoples what he described as the over-all strategic concept of "the safety and welfare, the freedom and progress of all the homes and families of all the men and women in all the lands."

For the United States to ignore or fritter away its "clear and shining" opportunity would be to "bring upon us all the long reproaches of the after-time," he added.

Turning to the Far East, Mr. Churchill called the outlook there "anxious," especially in Manchuria, despite the aspects of the Yalta agreement, to which he was a party.

He defended the agreement on the ground that the war with Germany was then expected to last until the autumn of 1945, with the war against Japan calculated to endure eighteen months after that.

Mr. Churchill gave his listeners the impression that he and President Roosevelt would not have dealt so generously with Marshal Stalin, had they realized that collapse of the Axis was near at hand.

War and tyranny were the twin evils Mr. Churchill saw threatening the world today. He looked for the hunger and distress now afflicting so much of the world to pass fairly quickly, and for "the inauguration and enjoyment of an age of plenty."

"Nothing can stand in the way of such an outcome," he said, except "human folly or sub-human crime."

Mr. Churchill described himself as a "private visitor" with no official mission or status of any kind, and as a man whose early private ambitions had been satisfied beyond his wildest dreams.

He said that Mr. Truman had granted him full liberty "to give you my true and faithful counsel in these anxious and baffling times."

In his introduction the President said that he and Mr. Churchill both believed in freedom of speech, adding:

"I know he will have something constructive to say."

When Mr. Truman later took the platform to acknowledge the doctorate of laws which Westminster conferred on him, as well as on Mr. Churchill, he told the audience that it was "your moral duty and mine to see that the Charter of the United Nations is implemented as the law of the land and the law of the world."

The President, however, made no direct reference to the "fraternal association" Mr. Churchill suggested.

"We are either headed for complete destruction or are facing the greatest age in history," Mr. Truman said, adding:

"It is up to you to decide, and **up to me to see that we follow that path toward that great age and not toward destruction.**

"The release of atomic energy has given us a force which means the happiness and welfare of every human being on earth or the destruction of civilization.

"I prefer to think we have the ability, the moral stamina and the energy to see that the great age comes about, not destruction."

Churchill Drops Serious Note

When it came Mr. Churchill's turn to thank Dr. Franc Lewis McCluer, the faculty and trustees of Westminister College for the honor they conferred on him, he dropped the serious tenor of his earlier address and made the following remarks:

"Mr. President, President McCluer, Members of the Faculty: I am not sure that I may say fellow-members of the faculty. I am most grateful, and through you to the authorities of the State of Missouri and to the college authorities, for their great kindness in that conferring upon me another of these degrees, which I value so highly and, as I was saying only the other day at Miami, which have a double attraction to me, that they do not require any preliminary examinations.

"I value very much this token of good-will which comes from this center of education in the very heart of the United States and in the State which is so dear to the heart of the President of this great country.

"I also thank you all here for the great patience, indulgence, kindness and attention to listen to what I had to say, for I am quite sure it will have been right and wise to say at this juncture. I am very glad to have had this opportunity and am grateful to all who have come here and assisted me to discharge my task.

"I am, of course, unswerving in my allegiance to my own king and country, but I can never feel entirely a foreigner in the United States, which is my motherland **and where my ancestors, forebears on that side of the family for five generations, have lived.**

"I was, however, a little puzzled the other day when one branch of the Sons of the Revolution invited me to become a member, on the grounds that my forebears undoubtedly fought in Washington's armies.

"I felt on the whole that I was on both sides then, and therefore I should adopt as far as possible an unbiased attitude. But I may justly tell you how proud is my love for this great and mighty nation and empire of the United States."

This was a gala day in Fulton and Jefferson City, the State Capital, where the President and Mr. Churchill left their train. In both towns the motor cavalcade drove slowly around the principal streets, which were lined with spectators.

Police estimated that the normal population of 8,000 turned out in Fulton and was augmented by some 20,000 visitors who had come from as far distant as St. Louis.

Dr. McCluer entertained the President and Mr. Churchill with the members of their immediate party at luncheon in his home on the campus before the ceremonies.

The President and Mr. Churchill marched into the gymnasium at the end of the long academic procession. Mr. Truman wore the hood indicating the honorary doctorate of laws conferred on him last summer by the University of Kansas City, while Mr. Churchill wore a scarlet hood indicating an Oxford degree.

Mr. Churchill's speech was received with marked applause in the passages where it dealt with the responsibility of this country to see that another World War was avoided, but the proposal for "fraternal association" brought only moderate handclapping.

March 6, 1946

ECONOMIC WAR DUE IF TRADE BARS STAY, TRUMAN WARNS U. S.

World Looks to This Country for Leadership in Cutting Barriers, President Asserts

CHOICE IS CALLED OURS

In Talk at Baylor University He Backs the ITO as Device for Preventing Conflict

By FELIX BELAIR Jr.

Special to THE NEW YORK TIMES.

WACO, Texas, March 6—President Truman asserted today that the United States must take the lead in reducing international trade barriers, or plunge the world into economic war and pave the way for future armed conflicts.

In an address at Baylor University here after receiving an honorary degree, the President, who arrived at 9:30 A. M. after a predawn flight from Mexico City, declared:

"We are the giant of the economic world. Whether we like it or not, the future pattern of economic relations depends upon us. The world is waiting and watching to see what we shall do. The choice is ours. We can lead the nations to economic peace or we can plunge them into economic war."

He said that while the leaders of both political parties were agreed on the indivisibility of the political and economic in American foreign relations, there were some who frowned on bipartisan support of foreign economic cooperation.

World Called at Turning Point

Now, as in 1920, the world has reached a turning point in its history, the President stressed. National economies have been disrupted by war; economic policies are in a state of flux, and in this atmosphere of doubt and hesitation, he warned, the decisive factor will be the type of leadership the United States gives the world.

The President recalled that negotiations would begin in April at Geneva for reduction of tariffs here and abroad, the elimination of other restrictive trade measures and the abandonment of discrimination in international commerce.

The success of these negotiations is essential, he said, to the establishment of the international trade organization, to the effective operation of the International Bank and the Monetary Fund and to the strength of the whole United Nations structure of cooperation in economic and political affairs.

"The negotiations at Geneva must not fail," Mr. Truman asserted.

"Isolationists" Are Warned

Congratulating the leaders of both political parties for having removed, for the time being at least, the subject of foreign economic policy from the political arena, the President said that he would welcome a continuation of bi-partisan support.

The chief executive then struck out against "those among us who would seek to undermine this policy for partisan advantage and go back to the period of high tariffs and economic isolation." To this group, he addressed the following warning:

"Take care, times have changed. Our position in the world has changed. The slogans of 1930 or of 1896 are sadly out of date. Isolationism after two world wars is a confession of mental and moral bankruptcy."

The President said that there was one thing that Americans valued even more than peace, and that was freedom — freedom of worship, freedom of speech and freedom of enterprise.

There is a definite connection between the first two of these freedoms and the third, he added, and throughout history, freedom of worship and freedom of speech have most frequently flourished where a considerable measure of freedom was accorded individual enterprise.

In the United States, the devotion to freedom of enterprise has deeper roots than a desire to protect the profits of ownership; it is part and parcel of what we call American, he asserted.

Recalling the "battles" in the economic war of the 'Thirties, the President said that from the Hawley-Smoot tariff policy in this country, the world went on to the British system of imperial preferences, and from there to the detailed restrictions adopted by Nazi Germany.

The world over, countries strangled normal trade and discriminated against their neighbors. Mr. Truman said that he would not argue that economic conflict was the sole cause of the depression of 1929, but he insisted it was a major cause.

The President stressed that unless this country led the way toward lower tariffs and abandonment of discriminatory practices, governments would be brought increasingly into international trade because of demands far more and stricter controls in retaliation for the curtailing or cutting off of foreign markets.

"The pattern of trade that is least conducive to freedom of enterprise is one in which decisions are made by governments," he asserted.

Under such a system, Mr. Truman warned, it was left for public officials to dictate the quantity of purchases and sales, the sources of imports and the destination of exports. This was the system of the seventeenth and eighteenth centuries, and the President said that "unless we act, and act decisively, it will be the pattern of the next century."

The nations of the world are being driven by post-war economic pressures in the direction of more rather than less regimentation, he said.

Countries seeking to reconstruct their industries are trying to control imports, he added, so as not to exceed exports, and those seeking to build new industries are trying to foster them through the same device.

Lack of available exchange he called still another cause for nations to curtail imports from countries whose currencies they did not possess. All manner and form of controls are being used, he said, including quotas, licenses and other practices that have for their purpose the limiting of imports in conformity with a central plan.

If this plan is not reversed, Mr. Truman predicted, the United States Government would be under pressure, sooner or later, to use these same devices in the fight for markets and for raw materials.

If the Government yielded to this pressure, he said, it would soon be telling every trader what he could buy and sell, and how much, and when and where.

The charter of the International Trade Organization was offered as an alternative to this course, Mr. Truman said. It would limit the freedom of governments to impose detailed administrative regulations on their foreign trade. It would require members to confine such controls to exceptional cases and to abandon them as soon as possible.

The President forecast a larger foreign trade, both imports and exports, under the new organization.

Business is poorer when markets ar small, he said, and good when markets are big.

He asserted that there was no thought that the Geneva meeting would attempt to eliminate tariffs or to establish free trade. All that was contemplated was a lowering of tariffs, removal of discriminations and the promotion of freer trade.

Tariffs would not be cut "across the board," the President said. The action would be selective, some rates being cut substantially, some moderately and some not at all. Concessions would be demanded for concessions granted, he added, and there was no thought of sacrificing one economic group for the benefit of another.

The Chief Executive was introduced to his university audience by Pat Neff, president of Baylor, as "just a plain, common everyday citizen with a soul and a heart and a liver just like the rest of us."

Earlier, Mr. Neff stood at the head of a welcoming committee in a pelting rain as the President's plane circled the field and taxied down the runway. Others on hand to greet Mr. Truman were Gov. Beauford Jester of Texas, Attorney General Tom Clark, Senator Tom Connally and Jesse H. Jones, former Secretary of Commerce.

March 7, 1947

NEW ROLE IS SEEN FOR EXPORT BANK

Foreign Traders Say Imports Will Be Stimulated Under New Lending Policy

BALANCED TRADE HELD AIM

Wants to Offset $7,000,000,000 Excess of Shipments Abroad Over Total Entries Here

By CHARLES B. CRISMAN

The Export-Import Bank is carving out a new niche for itself in the pattern of organizations already established and being established in the field of international lending, foreign traders pointed out last week. The bank's new role will be in the field of stimulating imports into the United States to fill the $7,000,000,000 gap between exports and imports.

This role is in perfect keeping with the functions for which it was formed, that of assisting domestic industry and foreign traders to finance exports and imports, it was pointed out. The bank has had, however, few opportunities up to the present time to exercise this function.

When its charter was extended in 1945 and its lending powers increased it was for the purpose of allowing the bank to carry out rehabilitation loans until the International Bank for Reconstruction and Development and the International Monetary Fund could become effective.

The Export-Import Bank has carried this load with commendable skill, according to commercial banking circles, but in the process it has depleted its funds to the point where it now has only $300,000,000 uncommitted resources, non-inclusive of the $500,000,000 earmarked for China.

New Function Seen

With the present possibility that the International Bank soon will begin to function, foreign trade circles pointed out, the Export-Import Bank will no longer be required to handle this type of reconstruction loan.

At the same time the enunciation of the Truman Doctrine of political loans and grants to other nations would also remove this type of loan from the bank, they said, and permit it to operate in the field for which it was originally intended.

How officials of the bank itself view this function has gradually become clear. William McChesney Martin Jr., chairman of the bank, pointed out the direction in which it was tending at the annual convention of the National Foreign Trade Council last November.

Pointing to the prospect of a continuing excess of exports over imports for the United States, he explained that the bank was very much aware of the need to build imports and suggested that private export-import banks could be established to help in this work with the Export-Import Bank itself acting as a kind of central bank.

It was reliably reported in New York several days ago that officials of the bank have recently approached New York bankers urging them to implement the plan suggested by Mr. Martin. According to banking sources, the idea was not received with too great enthusiasm because major banks dealing in international credit already cover the field.

A more direct approach to the same function of stimulating imports was revealed in a speech made by August Maffry, vice president of the Export-Import Bank, at the meeting of the Export Managers Club last week.

New Type Loan Made

Mr. Maffry pointed out that the bank has recently lent the relatively small sum of $2,500,000 to the Finnish-American Tarding Corporation of New York to finance sales promotion of Finnish products in the United States. Purpose of the credit, he said, was to enable a group of minor industries in the borrowing country to purchase in the United States equipment needed to expand production of a variety of products destined especially for the United States market.

The loan was contingent upon the corporation's ability to obtain additional capital from American and Finnish sources. According to Mr. Maffry, credit had been extended to it by three private banks since the loan was projected.

As he pointed out, the loan was to be used in developing the importation into the United States of products that had not been previously exported from Finland, such as ceramics, china, glassware, wood manufactured products and handicraft articles.

If this program is expanded with the help of private capital, he said, the operation will not only provide the means of repaying this and other credits to the country concerned, but will also lay the foundation for a permanently expanded market for United States products.

Foreign traders pointed out that both types of activity involve the cooperation of private capital with the government bank. This combination is necessary in that area of international trade, they said, where private capital would not be willing to venture alone and it would serve the very useful purpose of working toward a solution of unbalanced trade which promises to plague the United States for several years to come.

March 23, 1947

NEW BANK PUTS AID ON SELF-HELP BASIS

McCloy Explains International Reconstruction Unit Seeks an Expanding World Economy

PRIVATE FUNDS RELIED ON

Agricultural, Sociological and Labor Aims Also Discussed Before Life Underwriters

The International Bank for Reconstruction and Development is prepared to extend its facilities to those peoples who are willing to aid their own recovery through cooperative effort and thus create an expanding world economy, John Jay McCloy, president of that institution, declared yesterday in his first public statement on its program.

With other leaders in various phases of the nation's economy, including agriculture, labor and sociology, he addressed the seventh annual forum on current economic and social trends conducted by the New York chapter, American Society of Chartered Life Underwriters, held in Town Hall, 123 West Forty-third Street.

After stressing the need for the investment of capital on an international scale for productive purposes to achieve "stability, prosperity and progress" as a means to peace, Mr. McCloy announced that branches would be opened soon in foreign centers convenient to those nations that have applied for loans.

Bank's Functions Explained

He explained that "the size of the bank will be limited only by the confidence of the investor" in the prime investment market, and that operations would be subject to the limitations imposed in this country by the Securities and Exchange Commission. France, Poland, Czechoslovakia, the Netherlands, Luxembourg, Denmark and Chile were listed as nations that have applied for loans.

"The financing of the world's needs is not only an opportunity; it is the satisfaction of a desperate need," Mr. McCloy declared in his prepared address. "The United States today is in a position to contribute to a prosperous and expanding world economy by assuming leadership in international investment which its dominant productive position makes inevitable. The International Bank is the mechanism by which economic rehabilitation may be accomplished in the great part of the world where the economic community has been destroyed or demoralized."

Describing this international banking institution as essentially an activity of private capital rather than a governmental operation, the new president explained that the funds that would be required to repair the ravages of war might not be available in the private market without some form of international guarantee as that afforded by the International Bank.

Private Investment Stressed

"In the long run, however," he continued, "international investment of capital is primarily the function of the private market, not of public agencies. The founders of the bank recognized this when they wrote into the charter of the bank that one of its fundamental purposes is to promote private foreign investment, and that, to this end, no loan may be made by the bank when the loan is otherwise available to the borrower in the market on reasonable terms."

Although several of the executive directors of the institution "represent potential borrowers," according to Mr. McCloy, he explained that the charter of the bank forbids making any loan that is disapproved by a loan committee of officers of the institution.

The outlook in other phases of the nation's economy was presented by Dr. Herrell DeGraff, associate Professor of Land Economics at Cornell University; Walter W. Cenerazzo, organizer and president of the independent Watch Workers Union, and Dr. James H. S. Bossard, Professor of Sociology and director of the William T. Carter Foundation at the University of Pennsylvania. Stanley High, who acted as moderator of the forum, summarized the public's point of view.

April 19, 1947

WORLD BANK LENDS FRANCE $250,000,000

LOAN FOR 30 YEARS

Interest Is 3¼% With No Repayment Needed During First 5 Years

NEW REQUEST NOT BARRED

Funds Are for Aid in Economic Revival—French See Need for $600,000,000 More

By CHARLES HURD
Special to THE NEW YORK TIMES.

WASHINGTON, May 9—The World Bank began operations today by lending $250,000,000 to France to assist that country in its reconstruction and development of post-war economy. This was the first loan made by the $8,000,000,000 institution set up under the Bretton Woods Charter as an adjunct of the United Nations.

The loan papers were signed shortly after 5 P. M., at the bank's offices here by three persons. John J. McCloy, president of the bank, signed for the institution; Henri Bonnet, French Ambassador, signed for the French Government as guarantor of repayment, and Wilfrid Baumgartner, president of the French Credit National, signed on behalf of that Government corporation, to which the loan technically was made.

The loan runs for a term of thirty years, with no re-payment expected in the first five. It bears interest at the rate of 3¼ per cent, plus an additional 1 per cent a year on unrepaid balances. This premium payment, for the building up of a special reserve, was specified for all loans made by the bank in its Articles of Agreement.

The loan to France was made in the name of forty-four nations that are subscribers to the bank, and the money was lent against capital assets technically estimated to total more than $8,000,000,000.

Since, however, the only money that may be used at this time for loans by the bank consists of slightly more than $700,000,000 in United States dollars held by the bank, the loan actually is a credit in dollars advanced by the bank, with all subscribers to the bank bound to stand as surety in case of default.

The loan was notable also for the fact that, if the funds are claimed by France immediately, they will be taken from the working capital of the bank. In the near future, according to plans already being prepared, the bank plans to cover its loans by means of debentures to be sold in the open market.

The loan papers were signed within a few hours after the twelve executive directors of the bank approved the final details of the long negotiations that have preceded the culmination. France requested a loan of $500,000,000 last October, or twice the sum that was granted. However, the bank announced that it would consider, without present commitment, another application by France "later this year."

"Although the bank is not now prepared to make any commitments with regard to a further loan," an announcement said, "it will be willing to consider an additional application from France later this year. Any new application will be considered in the light of the funds which the bank will then have available for lending and of the progress made in carrying out the French economic and recovery program."

This announcement was taken by informed observers to mean that the bank, rather than desiring to limit France, wished first to learn the extent and terms of the money it could borrow in the United States market. Many other applications for loans are pending. A study is now being made on the basis of a questionnaire sent to financial institutions to test the reaction of investment circles to the bank's operations.

An official description of the French loan summarized its basis as follows:

"The loan is being made to assist France in the reconstruction of its war-torn economy and to finance the import of specific goods and equipment necessary to its economic rehabilitation. A portion of the proceeds will be devoted to the modernization of the steel industry, including a modern strip mill.

"The transportation system is to be improved by the purchase of locomotives and freight cars, cargo ships and canal barges, and commercial airplanes. Coal and oil, essential to industry and transport, figure largely among the prospective purchases, as do industrial raw materials, including semi-finished steel products and non-ferrous metals.

"Under the loan agreement, the bank will obtain full information concerning the goods to be purchased with the proceeds of the loan, and their utilization. France will be free to purchase in whatever markets are most advantageous."

Deferment for five years of any repayment was ascribed to the fact that "the French national recovery program calls for heavy imports during the next five years."

The loan was based, the bank stated, on France's evident need, plus "the recovery prospects of France," as well as a realization of the position of France in relation to the European picture as a whole.

A summary of the French economic position gave a reassuring picture. It stated that by the end of 1946 production had been restored to 90 per cent of the 1938 level and exports to 75 per cent of that year's rate.

This recovery was achieved, however, at the cost of heavy imports that reduced France's gold and "hard currency" holdings from $2,614,000,000 at the date of liberation to about $1,000,000,000, and had caused other borrowings abroad equivalent to $2,600,000,000.

At the same time, the expectation was voiced that France would achieve, in 1950, the restoration of equilibrium in the franc area. The crucial "gap" would occur between now and 1949, and the prospectus stated that it was "a serious one."

France was said to expect to balance her governmental budget this year. In the meantime, the summary added, it was expected that French industry would reach the 1938 level of production and achieve, by 1950, a production level 30 per cent greater than that of 1938.

May 10, 1947

JAPAN TO RESUME TRADING ON AUG. 15

Private Buyers to Be Admitted by That Time, Transactions Allowed After Sept. 1

By BURTON CRANE
Special to THE NEW YORK TIMES.

TOKYO, June 9—On Aug. 15 private international trade with Japan will be resumed and on Sept. 1 the initial deals may be consummated. Gen. Douglas MacArthur announced today.

General MacArthur hailed the move as "a step which partially lifts the economic blockade, a sound step, but a partial one."

"Japan's economy," he said, "will remain precarious until trade is completely restored to normal channels, which means private trade channels. While the present measure is merely a palliative, it is probably the best that can be done until we have peace. It will give some measure of relief to all concerned but it falls far short of a full economic solution. This can only be attained through the medium of a peace treaty and the better, not only for Japan, but for the world."

Private buyers will be permitted to enter Japan after Aug. 15, but to safeguard the interests of nations not officially represented here the first deals may not be closed until Sept. 15.

400 Buyers Expected

Accommodations are being arranged for 400 buyers who will be allocated by the Far Eastern Commission's Inter-Allied Trade Board. Final approval for their entry is a Headquarters responsibility. The Japanese will handle hotels, transportation and communications within Japan but because of short supplies here the traders will eat imported food. Entry will be p ermitted to banking, insurance and communications companies as rapidly as possible.

Because of previous commitments the United States Commercial Company will continue to handle the cotton textile and raw silk trades and the 1947 tea crop. It will also remain headquarters' representative for Government-to-Government sales in the United States.

Two important changes have been made from the preliminary details previously published. Originally it was proposed that foreign buyers might not talk price with the Japanese suppliers and that exchange rates could not be fixed. Now price discussions will be permitted and exchange rates are promised "as soon as conditions permit."

Rate "Unrealistic" Now

"It is believed," said today's announcement, "that at the outset any arbitrary rate would be realistic and unfavorable to some transactions because of the wide range of prices within Japan and consequently would restrict the total volume of trade. Since the objective is to develop the maximum amount of trade possible, it has been agreed that no exchange rates will be practicable until a flow of export trade in a wide range of commodities has been established.

"Official pricing will be determined by Headquarters commodity specialists, based upon world market standards, but this does not prevent individual traders from discussing prices with Japanese producers. Prices will be quoted in dollars, but sales will be consummated in any acceptable currency. Pricing will also be transferred to the Japanese at the earliest practicable date.

"The Japanese producer does not know the dollar or pound sterling cost of imported raw materials and hence is unable to quote in terms of those currencies. After sufficient transactions have been consummated to establish a relationship between yen production costs and selling prices in an acceptable currency a direct quotation on individual dealing will be possible.

Not Bound by Formulas

"Private buyers will not in general, be bound by pricing formulas, but will negotiate with headquarters pricing agencies in accordance with accepted trade principles."

Private deals, according to the announcement, will be licensed by the Japanese Government and validated by Headquarters, but Headquarters will not be a party to them. The principals will be the buyer and the Japanese Trade Board.

"Necessary safeguards," adds the announcement, "will be included to provide against undue advantage to Allied and neutral nationals now residing in Japan in connection with the closing of transactions."

Headquarters will not guarantee any goods, but will insist that the Japanese Government make prompt adjustments of all claims forwarded through the Allied powers.

The final paragraphs contain a warning that traders must not expect pre-war conditions and must be prepared to rebuild trade.

June 10, 1947

CONTROL OF TRADE LINKED BY TRUMAN TO FOREIGN POLICY

Signing Bill Extending Curbs, He Implies Use of Exports to Aid Cooperative Nations

HELP OF CONGRESS HAILED

President Says U. S. Objective Still Is End of All Barriers When Time Is Opportune

By HAROLD B. HINTON

Special to THE NEW YORK TIMES.

WASHINGTON, July 15—President Truman expressed the opinion today that Government controls of United States exports would be required for the indefinite future. His views were given in a statement accompanying his signature of the Second Decontrol Act of 1947.

He acknowledged the anomaly inherent in the channeling of exports out of this country at a time when its representatives are doing everything in their power to reduce world trade barriers. He promised sparing use of the powers granted to him by the act, as well as their abandonment at the earliest practicable moment.

The Second Decontrol Act continues until March 1, 1948, control over exports of commodities in short supply; control over imports of essential commodities which can only be obtained abroad; power to allocate railroad equipment, and authority to direct United States exports toward the foreign production of commodities needed in the United States, or in implementation of United States foreign policy.

The President emphasized this last aspect of the legislation in view of the Marshall Plan, intended to offer United States aid to foreign nations willing to cooperate in a common effort toward world rehabilitation. By implication, he envisaged the possibility of using the export controls to favor cooperating nations over those that will not cooperate.

Sees Unity on Foreign Policy

Another point he made was that Congress, by continuing the wartime powers enumerated, had again put in evidence its willingness to support the national foreign policy. He had held at least two formal conferences with leaders of the Republican majority in Congress to explain the vital necessity he saw of controlling United States foreign trade in directions appropriate to its foreign policy.

The bi-lateral trade agreements being negotiated by the Soviet Union with its satellite countries in the Balkans served to emphasize the President's point. He feels that the United States must preserve, despite its people's aversion to governmental economic controls, its power to meet economic competition in kind.

While Mr. Truman deplored the necessity of continuing the controls, he said that world shortages and inflation threats made them obligatory for a period that would last beyond next March 1. His statement left a strong presumption that the Chief Executive will ask for their further extension when Congress reconvenes next January.

On the purely economic side, the President said that haphazard distribution of United States products throughout the world, in a free market, would lead to shortages and higher prices at home and suffering from the neediest foreign cooperative nations, which would be unable to pay at the inflated levels that would result.

Against these developments in Washington, William L. Clayton, Under-Secretary of State, is striving at Geneva to establish an International Trade Organization dedicated to the demolition of world trade barriers as rapidly as possible.

The official position of the United States Government is in opposition to export controls, import quotas, excessive tariffs and similar obstacles to voluminous exchange of goods and services among the nations of the world.

The President sought to attest the Administration's sincerity in this field by his veto of the wool bill, which would have added special import fees to the existing tariff on wool, and he was upheld by Congress. His statement today repeatedly called attention to the temporary and emergency conditions which dictated his advocacy of further export controls.

He recalled that he had appointed on June 22 a non-partisan committee to study the effect on the domestic economy of exports shipped out in pursuance of foreign-aid programs. This committee, headed by Secretary of Commerce W. Averill Harriman, has the difficult task of determining whether such exports are of maximum benefit to foreign purchasers without unduly adverse effect on the situation in the United States.

THE PRESIDENT'S STATEMENT

"I have today approved H. R. 3647, extending until March 1, 1948, the authority of the Government to regulate the export of commodities which are in critically short supply here and abroad; to control the importation and domestic use of a small group of essential commodities which we must obtain from sources of supply abroad; to allocate transportation equipment of rail carriers; and to direct the delivery abroad of goods required for the production in foreign countries of commodities urgently needed in the United States, or required for carrying out our foreign policy.

"The bill differs only in detail from that requested in my message to the Congress on this subject. Thus, we have again demonstrated to the world our unanimity on matters affecting our international relations. This is particularly significant and timely at this moment when so much attention is focused abroad on our desire to assist nations willing to cooperate in the common objective of reconstruction.

"I wish it had not been necessary to request a continuation of these controls. But world shortages have by no means been dispelled and the threat of inflation has not been dissipated. The haphazard distribution of our produce throughout the world could only lead to higher prices at home and suffering for the neediest of our friends abroad.

"Our objective continues to be the removal of interferences with world trade. We shall, accordingly, use these controls sparingly and dispense with them as soon as conditions permit. I should be less than candid, however, were I not to say that I believe the need for some supervision of our foreign trade will continue beyond next February.

"Under this legislation, it will be the duty of the Secretary of Commerce to watch the effect upon the domestic economy of the exercise of these powers. This responsibility ties in closely with the work I requested him to undertake when, on June 22, I appointed a representative, non-partisan public committee headed by him to consider the effect upon our domestic economy of the exports we are now shipping abroad or may furnish as economic assistance to foreign countries. It is imperative that these programs of assistance be conceived and executed so as to be of maximum benefit to such foreign countries, without having an unduly adverse effect upon our domestic economy.

"I am gratified that the Congress has again demonstrated its willingness to support the achievement of our foreign policy objectives. Despite the aversion of our people to controls, I am confident that under these circumstances they will approve of their continuance."

July 16, 1947

NEW EFFORTS URGED TO AID WORLD TRADE

Foreign Commerce Executives Say Small Headway Is Made Toward Fundamental Cure

FOR INVESTMENTS ABROAD

Payments Compromise, Other Developments Held to Point Up U. S. Role as Creditor Nation

By THOMAS F. CONROY

The British crisis and the compromise represented in the new intra-European payments agreement indicate that little real headway is being made in the cure of fundamental causes of world commerce ills, according to views in foreign trade circles here last week. Trade barriers, bilateral treaties, restrictive quotas, import licenses and over-valued currencies continue to create increasingly serious dislocations untouched by steps taken so far.

At the same time, many believe last week's developments may bring more rapidly into sharper focus the rôle which the United States must play as a creditor nation, chiefly in the field of foreign private investment. "Give-away" can be replaced by constructive investment abroad if non-discriminatory treaties are negotiated by the State Department and our Government is willing to give tax incentives to American risk capital abroad, it was contended.

One phase of this was pointed up in the suggestion a few days ago by Walter Nash, Prime Minister of New Zealand, that the United States follow the example of Great Britain from 1870 on—to continue to export freely and leave the surpluses invested in foreign countries. The mechanics of how this was to be done were not explained, whether through Government channels, private investment, or the activities of American exporters themselves.

Conditions Different Today

However, it was pointed out there is a vast difference under the free enterprise conditions under which Britain invested capital abroad during the latter part of the last century and those of today. Potential American investments today are scared away and limited by restrictions in many foreign countries which discriminate against our capital, place control or management in jeopardy, prevent outgo of principal once invested and in many instances limit the amount of profits which can be withdrawn.

Despite these handicaps, a number of leading American companies are struggling to get around the dollar shortage by using local currency proceeds to build and expand factories and assembly plants abroad. Some are carrying out multilateral barter-type deals on raw materials, others are maintaining import departments to bring in varied imports, the proceeds of which will pay in part for equipment exported, and still others are carrying local currency balances abroad which may be subject to depreciation in value in the event of devaluation.

The head of one leading company engaged in foreign trade believes that more can be done by the United States to aid world recovery and commerce than the undertaking of stop-gap measures now being carried out. Differing from Point 4 of the Truman program in some respects, he suggested last week that the Government now bend its efforts toward creating a favorable business investment climate in five countries as a start.

The five countries he mentioned were Mexico, Colombia, Brazil, Italy and India. The specific things he urged were the negotiation of treaties by the State Department to create the favorable climate by negotiation of new treaties curbing discrimination and restrictions, and the granting of a tax incentive to private American risk capital to undertake the investments, which would cover the export of American equipment and know-how.

Stimulus on World Trade

Success in investment undertakings in these countries, he contended, would start the United States on its true role as a creditor nation and set an example that would have a powerful stimulus upon world commerce.

Meanwhile, foreign traders here felt that the new intra-European payments agreement would not do much to ease the dollar shortage or to aid in solution of their trade problems. An executive of one large company here, with factories in Europe, said the 25 per cent transferability clause would probably permit the purchase of materials to better advantage in Italy, France and Germany.

Another official with a large export business said the agreement "doesn't solve anything" with the exception that Belgium's position has been strengthened. He discounted the view that Britain's gold reserves or dollar balances would be affected to any appreciable extent.

Under the agreement, the United States abandoned its stand that proceeds of an estimated $700,000,000 in conditional grants be convertible into dollars, while Great Britain modified its stand with respect to bilateral trade. The agreement provided, instead, that 25 per cent of the credits or "drawing rights" [illegible] transferable by debtor countries. This yields a greater flexibility of trade, permitting the debtor nation to "shop" for its purchases rather than be required to make the purchase in the creditor country making the grant.

July 10, 1949

HOFFMAN DEMANDS ACTION BY EUROPE ON ECONOMIC UNITY

Tells Council of O. E. E. C. in Paris Integration Is Not an Ideal but a Necessity

INSISTS ON MORE TRADE

Would Eventually Sweep Away All Tariffs—U. S. Warns Aid May Be Halted

By HAROLD CALLENDER

Special to THE NEW YORK TIMES

PARIS, Oct. 31—Paul G. Hoffman, Economic Cooperation Administrator, called upon the Europeans today to demonstrate by early next year that they intend to move toward "an integration of the Western European economy."

He made this appeal in a speech to the European Marshall Plan Council, which was composed on this occasion of the Foreign or Finance Ministers of the European countries receiving dollar aid.

Mr. Hoffman insisted that the "integration" he urged was "not just an ideal" but "a practical necessity." He defined this integration as the formation in Europe of a single market within which quantitative restrictions on movements of goods and moneys "and eventually all tariffs" should be "permanently swept away."

Thus there would be created "a permanent freely trading area comprising 270,000,000 consumers in Western Europe," Mr. Hoffman said.

[Congress will not be asked for a third Marshall Plan appropriation by the Truman Administration unless the Western European governments can agree by January on a plan to integrate their economies, it was stated in Washington on high authority.]

Mr. Hoffman, urging "a far-reaching program to build in Western Europe a more dynamic expanding economy," said the first task was to overcome the dollar shortage. He urged greater incentives for private exporters simultaneously with efforts to prevent inflation. But he insisted that balancing of Europe's dollar trade must be linked with expansion and liberation of European economies.

Mr. Hoffman then urged, as a first step toward "integration," the coordination of national fiscal and monetary policies to prevent too divergent prices and costs.

Mr. Hoffman made it clear he approved steps toward freer trade taken by groups of countries—as proposed by the French, Italians and Belgians—if they did not result in raising new barriers against others. He again pleased the French by denouncing higher foreign than domestic prices for "fuel and basic materials." The French have protested against such double prices for German coal.

It was clear that his hearers thought that transformation of Western Europe into a free trade area was a large order even though the element of surprise was lacking.

The speech was regarded as urging a revolution in the economic organization of Europe, though not as an immediate goal or within any fixed period.

French officials professed to be pleased by the speech which, as Maurice Petsche, French Finance Minister, pointed out, coincided with much that M. Petsche had advocated. For this reason the conclusion was drawn that Mr. Hoffman implicitly had given his approval to the economically liberal bloc of the Continental nations—France, Italy and Belgium—that had found itself on the opposite side of the fence from Britain in recent disputes.

British officials made little comment. But in the British bloc of the planned economy states some contended Mr. Hoffman's proposals ran counter to their programs of restricted imports and consumption as a means of concentration on productive investments. They saw a basic conflict between their socialistic controls of economic life, including trade, and the free-trade Europe that Mr. Hoffman said should be the aim of current recovery measures.

Mr. Hoffman used the word "integration" fifteen times, or almost once to every hundred words of his speech. It is a word that rarely if ever has been used by European statesmen having to do with the Marshall Plan to describe what should happen to Europe's economies.

It was remarked that no such term or goal was included in the commitments that the European nations gave in agreeing to the Marshall Plan.

Consequently it appeared to the Europeans that "integration" was an American doctrine that had been superimposed upon the mutual engagements made when the Marshall Plan began—a doctrine that seems logical to Americans and to many Europeans but that European officials consider remote from the immediate practical issues.

What might be considered the first response to Mr. Hoffman's speech, even though prepared in anticipation of it, was given tonight when the Steering Committee of the Council decided to recommend that quantitative restrictions on one-half the imports in private trade of Marshall Plan countries be removed by Dec. 15.

It was characteristic of the hesitations and difficulties connected with even this partial liberation of trade that the committee reached agreement only by introducing an escape clause. It provided that countries unable to remove quotas to that extent by the deadline set should explain to the council their reasons for failing to do so.

Behind this ostensible agreement lies a half-concealed clash between the British and the French, the latter contending that the proposal by Sir Stafford Cripps, British Chancellor of the Exchequer, for such removal of quotas was disingenuous and one-sided, since the British Government controlled one-third of Britain's imports and Britain had excluded Switzerland, Belgium and Western Germany from the benefits of her own removal of quotas.

The French contended the reason Britain had excluded these three was that their manufactures competed most with the British. The French argued they would benefit less from the proposed measures because the foodstuffs they export were controlled imports in most Marshall Plan states. The French, therefore, were understood to have accepted today's tentative agreement with large reservations, which they expected to define tomorrow.

It was believed tonight the council would adopt recommendations to the member nations that would embrace some points in the Hoffman speech, Sir Stafford's proposal and the proposals of M. Petsche and Sean MacBride, Irish Minister of External Affairs, who urged a world economic conference to discuss surplus production.

M. Petsche advocates periodical meetings of the Finance and Foreign Ministers of the Marshall Plan countries and of the governors of their central banks; a monetary stabilization fund, a special European bank to coordinate investments, regional freer trade blocs and a link between the Marshall Plan council and Council of Europe.

M. Petsche insists the dropping of quotas is useful only if there is also internal financial and price stabilization and if, consequently, there is "equality of European competition." He was pleased that Mr. Hoffman supported him on this point and on the need for monetary consultation.

November 1, 1947

EUROPEAN ERP BODY VOTES FREER TRADE

Approves Moves to Facilitate Exchange and New Plan to Finance Action

COUNCIL DOUBTS EFFECTS

World Economic Disequilibrium Seen Dwarfing Group's Acts and Marshall Aid Itself

By HAROLD CALLENDER

Special to THE NEW YORK TIMES.

PARIS, Aug. 13—The European Marshall Plan Council adopted today proposals for freer European trade and a new payments plan to finance this trade.

But it did so with a growing feeling that all of its actions—and the Marshall Plan itself—were dwarfed by the proportions of the world-wide dollar shortage and the economic disequilibrium that it reflected.

Members of the Council have discussed a project for a review by its experts of this wider and more basic problem, and of the limitations of the Marshall Plan in relation to it. An analysis of the world situation, so dramatically reflected in the acute British dollar shortage, may be undertaken in September for presentation to the Council in October.

The freer trade proposals adopted, which were outlined in a dispatch last Tuesday, will depend for their efficacy upon the willingness of European Governments to apply them to a substantial list of commodities, upon the character of the currency devaluation expected in autumn and upon negotiations between countries where agreements provide for the payment of gold in the settlement of balances.

Specifications Wanting

The payments plan, based upon the compromise between Sir Stafford Cripps, British Chancellor of the Exchequer, and W. Averell Harriman, roving Marshall Plan Ambassador, on July 1, still lacks specifications of the credit-drawing rights that form its machinery. It lacks also the dollars that are to finance it.

As European officials have studied the problem of reconciling their dollar deficits with reduced dollar aid, they have been increasingly impressed by what some call the comparative futility of these debates over a few hundred million dollars in relation to the question of how or whether workable economic relations can be established between the United States and the rest of the world.

The British dollar deficit, now swollen to such proportions that Marshall Plan funds cannot cover it, has brought conflict into the European Council. But it has brought illumination also. It has compelled those who have not done so to consider the dollar shortage as exemplifying the economic, financial and social problems raised by the fabulous productivity of the United States and the relative decline of Europe from its former position as the manufacturing and financial center of the world.

One European official observed that when the Marshall Plan Council was asked to deal with the British dollar deficit it was asked to deal with a question that involved not only the countries represented in the Council but the whole sterling area in relation to the whole dollar area. How could continental nations settle the relations between the pound and the dollar? he asked, commenting that this may possibly be done by Washington negotiations in September but not in these meetings in Paris.

Other officials described the problem by recalling that the original conception of the Marshall Plan in Washington was as a device that would cost between $15,000,000,000 and $20,000,000,000 and would ease Europe's position for about four years, so that there would be time to prepare to deal with the basic disequilibrium that would remain when Europe's temporary needs had been fulfilled and its production had revived.

But after only a year of Marshall Plan aid, Europe's production has reached the pre-war level in general, the problem has shifted from that of producing goods to that of exchanging them, and the long dreaded crisis that had been expected at the end of the Marshall Plan has appeared some three years ahead of schedule and while dollars still are flowing.

Point 4 Plans Stir Interest

For this reason President Truman's suggestion for United States aid in developing backward areas has aroused deep interest in those European countries that have backward overseas territories. But they observe that the prospective productivity of those areas must result not only in their buying dollar goods but in their buying from Europe if Europe's position is to be improved.

A flow of United States capital abroad in the form of investments that, although not necessarily placed in Europe, would aid Europe is one possibility under consideration. The lowering of United States tariffs to enable Europe to earn more dollars is another.

There has lately been much discussion, notably in British circles, of increasing the dollar price of gold. It is estimated that if this price were doubled, this would automatically increase Europe's purchasing power by something more than $1,000,000,000 a year.

Nobody expects or desires the United States to go on pouring out dollars in the Marshall Plan manner, which would not solve the problem. Those dealing most closely with it mostly acknowledge they do not know all the answers, but they contend it is high time that the scope and character of the problem be understood by other than specialists

The experts argue that in a sense the Marshall Plan has worked too well since it has restored European production sooner than anticipated and thus brought into the present what had been considered a post-Marshall Plan problem.

August 14, 1949

FOREIGN TRADE ACT PASSED BY SENATE; 'PERIL POINT' LOSES

15 Republicans Join Democrats in Final Vote of 62 to 19—Bill Goes to White House

FIGHT FOR CURBS IS CLOSE

Administration Defeats GOP, 43 to 38, in Test—Barkley First Ballot Breaks Tie

By JOHN D. MORRIS
Special to THE NEW YORK TIMES.

WASHINGTON, Sept. 15—The Senate passed the Administration's Reciprocal Trade Agreements bill without change today by a bipartisan vote of 62 to 19.

The measure, which revives the President's authority to adjust tariffs in exchange for similar trade-stimulating concessions by foreign countries, had been passed previously by the House and now goes to Mr. Truman for his signature.

Nearly half the Republicans present supported Administration forces on the final ballot, but only after a hectic two and one-half hours of voting during which Mr. Truman's lieutenants narrowly defeated attempts to restrict the bill.

With party lines tightly drawn in several of the preliminary battles, Alben W. Barkley at one point cast his first vote as Vice President, breaking a tie to carry the ballot for the Administration.

Errors Snarl Tallies

Mr. Barkley, as presiding officer of the Senate, was also the central figure in parliamentary wrangles that resulted from clerical errors in tallies on two other votes.

The Republicans' main fight was for adoption of the Millikin "Peril Point" amendment, whereby the President would be required to make a public explanation to Congress if he cut duties below levels designated by the Federal Tariff Commission as threatening serious injury to domestic producers.

The proposal, opposed by the Administration on the ground that it would give undue emphasis to protectionism was rejected by 43 to 38. Three Democrats—Senators Edwin C. Johnson of Colorado, Joseph C. O'Mahoney of Wyoming and Elmer Thomas of Oklahoma—voted for the plan along with all Republicans present.

On passage of the bill, forty-seven Democrats and fifteen Republicans voted in the affirmative. The opposition consisted of eighteen Republicans and one Democrat, Senator Thomas of Oklahoma.

Effects Abroad Hailed

The action was hailed by Administration spokesmen as firm evidence that the United States was determined to continue its leadership in world economic affairs instead of heading back toward a high-tariff policy that would deprive friendly foreign countries of American markets needed to solve their dollar shortages.

The effect of the bill is to restore in full the Presidential powers under which this country's reciprocal trade program was developed by Cordell Hull as Secretary of State.

Congress first delegated its tariff-making powers to the President in the Reciprocal Trade Agreements Act of 1936, which was periodically renewed without restrictive modifications until last year when the Republican Congress enacted a stop-gap extension that contained the "Peril Point" requirement.

The stop-gap law, which expired last June 30, was opposed by the Administration as crippling a program that had been called the keystone of United States foreign economic policy.

The House early this session soundly defeated Republican efforts to write the "Peril Point" clause into the 1949 extension bill, and today's Senate action on that measure completed the Administration victory. Under its terms, the President's tariff-making authority would be revived until June 12, 1951.

President Truman's signature on the bill would clear the way for the signing of multi-lateral trade agreements recently drafted at conferences in Annecy, France. Action on these had been deferred pending Congressional passage of the act reviving the President's authority to put the decisions into effect.

Mr. Barkley's vote was necessary as the Senate's presiding officer during a battle over an amendment offered by Senator Joseph R. McCarthy, Republican of Wisconsin. The proposal called for the establishment of import quotas on furs if deemed necessary by the Tariff Commission to prevent serious injury to the domestic fur industry.

The amendment first was adopted, 42 to 40, and supporters sought to prevent its being brought up at some future date by invoking a parliamentary maneuver that entails a motion to reconsider, followed immediately by a motion to table that motion.

Democrat Changes Vote

The scheme backfired, however, when Senator Elbert D. Thomas, Democrat, of Utah, switched to the Administration side as the roll was called to determine whether the reconsideration motion should be tabled. This resulted in a tie of 41 to 41.

Announcing the tie, Mr. Barkley said:

"Under the Constitution the President of the Senate is entitled to vote, and he votes No."

That permitted a ballot on reconsideration of the McCarthy amendment and the outcome was announced as 41 to 40 for reconsideration, whereupon another roll call on the amendment itself was ordered, resulting in its defeat by 43 to 40.

This did not reckon, however, with the fact developed some time later that the clerk had been in error in adding up the votes for reconsideration of the amendment. Instead of being 41 to 40, it actually was 41 to 41.

The error became known during consideration of a subsequent amendment proposed by Senator Thomas of Oklahoma to limit the importation of petroleum. Mr. Barkley first announced that the oil amendment had been adopted, 42 to 41, but a few minutes later he reported that there had been an error in tallying the votes and that it actually had lost, 41 to 40.

Orders It Corrected

The Vice President ordered the official record to be corrected, bringing on a storm of protests by Senators McCarthy and Kenneth S. Wherry, Republican, of Nebraska, the minority leader.

Disclosing that an error also had been made in tallying the earlier vote on reconsideration of the McCarthy fur amendment, the two Senators argued that it, also, should be corrected. In the absence of tie-breaking action by the Vice President, the motion to reconsider the McCarthy amendment would have been defeated, 41 to 41, since it takes a majority to carry a motion.

Mr. Barkley contended that it made no difference, as he would have voted if he had known there was a tie.

The outcome of the tangle was that the correction on the oil amendment was made, causing its defeat, while the error on reconsideration of the fur amendment stood as the official count.

If the Republicans had succeeded in correcting the first error, the fur amendment could not have been reconsidered unless Mr. Barkley could have found some way to cast his vote and break the tie. Consequently, the provision would have gone into the bill.

In an attempt to clear up the tangle while the argument was going on, Senator Scott W. Lucas, Democrat of Illinois, the Majority Leader, obtained unanimous consent to correct the tally on adoption of the oil amendment. But when Mr. Wherry asked unanimous consent to correct the earlier error, he was blocked by an objection from Senator Walter F. George, Democrat, of Georgia, floor manager of the bill.

State and regional interests were involved in consideration of both the oil and fur amendments, and party lines consequently were largely ignored.

In the vote on the oil amendment, nineteen Democrats at first were among the forty Senators supporting it. But just before the result was announced, with the unofficial tally standing at 42 to 39 for the proposal, two Democrats who had voted for it arose and changed their votes. They were Senators James O. Eastland of Mississippi and J. Allen Frear Jr., of Delaware. The proposal consequently was defeated, 41 to 40, once the tally clerk's error had been corrected.

The vote regarded as the best test of high-tariff sentiment in the Senate came on a substitute bill offered by Senator George W. Malone, Republican, of Nevada. The proposal called for the establishment of tariff rates reflecting the difference between the production cost of imported items and that of comparable articles produced in this country.

It was defeated, 64 to 17. One Democrat, Senator Russell B. Long of Louisiana, voted for it.

Also defeated, 53 to 29, was an amendment by Senator Hugh Butler, Republican, of Nebraska, to require the renegotiation of trade agreements in which there is no "escape clause." There are thirteen such agreements, formulated before it became the practice to include in all pacts a clause whereby the United States could modify or withdraw tariff concessions if they threatened to cause serious injury to domestic producers.

A surprise proposa by Senator Eugene D. Millikin, Republican, of Colorado, to limit renewal of the President's tariff-making power to one year, was rejected by 49 to 33.

An amendment offered by West Virginia's two Democratic Senators, Harley M. Kilgore and Matthew M. Neely, lost on a vote of 61 to 19. It called for the exemption of hand-made pottery from provisions of the act.

Just before the voting started, Senator George read an appeal from former Secretary of State Hull for rejection of the Millikin "Peril Point" clause.

Mr. Hull wrote that under the original act "the interests of our industry, labor and agriculture were amply safeguarded, and the entire nation benefited greatly from the increase of commerce and the improvement of international relations brought about y the program."

September 16, 1949

DEVALUATION HITS AMERICAN EXPORTS

Foreign Traders as Result See Need to Reappraise Policies to Meet Competition

60% OF TRADE AFFECTED

Suggestion Made to Lower Prices as Way of Offsetting Effect of Currency Cuts

By THOMAS F. CONROY

Current export policies must be re-appraised by American foreign traders to meet the stark fact that United States goods will cost foreign buyers up to 44 per cent more in terms of their own currencies as a result of the wave of devaluation last week.

Exporters and shippers here said they were keenly aware that the initial impact of devaluation will mean greater competition for American exports from British and Continental producers. As the week ended, they were awaiting definite evidences of the extent of the competition in the new prices which foreign producers, especially those in sterling areas, were expected to quote in world markets.

At this stage, two aspects of the situation were cited in favor of our non-government export trade. These were:

1. That prices will advance in the sterling areas, cutting down the net price change attributable to devaluation to about half of the 30 per cent revision in the pound sterling.
2. That for some time at least American manufacturers and exporters will be able to make better deliveries than foreign producers.

Threat Is Seen

However, even allowing for these factors there seems little doubt that the 60 per cent of our foreign trade, which is still privately financed, the other 40 per cent or so comprising ECA goods, is now threatened. This may not be a factor immediately, although cancellations and suspensions of pending orders hung over the export field last week as foreign buyers sought to appraise conditions.

In some quarters, it was suggested that "pencil sharpening" by manufacturers and direct exporters to lower export prices is inevitable, and that a recasting of export policy may be required in relation to its value in keeping up factory production schedules. In other words, while export business has been profitable on its own for some years now, it may be that margins will now have to be trimmed to a point where exports carry themselves largely in relation to a company's total volume of business.

Bearing on these considerations is the fact that of itself foreign devaluation has its deflationary aspects so far as this country is concerned. For months prior to devaluation, prices in the United States had been trending lower than those in European markets and the sterling areas. Devaluation now will make dollar prices of some foreign raw materials cheaper than they were a week ago, although, of course, others have already been marked up so that there has been little or no actual change in dollar costs.

However, from a broad viewpoint it appears that "undervaluing" the pound will react against the price level here, at least temporarily. The dollar appears "overvalued" but how costs will be affected from both short run and longer-term prospects was still uncertain.

Perhaps the outstanding gain in the whole trade picture is that devaluation has re-established confidence in the value of the pound. By cutting deeply to $2.80, it was pointed out, Britain has greatly reduced the likelihood of a repetition of the "short-selling" tactics which undermined the pound at $4.03, and at the same time has eliminated the "three-cornered" manipulated deals in cheap sterling. Britain and the sterling areas will now receive the benefit of those dollar sales which previously only diminished blocked sterling but did not add to current account. This, of course, will strengthen Britain's reserve and over-all dollar position.

Outlook for Convertibility

Foreign traders also saw devaluation as a "preliminary" step to convertibility of currency in world markets. They agreed that progress in this direction may be slow, but convertibility and the development of multilateral trade were cited as the next objectives in the development of sound world commerce. Of interest in this connection were the feelers put out in Europe last week aiming at a single monetary system for all of Western Europe. Moreover, talk increased of re-establishment of the American gold standard.

Meanwhile, from the import side, it appeared the concensus that British and European producers will not be in position to rush any tremendous volume of goods into the United States for some time. There will be sharp gains in some lines as orders held up in anticipation of sterling devaluation are reinstated, but in many lines seasonal production schedules call for lines to be sold here for next year and 1951.

In other words, some time will be required for foreign producers to show what they can do in raising exports to the United States so far as prices and deliveries are concerned. It was already evident **that retail prices of many major foreign items will not reflect more than half of the pound devaluation of 30.5 per cent.**

Tariff reductions on many imports are now probable, however, because of the lower exchange value where duties are levied "ad valorem" on the basis of foreign market or export price, whichever is lower. Coupled with the 50 per cent reductions already made under the Reciprocal Trade Agreements Act, this will make actual duties on a wide range of foreign merchandise almost nominal.

But American merchandising methods and ability of the buyer here to reorder freely are major requirements in successful importing of foreign consumer goods and these will take time to develop successfully.

September 25, 1949

KEY ECONOMIC QUESTION: WILL WE RAISE IMPORTS?

Commitment to Act as Creditor Nation Likely to Mean Battle in Congress

By FELIX BELAIR

Special to THE NEW YORK TIMES.

WASHINGTON, Sept. 24 — **The significant progress made recently toward the political security and economic stability of the Western democracies leaves unanswered a larger question, the answer to which may implement or undermine every effort at international cooperation since San Francisco.**

The question that now puzzles the foreign economic policy makers of this and most other Governments is whether we, as a nation, are ready to assume the responsibilities that go with our position as the only big creditor in the world today. Are we prepared to buy enough of the world's goods and services to enable the economy of the Western world to stand on its own feet?

Chaos and War

Enough has happened or been narrowly averted in Europe since the war to indicate the broad problem that still remains. If economic stagnation and chaos turn whole peoples in hunger from the democratic way, the result would be to recreate a condition identified in the United Nations Charter as the root cause of wars.

The recent and continuing world-wide monetary adjustments have dramatized the inescapable if unpleasant truth that unless they are to get help from us ad infinitum in the form of gifts, the other nations of the world can only buy needed goods from us as we buy from them and provide the dollars for settling the accounts.

Paul G. Hoffman, Economic Cooperation Administrator, has placed at about $2.5 billion the value of Western European goods and services this country must buy annually to provide a self-sustaining economy for the Marshall Plan countries. The figure amounts to about 1 per cent of the gross national product of the United States at current level.

Elsewhere in the Government the figure is considered high. It assumes that Western Europe's only source of dollar income would be in the form of goods and services sold here and would be reduced to the extent dollars were supplied in the form of direct American investments in those countries. In any case, Mr. Hoffman has put the problem in its proper perspective.

Tests for Congress and Public

By joining in the agreements reached at the conference of Foreign and Finance Ministers of the United States, Great Britain and Canada, this Government answered the big question clearly in the affirmative. That answer has yet to be put to the test either in Congress or in the forum of public opinion.

Whether the Government's answer can be made to stick will not be known until Congress has been called upon to implement the agreements and until public opinion has registered for or against the inevitable complaints of domestic interests affected by the foreign competition that the agreements would make possible.

However, if past performance is any indication of what may be expected, the decision will not be known until the pressure groups have lost or won in the biggest battle of the Congressional lobbies since the Smoot-Hawley Tariff Act helped pave the way for the present disequilibrium in world trade.

U. S. Promised Help

In the tripartite conference agreements the United States said, in effect, that in return for Britain's declaration of intention to help liberate world trade from the quantitative restrictions now confining it to bilateral deals, this Government would recognize its creditor position and facilitate imports from and capital investment in England and Western Europe.

Unless this country is to become a net importer of products from abroad, it is difficult to see how other countries will be able to buy from us the things they need.

Existing public policies that impede or prevent such an arrangement must be re-examined. And if those responsible for foreign economic policy had their way, one of the first to be changed would be the present merchant marine policy whereby foreign countries are deprived of the dollars they formerly earned from us for carrying our ocean freight.

Cost to the Taxpayer

Under the present system, the American taxpayer finances the total cost of merchant-marine construction and half the operating cost and pays the bill for hauling half the Marshall Plan supplies to Europe. A more realistic policy might limit United States merchant-marine operations to those demanded by security and permit foreign lines to earn dollars from freights beyond that amount.

Although the merchant-marine policy points up the question of America's readiness to assume its creditor obligations, it presents no unique situation. The story is much the same when any other domestic interest feels the pinch of foreign competition. Some Congressional district makes a protest and the reverberations soon fill the Senate and House chambers.

What is overlooked in the reception usually given the protests is that the dollars thus earned through purchases here of foreign goods and services must inevitably find their way back to the United States

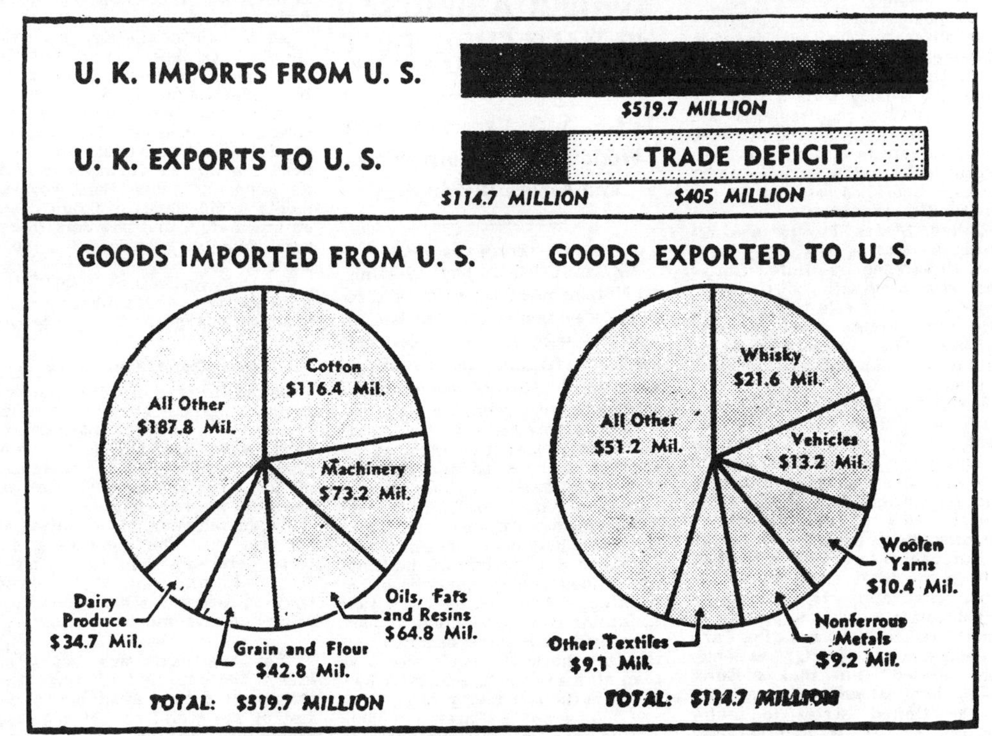

The figures in the chart are at the pre-devaluation rate—$4.08 to the pound.

in payment for some other goods or services or in liquidation of debt.

Capital Needed Too

While the official emphasis just now is on the need for larger imports from abroad, this Government is not overlooking the need to revive the flow of private capital for foreign investment. There will be no large-scale underwriting of foreign bond issues such as was tried after the first World War. Instead, direct investment through the Export-Import Bank and the International Bank for Reconstruction and Development will be pushed.

If through so-called project loans, a demand for the goods and services of all Western countries can be built up in the underdeveloped areas and even in some highly industrialized nations, a substantial contribution will have been made toward closing the "dollar gap." But if the standards of the Export-Import Bank are any indication, there will be no grab bag.

The advent of the national labor unions into the international economic picture through interest in maintaining domestic employment levels and income standards may complicate the working out of an answer to the long-range, balance-of-payments problems. But for the pressure on Congress from the maritime unions, the merchant-marine policy might have been long since corrected.

They will be heard from again whenever unemployment here can be plausibly attributed to any expansion of imports into the United States. This time, however, the Government expects to be ready with the answers to the protests.

Business for Dollar Study

Meanwhile there are encouraging signs that organized American business may pursue a more enlightened policy than characterized its representations to Congress in the drafting of the 1930 tariff law. One such came recently from the National Association of Manufacturers in the form of a study of possible solutions to the universal dollar shortage and our creditor position. The association concluded that the United States ultimately must buy more than it sells abroad.

As this Government now views the problem, the question remaining to be answered in the next twelve to eighteen months is whether the public will learn in time that it is better to give the rest of the democratic world a chance to earn its way than to risk its bankruptcy and get nothing in return but grief.

September 25, 1949

EUROPEANS RESENT U. S. MARKET BARS

Protectionist Psychology of Business Men Seen as Curb Despite Government Policy

By MICHAEL L. HOFFMAN
Special to The New York Times.

GENEVA, March 10—Europeans sometimes despair of ever being able to earn their dollars honestly by selling a good product at a good price in the United States market.

According to steel experts here, private pressure by United States steel interests, unreasonable customs requirements and building codes inspired by protectionist psychology are combining to keep European sellers from getting a small share in the United States market for a few types of steel.

European producers neither could nor desire to compete over the entire range of steel products. But with present prevailing prices and costs they could lay down steel of a number of types in Eastern ports at prices, after paying transportation costs and duty, that would be under current United States prices. Only in many cases they cannot.

The case of bars for reinforcing concrete is cited. A Luxembourg producer had a good offer for 10,000 tons of these bars. He discovered that he could fill the order except for the fact that every single little bar would have to be stamped with the word "Luxembourg." Stamping involves an additional process in manufacture. This producer could not, physically, stamp more than 500 tons in the time it took him to manufacture 10,000 tons, and he had to turn down the order.

In the same product, according to European steel men, United States underwriters' codes and building codes have all conspired against the European producer. Virtually all of them require that concrete reinforcing bars be made of open hearth—or electric furnace steel and ban the use of Bessemer process steel.

Europeans maintain that there is no difference whatever between Bessemer steel and other steels as far as their use for this purpose is concerned. They believe that the United States requirements are inspired wholly by a desire to keep European steels, which are to a considerable extent made under the Bessemer process, out of the United States market.

United States buyers are reported as stating that they have been threatened by United States steel suppliers with "difficulties" in getting the steels they want if they buy foreign steel for any purpose. These pressures are informal and unwritten — but effective.

Europeans know perfectly well that the United States Government, whose announced policy is to encourage Europe to earn its way in dollar markets, cannot be held responsible for all these obstacles. Most of them are simply business tricks, equally well known to Europeans, to protect a market.

It is the total effect of an attitude that supports, encourages and ultimately justifies private or public policies of treating any product marked "foreign" as somehow tainted, that makes Europeans skeptical about the capacity of the United States to follow through on its well-intentioned pledges to cooperate in building a strong non-Communist world economy.

March 11, 1950

KOREAN WAR HELPS TO HALT SURPLUSES

But F. A. O. Experts Caution World to Act to Curb Prices and Assure Distribution

Special to The New York Times.

LAKE SUCCESS, Oct. 19—United Nations members received a report today saying that the Korean conflict—with its heavy demands for foodstuffs and supplies—had incidentally brightened economic conditions in most countries.

This improvement in the global economic picture was reported by experts of the Food and Agriculture Organization in their annual survey of the "world's outlook." Their findings were summed up in the wry judgment of Norris E. Dodd, director general of the United Nations' agency, that the bitter fighting in Asia and the expansion of armaments production apparently had been more beneficial to the international food situation than all the peaceful efforts undertaken in the last four years.

"This is not a flattering commentary on international statesmanship," Mr. Dodd said, "but by all means let us take full advantage of this by-product of a troubled situation, and hope that in the future we can do better in developing methods that will work in an atmosphere of international good-will."

As a result of the Korean crisis, the F. A. O. experts predicted, the demands on producing and importing countries would be so strong in the next two years that all threat of unmarketable surpluses would fade. They cautioned however, that prices would go so high on some products that governments might have to clamp down on speculators and hoarders to assure fair distribution for consumers.

In the agricultural field, the price of wool and rubber already has risen "dangerously," the report said.

Sees Trade Stimulated

Before the war in Korea, the experts said, currency difficulties "loomed as a great barrier" to world-wide distribution of supplies, particularly in the instances of soft-currency nations such as those in Western Europe.

As an outcome of mobilization for war and the stepped-up defense program of the United States, it was said that "world trade in food and other agricultural products should be stimulated."

"For the next two years at least," the report predicted, "the amount of dollars available to the rest of the world should continue to increase." By the middle of next year, it added, United States military spending should reach $30,000,000,000 and the gross national income should approach an annual rate of $300,000,000,000. As a consequence, the demand for imports into the United States of raw materials and manufactured goods, as well as foodstuffs, should rise "appreciably," the experts said.

Many countries, the F. A. O. report stated, will be unable to cope with the increased United States demand for products since many of the commodities take time to produce and output cannot be raised rapidly.

Within the next few months other products besides wool and rubber will be affected by the increased demand, the report said.

One approach, the experts asserted, would be to place items in short supply under some form of international control. Aside from products already in "extreme scarcity," the report posed the question of what arrangements should be made to prevent the exhaustion of cereals, livestock products, cotton, tobacco and other commodities. While these commodities were not necessarily in short supply national stockpiles could be drained rapidly, the specialists cautioned.

The report asked that consideration be given to what action the agency should take in the United Nations' efforts to forestall civil disturbance and war. It suggested that the F. A. O., with the approval of members of the United Nations, might make preliminary studies of land reforms, a basic problem in Asia.

October 20, 1950

A Crisis in Raw Materials Found Imperiling Security

By FELIX BELAIR Jr.

Special to The New York Times.

WASHINGTON, June 23—The President's Materials Policy Commission reported today that developing shortages and mounting costs of raw materials had raised grave questions for the nation's security and living standards and called for coordinated development and use of resources by all free nations.

After an eighteen-month study of American material needs and supplies over the next twenty-five years, the commission found that the United States had already crossed the great industrial divide into the status of a raw-materials deficit nation. By 1975, it said, we will be importing about one-fifth of our industrial needs at a cost of about $3,000,000,000.

The group predicted that the need for industrial raw materials would increase 50 to 60 per cent by 1975 to support a doubling of the gross national product to an annual rate of $566,000,000,000, a population of 193,000,000 and a 20,000,000 increase in the "working force" to 82,000,000. It said this annual production rate would be no more than the average increase each year for the last century.

Solution Held Possible

The commission denied any "alarmist" intentions in citing the gradual shrinkage of our national resources. Its attitude was one of "serious concern," but it reported that with a proper combination of initiative, prudence and cooperation abroad, the problem could be solved.

The commission, headed by William S. Paley, chairman of the board of the Columbia Broadcasting System, was directed by President Truman to investigate and report on the long-term aspects of the materials problem as distinct from emergency aspects. It neither overlooked the possibility of war nor assumed that war was inevitable.

War in the next twenty-five years would alter the projected pattern of materials supply and demand swiftly and drastically but, even if permanent peace should prevail, according to the report, an increase in living standards abroad to the level of the United States would increase the demand for materials sixfold.

One of the earliest conclusions of the commission was that "there is no such thing as a purely domestic policy toward materials that all the world must have; there are only world policies that have domestic aspects."

Truman Praises Group

In a letter to Mr. Paley, President Truman congratulated the group on its report and "the far-sighted appraisal of the material needs and resources of the United States in relation to the needs and resources of the whole free world."

"The conviction you have expressed that this nation, despite its serious materials problems, can continue to raise its living standards and strengthen its security in partnership with other freedom-loving nations should be heartening to people everywhere," he declared.

More than seventy recommendations were advanced by the commission, ranging from scrapping outmoded laws that prevent or hinder other countries from selling us the materials needed for peace and war to financial aid and incentives to exploration and development of undiscovered resources here and abroad.

Prospectors loans, leasing privileges and special tax concessions were recommended for those willing and able to ferret out domestic sources of vital industrial materials.

The report challenged the principle of a high protective tariff as obsolete and denounced the "Buy America" Act as a "relic of depression psychology." It condemned the whole theory of economic self-sufficiency as defeatist and the idea of protecting domestic industries against cheap foreign labor as "a self-imposed blockade."

This line of argument ended with a recommendation that the Execu-

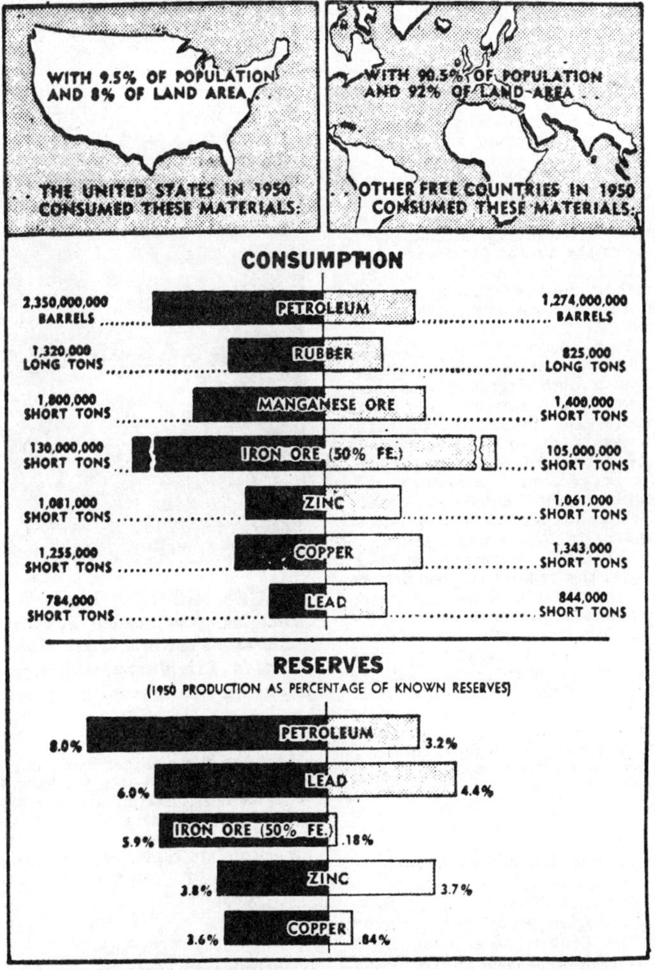

The United States, the largest consumer of materials in the free world, also is using up its reserves faster than other countries. This chart, based on the President's Commission report, compares details of both the consumption and reserves.

tive branch be empowered to cancel tariffs, entirely aside from any reciprocal arrangements, whenever there was a critical need for a foreign material.

'Buy American' Act Decried

The "Buy American" Act, still on the books despite a two-year effort to have it removed, forbids Federal purchases overseas except where domestic supplies of the same material are unreasonably priced or in insufficient quantity or quality.

An administrative interpretation has placed the test of reasonableness of price at 25 per cent above the domestic market, and this was recently written into a new law governing even foreign contracting for stockpiling here.

New and more restrictive Federal-state arrangements were urged to conserve forestry reserves. Arrangements for expansion of electric power supplies along lines negotiated between private companies and the Atomic Energy Commission were recommended.

The report made it clear that mounting costs of industrial raw materials rather than the depletion of supplies was the essence of the materials problems. The danger was not so much that we might get down to our last barrel of oil but that more man-hours of labor and capital investment would be required to obtain and transform it into useful goods.

To this end the report called for improved Federal arrangements to promote technological advances. Ultimately, the great hope of reversing the present trend of rising real costs of material production lay in the harnessing of expanded power facilities to these improved techniques with resulting lower unit costs, the report said.

Breakdown of Materials

Among major classifications of raw materials, the commission said, something like this might be expected in the United States in 1975 as compared to 1950:

¶Demand for minerals as a whole, including metals, fuels and nonmetalics, will rise the most, about 90 per cent or nearly double the 1950 rate.

¶Demand for iron, copper, lead and zinc might rise only about 40 to 50 per cent. But other indicated increases include bauxite for aluminum, 400 per cent; fluorspar, 300 per cent, and magnesium, 1,800 to 2,000 per cent. In addition to steel making, fluorspar is used for refrigerants, plastics, propellent gases, oil refining, aluminum refining and in fluoridation of water.

¶Demand for timber will rise least of all materials, about 10 per cent.

¶Requirements for agricultural products will rise about 40 per cent. One study showed that agricultural output could be increased by 200 per cent if all farmers used fertilizer to the economic limit and used all other known good farming practices. But it said millions of independent operators would not do so.

¶Total energy supply must be doubled in the period. Electric supply must increase 260 per cent to 1,400,000,000,000 kilowatt hours. Liquid fuel output would have to more than double, even without a war, and natural gas supplies would have to be tripled.

¶Coal demand would have to climb 60 per cent and "all signs point to a re-emergence of coal in stronger and stronger demand, as supplies of petroleum and natural gas inevitably begin to decline and grow more costly."

Illustrative of the appetite of the American industrial maw, the report said that "the quantity of most metals and mineral fuels used in the United States since the first World War exceeds the total used throughout the entire world in all of history preceding 1914."

June 24, 1952

PRICE IS HELD KEY TO IMPORTS BY U. S.

Management Men Told Nation Can Use Substitute Materials if Cost Is Too High

This country will take an increasing supply of raw materials from foreign nations only if prices are in line and investment conditions abroad are advantageous, Dr. Edward S. Mason, dean of Harvard University Graduate School of Public Administration, declared yesterday. He spoke before the American Management Association's annual finance conference in the Roosevelt Hotel.

Dr. Mason is a member of the President's Material Policy Commission. He warned against misinterpretation of the "most widely quoted finding" in the commission's recent report. The committee found that the United States in the last decade has become more dependent on foreign sources for raw materials.

This does not mean, Dr. Mason emphasized, that the United States is becoming a "have not" nation or that it must import regardless of the prices of imported raw materials.

"In fact," he said, "there are available domestic substitutes for most raw materials. Consequently our dependence on foreign sources of supply will increase only if materials are forthcoming from these sources on reasonable terms."

Dr. Mason called on private investors as well as the United States and foreign Governments to make a joint effort to remove obstacles to mineral resources development abroad by American investors. An increase in American investments abroad soon will become almost a necessity, he declared.

New variable annuity plans represent the first really significant attack on the depreciation of the pension dollar, according to J. H. Schreiner, vice president of Towers, Perrin, Forster and Crosby, Inc. Mr. Schreiner described the new plans recently set up by his organization and the Teachers Insurance and Annuity Association of America.

Both plans, he said, are based on the premise that there is a substantial relationship between the cost of living and the average of common stock values.

November 21, 1952

Lower U. S. Trade Barriers Urged to Uphold Allied Unity

Lewis W. Douglas, in Report to President, Fears Ties Will Remain 'Precarious' Unless Currencies Are 'Unfettered'

By JOSEPH A. LOFTUS
Special to THE NEW YORK TIMES.

WASHINGTON, Aug. 24—Lewis W. Douglas, after a study of world trade problems for President Eisenhower, has reported that the unity of the free world will rest on a "precarious and fragile" base until the United States lowers the barriers to commerce.

The report by the former Ambassador to Great Britain said that one of the most necessary measures was to make sterling more fully convertible into other currencies, particularly dollars. It urged speed to bring about such a transferability of sterling—the medium of exchange for the United Kingdom and wide areas of the world in her sphere of activity.

The White House made public the report today, along with a reply from President Eisenhower and a letter from the General referring the report to Clarence B. Randall, chairman of the newly established Commission on Foreign Economic Policy.

The President told Mr. Douglas that his report "strikes me as a most valuable contribution toward illuminating the still dark corners of this highly significant matter."

"It has in it a vein of candor, both with respect to the United Kingdom's position and our own, which is, I think, refreshing and very useful," he declared.

The report, after citing what Mr. Douglas believed to be the major causes of the imbalance between sterling and the dollar, said that a review of these causes "makes it crystal clear that monetary measures alone cannot produce the solution that is needed to neutralize the increasingly persistent tendency of the United States payment position to be in surplus with the rest of the world."

The former envoy cited corrective measures taken so far by Great Britain and the United States and said more remained to be done by both nations.

"For thirty years," he continued, "the barriers that we have erected against imports into the United States have been incompatible with, and have operated against, the re-establishment of international economic and financial health and equilibrium.

"Long ago we became the world's greatest creditor. We can no longer pursue the protectionist policies of a debtor nation and hope to escape from governmental intervention, restrictionism, state planning and discrimination against American products in the international markets."

The report observed that under the most favorable circumstances time would be required to pass laws for establishing a freer American trade policy, but said that it would be unfortunate if in the meantime nothing was done to continue the progress already made toward freer trade.

Accordingly, it made these suggestions:

¶The United States Government should make a prompt announcement that it is the determined policy of this nation to work toward a simplification of our customs practices and toward a progressive, vigorous relaxation of foreign trade restrictions.

¶The private investment of dollars in foreign countries should be increased. For example, the provisions of loans by the International Bank could define terms upon which the investment of private funds might be made with reasonable immunity against most political hazards, such as expropriation.

¶American banking houses might consider participating in sterling loans made by London banks with some sort of British guaranty of a rate of exchange.

¶Finally, we should seek to develop measures to abate violent fluctuations in the prices and volume of the major raw materials that enter into international trade.

Special Deputy to Dulles

Mr. Douglas, serving as a special deputy to John Foster Dulles, the Secretary of State, began his study shortly after the British-American talks in Washington last March on economic and financial problems.

In spite of present limitations a larger part of world trade is conducted in sterling than in any other currency. The national interests of the United States are deeply affected by the status of this sterling and the financial strength of the sterling area, the report said.

"It is doubtful," Mr. Douglas said, "whether the world can recover a high degree of economic freedom or whether American exports—so important to large segments of our country—can enter foreign markets without benefit of continued American subventions and subsidies, unless sterling makes further progress toward its own emancipation.

"If further progress is not made toward the removal of restrictions on trade and a more unfettered exchange of currencies, it is quite likely that, despite any international political institutions that have been erected or that may be erected in the future, the unity of the free world will remain precarious and fragile. On these points American national interests are vitally concerned."

The New York Times

ISSUES REPORT: Lewis W. Douglas, who headed mission that studied world trade problems for President Eisenhower.

Greeted Warmly in London

Special to THE NEW YORK TIMES.

LONDON, Tuesday, Aug. 25—The Douglas report was greeted by the London press today with warm approval, though The Daily Herald, the Laborite paper, doubted that it would be heeded in the United States. This country has been calling for a liberalization of United States restrictions on imports and the report falls into line with the Government's goal of "trade, not aid."

The conservative Daily Telegraph "commended the report to the American people," saying, "Mr. Douglas has rendered his country and ours a good service." The newspaper asserted that a permanent monetary balance between Britain and the United States could be achieved only by following the course Mr. Douglas had pointed out.

In its leading editorial, The Financial Times said the report "seems to go out of its way to reinforce several of the major points made in the official communiqué of the Commonwealth economic conference last December." The conference indicated that United States support would be necessary if sterling convertibility were to be re-established. But, The Financial Times continued, the conclusions of Mr. Douglas may be ignored by Congress because President Eisenhower, despite his recommendation of its conclusions, has chosen to adopt "a position of impartial arbiter."

The Daily Herald also voiced a fear that Mr. Douglas would be unheeded. "If so," an editorial said, "America will get badly hurt, for the rest of the free world will be forced to discriminate harshly against her products. The postwar unity which owes so much to American statesmanship is being imperiled by American commercialism."

Ottawa Pleased, Surprised

OTTAWA, Aug. 24 (Canadian Press) — Trade Department officials greeted Mr. Douglas' report with pleased surprise today.

"It couldn't have been better timed," one Canadian official said, noting that Canada had frequently cautioned the United States against protectionist policies.

The official noted that the report came at a time when a commission—Mr. Randall's—was being established in the United States to examine foreign trade policies.

Another official said that Canada on a number of occasions had declared in notes to the United States that unless Washington followed a policy of fewer restrictions against foreign imports, the United States' internal economy would eventually be adversely affected.

The United States has agreed, the official said, but has not followed up this agreement with action. Restrictions have increased on the importation of dairy products from Canada and there has been agitation to limit further imports of Canadian oats, lead, zinc and frozen fish fillets.

August 25, 1953

3-YEAR TRADE ACT EXTENSION AND 15% TARIFF CUTS BACKED IN RANDALL BOARD'S REPORT

CONCESSIONS MANY

'Buy American' Waiver Asked—Rigid Farm Price Props Decried

By CHARLES E. EGAN

Special to THE NEW YORK TIMES.

WASHINGTON, Jan. 23—President Eisenhower and Congress were told today by an agency of their own creation that the nation's "awesome" responsibility for leadership could not be discharged without correcting "distortions in our economic relations with the rest of the world."

Both the diagnosis and the remedy for the ills now besetting the international trade of the free world were set forth in a ponderous report by the Commission of Foreign Economic Policy.

The study group was created by Congress at the request of the President last summer, with seven members appointed by General Eisenhower and five by the Senate and House of Representatives, respectively. It is headed by Clarence B. Randall, chairman of the board of directors of the Inland Steel Company.

In its report the commission sought to point the way toward a relatively freer world trade in which all free world currencies would be interchangeable and the skills and resources of all components could be released from present artificial restrictions.

Liberal Approach Evident

More than a score of recommended corrections in policy and legislation stamped the document as a liberal approach to the economic dislocations growing out of the war. Among its major recommendations were these:

¶ Congress should authorize a three-year extension of the Reciprocal Trade Agreements Act and for a relatively longer period on the basis of results of concessions observed during the initial period. The President should be authorized to cut tariff rates by 5 per cent in each of the three years—for a total of 15 per cent.

¶ The President also should be authorized without any reciprocal agreement to cut tariff rates by 50 per cent under Jan. 1, 1945, on products not being imported or, imported only in negligible quantities, and to reduce to a 50 per cent ad valorem rate any import duty higher than that.

¶ Congress should authorize the President to waive the "buy American" statutes for countries that treat United States bidders on contracts on a basis of equality with their own nationals. Pending corrective legislation, the President would direct Federal purchasing agencies to treat foreign bids that meet other standards on the same price basis as those of Americans.

¶This Government should make an all-out diplomatic effort to create a more hospitable climate abroad for private United States investment capital. It should make sharp reductions in tax rates on American earnings on investments abroad, and should extend Government guarantees of private investments to cover risks of foreign revolutions and wars.

¶The Government should agree to a larger trade between Eastern and Western Europe in peaceful goods, to improve living conditions in the West but subject to the embargo on trade with Communist China and North Korea.

¶Every encouragement should be given to free foreign governments in making their foreign exchange again convertible into the money of other free nations. This Government should promote a "more active utilization than heretofore" of the $3,300,000,000 gold and dollar reserves of the International Monetary Fund to this end. The Federal Reserve System should explore the provision of "stand-by credits" for Western Europe's central banks for the same purpose.

¶Congress should repeal legislation requiring shipment of 50 per cent of Government-financed seagoing freight in American bottoms to give foreign shipping a chance to earn dollars from this source. A direct subsidy of United States shipping should be substituted as necessary.

¶The Government should abandon high and rigid agricultural price supports at home that tend to force accumulation of surplus farm products and to prevent their movement in international markets because of domestic prices pegged above the world level.

In the many findings and recommendations of the report there was little that had not been proposed at one time or another by private or Presidential study groups since World War II. Its separate chapters and recommendations were peppered with dissenting opinions of two or more members.

'Dollar Gap' Stressed

The same "dollar gap" that engaged the attention of the Presidential commissions headed by Gordon Gray, president of the University of North Carolina, and by Nelson A. Rockefeller, as well as by the Government's own Economic Cooperation Administration was found to be still at the root of the trouble.

But the report was the first effort of its kind undertaken during a Republican Administration and it made a significant contribution to the study of foreign economic policy in showing that, given the same sets of economic or monetary facts, competent experts usually find agreement on the cause and cure of any maladjustment.

In the field of tariffs and reciprocal concessions in foreign trade, the report reflected compromises in an effort to obtain unanimity. While conceding the need of customs simplification to enable foreign exporters to plan ahead their sales in the United States market, the report retained the "peril point" and "escape clause" provisions of the present law.

The report was eloquent in its portrayal of the "dollar gap," or the inability of trading nations abroad to earn enough dollar exchange to buy needed goods and services available only in the United States. While there was much the United States might do to solve this problem, the report pointed out, there was more that could be undertaken only by the nations themselves.

Cooperation Found Implicit

Thus the report said:

"The commission has concentrated upon measures which it recommends, to the Government of the United States. But implicit in all that it recommends is the necessity for like action by other nations. The United States cannot do this job alone.

"Our actions must be matched by comparable efforts on the part of the other nations of the free world. Only by acting together can we develop a system of international economic relations that our mutual welfare and security so urgently requires."

This philosophy of the majority members was brought to bear with special emphasis in the section of the report dealing with the need for greater American overseas investment of venture capital.

America's foreign friends might as well face up to the fact, in the majority view, that United States Government capital was inadequate to the need abroad and that main reliance must be on private capital. It was thus up to friendly free nations to create the conditions required for investment of private American funds in foreign plants and securities.

They had also to face squarely the fact that large-scale economic grants were a thing of the past, the commission said. It recommended that any such assistance, other than technical aid, must now take the form of loans, while any military assistance should take the form of gifts, so as not to impose an undue burden on local economies.

The report took sharp exception with what it called a disposition in some quarters to insist that the dollar problem had already been solved because United States exports, exclusive of military shipments, had come into balance and because foreign countries had in the last year increased their gold and dollar reserves by more than $2,000,000,000.

The fact was, the commission explained, there was still at the end of last year a "concealed dollar gap" of between $2,000,000,0000 and $3,000,000,000 which would be worsened by an economic recession here or any deterioration in Europe's "terms of trade." These "terms" are good or bad depending on whether the price or raw materials entering into Europe's manufactured products are relatively cheap or expensive.

Actually, it was explained, Europe's continuing shortage of dollars or capacity to earn them was covered up by "extraordinary" United States expenditures on the Continent of about $5,000,000,000 a year for military and civilian establishments, so-called off-shore procurement and stockpiling operations.

Presidential Discretion Urged

The commission proposed that the "escape clause" and "peril point" provisions of the existing Reciprocal Trade Agreements Act should be retained. But the

President, now authorized to disregard recommendations of the Federal Tariff Commission on the two provisions, would be permitted to disregard recommendations only when he found that the national interest of the United States required it.

In dealing with agricultural aspects of the total foreign economic problem the commission started out with a denial of any conflict between the requirements of a sound domestic agrarian program and the needs of a rounded system of trade and payments. It said the conflict was not in our farm policy but in its implementation.

"A dynamic foreign economic policy as it relates to agriculture cannot be built out of a maze of restrictive devices such as inflexible price - support programs which result in fixed prices, open or concealed expert subsidies, import quotas at home and abroad, excessive use of tariffs here and abroad, exchange restrictions, and state trading," the report declared.

The commission urged that this nation move as quickly as feasible toward the elimination of such devices in our own farm program. It warned especially against inflexibility of high price supports, which it said only resulted in pegging domestic prices above the world level and encouraged accumulation of surplus supplies that could not then move into world markets.

The commission said that this country's tariff policies over recent years belied the label of a "high tariff country," which it has borne internationally. This country, the report declared, is no longer among the high tariff countries of the world. Indeed, taken by and large, "our trade restrictions are certainly no more of a cause of payment imbalance than the rigidities maintained by other nations."

Labor Standards Considered

A new concept of eligibility for tariff concessions was put forward by the commission in its discussion of labor standards in international competition. The group suggested that United States representatives in negotiating a reciprocal trade agreement make it clear that no tariff concessions would be granted on products made by workers who received wages that were substandard in the exporting country.

This recommendation, according to those close to the commission, was based on the conviction that this country could help to spread the philosophy of the American Fair Labor Standards Act abroad by adhering to the commission's suggestion.

It was held that before the Government made a concession on a tariff rate for a given product it should require proof that the industry producing the product in a foreign country was not using labor paid subnormal wages and working under "sweat shop" conditions.

The report was shot through with notations of dissent or mild disagreement by various members of the commission. Only Representatives Daniel A. Reed, Republican of upstate New York and chairman of the House Ways and Means Committee, and Richard M. Simpson, Republican of Pennsylvania and a senior member of the Ways and Means Committee, balked at the entire report.

In a letter noting their dissent from the commission's general conclusions, the two Representatives announced that they would draw up their own report. They declared the majority report had been hastily prepared and was inadequate. They said they would submit to the commission some time before March 6, "alternative recommendations, and a statement of principles upon which they are based."

Senator Eugene D. Millikin, Republican of Colorado, chairman of the Senate Finance Committee, registered reservations and dissents on a number of the report's findings and recommendations. He set forth his views in a letter to Mr. Randall, which was printed at the end of the report.

Representatives Reed and Simpson, in their letter of dissent, declared that the commission's report contributed "little to a solution of the over-all problems which this country faces with respect to its foreign policy."

"It adds nothing to the views of the members of the commission previously published and well known before their selection," the letter asserted.

The mandate of Congress to the commission, the Representatives said, called for submission of the report by March 6.

"Yet the report is now submitted six weeks before the deadline set by Congress with the complaint that adequate time was not permitted, the letter continued. "However, of the seven months available, less than four months had been fully used, when the report was frzen and submitted to the members of the commission with only one week allowed for development of their dissents.

"No comprehensive study of facts, conditions, and problems was made. The only witnesses allowed to appear at public hearings held by the commission in the United States were representatives mainly of recognized pressure groups whose views were known in advance.

"Witnesses in the United States were allowed two days for appearances; those appearing at private hearings in Europe, whose primary interest was to obtain help for foreign contries, were allowed four days.

"Several days of executive hearings were also held at the commission. There is no evidence in the report of serious consideration of the exhaustive studies prepared and submitted by many affected domestic industries. Spokesmen for industries vitally affected were not permitted to testify."

January 24, 1954

Experts Say Randall Report Fails as World Trade Policy

Special to The New York Times.

PRINCETON, N. J., March 22—The Randall Commission report, which is expected to provide the basis of President Eisenhower's foreign economic policy, was criticized today as inadequate by a group of seventeen economics experts.

They scored the report for what they called "its want of basic philosophy and for its failure to assert American leadership or to enlighten the American people as to their international responsibilities and opportunities."

The criticism, contained in a 25,000-word report published today, was the result of a two-day conference sponsored here last month by Princeton University's International Finance Section and Center of International Studies. The critique will be mailed to 2,500 individuals and groups throughout the country.

The Randall Commission report, presented to the President on Jan. 23, had criticized United States foreign economic relations and called for freer world trade, with a greater interchange of currency, the removal of artificial trade barriers and a lowering of tariffs.

The commission was headed by Clarence B. Randall, chairman of the Inland Steel Company, and was formally called the Commission on Foreign Economic Policy. It had seventeen members — ten members of Congress and seven leaders in business, labor and economics. Its recommendations are now being drafted as proposals for Congress.

Although the Princeton report agreed with the Randall Commission in certain respects, it struck at what it termed the "lack of optimism and the lack of confidence in the American economy."

"There is no emphasis [in the Randall report] on the possibility of American consumers' and producers' standing to gain from freer trade and large imports," the economists declared.

They also expressed disappointment with the commission for having given "no consideration to the problem of United States policy toward the economic and political integration of Western Europe, or toward Japan," a nation of "great political and economic importance to the United States."

"An even more serious omission of the report," they continued "was its failure to discuss, more than incidentally, the question of whether the United States should be concerned with the attempts to facilitate the economic development of the so-called underdeveloped areas and, if so, what are the most effective means of doing so."

The conference agreed with several of the Randall Commission's recommendations on trade policy, with the statement that if they could be enacted in their entirety in the next two years "the result would constitute the biggest single step toward a more liberal commercial policy" since the Trade Agreements Act of 1934.

Gradual Approach Lauded

The group found, however, "no sense at all that the problem is more than one of the rest of the world's trade and payments with the United States."

While it praised the gradual approach to tariff reductions, the conference criticized the "year-by-year approach in the recommendations of the Randall report" for two reasons:

1. "Setting up tariff reductions on a calendar basis would inhibit practically all imports of the affected goods for a considerable time prior to each successive reduction."
2. "Most of those who would support a series of gradual tariff reductions would probably also be willing to support one major reduction all at once, whereas those who opposed reductions would have a longer period to press Congress into passing a law suspending execution of the second and third reductions."

Almost unanimously the conference stated that "in building the report around the dollar-gap problem, the Randall Commission has taken too narrow a focus."

The "dollar gap" is the difference between the dollars that foreign countries have or are likely to earn and the dollars they need to buy goods and services.

The Randall report stressed the need for measures to close this gap to encourage trade, since most foreign nations lack enough dollars or dollar credits.

The Princeton group also said the commission had not dealt with the problems of an American business slump on other countries, although "the outside world is extremely apprehensive of an employment slump in the United States" and such a fear "figures importantly in foreign thinking about the desirability of freer trade and payments."

Areas of Criticism Cited

The critique discussed several major areas in which it believed the commission had been "weak" or had not gone far enough in the right direction.

It termed the treatment of foreign aid "weak, confusing and unimaginative," and called for a combination of "pragmatic and flexible attitudes" with "rigorous thinking on the level of operational problems."

It agreed with the Federal commission, however, that "an increase in private transactions would cushion the shock of any decline in foreign aid," and stated that the Government should promote private capital investment in foreign nations by every possible means.

It stressed that foreign economic policy should not be "primarily concerned with solving the world's dollar problem," but with the underlying conditions in this country and abroad—economic, political, social and psychological—of which the dollar gap was symptomatic.

"It would not require revolutionary increases in the flow of American imports for American foreign investments to close the gap completely," the economists declared. The gap cannot be measured quantitatively, they added, because "so much of it is suppressed by import barriers."

"The lack of continuity in American commercial policy" was called a major obstacle to expanded trade, and the conference expressed disappointment that the Randall commission had not recommended a ten-year extension of the reciprocal trade law. The commission had advised a three-year extension.

The experts also criticized the escape clause and peril point provisions in the existing law. These are provisions by which the President is authorized to disregard Federal Tariff Commission findings and to act in the national interest on specific tariffs. "Though not often invoked in the past," the economists said, "they remain an effective barrier to imports because they add to the uncertainty which discourages foreign exporters from making investments in the United States."

Cautious On Convertibility

On the question of converting one currency into another for trade, the conference stated that convertibility "should not be pressed at the price of a general tightening of quantitative import restrictions."

"A free [currency] market rate is not desirable," it said, "in that it would probably result in a rate well below what would otherwise be the equilibrium rate in the next two or three years, would probbaly result in a serious deterioration in the trade of the country freeing its rate and would generate serious internal inflationary pressures."

The Randall report had advocated a gradual move toward convertibility together with the removal of restrictions on trade and payment. It also had proposed a "floating rate" of currency convertibility rather than letting each nation's money find its own level on the world market.

The conference closed its report with a statement that the Randall report was not "a document from which the nation could derive inspiration or on which it could rest for any length of time."

Participating in the conference were Edward M. Bernstein of the International Monetary Fund, Harlan Cleveland, H. Van B. Cleveland of the Committee for Economic Development, William Diebold Jr. of the Council of Foreign Relations, Prof. John K. Galbraith of Harvard University, Theodore Geiger of the National Planning Association, and D. Gale Johnson of the University of Chicago.

Also, Wilfred Malenbaum of the Massachusetts Institute of Technology, Stacey May of the International Basic Economy Corporation, Judd Polk of the Council on Foreign Relations, Thomas C. Shelling of Yale University, Herbert Stein of the Committee for Economic Development, Robert Triffin of Yale University, Prof. Jacob Viner of Princeton University, and Clair Wilcox of Swathmore College.

Klaus Knorr, a member of Princeton's Center of International Studies, and Gardner Patterson of the International Finance Section prepared the published report.

President's Plans Awaited

WASHINGTON, March 22 (AP)—President Eisenhower will send Congress a special message next week on tariffs and foreign trade policy.

The President's plans were disclosed today by Republican Congressional leaders after their regular Monday morning conference at the White House.

Speaker Joseph W. Martin Jr. said that the leaders, at next Monday's conference with the President, would go over the message with Mr. Randall. He added that General Eisenhower had not indicated whether his message to Congress would be based on the majority recommendations of the Randall group. Dissents had been registered by some members.

March 23, 1954

World Trade Is Improving Despite Post-Korea Strains

GATT Study Calls Balance Better Than at Any Time in Post-War Period—No Ill Effect Seen in U. S. Adjustment

By MICHAEL L. HOFFMAN

Special to The New York Times.

GENEVA, July 8—International trade was by the end of 1953 "far better balanced than at any time during the post-war period." This conclusion was reached by the secretariat of the General Agreement on Tariffs and Trade (GATT) in a report published here today.

Trade probably is even better balanced today. The forces that have undone the great distortion in the pattern of international prices caused by the repercussions of the Korean war still seem to be at work. United States economy has been behaving in an exemplary fashion from the point of view of its impact on world economy.

This study is mainly the work of Dr. Hans Staehlen, a United States economist on the GATT staff.

What made 1953 a good year? First of all, trade among the three great industrial areas of the world (North America, continental Western Europe, and the "European sterling area," which includes Britain, Ireland and Iceland), expanded. At the same time, prices of the principal raw materials have reverted to about the same relationship to prices of manufactures that prevailed before the Korean commodity boom, that is, to the 1950 pattern.

Furthermore, continental Western Europe and the European sterling area, which have had great difficulty financing their imports from North America, enjoyed a three-way shift of trade that eased that problem. They bought less raw material from the United States and Canada, found more raw materials in non-dollar areas, and steadily expanded their sales of manufactures to North America.

Forecasts of a collapse of world trade on the advent of a United States recession turned out to be monumental miscalculations. "Up to the end of 1953," the GATT report cautiously states, "the downward adjustment in United States business conditions which had been evident during the second half of the year failed to produce the depressing effects upon international trade that had been widely expected."

Countries producing mainly primary products have suffered from the fall of the high post-Korean prices of their products. They had to cut their imports from industrial areas and from each other. They cut mostly in the category of finished consumer products.

Lesson to Producing Areas

There is a warning for the industrial countries in this experience, the report suggests. They have been able to sell less to such primary producing areas as Latin America, African territories and the countries of Southeast Asia than in 1951. "The loss they suffered in the nonindustrial markets is likely to be at least partly permanent."

Because they could not maintain imports, many of these countries are encouraging home production of consumer goods. They are unlikely to open their markets as freely again to United States and European manufacturers.

The report provides strong evidence of the advantages that accrue to business from the establishment of policies of non-discrimination and free interchangeability of currencies.

Although trade between industrial and primary producing areas in general declined, trade between certain industrial regions and the primary producing areas most intimately associated therewith by currency and commercial ties actually increased.

July 19, 1954

FIGHT OVER TARIFF HOTTEST SINCE '29

Hawley-Smoot Days Recalled as Protectionists Combat Lowering of Trade Bars

ISSUES ARE CONFUSED

GATT and Relief Measures for Japan, Switzerland 'Crowd' the Basic Bill

By **BRENDAN M. JONES**

Veteran foreign traders had to reach back to 1929 last week for a parallel to the debate that has broken out over the Eisenhower trade program.

It was in that year that another great debate began. Out of it came the Hawley-Smoot Act, which sent up a high protective wall around depression-struck American industry.

The present dispute in and around Congress over President Eisenhower's proposals for a further lowering of that wall has reached an intensity unequaled since the Hawley-Smoot days, it was noted.

Last week confusion was added to controversy in the Senate Finance Committee's closing hearings on three-year extension of the Reciprocal Trade Agreements Act with new tariff-cutting powers for the Administration.

New World Group an Issue

It arose from suspicions that the Administration was attempting to get Congress to approve United States membership in a new world trade organization through obscure provisions of the trade act extension. Credit for arousing these suspicions has been claimed by a leading protectionist group.

The result has been further delay in Senate action on the trade bill. The measure, passed by a narrow margin in the House, had been meeting increasing opposition in the Senate.

It has been evident that it faced drastic amendment to exempt such industries as textiles from further tariff reductions. With many other parts of the Eisenhower trade program yet to be introduced in Congress, delay on this key measure may postpone consideration of such matters as customs simplification and reduced taxes on foreign investments.

Trade Bills Crowd In

The timing of Administration tariff measures has been a factor in building up the controversy. The reciprocal trade issue, postponed from last year, now seems to be crowding other tariff-cutting projects.

Shortly before the presentation of its trade program to Congress in January, the Administration pressed for a tariff-cutting agreement with Japan. This stirred a storm of protest from numerous industries.

Hearing has followed on hearing. Those on Japan no sooner ended than others opened on the reciprocal trade bill. Tomorrow another round of hearings will begin on proposed tariff reductions to compensate Switzerland for last year's watch-duty increase, and on a second list of goods to be added to the more than 150 figuring in the Japanese negotiations.

The injection of the issue of the world trade organization into the tariff debate came with the announcement last week of the long-awaited revision of the General Agreement on Tariffs and Trade. This revision, which basically makes it more difficult for GATT countries to obtain waivers on their trade and tariff concessions, has been a major part of the Eisenhower trade program.

This country and thirty-three others that account for more than three-fourths of the world's trade entered into the general agreement as a kind of temporary world tariff truce. After seven years they agreed at Geneva this month to put the arrangement on a more lasting and effective basis.

Included in the revision was a new Organization for Trade Cooperation to administer the revised rules. This quickly became the target of renewed protectionist opposition in Washington.

Prompted by protectionist telegrams, Senate committee members immediately raised the question whether the trade agreements act extension would commit the United States to GATT membership without prior approval of Congress.

The question was brought up despite the fact that the Administration had said it would ask Congress to approve United States membership in the new organization in a few weeks. Secretary of State John Foster Dulles, as final witness in the committee hearing, was called on to clarify matters.

The Secretary explained that the trade act extension did not commit this country to GATT. On the matter of whether the trade extension bill "implied" such adherence, he said that it should be considered along with the GATT bill.

Out of this confusion it was concluded that the State Department should promptly provide the committee with a report stating the relationship of the two bills.

It long has been quite evident that the matter of the United States tariff and trade policies are related to the similar world-wide policies represented by GATT. All recent reciprocal trade agreements entered into by this country have been under the auspices of the general agreement.

United States adherence to GATT has been one of the main targets for the protectionists. They have questioned its constitutionality on grounds that Congress alone has power to set tariffs. The trade agreements act represents a delegation of this authority to the President.

Suggesting that United States tariff policy would somehow be directed by a foreign organization is an effective tactic for arousing greater opposition to tariff reductions. It remains to be seen how effectively the President will rally support for his threatened program.

Last week he made it clear that more than ever he considered his trade policy proposals a vital contribution to the strength of free-world nations.

March 27, 1955

EISENHOWER SIGNS 3-YEAR TRADE ACT, HAILS 'MILESTONE'

Asks Approval of U. S. Entry Into World Organization for Aid to Commerce

PRAISES CONGRESS UNITY

By **CHARLES E. EGAN**

Special to The New York Times.

WASHINGTON, June 21 — President Eisenhower signed today the bill extending for three years the Reciprocal Trade Agreements Act.

He used the occasion to urge Congress again to approve American entry into the Organization for Trade Cooperation. Thus supplemented, the President said, the new trade act "can contribute significantly to economic growth and economic well-being throughout the free world."

The Organization for Trade Cooperation was created this year at the international trade conference in Geneva to administer policies of the parent organization, the General Agreement on Tariffs and Trade. In the latter group thirty-four countries of the free world have combined to seek mutual reductions in tariffs and other barriers to international trade.

The President called the new law "a significant milestone" in the nation's foreign economic policy.

Signs With Nine Pens

Even greater import was read into the act by Clarence B. Randall, chairman of Inland Steel Corporation and head of a Presidential commission on foreign economic policy.

Mr. Randall said the renewal measure "may give the final push necessary for the establishment of the convertibility of currencies which the world needs so urgently."

A primary objective of United States foreign economic policy since the end of World War II, currency convertibility means the ability freely to exchange one currency for another.

The President signed the reciprocal trade measure before a gathering of Congressional leaders of both parties and of members of the Senate Finance and House Ways and Means Committees. He used nine pens in signing.

The act gives the President authority to cut tariffs on goods from countries that reciprocate the concessions. He can make reductions up to 5 per cent a year in each of three years, after negotiations with countries affected.

A three-year renewal of the Reciprocal Trade Act was made the cornerstone of the foreign-trade program urged on Congress by the President in January, 1954. Last year Congress balked at renewing the act for more than a single year and this year the proposal provided the grounds for a great battle in which the bill was under debate from mid-January until ten days ago in both House and Senate.

President's Statement

The President issued the following statement today as he signed the new law:

"Enactment of the Trade Agreements Extension Act of 1955 is an important milestone in the development of our country's foreign economic policy. Supplemented by early approval of United States membership and participation in the proposed Organization for Trade Cooperation, the act can contribute significantly to economic growth and economic well-being throughout the free world. In this way it will materially strengthen the defense and capabilities of our friends abroad, and advance the mutual security of us all.

"I am particularly gratified that this measure was supported by overwhelming majorities in both political parties. This bipartisanship demonstrates anew our unity in dealing with matters affecting our relations with other countries."

Interested groups agreed that the President's attitude toward future tariff changes would prove the measure of success or failure of the new bill. Under Senate amendments in the act the "escape clause" by which industries previously have been able to petition for tariff increases has been broadened.

Whereas, under previous regulations, the industry had to prove it was suffering generally because of imports it now can petition for relief if only a segment of the industry is being adversely affected.

Another provision, under which an industry can claim protection on the grounds that it is essential to national security, is regarded with suspicion by foreign traders. Although the President will be the final judge of the security factor, the Office of Defense Mobilization must examine all claims and make recommendations to him.

Foreign Objections Stated

Representatives of some foreign nations, among them spokesmen for British, French, German and Japanese interests, agreed that the two clauses were major detriments to any concerted drive by their countrymen to develop the United States market.

Instead of being able to plan three years in advance, they said, manufacturers in their countries will operate much as they now are doing through fear that if they undertake an extensive drive for trade here domestic interests will invoke either the escape clause or the national security argument to curb the foreign sales.

Charles P. Taft, president of the Committee for a National Trade Policy, representing business men who supported the Administration's original program, said that the new law "unfortunately . . . provides some new loopholes for . . . a flood of new pressures on the President."

O. R. Strackbein, chairman of the Nation-Wide Committee of Industry, Agriculture and Labor on Export-Import Policy, and a bitter foe of the Administration's liberal trade views, said that the test of "the unhappy trade bill of 1955 will come with administration of the escape clause."

June 22, 1955

JAPAN SETS OIL IMPORTS

Nation Allots 60% of Trade Budget Over 6 Months

TOKYO, Oct. 28 (AP)—Japan will spend 60 per cent of her import budget of $47,000,000 for oil imports from October to March, the Ministry of International Trade and Industry announced today.

The ministry allotted $3,000,000 in foreign exchange to buy mollasses from Formosa and the Philippines.

The Economic Planning Board reported, meanwhile, that Japan had a record rice crop this year, estimated at 372,400,000 bushels, and that her exports climbed to a new post-war high in September. Steel and textiles largely accounted for the high September figure of $149,000,000, which left an export balance for the month of $82,000,000, the board said.

October 28, 1955

SOUTH AMERICANS ARE ENCOURAGED BY RECENT GAINS

But Governments Still Face Problem of New Capital and Inflationary Trends

TRADE UNITY IS PUSHED

Efforts Are Made to Develop Intra-Continent Commerce —Stable Prices Sought

Special to The New York Times.

RIO DE JANEIRO—The year 1955 brough a fair amount of economic housecleaning and many encouraging developments to the South American republics.

But the governments still had to brace themselves against the traditional problems of dollar gaps, a dangerous inflation in a majority of the countries and insufficient foreign and domestic investments. An added serious element last year was a slump in some world commodity markets and the attendant worries about slipping prices and gathering surpluses.

Two developments kept the dollar gap open and encouraged inflationary trends. They were the immense demand for imports as part of industrial development, and the increase in consumer goods purchases resulting from increased incomes.

Farm Output Lags

The dollar gap and inflation were most evident in Chile, Brazil, Bolivia and Uruguay. In some republics the absence of consistent financial policies helped to worsen the situation.

With populations rising unceasingly agricultural production per person became lower than in the pre-war years when industrialization and its lures to the labor force had not reached its present-day importance.

On the favorable side of the ledger was the fact that South American Governments and their Central American neighbors were slowly becoming convinced of the need for close co-operation to face the problems of trade and development.

Brazil, Colombia and the Central American producers have not been able yet to get together on a comprehensive coffee-growing, marketing and pricing program but some progress was made in that direction last year.

With the threat of African competition, the menace of overproduction and relatively low prices, it is becoming clear that nations whose economies largely depend on coffee must get together to work out a joint approach.

Joint Planning Spurred

The conference of the United Nations Economic Commission for Latin America, held in Bogota, Colombia, last August and September, also appeared to provide the stimulus for joint planning in other fields. These range from foreign trade to turning into reality the great promise of the use of atomic energy on this power-starved continent.

Other governments noted with interest Brazil's successful pioneering in establishing a system of multilateral trade and free convertibility with a group of European nations patterned after the European Payments Union. The United Nations conference adopted a resolution urging member nations to study the possibility of streamlining Latin-American trade along these lines.

These continent-wide efforts accompanied by local housecleaning in several republics, are being accomplished with a greater or lesser degree of success.

Thus Argentina, emerging from the revolution that ousted President Juan Perón, still is trying to assess her economic situation after ten years of ruinous Perónist policies.

Colombia imposed strict curbs on imports in an effort to balance her foreign trade.

Chile, in the midst of skyrocketing inflation and labor troubles, has been receiving outside advice from a United States concern of consultants. But President Carlos Ibanez del Campo may have trouble in implementing the recommendations.

Brazil is awaiting the inauguration of a new administration at the end of the month to try to solve her problems of inflation, mismanagement and falling exports.

Peru has been thriving since freeing her foreign trade a year ago.

Foreign Investments Rising

South Americans have been encouraged by the slowly but steadily growing foreign interest in investments in their republics. European capital has been coming into Brazil, Argentina, Peru, and Venezuela. Private United States investors, the Export-Import Bank and the International Bank for Reconstruction and Development are making loans available at a greater rate than in past years.

Thus in fiscal 1955 the Export-Import Bank lent Latin America $284,000,000, while the total authorized credits for the area stood at more than $1,500,000,000.

Having realized in the post-war years that foreign investments were a prerequisite for the healthy development of their economies, the Latin American nations have been eager to make themselves attractive as investment markets.

Liberal legislation in most republics provides interesting terms for industries desirous of opening branches in South America, though current foreign exchange regulations in Brazil, expected to be changed soon, have been slowing down this type of investments.

Peru, Bolivia and Colombia have liberalized petroleum legis-

TRADITIONAL: A small South American coffee-grower and his sons examine the beans lying in crude drying areas.

lation that has attracted foreign capital and technicians. Only last month the Cities Service Company signed a contract for the joint exploration with the Colombian Government of more than 2,000,000 acres of potential oil land. But Brazil, which spends more than $300,000,000 annually on oil imports, still bars foreign companies.

Oil production on the Continent is growing steadily, and the output of electric power last year rose considerably.

Three South-American nations received late last year strong economic aid from the United States in the form of the sale of $78,000,000 worth of surplus agricultural products payable in local currencies on excellent terms. Brazil received wheat, Argentina, oils and fats and Colombia, wheat and cotton oil.

Many local economists saw this as a mixed blessing—there is fear in Latin America that the United States will launch a major program of dumping surpluses abroad at prices with which Latin-American producers cannot compete.

Thus Brazilians who were happy to get United States wheat in the surplus deal, become unhappy at the thought that Colombia has taken United States cotton on the same terms, thus cutting off the potential sale of surplus Brazilian cotton.

Taken as a whole, the outlook for South America for 1956 seems more encouraging than in previous years—provided that investments grow and the prices of raw materials and commodities remain stabilized at sound levels.

January 5, 1956

Hamilton Wright

MODERN: The Cardon oil refinery in Venezuela, which has capacity of 170,000 barrels a day, handles crude petroleum brought by pipeline and tanker from Lake Maracaibo fields.

EAST-WEST TRADE ROSE 24% IN 1955

U. S. Says Underdeveloped Lands Welcome Red Bids

By EDWIN L. DALE Jr.
Special to The New York Times.

WASHINGTON, Oct. 9—The Government reported today that trade between the Communist bloc and the rest of the world rose by 24 per cent in 1955.

The data appeared in a report on the Communists' economic drive aimed at the underdeveloped countries.

The report covered activities ranging from trade to trade fairs, from economic aid to goodwill missions. It said the drive presented "many, complex and formidable issues." And it reported that, on the whole, the reception of the Communist offensive in the underdeveloped countries had been good.

The report did not touch on the subject of what should be done about the problem. It said merely that "the mutual security programs of the United States are meeting this challenge by improving the economic growth and military security of our partners in the free world."

The report, covering the year 1955, was required by the Battle Act, which is the legal basis for controls over trade in strategic goods with the Communist bloc.

Trade between the Communist bloc and the rest of the world, according to the report, rose from $3,600,000,000 in 1954 to $4,460,000,000 in 1955, an increase of 24 per cent. However, this trade accounted for only 2.6 per cent of the total trade of the non-Communist world.

Eight countries increased trade with the Communist bloc to more than 10 per cent of their total trade. They were Afghanistan, Egypt, Finland, Hong Kong, Iceland, Iran, Turkey and Yugoslavia.

In 1956, the report continued, the Communist countries offered credits of nearly $600,000,000, most of them to Yugoslavia, Egypt, Afghanistan and India.

The number of Soviet bloc exhibits in trade fairs jumped from 125 in 1954 to 288 in 1955, the report said. These exhibits were displayed in 149 fairs and exhibitions last year, compared to only sixty in 1954.

The report said that, because of the surge of economic growth in the Soviet Union itself, the country "can probably export machinery, raw materials and skilled technicians in substantial quantity" without undue strain on domestic development.

Pacts Believed Fulfilled

The United States report examined many individual agreements and concluded that "the bloc countries appeared, in general, to have provided goods of acceptable quality and to have fulfilled the terms of trade contracts."

The report covered a wide range of individual deals between Communist countries and underdeveloped nations, such as the arms - for - cotton arrangement with Egypt and the Soviet offer to purchase Burmese rice.

The aim of the Communist drive, the report said, is to extend in the underdeveloped part of the world "the areas of the Communist bloc's political, economic and cultural influence."

But the report added: "It remains to be seen whether this pattern of exchange will be of continuing benefit to the less developed nations."

The trade section of the report pointed out that, despite the steady growth in East-West trade, trade within the bloc remained at about 80 per cent of the total trade of the Communist countries, about the same as in 1954.

Trade with Communist China, the report showed, rose from a total of $669,400,000 in 1954 to $805,800,000 in 1955.

It also said free world exports to Communist countries rose by 15 per cent in 1955, to a total of $2,030,000,000, while imports rose much faster, by 32 per cent to a total of $2,430,000,000.

October 10, 1956

EUROPEANS UNITE IN CUSTOMS UNION AND ATOM AGENCY

Signing of 2 Pacts in Rome Paves Way for Forming 6-Nation Federation

By ARNALDO CORTESI
Special to The New York Times.

ROME, March 25—Statesmen of six West European nations signed today the birth certificate of a European federation of states. The signing took place in the Hall of the Horatii and Curiatii on Rome's Capitol Hill.

The six countries are France, West Germany, Italy, Belgium, the Netherlands and Luxembourg.

The documents attesting to the birth of a new grouping of six European countries were two international treaties and several annexes. One treaty provides for the creation of a European common market, in which goods and persons will ultimate-

Associated Press Radiophoto

UNITY: Italian Premier Antonio Segni, left, and Chancellor Konrad Adenauer of West Germany in Rome after signing European common market and nuclear energy pool treaties with four other nations. Behind them is Corrado Baldoni, Italian protocol officer.

ly move unrestricted by tariffs or other barriers.

A second creates a European atomic pool for the development and exploitation of nuclear energy.

Machinery Is Established

Accompanying these provisions, which are largely economic, are some political stipulations. The two treaties establish the international machinery that will develop in due course into the organs of a central European government.

This machinery is due to include a Court of Justice, a rudimentary Parliament and the embryo of a future European Cabinet. In other words, the two treaties resume the task of building a united Europe at the point where it was halted with the defeat of the European Defense Community project.

The treaties crown the efforts made by the six West European countries to find a substitute for the European Defense Community project. That plan was defeated by a voting technicality in the French National Assembly Aug. 30, 1954.

Unity Will Be Gradual

The six nations seeking unity met in Messina, Sicily, in June 1955 and decided that the ideal of united Europe was not to be abandoned. For the next twenty months they sought to establish the two organizations covered by the treaties signed today.

The new treaties do not go as far as the European Defense Community project. This was largely military in scope and was aimed at creating an integrated European army.

The treaties signed here aim rather at bringing the six European nations together, first of all economically by incorporating them all in a single market and making them all dependent on the same sources of nuclear energy. Then the organs of a central European government created by the treaties will come into play, gradually, drawing the nations still closer together.

The Assembly and Court of Justice established under the two new treaties will apply to the European coal and steel community established in 1953 by the same six signatory nations. To attain this end a special convention amends the treaty that established the coal and steel community.

The transition will be made slowly and gradually. Even the process of eliminating tariff almost certainly will not be completed before 1970.

Even greater is the importance that some deplomats attach to getting the French and West German economies integrated in the same economic unit. These diplomats believe it will make a war between France and Germany as impossible as a war between Paris and Marseilles.

The principal signers of the two fundamental treatries and annexes were Dr. Konrad Adenauer, Chancellor of West Germany; Christian Pineau, French Foreign Minister; Paul-Henri Spaak, Belgian Foreign Minister; Dr. Joseph M. A. H. Luns, Netherlands Foreign Minister; Joseph Bech, Premier and Foreign Minister of Luxembourg, and Antonio Segni, Premier of Italy.

A second delegate also signed for each country. In Italy's case the second delegate was Dr. Gaetano Martino, the Foreign Minister.

The six signatory states have a combined population of 160,000,000. They represent, therefore, considerably more than one-half of free, or non-Soviet, Europe.

Rome Mayor Hails Accord

Senator Umberto Tupini, Mayor of Rome, started the signatory proceedings with a speech welcoming the delegates and underlining the importance of what they were about to do. He said they were preparing for Europe "a century of union in peace, freedom and prosperity."

He was answered first by Dr. Martino, then by Dr. Adenauer and then in turn by the heads of all other delegations.

All who spoke underlined that, though European unity had been born, much remained to be done if it was to be kept alive. Dr. Adenauer added that "it is painful for us Germans not to be able to participate in a united Europe as a united Germany, but we have not yet given up hope."

Mr. Spaak said he could hardly contain his enthusiasm and optimism that European unity had taken its initial step.

M. Pineau said he felt certain arrangements could be worked out whereby Britain would associate herself with the common market, or European Economic Community, as it is officially called. Then he added:

"We have created not a small isolated Europe but a great Europe. Our union and our strength will inspire respect in anyone who might be tempted to disturb our peace."

Mr. Bech said the idea of European unity no longer belonged to a few lofty spirits but was shared by the peoples of all European countries. Dr. Luns said that growing prosperity and progress would come to Europe as a result of the treaties.

Almost all speakers had warm words of praise for the part played by M. Spaak in making European union possible.

When the speeches were finished the actual ceremony of signing began. The treaty for the common market or European Economic Community as it is officially called, was placed in front of M. Spaak, who sat at one end of the table. He signed it, quickly followed by the second Belgian delegate.

Then the treaty for the atomic pool, or the European Atomic Energy Community as it is officially called, was placed before M. Spaak, while the common market treaty continued to move from delegate to delegate. So the two treaties moved from the Belgians to the French, to the Germans and to Signor Segni who was sitting at the center of the table.

Then they continued to Dr. Martino, who was sitting at Premier Segni's left and to the Dutch and the Luxembourg delegations.

When all had signed, Mayor Tupini gave each delegate a specially struck gold medal to commemorate the event.

In the evening delegates participated in a reception at Palazzo Venezia where Benito Mussolini once had his office.

Earlier in the day all delegates were present at the final burial of Dr. Alcide De Gasperi, former Italian Premier who worked hard to achieve European unity. He is buried in the Basilica of St. Laurence outside the walls where a monument to him also was dedicated. Dr. De Gasperi died Aug. 19, 1954.

Crowd Gathers Outside Hall

Despite a drizzle that fell all day, a sizable crowd gathered on Capitol Hill while the European treaties were being signed.

Some Communists in the crowd tried to create a commotion but they were quickly set upon by the rest of the watchers. Some Communists were manhandled and some were taken into custody by the police.

Completion of the signing ceremony was announced to the crowd by the pealing of two historic old bells in the Capitoline Tower. The ringing of the bells brought cheers from the crowd.

March 26, 1957

The World Trade Issue

A Shortage of 'International Liquidity' Is Behind Surge of Economic Comment

By EDWIN L. DALE Jr.

Special to The New York Times.

WASHINGTON, June 9 — A complicated thing known in economists' jargon as "insufficient international liquidity" is behind the sudden surge of comment about the economic problems of the Free World.

News Analysis

It is at the heart of the economic portion of the talks between President Eisenhower and Harold Macmillan, the British Prime Minister. It is the problem that gave rise to recent speeches by Adlai E. Stevenson and Dean Acheson.

So far it is a problem that has mostly led to talk, with few concrete proposals. British officials stressed today that Mr. Macmillan himself was not now ready to make any proposals but merely wished to get the United States Government thinking about the problem.

In its broadest sense, the liquidity problem underlies the associated problems of keeping world trade growing and helping the under-developed countries to start the slow process of economic growth.

"Insufficient liquidity" for a corporation or a family means simply not enough cash to finance the volume of business or of consumption that the firm or family would like to undertake.

In the international sense, it is usually described as an insufficiency of gold and dollar holdings, outside the United States, to finance world trade and investment.

All sides are agreed that the problem is not of immediate urgency. Even Mr. Stevenson calls it a "creeping crisis." But as the British and others see it, the potential problem is something like this:

Suppose there should be a prolonged American recession, with a resulting drop in American imports. Or suppose there should be a general industrial recession throughout the Western World. Or suppose there should be another Suez situation with its "crisis of confidence" for such a key currency as the pound sterling.

In any of these events a number of countries, from Britain through Brazil, would find their relatively meager hard currency freely exchangeable in international transactions and gold reserve quickly depleted.

They would, quite literally, have not enough money in the bank to pay for their accustomed volume of imports.

Their only recourse would presumably be to shut off imports, either by physical controls on the movement of goods or by financial controls on the means of paying for them. But obviously one country's action of this kind would hurt its trading partners. The result would be a spreading of controls, a sharp contraction in trade, and impoverishment for everybody.

The issue of liquidity has arisen now for three reasons.

First, world trade has been expanding vigorously with no comparable growth in world financial reserves. A smaller world cash balance is financing a much bigger volume of business.

Second, twice in the last eighteen months the British discovered just how slim a margin of reserves was behind the pound, which finances at least 40 per cent, and probably more, of world trade. The Suez crisis in late 1956 and the franc crisis in September, 1957, both caused runs on the pound that came near creating a disaster for Britain.

Third, a combination of the American recession, a mild business slowdown in Europe and general over-supply has cut sharply into the demand for the products of the one-crop under-developed countries — copper, rubber, wool, tin, oil, coffee and others.

The reserves of important importing countries, ranging from Brazil to Australia and from Malaya to Chile, have been seriously depleted from this cause and, in some cases, from over-ambitious development programs as well.

So far, emergency devices of various kinds have prevented these problems from developing into full fledged crises. The International Monetary Fund and the United States Export-Import Bank have bailed out one situation after another.

But the feeling of those who are worried about the problem is that the resources of these two institutions are not unlimited, and that something more should be provided. If the world was and felt more liquid, these benefits would flow, according to the argument:

¶The British would not have to fear a run on the pound because no runs would occur as long as world traders and financiers knew that the pound was fully defended by ample reserves of gold and dollars.

¶The growth of world trade could proceed without fear of interruption from insufficient money in the bank by key importing nations.

¶The under-developed countries would have more of a financial cushion behind their development programs, which inevitably involve some excess of imports over exports in at least their earlier stages.

How, then, can the problem of insufficient liquidity be solved? A number of proposals have been made from such sources as The Economist of London, ranging from an increase in the dollar price of gold to wholly new international institutions.

But the proposal that appears to be receiving the most attention within governments — though none has yet reached a firm conclusion—is relatively simple. It is to increase substantially the resources of the International Monetary Fund. This would mean, among other things, another big injection of United States dollars into the fund.

The United States Government has not accepted the existence of a liquidity crisis. The position of both the Treasury and the State Department is that people who try to live beyond their means are always "illiquid" and that the best solution is to stop being profligate.

What is more, all sides, including the British Government, agree that there is no immediate problem. British reserves have been doing remarkably well for the last six months, having at last passed the $3,000,000,000 mark. World trade has survived the early stages of the American slump remarkably well.

But the United States Government does see a problem for the under-developed countries. And it has no wish to see the kind of spreading of depression that occurred in the industrial West in the Nineteen Thirties.

The merit of an approach like bolstering the reserves of the Monetary Fund, as many officials see it, is that it would kill both birds with one stone—the general problem of liquidity for the world as a whole and the special balance of payments problem of the under-developed countries in particular.

June 10, 1958

NEW ERA IN TRADE DAWNS IN EUROPE

Six-Nation Common Market Presents Opportunity and Challenge to Members

By HAROLD CALLENDER
Special to The New York Times.

PARIS, Jan. 1—The six-nation common market, which began to take economic effect today, offers to its members both an opportunity and a challenge.

The opportunity is that of a great single market where tariffs and other barriers will gradually be eliminated over a transition period of twelve to fifteen years. France, for instance, will be able to sell in the other countries of the common market — West Germany, Italy, Beligum, the Netherlands and Luxembourg — at diminishing tariff rates and finally without any tariffs. French buyers will eventually be as free to buy in the five other nations as in France.

The challenge is that within this great market French producers must compete with those of five other nations, above all with the highly organized economy of West Germany. They must compete not only in the five other countries but in France herself. For West Germans, for example, will have the same access to the French market that French producers have.

When the common market is fully effective, a French textile manufacturer must treat German textile rivals as if they were Frenchmen, a German chemical producer must treat French chemical industries as if they were German. In the field of trade there will no longer be any national distinctions.

Producers in the six nations have long since planned for both the new opportunities that will open up and for the new competition they will face. Modernization, cutting of costs and amalgamations have been contemplated and it is reported that trade plans reach across frontiers in cartel-minded Europe.

A writer in L'Express told of a small manufacturer of metallic products in Paris who was content with his profits but was lured into the West German market by an agent. He found the Germans would buy large quantities of his goods at prices slightly below those he demanded. He was depressed, but an expert showed him how to modernize his family factory and cut costs so he could easily produce at the German prices. This was a new idea to him, but he jumped at it and his factory expanded.

This is typical of what may happen in France and elsewhere when tariffs among the six nations fall and finally disappear. There will be widespread "reconversions" by producers able to face competition. The devaluation of the franc, reducing costs in terms of the currencies of the five other nations, will facilitate French exports if not offset by inflation.

Not all producers will be able to stand the pace, and badly equipped or high-cost concerns will have to reorganize, combine with others or go out of business when deprived of the protection they now enjoy.

To the other nations of the common market West Germany has lately sent about 29 per cent of her exports, France 24 per cent, Italy 23 per cent, Belgium and Luxembourg a total of 45 per cent, the Netherlands 38 per cent. The common market probably will expand this internal trade, yet its member nations will still require foodstuffs, raw materials and fuel from the rest of the world and will need to export beyond the common market.

It is assumed that the greater tariff-free market will develop larger-scale production and greater aggregate output, as in the United States. In that case the six nations might become more formidable competitors in the world market.

Producers in other countries have considered this possibility while calculating the extent to which they will be handicapped in exporting to the six nations.

British Face Problems

The British have been especially troubled by these problems. Britain will no longer compete on equal terms with West Germany in France, Italy or the Low Countries, where British exports must face the common tariff of the common market while German exports will enter free.

Meanwhile West Germany, by virtue of the stimulus of a free market in Europe containing 160,000,000 people, may grow stronger as a competitor with British manufacturers in South America, for example.

In a dispatch yesterday on the common market it was said that the immediate discrimination against outside nations would be in import quotas. There will be some discrimination in tariffs also, but only by Belgium, the Netherlands and Luxembourg, which will not extend to outside nations the 10 per cent tariff cut they will make for the other common market nations.

This is because their tariffs are lower than the prospective common market tariff. Since their tariffs are low, the discrimination will be small. It will be greater when their tariffs rise to the level of the common market tariff when this tariff takes effect. The common market tariff is to be approximately the average of the present tariffs of the six nations.

January 2, 1959

TRADE BARRIERS STIR U.S. PROTEST

Concern Rises Over Payments Balance

By E. W. KENWORTHY
Special to The New York Times.

WASHINGTON, Oct. 31—In Tokyo this week Under Secretary of State Douglas Dillon delivered a blunt warning to the other contracting nations in the General Agreement on Tariffs and Trade: Stop discriminating against United States imports or Congress will get Smoot-Hawley after you.

Of course Mr. Dillon did not use such undiplomatic language. What he actually said was: "Either we move ahead to get rid of outmoded trade restrictions or we can expect a resurgence of protectionism and restrictive action."

Mr. Dillon's warning was the latest in a series delivered by the United States Government in the past few weeks, and his fellow ministers knew that the warning was not an idle one.

What the United States has been saying is that the time has now come when the industrialized nations of Europe and Japan should "do away altogether" with the discriminations and restrictions against United States imports.

Even Break Sought

The United States recognizes that many less developed nations must continue to control imports because of their trade deficit. But the United States contends that these nations should give dollar imports an even break with imports from other countries, and not single them out for special limitations.

This is the substance of the United States argument:

GATT was set up twelve years ago to encourage world trade through multilateral credit and non-discriminatory trade practices.

The general application of these principles had to be postponed because of the situation in which most industrialized nations found themselves after World War II. They had to import heavily from the United States to reconstruct their plants. They were unable to pay for imports with exports. They consequently had severe balance of payments problems. To protect their slender gold and dollar reserves, they imposed strict exchange controls and quantitative and other restrictions on dollar imports, particularly of consumer goods.

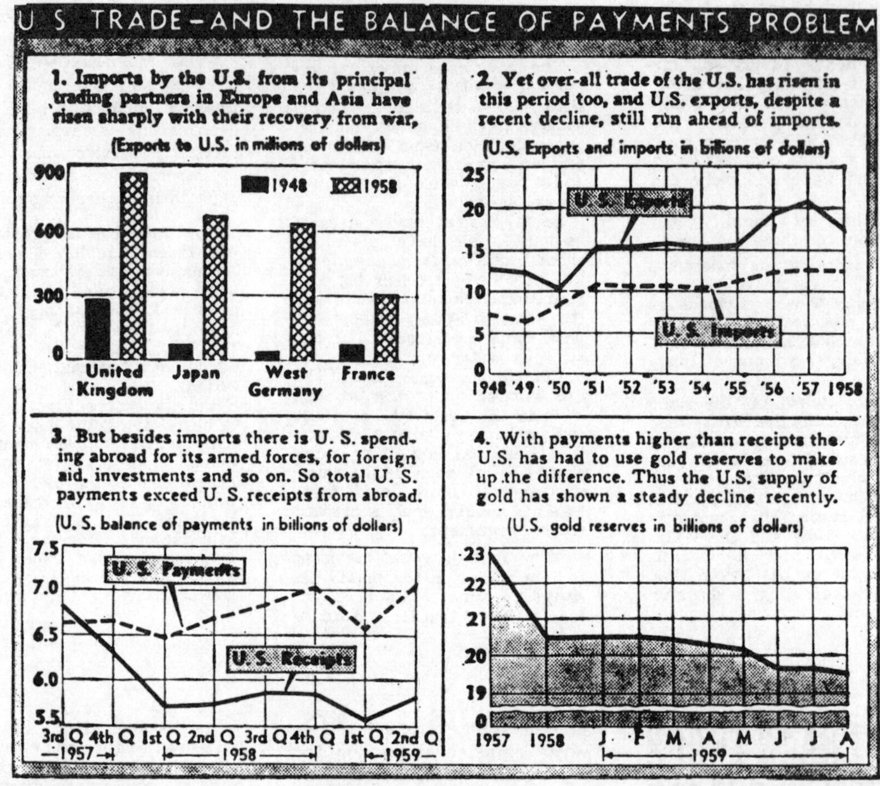

American Concessions

The United States recognized the necessities of this situation. It made concessions in trade negotiations, acquiesced in exemptions to GATT principles, granted benefits for which it received no compensating treatment. In addition, it helped to close "the dollar gap" of other nations by supplying billions of dollars in grants and loans under the foreign aid program.

In the past two years there has been a complete reversal in this situation. Europe and Japan have made a complete recovery. They have substantial gold and dollar reserves. Last December the European nations made their currencies completely convertible in international trade. Their manufacturing industries are competitive with United States industries. They have enjoyed a great increase in exports to the United States.

On the other hand, United States, although it still has a favorable trade balance, is running a deficit in its over-all balance of payments because of continued heavy dollar outflow on foreign aid and military expenditures abroad. This deficit amounted to $3.4 billion last year and is expected to reach $4 billion this year.

Therefore, the United States contends that other nations can no longer find justification in the balance of payments situation for continued exchange controls and discrimination against dollar imports.

Just before the GATT ministerial meeting opened this week, the International Monetary Fund gave complete support to the United States position that there is no sound financial excuse for restrictions on this country's trade.

How extensive are these discriminations and what form do they take? What would their removal mean to the American economy and world prosperity? What are the prospects that they will be removed?

As their payments position has improved over the last two years, a number of countries have eased, piecemeal, their restrictions against dollar imports. In the first six months of this year, the principal European trading nations accelerated the dismantling of controls on dollar trade.

Nevertheless, twenty-five of the thirty-seven GATT members still have import restrictions, which they justify on the balance of payments argument, and twenty-one of these nations specifically direct the restrictions against particular currencies, usually the dollar.

The restrictions are legion in number, and many of them reveal how nimble in contrivance is the commercial mind. The most common restrictive device is licensing, and it has infinite variations.

Import Licensing

Some countries have lists of goods for which import licenses are required, others have lists of "prohibited goods" for which licenses are not issued, some have lists of countries from which licensed imports may not be imported. Others license the expenditure of foreign currencies generally, or dollars particularly, on an annual, semiannual or even quarterly basis.

Under the licensing system, discrimination against dollar imports is often not specifically set out in regulations, and the extent of the discrimination becomes apparent only when the numbers of licenses granted are actually known and totaled.

Another discriminatory practice is the bald-faced quota. For example, Britain limits American tobacco to 61 per cent of all imported tobacco. Some quotas

DOUGLAS DILLON

The New York Times
Under Secretary of State.

are not so open. Thus, France does not disclose the size of quotas except on a few items, notably automobiles and whisky. Dollar whisky and automobiles get comparatively rough treatment.

Finally, there is the device of internal taxes high enough to discourage the purchase of imports. For example, French internal taxes on automobiles are particularly high on cars of more than a certain horsepower—and only Detroit sires that horsepower.

Incidentally, there is also such a thing as discriminatory liberalization. France has recently removed import restrictions on all automobiles—except those of less than 3,000-cubic-centimeter cylinder capacity. The only American cars that will not qualify for this liberalization are the new "compact" cars. France will license these under a $3,000,000 quota.

U. S. Has Quotas

It should be noted that the United States is not simon-pure, but only comparatively pure. It has some quotas—on oil, lead, zinc, wool goods, velveteen, steel, flatware and so on. And these quotas are not imposed because of the current balance-of-payments deficit, but to protect United States producers.

United States exports are now running at an annual rate of $17,000,000,000. Of this, Canada, which does not restrict dollar imports, accounts for $3,000,000,000 to $4,000,000,000.

No one can estimate with any accuracy the increase that would follow the removal of all discriminations by industrialized countries. This would depend upon many factors, varying from product to product—comparative quality and price, availability of spare parts and servicing, cost of maintenance. For example, the price of gasoline would probably operate as effectively against imports of Detroit's gluttons as any quota system.

But of one thing government economists here are convinced. And that is that the present trade prosperity of many European nations and Japan is, as Mr. Dillon said this week, "inherently unstable and cannot be long maintained."

Three Factors

Officials here remark that this prosperity is sustained in part by three conditions that are fundamentally unjust to the United States and which Western Europe and Japan cannot count on indefinitely.

First, Europe and Japan are not doing their part in supplying credits to under-developed countries.

Second, they are relying on United States foreign aid to finance much of their exports to such countries.

Third, they are continuing to discriminate against United States imports.

The Administration hopes to rectify the balance-of-payments deficit through an increase in exports. It does not intend to rectify it through raising United States tariffs. It fears, however, that unless Europe and Japan increase their aid to under-developed countries and end their discriminations against dollar trade, Congress may seize the tariff stick.

There are reports here that Britain and Japan are going to lead the way by ending many dollar restrictions. Fortunately, there appears to be substance in these reports.

November 1, 1959

EUROPE RUSHES AHEAD AS THE '6' AND '7' STRIVE FOR ERA OF FREE TRADE

LIBERALISM GAINS

A New Economic Spirit Is Evident Despite Split Into Blocs

Special to The New York Times.

LONDON—Contemporary citizens have already marked down 1959 as the year when Europe split itself into two trading blocs—the year of "Europe at Sixes and Sevens."

But economic historians may have a different label. To them —depending on which way things go from here—1959 may be the year of the turning point in the Western world toward the principle of complete free trade in nonfarm goods.

It is possible, in short, that contemporaries have been missing the forest for the trees. The forest, it may be, is not the Common Market of the Six and the European Free Trade Association of the Seven, but the decision of these thirteen major industrial nations to abolish by 1970 all import barriers against a significant group of foreign competitors.

True, the decision to wipe out the barriers is limited and potentially discriminatory against outsiders. True, agriculture is firmly excluded. True, the origin of the movement was more political than economic.

Liberalism at Work

But a traveler through Europe toward the end of the year could not help getting the impression that a spirit of genuine trade liberalism was at work—a spirit dictated mainly by plain self-interest.

Just as Britain began a whole new era of free trade and rapid economic advance 120 years ago with repeal of the corn laws (tariffs on imported farm products), so Western Europe as a whole at the beginning of the Nineteen Sixties may be doing the same thing for manufactured goods.

The era of free trade begun by Britain in 1840 came to a close early in this century with the first erection of tariff barriers. Is the age of protectionism, in turn, now approaching its demise?

This is a question that certainly cannot be answered affirmatively yet. Despite an astonishing amount of support for free trade by industry —industry that, in the age of technology, needs duty-free imported semi-manufactured materials and components, and needs markets bigger than European national markets—Governments have "backed into" free trade almost inadvertently.

Political Reasons

They were forced into it by a series of events—chiefly the formation of the European Common Market by Belgium, the Netherlands, Luxembourg, West Germany, France and Italy — that took place for essentially political reasons.

But the question being asked by economists and officials and business men as 1959 ended was this:

Will the experience of limited free trade prove so appealing that peoples and Governments will ask for more? In short, will the almost inadvertent experiment in tariff-cutting lead to broader results than the original authors foresaw?

A series of key decisions over the next two years will help to supply part of the answer.

The Six of the Common Market must make decisions on tariffs on a list of seventy important items — the so-called "List G"—that were not decided at the time of the signing of the Rome treaty. These decisions could be either liberal or protectionist.

The Six also must decide on how much, if at all, the benefits of their internal tariff cutting will be extended to outsiders. This is intimately involved in a series of proposals for accelerating the Common Market that are awaiting decision.

The Six, the Seven (Britain, Sweden, Denmark, Norway, Portugal, Switzerland and Austria) and the United States will face, early in 1961, a major negotiation in the General Agreement on Tariffs and Trade in which all sides will try to bargain tariffs downward. The success or failure of these negotiations will depend in great part on how extensive the liberal spirit really is.

But no matter how these decisions go, a partial dismantling of trade barriers is firmly under way. Straws are already in the wind.

Restrictions Fading

Quantitative restrictions on internal trade in Europe are now almost gone. Payments are free. Only tariffs remain, and the Six and the Seven have begun the process of eliminating those within each bloc.

The important thing is the amazing results already achieved. Intra-European trade, measured by exports of European countries to one another, rose from $9,770,000,000 in 1950 to an annual rate of $21,600,000,000 by the second quarter of 1959.

This growth in trade among industrial nations was far greater than the growth of trade between them and the countries producing raw materials. Foreign goods are already a fairly common sight in the shops of Europe, even before the Common Market and Outer Seven have made any significant tariff cuts.

One result of this huge expansion in trade has been to make business in Europe export-minded. And to be export-minded is to be free-trade-minded.

Belgium's exports are the equivalent of 40 per cent of her gross national product. The German and British automobile industries export roughly half their output. Even in France, the role of foreign trade in the total economy has been creeping upward, from about 10 per cent before the war to nearly 15 per cent now. (In the United States it is less than 5 per cent.)

It is these hard facts—and their accompanying indication of where self-interest lies—that makes the dream of complete free trade in manufactured goods seem not wholly impossible.

Where does the United States fit into all of this? The answer is that a great many people in Europe would be happy to see this nation join the parade, but everyone realizes that such a move is not now in the cards.

The reasons are familiar. In brief, the United States is simply not free-trade-minded, at least not now. There remains a deep and genuine fear of import competition.

But by not joining the parade, the United States will almost certainly have to resign itself to discrimination against exports. For Europe has shown few signs yet of willingness to reduce barriers to the United States. "gratis" that is.

Europe is moving toward internal free trade, but it is doubtful that Europe will give the same privileges to American goods without important tariff reductions in return.

The outcome of it all is impossible to forecast. But it is already clear from the results in Europe to date that freer trade pays off.

Those results, in a word, are prosperity, economic growth, higher standards of living. Europe at the moment is growing considerably more rapidly than the United States.

January 12, 1960

7 Latin Nations Sign Pact To Form Common Market

By JUAN de ONIS
Special to The New York Times.

MONTEVIDEO, Uruguay, Feb. 18—The foreign ministers of seven Latin-American countries signed today a treaty for a free trade zone linking their nations' economies.

The countries involved are Argentina, Brazil, Chile, Mexico, Paraguay, Peru and Uruguay.

The treaty provides for the elimination over a twelve-year period of all trade restrictions on at least 75 per cent of the trade within the area. Any Latin-American country may join the treaty group.

At the signing ceremony, in the Red Room of Government House, Foreign Minister Horacio Lafer of Brazil said the treaty "opens a new path" in Latin America toward higher production and living standards. Foreign Minister Homero Martinez Montero of Uruguay said the treaty reflected a conviction that Latin-American countries could grow faster economically by cooperation than by isolation.

The negotiations on the treaty started last September and were assisted by the United Nations Economic Commission for Latin America and the Inter-American Economic and Social Council of the Organization of American States. The United States also offered encouragement.

Treaty Is Popular

The idea of a free trade area, or common market, is popular with most Latin Americans and the treaty has been hailed in the hemisphere's press.

The delegates agreed that the United States could contribute to the success of the treaty in the following ways:

¶By supporting the treaty when it is submitted for approval to the organization administering the General Agreement on Tariffs and Trade.

¶By offering constructive criticism in inter-American conferences on integrating the trade zone into the hemisphere's trade and investment structure.

¶By distributing information on the agreement and its implications for investments.

¶By providing loans to private Latin-American industrialists seeking to expand their enterprises to take advantage of the market of 140,000,000 persons that would be created by the treaty.

Latin-American industrialists fear that only foreign corporations will have enough capital to take advantage of the new market unless the area's companies receive loans.

The treaty must be signed by three signatory nations to go into effect. Delegates expect this stage to be reached by early next year.

In the meantime, the treaty establishes a provisional free-trade association of the seven signatories with offices in Montevideo, the eventual seat of the treaty's secretariat.

As soon as the treaty goes into effect the members will hold the first of twelve annual conferences to negotiate reciprocal trade and tariff concessions.

Each country will present a list of goods on which it will reduce tariffs at least 8 per cent and on which it will ease other restrictions for members of the zone.

Each year an additional 8 per cent reduction must be granted, although the goods on the lists may be changed. Every three years a common list of irremovable goods representing 25 per cent of the area's trade must be established.

The treaty exempts agricultural and livestock trade to protect such activities as the subsidized wheat programs in Brazil and Chile from Argentine competition.

February 19, 1960

DEBATE ON JAPAN TRADE

Rising Imports Stir Fears in U. S. Industries And Raise Difficult Foreign Policy Issues

By RICHARD E. MOONEY
Special to The New York Times.

WASHINGTON, March 18—Baseball gloves, transistors, plastic raincoats, Diesel locomotives, men's suits, zori sandals. Those are the things that touchy trade relations are made of.

Each of those items, currently or in the recent past, has been imported to the United States from Japan in such quantities as to set off yells from competing American industry.

The matter is alive right now because two labor unions have joined their industries in protest, threatening to have their members boycott the offending products. One of the boycotts—against transistors—was postponed this week. The other—indirectly against suits—may be called off soon. But the issue remains.

Japan is the United States' second-ranking trade partner. We buy more from Japan than from any other country and sell more to Japan than to any other country, save Canada in both respects. Last year, Japan bought $1,300,000,000 worth of American goods and the United States bought $1,100,000,000 of Japanese.

Textile Sales

The things Japan buys here are primarily basic materials—cotton, scrap iron and such—and the machinery with which to make them into finished products. The things she sells here are the finished products and fish.

The biggest single category of Japanese sales to the United States is textiles and clothing—$252,000,000 last year. Next comes a category called "electrical machinery"—$102,000,000 last year. It ranges from a flood of button-sized transistors to a few pieces of heavy equipment. Another big item last year was $77,000,000 of rubber shoes, mostly those things held on by a thong between the toes.

President Kennedy made the point at a news conference ten days ago that sometimes a protested import amounts to only a tiny fraction of the competing product in this country.

That is true in the case of men's suits. The United States imported about 40,000 from Japan last year while American suit makers turned out 20,000,000. It was true of cotton shirts just a few years ago, but last year's imports from Japan came to 1,200,000 dozen, against domestic production of 12,000,000 doben, or 10 per cent—and there were imports from Hong Kong and elsewhere on top of that.

Japan's natural advantage is her huge labor supply and relatively lower standard of living. Japanese labor costs are lower than American, though generous fringe benefits in Japan make this advantage smaller than appears in a straight comparison of hourly wage rates. Japanese skills and productivity, while rising, are nonetheless lower than this country's, and that cuts her advantage, too.

The Arguments

The arguments for limiting the entry of foreign goods are as follows:

(1) Every imported competing product is one less bought from an American factory, which means fewer jobs for Americans, less vitality for American business and less readiness to meet the production demands of a war if one should come. We are sowing the seeds of our own destruction, economic if not political.

(2) The Government has contributed to the import problem, so the least it can do is help to relieve it. The "contributions" include the liberaliation that has occurred these last twenty-five years, the post-war foreign aid that built and is still building modern foreign factories and the more recent subsidy on sales of American cotton to foreign manufacturers.

(3) Foreign countries have been far less liberal than the United States. If they will not open up to American goods, the United States must tighten up on theirs.

On the other side, arguing for greater American liberalism, are these points:

(1) Foreigners must sell here to earn dollars so they can buy here, and they buy much more than they sell—a near-record of $5,000,000,000 more last year.

(2) The United States is and wants to be the leader of the free world. The world's economic viability depends on expanding international trade. We are the richest member. We cannot afford allies in distress. We must take a generous position.

(3) When it comes to particular industry appeals for protection, imports are often more blamed than blameable. In the case of transistors, for instance, rising imports may be less to blame for unemployment among electronic workers than the slackness in demand for television sets that has existed for several years.

Administration's Position

The Kennedy Administration's stated position on trade is liberal. The President's balance of payments message to Congress said flatly that "protectionism is not a solution." But his policy has yet to face a major test, and some advocates of liberalism are a little uneasy.

Finally, the liberals are disappointed that the Administration has not accepted their preferred legislative remedy from import problems—a depressed areas type of program that would earmark Federal aid specifically to redevelop or redirect industries and workers who really are suffering because of imports.

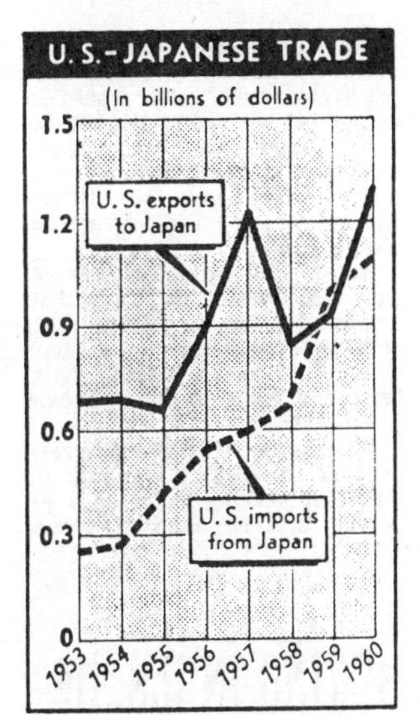

The Administration's liberalism lies in its broader policies. Its most important assault on import competition is its effort to nip the price problem in the bud, by restraints on inflation and by incentives to more productive mechanization of industry here.

Relevant to the present question, the United States has two major points to make: That other countries' domestic wage and working standards are too low, and that their barriers to foreign trade—from here, but particularly from Japan—are too high.

March 19, 1961

U. S. Now in a 'Lethargic Sleep,' Khrushchev Tells Tokyo Group

Soviet's Rockets Fly Better, He Boasts—Japanese Mission Gets a $100,000,000 Contract to Build Ships for Moscow

Special to The New York Times.

MOSCOW, Aug. 22—Premier Khrushchev asserted today that the United States was "in a state of lethargic sleep."

The Russian leader made his remarks in complaining to a group of visiting Japanese business men that the United States refused to trade with the Soviet Union.

"But though America does not trade with us, our rockets fly better than theirs," the Premier declared. "This shows we can live without trade with the United States."

"America produces good electronic machines," he went on, "but again our rockets hit the target more accurately than the American ones; and it is Soviet electronic equipment that was used in our missiles."

Mr. Khrushchev's remarks were quoted by Tass, the Soviet press agency.

Reception in Crimea

The Premier received a delegation of prominent Japanese business men at his villa, a two-story country house in a park near the South Crimean coast.

Mr. Khrushchev told the Japanese delegation that the United States eventually would be compelled to trade with the Soviet Union. He said Japan should start doing business with his country before the United States became "a dangerous competitor."

Before the Japanese delegation left by air for Yalta this morning, it was announced here that the businessmen had concluded during their stay long-term contracts worth well over $100,000,000.

Yosomatsu Matsubara, president of the Hitaci Shipbuilding and Engineering Company, reported that he negotiated contracts that called for the Soviet Government to buy ships from Japan worth $100,000,000.

According to Japanese sources the contracts, involving three Japanese shipbuilding companies, cover the delivery of twelve 35,000-ton tankers, five 12,000-ton freighters, twelve barges, six drag suction dredgers and two floating cranes.

The contract terms were understood to include deferred payment over six years of 70 per cent of the total value of the contracts.

Siberian Timber to Japan

The contracts presumably will be subject to inspection by the Japanese Government.

Japan's trade with the Soviet Union, as in the case of the United States, is governed by regulations that restrict the sale of strategic items to Communist countries.

Tass quoted Mr. Khrushchev as having added in his remarks to the Japanese delegation: "The same may be the case with you."

The Premier said: "We are for trade and peace and not repeat not for war. Though we have stronger means of warfare, we shall do everything in our power for the development of our trade from year to year."

Yoshinari Kawai, a machinery manufacturer who heads the thirty-man delegation from Tokyo was quoted by Tass as having said that artificial roadblocks could not be tolerated in trade.

"We have had difficulty in switching over to new lines right away," Mr. Kawai said, according to Tass, "because we were oriented toward the United States after World War II. But we shall exert every effort to take the correct road."

August 23, 1962

BUYING IN U.S. UP FOR PUERTO RICO

Aide Says Commonwealth Will Be 3d Best Customer

By CLAYTON KNOWLES

Special to The New York Times

SAN JUAN, P. R.

A leading Puerto Rican Government spokesman predicts that the commonwealth, now the mainland United States' fifth best customer, will pass West Germany and the United Kingdom to take over third place by the end of 1964.

Joseph Monserrat, the Labor Department's director of migration, noted that Puerto Rico already is the mainland United States' best customer on a per capita basis.

With a population of 2.4 million and per capita income of just $717, Puerto Rico purchases $400 worth of goods a person from the United States each year.

Mr. Monserrat startled the recent Conference on Automation, Education and Collective Bargaining here by reporting that Puerto Rico now is spending nearly $1 billion a year for United States products.

The only nations buying more are Canada, $3,829,715,000; Japan, $1,413,840,000; West Germany, $1,075,942,000, and the United Kingdom, $1,074,787,000. Yet per capita spending by Canada, for example, comes to only $211.

Mr. Monserrat stressed that the "multiplier" effect—the generation of additional income from Puerto Rican buying—actually generated another $1 billion in gross income for the United States. Headquartered in New York, Mr. Monserrat is Puerto Rico's leading spokesman on the mainland.

Northeast Does Best

Of the $958 million in Puerto Rican purchases in the United States, the Northeast does best with major sales to the commonwealth exceeding $233 million. Next come the north-central states with $216 million in major exports; the South with $202 million and the Western states with $96 million.

New York State sells $100 million in goods to Puerto Rico each year, sales that generate 12,000 jobs. California is next with $75 million in sales and 8,500 jobs, but other Eastern states rank high.

Pennsylvania's sales hit $47 million and jobs 5,800; New Jersey's sales come to $39 million and 4,400 jobs; Connecticut's are $25 million and 4,000 jobs and Massachusetts $26 million and 3,300 jobs.

Puerto Rico is the Port of New York's second largest customer. Topped only by Japan, the port moves 800,000 tons of goods destined to or from Puerto Rico each year.

The commonwealth's contributions to the growth of the United States economy involves more than just buying, Mr. Monserrat said. He noted that 654,000 Puerto Ricans have migrated to New York City, making it the world's largest Puerto Rican city. San Juan, the commonwealth's capital and largest city, had a population of 432,000 in the 1960 census.

Mr. Monserrat said a Labor Department study here indicated that Puerto Ricans in New York City earn more than $525 million a year and pay $90 million in taxes.

Farm Workers

A small army of 14,000 Puerto Rican farm workers help harvest major crops in 13 states each year.

In predicting that Puerto Rico soon would be buying more from the United States than West Germany or the United Kingdom, Mr. Monserrat made only one slight qualification that the steady rise in Puerto Rico's economic growth continue without a break.

He noted that Puerto Rico buys more from the United States today than Brazil, Uruguay, Argentina and Paraguay combined; or Chile, Bolivia, Peru, Ecuador and Colombia combined. It buys more even than all of the six Central American states and the rest of the Caribbean islands put together.

He said that Puerto Rican purchases from the United States actually exceed the total buying from the same source by Spain, Sweden, Denmark, Norway, Austria, Finland, Portugal and Ireland.

"There is even more than that to it for the United States," Mr. Monserrat declared. "All but a tiny fraction of all shipments to Puerto Rico from the United States must be shipped in United States ships or planes and so the United States benefits to the tune of another $70 million in gross income."

January 5, 1964

A TARIFF DILEMMA CONFRONTS TOKYO

Japan Wants Trade Ties, but Seeks Protection

Special to The New York Times

TOKYO — The coming year is a critical one for Japan's economy as the nation opens her doors to increased competition from abroad while continuing intensive efforts to expand her exports.

As a nation that must trade to live, Japan is aligned with the United States and other nations pressing for a general lowering of tariff barriers and other restrictions on trade.

But as a nation that has industrialized in somewhat haphazard fashion, at a sometimes headlong pace, she believes it vital to protect certain weak sectors.

How to reconcile the two approaches is one of the major problems facing economic and financial officials.

Japanese exports continue to increase at a healthy rate in 1963, with a gain of about 10 per cent of a total of approximately $5.550 billion forecast for the fiscal year ending March 31. There seemed little doubt that the growth would continue throughout 1964.

Heavy Reliance on U. S.

However, the division of the export market caused some concern because of Japan's continued heavy reliance on the United States as a customer. About 30 per cent of Japan's exports go to the United States, about 20 per cent to other industrialized countries, and about 50 per cent to what are generally considered non-industrialized nations. Most of the expansion recently has been concentrated in trade with the United States and Europe. Western European countries account for about 10 per cent of Japanese trade.

The emergence of a number of economic irritations between Tokyo and Washington last year prompted demands here for a more independent trade policy. There was talk of increased trade with Communist-bloc countries, including China, despite official recognition that Japan could expect little in return for her shipments and that most of her exports would have to be on a deferred-payment basis.

Trade with the Communist countries amounted to only 4 per cent of Japan's total, and prospects of expansion to even as much as 7 or 8 per cent appeared dim. The Japanese are well aware that Peking could shut off trade at any moment for political reasons, as was done in 1958.

Japanese economic leaders, themselves maintaining a restrictive economy, protest vigorously against what are called 'protectionist' American policies. Nihon Keizai Shimbun, an influential economic journal, said recently that the Japanese had to combat restrictions by tariffs. Direct restrictions of imports and restrictions of exports through what are euphemistically called "voluntary restraints" and in fact are forced upon Japan under strong outside pressure.

U. S. Protests Noted

According to Nihon Keizai Shimbun, sharp protests from American competitors have arisen whenever the Japanese have succeeded in introducing effectively such articles as cheap blouses, toys, metal table flatware and transistor radios in the American market. "Such outcries have compelled Japan to compromise in the form of exercising 'voluntary restraints' on controversial items," the newspaper said.

Consequently, it declared, Japanese manufacturers and traders are forced to do business under constant fear of an American tariff raise."

There was irritation here last August when a new three-year cotton textile trade agreement provided only minor increases in Japan's shipments, and reports that similar restraints were in prospect for woollen goods drew hostile reactions.

The Japanese have been incensed at charges by United States Steel interests that Japan was "dumping" steel products, and suggestions that an American mision be sent here to investigate were sharply rejected.

The death of President Kennedy deferred for two months the high-level economic conference at which the Japanese hoped to take up some of their complaints with United States Cabinet officials. The rescheduled meeting, to be held late this month, has taken on new significance here because it will presumably enable the Japanese to ascertain whether the Johnson Administration is likely to be more 'protectionist' than that headed by President Kennedy.

Exports to U. S. Rise

Despite the irritations, it is noted by economic observers that Japanese-United States trade has shown a healthy rate of growth, with American restrictions having a much less "stultifying" effect than has been charged. An increase of 6.6 per cent in Japanese exports in the first nine months of 1963 was cited, with an enormous rise in iron and steel shipments.

Japan turned increasingly to Western Europe in 1963 and noted with satisfaction that much of the old suspicion that her goods were based on cheap labor had been eliminated. A general easing of restrictive practices toward Japan was noted, although France and Italy continued to retain curbs on large numbers of Japanese items.

Japanese businessmen and Government officials also sought diligently to improve their trade position in Latin America, Southeast Asia and Africa. But in all these areas fundamental difficulties were posed by problems of payments, political instability and the lack of suitable imports to balance the shipments of Japanese goods.

With the future of the European Common Market uncertain, there seemed little disposition here to look publicly toward specific aspects of the Kennedy round of tariff talks slated for Geneva in May. But there were signs that the Government planned to readjust upward some tariffs to protect weak elements in the Japanese economy prior to entering a conference that could produce across-the-board tariff cuts.

January 13, 1964

HODGES FORESEES NEW SOVIET TRADE

Calls 'Political Feeling' Only Bar to Wider Exchange

By EDWIN L. DALE Jr.
Special to The New York Times

WASHINGTON, March 10 — Secretary of Commerce Luther H. Hodges said today that "we are now at the stage where we could go a long way toward "normalizing trade relations" with the Soviet Union.

Mr. Hodges told a news conference that the main barrier to such a change was "political feeling" in this country, and that "more education" was required to alter that feeling. He called the present United States policy "schizophrenic."

The occasion for the news conference was the release of details of last week's agreement in Moscow under which large American ships will be permitted to unload wheat at Odessa.

Mr. Hodges praised the "extremely cooperative attitude" of the Soviet authorities, but said he had "no idea" why they had changed their minds about such vessels.

The Secretary revealed that subsequent talks in Moscow between Clarence D. Martin Jr., Under Secretary of Commerce for Transportation, and Aleksei N. Kosygin, Soviet First Deputy Premier, on trade matters had not reached the point of specific negotiations.

In discussing the "normalization" of trade relations with the Soviet Union and other Communist countries, Mr. Hodges indicated he might eventually favor a change in the present law that imposes tariffs on goods from Communist countries, except Poland and Yugoslavia, more than twice as high as those on goods from non-Communist countries.

He also indicated he favored a narrowing of the present embargo list of goods barred from export to the Communist countries.

However, he said, such normalization will have to be part of a "total settlement" including such matters as repayment by the Soviet Union of wartime lend-lease debts.

March 11, 1964

LEADERS APPROVE 'ACTION PROGRAM' FOR THE AMERICAS

Johnson Pledges Support of U.S. for Common Market —Farm Progress Urged

By JAMES RESTON
Special to The New York Times

PUNTA DEL ESTE, Uruguay, April 13 — The Presidents of the American republics approved unanimously today a declaration of purpose and "action program" designed to achieve the economic integration of the Americas.

Bolivia was the only nation absent from the second conference ever held by the Presidents, and Ecuador raised the only objection to the final communiqué.

President Otto Arosemena Gómez of Ecuador, the youngest chief of state in the meeting at the age of 42, indicated his intention of adding a reservation to what will be known as "The Declaration of the Presidents of America." His main objection was that it did not call for more economic assistance from the United States.

The Presidents proclaimed "the solidarity of the countries they represent and their decision to achieve to the fullest measure the free, just and democratic social order demanded by the peoples of the hemisphere."

Objectives Listed

The declaration summarized the decisions of the Presidents in the following terms:

¶"Latin America will create a common market." It added: "The President of the United States of America, for his part, declares his firm support for this promising Latin-American initiative."

¶"We will lay the physical foundations for Latin-American economic integration through multinational projects so as to open the way for the movement of both people and goods throughout the continent."

¶"We will join in efforts to increase substantially Latin-American trade earnings."

¶"We will modernize the living conditions of our rural populations, raise agricultural productivity in general and increase food production for the benefit of both Latin America and the rest of the world."

¶"We will vigorously promote education for development."

¶"We will harness science and technology for the service of our peoples."

¶"We will expand programs for improving the health of the American peoples."

To meet these expensive and

ambitious objectives, the chiefs of state also declared their intention to "limit military expenditures in proportion to the actual demands of national security in accordance with each country's constitutional provisions."

They also expressed the hope that the treaty on the banning of nuclear weapons in Latin America "may enter into force as soon as possible."

The conference participants reached no spectacular new decisions. The United States did not come forward with an offer of large-scale aid, as some officials in this part of the world had hoped.

President Johnson did commit himself to more assistance for opening up the inner frontiers of the continent, however, and he indicated a willingness to consider a new system of trade preferences, not for Latin America alone but for all developing countries, provided the other rich and industrialized countries of the world did the same.

There was, therefore, some criticism here that the specific programs proposed were not equal to the problems discussed, but there was general agreement on certain important though intangible advances.

Progress Made

For one thing, the ideas of economic integration, regional development and trade preferences for the poor nations, all of which have been discussed at length by the technicians of the various governments and hemispheric organizations, have now been raised to the highest level of political decision.

A beginning has been made on common discussion by the Presidents of common problems, and Latin America has had a chance to see a few leaders of continental scale, among them President Eduardo Frei Montalva of Chile, who played an important part in today's tense debate on the final communiqué, and President Fernando Belaunde Terry of Peru, who is fighting for the opening up of the continent's formidable mountain frontiers.

Controversial Issues Avoided

Some of the most controversial political issues of the hemisphere were omitted from the agenda. Though the population of Latin America is rising faster than that of any other region of the world, and is expected to increase from 200 million to 300 million in the next 10 years, the population question was scarcely mentioned publicly.

Nor was there much discussion of Fidel Castro's Cuba or the threat of Communist subversion during the President's private meetings today. There were many ominous warnings that Latin America must create a revolution in freedom or have one forced upon it by totalitarian means, but a decision was reached to play down these divisive political issues to concentrate on the positive hopes of economic integration and continental development.

Nevertheless, President Arosemena of Ecuador did break the drone of generalities this morning by complaining that the United States had done more for its defeated enemies in the last war than for its neighbors and allies on this continent.

He referred at the end of his speech to José Enrique Rodo, an eloquent Uruguayan who wrote a book in 1900 entitled "Ariel," in which he scalded the United States as a materialistic society and worse.

This created a stir in the little Victorian conference hotel by the sea, and President Arosemena carried the issue further during the afternoon by suggesting that the "declaration" and "action program" before the Presidents could not represent the wishes of the peoples of Latin America unless they were amended to call for more United States aid and better prices for Latin-American products.

This was immediately opposed by the Presidents of Costa Rica, Venezuela, Colombia, Mexico and by President Frei of Chile, who made an eloquent appeal to President Arosemena to settle for "attainable reality" and not "clutch for the moon."

President Frei had lunched with President Johnson earlier and praised him for the spirit of cooperation shown by the United States Government. He told Mr. Johnson frankly that he was sorry an issue had been raised by political leaders in Washington about committing $1.5-billion to Latin America in the next five years.

President Frei said it was better that Mr. Johnson had "not come with dollars." The purpose of the conference was to talk principles and "not amounts," he said. He urged the Ecuadorian President to go along with the communiqué.

President Arosemena replied that he had been "impressed and moved" by the appeals. He explained that he had not meant to be "disruptive," according to officials who were in the private meeting, but in the end he insisted that, while he would sign the document, he must add his own reservations calling for more aid from the United States.

Market to Begin in '70

The "Action Program" approved this afternoon committed the Presidents to establish progressively, beginning in 1970, the Latin-American common market, which should be substantially in operation within a period of no more than 15 years.

"The Latin-American common market will be based on the improvement of the two existing integration systems, the Latin American Free Trade Association and the Central American Common market," the statement said. The Presidents added that they would "encourage the incorporation of other countries of the Latin-American region into the existing integration system."

There has been great emphasis here on the need to improve the means of communication among the countries of the continent, and on the urgency of moving forward on regional projects common to several but not all Latin-American countries.

Modernization Urged

Thus the action plan stated that the economic integration of Latin America demands a vigorous and sustained effort to complete and modernize the physical plant, equipment and communication structure of the region.

"It is necessary to build transport systems to facilitate the movement of persons and goods throughout the hemisphere, to establish an adequate and efficient telecommunications system and interconnected power systems, and jointly to develop international watersheds, frontier regions and economic areas that include the territory of two or more countries," the statement asserted.

One of the projects now under urgent study is to complete a communications satellite network and build ground stations that would provide continent-wide television and even enable a citizen of one country to make a telephone call to another country without paralyzing his lungs.

April 14, 1967

U.S. TRADE ATTITUDE FEARED IN GENEVA

American Dislike of Assuring Full Employment Looked on as Heresy in Parley

By MICHAEL L. HOFFMAN
Special to THE NEW YORK TIMES.

GENEVA, April 12—The opening speeches at the Geneva Trade Conference have accentuated the wide and growing gap between the United States and the rest of the world in all that pertains to economic philosophy and organization.

With the possible exception of Canada, none of the other countries represented here conducts its internal affairs with the economic philosophy that the maintenance of private enterprise is the primary objective of public policy. Indeed, in most of the rest of the world, the argument that a policy is judged by its effects on the institution of private enterprise—which no American representative can ignore—is a collection of words with no relation to political realities.

By a wise maneuver, resulting in the postponement of his first statement to Monday, at the end of the introductory series of addresses, Clair Wilcox, acting head of the United States delegation, has gained a useful opportunity to reassure the delegates that, despite differences in national economic policies, the United States is determined to reach agreement on tariffs and on a new world trade organization charter.

U. S. Looked on as Doctrinaire

Most of the other delegates need reassuring. In a number of ways their speeches have reflected the belief of many delegates that, since the London conference of this preparatory committee adjourned in December, the United States has withdrawn further into its psychological shell of free-enterprise dogma.

Dr. H. C. Coombs, whose personal influence among delegates is greater even than his position as head of the Australian delegation would indicate, laid special stress in his first speech on the need to create a structure that nations with all types of economic organization could join.

This was not just a polite reference to the absent Soviet Union, with which Australia is not notably chummy. It was repeated by other speakers, and it represents real concern lest the American urge to impose the United States economic philosophy on the rest of the world should endanger the success of this unprecedented effort to bring order into international trade.

The measure of the distance separating American thinking from that of other democratic countries is being found by some delegations in the fact that even the National Foreign Trade Council, supporter of the basic ideas embodied in the draft trade charter, in its comments on the work of the London conference, suggested dropping the chapter on full employment. The council's reason was that the maintenance of employment is a function of private enterprise, not of government.

Job Level Seen as Paramount

This seems like purest heresy to British, French and other Europeans, as well as to most delegates from the British dominions. It is no longer a party issue in most democratic countries that maintenance of full employment is one of the main functions of government.

There would not be the slightest chance that anybody but the United States, and possibly a few Latin-American countries, would join the Internatiolal Trade Organization if it did not also concern itself with the problem of stabilizing effective demand throughout the world. And that objective inevitably entails that member Governments accept responsibility for maintaining employment.

These differences of national background will plague this conference and any organization that emerges. None of the leading delegates considers, however, that they are likely to wreck the program.

The underlying forces making for agreement are so strong that, as one European representative put it, only if the United States acts like the Russia of the economic world, refusing to see the others' interests or points of view, is a breakdown to be feared.

April 13, 1947

23 COUNTRIES SIGN NEW TRADE PACTS

6 Nations, Including U.S., Agree to Put Geneva Agreements Into Effect on Jan. 1

EASTERN BLOC STILL SPLIT

Soviet Union and 7 Others Refuse Bids to Conference at Havana to Form ITO

By MICHAEL L. HOFFMAN
Special to THE NEW YORK TIMES.

GENEVA, Oct. 30—Twenty-three nations signed the final act of the Geneva Trade Conference in the Council Room of the United Nations Palace in Geneva at 10 A.M. today.

In a ceremony lasting one hour and a half, plenipotentiaries of countries representing three-quarters of the world trade solemnized the end of the longest economic conference in history with markedly little oratory or fanfare. It was the 203d day of the conference.

Six countries, Belgium, Canada, Luxembourg, the Netherlands, the United States and the United Kingdom also signed a protocol binding their governments to put the new tariff schedules attached to the general agreement on tariffs and trade into effect Jan. 1.

This protocol will become binding when France and Australia sign. France will sign probably in New York within ten days while approval of the tariff schedules by the Australian Cabinet the day before yesterday assures that country's signature in time to meet the Nov. 15 deadline.

Brazil Encounters Difficulty

It was learned today that Czechoslovakia also would sign the protocol shortly but that Brazil, which had intended to become the "key" country by signing in Geneva, had found last-minute constitutional difficulties about signing without parliamentary ratification.

Winthrop G. Brown of the United States State Department, who literally snatched the Anglo-American tariff accord and thus the whole conference back from what seemed like certain failure twice, signed for the United States.

Though many delegates had already hurried home to prepare for the Havana meeting Nov. 21, the gorgeous black and gold council chamber was comfortably full for the ceremony. There was a ripple of laughter when the much-discussed document was brought in by the secretariat at Chairman Max Suetens' request.

The document stands about eighteen inches high and weighs nearly forty pounds. It contains 2,040 pages bound under one cover and nineteen complete tariff schedules covering more than 10,000 items.

Chairman Suetens' address reviewed the long history of the meeting and contrasted its success with the failures of former tariff conferences.

"The signing of the final act today," he said, "marks the completion of the most comprehensive, the most significant and the most far-reaching negotiations ever undertaken in the history of world trade."

The chairman also announced the names of thirty-two countries that had accepted invitations to the Havana Conference, and eight countries that had refused. The latter list perhaps is most interesting. It includes the Soviet Union, the Ukraine, White Russia, Yugoslavia, Bulgaria, Saudi Arabia, Ethiopia and Siam.

Eastern Split Continues

Czechoslovakia has accepted and Poland is still expected to accept, the Eastern bloc seems destined to continue its split on the vital question of trade cooperation with the rest of the world.

In addition to signing the general agreement and the protocol several nations exchanged notes confirming adjustments in previously existing treaties or agreements necessitated by the completion of the multilateral accord. The United States had to sign supplementary agreements with seven countries with which trade agreements are now in force.

Canada, Britain and South Africa also exchanged notes today releasing each other from obligations to maintain imperial preference margins in any future negotiations with non-empire countries. These notes were exchanged secretly, however, and not as part of the general signing ceremony.

Though twenty-three countries signed the final acts they represented only nineteen customs areas. Belgium, the Netherlands and Luxembourg, members of the Benelux customs union, signed separately, as did Syria and Lebanon and Pakistan.

As the delegates dispersed to reassemble in three weeks in Havana, the dominant mood was one of confidence in the ability of this group to lead the United Nations successfully through the final stages of the formation of the International Trade Organization. Chairman Suetens said today's signature was irrefutable proof that the basic idea of the trade organization was right and that it could work.

October 31, 1947

TARIFF CUTS AFFECT 60% OF U. S. TRADE IN 23-NATION PACTS

Geneva Accords Yield Gains to America Affecting About $1,500,000,000 of Sales

OUR DUTIES GO TO '13 BASIS

British Imperial Preferences Reduced—New Scale Seen as a Long-Term Help

Tariff reductions ranging up to 50 per cent of present rates on major imports, and affecting 60 per cent of United States trade, were disclosed yesterday by State Department sources in a conference at 2 Park Avenue.

An analysis by these sources of the general trade and tariff agreements signed in Geneva by twenty-three nations shows that foreign countries concerned were making concessions or "bindings" to maintain present duties that would affect about one and a half billion dollars of United States exports.

The American reductions, estimated as bringing the general level of United States tariff schedules to the lowest point in thirty-four years, cover some 45,000 items listed in 1,350 pages. The pacts are designed to give long-range stimulus to international trade through the removal of artificial trade barriers. The signatory countries conduct from 65 to 70 per cent of the world's trade.

Revisions Effective Jan. 1

The United States tariff revisions will become effective Jan. 1. It was indicated that a Presidential proclamation would be issued early in December, setting forth the items on which tariff cuts would be made effective. Simultaneous reductions in tariffs and trade concessions will be made effective then by the United Kingdom, Canada, Australia, France and the countries composing the Benelux customs union—Belgium, the Netherlands and Luxembourg

The text of the general agreement on tariffs and trade provides that the countries signing the protocol, or provisional application, will, so far as their laws permit, put the new duties into effect in January.

To date the United States, Britain, France, Australia, Canada, Belgium, the Netherlands and Luxembourg have signed the protocol. For these countries not only the new tariffs but also the rules of international commercial conduct embodied in the draft charter of the International Trade Organization go into provisional effect at that time. Substantive parts of the agreement are subject to change, according to the outcome of the Havana Conference, opening tomorrow.

The nations making the chief concessions are Canada, the United Kingdom, France and the Benelux countries.

Additional nations will make the pacts effective in accord with the specific legislative and constitutional requirements of their own countries not later than June 30, 1948. Their action will be followed by additional Presidential proclamations adding to the items coming within the scope of the pacts.

Wool Tariff Cut 25 Per Cent

Among the outstanding reductions in the United States tariff from present levels are:

Wool, 25 per cent, or from 34 cents a pound to 25½ cents; Scotch and Canadian whisky, 40 per cent, or from $2.50 to $1.50 a gallon; beef and veal, 50 per cent; butter, 50 per cent, depending upon quota; sugar, 33 1/3 per cent; rayon and staple fiber, 20 per cent, and copper 50 per cent.

Rubber and newsprint are held to their present "free" basis. Woolens and worsteds are reduced to 25 per cent from 35 to 45 per cent, with the right to increase them reserved if imports rise to 5 per cent of United States production. Cattle has been maintained at present duty levels, but the import quota has been increased.

Other products showing major tariff cuts included all softwood lumber, portland cement, wheat and wheat flour, bauxite, quicklime, high-quality furs, jute, burlap, manganese ore, textile machinery, photograph film, steel products and electrical items.

The over-all tariff reductions, according to State Department sources, will affect $500,000,000 in United States imports. The concessions granted by the fifteen nations with whom the United States has direct signatory pacts will affect also $500,000,000 in exports from the United States, as measured in 1939, the last pre-war year. The "bindings," or maintenance of present tariff rates in the pacts will cover an additional $900,000,000 in trade, it was added.

In estimating that the United States tariff level on Jan. 1 will be the lowest in thirty-four years, analysts said it would bring the new basis to that of the Underwood Tariff of 1913. This tariff had a general level of about 16 per cent of the value of imports subject to duty, which was estimated to be about the same as that to be established under the Geneva pact. No comment on this phase was made at the conference yesterday.

British Empire preferences were reduced substantially. The agreement also calls for a ban on import quotas by foreign countries, except under certain specified conditions. State Department officials indicated, however, that while the agreement was viewed as the longest step in history toward the removal of trade obstacles, the short-range outlook for international trade was affected by dollar shortages and the continuance of import regulation in many countries for the sake of stabilizing their economies.

Concessions Granted to U. S.

Among the major concessions granted on United States exports were:

Reductions on American automobiles in almost every one of the twenty-three countries. There were widespread reductions on United States electrical appliances, radios, refrigerators, and office and agricultural machinery.

England bound to the free list United States wheat, raw cotton and a total of 77,000,000 pounds of ham a year. France reduced the duty on United States wheat by two-thirds, on lard by 59 per cent, on canned fruit by 50 per cent, and on automobiles by nearly half. The United Kingdom duty and Empire preference on canned salmon was cut 50 per cent. Canada, England, Australia and New Zealand allowed tariff or preference cuts on American tobacco. Concessions were made on aircraft by Canada, France, Australia, Czechoslovakia and other nations.

Major concessions also were obtained on trucks, motorcycles and parts. Concessions were granted on American apples, oranges, grapefruit and dried fruits.

A number of British Empire preferences were wiped out entirely, while others were reduced substantially, thus placing the United States exporter on a more competitive status in he markets of the various British Commonwealth nations.

Reciprocal Tariffs Supplanted

The Geneva agreement, which runs three years, replaces the reciprocal trade pacts between the United States and seven other countries, the latter consisting of Canada, England, The Netherlands, Cuba, Belgium, Luxembourg and France.

Under the agreement, the "most-favored nations" clause is accepted by all the participating nations.

Trygve Lie, General Secretary of the United Nations, last night hailed the General Agreement on Tariffs and Trade "as a substantial step on the part of the United Nations toward the establishment of economic well-being and prosperity, which are among the cardinal aims of the United Nations."

Declaring that the signatory countries represent a substantial majority of world trade, and that the reductions they have granted cover the greater share of their imports and exports, he added:

"It can, therefore, be safely said that an initial successful attack has been carried out in a key sector of international trade.

"Under the future international organization, the establishment of which is to be one of the principal purposes of the forthcoming Havana Conference, it is intended that this work on the reduction of trade barriers will be carried on so that it may include an ever-enlarging percentage of the trade of nations."

Foreign traders here hailed the General Agreement on Tariffs and Trade as a major step toward the reduction and elimination of trade barriers, although they expressed the belief that its chief benefits would be of long rather than of a short-range character.

The National Foreign Trade Council said:

"We welcome the announcement of the general agreement on trade and tariffs negotiated at Geneva, Switzerland, as a major advance toward the lowering of barriers to American export and import trade, taken despite admittedly difficult economic conditions throughout most of the world.

"The full benefits of the agreement cannot be expected to become immediately effective, but as recovery and stabilization programs are put into operation, the improvement of commerce due to the reduction of trade barriers should be widely felt. The agreement serves substantially to stem the tide of restrictive devices, resorted to during the post-war economic emergency. An exhaustive analysis of the agreement is to be carried out by the Council and a formal statement issued at a later date."

Speaking for importers here, Morris S. Rosenthal, president of the National Council of American Importers, praised the Geneva trade pacts "as the most significant step taken since 1930 in eliminating trade barriers in the form of excessive duty rates."

Importers' Duties Stressed

"The composite effect of the modification in duty rates," he said, "provides a new tariff structure. American importers must assume a heavy responsibility to give full effect to the objectives of the tariff reductions by taking all necessary steps to speed up the volume of imports of desirable materials and consumer goods as rapidly as greater supplies become available at more reasonable prices.

"In those cases where high tariffs have long burdened the American consumer with no compensatory benefit to any efficiently operated domestic industry, the reduced duties ultimately will be passed on by importers, to the advantage of the consuming public."

The general provisions of the agreement are divided into three parts. Part I gives legal effect to

the tariff concessions set out in the schedules of the agreement and, in addition, lays down the basic rule of non-discrimination in tariff and customs matters generally.

Part II deals with barriers to trade other than tariffs, such as quotas, protective excise taxes and restrictive customs formalities. These provisions are intended to prevent the value of the tariff concessions from being impaired by the use of other devices, and also to bring about the general relaxation of non-tariff trade barriers, thus assuring a further quid-pro-quo for the action taken with respect to tariffs.

Part III covers procedural matters and other questions relevant to the agreement as a whole. Included in Part III are provisions setting out the relationship between the agreement and the proposed charter for an International Trade Organization, to be acted on in Havana beginning Friday.

Six Months' Work Fruitful

Special to THE NEW YORK TIMES.

GENEVA, Nov. 17—The extensive changes in tariffs are designed to ease greatly the existing unbalance in world trade.

This most extensive and deepest slash in world trade barriers is the result of six and a half months of bargaining in the Geneva Trade Conference.

In the case of the United States alone, more than three-quarters of more han 1,800 items in the tariff, many of which have as many as fifteen subclassifications, have been either reduced or bound. Some countries, notably France, have produced entirely new tariffs, which by their terms are not comparable with previous import regulations.

Among the benefits for United States farmers obtained by the American team were removal of the 20 per cent Canadian duty on most types of fresh fruits, the complete removal of British preferences on dried fruits—apples being bound on the British free list—and a flat 10 per cent duty without quotas (after the transition period) on all dried fruits in France.

November 18, 1947

31 NATIONS PUBLISH DUTY CUTS AIMED AT SPURRING TRADE

80% of Global Sellers Take Part in Common Revisions Downward of Customs

ANNECY SUCCESS HAILED

U. S. Gets, Gives Concessions —Signing of Protocol Begins Today at Lake Success

By MICHAEL L. HOFFMAN

Special to THE NEW YORK TIMES.

GENEVA, Oct. 9—Thirty-one countries representing twenty-eight customs areas released new customs tariff schedules today incorporating the results of the summer-long trade conference held at Annecy, France.

The protocol, the signature of which will start in motion the process of putting new, lower duties into effect on some 7 per cent of total world trade, becomes open for signature at Lake Success tomorrow.

For the second time in two years the United States will make a significant reduction in import duties, in furtherance of its policy of attacking trade barriers in all forms throughout the world. This would have been a significant event in any case, although less trade is affected than by the basic multilateral accord signed at Geneva in 1947.

The United States action is doubly significant because of the Washington financial talks of last month when attention was concentrated on the necessity for the United States, as the world's principal creditor nation, to move away from its traditional policy of high import barriers.

[The State Department, hailing the Annecy accords, said that the United States had obtained concessions on a segment of United States exports that in 1947 amounted to more than $500,000,000. In return, the United States granted to other countries concessions on a segment of United States imports that in 1948 amounted to more than $143,000,000.]

Trade System Broadened

The general significance of the completion at Annecy of the "second round" of trade negotiations is that they broaden and strengthen the trading system established by the free nations of the world, incorporated in the General Agreement on Tariffs and Trade.

The agreements have confirmed the success of an entirely new technique of negotiating tariff reductions. This technique and the framework of the principles of commercial policy within which the member nations agree to operate emerge from the Annecy meetings as a proved method of international cooperation on a practical economic level, the like of which has never been seen before.

Twenty-three nations adhering to the agreement, together with ten that will shortly join, form a kind of club, the price of admission to which is demonstrated willingness to carry out in good faith a reduction of trade barriers and adherence to common rules of conduct in international trade matters.

Member Nations Listed

Together, these thirty-three countries account for more than 80 per cent of world trade. The twenty-three original members are Australia, Belgium, Brazil, Burma, Canada, Ceylon, Chile, China, Cuba, Czechoslovakia, France, India, Lebanon, Luxembourg, the Netherlands, New Zealand, Norway, Pakistan, South Africa, Southern Rhodesia, Syria, the United Kingdom and the United States.

The ten new members, all of whom have completed negotiations with each other and with some or all of the old members, are Denmark, the Dominican Republic, Finland, Greece, Haiti, Italy, Liberia, Nicaragua, Sweden and Uruguay.

Admission to the "club" is by no means automatic. Colombia, which negotiated at Annecy, failed to complete negotiations with enough countries to warrant applying for membership. If Colombia had applied, there is reason to believe that the necessary two-thirds approval of the old members could not have been obtained.

The schedules of duties of the participating countries, lowered or bound under the Annecy protocol, fill more than 200 pages of small type. The United States has granted reductions or bindings on a wide variety of items, although a relatively small part of its total imports is affected. These include steel cutlery, forgings, plywood, bacon, hams, butter, cheese, macaroni, several fruits, cocoa and chocolate, rum, aquavit, vermouth, matches, silver, jewelry, works of art and umbrellas.

The most controversial items in the new United States schedules, judging from the record of negotiations in Annecy, are the concessions on butter and lemons.

In negotiations with Denmark, the United States agreed to permit the entry of 10,000,000 pounds of butter at seven cents a pound duty during the summer months. Previously, a rate of fourteen cents a pound had applied during those months, with the quota for the period Nov. 1 to March 31 permitting entry at a seven-cent rate.

The ability to sell luxury quality butter in the United States market was regarded by Denmark as essential to her entire recovery program.

In negotiations with Italy, the duty on lemons was lowered from two and one-half to one and one-quarter cents a pound, with the reservation that if imports exceeded 5 per cent of the total United States production during any one year, the duty would be doubled on all excess over that quantity.

The widest world interest will be in the Italian tariff, which is entirely new, having been changed from the old pre-war basis of specific duties to a tariff expressed almost entirely in ad valorem terms. It is unquestionably a "high tariff" judged by the average rates of duty. Most manufactured products must pay from 25 to 40 per cent duty. Duties are high both on raw materials and finished products.

Even so, traders will welcome the simplification and clarification of the tariff of this important trading country so that they will know where they stand.

The third series of negotiations for Sept. 1950 is already being planned, Eric Syndham-White, executive secretary of the Interim Commission for the International Trade Organization, said here today. Means for incorporating Western Germany into the trade system is the most important single problem to be settled in advance.

October 10, 1949

FREE-TRADING HOPE GAINING IN GENEVA

True Multilateral Concepts Win Ground as Officials of 20 Nations End Talks

Special to THE NEW YORK TIMES.

GENEVA, April 4—The contracting parties to the General Agreement on Tariffs and Trade ended a six-week session here today that, in the opinion of trade officials of the twenty participating countries, has strengthened the multilateral system of settling trade policy disputes.

While the machinery established under the Geneva Agreement of 1947 to bring order into the chaos of conflicting national trade policies has met only minor tests at this session, it has met them well, the delegates believe.

The session also has taken decisions that will make major tests of this machinery inevitable at the fifth session, to be held during the third round of tariff negotiations in England this autumn. At the closing session, the date for the fifth meeting of the contracting parties w s set for Nov. 2, at Torquay, where the tariff conference will have convened by the end of September.

Tariff Stability in Offing

Among the most important practical actions taken at this session was a decision to prolong the tariff concessions granted as a result of the Geneva and Annecy negotiations until Jan. 1, 1954. This decision will be made formal only after the end of the Torquay conference. It means that, after having incorporated the concessions to be negotiated at Torquay a series of tariff schedules for some forty countries will emerge that will be binding until 1954, bringing a degree of stability in world tariffs never before even attempted.

The contracting parties also took an important decision of principle in response to the complaints of European low-tariff countries. The latter's contention was that their commerce was being damaged by the reciprocal removal of quantitative restrictions among the countries participating in the Marshall Plan, leaving them face to face with high French and Italian duty walls while opening their own markets to exports from those countries.

Disguised Protection a Target

The contracting parties decided that the low-tariff countries might exact concessions from the high-tariff countries on the basis of an agreement to bind the existing low duties, and that the high-tariff countries not bargaining in good faith on this basis might be declared in violation of the General Agreement and suffer retaliation.

A series of decisions and recommendations were elaborated, clarifying the provisions of the General Agreement forbidding the use of quantitative restrictions on imports and exports except under certain specific circumstances. On both the import and export sides, the work done here is expected to reduce considerably the use of trade controls imposed for balance-of-payments reasons as a form of disguised protection of the domestic industries competing with imports. The United States delegation initiated this work, and is especially gratified at the outcome.

A general review of quantitative restrictions — the basic question whether the non-Communist world really does or does not intend to make a serious effort to establish nondiscriminatory multilateral trade—has been put off until the Torquay meeting. Only a few countries were prepared to bite into this problem now.

April 5, 1950

U. S. PARES TARIFFS ON 16% OF IMPORTS

Reciprocal Cuts With 17 Lands Cap Torquay Agreements to Foster World Trade

By FELIX BELAIR JR.

Special to THE NEW YORK TIMES.

WASHINGTON, May 8—A major revision of the United States tariff structure providing lowered rates on dutiable imports that accounted for about 16 per cent of the 1949 value of total United States purchases abroad was announced by the State Department today under the Torquay Protocol.

An analysis of the agreements covering reciprocal concessions between the United States and seventeen foreign countries showed 1,325 tariff items that were either sharply reduced or "bound" at previously negotiated low levels or in their duty-free classification.

The agreements were described by the State Department as "a very substantial advance in the field of international trade relations" notwithstanding Britain's refusal to modify her imperial-preference tariff system prescribing a substantially lower set of duties for Commonwealth countries than for all others.

A statement by the Department on the results of eight months of negotiation at Torquay, England, said on this point that "the United States was not able to find a basis for expanding the existing range of concessions in the General Agreement with regard to Australia, Cuba, New Zealand, the Union of South Africa, the United Kingdom and India."

The failure of the conference to effect any narrowing of the margins of empire-preference rates stamped the meeting a failure on balance in the estimate of many economists in and out of Government service. However, the State Department noted in this connection:

"This situation does not affect the continued participation of these countries as parties to the General Agreement nor the maintenance of the concessions which they negotiated at Geneva and Annecy. Neither does it preclude further negotiations with them at some future time when conditions are more favorable."

At a background conference on the documents, a spokesman for the Department said this "might be only a pious hope" but that the objective of substantial modification of the British system had not been abandoned.

1949 Basis Not Normal One

On the basis of 1949 foreign trade, it was estimated that tariff concessions received by the United States in the negotiations would facilitate exports of items in which this country had a total trade of about $1,100,000,000. On the same basis, concessions to this country at Torquay applied to items of which the United States had total imports of about $500,000,000.

The department acknowledged, however, that this estimate of exports was far above anything that might be expected under more normal trading relations, and suggested that under such conditions the two sets of concessions would about balance.

The point of all this was that 1949, the latest year for which detailed trade figures are available, was anything but normal and that without financing by the Economic Cooperation Administration and other foreign-aid programs, United States exports would have been less than half the volume they attained in that year.

Of the seventeen countries with which the United States exchanged concessions at Torquay, five were becoming parties to the General Agreement on Tariffs and Trade for the first time. They were Austria, Western Germany, Korea, Peru and Turkey.

The twelve other countries were contracting parties at the Geneva or Annecy conferences in 1947 and 1949 and included Belgium, Brazil, Canada, Denmark, the Dominican Republic, France, Indonesia, Italy, the Netherlands, Norway, Luxembourg and Sweden.

In addition to new tariff concessions exchanged, the conference at Torquay agreed to the extension until Jan. 1, 1954, of the validity of the concessions exchanged at the Geneva and Annecy meetings. This and other countries are expected also to benefit indirectly from the generalization of concessions for which the General Agreement provides, in addition to those directly negotiated.

Because, outside the General Agreement, the United States has pursued a policy of generalizing concessions made to any country, the Soviet Union and its satellite nations are eligible to receive all those exchanged by this country at Torquay.

May 9, 1951

U.S. SIGNS ACCORDS ON REVISED GATT

But Washington Will Limit Its Role in Organization Administering Pacts

By MICHAEL L. HOFFMAN
Special to The New York Times.

GENEVA, March 21—The United States signed here today the documents necessary for its adherence to the revised General Agreement on Tariffs and Trade (GATT).

It thus became the first Government to commit itself firmly to the continuation, at least until Dec. 31, 1957, of the world tariff truce effected through general agreement.

It also thus indicated the intention of the Eisenhower Administration to continue to adhere to the system of trade rules embodied in the revised general agreement.

Erich Wyndham-White, executive secretary of the GATT administrative organization, described the general agreement as "a fair trading system supported by a code of international conduct effectively administered by a strong organization."

Samuel C. Waugh, Assistant Secretary of State for Economic Affairs, signed the six protocols involved on behalf of President Eisenhower. He said the United States Administration had reviewed the results of the world trade conference that produced the revised agreement "with considerable satisfaction."

These results have been reviewed within the last two weeks by all branches of the Administration, Mr. Waugh added. "Complete unanimity" has been reached among the various deparments on the desirability of United States participation in the general agreement, Mr. Waugh declared.

Mr. Waugh also signed a protocol establishing the Organization for Trade Cooperation. He made it clear that the President, through him, was not committing the United States Government to the trade cooperation organization to the same extent as was done in signing the documents relating to the General Agreement. This is because the President has full powers under the Reciprocal Trade Agreements Act to commit the United States to a trade agreement. The joining of the proposed organization, however, has to be approved by Congress.

The agreement for the establishment of the Organization for Trade Cooperation was published here today, along with the other documents emerging from the recent conference. The organization would be comparatively simple, consisting of a secretariat, an executive committee of seventeen members and an assembly that would consist of all the Governments adhering to the general agreement.

Other Governments could become associate members of the organization, but without the right to vote on matters involving the interpretation or administration of the tariffs and trade agreement.

Two important points about the organization appear clearly from the text. The first is that it is designed to deal promptly with trade disputes or complaints made by one Government against another for violations of the general agreeement rules. The second is that provisions for the implementation of the organizational agreement are such that the organization will not be established unless the United States joins it.

This second point is what leads all who have participated in the formation of the organization to emphasize that this is a take-it-or-leave-it proposition. Either the United States will join this system or there will be no effective world trading system devoted to the maintenance of order in world trade, they believe.

Other Governments have made it clear that should the United States not come in wholeheartedly, with Congressional backing, they would consider its formal adherence to the tariffs and trade agreement as offering no real assurance against arbitrary and unilateral charges in tariffs and other aspects of trade policy.

March 22, 1955

Japan a Full Member of GATT

TOKYO, Saturday, Sept. 10 (AP)—Japan became today the thirty-fifth full member of the General Agreement on Tariffs and Trade (GATT). She was accepted thirty days ago after a favorable two-thirds majority vote of members.

September 10, 1955

GATT, AT AGE OF 10, HAS BIG PROBLEM

Trade Pact Nations Ponder Whether Europe Pool Will Violate Obligations

1957 MEETING GOING ON

Organization Marks Tenth Anniversary This Week —37 Members Now

Special to The New York Times.

GENEVA, Oct. 27 — In a cluttered cosmos of international organizations, the General Agreement on Tariffs and Trade shines faintly. Yet it influences commercial tides in thirty-seven of the world's largest trading nations.

Strictly speaking the GATT which is ten years old this week, is not an organization at all. It is rather a code of conduct, a contract pledging thirty-seven nations to the belief that tariffs and discriminatory trade policies obstruct economic progress.

Reducing tariff barriers is the agreement's first order of business, but not its only one. Rules and precepts also are laid down on import and export restrictions, taxation and trade regulations, and balance-of-payment problems.

At annual meetings like the one now in session, member nations negotiate reciprocal trade concessions and examine complaints. Almost any subject bearing on international trade is liable to come up at the private sessions.

The agreement was never meant to be an independent entity. Ten years ago it was conceived as an adjunct to the proposed United Nations International Trade Organization. But the organization never materialized, mainly for lack of United States participation. This left the general agreement to do what it could about stabilizing and freezing tariff levels before the advent of a post-war boom.

Cuts Achieved

Concerted attacks on tariffs were opened by the GATT nations in 1947 and 1949 and considerable reductions were achieved. In the winter of 1954-55, when it became clear that ambitious projects for international trade cooperation through the United Nations were unavailing, the GATT nations drafted an Organization for Trade Cooperation to administer their agreement and give it a permanent legal existence.

Again the United States demurred, although it had worked long and effectively within the agreement to promote liberal, multilateral trade. Congressional opponents claimed that the O. T. C., by making recommendations on international trade, would collide with the United States freedom to determine its own policies. To date the organization has not been ratified by Congress.

"This failure to ratify the agreement has signified the abdication of leadership by the United States in the field of commercial policy on the international plane," Canada's delegate, L. D. Wilgress, said today.

A lack of vigorous enforcement powers has limited the achievement of the agreement. Fifteen of the thirty-seven nations refuse to grant full nondiscriminatory treatment to one of the members, Japan. Some nations have turned from tariffs to quantitative restrictions for protection (the United States among them, in an effort to cope with mounting agricultural surpluses.) The GATT has recently intensified its campaign against this device.

Trade ministers from the GATT nations are in Geneva this week to discuss the consequences of six European nations' decision to form a common market in association with their overseas territories. This presents the GATT with its newest and thorniest problem: will the six, all members of the agreement, create a new preferential area in violation of their individual obligations to other members?

The trade ministers do not wish to interfere with the political unity that may grow out of the common-market scheme. Their overmastering concern is to assure that the common market will be "outward-looking," with liberalism prevailing over protectionism. And that, by common consent, is the GATT's goal.

October 28, 1957

PRESIDENT IS TOLD TARIFF BARRIERS ENDANGER WEST

Long-Secret Report Warns of Economic Disintegration Without 50% Reduction

By FELIX BELAIR Jr.

Special to The New York Times.

WASHINGTON, Jan. 7—A long-secret report has warned President Kennedy that "disintegration of the Free World economy into separate trading systems" may result unless Congress authorizes 50 per cent cuts across the board in tariff rates.

The report, compiled by a task force studying foreign economic policy, said the failure of the United States to liberalize trade would have "political consequences of a most serious order."

These, it said, would be in addition to "a formidable competitive disadvantage" to American exporters implicit in the growing European Common Market.

The report also proposed a virtual scrapping of the existing embargo on exports of strategic materials to nations of the Communist bloc. It favored a new policy that would acknowledge the mutual advantages of expanding East-West trade and that would invite the Soviet Union to join in a code of fair practices for international trade.

Basis of Program

Although it was submitted to Mr. Kennedy as President-elect just before his inauguration, the report remains the basic rationale for the liberalized trade program he plans to ask Congress to approve at this session. The program would replace the expiring Trade Agreements Act.

The present trade agreements legislation requires that the President obtain concessions equal in value to the concessions the United States makes in the area covered by negotiations. It takes no account of concessions with respect to non-tariff trade barriers that this country might seek.

The new program would give the President authority for the first time to negotiatate whole categories of tariff rates with a view to their reduction. It would also enable him to seek trade concessions in return for commitments not restricted to the trade field.

The task force was headed by George W. Ball, who later became Under Secretary of State. Other members of the group included college professors and private consultants, many now holding high Administration posts.

Apparently reluctant to risk rejection of the new trade program during the first Congressional session of his Administration, the President did nothing, except in the field of foreign aid, about the report's many urgent and sweeping recommendations. Most of the aid proposals have since been carried out, but without adoption of the scope of expenditures proposed.

Britain's decision to seek membership in the European Common Market, a continuation of the United States' balance-of-payments deficit last year, and the expiration of the trade agreements legislation next June, decided the President on an immediate course of action on the new program. The balance of payments is the measure of payments into and out of the country by individuals, business and governments.

The task force proposed Presidential authority to negotiate mutual trade concessions by cutting present tariff rates as much as 50 per cent. The cuts would be made in annual steps through 1966. The task force also proposed these further legislative authorizations:

¶"Assistance to labor and industry in adjusting to tariff reductions to replace the 'no serious injury' principle."

¶"Revision of the existing peril point provision so that it (A) is a device for determining what individual tariff rate adjustments should be made within a given category, and (B) goes into operation only after negotiations are completed on average reductions for each category." A peril point, determined by the Tariff Commission, is the level below which the tariffs cannot be cut without causing serious injury to domestic industry.

¶"Revision of escape clause standards [under the Reciprocal Trade Agreements Act] so that the clause applies only when (A) injury occurs to an industry as a whole, and (B) adjustment to the increased imports cannot readily be made.

¶"Trade adjustment assistance

that would come into effect after a finding by the Tariff Commission of injury under the escape clause.

¶"Authority for the President to reduce or remove duties, import taxes and quotas on articles produced principally by the less developed countries.

¶"Authority to make or receive types of reciprocal concessions other than tariff reductions in trade negotiations.

¶"Revision of the national security provisions of trade agreements legislation to permit reduction of duties and an increase in quotas; use of measures other than tariffs to protect national security interests; relaxation of import restrictions, in concert with other members of the Organization for Economic Cooperation and Development, to accommodate trade with a country under Soviet economic pressure.

¶"Amendment of the Battle Act to safeguard normal trade against the disruptive practices of the Communist bloc.

¶"Authority for the President to suspend the embargo on furs and to suspend discriminatory tariff treatment for Soviet bloc imports."

Because of the operation of a modified concept of existing "peril point" and "escape clause" provisions, the report found that it would be possible to make uniform 50 per cent cuts in all negotiable categories of tariff rates.

For that reason it proposed that "the new legislation should provide authority to make greater than 50 per cent reductions on certain items on which there is now a high level of tariff protection."

At the time the report was submitted, its authors considered it unlikely that Britain and the six other countries in the Free Trade Association would seek membership in the European Common Market. Britain's decision to do so presumably underscores the arguments for broad Presidential tariff powers.

"This tariff-cutting authority is necessary," said the report, "if we are to match the reductions to be made in the internal tariffs of the European Common Market and the Free Trade Association. In that way we could receive the benefits of the generalization of these reductions on a most-favored-nation basis." All nations having most-favored-nation provisions in agreements with the United States get and receive concessions on a basis of equality with any other nation.

"Since those two trading groups will have reduced their tariffs by 50 per cent across the board by 1966," the report said "The United States, armed with the authority we propose, would be able to prevent divisions of the industrial countries of the Free World by widespread trade discrimination."

As explained in the report, "the peril point mechanism serves as a limitation on the tariff-cutting authority of American negotiators in trade agreement negotiations." Under the Trade Agreements Act the President must explain to Congress any cuts below a peril point.

The escape clause mechanism, on the other hand, comes into play after tariffs have been reduced if the Tariff Commission determines that increased imports following a reduction cause "serious injury."

"The task force is of the strong opinion that the 'no serious injury' doctrine should be substantially abandoned," said the report. "The United States should recognize frankly that the liberalization of trade essential to a prosperous Free World will require that tariffs be reduced to the point where it will be necessary to accept some temporary and local injury to certain American firms, industries and communities."

To mitigate such possible hardships, the group proposed the inclusion of "trade adjustment provisions" in any authorizing legislation. But it suggested that this relief take the form of higher tariff rates only in extreme cases, such as when producers and workers in an industry are being displaced by competitive imports faster than the workers can be absorved into alternative employment.

Such tariff relief could be applied by the President even where displaced workers were already receiving relief compensation, but it was recommended that such relief be of "limited duration" and progressively reduced.

Federal Loans Backed

A trade adjustment program should rely in the main on Federal loans to finance industry relocation, accelerated tax write-offs, and related procedures, the report said.

These would include retraining of workers, additional unemployment compensation, early retirement benefits and the like. Such benefits would be available "without regard to whether or not the affected industries or workers are located in areas of substantial labor surplus."

The study group suggested that unilateral tariff concessions to under-developed areas be conditioned on parallel concessions to such areas by other industrialized countries. Such concessions could take the form of reduction or removal of consumption taxes or other restrictions on imports of tropical products, raw materials or materials in the early stages or processing and "certain light manufactures.

Such concessions would not only promote export earnings of under-developed areas, according to the report, but would tend to remove discriminations implicit in preferential trading systems maintained by Britain and the Common Market countries for their former overseas possessions.

To further the purpose of trade liberalization, the report urged abolition of the following provisions of the Tariff Act of 1930:

¶"The provision relating to cost-of-production criteria in fixing and raising of duties.

¶"The provision requiring the use of American selling price in fixing the valuation of certain products.

¶The provision directing customs officers to apply the highest rate of duty when alternatives exist."

Commodity Plan Suggested

Without committing itself to any particular method of approach, the task force said the time had come for the United States to consider ways of stabilizing the export income of under-developed areas producing a single raw material. Commodity stabilization agreements as well as loans to offset income fluctuation were suggested as worthy of exploration.

The report warned in this connection against "commodity agreement techniques that support prices at artificially high levels." It went on:

"The task force feels that much greater consideration should be given to the possibilities of using the resources of the International Montetary Fund for short-term loans to cushion income fluctuations resulting from cyclical variations in production conditions or on the terms of trade of raw material producing countries."

A complete alteration of United States policy on trade with Soviet bloc countries was recommended by the task force. It held this to be imperative not only because the present policy was outmoded and negative but also because it had begun to affect our relations with other industrialized countries as well as with the under-developed areas.

The problem will not go away because Americans consider trade with Communist countries to be "immoral, dangerous and of doubtful economic benefit," said the group. It said such trade would become vastly more important in this decade than in the last because other Western countries had found such trade to be advantageous.

"As a result," said the report, "our Allies have refused to follow docilely the tariff discriminations and export limitations on Communist trade imposed by United States law."

European Trade Cited

Meanwhile, because the United States has refused to face the issue, trade between the Soviet bloc and Western Europe has been developing largely on Soviet terms, the group said. It said the time had come for the United States to give direction to this inevitable development.

It called for "a positive response to Khrushchev's high-sounding trade overtures" and said "the Soviet should be invited to trade with Free World countries on the basis of a code of fair practices designed to remove the distortions and disruptions arising from monopolistic state commerce."

"The code should serve as a model for industrialized and under-developed countries in the negotiation of bilateral treaties or multilateral trade arrangements with the bloc," said the report.

"For example, detailed ground rules, coupled with an effective complaints procedure, would seek to regulate disruptive price undercutting and dumping by reference to comparative world price and cost criteria, rather than to the totally unrelated and unascertainable conditions prevalent in the Communist home market; to provide meaningful reciprocity in conditions governing access to Communist markets; to obtain Soviet commitments to purchase specified quotas of goods in lieu of an otherwise futile most-favored-nation treatment undertaking; to end the wholesale pirating of Western patents, know-how, and technology; and, in general, to ensure that trade and competition are conducted on the basis of commercial considerations."

The report reasoned that "failing East-West agreement, the United States and its industrialized Allies would still possess the economic advantage needed to secure observance of the rules, assuming that a uniform and coordinated policy toward Soviet bloc trade is established through consultation with O. E. C. D. and the G. A. T. T. [General Agreement on Tariffs and Trade]"

On the general question of East - West trade the report continued:

"To blunt the dangers and exploit the opportunities inherent in the bloc's expanding economic commitments, we must persuade other free enterprise countries to take constructive and coordinated action.

"What is needed first of all is some measure of conviction on their part that we are genuinely prepared to recognize the potential economic advantages of expanded East-West trade.

"Only then will we be in a position to assert positive leadership in the formulation and enforcement of safeguards necessary for the protection of the common interest in stable world trade."

Members of Panel

The members of the task force were:

CHAIRMAN — George W. Ball, now Under Secretary of State.

SECRETARY OF COMMERCIAL POLICY—Myer Rashish, formerly staff director of the Subcommittee on Foreign Trade Policy of the House Ways and Means Committee.

CONSULTANTS ON COMMERCIAL POLICY—

Robert E. Asher, senior staff member of the Brookings Institution; William Diebold, member of Council on Foreign Relations; Richard Gardner, Deputy Assistant Secretary of State for International Organization Affairs; Don D. Humphrey, professor at the Fletcher School of Law and Diplomacy, Tufts University.

Also Jerome Jacobsen, president of International Economic Consultants, Inc.; Stanley D. Metzger, professor, Georgetown University Law Center; William T. Phillips, Professor of International Economics, The John Hopkins University.

Also Samuel Pisar, consultant, Senate Committee on Interstate and Foreign Commerce; Seymour J. Rubin, general counsel of the Agency for International Development, and Raymond Vernon, professor, Graduate School of Business Administration, Harvard University.

SECRETARY for FOREIGN AID—George S. Springsteen, senior economist, Development Loan Fund.

CONSULTANTS ON FOREIGN AID—

Robert R. Bowie, director, Harvard University's Center for International Affairs; Harlan Cleveland, Assistant Secretary of State for International Organization Affairs; J. Kenneth Galbraith, Ambassador to India.

Also Lincoln Gordon, Ambassador to Brazil; Max F. Millikan, director, Massachusetts Institute of Technology's Center for International Studies; Robert R. Nathan, president of Robert R. Nathan Associates, and Walt W. Rostow, chairman of the State Department's Policy Planning Council.

January 8, 1962

PRESIDENT URGES A WORLD PARLEY TO EASE TARIFFS

Tells Diefenbaker He Wants to Take Full Advantage of New Trade Act

By The Associated Press

WASHINGTON, Oct. 19 — President Kennedy, bolstered by his new Trade Expansion Act, proposed today an international conference of ministers next year to seek ways to cut down obstacles to world trade.

He suggested February or March. No site was named.

Taking part would be representatives of countries that have signed the General Agreement on Tariffs and Trade. The conference actually would be a special meeting of adherents to the General Agreement.

Mr. Kennedy's proposal was made in an exchange of letters with Prime Minister John Diefenbaker of Canada. Mr. Diefenbaker had congratulated the President on the new law and suggested a ministerial meeting.

Delegation Instructed

The Prime Minister, disclosing Mr. Kennedy's reply in Ottawa today, said he was instructing Canada's delegation to next week's GATT meeting in Geneva to seek a special meeting next year.

The Trade Expansion Act gives the President new power to cut tariffs. Its passage on Oct. 4 was one of Mr. Kennedy's major victories in the last session of Congress.

Mr. Diefenbaker suggested that "all like-minded nations" meet soon "to consider how the great problems of trade facing us today can be dealt with to the mutual advantage of all."

President Kennedy replied that "perhaps we might join forces" in recommending a meeting of the ministers of countries taking part in the General Agreement.

A 'New Approach'

"I would like to take full advantage of the authority which the Trade Expansion Act confers upon me,' Mr. Kennedy said, "and I am eager to explore with other like-minded nations as soon as possible the problems and prospects for a new approach to the reduction of obstacles to world trade."

The President hopes to use his new tariff-cutting power to bargain with other nations that have barriers against United States goods. Under his plan barriers would fall and trade would expand.

Mr. Diefenbaker first suggested an international conference on world trade when he addressed the conference of Prime Ministers of the British Commonwealth in London last month. His proposal was part of a speech attacking Britain's plan to join the European Economic Community or Common Market.

United Press International

EXPRESSES HOPE: Walter W. Heller, chairman of the President's Council of Economic Advisers. He said business should improve.

October 20, 1962

Groundwork Is Laid For New Trade Talk

By RICHARD E. MOONEY

Special to The New York Times

WASHINGTON—The "Kennedy round" has begun.

The Kennedy round, so named in honor of the sponsor of the Trade Expansion Act of 1962, is the next big round of international trade and tariff negotiations. The actual negotiations will begin early next year if the sponsor has anything to say about it. But the preliminaries—extremely important in themselves — are under way in earnest already.

The crucial questions that must be settled before the negotiations begin are, in essence, the rules of the game.

What will be negotiated — agricultural products as well as industrial?

How?

What is to be done about trade curbs other than tariffs —internal taxes and various national laws and regulations that can have as much effect as any tariff, if not more.

And what is General de Gaulle up to anyway?

The framework for negotiations is the General Agreement on Tariffs and Trade—GATT as it's called. This agreement sets an outline for the conduct of international trade relations. Its signatories are the United States and 43 other countries, divided roughly half-and-half between "advanced" and "less developed" countries. In any negotiation, some members may choose not to play, and nonmembers may join in.

New Office Set Up

A special feature of the new United States law is the creation of an office of Special Representatives for Trade Negotiations with Cabinet-level status. The idea for the new post came from Congress, as a stand-off to the protectionist bloc's suspicions that the State Department might use the new authority to negotiate away Detroit, Pittsburgh and Akron, not to mention Lowell, Mass., if given half a chance. In practice, the post has had a different effect.

The job, and a White House office, went to Christian A. Herter—a prestigious name, not exactly a stranger around the State Department, and something of a committed trade "liberal" himself. As deputy, Mr. Kennedy named William T. Gossett from the Ford Motor Company, where he was vice president and general counsel.

In theory, this pair and a small staff—it is still fewer than a dozen—were to be in charge. On paper, they are. But in fact, most of the detail work is still done by the State Department, and detail becomes policy in this field without much strain.

Thus, the effect of the job has not been any real change in State Department influence, but it has been the creation of a new and more liberal influence in the White House.

The prime example of its effect to date is the way Mr. Herter insisted on, and succeeded in getting, the President's authorization to reject woolen industry demands for an international agreement to control wool textile trade. Mr. Herter said, in effect, that to honor these demands would jeopardize the whole Kennedy round.

At the State Department, top-echelon authority on international economics is in the hands of Under Secretary George W. Ball, but as No. 2 to the Secretary Mr. Ball cannot spend full time on trade. The Assistant Secretary for Economic Affairs is G. Griffith

TO AID AT TALKS: W. Michael Blumenthal, who will assist Christian A. Herter at tariff negotiations scheduled next year.

Johnson Jr., an economist and former vice president of the Motion Picture Association.

The chief operative in this apparatus is one stop further down—W. Michael Blumenthal, a 37-year-old former vice president of Crown Cork International Corporation, now deputy to Mr. Johnson.

Mr. Blumenthal was chief United States negotiator for last year's cotton textile trade agreement that the woolen interests want duplicated for them. In the Kennedy round preparations, he led the United States delegation at the first GATT "working party" talks in Geneva last month, and is right now cruising European capitals on a soundings mission en route to a coming second round.

Key Role in Planning

There are, as indicated, several layers of authority above him, but Mr. Blumenthal stands well with all of them and is himself a participant and a mover in policy planning, right up to the Presidential level.

The bosses do not stay put, either. Mr. Herter has been to Japan this month and may go to Canada soon. Mr. Gossett is bound for Mexico City, for the International Chamber of Commerce annual meeting, where his target is European business interest; next month Geneva, for the high-level trade ministers' planning session for next year's bargaining.

Accompanying Mr. Blumenthal on his tour is the head of one of the European outposts of United States trade policy planning—John W. Tuthill, a career foreign service officer serving now in Brussels as United States Ambassador to the Common Market. The other outpost is Paris, where John M. Leddy, another career man, is representative at the 20-nation Organization for Economic Co-operation and Development.

Nor are all the travelers Americans. A procession of Common Market officialdom has been shuttling to Washington, and isn't finished yet.

The industrial powers represented in the Common Market and O.E.C.D. are the United States's principal adversaries—or "partners" — in the coming trade talks, but no policy is planned without thought for the less-developed countries. The basis for this thought is not all humanitarian. Under United Nations sponsorship, at the urging of the Communist bloc and the less-developed countries, a "World Trade Conference" is being planned for the same time as the GATT negotiations.

It is the United States's hope that the GATT negotiations will produce the beneficial results for less-developed countries and their exports that these countries will be demanding at the United Nations conference. Another Johnson deputy — Isaiah Frank, also a career man — is attending to planning for the United Nations talks.

And so the Kennedy round goes 'round.

April 19, 1963

COMMON MARKET APPROVES ACCORD ON KENNEDY ROUND

Six Members Meet Deadline on Goods to Be Excepted From Key Tariff Talk

By EDWARD T. O'TOOLE
Special to The New York Times

BRUSSELS, Sunday, Nov. 15—The European Economic Community won a race against the clock early today as ministers of the six member nations reached agreement on a common negotiating position for the Kennedy round of tariff discussions.

The agreement came after an all-night session of hard bargaining. It had capped four days and nights of wrangling over which of the Common Market's industrial imports should be excepted from the sweeping tariff cuts that are the goal of the Kennedy round.

Some time later today, after a few technical points are cleared up, a courier will fly to Geneva to submit the European Community's list of proposed exceptions tomorrow.

Other Lists to Be Offered

The list will be received by officials of the General Agreement on Tariffs and Trade with lists of proposed exceptions prepared by the United States and by other major industrial powers in the non-Communist world.

By observing the deadline, the negotiating nations will give great impetus to the trade-expansion effort, which has been virtually stalled since summer.

The Kennedy round, named for the late President because of his association with the Trade Expansion Act adopted by Congress, is widely regarded as the most important liberalization effort in modern history. The act authorizes United States participation in the negotiations.

Big Expansion Foreseen

The primary objective is to make simultaneous tariff cuts on all possible industrial products involved in world trade. The reductions are to be reciprocal, with the goal 50 per cent across the board.

In previous negotiations the elimination of barriers has been most gradual, with reductions made on a product-by-product basis.

Should the across-the-board reductions materialize, they would result in a few years in an expansion of trade that would amount to billions of dollars.

Trade officials of West Germany, Italy, France, the Netherlands, Belgium and Luxembourg have been working here in the unofficial capital of the community to condense their separate lists into a single list that will be representative of the bloc.

The starting point for this intramural tug of war was a basic list prepared by the Common Market's Executive Commission. Of modest proportions, it embraced special imports that added up to about 12 per cent of the community's imports that bear tariffs. This would have left 88 per cent of the Common Market's industrial imports as candidates for the across-the-board cuts.

However, France, Italy and Belgium offered separate lists of additional exceptions that, if all had been added to the original schedule, would have expanded it to unmanageable proportions.

Another consideration that put pressure on the secret bargaining sessions was a realization that nations such as the United States and Britain would submit modest lists. A long community list would have reflected adversely on the Common Market, and if there is one thing on which the European Community has prided itself above all others, it has been its liberal approach to international trade.

The consensus among analysts was that the Economic Community's list would turn out to be about eight percentage points greater than the list recommended by the Executive Commission. This will mean exceptions embrasing about 20 per cent of imports subject to tariffs.

It was felt that this would make the list substantially longer than those of the United States and Britain, among others, but not too long to be rejected by the Ministerial Council of GATT, under the auspices of which the Kennedy round is to be held.

The Ministerial Council is in charge of setting up the ground rules that will govern the tariff-cutting procedures. The negotiators are scheduled to get down to business in January.

It was generally agreed in the GATT Council last spring that only those imports that affected strategic or other vital national interests were to be acceptable as exceptions.

Experienced observers concurred in the view that while the negotiators on the Kennedy round still had a long, hard road to climb, the submission of exceptions lists by the chief missions would signal that a start had been made.

Should the Kennedy round proceed to a successful conclusion, one minister remarked, the increase in trade that would result would do more to integrate the economies and governments of the non-Communist nations than all other alliance plans combined.

Problem in Exceptions

By RICHARD E. MOONEY
Special to The New York Times

PARIS, Nov. 16—The United States, Britain and the major European countries outside the

Common Market have prepared lists of exceptions for the Kennedy round of tariff negotiations that will make the Common Market's demands seem big.

To some extent the difference will be a statistical apparition. The ensuing bargaining will be an exercise in statistical contortion, with each country seeking a better deal than its neighbor.

Monday is the day when the dozen-odd major participants in the Kennedy round have agreed to meet in Geneva and exchange secret lists of the products on which they do not want to make full-scale, across-the-board tariff cuts.

Switzerland and two or three of the Scandinavian countries are expected to submit, in effect, blank sheets of paper. That is, they are expected to offer to go all the way with any agreed general reduction, provided they are satisfied with what they will gain in return.

The United States plans to submit a list that covers, by United States estimate, less than 10 per cent of American imports subject to tariffs. Britain's list is said to be smaller and Japan's twice as large.

Finally, there is the Common Market, or European Economic Community — West Germany, France, Italy, Belgium, the Netherlands and Luxembourg.

On its face the list the Common Market submits will be substantially greater than that of the Americans. But to understand its proposal—in fact, to understand the Kennedy round — it must be noted that there are many ways to compute the values involved.

If the United States were to compute the value of its list by a method that has been suggested over here, it would be much larger than Washington acknowledges, and not so different from that of the Common Market.

The point here is oil. The United States is not offering to bargain on oil imports, which are controlled by executive order. But neither does Washington count oil on its exceptions list, because most United States oil imports come from countries that are not in this part of the negotiations.

This single omission involves more than 10 per cent of American imports.

A similar case might be made against the European Community's position on steel. It is not likely to be on the European exceptions list, but the tariff is being raised for the bargaining so that the cut will not cut so deep.

The countries that intend to enter this part of the negotiations, aiming in theory at a 50 per cent general reduction in their tariffs on manufactured goods, subject to exceptions, are the United States, the six Common Market countries and Britain, Japan, Switzerland, Sweden, Norway and Denmark. Canada is participating, too, but not across the board.

November 15, 1964

Once More, the Kennedy Round

Complex Talks Fare Well Despite Lack of Written Rules

Special to The New York Times

PARIS—The Kennedy Round is about to begin in Geneva—again.

It has already begun three times in the last 20 months, each time a little more realistically. In the next 12 months it might even reach a successful conclusion—maybe.

The Kennedy Round is the biggest, broadest negotiation on the terms of international trade that has ever been held. But 20 months of intense haggling has established a few things that it is not.

¶It is not going to be a 50 per cent reduction of all tariffs "across the board," as it was advertised to be when the Kennedy Administration pushed the authorizing legislation through Congress three years ago.

¶It is not going to open up trade in farm products so significantly as trade in industrial products, although the United States insists officially that it must do both.

¶It is not a simple proceeding. It is, in fact, unbelievably complicated, much more so than anyone anticipated.

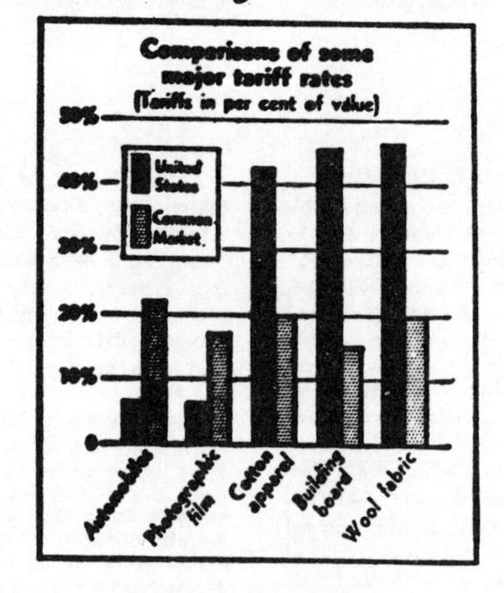

CHRISTIAN HERTER
The U. S. representative for trade negotiations:

"By lowering trade barriers we show that in a competitive system, with efficiency and range of choice, all parties benefit."

Enthusiasm Varies

Trade negotiations have never been conducted this way before, which is one of the two reasons that progress has been so slow. The other is that some of the participants, principally France and thus the European Common Market, are distinctly less enthusiastic about the idea than some others, principally the United States and almost everyone else, rich and poor.

The Kennedy Round is different because it is so all-inclusive.

Potentially, there may be 50 or more countries involved in the final deal, where previous multination negotiations have wound up with only a dozen or so.

The subject matter is also broad, covering potentially all trade restrictions, tariffs and nontariff obstacles alike, on the products of both factory and farm.

Acknowledging the bulk of the project and the endless impossibility of negotiating all the way through on an item-by-item basis, it was informally agreed by the major negotiators —Europe and the United States —that a set of broad rules should be written. The rules would then be applied and the negotiation would be done.

At least, this was the theory. It has not worked. Today, 20 months later, there are almost no rules.

But the failure to write rules has not meant failure for the negotiations. On the contrary, the talks are proceeding rather well—much better, in fact, than seemed likely in the dark days of last spring, when the rules business seemed impenetrable.

Instead of rules, there are some "hypotheses," and they are important.

First, there is an unwritten hypothesis that the negotiations shall go through. All parties agree that there should be a deal and that the whole pro-

cedure should not be abruptly cut off. This could change, but it is commonly accepted now.

Second, there is a so-called working hypothesis that there should be a 50 per cent cut in tariffs. This does not mean that 50 per cent will be the amount of the final cutting. It is, rather, the theoretical maximum. The final composite average will be less, probably substantially less, but still much more than any worldwide cut ever negotiated before.

Some Little Lists

On the basis of the 50 per cent hypothesis, the major negotiators have prepared exceptions lists—that is, lists of items whose tariffs they do not want to cut by 50 per cent. And it is on the basis of these lists that the Kennedy Round is about to begin again.

The first beginning was in the spring of 1963, when the major countries agreed to negotiate and made big, bold commitments. The second beginning was a year later, when they met again, acknowledged that they had not written the rules that had been promised, but swore to try again. The third was just two months ago, when they proceeded to tender their exceptions lists anyhow.

Now comes the fourth, later this month. Having presented their lists to each other—all rather short lists—they will start now to try bargaining each other down.

And then there is agriculture. The settlement of basic policy on grain prices inside the Common Market—Germany, France, Italy, Belgium, the Netherlands and Luxembourg—has at least and at last provided a specific basis for negotiations.

But these agricultural negotiations are still in the rule-making stage themselves. Previous experience with rule-making, for industrial goods, has led to no great expectations for farm goods.

And if the Kennedy Round turned out to be mostly a deal on industrial trade, there would be no great surprise in Geneva.

January 15, 1965

U.S. Denies Plan to Overlook Common Market in Tariff Talks

By EDWIN L. DALE Jr.

Special to The New York Times

WASHINGTON, Oct. 11 — The State Department said today that the United States had no thought of trying to conclude a tariff-cutting deal in the Kennedy round of trade negotiations without the European Common Market.

The formal statement of United States policy was prepared in response to a story from Paris in this morning's Washington Post. The story said that the United States had begun explorations with Britain and other countries of the possibility of proceeding in the Kennedy round without the Common Market.

Today's statement made clear that no such explorations had taken place, and also aimed at setting at rest informal speculation that such a plan might be a good idea.

"The United States Government," the statement said, "was neither issued instructions for, nor received reports of, any 'conversations' exploring the possibility of completing the Kennedy round without the European Economic Community. It is not considering such soundings.

Government Policy

"The policy of this Government is to work in as close a partnership with the European community as proves to be possible. To this end we are continuing the Kennedy round discussions in Geneva with the European Commission.

"We expect that the E. E. C. will resolve its internal difficulties and we anticipate that the European community will continue to play a key role in bringing the negotiations to a successful conclusion."

There are several reasons that the Government has not considered the idea of a tariff-cutting deal without the Common Market. Even though the Common Market has proved an extremely difficult negotiating partner.

One is that the major purpose of the Kennedy round in the first place, and the U.S. Trade Expansion Act of 1962 that led to it, was to knock down the tariff wall around the Common Market. The lower this wall, the less discrimination the European customs union imposes against outsiders. Thus the Common Market tariff is the key to the negotiations.

A second reason is that any deal without the Common Market would involve a major break with the principle that has governed world trading relations ever since World War II — the principle of "most favored nation." Under this principle a nation's tariff applies equally to imports from all sources. Any deal excluding the Common Market would involve a two-tier set of tariffs—higher for goods from community members and lower for everybody else.

In addition, the Government remains confident that the present internal crisis in the Common Market will be resolved some time after the French presidential election in December. At that point the community will presumably be in a position again to negotiate in Geneva, on both industrial and agricultural products.

October 12, 1965

New Common Market Accord Speeds Tariff Talks in Geneva

BRUSSELS, June 14 (Reuters)—The European Common Market's ruling Council of Ministers reached agreement here today on major industrial and farm issues, thus enabling the Kennedy round of tariff-cutting talks in Geneva to proceed.

The Geneva negotiations have been held up for the last year because of the lack of agreement among the six Common Market countries—France, West Germany, Italy, Belgium, the Netherlands and Luxembourg—and because of their seven-month internal crisis, which ended last January.

The negotiations must be concluded before July 1967 — the date President Johnson's authority to make 50 per cent tariff cuts expires.

The most important agreement today was one on world grain arrangements.

Plan Is Outlined

The Common Market now is expected to offer the following plan at the Geneva negotiations:

¶A world reference price for wheat to be fixed at a level equal to the present Canadian price, plus $2.50 to $3.50 a ton.

¶Support for grain production to be kept at their present levels in all major producer countries.

¶Self-sufficiency levels for grain production to be fixed for all producer countries. Any production above these levels would be considered as a surplus. In the case of the Common Market, this level would be equal to 90 per cent of total consumption, plus net commercial sales and an acceptable amount of stock.

Surplus production above this level would be sold at low prices or given away to developing countries in need of food aid, such as India.

Every producing country or economic unit would be responsible for financing its own donations to developing countries.

The Common Market's disposal of surpluses would be financed by the trade bloc's agricultural fund in accordance with a system to be worked out.

Observers said the 90 per cent self-sufficiency level for grains left the door open to imports from other countries such as Canada and the United States.

It was a compromise between France, the economic community's major grain-producer, which did not want production limited, and the main importing countries, such as West Germany and the Netherlands, which did not want Canadian and American grains shut out.

The council also agreed on a program of aid to the community's paper pulp industry over a period of 10 years.

It also decided that the United States tariff offer on chemical products was unsatisfactory and had to be substantially improved, if effective negotiations were to be held on this subject in Geneva.

The United States has offered to abolish its selling-price system, but to raise tariffs at the same time. According to the "six," this would mean that the United States protective barrier on imports of chemical products would be practically as high after the tariff cuts were made in the Kennedy round as at present.

The problem has been referred back to a Common Market committee, which will make suggestions how the American offer can be improved.

On aluminum, the Common Market's external tariff of 9 per cent would be maintained, but a community quota of 100,000 tons at a reduced tariff of 5 per cent would be opened each year for imports from nonmember countries.

On paper pulp, the Common Market's external tariff would be reduced from its present level of 6 per cent to 3 per cent, with the possibility of its complete suspension later.

On newsprint, the Common Market's external tariff of 7 per cent would be maintained but duty-free quotas of 420,000 tons a year would be opened by the community for imports from nonmember countries.

June 15, 1966

DUTY CUTS LISTED ON 6,000 PRODUCTS ENTERING THE U.S.

Consumers Expected to Pay Lower Prices Eventually on Some Imported Items

By EDWIN L. DALE Jr.
Special to The New York Times

WASHINGTON, June 29—The Government disclosed today tariff reductions ranging up to 50 per cent on about 6,000 imported products.

The listing came as President Johnson approved the final results of the Kennedy round of trade negotiations and authorized United States signature for the agreement tomorrow in Geneva.

The tariff reductions will take place in five annual steps, the first one on Jan. 1, 1968, and the last one on Jan. 1, 1972. Thus the effect will be gradual, but in the end it will be substantial for both consumers and industry.

Some Big Cuts

For consumers, to cite some examples, there are big duty cuts on such imported items as champagne, Scotch whisky, brandy, perfume, bone chinaware, sewing machines, television sets, record players, motorcycles, automobiles, yachts, binoculars, luggage, handbags, shotguns, wigs and cameras.

Most of the reductions will cut the present tariff in half. Where the present tariff is already low, as on automobiles, the effect on the price to the consumer will not be large. For example, on a $2,000 foreign car, the present duty is $125. This will be reduced to $60 by 1973.

Where the duty is relatively high, however, on such products as binoculars, lamps and perfume, the customer will probably eventually pay lower retail prices on imported items.

Taxes Noted

In the case of imported alcoholic beverages, the duty has far less effect on the price than domestic taxes — Federal, state and local. However, the duty reductions are still of some importance. For example, the tariff on Scotch whisky was reduced from $1.02 a gallon to 51 cents.

Among consumer products, the chief area where tariff reductions were relatively small or nonexistent was in wearing apparel. Only modest reductions were made in cotton, apparel items and in most types of footwear. No reductions at all were made for woolen goods.

The domestic wool textile industry is one of the relatively few cases of an industry that is already clearly suffering from import competition, from such countries as Japan, Britain and Italy. So woolens were put on the United States "exceptions list" in the Kennedy round. Other nations did the same thing for other items.

The American shoe industry also has complained of import competition. Thus the duty on men's leather shoes was reduced to only 8.5 per cent from 10 per cent. For cheap footwear, generally valued at not more than $2.50, the duty reduction was to 15 per cent from 20 per cent.

Today's announcement of tariff cuts came from William M. Roth, the President's Special Representative for Trade Negotiations. While the announcement itself gave few details for individual products, the new tariff schedules—covering all the approximately 6,000 items listed—were made available for inspection.

The announcement said that tomorrow's signing in Geneva by all the nations that took part in the Kennedy round "concludes the most comprehensive assault on barriers to international trade that has ever taken place."

Based on 1966 imports, the United States reduced duties on goods entering the country worth $7.5-billion to $8-billion. Foreign countries reduced their duties on products the United States exports to them in about the same amount.

About one-third of United States imports—items (such as coffee) that are not produced in this country—are duty-free. Thus the tariff cuts covered the bulk of the dutiable imports, though not all items were reduced by as much as 50 per cent.

Nontariff Barriers

The main elements of the Kennedy round agreement had been previously disclosed. Today's announcement elaborated on some of them.

For example, some details were disclosed concerning a new international antidumping agreement. This sets procedures for all nations to follow before they can apply special duties based on the allegation that an import is entering at "less than fair value."

Antidumping duties come in the category of "nontariff barriers" to trade. While the Kennedy round results in this area were modest, other accomplishments included a European agreement to reduce extra-high road taxes on heavy American-made automobiles, a modification by Switzerland in regulations on imported canned fruit and abolition by Canada of a restriction barring imports of fresh fruits and vegetables in three-quarter-bushel baskets.

The United States, in turn, promised to ask Congress to repeal this nation's chief nontariff trade barrier—a special system of customs valuation for some types of organic chemicals that has the practical effect of greatly increasing the tariff.

If Congress agrees and repeals this barrier, known as the American Selling Price, other major trading nations are committed to make further reductions in their tariffs on chemicals.

In the case of agriculture, reductions of tariffs and the numerous other barriers affecting trade in this sector were less significant in the Kennedy round than in the case of industrial products. However, today's announcement said, "The United States achieved a wide range of concessions from its principal negotiating partners which should improve export opportunities for such products as soybeans, tallow, tobacco, poultry and horticultural products, including citrus and canned fruit."

As previously disclosed, the Kennedy round included a new international grains agreement that would raise the minimum world trading price for wheat and would involve other developed countries besides the United States in the supply of food to poor countries. The lengthy trade negotiations at Geneva were given the name of "Kennedy round" because the Trade Expansion Act, which authorized America's participation, was passed in 1962 during the Kennedy Administration. The talks were sponsored by the General Agreement on Tariffs and Trade.

June 30, 1967

KENNEDY ROUND SUCCEEDS; 50 NATIONS TO CUT TARIFFS, LIBERALIZING WORLD TRADE

DUTIES DOWN 33%

Program of Food Aid for Hungry Lands Also Provided

By CLYDE H. FARNSWORTH
Special to The New York Times

GENEVA, May 15—The major trading nations reached agreement tonight in the Kennedy round of tariff negotiations, paving the way for the most ambitious attempt ever made to achieve the liberalization of international trade.

After more than four years of negotiations, nearly 50 countries, accounting for about 80 per cent of world trade, agreed to an average one-third cut in their tariffs, liberalization of trade in agriculture and a program of food aid for the hungry nations.

The agreement probably will lead to a sharp increase in world trade. It also could mean, over the five-year staging of the tariff cuts, somewhat lower prices for much imported merchandise.

An American who goes to buy a new Volkswagen five years from now will pay about $30 less for the car—assuming the dealer passes along the entire amount of the tariff cut. This is about 2 per cent of the retail price and could be offset by other factors, such as auto safety standards, that may drive prices up by then. The United States tariff on Volkswagens, under the Kennedy round terms, is to be cut in half by 1972—to 3¼ per cent from 6½ per cent.

$40-Billion of Trade

Trade in the products on which concessions have been agreed amounts to some $40-billion. This is about eight times more than the previous round of world tariff cutting negotiated in 1960-61.

The agreement was announced at midnight tonight at the Italian-style Villa le Bocage, overlooking Lake Geneva, which is the headquarters for the organization that supervises the General Agreement on Tariffs and Trade. The GATT organization acted as the host to the trade talks.

Negotiators, who only a few hours earlier had been haggling over the amount of traffic reductions in chemicals, tobacco and canned peaches, congratulated each other and the GATT director-general, Eric Wyndham White. His package of compromises, submitted this morning, served as the general framework for the agreement.

The precise terms of settlement were not known. According to the United States chief negotiator, William M. Roth, they will not be made known until President Johnson signs the agreement some time in June.

Tribute to Kennedy

The Kennedy round is so called because legislation authorizing American participation in the talks was passed by Congress in 1962, during the Administration of President Kennedy.

Mr. Wyndham White told newsmen tonight that the results are a "fitting memory to a great President who was lost to the world too soon."

Mr. Roth said the United States had given or received concessions on products involving $16-billion of American trade. The United States won concessions on agricultural products acounting for $2-billion of American exports of which $650-million was in grains.

Total American exports last year were $27-billion, and American imports were $19-billion.

Winning the agricultural concessions, mainly from Europe's Common Market, which was the great antagonist of the United States in the trade talks, had been one of the major difficulties throughout the long, drawn-out negotiations.

Though the Kennedy round should theoretically lead to lower prices—because it means the slashing of tariffs by the major trading nations—inflation in the United States and Western Europe may hide the effects. Also, there is a question of how much the middleman will pass on to consumers.

Weary Delegates Nap

Mr. Roth said he was finally convinced there would be agreement tonight at 9:25 P.M. when Jean Rey, the chief negotiator for the Common Market, telephoned to make an appointment with him at the Hotel Richemond. Both Mr. Roth and his second in command, W. Michael Blumenthal, were taking naps at the time after all-night negotiations yesterday and talks throughout most of the early part of the day.

It was at this appointment that Mr. Rey, a member of the Common Market's commission and the man considered likely to be the next commission president, said he accepted the Wyndham White compromise proposals with certain alterations that proved satisfactory to Mr. Roth.

After their talks a 650-word communiqué was drawn up. The whole Kennedy round had hinged on agreement by the two giants of international trade.

Mr. Roth estimated the size of the tariff cuts at 33 to 35 per cent. Mr. Rey said he guessed they were somewhere between 35 and 40 per cent.

The Common Market commissioner described the results in the industrial sector as excellent and those in agriculture as "more modest."

The precise date for the first tariff cuts to take effect has not yet been fixed. Most likely it will be either next Jan. 1 or July 1, 1968.

Farm and Chemical Issues

The major issues between the United States and the European Economic Community (as the Common Market calls itself) involved both the agricultural concessions the United States demanded from the community and the community's demands that the United States Congress get rid of the American Selling Price system of computing highly protective duties on chemical imports.

Neither side got all it wanted. The Americans won only modest concessions in agriculture, while the Common Market got no assurance that the A.S.P. system would be repealed.

The Common Market originally had conditioned all its tariff cuts in chemicals on repeal of the American Selling Price. This was totally unacceptable to the United States, which offered to cut most of its chemical tariffs by 50 per cent.

It is believed that the compromise worked out left the Common Market making three-fifths of its chemical tariff cuts of 50 per cent conditional on repeal of the A.S.P. system and two-fifths automatic.

The world food aid program, representing the biggest multilateral commitment yet undertaken to feed hungry nations, also presented problems to the very end of the negotiations.

The industrial countries agreed to set aside or buy in world markets annually four and one-half million tons of wheat or other grains worth about $350-million to give to the hungry nations.

The United States pressed for the program both to get other nations to share the food-aid burden and to remove grains from commercial markets so that American farmers could sell more.

The European nations and Japan objected at first to the idea, but then they slowly swung around. However, Japan held out until the last 24 hours of the negotiations, when she agreed in principle to participate but with certain conditions. The final sealing of Japanese participation in the program has been left for further negotiation.

Japan's contribution would be about 5 per cent. The United States would contribute 42 per cent; the Common Market's six members (France, West Germany, Italy, Belgium, the Netherlands and Luxembourg), 23 per cent; Britain 5 per cent; the four Nordic countries of Sweden, Norway, Denmark and Finland, about 3 per cent; Switzerland 0.7 per cent, and Argentina 0.5 per cent. The percentage contributions of other countries are not yet known.

The developing countries did not fare too well in the negotiations, though they certainly got more out of the Kennedy round than in any previous efforts to liberalize trade.

The communiqué issued tonight by Mr. Wyndham White

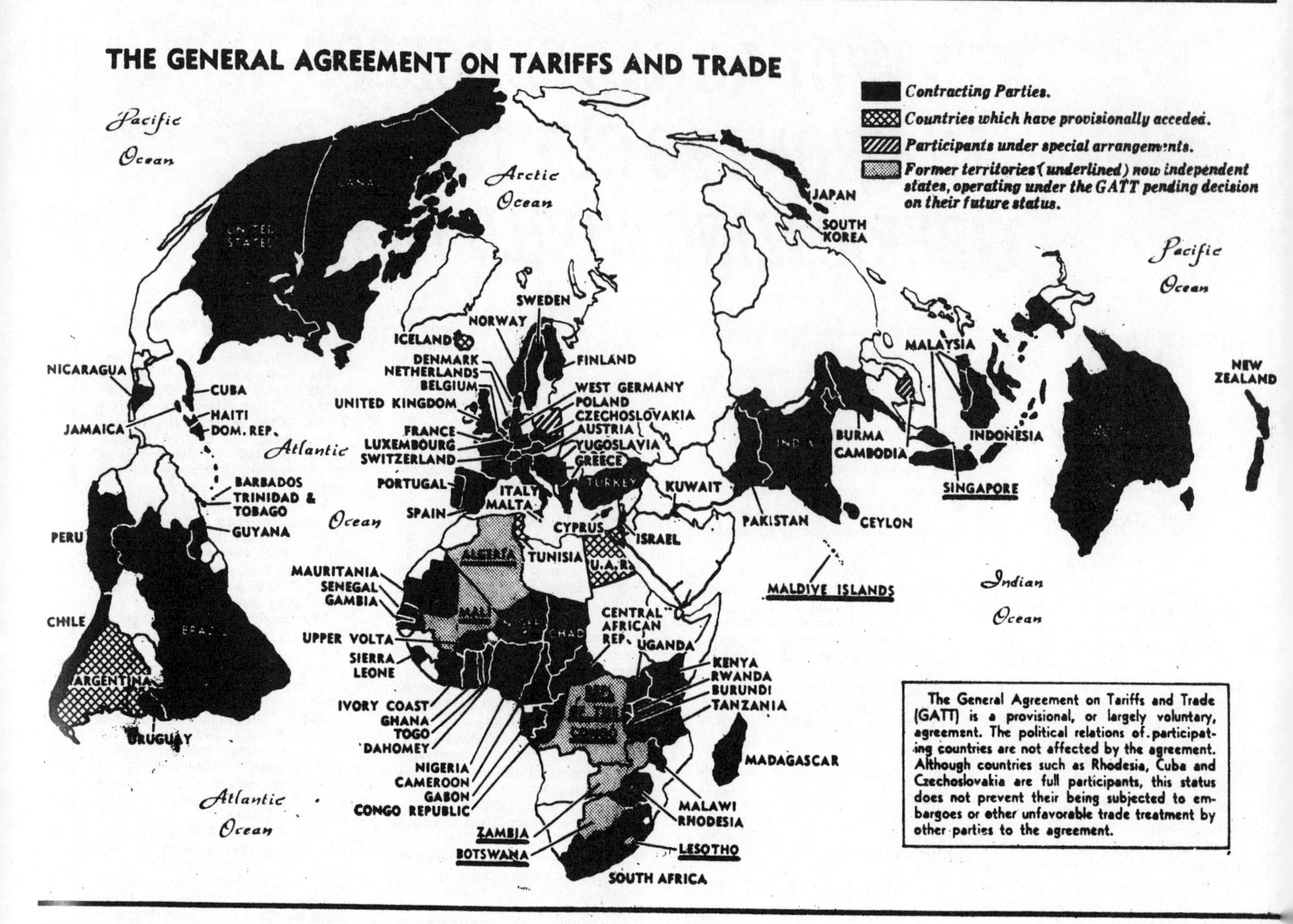

The General Agreement on Tariffs and Trade (GATT) is a provisional, or largely voluntary, agreement. The political relations of participating countries are not affected by the agreement. Although countries such as Rhodesia, Cuba and Czechoslovakia are full participants, this status does not prevent their being subjected to embargoes or other unfavorable trade treatment by other parties to the agreement.

SPANS THE WORLD: General Agreement on Tariffs and Trade encompasses 86 nations, but about 50 took part in Kennedy Round of tariff-cutting

May 16, 1967

said that for many tropical products it was "not possible to reach agreement at this stage on the elimination or reduction of tariffs because of the existence of preferential arrangements."

Former Colonies a Factor

This referred to the fact that the Common Market could not make concessions because it would disrupt the preference system worked out with former African colonies of Belgium and France.

The United States had conditioned offers it made in tropical products on action by the Common Market.

The communiqué said the developed countries had declared their willingness to try to improve access for other products exported by developing countries such as handicrafts and hand-loomed fabrics.

Tonight's agreement was one of principle in which many of the details remain to be worked out. The results have to be codified and embodied in legal instruments. This could take weeks.

But there is no doubt now that the agreement will be ready for signature by President Johnson before June 30, the expiration date of the special White House negotiating powers under the Trade Expansion Act of 1962.

Nuisance duties—tariffs of 5 per cent or less—have been lopped off by the United States during the Kennedy round on many products traded with Canada. To a large extent this makes the United States and Canada one big free trade area.

Drivers carrying loads of Portland cement between Windsor, Ont., and Detroit now have to stop at the border, fill in all sorts of customs forms and pay a duty of 3 per cent. When the Kennedy round takes effect, this duty will vanish.

The Kennedy round could also smooth the transition if Britain successfully negotiates entry into the Common Market. It also could make Britain's negotiating task easier. If she is unsuccessful, she would still have the greater access to the community's markets provided by the tariff cutting. It was for all these reasons that the British had been among the strongest supporters of the Kennedy round.

One major aim of President Kennedy had been to put solid economic foundation under the Atlantic alliance. The Administration feared that the formation of trading blocs in Europe would slow down trade growth with the United States and, in the long run, damage political relations.

Throughout the tremendously complicated negotiations, Washington badly wanted agreement because of these political considerations. At the same time, however, the American negotiators had to strike what they considered a fair commercial bargain.

The major confrontation came with the Common Market, negotiating as a powerful economic unit. It was a confrontation of equals. In international trade, in fact, the Common Market ranks even higher than the United States.

There were some doubts in the earlier stages of the negotiations whether the Common Market would even be able to participate.

Before negotiating agricultural concessions, the Common Market had to come up with its own farm rules. This brought on a serious crisis, resolved after the Germans agreed to finance the bulk of the community's farm program, provided the French supported the Kennedy round.

May 16, 1967

GATT WILL WEIGH EASING FOR TRADE

Refuses to Commit Itself to an Attack on Barriers

By VICTOR LUSINCHI
Special to The New York Times

GENEVA, Feb. 27—The International trading community refused today to commit itself to the launching of another major attack on barriers to the free flow of trade in 1971.

Instead, the 76 member nations of the General Agreement on Tariffs and Trade agreed to consider what "appropriate actions" might be taken in an effort to liberalize trade in agricultural and industrial products.

The shying away by major trading powers from a commitment to undertake what has been called a "second Kennedy round" of trade negotiations in 1971 is widely viewed as a setback for Olivier Long, the GATT director general.

The executive head of the world's leading trade organization had urged at the outset of its 26th general assembly that the member states undertake to complete the necessary preparatory work in time to get the next large-scale international negotiation in the lowering of trade barriers under way in 1971.

'Appropriate Actions'

But in their final statement at the end of their two-week session the GATT nations even avoided using the word "negotiation" because the European Economic Community in particular considered the term too strong.

The term "appropriate actions" was preferred because "negotiation" smacked too much of a major international confrontation like the one that was named after John F. Kennedy, the late President of the United States. Legislation he sponsored sparked the Kennedy round of tariff-cutting talks that were successfully concluded here in 1967.

GATT officials freely admitted that the session fell short of their "ideal."

They sought consolation in the phrase in the final statement that said the GATT nations agreed that the preliminary work should be completed in 1970 so that the next action to be taken could be considered at the next assembly.

This is expected to be held a year from now. It was unlikely, GATT officials said, that it could be scheduled earlier.

Mr. Long, a former Swiss diplomat, also failed to obtain the firm commitment he had hoped to see the GATT countries give not to introduce new trade barriers or intensify existing ones while the GATT preparatory work on action to further free trade is under way.

The Gatt countries did say that each of them "should refrain from aggravating the problems and obstacles to be dealt with." Such restraint, it was recognized, would help create a "favorable point of departure for future action."

GATT officials said these provisions in the final statement were "very important" even if they fell short of what Mr. Long had proposed.

Some GATT sources said that Mr. Long had asked for more than he expected to get in order to get more than he would have otherwise. But other sources held that the secretary general had overreached himself in a tactical move that failed.

Despite the uncertainty as to the next course of action, the GATT countries did reaffirm their "support for the maintenance of the multilateral trading system and their determination to move progressively toward the further reduction of trade barriers."

A major obstacle to the scheduling at this time of another large-scale international assault on trade barriers under GATT sponsorship is the negotiation that is soon to begin between, Britain and the six-nation European Economic Community, or Common Market.

Both Britain and the six disclosed at the GATT session their doubts over their ability to conduct this negotiation on Britain's proposed entry into the community and to participate concurrently in a major GATT trade conference. There is also some questioning of the wisdom of holding such a conference before it is clear to what extent the community, now composed of West Germany, France, Italy, Belgium, the Netherlands and Luxembourg, is to be expanded.

The United States does not believe that the Britain-Common Market negotiations should be allowed to delay the projected GATT attack on trade barriers. In fact, United States sources say it would even be preferable to obtain a general lowering of these barriers before the question of the community's expansion is settled.

The terms of an accord on the admission of the United Arab Republic to GATT were approved today, while this is considered to be tantamount to an acceptance of this country, the admission will not be formalized until after two-thirds, or 51, of the present member states have officially agreed.

Israel said it could not approve the accord with the U.A.R. because of this country's boycott of the Jewish state, its denial of free passage and its state trading practices.

Ray Defends E.E.C.

Special to The New York Times

BRUSSELS, Feb. 27 — The President of the European Executive Commission, Jean Rey, rejected today accusations that the Common Market is eroding international trade agreements by concluding preferential treaties with certain countries or areas.

He told a news conference at the Common Market's headquarters here that the accusations had "rather astonished" him since the volume of trade under these agreements does not exceed 10 per cent of the community's total trade.

February 28, 1970

16 Nations Offer to Speed Tariff Cut on U.S. Exports

Seek to Narrow American Payments Gap —Move Is Conditional on No New Import Bars by Washington

Special to The New York Times

GENEVA, May 1—Sixteen industrialized nations offered today to speed up tariff cuts on American exports to help ease United States balance of payments problems.

The offer was hailed by Eric Wyndham White, head of the General Agreement on Tariffs and Trade, to which the 16 nations belong, as an event of "historic importance." It marked, he said, a "spontaneous European reaction to try and assist the United States by taking positive action."

The 16 nations, the major trading partners of the United States, proposed to introduce next Jan. 1 a 22 per cent reduction in tariffs on American exports that are scheduled to come into effect a year later.

The GATT nations also noted "broad measures of agreement" to permit the United States to delay for a year tariff cuts it should introduce next Jan. 1.

Two conditions were implicit in the offer:

1. The United States must refrain from imposing "restrictions or surcharges on imports or a subsidy on exports."
2. A number of the 16 nations "attach special importance" to the repeal this year by the United States Congress of the American Selling Price system of evaluating the duty levied on some imports, primarily coal-tar chemicals.

Competitive Edge

Under the American Selling Price system, duties are levied on certain imports according to the wholesale price of the comparable American product rather than the lower price abroad, thus giving domestic prices a competitive edge.

The offer to advance tariff cuts was outlined in a two-page statement issued by Mr. Wyndham White after three weeks of consultations here among the representatives of the 16 nations. These nations are Canada, Japan, the members of the European Economic Community (France, West Germany, Italy, Belgium, the Netherlands and Luxembourg) and the members of the European Free Trade Association (Britain, Austria, Denmark, Norway, Sweden, Portugal, Switzerland and an associate member, Finland).

Set in Kennedy Round

The proposed tariff reductions are those scheduled under the so-called Kennedy round agreements, which were reached in 1967 after years of intensive negotiations among the GATT nations. The impetus for the negotiations was the 1962 Trade Expansion Act proposed by President Kennedy

If the tariff cuts go into effect early, they should ease the international payments deficit of the United States by stimulating several hundred million dollars in sales of American exports, swelling the flow of currencies to the United States. The payments deficit arises from the excess of dollars going abroad—primarily for imports, tourist trips and military operations—over those earned by American exports and visits by foreigners to the United States.

Mr. Wyndham White praised the readiness of Washington's trade partners to deal with the United States payments problems in a "constructive way that leaves unimpaired the high level of trade liberalization which we have reached."

He described the GATT proposal as a "modest counterpart to the good creditor policies" that the United States followed in the Marshall Plan and other aid to Europe after World War II.

He refrained in his statement from referring to any "conditions" to the offer. Instead, he said that the offer was based on "certain hypotheses."

If they were not fulfilled, he said, it would "call for reconsideration by governments of their decisions and policies and no doubt there would be further consultations."

A United States Government spokesman said that his nation appreciated the "constructive spirit" of the GATT offer.

The efforts it reflected, the spokesman said, "represent a noteworthy step toward trade cooperation and the recognition of the responsibility of all countries in dealing with balance of payments adjustments."

The terms of the proposal on tariff reductions were essentially those set by the E.E.C. nations. The E.F.T.A. nations had proposed that all the tariff cuts envisaged by the Kennedy round accord — those scheduled for 1971, in addition to 1970—go into effect next year.

May 2, 1968

New Frontier, European Style

THE AMERICAN CHALLENGE. By J.-J. Servan-Schreiber. Foreword by Arthur Schlesinger Jr. Translated by Ronald Steel from the French, "Le Défi Américain." 291 pp. New York: Atheneum. $6.95.

By DAVID CAUTE

WHEN "The American Challenge" was first published in Paris last year, it immediately became a best seller. In France no book since the war, fiction or nonfiction, has sold so many copies in its first three months. Nor was this phenomenal success confined to Mr. Servan-Schreiber's native France. Throughout Europe, and particularly in the countries of the Common Market, his book's dire warnings about the rapidly widening technological gap separating Europe from the United States were absorbed and quoted.

MR. CAUTE is Reader in Social and Political Theory at Brunel University, London. He is the author of "Communism and the French Intellectuals," "The Left in Europe" and of three novels, most recently "The Decline of the West."

What the author had done was to provide the new élites of the managerial society — politicians, journalists, civil servants, bankers, industrialists, professors, technicians — with an easily digestible manual combining statistical and technological evidence of Europe's relative economic decline with a simply presented program of political rescue. Perhaps it is this combination of qualities that leads Arthur Schlesinger Jr. to write in a brief foreword that, "If Europeans respond to his appeal by acting on this book as well as by reading it, 'The American Challenge' may do for European unity very much what Thomas Paine's 'Common Sense' did for American independence."

He, like de Gaulle, does not want France and Europe to succumb to American hegemony, to be by 1980 an economic backwater while the United States, Canada, Japan and Sweden move forward into the post-industrial age. There the similarity ends. Whereas de Gaulle has treated the U.S. as an aggressor to be kept at bay by means of diplomatic and economic barricades, Servan-Schreiber, on the contrary, welcomes American economic penetration of Europe as necessary and stimulating, and urges Europeans to take up the challenge by imitating American flair and flexibility.

To this end his book advocates: the creation of large European industrial units; an audacious approach in major penetrations of advanced technology in such areas as space exploration, supersonic flight, computer design and electronics; a closer integration of business, education and government; a revolution to revitalize the élites and produce more efficient systems of decision-making; and finally, at the political level, at least a measure of federal government in Europe.

Powerful European voices have been raised in support of Servan-Schreiber's thesis. Jean Monnet, architect, it is always said, of the European Economic Community and arch-technocrat and modernizer of postwar France, asserts that, "books like J.-J. Servan-Schreiber's ought to be taught in the schools." Gaston Defferre, the Mayor Daley (if you like) of Marseilles, calls "The American Challenge" "a cry of alarm that strikes us at the heart."

Photograph by Jack Nisberg. Courtesy Newsweek.
Jean-Jacques Servan-Schreiber.

This last remark reminds us that it was Servan-Schreiber's weekly magazine, L'Express, which early in 1965 ran an American-style campaign in favor of the presidential candidacy of "Monsieur X," who finally emerged in the grim form of the machine politician Defferre. This campaign was a measure of the great political and ideological distances that Servan-Schreiber had traveled since he supported Pierre Mendès-France in the mid-1950's. In those days L'Express provided a forum for leading intellectuals to express their opposition to the Anglo-French Suez expedition and the Algerian war. Drafted into the army, possibly as a reprisal, he emerged with a brilliant firsthand critique of the folly and brutality of France's last colonial war, "Lieutenant in Algeria."

But by the early 1960's, Servan-Schreiber had discarded old clothes for new. While his former hero Mendès-France moved further toward the left, Servan-Schreiber became, as Arthur Schlesinger Jr. calls him, "a European of the Kennedy generation." Old socialist dreams gave way to a hard-edged acceptance of the managerial society. To prove the point, Servan-Schreiber transformed both the content and format of his L'Express into the glossy guise of a French Newsweek. Vigorously trend-setting, he also became general director of a group publishing a monthly business magazine, L'Expansion.

Servan-Schreiber does indeed embody all the self-conscious modernmindedness of the Kennedy generation in America. The European politicians whom he most admires are Gaston Defferre and François Mitterand in France and Harold Wilson in Britain. Such leaders, Servan-Schreiber believes, combine the traditional attachment of the left to social justice and social mobility with an admirable grasp of modern economic and technological realities. Above all, they are not blighted by anti-Americanism. They appreciate—so his book's argument persuasively runs — that the old, fundamentalist suspicion of capitalist enterprise in all its forms condemns the European left to a sterile withdrawal from an active, decision-taking role in Europe's future.

Sensitive to the raw nerves of Europeans, he attempts to reassure patriots by arguing that "our only choice is whether we want to be a poor imitation of the United States, or seek our goals by following our own special genius."

But special genius looks like special pleading in a book that, in effect, says all along: copy the Americans. He attempts to placate left-wing critics by insisting that while expansion is the only basis for social justice, social justice is equally the condition for continuing growth. Yet there seems reason to doubt whether the United States stands today as a model to all the world of social justice. Servan-Schreiber has been compared to J. K. Galbraith. But did he ever read that economist's brilliant "The Affluent Society"?

So the events that have occurred in France during the last three months constitute a massive mockery of the attitudes and objectives for which Mr. Servan-Schreiber pleads in this book. He must have been equally as exasperated by the explosion of quasi-revolutionary, quasi-anarchist student violence which precipitated the French crisis, as by the solid vote of confidence in President de Gaulle and Premier Georges Pompidou by which the majority of the electorate expressed their reaction to it.

THE most conspicuous victims of

France's recent upheaval are precisely the modern-minded technocrats represented by Mitterand and Defferre. The students of the Sorbonne, despite their superficial physical defeat, have created a climate of thought and feeling that is likely to influence a large segment of the younger generation in Europe during the foreseeable future. This climate, with its emphasis on the existential, humanistic quality of revolt against oppression, brings the students closer to the fictional heroes of André Malraux than to the new-style managers, technocrats and educators who, with Servan-Schreiber, call for "systematic clarification of objectives, cost-effectiveness analysis," and who wish to "project competition into all decision-making areas."

No doubt much of what he says is good sense. No doubt many Europeans prefer to bury their heads in the sand rather than face up to the coming age of computers and integrated circuits. No doubt, too, the author feels justified in endlessly hammering home the same point. A pity, then, that Servan-Schreiber does not write with more subtlety and persuasion. Statistics are fine, but here they swamp the page; they swamp the brain; they strangle style; they give the impression that Servan-Schreiber is not so much an individual writer as a team of programed research assistants. Or is the belief that books should be written, not produced, merely one of the obsolete prejudices of an antiquated Europe?

July 28, 1969

FRANC IS DEVALUED TO 18C; BONN AND LONDON INTEND TO KEEP PRESENT PARITIES

ECONOMY IS AILING

Finance Minister Says the Government Had No Other Option

By CLYDE H. FARNSWORTH
Special to The New York Times

PARIS, Aug. 8—The Government decided today to reduce the value of the franc to 18.004 United States cents from 20.255 cents in an effort to bolster the ailing economy.

The action was taken this evening at a Cabinet meeting called by President Pompidou.

It followed some recent massive losses of French gold and dollar reserves. Finance Minister Valéry Giscard D'Estaing told a nationwide television audience tonight that the Government had no other realistic option.

The engineering of a recession to defend the currency would have been unacceptable, he explained. Without a devaluation, he added, the reserve coffers would have been empty by the end of the year.

Mr. Pompidou said he could not impose "unbearable sacrifices and massive unemployment" on the country.

Number in Dollar Off

The action increases the number of francs per dollar by 12.5 per cent, but the value of those francs — whether expressed in terms of dollars or in terms of gold—will decline by 11.1 per cent.

The West German Government welcomed the French action, calling it a vindication of Bonn's refusal to raise the value of the mark, and said the value would be maintained at 25 cents.

In London, British officials had no comment on the French move, but said the parity of the pound sterling would be maintained at $2.40, despite what financial experts saw as inevitable pressure.

The decision, which has important implications for France, the European Common Market and the free world's monetary system, came when most Frenchmen were on vacation.

Devaluation represents an attempt to improve a country's trade and over-all financial positions. A country's exports sell for less on foreign markets, becoming more competitive, and imports are more costly on domestic markets, generally encouraging citizens to buy domestic products.

Although long expected, the timing was a surprise. There had been no sudden bout of speculation. Currency markets were in their August doldrums.

Mr. Giscard d'Estaing disclosed that Mr. Pompidou had agreed to a devaluation on July 16. The Government held up taking the formal decision to take advantage of the August calm.

Devaluation means that Frenchmen will have to pay more for goods bought abroad, such as Italian refrigerators or British Cars.

Food costs will also rise, a result of Common Market agreements under which farm prices are pegged to the dollar. There is an increase in the guaranteed price to farmers, leading to higher prices for the consumer.

Foreign tourists who have long complained about the cost of Paris meals and hotel rooms will find their money goes farther in France. French tourists abroad will have to pay more to buy foreign currency.

The decision was taken less than nine months after President de Gaulle intervened to prevent a devaluation by what would have been nearly the same amount.

At that time there was feverish speculation, and at a Bonn monetary conference, French officials tried to bargain a small franc devaluation for an upward evaluation of the mark. The West German authorities refused to alter the mark's parity of 25 cents. French authorities then indicated they would devalue anyway, but General de Gaulle, who had earlier characterized devaluation as "the worst possible absurdity," was determined to hold the parity. The franc had become a symbol of French prestige.

Position Deteriorates

The new Government under Mr. Pompidou, faced with an ever-deteriorating financial position, was ruled by more practical considerations.

Although the French decision, which goes into effect on Monday, is expected to cause tremors on the currency markets, there was some hope that it would not lead to a rash of competitive devaluations.

Although monetary prospects remain uncertain, the French action was not expected to endanger the present relationship between the dollar and gold. For 35 years, gold has been worth $35 an ounce in officials transactions between governments.

A Paris monetary official said the rate of devaluation was within what was considered to be the "safe limit" that would have the least possible effects on other currencies.

There are, however, countries such as Denmark and Belgium that have suffered badly in recent rounds of speculation. They might be hard pressed to hold the parity line.

Some observers felt that the French action had reopened the question of the West German mark.

Because of its abilities to control inflation, West Germany has what many monetary specialists believe is an undervalued currency. Cited as evidence are its continued trade surpluses, amounting to $4,-billion a year.

The franc had long been a devaluation candidate. Now that the French Government has acted, the mark stands almost alone among major currencies as a problem, according to specialists here.

While causing monetary problems, the French action will be of benefit to thousands of tourists in France, who will enjoy cheaper vacations. For Frenchmen traveling abroad, however, it will be more expensive.

New Parity Set

The devaluation means that if a Frenchman wants to buy foreign currencies, it will cost him 12.5 per cent more. His francs, on the other hand, will be worth 11.1 per cent less.

It takes 4.93706 francs to buy a dollar now. The new rate will be 5.55419. The franc's new value is placed at 0.160 milligrams of gold, down from 0.180 milligrams, where it had stood since the last devaluation on Dec. 26, 1958. There have been eight French devaluations since World War II.

France did not consult beforehand with her Common Market partners or with Washington. Key European monetary officials heard about the decision only a matter of hours before the formal announcement was made.

Under rules of the Common Market, members are supposed to inform their partners beforehand of major monetary decisions. When the British Labor Government devalued the pound in November, 1967, key countries had been informed a few days earlier.

Mr. Giscard d'Estaing said the Government would consult with her Common Market partners and with countries of the franc zone over the weekend.

Most of the major industrial countries said tonight they would maintain their exchange rates. While the problem of the mark has now been isolated, there was some feeling that the British pound might be in for some hard days ahead.

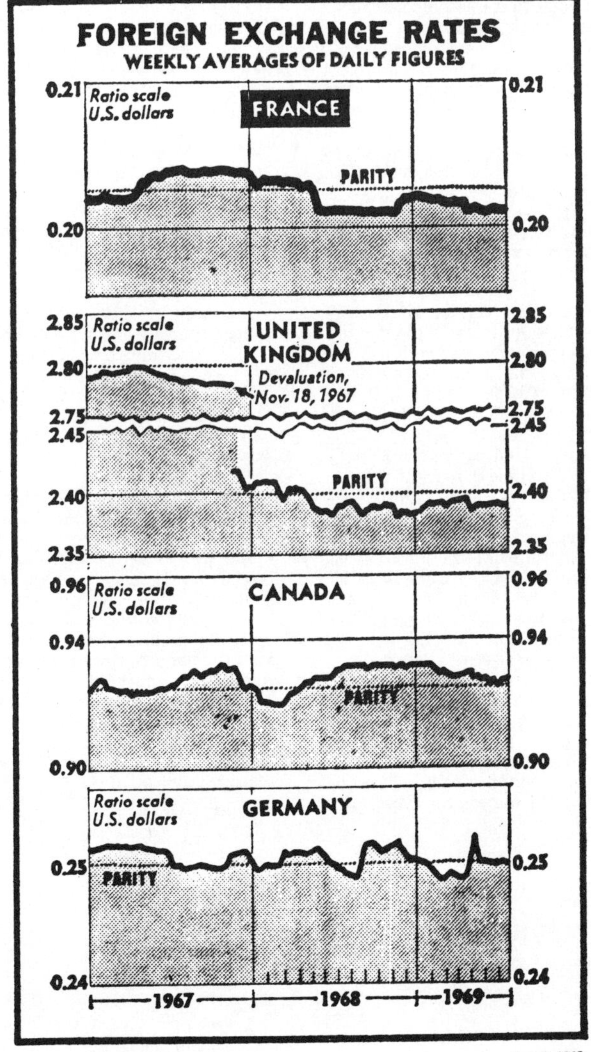

The British recovery effort has been slow since the 1967 devaluation.

A country lowers the value of its currency to improve its trade and over-all financial position. Imports become more expensive. Exports are cheaper or more profitable.

France has had financial troubles since national strikes last May and June resulted in wage levels rising sharply and the cost of living also increasing.

This, in turn, decreased France's international competitiveness. It led also to massive outflows of capital because many Frenchmen expected the events would lead inevitably to devaluation.

The cost of living has been rising in France at an annual rate of between 6 and 7 per cent. While exports in the first six months of 1969 rose 27 per cent, imports rose by 35 per cent.

The trade gap and outflows of capital led to reserve losses in the final six months of 1968 of $500-million a month and in the first half of this year of $300-million a month.

Before the May-June crisis, France had reserves of more than $7-billion. The latest offically reported reserves were $3.5-billion. Undisclosed are more than $1-billion of short-term borrowings from foreign central banks that represent a lien against these reserves.

Making the situation all the more serious was the high rate of French economic activity—overheating as economists say—which was bringing in imports at a faster than normal rate.

This was caused by a consumption boom, a result of an inflation psychology that led Frenchmen to buy now—everything from television sets to cars — rather than wait until priees climbed some more.

Mr. Pompidou had pledged that he would not lead France into a recession.

An economic decline might have slowed consumption and imports, but it would have almost certainly aggravated social problems.

Backdrop of Unrest

Against the backdrop of the worker-student unrest of May-June last year, this would have been politically dangerous for any new Government.

However, as Premier Jacques Chaban-Delmas and Mr. Giscard d'Estaing pointed out tonight, the devaluation will be accompanied by measures intended to cool off economic activity somewhat.

Foreign-exchange controls are to remain in effect. There will be further budget cuts. Credit restraint is to continue. Details of the program are to be announced in a few days.

Monetary specialists here said they expected one result of the devaluation would be to return much of the capital that had left the country earlier to France.

Another beneficial effect is expected to come in what trade experts term leads and lags. Anticipating a devaluation, many foreign companies were delaying purchases from France and trying to speed up sales and payments from France. These distortions affected the trade and balance-of-payments figures. With devaluation out of the way, the trading patterns should revert to normal.

Some Expected Step

Signs that some persons expected devaluation were seen not only in the flight of French capital abroad but also in discounts that had already appeared in franc quotations.

French bank notes, for example, had been traded in Switzerland for between 10 and 15 per cent under parity. Discounts on the franc of about the same proportions had also appeared in dollar securities quoted on the Paris Bourse and in the French gold market.

Mr. Giscard d'Estaing cited these discounts, saying it was necessary to restore the franc to its "real value."

The Finance Minister said that only eight persons knew of the devaluation decision that President Pompidou had taken on July 16.

Nevertheless, there had been some rumors of impending devaluation on the Paris Bourse. A sharp increase in the rate of capital outflow in the last week of July also pointed to the possibility that word might have leaked out.

August 9, 1969

BIG TRADE NATIONS FEAR RISING CURBS

2-Day Geneva Talks Fail to Stem Protectionism

By CLYDE H. FARNSWORTH
Special to The New York Times

GENEVA, Aug. 1—The major industrial nations sought today to prevent a tide of protectionism from engulfing world trade.

After two days of informal talks, delegates from the United States, the six-nation West European Common Market, Britain and Japan failed to come up with specific solutions to problems that have caused trade relations to deteriorate over the last few months.

But they undertook to study new approaches and hold off taking any hasty action that might get off protectionist chain reactions.

"We all decided to do some talking back home over the whole complex of problems that need attention and to continue the multilateral discussions," said one delegate privately.

Observers said these were probably the best results that could have been achieved after the relatively brief encounter.

Informants said the Nixon Administration gave assurances that the President would veto the proposed trade bill now in the House Ways and Means Committee if it restricted other imports besides textiles.

Shoes Also Included

The latest version of the bill forcing quota restraints on imports of shoes as well as textiles. In addition, it makes it easier for other domestic industries to seek increased protection.

Other trading nations have served notice that they will retaliate against American exports to the extent that their markets are reduced in the United States.

The trade bill provided a sense of urgency in the Geneva talks. In its present form, it would be the most protectionist piece of legislation in the United States since World War II.

The British delegation sought to take some of the heat out of the situation by reviving the idea of voluntary restraints on textile exports.

The Nixon Administration supported quotas on imports of textiles made from man-made fibers and wool after talks between the United States and Japan broke down over the issue of voluntary Japanese restraints.

If the Japanese could be induced to make new concessions, informants said, the Nixon Administration might tell Congress that there was no need to enforce quota restrictions.

Next Move Up to Japan

The only indication from Japanese sources was that they would continue their strong resistance against voluntary restraints, but observers pointed out that for the time being the ball had been bounced back to Tokyo.

While textiles are the most pressing problem, the American delegation insisted that the discussions be broadened to include points of contention between Washington and the European Economic Community.

A 13-line communiqué issued after the meeting mentioned agriculture and preferential agreements in addition to the trade bill and textiles as problems that were discussed.

Washington has long contended that the European trade bloc composed of France, West Germany, Italy, Belgium, the Netherlands and Luxembourg has been following protectionist policies in agriculture, resulting in reduced American farm sales to western Europe over the last three years.

The Common Market maintains that its policies were put into effect to ease social problems for its relatively large number of farmers, more than 15 per cent of the population compared with less than 5 per cent in the United States and Britain.

Americans also complain that preferential agreements between the Common Market and the countries of the Middle East and North Africa discriminates against American exports and violates principles of the General Agreement on Tariffs and Trade under which mutual tariff concessions are granted only under special circumstances.

It was the director general of the G.A.T.T. organization, Olivier Long, who called the meeting of the major trading nations today and yesterday.

The sessions were closed to reporters and no delegation issued any statements afterward. As one delegate put it, "the less said in public the better are the chances for success."

August 2, 1970

U.S. SUSPENDS CUT FOR PIANO TARIFF

Nixon's Action Opens Way for Industry to Obtain Adjustment Assistance

By EDWIN L. DALE Jr.
Special to The New York Times

WASHINGTON, Feb. 24 — President Nixon opened the way for the first time today for a United States industry to obtain "adjustment assistance" from the Government on the ground it was being injured by imports.

The industry is a small one, the piano industry. It did not ask for adjustment assistance but rather relief in the form of higher tariffs.

On the tariff side the President decided to give very little relief. He merely suspended for three years tariff reductions due for 1970, 1971 and 1972 that had been negotiated in the "Kennedy Round" of trade negotiations, thus holding the tariff at 13.5 per cent where it was at the end of 1968.

But the President did accept the finding of a 3-2 majority of the Tariff Commission that imports, almost entirely from Japan, were threatening the industry with serious injury. And thus he invited the industry to apply to the Commerce Department, and its workers to apply to the Labor Department for a still unspecified relief in the form adjustment assistance.

Various Forms of Aid

Under the Trade Expansion Act of 1962, which first provided for adjustment assistance, the help can take the form of loans or other financial assistance, technical aid and some forms of tax relief. But no one knows how it will work out in practice.

The industry itself will first have to decide whether to apply for help and in what form. It is supposed to draw up a plan that might, as one example, involve switching to production of some other musical instrument.

In a statement today the President said:

"The piano industry is one in which some firms are operating at reasonably good levels while others are experiencing difficulties. The case thus does not call for large scale tariff relief. It is the kind of case for which adjustment assistance was meant to apply: to help industries become more competitive through economic means, rather than by erection of a high tariff wall to prevent imports. The temporary suspension of tariff reductions will help provide time for industry to utilize effectively its adjustment assistance.

Could Ease Price Rises

"The combination of adjustment assistance and a suspension of the Kennedy Round tariff reductions should provide the means for relieving the severe impact of imports on the domestic industry and its workers, at the same time, it should avoid price increases for consumers during this period when we are attempting to deal with a general inflationary problem."

The workers are entitled to special unemployment benefits and retraining assistance.

Not only was today's ruling a "first" for adjustment assistance for an industry, but it was also the first time any President since the 1962 act was passed has been confronted with a case under the "escape clause" of the act. All previous appeals for relief had been turned down by the Tariff Commission, usually on the ground that the industry either could not prove injury from imports or that it could not prove the rise in imports was caused by past tariff reductions.

February 25, 1970

PRESIDENT WARNS HE WILL VETO BILL ON IMPORT QUOTAS

Says at News Conference That Legislation Should Apply Only to Textiles

By JAMES M. NAUGHTON
Special to The New York Times

WASHINGTON, July 20—President Nixon threatened today to veto trade legislation if it imposes mandatory quotas on any imports other than textiles.

At an impromptu news conference this afternoon in his office, the President told White House reporters that he could not sign a trade bill that has already won the approval of the House Ways and Means Committee.

In its present form, the bill would also impose quotas on imported shoes, would foreclose a shift from a quota system to tariffs on oil imports, and would ease the task of other industries in seeking relief through quotas or other import limitations.

Jokes With Reporters

Mr. Nixon, in effect filling in at the usual afternoon briefing for the White House press secretary, Ronald L. Ziegler, joked with reporters as he stood behind a spotless desk taking questions on a variety of foreign and domestic issues.

In nearly every instance, the President was conciliatory with his replies. He sought, for example, to reassure the South that new efforts to achieve desegregation of schools this fall would not involve "coercion" by Justice Department "vigilante squads," while asserting that it was in the South's interest to end its dual school systems.

Mr. Nixon also sought to soothe antiwar dissidents, maintaining that he, too, sought peace on the nation's campuses but that he could not afford to take the "easy and sometimes tempting road" of unilateral withdrawal simply to quell domestic unrest.

Warning to Congress

The President's harshest words were for the Democratic-controlled Congress. He reissued his warning that the voters would oppose the Congress if it continued to imperil a stable economy by appropriating more funds than his Administration has sought.

Reacting strongly to the Ways and Means Committee's decision to broaden the Administration's request for a quota only on textile imports, Mr. Nixon said that such a restrictive policy would mean the loss of more jobs than it would protect and would be "highly inflationary."

He said that if the bill that emerges from Congress went beyond his proposals, "I would not be able to sign the bill because that would set off a trade war."

The only announcement Mr. Nixon made at the news conference was that he would hold what he described as a "major" meeting on the 1972 budget when he goes to his Western White House in San Clemente, Calif., later this week.

The President said he was seeking a balanced budget in 1972, but that he could not promise one unless the economy improves and Congress shows some "restraint" on spending for the fiscal year 1971.

In response to a suggestion by Senator Mike Mansfield of Montana, the Senate majority leader, that budget deficits could be held to a minimum by cutting defense spending, the President said:

"I know it is fashionable to suggest that, as we face these increased spending programs in the domestic field that Congress seems intent upon enacting, that we can just take it out of defense. Well, there is very little left to take out of defense."

Most of the 35-minute news conference dealt with attempts by Mr. Nixon to clarify the Administration's position on controversies that have arisen in recent days.

The President said he was not surprised that one of his stanchest Southern supporters, Senator Strom Thurmond, Republican of South Carolina, had reacted angrily in a speech last week to reports that the Justice Department would send 100 lawyers into the South to assure the continued desegregation of public schools.

Mr. Nixon said the lawyers would not be "vigilante squad" forcing the compliance of the desegregation efforts. At the same time, he said he believed that "we finally get what the people in the South have wanted, a one-nation strategy" that treats Southern and Northern school systems alike.

On the issue of domestic dissent, the President noted that there had been testimony last week before the Presidential Commission on Campus Unrest that the quickest way to peace at home was to achieve peace in Vietnam.

"That of course is not news," Mr. Nixon said, expressing doubt that an end to the war would completely satisfy the young dissidents.

The President began the impromptu session by stating that it would be on the record, but that no tape recordings could be made. That way, he said, "no requests of equal time will be honored," a joking reference to Democratic party demands for equal time to answer his televised statements.

Later tonight, Mr. Nixon had another surprise. Without any advance notice, he left the White House to attend the baseball game at Robert F. Kennedy Stadium between the Washington Senators and the Milwaukee Brewers.

July 21, 1970

4,390 Economists Urge Nixon to Veto Trade Bill

Petition Assails Import-Restricting Plan Now Before House—Move Parallels Smoot-Hawley Protest of 1930

By EDWIN L. DALE Jr.
Special to The New York Times

WASHINGTON, Sept. 18 — A group of 4,390 economists urged President Nixon today to veto the import-limiting trade bill if it reaches him in the version now pending before the House.

The statement supported by the economists had a parallel 40 years ago — a petition by more than 1,000 economists to Herbert Hoover to veto the Smoot-Hawley tariff bill, which sharply raised tariffs. President Hoover signed the bill and, partly because of the resulting higher tariffs, United States and world trade declined sharply during the nineteen-thirties.

Although an exact check has not been made, about 15 of the 1930 signers also signed today's statement, including former Senator Paul H. Douglas, Democrat of Illinois. Most of the original signers are dead.

At a news conference this morning, Mr. Douglas said the bill now in the House was worse than the Smoot-Hawley measure. The present legislation calls for quotas that definitely limit imports; the earlier legislation set high tariffs that allowed imports at a steep price.

A spokesman for the National Commission on Trade Policy, which sponsored the news conference, said the bill would probably pass the House if it goes to the floor under a rule that forbids amendments. It is expected to be voted out of the Rules Committee Tuesday.

In the Senate today, Senator Ernest F. Hollings, Democrat of South Carolina, introduced the trade bill as an amendment to the Administration's family assistance plan and the Social Security bill. But its fate in the Senate is up in the air since that body has few rules about amendments.

Also listed as sponsors of to-

New York Times.

Copyright, 1930, by The New York Times Company.

NEW YORK, MONDAY, MAY 5, 1930.

1,028 Economists Ask Hoover To Veto Pending Tariff Bill

Professors in 179 Colleges and Other Leaders Assail Rise in Rates as Harmful to Country and Sure to Bring Reprisals.

Special to The New York Times.

WASHINGTON, May 4.—Vigorous opposition to passage of the Hawley-Smoot tariff bill is voiced by 1,028 economists, members of the American Economic Association, in a statement presented to President Hoover, Senator Smoot and Representative Hawley by Dr. Claire Wilcox, associate professor of economics at Swarthmore College, and made public here today. They urge the President to veto the measure if Congress passes it.

Economists from forty-six States and 179 colleges, among them Irving Fisher of Yale, Frank W. Taussig of Harvard, Frank A. Fetter of Princeton, Wesley C. Mitchell of Columbia, J. Laurence Laughlin of the University of Chicago and Willford I. King of New York University join in the statement.

Arguing against increased tariff rates they declare that the pending ... of high tariff proponents that higher rates will give work to the idle. Employment, they state, cannot be increased by restricting trade, and American industry, in "the present crisis, might be spared the burden of adjusting itself to higher schedules of duties."

They urge the administration to give regard to that "bitterness which a policy of higher tariffs would inevitably inject into our international relations."

The text of the statement is:

"The undersigned American economists and teachers of economics strongly urge that any measure which provides for a general upward revision of tariff rates be denied passage by Congress, or if passed, be vetoed by the President.

"We are convinced that increased restrictive duties would be a mistake.

ROOSEVELT SUBMITS LONG-RANGE PLAN TO AID EMPLOYMENT

Governor, in a Letter to Local Executives, Advises Preparing for Fall and Winter.

"CORNER NOT YET TURNED"

He Offers a Five-Point Program for Fact-Finding and Joint Stimulation of Industry.

BUILDING GAIN SEEN HERE

Merchants' Survey Finds That It Is Reflected in Improvement in the Metals Trades.

PARALLELS: This article from The New York Times of May 5, 1930, told how leading economists had urged President Hoover to veto the Smoot-Hawley tariff bill, which sharply increased tariff rates. Mr. Hoover rejected their advice. Yesterday, more than 4,000 economists urged President Nixon to oppose a new trade bill, which limits imports.

day's statement were four former chairmen of the President's Council of Economic Advisers, under both Republican and Democratic Administrations. One original sponsor, Jacob Viner, of Princeton University, was, like Senator Douglas, a signer in 1930, but he died last week before the new statement was published.

The present trade bill is not the same as the Smoot-Hawley measure, though both have import-limiting provisions. The Smoot-Hawley tariff, following the tradition of more than a century, actually fixed the tariff on thousands of products, mainly at a higher level than before.

The bill approved this year by the House Ways and Means Committee directly affects only five items. Chief among them are shoes, textiles and oil. But the bill contains provisions under which it would become easier for other industries to obtain relief from imports through a process of petition to the Tariff Commission, though the President would have the ultimate power of decision

Caution Expressed

The bill does not, in the main, return to the practice, finally abandoned in 1934, of Congressional tariff-setting. But it is still opposed vigorously by the free-trade forces, though it has strong support from a number of industries and partial support from organized labor.

Today's statement was organized by the Committee for a National Trade Policy, the oldest of the organizations supporting freer trade. Its chairman is Charles P. Taft.

The statement said, "We now seem on the threshold of another massive mistake, which would seriously damage the trade agreements system that, since 1934, has replaced the anarchy of the nineteen-twenties and early thirties."

It continued: "Import controls would be an unproductive and irresponsible answer to the problems and needs of industries and workers seeking Government help against foreign competition. There are serious adjustment problems at home and considerable cause for irritation at the treatment accorded to our exports abroad. But the right answer does not lie in triggering a trade war. That would only make a bad situation worse.

"We therefore urge Congress to reject import controls—direct or indirect, explicit or implicit. The bill reported out by the House Ways and Means Committee provides for and encourages such controls. If such a bill is passed by Congress, we urge the President to veto it."

The former chairmen of the Council of Economic Advisers who sponsored the statement were Gardner Ackley, Walter W. Heller, Leon H. Keyserling and Raymond J. Saulnier.

John W. Hight, executive director of the Committee for a National Trade Policy, said "fewer than 10" of the 10,000 economists to whom the statement was sent specifically opposed it. More than 4,000 have endorsed it. The rest did not reply.

September 19, 1970

O.E.C.D. PROPOSES LIBERAL TRADE

Sees Easier Policy as Way of Combating Inflation

PARIS, Nov. 16—An international organization's tough proposals to restrain global inflation, including a suggestion that full employment be demoted as a policy priority, drew a lukewarm reaction today from major industrial nations.

The controversial and as yet unpublished report of the Organization for Economic Cooperation and Development was the subject of a ministerial meeting of the member nations as they continued their efforts to devise a concerted approach to the inflation menace.

The O.E.C.D.'s report advocated more liberal trading policies, including acceleration of the Kennedy round tariff cuts, elimination of government procurement policies that give preference to domestic suppliers, and stronger direct government action on the wages-and-price front among its other recommendations.

"Giving a higher priority to price stability," it said in a key passage, "means giving lower priority to something else. Over the long run, this need not be necessarily economic growth and employment, although in a number of countries this may temporarily have to be the case."

The report went on: "Until a better price performance has been achieved, it may be necessary to being about or maintain a larger margin of unused resources than has been regarded as normal or acceptable in the past."

In another key passage the report, drawn up by the O.E.C.D.'s economic staff in Paris, said that in the short term "recourse to some form of price or wage controls may be justified in the framework of a suitable over-all program to deal with an acute inflation."

Wage and price controls have been rejected by the administrations of the United States and Britain. Price controls already exist in Scandinavia.

November 17, 1970

NIXON PROPOSES FUND-FLOW STUDY

Examination of Short-Term Movements of Capital in Leading Nations Asked

By EDWIN L. DALE Jr.
Special to The New York Times

WASHINGTON, Feb. 25 — President Nixon proposed today an "intensive examination" by the leading industrial countries of massive movements of short-term capital funds from one country to another.

In his State of the World Message to Congress, the President also labeled last year's House-passed trade bill "protectionist" and reaffirmed that, "This Administration is committed to the principles of free trade" as "indispensable to our domestic economic health and a successful U. S. foreign policy."

In the monetary section of the message the President noted that 1970 "was one of the most tranquil years for the international monetary system in a decade."

But he said the events of the last few years had raised the problem of how to "handle large-scale shifts of liquid capital without exchanges crises or losses in the ability of individual nations to pursue their own monetary policies."

He continued: "It has become clear that very large amounts of money can be attracted to any major country whose money and credit markets are tighter than the comparable markets in the rest of the world. We need an intensive examination to determine whether there is a need to reinforce the present techniques and procedures of international monetary cooperation to enable us better to cope with such movements."

Support Reaffirmed

The President also reaffirmed his support for "orderly exchange-rate adjustments" as an important means of reducing balance-of-payments surpluses and deficits and avoiding monetary crises.

"We welcome continued work in this area by the International Monetary Fund and other bodies, with particular attention to the possible need for amendments to the I.M.F. articles of agreement to achieve the needed evolutionary improvements in the present system," he added.

In the trade section the President emphasized that "other countries can no longer proceed on the facile assumption that, no matter what policies they pursue, liberal trade policies in the United States can be taken for granted."

He pointed in particular to the policies of the European Common Market and Japan and said, "We and other countries shall all move toward freer trade together or we shall all retreat to protectionism together."

The E.E.C. is made up of Belgium, France, Italy, Luxembourg, the Netherlands and West Germany.

The President noted that he had approved increasing use of the technique of "adjustment assistance" for United States companies and workers injured by imports and added, "We have therefore demonstrated that there are several viable alternatives to legislated import restrictions, and that we can and will use them effectively."

February 26, 1971

Nixon Sees Strong Rivalry From 4 Other 'Economic Superpowers'

By JOHN HERBERS
Special to The New York Times

KANSAS CITY, Mo., July 6 —President Nixon said today the United States would face severe economic competition from the Soviet Union, China, Western Europe and Japan in the next few years and needed to institute internal reforms to meet the challenge.

"We now face a situation where the four other powers have the ability to challenge us on every front," he said, "and this brings us back home for a hard look at what we have to do."

The President said that the United States must concentrate on building a nation that was "healthy" in its environment, in its economy and in the moral and physical strength of its people.

Mr. Nixon spoke to a group of about 130 newspaper and broadcast editors from 11 middle Western states in one of a series of such meetings Administration officials have held around the country to explain and promote the Nixon programs.

On Way to Coast

He stopped here on his way from Washington to the summer White House in San Clemente, Calif., where he will spend about two weeks working on the budget and conferring with aides on foreign affairs.

The meeting here was billed as an explanation of the Administration's domestic policies, but Mr. Nixon said that national and foreign policies were so intertwined that they could not be separated.

At one point he said that the United States was reaching the period of "decadence" that brought down Greece and Rome, but in the next breath he said that he believed the United States had the strength and courage to meet all challenges.

He said he was reminded of this when he viewed the National Archives Building in Washington.

"Sometimes when I see those columns I think of seeing them in Greece and in Rome," he said. "And I think of what happened to Greece and Rome, and you see only what is left of great civilizations of the past—as they became wealthy, as they lost their will to live, to improve, they became subject to the decadence that destroys the civilization."

"The United States is reaching that period," he said.

Then, however, he warned against creating a "sense of defeatism" by stressing the nation's divisions and alienations and the belief that "this is an ugly country." He said that he believed the country had the basic spiritual and moral strength to continue as a great world leader.

"I honestly believe that the United States has in its hands the future of the world for the next 25 years," he said.

That was the ending of his speech. Most of it pertained to the rise of economic powers in the world and the challenge they presented to America.

While the United States has been preoccupied with Vietnam, some profound changes have taken place in the world, and change will be even faster in the future, the President declared.

He said that there were five "great economic superpowers" that would "determine the economic future and, because economic power will be the key to other kinds of power, the future of the world in other ways in the last third of this century."

Mr. Nixon spoke of the rapid development of the four outside the United States. He said that relations with the Soviet Union had moved from confrontation to negotiation in his Administration, that he had moved to end the isolation of China because that country had become "creative and productive," and that Japan and Western Europe were increasingly providing tough, if friendly, competition.

Thus, the United States "has a challenge such as we did not even dream of," he declared.

From this, he concluded that the first step to effective world competition was to have a healthy and strong country; and that the way to do this was to follow the Nixon domestic policies, return to "moral and spiritual strengths," and preserve free enterprise.

On domestic policies, he said that sharing Federal Revenues with state and local governments would strengthen local political leadership and that the support being given to law enforcement officials meant "the era of permissiveness in law enforcement has come to an end."

Assails Price Controls

He delivered a strong statement against wage and price controls, saying that such steps were alien to the American system of free enterprise.

The President viewed the problem of drugs as essentially a spiritual one.

"When society comes to a point where there is negativism and defeatism and a sense of alienation, it is inevitable that younger people will give up and turn to drugs and other kinds of acts that are destructive of society," he said.

Mr. Nixon repeatedly stressed the need for "moral health."

"I don't want to sound here like a moralist or a preacher although I have great respect for preachers and moralists," he said. "This nation needs moral health."

The President was greeted here by a crowd of several hundred people that filled the streets around the downtown Holiday Inn, where the meeting was held.

Before leaving Kansas City Mr. Nixon telephoned former President Harry S. Truman at his home in Independence, wished him well and inquired about the health of Mrs. Truman, who was reported in the hospital for a check-up.

United Press International

President Nixon shaking hands with members of band that welcomed him in Kansas City

July 6, 1971

Trading Partners of U.S. Hurt by Import Surcharge

Survey Finds Nixon Economic Program, Including Decision to Float Dollar, Stirring Resentment Abroad

By BRENDAN JONES

Most of the United States' main trading partners have been hurt in some degree by the international measures—primarily the 10 per cent surcharge on imports—included in President Nixon's economic program.

The surcharge, combined with the decision to let the dollar float downward in exchange markets while other currencies are pressured upward, has also caused considerable resentment abroad at what is regarded as a one-sided American action.

Although in some countries, notably West Germany, there is a feeling that the surcharge may not be as damaging as first feared, in many there is worry that its effects could severely check business and perhaps contribute to recession.

Trade War Feared

There is fear, too, that the American surcharge and general currency-value uncertainties could be the spark that might set off cut-throat competition among nations grimly determined to maintain trade in any and all markets, especially the United States.

These are some of the highlights of a 15-country survey just completed by New York Times correspondents on the effects of the American economic policies on international trade. The countries covered accounted for more than 75 per cent of the $40-billion of United States imports in 1970.

The survey showed that, slightly less than a month after the Administration's surcharge and monetary actions, most countries have not yet been able to calculate the full effects of the measures on their trade.

It was evident in the survey, however, that the surcharge particularly—as designed and expected—is having upsetting worldwide repercussions.

Surcharge Assessed

In a number of countries—Canada, Mexico, Italy, Japan and West Germany—it was found that the main adverse effects of the surcharge are being felt by small and medium-sized industries.

These are mainly concerns producing sundry goods—footwear and light manufactures—or specialized products such as optical or surgical instruments.

One West German executive of a small surgical instrument manufacturer said that the American surcharge, together with the higher floating value of the mark, "will strangle us to death."

A Brazilian official remarked that "it is now a case of push or be pushed" for countries scrambling for trade as a consequence of the surcharge-monetary turmoil. A British manufacturer termed the surcharge "a bloody nuisance."

So far, the reports indicated there has not yet been any widespread wave of unemployment caused by the surcharge. But there have been some layoffs in Japan and cutbacks in working hours in West Germany that might be the start of a trend.

1970 Exports to U.S. from Countries Surveyed

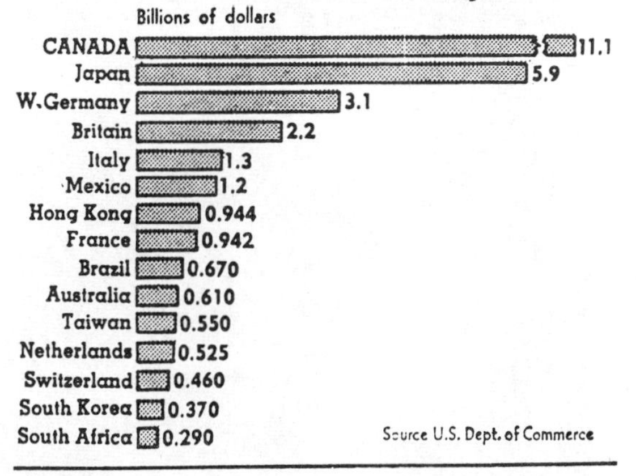

The New York Times Sept. 13, 1971

Swiss Affected

In Switzerland, watch imports have been hard hit by the surcharge and there is unemployment in the industry for the first time in years.

In Britain and other West European countries—and Canada—the proposed American 10 per cent investment tax credit on new industrial equipment is regarded—in addition to the surcharge—as the most disturbing new trade barrier.

The credit would not apply to imported equipment and would thus be a discriminatory measure against which other countries might retaliate.

Ironically, The Times survey also indicated that the surcharge seems to be having more adverse effect on imports from Western Europe, where the United States enjoys a trade surplus, than on Far Eastern countries whose competitive exports the levy was largely designed to check.

There is evidence also that the surcharge is having a kind of chain reaction on trade between other countries.

Australia, for example, is a major supplier of raw materials to Japan. But Australians, although not directly feeling the surcharge too much, see Japan's loss of exports as a loss for them, notably in such exports as wool.

Importers Protest

The United States surcharge—a full 10 per cent addition on top of regular ad valorem duties for most dutiable imports—became effective Aug. 16. The sudden impact, especially on goods tied up by the West Coast dock strike or already in bonded warehouses, brought vigorous protests from importers.

As a result of these, a measure of relief was granted on Sept. 1, which exempted goods in transit before Aug. 15 as well as those strikebound or in bond if they are cleared by Customs before Oct. 1.

The surcharge does not apply to duty-free imports such as green coffee, iron ore or newsprint, nor to those under import quotas such a crude oil, cotton textiles and beef.

However, roughly 60 per cent, or $24-billion to $25-billion, of American imports are subject to the surcharge. This amount represents about 8 per cent of total world exports by other than Communist countries.

In many of the countries surveyed there is appreciation that the American trade measures are designed to spur needed realignment of major world currencies.

But in developing countries, especially, it is asked why solution of this problem, primarily one for the developed countries, should entail harm to their exports.

Resentment against the American action in many cases is combined with a determination "to beat the surcharge," to compete more vigorously.

But there is sentiment also that the sooner the surcharge is ended and monetary stability attained, the better off all countries will be.

Following are some of the main points in the survey reports:

CANADA

OTTAWA — Precisely how much the American surcharge will hurt Canadian exports is unclear, but there are unmistakable grounds for concern, particularly for the effects on comparatively new manufacturing industries and on employment.

Although Canada is the United States' chief trading partner and source of a fourth of American imports, there might seem to be little cause for Canadian worry about the surcharge.

The import levy does not apply to three-fourths of Canadian exports to the United States. The bulk of these enter duty-free or under quotas.

Autos Also Exempt

Also exempt are autos, which cross the border duty free under the 1965 Canadian-American auto trade pact. And if repeal of the American 7 per cent auto excise does switch buyers to North American makes, Canada's auto plants are likely to share in the increased production.

Some $2.5-billion of Canadian exports, however, are subject to the surcharge. A good part of these are the products of industrial plants concentrated in Ontario and Quebec. Development of this so-called secondary industry has been a major Canadian policy aim.

These industries have borne the brunt of the 1970 business recession and also the adverse trade effects of an upward floating Canadian dollar. They will be hurt most by the new American import levy. Thus, there is an added worrisome aspect for Canadians in that 85 per cent of their finished manufactures go to the United States.

Some Ottawa economsts have advised "adjustment," letting barely profitable manufacturers go under. The Government, however, a year or less away from an election, has just announced an $80-million employment support fund—in effect, a subsidy—for exporters hit hard by the surcharge.

As for employment effects, Ottawa fears that the surcharge will nip in the bud the long-awaited decline in the national employment rate, which in July was 6.3 per cent.

Particularly worrisome is that unemployment will be aggravated in Quebec, where it has been chronically higher (8.6 per cent in July) and where it contributes to the social unrest that fuels the separatist movement.

JAPAN

TOKYO — The heaviest blow of the surcharge will be sustained by Japan's small and medium-sized enterprises that turn out sundry goods. The surcharge also has raised a formidable barrier to textile exports.

Larger, highly-efficient industries—autos, steel and cameras—are optimistic, however, that their competitive power will make it possible for them to absorb the impact of the surcharge in a short time.

But the immediate prospect is that the combination of the surcharge and the higher exchange rate of the yen will sharply reduce total Japanese exports by about 12 per cent of last year's $19.4-billion total.

The Ministry of International Trade and Industry estimates that exports to the United States will decrease on an annual basis by $1.67-billion. A decline of $710 million in exports to other countries is expected to result from the side-effects of the surcharge and currency revaluations.

For sundry-goods producers, which have shipped about half of their annual $2-billion of exports to the United States, the surcharge and yen revaluation are expected to cut sales by as much as 50 per cent.

Japan's auto industry, however, is hopeful that it will be able to attain about 90 per cent of the 600,000-unit export set for this year.

The steel industry is confident that it can absorb the surcharge on its own exports, but it is worried about the indirect impact of the levy on the domestic industries which are impartant steel users.

So far, the major action move affecting employment has been the announcement by Mitsubishi Metal Mining, Japan's largest copper refiner, of a 10 per cent reduction in its 1,000-worker forme. The Labor Ministr yaaid that 50 enterprises have suspended their plans for hiring fresh graduates of high schools next spring.

WEST GERMANY

BONN — West German businessmen still show restraint in making precise statements about the repercusions of the American surcharge. There appears to be growing sentiment that they will be less harsh than originally feared, that sales will dip but not slump.

Over-all, the prospect is that the expected sales dip will tend to accentuate the present domestic trend toward shrinking business, if not a recession.

After two years of hectic busines boom, with swiftly rising prices and wages, domestic demand has been falling off noticeably in the past few months.

Thus, the most-heard forecast here is that dwindling sales in the United States will cause lay-offs and short-hour work in at least some major industries.

According to the Federation of German Industries in Cologne, about 90 per cent of West Germany's sales in the United States will be affected by the surcharge.

Autos, the most important item, however, are expected to escape some of the brunt of the import levy with prospective repeal of the American auto excise tax.

By far the hardest hit German industry are the makers of surgical instrument, mostly small family enterprises in Baden-Wurttemberg.

Of 280 such small and medium-sized companies, more

than 200 sell at least 80 per cent of output to the United States and some produce only for American customers.

BRITAIN

LONDON—No exact estimates have yet been made on the impact of the American surcharge on British exports, but it is widely assumed that it will cut profits if nothing else.

The United States is Britain's main export market, accounting for $2.2-billion of sales last year, or about 12 per cent of total exports.

About 40 per cent of the exports to the United States are machinery and transportation equipment, chiefly autos, while 25 per cent is manufactured goods.

The greatest impact of the surcharge thus is seen in the machinery and auto industries. In addition to the surcharge, the proposed American 10 per cent investment tax credit that will apply only to domestically-produced capital goods will result in a marked competitive disadvantage for foreign-made equipment.

While some auto makers are hopeful about holding markets for sports cars, others expect to feel some pinch in sales because of the surcharge.

British complaints about the American import levy have been inhibited by the fact that Britain itself resorted to a surcharge in 1964-66 as a means of correcting a payments deficit.

"More monetary sense was less trade nonsense" has become an official slogan among members of the Confederation of British Industry, which is roughly equivalent to the American National Association of Manufacturers.

The comment reflects the bitterness of many manufacturers here that the American surcharge is being used as a lever to bring about monetary and currency realignments.

"It's all just intended to make Japan see some sense, isn't it?" a chemical producer asserted. "In the meantime, we all have to suffer."

In contrast to the announced plant closings, layoffs and predictions of falling business in Italy, West Germany and Japan, British manufacturers have been quiet. Detailed studies await the resumption of full-scale business activity this month after the vacation period.

United Press International

In Japan, auto, steel and camera industry should have enough competitive strength to overcome the surcharge. But many small firms face a 30 to 50 per cent loss of exports.

ITALY

ROME—No reliable estimate is available on how the surcharge and other factors will affect Italian imports.

The American market, however, is Italy's third largest export outlet, after West Germany and France, and there is general worry over the effects on the major items of this

Fiat assembly line in Turin. Italian motors, footwear and textiles are the goods most affected by the import tax.

trade — footwear, textiles and autos.

Although Italian Government officials recently have exhorted industry to look for alternative markets, there is considerable fear that there will be cut-throat competition with other nations equally affected by the American protectionist moves, such as West Germany and Japan.

From Piedmont to Florence, entire plants, sometimes entire towns, depend on the American market. This is particularly true of the footwear industry, which is based on hundreds of small and medium-sized factories in and near such centers as Varese, Bologna and Florence.

Last year, Italy exported 80-million pairs of shoes (including sandals) to the United States, two-fifths of its entire footwear sales abroad.

Elio Camagna, president of the Italian Footwear Manufacturers Association, said, "The United States measures make it almost impossible to hold the positions that our industry has conquered. The consequences will be very grave."

MEXICO

MEXICO CITY—Because of this country's close economic ties with the United States, Mexico is bound to be badly hit by the American import surcharge.

The United States is overwhelmingly Mexico's largest trading partner, buying more than 70 per cent of Mexico's exports and supplying 63 per cent of its imports.

The American trade restrictions have dealt a blow particularly to Mexico's efforts to balance, which has been deteriorating in recent years to a minus last year of $865-million.

Mexico's trade balance with the United States-$833-million of exports $1.565-billion of American imports—further intensifies Mexican complaints against the surcharge measures.

According to Finance Minister Hugo Margain, more than 50 per cent of Mexican exports to the United States—some $480-million worth— are affected by the surcharge, although it is not clear how much can be passed on to American importers and consumers.

The maximum loss for the balance of this year—roughly three months— is estimated at $48-million. Newly-developed border industries, as well as Mexico's young industrial sector, have been badly hit by the surcharge on semi-manufactured goods.

Among the products most affected are processed foods. Some unemployment is expected to result from the drop in exports of these products and of manufactured goods.

With the peso floating in close relations to the American dollar, Mexico, however, hopes to gain in tourism as a result of an upward revaluation of European currencies. More Americans, it is thought, visit Mexico because of the higher costs of European vacations.

Tourism is an essential part of the Mexican economy and, as the largest dollar earner last year, brought in $575-million.

A typical view of the surcharge action by one Government official was:

"There was no reason why developing countries should suffer from a measure directed at developed nations."

HONG KONG

HONG KONG—Washington's new trade barriers are regarded here generally with equanimity as not presenting any insurmountable obstacle to Hong Kong's export to the United States, its biggest single market.

As long as the colony's main competitors face the same conditions in entering the American market, Hong Kong business men and leaders express confidence that the extra costs can be absorbed and competitivenes maintained.

The main Hong Kong exports to the United States are finished and unfinished textile manufactures and half of these are made of cotton. As such, they come under the cotton import quota and are exempt from the surcharge.

One Hong Kong exporter said, "We will only have to watch out for American products being able to sell better under the protection of the surtax, but I don't really think we will be beat out on this."

He added that the surtax costs "could be absorbed at various places along the line and the price to the consumer will rise very little, if any."

FRANCE

PARIS—Only 6 per cent of French exports go to the United States, so the surcharge is regarded as "annoying, but certainly not catastrophic."

The American market, however, has been the biggest growth market for French exports this year. The French therefore find the American surcharge an irritation when they are in the midst of a campaign to redress a substantial trade deficit with the United States — roughly a two-to-one imbalance.

French business leaders expect the surcharge to have a marginal effect on their exports. But they are more worried about the indirect effects, which they feel will deflect more Japanese and West German products into domestic markets and increase competition for French products in foreign markets.

Steel is expected to be the main French product affected by the surcharge. For other leading items such as wines and perfumes, the import levy is either negligible or not considered a threat to French quality and distinction.

BRAZIL

RIO DE JANEIRO—Although all of Brazil's major exports to the United States — coffee, iron ore, cotton, sugar and cocoa — are not touched by the surcharge, the import levy nonetheless has aroused complaints.

The reason is that Brazil has just recently begun to increase production and export of a wide range of manufactured products. These include shoes, ready-made clothes, office equipment, tools and canned corned beef.

The surcharge, therefore is a blow to Brazilian aspiration for diversifying trade. Ministry of Finance officials estimate that the surcharge will affect some $160-million of Brazilian exports, or about 6 per cent of the total.

One main alternative cited by business men is to find more markets in Europe, where currency revaluations have made Brazilian products more attractive in price.

The Brazilian cruzeiro is tied to the dollar, and has depreciated in terms particularly of the German mark and Japanese yen.

AUSTRALIA

SYDNEY—As far as Australian exports to the United States are concerned, most of them are exempt under duty-free or quota status given raw materials such as mineral ores.

However, as Japan is Australia's leading customer — taking 25 per cent of all exports — there is definite anxiety here that losses of Japanese export markets because of the surcharge and revaluation of the yen will soon be felt in reduced trade by Australia.

Because long-term agreements for export of Australian minerals to Japan are covered by contracts written in terms of dollars, it is estimated that the losses from currency value changes could add up to as much as $100-million.

Most of the contracts do not have renegotiation clauses, but some Japanese buyers have indicated willingness to make price adjustments.

Australian press comment on the American economic policies has been generally unsympathetic, with one nationally-circulated newspaper calling it "blackmail."

TAIWAN

TAIPEI—Officials here have been more concerned with the effects on trade of the United States West Coast dock strike than with the new surcharge. Most exporters, however, express optimism about being able to adjust to what may be tougher competitive conditions.

The Government has shunned criticism of the Nixon policies and concentrated in urging exporters to increase productivity, lower costs and diversify markets. It has offered to provide loans to tide over companies hurt by the dock strike and the surcharge.

So far, most economic indicators are holding up, among them production of synthetic fibre and plastics. Factories are running full blast on full order books.

Revaluation of the Japanese yen is seen as likely to make Taiwan more attractive to Japanese investors seeking a lower-cost production environment. The higher yen costs may also make American raw materials more competitive with those from Japan, presently Taiwan's main supplier.

THE NETHERLANDS

THE HAGUE—Dutch brewers who have successfully gained markets in the United States appear to be the most likely to suffer losses because of the American surcharge.

But apart from some worry over exports of flower bulbs and canned hams, the Dutch feel that much of their goods such as chocolates and liquors are "status" products that will not suffer from some rise in prices.

Combined with the surcharge, however, the rise in value of the Dutch guilder has given exporters cause for concern about surviving against competitors.

While hoping that the surcharge will not last too long, they are looking to cost-sharing arrangements with importers and also profit-trimming.

SWITZERLAND

GENEVA—According to Government sources here, 93 per cent of Swiss exports to the United States — machinery, watches, chemicals, textiles, shoes and cheese—are subject to the surcharge.

Watch exports have been hardest hit by the surcharge while machinery exports are expected to be hurt by the United States investment tax credit. In addition, the rise in the Swiss franc has added to competitive problems for exporters.

Switzerland's economy has been booming and with the import of some 500,000 foreign workers, there has been negligible unemployment. No one anticipates any real unemployment problem, but the Nixon program is expected to take a lot of zip out of the boom.

SOUTH KOREA

SEOUL — The surcharge already has resulted in a drop

of about $30-million in South Korea's exports during August as compared with the previous month.

According to revised estimates by the Korean Traders Association, the surcharge-caused loss this year will amount to at least $50-million, or 7.5 per cent of the $670-million goal set for exports to the United States in 1971.

Some 95 per cent of Korea's exports to the United States—plywood, noncotton textiles, wigs and electronic products—are affected by the surcharge.

So far, there have been no repercussions on employment and export industries are taking a wait-and-see attitude in the hope that the world trade situation may be settled soon.

Because of yen revaluation, the Government is planning to diversify import sources to decrease dependence on Japan, which accounts for 40 per cent of Korean imports.

SOUTH AFRICA

JOHANNESBURG—In face of the confused world currency situation and the American surcharge, South Africa finds herself in the position of having to meekly wait while other countries determine the value of its chief product—gold.

Uncertainties about the future role of gold—as well as its price — in monetary terms has brought a fall in gold mining shares and official pleas for a direct devaluation of the dollar.

But meanwhile, the South African currency, the rand, has been floating with the dollar and, without its old tie to sterling, has depreciated about 2 per cent.

The American surcharge is expected to affect some $70-million of South African exports on an annual basis.

September 13, 1971

NIXON PANEL ASKS FREE TRADE MOVES

Urges Negotiations to End All Barriers in 25 Years—Labor Members Dissent

By EDWIN L. DALE Jr.
Special to The New York Times

WASHINGTON, Sept. 13—A Presidential commission, calling for a "new realism" in the nation's foreign economic and trade policy, said today that "the time has come to begin immediately a major series of international negotiations" with the long-term aim of "elimination of all barriers to international trade and capital movements within 25 years."

The basic thrust of the report of the 27-member Commission on International Trade and Investment Policy was in the direction of freer trade here and abroad. The two members from organized labor dissented from the entire report, calling for controls on the inflow of goods and the outflow of capital and technology.

The report, consisting of 307 pages and 147 recommendations, was presented to President Nixon today by the commission chairman, Albert L. Williams, former president of the International Business Machines Corporation. Mr. Nixon named the group in May, 1970, and it has been at work ever since.

The report had actually been in the White House since July 14. Two of its recommendations came close to the decisions announced by the President in his new economic policy Aug. 15.

One was "a uniform import tax and export subsidy" to induce upward revaluations of the exchange rates of leading foreign currencies. The President adopted just the import tax.

The other was unspecified measures to control domestic inflation going beyond "fiscal and monetary policies alone." The commission urged "measures designed to moderate wage and price increases," and the President adopted a 90-day freeze.

The commission acknowledged a "crisis of confidence" about the nation's foreign trade caused most of all by "the increased pressure of imports in the U. S. market."

The report recommended a vastly improved system of "adjustment assistance" to groups of workers and smaller companies injured by import competition, with only relatively rare resort to restraints on imports.

Foreign Investment Backed

Foreign investment by United States companies, the commission concluded, serves the interests of the United States and should not be impeded.

"The commission believes," the report said, "that freedom of U.S. enterprises to establish foreign facilities should be maintained even if it is occasionally associated with shifts in production and jobs. To attempt to control foreign investment is both undesirable and ineffective."

In general, the report said, "The commission is in agreement that the long-term interests of the United States are best served by a trading system containing as few restrictions or Government interventions as possible."

While individual members dissented on a number of specific recommendations, only the two labor members refused to endorse the report. They were I. W. Abel, president of the United Steelworkers of America, and Floyd E. Smith, president of the International Association of Machinists and Aerospace Workers.

Their dissent essentially recapitulated a policy statement adopted earlier this year by the executive council of the American Federation of Labor and Congress of Industrial Organizations calling for far more controls on the goods coming into the United States and on investments abroad.

The report's advocacy of new and sweeping international negotiations was decided upon before the President's measure of Aug. 15 made such negotiations almost inevitable. The commission made the following major points:

¶The negotiations should be "comprehensive," not limited to trade and tariffs but also to include monetary problems such as exchange rates, rules governing foreign investment and the sharing of defense burdens.

¶The negotiations should seek "reciprocity." This should be sought "in terms of the whole set of negotiations rather than as an objective to be achieved within self-contained compartments of trade, investment or finance."

¶The United States "should more than in the past use its bargaining power in the defense of its economic interests."

Among the objectives the United States should seek to achieve, the report said, were "reform of the international monetary system," reduction in the import-limiting effects of the agricultural program of the European Common Market, an ending to the Common Market's special trade deals with a number of nonmember countries, a reduction in nontariff obstacles to trade and creation of new rules to limit the export subsidies of various countries.

Basic Elements Backed

The report concluded that the United States should seek to preserve the basic elements of the "multilateral trade and payments system" that had prevailed for a quarter century, including such institutions as the General Agreement on Tariffs and Trade and the International Monetary Fund.

It suggested that the GATT rules governing trade be made more explicit in such areas as export subsidies, with the initial agreements to include, if necessary, only "key countries."

The 27 commissioners included representatives from business, agriculture, finance, labor and the universities. It was clear that on a number of issues their thinking was far from identical, though a majority was found for every recommendation.

However, the commission reported that it was "unable to reach a consensus" on one present major recommendation of the President—a system of tax incentives for exports known as DISC, or domestic international sales corporations. This is part of the President's tax package pending before Congress.

The following were some of of the commission's many recommendations:

¶Decisions on "adjustment assistance" for workers and smaller companies—which includes such things as cash grants and technical assistance—should be made by the President and not require a finding of import injury by the Tariff Commission.

¶Present controls limiting the outflow of capital from the United States should be "phased out progressively over the next three to five years."

¶Antitrust laws should be changed to permit mergers "if the firm in question is encountering serious difficulty because of import competition."

¶"Orderly marketing agreements" covering several countries, such as the one now in effect for cotton textiles, should occasionally be used to solve trade problems, but only where there is a "severe domestic adjustment problem in more than one importing country."

Government Procurement

¶New international rules should be established on the access of foreign-made products to government procurement, with the United States denying such access to products of countries not living up to the rules.

¶The antidumping act should be enforced more rigorously "as a remedy to unfair competition." This act imposes special duties on goods sold in the United States market at prices below those in the home market of the exporting country.

¶If the United States adopts a "value-added tax," a form of sales tax used by other countries, "its adoption should be based primarily on domestic tax policy considerations," not on its impact on exports and imports. Such a tax is rebated on exports and imposed at the border on imports and is believed by some to help a nation's foreign trade position.

¶New international rules should be negotiated on the possible trade-distorting effects of national antipollution laws and regulations, with the aim of avoiding "artificial nontariff barriers to trade."

¶No special free-trade agreement should be established with Canada.

¶The list of goods barred for export by the United States to the Communist countries should be aligned more closely with that of the other industrial countries but "careful review" of transfers of technology and production processes should be maintained.

And, as proposed by the President, the United States should adopt a system of zero tariffs for many manufactured and semimanufactured goods from the less developed countries, though there were numerous reservations on this issue from individual commissioners.

September 14, 1971

GATT Group Urges U.S. To Drop Surcharge Soon

Report by 55-Member Council Asserts That Surtax Has Had Serious Effects — Method Termed 'Inappropriate'

By THOMAS J. HAMILTON

Special to The New York Times

GENEVA, Sept. 16 — The 55-member council of GATT adopted unanimously today a report holding the 10 per cent United States import surcharge "not compatible" with the General Agreement on Tariffs and Trade. It urged the United States to remove it "within a short time."

The report said the surcharge had had "serious effects" on the trade of other GATT members and was therefore "inappropriate" for remedying the United States balance-of-payments deficit.

However, the stronger language used in the body of the report was hidden from sight in the only part made public today by the GATT council, the page and a half of its conclusions.

Herbert F. Propps, the United States representative, joined in the unanimous decision taken without a vote, although he said this did not affect Washington's position.

Surcharge Kept on Agenda

Emphasizing that it had not finished its consideration of the surcharge, the council said that in view of its "importance and urgency" it would be kept on its agenda for "close review." The working group will be reconvened in the light of developments, it said.

A GATT spokesman said that Erik Trane of Denmark, president of the council, would ask the working group to submit a second report to the annual meeting here of the 80 members of GATT on Nov. 6. However, the working group may be reconvened earlier, the council said.

The 11-page body of the report stated flatly that the other members of GATT were entitled to make countermeasures against the surcharge, although the council members did not plan to do so.

But the last sentence of the conclusions limited itself to the ambiguous statement that the council's consideration of the surcharge "in no way prejudices the rights of contracting parties under the General Agreement."

A GATT spokesman said tonight that this actually was a threat to take countermeasures if Washington did not remove the import surcharge promptly.

However, Mr. Propps told the council that the United States favored this statement. Theoretically it might entitle Washington to take action of its own in reply to any countermeasures adopted subsequently by other GATT members.

Both the conclusions and the report contained Mr. Propps's body of the working group's assertion that the import surcharge was less damaging to world trade than quantitative restrictions on United States imports.

I.M.F. Report Cited

Mr. Propps, who is the White House assistant representative for international trade negotiations, argued that the United States would have been entitled to apply quantitative restrictions in view of an International Monetary Fund report holding that the currency crisis required action.

However, the I.M.F. report, which remained secret, held that the proper remedy was a readjustment of currency parities.

According to some sources, Washington had intended to put up a fight against adoption of the working group's report if the entire report had been made public.

A GATT spokesman explained the withholding of the body of the report on the ground that it contained the I.M.F. study, which was to remain secret. However, it was disclosed that the decision to release only the milder conclusions had arisen from a desire not to make the situation any worse for the United States, which found itself isolated in both the working group and the council.

One member of the group said tonight that Washington's decision to go along with the unanimous decision was wise because such a move would have caused the majority to make the criticisms much stronger.

Developing Countries Move

Some of the strongest language in thec onclusions resulted from the intervention of the developing countries, which obtained the inclusion of a paragraph stating that the working group had taken up with the United States the feasibility of exempting more imports from developing countries from surcharge.

It cited the recent endorsement by GATT, with United States support, of a general system of preferential tariffs on exports of the developing countries.

'The working party," the conclusions said, "fully understood the keen desire and the urgent need of developing countries to expand their imports, as well as the importance of the United States market to them, and generally agreed that, in spite of the exemption of many raw materials and primary products normally exported by them, the import surcharge significantly affected the export interest of the developing countries."

After naming this factor as an additional reason for the prompt removal of the surcharge, it added:

"In the meantime, the United States should keep the situation under constant review so as not to overlook any possible opportunity of adding to the exemptions list products of particular export interest to developing countries."

The device of making public only the conclusions and not the body of the report suppressed the fact that the working group, over United States protests, had also attacked two other provisions of President Nixon's program: the decision not to permit foreign-manufactured equipment to qualify for the tax credit on improvements to equipment, and the privileged tax incentive for exports under the Domestic International Sales Corporations proposal.

The United States had contended that these should not be considered by GATT because neither had gone into effect since neither had been approved by Congress.

In response to questioning a GATT spokesman conceded today only that there had been "an exchange of views" on both.

But reliable sources said the working group, with only one member dissenting, had condemned both actions as "discriminatory" and "inconsistent with the General Agreement.

According to these sources, the British representative on the working group, Robin Grey, of the Department of Trade and Industry, said these two provisions would give the United States "an illusory short-term benefit." Mr. Grey, however, was said to have warned that if they were adopted by Congress they risked "further undermining the whole structure of GATT."

The GATT council also withheld annexes to the working group's report, including a United States paper showing that other GATT members had taken no counteractions when 11 members of GATT, including three American allies — Britain, Canada and France — imposed import surcharges.

Surcharges Detailed

The paper said that in 1964 Britain imposed a 15 per cent surcharge, later reduced to 10 per cent, and that in 1962 Canada imposed a 5 per cent surcharge, later increased to 10 per cent and finally to 15 per cent. The French surcharge was imposed in 1968, but was promptly removed in response to charges that it was contrary to GATT rules.

According to one participant in today's decisions, the working group understated the case when it said in its conclusions that the surcharge, it not removed within a short time, would have far-reaching effects on the world economy and world trade and would slow down GATT's efforts to liberalize trade policies.

Recent declarations by United States representatives show that the United States intends to to use the surcharge as leverage in an attempt to obtain a general reduction in tariffs on American exports, he said.

Countermove in Canada

He added that this had produced a countermove in Canada, where the Trudeau Government had introduced a bill authorizing subsidies exports to the United States, and that other countries heavily dependent upon the American market would follow.

The result, he said, is a dangerous threat to GATT's attempts since its inception to end subsidies and promote a steady reduction in tariffs and other obstacles to international trade. The difficulty, he said, is that GATT as an organization is powerless to affect the course of events.

Regardless of when GATT takes up the issue again, he said, the reaction to the surcharge and other parts of Mr. Nixon's program will be decided by the principal trading countries themselves.

September 17, 1971

The New Big 5

Nixon Stresses Developing Relations With Emerging Economic Superpowers

By LEONARD SILK

Economic Analysis

Shortly before the turn of the year, William L. Safire, Special Assistant to President Nixon, told a New York Law Journal Forum that the first of the great changes he foresaw for 1972 would be "a growing awareness of the economic root of international power. Our eyes will become accustomed to the new Big Five in world affairs—the United States, the Soviet Union, the Common Market, mainland China and Japan." What do these portentous words mean? Are they simply inflated rhetoric or do they signify a coming development in United States foreign economic policy whose importance has not yet been appreciated?

The Safire statement repeats a theme that the President himself voiced in Kansas City, Mo., last July 6. Mr. Nixon then declared that there were "five great economic superpowers"— the same named by Mr. Safire — that would "determine the economic future and, because economic power will be the key to other kinds of power, the future of the world in other ways in the last third of this century."

"We now face a situation," said Mr. Nixon, "where the four other powers have the ability to challenge us on every front, and this brings us back home for a hard look at what we have to do."

Domestic and foreign policies were so intertwined, he said, that they could not be separated. Mr. Nixon warned that the United States was reaching the period of "decadence" that had brought down Greece and Rome.

In the past, he said, decadence had resulted from growing national wealth. This had caused earlier great civilizations to lose "their will to live, to improve." But he thought the United States had the strength and courage to meet all challenges.

In that Kansas City speech, delivered only five weeks before the President launched his new economic policy, he linked national health and strength to the free-enterprise system. He delivered a strong indictment of wage and price controls, declaring that such steps were alien to the American system of free enterprise.

On Aug. 15, Mr. Nixon froze wages and prices and subsequently adopted Phase Two controls.

But at the recent American Economic Association convention in New Orleans, Prof. Paul A. Samuelson, America's first Nobel Prize winner in economics, predicted that the Administration would end wage and price controls before the November, 1972, election.

And Assistant Secretary of the Treasury Edgar R. Fiedler said that the best time to get rid of wage-price controls would be before the economy gets back to full employment.

Since Administration economists apparently now regard a rate of unemployment of 5 per cent as tantamount to full employment, rather than 4 per cent as was customary in the past, this could mean suspending controls almost any time in the coming year, assuming even a modest decline in unemployment from the recent 6 per cent rate.

President Nixon himself, in a television interview last Sunday, said that the Johnson Administration's low unemployment rate had been achieved "at a cost of 300 casualties a week" in Vietnam; but he would continue to wind the war down.

Statement Challenged

Declaring that his system of wage-price controls was intended "to break the inflationary psychology," Mr. Nixon also took issue with a statement of Paul W. McCracken, former chairman of his Council of Economic Advisers, that wage-price controls might be needed for years to come.

The restatement of the "five great powers" theme may foreshadow a return by the President to the true free-enterprise creed in 1972. But this need not mean a diminution in White House support for aids to business, especially in the international arena.

In his recently released foreign trade study, Peter G. Peterson, assistant to the President for International Economic Affairs, suggested a number of additional Government aids to business, including help on research and development outlays and exemption from the antitrust laws if needed to spur exports.

The foreign economic policy implications of the "five great powers" concept do not all go in the same direction.

Toward the Common Market and Japan, the concept appears to mean the sort of tough and highly competitive attitude expressed frequently by John B. Connally, Secretary of the Treasury, and by Mr. Peterson.

But toward the Soviet Union and mainland China — foes though these countries may be in the Communist world—Mr. Nixon has adopted a friendly view and has stressed his hopes for growing trade.

United States-Soviet relations, he said in his Kansas City speech last July, have moved from confrontation to negotiation. And he added that he had moved to end the isolation of Communist China because that country had become "creative and productive."

In straight economic terms, it is difficult to see United States trade with Communist China amounting to a great deal for years to come. Despite its enormous population of between 750-million and 850-million, China's gross national product is estimated by Western experts at only about $80-billion—about 7 per cent of this country's. China's exports are chiefly textiles, agricultural materials and foodstuffs.

Peking has signaled its interest in trading with the United States, although it can get most of what the United States could offer elsewhere—for instance in Japan or Western Europe. Nevertheless, China would doubtless like to get certain American products because of their superior quality.

The significance of Mr. Nixon's interest in developing trade with China is certainly more political than economic.

Although the Soviet Union is a far greater industrial power than China, the same logic holds: Mr. Nixon intends to use economic means for political ends. Toward both great Communist states, he is seeking to normalize relations.

Thus, the "five great powers" concept implies that Mr. Nixon is heading into a year of important economic maneuvering among the other four great powers.

The curious paradox is that this champion of the free-enterprise creed will be working for closer economic relations with Communist China and the Soviet Union as he toughens his response toward the growth of economic power in Western Europe and Japan.

January 5, 1972

The Gentleman From Texas

By JAMES RESTON

WASHINGTON, Jan. 22—The spunkiest character in Washington these days is the Secretary of the Treasury, John B. Connally. You may not like his politics or his economics, and the other financial ministers of the world clearly don't like his rough tactics, but if you really want to understand the state of the nation, Mr. Connally is a better source than most.

He is tossing away those computerized Treasury speeches and telling American business and American labor to get off their respective duffs.

"The rest of the world is at work while we're worrying," he told big-business leaders at the U.S. Chamber of Commerce on State of the Union day here. "They're out-working us, they're out-thinking us, and they're out-planning us."

Though Mr. Connally came up here from Texas with a reputation as a big-business lawyer, he is now shouting at big business like a latter-day Lyndon Johnson to stop whining about the uncertainty of wage-and-price controls and longing for protection against foreign competition.

"Those of you who work in the international field," he told the U.S. Chamber, "know full well what I'm talking about. Somehow you have to lead a resurgence of the American spirit of work. We have to return to our puritanical system of work if we are going to survive."

Well, it's not a bad sermon on the weekend when the British, the Irish, the Danes and the Norwegians sign their intention to join the European Economic Community and turn it into a vast competitive trading unit of 256-million people, the largest in the world.

President Nixon noted this in his State of the Union address as one of many new economic challenges to the United States. Peter G. Peterson prepared a superb report for the President's Council on International Economic Policy on the problem, but it is Mr. Connally who is really running interference for economic, trade and monetary reform and taking on the protectionists in Congress, Big Business and Big Labor.

The facts are fairly obvious. For most of this century, the United States could pay higher wages, work shorter hours, afford Social Security benefits, tolerate strikes and still outproduce and outsell all others, and the reason was quite clear. The U.S. led every other nation in technology, mass production, distribution, salesmanship, management and capital investment.

Besides, the United States had its own empire, which could employ and supply its people without worrying about overseas markets.

But what economic scholars have been saying for years, and now even the Republican Administration is saying, is that the other industrial nations of the world have now mastered the arts and techniques of the industrial and scientific revolutions. The President and Mr. Peterson are saying, rather gently, that this is a real problem. Mr. Connally sees the same facts more urgently and is making a frontal attack on the protectionists.

It is a fascinating exercise by a bold, ambitious and self-confident Democratic politician in a Republican Administration. Mr. Connally went to the House for the State of the Union address and listened to the President's main theme that this is a "good country" on its way to peace and prosperity. Then he drove downtown to the U. S. Chamber and emphasized the opposite—not that all was well but that we were in more trouble at home and in the world than we realized.

The facts of America's declining position in the world of production, trade and money clearly support Mr. Connally's urgent rhetoric. In 1950, the U. S. gross national product amounted to 40 per cent of the G.N.P. of the whole world; now it is about 30 per cent.

During the 1960's, U. S. exports of manufactured goods increased by 110 per cent, but West Germany did even better, and Japanese exports increased by 400 per cent. The Peterson Report suggests the reasons for the decline.

"They include," it says, "the emergence of discriminatory trading agreements abroad, the development by some of our partners of export development programs more aggressive than ours . . . a marked deterioration in American competitiveness aggravated by a rapid rise in U.S. labor costs per unit of output.

But this is not all. The European Economic Community countries already exceed the U. S. in steel production, and Japan will almost certainly surpass both of them by 1975. U. S. imports are now exceeding U. S. exports for the first time since 1893. And on top of all this, organized labor in the United States, which used to be for free trade, is now arguing for protection.

All this worries the President, the State Department and Peter Peterson, but Mr. Connally is the boldest and loudest voice around here on the problem. He is shouting out what he thinks, and this could have political implications on the Vice Presidency next November, even though Spiro Agnew is almost the only other character in Washington who speaks his mind.

January 23, 1972

Return to Reason on Trade

The one good thing to be said about America's deteriorating trade and payments position in 1971 was that it helped to shake the Administration out of the lethargy of its old game plan. Last year brought the United States its first foreign trade deficit since 1888, the year of the Great Blizzard. In 1971 the trade deficit was $2.047 billion and in 1888 a mere $37 million.

A dollar isn't what it used to be, though. Measured by what it could buy in 1888, a dollar is now worth less than a quarter. But if the dollar has shrunk, the economy has grown. In constant dollars, the gross national product was fifteen times as big last year as it was in 1888. In neither the year of the Blizzard nor that of the Wage-Price Freeze were small trade deficits disastrous for the economy.

Obviously, the 1888 trade deficit proved to be a flash in the pan. Will the trade deficit in 1971 turn out to be the start of a trend? Some economists contend that the United States has now become a "mature creditor" economy and can normally expect trade deficits to be covered by the flowback of earnings from foreign investment.

Such expectations may be premature; the odds are that the American trade surplus will return next year, with the devaluation of the dollar and stronger demand in some of this country's largest markets—such as Canada and Japan—to spur American exports. And, if inflation is kept under reasonable control, the breakneck pace at which United States imports have been growing should slow down.

Indeed, the Administration appears to have regained much of its cool on trade as a result of the realignment of currencies. Secretary of the Treasury Connally and the President's trade adviser, Peter G. Peterson, who is now replacing Maurice H. Stans as Secretary of Commerce, have lashed out against the Hartke-Burke bill, which would put quotas on all imports and impose heavy penalties on American foreign investment. Their efforts represent a welcome move away from the protectionist fever President Nixon himself helped to generate in Congress by his drive for "voluntary" textile quotas, to make good his campaign promise to the textile industry. The President's Council of Economic Advisers says it still favors the textile agreement, which the Administration bludgeoned four Asian countries into accepting. The council acknowledges, however, that in general such "voluntary" quota agreements have "serious disadvantages" and foster "cartels."

The Hartke-Burke bill would be far worse. It would pile extra costs on American consumers, reduce competition, worsen inflation, damage United States export industries by drastic slashes in import levels, hamper foreign investment and world economic development, and almost certainly provoke a trade war. Nevertheless, the bill has strong support from some industries and from the A.F.L.-C.I.O., although at least two major unions —the United Auto Workers and the Teamsters—are still holding out against it.

An important test of the character and understanding of Democratic candidates for the Presidential nomination will be their ability to withstand labor pressure for the protectionist Hartke-Burke bill — and their ability to formulate trade and monetary policies that better serve the nation's true economic and political interests.

February 1, 1972

Peterson Urges Settlement Of Differences With E.E.C.

By GERD WILCKE

A somber picture of the problems facing the United States and its key commercial partners was drawn yesterday by a number of prominent executives who were, or still are, responsible for shaping the country's foreign economic policy.

Peter G. Peterson, the outgoing Secretary of Commerce, urged that Europeans and Americans redefine their special relationship in the wake of President Nixon's "bold" Soviet and Chinese initiatives and the repaid growth of economic power in the European Common Market.

He said that unless the two sides reconciled their differences recent developments "could easily stimulate increasing bitterness and pressure for unilateral, increasingly isolationist, and, I believe, self-destructive confrontations."

George W. Ball, a former Under Secretary of State and now a senior partner of Lehman Brothers, cautioned that multinational companies and individual governments were on a collision course.

At the same time, Mr. Ball criticized organized labor for backing protectionist legislation aimed at curbing the overseas activities of United States companies.

Mr. Peterson and Mr. Ball were among several noted speakers invited to address a meeting on international trade sponsored by The Conference Board, an independent business-research organization. The two-day meeting opened yesterday at the Waldorf-Astoria Hotel.

Mr. Peterson, who will continue to serve in the Nixon Administration on a special White House assignment, noted that the United States would enter a series of important trade and monetary negotiations this year with other industrialized nations.

He suggested that the negotiating partners consider preparing a set of principles that could lead toward long-term agreements.

The principles, he said, might include a commitment to monetary reforms, a commitment to accept rules and procedures for arbitrating commercial disputes, the role of less-developed nations, principles underlying security and burden-sharing, and cooperative undertakings in energy, health, drugs, space, pollution and crime.

"In short," Mr. Peterson said, "if only to help the United States clarify its own thinking, perhaps we should explore what are the principles that we believe should continue to make our relationship a special one."

Mr. Ball said that it could be expected that there would be increasing efforts to impose restraints at the national level, or in Europe at the community level, that could seriously impede the operations of multinational companies.

January 19, 1973

Nations' Economic Might: New Concept Is Emerging

By LEONARD SILK

Economic Analysis

Historical eras are marked off by changes in concepts. The period of colonial expansion of the great European powers was a quest for "wealth"—defined as gold and treasure. The end of that era was marked in 1776 by Adam Smith's "Wealth of Nations," in which he defined wealth not as precious metals but as the ability of the people of a nation to produce useful goods and services.

Today, with the initialing of the agreement to end the war in Vietnam, the world appears to be passing from a period of confrontation between the Communist and capitalist powers into what President Nixon, in his second inaugural address, foresaw as "a structure of peace that can last, not merely for our time, but for generations to come."

The new era, if it is to come, is unlikely to result from some outburst of national morality or from a new willingness of sovereign nations to subordinate their interests to those of others. Rather, it will depend on the deployment of power in some form to insure world stability.

Dramatically—and tragically—the old bipolar, cold-war era, and its concept of power, foundered on the inability of the United States, one of the world's two superpowers, to prevail over North Vietnam, which stood near the bottom of the cellar in the rankings.

The traditional concept of national power had two basic elements:

¶The resources a nation could pour into military goods and manpower, as measured by its total defense expenditures.

¶The economic capability of the nation to produce goods and services, as measured by its gross national product.

In the prenuclear age, a capability was considered an even better measure of its power than current defense outlays—since in a long war it could shift resources from civilian to military use and thereby mount and sustain a bigger military force than its rivals.

This was the secret of the successful American effort in World War II. Indeed, this formula for power was first demonstrated by the way the North crushed the South in the American Civil War.

The nuclear age seemingly downgraded the significance of a nation's underlying economic capabilities:

What would count in wars that were expected to last a few days (or perhaps only minutes) were forces in being — nuclear weapons immune from attack and ready for instantaneous response to any threat.

Vietnam—"America's longest and most difficult war," as President Nixon called it last week—altered the concept of national power by its incredible length and by its inconclusive outcome. It demonstrated the constraints and limitations upon the use by a superpower of its full military and economic capabilities. Obviously, those constraints were not physical but political and social, both at home and abroad.

3 Trends Inderact

The constraints are linked to three interacting trends in the world. Seyom Brown, a Senior Fellow at the Brookings Institution in Washington, describes these trends in the current issue of Foreign Affairs. He says that:

¶The cold-war coalitions have started to disintegrate. The smaller powers strike postures of independence while the superpowers find the fidelity of their allies questionable and reduce their own commitments. At his second inauguration, President Nixon said: "The time has passed when America will make every other nation's conflict our own or make every other nation's future our responsibility or presume to tell the people of other nations how to manage their own affairs."

¶Nonsecurity issues — primarily economic — have risen to the top of the diplomatic agenda. To be sure, security issues remain important, but the ability of the United States on one side or the Soviet Union on the other to prevail over allies by threatening to withdraw military protection is decreasing. Europe unites, expands its sphere and forms coalitions with nonaligned countries and the Soviet bloc. So doth the United States. Even the Warsaw Pact countries, though still in the Soviet grip, form new coalitions to reduce the dominance of their superpower.

¶Friendships and adversary relations have grown more complex and ambiguous. At the height of the cold war each of the two superpowers, while competing for allies around the globe, made sharp distinction between friends and enemies. Nonaligned countries—especially India, Egypt and Indonesia—played the field, but theirs was considered an untenable policy over the long run.

In the new multipolar era, precisely that posture of nonaligned flexibility, says Dr. Brown, "seems to be serving as the model for ealistic diplomacy.

Flexibility Found

President Nixon has put forth his own doctrine of flexibility in his concept of "the give great powers." These are the United States, the Soviet Union, the People's Republic of China, Japan and the European Economic Community.

The President voiced this concept for the first time on July 6, 1971, in Kansas City when he declared that the five great powers would "determine the economic future and, because economic power will be the key to other kinds of power, the future of the world in other ways in the last third of this century."

Critics of the President feel that his five-great-powers concept is too narrow—and that it underrates the significance of the role that many other nations will play as the century wears on.

The President's list does not include Canada, India, Brazil, Spain or Mexico.

Role of Countries

The Nixon concept is also held by his critics to underrate the importance of the underdeveloped countries of Latin America, Africa and Asia to the future stability of the world.

Walter Salant of Brookings feels that the President has overstressed the power of nation states and has neglected the power of "transnational" institutions—especially multinational corporations but also various types of labor, environmental, technological, scientific, religious and cultural communities that are creating their own global networks and which either support or tug against national policies.

In such a world of multiple and cross-cutting coalitions, Dr Brown contends that the essence of power itself is changing from the direct use or threat of military force to gain national ends to various other kinds of promises or threats.

The basic promises are offers of economic exchange, trade, investment or technical cooperation. The basic threats are to withdraw such support or cooperation.

Pattern of Future

In the new era, Dr. Brown suggests, nations with the most influence are likely to be those that are "major constructive participants in the widest variety of coalitions and partnerships." Such countries would have the largest supply of usable political currency—in effect, promissory notes that say: "We will support you on this issue, if you support us on that issue." Nations will be driven to work together to get scarce energy resources—or valuable technology.

To be sure, the old system—the threat or use of military power—will still be there and will be of decisive importance if issues over aggression or national survival again develop.

But it is the diminished fear of such threats that is forcing scholars—and Presidents, generals and businessmen—to rethink the concept of the power of nations in the post-cold war, post-Vietnam era. This rethinking leads to the conclusion that economic weight and flexibility are becoming the dominant elements of national power.

The New York Times/Jan. 24, 1973

Trends in U.S. Trade

(In billions of dollars)

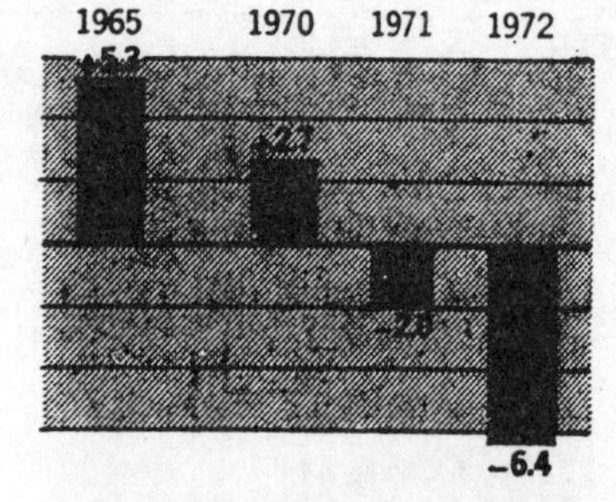

Growing Deficits With Major Countries...

Japan

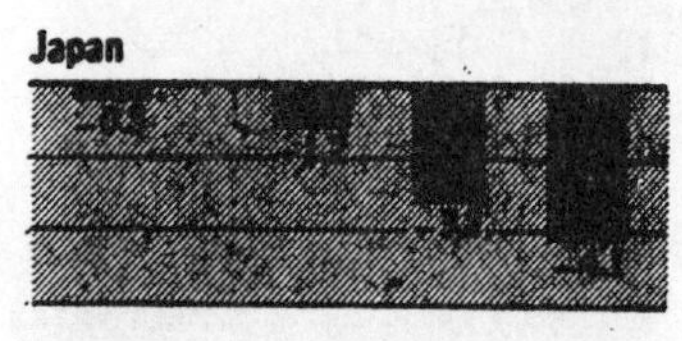

Canada

Expanded European Economic Community

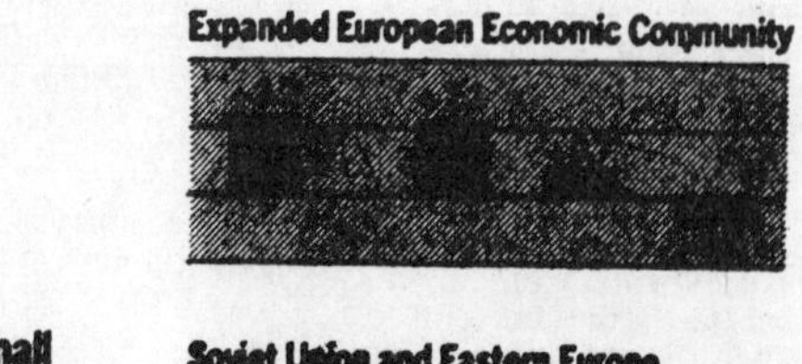

... small Surplus With Communists...

Soviet Union and Eastern Europe

Rest of World

... and Sharpest Setback in Trade With Less-developed Nations

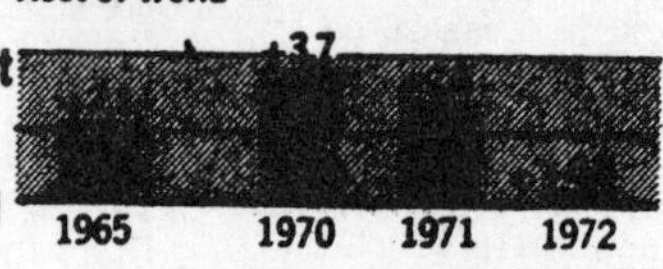

Source: U.S. Department of Commerce

February 15, 1973

NIXON ASKS POWER TO CUT, RAISE OR CANCEL TARIFFS AND TO SET IMPORT CURBS

URGENCY STRESSED

Message Says Peace Can Be Undermined by Economic Strife

By EDWIN L. DALE Jr.
Special to The New York Times

WASHINGTON, April 10—President Nixon sent Congress today a comprehensive trade bill that would give him sweeping new authority both to raise and lower United States tariffs and other trade barriers as a prelude to forthcoming international negotiations.

The President said his new "Trade Reform Act"—which is nearly a half-inch thick and 124 pages long—"calls for the most important changes in more than a decade in America's approach to world trade." The last big legislative change was the Kennedy Administration's Trade Expansion Act of 1962.

Although the bill would give the President new powers to curb imports in a variety of circumstances, Mr. Nixon said its main purpose was "expanding trade and expanding prosperity, for the United State and for our trading partners alike."

He also emphasized the urgency of negotiations on trade because "our progress toward world peace and stability can be significantly undermined by economic conflicts which breed political tensions and weaken security ties."

Highlights of Bill

Following are some of the highlights of the bill:

¶The President would be given unlimited authority, as part of international agreements, to raise, lower or eliminate tariff duties on imports.

¶He would be given a variety of techniques to reduce United States nontariff barriers — ranging from import quotas to health and safety regulations—in return for similar foreign actions. Under one new technique, either house of Congress could veto the final result.

¶There would be a new, more rapid procedure by which domestic industries damaged by rapidly rising imports could get relief, but the President would retain the ultimate discretion as to whether to grant relief by limiting imports.

¶There would be a new procedure — including the right of Congressional veto—for entering trade agreements with Communist countries and granting them much lower tariffs through the most-favored-nation principle.

¶The President would have new powers to impose import restrictions on goods from countries engaging in such unfair trade practices as putting limitations on goods from the United States or subsidizing their own exports.

¶There would be wholly new authority for the President to impose sweeping import taxes or quotas in cases of serious deficits in the nation's balance of international payments, and to reduce all or most tariffs in the opposite situation—a major surplus in the United States balance of payments.

¶There would be authority to drop tariffs to zero on most manufactured and semi-manufactured goods from most developing countries, to aid their exports and, thus, their economic development.

Most of the basic provisions of the trade bill had previously been disclosed in broad outline by the President and other officials. However, many details were disclosed today for the first time.

The outcome of the legislation in Congress is wholly uncertain. However, Representative Wilbur D. Mills, Democrat of Arkansas, Chairman of the House Ways and Means Committee, said his committee would begin hearings on the bill May 7 and added that he hoped that a trade bill could pass the House by August.

Mr. Mills said of the President's message, "He is asking for more of a grant of authority than we have given any other

Associated Press

Peter M. Flanigan, Presidential aide on trade, and Secretary of the Treasury George P. Shultz, rear, during the news conference on the President's trade proposals.

President. This is a touchy subject in Congress right now. But it is essential if we are to move forward. I'm for it."

The President conceded in his message that he was asking for an unusually large grant of authority. But he said:

"The key to success in our coming trade negotiations will be the negotiating authority the United States brings to the bargaining table. Unless our negotiators can speak for this country with sufficient authority, other nations will undoubtedly be cautious and noncommital—and the opportunity for change will be lost. . . . Unfortunately the President of the United States and those who negotiate at his direction do not now possess authorities comparable to those which other countries bring to these bargaining sessions."

The President now has no tariff-cutting authority at all. Under the new bill he would have authority for five years to enter international agreements, with the possibility of unlimited tariff cuts, but, he said, he wants to complete the forthcoming round of trade negotiations by 1975.

The negotiations are scheduled to begin formally in September with a ministerial-level meeting of the major trading nations in Tokyo. This meeting will probably take place even if Congress has not yet passed trade legislation, but serious negotiating will almost certainly have to await a United States trade bill.

Apart from the complex trade legislation itself, the President disclosed his intention to propose relatively minor changes in the taxation of profits earned abroad by American corporations, a highly controversial issue.

Mr. Nixon called the present system of taxation — which among other things taxes overseas earnings only after they are remitted to the United States — "fundamentally sound" and said, "We should not penalize American business by placing it at a disadvantage with respect to its foreign competitors."

He urged, however, that overseas profits be taxed by the United States as they are earned in cases where a major portion of the production of an American-owned foreign plant is sent back to the United States, which is not a typical situation, and where the investment was made to take advantage of "major tax inducements" granted by foreign countries to attract investment.

Organized labor has supported far tougher taxation of the multinational corporations, and has also backed much tougher restraints on imports than the President proposed. In an early reaction today Paul Jennings, President of the International Union of Electrical, Radio and Machine Workers, said the President's program "does not go far enough" and shows only a partial recognition of some aspects of the nation's complex trade crisis."

Apart from its many innovations, the trade bill contains many, largely technical changes designed to improve portions of the nation's underlying trade law that dates to the early nineteen-thirties.

April 11, 1973

Nixon Seeks Trade Concessions For Soviet Not Tied to Exit Fees

By BERNARD GWERTZMAN

Special to The New York Times

WASHINGTON, April 10 — President Nixon asked Congress today to permit him to grant trade concessions to the Soviet Union without linking them to the lifting of its restrictions on free emigration or Jews and other Soviet citizens.

As part of the message accompanying a trade reform bill Mr. Nixon directly opposed the plan of Senator Henry M. Jackson, Democrat of Washington, which is backed by 75 other Senators and a majority of the House of Representatives.

Mr. Jackson would link the granting of most favored-nation status, allowing lower tariffs for Soviet goods, to the removal of the travel barriers and high exit taxes on those seeking to go to Israel and other countries.

In a message accompanying his bill Mr. Nixon said: "In the case of the Soviet Union, I recognize the deep concern which many in the Congress have expressed over the tax levied on Soviet citizens wishing to migrate to new countries."

"However," he continued "I do not believe that a policy of denying most-favored-nation treatment to Soviet exports is a proper or even an effective way of dealing with this problem."

Senators Are Not Swayed

Mr. Jackson was unmoved by Mr. Nixon's plea as he and the other Senators formally introduced on the floor of the Senate an amendment that would bar most-favored-nation treatment or Government-backed export credits to any Communist country that restricted free emigration or imposed more than nominal taxes on exit visas.

In a statement, Mr. Jackson described the Administration's efforts to seek trade concessions for the Russians as a form of "economic assistance" and said his amendment "will enable the Congress to insure that its insistence on the right of free emigration is and will remain a condition of American economic assistance to the Soviet Union and the countries of the Eastern bloc."

The statement by Mr. Nixon was his first public comment on the extremely sensitive issue, which has aroused considerable attention on Capitol Hill and Jewish organizations.

"My proposed legislation would grant the President authority to extend most-favored-nation treatment to any country when he deemed it in the national interest to do so," Mr. Nixon said.

"Under my proposal, however, any such extension to countries not now receiving most-favored-nation treatment could be vetoed by a majority vote of either the House or the Senate within a three-month period," he added.

In the last two years Moscow has eased travel restrictions considerably, with 15,000 Jews permitted to go to Israel in 1971 and 30,000 in 1972; the figure for this year is estimated at 35,000.

Moreover, a few weeks ago, after a trip to Moscow by the Secretary of the Treasury, George P. Shultz, the Russians waived a controversial exit t for many Jews. The tax, made official last summer, was based on educational level attained, and was bitterly denounced by Jewish groups in the United States.

The Administration indicated apparent easing of emigration curbs is due to its efforts at "quiet diplomacy."

The administraiton indicated that despite the Congressional sentiment, it planned to press for passage of the most-favored-nation provision, which it promised the Soviet Union when a comprehensive Soviet-American trade agreement was signed last fall.

Linked to Repayments

Under that accord Moscow does not have to make further payments on a $722-million Lend-Lease debt if it is not given most-favored-nation treatment by 1974.

Mr. Nixon, in his trade reform legislation sought to mollify the Congressional concern by providing that either house could veto a trade agreement if it acted within 90 days. Moreover, Mr. Nixon said that any concessions to the Russians would be limited to three years and would have to be renewed at that time, providing another chance for Congress to act.

At present, the Administration extends most - favored nation treatment to two Communist countries—Poland and Yugoslavia—and has promised it to Rumania and Hungary as well as to the Soviet Union.

Most-favored nation treatment allows exports to enter the United States at the lowest tariff rate charged any other country.

April 11, 1973

HOUSE PANEL TIES SOVIET EMIGRATION TO TRADE BENEFITS

Requires Moscow First to Relax Minority Curbs—Administration Setback

By MARJORIE HUNTER
Special to The New York Times

WASHINGTON, Sept. 26 — The House Ways and Means Committee voted today to deny any new trade privileges to the Soviet Union until it eases its emigration policies for Jews and other minorities.

The committee's action was a major setback to the Nixon Administration and to the American business community. The restriction, adopted by voice vote, was attached to a major foreign-trade bill that is now under consideration by the committee.

Kissinger Plea Undercut

The committee acted about an hour after Secretary of State Kissinger, at a news conference in New York, repeated the Administration's contention that over the long run more could be accomplished to ameliorate the lot of Soviet Jews and others by quiet diplomacy.

[In Nairobi, Kenya, Secretary of the Treasury George P. Shultz said that expanding trade with the Soviet Union would be set back if Congress denied tariff cuts, The Associated Press reported.]

Curb on Nixon's Power

The amendment would deny President Nixon the right to grant "most-favored-nation" status to the Soviet Union or any other Communist country until he certified to Congress that the country involved did not restrict emigration.

While the restriction would apply to all Communist countries, including China, it was principally directed at emigration policies of the Soviet Union.

The amendment was cosponsored by Representative Wilbur D. Mills, Democrat of Arkansas, the committee chairman, and Representative Charles A. Vanik, Democrat of Ohio. It was similar to one proposed in the Senate by Henry M. Jackson, Democrat of Washington.

The dispute over Soviet emigration policies intensified in the late summer of 1972, when Moscow imposed heavy exit taxes, ranging into the tens of thousands of dollars, on Jews seeking to leave the country for Israel.

Russians Shelve Tax

The Soviet Union has now shelved the taxes and is allowing Jews to leave at the rate of about 30,000 a year. However, there is a large backlog of would-be emigrants.

While the easing of the exit tax last spring appeared for a time to dampen the chances for Congressional approval of the proposals by Representatives Mills and Vanik and by Senator Jackson, the highly emotional issued flared again in recent months, with evidence of renewed Soviet repression against such dissenting intellectuals as Andrei D. Sakharov, the physicist, and Aleksandr I. Solzehenitsyn, the novelist.

As recommended today, the House amendment would prohibit the President from giving most-favored-nation tariff treatment—the allowing of any favorable agreements that were extended to any other country—to a nation that denied Jews or other citizens the opportunity to emigrate, that imposed more than nominal emigration fees, or that imposed fees strictly on the basis of the country to which a person wanted to emigrate, such as Israel.

Certification Required

Under the amendment, the President would be required to certify to Congress every six months that the countries receiving most - favored - nation treatment maintained a policy of free emigration..

President Nixon had strenuously opposed the restriction, arguing that it could jeopardize efforts to establish better relations with the Soviet Union.

But while defeated today on the issue of trade restrictions, the Administration won a partial victory when the committee struck from the House amendment a provision that would have also denied trade credits or credit guarantees to the Soviet Union or other Communist countries that restricted emigration.

The move to strike the provision on credits was offered by Representative Herman T. Schneebeli, Republican of Pennsylvania, on the ground that the Ways and Means Committee had no jurisdiction over trade credits.

At present, the President has unlimited authority to grant trade credits.

Annual Veto Power Voted

WASHINGTON, Sept. 26 (AP) —The House Ways and Means Committee also approved an amendment by Representative James C. Corman, Democrat of California, giving Congress annual veto power against trade concessions.

The amendment would require the President to determine each year that the Russians and other Communist countries were meeting nondiscriminatory emigration requirements, and would permit Congress to veto any continued trade concessions.

Shultz Fears Trade Curbs

NAIROBI, Kenya, Sept. 26 (AP)—Secretary of the Treasury George P. Shultz said today that expanding trade with the Soviet Union would be set back if Congress, protesting the treatment of Jews and intellectuals, denied tariff cuts to the Russians.

Mr. Shultz, who will leave for Moscow Friday, said that the issue of Soviet dissidents was a matter "that has no direct connection with arrangements to buy or sell something."

"It's essentially a matter of the internal affairs of the Soviet Union," he added.

Mr. Shultz said that he did not mean to imply the Administration did not care about the plight of the Soviet Jews and intellectuals. But he noted that the two Governments had signed a trade deal, agreeing to lower tariffs. The Secretary is here for the annual meeting of the International Monetary Fund and the World Bank.

September 27, 1973

Surging Trade With China

By LESLIE GELB

WASHINGTON — United States trade with China this year is surging tenfold from the 1972 level. Exports to China will reach $840-million by year end while imports from China will total $60-million, according to officials of the White House, State Department and Commerce Department.

These experts say the thaw in political relations between the two nations paved the way for the dramatic trade increase. But they say it was mainly due to economic factors — the poor Chinese grain harvest in 1972 and the new Chinese desire to acquire Western technology.

Chinese and American leaders seem prepared to let their economic relations move forward more or less independent of political issues. This is in contrast to Soviet-American relations, where the leaders on both sides carefully intermix trade discussions with diplomatic talks.

President Nixon and Secretary of State Kissinger have used economics as a weapon in dealing with the Russians. Government officials acknowledge, for example, that they delayed the wheat deal in 1972 pending Soviet agreement on the strategic nuclear arms treaty.

The President and Mr. Kissinger are said to believe that a prime reason the Kremlin wants détente to work is the hope of gaining access to American trade, technology and credits.

Similarly, China has used the lure of profits in its contacts with Japan. A State Department official noted that Peking is holding up an airline agreement with Japan until the latter cancels her airline pact with Taiwan.

But in American-Chinese relations, both sides have tended to treat economic issues as subsidiary to the development of over-all political considerations, ranking officials assert.

Peking, they say, is mainly interested in détente with Washington to have a friend against the Russians and to further isolate the Government of Taiwan. Washington is said to be primarily interested in better relations with Peking to have another lever against the Soviet Union.

Mr. Kissinger and China's Premier, Chou En-lai, spent little time in their meetings three weeks ago talking about economics. Also, the Chinese Premier made no special issue of the fact that the Jackson Amendment, which would deny most-favored-nation trading status to the Soviet Union pending a change in Soviet emigration policy, also applied to China.

One White House official speculated that Chou En-lai might even be content about the denial of this trading status for his country so long as the Soviet Union suffered even more.

Nevertheless, a number of American officials describe as astonishing and unpredicted the extent to which trade with China has swollen. They had looked upon (and still basically regard) China's leaders as stoutly determined to preserve their country's self-contained economy. They were surprised about the speed with which China is increasing its reliance on foreign trade rather than seeking to develop products on its own.

In 1971 the U.S. trade was tiny and one-way—$4.9-million in exports to China. In 1972 the United States exported $60-million of goods to China and imported $30-million of goods. In 1973 the two-way trade total is ballooning to $900-million.

China's worldwide trade went from $4.7-billion in 1971 to $5.8-billion in 1972 and is approaching an estimated $7-billion in 1973. This represents about 4 per cent of China's gross national product, or about the same proportion as in the Soviet Union.

Of the estimated $840-million in this year's American exports to China, three-quarters is in agricultural products — wheat, corn, cotton and soybeans. The Chinese grain harvest in 1972 was described as very poor. China, therefore, turned to American exports of farm products as well as industrial products and advanced technology. The largest single transaction was the sale of 10 Boeing 707's for $150-million.

Two-thirds of China's exports to the United States was in the form of primary products — silk and hog bristles for toothbrushes and paint brushes. China also exported antiques, food specialities and light manufactured goods such as rugs.

The most pressing problem in Sino-American trade relations, Government officials say, is the deficit of almost $800-million that China is running.

So far, China has met this situation by using its trade surplus with nations like Singapore and Hong Kong to offset its deficit with the United States. Washington officials believe that China's over-all imports and exports are in balance but that this cannot last long.

China has a policy of paying for everything in cash—either American dollars or British pounds. Officials in Washington cannot estimate the size of China's foreign reserves in currency, but they assume these reserves will soon be exhausted.

This would put China in the position of either asking for credits (and going into debt) or trying to increase its exports. Peking has had a long-standing policy against incurring debt. It has modified this only to the extent of working out an extended payments arrangement with Japan for certain large purchases.

American officials predict China will move to increase its exports, but they foresee a multitude of obstacles.

First, there are legal problems. Private American claims against previous Chinese expropriation of property totals $197-million, and there are other claims as well. This means that China cannot hold a trade fair or open bank accounts in the United States without the risk of these claimants attaching Chinese goods and money.

Chinese Government funds in American banks totaling about $75-million have been blocked since 1950. Officials say that negotiations are under way to settle the private American claims and to unblock China's bank accounts.

Second, there is the problem of most-favored-nation status. This matter, according to Congressional sources, is not likely to be cleared up soon, and no exception will be made for China. Chinese exports to the United States, a State Department official says, would immediately increase about 15 per cent if this nondiscriminatory status were conferred.

Even then, officials maintain, Washington would seek a quid pro quo. In dealing with planned economies, Washington asks for structural changes in the way of doing business with America — for example, facilities for businessmen, shipping arrangements and port openings.

Third, another problem for China is learning how to make its products salable in open markets. This means finding out about competitive pricing, labeling laws and the like. Experts say this will take time.

American officials point out that China is "tough and meticulous" in its business dealings. But they hasten to add that all is moving along in a cooperative manner.

Last week the M. W. Kellogg Company, a division of Pullman, Inc., announced the signing of a $130-million contract to build five ammonia-producing plants in China. This follows a similar Kellogg deal for three such plants signed in September.

Perhaps more important, officials say, was the signing on Nov. 16 of a communiqué between the Chinese Government's trade council and the American-based National Council for United States-China trade. The communiqué called for the sending of a trade delegation to the United States in 1974 and the exchanging of trade missions and information in a systematic way.

The National Council was formed in May, 1972, with the Nixon Administration's blessing, to facilitate trade with China. It is a private, nonprofit organization with business corporations as members.

For the time being, however, most of the officials interviewed predict that over-all Sino-American trade will drop in 1974. They cite these reasons: a good Chinese harvest in 1973, which will probably take them out of the wheat market, and major transactions under way to buy plants from West Germany, France and Japan.

Another reason mentioned is that the Chinese will be busy over the next few years copying these plants. They want to learn the technology and then build plants on their own.

American officials insist that the expected drop in trade with China will not signal any change in détente.

Dwight Perkins, professor of Far Eastern economics at Harvard, agrees. "In the end," he says, "China will buy what it wants on economic terms, and politics won't affect this much."

December 2, 1973

CREDITS TO SOVIET BARRED AS HOUSE BACKS TRADE BILL

Representatives Also Reject Tariff Cuts for Russians Until Emigration Eases

By EDWIN L. DALE Jr.
Special to The New York Times

WASHINGTON, Dec. 11—The House of Representatives cast a resounding vote against the Soviet Union's emigration policies today and then approved and sent to the Senate the most comprehensive foreign trade legislation in at least 40 years.

In two separate votes the House decided by margins of 319 to 80 and 296 to 106 to deny lower tariffs or export credits to the Soviet Union unless the President can certify that the Russians do not restrict emigration, by high taxes or other means. At issue chiefly were Soviet restrictions on emigration of Jews.

The House had no chance to vote separately on the multitude of other provisions in the trade bill, which would open the way to new international negotiations aimed at lowering trade barriers generally and would also make numerous permanent changes in United States law. Some of these would open the way to new restraints on imports, including curbs to be imposed in cases where American industries could show these imports caused them iniury.

House Votes Israel Aid

In another action, the House approved by a vote of 362 to 54 legislation that would authorize the President to extend $2.2-billion in emergency military aid to Israel to rebuild her forces in the wake of the October war.

President Nixon has threatened to veto the trade bill, which he strongly favors in all its main provisions, if the anti-Soviet aspects remain.

In the Senate, which is not scheduled to take up the trade bill until after New Year's, more than 80 Senators have announced their endorsement of the restrictions on Soviet trade and credit approved by the House today.

Such restrictions, if enacted into law, could affect the flow of credit to the Soviet Union to finance potentially billions of dollars worth of projects and United States exports. But in the meantime, the flow can continue.

The vote in the House to approve the bill on final passage was 272 to 140, which represented a decisive defeat for the stand of organized labor.

Only last week, George Meany, president of the American Federation of Labor-Congress of Industrial Organizations, wrote a letter to every member of the House urging that "you vote to defeat the entire bill." Labor has supported entirely different trade legislation, centering on major new barriers to imports that it asserts have caused large-scale losses of jobs in the United States.

The merits or demerits of the myriad provisions of the bill became largely lost in the emotional question of Soviet emigration policies and other matters relating to "human rights" in the Soviet Union.

Representative Charles A. Vanik, Democrat of Ohio, who offered the key amendment linking the granting of export credits to a removal of Soviet restrictions on emigration, said that a vote for his proposal "will be a reminder to the world that this country is still the hope of free men everywhere."

Representative Ogden R. Reid, Democrat of Westchester, said: "This is not the time for economic expediency to take precedence over human rights."

The small band in opposition was led by Representative Barber B. Conable Jr., an upstate New York Republican, who argued that adoption of the restrictive provisions would be "mischievous and probably counterproductive."

The history of this unusual issue in brief, is as follows:

In October, 1972, President Nixon negotiated with the Soviet Union a trade agreement —as part of the over-all policy of improving relations — in which he promised to ask Congress to change a long-standing law that imposes very high tariffs on goods from most Communist countries, including the Soviet Union. The Soviet Union would be given "most favored nation," or nondiscriminatory, tariff treatment.

At about the same time concern began to mount about Soviet restrictions, including high taxes, on emigration of Jews. Support quickly sprang up behind a proposal by Senator Henry M. Jackson, Democrat of Washington, to deny any trade benefits to the Soviet Union until there was a policy of essentially free emigration.

Last April the President, after some debate within the Administration, decided to include the provision giving the Soviet Union most-favored-nation treatment as one section in the sweeping Administration trade bill.

In late September the House Ways and Means Committee, while approving the basic bill in its main essentials, included the restrictions on lower tariffs specified in the original "Jackson amendment." But it split evenly on whether to add an even more important provision —denying export credits that were intended to help huge exports of machinery and other capital goods from the United States to the Soviet Union. The rules committee permitted Mr. Vanik to offer this section as an amendment when the bill came up on the floor.

When war broke out in the Middle East, the Soviet Union gave extensive military aid to Egypt and Syria and President Nixon and Secretary of State Kissinger sought Soviet cooperation in achieving a cease-fire and an eventual peace settlement. On three occasions the President or Mr. Kissinger asked the House to defer action on the trade bill, fearing that the anti-Soviet amendments would be approved.

Last week, warned that basic support for the underlying bill might erode, the President asked the House to take up the bill but to drop the whole section dealing with Soviet trade. On Friday Mr. Kissinger supported the President's position.

After lightly attended and relatively listless debate in the House yesterday and early today, Mr. Vanik's amendment denying export credits was adopted by 319 to 80.

When Mr. Conable proposed an Administration amendment that would drop the whole section of the bill dealing with Soviet trade, he went down to defeat, 298 to 106.

The National Conference on Soviet Jewry and the American Jewish Committee promptly hailed today's results.

Jerry Goodman, director of the National Conference, said in an interview that he had spoken with Soviet Jews "and they are elated." Elmer Winter, president of the American Jewish Committee, said the vote in the House "expresses the decisive judgment of American public opinion."

Shock for Moscow Is Seen

Special to The New York Times

MOSCOW, Dec. 11—While the Soviet Union has cushioned itself for an unfavorable trend in Congress on expanded trade and credits, today's House of Representatives vote on the trade bill is expected to come as a shock to the Soviet leadership.

The vote came too late for a news of it to be included in Soviet newspapers or late evening radio and television broadcasts.

Earlier this fall Secretary of the Treasury George P. Shultz urged the Russians to bypass Congress and deal directly with American industry to maintain the momentum of Soviet-American trade. He suggested privately that the Administration was trying to put off a vote on trade legislation until early next spring because of the unfavorable trend in Congress.

Subsequently, fairly candid commentaries in such newspapers as Pravda have signaled the awareness of high Soviet circles that the situation had gotten beyond President Nixon's control.

December 12, 1973

U.S. Asks Quick Trade Accords

Piecemeal Accord Sought as World Talks Open

By VICTOR LUSINCHI
Special to The New York Times

GENEVA, Feb. 11—World trade negotiations opened here today with the United States urging that quick agreements be made wherever possible, without waiting for an over-all accord.

"We should start now to negotiate and work seriously, consolidating what we can, when we can," Harald B. Malmgren, leader of the American delegation, said at the opening of perhaps the most ambitious world trade talks yet undertaken.

Mr. Malmgren, President Ford's Deputy Special Representative for Trade Negotiations, said that the session should avoid leaving final decisions to "one big burst of energy" as was the case in the Kennedy Round of tariff-cutting negotiations.

The Kennedy Round, also held under the auspices of the General Agreement on Tariffs and Trade, was concluded in May, 1967. After four years of talks, the outcome was still in doubt through the final weeks of intensive bargaining as a deadline set by the expiration of the United States mandate for an accord approached.

Mr. Malmgren stressed that the United States did not want to see the new round of trade bargaining to extend inconclusively until 1980 even though the Administration now has a five-year negotiating mandate under the new Trade Reform Act.

"We should aim to start concluding trade agreements on specific subjects as soon as they are ready," he said. The meeting groups 90 nations, representing all leading trading nations except for the Soviet Union and China.

Harald B. Malmgren, leader of the U.S. delegation at conference, called for early serious negotiations.

The New York Times/Victor Lusinchi

Paul Luyten, Common Market chief at talks, said conference would deter isolationism.

At this curtain-raising session, which is expected to last three days, delegates are to list the questions to be taken up in the initial phase of the negotiations and fix a timetable for tackling them. An agenda is expected by July 1.

The divergent approaches of the United States and the European Common Market to tariff-cutting emerged immediately.

Mr. Malmgren proposed uniform across-the-board cuts as the "simplest, fairest, formula." Mr. Luyten said that the community preferred deeper cuts in high-tariff areas so as to achieve a "harmonization" of duties.

Mr. Malmgren said the aim should be for over-all tariff cuts equal at least to the average achieved at the Kennedy Round —about 33 per cent.

He also called for a quick start on lowering non-tariff barriers to trade, some of which could be dealt with without having to relate them to other issues. He mentioned widely divergent product standards and government subsidies as examples.

The new effort to break down trade barriers was officially set in motion in Tokyo in September, 1973, at a ministerial session of the 83-nation GATT, the agency that writes the rules under which some 85 per cent of international trade is conducted.

However, the actual negotiations were stalled by the delay of the United States Congress in passing the Trade Reform Act that gives the Administration the broad negotiating authority necessary to strike bargains.

Paul Luyten, the European Economic Community representative, said that the new round was important if only because the "simple fact that it is being undertaken will serve as a deterrent to isolationist and protectionist tendencies."

Similarly Kiyohiko Tsurumi of Japan said that in these difficult economic times there was a "danger that if all stood still we might be pushed to lean towards the adoption of various protectionist devices."

The "big three" of the negotiations—Europe, the United States and Japan—also stressed the importance for consumer countries of being assured of regular supplies of the raw materials and agricultural commodities they may need.

This is a relatively new idea in GATT and has arisen as a result of shortages that developed in recent years and resulting export restrictions.

Mr. Luyten said that trading nations had been used to thinking in terms of finding outlets for their products. "Now," he continued, "the problem of obtaining a sure supply of raw materials and of energy supplies is at least as important."

The entire oil question, however, is being left for discussion in other forums.

Aside from Mr. Malmgren, the United States was represented at today's session by four members of Congress.

They were Representatives Al Ullman, Democrat of Oregon and new chairman of the House Ways and Means Committee; William J. Green, Democrat of Pennsylvania and chairman of the international trade subcommittee, and Barber B. Conable, Republican of New York and a member of the international trade subcommittee, plus Senator William V. Roth, Republican of Delaware and a member of the Senate Finance Committee.

Their presence was viewed as an attempt by the Administration to emphasize its intention to work closely with Congress all through the negotiations.

February 12, 1975

THE MARSHALL PLAN
AT THE MID-MARK

CHAPTER 3
Foreign Aid

Dean Acheson, left, honors George C. Marshall, right, as Paul G. Hoffman looks on.
Courtesy The New York Times

MARSHALL PLEADS FOR EUROPEAN UNITY

AS 'CURE' FOR ILLS

Only Then Can Our Aid Be Integrated, Says the Secretary

HITS 'PIECEMEAL' BASIS

He Tells Harvard Alumni Our Policy Is Not Set Against 'Any Country or Doctrine'

By FRANK L. KLUCKHOHN

Special to THE NEW YORK TIMES.

CAMBRIDGE, Mass., June 5—The countries of Europe were called upon today by the Secretary of State, George C. Marshall, to get together and decide upon their needs for economic rehabilitation so that further United States aid could be provided upon an integrated instead of a "piecemeal" basis. This was important to make possible a real "cure" of Europe's critical economic difficulties he asserted in an address to Harvard alumni this afternoon after he had received the honorary degree of Doctor of Laws at this morning's commencement exercises.

General Marshall supported President Truman's statements in Washington earlier today that United States aid abroad was necessary. He declared that Europe "must have substantial additional help or face economic, social and political deterioration of a very grave character."

"There must be some agreement among the countries of Europe as to the requirements of the situation," he warned, adding that no American aid would be given to "any government which maneuvers to block the recovery of other countries." The Secretary emphasized that governments or parties or groups, seeking to make political capital by perpetuating human misery, would encounter "the opposition of the United States."

General Marshall was the recipient of several ovations as he participated in Harvard's first fully normal post-war graduation exercises. The first came when he moved to the platform before Memorial Church in the procession of 2,185 undergraduates, graduate students and the honor group who were to receive degrees. The second ovation came when James B. Conant, president, conferred an honorary degree upon him.

The biggest ovations came just before and after he spoke, with applause interlarded when the Secretary said American help would be withheld from those making capital of trouble in Europe.

General Marshall was one of the last to speak this afternoon. Gen. Omar N. Bradley, administrator of veterans' affairs, who also received a Doctor of Laws degree, had asserted that the expenditure of $12,000,000,000 for veterans' education was a good investment for the United States and Dr. Conant had called for the raising of $90,000,000 to increase Harvard's activities.

"Friendly Aid" Stressed

After asserting that no "assured peace" or political stability was possible without the aid of the United States in effecting a return to normal economic health in the world, General Marshall said that "the initiative, I think, should come from Europe." This country should restrict itself to "friendly aid" in the drafting of a European program and later in supporting this program "as far as it may be practical for us to do so," he added.

He held it to be essential that several and, if possible, all European states should effect what he termed a "joint" program. It would be neither "fitting nor efficacious" for us to draw up a unilateral program and then foist it upon possibly unwilling governments and nations, said the General.

Economic rehabilitation in Europe would require "a much longer time and greater effort" than had been officially foreseen, he continued. Then he stressed that the United States was willing to give "full cooperation" to countries willing to assist in steps toward European recovery, and denied that the policy of the United States was directed against "any country or doctrine."

For American Understanding

In a few brief words after his prepared talk, Secretary Marshall said that he regarded full understanding by the American people of foreign problems and the aims of American policy to be of high importance.

He already had expressed the fear that the enormous complexity of problems and the mass of facts available were confusing people.

The dislocation of the entire fabric of European economy through the breaking up of commercial ties and the elimination of private banks, insurance companies and the loss of capital, probably was even more serious than the destruction of physical property of all sorts and the losses in manpower, he explained.

The Secretary said that one important factor leading to the threat of a complete "breakdown" in Europe was the fact that the cities were no longer producing much that the farmers wanted and that, as a result, the farmers were making little effort to raise enough to feed the cities. Thus, with city people short of food and fuel, he added, "the Governments are forced to use their foreign money and credits for necessities instead of reconstruction."

The Secretary, who was presented to the Harvard alumni by Gov. Robert F. Bradford, returned to Washington by air after the ceremonies.

General Bradley, in the uniform of a full general with four rows of ribbons, devoted himself largely to one facet of the country's program, his own.

"In the United States, of the 2,300,000 students in colleges, 1,200,000 are veterans, getting their education mostly at Government expense," he said. "Within twenty months after the close of the war, the American people had already invested nearly $2,500,000,000 in the (educational) program. By the time it is completed, the program may have cost a total of $12,000,000,000, or barely enough to have run the war for several weeks."

"There are times when it may be more dangerous to spend too little than to spend too much," General Bradley continued. "For example, if ever we should expose our people to sickness, our resources to waste, our economy to depression and our nation to aggression in a panicky effort to save dollars, we may some day have to ask ourselves if such savings were worth the cost.

"If we offer youth a fair chance to make its way in the nation we need not fear political deflection to either the left or right. We cannot meet the challenge of rival ideologies with labels and reaction. We must offer these young veterans progress and the opportunity for constant self-betterment throughout their busy lives."

General Bradley obtained a laugh from his audience when, referring to his honorary degree, he said:

"Like thousands of other veterans, I appear to be getting my education as a result of the GI bill."

THE SECRETARY OF STATE HONORED AT HARVARD

Gen. George C. Marshall wears a plain business suit as he walks in academic procession before receiving Doctor of Laws degree. Accompanying him is Prof. Edmund M. Morgan. Associated Press Wirephoto

June 6, 1947

HOUSE PASSES BILL FOR 590 MILLION AID IN EUROPE AND ASIA

Winter Help for France, Italy, Austria and China Voted by Voice in Roar of Approval

MARTIN WHIPS IT THROUGH

Democrats, Surprised, Fail to Get Record Tally—Measure Sent to Congress Conferees

By C. P. TRUSSELL
Special to THE NEW YORK TIMES.

WASHINGTON, Dec. 11—The House, by a voice vote, passed its $590,000,000 emergency relief bill for France, Italy, Austria and China today. The roar of "ayes" indicated support by an overwhelming majority. Democrats complained that the gavel of Speaker Joseph W. Martin Jr. had banged too fast for them to demand that the House go on record, member by member.

The completed House measure was sent to conference for adjustments of differences with the Senate. A principal contest was expected over the amount of the authorization. The Senate has approved $597,000,000 for the three European countries alone. This was asked by the Administration as "an irreducible minimum" if the program to combat communism this winter was to have full effect. A $60,000,000 authorization for China by the House cut its European assistance total to $530,000,000.

Conferees will meet tomorrow morning. Their announced timetable is to adjust all differences in time for presentation for final Congressional ratification next Monday. While the House, after six days of consideration, added many provisions not contained in the Senate measure, leaders looked with apparent confidence to prompt compromise.

Appropriations Debate Set

By Tuesday, unless plans miscarry, the actual appropriations to run the program will go under House debate. Members of the Appropriations Committee predicted openly that that body would recommend a total materially less than that authorized by either house.

Before passing its bill late this afternoon, the House rejected, also by voice, a proposal that it be returned to the Foreign Affairs Committee "for further study." The motion was made by Representative Glen D. Johnson, Democrat of Oklahoma, who opposed the bill. Its defeat was the signal for the final decision.

When the roaring voice vote was taken, Speaker Martin banged his gavel and declared the bill passed. He said later that he observed no one standing to seek recognition for a demand either for a standing vote or a recorded count. Differences persisted in corridor discussion over whether the Democrats were caught napping or lacked enthusiasm for a roll call as much as they said the Republicans did.

It was predicted, however, that when the finally adjusted measure was called up for ratification, a recorded vote would be taken.

During four days of amendment contests in the House, nearly fifty proposed revisions were offered, and twenty were accepted. Yet, it was contended widely the Senate and House programs were "not too far apart."

Some of the amendments voted into the House measure were declared by handlers of the bill to be so "crippling" that they possibly would make the program impotent. There was, however, wide difference of opinion as to effects.

It appeared that many of the amendments would be "lost" in conference.

Restriction Voted on Grain

One amendment, sponsored by Representative August H. Andresen, Republican of Minnesota, seemed to promise much conference attention. It would provide that no American wheat, wheat flour or cereal grain be made available to the foreign relief program unless the President did these things:

Surveyed the requirements of countries which are dependent upon the United States for a portion of such commodities.

Determined the requirements of American consumption during the next twelve months.

Then determined the total availability of these commodities for export, after allowing for a carryover of at least 150,000,000 bushels for domestic use in case of crop adversities.

The Foreign Affairs Committee was split sharply on this proposal. It was declared, on the one hand, that it would take two years to make such determinations, with an emergency situation at hand. Some $300,000,000 of the authorization was designed to provide grain foods, it was stressed. On the other hand, it was held that such determinations could be made promptly by the machinery of the Department of Agriculture and were important factors in the planning of emergency and long-range foreign aid.

Other Provisions Disputed

Also apparently due for conference contest were House-adopted provisions which called for these things:

Putting the program into immediate action—Secretary of State George C. Marshall recently set a deadline of "before Dec. 1" on effective availability of food, fuel and other commodities of the program—even before the time-consuming formalities of appropriation-making were completed.

The House bill provides that as soon as the President signs the bill the program could draw upon the Reconstruction Finance Corporation to the extent of $150,000,000. This would be paid back when the formal appropriations were approved.

Adding to the program shipments of "incentive goods" which were not in short supply in the United States in an effort to speed up production and other self-help in countries receiving aid. It was contended that western European workers, having nothing beyond food available to buy with their earnings, were working only to receive pay to cover this need.

Purchasing for the foreign aid program in such a way as to minimize impacts upon American resources and upon prices which continue to soar. No fault was found with this objective, but differences prevailed over how it could be carried out.

Permitting up to 25 per cent of the funds made available to be used to buy commodities abroad (to relieve domestic strain) and at the same time allowing such purchases to be made at levels 10 per cent higher than American delivery cost, if the commodities were in short supply here.

Buying for the foreign program be at levels prevailing in the markets concerned at the time of procurement.

Denying aid to countries which do not distribute, free of charge, food and other essentials to the needy and indigent.

The House bill, while requiring such free distribution, would insist upon recipient countries posting in a revolving fund for further self-help only the equivalent in local currency it received from sales of American commodities to their people. The Senate measure would require that the recipient countries post local currency to cover the cost of everything received from the United States.

Other Congressional additions to the original Administration program, it was indicated, might step in to make conference adjustments more difficult.

Managers of the House bill, however, expressed relief over the fact that some of the proposed amendments were voted down.

Among these was one, offered by Representative Vito Marcantonio, American Labor party of New York, under which $1,500,000,000 of American money would be turned over to the United Nations to give relief to countries, regardless of the race, creed or political opinion of their people. The U. N. Security Council, where the veto prevails, it was pointed out in debate, would select the countries to be aided under such an arrangement.

This proposed amendment appeared, from the voice vote that killed it, to have won the support only of Mr. Marcantonio and Representative Adam C. Powell Jr., Democrat, of New York.

Representative John Taber, chairman of the Appropriations Committee, told the House today that the Administration had not yet sent to Congress the "justifications" for the voted $60,000,000 relief fund. The committee would not recommend, he said, until they arrived and were considered.

It developed in debate that the Administration's program for helping China had not yet been worked out, and that the "justifications" would be considerably delyaed.

House Conferees Are Named

WASHINGTON, Dec. 11 (AP)—Speaker Martin named Representatives Charles A. Eaton of New Jersey, John M. Vorys of Ohio, Karl E. Mundt of South Dakota, all Republicans; Sol Bloom of New York and John Kee of West Virginia, Democrats, to work with the Senate conference committee, headed by Senator Arthur H. Vandenberg, Republican, of Michigan, on differences between the two aid bills.

December 12, 1947

TRUMAN ASKS $17 BILLION TO RESTORE EUROPE; MARSHALL SAYS PEACE MUST AWAIT RECOVERY; CONGRESS VOTES STOP-GAP AID, LATER ADJOURNS

PRESIDENT IS GRAVE

Warns Poverty and Fear of Tyranny Will Grip All if Europe Falls

URGES SWIFT ACTION

Asks $6,800,000,000 for 15 Months From April 1, and New ERP Agency

By FELIX BELAIR Jr.
Special to THE NEW YORK TIMES.

WASHINGTON, Dec. 19—President Truman asked Congress today to authorize a 1948-51 European Recovery Program costing $17,000,000,000 to halt the march of "selfish totalitarian aggression" and to maintain a civilization in which the American way of life is rooted.

In a message outlining the largest program of expenditure in the nation's peacetime history, the President urged haste in completing legislative action so that the program might begin on April 1. He asked that $6,800,000,000 be appropriated for use in the ensuing fifteen months. Appropriations for the three years following would be considered subsequently on an annual basis.

THE PRESIDENT GREETS GEN. MARSHALL

Mr. Truman welcoming the Secretary of State at National Airport upon latter's arrival from Foreign Ministers' Conference.
The New York Times (by Tames)

Justifying his program on political as well as economic grounds, the President warned that if Europe failed to recover, its people would be driven by want to surrender their rights to totalitarian control and that such a turn of events "would constitute a shattering blow to peace and stability in the world."

Holds World Freedom at Stake

"It might well compel us," he added, "to modify our own economic system and to forego, for the sake of our security, the enjoyment of many of our freedoms and privileges."

Considerably more than the future of the people of Western Europe was involved in the "grave and significant decision" he was asking Congress to make in favor of the so-called Marshall plan, the President said. It would also determine whether the free nations of the world could look forward to a peaceful and prosperous future as independent states or "whether they must live in poverty and in fear of selfish totalitarian aggression."

As President Truman described it, the substance of his proposal was that America finish the job for which he said $15,000,000,000 had been spent by us throughout the world since surrender of the Axis powers. That job would not be easy but was well within this nation's means, Mr. Truman continued, noting that it would take less than 3 per cent of the national income during the life of the program.

Predicts Further Incitements

Political as well as economic obstacles would be encountered in helping to put Western Europe and occupied Germany back on their feet and the President reminded that Communists and Communist-inspired groups were opposed to recovery on the Continent as a matter of policy.

"We must not be blind to the fact that the Communists have announced determined opposition to any effort to help Europe get back on its feet," the President said. "There will unquestionably be further incitements to strike, not for the purpose of redressing the legitimate grievances of particular groups, but for the purpose of bringing chaos in the hope that it will pave the way for totalitarian control."

The President said satisfaction of the import requirements of 270,000,000 Europeans would call for some self-denial on the part of Americans. It would not be possible to satisfy this demand entirely because of short supplies here and throughout the world, and the program of aid had been scaled down materially to reflect these realities and to eliminate non-essentials.

But he pointed out that a total cost of the program, amounting to about 5 per cent of the expenditure for the war effort, was "an investment toward the peace and security of the world and toward the realization of hope and confidence in a better way of life for the future." Viewed in that light, he said, the cost was small indeed.

To carry out the long-range program of loans and grants-in-aid, the President proposed a new and separate Federal agency to be called the Economic Cooperation Administration. Neither the President nor the supporting data he transmitted from a dozen Government agencies described the new organization as "independent."

State Department Powers Urged

The new agency with its single Administrator and Deputy Administrator at the top would come under the policy jurisdiction both of the State Department and the National Advisory Council. The chief foreign representative of the Economic Cooperation Administrator would take orders from his immediate chief as well as the Secretary of State.

Rejecting recommendations of the committee of private citizens headed by Secretary of Commerce W. Averell Harriman that the broadest possible powers be vested in a single Administrator, Mr. Truman said the news agency "must work with, rather than supplant, existing agencies."

"The Administrator must be subject to the direction of the Secretary of State on decisions and actions affecting our foreign policy," the President declared.

In addition, the Department of Agriculture would continue in charge of the procurement and allocation of food and the Department of Commerce in the allocation of commodities and products in short supply and administration of export controls.

It was clear from the 241-page analysis of the program transmitted by the President that while the new Administrator might propose, it would be for other agencies to dispose. The National Advisory Council would decide whether aid to a particular country should be in the form of a loan or grant and the State Department would determine whether the proposed aid was in line with our foreign policy and, therefore, whether it should be forthcoming at all.

It was indicated in the supporting data that "much" of the foreign aid would be made in the form of non-repayable grants. How much was not indicated except that the yardstick of determination would be the ability of beneficiaries to repay without jeopardizing recovery progress.

The voluminous explanatory report on the program completely abandoned the original formula that the type of aid requested would largely determine whether a loan or grant would be made. This concept was that grants should be provided for food, fuel and fertilizer, since these categories would be rapidly consumed without any visible effect on recovery progress.

The $17,000,000,000 requested in the form of a Congressional authorization by the President was a rounded sum. As the supporting data explained, the actual cost of the program to the United States Treasury might go as low as $15,111,000,000 or as high as $17,758,000,000, depending on the behavior of prices here and in world markets during the four years.

Neither did the over-all estimate include $822,000,000 for Western Germany, to be sought in a separate appropriation for the Army Department. Moreover, the round sum asked by Mr. Truman assumed about $4,100,000,000 of financing under the plan by the World Bank, private loans, aid from other Western Hemisphere countries and credits remaining from unexpended appropriations.

Bars Gifts to Those Able to Pay

Actual management and collection of loans certified by the Economic Cooperation Administrator and approved by the National Advisory Council, would be undertaken by the Export-Import Bank, under the program.

President Truman recommended in this connection that no grants should be made to countries able to pay cash for all imports or to repay loans. At the same time, he reminded that if the participating nations of Europe became burdened with debt obligations under the European Recovery Program, participation by the World Bank and through a revival of private financing would be retarded.

The President's message and the draft legislation he submitted left the way open for European countries other than the sixteen that joined in the Committee of European Economic Cooperation at Paris to participate in the program.

The eventual entry of Spain and Czechoslovakia has been mentioned as a possibility by Administration officials. However, any new participants would first have to be accepted by the sixteen nations comprising the committee of European Economic Cooperation. After that, it would be a matter for the United States Senate through implementing bilateral treaties with each of the participants.

Self-Help Requirement Stressed

While the President went to some lengths in his message to explain this nation's interest in the European Recovery Program, he was no less insistent that the participating nations must do their part in specified ways. He said the first requirement was that each country of Western Europe and all of them collectively "should take vigorous action to help themselves."

Among action programs required of the beneficiary nations, the President mentioned financial and monetary measures to stabilize currencies, maintain proper rates of exchange and restore and maintain confidence in monetary systems. Also included was cooperation with other participants in reduction and elimination of trade barriers and toward efficient use of resources.

Recipients of grants would be required to increase their output of strategic materials in short supply in this country for purchase by the United States. This program of stockpiling here would be facilitated by a stipulation requiring the deposit in a special fund of the currency equivalent of the grant-in-aid. Strategic resources development for purchase by this Government would be among the purposes for which the fund would be available.

Officials estimate some $250,000,000 of short materials might be acquired annually by the United States in this way.

December 20, 1947

Britain's Clutch on Sterling Area Held Inconsistent With ERP Goal

U. S. and Western Europe May Use Pressure to Have London Drop Role of Banker for the Empire—Hard Fight Ahead

By MICHAEL L. HOFFMAN

Special to THE NEW YORK TIMES.

PARIS, March 18—Britain may be forced by pressure from her Western European neighbors and the United States to abandon her efforts to maintain her position as banker for the British Commonwealth and other sterling-area countries, in the opinion of many of the best-informed experts who have been attending the second Paris Conference on the European Recovery Program.

Among the steps the British may be urged and eventually forced to take are the definitive blocking of existing sterling balances to reduce the ability of India, Egypt and other non-European countries to buy British goods that might otherwise go to Europe; the cessation of the conversion of sterling into dollars for sterling-area countries, and the extension of sterling loans to France and possibly other Continental countries.

In effect, Britain would be required to declare herself bankrupt and to start over again with a drastic shift in the orientation of her economy and financial system away from the Commonwealth and toward Europe.

The struggle over the role of the pound sterling in the emerging world of the union of Western Europe, ERP, and the prolonged East-West political and military tension is the big behind-the-scenes issue at this conference. It has not been referred to publicly, but it dominates the thoughts of men who will finally decide what concrete meaning can be given to the fine phrases of the Foreign Ministers.

It would be premature to forecast just what form the attack on the cidatel of sterling, not long ago the world's strongest and still the world's most widely used international currency, will assume. United States and Continental experts have, however, arrived at some common conclusions which, when they began exchanging views here, made it obvious that sterling is now Europe's No. 1 problem.

First, there is a basic inconsistency between Britain's participation in the European Recovery Program and Britain's position as banker for the sterling area. As that banker, Britain last year had to furnish more than $1,000,000,000 to other sterling countries to cover their deficits in trade and financial transactions with the Western Hemisphere. Under the Marshall Plan, Britain's dollars are supposed to be geared in with Europe's overall dollar requirements.

Second, the British have not succeeded in the past six months in getting the rest of the sterling area to pay its way in dollars. In fact, the situation has worsened. In the end, the United States cannot allow recovery program dollars to be used to finance the sterling area instead of Europe.

Third, France is moving from a position of surplus in her balance of payments with the sterling area as a whole to a position of deficit of about £100,000,000 annually. Unless France gets sterling credits, she will have to buy with dollars the things she could obtain in the sterling area.

It would be the negation of everything that ERP stands for if France, for example, had to use recovery dollars to buy coal in the United States when Britain had coal for sale against sterling. Therefore, Britain must be prepared to grant credits to the ERP countries at the expense, if necessary, of the sterling area.

Fourth, abolishing the sterling area in its present form will not alter the underlying problems of the sterling-area countries. Instead of furnishing dollars by way of Britain, the United States may have to take over the direct responsibilities that Britain, as the center of the sterling area, has formerly shouldered for countries like India, Egypt, Australia and New Zealand.

The political and economic implications of this shift are so great that harassed experts here are not even trying to figure them out now, but none of them believes the United States is well equipped for the job.

It is taken for granted that the British will fight to the last ditch against efforts to draw logical conclusions from these basic considerations. The British are weak on paper, but are vigorous and skilled negotiators when defending their centuries' old position as the world's bankers. Foreign Secretary Bevin has already warned the conferees that Britain's "traditional" links with the Commonwealth "will be maintained."

A growing body of opinion in the State Department and in continental Governments sees the British struggle to defend sterling as the greatest menace, outside communism itself, to the success of the European Recovery Program.

March 19, 1948

FOREIGN RECOVERY PROGRAM SENT TO PRESIDENT

AID VOTED SWIFTLY

House Passes, 318-75, $6,098,000,000 Bill for Europe, East

SENATE IS ALSO QUICK

Conference Compromise Unchallenged—Spain Ignored in Action

By FELIX BELAIR Jr.
Special to The New York Times.

WASHINGTON, April 2—Congress passed and sent to the White House today a $6,098,000,000 foreign aid program without precedent in peacetime history. Built around a four-year program of European economic recovery for which it authorized $5,300,000,000 in the first twelve months, the measure provided supplemental military assistance for China, Greece and Turkey.

Final action by the two legislative branches came on adoption of a conference report resolving differences between the House and Senate versions. The House acted first, approving the report by a vote of 318 to 75 with less than 15 minutes of explanation. The Senate followed suit soon afterward by a voice vote.

Only minor changes were made in the legislation by the legislative negotiators in the final meeting which adjourned a few minutes before last midnight.

Total aid to China was held to the $463,000,000 originally authorized by the Senate but the committee increased the amount of military assistance to $125,000,000 and cut economic aid to China to $338,000,000.

A total $275,000,000 was authorized for military aid to Greece and Turkey. This was supplemental to the $400,000,000 voted to those countries last year. It was intended to bolster the government's battle against Communist aggression in the one country and the threat of it over the Dardanelles questions in the other.

In the House, Representative John Vorys, Republican, of Ohio who managed the legislation on the floor, said it is to enable the United States to "wage peace while preparing for war," voting for the bill were 167 Republicans and 151 Democrats. Against it were sixty-two Republicans, eleven Democrats and two American Laborites.

No effort was made to restore Spain to the list of nations eligible to participate in the European Recovery Program.

Senate adoption of the conference report was even more perfunctory. Chairman Arthur H. Vandenberg of the Foreign Relations Committee explained such changes as had been effected since the measure left the Senate in piecemeal fashion. Senator Scott W. Lucas, Democrat, of Illinois, was all set to make a foreign policy speech, but was dissuaded by Senator Vandenberg to delay it until the measure was passed.

Administrator to Have Charge

Although slightly beyond the April 1 deadline set by the Administration, final action on the legislation was well ahead of the crucial elections in Italy in which the Communists are expected to make their major bid for power.

As finally agreed to, the measure placed the recovery program under the direction of an Economic Cooperation Administrator at the head of an independent agency to be called the Economic Cooperation Administration. The administrator will draw a salary of $20,000 a year, and is to be assisted by a deputy administrator at $17,500. A special representative abroad will draw the same pay as a chief of mission.

Intended by the Administration to be administered by the State Department, the program was removed about as far as possible from the working jurisdiction of that agency. The Secretary of State is permitted only to appeal to the President in matters of foreign policy if he disapproves the decision of the administrator.

The measure authorizes an appropriation of $4,300,000,000 and directs the administrator to raise the other $1,000,000,000 from sale of notes to the Treasury Department. The smaller amount is earmarked for loans through the Export-Import Bank and for guaranteeing the convertibility of foreign currencies into dollars for the benefit of American enterprises investing funds in furtherance of the program.

Pending Congressional action on an appropriation bill, the omnibus measure makes available $1,000,000,000 from the Reconstruction Finance Corporation for loans and grants to the sixteen western European countries that are to participate in the recovery program.

Additional amounts of $50,000,000 each to China, Greece and Turkey are made available from the same source pending action on the appropriation.

Although assisted by a Public Advisory Board, the Economic Cooperation Administration has the final voice "in consultation with" the National Advisory Council in determining whether assistance to participating nations should be in the form of loans or grants or a combination of both.

The Bretton Woods Agreement Act is amended to make the administrator a member of the National Advisory Council along with the Secretaries of the Treasury, State, and Commerce, the chairman of the Federal Reserve Board and the head of the Export-Import Bank. The Council is the top coordinating agency for Federal financial policy in the international field.

The administrator is authorized in determining the form of assistance to consider "the character and purpose of the assistance and whether there is reasonable assurance of repayment, considering the capacity of such country to make such payments without jeopardizing the accomplishment of the purposes of this title."

Although called upon to administer the loans, the Export-Import Bank is absolved from responsibility for terms and conditions which will be prescribed by the Administration in consultation with the National Advisory Council. Neither are loans supervised by the bank to be held against its maximum lending authority under its organic act.

In agreement with participating countries, the Administrator is authorized to require repayment of loans or grants in strategic materials in short supply in this country so as to facilitate stockpiling of critical items. He is empowered also to direct the Secretary of State to negotiate agreements for the development of such materials in dependent areas of the participant countries.

In procuring commodities and equipment, the Administrator is instructed:

"1. To minimize the drain upon the resources of the United States and the impact of such procurement upon the domestic economy, and

"2. Avoid impairing the fulfillment of vital needs of the people of the United States."

The Administrator is instructed to satisfy any demands for petroleum from resources outside the United States. He is required to purchase the surplus agricultural commodities of this country except where one participating country has a surplus available for transfer to another participant or where the surplus here is required domestically.

Although the measure commits the United States conditionally to participation in a four-year program through June, 1952, it makes it necessary for Congress to authorize and appropriate every year. In other words, besides providing the money for each year's commitments Congress will have to renew the basic authorization.

While seeking to restrict trade between eastern and western Europe in materials subject to United States export controls, the final draft of the bill modified the Administrator's embargo authority over exports to Russia. The law as it went to the President provides:

"The Administrator is directed to refuse delivery insofar as practicable to participating countries of commodities which go into the production of any commodity for delivery to any nonparticipating European country which commodity would be refused export licenses to those countries by the United States in the interest of national security.

Pledges of Self-Help Included

"Whenever the Administrator believes that the issuance of a license for the export of any commodity to any country wholly or partly in Europe which is not a participating country is inconsistent with the purposes and provisions of this title, he shall so advise the department, agency or officer in the executive branch and, if differences of view are not adjusted, the matter shall be referred to the President for final decision."

To prevent a repetition of Lend-Lease experience and the continued delivery of materials long after termination of the assistance program, the measure provides that deliveries shall terminate automatically on cessation of any aid program.

Congress adopted and wrote into the authorizing legislation the pledges of self-help and mutual aid by the sixteen participating countries through the Paris report of the Committee for European Economic Recovery.

Providing generally that all participating countries shall put their houses in order economically and financially, the pledges will be embodied later in a multilateral treaty between the United States and the continuing European organization.

Renewal of the pledges through the treaty will be a condition precedent to any aid from this country, as will a separate bilateral treaty between the United States and each of the participants. The latter will be intricate and specific, whereas the multilateral pledges will be general.

Failure of any participant to live up to its pledges and more specific commitments is made justification for termination of further aid, and the continuity of assistance to European countries is made contingent on the continuity of self-help and cooperation all around.

The legislation contains a blanket termination clause designed to anticipate political conditions beyond the control of participant nations, such as a loss of or limitation of sovereignty through Communist aggression. To remedy this, it is provided that aid may be terminated when, "because of changed conditions, assistance is no longer consistent with the national interest of the United States."

Within three months of the effective date of the legislation all employes of the Economic Cooperation Administration must be screened by the Federal Bureau of Investigation for loyalty to the United States and must be certified as such by the Secretary of State or the Administrator, acting independently or on the basis of the FBI findings.

The omnibus foreign aid measure contains provision for a $60,000,000 contribution to the International Children's Emergency Fund of the United Nations and $20,000,000 for rehabilitation in the free territory of Trieste. The latter funds are authorized either from ERP or the unappropriated balance of the European interim aid authorization.

April 3, 1948

U.S. WARNS BRITAIN ON MARSHALL PLAN

Says Aid Must Not Be Used Solely to Underwrite Sterling Area Financing

By HERBERT L. MATTHEWS
Special to THE NEW YORK TIMES

LONDON, April 9—Britain has been warned again by the United States that Marshall Plan aid must not be used to underwrite the sterling area, it was learned today.

Moreover, it appears to have been made clear that there is a strong feeling in some circles in Washington that Britain must exercise tighter controls over the drain of dollars from the sterling area. Last year the drain amounted to more than £1,000,000,000 and the Washington circles are said to feel this was too large.

Finally, there are signs of new United States pressure to induce Britain to do something more drastic about her enormous wartime sterling debts, which are leading to a certain amount of unrequited exports from Britain.

These warnings have not yet been formalized. They are more like storm signals of what to expect when the European Recovery Program Administrator, Paul Hoffman, and his European representative get to work.

British Back U. S. View

The British conceded that point and they have pledged themselves to use Marshall Plan aid only for their own reconstruction and for European trade. In the last analysis the United States and Western Europe must rely to a great extent on British good faith and fair play.

It is felt that the new Economic Cooperation Administration is in a position not only to control the use of its aid up to a point, but to help Britain keep other members of the sterling area in line.

British officialdom has not shown any signs of agreeing with the United States contention that Britain can devise tighter control over the sterling area or can adopt a different system of control. The sterling area has been described as "weak and soggy" in its present form and United States officials feel it can be made much stronger.

In any event, Marshall Plan aid by itself would not be enough to prevent a decline in the sterling area's dollar and gold reserves. On that basis alone United States quarters here believe Britain must take new measures.

Britain's gold and dollar reserve position improved during the first quarter of this year to the extent of £40,000,000 (about $160,000,000), Sir Stafford Cripps, Chancellor of the Exchequer, informed the House of Commons.

The South African loan of £80,000,000 was the major factor in offsetting the drain on the reserves of the sterling area, he said in a written answer to a question.

Reports Disturb Britons

Britons have been disturbed in recent weeks by reports that the State Department on the one side and the Western European nations on the other feel that the sterling area represents a potential threat to proper functioning of the aid program. There has been much heart-searching in the British

Treasury, the Bank of England and other offices about this question.

However, as matters stand today there is no outward intention to do anything more than to try to make the existing arrangements work better and as time passes to apply any new measures that may seem possible. All along the line a keener watch is being kept to make sure that agreements are honored and any loopholes closed.

In general, British officials seem convinced that the State Department does not want to see the sterling area disintegrate, even though it is known that some individuals in the State Department would be glad to see such a result. The British feel that most economists and financiers would agree with them on the necessity of maintaining the sterling area if only for the reason that there is no substitute for sterling as international currency.

United States circles here believe a collapse of the sterling area might cause a shattering blow to the world economy. The impression given is that there is no objection to the sterling area as such, but that it must maintain itself and not rely on United States dollars and imports to Britain.

April 10, 1948

EUROPE'S INDUSTRY SET FOR DIRECT AID

U. S. Business Leaders Taking First Steps Toward Backing of Emergency Relief Plans

STUDY VOLUNTARY SHARING

ECA Help Thus May Be Either by Engineering Cooperation or Credits and Materials

By HARTLEY W. BARCLAY

Direct aid to European industry by American business will be one of the first steps taken to back up emergency relief plans, industrial leaders revealed here yesterday.

Because the foreign-aid bill guarantees dollars for United States investments up to $300,000,000 to carry forward the program business leaders here are getting ready to provide services in Marshal' Plan countries heretofore unavailable.

Present plans include voluntary sharing of products, equipment, engineering methods, skilled managerial personnel and the "know-how" of distribution, spokesmen disclosed. These will be made possible by an early revision of governmental restrictions on commercial cooperation between the United States and companies in the Marshall Plan nations, it was learned from reliable sources.

The Economic Cooperation Administration will therefore be enabled to provide two forms of economic aid, wherever conditions of the ECA are acccepted. One form of aid will be credits and materials; the second form will be management and engineering cooperation through expanded trade relations of private companies. All of this will be accomplished without necessarily reimposing any general economic controls.

Prepared for Sacrifices

While the activities of the Economic Cooperation Administration have not been set by even major policy and procedural decisions, business and industrial leaders have reached the conclusion that voluntary sacrifices will have to be made here to cement permanent improvements in European economic reciprocal relations with American industry.

Five steps will have to be taken to cooperate in the economic recovery activities in Europe. These will include: (1) Make an audit or take an inventory of inquiries from European companies on which action has been held up pending decisions on the final shape of the Marshall Plan, (2) Offer specific proposals for construction of plants or exchange of products to spur trade, (3) Supply managerial and engineering executive manpower to help install whatever American business methods they desire at the earliest possible moment, (4) Transfer blocked machine tools and equipment previously destined for Russia or satellite countries to buyers in Marshall Plan nations where desired, and (5) Install a voluntary allocation system for routing scarce tools, equipment and supplies to European industry to meet immediate necessities.

Industrial executives said they were convinced that this constructive leadership by American industry would be given serious consideration for prompt approval in Washington as rapidly as individual plans were received by Government officials.

They added that they envisage the set-up of the new ECA as a sort of voluntary "Peace Production Board" organization combined with many of the principles of business promotion formely advanced by the Committee for Economic Development during the post-war period here. This type of a combination would meet the greatest need of European business, which is, they explained, improvement of methods, installation of time and cost-saving techniques, better utilization of manpower, less waste of materials, elimination of long-standing obsolescence in applications of power, tools, handling methods and assembly techniques, and improvement of sales and distribution methods.

U. S. Stimulation Needed

Beyond this, they added, European business needs a stimulant for the initiative of the business management executives. Many of these people are still depressed from war experiences and need the encouragement and enthusiasm which American business can provide. In the absence of this stimulant black markets have thrived, and in some countries the only way to conduct trade is to deal in black markets, which now must be eliminated.

One spokesman who had just returned from a tour of European business centers disclosed that many Marshall Plan nation business executives want to break away from many post-war business practices which have been evolved to meet extreme scarcity situations. Transations involving "under-the-table rebates" and "round-about" money payments have spurred inflation.

Speaking from extensive experience in European business activities, executives pointed out that the American ideal of continuous "modernization of industry" provides one of the vitally necessary answers to Europe's present needs. Ancient practices of production, rooted in tradition and far too expensive when compared to American methods, will be replaced as more and more of the Continental manufacturere visit the United States, receive exchange visits from American manufacturers and step up their output with American "know-how."

Prior to World War II most of these same European manufacturers had little desire to make use of many American methods and placed their reliance upon political trade treaties, subsidies and other artificial devices of government and business reciprocity. While not ready to accept all of the American ideas even now, there are many principles which they want. Among these they listed: (1) continuous assembly methods; (2) synthetic chemicals production; (3) mechanized agricultural equipment; (4) automatic machine production; (5) mechanical materials handling methods, and (6) modern incentive and time and motion systems.

American manufacturers revealed that they expect these valuable adjuncts to economic recovery will be "offered but not imposed" upon European business. They said the methods would be available if foreign business establishments wanted them.

A further advantage of the technique is that these methods will enable European countries to make the greatest possible use of their own reserves of materials, manpower and productive facilities. If several of the major industrial regions can step up their output one-third in one year instead of four years, as has been envisaged from other sources, this improvement would completely rehabilitate the economy of regions where the methods are used.

Meanwhile, to emphasize their argument, many leading executives in industry have already offered, by letters to Paul G. Hoffman, newly appointed ECA administrator, to volunteer for active service in his agency in order to assure all possible assistance in the program now under way through governmental channels.

April 11, 1948

What We Must Do Next in Europe

Foreign Ministers of the Western Union nations during their recent quarterly session in The Hague. From the left are Bevin, Britain; Bidault, France; Baron van Boetzelaer, The Netherlands; Spaak, Belgium, and Dupong, Luxembourg Premier. Bidault has since been replaced as Foreign Minister by Robert Schuman.

By HAMILTON FISH ARMSTRONG

A YEAR ago Western Europe was like a beleaguered medieval city, measuring her capacity to hold out by months and scanning the horizon for signs of possible succor. Plundered, scarred and exhausted in a long campaign, liberated at last, she saw a new foe massing in the East. She felt the pressure of its agents in her streets and heard their boasts even in the governing circles that should have been the centers of the new resistance.

America's veins were pulsing with the life blood that Europe needed. Would the transfusion be offered? In our times, free will is so limited that the opportunity to exercise it on a grand scale was exhilarating. Some of us had no doubt that as soon as Americans understood the choice which Europe was facing they would assume all the costs and risks necessary to enable her to remain within the stream of Western civilization. So it proved. Within a year ERP had been suggested, debated, adopted and put into operation.

As a result, Europe west of the Iron Curtain today lives, works and is not Communist. In Italy, France and Greece, where a year ago communism was advancing, it still has not been defeated, but it has suffered severe defeats. In the other countries it is increasingly on the defensive. And Eastern Europe, forbidden by Moscow to participate in the revival of the West, watches its progress enviously and with restless memories of lost personal and national freedom.

This is no mean achievement for one year of American foreign policy.

A year ago the problem of Europe was economic and social. This year it is political and military.

This year's problem grows directly out of last year's. As the path of economic salvation for the Western nations becomes clearer under ERP the risk that the Soviet Union will intervene to frustrate their progress along it becomes greater. For if the Western nations are healthy they will be immune to Communist infiltration and continue to magnetize Eastern Europe. What is more, their strength, added to that of the United States and other faithful members of the United Nations, can make the barrier against Soviet aggression absolute.

We are as concerned to bring about this result as the Kremlin is to prevent it. So far the advantage has been ours. The nations of Western Europe disregarded Soviet threats of retaliation, accepted our aid, turned their backs on communism and threw in their lot with us. Now that, as we hoped and planned, they are in our camp, we must help make them able to stand up to the threat of Communist aggression from without just as last year we helped make them able to stand up to Communist revolution from within.

The essence of our decision to do this is not military so much as political, in the sense that an understanding of the broad movements of history is political. Yet it must be substantiated by both political and military action.

WE must reiterate in terms specifically applicable to the present emergency the general pledge of support against aggression which we have already given all our fellow-members of the United Nations. We and those who will reciprocate this more specific pledge must bring our plans for the use of our joint forces against aggression to the same pitch of readiness which they would have reached if the Military Staff Committee of the U. N. Security Council had been permitted to function. And we must supply them, to the extent of our capacity, with arms and materials, so that they may be ready to do their part under those plans effectively.

These actions should all be taken now. They constitute a confirmation of the policies we

HAMILTON FISH ARMSTRONG has been editor since 1928 of Foreign Affairs, published by the Council on Foreign Relations. From 1942-44 he was a member of the State Department's Committee on Postwar Foreign Problems. He recently returned from a tour of Europe.

adopted when we joined the United Nations and voted ERP. They extend those policies only in that they make them more precise.

It always seems more risky to be precise than general—at the start. Actually, the maximum risk would be to retain the obligations of the Charter without arranging the collaborative means for carrying them out successfully, and to continue building up Europe with American goods and money without assuring her a breathing spell of safety in which to turn them to effective account.

THE first objective, of course, is to avert war, by making plain to a potential aggressor that if he takes the final plunge he will be sure of finding powerful forces ranged against him. The second is to make certain that if this deterrent fails and war nevertheless comes, those forces will be brought into such instant and harmonious operation that they will be assured of victory.

European statesmen differ about what are the potential risks of war today, but not about the fact that a risk exists. The fear in Foreign Office circles in London is that Stalin may be as ignorant of the temper of the West as Hitler was, and that he may blunder as badly in estimating its limits. French and other Continental leaders worry not only about this possibility but about the risk of a deliberate Soviet attack.

The French line of reasoning runs as follows:

A year ago everything seemed to favor the fulfillment of Soviet ambitions. Looking at Western Europe, members of the Politburo saw a power vacuum. Looking at the United States, about to indulge in one of its mysterious political orgies, they figured that party leaders would never be able to agree on a program of European aid, and that even if they did its progress would soon be disrupted by the economic crisis which, according to Marxist prophecy, was about to overwhelm the capitalist world. Already in March, President Truman had announced a policy of military aid for Greece and Turkey. Moscow counted on his getting his fingers burned. All these events would fan a recrudescence of American isolationism.

THIS year, by contrast, members of the Politburo look out on a very different world scene.

In Western Europe, a defensive coalition was formed by Britain, France and the Low Countries at Brussels on March 17, 1948. The American policy of strengthening resistance to communism around the whole Soviet periphery has been pushed more vigorously than Moscow expected, and has been more successful, notably in Italy, Greece and Turkey. Moscow also counted on regimenting life within her own zone of Europe quite easily. But Yugoslavs, Czechs, Poles and others are not the *mujiks* that the Russian revolutionaries had to deal with, but lettered peoples proud of their nationality and experienced in independence.

NOR have American affairs marched according to the Kremlin schedule. Bipartisan support of an active foreign policy did not founder on the rocky approaches to the Presidential campaign. ERP was voted and is pumping blood into the wasted veins of Europe. Rearmament has begun. The demands of these two programs have at least postponed any business depression. Revolutionaries who joined with well-meaning citizens under Mr. Wallace's umbrella, borrowed from Neville Chamberlain's bankrupt estate, seem unlikely to receive the help they counted on from unemployed and restless labor in a period of economic stagnation.

The contrast in these two pictures is taken in Paris to indicate that whereas a year ago the Russian rulers might have felt content to move forward on the current of world events without themselves making an aggressive move and without much risk of war, today they can hardly count on that sort of progress. Hence, in this reasoning, unless the Soviet program excludes war as an instrument of policy, why would not this year or next be a more propitious time for the Kremlin to act than a year or so from now, when the counter-measures of the democracies will have decisively turned the balance in their favor?

IT will be noticed that the effect of the atomic bomb on Russian calculations has not been mentioned. Obviously the men looking out from the windows of the Kremlin are taking it into account, but on the Continent there is a question whether it encourages the Russians to make war or seems to them a reason to postpone it.

Soviet strategists must guess that the present American supply of bombs is small. But they know it will grow steadily in numbers and in effectiveness per unit. They expect to develop the bomb themselves. But America will have acquired a tremendous head-start both in numbers and quality.

Probably they feel confident that we are not meditating a preventive war, even assuming we were sure that the atom bomb would bring us victory. Indeed, as things stand, they probably would count on their armies being able to occupy the capitals of Western Europe, at any rate to the Channel and the Pyrenees, before we made up our minds to use the bomb; and they would figure that, once there, their armies would be safe from the bomb. On the technical problem of the effectiveness of the bomb against communications between armies of occupation and their base they probably keep as open a mind as do some American authorities.

But here a doubt must assail them. As tension between East and West grows, and as Western cohesiveness and strength increase, will not the peoples of the Western world feel tempted to put an end somehow to the uncertainty in which the Soviet Union is compelling them to live? Will they not rebel against the perpetual drain on their resources required to keep ahead of Soviet military preparations? Will they not reach the point of exasperation where they will use the bomb against their tormentors, with or without special provocation and warning, or make demands which will lead to a showdown in which they will use the bomb as a matter of course?

RUSSIAN leaders may not dare answer these questions with a confident negative. This possibility has made statesmen on the Continent feel that, on the whole, the bomb increases the temptation for the Soviets to seek a showdown in the near future rather than risk waiting to see whether the Western world will seek one later.

Certain English Conservatives with a good record of political forecast see merit in the French analysis. But the tendency in official circles in London is to label it "too French"—by which the speaker may mean either "too logical" or "too emotional."

British officials cite the fact that, so far, there are no intelligence reports of special military preparations just inside the Soviet border. More important, they believe that Soviet Russia is too weak internally to risk war, and has run into too many difficulties in the territories she has recently brought under her sway to care to add to them. Anyway, they say, the Russian method is to deal with one big problem at a time. With the Cominform split already complicating Moscow's handling of the German problem, they do not see much likelihood that the Politburo would launch out on a great aggressive venture which would be sure to end, even if it did not begin, as a world war.

ONE further consideration seems pertinent. Mr. X. stated in "Foreign Affairs" that the American Government's effort to contain Soviet expansion at all points aims to build up an increasing strain on the Kremlin's foreign policies. As ex-Secretary Stimson put it, the American object is to make the Soviet leaders change their minds or lose their jobs. If the Soviet leaders understand that this is the adopted American policy, will they wait passively for it to become effective? If Stalin wanted or expected peace, would he have taken Ambassador Bedell Smith's very serious démarche of May 4 as a mere excuse for launching a propaganda campaign in the course of which he hurled Mr. Wallace in President Truman's face?

THE British do not ignore the long-run implications of a line of thought like this, and, of course, they are worried about what a dictator might do with the atomic bomb when he secures a supply. They simply feel that the chance of a blunder by the Kremlin or a Soviet commander in Germany, Austria or elsewhere is sufficiently acute to justify every possible precautionary move on our side, without losing sleep over the minor chance, as they see it, that Stalin may overnight order a sweep toward the Atlantic.

The European debate as to whether the risk of war issues chiefly from Soviet calculations or miscalculations interests the United States less than the fact that there is a risk. President Truman and Secretary Marshall gave renewed recognition to the fact that the risk exists when they welcomed the Brussels Pact and promised American help to make it successful. The Vandenberg Resolution of June 11 has now authorized them to carry out that promise, and the first discussions of how to link the United States and Canada with the West European defense system have been held in Washington with representatives of the five Brussels Pact nations.

WHILE we discuss the form of our political guarantee of the European democracies, we can press forward with *de facto* cooperation. One advantage of informal staff talks with European military leaders is that our own military leaders will have to clarify their opinions regarding various projects for the defense of Europe. Europeans are not interested in hearing about how their countries might be liberated after some years of conflict. What they want to know is how much aid we can give them in defense at the start.

Our various military services are supposed to be somewhat at cross-purposes about the feasibility of defending Western Europe and about the methods to be used in the attempt. It will be salutary for them to discuss the problem on the assumption that for political reasons that attempt is going to be made.

How to supply American arms to Europe at this stage is a more difficult problem. Presumably our Government could declare certain stocks surplus or out of date, and could sell them to our friends in Europe or lend-lease them. But the major part of the answer must be an effort by American industry, and by European industry supplied in part with American raw materials, to provide at an accelerated pace and in accordance with an agreed priority rating, the particular equipment most needed for joint operations.

MEANWHILE, the British welcome the bomber squadrons which we are stationing at British airfields for "training" purposes, but wish the system could be extended to France and the Low Countries. They also are particularly anxious for the French forces to be better equipped. They think France might be less reluctant to permit a controlled German recovery, and the full integration of the Ruhr industry with West European recovery plans, once she has regained her military strength and once she is assured that the United States as well as Britain will be her partner from the start in opposing any Russian attempt to make use of a revived Germany in an attack on the West.

For it must be understood that the French fear today is not so much of Germany alone, as in the past, but of Germany as a partner and spearhead of Russia. French leaders think that Americans like General Clay ignore this danger in their preoccupation with the direct Soviet danger. Once the German war potential has been restored, even under Western supervision, the French see no possibility of outbidding Moscow for Germany's favor. What can the West offer Germany? Nothing, unless the Saar and frontier rectifications at the expense of France. What can Moscow offer Germany? In the East, the former German territory which is now Polish, and in the West —the West.

BEFORE the time for such unequal bargaining comes, France must be as strong as possible herself and joined in partnership with great allies. She sees no chance for ultimate peace and safety except in a group which possesses power superior to a Russo-German combination, and she feels that she must delay German recovery, even to the detriment of West European recovery, until that group takes shape.

On this more general score, then, as well as with a view to the immediate military situation, there is a strong argument for early American participation in the organization of the nations of Western Europe for defense against aggression.

The need goes beyond our participation in an observer role in the military committee of the Brussels Treaty powers, and beyond whatever arms we may be able to give those powers at short notice. It is important to avoid any misunderstanding by our people or by the Europeans as to the nature of the action we are taking to build up a defense system against possible Soviet aggression. And it is vital that the Soviet Union understand just what we are doing and intend to do. The United States must assemble the whole of its influence to prevent war. It must not hazard being sucked into war, as Britain was in 1914 under Sir Edward Grey, without having made plain to its possible antagonists the full measure of the risk they run.

EUROPEAN leaders have recognized the difficulty of our taking action on a political guarantee before the new President and Congress are elected, and have deeply regretted it. They are certain that once the United States has given a specific undertaking to support the European democracies against aggression, the risk of aggression, either blundering or deliberate, will be enormously reduced. A promise by the United States to be in a war against aggression from the start, instead of after it has already been halfway lost, as in 1917 and 1941, will go far to make sure, in European eyes, that the promise will not be put to proof.

But now that a special session of Congress has assembled it is possible to do almost at once what a few weeks ago seemed impracticable. We can have *de facto* cooperation; and we can add to the psychological impact of a formal declaration of policy in the shape of a treaty approved by the Senate.

Approval of an agreement associating the United States in the defense of Western Europe, in harmony with the Vandenberg Resolution, would not be grist to the campaign mill of either Republicans or Democrats. Leaders on both sides supported that resolution, and the policy which it is designed to implement could not have become our national policy without the cooperation of both. Advantage would accrue not to either party but to the nation.

THE gravity of the present emergency should persuade Senate leaders of both parties to set controversial issues aside long enough to act on it; and if they act on it, they are bound to support it, for no association could be imagined which more closely affected our national security in the precise connotation of their own declaration.

Last autumn, I suggested that the failure of all efforts to give substance to the enforcement provisions of the Charter made supplementary security measures necessary, and that those members of the United Nations who were anxious to carry out their obligations of mutual self-defense against aggression should agree to do so voluntarily even in cases when a veto prevented the Security Council from ordering it. They might make the commitment in a special protocol open to all U. N. members, or in a series of regional treaties on the model of the Rio treaty of Sept. 2, 1947. Either method of arranging group defense would be authorized by Article 51 and other articles of the Charter.

Given the present precarious situation in Berlin, where some Russian move, either intentional or blundering, might require us at any moment to make almost instantaneous decisions involving war, delay in acting along one or other of these lines is increasingly risky.

The natural tendency will be to follow the easier course of underwriting by treaty the five members of the Brussels Pact. But if we bear in mind the interests of the United Nations as a whole, with which our own long-term interests are so closely bound up, we may well decide to emphasize our intention to carry out our world-wide commitment under the Charter to resist aggression, whatever its source and against whomever it may be directed, instead of limiting that commitment by implication to nations with which we have signed special group agreements.

WE can do this by signing a general protocol open to all faithful members of the United Nations, those now directly menaced and others as well. The phraseology of the agreement can be simple, and so can the procedure by which it is to be brought into operation in case of need. While this is being settled, we shall be showing our practical support for the Western European security pact by participating as an observer in the discussions of its military committee and by arranging to sell or "lend-lease" them certain categories of arms and to help them manufacture others.

Then Congress can add to these physical preparations to deter and if need be defeat aggression, the immense weight of an unmistakable political guarantee. If in these circumstances war should come, we need not feel that we have omitted any practicable step in harmony with the Charter to ward off such an untold calamity, or to survive it.

FOREIGN AID BY U. S. COST $18,200,000,000

WASHINGTON, Aug. 4 (AP)—President Truman today sent to Congress a report showing this country furnished $18,200,000,000 in post-war foreign aid up to Jan. 1, 1948

The report was prepared by the national advisory council on international monetary and financial problems. It shows the gold and dollar assets of other countries dropped from $23,000,000,000 in 1945 to $17,800,000,000 at the end of 1947.

The report covers foreign financial operations prior to the European Recovery Program. It indicates that western European nations taking part in the Marshall Plan lost more than one-fourth of their total reserves between the war's end and the start of that program.

"The consequence of this decline in gold and dollar balances was that most countries of the world in 1948 had inadequate resources in gold and foreign exchange to maintain working balances * * * for their note issues," the council said.

It estimated the total gold and dollar resources of the Marshall Plan countries last year at $7,500,000,000, compared with $10,300,000,000 in July, 1945.

The council was created by the Bretton Woods Agreements Act to advise the Government on foreign lending. Its members are Secretary of Treasury Snyder, chairman; Secretary of State Marshall, Secretary of Commerce Sawyer, Chairman Thomas B. McCabe of the Federal Reserve Board, Chairman William M. Martin Jr., of the Export-Import Bank of Washington, and Economic Cooperation Administrator Paul G. Hoffman.

August 5, 1948

EUROPE MAKES BID FOR LONGER ERP AID

Marshall Plan Nations Doubt Self-Sufficiency Can Be Won by '52 Without New Help

ALLOTMENT HITCH ARISES

Hoffman Says $150,000,000 Fund for Liberalizing Trade Cannot Be Diverted

By LANSING WARREN
Special to THE NEW YORK TIMES.

PARIS, Sept. 1—Amid suggestions that the Marshall Plan was in danger of being compromised, two top officials of the European Council of the plan issued today a statement that was regarded as a supreme appeal to the United States for more extended dollar aid.

The stringency was made more acute since the device by which the latest schedule of allotments was made acceptable was the use of a special $150,000,000 pool set aside to assist in liberalizing European trade. A letter from Paul G. Hoffman, Economic Cooperation Administrator, sent late tonight to the European Council, declared that this could not be done. Mr. Hoffman's note expressed satisfaction that agreement had been reached, but added that the fund "cannot at this time be made a part of the individual country programs."

It was only by increasing the general allotments by the amount of this fund that the mediators achieved acceptance of the accord without the reservations that most nations had made about the plan in their individual statements. Hope was expressed tonight in council circles that a way might yet be found to make it possible to use these funds, perhaps by providing that they should be reconstituted at a future date.

Drop in Exports Blamed

Today's report was issued on behalf of Robert Marjolin, French secretary general of the council, and Baron Snoy of Belgium, its chairman. It said that after one year of the Marshall Plan, Europe's recovery was slackening instead of progressing. Recovery is said to be gaining less than the reductions in United States aid, so that at the present rate self-sufficiency cannot be attained by the time aid is scheduled to cease in 1952.

Noting the aforementioned facts and putting the blame on the sudden drop this year in Europe's exports to the dollar zone, Mr. Marjolin, who declared he was also speaking for Baron Snoy, said at a press conference that this grave situation made the dollar problem the "fundamental question of the whole free world today."

"Europe," he said, "is not now on the road to viability, but this is not solely a European problem. It is a problem for the United States and also for the whole free world. It is our conviction that the fundamentals of this problem must be reconsidered at a very early date and that this organization will have to concentrate its efforts to this end."

His statement made it plain that Europe would require greater dollar aid or that, by some means not yet devised, it must succeed in improving its balance of trade with the United States. Taken in conjunction with the call of the Council of Europe's Economic Committee for a reduction of United States tariffs and for the convertibility of currencies, the Marshall Plan Council's report constitutes an urgent appeal for an extension of dollar assistance.

Situation Seen as Serious

In council circles there was no effort to conceal the fact that the situation was considered very serious and that unless some remedy could be found next week in Washington, the whole Marshall Plan might be compromised.

M. Marjolin stressed today that the solution endorsed last night did not come up to the estimates of minimum needs. He hailed the decision to accept the plan as evidence of European solidarity in a time of difficulty.

In the report that M. Marjolin and Baron Snoy made to the council, it was declared that Britain's position had worsened considerably more than the others and that the United Kingdom would be less able than any other country to cover its 1949-50 deficit in gold and dollars. It was Britain's refusal to accept the original figures that had held up the council's accord.

"We have paid very special attention to Britain's position not only in view of the welfare of the populations of the sterling area, but also because of the immense part played by the sterling area in the European and world economy," said the report. "This is a problem for which our organization can find no solution, but to which it was our duty to draw particular attention."

Hoffman Gratified by Accord

WASHINGTON, Sept. 1 (UP)—Administrator Paul G. Hoffman said today he was gratified by Western Europe's division of Marshall Plan funds for fiscal 1950, but he cautioned that Congress still must approve an appropriation.

Britain Views Accord as Fair

Special to THE NEW YORK TIMES.

LONDON, Sept. 1—British reaction today to the tentative allocation of Marshall Plan funds announced in Paris yesterday was that the decisions were fair and statesmanlike even though the results would present problems for the United Kingdom.

It was said in official quarters that the report showed no evidence of discrimination against any country and that it would not be challenged. Problems are anticipated in connection with the imports program for 1949-50, which will depend partly on the outcome of the coming talks in Washington.

September 2, 1949

CONGRESS APPROVES FOREIGN AID FUNDS, REJECTING ANY CUT

House, Senate Quickly Support Accord Conferees Reached in Two Months of Debate

TOTAL IS $5,809,990,000

An Effort to Kill Provision for $150,000,000 in Loans to Member Nations Defeated

By FELIX BELAIR Jr.
Special to THE NEW YORK TIMES.

WASHINGTON, Sept. 29—A foreign aid appropriation of $5,809,990,000 got final Congressional approval tonight. The measure includes $3,628,380,000 for European recovery in the current fiscal year and $150,000,000 of additional loan authorizations for Marshall Plan countries from the Export-Import Bank. It now goes to the White House for President Truman's approval.

The joint conference committee agreement on the bill was first approved by voice vote in the House in the early afternoon. It was then voted favorably by the Senate just before that body recessed at 6:51 P. M.

Senate approval of the conference agreement came unexpectedly on a motion by Chairman Kenneth McKellar of the Appropriations Committee. There was no discussion. Senator McKellar earlier had indicated that he would let the bill go over until tomorrow.

In addition to Economic Cooperation Administration funds for the current year, the measure provides $1,074,000,000 already obligated by the agency in the final quarter of the fiscal year 1949-1950; $45,000,000 for the Greece-Turkey aid program; $912,500,000 for government and relief in Army-occupied areas, and $110,000 for the joint Congressional foreign aid "watchdog" committee.

House action came after an effort to kill a provision for $150,000,000 of Export-Import Bank loans to participating countries was defeated on a roll call vote of 177 to 123. Representative John Taber, Republican, of New York, led the fight against the loan provision but his argument was directed mainly against British socialism.

It was evident early in the debate that few votes would be changed by what was said on the floor today in the face of an overwhelming desire to speed the measure on its way to the Senate. More than two months have been spent in haggling by conferees for the two legislative bodies.

Although one of the conferees for the House, Representative Taber said that he would vote against adoption of the conference report as well as the $150,000,000 loan provision. The latter would have the effect of increasing Marshall Plan disbursements by $24,000,000 a month above the average for the first seventeen months of the program, he asserted.

"We should cut down on unnecessary gratuities and try to place this operation on a business-like basis which would wind up at the end of four years," Mr. Taber continued.

Federal Deficit Is Stressed

Finally, he declared that "the whole question is whether we intend to maintain the Socialist Government in power in England" and make it possible for that Government to continue a food subsidy costing $2,000,000,000 a year with socialized medicine costing another $1,000,000,000, while the United States faced a deficit of $5,500,000,000 on the Federal budget.

Representative Francis Case, Republican, of South Dakota, criticized the conference committee's compromise that left it to the discretion of the ECA Administrator to determine whether $25,000 could be spent to advantage on a re-examination of the German reparations plants question.

Out where he came from, Mr. Case told the House, it was axiomatic that "he who pays the fiddler can call the tune." He suggested that Britain and France should be required to release for retention in Western Germany additional industrial units that had been marked for dismantlement as reparations.

No effort was made to bring the question to a vote. Representative J. Vaughan Gary, Democrat, of Virginia, who was in charge of the bill, suggested that if the reparations plants issue was reopened for a third time the United States might get a reputation like Russia's of not sticking to its agreements.

More Recovery Funds Allocated

Still operating under the joint resolution permitting Federal agency spending at last year's rate pending action on specific appropriations, the Economic Cooperation Administration authorized $91,802,000 of new spending for European recovery today. This included a $40,000,000 grant to Britain for buying Canadian wheat. Britain got $10,000,000 for the same purpose yesterday.

Under agreements reached at the recent tripartite dollar talks, Britain is permitted to use ECA funds in spending up to $175,000,000 for Canadian wheat this year, provided $30,000,000 of other ECA grants are used by the British in purchasing United States wheat.

Britain also received the agency's approval today to buy $14,410,000 worth of Canadian aluminum and aluminum products; $2,600,000 worth of American nonfarm tractors; to spend $1,500,000 for United States farm equipment; $1,000,000 for manilla fiber from the Philippines, and $1,490,000 for tractors and other farm equipment from the United States and Canada.

At the same time, it was ruled that musical instruments, toys and sporting goods were not essential to European recovery and therefore ineligible for Marshall Plan grants.

The new ineligible list also included automobiles valued at $3,000 or more or convertible type cars regardless of value; automobile radio; beverages, cameras and equipment including film; clothing; confections, household equipment; jewelry and precious metals and stones and draperies.

The ECA also announced today its approval of an expenditure of about $57,000,000 in French counterpart funds to finance that country's investment program for October. Counterpart funds in local currencies are required to be deposited by recipient countries in proportionate amounts to grants received under the Marshall Plan.

Of francs involved, about 6,800,000,000 will be used for coal mines; 7,500,000,000 for electric power installations; 3,000,000,000 for war damage reconstruction; 500,000,000 for private industry, and 2,100,000,000 for the development of overseas territories.

Overseas development projects approved by the agency include road building in French West Africa, French Equatorial Africa, Madagascar and New Caledonia, improvement of port facilities at Casablanca and electrification in Algeria.

September 30, 1949

2 FOREIGN AID ACTS PUT INTO OPERATION

Truman Approves the Mutual Defense and the Economic Assistance Measures

By HAROLD B. HINTON
Special to THE NEW YORK TIMES.

WASHINGTON, Oct. 6—With President Truman's signature today, the long debated project to supply military assistance to foreign countries to the amount of $1,314,010,000 by next June 30 became law. The new statute is called the Mutual Defense Assistance Act of 1949.

In giving it his approval, President Truman said that the measure "will strengthen the peace of the world." He predicted that it would promote the economic welfare of the world's free nations and restore their confidence in the future by removing the shadow of fear of armed aggression against them.

The President also signed the $5,809,990,000 foreign economic aid bill. He made no comment on this measure.

Of the military bill, the President's statement said:

"This act is necessary only because of the unsettled conditions of the world today which we, in concert with many other nations, are striving to overcome.

"It is my belief that we shall be successful in these efforts to achieve international understanding and to establish, in accordance with our national policy, effective international control and reduction of armaments, through the United Nations."

The document signed by the President is merely an authorization, however. Congress must still vote the exact amount of money to be expended. The State and Defense Departments hope that hearings before the Appropriations Committees of the House and the Senate will start early next week.

In its final form, the act requires President Truman to approve plans for the "integrated defense" of the North Atlantic area before the last $900,000,000 of the projected supplies can be shipped across the ocean. Only the first $100,000,000 can be spent, once the appropriation is approved, prior to a Presi-

TRUMAN SIGNS FOREIGN ARMS AID BILL

The Chief Executive affixing his signature to the Mutual Defense Assistance Act of 1949. The New York Times (by Bruce Hoertel)

dential finding that an "integrated defense" is planned.

The professional military men who will undertake to formulate strategic defense plans of a character that will enable Mr. Truman to make his finding started on their task shortly after the bill was signed. They are the ten members of the Military Committee established yesterday by the Defense Committee of the North Atlantic Treaty organization.

Of the twelve signatory powers, Iceland and Luxembourg did not elect to appoint members of the Military Committee, although they were represented on the Defense Committee yesterday.

Military Committee Personnel

Gen. Omar N. Bradley, chairman of the United States Joint Chiefs of Staff, was chairman at the initial meeting today. The members, in addition to General Bradley, were the following:

Lieut. Gen. Etienne Baele, Chief of Staff of the Belgian Army; Lieut. Gen. Charles Foulkes, chairman of the Chief of Staff Committee of Canada; Maj. Gen. Eric C. V. Moeller, Chief of Staff of the Danish Army; Gen. Charles Lecheres, Chief of Staff of the French Air Force; Lieut. Gen. Efisio Marras, Chief of Staff of the Italian Army; Vice Admiral Jonkheer E. J. Van Holthe, Chief of Staff of the Netherlands Navy; Lieut. Gen. Bjarne Oen, Commander in Chief of the Norwegian Air Force; Gen. Anibal Valdez Passos Souza, Commander in Chief of the Portuguese Army, and Gen. Sir William Morgan, chairman of the British Joint Services Mission.

A sort of executive committee, called the Standing Group, was appointed to function continuously in Washington. It is made up of General Bradley, General Morgan and Lieut. Gen. Paul Ely, for France. The Standing Group will hold its first meeting in the Pentagon Building on Monday.

The Standing Group will set up immediately a staff to start work on the fundamental questions on which it must offer recommendations. It is hoped to secure, in the reasonably near future, agreement of the North Atlantic Council on prime decisions that must be reached before President Truman can certify that an integrated defense plan exists.

One of the first of these must be the frontiers of the area to be defended by arms in the event of attack. This will probably be the thorniest of the major issues to be settled.

Assignment of Roles

From this will grow the assignment of roles and missions. For example, it would be logical for France to concentrate on ground forces, and not to branch out in a naval building program, since the United States and the United Kingdom already possess overwhelming naval strength between them.

It is hoped to avoid the natural tendency of each military establishment to wish to build up for itself ground, sea and air forces.

Each of them must obviously maintain sufficient force, of rounded complexion, to maintain internal security and to defend itself against the first shock of a surprise attack.

Certain divisions of military labor are well indicated, however. The United States and Great Britain will probably be assigned the defense of deep-sea lanes. France will get the responsibility for providing the main force of ground troops.

Strategic bombardment will presumably be assigned to the United States. To Great Britain might go the medium, or tactical bombardment in direct support of ground forces.

It was pointed out today that the Western European Union staff took fifteen months from the date of formation to agreement on a defense plan involving only five countries and a relatively limited terrain. The Standing Group must act much more swiftly, for it is intended to have the weapons and equipment either in the hands of the Western European military establishment or in process of manufacture, by next June 30.

PRESIDENT'S STATEMENT

WASHINGTON, Oct. 6 (AP)—Following is the text of President Truman's statement on the signing of the Mutual Defense Assistance Act of 1949:

I have just signed the Mutual Defense Assistance Act of 1949. This is a notable contribution to the collective security of the free nations of the world. It is one of the many steps we are taking with other free peoples to strengthen our common defense in furtherance of the principles of international peace and order enshrined in the Charter of the United Nations.

The dominant objective of our foreign policy is to create peaceful and stable conditions throughout the world, so that men may lead happier and more fruitful lives. This objective cannot, however, be achieved if the economic efforts of free men are overshadowed by the fear of aggression.

By strengthening the common defense, this act will do much to allay that fear. The security which this act offers will aid in promoting the economic welfare of the free nations and in restoring their confidence in a peaceful and prosperous future.

Since the ratification of the North Atlantic Treaty, the countries of the North Atlantic community have made considerable progress in working together for their mutual security. Their combined activity will do much to increase the effectiveness of the assistance to be provided under this act. Further progress in these arrangements for the common defense will make it possible to provide the full measure of protection which this act offers to this country and other nations.

Recent developments in the field of armaments have strengthened the free nations in their adherence to the principle of a common defense—the principle that underlies this act. By emphasizing the common determination of free nations to protect themselves against the threat or fear of aggression, the Mutual Defense Assistance Act will strengthen the peace of the world.

This act is necessary only because of the unsettled conditions of the world today which we, in concert with many other nations, are striving to overcome. It is my belief that we shall be successful in these efforts to achieve international understanding and to establish, in accordance with our national policy, effective international control and reduction of armaments, through the United Nations.

We, as Well as Europe, Must Do Our Part

It won't be easy, Mr. Hoffman warns, but unless the Marshall Plan succeeds the outlook is bleak.

By PAUL G. HOFFMAN

AS Administrator of the Economic Cooperation Administration I have visited many foreign countries in the last eighteen months. Two impressions and one firm conviction stand out vividly in my mind

These are the impressions:

First, the world is going through a period of rapid and violent change. We are compressing into this first decade of the atomic era political, economic and social developments that will influence and perhaps determine the course of history for a century.

Second, the free world is looking to the United States for leadership.

This is the conviction:

I am convinced that the American business community has within its hands the opportunity and the capacity to insure the ultimate success of the Marshall Plan. To do so, moreover, is as much in its own economic self-interest as in the broader altruistic interest of world peace.

The question all of us have to face is whether it will be a hundred years of peace in which free men can build a better world, or whether it will be a new dark age of enslavement. We alone have that combination of economic and financial resources, military strength, and moral force which can assure the preservation of free institutions.

I WAS in northern China just before the Communists triumphed there.

I was in South Korea the day the United Nations recognized a new Government there. I saw at first hand the splendid effort of a newly liberated people to establish a democratic Government. I observed the difficulties faced by the leaders of this new republic in South Korea, difficulties even greater than those faced by our founding fathers.

Two months ago I was in Greece, where battles have been raging amid monuments of a timeless past. It looks now as though the Greek Government has won its fight. Just before I arrived in Greece Government troops had driven the guerrillas out of the Vitsi-Grammos region, their last stronghold.

It is not until you leave the comparative safety and comfort of America and spend time in countries such as China, Korea, and Greece that you get the feel of the wicked force that stems from the Kremlin.

As a protector of the weak and oppressed, Russian communism is a gigantic fraud. The last trace of idealism has been squeezed out of it. The Kremlin has long since abandoned the Marxist credo that each should contribute according to his ability and each be rewarded according to his needs. In place of that credo the Soviet Union has substituted a ruthless economic system which gives rich rewards to the party favorites and imposes drastic penalties on those who are out of favor or who through no fault of their own cannot maintain production standards set by the commissars.

If the masters of the Kremlin were content to carry on their ruthless and godless experiment in Russia alone, the outside world might be concerned but there would be little it could or should do about it. It would be a Russian problem to be solved by the Russians. But that is not the situation.

THE evidence is crystal clear to me that the Kremlin seeks nothing less than world conquest. It was hard for me to believe this, but I am utterly persuaded that it is true.

This drive of the Kremlin for world conquest can be stopped if the United States remains strong and prosperous, if Western Europe becomes strong and prosperous, and if the free nations of the Western Hemisphere and Western Europe remain united.

Looking back at the accomplishments of the last two and a half years, I think we have much to give us confidence. Thanks to the Truman Doctrine, the Marshall Plan and the Atlantic Pact, communism has not only been contained in Europe but it has been set back on its heels. And despite the Kremlin's gloomy predictions of depression in the United States, disaster

ECA Director Paul G. Hoffman tells Washington newsmen of the self-help program for the Marshall Plan nations.

PAUL G. HOFFMAN, head of the Economic Cooperation Administration, has a long-time knowledge of America's business affairs gained as a public official and director of many corporations.

in Europe, and disunity among the free peoples, and despite their best efforts to make those predictions come true, the United States remains strong and prosperous, the free nations of Western Europe are getting stronger, and, most important of all, we, the free peoples, are united.

But ahead there are grave and threatening problems. Communism will never cease to be a danger in Europe until the European economy rests on a sound basis.

MANY of the things that must be done can be done only by the Europeans themselves. They must integrate their separate economies. And they must sharply increase productivity as a foundation on which to build a higher standard of living. But there is one problem of pressing importance, the solution of which rests largely with the United States.

World trade, and especially the trade of the United States with Western Europe, is fundamentally out of balance. Other countries are simply not earning enough dollars to pay for what they must import from us and which they must have to maintain the primary condition of freedom, namely, a reasonable standard of living. They have an acute "dollar shortage." We in the United States, on the other hand, have a vast export surplus which we have maintained for thirty years at the taxpayers' expense.

Our problem, Europe's problem, and the problem of many other countries in the world, is therefore the problem of the "dollar gap." This is the basic economic problem of our time but it is not new. It has been with us, largely unrecognized, for thirty years.

IN the twenty-five peacetime years since 1919 (omitting 1941-45), the United States exported goods and services worth $170 billion. During that period we imported goods and services valued at only $118 billion. This means that during those twenty-five peacetime years we exported $52 billion of goods and services more than we imported.

Most of this huge difference between our exports and imports was paid for by the United States taxpayer and sent abroad for relief and reconstruction. Part was financed privately by United States citizens in the form of investments that were largely defaulted because of inability to transfer principal and interest in dollars. And for still another part of the difference between our exports and our imports we accepted gold and other dollar assets. The gold is buried in Kentucky.

The reasons for the acute worsening of the dollar shortage since the war are not far to seek. Britain and several other European countries lost permanently most of their overseas investments during the war. Moreover, they lost, though perhaps temporarily, most of the dollar revenues from shipping, insurance, and brokerage.

A third sharp loss of dollar income to Europe resulted from the physical disruption and loosening of political ties in the Far East, accompanied by the development of synthetic materials in the United States. American purchases of rubber, silk, tin, jute and other raw materials from the Far East have only partially recovered since the war, and the flow of dollars available to Europe through triangular trade has been correspondingly reduced.

In addition, East-West trade within Europe has so shrunk that Western Europe, formerly able to obtain needed food and raw materials from Eastern European countries in exchange for manufactures, has been obliged to buy its food and raw materials increasingly in the Americas, where its possibilities of payment with manufactured goods have been less good.

IN trade with the United States, Western Europe had a deficit of $4.2 billion in 1946, $5.4 billion in 1947, and $3.5 in 1948. These deficits were financed largely by United States grants and loans, including ERP funds.

As kingpin in the free world's economy, as the free world's major creditor and supplier, as a world leader, the United States has an inescapable duty and responsibility to lead the way toward a fundamental solution of the dollar shortage that will provide a solid economic foundation for the free world. The dollar gap can be easily closed —there is no great difficulty in doing that. Cut off United States aid, and Europe's imports would fall to the level of her exports, that is to say, from $4.5 billion to $1.5 billion. But this would be a vital blow to Europe's reconstruction effort. Food rations in many countries would fall below subsistence level. In the resulting unemployment, hunger and misery, communism would breed.

THE problem, therefore, in this dangerous and divided world of today is not just to balance Europe's dollar trade, but to balance it at a high level to allow Europe to remain free.

The people of the United States have already determined that it is not in their interest to allow the dollar gap to be closed at a level that would mean anarchy in Europe. This is the reason for the Marshall Plan. This is also the reason why the Marshall Plan is not just another relief and reconstruction job but an effort to root out the fundamental causes of imbalance in Europe's dollar accounts. It is the reason why Marshall Plan funds are used in every way possible to increase productivity, increase efficiency, and organize European economic life so that it may be self-supporting and at the same time provide a decent standard of living for its people.

The Marshall Plan will and should definitely end in 1952. Assuming that American exports to Western Europe will not be subsidized thereafter by direct gifts and loans to European countries, and assuming that we do not wish trade stabilized at a disaster level, only one course remains for closing the dollar gap: Europe must greatly increase its sales in the American market. This means that both Europe and the United States must take every step possible to increase United States imports from Europe.

WHAT are some of the things that must be done?

Let us consider first what Europe must do.

To increase productivity and bring down costs and prices, European manufacturers must make a vigorous effort not only to modernize their plants, but also to bring about more constructive relationships between workers and management. As an essential element in Western Europe's cost-lowering program she must establish a Europe-wide market without trade, tariff and exchange barriers so that large-scale European industry will have available a mass market and so that Europe-wide competition can exercise a continuous discipline on costs and prices.

Europe must develop new and aggressive merchandising techniques (advertising, promotion, market surveys) and adapt products in style, design, packaging, etc., for the American market.

Europe must provide adequate credit facilities for foreign trade, and adequate guarantees against loss.

There are many other things that Europe can do to increase its exports to the United States, but those perhaps are the principal ones.

WHAT must we in the United States do to increase our imports from Europe?

The most important thing, as stated earlier, is for us to remain strong and prosperous. Even a small reduction in the rate of our production and consumption in the United States affects imports sharply.

Second, we must encourage private capital to flow in a large annual stream into foreign investment, not only in Europe but in less developed regions of the world.

Third, we must continue to lower our tariff barriers. Through the Reciprocal Trade Agreements Act we have been for fifteen years lowering the tariff walls we built around ourselves. But many American tariff rates still remain high and, in some cases, prohibitory on a wide range of products, many of which are non-competitive with United States goods.

Fourth, we must revise our customs procedures. Many who would increase their sales in our market complain that unwarranted delays and complications and costs connected with the appraisal, assessment, and marking of imported goods make it difficult or impossible to increase trade. Fortunately the United States Treasury has been studying this problem for two years and specific relief is under way.

Fifth, we must ease existing Federal, state, and local laws that prohibit the purchase with public funds of imported products or products made in the United States of foreign materials. These restrictions, originating in an earlier day when United States interests in a large world trade were less marked, today run counter to our national interest.

Sixth, we must recognize that imports do not hurt us, but enrich us, both as individuals and as a nation. They bring us goods that we could not otherwise have or afford. They enable us to export an equal value of things we produce best at lower cost. They can reduce the high taxes we are now paying for foreign aid and for national defense. They can help insulate Europe and the world against communism, strengthen our allies, bring better living to all of us.

The winning of the peace itself is involved in this question of expanded imports. The primary condition of peace is continued unity of the nations of the free world. This unity can be maintained only if relationships between Western Europe and the United States are put on a business basis, with Europe paying for what it buys from us with what it sells to us. No peace and unity can rest upon the tensions of a creditor-debtor relationship.

OUR new role as the world's largest creditor nation seems glamorous as long as it is considered only in generalities. But when we begin to discuss it in specifics, as I have been doing, the hardships, the responsibilities of the role appear. I know full well that the acceptance of larger imports which our national and international interests require may in certain cases adversely affect particular interests in the United States. But dare we in our new role continue to subject the whole American people to several billions of dollars of taxes each year in order to protect these special groups? And much more importantly, dare we endanger the peace of the world by so doing?

It will not be easy for the United States to play wisely and well its new role as a leader of the free world. But the stakes we are playing for are tremendous. If we falter in that leadership, if we think only in terms of immediate advantage, and if we permit narrow and sectional interests to control our actions, the outlook is bleak indeed. If, on the other hand, we do play our new role wisely and well, the Atomic Era can well be the Golden Age men have dreamed of through the centuries.

November 13, 1949

A CURRENCY UNION IN MARSHALL PLAN TO START IN 90 DAYS

Hoffman, E. C. A. Chief, Tells House Committee He Will Ask Dollar Pool for Europe

TRADE CLEARANCE IS AIM

Exchange Will Be Multilateral, Replacing Present System of Commodity Purchases

By FELIX BELAIR Jr.
Special to THE NEW YORK TIMES.

WASHINGTON, Jan. 13—Paul G. Hoffman, Economic Cooperation Administrator, told the House Foreign Affairs Committee today that a European currency union for clearing payments among Marshall Plan countries would be "set up and operating" within ninety days.

The ECA chief told the committee further that he would ask Congress soon for authority to use part of the $3,100,000,000 Marshall Plan appropriation suggested by President Truman to provide a "dollar pool" from which the central clearing agency could settle current trading accounts of the participating countries.

The prospect held out by Mr. Hoffman was the most optimistic forecast yet presented to a Congressional unit for early solution of the payments problem, which remains the chief obstacle to a liberalization of trade in Western Europe. He appeared before the House group in support of the Administration's Point Four program of technical assistance to underdeveloped areas.

The magnitude of the yet to be appropriated ECA funds that would be diverted for use as "free dollars" by the proposed clearing agency was not indicated by Mr. Hoffman. Unofficial estimates here place the amount between $400,000,000 and $500,000,000 but not even the Organization for European Economic Cooperation in Paris has yet attempted a working figure.

For one thing, the experts of ECA and the OEEC can only guess at the volume of intra-European trade that would result from liberalizing trade and payment practices through establishment of a multilateral clearing agency accompanied by gradual abandonment of quantitative restrictions such as import quotas and a lowering of tariff rates.

All that is definitely known and agreed on both sides of the Atlantic is that the proposed clearing arrangement would require substantially fewer dollars than are now devoted to the intra-European payments plan. This device, which provides for clearances only on a bilateral basis, will cost about $800,000,000 during the current fiscal year.

But where the latter scheme utilized commodities purchased with ECA dollars as a medium of settlement, the new currency union would require free dollars at the disposal of the clearing agency or use in canceling out deficits and surpluses in current accounts of the participating countries.

Under the existing payments scheme, the combined deficit of the net importing Marshall Plan countries is made up by conditioning grants of ECA aid to the net exporting countries on their extension of a like amount of credit to the countries to whom they are net exporters. Because of its bilateral limitations the plan has not worked too well.

See Help in Point Four

Mr. Hoffman sought at the outset of his testimony to "disqualify" himself as an expert on the Point Four program. He said that that program could pick up where the Marshall Plan leaves off in July, 1952, but suggested it could not substitute for economic integration of Western Europe as a means of raising living standards there.

At the same time, Mr. Hoffman was not discounting the potentialities of a technical assistance program. He likened the undertaking to the rural rehabilitation program started by ECA in China, and said the Communists would not be in control there now if expenditures on rural development had been started five years earlier.

"Wherever these programs operated," said Mr. Hoffman, "the attitude of the people changed so that the only opposition encountered by the Communist forces from civilian groups came in those areas where these rural development programs had been operating."

The ECA chief warned the committee, however, that "you cannot

TESTIFYING ON POINT FOUR PROGRAM

Paul G. Hoffman, ECA Administrator, before the House Foreign Affairs Committee. The New York Times (Washington Bureau)

export American know-how, but only try to create the conditions under which other peoples want to import it." More explicitly, Mr. Hoffman explained, "you cannot ram assistance down people's throats."

Plans 'Highly Successful'

The technical assistance programs of the ECA for Marshall Plan countries had been highly successful, Mr. Hoffman told the committee, because the agency had merely let it be known that the assistance was available if wanted. Productivity teams from the principal participating countries had visited industrial plants here with profitable results to their home industries, he said.

In like manner, ECA had let it be known to Marshall Plan countries that it had $15,000,000 available for development projects in their overseas dependencies. Mr. Hoffman said this method plus a variation of the "hard-to-get" attitude of his agency had brought in a number of worth-while plans from the participating countries.

One such program, he said, involving only a small expenditure by ECA in Africa might easily result in driving a wedge into the international cartel in industrial diamonds in the procurement of which he said American industry had long been at the mercy of British and Belgian interests.

Mr. Hoffman said ECA now was considering plans for development projects in South Africa calling for an ECA outlay of $20,000,000 and added that he would be "very much surprised" if the resulting expenditure by participating governments in their own currencies did not run as high as $200,000,000 or $300,000,000.

Cites Taxpayers' Load

Mr. Hoffman was emphatic in advising the House group that any American aid to Europe after termination of the Marshall Plan should be on an individual country basis. He indicated there might be a few countries, such as Greece, that would require aid after the present program ended, but said this should not be used as an excuse for continuing the present load on taxpayers here.

The ECA already has notified participating governments that another estimated $150,000,000 would be withheld from allocation as grants during the current year in order to set up an incentive fund to countries undertaking financial risks in liberalizing trade and payments restrictions.

In adddition to Mr. Hoffman, the House group heard supporting testimony for the Point-Four program from a representative of the Congress of Industrial Organizations.

Donald Montgomery, director of the Washington office of the United Auto Workers said he spoke for the entire CIO in endorsing the proposal but said the organization was opposed to guarantees that would be required from beneficiary areas under a measure suggested by Representative Christian A. Herter, Republican of Massachusetts.

The CIO witness described provisions in the Herter bill as amounting "to onerous and humiliating conditions of special favoritism for United States corporations."

January 14, 1950

3.2 Billions Aid Bill Signed, Truman Calls It 'Peace Step'

By ANTHONY LEVIERO
Special to The New York Times.

WASHINGTON, June 5—President Truman today signed into law the bill that authorizes $3,200,000,000 for five foreign-aid programs. He declared that it was "a memorable step forward in our program for peace."

Members of the Senate Foreign Relations Committee and of the House Committee on Foreign Affairs, and representatives of the State Department, the Economic Cooperation Administration and other Federal departments were ranged behind the President as he put his signature on what is now officially the Foreign Economic Assistance Act of 1950.

As is customary, on the signing of an important bill, the President used several pens in writing the word "approved," the date and his signature. Then he distributed the pens among the principal witnesses.

Dean Acheson, Secretary of State, headed his department's delegation. Congress was represented by the following members:

Senator Tom Connally, chairman of the Foreign Relations Committee; Senator H. Alexander Smith, Republican of New Jersey, a member of the committee; Representative John Kee of West Virginia, chairman of the Foreign Affairs Committee; Representative Charles A. Eaton, Republican of New Jersey, senior minority member and the committee's former chairman; and Representatives James P. Richards, Democrat of South Carolina, and Frances P. Bolton, Republican of Ohio, members of the committee.

Mr. Truman paid tribute to the "forward-looking members of the Congress of both political parties" who had supported the measure through some sharp debate in sustaining the bipartisan foreign policy.

He called the bill a "typically American enterprise" in the effort to build a peaceful and prosperous world.

While the measure authorizes the programs and the sum of $3,200,000,000, it still is subject to enabling actions by the Appropriations Committees of the House and Senate. They have not yet acted, and they could recommend a smaller or a larger amount. Then the recommended figure would be subject to final action by the full House and the Senate.

As in the case of the legislative processes before the two Foreign Affairs Committees, the final authorized aid figure is expected to encounter attacks by the economy groups as well as by others who object to certain features of the proposals.

Five distinct programs, including the primary European Recovery Program, are encompassed in the bill that was signed today. One of these, which authorizes $35,000,000 for the purpose, finally gives a start to the "bold new program" or the Point Four undertakings, which President Truman first enunciated in his inaugural message in January, 1949. This set-up will provide American technical assistance designed to help backward countries to develop their resources and thus to become self-sustaining and free members of the free world community.

The act also would provide $100,000,000 for economic aid to the Republic of Korea; $94,000,000 for the people of "non-Communist China," and other pepole in that area; $27,450,000 for help to Palestine refugees, and $15,000,000 for the United Nations program on behalf of children.

In a formal statement on the bill, Mr. Truman expressed confidence that the third year of the foreign-aid programs would encourage increasing cooperation by the recipient countries, would greatly increase their collective strength, and that it would "bring closer the day when they can contribute on a self-sustaining basis to the economic growth of all free nations."

He called attention to the results of American aid in the Far East, particularly in supporting an independent Korea, and millions of people who recently won independence.

The President said too, that the Point Four Program was nothing new, since it was in keeping with American traditions of free enterprise, and that similar activities of the past would now be placed on an organized and sustained basis. By helping to raise the standards of living in backward regions, Mr. Truman added, "we shall make a tremendous contribution to the strength of freedom and the defeat of Communist imperialism."

More than Government action was necessary in the Point Four program, the Chief Executive said, in pointing out he expected continued work in this field by private groups and expanded business investment by Americans in the areas marked for assistance.

In a separate statement Vice President Alben W. Barkley declared that the Palestine refuge program "will contribute to the general economic betterment of the Near East and hence to the strength and stability of that area."

June 6, 1950

GRAY REPORT ASKS 3 MORE YEARS' AID AS EUROPEANS ARM

Survey of Foreign Economic Policies Made for President Says This Would Benefit Us

IS APPROVED BY TRUMAN

It Calls for Increased Help to Undeveloped Areas, Pacts to Get Scarce Materials

By JOSEPH A. LOFTUS
Special to THE NEW YORK TIMES.

WASHINGTON, Nov. 1[illegible] — United States aid to Western Europe should go on for three or four more years while the free world's defenses are made stronger there, President Truman was advised today in a special report.

Aid to underdeveloped areas on a more intensive scale also is imperative, the report said. These programs, it added, are consistent with this nation's own interest as well as the welfare of others.

The report submitted by Gordon Gray, president of the University of North Carolina and former Secretary of the Army, brought into focus the tremendous weight of economics in the nation's foreign policy.

Mr. Truman, who commissioned Mr. Gray last spring to re-examine our foreign economic policies, said:

"The guiding concept of Mr. Gray's report is the unity of foreign policy in its economic, political, military and informational aspects. Our national security can be assured only through effective action on all these fronts. I fully endorse Mr. Gray's statement on the basic objectives of our foreign economic policy."

The report did not estimate precisely the amount of aid that would be necessary for Western Europe during the rearmament period, but said it "should be substantially less than we have been spending for these purposes during the past year."

"This would be apart from military equipment," it continued. "The dollar amount of aid to Europe in the past year was close to $2.5 billion."

In recommending a policy on aid for underdeveloped areas, the report said private investment "should be considered as the most desirable means of providing capital, and its scope should be widened as far as possible." Stimulants and safeguards were recommended for the private-investment approach.

The report added, however, that "a heavy reliance on public lending must be recognized as essential for an aggressive development program" under present conditions.

The proposed aim was a net outflow of capital to underdeveloped areas in the range of $600,000,000 to $800,000,000 a year, of which half or more would be supplied by the World Bank from sources other than the United States Treasury.

Grants Included in Plan

Provision of this money for the development program would require "continued vigorous efforts" by the World Bank "supplemented by the Export-Import Bank," the report said.

Grants would be used where development urgently needed by the United States could not be soundly financed by loans.

"It seems probable that a needed, feasible, and effective program (of grants) would require funds of up to about 500 million dollars a year for several years, apart from emergency requirements arising from military action," the report said. "This compares with present funds of about 150 million dollars a year for those purposes."

With respect to lending, recommended steps included the following:

1. An increase in the lending authority of the Export-Import Bank from the present three and one-half to a total of five billion dollars, to make advance planning effective.
2. A general policy of permitting United States loans to be spent outside as well as within the United States. In this way, those receiving the loans could buy goods wherever they were cheapest, and other industrial countries would have an opportunity to expand exports and dollar earnings if they were sufficiently competitive.

"This would also be in the interests of the United States," the report said, "it would tend to help relieve inflationary shortages at the present time, and in the longer run to support export markets for United States goods which are likely to be most readily available."

Japan's Importance Stressed

With respect to Japan, Mr. Gray said that under stable, democratic conditions, her potential contribution would be extremely important for economic growth, the improvement of living standards and the maintenance of peace in the region. By the fiscal year 1952, with a continuation of present favorable trends, Japan may be self-supporting and may possess substantial dollar and possibly commodity reserves, although living standards will still remain below the pre-war level, the report added.

Mr. Gray recommended "further appropriations for Japanese aid should be carefully considered and measured against the effect of the favorable circumstances brought about by current developments, and also in the light of other recommendations in this report that would increase Japanese export opportunities." "However," he went on, "should Japan for any reason prove unable to increase production for export, it might need external aid."

The report also made recommendations on what should be done about the procurement and export of goods in short supply, what should be done to promote United States international trade and financial objectives, and how the foreign economic programs should be administered.

The problem of the procurement and export of materials in short supply is this:

The United States imports many minerals and other commodities vital to national security and to our economy that are produced predominantly in the underdeveloped areas.

Rearmament here and abroad greatly increases the demand for these commodities. An unchecked scramble for supplies and the inevitable effects on prices would have serious consequences for the rearmament programs, for our own economy and those of friendly nations.

Such a scramble would affect adversely the balance of payments positions of many Western European countries and Japan, and would introduce an element of instability into the economies of exporting countries.

Exports of manufactured goods are also likely to be inadequate to meet all demands, and measures may be required to see that the high priority needs of friendly nations are met.

Mr. Gray, therefore, recommended that:

1. In addition to necessary measures within the United States, international arrangements should be made to channel supplies of scarce materials among the free nations in the way that would be most effective in the common defense.
2. Export controls should be used to assure the delivery of goods required by other countries for purposes that support broad United States interests.
3. Efforts should be intensified to effect a rapid expansion in the output of scarce materials, not only through the provision of capital funds and equipment, but also through procurement activities such as long-term contracts.

Question of Morale Noted

Mr. Gray warned that there was cause for concern about the morale of peoples in many parts of Western Europe and the underdeveloped areas. Foreign economic policies and programs, he said, "must be part of a total policy which can generate greater unity, hope and support for freedom now, while providing the basis for gradual economic improvement in the future."

Economic stagnation, political unrest and extreme poverty of most underdeveloped countries, his report stated, "represent a growing threat to the rest of the free world."

"In general," it continued, "the requirements for adequate economic development are beyond their internal capabilities—in some cases because of inadequate material resources, but more generally because of insufficient technical and administrative ability and the corrosive effects of poverty itself."

In the case of Western Europe the problem has changed in a few months from one of finding export markets to one of producing sufficient goods and services to meet the new military needs and minimum civilian needs, plus the exports necessary for self-support.

It is also necessary to increase the production of raw materials. It is not simply a matter of buying existing supplies; new capital must flow into the countries producing raw materials so that more will be produced.

Major adjustments also were needed in some of our own national policies, the report added. A freer flow of imports would be of general benefit in many ways, and at present "there exist unreasonable obstructions to such a flow."

For example, he said, administration of price, allocation, and export controls should take foreign programs into account if they were not to impair the progress toward our international objectives.

November 13, 1950

EUROPEANS OBJECT TO U.S. STOCKPILING

Marshall Plan Council Weighs Members' Desire for Equal Raw Material Allocation

Special to THE NEW YORK TIMES.

PARIS, Dec. 1—At a meeting today of the European Marshall Plan council at the ministerial level, an effort was made to reconcile United States stock-piling of strategic materials with the European desire to allocate them to insure adequate supplies for all consumers and to prevent further price increases.

This entailed consideration of the rôle in raw material control that should be played by the North Atlantic Treaty Organization, as an expression of the military interests of the Atlantic coalition, and the rôle that should fall to the Marshall Plan council as a medium of economic cooperation within Western Europe and between it and the United States.

The latest Korean crisis has emphasized the need of stockpiling by the United States against which Europeans had contemplated protesting on the ground that it raised prices for them by limiting supplies. United States officials insist that nonferrous metals, at least, shall be apportioned by the Atlantic treaty authorities, not by or through the Marshall Plan council.

Some Continentals, like the Swiss and the Swedes, who are in the Marshall Plan council but not in the Atlantic treaty, objected to this United States policy regarding raw materials vital to industry. The staff of the council proposes conferences in Paris with the major nations producing these raw materials in order to arrange for their allocation.

The Europeans said tonight that United States officials had shown today less resistance than previously to the pleas for fuller consideration of European needs of materials, the prices of which are determined by the United States, either as main producer or as the main buyer.

William C. Foster, Economic Cooperation Administrator, who addressed the council today, said he welcomed the opportunity to cooperate with it on raw materials.

Mr. Foster urged Europeans to increase their gross output from $160,000,000,000 annually to $260,000,000,000. He suggested this could be achieved before the end of the Marshall Plan—but he added that "at least great strides" toward it could be made in that period, which is only eighteen months.

December 2, 1950

TRADE GROUP ASKS ERP AMENDMENTS

European Recovery Program Urged to Make More Use of Private Enterprise

NORMAL TRADE CHANNELS

National Council Recommends Also That U. S. Aid End When 1938 Level Is Reached

Greater use of private enterprise facilities in the European Recovery Program is urged by the National Foreign Trade Council in communications sent to Senator Vandenberg, chairman of the Senate Committee on Foreign Relations, and Representative C. A. Herter, vice chairman of the House Committee on Foreign Aid, it was announced over the week-end.

The recommendations of the Council, which represents all branches of American foreign trade, include a series of suggested amendments to Senate Bill S. 2202, introduced by Senator Vandenberg. One of them would set the 1938 level of production as the normal level of recovery upon which outside aid to each country should be terminated.

In addition to stress on private enterprise and maintenance of normal trade channels, these recommendations include: Elimination of the 5 per cent guaranty provision of the bill; protection against nationalization of properties; fair treatment of American business; no disclosure of names of holders of private foreign funds here; a check of ERP operations by a joint Congressional committee and measures to determine when ERP expenditures should cease.

With respect to the utilization of private enterprise facilities, the letter to Senator Vandenberg, signed by Robert F. Loree, chairman of the council, declared:

"In my opinion, S. 2202 relies entirely too much on Government operation and administration of the proposed recovery program.

"It is true that the bill contains a section, 11 (b) (3), which provides for a limited Government guarantee of American investments made in connection with projects approved by the administrator of the program. But even this provision merely authorizes but does not direct that private investment be used in operation of the program.

"Moreover, there is no provision requiring that facilities provided by private enterprise be utilized in carrying out the program. Possibly the bill contemplates that such facilities will be used by the administrator in procurement, processing and other operations involved in the operation of the program, but nowhere is there provision requiring that such facilities be so used.

Directions for Funds

"Specifically, I would suggest a new numbered paragraph be included after paragraph (5) in section 11 (a) of the bill to read somewhat as follows:

" 'In arranging for the performance of the functions set forth in paragraphs (1) to (5) of subsection (a) of this section, the Administrator shall, to the greatest extent practicable, utilize the facilities provided by private industry and trade.' "

Mr. Loree also noted there is no specific direction to the Administrator in S. 2202 to use funds provided through private investment channels or to seek to use International Bank funds.

Referring to the provision of guarantees to American private investments which may be made in connection with the program, Mr. Loree said he did not regard it as satisfactory to place a definite limitation of 5 per cent or any other specification of percentage on the amount of total funds appropriated under the act which could be used for such guarantees.

"The proportion of the funds appropriated which could be used for such guarantees should be left entirely to the discretion of the Administrator," Mr. Loree wrote. "Nor do I think that the guarantee to American investments under the program should be limited to the actual amount of dollars invested in a project."

As regards the provision in S. 2202 relating to disclosure and use in this country, in connection with the recovery program, of foreign assets, Mr. Loree expressed the belief that such provision is neither necessary nor desirable.

March 8, 1948

EUROPEANS AGREE ON DOLLAR DIVISION

Britain Accepts $962,000,000 as Marshall Plan Share but Calls It Inadequate

OTHERS PROTEST AID CUTS

Report to Washington Will Stress That Trade Deficit With U. S. Is Increasing

By HAROLD CALLENDER
Special to THE NEW YORK TIMES.

PARIS, Aug. 31—The prolonged deadlock among the European Governments over the division of this year's dollar aid was broken late tonight when the Marshall Plan Council reached a reluctant and belated agreement.

This was made possible when the British, who had indignantly rejected an offer of $842,000,000 as their share, accepted instead $962,000,000 while emphasizing its insufficiency to meet their dollar needs.

The total allotments came to nearly $3,780,000,000 and it is hoped Congress will appropriate this much.

All other recipients except Belgium and Trieste likewise protested that the dollars allotted to them were far from enough and could not be further reduced.

The continentals as well as the British have suffered heavy losses of dollar export revenues in the second quarter this year and expect further losses. This applies even to Belgium, the most prosperous of the European exporting countries.

Dollar Needs to Be Stressed

It was therefore expected that a report to be made to the Economic Cooperation Administration would reveal and underline the inadequacy of the Marshall Plan dollars, which are expected to be reduced by about $1,000,000,000 in the very year when the economic situation calls for more, not fewer, dollars to keep Europe from falling behind.

This coincidence of reduced dollar aid and a suddenly increased dollar shortage is considered merely an unexpectedly dramatic symptom of an underlying dollar problem that the Marshall Plan could not cure even if the aid granted under it were not reduced in the second and subsequent years of the plan.

This more fundamental dollar shortage is attributed to Europe's inferior productivity as compared with that of the United States, and to the unwillingness of the United States so far to import more than it exports.

One high European official said today that Europe's dollar shortage could not be overcome until the United States drastically reduced its tariff to enable Europeans to sell more voluminously in the United States market. The Europeans hesitate to say this officially for fear of offending Congress, to which they must look for dollar aid.

Franker Dealings Foreseen

But the bitter rivalry for the diminished dollars that long deadlocked the Marshall Plan Council is expected to contribute to greater frankness in the future regarding the deeper causes of Europe's plight. Some officials consider that the dollar crisis of this summer has been fortunate in that it will compel a new measure of realism in United States-European financial and economic discussions.

French officials pointed out that in the final allotment France's share of dollars had been cut nearly $200,000,000. This means France will have to spend more for imports. This additional expenditure will add to the already existing acuteness of France's budget problem, which will require heavy new taxes that will be politically difficult to levy.

Thus the dwindling Marshall Plan dollars may contribute to an internal crisis in France, which lately has been close to financial stability because of United States aid.

To win British agreement to the division of dollars, the mediators, Baron Henri Snoy of Belgium and Robert Marjolin of France, decided to give Britain $120,000,000 more by using up a pool of $150,000,000 that had been set aside, at United States suggestion, to compensate for gold losses or for reconstruction projects like international electrical power plants. They thus scraped the bottom of the dollar barrel.

Their report, adopted in its essentials tonight, must be approved by the Economic Cooperation Administration to become effective.

The Greeks mentioned this pool in accepting the division on two conditions—that they not be asked to contribute to a new pool and that they should obtain compensation for their loss of dollars through grants of European currencies under the trade payments plan. It is expected others may seek similar offsets to the dollars that were taken from them in the final division.

Following is the distribution of dollars by countries as agreed upon:

(In Millions of Dollars)

	Proposals for 1949-50	Allotted for 1948-49
Austria	174	215.2
Belgium-Luxembourg	312	247.9
Denmark	91	109.1
France	704	980.9
Trieste	17	17.8
Greece	163.5	144.8
Ireland	47	78.3
Iceland	7	5.2
Italy	407	555.5
Norway	94	83.3
Netherlands & Indies	309	469.6
Portugal	33	...
Sweden	48	46.6
Britain	962	1,239
Turkey	61	39.7
German Bizonal Area	261.7	410.6
French Zone, Germany	86.5	99.2

September 1, 1949

THE PRESIDENT SIGNING THE FOREIGN AID BILL

Looking on are (left to right) Senator Tom Connally, William C. Foster, Deputy E. C. A. Administrator; Representatives John Kee and James P. Richards, Secretary of State Dean Acheson, Philander P. Claxton Jr., State Department aide, and Representatives Frances P. Bolton and Charles A. Eaton.

The New York Times (by George Tames)

TRUMAN, 32D PRESIDENT, IS INAUGURATED; CALLS ON U. S. TO LEAD DEMOCRATIC WORLD; DENOUNCES COMMUNISM, PLEDGES U. N. AID

PEACE A MAJOR AIM

Truman Says America Will Not Waver From Fight on Aggressor

TO STRENGTHEN FREE

Proposes Sharing U. S. Scientific Gains With Undeveloped Areas

By ANTHONY LEVIERO
Special to THE NEW YORK TIMES.

WASHINGTON, Jan. 20—Harry S. Truman denounced communism as a false doctrine and outlined a four-point program for American world leadership, and peace, as he assumed the Presidency in his own right in the most impressive inaugural of American history.

Thus with a positive statement of American aspirations, the thirty-second President of the United States concluded the traditional ceremony on Capitol Hill which reached a tremendous global audience on the radio waves.

He took the oath of office before a throng of more than 100,000 of his fellow countrymen at 12:29 P. M., a few minutes after Senator Alben W. Barkley of Kentucky took a similar oath and became the Vice President.

Unlike many of his predecessors, whose inaugural addresses were in the nature of philosophical discourses, the plain-spoken Missourian delivered a major policy statement. It was replete, like virtually all his speeches, with concrete statements and proposals.

Calls for Just Settlement

Mr. Truman drew a sharp, straight line between democracy and communism, without the slightest trace of the softening toward Russia which some observers had been suspecting recently.

The Chief Executive asserted that democracy was a vitalizing force, sustaining the initiative which was in our hands, and that we would not be moved from our faith by the Soviet political philosophy.

President Truman explained he was not making his strongly contrasting definitions of democracy and totalitarianism merely to be argumentative. He saw communism as a threat to world recovery and lasting peace, he said, and he was offering what he proclaimed to be a constructive program for all nations.

He did not leave Russia and her satellites out of his hopes. Although he mentioned none of them by name, as he neared the end of his address he expressed a belief that the countries under Communistic regimes would "abandon their delusions and join with the free nations of the world in a just settlement of international differences."

Would Share Progress

The heart of his aims Mr. Truman set forth in one, two, three, four fashion. First he reiterated unwavering support of the United Nations and here he made a friendly gesture to such nations that are aborning, as Israel, Korea and Indonesia. He said they would strengthen the United Nations as they themselves became strong with the nourishment of democratic principles.

As his second point, Mr. Truman reiterated this country's determination to work for world recovery by giving full measure to the European Recovery Program and promoting trade for all the world's markets.

On the North Atlantic Security Plan, which is now crystallizing, Mr. Truman focused his third point. He said, "We will strengthen freedom-loving nations against the dangers of aggression," but only within the recognized framework of the United Nations Charter and in the pattern of the Western Hemisphere arrangement.

In his fourth point Mr. Truman proposed a wholly new program, still to be expounded in detail, for sharing American scientific and industrial progress with the rest of the world. He made the proffer on a global scale, but it was understood that it was intended primarily for the colonial areas of Africa and Asia.

The great crowd liked what the President said, and applause was perhaps strongest when Mr. Truman stated, in connection with the North Atlantic Security Plan, that if we make it sufficiently plain that we would meet a threat with overwhelming force, "the armed attack might never occur."

Sensing that clapping with hands gloved against the cold did not carry well, the crowd began pounding their approval with their feet on the plank flooring of their seats. Thereafter for about a dozen times the dulled handclapping was almost drowned by the rumble from the raw lumber.

The ceremony of the Presidential oath, scheduled for noon, was delayed twenty-nine minutes, apparently because in the rotunda of the Capitol there were so many amenities to be exchanged among a great assemblage of statesmen and diplomats.

The signal that the ceremony would soon begin came when the Marine Band at 12:14 P. M. played "Hail to the Chief." Chief Justice Fred M. Vinson, in judicial robe and skull cap, first came into view on the inaugural stand in front of the Capitol. Soon Mr. Truman and Mr. Barkley were seen.

Associate Justice Stanley Reed, clad like Justice Vinson, swore in Senator Barkley at 12:23 and six minutes later Mr. Truman took the oath from Chief Justice Vinson.

More than 100,000 persons, it was estimated, were in the plaza and in the visible environs, and as each of the nation's leaders was confirmed in office he was warmly applauded.

Procession 7½ Miles Long

About 100,000,000 more people listened in on the ceremony on the radio throughout the nation, it was estimated, and the Voice of America beamed it to many more millions abroad in many tongues. For the first time television was at hand for the national ceremony and through this medium, it was said, 10,000,000 more were added.

It seemed plausible therefore that today's ceremony was presented to more people than all, combined, who could have attended the previous forty inaugurals.

Perhaps a million people could have been counted, too, in the close-packed ranks along Pennsylvania Avenue later as the former farm boy and the Kentuckian who came from a log cabin rode triumphantly from the Capitol to the White House reviewing stand.

Apart from the solemnities of ceremony and the serious speech, the great spectacle took on a tone of national joy and carnival. The parade route was one-and-a-quarter miles long and over it moved a procession seven and a half miles long.

Up front was the Missourian from a town called Independence and way back at the end was a steam circus calliope. Between them was the flavor, the glamour, the humor, the shadings of dialect and dress of the nation. In essence it was the American spirit and it moved forward buoyantly to the music of many bands.

Governor Thurmond Pays Respects

The basic unity of it all was attested when Gov. J. Strom Thurmond of South Carolina, leader of the State's Rights movement that had bitterly divided the Democratic party, passed by in review before the confirmed leaders.

The crowning touch of simplicity came just at 3 P. M., when Mr. Truman and Mr. Barkley arrived at the reviewing stand. They were top-hatted and frock-coated according to custom, but the day was cold. Somebody placed a stack of sandwiches and cardboard containers of coffee before them.

At the moment the cadets of West Point, smart in their gray capes and in the rhythm of their march, were passing in review. Mr. Truman and Mr. Barkley faced each other, touched their cups together and drank their coffee, in a silent toast. Then they munched sandwiches as the cadets were marching by.

For a brilliant occasion Mr. Truman had a cold but brilliant day. Only a few weak streaks of clouds were in the northern sky as the oaths were administered. The temperature ranged between thirty and the low forties. There was a wind with a sharp edge that chilled the crowds and kept the flag on the portico of the Capitol rippling continuously.

The action was not all in splendid floats, and prancing, bare-legged drum majorettes, and parading politicians and fraternal organizations, however.

The speech of the President, with its overtones of concern for the common welfare and world peace, was strongly accented by the military power of the nation.

Military Power Accented

Of the atomic bomb there was only a simple reminder, but stressed as Mr. Truman voiced it, in his statement that this country had made every effort "to secure agreement on effective control of our most powerful weapon * * *"

Overhead, though, roared one of the greatest air armadas that has ever coursed over the capital—about 700 planes, led by five of the B-36 monsters capable of intercontinental action.

For the ambassadors and attachés of many nations, in their bright uniforms and silk hats on the inaugural stand, as well as for everybody else, they came in impressive and precise patterns over the trees screening the Library of Congress and passed over the Capitol Dome. The giant bombers were followed by flashing jets and by lumbering transports like those that are feeding Berlin.

The precision of the air squadrons was matched on the ground by the military and naval cadets, the soldiers and sailors, the cadets from the private military schools.

Equally eloquent was another kind of strength—the people who did, and the people who did not, vote for Truman packed literally every inch along the avenue except at the few cross streets kept open for traffic. They had come from every part of the nation. The 40,000 seats were filled and every inch of standing room was packed with old and young, white and black, from the curb to building fronts. Hundreds of simple periscopes were thrust above the heads of those in front by those at the rear for a glimpse of the carnival-like procession.

January 21, 1949

Iran to Rebuild Her Entire Economy in 7 Years With U. S. 'Know-How'

First Nation to Announce Complete Social as Well as Industrial Program Under Point Four—The Cost to Be $650,000,000

By HARTLEY W. BARCLAY

Iran has become the first foreign country to announce a complete industrial, social and economic development plan to take full advantage of Point Four of President Truman's program of aiding backward nations with American know-how. An increase in Iranian agricultural and industrial output of more than 200 per cent during the next seven years is the goal.

Iranians are beginning construction and improvement projects requiring total expenditures of $650,000,000 during this period. With the use of their own funds from oil royalties that exceed $50,000,000 this year and internal loans, it is possible that work will be completed without outside financial aid. The engineering program and objectives were announced here yesterday by Clifford S. Strike, president, Overseas Consultants, Inc., 51 East Forty-second Street, engineers for Iran.

For the first time in any foreign country a team of experts from the largest engineering organizations in the United States has been employed to insure that the most up-to-date methods will be used in a national development project. New York engineering companies retained to advise on future work as participants in Overseas Consultants, include the American Appraisal Company, Coverdale & Colpitts, Ebasco Services, Inc.; Ford, Bacon & Davis, Inc.; Jackson & Moreland, Madigan-Hyland, F. H. McGraw & Co., Sanderson & Porter, Standard Research Consultants, Inc.; Stone & Webster Engineering Corporation and the J. G. White Engineering Corporation.

The basis for the program, described by these engineers as "the largest industrial development program in one country in history," is to rebuild the entire economy of Iran from the "bottom up." The first aim of the program is to strengthen the social foundations of Iran at "the workers' level." Textile mills, mechanized agriculture, equipment plants and chemical plants follow later.

The steps starting immediately, however, involve vast construction activities in which million-dollar sub-contracts will be open to American bidders, in competition with British, Dutch, Belgian, Italian and other European companies. Because of the availability of American machinery, tools and supplies, however, it is expected that 60 per cent of dollar funds will be spent for American services, equipment and materials.

These are needed to install the physical basis for social improvement, through vast housing, waterworks, sanitation, hospital, school, sewer, food plant, and agricultural facilities. Chemicals and drugs will be required immediately to fight diseases and vermin rampant throughout Iran.

In a five-volume report just completed by Overseas Consultants, after more than eight months work by more than thirty-five American experts, steps of social improvement received priority over industrial construction. Immediate aims include raising educational standards, improving agricultural methods, tax law administration reform, installation of roads, streets, airports and docks, homebuilding, and eventually the transfer of many government owned industries to private ownership.

The purchasing for the seven-year program will be conducted by Iran.

Overseas Consultants is considering applications from technicians seeking employment as staff members. The "nucleus" group, to comprise a resident advisory staff in Iran, will leave for Teheran this month. Max W. Thornburg, vice president of Overseas Consultants, will supervise the Teheran office. There is no United States Government financing required for this activity.

Overseas Consultants recommended complete reform of the Iranian educational system to improve standards of public honesty.

Although nearly 80 per cent of Iran's population is supported by agriculture, only 10 per cent of the country's arable land is under cultivation. Large quantities of farm machinery is to be introduced.

Peasants are to be established as independent farm operators in areas such as the Gurgan Plain. Much Government-owned land will be irrigated.

Housing plans call for setting up a Central Housing Authority, with broad plans for financing and construction.

The report asks for $7,950,000 in foreign exchange for the purchase of materials to repair locomotives and purchase eighteen new Diesel locomotives and thirty new passenger cars. Funds for railroad capital improvements are available from current sources.

In the road-building program now scheduled, purchases of $2,000,000 in construction machinery are listed.

Recommendations were made for extension of telephone and telegraph lines and facilities and for two new radio stations.

More than $20,000,000 in electric power plant construction was recommended.

The present work shifts of 10 to 12 hours in the textile industry are to be changed to eight-hour shifts.

The industrial program includes a new cement mill, chemical and fertilizer plant expansions, completion of enlarged soap works, new facilities for making insecticides, improvement of soda ash works, construction of a small chlorine plant for water purification uses, and possibly a carbon black plant.

The seven-year plan as a national program will be supervised by Iranian councils composed of elder statesmen, and an Iranian managing director, Dr. Mosharaf Naficy. All were appointed by the Iranian Parliament and by royal decree. Shah Mohammed Reza Pahlevi, who has been a driving force behind the project, is supporting administration of the project.

October 12, 1949

VAST AID PROGRAM TO BAR RED GAINS SENT TO PRESIDENT

Report by Rockefeller Board Asks New Agency to Direct Program of Development

PROJECT IS WORLD-WIDE

By ANTHONY LEVIERO
Special to THE NEW YORK TIMES.

KEY WEST, Fla., March 11 — The International Development Advisory Board recommended to President Truman today the creation of a great new agency that would utilize billions of dollars for the improvement of under-developed areas as a foil to Soviet imperialism.

Twenty-three United States agencies now handling aspects of foreign economic operations, as well as American connections with thirty-three international agencies would be concentrated in a new agency called the United States Overseas Economic Administration.

The new agency would start with an appropriation of $500,000,000 and direct the use of billions in private capital and lesser Government funds in a vast expansion of President Truman's Point Four program of aid to under-developed regions.

Latent resources would be developed, standards of living would be raised and food production stimulated in unexploited regions of Latin America, Africa, the Middle East, Asia and Oceania.

The proposed program of economic action in poor areas susceptible to Communist infiltration would compare in scope to our domestic mobilization and foreign military aid programs. The new agency would function as a sort of economic general staff that would employ economic forces to attack hunger, poverty, disease and illiteracy.

At stake, as the board headed by Nelson Rockefeller noted, are the 1,075,000,000 people of the under-developed areas who outnumber the populations of both the free, highly industrialized areas and the regions "controlled by Soviet imperialism." It is the supreme aim of the proposed program to win over these people and their resources to the side of freedom.

The plan was conceived by Mr. Rockefeller and twelve fellow members of the board who represent labor, business, education, agriculture and other aspects of American life.

President Truman has sent copies of the report to the chairmen of the foreign relations committees of Congress and to ranking Republicans. He stated that the report of the Rockefeller board would help Congress in considering the new legislation for foreign defense and economic assistance that he would send to Capitol Hill soon for the 1952 fiscal year that begins July 1.

Thus, President Truman did not say he accepted the plan in every particular, nor did he ask Congress to enact it as it was presented to him. Nevertheless, in a letter of appreciation to Mr. Rockefeller, Mr. Truman said he was "impressed" by it and that it demonstrated why a lasting peace could be attained only by "a wise combination of strong military defenses and an effective campaign of international economic development."

It was learned that Mr. Truman wished to avoid a blanket acceptance of the plan pending further study. He accepted it in principle, however, but might reject some of its details.

Mr. Truman also sent the report for study to the Economic Cooperation Administration, which would be swallowed up by the new agency, to seven Cabinet members concerned with foreign aid programs, to the Office of Defense Mobilization, the Defense Production Administration and the Budget Director.

"Economic stagnation is the advance guard of Soviet conquest," said Mr. Truman in his letter to Mr. Rockefeller. He remarked that "economic development is the spearhead of the forces for freedom."

Nine Points of Action

The program was conceived around nine points of economic action and organization, and its architects proposed the use of funds aggregating $4,500,000,000. Much of this money would be used in a year's time after the program got going and it would be utilized on that scale annually.

But virtually all of it would be used productively, with returns for American investors, in bringing natural resources out of the ground, in the production of critical materials needed for our mobilization program and in food production.

The breakdown of this huge sum was as follows:

United States Overseas Economic Administration	$500,000,000
Private investments in existing productive facilities abroad to produce critical material urgently needed now...	2,000,000,000
Private capital for general investment abroad.	1,000,000,000
Proposed new International Development Authority, in which all free countries would participate, for constructing foreign public works (United States share $200,000,000)......	500,000,000
Funds of the Export-Import Bank to be earmarked to underwrite new foreign debt obligations purchased by United States investors, in the sum of.....	100,000,000
International Finance Corp., to be created as an affiliate of the International Bank for Reconstruction and Development, would issue nonvoting stock to member countries and make loans in local and foreign currencies to private enterprise. United States would subscribe $150,000,000 of its authorized capital of	400,000,000
	$4,500,000,000

Thus on this grand scale the board proposed the fruition of the President's vision, that began as a mere idea without body and prosaically designated "Point Four" in his Inaugural Address of January, 1949.

Using merely the $500,000,000 appropriation for the new agency for comparative purposes, the size of the program might be appreciated by considering it in relation to current Point Four expenditures. These consist of the $34,500,000 directly appropriated for the program in State Department funds, and $50,000,000 allocated by the Economic Cooperation Administration for Point Four-type assistance.

Ever since his inaugural Mr. Truman has persistently urged the Point Four program. Early critics scorned it as a program without a plan. The President insisted that it could be implemented to transform the world into a new-day utopia based on the American concept of industrial and agricultural development and free enterprise.

Over and over again he has discussed the plan with visitors to his office, spinning his big globe and pointing to places such as the Tigris-Euphrates Valley of the Middle East. In that valley, he said, millions of acres could be made fertile by irrigation and support 2,000,000 to 3,000,000 persons settled on new farms.

In proposing to place a great fiscal foundation under the plan, the Rockefeller Board said it would mean much more than production of food and raw materials. It went on to say it would bring the American kind of Bill of Rights and living standards to a great many people, including about 500,000,000 in under-developed areas who have won national independence since the end of World War II.

Recommendations of Board

The nine recommendations of the board embodied the half-billion-dollar appropriation; creation of the super-agency; drafting of a specific economic program for each country qualifying for Point Four aid; an all-out food production drive, especially for areas such as Burma, Thailand and Indo-China, which "are most directly exposed to possible Soviet aggression"; the program to stimulate strategic materials production abroad; assurance of essential imports to underdeveloped countries; creation of the International Development Authority; a program of stimulating local cooperation by assisted countries to engender the feeling that they have a stake in Point Four, and a plan at home to encourage private American investments abroad.

If the new agency is created as recommended, the overseas economic administrator would be a man invested with great authority, commensurate in the foreign economic field with the power of Charles E. Wilson, Director of Defense Mobilization. The board recommended that the administrator should be made a member of the topmost policy-making agencies—the National Security Council, the National Advisory Council on international financial and monetary policy, and an ex officio director of the Export-Import Bank.

The Budget Bureau "should initiate action," said the board, to see that foreign procurement, export licensing, foreign mineral production, Export-Import loan operations, activities of the United States executive director of the international bank and activities of United States representatives in international agencies are made consistent with and responsive to the programs of the new administrator.

The board, formed by the President last fall to survey the problems of under-developed areas in line with the interests of the democracies, apparently recalled the early debate when the creation of the Economic Cooperation Administration was pending before Congress. It was contended then that E. C. A.'s authority and responsibilities would conflict with those of the Secretary of State.

In its report the Rockefeller board states that the responsibility between the new agency and the State Department should be clearly stated as "the responsibility of the State Department for United States foreign policy must not be diluted." It recommended that the overseas administrator should be guided in foreign policy by the Secretary of State and that he should consult frequently with the Secretaries of Defense, Treasury, Commerce, Labor, Agriculture and Interior and the Office of Defense Mobilization.

The board said that while on the whole our economic assistance programs have been handled well, new financing tools should be devised to eliminate any emphasis of "giveaway." Local investment in Point Four programs would be required wherever possible and in no case would the International Development Authority "make grants covering the full cost of any project."

"No miracles should be promised—none can be expected," said the board. But he concluded on a note of optimism that the present economic pattern under-developed regions could be revolutionized "through a consistent investment flow from the Western industrialized world of three billion dollars a year." If its program is carried through, said the board, free countries would be strengthened against any possible aggression and could build a lasting peace.

March 12, 1951

POINT FOUR ACTION DECLARED SCANTY

Analysis of 3 Studies Shows United States Is Expected to Do Most of Financing

Little has been done "of a concrete nature" to carry out the underlying goals of President Truman's Point Four program to aid underdeveloped areas of the world, the National Industrial Conference Board asserted in a statement released for publication today.

The board's comment was made in an analysis of three major reports on foreign aid. These are "Measures for the Development of Underdeveloped Countries," a United Nations document; "Partners in Progress," a Rockefeller Foundation report, and the Gray Committee's report to the President on foreign economic policies.

The analysis noted that it should be remembered that the reports were "merely recommendations" to the United States or to the United Nations.

"They are not yet official policies," it said. "Either directly or by implication, however, they look to the United States to supply a major part of the financing, private or governmental."

Aim to Raise Per Capita Income

The board commented that of the three the United Nations report was "easily the most ambitious" in terms of outside financing. It was also described as the most specific in its aim—"that of raising the per capita income of the underdeveloped nations by 2 per cent a year."

The board added that it was "the most outspoken about the social and political difficulties that development programs must face in the backward nations themselves."

"The Gray report gives the lowest recommendations for dollar assistance to underdeveloped areas," the board went on. "The question of the amount of aid to be sent abroad, if any, was only part of this committee's task, and it is the Rockefeller report which expands on this theme. The Rockefeller proposals fall somewhere between the United Nations and the Gray reports in the amount of assistance proposed.

New Sources of Raw Material

"The Rockefeller report, more than either of the others, and particularly more than the United Nations—bears the earmarks of the post-Korean world crisis, especially in its emphasis on the development of new and greater sources of raw material. This report also differs from any other on this subject in that it is obviously directed at popular consumption as well as for policymakers."

The analysis added that if the private and government investment program envisaged in such a moderate report as "Partners in Progress" were to be put into effect "more than $2,800,000,000" would have to be earned by foreign countries in 1960 to pay interest and dividends on dollars invested in their countries.

This estimate, the analysis explained, rests on the assumption that the program would be put into effect in 1952 and that the first investment returns would be in 1953. From a total of $1,700,000,000 in interest and dividends actually received in 1950 the amount would gradually increase to a projected $2,800,000,000 in ten years.

August 13, 1951

KENNEDY SETS UP U. S. PEACE CORPS TO WORK ABROAD

Creates Pilot Plan and Asks Congress to Establish a Permanent Operation

RECRUITS TO GET NO PAY

President Aims to Have 500 on Job by the End of '61—Training Will Be Pushed

By PETER BRAESTRUP
Special to The New York Times.

WASHINGTON, March 1 — President Kennedy issued an executive order today creating a Peace Corps. It will enlist American men and women for voluntary, unpaid service in the developing countries of the world.

The order set up the Peace Corps on a "temporary pilot basis." President Kennedy also sent Congress a message requesting legislation to make the corps permanent.

Announcing the move at his news conference, the President described the Peace Corps as a "pool of trained American men and women sent overseas by the United States Government or through private organizations and institutions to help foreign governments meet their urgent needs for skilled manpower."

The President's expressed hope was to have 500 to 1,000 Peace Corps workers "in the field by the end of this year."

Shriver Heads Planners

The Administration's planning effort on the Peace Corps has been headed since late January by R. Sargent Shriver, a Chicago business man and civic leader who is the President's brother-in-law. The President said today that a decision on who would head the agency would be made "in several days."

Life in the Peace Corps, the President stressed, "will not be easy." Members will work without pay but they will be given living allowances. They will live at the same level as the inhabitants of the countries to which they are sent.

The President emphasized that "we will send Americans abroad who are qualified to do a job," particularly those with technical skills in teaching, agriculture and health.

"There is little doubt," the President said in his subsequent message to Congress, "that the number of those who wish to serve will be far greater than our capacity to absorb them."

President Kennedy first broached his version of the Peace Corps idea in a campaign speech at San Francisco last Nov. 2. Previously, Senator Hubert H. Humphrey, Democrat of Minnesota, and Representative Henry S. Reuss, Democrat of Wisconsin, among others, had advocated such a plan.

In his San Francisco speech, Mr. Kennedy suggested that membership in the Peace Corps could be an alternative to the military draft.

Today President Kennedy said in his message that there would be no draft exemptions for members of the Peace Corps.

White House aides said that as a practical matter, draft boards would probably grant deferments to members of the Peace Corps.

White House spokesmen outlined the Peace Corps operation as follows:

The initial cost for the fiscal year ending June 30 will be paid out of foreign aid funds that have already been appropriated.

LED CORPS PLANNING: R. Sargent Shriver, President Kennedy's brother-in-law. He has headed the peace corps effort since late in January.

For the following years, a special appropriation will be required from Congress. The cost for a worker a year is estimated at $5,000 to $12,000—including training, transportation, living allowances, medical care and administrative overhead.

The State Department will be in charge of the program.

Personnel for the corps will also be made available through private universities, voluntary agencies and United Nations bodies.

In the case of voluntary agencies, private institutions have the option of using their own recruitment system. Overseas, a small number of liaison officers from the Peace Corps or the International Cooperation Administration will provide administrative support. Fifty to sixty persons will be employed at headquarters in Washington.

Screening will be rigorous, including security clearance by the Federal Bureau of Investigation.

Regional training centers will be set up at universities throughout the country to receive recruits after the school year ends. Each recruit will get three to six months of training in language, culture and work skills. In the pilot stage, in particular, applicants with language qualifications will be favored.

Negotiations are under way with foreign governments on service by the corps. Brazil, Colombia, Nigeria, Pakistan and the Philippines may become the first host nations.

The Administration will prohibit any use of the Peace Corps for religious missionary purposes. Nor will the Central Intelligence Agency be involved in any way.

March 2, 1961

PROJECT TO SLASH FOREIGN AID STIRS CONGRESS BATTLE

Advisory Committee's Plea 'for a Reduction Presents Kennedy With Dilemma

PASSMAN FOR A 50% CUT

Officials Believe Tax Bill and Deficit Will Cause Record Retrenchment

By FELIX BELAIR Jr.
Special to The New York Times.

WASHINGTON, March 24—The toughest foreign aid fight in Congress in more than a decade was shaping up today after an advisory group's report to President Kennedy that this Government was trying to do "too much for too many" and should retrench.

Although unanimously agreed that foreign aid was "essential to the security of our nation," the 10-member panel voted 9 to 1 for a smaller economic and military aid program. In the lone dissent, George Meany, president of the A.F.L.-C.I.O., called for an expanded program and a voice in policy decisions.

The upshot of the report was to confront President Kennedy, now preparing a special message to Congress for delivery later in the week, with a risky choice of appearing to disregard his own committee's proposals or, by adopting them, to invite a chopping-block operation on his budget estimate of $4,945,000,000 for aid in the fiscal year ahead.

Big Cutback Expected

This amount had been shaved $200,000,000 by aid officials before the advisory group reported. The amount represents undisbursed funds for development loans in the current fiscal year. The Agency for International Development is trying to find ways of cutting the budget estimate further but all indications are that it will remain close to $4,700,000,000.

President Kennedy asked Congress last year for $4,900,000,000 and Congress cut the amount about $1,000,000,000. Representative Otto E. Passman, head of the House Appropriations subcommittee handling foreign aid, served notice just before the advisory group's report that he planned to cut the President's figure this time by $2,400,000,000, or about 50 per cent.

Application Must Wait

Administration officials generally agree that the combination of a large budget deficit now in prospect and the proposed tax cut will fortify Mr. Passman's position and result in the biggest cutback in foreign aid funds in recent years.

This predicament, they believe, has been worsened by the

advisory committee's suggestion that, if the administrative criteria it recommends for tying aid more closely to United States security requirements were in effect now, "present programs would be reduced by about $500,000,000." It said the same criteria would mean further reductions later "as these programs were phased further down or out."

The estimate, supplied to the committee by the Agency for International Development, was admittedly more decorative than meaningful. The advisory group readily acknowledged that its criteria could not be applied now or a year from now because they would mean the acceptance of intolerable foreign policy decisions.

But because Gen. Lucius P. Clay, the committee chairman, failed to explain at a news briefing that the estimate was no more than an expression of an ideal that might take years to realize, most published accounts of the report said it found the present $3,900,000,000 aid program at least $500,000,000, "too big."

In Congress Democrats and Republicans alike accepted the committee conclusion as an invitation to cut the new aid appropriation to the bone. Its impact was the greater, one Democratic supporter of aid programs pointed out, because most members of the advisory group were well known for their advocacy of amply-financed programs.

Created by President Kennedy last December as the Committee to Strengthen the Security of the Free World, the group was charged with determining whether foreign aid was contributing materially to the security of the United States and to the "political and economic stability of the free world."

The Major Conclusions

Among its major conclusions and recommendations were the following:

¶Military and economic aid to most countries should be curtailed and in many it should be abolished because the recipients are not important to United States security. The cutbacks, including aid to some countries bordering the Chinese Soviet bloc, should be over a three-year period.

¶Total military aid programs should be cut to $1,000,000,000 "in a few years" instead of by 1968 as planned by the Defense Department. The current year's appropriations total $1,440,000,000.

¶The kind and extent of United States aid should be decided on "economic" rather than "political" grounds "except where paramount military security or other extraordinary circumstances are involved." This Government should establish "sound bench marks for its own performance" and not be swayed by "the vagaries of the ephemeral world opinion."

¶To the extent possible by cooperation of other free world donor countries, all economic aid programs should be placed under international management such as could be provided by the World Bank affiliate, the International Development Association.

¶No aid should be given to help establish "Government-owned industries and commercial enterprises which complete with existing private endeavors." Too much aid has been given in disregard of this country's dedication to the private enterprise system. General Clay said this was not a matter of "doctrine or ideology" but of "hardheaded economics."

¶Other advanced nations should carry a larger share of the aid burden and the surest way of bringing this about was for the United States to cut down its aid program.

¶Terms and conditions of United States development loans should be flexible, with higher interest and shorter maturity for countries able to carry them. Also, other development lending countries must be required to bring their terms and conditions more in line with more liberal United States loan terms. Otherwise, this Government's loans are helping to pay the debt service on hard loans of other countries.

¶Thus the $350,000,000 United States technical assistance program is too big for the skilled manpower available to carry it out and should be curtailed.

¶Aid to new African republics, except the Congo, should be reduced and terminated, except for surplus agricultural commodities and small training programs in countries where the United States has military bases. Economic aid to the Congo should be limited to matching whatever amount is provided by all European countries. Military aid should be ended or confined to internal security weapons.

As a general rule the committee avoided mentioning the names of countries receiving unjustified amounts of aid and not making wise use of it. Exceptions included Spain, Portugal and Indonesia.

The committee said the Iberian countries should get less rather than more aid because they were "already more than adequately compensated" for United States military base rights. In the case of Indonesia, the report said, "we do not see how external assistance can be granted to this nation by free world countries unless it puts its internal house in order, provides fair treatment to foreign creditors and enterprises, and refrains from international adventures."

In addition to General Clay, committee members who signed the report included former Secretary of Defense Robert A. Lovett; Edward Mason, Harvard University economics professor; Eugene Black, former head of the World Bank; Robert B. Anderson, former Secretary of the Treasury; L. F. McCollum, president of Continental Oil Company; Herman Phleger, San Francisco attorney and former legal adviser to the State Department; Clifford Harden, chancellor of the University of Nebraska, and Dr. Howard A. Rusk, associate editor of The New York Times.

March 25, 1963

PRESIDENT URGES FOREIGN AID FUND OF $3.38 BILLION

Request, Lowest in History of Program, Is Called the Necessary Minimum

PLEA MADE ON VIETNAM

Johnson Says He May Ask for More Money Later if New Situations Arise

By FELIX BELAIR Jr.
Special to The New York Times

WASHINGTON, Jan. 14—President Johnson sought today Congressional approval for a $3.38 billion foreign aid authorization for the next fiscal year.

He said the program was designed to promote a world of stability, freedom and peace along with the security and well-being of the United States.

In a special message describing his program for the fiscal year 1966, beginning next July 1, the President reminded Congress that "this minimum request is the smallest in the history of foreign aid." He said it was "the lowest aid budget consistent with the national interest."

His request included $2.21 billion for economic loans and grants and $1.17 billion in military assistance to help independent developing nations remain free while acquiring the benefits of modern knowledge.

Reds' Aid Efforts Cited

The total cost would be $136 million less than the White House requested last year and the lowest since the first Marshall Plan installment of $7.4 billion in 1948.

Mr. Johnson said that the $500 million earmarked for military aid and supporting assistance to South Vietnam and Laos in the new fiscal year might not be enough.

Therefore he asked for an additional "open," or standby, authorization in these categories of aid, to be used only in Vietnam. Any such added amounts would be justified to the Congressional authorizing committees whenever an appropriation was requested, he said.

The President sought to counter criticism that the aid program was too widely scattered over a large number of countries. He said that the plan for the new year was both selective and highly concentrated.

Mr. Johnson declared that the Soviet Union and Communist China were trying to outdo each other in promises of aid so as to increase their influence in Asia, Africa and Latin America.

"If, during the year, situations should arise which require additional amounts of United States assistance to advance vital United States interests, I shall not hesitate to inform the Congress and request additional funds," he said.

The estimates submitted by Mr. Johnson reflected a conscious effort to tailor the aid program as nearly as possible to Congressional apathy toward it.

Mr. Johnson's tactic of insisting on a "bare bones" program, designed to invite a minimum of cuts, worked well last year, when it was used for the first time. Then the President asked for $3.5 billion and Congress appropriated all but $250 million.

Requests Called Realistic

The President explained at the time that his request was based on a more realistic estimate of performance that could be expected in recipient countries under self-help and economic reform criteria of the program. He said that in the past aid officials had based requests on what they hoped could be achieved rather than realistic performance expectations.

The new program also showed an effort to avoid any new departures that might provide a rallying point for its opponents.

The message made no mention of a long-term authorization for either economic or military aid. Aid officials, backed by Senator J. W. Fulbright, Democrat of Arkansas, chairman of the Senate Foreign Relations Committee, have been promoting the plan as a means of reducing antagonism over the legislation.

Under this proposal, Congress would make an authorization for five years, setting ceilings on programs for that period. Then debate in both houses would be limited largely to the annual appropriation bills providing the money.

Decision Is Pending

While officials confirmed that this proposal had been abandoned, they said the President had yet to resolve another area of controversy. This is whether the total aid program should be presented in an omnibus bill, as in the past, or split up into two or more measures that would at least separate economic aid from military aid programs.

The President's message emphasized these points:

¶Of the $369 million asked for supporting assistance, 88 per cent would be used in Vietnam, Laos, Korea and Jordan. (Under the supporting assistance program, the United States helps 11 nations on the periphery of the Communist bloc to support larger military establishments than they could support alone.)

¶Except for Laos, which gets no military aid, the 11 countries, stretching in a great arc from Greece to Korea, receive nearly 75 per cent of all military aid funds. While helping these countries to survive, the money also contributes to American security because it helps maintain 3.5 million men under arms without whom more Americans would have to be stationed overseas at greater cost.

¶The $780 million requested for making long-term development loans would be "concentrated where it will contribute to lasting progress." About 65 per cent of the money would continue going to seven countries that have demonstrated a capacity to help themselves, eliminate waste and avoid expenditures of "unnecessary armaments and foreign adventures." They are India, Nigeria, Pakistan, Tunisia, Turkey, Brazil and Chile.

¶The $580 million requested in loans and grants for the Alliance for Progress with Latin-American countries is $70 million above the appropriation for the current year. But the "governments and people of Latin America are accepting increasing responsibility for their own development" and "the failure of Castroism is becoming clearer each day."

Congressional reaction to the 3,500-word message followed the usual pattern. In both the Senate and House those who have always opposed the program continued to do so vocally. Those who usually support it adopted a wait-and-see attitude, pending submission of specific legislation.

Had Mr. Johnson split the difference between the amount he sought last year and what he got then, he would have placed his authorization request today at $3,375 billion, just $5 million less than his actual proposal.

Most items he requested today were larger than what Congress finally approved last year but were significantly less than what was asked then. Notable exceptions were the amounts asked today for the Alliance for Progress, the President's contingency fund and voluntary contributions to international organizations and programs.

Last year, $550 million was requested and Congress appropriated $510 million for the Alliance for Progress. The new request is $580 million.

Integrated Program

For the contingency fund, the President asked this year for $50 million, a record low. Since the advent of Communist-inspired insurgent movements, the Administration has been asking for about $150 million for this purpose each year. Last year Congress cut this asking figure to $99 million.

This year, $155 million was requested for international organizations and programs, compared with $134 million asked and appropriated last year. Aid officials attributed the increase entirely to the American commitment to the Indus River Basin Development Fund administered by the International Bank for Reconstruction and Development.

The President indicated that, however packaged in Congress, the two forms of aid, economic and military, must continue as integrated part of a single concept.

"Military security in the developing world will not be sufficient to our purposes unless the ordinary people begin to feel some improvement in their lives and see ahead to a time when their children can live in decency," Mr. Johnson said.

He emphasized the importance to American security and well-being of promoting and maintaining independent free societies.

"Here is our difference with the Communists -- and our strength. They would use their skills to forge new chains of tyranny. We would use ours to free men from the bonds of the past."

He stressed that private institutions and private enterprise had an increasing role to play in helping underdeveloped countries, as did other non-Communist nations.

Proposes Tax Credit

To mobilize additional American private capital and skill in support of this effort, the President said he would again ask Congress to approve a 30 per cent investment tax credit. He said he would also propose continuing and expanding the investment guarantee program insuring American investors against loss from expropriation, revolution and other risks.

Mr. Johnson said that this Government would continue to work through international organizations to provide development of multilateral assistance.

To this end, and apart from the substantive aid program, he urged Congress to approve promptly the three-year authorization of $750 million that constitutes the United States contribution to the fund for special operations of the Inter-American Development Bank.

In the new fiscal year, 85 per cent of American development loans in Asia and Africa will be subject to consortiums and consultative arrangements with other donors. This Government, therefore, plans increasing use of such devices with a view to focusing all development aid on the most productive targets, Mr. Johnson said.

He said that since 1960 new commitments of bilateral economic assistance by other donor countries had been increased 50 per cent. "We are continuing to urge other donors to give more aid on better terms," he said.

January 15, 1965

FULBRIGHT QUITS AS FLOOR LEADER FOR FOREIGN AID

Arkansan Against Combining Authorization on Military and Economic Funds

By FELIX BELAIR Jr.
Special to The New York Times

WASHINGTON, Jan. 27 The chairman of the Senate Foreign Relations Committee, Senator J. W. Fulbright of Arkansas, disclosed today that he was dropping his role as floor manager and chief defender of the Administration's $3.38 billion foreign aid legislation.

The refusal of the committee chairman to shepherd the controversial measure through the Senate for the first time in its 15-year history placed in jeopardy its chances of getting through the Senate without substantial cuts and important policy restrictions.

The immediate cause of Senator Fulbright's decision was President Johnson's unannounced rejection of the Senator's demand that the economic and military programs be covered in separate authorization bills.

$3.38 Billion Total

The Administration has asked $2.21 billion for economic-development loans and grants and $1.17 billion for military aid to friendly non-Communist governments.

Basically, however, Senator Fulbright believes that the traditional form of extending foreign aid through bilateral agreements with recipient governments has outlived its usefulness and could make as many enemies as friends for this country.

He believes this is an inescapable result of the debtor-creditor relationship that the bilateral system entails.

He thinks further that all United States development loans should be made available through multilateral institutions like the International Bank for Reconstruction and Development and its subsidiary International Development Association or the Organization for Economic Cooperation and Development as well as United Nations agencies.

Letter Told of Views

The Senator explained to friends that despite his reservations he was not opposing the principle of foreign aid, and that he expected to vote for the

Administration bill and might introduce it. He said, however, that he could not play his accustomed role feeling as he did about the catchall form in which the program was being presented to Congress.

Senator Fulbright, a Democrat, warned of the course on which he has now decided in a letter to Secretary of State Dean Rusk last October. He said he would have to ask another member of his committee to handle the bill on the floor unless the Administration was prepared to separate the economic and military programs by having them authorized in different bills.

Who would take over the task was an open question today. Senator John J. Sparkman, Democrat of Alabama, filled the role when Senator Fulbright was campaigning for re-election two years ago, but he has indicated his reluctance to do so again. Senator Mike Mansfield of Montana, the majority leader, is the next ranking Democratic co mitteeman, but he shares Mr. Fulbright's view.

The next in line is Senator Wayne Morse, Democrat of Oregon. He has led the fight to cut the Administration's requests in the last two years, and has initiated more amendments than any other member to restrict the President's freedom of action in using the aid program as an instrument of United States policy.

Senator Russell B. Long of Louisiana, recently elected Democratic whip, follows Mr. Morse in seniority on the committee, but he has voted consistently to cut the Administration's requests and has sided with Mr. Morse on most restrictive amendments.

This issue between Senator Fulbright and the Administration is not expected to mushroom into any antagonism between Congress generally and the President over his total legislative agenda.

In his letter to Secretary Rusk, Senator Fulbright called for three separate authorizing bills to replace the single package of past years. One would deal with military aid, another with grant aid and a third with all lending operations.

He made clear that his insistence on separate programs for military and economic aid was a minimum demand, believing that if this were done it would be possible later to break the omnibus legislation down further into three and possibly four measures.

A Triumph for Morgan

The White House has yet to make known the President's decision to continue the single-package method of presenting the aid program except to Administration officials immediately concerned. President Johnson sent his special assistant, McGeorge Bundy, and the foreign aid administrator, David E. Bell, to intercede with Senater Fulbright but to no avail.

Senate and House committeemen first knew of the President's decision when representatives of the Agency for International Development began briefing the staffs of the Senate Foreign Relations Committee and the House Foreign Affairs Committee on the omnibus measure Monday and yesterday.

The continuation of the traditional approach was a personal triumph for Representative Thomas E. Morgan, Democrat of Pennsylvania. Mr. Morgan, chairman of the House Foreign Affairs Committee, convinced the President at a White House conference last year that drastic cuts in economic-aid funds were certain unless these programs were combined in the same bill with military aid.

Mr. Morgan and key Democrats of his group told the President that because of substantial unemployment in their districts they could not justify their support of his full exconomic foreign aid request except by explaining to constituents that the economic and military programs were interdependent.

Informed by his committee staff of the Administration's decision not to split the programs, Senator Fulbright began explaining his position to colleagues. He expects to make a detailed explanation to the Senate, probably next week in a floor speech that will make these points:

¶The legislation has become the catchall in recent years for dozens of amendments and pronouncements on foreign and domestic policy.

¶The annual Congressional debate on intricate and delicate relations with foreign nations creates doubt and confusion at home and abroad about the constancy and direction of United States foreign policy.

¶Foreign aid authorizations should cover at least two years. Limiting these to one year while asking a four-year authorization for the disarmament agency is a confession of uncertainty and a lack of conviction about the purposes of the aid program.

¶While the President's Foreign Aid Message this month stressed that two-thirds of all development loans go to seven countries and two-thirds of military aid goes to 11 countries, United States aid programs involving more than $1 million, including surplus - food shipments, were operating in more than 90 countries on Jan. 1. This indicates that any country willing to accept United States aid gets some.

¶Military aid should be limited to countries that can contribute something to the defense of the United States. This aid is now given, however, because there is some political reason for cultivating the generals, the admirals or the government in power. However legitimate these political reasons for the giving of aid, it should not come from military-assistance funds.

¶The first step in correcting this practice is to put foreign military aid under the national-defense budget. Then the Department of Defense would extend the aid where it would do the most good for the United States defense. The Secretary of State could have veto power over giving aid to certain countries, but should not have authority for political reasons to pressure the Secretary of Defense into aid allocations that do not help the national defense.

Senator Fulbright is expected to say further that to be effective, aid must be accompanied by guidance to help recipient countries develop healthy economies, reasonably stable political conditions, and societies in which the rule of law is respected, in which there is freedom of speech and of the press and where the state exists to serve the individual, rather than the other way round.

January 28, 1965

U.S. Aid Problems And Plan

By FELIX BELAIR Jr.
Special to The New York Times

WASHINGTON, Feb. 5—The "new and daring direction" that President Johnson promised to give the foreign aid program was pointed this week to a return toward the drawing boards and the building blocks of economic development.

No other conclusion was possible from the foreign aid message in which he described the appalling conditions of the poorer nations as "a challenge to our own security" and then proposed to remedy them with one of the smallest appropriations for economic and social improvement abroad in the past 20 years.

It took a lot of reading between the lines but what the President seemed to be saying to Congress was that it was futile to invest large sums to bring about viable economies in the developing nations unless and until something was done first about the human resources on which viability must ultimately depend.

Worldwide Attack

In his aid message to Congress on Tuesday, Mr. Johnson requested a combined military and economic foreign assistance program totaling $3.86-billion for the fiscal year beginning July 1. In a follow-up the next day, he asked Congress to devote $524-million of already budgeted funds to launch a worldwide attack on ignorance and disease and called on all nations to join the battle.

Put another way, unless malnutrition and hunger could be reduced and eliminated among people of the developing countries there was little point in trying to bring about economies with a growth rate of four or five per cent a year because the malnourished children of today would be the mentally and physically retarded adults of tomorrow.

That is why the President talked about attacking "the root causes of poverty" in the poorer nations and why he proposed to devote about $1-billion of foreign aid funds in fighting hunger, disease and ignorance.

It is true that this investment in expanded local food production, health and education programs would add less than $400-million to the amount already programmed for such activities by the Agency for International Development (A.I.D.) in the current fiscal year.

Reduction Questioned

It is also true that many would question whether this additional sum constitutes the "bold and daring response" to the misery and suffering he described. Some Senators and Representatives also privately questioned whether a genuine commitment to the principle of economic development would justify the $115-million reduction he proposed in development loans under this year's total.

Apart, however, from the disparity between objectives enunciated by the President and the financing proposed for attaining them there can be no doubt that agriculture, health and education in the developing countries will claim more time and energy of A.I.D. in the year beginning July 1 than in the past. Neither is there any doubt that industrialization of such areas will claim less.

In this connection the President's message as expanded by

follow-up message on health and education may prove as important for what it left unsaid as for what it said. It also disclosed a vast difference between the President's thinking about development and that of some other recognized experts in the field.

Writing in the December issue of Foreign Affairs, for instance, George D. Woods, president of the World Bank, said that developing countries "could put to constructive use" between $3-billion and $6-billion a year of outside aid in the next five years, more than is currently available from donor countries.

He suggested that unless something was done about it by the rich industrial nations the already lagging pace of development would lose momentum and the poor countries would "retreat into an isolation of despair." His forecast carries an ominous note. For it was to prevent the modern "revolution of rising expectations" from exploding into violent upheavals that economic development was invented.

Need for Self Help

The President's message did not speak to this point. But he did say of the same developing nations that "they must supply most of the capital, the know-how and the will to progress. If they do we can and will help. If they do not, nothing we can supply will substitute."

Among aid officials, efforts to explain away this apparent conflict were not completely convincing. They said that, as a matter of fact, the underdeveloped countries were running out of acceptable or "bankable projects." Some said that while projects could be undertaken, there were not sufficient technical personnel available in the poorer countries to operate them on completion.

But nobody would say that George D. Woods didn't know what he was talking about or that the amount he mentioned could not be used constructively.

Words and Music

The President's message might have been received with more enthusiasm by some Congressional supporters of the aid program if it acknowledged that the $550-million cost of supporting the economy of South Vietnam prevented financing as much economic development as the Administration would like.

As one Senator remarked after hearing the President's message: "That sure was a real concert—it's too bad the lyrics didn't fit the music."

The President's proposals that foreign aid programs be authorized in advance for each of the next five years and that military and economic assistance programs be considered in separate legislative vehicles had less than their expected impact in Congressional quarters.

U.S. AID—WHERE AND WHY

President Johnson's message to Congress last week on the foreign aid program focused on the underdeveloped nations. Diagram shows current allocations of economic aid to these regions.

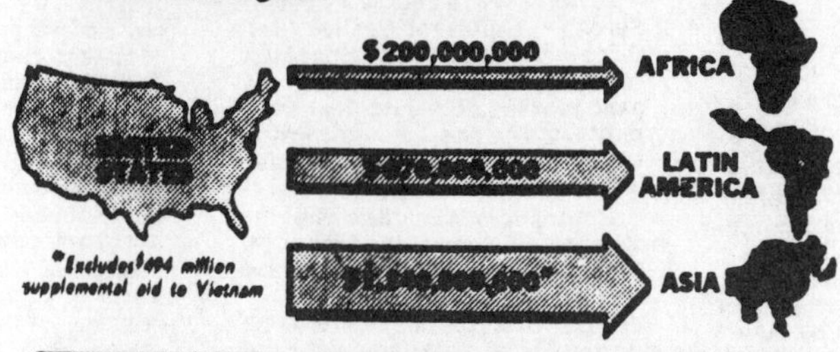

The President pointed to some of the major problems confronting these regions. Quotations are from the President's message.

"I propose to cooperate in worldwide efforts to deal with population problems."

Annual rate of population increase

"I propose to assist the progress of education."

Literacy rates—percentages of persons over 15 able to read or write

AFRICA, LATIN AMERICA, ASIA

UNITED STATES

97.6%

"I propose to combat malnutrition."

Changes in per capita food production (1951=100)

AFRICA, LATIN AMERICA, ASIA

Economic aid will be increased in the new budget, partially reversing a trend in recent years in which over-all aid expenditures has been declining.

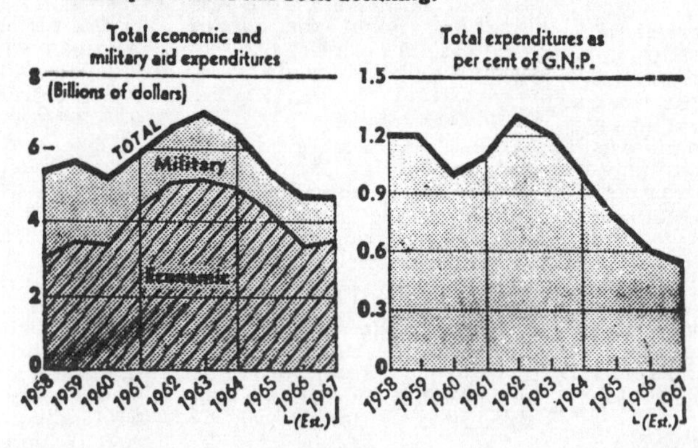

Washington: Revolt in the Senate

By JAMES RESTON

WASHINGTON, July 21 — The Senate has been nibbling President Johnson's foreign-aid bill to pieces this week. It has not only reduced the money substantially, but made the terms of development loans harder, and refused to authorize the program for more than a year.

The reasons for this are more complex and interesting this year than ever before. The Senate is particularly money-conscious these days. The House has just passed a $58.6-billion bill for defense — the largest money bill in peacetime history. The cost of Vietnam, according to Senator Richard Russell, is now running at a rate of almost $2 billion a month, and both the debt and the inflation are troubling the Senators.

Pressures at Home

The Senators are being told, too, that these costs are interfering with the solution of problems at home. High interest rates are creating a slump in the housing market. The riots in the city slums are raising demands for substantially larger Federal expenditures to deal with the social and economic ills in the American cities, and all this encourages cuts in the foreign-aid program, which has no effective lobby in the American electorate.

Nobody in the Senate debate has denied that the need for foreign aid is increasing, as the population of the hungry nations increases, but this aid program has been going on for eighteen years now and a defeatist mood has come over the Senate. Senator Robert Kennedy of New York goes further: he thinks the mood is not only defeatist but isolationist.

Whatever the word, one reason for the flood of Senate amendments cutting the aid and restricting the President's authority to plan long-range aid is the disappointing results of the aid in the past decade. In these last ten years, the rich industrial nations have put over $51 billion into the underdeveloped nations, plus another $30 billion in private capital; and the gap between the rich and poor nations during this period has not only widened, but the poor nations as a whole have actually had less economic growth in this decade than in the previous ten years.

Part of this is due to the decline in the prices of their raw materials, part of it to the costs of their rising debts, and part to their soaring populations, but the result here is a fear that even these vast bills for aid are not only useless but endless.

Beyond this, however, there is another factor in the revolt in the Senate. This is not only a revolt against foreign aid—it has always had grudging support at best—but it is also a revolt against Lyndon Johnson.

Restraining Johnson

There is a strong feeling in the Senate, mainly as a result of Vietnam, that the President has a way of stretching small commitments into very large commitments; that he is fascinated with the exercise of power; that he is determined to retain an American "presence" in all the critical trouble-spots in the world, and is now talking more and more of an elaborate American policy of security for all of non-Communist Asia.

This is why the chairman of the Foreign Relations Committee, Senator J. W. Fulbright of Arkansas, has been acquiescing to so many changes in the foreign-aid bill he is expected by the President to defend, and why he has reversed himself and insisted on limiting the President's foreign-aid authority to a single year.

'Manifest Destiny?'

"Is this foreign aid," he asked the Senate this week, "merely a tool and a part of a new policy of manifest destiny designed to establish our paternalistic control in Asia, or is it not? I do not know. But I think the question is sufficiently serious to warrant the consideration of the Senate, and that we should be very careful about expanding our aid commitment beyond a year."

This goes beyond the suspicions of most of the Senate, but the suspicions are there. The political costs of Vietnam are now beginn·‘g to be felt. To all the normal doubts and disappointments about this program, there is now being added the feeling that the President's power is too great and needs to be restrained, and a further reason for the present trouble is that the President has not backed the bill with his usual vigor.

July 22, 1966

Aid Bill Approved, Lowest in 9 Years

By The Associated Press

WASHINGTON, Oct. 7—The House and Senate quickly passed a $2.94-billion foreign aid appropriation today, sending it to President Johnson a day after the compromise was whipped together

House passage came first, on a 189-to-89 roll-call. The Senate sent it along to the White House by voice vote less than two hours later.

The figure is $443.4-million less than Mr. Johnson had asked and is the lowest financing for the program in nine years.

Yesterday, after House and Senate conferees agreed on the figure, it was described by William S. Gaud, administrator of the Agency for International Development, as "pretty hard to swallow."

But Representative Otto E. Passman, Louisiana Democrat who is the bill's floor manager in the House, said just before it passed that it would be "a distinct act of dishonesty and deceit" to contend that the bill cut the aid program.

Mr. Passman said the program had been so fragmented that it was impossible to keep up with its costs. He said appropriations and authorizations for other programs not directly identified as foreign aid increased the total program for the current fiscal year, which began July 1, to beyond $10-billion.

That amount, Mr. Passman said, is the highest since the aid program started.

The total was worked out in less than an hour yesterday by Senate-House conferees just after Mr. Johnson had told a news conference that every spending increase Congress voted made the need for a tax increase more likely. He has repeatedly urged Congress to hold down spending increases.

The over-all total was the Senate figure instead of the House's original $3.05-billion.

The compromise restored $25-million the Senate had pared from the fund for development loans under the Latin American Alliance for Progress. But it included a House-voted cut of $25-million in the military support program.

In the final bill is a requirement that 90 per cent of steel purchased with aid funds must be obtained in the United States —a provision designed to cut down on purchases of steel from Japan.

Also in the bill is a ban against aid to nations that deal with Cuba and North Vietnam.

This is the first time the aid money bill emerged under $3-billion since 1957, when it was $2.77-billion. The record low was $2.70-billion in 1955.

House Gives Ground

The approval concluded a turbulent year for the aid program, which became a target of a variety of Congressional frustrations, ranging from the war in Vietnam to inflation.

Much of the unhappiness centered in the Senate Foreign Relations Committee, headed by Senator J. W. Fulbright, who argued that aid was a factor in the United States entanglement in Vietnam.

Thus, one of the key disputes was over Mr. Fulbright's insistence that at least 10 per cent of the development loan funds be channeled through the World Bank or similar international organizations.

The Arkansas Democrat contended that by moving away from the bilateral basis of foreign aid the United States would be insulated from such entanglements and that overall the program's purposes would be better served.

In the past the House had refused to permit such transfers of aid funds. But this time it gave a little ground.

The House refused to require that at least 10 per cent of development loan funds be administered by international organizations. But it agreed to leave the decision up to the President.

Mr. Fulbright told the Senate today he was "very pleased" and called this action "a start."

It was understood that without this provision Mr. Fulbright would have voted against the aid appropriation. He repeated his assertions that unless the aid program was given a more multilateral character he would not be able to support it at all.

October 8, 1966

House Panel Divided On Aid Bill Secrecy

By FELIX BELAIR Jr.
Special to The New York Times

WASHINGTON, March 24 — A major controversy over "the public's right to know" about the Administration's presentation of the President's request for foreign aid is emerging in the House Foreign Affairs Committee.

Representative Paul Findley, Republican of Illinois, has demanded a committee vote on the issue of open or secret sessions for testimony on the combined economic and military aid program. The vote is expected to be taken by the committee on Tuesday.

Underlying the demand of the Illinois Representative for opening all committee meetings is the conviction of some members that American taxpayers have a right to know how their money is being spent and whether the foreign aid program is succeeding or failing in its objectives.

But Mr. Findley's principal concern is that at a time when the Administration has revealed all the underlying economic aid figures ($2.5-billion) for the first time in 20 years on a country-by-country basis, the House panel insists that its hearings must be closed whenever political relations between the United States and a friendly country may be compromised by critical testimony of American experts.

Chairman's Aim Is Speed

Arrayed against Mr. Findley and his supporters — Democratic and Republican—is the House Committee's chairman, Representative Thomas E. Morgan of Pennsylvania. It is Dr. Morgan's job to see to it that hearings on the Administration's bill are completed as quickly as possibly.

It is his position that unless witnesses from the State Department and the Agency for International Development can be heard in closed sessions the result will be a doubling of the time required for completion of the hearings.

Both sides agree that certain things cannot be said in a public hearing about how well or how badly aid recipients are using loans and grants under the foreign aid program.

But where Dr. Morgan has insisted on more secret than open sessions to protect the amicable relations of this nation with underdeveloped countries, Mr. Findley has been seeking "as many open hearings as possible even though some of these may have to be followed by executive sessions to hear talk of so-called delicate matters."

Some of these questions on "delicate matters" have touched during the last week on "the honesty and integrity" of certain officials of Latin-American governments involved with the United States in the Alliance for Progress, according to some members of the House panel.

Testimony on Alliance

The House committee's most recent closed meeting was last Thursday, when it heard testimony on the Alliance for Progress by the Assistant Secretary of State for Inter-American Affairs, Covey T. Oliver, who also is the United States coordinator for the Alliance for Progress with Latin-American countries.

Mr. Oliver resumes the stand Monday—also in executive session. Then follow two more days of closed door hearings on the controversial economic aid programs in Vietnam. James P. Grant, chief of A.I.D.'s new Vietnam division, is scheduled as the principal witness.

Traditionally A.I.D. officials have testified in open session of both the House and Senate committees. They still do except when accompanied by a political officer of the State Department, in which case the department insists on closed sessions.

Although A.I.D. "broke out" all its authorization and appropriation requests on a country-by-country basis this year, the Pentagon continues to insist all military aid figures must remain classified. This has been a source of irritation to foreign policy committeemen on both sides of the capitol.

Adding to the Senate group's resentment has been the refusal of all top officials of the Pentagon to appear either in open or closed sessions of the Senate Foreign Relations Committee.

Apparently taking his cue from the new Defense Secretary, Clark M. Clifford, Paul H. Nitze, the Deputy Secretary of Defense, informed the committee last week that he would also be unable to appear. He did not foreclose the possibility of an appearance later, however.

The Pentagon offered as substitute witnesses Paul C. Warnke, the Assistant Secretary of State for International Security Affairs, and Vice Adm. Luther C. Heintz, director of military assistance, under Mr. Warnke.

The Senate committee chairman, J. W. Fulbright, Democrat of Arkansas, promptly served notice that he would settle for nothing less than Mr. Clifford on the witness stand and that there would be no military aid bill at this session unless he changed his mind.

President Johnson's request for the fiscal year beginning next July 1 included $2.5-billion for economic aid and $540-million for military assistance grants. The latter excludes a request for $120-million in separate legislation for a limited credit sales program for the underdeveloped countries.

The difficulties awaiting the President's request during the current session were acknowledged today by the A.I.D. administrator, William S. Gaud, during a televised interview on the Metromedia news network.

Expects "Cliff Hanger"

Reminded that the House last year "came within eight votes of voting down the aid program altogether," Mr. Gaud said:

"I think we'll go through one of those 'cliff hangers' that we go through every year. . . . I think we will have tough sledding on the hill. But I don't believe myself that Congress will cut down the foreign aid program."

Mr. Gaud added that the circumstances of a Presidential election year would not have any effect on the aid program. As he put it:

"President Kennedy had always supported foreign aid and so has Senator McCarthy supported economic aid—the program that I'm concerned with.

"Similarly, on the Republican side, Governor Rockefeller, if he decided to run, has always supported foreign aid. Mr. Nixon has supported foreign aid in the past—so I don't see that any of the major candidates are out to cut the program. And I don't think that either side would be anxious to kill the program in an election year and take on an issue of that kind."

At the same time, Mr. Gaud acknowledged that Congress cut the President's request last year by about $1-billion and that the real danger this time was not that the economic aid program would be killed but that it might be "crippled."

March 25, 1968

Johnson Stressing Inter-American Bank in Policy on Latin Aid

By BENJAMIN WELLES
Special to The New York Times

WASHINGTON, June 2— President Johnson appears to be turning increasingly to the Inter-American Development Bank as his chosen instrument for United States policy in Latin America.

This shift, United States and Latin-American observers say, reflects the increasing resistance of Congress to financing direct foreign aid at anything approaching previous levels and its willingness to work through international agencies.

A major reason is the growing feeling in Congress that American aid, when distributed through such agencies, not only promotes cooperation between countries but also spares the United States criticism when things go wrong.

On the other hand, aid distributed through the United States Agency for International Development has become such a fixed feature throughout most of the underdeveloped world that any reduction or postponement is often seized on by anti-American politicians to assail "United States meddling" in their internal affairs.

Less Interference Likely

An additional benefit in the use of the Inter-American Development Bank, in Mr. Johnson's eyes, is the fact that Congress is less prone to interfere in the day-to-day spending of United States funds by international agencies than by the Government's own aid agency.

The Long-Conte amendment to the foreign aid bill, which recently obliged the Administration to slash aid to Peru, thereby causing widespread criticism of the United States in Latin America, is held up as an example of well-meaning but diplomatically disastrous Congressional interference.

Mr. Johnson's growing support for the bank is shared by a number of Congressional leaders interested in Western Hemisphere affairs. As one mark of support, Congress recently raised the United States share of the "soft loan window," thus enabling the bank to finance $300-million in multinational projects over the next three years.

The soft loans—those made at low interest rates over long periods to help underdeveloped governments — finance socially necessary but financially unremunerative projects such as roads, schools, hospitals and sewage plants.

Bank Founded in 1959

The members of the Inter-American Development Bank are the United States and most of the independent countries of Central and South America. It was founded in 1959 to finance economic and social development projects. It has made 448 loans totaling $2.3-billion for Latin - American development, and only two loans have failed.

President Johnson, informants say, is eager to leave office with a success in United States relations with Latin America.

But the hostile mood of Congress toward foreign aid, spurred in large measure by irritation over Vietnam, has resulted in sharp cuts in aid programs, including the usually sacrosanct Alliance for Progress.

For the year that starts July 1 Mr. Johnson is asking for $648-million for the alliance out of total foreign aid requests of $2.5-billion. But in each of the last three years Congress has slashed such "gross obligational" authority for the alliance. It authorized $684-million in fiscal 1966, $572-million in fiscal 1967, and $515-million in fiscal 1968, which ends June 30.

Special Attention for Clark

Against this background there was special significance in a White House ceremony April 23 that marked United States ratification of the amended Charter of the Organization of American States. As the capital's entire Latin-American diplomatic colony watched and the television cameras whirred, Mr. Johnson placed his arm around Edward A. Clark, his old friend from Texas and former Ambassador to Australia, and handed him his commission as the new United States executive director on the board of the Inter-American Development Bank. Mr. Clark succeeded W. True Davis, a Treasury official whose policies frequently conflicted with those of the State Department.

"Ed Clark likes to play the Texas country boy and he has little background in South America," an astute Latin-American diplomat observed, "but he was an effective ambassador in Australia, he's smart and he's very close to L.B.J. When Johnson appointed him, the bank got the message."

And Mr. Johnson has invited a large delegation to the White House for a ceremony Tuesday marking the recent approval by Congress of the bank's decision to increase its capitalization for "hard" loans from $2.1-billion to $3.1-billion. The United States share of the increase will be $412-million, reflecting the 42 per cent United States share in the bank's voting rights.

Mr. Johnson has also offered Mr. Clark use of a Presidential jet for an indoctrination tour of Latin-American countries. No date has been set, but it is expected that Mr. Clark will be accompanied by Covey T. Oliver, Assistant Secretary of State for Inter-American Affairs and coordinator for the Alliance for Progress.

In the April 23 ceremony, Mr. Johnson urged the formation of a task force, to be headed by a Latin American, to take responsibility for drawing up a five-year plan to speed the development of roads, bridges, power grids and other multinational development projects throughout Latin America.

A source of irritation to Mr. Johnson, it is said, is the bickering that erupts periodically between the United States and individual Latin-American nations, much of it caused by the fears of American officials that Congress will criticize their agencies unless they make aid recipients "toe the line."

The recent disputes, for instance, between the United States and Colombia over aid terms that Colombia found humiliating, and between the United States and Peru over Peru's decision to spend its scant dollar reserves on French Mirage jet fighters, which have revived fears of United States "domination" in Latin-America, are said to have disturbed the President. He was also critical of the long delay in electing Galo Plaza Lasso of Ecuador to be secretary general of the Organization of American States.

The appointment of Mr. Clark is viewed by observers here as a move to strengthen the "Latin-American team," which also includes Mr. Oliver and Sol M. Linowitz of New York, United States delegate to the O.A.S.

June 3, 1968

Aid to Developing Nations Shifting to Private Sector

By SEYMOUR TOPPING

The world pattern of economic aid to the developing countries of Asia, Africa and Latin America is undergoing a fundamental change.

Most of the major donor nations are leveling off or reducing their governmental economic and technical-assistance programs.

In Western and Communist countries, popular support for foreign aid is diminishing because of competing domestic needs, international payment problems and doubts about the effectiveness of governmental programs.

The developing countries are being advised by the United States and other Western countries to rely more on private business as a source of foreign credits and investment. Thus their planning must be revised at a time when expanding populations are widening the gap between what capital is needed and what is available.

This trend is discernible in reports by correspondents of The New York Times abroad and in this country.

United Nations officials expect the trend to be accelerated by the action of Congress in slashing the Administration's budget for foreign loans and grants to the developing countries.

Senate and House committees last week cut President Johnson's request for $2.54-billion to $1.6-billion, $300-million less than last year's authorization.

Congress also shelved two requests meant to induce matching contributions from other nations. These were $200-million for the Asian Development Bank and $160-million for the World Bank's International Development Association, which offers loans on easy terms.

The United States regularly provides about half of the new funds made available in the West to the developing nations, but its contribution in terms of national wealth is less than the average among the major donors.

U Thant, the United Nations Secretary General, observed in a recent report that a "climate of fatigue and disenchantment" had been gradually taking hold in international aid.

The leaders of some developing nations attribute the slowdown to the lessening of East-West tensions.

In the late fifties and in the first part of this decade, the United States and the Soviet Union heavily emphasized aid programs in the competition for ideological influence among the uncommitted nations. Today, American and Soviet aid programs are regarded in some countries as complementary rather than competitive.

Soviet Aid on Decline

Moscow and Washington have learned, sometimes painfully, that aid is not always an effective lever of influence.

Moscow supports Cuba with about a million dollars a day, but Premier Fidel Castro continues to flay the Soviet Union for refusing to back violent revolutionary action throughout Latin America.

The United States, to avoid the backlash of nationalist charges that aid represents political intervention, has been putting more of its assistance funds into multilateral channels, such as the Asian Bank and the Inter-American Development Bank.

In 1967, new Soviet aid committments for economic development declined to $70-million. There is a back-up in the Soviet aid pipeline of $3.9-billion in unused credits.

Analysts in Moscow believe that the cutback in United States aid has made it easier for the Russians to reduce their outlays.

However, when there is an important political advantage

to be gained, Moscow has not hesitated to spend. As part of its penetration of the Mediterranean region, Moscow extended last March a $200-million loan to Turkey for indistrial development, in competition with the American program.

The Soviet Union and the United States recognize a common security interest in extending aid to such countries as India and Indonesia, whose governments are in ideological opposition to Communist China.

Communist China has sought in its propaganda to exploit economical stagnation and political instability in the "have not" countries to mobilize a common front against the Soviet Union and the United States, which Peking lumps together as allied bourgeois "have" nations.

Peking's Effort Is Modest

Communist China, despite the internal upheaval of its Cultural Revolution, appears to be sustaining its modest economic aid program for Albania and countries in Africa and Asia.

Japan and West Germany are the only major donor countries that are significantly increasing their aid programs.

Koichi Komura, a senior Japanese aid official, says his Government has had to overcome strong feelings among Japanese that economic aid should go first to "pockets of stagnation" that mar the generally prosperous domestic scene. Similar sentiments are being voiced in every major donor country. United States opponents of aid programs have cited the need for more money for the poverty programs.

Japan, now the third largest industrial power, has been under strong pressure to increase her development aid. Unlike the other major donors, Japan, which is under United States military protection, does not bear a large defense burden.

Japanese aid this year will total about $885-million, nearly 1 per cent of the country's gross national product.

In 1961, at the suggestion of the United States delegate, Adlai E. Stevenson, the United Nations designated the sixties as the Development Decade, in which the richer nations would contribute 1 per cent of their national income to aid, loans and private investment in the developing countries.

In 1967, the United States contributed about one-seventh of 1 per cent of its income. The percentage declined this year.

In 1967, Bonn budgeted $553-million for aid, an increase of only $67-million, but West Germany is a leader in private investment in the developing countries. The level of British Government aid is holding steady, although devaluation this year cut the dollar level to $492-million from $574-million.

France contributes 1.6 per cent of her national income to aid, the only one of the major donors to exceed the 1 per cent goal of the United Nations. However, 90 per cent of this aid, which totals more than $1-billion, comes from private sources and a further reduction in the governmental program is expected. There is a similar emphasis on private sources in the Italian aid program, which is at a level of about $600-million.

Planners in Washington and other Western capitals, anticipating continued curtailment of government aid, are projecting new programs that put greater emphasis on stimulating private investment. These programs will utilize such incentives as government export credits, guarantees on investment involving risk, and public corporations utilizing mixed private and public funds.

Officials of international aid agencies believe that it will be some years before many of the developing countries will be able to adjust their economies so as to attract and absorb more private capital.

Surveying the prospects for the developing countries, Mr. Thant said recently: "We are not winning the war on want. The opportunity gap for many, if not most, of the nations and individuals of the world is growing wider, and inequality is increasing."

August 5, 1968

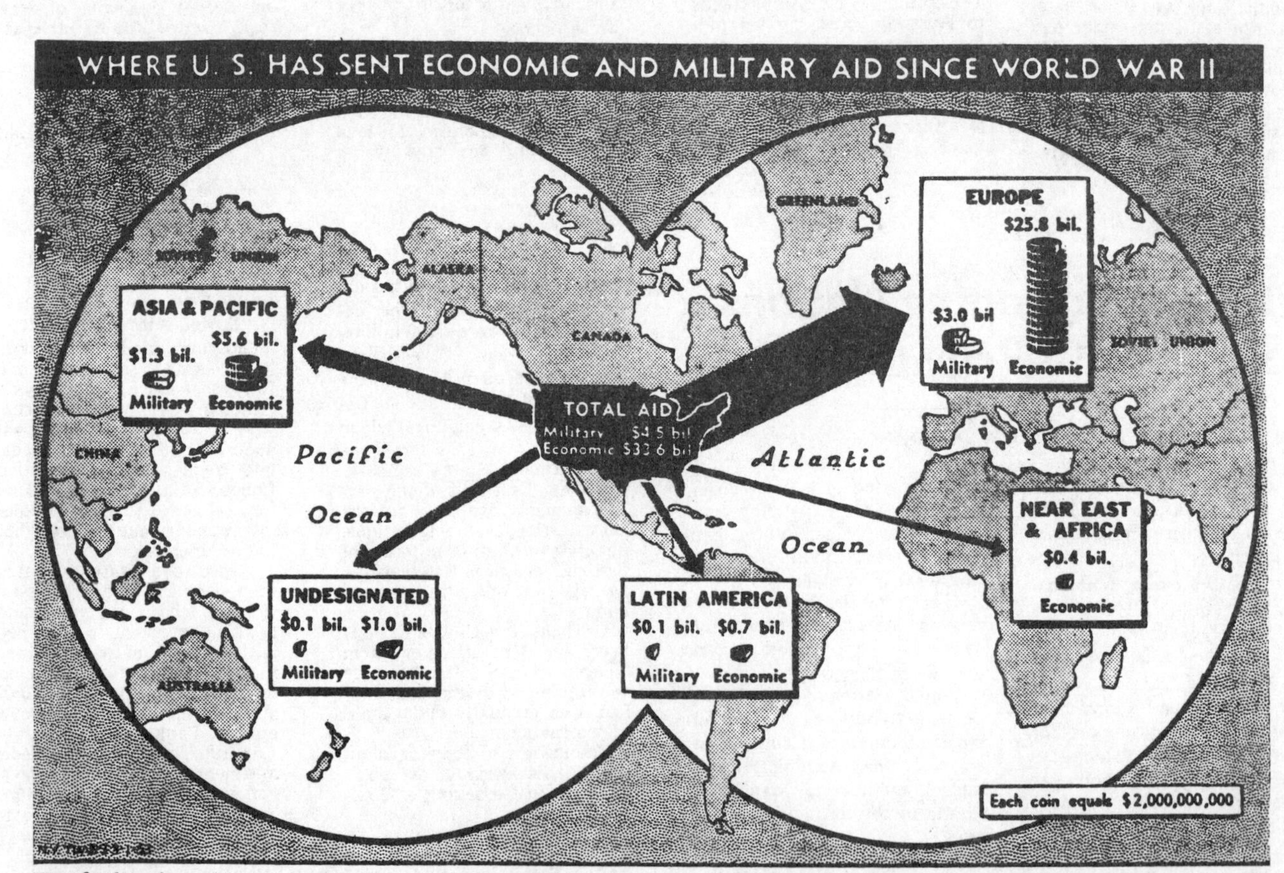

The forthcoming visit of British Foreign Secretary Eden and Chancellor of the Exchequer Butler has stirred speculation that the British may ask for further U. S. aid. Map above shows where U. S. sent aid between the end of World War II and last June 30. Of the European total of $29 billion, the United Kingdom received $7.2 billion. Congress authorized foreign aid in the current fiscal year of about $5.8 billion, which would raise the over-all total to more than $40 billion. Figures were compiled by Commerce Dept.

March 1, 1953

FOREIGN AID PLAN TAKING NEW FORM

Hollister Heads Successor to F. O. A. — $51 Billion Spent Since War's End

By DANA ADAMS SCHMIDT
Special to The New York Times.

WASHINGTON, June 30—The foreign aid program, under which the United States has spent some $51,000,000,000 since the end of World War II, will be under new management beginning tomorrow.

John Baker Hollister of Cincinnati, a former law partner of the late Senator Robert A. Taft and until today executive director of the Hoover Commission, will be sworn in by President Eisenhower tomorrow morning as director of the International Cooperation Administration. He replaces Harold E. Stassen, appointed special assistant to the President for disarmament. Under Mr. Stassen's Sdirection all foreign aid programs had been concentrated in the Foreign Operations Administration.

The Eighty-third Congress last year voted to put an end to that unit as an independent agency as of today and to end economic or development assistance gradually in the ensuing two years.

President Eisenhower accordingly has set up the new agency as part of the State Department. Present indications are that the Eighty-fourth Congress, far from ending economic aid programs, will vote more than its predecessor. The Administration has asked for $3,400,000,000 for 1955-56, about one-third of it in various forms of economic assistance.

Scope of Agency Limited

Whereas Mr. Stassen had over-all direction of the program and sat in the Cabinet and National Security Council, Mr. Hollister will administer only the economic side. He will appear at Cabinet and National Security Council meetings only when his program is at issue.

In practice the Defense Department for some time has administered military aid programs, and this situation has now been formalized by the President's order. The Departments of State and Defense are directed to coordinate military and non-military programs, but no over-all coordinator has been named.

This latest phase in the foreign aid programs comes at a time when several concepts of foreign aid appear to have taken firm hold in the Executive Branch and on Capitol Hill. Among these are the following:

¶That foreign aid programs are an integral part of United States foreign policy and are likely to remain so for some time to come.

¶That military aid alone will not stop communism.

¶That military aid must be buttressed with economic assistance, especially in underdeveloped countries, to enable the recipients to carry their defense programs.

Lend-Lease and Aid Costs

During and immediately preceding World War II the United States dispensed about $41,000,000,000 in the form of lend-lease and relief.

From the end of the war until March of this year aid actually delivered abroad totalled $50,026,000,000, and by today it is estimated to have reached $51,000,000,000.

The Mutual Security Act of 1951 gathered all aid programs under one coordinating director. This centralizing trend was completed by President Eisenhower's Reorganization Plan Number 7 on June 1, 1953, which brought technical economic and military assistance as well as the previously separate program for Latin America under the single authority of Harold E. Stassen.

Of the full aid deliveries of $50,026,000,000, a total of $26,262,000,000 was dispensed before the outbreak of the Korean war. About one third of the totals before and after Korea were in the form of repayable credits.

The biggest beneficiaries in non-military aid throughout the period have been Britain, with $6,915,000,000; France with $5,349,000,000, and Germany, with $3,856,000,000.

July 1, 1955

DULLES PROPOSES A FUND FOR LOANS FOR ECONOMIC AID

2 Billions Reported Sought by Administration to Start a Long-Range Program

SENATORS HEAR APPEAL

Separate Outlay for Weapons Urged, Coming Under the Nation's Defense Budget

By WILLIAM S. WHITE
Special to The New York Times.

WASHINGTON, April 8—The Eisenhower Administration presented to Congress today a fundamentally altered Mutual Security Program that would commit this country to foreign aid for indefinite years.

In the face of warnings that the whole aid policy would be in great Congressional trouble unless a new approach were devised, John Foster Dulles, the Secretary of State, offered proposals involving several departures.

One was the establishment of a special economic development fund with "a capital authorization sufficient for several years" to extend economic aid on a loan basis. Outright aid grants—that is, nonrepayable ones—would be extended only to meet emergency situations. This fund ultimately might be extending assistance at the rate of as much as $750,000,000 a year.

Authorization Sought

It was understood that the Administration was considering asking Congress almost immediately for an authorization of perhaps $2,000,000,000 to set this fund going and keep it going for three or four years. Initial annual outlays would be less than the probable maximum of three-quarters of a billion dollars.

It was understood also that the President would send to Congress within a few days a speccial message conceding that some relatively small savings—perhaps $200,000,000—could be shaved from the Administration's foreign aid budget. This is estimated at $4,400,000,000.

Mr. Dulles also proposed a sharper definition alike of military and economic assistance. Hereafter, military aid would be comprised only of the actual "hardware" plus the monetary assistance to an associated country directly required for it to maintain its armed forces. All the rest, including some assistance now regarded as supporting military defense, would be economic aid.

Military Aid Separated

This would be handled in the new development fund or under the existing technical assistance programs.

Military aid would be bracketed into the regular budget of the Defense Department and taken out of the foreign aid budget. The President and State Department would continue, however, to give final policy guidance to military as well as all other types of foreign aid.

The intention here is to obtain a permanent Congressional authorization for military aid in principle. Then, the Administration would need to ask annually only for appropriations and not each time for renewed authority. Two annual issues would thus be cut to one.

Moreover, military aid is always the largest single sum in any foreign aid bill. If this is taken out of such bills and the revolving economic development fund is approved, new aid appropriations requests would be in terms of hundreds of millions rather than in multi-billions.

Mr. Dulles placed his proposals before the special Senate committee to study the foreign aid program, made up of members of the Foreign Relations and Armed Services Committees.

The reception for this remodeled foreign program was much more friendly, though still noncommittal, than a good many in the Administartion had expected. Not all the Secretary's hearers, however, were convinced.

One skeptic was Senator Richard B. Russell, Democrat of Georgia, perhaps the special committee's most powerful single member as chairman of the Armed Services Committee.

What Mr. Dulles unfolded was a plan that would grant two major concessions to Congress—the virtual end of economic grant aid and an administrative reshuffling that would take military aid out of the mutual security bill and put it into the Pentagon's bill.

But the Secretary's revision also would require a major concession from Congress—a grant to the Administration of long-term authority of a sort never before given.

The Republican Senate leader, William F. Knowland of California, commended the Administration for emphasizing loans rather than grants. He predicted, however, that Congress still would cut about $1,000,000,000 from the Administration's total budget estimate.

Mr. Dulles' testimony and his colloquies with the Senators made it plain that he sought to avoid the necessity thereafter of receiving Congressional approval for individual economic aid projects.

This, he said in effect, is required for a more rational administration. Present law, he asserted, has sometimes forced "scandalous inefficiency" in obligating and spending foreign aid funds because of Congressional restrictions.

The Administration now comes to Congress for direction on what country is to have what projects. Under the new approach Congress would authorize the money, but the Administration would be enabled to obligate it with much greater flexibility—or, as Mr. Dulles said, "without geographical predisposition."

The precise sort of economic development fund to be set up, he told the committee, is not yet some of the characteristics of a bank, he said, and it "might usefully join" with the World Bank and the Export-Import Bank "in financing particular projects."

The fundamental point was that the arrangement would tend to drown charges of "giveaway" and to put the bulk of economic aid on something approaching a straight business loan basis.

This aspect of the new program was manifestly pleasing to such diverse committeemen as Senators J. William Fullbright, Democrat of Arkansas, and Homer E. Capehart, Republican of Indiana. Mr. Fullbright is an old internationalist leader; Mr. Capehart has been a sharp critic of foreign aid.

Pleasing to the committee generally, too, was the proposal to put military aid under the domestic military budget.

This rearrangement, nevertheless, did not placate Senator Russell, the chief spokesman in the Senate on military affairs.

Mr. Russell told Secretary Dulles that despite the expenditure of "a great deal of money" the West's defense was weaker than five years ago, "especially with regard to the North Atlantic Treaty Organization."

Mr. Russell suggested that the recent revolutionary change in Britain's defense strategy, plans for heavily reducing conventional weapons and forces, has lessened the free world's total strength.

Mr. Dulles refused to concede that there had been any weakening of the West's deterrent power, which he considered to be the heart of the matter.

Mr. Dulles conceded to Mr. Russell that he could not "put a date" on any probable termination of the foreign aid policy.

Reuben B. Robertson, Deputy Secretary of Defense, assured the committee that the military would continue to rely fully on the State Department for guidance in the military aid program.

Mr. Dulles' new plan depended in part on foreign aid studies made by commissions headed by Benjamin F. Fairless, former chairman of the United States Steel Corporation, and Eric A. Johnston. Mr. Johnston is president of the Motion Picture Association.

April 9, 1957

PRESIDENT OFFERS REDUCED AID PLAN; PUTS IT TO PEOPLE

A BIG CUT OPPOSED

Eisenhower Declares Slash Would Be a Risk to Peace

By W. H. LAWRENCE
Special to The New York Times.

WASHINGTON, May 21—President Eisenhower asserted tonight that a Congressional economy drive that would cripple his reduced $3,865,000,000 mutual assistance program would be a reckless gamble with peace and freedom.

He spoke in strong terms to the nation by radio and television after he had placed the foreign aid program before Congress formally in a special message.

He sought to counteract the strong bipartisan sentiment in both houses for a sharp reduction in this program and in regular defense spending.

Initial reaction indicated he had gained little, if any, ground.

General Eisenhower warned that the cost of peace was high. But the cost of war is greater, he asserted, and "paid in different coin—with the lives of our youth and the devastation of our cities."

'The Price of Peace'

"The road to this disaster could easily be paved with the good intentions of those blindly striving to save the money that must be spent as the price of peace," he declared.

"To cripple our programs for mutual security in the false name of 'economy' can mean nothing less than a weakening of our nation. To try to save money at the risk of such damage is neither conservative nor constructive. It is reckless.

"It could mean the loss of peace. It could mean the loss of freedom. It could mean the loss of both.

"I know that you would not wish your Government to take such a reckless gamble. I do not intend that your Government take that gamble."

The program submitted today was $535,000,000 less than the President estimated in his January budget message. He declared the reduced sum was "a reasoned figure" and was, indeed, a "minimum figure * * * considering the issues at stake."

The President's new proposal that the bulk of future economic assistance to foreign countries be in the form of loans rather than grants drew bipartisan support. One of those who spoke out in support of this approach was Senator Lyndon B. Johnson of Texas, the Senate majority leader. He said he had been urging the Administration since January to propose a loan program.

Loan Program Backed

Senator Homer E. Capehart, Indiana Republican, gave his backing to the loan program and to the President's suggestion that future military assistance appropriations be lumped into the regular Defense Department budget.

The President broke down his program among these items:

	In millions
Military equipment and services	$1,900
Defense support	900
Development loan fund	500
Technical cooperation program	152
Emergency assistance	300
Nonmilitary programs, including peaceful use of atom	113

The Congressional reaction was mixed, but the bipartisan move for economies remained strong in the Congress, with the prospect that the President's program will be cut at least $500,000,000.

Senator Styles Bridges of New Hampshire, the senior Republican of the Senate, forecast authorized appropriations of no more than $3,400,000,000. Others suggested the total probably would be smaller.

Second Eisenhower Speech

This was the second of two speeches by the President seeking to rally support for his big budget. The reaction of the first one, last week, was so mild it convinced many top Administration strategists that General Eisenhower was fighting a losing battle. The White House declined any breakdown on the mail response to the Presidential message, but did say the President was satisfied he had attained his objective.

But on Capitol Hill there was little evidence that the people had thrown their weight behind the President, and there was no slackening of the economy campaign.

In his speech tonight, the President recognized that of his mutual assistance program was vulnerable to the economy drive because it operated long distances from home and was less visible than programs carried on at home.

But General Eisenhower argued that the efforts to help free nations to resist international communism by building up their military and economic strength accomplished more than any other programs "dollar-for-dollar in securing the safety of our country and the peaceful lives of all of us."

He said that it was "no accident that those who have most intimately lived with the horrors of war are generally the most earnest supporters of these programs to secure peace."

"I know of no more sound or necessary investment that our nation can make," he continued. "I know of no expenditure that can contribute so much—in the words of the Constitution—to our 'common defense' and to securing the blessings of liberty for ourselves and our posterity."

Lower Taxes Cited

In his message and in his speech, the President took note of the sentiment in Congress and among the people for lower taxes.

"We live at a time when our plainest task is to put first things first," he said. "Of all our current domestic concerns—

lower taxes, bigger dams, deeper harbors, higher pensions, better housing—not one of these will matter if our nation is put in peril. For all that we cherish and justly desire—for ourselves and for our children—the securing of peace is the first requisite."

In his message to Congress, he said there was "only one sound way for us to achieve a substantial tax reduction." This, he said, is to succeed in waging peace, thereby permitting a substantial cut in our heavy military expenditures. But a substantial cut in such expenditures now "in the face of present world conditions would be foolhardy," he asserted.

The president spoke from his White House office with the aim, he said, of bringing the facts to the people of what mutual security programs mean to them in their daily lives.

Bipartisan Program

The program, he noted, was a bipartisan one, suggested by a Democrat President, Harry S. Truman, and enacted by a Republican Congress. In eight years, he said, the nation had furnished direct military assistance to our allies costing $17,000,000,000, while the foreign nations themselves spent $107,000,000,000. He used charts to illustrate what this "united effort" had achieved.

"In 1950, the strength of our allies totaled 1,000 combat vessels, 3,500,000 men in the ground forces and 500 jet aircraft," General Eisenhower recalled. "Now, in 1957, they have: 2,500 combat vessels, 5,000,000 men and 13,000 jets."

He contended this effort had saved Iran for the free world, rescued Guatamala from Communist infiltration and encouraged Yugoslavia to remain independent of Kremlin domination.

In putting forth his loan program, he said it would cost $500,000,000 in the first year, but about $750,000,000 a year for each of the next two years.

"In this whole program," he went on, "we do not seek to buy friends. We do not seek to make satellites.

"We do seek to help other peoples to become strong and stay free—and learn, through living in freedom, how to conquer poverty, how to know the blessings of peace and progress."

The President argued the importance of combining the foreign military assistance program with the regular Defense Department budget. Such an act, he said, would "fittingly recognize that our own security requires continuance of these parts of our own military effort as long as Communist imperialism remains a menace to free peoples."

"This would also enable the Congress to consider simultaneously appropriations both for our own armed forces and for assistance to friendly forces," he continued. "In this way, these two interrelated elements of our military budget can be better integrated and balanced, and the effectiveness of both increased."

Last Year's Savings

The President noted that $500,000,000 of the $3,800,000,000 voted by the Congress last year had been saved during the current fiscal year. He asked the Congress to carry over this sum as additional authorized spending during the 1958 fiscal year, beginning in July.

It was this saving, he added, that made possible the $535,000,000 reduction between his January budget estimate and the mutual assistance program submitted today.

These savings resulted, he said, from a "reduction in spare parts requirements based on experience in the actual use of our equipment by the forces we are assisting, reduced needs resulting from better planning with our allies, and a continuing improvement of the administration of the program."

May 22, 1957

AID BILL IGNORES 'NEW APPROACH'

Money Grants Are Reduced as in Past Years but 'Bold Program' Is Out

By EDWIN L. DALE Jr.
Special to The New York Times.

WASHINGTON, Aug. 31—The annual foreign aid hassle is over once again.

After this year's unusually heavy cloud of smoke cleared away, the results could be summarized this way: the Administration did better in getting dollars than in selling new ideas.

Emerging from the verbal underbrush about authorizations, appropriations and re-appropriations came a money figure cut only a little more than the average reduction of recent years.

The Administration will have about $3,400,000,000 to use for mutual security in the present fiscal year, a cut of a little more than $1,000,000,000 from what President Eisenhower wanted.

Not only is this an average sort of cut but also almost exactly half of it came in the military "hardware" request. This is the part of foreign aid that has the biggest backlog of unspent funds, and in which requests and actual needs have proved in the past to be farthest apart.

Funds Left Over

What is more, the dollar cut in the "working diplomacy" part of the foreign aid request was rather slight. The Administration will have close to what it asked for in "defense support" (subsidies for a small group of allies that maintain large armed forces beyond their economic capacity to support) and "special assistance" (the catch-all but crucial category that provides emergency aid in such situations as Jordan and Poland).

That covers three of the five functions foreign aid is now performing. A fourth, technical assistance, was cut, but the program will be able to carry on at about the same level as in the last fiscal year.

When the fifth category is assessed, however, the problem of the Administration's failure to sell new ideas and concepts begins to emerge. This is a category that has had varying names in the past, but comes down to this: aid for the vast array of underdeveloped nations, mostly not allied with the United States, to spur their economic development.

A series of expert reports to the Administration and to the Senate earlier this year advocated something in the nature of a "bold new program" in this area, with suggested annual aid figures running $1,000,000,000 and upward.

Loan Fund Slashes

It asked for a new development loan fund with a three-year capitalization of $2,000,000,000. It wanted both authorization of the fund and a three-year initial funding enacted this year, on the widely accepted premise that development aid simply cannot work on a year-to-year basis.

The Administration got practically nothing of what it requested in this area.

(1) Of the $500,000,000 asked for the fund for its first year, Congress approved $300,000,000—a cut of 40 per cent.

(2) The Administration had asked that the second and third year financing, $750,000,000 each year, be authorized now in the form of loans from the Treasury. Congress simply authorized a possible appropriation next year of $625,000,000.

Thus the "long-term" feature of the fund was largely lost, and its financing was cut drastically.

Another important conceptual change in the program fared equally badly.

The Administration wanted a permanent authorization for both military aid and defense support. This would mean that each year it would make a simple appropriation request, to be included in the regular defense budget. No authorization bill for this part of the aid program would be needed, thus removing one stage of the annual cutting process. This request was flatly rejected.

'No-Year' Programs

The Administration did achieve a limited success in one other requested change. It had asked that much of the program be appropriated on a "no-year" basis—as, for example, military aircraft procurement is appropriated. Under this system, funds not committed or obligated in the fiscal year for which they were appropriated remain available indefinitely, thus eliminating the need to ask for "re-appropriation" of funds not used during a given fiscal year.

Congress granted full no-year status to the $300,000,000 voted for the new development loan fund, and it appropriated military aid funds for eighteen months instead of the usual twelve.

Probably the worst aspect of the failure to achieve the bulk of the new approach, from the Administration's point of view, is that it will have to go through the same old struggle over foreign aid again next year—without much in the way of a shiny new package to make the program more attractive.

September 1, 1957

PRESIDENT'S UNIT URGES RISE IN AID OVER LONG PERIOD

Study Board Asks 3.4 Billion Annually to Help Allies Meet Enduring Menace

By FELIX BELAIR Jr.
Special to The New York Times

WASHINGTON, March 17—A long-range program providing about $2,400,000,000 a year in military aid abroad and economic assistance averaging about $1,000,000,000 annually was recommended today by a Presidential study committee.

The group recommended to President Eisenhower an immediate $400,000,000 increase in his $1,600,000,000 request for foreign military aid under the Mutual Security Program for the 1960 fiscal year. The President requested the $1,600,000,000 sum in his recent message to Congress asking for a total of $3,930,000,000 for all foreign aid in the fiscal year 1960.

A Preliminary Report

The Presidential committee said that it was equally important that Congress and the nation face the fact that it was engaged in a long-term struggle for survival against Communist imperialism. It demanded a long-term legislative commitment to provide continuity in the programs of authorization and administration.

"The choice our country faces is very real and near at hand," said the committee's preliminary report. "In our fascination with our own mistakes, and the constant use of foreign aid as a whipping boy, we may be gradually choking this vital feature of our national security policy to death."

The ten-member survey group, designated as the President's committee to study the United States Military Assistance Program, was appointed by President Eisenhower last November. It is headed by William H. Draper Jr., chairman of the board of the Mexican Light and Power Company in Mexico City and a former Under Secretary of the Army.

Eisenhower Asked Study

President Eisenhower had asked the study group for an interim report in time to bear on the current Congressional debate and committee studies of the Administration request for foreign aid funds. In his recent message the President said that he was aware of the group's forthcoming report and proposed to consider it in further recommendations to Congress later.

Meanwhile a dispute about the secrecy over the proposed allotments of military aid abroad almost disrupted a House committee hearing today on the President's fund request.

In its interim report to the President, the Draper study group pointed out that the $1,600,000,000 requested for military aid in the fiscal year beginning next July 1 would produce a spending level for "military hardware" of no more than $1,850,000,000 in that year and lesser amounts in the two succeeding years.

The higher expenditure level over current appropriations has been possible because of drawings on unexpanded balances of past appropriations. These unexpended balances have been gradually reduced from some $8,000,000,000 a few years ago to about $2,500,000,000 in prospect at the close of the current fiscal year.

Of the expenditure level for military hardware now in prospect, the report said, "they would not permit the United States to make the contribution necessary for the modernization of NATO forces now under way, and to help maintain effective forces in other parts of the world."

Because of the reduction in cording to the report, current appropriations could no longer be supplemented from this source. In future, military aid the unexpended balances, accordeliveries will just about equal the amount of current appropriations, it said.

"We view with concern the projected sharp decline in the rate of deliveries below the $2,400,000,000 average level of recent years," said the committee.

The committee proposed to examine the problem of economic aid more fully in its final report to the President, but said that, meanwhile:

"We believe that loans for economic development under the Mutual Security Program will probably be needed at a rate of at least $1,000,000,000 a year by fiscal year 1961."

Today's clash in the House Foreign Affairs Committee developed when the chairman, Representative Thomas E. Morgan of Pennsylvania, a Democrat, called for the hearing room to be cleared of press and public. He made the request so the committee could hear testimony in secret from C. Douglas Dillon, Under Secretary of State, about the amounts of military aid being allotted to various countries.

Representative Wayne L. Hays, Democrat of Ohio, entered a vigorous objection and threatened to divulge all the figures on the floor of the House if the chairman insisted on an executive session.

Mr. Morgan insisted that the information was "classified" and that he had decided it should be heard only in closed session.

Associated Press Wirephoto

REPORT ON FOREIGN AID: President Eisenhower and William H. Draper Jr., head of Presidential study group, discuss foreign military and economic assistance at White House. Group recommended an immediate foreign military aid increase of $400,000,000.

March 18, 1959

CONGRESS PASSES 3.5 BILLION IN AID; FUND BATTLE DUE

Authorization Bill Is Short of Presidential Request by 353 Million

By RUSSELL BAKER
Special to The New York Times.

WASHINGTON, July 22—Congress passed and sent to President Eisenhower today a $3,556,200,000 mutual security authorization for the 1960 fiscal year. It falls $353,200,000 short of the amount sought by the President.

The bill, a compromise between differing Senate and House versions, was passed quickly through both houses this afternoon without change or significant debate.

The Senate acted by voice vote. The House approved the measure by a roll-call vote of 257 to 153.

Passage of the authorization measure sets the stage for the opening of the second major phase of the annual foreign aid battle, the fight for an appropriation bill.

Fund Cut Probable

The authorization merely sets a ceiling on the amount of money to be available for the program. The appropriation is the amount of money Congress actually empowers the Administration to spend. It is normally well below the ceilings set in the authorization bill.

The struggle over the appropriation is always the most difficult for the Mutual Security Program.

Broadly, this is because the authorization bill is handled by committees essentially sympathetic to the State Department's problems—the Foreign Relations Committee in the Senate and the Foreign Affairs Committee in the House.

The appropriations committees, by contrast, have historically been less concerned with the problems of diplomacy than with the emotions of the taxpayer.

Less Military Aid

The authorization bill approved today carries $1,400,000,000 for military assistance, or $200,000,000 less than President Eisenhower had said was the minimum requirement. It also provides that for the next two fiscal years, 1961 and 1962, military assistance shall be included in the Pentagon's defense budget and need not go through the annual Mutual Security authorization process.

The bill also authorizes an appropriation of $700,000,000, as requested by the President, for the Development Loan Fund during the present fiscal year. It authorizes an appropriation of $1,100,000,000 for the development Loan Fund in the 1961 fiscal year.

Spending limits in other major categories are $179,500,000 for technical cooperation, $247,500,000 for special assistance, $751,000,000 for defense support and $155,000,000 for the President's contingency fund.

July 23, 1959

PRESIDENTIAL UNIT WARNS ON CUTTING MILITARY AID PLAN

Draper Panel Disputes View Program Is Overbalanced in Less-Developed Lands

URGES GREATER OUTLAYS

Decline in Shipments Would Imperil the Free World, Final Report Declares

By E. W. KENWORTHY
Special to The New York Times.

WASHINGTON, Aug. 20—A Presidential committee took issue today with Senators who believe that the Administration attaches too much importance to military and not enough to economic aid in less-developed countries.

In a fourth and final report, the Committee to Study the United States Military Assistance Program said:

"The committee believes that the impression held in some quarters to the effect that our military assistance program is too great in relation to the economic development assistance program is not justified."

The ten-member bipartisan panel is headed by William H. Draper Jr., former Assistant Secretary of the Army and onetime Ambassador to the North Atlantic Treaty Organization.

When the President set it up last November, his instructions included a request for a "critical appraisal" of the relative emphasis to be given to military and economic aid in less-developed areas.

Letter Sent to President

A factor in establishing the committee was a letter sent by eight Senators to the President last Aug. 25. In it, they expressed the conviction that there was a "serious distortion" in the relative importance assigned to the two types of assistance. They asked that a study be made.

In its report the committee said:

"Any marked decline in the level of general military-aid deliveries at this time for less-developed areas would represent a serious danger to the security of the free world."

Many advocates of increased development aid would achieve their objective through cuts in military assistance, it noted. However, it said, it regarded this as a "dangerous" expedient, and warned that economic and military aid should not become competitors for "resources within preconceived limitation."

Much of the final report was devoted to an extension of arguments for the recommended increase in military aid.

The President submitted this proposal to Congress without recommendation, but said he would review the situation after Congress had completed action on the mutual security bill. In view of the deep cuts in prospect, it was believed that the President might ask a supplemental appropriation for military aid early in 1960.

In submitting the report to Congress, President Eisenhower said he agreed with the committee "concerning the dangerously low level of appropriations authorized for the military assistance program for fiscal 1960."

In its first report last March 17, the committee proposed that the President's request for military aid be increased from $1,600,000,000 to $2,000,000,000 for the fiscal year that began last July 1.

It urged then that about three-fourths of the increase be used to supply intermediate-range ballistic missiles to Atlantic treaty allies, and the remainder for increased air strength, replacement of obsolete equipment and weapons modernization in the Far East.

In the authorization bill, which sets a top limit for appropriations, Congress cut the President's military aid request from $1,600,000,000 to $1,400,000,000. On the appropriation bill the House voted only $1,300,000,000, or $400,000,000 below the President's request.

The Senate has not yet acted but the prospect there is for a final appropriation of not much more than $1,300,000,000.

The Draper committee warned that this level of military aid "falls far below" what was needed.

When the Administration came in, it said, there was a carryover of unexpended funds for military assistance amounting to more than $8,000,000,000. This provided a "pipeline" for deliveries of weapons requiring a long "lead time" in production, it declared.

Because of the size of the carryover, President Eisenhower cut President Truman's request for military aid in the 1954 fiscal-year budget from $5,500,000,000 to $3,500,000,000. John Foster Dulles, late Secretary of State, said the revised figure would maintain a balance between "our economic health and our military effort." Congress gave the President only $3,200,000,000.

Despite these cuts, the carryover was still large enough so that deliveries of weapons and supplies were maintained at an average rate of $2,500,000,000 a year.

However, since the 1954 fiscal year, the committee noted, "annual deliveries have exceeded annual appropriations."

Decline in Funds

In fact, over the last four years, it said, while deliveries have been maintained at $2,500,000,000, appropriations have averaged only $1,500,000,000. As a result, by last June 30, there was only about $2,500,000,000 in carry-over funds.

This "is close to the minimum amount required to finance the production of items required to maintain the rate at which deliveries have been flowing," the committee warned.

By implication the committee criticized the President for having asked too little and Congress for having cut the President's requests.

The President asked $1,800,000,000 for military aid for the 1959 fiscal year, and Congress voted only $1,500,000,000. For 1960 he asked $1,600,000,000.

For 1960 and 1961, the committee said, the minimum needed to keep supplies flowing will be $2,000,000,000 a year.

If Congress appropriates less than $1,400,000,000 this year, it warned, there will be a decline of 40 per cent or more in deliveries in 1962.

"Reduction of the pipeline to a level which will no longer permit provision of modern weapons [for NATO countries] entails risks that are militarily unacceptable," it asserted.

At the same time the committee urged that the Administration encourage larger defense expenditures by other industrialized countries of the alliance.

It also recommended more vigorous measures to inform the American people of the relationship between foreign aid and the national interest.

"Unjustified attacks" on the program should be answered "publicly, promptly and forcefully," it declared.

In its second report June 3, the committee recommended that the military-aid program be included in the Defense Department budget and given continuing authorization for more than one year. The Administration accepted both recommendations, and Congress adopted them in the authorization bill.

In the third report on July 13, the committee recommended that the Development Loan Fund receive a lending authority of $1,000,000,000 a year for five years. The State Department favors that, but the Treasury and the Budget Bureau do not and Presidential approval is unlikely.

Besides Mr. Draper, the members of the committee are:

Gen. Alfred M. Gruenther, president of the American Red Cross; Admiral Arthur W. Radford, former chairman of the Joint Chiefs of Staff; Gen. Joseph T. McNarney, former commander of United States forces in Europe; George C. McGhee, former Assistant Secretary of State; John J. McCloy, former Under Secretary of War, and Marx Leva, former Assistant Secretary of Defense.

Also, Dillon Anderson, former assistant to the President for national security affairs; James E. Webb, former Under Secretary of State, and Joseph M. Dodge, former chairman of the Council on Foreign Economic Policy.

August 21, 1959

PRESIDENT SEEKS OVERHAUL OF AID, ASKS $3.2-BILLION

Requests for Economic and Military Programs Are Up by Almost $800-Million

REFORMS TO BE MAJOR

2 New Bodies Would Replace A.I.D.—Aim Is to Enable U.S. to Reduce Its Role

By FELIX BELAIR Jr.
Special to The New York Times

WASHINGTON, April 21 — President Nixon proposed a major revision of economic and military foreign aid today and asked Congress to provide $3.2-billion for the programs in the fiscal year beginning July 1.

The request was almost $80-million more than was provided for the current fiscal year, when Congress voted a regular appropriation of $1.94-billion and $500-million in supplementary appropriations, chiefly for military and other aid for Indochina and the Middle East.

In an 8,000-word special message to Congress, on which the White House issued a summary, the President said that his proposals would bring about greater efficiency and help other nations to "increasingly shoulder their own responsibilities so that we can reduce our direct involvement abroad."

Loans, Research, Training

Mr. Nixon proposed to replace the Agency for International Development with two bodies — an International Development Corporation that would make loans to poorer countries and an International Development Institute to carry on research into development problems in such countries, to train technicians and to provide American advisers on development.

The development corporation would be equipped with a three-year authorization of $1.5-billion and with authority to borrow $1-billion more from the public or the Treasury within that period. It would have $655-million available the first year.

Military Aid Would Rise

The proposed institute would have a three-year authorization of $1.27-billion and an initial appropriation of $385-million. It could make some grants for technical assistance to the poorest of what Mr. Nixon termed lower-income countries but, for the most part, would make loans on easy terms.

A significant expansion of military aid—renamed international security assistance—is contemplated in the President's plan. He requested $1.99-billion, including $705-million of grant military aid, $510-million for credit sales of arms and $778-million for economic assistance.

The security assistance request is about $500-million more than the regular appropriation last year, but about the same as the total appropriated, including the large supplemental funds approved for use in Indochina.

Evidently indifferent to Congressional warnings, the President proposed to split what formerly was omnibus legislation into bills covering international security and economic development. White House officials had been assured by the House Foreign Affairs Committee's chairman, Representative Thomas E. Morgan of Pennsylvania, that the two would be combined when they reach that group.

The broad outlines of the revamping were given in the President's report to Congress last September in which he adopted the principal recommendations of a White House study group headed by Rudolph A. Peterson, former chairman of the Bank of America.

Key members of the House and Senate committees on foreign policy indicated then that

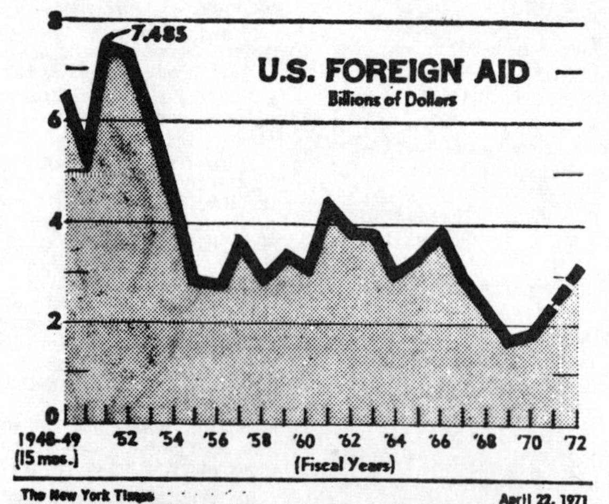

Chart begins with 15-month period marking the start of Marshall Plan aid. Part of the decline of 1968-70 was caused by the shift of military funds earmarked for countries in Indochina to United States defense budget.

they had serious reservations, largely because of the proposed recall of United State aid missions abroad and the channeling of more development funds through the International Bank for Reconstruction and Development.

President Nixon, stressing his commitment to an effective foreign aid program for the nineteen-seventies, said the United States could make no better investment for peace than "to participate fully in an international effort to build prosperity and hope for a better tomorrow among all nations."

"Foreign assistance is quite clearly in our interest as a nation," he added.

"We are people whose sons have died and whose great statesmen have worked to build a world order which insures peace and prosperity for ourselves and for other nations.

"We are aware that this world order cannot be sustained if our friends cannot defend themselves against aggression, and if two-thirds of the world's people see the richer third as indifferent to their needs and insensitive to their aspirations for a better life."

Rounding out the proposed economic-assistance structure are two existing agencies, the Overseas Private Investment Corporation, which insures United States investors against loss for political upheavals or expropriation, and the Inter-American Social Progress Institute, designed for Latin-American problems.

To Raise Export Earnings

Under security assistance, Mr. Nixon asked for a separate item of $100-million for his contingency fund. This could be used for military aid, development or humanitarian relief "when sudden crises in the international community require us to act promptly and decisively."

The $3.2-billion total for aid takes no account of separate amounts asked for international organizations a year ago but side-tracked by Congress in the rush for adjournment.

In the context of progress toward a development program for the seventies, Mr. Nixon reported that industrialized countries "have now agreed on comparable systems of tariff preferences for imports from the lower-income countries."

He described the plan as "a major step in the crucial international effort to expand the export earnings of these countries, and hence to reduce their reliance on external aid." European Common Market members plan to put tariff preferences in effect July 1 and Japan is expected to follow about Oct. 1, he said.

The reforms outlined include provision for a coordinator of development assistance responsible directly to the President and serving simultaneously as chairman of the development and investment corporations and of the Institute for Technical Assistance.

The post is the Administration's answer to Congressional opposition to the diffusion of accountability to House and Senate committees.

The plan also calls for a coordinator for security assistance "to be established at a high level in the Department of State." The Defense Department would have primary responsibility for administering the military assistance and credit sales but the supporting economic assistance would be under the State Department.

It was clear from the President's message that both military and economic loans and grants would be more concentrated among countries in which the United States has a "special interest." What was not so clear was who would ultimately determine the area of that interest.

April 22, 1971

U-69272
BRINK'S
A SUBSIDIARY OF
PITTSTON
7861-HB
Schools Open
DRIVE CAREFULLY

CHAPTER 4
Monetary Policy

Loading of silver bullion in New York City's financial district.
Courtesy Gene Brown

TREASURY SETTLES RIFT WITH RESERVE OVER BOND POLICY

Agreement to Curb Inflation Provides Long-Term Issue With 2¾% Interest

TRUMAN HAILS ACCORD

Sees a 'Very Important Step Forward'—Finance Chiefs in Congress Gratified

By JOHN D. MORRIS
Special to THE NEW YORK TIMES.

WASHINGTON, March 3—The Treasury and the Federal Reserve Board announced the settlement today of their long-standing dispute over management of the national debt.

The agreement is designed to curb the inflationary effect of the Treasury's bond-selling activities without damaging the Government's credit standing or unduly raising the cost of financing the debt.

It entails the issuance of a new series of nonmarketable long-term bonds bearing an interest rate of 2¾ per cent. The interest on present long-term bonds is 2½ per cent.

Secretary of the Treasury John W. Snyder and Thomas B. McCabe, Chairman of the Federal Reserve Board, announced the settlement in a brief joint statement, as follows:

"The Treasury and the Federal Reserve system have reached full accord with respect to debt-management and monetary policies to be pursued in furthering their common purpose to assure the successful financing of the Government's requirements and, at the same time, to minimize the monetization of the public debt."

Announces New Issue

Secretary Snyder simultaneously announced plans for floating the new 2¾ per cent bonds but gave no indication of the prospective size of the issue. The new bonds will be offered in exchange for outstanding 2½ per cent bonds of June 15 and Dec. 15, 1967-72.

The aim is to reduce the sale of bonds by holders to Federal Reserve Banks, which are required to buy them at prices for which they were originally sold by the Treasury and thus maintain the market for them at the same par levels. Through such sales, the country's banks and other financial institutions, holders of a large amount of the securities, provide themselves with cash reserves on which to make loans. Inflationary forces are consequently built up by the increased circulation of money.

In making the 2½ per cent bonds exchangeable for securities bearing a slightly higher interest rate, the Government now hopes to encourage banks and other long-term investors to retain their holdings in Government securities instead of converting their bonds to cash and adding to inflation.

Holders of the new 2¾ per cent bonds will not be able to sell them to the Federal Reserve or anybody else. However, they will be given the option of exchanging them for marketable Treasury notes bearing terms to be announced March 19. Whether the new notes would be salable to the Federal Reserve at par was a question that officials declined to answer at this time.

Truman Voices Gratification

President Truman in a statement issued at Key West, Fla., where he is vacationing, expressed gratification at the Treasury-Federal Reserve agreement.

The settlement was regarded by informed circles here as a clear compromise of the Treasury and Federal Reserve differences, with the latter's position perhaps prevailing slightly.

Secretary Snyder had previously stood fast for full support of the Government bond market at current levels by the Federal Reserve and the maintenance of low-interest rates. He put great emphasis on the fact that higher interest would increase the cost of financing the national debt and expressed skepticism that small increases would have any appreciable effect on inflation.

Spokesmen for the Federal Open Market Committee, consisting of members of the Federal Reserve Board and presidents of Reserve banks, had pressed for gradual withdrawal of the "artificial" support of the Federal bond market until the price of securities reached levels dictated by supply-and-demand factors. This would require higher interest rates on future issues to make bonds readily marketable by the Government.

RESOLVE FINANCE POLICY DISPUTE

John W. Snyder
Secretary of the Treasury

Thomas B. McCabe
Federal Reserve Chairman
The New York Times

The compromise apparently eliminated the main assignment given by President Truman only last Monday to a special group of economic advisers. The President then asked Secretary Snyder, Chairman McCabe, Charles E. Wilson, director of Defense Mobilization, and Leon Keyserling, chairman of his Council of Economic Advisers, to devise methods of curbing excessive bank credit without interfering either with the Treasury's monetary policies or with support of the market by the Federal Reserve.

The President said in today's Key West statement, however, that consideration of other aspects of the problems outlined to the group would continue to go forward as originally planned.

These include consideration of voluntary credit-curbing actions by banks, direct Government controls and new legislation to enable the imposition of additional reserve requirements on banks.

The extent to which holders of 2½ per cent bonds respond to the Treasury's invitation to exchange them for nonmarketable securities bearing interest of 2¾ per cent is expected to determine to a large degree whether further measures are necessary.

An intelligent forecast of the success of the forthcoming bond issue in accomplishing its purpose seemed to be impossible at present, since important details of the issue were withheld by the Treasury.

For example, the Treasury announced that the new securities would be offered for "a limited period" but gave no indication of how many of the presently outstanding 2½ per cent bonds would be accepted for exchange.

About $60,000,000,000 of Government securities are in the hands of banks and institutions. The extent to which they are withdrawn from the market by exchanges for the new bonds will be the deciding factor with respect to the anti-inflationary effect.

Details of the new issue are to be announced March 19.

The Treasury's announcement of the new issue said:

"The Secretary of the Treasury announced today that there will be offered for a limited period a new investment series of long-term nonmarketable Treasury bonds in exchange for outstanding 2½ per cent Treasury bonds of June 15 and Dec. 15, 1967-72, the details of which will be announced on March 19.

"The new bonds will be issued in registered form only, with appropriate maturity, and will bear interest at the rate of 2¾ per cent per annum payable semi-annually. They will not be transferrable or redeemable prior to maturity; however, owners of such nonmarketable bonds will be given an option of exchanging them prior to maturity for marketable Treasury notes bearing terms to be announced in the official offering.

"The new nonmarketable 2¾ per cent Treasury bonds will be acceptable at par and accrued interest in payment of Federal estate and inheritance taxes due following the death of the owner. They will not be acceptable in payment of Federal income taxes.

"The offering of this new security is for the purpose of encouraging long-term investors to retain their holdings of Government securities, in order to minimize the monetization of the public debt through liquidation of present holdings of the Treasury bonds of 1967-72.

"The Secretary stated that he planned to open the subscription books on Monday, March 26, and that the full terms of the offering and the official circular would be made available on March 19. The subscription books will remain open for a period of about two weeks, although the Secretary will reserve the right to close the books at any time without notice.

"The Secretary indicated that a special offering of Series F and G bonds, or an offering similar to the 2½ per cent Treasury bonds, Investment Series A-1965, will probably be made available for cash subscription at a later date when it appears that a need therefor may exist."

Several Democratic leaders of Congress made statements expressing gratification at the compromise.

Comment by Spence

Representative Brent Spence, Democrat of Kentucky, chairman of the House Banking and Currency Committe, said:

"The concurrence of the Treasury and the Federal Reserve Board in a financing and monetary program is most satisfying. The way is cleared for the soundest possible debt management operations. I congratulate the Treasury and Federal Reserve officials who brought the agreement about."

Senator Burnet R. Maybank, Democrat of South Carolina, chairman of the Senate Banking Committee, commented:

"The importance of this agreement cannot be overemphasized, both as a guide to Federal financial operations and as a stimulus to our entire defense mobilization effort. It should be productive of confidence in the safety of our economy."

March 4, 1951

WIDER ROLE SEEN FOR MONEY POLICY

Many Nations Seek Changes to Aid Economic Expansion, Reserve Review Asserts

Monetary policy appears slated for even larger roles as an instrument to foster balanced economic expansion, according to the latest monthly Review of Credit and Business Conditions by the Federal Reserve Bank of New York.

The Review shows that in the last few years monetary policies in the world's industrial countries, as well as some of the nations less developed industrially, have met with success in combating inflationary forces and adverse payments positions. As a result, it said there is a growing desire in many countries to undertake institutional and legal changes that would augment its effectiveness.

Explaining that a monetary policy can be flexible and quickly adapted to counter incipient disturbances, the Review also said it is necessary to employ other types of measures in conjunction with it to rectify serious imbalances.

It is still true, the Review said, that in most primary-producing countries monetary measures play a largely subsidiary role relative to other measures in combating inflationary conditions and balance-of-payment disorder. It is explained that this resulted largely from the undeveloped state of the market and the financial mechanisms upon which the effectiveness of monetary control must rest.

"The enlarged role of financial, as distinct from barter, transactions has been a prominent feature of many primary producing countries over the post-war period," the Review continued. "This development has of course increased the potential usefulness of monetary policy.

"In some cases, these market and financial developments have come not merely as normal consequences of economic expansion and diversification, but also as the result of conscious efforts on the part of Governments and monetary authorities to foster such developments."

The Review showed that Canada has taken action to enlarge the role of money market transactions and that India has increased the opportunities for commercial bank rediscounting of commercial paper. Also, it said a number of countries now are attempting to establish central banks.

The scope for monetary control employment undoubtedly will be broadened in the developing countries by the growth of financial markets, the Review said. For the world's more mature economies, it said there probably will be opportunities for its more intensive use.

October 5, 1954

Top U.S. Fiscal Agencies Report Continued Harmonious Relations

Treasury and Federal Reserve, Once at Odds, Tells of Gains Under 'Full Accord' Pact—Depression Held Avoided

By JOHN D. MORRIS

Special to The New York Times.

WASHINGTON, Dec. 2—The Federal Reserve Board and the Treasury, once bitterly at odds, emphasized anew today that they were now working in harmony toward a common goal.

Their goal is to promote financial stability and growth of the national economy through the use of complementary monetary and debt-management powers. They reported considerable progress in that direction since the "full accord" agreement of 1951.

The two agencies presented the picture of harmonious achievement in separate statements replying to questionnaires prepared by the Economic Stabilization subcommittee of the Joint Congressional Committee on the Economic Report.

The subcommittee, headed by Senator Ralph E. Flanders, Republican of Vermont, will review Treasury and Federal Reserve policies at public hearings next Monday and Tuesday.

The Treasury, in an unsigned statement, said that the independent Federal Reserve System had been free to pursue "a flexible credit policy conducive to stability and economic growth."

"We have worked very closely with the Federal Reserve Board, with the Federal Reserve Bank officials and with their staffs all along the line," it added.

"We know of no occasion in the past two years when debt management decisions were not completely consistent with Federal Reserve monetary policy."

The Federal Reserve Board, answering the questionnaire through its chairman, William McChesney Martin Jr., was less specific on the point of cooperation with the Treasury, but the entire tone of its report reflected harmonious relations.

The two agencies agreed that credit and monetary policy had exerted a wholesome restrictive influence in the 1952-53 period of inflation, and a desirable cushioning and sustaining influence in the economic decline that followed.

"In so doing," Mr. Martin said, "it [the policy] made a necessary and positive contribution to stable economic growth."

Before the "full accord" agreement of March 4, 1951, the Federal Reserve's power to influence the supply of money and credit was inhibited by a wartime commitment to support the prices of goverment securities through purchases in the open market.

Since then the Federal Reserve has been free to make such purchases and sales for the purpose of expanding or contracting credit and without regard to maintaining Goverernment bond prices at face value.

As a consequence, its authority to set reserves that member banks must maintain and to fix rates on its loans to banks also became effective instruments in regulating credit.

Depression Held Avoided

With these powers restored, the Federal Reserve, by restraining credit in 1952 and early 1953, helped keep demands for goods within the limits of the country's capacity to produce, Mr. Martin said, adding:

"The boom was checked without collapse and was followed by an orderly and moderate downward adjustment in activity. The adjustment was eased by progressive action to ease credit markets, as well as by tax reductions and other fiscal measures. It has not developed into a disastrous depression, as many quite reasonably feared."

The Federal Reserve is still pursuing a policy of "active ease" in the credit market, and Mr. Martin's report gave no hint of a prospective change.

The Treasury indicated that it would take no major steps in the meantime toward concentrating more of the national debt in long-term bonds with relatively high interest rates.

"During the transition to a lower level of Government spending," the Treasury said, "it has been important to economic stability that the Treasury not put out any long-term bonds which would interfere with the availability of long-term funds for capital investment.

"Under circumstances such as these, improvement of the structure of the public debt may be slowed temporarily."

Mr. Martin devoted a long part of his report to a defense of the Federal Reserve's practice of confining its market operations to short-term Government securities.

He emphasized, however, that the technique was experimental and subject to change after experience "in other more normal periods of Federal Reserve operations."

In reply to one of the questions, the Treasury frowned on the idea of charging banks interest on its deposits.

December 3, 1954

'ACTIVE' EASE OUT AS RESERVE POLICY

Board Drops Adjective From Description—Adopts More Neutral Credit Stand

SOUNDS NOTE OF CAUTION

Loans May Become Slightly Harder to Get and Interest Rates May Edge Up

By JOHN D. MORRIS

Special to The New York Times.

WASHINGTON, Dec. 16—Borrowers may find loans slightly harder to get and interest rates slightly higher as a result of a recent "shift in policy emphasis" by Federal Reserve System authorities.

Well-posted sources stressed, however, that the Federal Reserve had not abandoned its eighteen-month-old "easy money" policy. Rather, it was explained, authorities have decided to take a relatively neutral position, for the time being at least, in buying and selling Government securities to influence the supply and cost of credit.

This decision apparently reflects a high degree of satisfaction with general business conditions and confidence that the upward trend will continue. At the same time, the decision sounds a note of caution regarding the possible resumption of inflationary pressures.

Since May of 1953, the Federal Reserve has pursued what it has called a policy of "active ease" in the money market. Its chief instrument in this policy has been the purchase of Government securities, which increases the amount of cash bank reserves available for lending.

Word 'Active' Is Dropped

The word "active" has now been dropped from the description of the policy, but sources close to the Federal Reserve Board minimized the action both as to its immediate effects and, especially, as to its significance as a guide to possible future policy changes.

The shift of emphasis was agreed upon early last week at a meeting of the Reserve System's Open Market Committee, which sets policy for buying and selling Government securities. The committee consists of the six members of the Federal Reserve Board and the presidents of five of the twelve Federal Reserve banks.

Officially, the board will not confirm that such a decision was taken, although reliable Government sources have so reported.

Elliott Thurston, assistant to the board, answered all questions today by citing remarks made before the Bond Club in New York yesterday by William McChesney Martin Jr., chairman of the board.

"Monetary policy must be tailored to fit the shape of a future visible only in dim outline," Mr. Martin said. "Occasions are rare when the meaning of developing events is so clear that those who bear the responsibility can say, 'As of today, our policy should be changed from restraint to ease.'

'True for Shift in Emphasis'

"What is true for a change in policy is also true for a shift in policy emphasis: it rarely is decided upon in a single day. More typically, the outline of a shift in policy emphasis emerges gradually from a succession of market developments and administrative decisions.

"It is a poor subject for the photo-flash camera to capture as a clearly defined still life, or for a news story to etch in spectacular outline * * *

"One of the problems that confronts the developers of policy is the difficulty of forecasting in advance the various factors that will exert an impact on bank reserves. The Open Market Committee clearly recognizes that uncertainty, and consequently gives particular attention to whether it would be better in day-to-day operations to lean in the direction of restraint or ease.

"However, changing shifts in policy emphasis do not necessarily mean that a change in policy direction is emerging, much less that a new policy has been adopted. They may be useful signals, nevertheless, in thoughtful analysis. For by the time the facts of a developing economic situation are sufficiently clear to lead to the adoption of a changed policy directive, this much usually will be apparent:

"The day-to-day allowances that have been made for uncertainties in the forecast of reserve availabilities will have begun to be increasingly resolved in the direction indicated by a changed policy decision."

Treasury Bill Rate Up

Signs of a shift of policy emphasis are already emerging. They include a rise in the interest rate on ninety-one-day Treasury bills to the highest point since January. The present annual rate of 1.247 per cent compares with 1.087 per cent last week and 1.336 per cent reported on Jan. 11. It is still below the levels of a year ago.

The price of Treasury bills, which controls their interest rate, is determined weekly by competitive bidding. Price declines, as reflected in higher interest yields, provide a significant sign of a tightening of credit.

The weekly report of the Federal Reserve Board showed today that the Reserve System for the second successive week had neither bought nor sold Government securities. This the Federal Reserve did nothing to ease the apparently tightened credit situation.

December 17, 1954

U. S. HOLDING CURB ON MONEY SUPPLY

Federal Reserve Restraints Get Credit for Limitation Despite Soaring Loans

By EDWIN L. DALE Jr.

Special to The New York Times.

WASHINGTON, Sept. 25—Despite this year's soaring consumer, business and mortgage credit, the nation's total supply of money has so far been held under control.

The figures on money are being watched closely. If the growth in the money supply can be held to the amounts needed to support a normally prosperous and growing economy, then it is believed the "boom" can be expected to level out without inflation and a subsequent "bust."

Restraints imposed by the Federal Reserve are generally credited with keeping the money supply within bounds. The results to date have encouraged Administration officials in their hope that the boom can be prevented from "running away."

The political implications are obvious: If the Administration, working with the Federal Reserve, can maintain prosperity for at least another year, without a big rise in prices, Republican election prospects take on an extra glow.

Evidence is strong that what money there is has been turning over faster—that each dollar is doing more work. This situation, by adding to total spending, can produce inflation just as well as an additional supply of dollars.

But the increase in turnover is, in part, an inevitable result of the working of Federal Reserve restraint. It was expected. And—again because of the way the system works—there is a limit to it. That limit may be approaching now, according to officials in the monetary field.

2% Yearly Increase Shown

The latest figures for the total supply of money—currency and demand deposits—is $132,900,000,000 at the end of July, adjusted for seasonal factors. This was only $1,700,000,000 higher than at the end of January, or a rate of increase of about 2 per cent a year. This is actually somewhat less than the rough figure used by many economists of 3 per cent a year to keep the economy healthy and growing.

The money supply in the last half of 1954, however, shot up at a rate of 5 per cent, and so nobody is worried about a shortage. The aim of the Federal Reserve is to keep the growth down in the face of a tremendous demand for loans.

It is through the process of lending by the banking system that the money supply grows. The procedure is a bit complicated. It begins with the Federal Reserve, which has the power to create "reserves" for the banking system.

For each dollar of new reserves created, the banks as a group can add a dollar of new cash or six dollars of new deposits to the money supply. This creation occurs through the banks' loans and investments—and if the demand for credit is there, the additional money creation will always result.

The Federal Reserve, ever since spring, has been tightening up by refusing to supply all the new reserves that the thirsty banking system—and the economy—wanted. But the initial effect has not been to curb loans to businesses and people; it has been to force the banks to sell some of their "gilt-edged" investments, chiefly United States Government securities, to get the money to keep up the more profitable lending end of their business.

When a bank sells a Treasury bill or note to, say, a corporation, that corporation's deposits go down, and so does the total money supply. When a new loan is made, deposits and the money supply go up. Thus the story of this year has been a roughly stable money supply despite a rapid growth in loans by the banks.

Bank loans since the end of last year have risen by about $7,000,000,000, while bank holdings of Government securities have fallen by more than $6,000,000,000.

September 26, 1955

Reserve Easier on Money

Pressure Being Relaxed

By EDWIN L. DALE Jr.

Special to The New York Times.

WASHINGTON, Oct. 23 — The Federal Reserve System has decided to ease the toughness with which it has been applying its tight money policy.

The decision does not involve, as yet, any change in the basic policy of restraint. But it is a significant switch toward less pressure on the nation's banking system. It could mean some lowering in short-term interest rates and some easing in the availability of credit.

The decision has been taken, according to authoritative sources, for these related reasons:

¶The Federal Reserve is aware of some of the factors indicating a slackening in general business activity in the months ahead. It believes that the basic business picture is still strong, but it is also aware of the "downside" factors that have lately received such prominence.

¶The Federal Reserve feels that many of the results its policy was designed to achieve have occurred or are occurring. It believes that the dangerous exuberance of the boom, with its inflationary results, has largely evaporated.

¶The Federal Reserve is aware of the market switch in business psychology — as distinct from business statistics—away from optimism and toward pessimism. This psychological switch is another reason why inflationary pressures appear much less formidable. The recent sharp decline in the stock market is probably the best evidence of this change. The Stock Market today regained some of its losses.

One official described the change in emphasis of Federal Reserve policy in these terms:

"We have, as everybody knows, been leaning against the wind rather heavily—the wind being, of course, boom and inflation. Now I think we'll just lean a little heavily, while not changing the direction in which we are leaning."

A basic change in policy would involve a reduction in the Federal Reserve's discount rate. This is the rate it charges member banks that are forced to borrow from the Federal Reserve. This is not yet in sight.

Instead, the change will be much more subtle. It will work something like this:

Each week the Federal Reserve buys or sells short-term Government securities in the open market. A purchase adds funds to the banking system and a sale reduces them.

Also each week a number of other factors, not under the Federal Reserve's control, affect the funds (called reserves) available to the banks. Each week, therefore, the Federal Reserve sets a sort of target for the reserves it wants available for the banks and conducts its own buying or selling in such a way that, with the other factors, the desired result will be achieved as closely as possible.

Target for Reserves

Under the tight money policy as carried out up to now, the target each week appears to have been about $500,000,000 of "net borrowed reserves." This means that the banking system as a whole is forced to be a net borrower from the Federal Reserve by this amount. When the banks are this heavily in debt "at the Fed," they are restrained in their own lending and investing.

Under a policy of lessened pressure, the target for net borrowed reserves will presumably be set somewhat lower. This will correspondingly ease the pressure on the banks.

What the technicians call "the direction of error" is another way of describing the shift. In its weekly calculations, the Federal Reserve knows that it can never guess exactly what the impact on bank reserves of the forces other than its own operations will be. Thus its own buying and selling involves some estimating, and guesswork.

When the tight-money pressure is heavily on, the instructions to the day-to-day operating officials are to "make your errors on the side of tightness." It is probable—though the official orders are secret—that current instructions have been changed to "make your errors on the side of ease."

In practical terms, this could mean that some weeks would see net borrowed reserves down to $100,000,000 or lower.

October 24, 1957

Government Economy

A Study of a New Fordham Series That Includes Monetary Policies

By EDWARD H. COLLINS

What is perhaps the most important work dealing with the problem of Government economic controls to make its appearance in recent years is also probably the shortest. It runs to but eighty-eight pages.

For this happy combination of virtues major credit must go to the members of the Department of Political Philosophy and Social Sciences of Fordham University, and particularly to the Rev. William T. Hogan. The latter appears to have played a leading part in starting last year a new annual series of lectures in the social sciences in memory of the late Moorhouse I. X. Millar, chairman of the university's Department of Philosophy and the Social Sciences for thirty-years prior to his death.

Major Contribution

For purposes of the present discussion, the major contribution of the Department of Political Philosophy would be the inspired judgment it displayed in choosing Dr. Arthur F. Burns as the economist to initiate the new lecture series. Dr. Burns, who is now president of the National Bureau of Economic Research, is best know to the public, perhaps, as the first chairman of the President's Council of Economic Advisers under the Eisenhower Administration.

Each of the four Millar lectures by Dr. Burns has now become a chapter in a book freshly off the Fordham University Press. The title of the book, "Prosperity Without Inflation," suggests its general scope, but is otherwise not too important. What is important is the fact that the one man who is pre-eminently qualified to discuss the recent price inflation in terms of future Government stabilization policy has done so, and has done so with the intelligence and scholarship that we have long since come to expect of him.

Monetary Policy

Of outstanding interest — particularly when it is considered in the light of plans recently announced for the establishment of a new Monetary Commission — is the author's third chapter, titled "The New Environment of Monetary Policy."

The heavy emphasis that the

Government has recently placed on restrictive credit policy, notes Dr. Burns at the outset of this chapter "has served to bring us back to the best thought that ruled on the subject of inflation during the 1920's. In the meantime the economic world has changed profoundly."

There is not room here to list all the "environmental" changes enumerated by Dr. Burns, or even any considerable part of them. But one or two typical examples may be cited as illustrations of the manner in which "the economic area over which a restrictive policy can nowadays be effective" has been shrinking.

One might begin by pointing to the enormous expansion of Governmental activities over the last thirty years. In 1929, for example, all forms of Federal spending came to only about 2.5 per cent of the nation's total output, and the combined expenditures of all Government units were less than 10 per cent.

Federal Expenditures

Federal expenditures alone reached 21.3 per cent in 1953 and were still 17.4 per cent as recently as 1956. The combined total of all Government spending in 1956 was $104 billions, or "a little over 25 per cent of the nation's total output." The point here, as Dr. Burns puts it, is that "Federal expenditures * * * are practically unaffected by the level of interest rates or the availability of credit." State and local governments are not as completely immune to the effects of restrictive policies as the Federal government. Nevertheless, points out Dr. Burns, "the benefits to be derived from Government projects cannot be calculated in dollars, and this itself tends to blunt the influence of interest rates."

But the operations of part of the business world, at least, are similarly sheltered. In the first place, though corporations have for years relied, in the raising of funds, on internal finances to a greater degree than external, such reliance is far greater today than it was in the 1920's.

The differential in those days ranged from 10 to 20 per cent; over the last decade it has averaged 42 per cent. Though external financing has increased in absolute terms, steep tax rates and the rapid growth of amortizable loans have combined to reduce the influence of interest rates on corporate borrowing.

As a final example of the lessened authority of the Reserve Board on the monetary scene is the fact that commercial banks, on which the Reserve exercises a decisive influence, have been losing ground steadily to other types of financial intermediaries over which it wields no such authority. The assets of the commercial banks, which in 1922 exceeded those of all other comparable institutions (excluding the Federal Reserve Banks) had fallen to the point, in 1955, when they represented but 52 per cent of the assets of these same institutions.

January 6, 1958

EXPERT CAUTIONS ON MONEY SUPPLY

Top Economist Upholds Its Influence on Prices—Asks Change in Reserve Policy

By EDWIN L. DALE Jr.

Special to The New York Times.

WASHINGTON, May 25—The old-fashioned theory that the supply of money is the major influence on business and price levels is still true, Congress was told today.

Milton Friedman of the University of Chicago, a leading economist, impressed the Joint Congressional Economic Committee with his money theory.

He argued that the revolution in economic theory wrought by the late Lord Keynes had mostly gone astray, and that a refined version of traditional analysis was closer to the truth.

Lord Keynes, in the late Nineteen Thirties, downgraded the importance of money supply in explaining economic events. He gave major importance to changes in investment.

Mr. Friedman held that there were flaws in the Keynes analysis. He said the contradictions and expansions of money supply could be given as an explanation for the Depression of the Thirties.

In particular, he held that the history of the United States since the Civil War had demonstrated that changes in money supply were the main cause of both slumps and inflationary booms. He criticized the operations of the Federal Reserve System, which has ultimate control over money supply, since its establishment in 1913.

He said the ideal policy for the Federal Reserve would be automatic and mechanical—to increase the supply of money at a constant rate "month in and month out, year in and year out," regardless of business conditions.

For 3-4½% Rate

This rate should be 3 to 4½ per cent a year, with the money supply defined to include currency, plus demand and time deposits in banks, he suggested.

That would mean abandoning the current policy of "leaning against the wind," in which the Federal Reserve tightens money in booms and loosens it in slumps. Under this policy, the money supply recently has expanded rapidly during and soon after recessions, then has grown at a subnormal rate during later stages of booms.

According to Mr. Friedman, "leaning against the wind" is difficult because there is a lag between a shift in Federal Reserve policy and its effects on the economy.

Monetary changes have been "the primary source of deep depressions," he testified. During questioning by committee members, Mr. Friedman also made these points:

¶He does not "view seriously" the recent outflow of gold. The United States has been giving up gold in exchange for goods and services, he noted.

¶It is important that the annual percentage increase in money supply be selected with an aim of "reasonably stable prices."

¶Congress should abolish the discount rate and variable reserve requirements as weapons of Federal Reserve control over money, and limit the Federal Reserve to open market purchases and sales of Government or other securities.

The hearing was part of the committee's broad investigation of economic growth, inflation and unemployment.

May 26, 1959

Analysis by Morgenthau of Monetary Agreements

Special to THE NEW YORK TIMES.

BRETTON WOODS, N. H., July 22—The text of Secretary Morgenthau's radio broadcast tonight marking the completion of the international conference was as follows:

I am gratified to announce that the conference at Bretton Woods has completed successfully the task before it.

It was, as we knew when we began, a difficult task, involving complicated techical problems. We came here to work out methods which would do away with the economic evils—the competitive currency devaluation and destructive impediments to trade—which preceded the present war. We have succeeded in that effort.

The actual details of a financial and monetary agreement may seem mysterious to the general public. Yet at the heart of it lie the most elementary bread and butter realities of daily life. What we have done here in Bretton Woods is to devise machinery by which men and women everywhere can exchange freely, on a fair and stable basis, the goods which they produced through their labor. And we have taken the initial step through which the nations of the world will be able to help one another in economic development to their mutual advantage and for the enrichment of all.

'Faced Differences Frankly'

The representatives of the forty-four nations faced differences of opinion frankly, and reached an agreement which is rooted in genuine understanding. None of the nations represented here has had altogether its own way. We have had to yield to one another not in respect to principles or essentials but in respect to methods and procedural details. The fact that we have done so, and that we have done it in a spirit of good-will asd mutual trust, is, I believe, one of the hopeful and heartening portents of our time.

Here is a sign blazoned upon the horizon, written large upon the threshold of the future—a sign for men in battle, for men at work in mines, and mills, and in the fields, and a sign for women whose hearts have been burdened and anxious lest the cancer of war assail yet another generation—a sign that the peoples of the earth are learning how to join hands and work in unity.

There is a curious notion that the protection of national interest and the development of international cooperation are conflicting philosophies—that somehow or other men of different nations cannot work together without sacrificing the interests of their particular nation. There has been talk of this sort—and from people who ought to know better—concerning the international cooperative nature of the undertaking just completed at Bretton Woods.

National Interests Cited

I am perfectly certain that no delegation to this conference has lost sight for a moment of the particular national interest it was sent here to represent. The American delegation, which I have the honor of leading, has been, at all times, conscious of its primary obligation—the protection of American interests. And the other representatives have been no less loyal or devoted to the welfare of their own people.

Yet none of us has found any incompatibility between devotion to our own country and joint action. Indeed, we have found on the contrary that the only genuine safeguard for our national interests lies in international cooperation. We have come to recognize that the wisest and most effective way to protect our national interests is through international cooperation—that is to say, through united effort for the attainment of common goals.

This has been the great lesson taught by the war, and is, I think, the great lesson of contemporary life—that the peoples of the earth are inseparably linked to one another by a deep, underlying community of purpose. This community of purpose is no less real and vital in peace than in war, and cooperation is no less essential to its fulfillment.

World Accord Called Vital

To seek the achievement of our aims separately through the planless, senseless rivalry that divided us in the past, or through the outright economic aggression which turned neighbors into enemies would be to invite ruin again upon us all. Worse, it would be once more to start our steps irretraceably down the steep, disastrous road to war.

That sort of extreme nationalism belongs to an era that is dead. Today the only enlightened form of national self-interest lies in international accord. At Bretton Woods we have taken practical steps toward putting this lesson into practice in monetary and economic fields.

I take it as an axiom that after this war is ended no people—and therefore no government of the people—will again tolerate prolonged or widespread unemployment. A revival of international trade is indispensable if full employment is to be achieved in a peaceful world and with standards of living which will permit the realization of man's reasonable hopes.

What are the fundamental conditions under which the commerce among the nations can once more flourish?

First, there must be a reasonably stable standard of international exchange to which all countries can adhere without sacrificing the freedom of action necessary to meet their internal economic problems.

This is the alternative to the desperate tactics of the past—competitive currency depreciation, excessive tariff barriers, uneconomic barter deals, multiple currency practices and unnecessary exchange restrictions—by which governments vainly sought to maintain employment and uphold living standards. In the final analysis, these tactics only ssucceeded in contributing to world-wide depression and even war. The International Fund agreed upon at Bretton Woods will help remedy this situation.

Long-Term Aid Championed

Second, long-term financial aid must be made available at reasonable rates to those countries whose industry and agriculture have been destroyed by the ruthless torch of an invader or by the heroic scorched-earth policy of their defenders.

Long-term funds must be made available also to promote sound industry and increase industrial and agricultural production in nations whose economic potentialities have not yet been developed. It is essential to us all that these nations play their full part in the exchange of goods throughout the world.

They must be enabled to produce and sell if they are to be able to purchase and consume. The Bank for International Reconstruction and Development is designed to meet this need.

Objections to this bank have been raised by some bankers and a few economists. The institution proposed by the Bretton Woods conference would indeed limit the control which certain private bankers have in the past exercised over international finance. It would by no means restrict the investment sphere in which bankers could engage. On the contrary, it would expand greatly this sphere by enlarging the volume of international investment and would act as an enormously effective stabilizer and guarantor of loans which they might make.

Private-Loan Guarantee Sought

The chief purpose of the Bank for International Reconstruction and Development is to guarantee private loans made through the usual investment channels. It would make loans only when these could not be floated at the normal channels at reasonable rates. The effect would be to provide capital for those who need it at lower interest rates than in the past, and to drive only the usurious money lenders from the temple of international finance. For my own part, I cannot look upon the outcome with any sense of dismay. Capital, like any other commodity, should be free from monopoly control and available upon reasonable terms to those who would put it to use for the general welfare.

The delegates and technical staff at Bretton Woods have completed their portion of the job. They have sat down together and talked as friends, and have perfected plans to cope with the international monetary and financial problems which all their countries face in common. These proposals now must be submitted to the Legislatures and the peoples of the participating nations. They will pass upon what has been accomplished here.

Looks to World of Future

The result will be of vital importance to everyone in every country. In the last analysis it will help determine whether or not people will have jobs and the amount of money they are to find in their weekly pay envelopes. More important still, it concerns the kind of world in which our children are to grow to maturity. It concerns the opportunities which our children are to grow to maturity. It concerns the opportunities which will await millions of young men when at last they can take off their uniforms and can come home to civilian jobs.

This monetary agreement is but one step, of course, in the broad program of international action necessary for the shaping of a free future. But it is an indispensable step in the vital test of our intentions. We are at a crossroad, and we must go one way or the other. The conference at Bretton Woods has erected a signpost—a signpost pointing down a highway broad enough for all men to walk in step and side by side. If they will set out together, there is nothing on earth that need stop them.

July 23, 1944

Text of the Articles of Agreement Reached by 44 Countries at the Monetary Parley

Special to THE NEW YORK TIMES.

BRETTON WOODS, N. H., July 22—The text of the articles of agreement of the International Monetary Fund is as follows:

The Governments on whose behalf the present Agreement is signed agree as follows:

Introductory Article

The International Monetary Fund is established and shall operate in accordance with the following provisions:

Article I

PURPOSES

The purposes of the International Monetary Fund are

1. To promote international monetary cooperation through a permanent institution which provides the machinery for consultation and collaboration on international monetary problems.
2. To facilitate the expansion and balanced growth of international trade, and to contribute thereby to the promotion and maintenance of high levels of employment and real income and to the development of the productive resources of all members as primary objectives of economic policy.
3. To promote exchange stability, to maintain orderly exchange arrangements among members, and to avoid competitive exchange depreciation.
4. To assist in the establishment of a multilateral system of payments in respect of current transactions between members and in the elimination of foreign exchange restrictions which hamper the growth of world trade.
5. To give confidence to members by making the Fund's resources available to them under adequate safeguards, thus providing them with opportunity to correct maladjustments in their balance of payments without resorting to measures destructive of national or international prosperity.
6. In accordance with the above, to shorten the duration and lessen the degree of disequilibrium in the international balances of payments of members.

The Fund shall be guided in all its decisions by the purposes set forth in this Article.

Article II

MEMBERSHIP

Section 1. Original members.

The original members of the Fund shall be those of the countries represented at the United Nations Monetary and Financial Conference whose governments accept membership before the date specified in Article XX, Section 2(e).

Section 2. Other members.

Membership shall be open to the governments of other countries at such times and in accordance with such terms as may be prescribed by the Fund.

Article III

QUOTAS AND SUBSCRIPTIONS

Section 1. Quotas

Each member shall be assigned a quota. The quotas of the members represented at the United Nations Monetary and Financial Conference which accept membership before the date specified in Article XX, Section 2(e), shall be those set forth in Schedule A. The quotas of other members shall be determined by the Fund.

Section 2. Adjustment of Quotas

The Fund shall at intervals of five years review, and if it deems it appropriate propose an adjustment of, the quotas of the members. It may also, if it thinks fit, consider at any other time the adjustment of any particular quota at the request of the member concerned. A four-fifths majority of the total voting power shall be required for any change in quotas and no quota shall be changed without the consent of the member concerned.

Section 3. Subscriptions: Time, Place and Form of Payment

(a). The subscription of each member shall be equal to its quota and shall be paid in full to the Fund at the appropriate depository on or before the date when the member becomes eligible under Article XX, Section 4(c) or (d), to buy currencies from the Fund.

(b). Each member shall pay in gold, as a minimum, the smaller of

1. Twenty-five per cent of its quota; or
2. Ten per cent of its net official holdings of gold and United States dollars as at the date when the Fund notifies members under Article XX, Section 4(a) that it will shortly be in a position to begin exchange transactions.

Each member shall furnish to the Fund the data necessary to determine its net official holdings of gold and United States dollars.

(c). Each member shall pay the balance of its quota in its own currency.

(d). If the net official holdings of gold and United States dollars of any member as at the date referred to in (b) (2.) above are not ascertainable because its territories have been occupied by the enemy, the Fund shall fix an appropriate alternative date for determining such holdings. If such date is later than that on which the country becomes eligible under Article XX, Section 4(c) or (d) to buy currencies from the Fund, the Fund and the member shall agree on a provisional gold payment to be made under (b) above, and the balance of the member's subscription shall be paid in the member's currency, subject to appropriate adjustment between the member and the Fund when the net official holdings have been ascertained.

Section 4. Payments When Quotas Are Changed

(a) Each member which consents to an increase in its quota shall, within thirty days after the date of its consent, pay to the Fund twenty-five per cent of the increase in gold and the balance in its own currency. If, however, on the date when the member consents to an increase, its monetary reserves are less than its new quota, the Fund may reduce the proportion of the increase to be paid in gold.

(b) If a member consents to a reduction in its quota, the Fund shall, within thirty days after the date of the consent, pay to the member an amount equal to the reduction. The payment shall be made in the member's currency and in such amount of gold as may be necessary to prevent reducing the Fund's holdings of the currency below seventy-five per cent of the new quota.

Section 5. Substitution of Securities for Currency

The Fund shall accept from any member in place of any part of the member's currency which in the judgment of the Fund is not needed for its operations, notes or similar obligations issued by the member or the depository designated by the member under Article XIII, Section 2, which shall be non-negotiable, non-interest bearing and payable at their par value on demand by crediting the account of the Fund in the designated depository. This Section shall apply not only to currency subscribed by members but also to any currency otherwise due to, or acquired by, the Fund.

Article IV

PAR VALUES OF CURRENCIES

Section 1. Expression of Par Values

(a) The par value of the currency of each member shall be expressed in terms of gold as a common denominator or in terms of the United States dollar of the weight and fineness in effect on July 1, 1944.

(b) All computations relating to currencies of members for the purpose of applying the provisions of this Agreement shall be on the basis of their par values.

Section 2. Gold Purchases Based on Par Values

The Fund shall prescribe a margin above and below par value for transactions in gold by members, and no member shall buy gold at a price above par value plus the prescribed margin, or sell gold at a price below par value minus the prescribed margin.

Section 3. Foreign Exchange Dealings Based on Parity

The maximum and the minimum rates for exchange transactions between the currencies of members taking place within their territories shall not differ from parity

1. in the case of spot exchange transactions, by more than one per cent; and
2. in the case of other exchange transactions, by a margin which exceeds the margin for spot exchange transactions by more than the Fund considers reasonable.

Section 4. Obligations Regarding Exchange Stability

(a) Each member undertakes to collaborate with the Fund to promote exchange stability, to maintain orderly exchange arrangements with other members, and to avoid competitive exchange alterations.

(b) Each member undertakes, through appropriate measures consistent with this Agreement, to permit within its territories exchange transactions between its currency and the currencies of other members only within the limits prescribed under Section 3 of this Article. A member whose monetary authorities, for the settlement of international transactions, in fact freely buy and sell gold within the limits prescribed by the Fund under Section 2 of this Article shall be deemed to be fulfilling this undertaking.

Section 5. Changes in Par Values

(a) A member shall not propose a change in the par value of its currency except to correct a fundamental disequilibrium.

(b) A change in the par value of a member's curency may be made only on the proposal of the member and only after consultation with the Fund.

(c) When a change is proposed, the Fund shall first take into account the changes, if any, which have already taken place in the initial par value of the member's currency as determined under Article XX, Section 4. If the proposed change, together with all previous changes, whether increases or decreases,

1. does not exceed ten per cent of the initial par value, the Fund shall raise no objection,
2. does not exceed a further ten per cent of the initial par value, the Fund may either concur or object, but shall declare its attitude within seventy-two hours if the member so requests,
3. is not within (1.) or (2.) above, the Fund may either concur or object, but shall be entitled to a longer period in which to declare its attitude.

(d) Uniform changes in par values made under Section 7 of this Article shall not be taken into account in determining whether a proposed change falls within (1.), (2.) or (3.) of (c) above.

(e) A member may change the par value of its currency without the concurrence of the Fund if the change does not affect the international transactions of members of the Fund.

(f) The Fund shall concur in a proposed change which is within the terms of (c) (2.) or (c) (3.) above if it is satisfied that the change is necessary to correct a fundamental disequilibrium. In particular, provided it is so satisfied, it shall not object to a proposed change because of the domestic social or political policies of the member proposing the change.

Section 6. Effect of Unauthorized Changes.

If a member chang... the par value of its currency despite the objection of the Fund, in cases where the Fund is entitled to object, the member shall be ineligible to use the resources of the Fund unless the Fund determines; and if, after the expiration of a reasonable period, the difference between the member and the Fund continues, the matter shall be subject to the provisions of Article XV, Section 2 (b).

Section 7. Uniform Changes in Par Values.

Notwithstanding the provisions of Section 5 (b) of this Article, the Fund by a majority of the total voting power may make uniform proportionate changes in the par values of the currencies of all members, provided each such change is approved by every member which has ten per cent or more of the total of the quotas. The par value of a member's currency shall, however, not be changed under this provision if, within seventy-two hours of the Fund's action, the member informs the Fund that it does not wish the par value of its currency to be changed by such action.

Section 8. Maintenance of Gold Value of the Fund's Assets

(a) The gold value of the Fund's assets shall be maintained notwithstanding changes in the par or foreign exchange value of the currency of any member.

(b) Whenever (i) the par value of a member's currency is reduced or (ii) the foreign exchange value of a member's currency has, in the opinion of the Fund, depreciated to a significant extent within that member's territories, the member shall pay to the Fund within a reasonable time an amount of its own currency equal to the reduction in the gold value of its currency held by the Fund.

(c) Whenever the par value of a member's currency is increased the Fund shall return to such member within a reasonable time an amount in its currency equal to the increase in the gold value of its currency held by the Fund.

(d) The provisions of this Section shall apply to a uniform proportionate change in the par values of the currencies of all members, unless at the time when such a change is proposed the Fund decides otherwise.

Section 9. Separate Currencies Within a Member's Territories

A member proposing a change in the par value of its currency shall be deemed, unless it declares otherwise, to be proposing a corresponding change in the par value of the separate currencies of all territories in respect of which it has accepted this Agreement under Article XX, Section 2(g). It shall, however, be open to a member to declare that its proposal relates either to the metropolitan currency alone, or only to one or more specified separate currencies, or to the metropolitan currency and one or more specified separate currencies.

Article V

TRANSACTIONS WITH THE FUND

Section 1. Agencies Dealing With the Fund

Each member shall deal with the Fund only through its Treasury, central bank, stabilization fund or other similar fiscal agency and the Fund shall deal only with or through the same agencies.

Section 2. Limitation on the Fund's Operations

Except as otherwise provided in this Agreement, operations on the account of the Fund shall be limited to transactions for the purpose of supplying a member, on the initiative of such member, with the currency of another member in exchange for gold or for the currency of the member desiring to make the purchase.

Section 3. Conditions Governing Use of the Fund's Resources

(a) A member shall be entitled to buy the currency of another member from the Fund in exchange for its own currency subject to the following conditions:

1. The member desiring to purchase the currency represents that it is presently needed for making in that currency payments which are consistent with the provisions of this Agreement;
2. The Fund has not given notice under Article VII, Section 3, that its holdings of the currency desired have become scarce;
3. The proposed purchase would not cause the Fund's holdings of the purchasing member's currency to increase by more than twenty-five per cent of its quota during the period of twelve months ending on the date of the purchase nor to exceed two hundred per cent of its quota, but the twenty-five per cent limitation shall apply only to the extent that the Fund's holdings of the member's currency have been brought above seventy-five per cent of its quota if they had been below that amount;
4. The Fund has not previously declared under Section 5 of this Article, Article IV, Section 6, Article VI, Section 1, or Article XV, Section 2(a), that the member desiring to purchase is ineligible to use the resources of the Fund.

(b) A member shall not be entitled without the permission of the Fund to use the Fund's resources to acquire currency to hold against forward exchange transactions.

Section 4. Waiver of Conditions

The Fund may in its discretion, and on terms which safeguard its interests, waive any of the conditions prescribed in Section 3(a) of this Article, especially in the case of members with a record of avoiding large or continuous use of the Fund's resources. In making a waiver it shall take into consideration periodic or exceptional requirements of the member requesting the waiver. The Fund shall also take into consideration a member's willingness to pledge as collateral security gold, silver, securities, or other acceptable assets having a value sufficient in the opinion of the Fund to protect its interests and may require as a condition of waiver the pledge of such collateral security.

Section 5. Ineligibility to Use the Fund's Resources

Whenever the Fund is of the opinion that any member is using the resources of the Fund in a manner contrary to the purposes of the Fund, it shall present to the member a report setting forth the views of the Fund and prescribing a suitable time for reply. After presenting such a report to a member, the Fund may limit the use of its resources by the member. If no reply to the report is received from the member within the prescribed time, or if the reply received is unsatisfactory, the Fund may continue to limit the member's use of the Fund's resources or may, after giving reasonable notice to the member, declare it ineligible to use the resources of the Fund.

Section 6. Purchases of Currencies From the Fund for Gold

(a) Any member desiring to obtain, directly or indirectly, the currency of another member for gold shall, provided that it can do so with equal advantage, acquire it by the sale of gold to the Fund.

(b) Nothing in this Section shall be deemed to preclude any member from selling in any market gold newly produced from mines located within its territories.

Section 7. Repurchase by a Member of Its Currency Held by the Fund

(a) A member may repurchase from the Fund and the Fund shall sell for gold any part of the Fund's holdings of its currency in excess of its quota.

(b) At the end of each financial year of the Fund, a member shall repurchase from the Fund with gold or convertible currencies, as determined in accordance with Schedule B, part of the Fund's holdings of its currency under the following conditions:

1. Each member shall use in repurchases of its own currency from the Fund an amount of its monetary reserves equal in value to one-half of any increase that has occurred during the year in the Fund's holdings of its currency plus one-half of any increase, or minus one-half of any decrease, that has occurred during the year in the member's monetary reserves. This rule shall not apply when a member's monetary reserves have decreased during the year by more than the Fund's holdings of its currency have increased.
2. If after the repurchase described in (i) above (if required) has been made, a member's holdings of another member's currency (or of gold acquired from that member) are found to have increased by reason of transactions in terms of that currency with other members or persons in their territories, the member whose holdings of such currency (or gold) have thus increased shall use the increase to repurchase its own currency from the Fund.

(c) None of the adjustments described in (b) above shall be carried to a point at which

1. the member's monetary reserves are below its quota, or
2. the Fund's holdings of its currency are below seventy-five percent of its quota, or
3. the Fund's holdings of any currency required to be used are above seventy-five percent of the quota of the member concerned.

Section 8. Charges

(a) Any member buying the currency of another member from the Fund in exchange for its own currency shall pay a service charge uniform for all members of three-fourths percent in addition to the parity price. The Fund in its discretion may increase this service charge to not more than one percent or reduce it to not less than one-half percent.

(b) The Fund may levy a reasonable handling charge on any member buying gold from the Fund or selling gold to the Fund.

(c) The Fund shall levy charges uniform for all members which shall be payable by any member on the average daily balances of its currency held by the Fund in excess of its quota. These charges shall be at the following rates:

1. On amounts not more than twenty-five percent in excess of the quota: no charge for the first three months; one-half percent per annum for the next nine months; and thereafter an increase in the charge of one-half percent for each subsequent year.
2. On amounts more than twenty-five percent and not more than fifty percent in excess of the quota: an additional one-half percent for the first year; and an additional one-half percent for each subsequent year.
3. On each additional bracket of twenty-five percent in excess of the quota: an additional one-half percent for the first year; and an additional one-half percent for each subsequent year.

(d) Whenever the Fund's holdings of a member's currency are such that the charge applicable to any bracket for any period has reached the rate of four percent per annum, the Fund and the member shall consider means by which the Fund's holdings of the currency can be reduced. Thereafter the charges shall rise in accordance with the provisions of (c) above until they reach five percent and failing agreement, the Fund may then impose such charges as it deems appropriate.

(e) The rates referred to in (c) and (d) above may be changed by a three-fourths majority of the total voting power.

(f) All charges shall be paid in gold. If, however, the member's monetary reserves are less than one-half of its quota, it shall pay in gold only that proportion of the charges due which such reserves bear to one-half of its quota, and shall pay the balance in its own currency.

Article VI

Section 1. Use of the Fund's Resources for Capital Transfers

(a) A member may not make net use of the Fund's resources to meet a large or sustained outflow of capital, and the Fund may request a member to exercise controls to prevent such use of the resources of the Fund. If, after receiving such a request, a member fails to exercise appropriate controls, the Fund may declare the member ineligible to use the resources of the Fund.

(b) Nothing in this Section shall be deemed

1. to prevent the use of the resources of the Fund for capital transactions of reasonable amount required for the expansion of exports or in the ordinary course of trade, banking or other business, or
2. to affect capital movements which are met out of a member's own resources of gold and foreign exchange, but members undertake that such capital movements will be in accordance with the purposes of the Fund.

Section 2. Special Provisions for Capital Transfers

If the Fund's holdings of the currency of a member have remained below seventy-five percent of its quota for an immediately preceding period of not less than six months, such member, if it has not been declared ineligible to use the resources of the Fund under Section 1 of this Article, Article IV, Section 6, Article V, Section 5, or Article XV, Section 2(a), shall be entitled, notwithstanding the provisions of Section 1(a) of this Article, to buy the currency of another member from the Fund with its own currency for any purpose, including capital transfers. Purchases for capital transfers under this Section shall not, however, be permitted if they have the effect of raising the Fund's holdings of the currency of the member desiring to purchase above 75 per cent of its quota, or of reducing the Fund's holdings of the currency desired below 75 per cent of the quota of the member whose currency is desired.

Section 3. Controls of Capital Transfers

Members may exercise such controls as are necessary to regulate international capital movements, but no member may exercise these controls in a manner which will restrict payments for current transactions or which will unduly delay transfers of funds in settlement of commitments, except as provided in Article VII, Section 3(b), and in Article XIV, Section 2.

Article VII

SCARCE CURRENCIES

Section 1. General Scarcity of Currency

If the Fund finds that a general scarcity of a particular currency is developing, the Fund may so inform members and may issue a repart setting forth the causes of the scarcity and containing recommendations designed to bring it to an end. A representative of the member whose currency is involved shall participate in the preparation of the report.

Section 2. Measures to Replenish the Fund's Holdings of Scarce Currencies

The Fund may, if it deems such action appropriate to replenish its holdings of any member's currency, take either or both of the following steps:

1. Propose to the member that, on terms and conditions agreed between the Fund and the member, the latter lend its currency to the Fund or that, with the approval of the member, the Fund borrow such currency from some other source either within or outside the territories of the member, but no member shall be under any obligation to make such loans to the Fund or to approve the borrowing of its currency by the Fund from any other source.
2. Require the member to sell its currency to the Fund for gold.

Section 3. Scarcity of the Fund's Holdings

(a) If it becomes evident to the Fund that the demand for a member's currency seriously threatens the Fund's ability to supply that currency, the Fund, whether or not it has issued a report under Section 1 of this Article, shall formally declare such currency scarce and shall thenceforth apportion its existing and accruing supply of the scarce currency with due regard to the relative needs of members, the general international economic situation and any other pertinent considerations. The Fund shall also issue a report concerning its action.

(b) A formal declaration under (a) above shall operate as an authorization to any member, after consultation with the Fund, temporarily to impose limitations on the freedom of exchange operations in the scarce currency. Subject to the provisions of Article IV, Sections 3 and 4, the member shall have complete jurisdiction in determining the nature of such limitations, but they shall be no more restrictive than is necessary to limit the demand for the scarce currency to the supply held by, or accruing to, the member in question; and they shall be relaxed and removed as rapidly as conditions permit.

(c) The authorization under (b) above shall expire whenever the Fund formally declares the currency in question to be no longer scarce.

Section 4. Administration of Restrictions

Any member imposing restrictions in respect of the currency of any other member pursuant to the provisions of Section 3(b) of this Article shall give sympathetic consideration to any representations by the other member regarding the administration of such restrictions.

Section 5. Effect of other international agreements on restrictions.

Members agree not to invoke the obligations of any engagements entered into with other members prior to this Agreement in such a manner as will prevent the operation of the provisions of this Article.

Article VIII

GENERAL OBLIGATIONS OF MEMBERS

Section 1. Introduction

In addition to the obligations assumed under other articles of this Agreement, each member undertakes the obligations set out in this Article.

Section 2. Avoidance of Restrictions on Current Payments

(a) Subject to the provisions of Article VII, Section 3(b), and Article XIV, Section 2, no member shall, without the approval of the Fund, impose restrictions on the making of payments and transfers for current international transactions.

(b) Exchange contracts which involve the currency of any member and which are contrary to the exchange control regulations of that member maintained or imposed consistently with this Agreement shall be unenforceable in the territories of any member. In addition, members may, by mutual accord, cooperate in measures for the purpose of making the exchange control regulations of either member more effective, provided that such measures and regulations are consistent with this Agreement.

Section 3. Avoidance of Discriminatory Currency Practices

No member shall engage in, or permit any of its fiscal agencies referred to in Article V, Section 1, to engage in, any discriminatory currency arrangements or multiple currency practices except as authorized under this Agreement or approved by the Fund. If such arrangements and practices are engaged in at the date when this Agreement enters into force the member concerned shall consult with the Fund as to their progressive removal unless they are maintained or imposed under Article XIV, Section 2, in which case the provisions of Section 4 of that Article shall apply.

Section 4. Convertibility of Foreign Held Balances

(a) Each member shall buy balances of its currency held by another member if the latter, in requesting the purchase, represents

1. that the balances to be bought have been recently acquired as a result of current transactions; or
2. that their conversion is needed for making payments for current transactions.

The buying member shall have the option to pay either in the currency of the member making the request or in gold.

(b). The obligation in (a) above shall not apply

1. when the convertibility of the balances has been restricted consistently with Section 2 of this Article, or Article VI, Section 3;
2. when the balances have accumulated as a result of transactions effected before the removal by a member of restrictions maintained or imposed under Article XIV, Section 2; or
3. when the balances have been acquired contrary to the exchange regulations of the member which is asked to buy them; or
4. when the currency of the member requesting the purchase has been declared scarce under Article VII, Section 3(a); or
5. when the member requested to make the purchase is for any reason not entitled to buy currencies of other members from the Fund for its own currency.

Section 5. Furnishing of Information

(a) The Fund may require members to furnish it with such information as it deems necessary for its operations, including, as the minimum necessary for the effective discharge of the Fund's duties, national data on the following matters:

1. Official holdings at home and abroad, of (1) gold, (2) foreign exchange.
2. Holdings at home and abroad by banking and financial agencies, other than official agencies, of (1) gold, (2) foreign exchange.
3. Production of gold.
4. Gold exports and imports according to countries of destination and origin.
5. Total exports and imports of merchandise, in terms of local currency values, according to countries of destination and origin.
6. International balance of payments, including (1) trade in goods and services, (2) gold transactions, (3) known capital transactions, and (4) other items.
7. International investment position, i.e., investments within the territories of the member owned abroad and investments abroad owned by persons in its territories so far as it is possible to furnish this information.
8. National income.
9. Price indices, i.e., indices of commodity prices in wholesale and retail markets and of export and import prices.
10. Buying and selling rates for foreign currencies.
11. Exchange controls, i.e., a comprehensive statement of exchange controls in effect at the time of assuming membership in the Fund and details of subsequent changes as they occur.
12. Where official clearing arrangements exist, details of amounts awaiting clearance in respect of commercial and financial transactions, and of the length of time during which such arrears have been outstanding.

(b) In requesting information the Fund shall take into consideration the varying ability of members to furnish the data requested. Members shall be under no obligation to furnish information in such detail that the affairs of individuals or corporations are disclosed. Members undertake, however, to furnish the desired information in as detailed and accurate a manner as is practicable, and, so far as possible, to avoid mere estimates.

(c) The Fund may arrange to obtain further information by agreement with members. It shall act as a center for the collection and exchange of information on monetary and financial problems, thus facilitating the preparation of studies designed to assist members in developing policies which further the purposes of the Fund.

Section 6. Consultation between members regarding existing internationl agreements

Where under this Agreement a member is authorized in the special or temporary circumstances specified in the Agreement to maintain or establish restrictions on exchange transactions, and there are other engagements between members entered into prior to this Agreement which conflict with the application of such restrictions, the parties to such engagements will consult with one another with a view to making such mutually acceptable adjustments as may be necessary. The provisions of this Article shall be without prejudice to the operation of Article VII, Section 5.

Article IX

STATUS, IMMUNITIES AND PRIVILEGES

Section 1. Purposes of Article

To enable the Fund to fulfill the functions with which it is entrusted, the status, immunities and privileges set forth in this Article shall be accorded to the Fund in the territories of each member.

Section 2. Status of the Fund

The Fund shall possess full juridical personality, and, in particular, the capacity:

1. to contract;
2. to acquire and dispose of immovable and movable property;
3. to institute legal proceedings.

Section 3. Immunity from judicial process

The Fund, its property and its assets, wherever located and by whomsoever held, shall enjoy immunity from every form of judicial process except to the extent that it expressly waives its immunity for the purpose of any proceedings or by the terms of any contract.

Section 4. Immunity From Other Action

Property and assets of the Fund, wherever located and by whomsoever held, shall be immune from search, requisition, confiscation, expropriation or any other form of seizure by executive or legislative action.

Section 5. Immunity of Archives

The archives of the Fund shall be inviolable.

Section 6. Freedom of Assets From Restrictions

To the extent necessary to carry out the operations provided for in this Agreement, all property and assets of the Fund shall be free from restrictions, regulations, controls and moratoria of any nature.

Section 7. Privilege for Communications

The official communications of the Fund shall be accorded by members the same treatment as the official communications of other members.

Section 8. Immunities and Privileges of Officers and Employes

All governors, executive directors, alternates, officers and employees of the Fund

1. shall be immune from legal process with respect to acts performed by them in their official capacity except when the fund waives this immunity.
2. not being local nations, shall be granted the same immunities from immigration restrictions, alien registration requirements and national service obligations and the same facilities as regards exchange restrictions as are accorded by members to the representatives, officials and employes of comparable rank of other members.
3. shall be granted the same treatment in respect of traveling facilities as is accorded by members to representatives, officials and employes of comparable rank of other members.

Section 9. Immunities from Taxation

(a). The Fund, its assets, property, income and its operations and transactions authorized by this Agreement, shall be immune from all taxation and from all customs duties. The Fund shall also be immune from liability for the collection or payment of any tax or duty.

(b). No tax shall be levied on or in respect of salaries and emoluments paid by the Fund to executive directors, alternates, officers or employes of the Fund who are not local citizens, local subjects, or other local nationals.

(c). No taxation of any kind shall be levied on any obligation or security issued by the Fund, including any dividend or interest thereon, by whomsoever held

1. which discriminates against such obligation or security solely because of its origin; or
2. if the sole jurisdictional basis for such taxation is the place or currency in which it is issued, made payable or paid, or the location of any office or place of business maintained by the Fund.

Section 10. Application of Article.

Each member shall take such action as is necessary in its own territories for the purpose of making effective in terms of its own law the principles set forth in this Article and shall inform the Fund of the detailed action which it has taken.

Article X

RELATIONS WITH OTHER INTERNATIONAL ORGANIZATIONS

The Fund shall cooperate within the terms of this Agreement with any general international organization and with public international organizations having specialized responsibilities in related fields. Any arrangements for such cooperation which would involve a modification of any provision of this Agreement may be effected only after amendment to this Agreement under Article XVII.

Article XI

RELATIONS WITH NON-MEMBER COUNTRIES

Section 1. Undertakings regarding relations with non-member countries

Each member undertakes:

1. Not to engage in, nor to permit any of its fiscal agencies referred to in Article V, Section 1, to engage in, any transactions with a non-member or with persons in a non-member's territories which would be contrary to the provisions of this Agreement or the purposes of the Fund;
2. Not to cooperate with a non-member or with persons in a non-member's territories in practices which would be contrary to the provisions of this Agreement or the purposes of the Fund; and
3. To cooperate with the Fund with a view to the application in its territories of appropriate measures to prevent transactions with non-members or with persons in their territories which would be contrary to the provisions of this Agreement or the purposes of the Fund.

Section 2. Restrictions on Transactions with Non-member Countries

Nothing in this Agreement shall affect the right of any member to impose restrictions on exchange transactions with non-members or with persons in their territories unless the Fund finds that such restrictions prejudice the interest of members and are contrary to the purposes of the Fund.

Article XII

ORGANIZATION AND MANAGEMENT

Section 1. Structure of the Fund.

The Fund shall have a Board of Governors, Executive Directors, a Managing Director and a staff.

Section 2. Board of Governors.

(a). All powers of the Fund shall be vested in the Board of Governors, consisting of one governor and one alternate appointed by each member in such manner as it may determine. Each governor and each alternate shall serve for five years, subject to the pleasure of the member appointing him, and may be reappointed. No alternate may vote except in the absence of his principal. The Board shall select one of the governors as chairman.

(b). The Board of Governors may delegate to the Executive Directors authority to exercise any powers of the Board, except the power to:

1. Admit new members and determine the conditions of their admission.
2. Approve a revision of quotas.
3. Approve a uniform change in the par value of the currencies of all members.
4. Make arrangements to cooperate with other international organizations (other than informal arrangements of a temporary or administrative character).
5. Determine the distribution of the net income of the Fund.
6. Require a member to withdraw.
7. Decide to liquidate the Fund.
8. Decide appeals from interpretations of this Agreement given by the Executive Directors.

(c) The Board of Governors shall hold an annual meeting and such other meetings as may be provided for by the Board or called by the Executive Directors. Meetings of the Board shall be called by the Directors whenever requested by five members or by members having one quarter of the total voting power.

(d) A quorum for any meeting of the Board of Governors shall be a majority of the governors exercising not less than two-thirds of the total voting power.

(e) Each governor shall be entitled to cast the number of votes allotted under Section 5 of this Article to the member appointing him.

(f) The Board of Governors may by regulation establish a procedure whereby the Executive Directors, when they deem such action to be in the best interests of the Fund, may obtain a vote of the governors on a specific question without calling a meeting of the Board.

(g) The Board of Governors, and the Executive Directors to the extent authorized, may adopt such rules and regulations as may be necessary or appropriate to conduct the business of the Fund.

(h) Governors and alternates shall serve as such without compensation from the Fund, but the Fund shall pay them reasonable expenses incurred in attending meetings.

(i) The Board of Governors shall determine the remuneration to be paid to the Executive Directors and the salary and terms of the contract of service of the Managing Director.

Section 3. Executive Directors.

(a) The Executive Directors shall be responsible for the conduct of the general operations of the Fund, and for this purpose shall exercise all the powers delegated to them by the Board of Governors.

(b) There shall be not less than twelve directors who need not be governors, and of whom

1. Five shall be appointed by the five members having the largest quotas;
2. Not more than two shall be appointed when the provisions of (c) below apply;
3. Five shall be elected by the members not entitled to appoint directors, other than the American Republics; and
4. Two shall be elected by the American Republics not entitled to appoint directors.

For the purposes of this paragraph, members means governments of countries whose names are set forth in Schedule A, whether they become members in accordance with Article XX or in accordance with Article II, Section 2. When governments of other countries become members, the Board of Governors may, by a four-fifths majority of the total voting power, increase the number of directors to be elected.

(c) If, at the second regular election of directors and thereafter, the members entitled to appoint directors under (b) (i) above do not include the two members, the holdings of whose currencies by the Fund have been, on the average over the preceding two years, reduced below their quotas by the largest absolute amounts in terms of gold as a common denominator, either one or both of such members, as the case may be, shall be entitled to appoint a director.

(d) Subject to Article XX, Section 3 (b) elections of elective directors shall be conducted at intervals of two years in accordance with the provisions of Schedule C, supplemented by such regulations as the Fund deems appropriate. Whenever the Board of Governors increases the number of directors to be elected under (b) above, it shall issue regulations making appropriate changes in the proportion of votes required to elect directors under the provisions of Schedule C.

(e) Each director shall appoint an alternate with full power to act for him when he is not present. When the directors appointing them are present, alternates may participate in meetings but may not vote.

(f) Directors shall continue in office until their successors are appointed or elected. If the office of an elected director becomes vacant more than ninety days before the end of his term, another director shall be elected for the remainder of the term by the members who elected the former director. A majority of the votes cast shall be required for election. While the office remains vacant, the alternate of the former director shall exercise his powers, except that of appointing an alternate.

(g) The Executive Directors shall function in continuous session at the principal office of the Fund and shall meet as often as the business of the Fund may require.

(h) A quorum for any meeting of the Executive Directors shall be a majority of the directors representing not less than one-half of the voting power.

(i) Each appointed director shall be entitled to cast the number of votes allotted under Section 5 of this Article to the member appointing him. Each elected director shall be entitled to cast the number of votes which counted towards his election. When the provisions of Section 5(b) of this Article are applicable, the votes which a director would otherwise be entitled to cast shall be increased or decreased correspondingly. All the votes which a director is entitled to cast shall be cast as a unit.

(j) The Board of Governors shall adopt regulations under which a member not entitled to appoint a director under (b) above may send a representative to attend any meeting of the Executive Directors when a request made by, or a matter particularly affecting, that member is under consideration.

(k) The Executive Directors may appoint such committees as they deem advisable. Membership of committees need not be limited to governors or directors or their alternates.

Section 4. Managing Director and Staff.

(a) The Executive Directors shall select a Managing Director who shall not be a governor or an executive director. The Managing Director shall be chairman of the Executive Directors, but shall have no vote except a deciding vote in case of an equal division. He may participate in meetings of the Board of Governors, but shall not vote at such meetings. The Managing Director shall cease to hold office when the Executive Directors so decide.

(b) The Managing Director shall be chief of the operating staff of the Fund and shall conduct, under the direction of the Executive Directors, the ordinary business of the Fund. Subject to the general control of the Executive Directors, he shall be responsible for the organization, appointment and dismissal of the staff of the Fund.

(c) The Managing Director and the staff of the Fund, in the discharge of their functions, shall owe their duty entirely to the Fund and to no other authority. Each member of the Fund shall respect the international character of this duty and shall refrain from all attempts to influence any of the staff in the discharge of his functions.

(d) In appointing the staff the Managing Director shall, subject to the paramount importance of securing the highest standards of efficiency and of technical competence, pay due regard to the importance of recruiting personnel on as wide a geographical basis as possible.

Section 5. Voting.

(a) Each member shall have two hundred fifty votes plus one additional vote for each part of its quota equivalent to one hundred thousand United States dollars.

(b) Whenever voting is required under Article V, Section 4 or 5, each member shall have the number of votes to which it is entitled under (a) above, adjusted:

1. By the addition of one vote for the equivalent of each 400,000 United States dollars of net sales of its currency up to the date when the vote is taken, or
2. By the subtraction of one vote for the equivalent of each 400,000 United States dollars of its net purchases of the currencies of other members up to the date when the vote is taken

provided, that neither net purchases nor net sales shall be deemed at any time to exceed an amount equal to the quota of the member involved.

(c) For the purpose of all computations under this Section, United States dollars shall be deemed to be of the weight and fineness in effect on July 1, 1944, adjusted for any uniform change under Article IV, Section 7, if a waiver is made under Section 8(d) of that Article.

(d Except as otherwise specifically provided, all decisions of the Fund shall be made by a majority of the votes cast.

Section 6. Distribution of Net Income.

(a) The Board of Governors shall determine annually what part of the Fund's net income shall be placed to reserve and what part, if any, shall be distributed.

(b) If any distribution is made, there shall first be distributed a two percent non-cumulative payment to each member on the amount by which seventy-five percent of its quota exceeded the Fund's average holdings of its currency during that year. The balance shall be paid to all members in proportion to their quotas. Payments to each member shall be made in its own currency.

Section 7. Publication of Reports.

(a) The Fund shall publish an annual report containing an audited statement of its accounts, and shall issue, at intervals of three months or less, a summary statement of its transactions and its holdings of gold and currencies of members.

(b) The Fund may publish such other reports as it deems desirable for carrying out its purposes.

Section 8. Communication of Views to Members.

The Fund shall at all times have the right to communicate its views informally to any member on any matter arising under this Agreement. The Fund may, by a two-thirds majority of the total voting power, decide to publish a report made to a member regarding its monetary or economic conditions and developments which directly tend to produce a serious disequilibrium in the international balance of payments of members. If the member is not entitled to appoint an executive director, it shall be entitled to representation in accordance with Section 3 (j) of this Article. The Fund shall not publish a report involving changes in the fundamental structure of the economic organization of members.

Article XIII

OFFICES AND DEPOSITORIES

Section 1. Location of Offices

The principal office of the Fund shall be located in the territory of the member having the largest quota, and agencies or branch offices may be established in the territories of other members.

Section 2. Depositories

(a) Each member country shall designate its central bank as a depository for all the Fund's holdings of its currency, or if it has no central bank it shall designate such other institution as may be acceptable to the Fund.

(b) The Fund may hold other assets, including gold, in the depositories designated by the five members having the largest quotas and in such other designated depositories as the Fund may select. Initially, at least one-half of the holdings of the Fund shall be held in the depository designated by the member in whose territories the Fund has its principal office and at least forty per cent shall be held in the depositories designated by the remaining four members referred to above. However, all transfers of gold by the Fund shall be made with due regard to the costs of transport and anticipated requirements of the Fund. In an emergency the Executive Directors may transfer all or any part of the Fund's gold holdings to any place where they can be adequately protected.

Section 3. Guarantee of the Fund's Assets

Each member guarantees all assets of the Fund against loss resulting from failure or default on the part of the depository designated by it.

Article XIV

TRANSITIONAL PERIOD

Section 1. Introduction

The Fund is not intended to provide facilities for relief or reconstruction or to deal with international indebtedness arising out of the war.

Section 2. Exchange Restrictions.

In the post-war transitional period members may, notwithstanding the provisions of any other articles of this Agreement, maintain and adapt to changing circumstances (and, in the case of members whose territories have been occupied by the enemy, introduce where necessary) restrictions on payments and transfers for current international transactions. Members shall, however, have continuous regard in their foreign exchange policies to the purpose of the Fund; and, as soon as conditions permit, they shall take all possible measures to develop such commercial and financial arrangements with other members as will facilitate international payments and the maintenance of exchange stability. In particular, members shall withdraw restrictions maintained or imposed under this Section as soon as they are satisfied that they will be able, in the absence of such restrictions, to settle their balance of payments in a manner which will not unduly encumber their access to the resources of the Fund.

Section 3. Notification to the Fund.

Each member shall notify the Fund before it becomes eligible under Article XX, Section 4(c) or (d), to buy currency from the Fund, whether it intends to avail itself of the transitional arrangements in Section 2 of this Article, or whether it is prepared to accept the obligations of Article VIII, Sections 2, 3 and 4. A member availing itself of the transitional arrangements shall notify the Fund as soon thereafter as it is prepared to accept the above-mentioned obligations.

Section 4. Action of the Fund relating to restrictions.

Not later than three years after the date on which the Fund begins operations and in each year thereafter, the Fund shall report on the restrictions still in force under Section 2 of this Article. Five years after the date on which the Fund begins operations, and in each year thereafter, any member still retaining any restrictions inconsistent with Article VIII, Sections 2, 3, or 4, shall consult the Fund as to their further retention. The Fund may, if it deems such action necessary in exceptional circumstances, make representations to any member that conditions are favorable for the withdrawal of any particular restriction, or for the general abandonment of restrictions, inconsistent with the provisions of any other articles of this Agreement. The member shall be given a suitable time to reply to such representations. If the Fund finds that the member persists in maintaining restrictions which are inconsistent with the purposes of the Fund, the member shall be subject to Article XV, Section 2(a).

Section 5. Nature of Transitional Period

In its relations with members, the Fund shall recognize that the post-war transitional period will be one of change and adjustment and in making decisions on requests occasioned thereby which are presented by any member it shall give the member the benefit of any reasonable doubt.

Article XV

WITHDRAWAL FROM MEMBERSHIP

Section 1. Right of Members to Withdraw

Any member may withdraw from the Fund at any time by transmitting a notice in writing to the Fund at its principal office. Withdrawal shall become effective on the date such notice is received.

Section 2. Compulsory Withdrawal

(a) If a member fails to fulfill any of its obligations under this Agreement, the Fund may declare the member ineligible to use the resources of the Fund. Nothing in this Section shall be deemed to limit the provisions of Article IV, Section 6, Article V, Section 5, or Article VI, Section 1.

(b) If, after the expiration of a reasonable period the member persists in its failure to fulfill any of its obligations under this Agreement, or a difference between a member and the Fund under Article IV, Section 6, continues, that member may be required to withdraw from membership in the Fund by a decision of the Board of Governors carried by a majority of the governors representing a majority of the total voting power.

(c) Regulations shall be adopted to ensure that before action is taken against any member under (a) or (b) above, the member shall be informed in reasonable time of the complaint against it and given an adequate opportunity for stating its case, both orally and in writing.

Section 3. Settlement of Accounts With Members Withdrawing

When a member withdraws from the Fund, normal transactions of the Fund in its currency shall cease and settlement of all accounts between it and the Fund shall be made with reasonable despatch by agreement between it and the Fund. If agreement is not reached promptly, the provisions of Schedule D shall apply to the settlement of accounts.

Article XVI

EMERGENCY PROVISIONS

Section 1. Temporary Suspension

(a) In the event of an emergency or the development of unforeseen circumstances threatening the operations of the Fund, the Executive Directors by unanimous vote may suspend for a period of not more than one hundred twenty days the operation of any of the following provisions:

1. Article IV, Sections 3 and 4(b).
2. Article V, Sections 2, 3, 7, 8(a) and (f).

3. Article, VI, Section 2.
4. Article XI, Section 1.

(b) Simultaneously with any decision to suspend the operation of any of the foregoing provisions, the Executive Directors shall call a meeting of the Board of Governors for the earliest practicable date.

(c) The Executive Directors may not extend any suspension beyond one hundred twenty days. Such suspension may be extended, however, for an additional period of not more than two hundred forty days, if the Board of Governors by a four-fifths majority of the total voting power so decides, but it may not be further extended except by amendment of this Agreement pursuant to Article XVII.

(d) The Executive Directors may, by a majority of the total voting power, terminate such suspension at any time.

Section 2. Liquidation of the Fund.

(a). The Fund may not be liquidated except by decision of the Board of Governors. In an emergency, if the Executive Directors decide that liquidation of the Fund may be necessary, they may temporarily suspend all transactions, pending decision by the Board.

(b). If the Board of Governors decides to liquidate the Fund, the Fund shall forthwith cease to engage in any activities except those incidental to the orderly collection and liquidation of its assets and the settlement of its liabilities, and all obligations of members under this Agreement shall cease except those set out in this Article, in Article XVIII, paragraph (c), in Schedule D, paragraph 7 and in Schedule E.

(c). Liquidation shall be administered in accordance with the provisions of Schedule E.

Article XVII

AMENDMENTS

(a). Any proposal to introduce modifications in this Agreement, whether emanating from a member, a governor or the Executive Directors, shall be communicated to the chairman of the Board of Governors, who shall bring the proposal before the Board. If the proposed amendment is approved by the Board the Fund shall, by circular letter or telegram, ask all members whether they accept the proposed amendment. When three-fifths of the members, having four-fifths of the total voting power, have accepted the proposed amendment, the Fund shall certify the fact by a formal communication addressed to all members.

(b). Notwithstanding (a) above, acceptance by all members is required in the case of any amendment modifying

1. The right to withdraw from the Fund (Article XV, Section 1);
2. The provision that no change in a member's quota shall be made without its consent (Article III, Section 2);
3. The provision that no change may be made in the par value of a member's currency except on the proposal of that member (Article IV, Section 5 (b).

(c). Amendments shall enter into force for all members three months after the date of the formal communication unless a shorter period is specified in the circular letter or telegram.

Article XVIII

INTERPRETATION

(a) Any question of interpretation of the provisions of this Agreement arising between any member of the Fund or between any member and the Fund or between any members of the Fund shall be submitted to the Executive Directors for their decision. If the question particularly affects any member not entitled to appoint an executive director it shall be entitled to representation in accordance with Article XII, Section 3(j).

(b) In any case where the Executive Directors have given a decision under (a) above, any member may require that the question be referred to the Board of Governors, whose decision shall be final. Pending the result of the reference to the Board the Fund may, so far as it deems necessary, act on the basis of the decision of the Executive Directors.

(c) Whenever a disagreement arises between the Fund and a member which has withdrawn, or between the Fund and any member during liquidation of the Fund, such disagreement shall be submitted to arbitration by a tribunal of three arbitrators, one appointed by the Fund, another by the member or withdrawing member and an umpire who, unless the parties otherwise agree, shall be appointed by the President of the Permanent Court of International Justice or such other authority as may have been prescribed by regulation adopted by the Fund. The umpire shall have full power to settle all questions of procedure in any case where the parties are in disagreement with respect thereto.

Article XIX

EXPLANATION OF TERMS

In interpreting the provisions of this Agreement the Fund and its members shall be guided by the following:

(a) A member's monetary reserves means its net official holdings of gold, of convertible currencies of other members, and of the currencies of such non-members as the Fund may specify.

(b) The official holdings of a member means central holdings (that is, the holdings of its Treasury, central bank, stabilization fund, or similar fiscal agency).

(c) The holdings of other official institutions or other banks within its territories may, in any particular case, be deemed by the Fund, after consultation with the member, to be official holdings to the extent that they are substantially in excess of working balances; provided that for the purpose of determining whether, in a particular case, holdings are in excess of working balances, there shall be deducted from such holdings amounts of currency due to other official institutions and other banks in the territories of other counries.

(d) A member's holdings of convertible currencies means its holdings of the currencies of other members which are not availing themselves of the transitional arrangements under Article XIV, Section 2, together with its holdings of the currencies of such non-members as the Fund may from time to time specify. The term currency for this purpose includes without limitation coins, paper money, bank balances, bank acceptances, and government obligations issued with a maturity not exceeding twelve months.

(e) A member's monetary reserves shall be calculated by deducting from such central holdings the currency liabilities to the Treasuries, central banks, stabilization funds, or similar fiscal agencies of other members or non-members specified under (d) above, together with similar liabilities to other official institutions and other banks in the territories of members, or non-members specified under (d) above. To these net holdings shall be added the sums deemed to be official holdings of other official institutions and other banks under (c) above.

(f) The Fund's holdings of the currency of a member shall include any securities accepted by the Fund under Article III, Section 5.

(g) The Fund, after consultation with a member which is availing itself of the transitional arrangements under Article XIV, Section 2, may deem holdings of the currency of that member which carry specified rights of conversion into another currency or into gold to be holdings of convertible currency for the purpose of the calculation of monetary reserves.

(h) For the purpose of calculating gold subscriptions under Article III, Section 3, a member's net official holdings of gold and United States dollars shall consist of its official holdings of gold and United States currency after deducting central holdings of tis currency by other countries and holdings of its currency by other official institutions and other banks if these holdings carry specified rights of conversion into gold or United States currency.

(i) Payments for current transactions means payments which are not for the purpose of transferring capital, and includes, without limitation:

1. All payments due in connection with foreign trade, other current business, including services, and normal short-term banking and credit facilities;
2. Payments due as interest on loans and as net income from other investments;
3. Payments of moderate amount for amortization of loans or for depreciation of direct investments;
4. Moderate remittances for family living expenses.

The Fund may, after consultation with the members concerned, determine whether certain specific transactions are to be considered current transactions or capital transactions.

Article XX

FINAL PROVISIONS

Section 1. Entry Into Force.

This Agreement shall enter into force when it has been signed on behalf of governments having sixty-five percent of the total of the quotas set forth in Schedule A and when the instruments referred to in Section 2(a) of this Article have been deposited on their behalf. but in no event shall this Agreement enter into force before May 1, 1945.

Section 2. Signature.

(a) Each government on whose behalf this Agreement is signed shall deposit with the Government of the United States of America an instrument setting forth that it has accepted this Agreement in accordance with its law and has taken all steps necessary to enable it to carry out all of its obligations under this Agreement.

(b) Each government shall become a member of the Fund as from the date of the deposit on its behalf of the instrument referred to in (a) above, except that no government shall become a member before this Agreement enters into force under Section 1 of this Article.

(c) The Government of the United States of America shall inform the governments of all countries whose names are set forth in Schedule A, and all governments whose membership is approved in accordance with Article II, Section 2, of all signatures of this Agreement and of the deposit of all instruments referred to in (a) above.

(d) At the time this Agreement is signed on its behalf, each government shall transmit to the Government of the United States of America one one-hundredth of one percent of its total subscription in gold or United States dollars for the purpose of meeting administrative expenses of the Fund. The Government of the United States of America shall hold such funds in a special deposit account and shall transmit them to the Board of Governors of the Fund when the initial meeting has been called under Section 3 of this Article. If this Agreement has not come into force by December 31, 1945, the Government of the United States of America shall return such funds to the governments that transmitted them.

(e) This Agreement shall remain open for signature at Washington on behalf of the governments of the countries whose names are set forth in Schedule A until Dec. 31, 1945.

(f) After December 31, 1945, this Agreement shall be open for signature on behalf of the government of any country whose membership has been approved in accordance with Article II, Section 2.

(g) By their signature of this Agreement, all governments accept it both on their own behalf and in respect of all their colonies, overseas territories, all territories under their protection, suzerainty, or authority and all territories in respect of which they exercise a mandate.

(h) In the case of governments whose metropolitan territories have been under enemy occupation, the deposit of the instrument referred to in (a) above may be delayed until one hundred eighty days after the date on which these territories have been liberated. If, however, it is not deposited by any such government before the expiration of this period the signature affixed on behalf of that government shall become void. And the portion of its subscription paid under (d) above shall be returned to it.

(i) Paragraphs (d) and (h) shall come into force with regard to each signatory government as from the date of its signature.

Section 3. Inauguration of the Fund

(a) As soon as this Agreement enters into force under Section 1 of this Article, each member shall appoint a governor and the member having the largest quota shall call the first meeting of the Board of Governors.

(b) At the first meeting of the Board of Governors, arrangements shall be made for the selection of provisional executive directors. The governments of the five countries for which the largest quotas are set forth in Schedule A shall appoint provisional executive directors. If one or more of such governments have not become members, the executive directorships they would be entitled to fill shall remain vacant until they become members, or until January 1, 1946, whichever is the earlier. Seven provisional executive directors shall be elected in accordance with the provisions of Schedule C and shall remain in office until the date of the first regular election of executive directors which shall be held as soon as practicable after January 1, 1946.

(c) The Board of Governors may delegate to the provisional executive directors any powers except those which may not be delegated to the Executive Directors.

Section 4. Intitial determination of par values.

(a) When the Fund is of the opinion that it will shortly be in a position to begin exchange transactions, it shall so notify the members and shall request each member to communicate within thirty days the par value of its currency based on the rates of exchange prevailing on the sixtieth day before the entry into force of this Agreement. No member whose metropolitan territory has been occupied by the enemy shall be required to make such a communication while that territory is a theatre of major hostilities or for such period thereafter as the Fund may determine. When such a member communicates the par value of its currency the provisions of (d) below shall apply.

(b) The par value communicated by a member whose metropolitan territory has not been occupied by the enemy shall be the par value of that member's currency for the purposes of this Agreement unless, within ninety days after the request referred to in (a) above has been received, (i) the member notifies the Fund that it regards the par value as unsatisfactory, or (ii) the Fund notifies the member that in its opinion the par value cannot be maintained without causing recourse to the Fund on the part of that member or others on a scale prejudicial to the Fund and to members. When notification is given under (i) or (ii) above, the Fund and the member shall, within a period determined by the Fund in the light of all relevant circumstances, agree upon a suitable par value for that currency. If the Fund and the member do not agree within the period so determined, the member shall be deemed to have withdrawn from the Fund on the date when the period expires.

(c) When the par value of a member's currency has been established under (b) above, either by the expiration of ninety days without notification, or by agreement after notification, the member shall be eligible to buy from the Fund the currencies of other members to the full extent permitted in this Agreement, provided that the Fund has begun exchange transactions.

(d) In the case of a member whose metropolitan territory has been occupied by the enemy, the provisions of (b) above shall apply, subject to the following modifications:

1. The period of ninety days shall be extended so as to end on a date to be fixed by agreement between the Fund and the member.
2. Within the extended period the member may, if the Fund has begun exchange transactions, buy from the Fund with its currency the currencies of other members, but only under such conditions and in such amounts as may be prescribed by the Fund.
3. At any time before the date fixed under (1) above, changes may be made by agreement with the Fund in the par value communicated under (a) above.

(e). If a member whose metropolitan territory has been occupied by the enemy adopts a new monetary unit before the date to be fixed under (d) (1) above, the par value fixed by that member for the new unit shall be communicated to the Fund and the provisions of (d) above shall apply.

(f). Changes in par values agreed with the Fund under this Section shall not be taken into account in determining whether a proposed change falls within (1), (2), or (3) of Article IV, Section 5(c).

(g) A member communicating to the Fund a par value for the currency of its metropolitan territory shall simultaneously communicate a value, in terms of that currency, for each separate currency, where such exists, in the territories in respect of which it has accepted this Agreement under Section 2(g) of this Article, but no member shall be required to make a communication for the separate currency of a territory which has been occupied by the enemy while that territory is a theatre of major hostilities or for such period thereafter as the Fund may determine. On the basis of the par value so communicated, the Fund shall compute the par value of each separate currency. A communication or notification to the Fund under (a), (b) or (d) above regarding the par value of a currency, shall also be deemed, unless the contrary is stated, to be a communication or notification regarding the par value of all the separate currencies referred to above. Any member may, however, make a communication or notification relating to the metropolitan or any of the separate currencies alone. If the member does so, the provisions of the preceding paragraphs (including (d) above, if a territory where a separate currency exists has been occupied by the enemy) shall apply to each of these currencies separately.

(h) The Fund shall begin exchange transactions at such date as it may determine after members having sixty-five per-cent of the total of the quotas set forth in Schedule A have become eligible, in accordance with the preceding paragraphs of this Section, to purchase the currencies of other members, but in no event until after major hostilities in Europe have ceased.

(i) The Fund may postpone exchange transactions with any member if its circumstances are such that, in the opinion of the Fund, they would lead to use of the resources of the Fund in a manner contrary to the purposes of this Agreement or prejudicial to the Fund or the members.

(j) The par values of the currencies of governments which indicate their desire to become members after December 31, 1945, shall be determined in accordance with the provisions of Article II, Section 2.

DONE at Washington, in a single copy which shall remain deposited in the archives of the Government of the United States of America which shall transmit certified copies to all governments whose names are set forth in Schedule A and to all governments whose membership is approved in accordance with Article II, Section 2.

SCHEDULE A

Quotas

	(In Millions of United States Dollars.)
Australia	200
Belgium	225
Bolivia	10
Brazil	150
Canada	300
Chile	50
China	550
Colombia	50
Costa Rica	5
Cuba	50
Czechoslovakia	125
*Denmark	*
Dominican Republic	5
Ecuador	5
Egypt	45
El Salvador	2.5
Ethiopia	6
France	450
Greece	40
Guatemala	5
Haiti	5
Honduras	2.5
Iceland	1
India	400
Iran	25
Iraq	8
Liberia	.5
Luxembourg	10
Mexico	90
Netherlands	275
New Zealand	50
Nicaragua	2
Norway	50
Panama	.5
Paraguay	2
Peru	25
Philippine Commonwealth	15
Poland	125
Union of South Africa	100
Union of Soviet Socialist Republics	1200
United Kingdom	1300
United States	2750
Uruguay	15
Venezuela	15
Yugoslavia	60

*The quota of Denmark shall be determined by the Fund after the Danish Government has declared its readiness to sign this Agreement but before signature takes place.

SCHEDULE B

Provisions with Respect to Repurchase by a Member of its Currency

1. In determining the extent to which repurchase of a member's currency from the Fund under Article V, Section 7(b), shall be made with each type of monetary reserve, that is, with gold and with each convertible currency, the following rule, subject to 2 below, shall apply:

(a) If the member's monetary reserves have not increased during the year, the amount payable to the Fund shall be distributed among all types of reserves in proportion to the member's holdings thereof at the end of the year.

(b) If the member's monetary reserves have increased during the year, a part of the amount payable to the Fund equal to one-half of the increase shall be distributed among those types of reserves which have increased in proportion to the amount by which each of them has increased. The remainder of the sum payable to the Fund shall be distributed among all types of reserves in proportion to the member's remaining holdings thereof.

(c) If after all the repurchases required under Article V, Section 7 (b), had been made, the result would exceed any of the limits specified in Article V, Section 7(c), the Fund shall require such repurchases to be made by the members proportionately in such manner that the limits will not be exceeded.

2. The Fund shall not acquire the currency of any non-member under Article V, Section 7(b) and (c).

3. In calculating monetary reserves and the increase in monetary reserves during any year for the purpose of Article V, Section 7(b) and (c), no account shall be taken, unless deductions have otherwise been made by the member for such holdings, of any increase in those monetary reserves which is due to currency previously inconvertible having become convertible during the year; or to holdings which are the proceeds of a long-term or medium-term loan contracted during the year; or to holdings which have been transferred or set aside for repayment of a loan during the subsequent year.

4. In the case of members whose metropolitan territories have been occupied by the enemy, gold newly produced during the five years after the entry into force of this Agreement from mines located within their metropolitan territories shall not be included in computations of their monetary reserves or of increases in their monetary reserves.

SCHEDULE C

Election of Executive Directors

1. The election of the elective executive directors shall be by ballot of the governors eligible to vote under Article XII, Section 3 (b) (iii) and (iv).

2. In balloting for the five directors to be elected under Article XII, Section 3 (b) (iii), each of the governors eligible to vote shall cast for one person all of the votes to which he is entitled under Article XII, Section 5 (a). The five persons receiving the greatest number of votes shall be directors, provided that no person who received less than nineteen percent of the total number of votes that can be cast (eligible votes) shall be considered elected.

3. When five persons are not elected in the first ballot, a second ballot shall be held in which the person who received the lowest number of votes shall be ineligible for election and in which there shall vote only (a) those governors who voted in the first ballot for a person not elected, and (b) those governors whose votes for a person elected are deemed under 4 below to have raised the votes cast for that person above twenty percent of the eligible votes.

4. In determining whether the votes cast by a governor are to be deemed to have raised the total of any person above twenty percent of the eligible votes the twenty percent shall be deemed to include, first, the votes of the governor casting the largest number of votes for such person, then the votes of the governor casting the next largest number, and so on until twenty percent is reached.

5. Any governor part of whose votes must be counted in order to raise the total of any person above nineteen percent shall be considered as casting all of his votes for such person even if the total votes for such person thereby exceed twenty percent.

6. If, after the second ballot, five persons have not been elected, further ballots shall be held on the same principles until five persons have been elected, provided that after four persons are elected, the fifth may be elected by a simple majority of the remaining votes and shall be deemed to have been elected by all such votes.

7. The directors to be elected by the American Republics under Article XII, Section 3 (b) (iv) shall be elected as follows:

(a) Each of the directors shall be elected separately.

b) In the election of the first director, each governor representing an American Republic eligible to participate in the election shall cast for one person all the votes to which he is entitled. The person receiving the largest number of votes shall be elected provided that he has received not less than forty-five percent of the total votes.

(c) If no person is elected on the first ballot, further ballots shall be held, in each of which the person receiving the lowest number of votes shall be eliminated, until one person receives a number of votes sufficient for election under (b) above.

(d) Governors whose votes contributed to the election of the first director shall take no part in the election of the second director.

(e) Persons who did not succeed in the first election shall not be ineligible for election as the second director.

(f) A majority of the votes which can be cast shall be required for election of the second director. If at the first ballot no person receives a majority, further ballots shall be held in each of which the person receiving the lowest number of votes shall be eliminated, until some person obtains a majority.

(g) The second director shall be deemed to have been elected by all the votes which could have been cast in the ballot securing his election.

SCHEDULE D

Settlement of Accounts With Members Withdrawing

1. The Fund shall be obligated to pay to a member withdrawing an amount equal to its quota, plus any other amounts due to it from the Fund, less any amounts due to the Fund, including charges accruing after the date of its withdrawal; but no payment shall be made until six months after the date of withdrawal. Payments shall be made in the currency of the withdrawing member.

2. If the Fund's holdings of the currency of the withdrawing member are not sufficient to pay the net amount due from the Fund, the balance shall be paid in gold, or in such other manner as may be agreed. If the Fund and the withdrawing member do not reach agreement within six months of the date of withdrawal, the currency in question held by the Fund shall be paid forthwith to the withdrawing member. Any balance due shall be paid in ten half-yearly installments during the ensuing five years. Each such installment shall be paid, at the option of the Fund, either in the currency of the withdrawing member acquired after its withdrawal or by the delivery of gold.

3. If the Fund fails to meet any installment which is due in accordance with the preceding paragraphs, the withdrawing member shall be entitled to require the Fund to pay the installment in any currency held by the Fund with the exception of any currency which has been declared scarce under Article VII, Section 3.

4. If the Fund's holdings of the currency of a withdrawing member exceed the amount due to it, and if agreement on the method of settling accounts is not reached within six months of the date of withdrawal, the former member shall be obligated to redeem such excess currency in gold or, at its option, in the currencies of members which at the time of redemption are convertible. Redemption shall be made at the parity existing at the time of withdrawal from the Fund. The withdrawing member shall complete redemption within five years of the date of withdrawal, or within such longer period as may be fixed by the Fund, but shall not be required to redeem in any half-yearly period more than one-tenth of the Fund's excess holdings of its currency at the date of withdrawal plus further acquisitions of the currency during such half-yearly period. If the withdrawing member does not fulfill this obligation, the Fund may in an orderly manner liquidate in any market the amount of currency which should have been redeemed.

5. Any member desiring to obtain the currency of a member which has withdrawn shall acquire it by purchase from the Fund, to the extent that such member has access to the resources of the Fund and that such currency is available under 4 above.

6. The withdrawing member guarantees the unrestricted use at all times of the currency disposed of under 4 and 5 above for the purchase of goods or for payment of sums due to it or to persons within its territories. It shall compensate the Fund for any loss resulting from the difference between the par value of its currency on the date of withdrawal and the value realized by the Fund on disposal under 4 and 5 above.

7. In the event of the Fund going into liquidation under Article XVI, Section 2, within six months of the date on which the member withdraws, the account between the Fund and that government shall be settled in accordance with Article XVI, Section 2, and Schedule E.

SCHEDULE E

Administration of Liquidation

1. In the event of liquidation the liabilities of the Fund other than the repayment of subscriptions shall have priority in the distribution of the assets of the Fund. In meeting each such liability the Fund shall use its assets in the following order:—

(a) the currency in which the liability is payable;

(b) gold;

(c) all other currencies in proportion, so far as may be practicable, to the quotas of the members.

2. After the discharge of the Fund's liabilities in accordance with 1 above, the balance of the Fund's assets shall be distributed and apportioned as follows:

(a) The Fund shall distribute its holdings of gold among the members whose currencies are held by the Fund in amounts less than their quotas. These members shall share the gold so distributed in the proportions of the amount by which their quotas exceed the Fund's holdings of their currencies.

(b) The Fund shall distribute to each member one-half the Fund's holdings of its currency but such distribution shall not exceed fifty percent of its quota.

(c) The Fund shall apportion the remainder of its holdings of each currency among all the members in proportion to the amounts due to each member after the distributions under (a) and (b) above.

3. Each member shall redeem the holdings of its currency apportioned to other members under 2 (c) above, and shall agree with the Fund within three months after a decision to liquidate upon an orderly procedure for such redemption.

4. If a member has not reached agreement with the Fund within the three-month period referred to in 3 above, the Fund shall use the currencies of other members apportioned to that member under 2 (c) above to redeem the currency of that member apportioned to other members. Each currency apportioned to a member which has not reached agreement shall be used, so far as possible, to redeem its currency apportioned to the members which have made agreements with the Fund under 3 above.

5. If a member has reached agreement with the Fund in accordance with 3 above, the Fund shall use the currencies of other members apportioned to that member under 2(c) above to redeem the currency of that member apportioned to other members which have made agreements with the Fund under 3 above. Each amount so redeemed shall be redeemed in the currency of the member to which it was apportioned.

6. After carrying out the preceding paragraphs, the Fund shall pay to each member the remaining currencies held for its account.

7. Each member whose currency has been distributed to other members under 6 above shall redeem such currency in gold or, at its option, in the currency of the member requesting redemption, or in such other manner as may be agreed between them. If the members involved do not otherwise agree, the member obligated to redeem shall complete redemption within five years of the date of distribution, but shall not be required to redeem in any half-yearly period more than one-tenth of the amount distributed to each other member. If the member does not fulfill this obligation, the amount of currency which should have been redeemed may be liquidated in an orderly manner in any market.

8. Each member whose currency has been distributed to other members under 6 above guarantees the unrestricted use of such currency at all times for the purchase of goods or for payment of sums due to it or to persons in its territories. Each member so obligated agrees to compensate other members for any loss resulting from the difference between the par value of its currency on the date of the decision to liquidate the Fund and the value realized by such members on disposal of its currency.

SENATE VOTES 61-16 TO ADOPT BRETTON ACT

U. S. FIRST TO DO SO

Bill Returns to House, but Acceptance of Minor Changes Is Assured

MAJOR AMENDMENTS FAIL

Taft Proposal to Ban Nations With Currency Curbs Is Defeated After Long Debate

By JOHN H. CRIDER
Special to THE NEW YORK TIMES.

WASHINGTON, July 19 — The Senate passed the Bretton Woods bill by a vote of 61 to 16 this afternoon assuring United States membership in the first international institution in history designed to maintain stable currency exchanges and provide cooperative long-term credits for reconstruction and development.

All that remained for this country to put its final stamp of approval on the agreements reached a year ago at Bretton Woods, by representatives of forty-four nations, was acceptance by the House tomorrow of several Senate amendments and the signature of President Truman, both of which were foregone conclusions.

Thus, after four days of Senate debate and a year of public discussion on the complicated proposals, which involve ultimate investment by this country of $5,925,000,000 in an International Monetary Fund to stabilize exchanges and remove restrictions on currency transactions and a Bank for Reconstruction and Development, the Senate passed the bill by more than a two-thirds majority of those voting, which would have been required had the bill been presented as a treaty.

Barkley Congratulates Taft

Passed by the House on June 7 by a vote of 345 to 18, the bill had been expected to pass the Senate, but its most ardent supporters had not looked for such an overwhelming majority, particularly in view of the battle against the bill waged for four days by Senator Taft, Republican, of Ohio, for which he was congratulated on the floor today by his principal opponent, Senator Barkley.

Nineteen Republicans and one Progressive voted for the bill, and only two Democrats, Senators Wheeler of Montana and O'Daniel of Texas, opposed it.

Among the Republicans supporting the measure were Senators White of Maine, the minority leader, and Vandenberg of Michigan, a leading Republican supporter of the United Nations charter which comes up for debate Monday.

Before the Bretton Woods agreements can be regarded as effectively ratified, nations having 65 per cent of the quotas of the $8,800,000,000 fund and subscriptions to the $10,000,000,000 bank must accept the agreements and deposit the initially required parts of their quotas and subscriptions by Dec. 31. Original capital of the bank will be $9,100,000,000, but $10,000,000,000 is its contemplated eventual capitalization.

United States Is First to Ratify

This country was the first of the participating nations to ratify the agreements. Administration leaders have said that once the United States acted the others would rapidly follow suit.

There appeared to be no doubt that the prerequisite ratification would be obtained by the end of the year, but experts predicted that it would take from six to eighteen months for the two institutions to begin functioning.

Most of the debating period from 11:15 A. M. until passage of the bill at 5:13 P. M. was used in discussing a proposal by Senator Taft, providing that no member shall be entitled to use the fund's resources until it had removed all exchange restrictions on current transactions listed in Sections 2, 3 and 4 of Article VIII of the Fund Agreement.

Mr. Taft asserted that his amendment would make certain that the fund actually was used for the purpose of removing exchange controls, which was one of its stated objectives.

"It would destroy the whole purpose of the plan," Senator Barkley replied. "No man who has been very ill is expected to get up and walk right away. These countries which have been the principal victims of the war are not out of bed yet. They are not even convalescent."

The Kentuckian then explained that the "sterling area," which Mr. Taft had said would be used by the British for restrictive purposes, was similar to the "dollar area," in that countries in the "sterling area" did their principal trading with Britain and kept balances in London, just as countries in the "dollar area" did most of their trading with this country and kept balances in American banks.

"There was no aspect of the prewar sterling area arrangement which was contrary to the purposes of this fund," Mr. Barkley added.

When Senator Aiken, Republican, of Vermont, asked why there was so much criticism of the British and Russians, Mr. Taft said that the United States did most of her trading with the British, and that the United Kingdom and Russia had the next largest quotas in the fund to this country.

Senator Tobey, Republican, of New Hampshire, said that the Taft amendment would "hamstring" the whole arrangement, adding that the Ohioan had not read all of the section of the fund agreement relating to exchange controls but only that part permitting them to be retained during a five-year transitional period under constant surveillance of fund officials.

What he omitted to read, Mr. Tobey continued, was that the agreement required all members to end wartime exchange controls as soon as possible and put the fund officials under obligation to see that this was done.

"I would not impugn the good faith of Great Britain," Senator Tobey asserted.

"I am not questioning their good faith," Mr. Taft replied. "I am merely saying that under the agreement they are permitted to do these things."

Senator Barkley said that the exchange controls were put on when "Britain was all that stood between the rest of the world and Hitler."

Barkley Urges Flexibility

There must be flexibility in the Fund plan, he added, to enable Great Britain to work her own way out from under these controls.

The amendment would, in effect "serve notice on Great Britain that she couldn't belong to the Fund," Mr. Barkley asserted. Moreover, he added, it would require a reconvening of the forty-four nations to adopt the proposed amendment to the articles of agreement.

Senator Tunnell, Democrat, of Delaware, accused Senator Taft of making an "untrue statement" when he denied the amendment would keep Great Britain out of the Fund, and the Ohioan insisted that what Mr. Tunnell said was untrue.

Mr. Taft described the agreements as anything but final, pointing to a number of "reservations" taken to them by some of the Bretton Woods delegates. He frequently referred to Great Britain as "our greatest customer" who has "become practically an economic isolationist."

Senator Barkley replied that the "reservations" were nothing more than statements of what some of the nations represented at Bretton Woods "wanted but didn't get."

The amendment was defeated, 53 to 23, with ten Republicans voting with the Democrats.

Senator Ball, Republican, of Minnesota, offered an amendment requiring that the American representative on the fund ask its board to impose restrictions on any member which after three years had not removed exchange restrictions.

He said that the proposal would require no acceptance by the other forty-three nations and would not even assure that the board would accept the American's recommendation, but Mr. Barkley opposed the amendment primarily on the grounds of the "parliamentary situation," which finds the House without a quorum so that if objection should be made in the House, the whole legislative process would have to be repeated. The House, he added, would only accept the minor amendments of the Senate Banking Committee.

Vandenberg Supports Ball

Senator Vandenberg supported the amendment, stating that he could not see how it could possibly interefere with "the launching of this great adventure."

The amendment was rejected 46 to 29.

Other amendments voted down were as follows:

Two by Senator Millikin, Republican, of Colorado, one to prohibit the "scare currency" section of the fund agreement from being used as an excuse for violating international obligations and another to strike out entirely "the "scarce currency" section which gives the fund authority to "ration" currencies which become in excessive demand.

Another Taft amendment to refer the bill back to committee with instructions to report it back without provision for the bank, on the grounds that the latter duplicates the Export-Import Bank.

One by Senator Langer, Republican, of North Dakota, to prevent the resources of the fund or bank from being used for making armaments.

July 20, 1945

28 NATIONS SET UP THE BRETTON WOODS BANK

FUND ESTABLISHED

$8,800,000,000 Will Be Employed to Stabilize World Exchanges

BANK HAS 9 BILLION

Plans Rebuilding Loans —Russia Absent but May Sign Later

By JOHN H. CRIDER
Special to THE NEW YORK TIMES.

WASHINGTON, Dec. 27—The International Monetary Fund and the Bank for Reconstruction and Development came into being this afternoon when representatives of twenty-eight nations signed documents confirming that their Governments had ratified the Bretton Woods Agreements and deposited the nominal initial payment toward expenses of the organizations.

Although representatives of the Soviet Union signed the first documents at Bretton Woods in July, 1944, Russia was not among the twenty-eight signers today. There was no official indication of what Soviet action would be, but most officials expected that the U.S.S.R. would qualify and sign by the Dec. 31 deadline.

The International Monetary Fund is a new kind of world currency pool to maintain stable conditions of exchange as an essential prerequisite for a high level of international trade.

The Bank is a medium for international sharing of risks in the making of loans for world reconstruction and development. The Fund will have $8,800,000,000 in gold and currencies at the start, and the Bank initial subscriptions of $9,100,000,000.

The agreements provide that the seat of the institutions shall be in the country having the largest quotas and subscriptions (the United States) and it is confidently expected that the two institutions will be situated in or near New York City, now generally recognized as the financial capital of the world, unless the United Nations Assembly decides to place them at some other point, together with all other UNO organizations.

Fred M. Vinson, Secretary of the Treasury, who was vice chairman of the United States delegation to the Bretton Woods conference, signed the two documents in behalf of the United States at ceremonies in a "conference room" of the State Department that formerly served as the Navy Department Library.

Hailed as Mission in Peace

"We can be thankful," he said, "that the history we are now writing is not another chapter in the almost endless chronicle of war and strife."

He added that, on the contrary, it was "a mission of peace" for which the plenipotentiaries had gathered and, he said, "not just lip service to the ideals of peace—but action, concrete action, designed to establish the economic foundations of peace on the bedrock of genuine international cooperation."

The two documents were signed by the Ambassadors or Ministers of the twenty-eight countries, including France, which only ratified the agreements last night. Four other countries were ready to sign but unable for various reasons to do so.

These were Mexico, whose Ambassador had been grounded by weather on a flight to Washington; Czechoslovakia, whose Ambassador was ill and planned to sign the documents later at his embassy; and Peru, whose Ambassador was not sure at the last minute whether the action of his home government constituted complete ratification.

The signing nations were as follows:

Belgium, Bolivia, Brazil, Canada, China, Colombia, Costa Rica, Ecuador, Egypt, Ethiopia, France, Greece, Guatemala, Honduras, Iceland, India, Iraq, Luxembourg, Netherlands, Norway, Paraguay, Philippine Commonwealth, Poland, Union of South Africa, United Kingdom, United States of America, Uruguay and Yugoslavia.

Denmark to Sign Later

Henrik de Kauffmann, the Danish Minister, answered to the call for Denmark and handed Acting Secretary of State Dean Acheson a note informing him of the intention of Denmark to adhere to the two institutions, which Denmark was permitted to do by action of the Bretton Woods conference. Denmark will sign and become a member of the Bank and Fund after a quota in the Fund and a subscription to the Bank have been assigned to her.

The nations signing today represented not only more than the 65 per cent of the quotas of the Fnud, but constituted more than a majority of the forty-four nations attending the Bretton Woods Conference. The Fund agreement provided that countries having 65 per cent of the Fund quotas must ratify the agreements before Dec. 31, 1945, if this institution was to be created.

The nations signing today represented holders of about 80 per cent of the Fund quotas totaling $8,-800,000,000. The bank subscriptions, although not exactly the same as the Fund quotas, were nearly so.

Ceremony Is Impressive

The ceremony in the old Navy library room was impressive, if not even solemn, so much so that cameramen's flash bulbs went off faster than ever at the novelty of a smile on the lips of the Agent General for India, Sir Girja Shankar Bajpai, as he wrote his name on the documents.

During most of the period of the signing, Secretary Vinson chatted with the Earl of Halifax, the British Ambassador, who sat on his left.

Mr. Acheson, who presided, said he hoped the ceremonies would "not be regarded in any narrow way," since "the significance of what we do reaches far beyond the creation of these institutions" and was "symbolic of the ever-increasing cooperation between the nations of the world to bring about peace and a better life for all men."

When the signing had been completed he announced:

"I am pleased to announce that the agreements are now in full force and effect."

He introduced several persons who, he said, had played a major part in bringing the institutions into being. The first was Harry White, Assistant Secretary of the Treasury. Mr. Acheson said of him that "no one had done more." Mr. White is generally regarded as the principal author of the Fund agreement and is expected to be named American representative on the Fund board.

Mr. Acheson introduced former Secretary of the Treasury Henry Morgenthau Jr., who, he said, had been in charge of all of the preliminary work on the Bretton Woods institutions. Mr. Morgenthau, who was head of the United States delegation to Bretton Woods and chairman of the conference, likened the institutions to "another tree planted by the late President Roosevelt, which will grow throughout the years."

Officials said they did not believe that the institutions could be organized and put on an operating basis in less than six months.

Denmark Accepts Plan

COPENHAGEN, Dec. 27 (AP)—**Denmark has accepted the Bretton Woods monetary stabilization plan,** the Danish Foreign Office announced today.

Ratified by Iran's Parliament

TEHERAN, Dec. 27 (AP)—The Iranian Parliament today ratified the Bretton Woods monetary stabilization agreement.

December 28, 1945

MONETARY FUND BIDS NATIONS DEVALUE IF OTHER STEPS FAIL; TRUMAN URGES FREER TRADE

HINT TO CRIPPS SEEN

Pound Is Not Mentioned, but Experts Feel Aim Is to Prod Britain

48 COUNTRIES AT PARLEY

President Calls on Delegates to Remove the 'Obstacles' That Handicap Commerce

By H. WALTON CLOKE

Special to THE NEW YORK TIMES

WASHINGTON, Sept. 13 — Devaluation of currencies was recommended by the International Monetary Fund today as remedial action for any of its forty-eight member countries that are unable to solve their dollar deficiency problems by other methods.

The Fund's recommendation was contained in its annual report made public today at the opening session of the institution's fourth annual meeting. Financial leaders of the member countries are attending. The report did not specifically mention the British pound sterling, but there was little doubt in the minds of experienced observers that it was focused on Britain's dollar crisis.

Although the report referred only to "deficit nations" in general, it was considered by a great many persons here to be added gentle pressure for sterling devaluation.

Financial leaders of the United States, Britain and Canada concluded discussions here yesterday of the British economic problems. There was no mention, however, of a sterling devaluation. In fact, Sir Stafford Cripps, Britain's Chancellor of the Exchequer, had previously rejected proposals along this line.

Truman Pleads for Stability

President Truman, attending a joint meeting of Fund delegates with those representing the International Bank for Reconstruction and Development, said a stable international economy would be the greatest boon to world peace. He also urged dropping the "obstacles" to world trade.

He expressed hope that the representatives of the forty-eight member countries would go home thinking in terms of "cooperation on a world basis for the welfare of the world as a whole."

The President's remarks gave emphasis to the principal theme of this meeting — international cooperation and how it could help the economic recovery of dollar-deficient countries.

Before President Truman left the platform Maurice Petsche, France's Finance Minister, gave him a gavel made from a tree at Bretton Woods, N. H., where the Bank and Fund were conceived in 1944. President Truman smilingly assured the Finance Minister that he would use the gavel on any future occasion where he might be called upon to preside.

Fund's Report Significant

The Fund's report assumes added importance when considered in the light of the program, aimed at solving the British financial problems, that resulted from the three-power conference. Some United States officials believe that pound devaluation eventually must be adopted.

Devaluation of the pound, now valued officially at $4.03, would mean in terms of foreign trade a lowering of the price of British-made products. This, in turn, would be expected to increase exports and result in more dollars for Britain.

The subject of the pound's devaluation is expected to come before the Board of Governors of the Fund at their closed sessions, but it will be part of a discussion of the desirability of a general revaluation by debtor countries to increase their exports and encourage trade.

The International Bank for Reconstruction and Development, sister institution of the Fund, also is holding its annual meeting. The Bank emphasized in its annual report, filed with its Board of Governors this morning, that it could not provide the answers "to all or even a major part of the world's financial ills" through its lending powers.

Eugene R. Black, president of the Bank, stressed that it was "beyond both the purpose and the power of the Bank, for example, to cure the 'dollar shortage.'"

The articles of agreement of both the Bank and the Fund were drawn up by the United Nations Monetary and Financial Conference at Bretton Woods, N. H., in July, 1944.

It is the purpose of the Bank to act as a lending agency to its member countries by making or underwriting loans for reconstruction and industrial development. The primary purposes of the Fund are to facilitate the growth of international trade and to eliminate foreign exchange restrictions that hamper such trade.

Camille Gutt, managing director of the Fund, presented the institution's report to its Board of Governors. He stressed in a speech to the board that no nation alone could solve the financial ills of the world. "A large international effort will be necessary to arrive at a real settlement," he said.

"Further measures of restriction and discrimination offer no permanently satisfactory solution to [trade] payments difficulties,"

PRESIDENT AT MONETARY CONFERENCE

Mr. Truman receives from Maurice Petsche, French Finance Minister, a gavel made from a tree at Bretton Woods, N. H., where international agreements were reached in 1944 to found the World Bank and the Monetary Fund. Associated Press Wirephoto the Fund declared in its report. "A constructive solution to the payments problem requires the deficit countries to do all they can to make more of their output available for export, and to offer these exports at prices which will call forth greater demand in dollar markets."

The Fund also stressed that prolonged dependence on restrictions and discrimination would be likely to divide the world economy into economic blocs, each with its own price structure and each tending increasingly to insulate itself from the rest of the world. Such insulation would be required to protect the bloc's own inconvertible system by trade restrictions and exchange controls.

"The task of increasing dollar exports cannot be delayed in the hope that it can be quickly completed by some extraordinary effort at the eleventh hour," the Fund said. "The magnitude of the dollar payments problem requires that every constructive means should be used to meet it," the report added.

"For the creditor countries, this means maintaining high levels of national income, reducing the barriers to trade, and facilitating the flow of international capital. For the deficit countries, it means the reduction of their export prices to a competitive level, in order to meet as much as possible of their payments problem through the expansion of trade on a multilateral basis."

The Fund emphasized that the deficit countries "cannot afford to forego any suitable instrument, including any necessary exchange adjustment that could expand their dollar exports."

Where a very large price reduction in a country's goods is necessary to expand exports, "it would in many cases seem possible only through an adjustment in the exchange rate," the Fund added.

The Fund warned, in an apparent reference to Britain's efforts to balance trade accounts by her austerity program and import restrictions:

"It may be preferable for a country to change an unsuitable exchange rate through the machinery of Fund consultation rather than to subject its economy to the risks of serious deflation and unemployment or to impose restrictions that keep imports so low as to endanger its well-being and efficiency."

The Bank's annual report did not command the attention of that of the Fund because of the topical content of the latter's 122-page message. Mr. Black stated that the Bank now had the resources to help finance "all of the sound, productive projects in its member countries that will be ready for financing in the next few years, that can appropriately be financed through repayable foreign loans, and that cannot attract private capital."

The Bank' report emphasized the role the institution might play in building up the world's underdeveloped areas, as set forth in President Truman's Point Four program announced in his inaugural address.

Mr. Black stressed that foreign development financing preferably "should be derived mainly from private sources." He also was severely critical of proposals for "fuzzy," long-term, low interest loans which, he contended, were nothing more than international subsidies of "a disguised grant to the borrower."

The Bank's report described the salient features of eight loans that it had made during the past year, aggregating $191,600,000. Thus far, the Bank has made loans totaling $716,600,000 in France, the Netherlands, Belgium, Denmark, Luxembourg, Chile, Mexico, Brazil, Finland, India and Colombia. Twenty more reconstruction and development projects are now under consideration.

One of these is a loan of "moderate size" requested by Yugoslavia. The final loan is expected to be less than $250,000,000 suggested. Last week the Export-Import Bank granted a $20,000,000 loan to Yugoslavia.

September 14, 1949

WORLD FUND TELLS NATIONS TO REMOVE TRADE LIMITATIONS

Reminds Members They Will Need Permission After Next March to Curb Exchange

GAINS IN RESERVES CITED

Britain Seen as High on List of Countries Body Considers Able to Lift Restrictions

By FELIX BELAIR Jr.

Special to THE NEW YORK TIMES.

WASHINGTON, May 27—The International Monetary Fund notified its forty-nine member nations today that they would be required soon to eliminate or substantially modify exchange restrictions and other forms of discrimination against the trade of nations.

In its second annual report on exchange restrictions, the Bretton Woods agency reminded members that its special permission was required under the articles of agreement for signatory nations to retain exchange restrictions beyond March, 1952. Rather than await the deadline, the fund said, it soon will start discussions with member countries.

Without mentioning any countries by name, the Fund made it clear in its unanimous report that Britain was high on the list of nations it considered financially able to relax their complex systems of exchange controls. With quiet acquiescence of the United States Government, Britain has used the device to discriminate against Western Hemisphere products that must be paid for in dollars.

The case for early general compliance with the spirit of the Fund's basic agreement of 1944 was stated broadly in a letter of transmittal to members and the Governors of the fund by A. B. Overby, acting chairman of the executive board and acting managing director of the institution.

Cites Gain in Payments

"During the past year there has been considerable improvement in the balance of payments and reserve position of many countries," Mr. Overby said. "This improvement has in a number of cases been accompanied by a relaxation of restrictions on current payments.

"Generally speaking, however, the fund believes that the general improvement in the international financial position of many countries which has taken place warrants further relaxation of restrictions and reduction of discrimination."

Because all members of the agency's executive board must approve the language of its public reports, the approach to exchange restrictions was not nearly as sharp as many of its permanent staff would have preferred. In terms of economic diplomacy, however, the report was notable for its candor.

Inertia, fear of the future, protection of vested economic interests from outside competition and political bargaining practices were given as the reasons why some member nations retained exchange restrictions beyond the time when they were needed for financial reasons.

Lag Seen in Some Countries

The report noted with approval such progress as had been made during the past year toward relaxation of discrimination in trade but added:

"In many countries, however, the extent of this action could not yet appear to have been commensurate with the financial improvement.

"Especially, the marked improvement of the gold and dollar positions of many countries would seem to remove the basis of most currency discrimination on current transactions, which continues to be practiced to a considerable degree."

Under existing practices, unwanted imports are kept out of a given country by the simple device of refusing to make exchange available for the purpose. The basic agreement of the Fund permitted use of the device during the first five years of its operation because the post-war financial positions of the signatories were too strained to pay for the goods that importers otherwise might bring in.

In the case of Britain, for instance, the device is employed to keep out United States and other dollar products that sometimes are available at lower prices than articles imported from the countries with which Britain has accumulated substantial sterling balances. The United States Government has "winked" at the practice until now, although Britain is bound by treaty and separate financial agreements not to discriminate against United States products.

The report explained in this connection that one of the immediate effects of the military activity in Korea was "to accelerate the already occurring general improvement in the world payments situation, especially vis-a-vis the United States." It added:

"The same factors tending toward the elimination of the so-called 'dollar shortage' have worked toward the disappearance of the distinction between 'hard' currencies and 'soft' currencies, and of the distinction among various 'soft' currencies.

"The sterling area, in particular, has greatly bettered its position vis-a-vis many countries whose currencies were previously relatively 'hard.' Sterling has emerged as a much 'harder' currency. The previous tremendous gulf between 'hard' and 'soft' currencies, which has been a very substantial obstacle to the restoration of convertibility, seemed to be narrowing markedly at the end of 1950."

The continued demand for sterling products around the world has meant that the "overabundance" of sterling was a thing of the past, the report observed. This improvement was offset somewhat by the increasing liabilities in sterling Britain was incurring in parts of the sterling area through imports and through gold and dollar acquisitions by its exchange equalization account from sterling area earnings, it noted.

"But countries are now much less anxious to dispose of their sterling holdings," the report said, "and there is much less willingness on the part of holders of sterling to offer it for sale at considerable discounts than was previously the case.

"The greater demand for sterling has facilitated the developing settlement of the sterling balance problem. To the extent that the holders of these balances now want to hold them, the problem tends to disappear."

At the same time, the fund pointed out that the improvement in the payments position of member nations, and the increase in gold and dollar reserves of countries outside the United States had not been shared by all nations.

The fund anticipated in its report that many countries otherwise able to eliminate or modify restrictions and discriminatory practices would argue that retention of these policies was needed to protect their economies against the impact of rearmament programs.

"Historical experience indicates that greater efficiency or productivity in the economic field is encouraged by an international economic environment relatively free from hampering restrictions and discrimination," the fund said in reply.

May 28, 1951

AIMS VINDICATED BY FUND AND BANK

Former, Especially, Was Viewed Dubiously Once—Both Fulfill Big Roles

By PAUL HEFFERNAN

The hunger for more capital, experienced by nations big and small, rich and poor, capitalist and socialist ever since the end of World War II, is knocking at the door of the twin institutions set up at Bretton Woods.

The International Bank for Reconstruction and Development and the International Monetary Fund are by no means running out of money. But almost overnight, it seems, the major problems surrounding the functioning of these institutions have undergone dramatic change.

Only ten years ago the question was seriously raised whether the World Bank, as a long-term lender of capital, could perform any significant service in the post-war world under the rules adopted at Bretton Woods. And the opinion was widely expressed that the function of tiding nations over temporary shortages of foreign exchange, assigned to the Monetary Fund, had no place at all in the post-war world.

It Was Dispensable

It was even proposed in responsible financial circles that the fund be liquidated, or, at most, be continued as a subsidiary activity of the World Bank.

Today there is no question about the functions being fulfilled by the Bretton Woods twins. Both are leaving their stamp on history in a big and probably a lasting way.

Since 1946, membership in the bank and fund has doubled. The member nations then numbered thirty-four; today they number sixty-eight. Russia and Communist China are the only large nations that are outside.

Of the European non-members, most are the Russian satellites—Czechoslavakia, Poland, Hungary, Rumania, Bulgaria and Albania. Switzerland and Portugal are the only sizable non-Communist European nations that do not belong. Outside of some principalities and sheikhdoms, the other non-members are New Zealand, Nepal, Cambodia, Laos, Yemen and Bhutan.

By June 30 of this year, the bank had made 204 loans totaling $2,828,700,000 in forty nations. The fund over the same period had permitted thirty-five nations to draw a total of $3,100,000,000 to cope with exchange crises. Twenty-eight nations have used the fund's resources more than once.

More Capital on Way

The first formal steps probably will be taken at the New Delhi meetings this week to increase the capital resources of both lending agencies. The bank's subscribed capital is now $9,510,400,000, of which $3,175,000,000 represents the subscription of the United States. The capital subscriptions to the fund total $9,193,000,000, of which the United States share is $2,750,000,000.

While both the bank and the fund now see a need for adding to subscribed capital, the need varies with the function. For the bank a substantial increment in capital would serve largely as a guarantee against enlarged lending. Like most of the present subscribed capital of the bank, the new subscriptions might not be required in cash for years if ever. The reason is that the bank raises its lending money by selling bond issues in the public market. Most of the capital subscription is a stand-by security fund to meet the bank's obligations only if borrowers should default. Adding to the capital of the bank, then, need impose no financial strain on any member nation.

With the fund the problem is different. The fund gets its money only from capital subscriptions. For years these were virtually untouched. Suddenly in 1955, demands on the fund became substantial and frequent. As a consequence, the fund's uncommitted holdings of gold and convertible currencies shrank by July this year to $1,400,000,000.

Per Jacobsson, managing director of the fund, fears that this working balance is not enough if the fund is to fulfill its function under present international economic conditions. Here is how Mr. Jacobsson viewed the problem in a recent study:

Fund Held Inadequate

"The physical volume of world exports fell by 7 per cent from 1937 to 1947, but in the next ten years increased by 90 per cent, a rate of expansion almost unknown in the past. The prices of goods moving in international trade increased by 140 per cent between 1937 and 1957. Fluctuations in the balance of payments which may require use of the fund's resources are therefore potentially much larger now than when the fund quotas were established.

"If any lack of confidence were to set in, the potential movements of funds connected with the shifts in the financing of trade would likewise be larger. The fund's ability to provide assurance to its members and to act quickly on a massive scale if emergencies arise depends upon its having adequate resources, which have been made available in advance of any specific emergency. It is doubtful whether, with world trade greatly expanded in volume and value, the fund's resources are sufficient to enable it fully to perform its duties under the Articles of Agreement."

The Monetary Fund may thus be said to have at last come into the function for which it was created at Bretton Woods. With the Bank, however, a significant modification from the original blueprint has taken place.

At Bretton Woods, the Bank was viewed largely as a clearing house for public financial transactions. Loans could be made only to government bodies or to borrowers having the backing of a government guarantee. But with the passing of the years, the accent on World Bank lending is passing to undertakings—public or private—where the payoff of the loan can be related realistically to the productivity of the project financed. More and more, the loans are being made not to central governments, but to government-backed agencies charged with the burden of earning the debt redemption money.

World Trade and Economic Development Up for Review in New Delhi

Fabian Bachrach
Eugene R. Black
World Bank

The New York Times
Per Jacobsson
Fund

Information Service of India

This is the Vigyan Bhavan Hall in the capital of India, which will be the scene this week of the meetings of the governors of the International Monetary Fund, the International Bank for Reconstruction and Development and International Finance Corporation. Shown here are the principal executive officers of the organizations listed above.

Robert L. Garner
Corporation

Hubert Ansiaux
Fund

Jean Van Houtte
World Bank and Corporation

October 5, 1958

Old-Fashioned Fiscal Soundness Gains Adherents Around World

By EDWIN L. DALE Jr.
Special to The New York Times.

WASHINGTON, Oct. 3—Sitting at their desks cluttered with problems as well as papers, high officials of the twin institutions of Bretton Woods, N. H.—the World Bank and International Monetary Fund—have been allowing themselves a feeling of satisfaction this week.

It is the feeling that all over the world, developed as well as underdeveloped, a rather old-fashioned principle is increasingly accepted. In a word, this principle is that governments can do the best for their people only if they keep their budgets in control and use high interest rates aggressively when times require it.

It is the principle called "fiscal and monetary soundness" by those who believe in it. The bank and fund, and most of the member-government finance ministers and central bankers, are certain the principle works, and they feel they have conclusive evidence from numerous countries over the last decade to prove it.

Europe, of course, is the main case in point, but not the only one. For example, there are already signs that the "austerity" programs in Colombia, Chile and Argentina are beginning to pay off in those countries, partly in terms of foreign willingness to invest in them.

Two Exceptions

In any case, the point was regarded here this week as no longer subject to much debate. Country after country was willing to agree that the principle was right, even if the admission was given grudgingly in some cases.

But there was one clear-cut exception and one partial and wholly ironic exception.

The clear-cut exception was Brazil. Brazil simply does not agree with the rest. She believes the theory is wrong and harmful, or at least so her representative said. Brazil at the moment is in serious financial trouble.

The other, quite special, exception was the United States.

The official representative of the United States at the bank and fund meeting, Robert B. Anderson, the Secretary of the Treasury, agrees with it thoroughly. So does President Eisenhower. So does William McChesney Martin Jr., the chairman of the Federal Reserve Board.

But a majority of Congress apparently is not convinced, at least not yet, about the high-interest-rate part of it. Thus, in one important respect, the United States does not agree with it.

And one reason Congress is not convinced is that there exists in the United States a body of sophisticated opinion that genuinely believes much of the theory of "fiscal and monetary soundness" is mistaken. It is perhaps a minority body of opinion, but it is by no means negligible.

This body of opinion believes high interest rates are unnecessary and harmful. Its spokesmen, including some economists, have given intelligent Democrats in Congress the ammunition they needed to back up intellectually what they favored politically in any event.

The showdown issue, of course, was the Treasury's request for abolition of the 4¼ per cent interest-rate ceiling on long-term Government bonds. If this legal problem had not arisen, the Administration and Federal Reserve could have acted in the classic and old-fashioned manner, no matter what individual Congressmen might have felt and said.

But inasmuch as the issue has arisen, Congress will have the final say. The prevailing belief among both Americans and foreigners at this week's bank and fund meetings was that Congress would soon grant what the Treasury has asked and that the United States would join the parade. But predicting the course of Congress is a hazardous occupation.

Consequences Clear

To those who believe in the principle, like Secretary Anderson, the consequences of Congressional failure to accept it are clear: Inflation resumed; loss of gold; a dollar foreigners do not want and will not take; ultimately a weakening of the entire national strength, including military strength.

But to the doubters, this is all ridiculous. There are ways—all ridiculous. There are ways, they insist, to escape the need for high interest rates and falling Government bond prices, they hold the hardships that result from "soundness" are termed unnecessary.

For example, some believe that the Federal Reserve could buy Government bonds from time to time, abandoning its policy of dealing only in short-term bills, and offset any effects on the money supply by raising bank reserve requirements. The argument is often made that the Treasury's problem of managing the national debt could be solved without higher interest rates if bond buyers could be assured of more stable prices, presumably through Federal Reserve action.

The problem, of course, is highly complex. It involves matters such as bank-reserve requirements, techniques of operations, capital against current expenditures of the Government, intricate analyses of the savings process and the sources of economic growth.

The crucial point for the world of the future, however, is not the specific arguments but the fact that a substantial body of opinion in the United States, some of it informed and sophisticated, refuses to accept what most of the world's governments have come to accept.

October 4, 1959

MONETARY GROUP CHIDES MEMBERS

International Fund Seeks End of Currency Bars as Agreed To in Charter

Special to The New York Times.

WASHINGTON, June 1—The International Monetary Fund told some of its member countries today, without naming them, that time was running out on their supposedly temporary post-war currency restrictions.

The fund has sixty-eight members, only eleven of which have assumed full obligations under the fund's charter to keep their currencies fully convertible with the currencies of other countries. The United States and Canada are the only major industrial countries among the eleven.

The remaining fifty-seven are still living under an exemption that was set up to see them through post-war difficulties. The exemption means that they may tighten their restrictions when they feel it is necessary, without seeking the fund's approval.

Some of the fifty-seven, most importantly Germany and Britain, have taken big steps toward full convertibility, but none have taken the formal step of placing themselves in the position where their restrictions would be subject to approval of their fellow members.

Board Issues Statement

The fund's eighteen-man board of executive directors said in a statement today: "There has been in recent years a substantial improvement in the balance of payments and reserve positions of a number of fund members which has led to important and widespread moves to the external convertibility of many currencies."

"It seems likely," the directors said, "that a number of members either have reached or are nearing a position in which they can consider the feasibility of formally accepting the obligations" of maintaining supervised convertibility.

The message was conditioned with advice to members that they should not undertake these obligations unless they were in condition to stick to them.

The directors' statement was not expected to touch off a landslide of activity. Rather, the statement comes at a time when convertibility actions are increasingly likely to be taken of their own accord, perhaps by Germany, Britain and some other countries which have shown partciular economic vigor in recent years.

Countries which enjoy the exemption from fund approval for their currency restrictions must consult with the fund each year on the restrictions they maintain. Nations that do not enjoy the exeption have not been required to consult, but today's statement imposes that requirement on them.

June 2, 1960

OUTFLOW OF GOLD AT RECORD HEIGHT

Focuses Attention on U. S. Willingness to Put Its Fiscal House in Order

A record outflow of gold last year has focused attention on the willingness of the United States to put its fiscal house in order and the ability of her industry to compete in world markets.

By no stretch of language could the $2,300,000,000 drop in the United States monetary gold stock be described as a "run on the dollar." Foreign countries failed to liquidate existing dollar holdings as they had briefly during the sharp Korean war inflation. What is more, they continued to add to their short-term dollar assets. During the first nine months of 1958 these were increased more than $400,000,000.

In addition, the free world outside the United States added an estimated total of $C00,000,000 to its monetary reserves from newly mined gold and some shipments from the Soviet Union.

Free World Stronger

The free world gained strength in part because the United States declined to export its recession. In contrast to previous downturns, imports were held at a level only 3 per cent below that of 1957, based on data for the first three quarters. Raw materials imports remained large while imports of certain manufactured goods — notably small foreign cars—jumped substantially.

Exports, on the other hand, fell back from their 1957 heights to their more normal pre-Suez level. The 18 per cent drop reflected not only the end of emergencies boosting the demand for American petroleum and farm products but a moderate decline in Europe's own economic activity. This appeared to hurt imports from the United States more than proportionately.

Because of the greater decline of exports than imports, the balance of payments surplus accruing to the United States last year from merchandise trade dropped to an annual rate of $3,500,000,000 from $6,300,000,000 in 1957.

Spending by Tourists

The spending of a record number of United States tourists abroad, payments for shipping and insurance charges to concerns overseas, United States economic aid and loans, and a rising outflow of private American capital more than offset this surplus.

In addition, the recovery of British gold and dollar reserves after the Suez crisis and the 1957 "bear raid" on sterling brought back to Western Europe funds that had fled the area to the United States in fear of sterling devaluation.

Two other influences affected the size of the gold outflow from the United States. One was the fact that most of the payments gains were recorded by Western European nations, countries that traditionally maintain more of their reserves in gold than in dollars.

During the first nine months of 1958 Western European nations bought $2,000,000,000 of gold from the United States. Britain alone bought $800,000,000 worth. In part this reflected the improvement in her position with regard to raw-material supplying nations. For much of the year raw material prices declined while the price of Britain's exports held firm.

Another factor that may have influenced foreign decisions to buy gold rather than dollars was the decline in the yield of short-term United States Government securities the first half of the year, influenced by the Federal Reserve's policy of credit ease to combat the recession.

Currency Interdependence

If the gold outflow has reflected increased European strength rather than dollar weakness, it has emphasized to some who may have forgotten the interdependence of all free world currencies.

With the country's gold stock still $20,500,000,000, it amounts to more than half the free world's official gold holdings and exceeds by about $8,000,000,000 the 25 per cent gold coverage required against the note and deposit liabilities of the Federal Reserve System.

This $8,000,000,000 of "free" gold represented more than 57 per cent of the $14,000,000,000 of short-term dollar liabilities to foreign countries — about the same amount as held by foreign monetary authorities to meet exchange requirements or to intervene in foreign exchange markets. The remainder is held by foreign banks, businesses and individuals largely for financing international transactions.

A leading banker-economist observed recently, however, that the strong technical position of the dollar, like every other currency, depends ultimately on a sound and stable domestic economy. Roy L. Reierson, vice president and chief economist of the Bankers Trust Company, commented:

"Through most of the postwar era, the rebuilding of European economies and the corrollary strains on their exchange positions conferred on the United States dollar a key role in international trade almost independently of policies followed at home. This advantage cannot be expected to last indefinitely."

Two hazards, Mr. Reierson suggested, are emphasized by increasing sensitivity of the dollar to world opinion: the hazard to confidence resulting from continued large and uncontrolled Government deficits and the possibility that United States producers may price themselves out of world markets.

The New York Times

OUTWARD BOUND: *Armed guards take charge of gold bars to be moved in an armored car. During last year, the U. S. gold stock dropped more than $2,000,000,000.*

January 12, 1959

Why Dollars Go Abroad

Outflow of 'Volatile' Private Capital Reflects Sluggishness of U. S. Economy

By EDWIN L. DALE Jr.
Special to The New York Times.

PARIS, Nov. 17—A mass movement of "volatile" private capital, both American and foreign, across the Atlantic to Europe has drastically worsened the United States balance of international payments this year, mostly since June.

This factor, still partly obscured in the official figures, is the major reason behind yesterday's sweeping orders by President Eisenhower aimed at reducing the deficit in the balance of payments. Three recent comments by European bankers give an idea of what has been happening.

News Analysis

A Swiss banker said: "We worked overtime all summer taking on and handling new American accounts. These people wanted their money in Europe."

A British banker commented: "The flood of money coming in here because of our high interest rates was swollen recently by money coming in to buy gold. A good deal of both is American, and a good deal more is foreign money which had been invested in New York."

A German banker declared: "Money is so tight here that many of our big firms have been borrowing abroad, including in New York."

If conditions were different—if those three statements could not have been made—the deficit in the United States balance of payments this year would probably have been no higher than $2,000,000,000, instead of almost $4,000,000,000.

The mass movement of volatile private capital, which has disrupted the situation, has been caused by three principal factors.

U. S. Economy Sluggish

The first and second are related, both stemming from the sluggish, recession-like performance of the United States economy.

This performance has meant, first, low interest rates in the United States. With Europe booming, rates have been high in some centers here, London and Frankfurt above all. Money seeking an interest return came east to Europe, while European borrowers sought loans in New York.

Second, the sluggishness of the American economy, with its rather dim outlook for the near future, has meant a weak performance by the New York stock market. With European currencies now as hard as the dollar, with the United States no safer than Europe in the missile age and with European stock markets booming until early September, both foreigners and Americans did not hesitate to sell stocks in New York and buy in Europe.

Finally, there was distrust of the dollar. As more capital flowed out, the bigger the United States payments deficit became, and the bigger the gold loss. Every gold loss figure was prominently published.

The movement "fed on itself." Other foreigners and Americans pulled their money out of New York and sent it abroad, some to buy gold.

This movement of capital is not directly related to the continuing "invasion" of Europe by American companies. The number of deals and agreements continues to mount, but they involve a remarkably small outflow of dollars, at least up to now.

As an illustration, the offer by the Ford Motor Company to buy out its British minority shareholders for $364,000,000 would cost the United States balance of payments in that one transaction about as much as the entire flow of corporate dollars to the European Common Market in 1959 and 1960.

New corporate dollar investment in all Western Europe last year was $466,000,000—a relatively small item in a payments deficit of $3,800,000,000.

The problem this year has been one of individual funds and short-term bank lending funds. Will this mass outflow, costing as much as $2,000,000,000 this year in the United States payments accounts, continue?

The word "volatile" provides part of the answer. What goes out can come back. A great deal of it will certainly come back—with a big "plus" for the United States balance of payments—when the American economy shows an upturn.

There are already a few faint signs that the flow may be slowing down. If so, the reasons are probably that interest rates in Europe have begun to decline, and European stock markets have, on the whole, stopped rising.

Improvement Expected

It is not impossible, in the view of some students of the problem, for the United States deficit, running at a rate of $4,300,000,000 a year in the July-September quarter, to drop almost to zero for a while next year if the capital flow should be reversed.

President Eisenhower's measures were aimed at tackling the more permanent items of the deficit. They were presumably taken for two reasons.

One is that, even with all the "volatile" items removed, there remains a deficit of about $2,000,000,000, despite a major increase this year in the United States surplus of exports over imports.

The combination of United States military expenses abroad, foreign aid, tourists expenditures, remittances abroad of dollars by United States immigrants and "true" long-term corporate investment abroad remains larger than the export surplus.

The second reason is that the decisions may help confidence in the dollar, and thus help cut down the "volatile" outflow.

The measures are expected to save about $1,000,000,000 a year, starting next year. If they do, they will cut the "true" deficit almost in half. They will give some pain abroad, but it is easily sustainable pain in the present state of European business.

However, if for any reason the volatile capital outflow should continue, the measures will be only a drop in the bucket.

November 18, 1960

GOLD SOARS AGAIN ON LONDON BOARD

Price Rises to About $35.60 in Active Trading for the Largest One-Day Gain

MARKET TERMED 'WILD'

Decline in Confidence in the Dollar Called a Factor—Zurich Demand Noted

By THOMAS P. RONAN
Special to The New York Times.

LONDON, Oct. 19—The dollar price of gold moved up again today on the London bullion market after one of the busiest sessions the market has seen since it reopened on March 22, 1954.

"It was a pretty wild market," one of the major dealers said.

Because the market was so active, he said, it was difficult to say just what the top price was but it was about $35.60 a fine ounce. It might be more accurate, he added, to say it was in the $35.55 to $35.65 range.

Rise Sets a Record

Not only was this the highest price since the London market reopened in 1954, but it was the largest price rise ever recorded in one day. The 8-cent-an-ounce rise yesterday to $35.33 was the previous biggest one-day gain.

Again most of the demand came from the Continent and particularly from Zurich. Market sources said that a decline of confidence in the stability of the United States dollar undoubtedly contributed to the demand but that there were other reasons. "An accumulation of circumstances" was the way one source put it.

Dealers here are inclined to accept reports from Zurich that Swiss bankers have advised their foreign customers to buy gold for deposit there. This would save the customers the 1 per cent commission charged in Switzerland on deposits of foreign funds.

The Swiss Government directed the imposition of that charge last summer and decreed that no interest be paid on foreign funds deposited in Switzerland. These moves were to stem the inflow of "hot" money, that is money attracted by favorable interest rates.

Gold Price Rise Foreseen

This advice, it is thought, proved more palatable because of the growing belief in Europe that the United States Treasury would be forced to increase the price at which it buys and sells gold. This is $35 a fine ounce plus a commission of ¼ of 1 per cent.

This belief has persisted despite the repeated denials by United States authorities that they would do so. The continuing loss of gold from United States reserves and the deficit in the United States' balance of payments, that is in its over-all dealings with the rest of the world, have encouraged this belief.

Other factors believed to be contributing to the demand for gold were uncertainty about the economic situation in the United States and other parts of the world and the downward trend in stock markets on Wall Street, here and on the Continent.

It is thought that investors, wary of putting their money into stocks, are turning to gold partly because they consider it a safe investment and partly because they are speculating on a price increase.

Most of the dealing in gold is

through banks, and consequently it is not known here just who is placing the orders.

The London Times said editorially this morning that there was nothing to prevent the United States Federal Reserve authorities from intervening in the market to bring the price down.

But it noted that this had not been their custom, and said they might feel "that to risk prestige in one direction is no improvement in risking it in another. These authorities might feel that the United States' gold reserves, despite the losses, were still ample enough to ride out a short-lived speculative cycle, the paper said.

U. S. Gold Stock Dips 21 Million

Foreign governments and central banks purchased $21,213,-971 in gold from the United States Treasury last Friday, according to the Treasury's daily statement published yesterday. At $18,582,768,426, the monetary gold stock now is down about $873,000,000 since the first of the year.

October 20, 1960

BONN NOMINATED TO INCREASE AID

Big West German Reserves of Gold Held Basis for Rise in Foreign Assistance

By PAUL HEFFERNAN

If the United States has lost $6,000,000,000 of monetary gold since 1948, where has the gold gone?

If the United States ever is to reduce its financial aid to needy and underdeveloped nations, what other Free World nation is best suited to pick up the tab?

The answer to both questions is the same—Western Germany.

In 1948, when the United States had $24,000,000,000 of gold, the West German Federal Republic had negligible gold reserves. Today, with United States gold reserves down to about $18,500,000,000, those of West Germany total $6,500,000,-000.

United States money, to the extent that it reflects the productivity and balance of the basic United States economy, is about as strong today as it was in the world-wide "dollar shortage" of less than a decade ago. The chief measure of relative national productivity is the extent to which sales abroad exceed purchases from abroad. If the United States is losing gold it isn't for this reason. The United States is selling abroad in excess of $3,000,000,000 a year more in goods and services than it is buying.

Leakage Is Source

The gold drain rather comes from things such as extraordinary financial aid and fringe "leakage." The "leakage" gets scant attention because it consists mainly in the losses sustained by United States investors abroad, whether in property expropriated or in debts not paid. In Cuba, for example, more than $1,000,000,000 of United States property has been expropriated during the last year and most of the normal United States income from that country has been cut off.

It is the element of "leakage" that urges the nomination of Western Germany, with its embarrassment of swollen monetary reserves, to follow the lead of the United States as a generous Free World financier of underdeveloped economies. This is not only a mandate of economics but a compulsion of equity.

The reason lies in the fact that Germany's overswollen hoard of gold adds up, by and large, to what was forgiven Germany in the way of indebtedness by the United States Government and by private investors—mostly from the United States—after World War II.

Before the war, Germany owed to the outside world 13,-500,000,000 marks payable in gold. By reason of the willingness of Germany's creditors to forego full enforcement of the gold clause, the German debt was cut to 9,600,000,000 Deutsche marks. It was reduced further to 7,300,000 as a consequence of the decision of creditors at the London debt conference to forgive one-third of the accumulated interest arrears. Moreover, future interest payments were reduced to 75 per cent of the original contractual rate.

The total saving to Germany from such sources — that is, from the savings of foreign investors and the debt contract income due them — came to 6,200,000,000 Deutsche marks or about $1,500,000,000.

Another windfall — this one amounting to 9,000,000,000 Deutsche marks—came to Germany when the United States Government reduced its claims for post-war aid from 16,-000,000,000 to 7,000,000,000 Deutsche marks. The United States money equivalent to this debt forgiveness was about $2,-200,000,000.

The earning power of this $3,700,000,000 total of forgiven debt capital figured at 5 per cent interest over the last eight years equals about $1,500,000,-000 more, swelling the total German windfall stemming from creditors' gifts to more than $5,000,000,000.

Windfall Compounded

If accounts could be struck there, the base for Germany's financing foreign aid would be striking enough. But the windfall has a way of compounding itself. A great part of the post-war debt forgiven by the United States Government had a counterpart paid by internal German interests to the Bonn Government in satisfaction of advances granted by the Bank fuer Wiederaufbau, a state reconstruction agency. These counterpart funds have since been loaned out at high interest rates.

An instance of how debt capital forgiven by the United States was reloaned by West Germany at a high rate is the loan of 300,000,000 Deutsche marks — about $75,000,000 — granted by Germany to Greece largely to repay post-war debts owed by Greece to German industrial interests.

West Germany saw fit to charge Greece 6 per cent for the financial accommodation at the same time that Greece asserted it was unable to resume interest payments on bonds payable in United States dollars and British sterling that have been in default ever since German armies overran Greece in 1941. Much of the money was borrowed originally by Greece from private investors in the League of Nations era following World War I to reimburse the United States Government for outlays made in resettling Greek refugees from Turkey.

So go the incredible financial miscarriages of the post-war period. The war victor pays reparations to the loser by forgiving debt. The loser lends out the forgiven debt capital in the land he ravaged. The victim of the ravagement pays 6 per cent to the war ravager for the use of capital donated by the war victor. Finally, the war victim keeps defaulting on what he owes to those interests—both war allies and private investors —who repatriated his refugees of World War I and redeemed him from the disgrace of military conquest in World War II.

West Germany was not the only European nation to benefit from the forgiveness of debts owed to the United States Government. The specially privileged position of the Bonn Republic stems from the fact that the private debts of German business enterprises to non-German private investors also were scaled down, a windfall not shared by most beneficiaries of Marshall Plan aid. This distinctive $1,500,000,000 of private debt capital assigned by non-German creditors to German debtors, augmented by interest earnings, would seem to constitute a suitable European fountain for diffusing financial aid to the under-developed world.

October 30, 1960

EUROPEANS URGED TO USE IDLE FUNDS

Dillon Calls for Shift From Reliance on New York as Source of Capital

CITES U.S. DOLLAR DRAIN

Monetary Meeting in Rome Hears Bid for Steps to End Payments Deficit

By PAUL HOFMANN

Special to The New York Times.

ROME, May 18—Secretary of the Treasury Douglas Dillon urged prosperous Western Europe today to "mobilize its own capital resources" rather than rely on the New York money market.

Every nation with a stake in stable international finances has a strong interest in the "elimination of the lingering United States payments deficit," he said.

Discussing the international capital market, Mr. Dillon said that he would be "uneasy" so long as almost all of the world must look to the United States as its principal if not only source of capital for development.

The balance of payments is the relationship between a nation's total payments to foreigners and total receipts from foreigners.

Sees Idle Funds in Europe

The Secretary insisted that huge amounts of money were idle in Europe for lack of institutions and techniques to put them to work. He emphasized that America's role as banker for the rapidly growing European economy might at this time strain the United States' financial position.

Mr. Dillon advocated the development of a "broader, more fluid international market for capital" as an essential part of the United States' effort to defend the dollar in the interest of the West as a whole.

Mr. Dillon addressed more than a hundred leading American and European financial executives at the end of the four-day ninth annual monetary conference of the American Bankers Association here.

Confidence in Dollar Noted

American conference sources said that confidence in the United States economy and in the stability of the dollar had prevailed in the discussions behind closed doors.

According to one report, representatives of central banks of West European countries participating in the Rome meeting reached an informal agreement that present exchange rates should be maintained and that there should be no devaluation or revaluation of any currencies at this time.

Mr. Dillon's address was cautiously optimistic.

He emphasized that the United States was determined and able to continue giving essential military assistance and economic aid abroad. "Even as we meet today, American troops are deploying in Thailand in response to a request for assistance" against Communist aggression, he said.

The Secretary recalled that the non-Communist world's monetary system rested on the full acceptability of the dollar as a supplement to gold in financing world trade with "no practicable alternative in sight."

Mr. Dillon singled out "the current $25,000,000 borrowing by the European Coal and Steel Community" as a case of a financing operation that could and should be performed in Europe.

The Secretary said that many European borrowers would come to New York even if United States interest rates were higher, because they could not raise money in Europe. He warned that dollars saved in unessential defense and aid and dollars earned in trade "could too easily be drained away in an accelerating outflow of American capital."

Mr. Dillon emphasized he did not suggest that the United States should cease to export capital. Money going abroad in search of higher gross return "will in the long run serve the investor, the United States and the recipient country alike," he said.

Legislation Backed

However, the Secretary backed proposed legislation to bar the flight of American dollars into foreign tax havens. He also said that the overcrowding of the New York money market by Western European borrowers was unfair to underdeveloped countries that hoped to attract American investors.

Mr. Dillon noted that residents of only a few West European countries today were free to invest abroad wherever and in whatever form they wished, and he urged European governments to ease restrictions on external capital flow.

American conference sources said that Mr. Dillon's recommendations were received with great interest by the European bankers present. These sources emphasized that American financing houses could play a useful role in partnership with European banks in developing new mechanisms and methods for mobilizing European funds.

Views on Kennedy Action

Most European experts who had attended the conference were described as "favorable" to the resolute intervention of the United States Administration in business as exemplified by President Kennedy's action to prevent an increase in steel prices.

However, many of the European conference participants were reported to be worried about the ability of the United States to maintain the level of its industrial costs and suggested increased Administration initiative in collective labor-management bargaining.

Swiss bankers here were in contrast to the majority of the European participants by their markedly more sober appraisal of the American economy, United States sources said. The Swiss were said to be unfavorably impressed by recent declines on the American stock markets and tended to consider United States economic expansion at an end for the time being.

May 19, 1962

U.S.-BRITISH PACT TO CUT GOLD LOSS

Plan Calls for Exchanging Each Other's Currencies to Be Used as Reserve

$50,000,000 IS SWAPPED

London Has Agreed to Keep Dollar Stock Instead of Converting to Metal

Special to The New York Times.

PARIS, June 3—As if by the wave of a magic wand, Britain and the United States last Thursday increased each other's gold and foreign exchange reserves by $50,000,000. They did it by swapping each other's currencies, with each currency counted as reserves by the other.

In making the swap, they put in place the keystone of a daring new international system designed to help protect United States gold reserves. Highly authoritative sources called the United States-British agreement a "major break-through" in setting up the new system.

Among other things, this is the first time that Britain has agreed to hold on to a sizeable amount of dollars without converting them immediately into gold.

Move Is One of Series

The essence of the new system is a series of currency swaps between the United States and the main European countries. For the United States, the result is that foreign currency holdings can, if desired, be used to "pay for" part of the deficit in the international balance of payments instead of having most of the shock taken by the gold reserves.

Assuming continued gradual improvement in reducing the payments deficit, it now seems possible that United States gold losses for the rest of this year will be extremely modest.

No one intends to carry the new system of creating reserves out of thin air to excessive limits. The maximum being talked about is a sum equal to 1 per cent of the domestic money supply of the participants in the scheme. This could mean creation of foreign currency holdings by the United States of nearly $1,500,000,000.

New Power Created

With this "mass of maneuver," the United States authorities at any time, by intervening on the foreign exchange markets, can choose to diminish the gold-effect of the payments deficit.

For example, suppose interest differentials or some other factor should cause another large flow of funds to London. Normally this results automatically in the Bank of England taking in dollars, which it promptly converts to gold. That happened in the first quarter of this year.

Now, if the Federal Reserve so decides, it can sell pounds in the market during such a period. The effect would be fewer dollars taken in by the Bank of England and reduced United States gold losses.

In such a situation, the effect on Britain of her payments surplus, expressed in the inflow of funds, would be a reduction in her liabilities — the pounds held by the United States authorities—instead of an increase in her assets. For the United States the effect of the payments deficit would be a reduction in foreign exchange assets instead of a reduction of gold assets.

When the United States moves back into balance of payments surplus, it is already the announced policy to build up foreign currency holdings further by outright purchases in the foreign exchange markets. In that situation, for the European countries in deficit, the deficit would produce an increase in their liabilities instead of a decrease in their assets. Once again, total world reserves would rise.

It is being stressed on all sides that the new system is planned to be modest in size, certainly at this stage. It is also stressed that the system is not designed as a substitute for correction of the United States payments deficit.

But it does represent a co-operative effort to help preserve the United States gold stock, which in the end is the backstop for world monetary order.

June 4, 1962

PRESIDENT SIGNS GOLD-COVER PLAN

Action Repeals Requirement for Backing of Deposits

By EILEEN SHANAHAN
Special to The New York Times

WASHINGTON, March 4 Legislation partially repealing the gold-cover requirement for United States money was signed into law by President Johnson today.

The new law, which was enacted in the exact form that the Administration asked for, will release about $1.8 billion worth of gold for use in meeting foreign demands for it and for providing support for the expanding money supply needed by an expanding economy.

The measure releases this amount of gold by repealing the requirement that the Government hold an amount of gold equal to 25 per cent of the reserve deposits placed with Federal Reserve Banks. The companion requirement of a 25 per cent gold cover for most paper money in circulation still stands.

If both aspects of the gold-cover requirement had continued in force, a limit to further expansion of the domestic money supply would soon have been reached.

As of last week, the $14.9 billion in gold owned by the Treasury amounted to 27.8 per cent of the paper money in circulation and bank deposits with the Federal Reserve.

With the gold requirement against Federal Reserve deposits now removed, the ratio of available gold to the money for which gold backing is still required is now about 42 per cent. This means that the United States now has considerable leeway to meet foreign demands for gold and to supply gold backing for currency out of the existing stock of gold.

Foreign demands for gold have arisen out of the fact that the United States has been spending more abroad than it takes in from foreign sources, thus running an international payments deficit and leaving dollars in the hands of foreign governments and central banks, which sometimes turn them in for gold at the fixed price of $35 an ounce.

Some level of continuing foreign demand for gold will presumably persist as long as there is a payments deficit.

The Administration pressed Congress today for action in two separate areas designed to help reduce the payments deficit.

Undersecretary of the Treasury Frederick L. Deming went before the House Banking Committee to request an indefinite extension of the present emergency authority banks have to pay higher interest rates on time deposits of foreign central banks than on domestic deposits.

The higher interest rate is designed to keep the deposits in United States banks.

Deputy Attorney General Ramsey Clark appeared before the House Antitrust subcommittee to ask for limited exemption from antitrust prosecution for banks acting jointly in compliance with the Administration's program to reduce the volume of foreign lending by banks.

Subcommittee members indicated they felt the exemption was too loosely drawn and would require some amendments.

March 5, 1965

CAPITAL DIALOGUE HEARD IN ZURICH

Impact of U.S. Concerns on Supply of Funds Debated

By RICHARD E. MOONEY
Special to The New York Times

ZURICH—The crush of American companies trying to raise money in Europe for expansion of their overseas operations led a British investment banker to observe last week that "the patient"—the financial markets on this side of the ocean—is suffering from "high blood pressure."

In reply, an American investment banker stationed here commented: "Before further preparations take place for the funeral, may I point out that the patient is taking a short stroll outside the clinic."

The root of this dialogue is Washington's curbs on the outflow of capital. "Voluntary" in name only, the curbs have forced American companies to seek funds abroad.

They continue to borrow heavily, through private channels and in unknown amounts, from the American and European banks here and from other institutional and individual investors. Publicly, they have sold about 30 issues of bonds and convertible debentures in the last nine months, for a total of $700-million.

The visible borrowings—the public issues of bonds and debentures—have been an increasingly sore point in European financial circles for several months.

Complaints Noted

Many bankers have complained that these issues, most of them by American giants, were skimming the cream of the available money and making it harder for European companies to raise funds.

An official of the Common Market's Executive Commission in Brussels, Claudio Segré, has been trying to arouse interest in a new plan to sell stock in American companies' overseas interests when they need funds, instead of more and more bonds. He has some support among financiers here, but no takers yet among the American companies.

As the British and American bankers indicated, the bond and debenture markets have recently been unsettled, to say the least. When the Chrysler Corporation tried and failed to place a $50-million issue in mid-March, the reaction in some quarters was that the Americans had finally destroyed themselves and Europe, too. The drop in prices on the New York Stock Exchange hit the convertible issues at the same time.

Since then, W. R. Grace & Co. has sold an issue postponed by the earlier congestion. The market for outstanding issues has improved, but the line of borrowers planning to test the market soon remains unusually short.

A London banker, Siegmund Warburg of S. G. Warburg & Co., is the latest to suggest some form of control for the flood. He proposed that the principal European central banks, or the Bank for International Settlements, take charge and patrol both the timing and the size of issues.

Mr. Warburg conceded that the central banks might be unwilling to tangle with this. The settlement bank has been nominated before, and is not interested. Another idea sometimes advanced is that the European banking community itself undertake the project.

There is considerable doubt that it would work in any of these forms. Zurich bankers point out that their Government does not permit them to underwrite any issues that are originated outside Switzerland, but that at least half the sales are done through here. In other words, this big slice of the business would not even be represented in any control committee.

It is generally agreed that only Washington could wield effective control, and that it will not, for obvious reasons. United States controls on foreign borrowing, coupled with the existing curbs on funds flowing out, would amount to a virtual embargo on United States investment abroad.

Reports of official protests to Washington on this subject have been somewhat exaggerated. The protesting has been limited to questioning in one of the international groups of financial officials who meet each month to survey the international monetary situation. The Swiss and Belgians have been asking the most questions.

Canada Nudged by U.S.

Washington has already exerted some control, however, in nudging Canada to stop Canadians from buying these issues with funds they pull out of New York. There are no statistics on how much of this had been going on, but in any amount it was no help to the United States balance of payments.

Canada, which enjoys exemption from the interest equalization tax for Canadian borrowings in the United States markets, had little choice but to follow the nudge. There will be some effect from closing off this source of funds, but the amount is unpredictable.

Actually, Chrysler's failure may turn out to have been an effective regulator itself. Julian Pierre Kozul, European vice president of the First National City Bank of New York, observed in a speech here Friday that some borrowers had been acting like hoarders. Some, he said, "have asked for amounts which cover far more than their current needs."

Mr. Kozul noted that until the recent blow-up, the market had been digesting these issues in much greater volume than many Europeans believed possible. He thought that the European capital market would continue "fairly tight" now, but expected that there would still be several hundred million dollars more of American issues before the year is out.

April 3, 1966

BRITAIN DEVALUES POUND TO $2.40 TO AVERT A NEW ECONOMIC CRISIS; SEVERE RESTRAINTS ARE IMPOSED

REDUCTION IS 14.3%

Curbs Include a Basic Interest Rate of 8% and Spending Cuts

By ANTHONY LEWIS
Special to The New York Times

LONDON, Nov. 18—Britain devalued the pound tonight.

The official value was lowered 14.3 per cent, from $2.80 to $2.40. The announcement was made at 9:30 P.M. (4:30 P.M., New York time) and the new rate was effective immediately.

The devaluation meant that a long struggle to maintain a chronically weak currency at the rate set in 1949 had ended in defeat for the Labor party Government. The consequences for the British people and for the world monetary system just began to be sensed tonight.

The move was made in an attempt to lower the cost of British goods in foreign countries in the hope that exports would rise, and to increase the price of imports in the hope that they would be reduced. The result would be a better balance between exports and imports.

Rumors a Factor

A secondary consideration in the decision to devalue the pound was the hope that the move would end the uncertainty and talk of devaluation that have been common in financial circles recently.

The politics as well as the economics of Britain will be shaken by the decision. It represents a devastating blow to the Government, and especially to Prime Minister Wilson and his Chancellor of the Exchequer, James Callaghan.

Along with the devaluation the Government, ordered all banks and stock exchanges to remain closed Monday. It also outlined stringent measures designed to slow the economy: higher interest rates and taxes and reductions in Government spending.

At the same time Britain sought huge new international credits totaling $3-billion. The money will be used to replenish her depleted reserves of gold and dollars and to give strength to sterling in the days of readjustment ahead.

Of the total borrowing, $1.6-billion has been pledged by some of the world's leading central banks. The United States is in the pool, but it was not known tonight whether France had agreed to join.

The remaining $1.4-billion has been requested from the International Monetary Fund. A statement from the fund tonight said that Britain had been assured of "prompt and sympathetic consideration" and that a "favorable decision" was expected in a few days.

The lending arrangement was worked out with central bankers in the Group of Ten — the leading countries in world monetary affairs—who were meeting in Paris this week.

The urgent effort was to stop the deterioration of confidence in a major world trading currency. The pound is second only to the dollar in its use for international transactions and its place in many national reserves.

The pound was weak, basically, because Britain continued to import more than she exported.

Drain Turns to Panic

In the last week, events turned the chronic drain into panic. A record trade gap of $300-million was reported for October. As rumors of loans and devaluation circulated without official action, large amounts of Britain's reserves of gold and foreign currencies were poured out in an effort to keep the pound up to the official rate despite selling pressure.

The United States and Britain's friends in Europe were informed a few hours before the devaluation announcement. Their reactions quickly began to indicate what would happen in the world monetary system.

Ireland announced that she would devalue as Britain had, and Israel said she would make an announcement tomorrow. Denmark and Finland said they would devalue to some extent, and Norway may follow suit.

The countries in the sterling area, those that use the pound for trading, will differ in their reactions. In the old days they would have devalued almost automatically with Britain. Now such countries as South Africa and the rich Arab states are economically stronger than Britain.

No Market Devaluation

The Common Market's six members — France, West Germany, Italy, Belgium, the Netherlands and Luxembourg—will not devalue, demonstrating the very strength that makes Britain want to join the market.

The devaluation announcement was a sudden and dramatic turn after days of official silence in the midst of chaos in the financial markets.

Although the experts knew

United Press International Cablephoto

AT 10 DOWNING STREET: Prime Minister Wilson as he waved good-by to guests yesterday in London. Later, his Labor Government's decision to devalue the pound was announced by James Callaghan, Chancellor of the Exchequer.

that devaluation was a real possibility after years of abstract discussion, the actual news came as a surprise. The British Broadcasting Corporation continued for an hour with a Doris Day movie on television. Early editions of Sunday newspapers had such headlines as "Why Are We Waiting?"

For three years, since the Labor party took over the Government, it has asked the British people for sacrifice to maintain the value of the pound. In a moment tonight, all the sacrifice — unemployment, lagging wages and a stagnant economy —seemed a wasted effort.

Devaluation Rejected

Moreover, Mr. Wilson and Mr. Callaghan had repeatedly rejected the prospect of devaluation.

On July 24 the Prime Minister said that those who started rumors about devaluation were "wasting their time." The same day the Chancellor said that to devalue would be to "break faith" with governments abroad and "bring down the standard of life of our own people."

The possibility that the Labor party itself would turn against the authors of the old policy could not be excluded. Under the parliamentary system Mr. Wilson could be forced from office by losing the support of his own party.

Edward Heath, the Conservative leader, was quick to denounce the Government tonight. He pointed out that the last devaluation of the pound, from $4.03 to $2.80 in 1949, also took place under a Labor government.

NEWS OF THE WORLD

DEVALUED—AND BANK RATE 8%

SUNDAY EXPRESS

The three fatal errors

IT'S DEVALUATION—BY 14.3 PER CENT

POUND IS DEVALUED: IT'S DOWN 14%

The People

'I saw the last days of THE MOST EVIL MAN ON EARTH'

SUNDAY TELEGRAPH

THE POUND DEVALUED BY 14.3 p.c.

Spending Cuts:

Huge Loan:

Bank Rate 8 p.c.

Sunday Mirror

How the nation knows the grim facts—official

DEVALUATION AND A LOAN!

United Press International Cablephoto

TODAY'S HEADLINES: London papers report the news

Move Is Condemned

"I utterly condemn the Government for devaluating the pound," Mr. Heath said. "Twice in 20 years disastrous Socialist policies and incompetent Labor ministers have brought about devaluation, created hardship at home and discredited Britain abroad."

A Liberal member of Parliament, Richard Wainwright, called for a new Chancellor of the Exchequer. He said devaluation had come about "in the worst possible way—in a great scramble, surrounded by something close to panic."

The Sunday Express, a Conservative newspaper, said in an editorial: "What should Mr. Wilson do next? Just one thing. Quit."

The pro-Labor Sunday Mirror said devaluation stood for "disaster and disillusion."

The other measures announced by the Government tonight made it clear that the public would have to suffer as part of the price of economic readjustment. These were the major directives:

¶The country's basic interest rate, the bank rate, will rise to an extraordinary 8 per cent from 6½ per cent in an effort to slow down economic activity. In addition, banks will have to limit their loans except for such urgent needs as exports.

¶The Government will cut defense spending next year by more than £100-million, or $240-million at the new rate. Domestic public expenditure will be slashed by the same amount.

¶A large rebate now given to all manufacturing industry on the Selective Employment Tax, a flat tax on every worker employed, will be canceled except in distressed regions. A special export rebate will also be dropped.

¶The corporation tax, the Government warned, will be increased in April from 40 to 42.5 per cent. It said a "strict watch" would be maintained to prevent undue increases in dividends.

Freeze Omitted

The one glaring omission from the list of measures was a freeze on wages. Experts have long warned that any devaluation would produce great pressures for higher wages to match the inevitably rising cost of living. But wage increases would kill the aim of keeping exports less expensive in foreign currencies.

The Treasury statement tonight said only that it was "essential" to avoid large wage claims and settlements lest "industrial costs go up once more and the competitive benefits of devaluation be frittered away." It said talks on this matter with labor and industry would begin at once.

At present there is no legal freeze on wages. The Trades Union Congress, parent body of British unions, is supposed to keep some control on increases, though its ability to do so seems doubtful. The Government's Prices and Incomes Board can delay rises briefly while investigating them.

Some thought the Government would inevitably move toward a wage freeze like the one it imposed for six months after the crisis in July, 1966. The theory was that it was merely trying tonight to avoid too much bad news for its union supporters at once.

One of the agonizing questions for the Government was what effect the debilitating drama of the last week, ending in the humiliation of tonight, would have on its already tattered hopes of entering the Common Market.

A Foreign Office spokesman said tonight that devaluation would "not affect our determination to join" and would "put beyond doubt our ability to accept the obligations of membership."

French Opposition

To say that France will not agree with that appraisal is to understate the situation. The French, who have been using all possible means to block the British application, can be expected to say that the devaluation shows that Britain is in much too weak an economic position to be considered.

Others in the community will argue, however, that Britain has taken the painful step urged on her by the market's economists.

The Council of Foreign Ministers of the market is meeting on Monday to consider the British application. From London's point of view the timing could hardly be worse.

Mr. Callaghan will appear in the House of Commons Monday to discuss the devaluation. On Tuesday Mr. Wilson is expected to appear at a long-scheduled meeting of Labor Parliamentary members of economic policy.

November 19, 1967

FEDERAL RESERVE RATE UP; 6 IN COMMON MARKET MOVE TO BACK A LOAN TO BRITAIN

DOLLAR DEFENDED

Rise to 4.5% Follows Bank of England Step —Canada Also Acts

By H. ERICH HEINEMANN

The United States increased its official lending rate yesterday to 4.5 per cent from 4 per cent in a move designed to protect the dollar in the wake of Britain's financial crisis.

The increase was in the discount rate—the interest rate at which the Federal Reserve System, the nation's central bank, lends to its member commercial banks. It is one of the basic interest rates in the country's economy.

The increase is expected to raise the cost of borrowing money throughout the country, especially if, as many bankers expect, the Federal Reserve now moves to tighten somewhat the essentially easy money policy that it has been following so far this year.

In some cases, interest rates in the United States are already at their highest levels since the Civil War.

Rise in Loan Costs Seen

The basic cost of loans to business, now 5.5 per cent, is expected to rise, although probably not right away, since business-loan demand has been sluggish lately.

Interest rates on home mortgages, which now average 6.5 per cent, are also expected to move up. However, interest rates on other consumer loans—for automobiles, appliances, vacations or what have you—may be more sluggish, if only for the reason that many of them are already pressing against legal ceilings.

In Ottawa, the Bank of Canada raised its basic lending rate to 6 per cent from 5 per cent, also as a defensive move, following Britain's devaluation of the pound and the increase in her bank rate to 8 per cent from 6.5 per cent.

Ample Credit Stressed

Federal Reserve officials were frankly uncertain yesterday about what would happen when financial markets opened for business this morning.

The Federal Reserve stressed that it had ample credit available for any individual banks that might be subject to unusual withdrawals. "Borrowing by member banks [from the Federal Reserve] for purposes of making adjustments to market pressures is an appropriate use of the discount mechanism," it said.

It was suggested that the 8 per cent lending rate set by the Bank of England would lead to some "very attractive" interest rates in London.

This factor could lead to a substantial outflow of dollars from the United States, bankers suggested yesterday.

In a formal statement, the Federal Reserve noted that it had acted "to assure the continued orderly functioning of United States financial markets and to maintain the availability of reserves on the banking system on terms and conditions that will foster sustainable economic growth at home and a sound international position for the dollar."

Bankers interpreted this statement, which in part simply reaffirmed long-standing policy objectives of the Federal Reserve, in several ways:

¶ If any unusual outflows of funds should develop in the next few days, the Federal Reserve would move swiftly to offset such losses by pumping new funds into the economy.

¶ In the long term, if dollars should continue to flow abroad, the Federal Reserve would move to restrict the availability of funds, which would force short-term interest rates upward and would serve as a counter to the magnet of the percent bank rate in London.

¶The financial turmoil touched off bw the British devaluation may have served to resolve the current debate within the Federal Reserve System over monetary policy in favor of slightly tighter money, resigned to moderate inflationary pressures that many observers believe are already starting to get out of hand.

Technically, the Federal Reserve's action—which was actually taken on Saturday night, but was not announced until 2 P.M. yesterday—came in the form of unanimous approval by the seven-man Federal Reserve Board of requests by 10 of the 12 regional Federal Reserve Banks to increase their discount rates, effective this morning.

Announcement Delayed

Several of the regional banks had requested an increase on Saturday, but the board elected to delay its announcements so that more banks could join, including the Federal Reserve Banks of New York, which is the largest of the 12.

As of last night, only the Federal Reserve Banks of Philadelphia and St. Louis had not acted, and they were expected to join in the increase shortly.

The Federal Reserve Banks that did act yesterday, in addition to New York, were those in Atlanta, Boston, Chicago, Cleveland, Dallas, Kansas City, Minneapolis, Richmond and San Francisco.

The discount rate had been at 4 per cent since April 7, when it was reduced from 4.5 per cent, in a move that was made to bring it into line with sharp drops that had already occurred in interest rates in the open market.

Since that time interest rates have reversed their course and have climbed sharply, particularly on long-term loans, as corporations have borrowed in record amounts to rebuild holdings of cash and short-term securities that were depleted in last year's money squeeze.

In raising the discount rate, the Federal Reserve refrained from making any change in the maximum interest rate of 5.5 per cent that commercial banks are allowed to pay on certificates of deposit of $100,000 or more.

Such certificates are a major source of lendable funds for the nation's largest banks, and bankers immediately voiced concern about the possibility of being placed in a squeeze similar to the one they faced last fall—when more than $3-billion flowed out of the money-center banks into higher-yielding investments in the open market.

Banker Comments

Rudolph A. Peterson, president of the nation's largest bank, the Bank of America, in San Francisco, said in a statement that "we are of course hopeful that Federal authorities will also take whatever steps are necessary to allow commercial banks to remain competitive."

Other bankers said that the timing of an increase in the 5.5 per cent prime rate, the basic interest charge on bank loans to business, would depend in part on how rapidly rates on certificates of deposit rise to the ceiling.

Banks are now paying 5.5 per cent for certificates of deposit of six month terms or longer, but those of shorter maturity carry lower rates.

In its statement the Federal Reserve made no mention of any moves that might be pending in the form of further support for the devalued pound.

But indications were that an announcement would be forthcoming fairly soon, almost certainly including an increase in the reciprocal currency arrangement, or "swap" line, that the Federal Reserve has with the Bank of England.

Under such arrangements, the Federal Reserve has reciprocal borrowing rights with its overseas partner. It can borrow pounds, and the Bank of England can borrow an equivalent amount of dollars.

At present, the United States swap line with the Bank of England is $1.35-billion, out of a total of such lines of credit outstanding of more than $5-billion.

No figures have yet been published, but it is assumed that the Bank of England largely exhausted its available borrowing facilities in trying to support the pound last week.

On the domestic front, the increase in the discount rate appeared to leave the debate over the need for a tax increase to head off inflation about where it had been: mired in political differences between the White House and Capitol Hill.

Federal Reserve officials took the view yesterday that, if anything, the need for a tax increase was now greater than ever before, because British exporters would now be able to cut their prices in world markets.

Canada Raises Rate

Special to The New York Times

TORONTO, Nov. 19—Canada moved today to protect herself from any possible financial backlash resulting from the weekend devaluation of the British pound.

The Bank of Canada, the country's central bank, raised its interest rate to 6 per cent from 5 per cent in a defensive adjustment to increases its official interest rates in the United States and Britain. The object was to avert any heavy shift of funds from Canada to other markets in search of a higher return.

At the same time Louis Rasminsky, governor of the Bank of Canada, reassured the country that the move toward increased interest rates did not necessarily mean that the availability of credit would diminish.

Mr. Rasminsky said, "It would continue to be the policy of the bank to facilitate the provision of adequate credit to meet the needs of sound economic expansion."

The bank has been adding to the money supply at a fairly generous pace in recent months and financial sources forecast there would be no change in that policy.

November 20, 1967

GOLD BUYERS AIM ATTACK AT DOLLAR

In London, Pool Fully Meets Huge Demand for Metal—Commons Backs Wilson

By JOHN M. LEE

Special to The New York Times

LONDON, Nov. 22—The gold market was rocked today by extraordinary buying in a bearish appraisal of the strength of the United States dollar.

Traders talked of "the London gold rush." Some said they saw an effort by President de Gaulle to weaken the international role of the dollar. The heavy demand followed disclosure that France had stopped contributing to the international gold pool, which supports the United States gold price.

[France said she might be willing to contribute $230-million to the $1.4-billion loan Britain was to receive through the International Monetary Fund. Page 67.]

Surge of Buying

Although buying was said to have been the heaviest since the market reopened in 1954 after World War II, the demand was fully met as usual by the pool and the price was unchanged at its ceiling of $35.19⅞.

Other markets were also hectic. The devalued pound was in strong demand in foreign exchange trading and held at its support ceiling of $2.42.

The Labor Government won a vote of confidence in the House of Commons tonight on its decision to devalue the pound.

The stock market recouped all of yesterday's loss in a tremendous surge of 9.3 points on the Financial Times index to 420.6, just short of last Thursday's record of 420.7.

In the House of Commons tonight, James Callaghan, Chancellor of the Exchequer, offered assurances that the International Monetary Fund's $1.4-billion stand-by credit would be forthcoming, despite rumors to the contrary. He said $1.5-billion of the $1.6-billion sought in stand-by credits from central banks had been already agreed.

Mr. Callaghan earlier announced that the remaining balance of Britain's portfolio of dollar securities, which had been put in liquid form and still held in the United States, had been transferred to Britain's foreign exchange reserves. The value of the portfolio was recently estimated at $504-million. The addition to British reserves represents an outflow in the United States balance of payments.

Desirable Commodity

With the pound devalued to $2.40 from $2.80 and backed by extremely high interest rates and huge international loans, the dollar has become the target for speculators.

"In times of currency uncertainties," a banker commented, "there is no commodity in the world as desirable as gold." Gold mining shares were in strong demand for the second day.

For the last two days, the dollar had been firm against Continental currencies on the assumption that British devaluation would not seriously affect United States trade or worsen America's balance-of-payments deficit.

But the dollar came under pressure today and the market was described by dealers as "extremely nervous." Rumors were in good supply.

Dealings Secret

Some reports said American citizens were selling dollars for gold, in violation of United States law, but these reports could not be confirmed. The London gold market, largest in the world, is shrouded in secrecy concerning buyers, sellers and volume figures.

One of the few facts to emerge from the market is the price at the daily "fixing," or price setting. By design, this figure varies only slightly between $35.10 an ounce and $35.20.

These figures are the market equivalents of the $35 an ounce at which the United States stands ready to buy or sell gold in dealings with foreign national banks.

This unique commitment makes the dollar useful as a reserve currency and a supplement to gold and it provides the ultimate base of the international monetary system.

An increase in the price because of exceptional switching out of dollars and into gold, or for whatever reason, means devaluation of the dollar and world monetary chaos.

In a cooperative effort to avoid such a calamity, eight leading banking nations formed the gold pool in 1961 as an underpinning to the market. The pool supplies gold when demand is high and buys gold on the rare occasions when demand is slack, all with a view toward maintaining stability.

The gold pool uses the Bank of England as its agent in the London market. The bank, which represents also South African mine production, determines the daily rate after receiving, through its agent, the bids of five bullion dealers who gather at N. M. Rothschild & Sons, merchant bankers, each weekday morning for the daily "fixing."

Eight Members

The countries that formed the pool were Belgium, France, Italy, the Netherlands, Switzerland, West Germany, Britain and the United States. With France providing only 9 per cent of the pool, her withdrawal hardly spells disaster.

But dealers were distressed at the psychological implications of a valuable symbol of international monetary cooperation having been tarnished, with ill effects for the dollar.

They expressed confidence, however, that the dollar would withstand the assaults. They noted that the dollar was a strong currency in a weak phase, whereas the pound was a weak currency in a weak phase.

Mr. Callaghan was tense as he ended the debate on devaluation. He said he was "split-minded" over whether the Government had done enough to restore the economy through devaluation, spending cuts and economic restraints. He said the Government "may well have to take further steps" as exports and economic growth accelerate.

"Devaluation is no substitute for greater effort and higher productivity," he said, noting that the effect was to take pressure off the exchange rate. "We have got ourselves a breathing space. That is all."

November 23, 1967

7 Nations' Banks to Press For a Stable Gold Market

By CLYDE H. FARNSWORTH
Special to The New York Times

BRUSSELS, Nov. 26 — The governors of seven central banks, forming the so-called Gold Pool, met secretly in Frankfurt this afternoon to "insure orderly conditions" after a week of feverish speculative activity.

A communiqué issued in Washington and made available here said the seven central banks had enough gold and foreign-exchange reserves to guarantee the fixed-price of $35 an ounce for gold.

The public declaration was viewed as a major attempt to bring reason to bear in the highly agitated markets.

[President Johnson returned from Texas to Washington for a meeting with Secretary of the Treasury Henry H. Fowler Monday on the gold speculation.]

The Gold Pool was formed after similar speculation in 1960 pushed the price of gold in the London bullion market to more than $40 an ounce.

The central banks in the pool are those of the United States, Britain, Belgium, the Netherlands, Italy, West Germany and Switzerland.

The seven central banks combined have slightly over $27-billion worth of gold—more than enough to meet any conceivable speculative demand and hold the price.

The statement issued tonight indicated that the seven were prepared to throw these resources into the fight to maintain the gold price—and, therefore, the existing pattern of exchange rates among the leading currencies.

In the past, such joint efforts by the major countries have succeeded in stopping speculative attacks on currencies. There has been no precedent since World War II for the present gold-buying wave, but so far its volume is less than $500-million.

France was one of the original members of the Gold Pool but withdrew early last summer. The disclosure of her withdrawal last Monday, after the 14.3 per cent devaluation of the pound sterling, touched off the intense round of gold speculation.

During the week there were rumors, later officially denied, that Italy and Belgium had also pulled out of the group.

Hoarders from Europe, the Middle East and, according to some reports, the United States were counting on Washington's being forced to raise the official price of gold.

President Johnson said during the week that this was out of the question. It would have the effect of devaluing the dollar.

The Gold Pool acts to keep the price down by supplying private demand from government stocks. Before France withdrew, the United States furnished half the gold in this stabilizing operation. The Federal Reserve System, the American central bank, has taken over France's share, lifting the total American contribution to 60 per cent.

The communiqué tonight said the pool would welcome the participation of other central banks. The statement was issued by Secretary of the Treasury Fowler and the Federal Reserve Board chairman, William McChesney Martin Jr. It said the central bankers had made decisions on "specific measures to insure by coordinated action orderly conditions on the gold and foreign exchange markets.

It added that "the volume of gold and foreign exchange reserves" at the disposal of the seven banks guaranteed the success of their effort.

The United States is anxious to keep the price of gold from rising because a higher price would undermine the present monetary system of the Western world and reward countries like the Soviet Union, South Africa and France, which have big stocks. Most of the newly mined gold in the world comes from South Africa.

The monetary system is based on the willingness of the United States Treasury to buy and sell gold in transactions with foreign governments at $35 an ounce. Since only the United States stands ready to do so, the dollar becomes a "reserve" currency. Other countries can hold it in their reserves, knowing they can always exchange it for gold.

TEXT OF COMMUNIQUE

WASHINGTON, Nov. 26 (Reuters) — Following is the text of the Communiqué issued today by Secretary Fowler and Chairman Martin:

The Governors of the central banks of Belgium, Germany, Italy, the Netherlands, Switzerland, United Kingdom and the United States convened in Frankfurt on Nov. 26, 1967.

They noted that the President of the United States has stated:

"I reaffirm unequivocally the commitment of the United States to buy and sell gold at the existing price of $35 per ounce."

They took decisions on specific measures to insure by coordinated action orderly conditions in the exchange markets and to support the present pattern of exchange rates based on the fixed price of $35 per ounce of gold.

They concluded that the volume of gold and foreign exchange reserves at their disposal guarantees the success of these actions; at the same time, they indicated that they would welcome the participation of other central banks.

November 27, 1967

7 NATIONS BACK DUAL GOLD PRICE, BAR SELLING TO PRIVATE BUYERS; PLEDGE SUPPORT OF THE DOLLAR

$35 RATE UPHELD

By EDWIN L. DALE Jr.
Special to The New York Times

WASHINGTON, March 17— The United States and six Western European countries agreed today to supply no more gold to private buyers, thus establishing a two-price system for gold.

One will be the official monetary price of $35 an ounce, which will remain and will be the price for transactions between governments. The other will be a free-market price, which will be permitted to fluctuate from day to day and will probably start, at least, higher than $35.

The seven nations, which make up the London gold pool, issued a communiqué at the close of a two-day meeting, called in the wake of the worldwide gold panic last week.

Steps Outlined

The communiqué announced the following steps:

¶The United States will continue to buy and sell gold at $35 an ounce in transactions with other governments.

¶The seven nations agreed to support the present pattern of exchange rates among currencies, meaning that the European central banks will continue to buy dollars on the foreign-exchange markets. As a result, dollar traveler's checks should again be convertible into foreign currencies — which they were not in some places last Friday.

¶They agreed not to sell any gold, even in official transactions, to countries that sell their gold on the private markets to make a profit.

¶They said that "the existing stock of monetary gold is sufficient" in light of the pending agreement to create a new kind of monetary reserve called Special Drawing Rights, and thus they "no longer feel it necessary to buy gold from the market."

¶They announced extra standby credits for Britain that will bring the total to $4-billion, including $1.4-billion already available from the International Monetary Fund.

¶The United States independently announced an expansion of $2.27-billion in its short-term "swap" lines of credit with seven other countries and the Bank for International Settlements. This brings the total of these credits, which are used to keep the international value of the dollar stable and preserve the United States gold stock, to $9.35-billion.

The results of the emergency two-day meeting were read to newsmen at 5:30 P.M. by William McChesney Martin Jr., Chairman of the United States Federal Reserve Board. The briefing session was held in the State Department auditorium, less than a block from the white marble Federal Reserve Building, where the central bankers had met.

The key officials at the meeting, apart from Mr. Martin, who was chairman, were the heads of the central banks of Belgium, West Germany, Italy, the Netherlands, Switzerland and Britain, plus Pierre-Paul Schweitzer, Managing Director of the International Monetary Fund, and Gabriel Ferras, General Manager of the Bank For International Settlements in Basel, Switzerland. Secretary of the Treasury Henry H. Fowler was present for most of the meetings, but Mr. Martin represented the United States.

Soon after the communiqué was made public, Mr. Schweitzer issued a separate statement giving the backing of the I.M.F. to the agreement and asserting it was "most important" that countries continue to support the present pattern of stable exchange rates.

This, not gold, is the essence of the world monetary system that has been going through its gravest crisis since World War II.

Pattern Was in Doubt

On Friday, the pattern of exchange rates, including the value of the dollar against other currencies, was in doubt. Now the pattern is expected to be maintained, at least in the days immediately ahead, and possibly indefinitely.

The Bank of England announced that the London gold market—by far the biggest in the world—would be closed until April 1. However, world foreign-exchange markets will be open for business tomorrow, giving a test of whether stability will be restored.

Today's historic agreement, announced on a gray and rainy day at a time of political turmoil in the United States, means that the world monetary stock of gold, now about $39-billion, will probably be frozen forever where it is. All newly mind gold, in the United States and elsewhere, will become a commodity like any other, fluctuating in price. Governments will not buy it or sell it, except between each other at $35.

American jewelers and other industrial users, it is expected, will continue to be licensed, but they will have to buy their gold at the free-market price at home and abroad. United States gold mines will no longer sell to the Treasury but directly to domestic users, presumably at the free-market world price.

The United States mining companies, which produce about $60-million of gold a year, will probably also be permitted to export gold.

New regulations will be issued by the Treasury tomorrow.

Thus gold is expected to become more expensive for consumers, at least while the free price exceeds the $35 monetary price.

United States producers account for a small part of the annual supply of newly mined gold. About four-fifths comes from South Africa.

France Was Absent

France was a conspicuous absentee from the weekend meeting. Under one aspect of the agreement, France will be unable to turn a profit from her large gold hoard. France dropped out of the gold pool last June.

She cannot sell her gold in the private market for dollars at a price higher than $35 an ounce and expect to replenish the gold by cashing the dollars at the United States Treasury. This would apply to all other countries as well.

Some observers viewed the agreement as a defeat for France, particularly if the basic international monetary system — with stable exchange rates and a fixed monetary price for gold of $35 per ounce — has been preserved, as seems to be the case.

No one knows where the free-market gold price will settle. It is expected to be higher than $35 an ounce, but some experts doubt it will be even as high as $40. In London, however, some experts suggested the price might open on April 1 at $45 an ounce.

A key part of part of the communiqué was this statement:

"The Governors agreed to cooperate fully to maintain the existing parities as well as orderly conditions in their exchange markets in accordance with their obligations under the articles of agreement of the International Monetary Fund."

The articles say, in effect, that countries' central banks must intervene in the markets to buy and sell American dollars in order to keep their own currencies within one per cent of parity with the dollar. Thus, the West German mark is kept close to 25 cents and the British pound is kept close to $2.40, by intervention if necessary.

With the international value of the dollar under some suspicion as a result of the crisis, it is possible that traders and dealers will be heavy sellers of dollars on the foreign-exchange markets in the next few days. But if these sales occur, the central banks of the European countries will be ready to buy up the dollars, thus holding exchange rates steady.

As a reinforcement for this commitment, the Federal Reserve announced tonight another big expansion of its short-term credit lines, known as "swaps," with a number of other central banks. These provide a means by which the Federal Reserve can borrow foreign currencies to "buy back" excess dollars held by other other central banks.

March 18, 1968

The Financial Crisis

The Nation's Money Is in Trouble, But Government Action Is Curbed

By RICHARD E. MOONEY

The American economy has never produced more than it is producing right now. The rate of unemployment has been below 4 per cent for more than two years. Business profits are higher than ever before.

Yet the chairman of the Federal Reserve Board, William McChesney Martin Jr., says that "we are in the midst of the worst financial crisis we have had since 1931." This is not a contradiction. Mr. Martin himself pointed out that this is not the depression all over again—it is "not a business crisis, but a financial crisis."

News Analysis

In other words, the nation's business is obviously not in trouble at the present time. The nation's money is.

The nation's business is in the eighth year of its longest uptrend in history. For a time last year some economic authorities thought it was ending, but it only slowed down a little and has speeded up since then.

Whole World Involved

How long it will last is impossible to predict. It has already astounded the experts by lasting as long as it has.

Properly managed it could keep on going. Improperly managed it could develop into too strong a boom, followed inevitably by a painful retrenchment—painful for the United States and for the whole world, because no country's economy is as powerful as this one's and every corner of the world is influenced by it.

The possibility of a retrenchment as disastrous as the great Depression of the 1930's is essentially zero. The whole economic community—government, the banks, business, labor, and the academic economists — learned from that experience. The country knows how to keep the economy within bounds now, which it did not know then.

What worries Mr. Martin, and President Johnson and many others here and abroad, is whether the country will do what it knows how to do.

The immediate threat is inflation. In the first half of the 1960's, the economy grew fast and prices held relatively stable. But in the last two years the price trend has been steadily upward, 3 to 4 per cent a year.

Payments Deficit Worse

Related to this is the balance-of-payments deficit. It has been a problem for 10 years, but until recently it appeared to be manageable, and it appeared to be shrinking. Six months ago it started to become sharply worse.

Inflation and payments deficits go hand in hand. When a country is booming and its prices are rising, imports rise and exports slacken.

The boom means greater demand for all goods, domestic and foreign. Thus, there is less reason for American producers to export and more attraction for foreigners to sell here. The higher prices mean that lower-priced foreign goods sell better here, and higher-priced American goods sell less well abroad.

The result: less money flows in from sales of exports, more money flows out to purchase imports, and the payments deficit grows. This is only a very partial explanation of the causes and effects of inflation and unbalanced payments, but it is a critical part.

The classic remedy for both aspects of the problem is to curb the boom. If economic expansion slows down, the pressures of inflation are lessened, imports are weaker, and exports are stronger.

Two Government Tools

The Government has two principal tools for accomplishing this. One is budget policy—taxes and spending. The other is monetary policy—interest rates and other restrictions on the availability of credit through the banking system.

There are, at times, reasons for using one tool rather than the other. Monetary policy can be used more quickly, for instance. A tax cut, or a tax increase, can be aimed more precisely or more broadly — at a specific sector of the economy or at everyone — but it takes longer.

However, when there is a general problem of inflation or recession, the economic consensus says to use both. To use only one is the same as if a man uses only one hand to lift a heavy load. The one has to work harder to accomplish the job.

This is the dilemma of United States economic policy right now. The Government is relying on monetary policy alone to curb economic activity. The Federal Reserve System has tightened up on the availability of bank credit, and interest rates have risen to extraordinary levels.

President Johnson proposed a whole year ago that Congress bring budget policy into play, too, with a tax increase. After a long standoff he agreed to do part of the job himself, with cuts in proposed spending cuts. But Congress has still not budged and shows no sign that it will, so the outlook is for still tighter monetary restrictions.

The psychological effect of this is as important as the practical effect. The policy-making machinery of the greatest economic power that the world has ever known is observed to be operating on only one cylinder, and the problems of inflation and the payments are not being solved.

April 23, 1968

The Dollar Escapes Europe's Currency Crisis

By GERD WILCKE

Was it a franc crisis?

Or was it a mark crisis?

Answers to these questions depended largely on whether they were posed in Bonn or Paris.

The most that could be said about the hectic developments that moved toward devaluation of the franc was that they were a triumph of nationalism. And the real question was whether Europe could afford this type of nationalism any longer.

The Germans, of course, dealt from a position of strength. The strength was documented in their balance of trade, in their international accounts.

The Germans could insist that right was on their side because no one in Bonn last week held a card big enough to beat them.

But wrong or right, the Germans knew they had the backing of financial markets, as attested by the tremendous flow of foreign funds to their country.

Somewhat surprisingly, Frenchmen saw no direct link between the recent crisis and the political turmoil in their country in May and June that led to the crisis. Unanimously, these Frenchmen pointed out that economic data for October indicated that France had overcome its internal difficulties deriving from the early summer events.

A common theory advanced by bankers and industrialists in New York was that the May-June events may have triggered the crisis, but that its basic root was the lack of a unified currency in the European Common Market.

Common Currency Needed

As one banker put it: "When you remove barriers to let Europeans trade freely, it's absolutely impossible to maintain an equilibrium in balances of payments without a common currency."

For the moment at least, the dollar seemed immune from attack. This was in sharp contrast to the two previous crises, the first following devaluation of the British pound almost exactly one year earlier, the second the run on the dollar last March.

There were reasons. Inflation in the United States had led to higher stock prices and a flood of investment money into the United States from Europe. The booming American economy had caused banks to pull dollars from their branches abroad and from dollars on deposit in European banks. Finally, the restrictions on American capital exports had produced a record volume of dollar borrowing by American and international companies in the so-called European bond market.

All of these things, plus the unwillingness of European central banks to acquire new gold, had led to a shortage of dollars and, for the moment at least, to a fairly comfortable position for the United States currency.

The French banker who criticized the lack of a common currency in Europe cited the analogy of the United States. The United States functioned as a common market, he said, only because it had a common currency, the dollar. Massachusetts or Connecticut, thus, might experience a trade deficit but the free movement of goods, capital and people offset the effect.

Europe, he continued, also was trying to have its own version of free interstate trade. This could not be done painlessly without the benefit of a common currency.

"This time the crisis is in France, the next time it may be Belgium, Italy or even Germany," he said.

The banker continued that the biggest lesson to be drawn from the current crisis would be for the six members of the European Common Market to sit down and work out a common currency.

He acknowledged, however, that the prevalence of nationalistic attitudes in Europe did not make it likely that there could be an early agreement. "In order to create a unified currency you will have to give up a certain amount of national sovereignty," he said.

The banker and a prominent industrialist agreed that aside from the lack of a common currency, another reason for the recent crisis was the lack of confidence in France itself.

The political upheavals of last May were only the beginning. Once they were settled, the Government introduced exchange controls that did not work because there was no machinery to administer them.

The eventual removal of the controls, itself a daring gesture, did little to restore confidence because the Government introduced an internal measure that created a kind of panic.

The measure, a significant increase in inheritance taxes, was coupled with discussions about a possible return of capital taxes.

To the French, who had been subjected

to capital taxes after World War II, this was a signal to start moving funds out of the country to the safer grounds of Switzerland, Germany and the United States.

"When money starts running out of your country, it's always a reflection of a lack of confidence, and Frenchmen feared there might be a recurrence of the May upheavals," the banker said.

For most of the week France—joined somewhat incongruously by its ancient allies, the United States and Britain—sought to demonstrate that it was not a franc crisis a all but a mark crisis.

The Germans, supported by Italy, Sweden, Switzerland and the Netherlands, resisted pressure to increase the value of their currency.

By the end of the poker game, the Germans had agreed to change their tax structure. This was aimed at making imports cheaper and exports dearer.

Flow of Funds Stemmed

They also agreed to stem the flow of foreign funds by forcing their banks to freeze all foreign deposits of a speculative and noncommercial nature and turn them over to the German central bank. The regulation, applicable to deposits of nonresidents made after Nov. 15, provided that the deposits would earn no interest for the banks.

This and a promise to make foreign deposits subject to licensing, the Germans hoped would discourage foreign speculators and take the pressure off the mark. During three recent days the Germans accumulated $1.77-billion in foreign funds.

Could all this happen to the dollar?

The French banker said international speculation was always focused on a currency that was most vulnerable at a given time. The crisis was mostly between the French franc and the German mark.

"All the funds that can be concentrated on this speculation game are currently tied up. However, once over, the speculation might turn to any other currency," the banker said.

The factors favoring the dollar at the moment were ephemeral at best. A decline in the stock market, for instance, could arrest the inflow of investment funds from Europe. A slowing of the economy could reduce the demand for Eurodollars.

The warning was clear. The dollar easily could be next.

November 21, 1968

Achilles Heel of Monetary System

Crisis Spurs Calls to End Shortcoming in Rules of the I.M.F.

By EDWIN L. DALE Jr.
Special to The New York Times

WASHINGTON, Nov. 20 — The latest international money crisis—the third in 12 months —has exposed once again what many regard as the Achilles heel of the otherwise successful international monetary system that was agreed upon by the leading nations almost 25 years ago. But while the vulnerability of the system is now widely recognized, there is only the barest beginning of official exploration of the most plausible remedy, which is already seen to present numerous problems.

News Analysis

The Achilles heel is that the monetary system provides for fixed, steady exchange rates between currencies for trade and other international transactions without any parallel binding obligation for nations to pursue policies that keep their international payments in balance at the exchange rate they have chosen.

Imbalance Is Inevitable

In the view of thoughtful critics the system makes it almost inevitable that from time to time one or another leading country "gets out of whack" with the others — yesterday Britain, today France and West Germany, tomorrow, perhaps, the United States. For one reason or another, a nation's balance of payments drifts into chronic deficit or chronic surplus.

It may be because one country's wages rise faster than the others'—as France's have this year. It may be because world demand changes and a country's traditional exports gradually decline and are not replaced rapidly enough. Britain, for example, used to export coal.

In some cases, a country gets into difficulty because it allows too large a deficit in its budget, with resulting domestic inflation and a worsening trade balance.

The causes, in practice, have proved infinite—from overseas expenditure on military purposes (the United States) to a slowdown in foreign investment in the country (Canada). Sometimes they prove temporary, but sometimes they do not.

The system provides a way out—devaluation of the exchange rate for a country in deficit or revaluation upward for a country in surplus. But this is invariably a painful move for domestic political reasons. In the case of devaluation, consumers pay more for imported goods and vacations abroad cost more. In the case of revaluation, the profits of the important export industries are reduced and the farm sector may be hit hard.

Devaluation Affects Trade

What is more, in the delicately tuned network of international trade and finance, a change in the exchange rate of a major currency, particularly a devaluation, can cause ripples into many other currencies because competitive prices in world trade are immediately affected. The danger is ultimate chaos and a drying up of trade.

This is how the man in the street in all countries could be affected. It is why the leading nations have so often fought so hard, through mutual credits and otherwise, to preserve the existing parities of the leading currencies.

In brief, the danger is that all currency values might become uncertain and that something approaching a worldwide depression could result. This is what happened in 1931.

As long as devaluation or revaluation is even barely possible under a fixed exchange rate system, it pays traders and bankers to hedge by selling a currency that might fall in value and buying one that might rise. If no change occurs, they have lost nothing.

Switches Intensify Problem

But their very act of switching their money greatly intensifies the problem in the short run. This is the anatomy of crisis in the present system.

The remedy most often proposed for this problem is to allow currencies to fluctuate more widely against one another than the narrow limits of the present rules.

The rules, written into the articles of agreement of the International Monetary Fund, say that each nation must buy and sell foreign currencies — in practice, dollars — as necessary to keep its own currency within 1 per cent of its declared value.

This is why West Germany has "taken in" almost $2-billion in dollars in the last few weeks. It sold marks for dollars to keep the mark from rising above its upper legal limit of 25.25 cents.

The proposal for a change would alter the rules to permit fluctuations of, say, 5 per cent on either side of parity. It is widely, though not universally, accepted that most leading nations' currencies are unlikely to be overvalued or undervalued by much more than this, and that a change of 5 per cent could make major difference in balances of payments without causing all the disruption of an official devaluation or revaluation.

The first objection to this proposal is obvious: It would require a change in the articles of agreement of the Monetary Fund, with preliminary negotiations and then parliamentary ratification by three-fifths of the members.

But apart from this obstacle, there is little agreement among the men who actually run the international system that more flexibility in exchange rates would be desirable.

Last September, for example, Pierre-Paul Schweitzer, the managing director of the I.M.F., said he thought such a system "would mean more speculation than we now have." Many foreign-exchange dealers and central bankers believe the system would be unworkable, though others are less pessimistic.

There are other problems. It is widely assumed that the dollar would continue to be the "key currency"—the one against which other currencies are valued. The dollar would be the currency bought and sold by central banks to keep their own currencies within the new limits. The following situation could then arise, using the pound, the mark and the dollar as an example.

Problem Is Posed

In "year one" of the new system, all three currencies are in equilibrium and trade is close to par in the foreign-exchange markets.

In "year two" Britain gets into trouble with her balance of payments while West Germany starts running a big surplus. The mark rises to its "ceiling" 5 per cent above the dollar and the pound drops to its "floor" 5 per cent below the dollar. At this point the pound has been effectively devalued against the mark by 10 per cent, but only 5 per cent against the dollar.

Then, finally, in "year three" Britain turns healthy and West Germany runs into difficulty. The mark drops to its floor and the pound rises to its ceiling. The mark will have fallen 10 per cent and the pound risen 10 per cent, with the result that the exchange rate between those two currencies will have changed by 20 per cent.

This is far more fluctuation than traders or bankers want to see. They could not set prices or invest with confidence. A seemingly modest flexibility of currencies of "only" 5 per cent turns out in practice to be as much as 20 per cent for most currencies —and 10 per cent for the dollar.

Several Methods Used

In any event, the leading officials are barely beginning to explore the desirability of "wider bands" within which currencies can fluctuate. In the meanwhile, international money crises have eventually been resolved by one of these methods:

¶ "In extremis" devaluation or revaluation (Britain last November, West Germany in 1961).

¶ Credits by the others, often massive, to help the country in deficit until its payments get better (Italy in 1963, Canada in 1968).

¶ National measures to improve the balance of payments the United States on numerous occasions starting in 1959), often measures restricting investment or other transactions or curbing foreign aid.

The current crisis will be revolved along these lines, singly or in combination. And the system of fixed exchange rates will undoubtedly last a while longer—at least until the next crisis.

November 24, 1968

Purchases of Mark Soar; Revaluation Mood Grows

U.S. Silent on Currency Though Shifts Would Affect Its Trade

By EDWIN L. DALE Jr.
Special to The New York Times

WASHINGTON, May 7—The United States Government is maintaining a discreet silence in what is now clearly another major international monetary crisis, but its interests are clear.

The ideal outcome from the American point of view would be the earliest and largest possible upward revaluation of the West German mark and the smallest and fewest possible devaluations of any other currencies, especially the British pound. No devaluations at all would be considered best.

The worst outcome, as seen by the United States, would be a period of currency chaos that wound up with either "floating" exchange rates or large devaluations, under emergency pressure, of the French franc, the pound or other currencies.

There is nothing that the United States is being asked to say or do, as far as is known. The dollar is not directly involved in the crisis and could be affected only if the crisis degenerates into exchange-rate chaos.

The basic interest of the United States arises from its trading position in the world and its still precarious balance of payments.

With United States exports and imports approximately in balance—after years of large export surpluses—the worst thing that could happen to the dollar would be a series of devaluations of currencies of other important trading nations.

A devaluation of the pound, for example, would make British goods cheaper than they now are in the Brazils, Japans and Indias of the world—markets where the United States and Britain compete.

By contrast, the United States could only gain on an upward revaluation of the mark. German exports in these same markets would become more expensive, and United States goods would thus become more competitive.

With the dollar at the center of the international monetary system, the United States is all but barred from revaluing, whether up or down. Thus a number of experts have been reaching the conclusion that exchange-rate changes by other countries, if they are to be made, must not be limited to devaluations.

If the pound went down one year, the franc the next, the lira the next and so on, the dollar could gradually be left "high and dry" and clearly overvalued. American trade would suffer from the misfortunes of other countries. And a clearly overvalued dollar could jeopardize the whole monetary system.

By contrast, if the few countries with chronic trade and payments surpluses—West Germany has long been the outstanding example—occasionally revalue their currencies upward, exchange rates can be brought into more realistic alignment without harming the trading position of the United States. That is why a German revaluation now could set a useful precedent.

May 8, 1969

MONEY AILMENT IS HARD TO CURE

Lands With Surplus Dollars Avoid a Run on Fort Knox

By CLYDE H. FARNSWORTH
Special to The New York Times

PARIS, April 4 — After a movement of billions of dollars into the strong currency nations of Europe last week, Western monetary authorities faced the unenviable task of trying to head off a new financial crisis without being able to tackle the basic cause of the disturbances.

For 20 years the United States has run balance-of-payments deficits, mainly through overseas military and aid spending, which have fed the world with a supply of dollars well beyond basic liquidity needs.

Private forecasts by some of the world's major financial institutions see little improvement at least through the first half of the nineteen-seventies.

Theoretically, the foreign governments should be able to turn in the surplus dollars for American gold.

A Limited Supply

Although the United States is a trillion-dollar economy with nearly $150-billion of overseas investments, it does not have enough gold in Fort Knox to meet the foreign claims.

If the foreigners demanded payment for their chips, they could precipitate a major crisis in international trade and payments. They don't want this any more than the United States does.

The situation has been compared by William F. Butler, vice president and chief economist of the Chase Manhattan Bank, to the man who had his head so firmly wedged in the lion's jaw that the lion could not bite down.

Efforts are concentrated on keeping the system hobbling along by attacking symptoms, and not the cause, of the disease.

One of these symptoms is the interest rate differential between the United States, where expansionary policies are being pursued to get the economy moving again and reduce unemployment, and Europe, where the chief goal of economic policy is still to curb inflation.

These differentials have caused a massive shift of funds from the vast and still little undersood Eurodollar market to the European centers—particularly to Frankfurt, but also to Zurich, Amsterdam, Brussels and, before last week's bank rate cut by the Bank of England, London as well.

The Eurodollar market, where foreign-owned dollars are lent at rates influenced by domestic American money rates, is a phenomenon of the surplus dollar situation, and has grown in stride with the American deficits.

As the dollars flow from the Eurodollar pool in to the foreign centers where they are converted into foreign currencies, the conversions have the effect of swelling the foreign countries' money supply, aggravating its problems in curbing inflation.

It is an external force ("A hydra-headed monster" is the label of France's Finance Minister Valéry Giscard d'Estaing), which European central bankers complain reduces their monetary sovereignty.

"Even in its anemic state," read a front-page headline in the liberal Roman Catholic Paris newspaper La Croix, "the dollar makes the law in Europe."

European monetary authorities, two weeks ago at important meetings in Paris, told their Washington counterparts that the United States had gone too far with its easy money policies. They wanted to see somewhat higher short-term interest rates in the United States and more reliance on fiscal measures to spur the economy.

For their part, the Americans thought the Europeans were keeping their interest rates too high.

As part of an international understanding, a sign of the close monetary cooperation that still exists despite the American deficits, the Europeans pledged to reduce their rates, while the Americans said they would continue trying to limit the downward pressures on short-term rates ("Operation Twist" as it is dubbed in the United States).

The American authorities also said they would try to mop up more of the surplus dollars in the Eurodollar market to nudge the foreign dollar rates upward.

April 5, 1971

Threat to Economic Integration

By LEONARD S. SILK

PARIS—"Confidence is suspicion asleep," said Benjamin Disraeli. After a remarkably quiet year in the international money markets, suspicion about the dollar has been reawakened by huge deficits in the American balance of payments. The United States ran a deficit of $10.7 billion to foreign central banks last year. During 1971's first quarter the deficit—as estimated by the Morgan Guaranty Bank—totaled $5 billion, a $20-billion annual rate.

Ask an American monetary official what would happen if this enormous deficit rate were to continue for a year, and his answer would be "nothing." He would contend that the world has been on a dollar standard since March 1968, when we stopped pegging the price of gold in the private market, and that foreigners will go on accepting dollars in settlement of our payments deficits—because, if they did not, the world's monetary system would collapse.

However, many Europeans feel that the Americans are living in a dream world if they think the present dollar outflow can continue indefinitely. One high French official, asked what he really thought would happen, shrugged and exploded, "Something!"

And last week Raymond Barre, vice president of the European Economic Community, said, "No one wants a crisis for the dollar, which would be a crisis for the entire international monetary system, but, under the pressure of violations of the fundamental rules of the system, the moment will come when it will no longer be possible to keep control over events."

At this point, the money game is stalemated. American officials say that foreign currencies—especially the Japanese yen and the German mark—are undervalued and should be raised. The foreigners say the deficit is America's, and the Americans should get it under control.

Some foreign economists say, "Devalue the dollar." The Americans say that this is impossible—other currencies are pegged to the dollar and would come down with it. Though the economists say this is not necessarily so, many European business interests would oppose the trading advantage that a dollar devaluation would give the United States—the same reason they oppose a European up-valuation.

Some governments are starting to hold German marks as reserves. The "good Europeans" are trying to create a new European money, but few expect that this can be achieved in the ten-year period sketched in Brussels; some think it will never happen. The idealists dream of a world money; William McChesney Martin wants a World Federal Reserve Bank.

But while the long money debate winds on, a solution that none of the economists want is emerging. That solution is a retreat from liberal trade and freely flowing investment back toward protectionism and national self-sufficiency.

In a sense, the protectionist virus is always present in the blood stream of every nation's industry. Monetary disorder, imbalances of payments and the resulting inability of some producers to cope with foreign competition because of an over-valued currency will activate the virus and produce a protectionist epidemic.

European liberals are dismayed over President Nixon's weak and confusing trade policy; "The United States has no trade policy," they say. They are astonished at the lengths to which the President is willing to go to deliver on a political commitment to restrict Japanese textile shipments—even to the point of threatening to block the agreement to restore Okinawa to Japan.

But they recognize that the Americans have been provoked, both by the Europeans and by Japan. The Common Market remains highly protectionist on agricultural products. One still hears in Europe one of General de Gaulle's maxims: "One eats what one produces, not what one imports." Whatever this may lack in French logic, it has the mystical quality that appeals to French farmers—and many others.

Similarly, Japan has been too slow in liberalizing and has moved only under extreme threats. The Europeans are now afraid that if the Americans exclude Japanese textiles or other goods, they will be inundated—and have to boost their trade walls against industrial goods.

The Europeans are afraid of a trade war—"You don't want a war when you are building a cathedral," they say. Some would prefer America to cut back its capital exports to Europe. One official proposes that the United States adopt multiple exchange rates, with a penalty rate on capital investment in Europe. The ghost of Hjalmar Schacht is still around.

A return to protectionism, capital controls, Schachtian exchange rates and all that would be a tragedy for the industrial nations of the West, both economically and politically. Yet there is no evidence that the Nixon Administration is prepared to provide the leadership to reverse the trend. Nor is there reason to expect that the Common Market or Britain, waiting outside its door, can do the job. Japan, insecure and inexperienced, cannot lead. Who can? International civil servants? Some will certainly try. But the truth is that, to get out of the box, the United States, Europe and Japan must all be prepared to move.

Action cannot come on the trade front alone, for the international money muddle, world inflation and the protectionist trend are all linked. If the political will is lacking to make a concerted effort, "something," as the Frenchman said, is bound to happen.

April 26, 1971

Europeans Bear Brunt In Crisis Of Dollar

By EDWIN L. DALE Jr.

WASHINGTON—Last weekend, when the latest international monetary flare-up was nearing its climax, John B. Connally Jr., Arthur M. Burns, Paul W. McCracken, George Shultz and Richard M. Nixon, as far as is known, got some sleep.

Karl Schiller, Karl Klasen, Jelle Zylstra, Nello Celio, Valery Giscard d'Estaing and Guido Carli—to name a few European financial authorities did not.

Therein lies what is "wrong" with the international monetary system, if anything is. The system is asymmetrics. It imposes more burdens on some than on others.

This is a viewpoint that is gaining adherents here and abroad, although no one seems to know quite what to do to make things more even.

The problem of the system, in this view, is not some imminent and ill-defined "collapse." It is not a "weak" dollar, whatever that may mean—the dollar, as a result of the crisis, lost slightly in value against only four of the world's 120-odd currencies and is still accepted everywhere.

•

It is not a failure of the system to accomplish its purpose, which is to permit one currency to be exchanged for another. After a few days' interruption, exchanges continued normally.

From Lima to Bonn, from Cairo to Berne, from Buenos Aires to Tokyo, from Belgrade to London, foreign governments have to cope from time to time with a decision that is as difficult, even grave, as any government can face short of going to war: whether to change the exchange rate of the currency. It is a decision, as we have just seen, that causes sleepless nights.

Only Washington is immune from this, because of the way the present world monetary system was built.

Economists can argue until they are blue in the face that a government that raises the international value of its currency is actually doing a good turn for its citizens. They may be right, but most of the millions who gain do not realize it, or understand it, and the sizable minority who lose, chiefly the vast exporting industries, are loud in their anger.

Economists may argue, too, that devaluations too long put off—as in the case of Britain from 1964 to 1967—cost the citizens dearly. Again, they are probably right. But none of this makes the decision to devalue easy for the government in power. Again, people do not understand. Everything from prestige to the cost of imported food is at stake.

The agonies in Europe this past weekend were very real. The calm in Washington was equally very real, despite headlines about a "crisis of the dollar." The difference is that the Europeans had to make decisions about exchange rates and the Americans did not.

In a complex world, it is as simple as that.

●

The exchange rate decisions were forced upon the Europeans through no real fault of their own. They had the unpleasant options of exchange controls (which many of them, to American applause, do not like because controls interfere with the free market); swallowing more dollars, with a consequent increase in their own money supply and hence a worsening of their inflation problem; or an upward change in the exchange rate. Four chose the route of the exchange rate, with great reluctance, two by the route of floating.

France-Soir

"Vous n'auriez pas autre chose que du dollar?"

"Don't you have anything else than a dollar?"

The situation was particularly unfair for the three small countries — Austria, Switzerland and the Netherlands. They had to make their decision, in effect, because West Germany, their largest trading partner, did, and West Germany had to make its decision because of an uncontrollable flood of dollars.

●

Most of the mature and intelligent Europeans involved do not charge this injustice —and that is what it is—to some kind of intentional American power-grab, or American evil, or, for most of the recent period, to poor American monetary and fiscal policy.

But they still feel the injustice. And they feel frustrated.

For they know that, in the end, there is one dominant set of facts: the American economy is huge enough to be of great importance to them, but international transactions are so small a part of the American economy that nothing they could do would really cause widespread difficulty here, even if they wanted to cause difficulty.

Taking American gold would do them no good. And there would be a great cost in terms of inconvenience and uncertainty in trying—even if it could be done—to remove the dollar's central role as a world-transactions currency. Yet as long as it has that role, the asymmetry on the key matter of exchange rates will remain.

So far as is known here, nobody has a real answer to this injustice — certaintly no answer that has won any kind of general acceptance. France has suggested the United States ought to raise the official $35-an-ounce price of gold, but her Common Market partners have opposed making any such demand.

●

Perhaps the most promising is the idea of "wider bands" around a currency's par value, to let market forces, rather than politicians, make small changes in exchange rates and perhaps to minimize vast flows of funds based on interest-rate considerations. But this is still not accepted by some important countries and many small ones.

Meanwhile, those — mainly Americans—who talk about the tolerability and workability of a dollar-based system, with its implied need for occasional revaluations and devaluations by others. tend to ignore the political problem for the Government's changing the exchange rate.

The chances are that the system will continue, and with it the implied injustice. At least the system works.

May 16, 1971

Dollar Hits 22-Year Low In Trading Against Mark

FRANKFURT, West Germany, May 21 (Reuters)—The dollar fell today to its lowest value against the Deutschmark since the West German currency was floated 10 days ago, foreign exchange market sources said. The level was also the lowest in 22 years, since September, 1949.

The drop reflected a growing belief that the West German central bank will intervene in the markets early next week in an effort to start pushing out of the country huge amounts of inflationary dollars, which poured in earlier this year and led to the recent monetary crisis.

The level was officially fixed today at 3.5030 marks to the dollar compared to Wednesday's rate of 3.5290. Markets were closed yesterday for Ascension Day.

Immediately after the official fixing, the rate eased further in quiet trading to 3.4970, more than 4 per cent below the official parity of 3.66 marks to the dollar.

So far, the floating of the mark — releasing it from its fixed margins against the dollar and letting it find its own level—has stopped the inflow but has not achieved its main purpose of pushing the dollars out again.

Judging from forecasts by a number of well-informed sources, the Federal Bank will intervene, probably Monday, by offering surplus dollars it was forced to buy up at the lowest fixed rate before floating at a price of somewhere around 3.45 marks, equivalent to a temporary revaluation of more than 5 per cent.

The aim of the move would be to provoke speculators who bought up marks for dollars in the days and weeks before the floating to get rid of them at an advantageous rate, and thus start the outflow.

Originally, the Federal bank was known to have opposed intervention, fearing that it could only lead to a new permanent upward revaluation of the mark in contradiction to Bonn's pledges to its Common Market partners to return to the old parity after an unspecified period of floating.

But according ot informed sources, Economics and Finance Minister Karl Schiller persuaded the bank to change its mind at a long meeting Tuesday night.

Mr. Schiller, who has staked his political career on bringing economic stability back to his country through the floating despite internal and external opposition, told a meeting of businessmen here today that the action had opened the way to a long-overdue reform of the international monetary system.

A response had long been needed to the United States policy of "benign neglect" for its balance-of-payments deficit, he added.

Finland Raises Discount Rate

HELSINKI, Finland, May 21 (Reuters)—Finland today announced that she had raised her discount rate to 8.5 per cent from 7 per cent. The increase is effective from June 1.

May 22, 1971

Connally Tells Bankers U.S. Will Defend Dollar

Burns, Also at Munich Meeting, Calls for a U.S. Incomes Policy

By CLYDE H. FARNSWORTH

Special to The New York Times

MUNICH, West Germany, May 28—Treasury Secretary John B. Connally Jr. voiced today the United States Government's determination to defend the dollar and said that other industrialized nations must respond by assuming greater world responsibilities.

In a tough speech to international bankers gathered in this capital city of Bavaria, the silver-haired Texan demanded that Western Europe, Canada and Japan "share more fully in the cost of defending the free world."

He also called on these nations to undertake more liberal trading arrangements to permit American exports to expand.

"No longer does the United States economy dominate the free world," Mr. Connally said. "No longer can considerations of friendship or need or capacity justify the United States carrying so heavy a share of the common burdens."

Mr. Connally spoke to the international monetary conference of the American Bankers Association. The heads of most of the world's major banks were present as well as leading monetary officials.

Also addressing the forum was Arthur F. Burns, chairman of the Federal Reserve Board, who once again stressed the need for an effective incomes policy in the United States to check wage and price increases.

The first reaction of West German officials at the meeting was that Mr. Connally was making a political speech for home consumption. They did not take his remarks very seriously.

There was an element of friction between American and German officials at the week-long conference. This arose because of the West German Government's decision earlier this month to stop supporting the dollar in the exchange markets.

One of the signs of the tensions was the absence at the gathering of West Germany's Economics and Finance Minister, Karl Schiller.

By detaching the mark from its fixed dollar peg and permitting it to float upward, Mr. Schiller, in effect, devalued the dollar in terms of marks.

German Inflation Curbs

The Germans acted to curb domestic inflation. They are also pressing for some fundamental changes in the monetary system—moves toward acceptance of greater currency flexibility.

Mr. Connally pointedly referred to the floating-mark experiment in his speech. "To revert to the use of exchange rates as a supplementary tool of domestic policy is fraught with danger to the essential stability and sustainability of the system as a whole," he said.

But he did indicate that the United States would support moves toward limited flexibility that are being studied now by the International Monetary Fund, the quarter-century-old monetary institution of the West

"The question of codifying a degree of additional flexibility with regard to exchange-rate practices is clearly relevant," Mr. Connally said. "De facto events have brought some elements of flexibility. But I doubt that any of us could be satisfied with the variety of responses to the imperatives of speculative pressures."

The New York Times

John B. Connally Jr.

United Press International

Arthur F. Burns

Monetary Flexibility

Flexibility essentially is the provision for permitting currencies to fluctuate across wider bands, for installing a system of more frequent parity changes and for legalizing temporary floats such as are now being carried out by Canada, Germany and the Netherlands.

Under the rules, currencies fluctuate within 1 per cent above and 1 per cent below their fixed parity against the dollar. There is no provision for a temporary float.

Both Mr. Burns and Mr. Connally also went on record for the first time in support for some form of institutionalized controls over short-term international dollar flows.

Differences in Germany

It was the massive movement of dollars into Germany that set off the Bonn Government's decision to float the mark. The powerful German Economics and Finance Ministry remains opposed to exchange controls of any sort. The Bundesbank, the central bank, with its coffers overflowing with dollars, is more favorable.

There has been a good deal of talk about controlling the dollar flows, but no one is quite sure yet what form, if any, international action along these lines will take.

The Bundesbank president, Karl Klasen, spoke at the meeting today about Germany's inflation problem, pointing out that the public had to be convinced that higher wages or profits did not automatically mean more purchasing power.

Alluding to remarks by the First Secretary of the Soviet Communist party, Leonid I. Brezhnev, at a recent party congress in Moscow, Mr. Klasen said this was a problem that was faced both by Communist and capitalist countries. Mr. Brezhnev had said: "One can only distribute and consume what has been produced, this is an elementary truth."

Swiss Bank's Statement

Special to The New York Times

GENEVA, May 28—The Swiss National Bank expressed today the "firm hope" that every effort would be made at the international level to re-establish and maintain stable currency exchange rates.

Stable rates are required for the "international division of labor that assures the growth of general prosperity," a bank statement said.

U.S. Gold Imports Up in April

WASHINGTON, May 28 (Reuters) — United States gold imports totalled $20,722,637 in April, up slightly from March imports of $19,983,954, the Commerce Department reported tonight.

Most of the imports were from Switzerland, which sold $12,453,155 of the metal to the United States in the latest month.

Exports contracted to $21,000 in April from $4,999,653 in March. The entire April gold sale was made to Venezuela.

April purchases brought total United States imports of gold for the year to $86,394,100 and sales brought total exports to $20,040,101.

May 29, 1971

U.S. BIGGEST USER OF 'PAPER GOLD'

'Spent' $337-Million Special Drawing Rights by May 31

By EDWIN L. DALE Jr.

Special to The New York Times

WASHINGTON, July 5—By the end of May the United States had become the world's largest user of Special Drawing Rights, or "paper gold," the International Monetary Fund reported today.

The United States by then had "spent" $337 million of its S.D.R.'s to purchase unwanted dollars from others. The May transactions included the transfer of $55-million of S.D.R.'s to Belgium and $150-million worth to the Netherlands. These are countries that do not traditionally retain large holdings of dollars or any other reserve currency.

The transfer to the Netherlands brought that country's holdings of S.D.R.'s very close to the upper limit of the amount she is required to accept, from the United States or any other country. This limit is three times a country's initial allocation. However, the Netherlands could voluntarily accept more than that amount.

Although the United States has used more S.D.R.'s than any other country, a number of others have used a bigger share of their initial allocation. The United States has used up only 21 per cent of its supply, which totaled $1,584,000,000, the largest of any country.

Other Developments Noted

The I.M.F. also reported these developments in its monthly survey of events:

¶The fund bought $70-million of gold from South Africa in June under the system for purchases under certain conditions. This was the first purchase since January.

¶Under a new system of "remuneration" of members with creditor positions in the fund, the fund distributed about $37-million in gold and S.D.R.'s in May to 39 countries.

¶The United States became a debtor in the fund in May for the first time since November, 1968, using part of its automatic drawing right.

¶Total world trade in the first quarter, measured by total exports, was up 11.5 per cent from a year earlier. Previously, the fund estimated that exports of the industrial countries alone showed a year-to-year rise of 12.5 per cent.

Canadian Reserves Off

OTTAWA, July 5 (Canadian Press) — Canada's foreign exchange reserves totaled $4.85-billion at the end of June, down $26.8-million from the record $4.88-billion at the beginning of the month, the Finance Department reported today.

The decline included a drop of $20.9-million in holdings of United States dollars by the Bank of Canada, the receiver general and the exchange fund account, and a reduction in Canada's reserve position in the International Monetary Fund.

Gold holdings remained unchanged at $791.6-million. Canada's reserves climbed rapidly from their normal level of about $3-billion to more than $4-billion at the end of May last year, when the Government decided to let the Canadian dollar find its own level in international exchange markets.

German Reserves Fall

FRANKFURT, West Germany, July 5 (Reuters)—West Germany's reserves fell by 1.7 billion marks to 60.1 billion marks in the week ended June 30, the Bundesbank said today.

Gross monetary reserves fell 1.8 billion marks to 62.9 billion marks. Currently there is no effective par value for the mark.

French Reserves Up

PARIS, July 5 (Reuters)—The Finance Ministry said today that France's gold and foreign currency reserves increased by 148 million francs in June — compared with a rise of 368 million francs in May—to total 29.5-billion francs.

The ministry said the authorities made no debt repayments in June. The French franc is equivalent to about 18 cents.

July 6, 1971

CHAOTIC TRADING WEAKENS DOLLAR

Central Banks Abroad Are Forced to Support Official Minimum Exchange Rate

PROP BY U.S. RUMORED

Possible Nixon Move Is Tied to Meeting With Economic Aides on Defense Budget

By H. ERICH HEINEMANN

The dollar weakened further yesterday in chaotic trading on world currency exchanges.

Central banks in Europe and Japan were forced to buy substantial amounts of dollars to hold the United States currency at its official minimum in their home markets.

In Zurich, the Swiss National Bank acted to discourage further inflows of funds by imposing a 100 per cent reserve requirement on new deposits of foreign funds and banning the payment of interest on them.

On both sides of the Atlantic, there were rumors in the financial community that President Nixon's meeting with his senior economic advisers, scheduled at Camp David in the Maryland mountains this weekend, would produce a United States initiative to shore up the dollar.

Subject Announced

However, the announced topic of the meeting is not international finance, but rather the defense budget.

In New York, bankers said privately that at least a temporary breakdown of the system of relatively fixed foreign-exchange rates that was negotiated at Bretton Woods, N. H., at the end of World War II appeared to be imminent.

As a result of earlier currency disturbances, three major currencies—the West German mark, the Canadian dollar and the Dutch guilder—are already "floating" in the international markets. That is, these currencies are trading without reference to any specific, defined par value.

In a sense, because these three currencies have all increased in value in relation to the dollar, it can be said that, bit by bit, the American currency is undergoing a piecemeal devaluation. Many bankers here expect additional currencies to float upward against the dollar in the weeks ahead.

To the extent that foreign currencies do appreciate against the dollar, this will naturally tend to be reflected in higher prices of imported goods for American consumers.

'Loss of Confidence'

Meanwhile, the Chase Manhattan Bank in New York, the third largest bank in the United States and a major force in international banking around the world, said that the tension in world foreign-exchange markets reflected "widespread loss of confidence in the dollar."

"Perhaps the most important reason for this," Chase said in an unusually blunt and forthright statement in its publication International Finance, "is the disappointing progress in achieving better economic, and particularly price, performance in the United States."

In the New York foreign-exchange market — which does the bulk of its business after the European markets have closed for the day — the dollar did regain some lost ground in relation to the German mark, the Dutch guilder and the Swiss franc. But this did not change the basic pattern of dollar weakness that had been evident earlier in Europe.

Indeed, reports from Europe indicated that the rebound reflected a temporary, technical shortage of dollars that had developed because traders had, in effect, sold too many dollars and needed to buy some of them back to cover short-term working-capital requirements.

Dispatches from major European financial centers all painted a similar picture. Here are some examples:

¶In Paris, the Reuters news agency said that the Bank of France might have taken in between $200-million and $300-million this week to keep the dollar from falling below its lower limit of 5.513 francs to the dollar (18.139 cents). Last week, France took special measures to limit the influx of dollars.

¶According to The Associated Press, the West German money market in Frankfurt has borne the greatest share of the flood of dollars that has sent the rate of the mark steadily higher since it was allowed to float freely last May. Reuters added that foreign-exchange dealers in Frankfurt estimated that the Bundesbank, the German central bank, bought $43.5-million in dollars this week, even though it currently does not have any official obligation to support the dollar.

¶In Brussels, according to The Associated Press, the National Bank of Belgium bought $11-million in dollars yesterday to keep the dollar above its floor of 49.625 Belgian francs to the dollar (2.015 cents per franc). However, in the free foreign-exchange market in Belgium the dollar dropped to 48.65 francs to the dollar (2.055 cents per franc).

The great uncertainty in the exchange markets at present is how stability and calm are to be restored. With the deficit in the United States international balance of payments now running at an annual rate of between $15-billion and $20-billion, there is a widespread belief that the postwar system of relatively fixed foreign-exchange rates has broken down. What will replace it, no one knows.

It was incorrectly reported in yesterday's editions of The New York Times that the Federal Reserve System had increased its reciprocal credit arrangements with the Swiss National Bank and the National Bank of Belgium by $1.1-billion. The actual increase was $500-million, with the Swiss credit line being increased to $1-billion from $600-million, and that with the Belgians to $600-million from $500-million.

August 14, 1971

NIXON SEVERS LINK BETWEEN DOLLAR AND GOLD

A WORLD EFFECT

Unilateral U.S. Move Means Others Face Parity Decisions

By EDWIN L. DALE Jr.

Special to The New York Times

WASHINGTON, Aug. 15 — President Nixon announced tonight that henceforth the United States would cease to convert foreign-held dollars into gold—unilaterally changing the 25-year-old international monetary system.

How many pounds, marks, yen and francs the dollar will buy tomorrow will depend on decisions of other countries. In some countries, the value of the dollar may "float," moving up and down in day-to-day exchanges. A period of turmoil in the foreign-exchange markets is all but certain, which means uncertainty for American tourists, exporters and importers.

The President said he was taking the action to stop "the attacks of international money speculators" against the dollar. He did not raise the official price of gold, which has been $35 an ounce since 1934.

Devaluation Denied

Mr. Nixon said he was not devaluing the dollar. But, he said, "If you want to buy a foreign car, or take a trip abroad, market conditions may cause your dollar to buy slightly less."

In addition to severing the link between the dollar and gold, the President announced a 10 per cent extra tax on all dutiable imports, except those that are subject to quotas, or quantitative limits.

The tax will thus apply to cars but not to coffee, to radios but not to sugar, to shoes but not to oil. Coffee and other items, such as bananas, grown in tropical countries are exempt because no duty is charged on them. Oil and sugar are exempt because they are under quota. The President said he had legal authority for the new surcharge.

Foreign Action Favored

The change in the world monetary system brought about by the President's decision to cease converting foreign-held dollars into gold is entirely uncertain. That was the word used by Secretary of the Treasury John B. Connally. What matters most is exchange rates among currencies and Mr. Connally said he did not know what would happen.

The purpose of Mr. Nixon's move was clear. The President said, "The time has come for exchange rates to be set straight and for the major nations to compete as equals." This means a desire for other countries to raise their currencies' value in terms of the dollar. In effect, therefore, the dollar would be devalued.

Mr. Connally said, "We anticipate and we hope there would be some changes in exchange rates of other currencies."

But this will depend on other countries. For 25 years non-Communist nations have maintained the international exchange value of their currencies by "pegging" them to the dollar. Their central banks would buy or sell their own currencies in daily trading in the foreign-exchange market to keep the value within one per cent either side of "par," expressed in a precise dollar amount for each unit of the other currency.

After Mr. Nixon's action tonight, they can still do so, if they so wish. But they are no longer obligated to do so under the rules of the International Monetary Fund. Their obligation to peg their currencies to the dollar was a counterpart of the United States's obligation to exchange dollars for gold. The United States has now renounced that obligation.

Referring to the 1944 conference in New Hampshire that established the I.M.F. and the present rules for monetary exchange, Arthur M. Okun, Chairman of the Council of Economic Advisers under President Johnson, said tonight, "We just ended the Bretton Woods system forever."

Mr. Okun said he could not say by what degree other currencies would rise in value relative to the dollar, but he was certain that they would rise.

Apparently more than 100 countries are going to have to make decisions within the next 48 hours as to what to do. In Europe, as it happens, most foreign-exchange markets will be closed tomorrow because of the Feast of Assumption, giving Governments and central banks a little more time to decide.

Although the President's unilateral action may cause difficulties in the nation's foreign relations, particularly with industrialized countries, he held out an olive branch. He said his action "will not win us any friends among the international money traders," but he added:

"In full cooperation with the International Monetary Fund and those who trade with us, we will press for the necessary reforms to set up an urgently needed new international monetary system. Stability and equal treatment is in everybody's best interest."

A Treasury statement said, "United States officials will promptly be meeting with their colleagues from other countries to explain the background and details of the President's program. They will develop United States proposals for both dealing constructively with the immediate repercussions of today's decision and employing . . . the opportunity opened by today's action for speeding the evolution in the international monetary system in directions that serve the common needs of trading nations."

The background of the President's action was a long series of deficits in the nation's balance of international payments. Recently, the picture darkened as one key element in the balance of payments, the trade balance of exports and imports, swung into deficit in the second quarter for the first time since an abnormal period in 1946 immedately following World War II.

Last week, the dollar was under heavy selling pressure in European foreign-exchange markets. Where it could weaken, it did — as in West Germany, which has a temporary "floating" exchange rate, following pressure last spring for an upward revaluation.

The President emphasized that, although imports might cost more as a result of his action, "if you are among the overwhelming majority who buy American-made products in America, your dollar will be worth just as much tomorrow as it is today."

Technically, the Treasury announced these steps:

¶The United States "notified the International Monetary Fund that, effective today, the United States no longer freely buys and sells gold for the settlement of international transactions." This withdraws a commitment made in 1947.

¶Use of monetary reserve assets, including gold and other assets such as drawing rights or "paper gold" on the International Monetary Fund, will be "strictly limited" to "settlement of outstanding obligations and, in cooperation with the I.M.F., to other situations that may arise in which such use can contribute to international monetary stability and the interests of the United States."

¶The President "requested" the independent Federal Reserve Board to cease the automatic operation of its system of "swaps" with other countries, which is a means of converting dollars into other currencies and temporarily averting conversion of foreign-held dollars into gold.

The statement said no "new decision" had been made regarding the present controls over the outflow of United States capital, such as investments by United States companies abroad and purchase by Americans of foreign securities, now subject to an "interest equalization tax." These restraints remain in effect, the statement said.

August 17, 1971

Move Toward Flexibility Is Regarded As Realistic

By ANTHONY LEWIS
Special to The New York Times

LONDON, Aug. 16—"This is the end of the myth," a financial expert said today as he discussed what the London papers called the dollar bombshell. He might have been talking about the myth of American omnipotence, but what he actually had in mind was an article of financial faith through most of the years since World War II —the notion that world economic well-being depended on tightly fixed rates of exchange between the major currencies.

The idea of "flexibility" has been gaining in the international monetary world. The Germans advanced it a long step earlier this year when they let the mark float without any fixed peg. But observers here consider it a much bigger event, and much more symbolic, that the President of the United States in effect has invited other major financial powers to devalue the dollar.

The British have been through currency crises so often that they looked on today's with a certain familiarity. Observers said that some of President Nixon's words sounded like those of Harold Wilson when he devalued the pound in 1967. There were, for instance, the attempt to blame "speculators" and the assurance that few citizens would notice the difference.

Considered Realistic

But the general impression here was that inside Mr. Nixon's soft verbal presentation was a hard policy of realism and change. In essence, as British sources see it, he has accepted what no President could easily accept—the fact that the dollar's value in the world must reflect what the markets think it is worth.

There was apparent confirmation of this tonight in the news conference given here by Paul A. Volcker, the United States Under Secretary of the Treasury.

He was asked whether the United States Government would object if other countries floated their currencies now, letting them rise in value relative to the dollar. That would have been monetary heresy in the past, but Mr. Volcker smiled and said, "I think we are in no position to object."

Devaluation 'Inevitable'

Many European authorities have felt for a long time that the dollar was overvalued. Thus, to buy American products, others had to exchange more pounds or francs or marks than they thought the items were worth, and American exports became less competitive. The American balance of trade—the balance of exports to imports — steadily worsened.

Eventually, as the British learned with so much pain, people lose confidence in an overvalued currency and try to unload it. That weakens confidence still further.

Sir Roy Harrod, the British economist, reflected expert opinion when he commented today, "Devaluation of the dollar in one form or another was inevitable."

But the form was believed to be highly significant. President Nixon could have fought to maintain the dollar's official value through even greater restrictions on imports and American spending abroad and through strict restraints on the movement of capital.

The Labor Government took that course from 1964 to 1967. It treated the pound's set value of $2.80 as a matter of national pride and took highly restrictive measures to hold the rate. In the end the effort failed and the pound was devalued.

That history convinced most economic observers here that it was wiser for a country to accept reality gracefully when its currency is overvalued.

Some careful readers of the President's speech — the full text appeared in several newspapers here—said that he had turned the old symbolism of a nation's currency upside down. Instead of insisting on holding the dollar's value, he said twice that it was "unfair" for other countries to insist on present parities.

Some London commentators chided the President for some passages in his speech that they considered political window-dressing.

One was an assurance to American buyers of American products that "your dollar will be worth just as much tomorrow." That was seen here as paralleling a widely-criticized assurance by Mr. Wilson in 1967 that "the pound in your pocket had not been devalued." One cartoonist showed the President telephoning Mr. Wilson today to apologize for stealing his lines.

The President's attacks on "speculators" also paralleled Mr. Wilson's. Informed observers doubted that currency speculators had had much of a role in the dollar's troubles.

'Just Prudential'

An officer in a major London bank said that the "vast bulk"

of recent movements from dollars to other currencies was "just prudential — ordinary commercial coverings by large firms."

Sir Roy, writing in The Evening Standard, said that financial advisers to big companies or investment bodies were bound to warn their principals against holding too much of a weakening currency.

But the British commentators viewed these passages in the Nixon speech as insignifican compared with the policy of accepting parity changes. Even the 10 per cent import surcharge, much as it may hurt sales of British cars and whiskey, was widely seen as a bearable short-term measure.

The Financial Times of London, in an editorial in tomorrow's issue, calls the surcharge "regrettable in theory but in practice a good deal better than direct controls"—meaning quotas. The editorial add that Mr. Nixon seems to have avoided the danger of "bringing in measures of protection which would provoke reprisals and so inhibit the future growth of world trade."

August 16, 1971

Nixon, in Illinois, Says His Policies Seek to Realign World's Currencies

By JAMES M. NAUGHTON
Special to The New York Times

SPRINGFIELD, Ill., Aug. 18—President Nixon declared today that the international elements of his new economic policy were designed to meet "the need to revalue the currencies of the world."

It was the first time since the President announced a set of domestic and international economic moves Sunday night that he flatly asserted a desire to change the value of the United States dollar in relation to other nations' currencies.

Mr. Nixon on Sunday, in imposing a 90-day wage and price freeze, asking for tax cuts and suspending the 25-year-old United States pledge to redeem foreign-held dollars in gold, declared that he wanted to "lay to rest the bugaboo of what is called devaluation." The effect of his action halting the convertibility of dollars to gold would be, he said, "to stabilize the dollar."

But today, Mr. Nixon cast the economic move in terms of a general shift in currency valuations during brief remarks he made in the Old State Capitol just before signing a bill to make Abraham Lincoln's family home a national historic site.

Standing in the center of the Hall of Representatives, where Lincoln began his political career, the President invoked "the legacy of Lincoln" to appeal for the third time in four days for a revitalization of American competitive spirit.

Need for Strength Emphasized

The United States must remain the most sound and powerful nation in the world to assure the peace of future generations, the President said. Then he added:

"I am rather sure that if Abraham Lincoln were standing again in this place, as he stood here 110 years ago, he would perhaps say some of the things I have tried to say. I am sure that he would say, as I will now say, that we can, at this point in our history, nobly save or meanly lose man's last, best hope on earth."

Mr. Nixon, who flew here from New York en route west on a five-state public tour, spoke to a bipartisan audience of Illinois officials and dignataries before signing the Lincoln Home Bill on a walnut desk used by the Civil War President to write his first inaugural address.

But there was a political flavor to the President's appearance later at the Illinois State Fair grounds, where some 150,000 people gave him a warm welcome, crowding around him as he shook hundreds of hands, viewed champion steers and sows and praised the productivity of American farmers.

Unpopularity Recalled

Even at the old State Capitol building, Governor Richard B. Ogilvie, a Republican, sought in his remarks to draw a timely parallel between Presidents Nixon and Lincoln.

"Lincoln faced criticism, misunderstanding and personal abuse," Mr. Ogilvie said. "He knew what it was to be unpopular because of decisions that had to be made and responsibilities that had to be met.

"You face these same troubles today, Mr. President," the Governor went on. "And you are facing them with the attitudes that served Lincoln well."

Associated Press

President Nixon, at desk once used by Lincoln, signs bill making Lincoln home a historic site. With him are Gov. Richard B. Ogilvie and Representative Paul Findley, right.

August 19, 1971

$13-BILLION GAIN SOUGHT TO SPUR PAYMENTS TO U.S.

Connally Issues Challenge on Improving Balance as Group of Ten Meets

EUROPEANS SKEPTICAL

Plan 'Ambitious,' Common Market Leader Says as London Talks Start

By JOHN M. LEE
Special to The New York Times

LONDON, Sept. 15 — Secretary of the Treasury John B. Connally told the United States' trade partners today they must help produce what he conceded would be a "stunning" $13-billion improvement in the American balance of international payments.

Mr. Connally issued this challenge as finance ministers of the leading economic powers, known as the Group of Ten, met to tackle the dollar crisis provoked by President Nixon a month ago.

The issue is what other nations can do or should do to help turn the American payments deficit into surplus. Washington is pressing for an upward revaluation of foreign currencies, trade liberalization and sharing of worldwide defense commitments.

'What Friends Are For'

To spur action, Mr. Nixon upset the basis of the existing monetary system by cutting the dollar loose from gold and raised the specter of trade protectionism by imposing a 10 per cent surcharge on American imports.

"We had a problem and we're sharing it with the world, just like we shared our prosperity," Mr. Connally said blandly for the television cameras as he left the afternoon meeting. "That's what friends are for."

Some of these friends, however, took exception to the Secretary's estimate of the size of the problem and thus of the steps required to rectify it.

Turnabout Is Criticized

Mario Ferrari-Aggradi, Italian Finance Minister and chairman of the Common Market Finance Ministers group, criticized the projected $13-billion turnabout as "too ambitious" and one that would disrupt world economies if achieved too quickly.

The $13-billion turnaround figure Mr. Connally mentioned is the swing from a projected payments deficit, which ran at a $9-billion annual rate in the first half, to a payments surplus of undefined size.

"I admitted it was a stunning figure," Mr. Connally said at a news conference, "but it is a very conservative figure."

He said it was not produced just for negotiating purposes but was a realistic figure and made no allowances to cover short-term money movements or for any net increase in long-term capital flows.

Time Scale Is Avoided

The Secretary gave no indication of the time scale he had in mind for achieving such an enormous swing but it would obviously take years. His aides said most of the improvement must come from merchandise trade.

The $13-billion figure used by Mr. Connally was interpreted by some persons at the meeting as the turnaround sought on current account, that is trade in goods and financial services, excluding long-term capital for aid and investment. The $9-billion figure is the annual rate of deficit in the basic balance of payments, that is, the current account plus long-term capital but excluding erratic short-term money movements.

Edgar Benson, the Canadian Finance Minister and chairman of the meeting, told newsmen, "it's fruitless to talk about amounts."

But if the difference still yawned wide, the atmosphere was still friendly. The Ministers set out their positions calmly for about two and a half hours in the ornate upstairs Music Room at Lancaster House; a former royal residence near Buckingham Palace.

Tonight, they reassembled for informal talks during a black-tie dinner given by Anthony Barber, Chancellor of the Exchequer. The meeting ends tomorrow with an all-day formal session. Little measureable progress is expected.

"We're feeling for procedure, for methods for a way to do it," Mr. Connally said, describing for newsmen the meeting's approach to the tangled trade and currency problems.

"It's too much to hope we'd do much more than get our positions out on the table," he continued, "and get a feeling of the firmness of the respective positions."

However, European foreign exchange markets were highly unsettled today by the prospect that the ministers might negotiate higher parities for strong currencies, and the dollar came under strong pressure.

The West German deutschemark was at a new high of 3.3670 to the dollar, up from yesterday's 3.3755. Today's rate depreciated the dollar against the mark by 8 per cent. The dollar fell also against the British pound, the Swiss franc, the Dutch guilder and the Italian lire. It was unchanged against the Japanese yen and the French franc.

The Bank of England entered the market this afternoon to limit the pound's upward float to $2.471 up from yesterday's 2.4676.

Other Devaluations

The new rate devalues the dollar against the pound by 2.9 per cent. Other effective dollar devaluation rates are 6.4 per cent against the yen, more than 6 per cent against the Canadian dollar and 5.7 per cent against the guilder.

However, Washington officials have talked in terms of substantial revaluations (and effective dollar devaluations) in the range of 10 to 20 per cent. Foreign exchange experts say such changes in this higher range would be needed if the improvements projected by Mr. Connally are to be realized.

Mizio Mizuta, the Japanese Finance Minister, was said to have told the meeting that while Japan appreciated that a major realignment of currency values was necessary, including gold, the Japanese economy could not stand up to a substantial revaluation of the yen.

All the members of the Group of Ten except the United States have urged an outright dollar devaluation through a modest increase, say 5 or 10 per cent, in the price of gold. The official posture of the United States is to oppose such a change. But there is growing conjecture in Europe that this is negotiable.

When asked by newsmen after the meeting about the gold price, Mr. Connally volunteered no new commitment but said simply "our position on this subject is well known."

Regarding the envisioned $13-billion turnaround, in the light of an official estimate on Monday that the United States basic balance of payments had run a first-half deficit at an annual rate of $9-billion, Paul A. Volcker, Treasury Under Secretary for Monetary Affairs, said the higher figure represented a turnaround from a higher deficit that might be achieved if the economy was running near its capacity.

Pressed for an estimate of the actual 1971 payments deficit, Mr. Volcker said $9-billion was "a good ballpark figure."

Arthur Burns, chairman of the Federal Reserve system who is attending the meeting with other Central Bank governors, said the American objective was to achieve "equilibrium in our balance of payments with a certain margin of safety."

However, the Italian minister, Mr. Ferrari-Aggradi, expressed the view of many Europeans that the immediate American objective should be a moderate deficit and that the mid-term objective should be equilibrium, or a zero balance, rather than a surplus.

The members of the Group of Ten meeting here today are the United States, Britain, Japan, Canada, Sweden and the five most important Common Market countries, West Germany, France, Italy, the Netherlands and Belgium. Switzerland attends as an observer.

Today's meeting marked Mr. Connally's first appearance at a Group of Ten meeting and he was easily the most sought out figure both by newsmen and ministers. He arrived just at the 3 o'clock starting time after others had assembled, but he took a moment for a few smiles and handshakes with newsmen. Afterward, while other ministers rushed out, the Secretary willingly stopped for television interviews.

Mr. Connally told newsmen he had tried to emphasize the magnitude of the American problem and also convince other ministers that they were unduly emphasizing the effect of the import surcharge. He said once again that this was a temporary measure but he gave no indication of its duration or of the exact moves needed to secure its removal.

America's trade partners are united in giving priority to removal of the surcharge, with Japan and Canada particularly adament. All also seem agreeable to some sort of realignment of parities to give American goods a price advantage, provided the United States makes its contribution by devaluing the dollar with a gold-price increase.

The sticking point is that Washington has declined to give any specific commitment on the surcharge and has reaffirmed its opposition to increasing the price of gold from its official $35 an ounce.

September 16, 1971

Forewarning on Dollar

Prophecy by Triffin Recalled as a New Money Is Backed

By LEONARD SILK

Economic Analysis

Twelve years ago a group of the world's leading economists gathered at Elsinore, Denmark—the scene of Hamlet's tragic story — to enjoy the autumn weather by the sea and condemn inflation. But on the first day of their meeting, Prof. Robert Triffin of Yale arose like Hamlet's father's ghost to warn the economists of a greater danger than inflation. The international monetary system, he said, could not go on expanding indefinitely, based as it was on gold and national currencies, especially the dollar.

A day would come, Professor Triffin predicted, when the monetary system would fall apart as it had done in 1931, dragging the world into deep depression, unless a new international money were created to supplant dollars and gold.

Last week at the International Monetary Fund's meetings in Washington, Professor Triffin had the pleasure, granted to very few Cassandras, of hearing the finance ministers of the major nations repeating his grim prophecy and calling for his own remedy as though they were listening to a voice in the air.

However, the more sophisticated ministers knew that the voice they heard was that of Mr. Triffin.

He had foreseen back in 1959 two evolving threats to the international monetary system.

The first derived from the difficulty of providing enough gold for an expanding world economy. Gold production and Russian gold sales were not keeping pace with the increase of world trade—and with the need of nations to increase their monetary reserves to cover their balance-of-payments deficits.

The second threat resulted from the first. To palliate the gold shortage, the capitalist nations were rebuilding the old gold-exchange system.

Increasingly, they were using United States dollars as monetary reserves, acquired through the deficits in the American balance of payments. But Professor Triffin warned that chronic United States deficits would inevitably undermine confidence in the dollar.

A dollar crisis would come when nations had acquired more dollars than they were willing to hold.

During the 1960's, the crisis was forestalled when the United States induced other nations to convert dollars into other forms of debt.

The master of this Fabian defense of the dollar was Undersecretary of the Treasury Robert V. Roosa.

But that defense could not last indefinitely. The first massive attack on the dollar standard came in March, 1968. It was staved off by the creation of the two-tier gold system, which prevented private holders of dollars from claiming official gold.

The second blow to the dollar came last May. It was brought on by the rush of hot money out of dollars and into German marks and other European currencies, partly as a result of interest rate differentials between the United States and Europe, partly because of rumors of an impending German upvaluation, but most fundamentally because of the widespread belief that the dollar had been weakened by a long series of American deficits in the balance of payments.

American Government officials went on insisting that the dollar was as strong as ever. Indeed, they had taken this line throughout the preceding decade.

American administrations have always been convinced that when they really wanted to, they could eliminate the deficit in the balance of payments.

Eisenhower Proposals

At the end of the 1950's, the Eisenhower Administration urged European nations to pick up more of the west's defense burdens, step up their own foreign aid and capital exports, and drop discrimination against dollar goods.

Nevertheless, the payments gap was not closed. Vietnam and a stepup in United States inflation widened the gap after the mid-1960's.

However, Professor Triffin had foreseen that the real trouble would begin not while the balance-of-payments deficits of the United States continued but when they were ended.

The reason was that "a successful readjustment of the United States balance-of-payments is bound to bring to the fore the latent crisis of international liquidity."

As the liquidity squeeze developed, the high pace of expansion in the world economy maintained since the end of World War II would slow down.

Nations would feel increasing pressure to clamp on trade and exchange restrictions or to engage in competitive devaluations.

These pressures would spread from country to country and might be aggravated by speculative capital movements "culminating in a financial panic a la 1931," said Professor Triffin.

The decision of President Nixon on Aug. 15 to suspend gold convertibility and float the dollar, together with his imposition of the 10 per cent imports surcharge, are intended to close the United States balance-of-payments gap and swing it into surplus.

The world now faces the necessity of finding a new source of liquidity other than dollars or gold. Special Drawing Rights, created as a supplement to gold and dollars as monetary reserves only last year, may ultimately replace them.

Some economists would prefer a system of floating exchange rates that would keep nations' payments in continuous balance, thereby obviating the need for monetary reserves to cover deficits.

But most proposals for international monetary reform being offered these days are a blend of these two key elements—new international monetary reserves and more flexible exchange rates.

Which route or combination of routes the world takes toward reform is a matter of politics more than economics.

Nations highly sensitive to the pressures of industrial interest groups at home will not let the international markets freely determine exchange rates. Similarly, nations anxious to bind their economies closer together—such as the European Common Market countries—want highly stable exchange rates but realize this means they must closely coordinate their monetary and fiscal policies.

The major monetary powers—the United States, West Germany, France, Britain and Japan—are not yet ready to choose either the course of closer integration or floating exchange rates.

"These two roads are very different and it is extremely difficult to determine in which direction the international monetary system will evolve," says Lawrence B. Krause of the Brookings Institution, in a new tract, "Sequel to Bretton Woods: a Proposal to Reform the World Monetary System."

Straddle of Routes

"At this juncture, however, the world can keep one foot on its path without much discomfort," says Mr. Krause.

Whether the world can actually straddle the two routes of greater flexibility of exchange rates and closer economic integration or whether it must choose one group or the other is the crucial issue for world monetary reform.

However, to reject both of those routes would mean the fracturing of the international monetary system and a growing trend toward protectionism, capital controls, and economic self-sufficiency for individual nations and regional blocks.

October 6, 1971

10-NATION MONETARY AGREEMENT REACHED; DOLLAR IS DEVALUED 8.57%; SURCHARGE OFF

NIXON HAILS PACT

He Makes a Surprise Appearance—Gold Goes to $38

By EDWIN L. DALE Jr.

Special to The New York Times

WASHINGTON, Dec. 18 — The world's 10 leading non-Communist industrial nations reached agreement tonight on a new pattern of currency exchange rates, including a devaluation of the United States dollar by 8.57 per cent.

Speaking to reporters as the negotiations ended, President Nixon said, "It is my great privilege to announce, on behalf of the finance ministers and the other representatives of the 10 countries involved, the conclusion of the most significant monetary agreement in the history of the world."

The new United States 10 per cent import surcharge will be removed next week. The surcharge was imposed, and the entire recent monetary turmoil began, with President Nixon's dramatic domestic and international economic measures of August 15.

Yen to Go Up

Several other currencies, led by the Japanese yen, will be revalued upward.

Treasury Secretary John B. Connally said that the over-all effect would be an effective devaluation of the dollar by 12 per cent. This figure is arrived at by allowing for United States trade with each of the countries. The Canadian dollar, which will continue to float in daily trading, was left out of the calculation.

A communiqué issued by the Group of 10, said that most foreign exchange markets would be closed on Monday, but Mr. Connally said the United States market would be open.

The dollar devaluation figure of 8.57 per cent used by Mr. Connally results from a proposed increase in the official price of gold from $35 to $38 an ounce. Congress, however, will not be asked to approve the necessary legislation to increase the gold price until the United States wins concessions from Japan, the European Common Market and Canada on trade matters.

However, foreign exchange trading—that is, the actual exchange rate of the dollar against the other currencies—will be conducted at levels as if the new gold price were already in effect.

As in all cases of changes in a currency's exchange rate, the percentage of dollar devaluation can be calculated in two ways. The figure used by Mr. Connally of 8.57 per cent will be the increase in the cost of a currency—such as the British pound, which did not change in value—to an American buyer. For a foreigner buying dollars, the devaluation will be 7.89 per cent.

The latter figure is the technically more correct of the two.

The Group of 10 communiqué left to each country to announce its new exchange rate. However, most of the rates quickly became known here.

For example, the Japanese yen will rise in value against the dollar by just 16.88 per cent with a new yen rate reported at 308 to the dollar. The 17 per cent upward revaluation of the yen comes in part through the devaluation of the dollar and in part through a revaluation of the yen.

The British pound and French franc will remain unchanged in terms of gold, meaning they will rise by 7.89 per cent against the dollar. The West German mark will be set at 3.22 marks to the dollar for an upward revaluation of about 12 per cent.

Associated Press

ANNOUNCING MONETARY MOVE: President Nixon speaking at the Smithsonian Institution in Washington. At right is Karl Schiller, Finance Minister of West Germany.

Lira and Kronor Revalue

The Italian lira and Swedish kronor will both be devalued slightly — 1 or 2 per cent against gold. This will still leave them significantly higher in relation to the dollar than before.

The Canadian dollar will continue to float. The Canadian Government pledged not to manipulate the rate through intervention by its central bank in foreign exchange trading. Mr. Connally said he expected the Canadian dollar to rise somewhat from its present value of almost exactly one United States dollar.

Besides the currency realignment, the agreement included another significant change. For the indefinite future, currencies will be allowed to fluctuate above and below their par values by 2.25 per cent, compared with only 1 per cent under the former monetary rules. It is hoped that this change will both ease the transition to the new exchange rates and reduce heavy flows of speculative funds.

Convertibility Unsettled

Under the agreement, dollars held by foreign central banks will continue to be inconvertible into gold or any other United States monetary reserve asset. That is, President Nixon's suspension of buying and selling of gold remains in effect.

The delicate question of ultimate convertibility of the dollar will be negotiated as part of a sweeping reform of the world monetary system. But meanwhile, ordinary trading, travel, and investment can proceed at reasonably known and fixed exchange rates.

The agreement—the first in history involving a multinational negotiation of exchange rates—was reached after two days of secret talks among finance ministers and central bank governors of the 10 nations in the 116-year-old red castle building of the Smithsonian Institution. Just before the final communiqué was issued, President Nixon appeared dramatically before nearly 400 representatives of the world press in the Art and Industries Building next door, accompanied by many of the ministers of the 10 nations.

United Press International

DISCUSSES MONETARY ACCORD: Treasury Secretary John B. Connally briefing newsmen at the Smithsonian Institution on international agreement. At the left is Dr. Arthur F. Burns, chairman of the Federal Reserve System.

Besides the United States, the countries in the Group of 10 are Britain, Canada, Japan, Sweden, Belgium, France, West Germany, Italy and the Netherlands.

Asking himself the hypothetical question of "who won and who lost," the President said "the whole free world has won."

Simultaneously with the removal next week of the 10 per cent import surcharge, the President will also end the "Buy American" aspect of the new business investment tax credit just enacted by Congress to help stimulate the domestic economy. As enacted, the bill provided that this special tax benefit would not apply to purchases of imported machinery and equipment as long as the import surcharge lasted.

The communiqué recognized that scores of nations, including such important trading nations as Australia, were not represented here. It said:

"The ministers and governors recognized that all members of the International Monetary Fund not attending the present discussions will need urgently to reach decisions with respect to their own exchange rates. It was the view of the ministers and governors that it is particularly important at this time that no country seek improper competitive advantage through its exchange rate policies. Changes in parities can only be justified by an objective appraisal which establishes a position of disequalibrium."

Despite this admonition, many countries including most of Latin America, are expected to devalue along with the dollar. There would presumably be no international objection to such a move.

December 19, 1971

Text of Communique on Monetary Talks

WASHINGTON, Dec. 18 (UPI)—Following is the communiqué issued by the ministers at the monetary meetings:

The ministers and central bank governors of the 10 countries participating in the general arrangements to borrow met at the Smithsonian Institution in Washington on 17-18 December, 1971, in executive session under the chairmanship of Mr. J. B. Connally, Secretary of the Treasury of the United States.

Mr. P. P. Schweitzer, the managing director of the International Monetary Fund, took part in the meeting, which was also attended by the president of the Swiss National Bank, Mr. E. Stopper, and in part by the Secretary General of the O.E.C.D., Jonkheer E. Van Lennep, the general manager of the Bank for International Settlements, Mr. R. Larre, and the vice president of the Commission of the E.E.C., Mr. R. Barre. The ministers and governors welcomed a report from the managing director of the fund on a meeting held between their deputies and the executive directors of the fund.

The ministers and governors agreed on an interrelated set of measures designed to restore stability to international monetary arrangements and to provide for expanding international trade. These measures will be communicated promptly to other governments. It is the hope of the ministers and governors that all governments will cooperate through the International Monetary Fund to permit implementation of these measures in an orderly fashion.

The ministers and governors reached agreement on a pattern of exchange rate relationships among their currencies. These decisions will be announced by individual governments, in the form of par values or central rates as they desire. Most of the countries plan to close their exchange markets on Monday. The Canadian minister informed the group that Canada intends temporarily to maintain a floating exchange rate and intends to permit fundamental market forces to establish the exchange rate without intervention except as required to maintain orderly conditions.

It was also agreed that, pending agreement on longer-term monetary reforms, provision will be made for 2¼ per cent margins of exchange rate fluctuation above and below the new exchange rates. The ministers and governors recognized that all members of the International Monetary Fund not attending the present discussions will need urgently to reach decisions, in consultation with the International Monetary Fund, with respect to their own exchange rates. It was the view of the ministers and governors that it is particularly important at this time that no country seek improper competitive advantage through its exchange rate policies. Changes in parities can only be justified by an objective appraisal

which establishes a position of disequilibrium.

Questions of trade arrangements were recognized by the ministers and governors as a relevant factor in assuring a new and lasting equilibrium in the international economy. Urgent negotiations are now under way between the United States and the Commission of the European Community, Japan, and Canada to resolve pending short-term issues at the earliest possible date and with the European Community to establish an appropriate agenda for considering more basic issues in a framework of mutual cooperation in the course of 1972 and beyond.

The United States agreed to propose to Congress a suitable means for devaluing the dollar in terms of gold to $38 per ounce as soon as the related set of short-term measures is available for Congressional scrutiny. Upon passage of required legislative authority in this framework, the United States will propose the corresponding new par value of the dollar to the International Monetary Fund.

In consideration of the agreed immediate realignment of exchange rates, the United States agreed that it will immediately suppress the recently imposed 10 per cent import surcharge and related provisions of the job development credit.

The ministers and governors agreed that discussions should be promptly undertaken, particularly in the framework of the I.M.F., to consider reform of the international monetary system over the longer term. It was agreed that attention should be directed to the appropriate monetary means and division of responsibilities for defending stable exchange rates and for insuring a proper degree of convertibility of the system; to the proper role of gold, of reserve currencies, and of special drawing rights in the operation of the system; to the appropriate volume of liquidity; to re-examination of the permissible margins of fluctuation around established exchange rates and other means of establish ing a suitable degree of flexibility; and to other measures dealing with movements of liquid capital. It is recognized that decisions in each of these areas are closely linked.

December 19, 1971

U.S. ORDERS DOLLAR DEVALUED 10 PER CENT; JAPANESE YEN WILL BE ALLOWED TO FLOAT; NIXON TO SUBMIT TRADE PLAN TO CONGRESS

GOLD TO BE $42.22

Controls on Lending Abroad Also Will Be Phased Out

By EDWIN L. DALE Jr.
Special to The New York Times

WASHINGTON, Feb. 12—The United States announced tonight a devaluation of the dollar by 10 per cent against nearly all of the world's major currencies.

The action was taken in an effort to halt the latest currency crisis, in which there has been a flight from the dollar in international monetary markets.

The devaluation will be greater than 10 per cent against the Japanese yen, which will float upward in foreign-exchange trading for an indefinite period.

This is the second devaluation of the dollar in 14 months.

Tonight's announcement by Secretary of the Treasury George P. Shultz contained two other elements:

¶The President has decided to submit to Congress comprehensive trade legislation with the aim of lowering trade barriers but with unspecified provisions for "safeguards" against disruption of domestic industries as a result of imports.

¶The United States will phase out three controls on investment and lending abroad that go back to 1963. They will be ended by the end of 1974 or earlier. They cover buying of foreign stocks and bonds, bank lending to foreigners and direct investments abroad by United States corporations.

The announcement by Mr. Shultz came shortly before 11 P.M. at an unusual late evening news conference. As he was completing the news conference, Prsident Nixon returned to the White House. Mr. Nixon had cut short his stay in San Clemente, Calif., and flew back to the capital tonight.

Change 'Acceptable'

Mr. Shultz's announcement said that "the proposed change in the par value of the dollar is acceptable" to "our leading trading partners in Europe." He told the news conference that he did not anticipate any changes in exchange rates by other leading countries apart from the float of the Japanese yen.

While emphasizing that each foreign government would speak for itself, Mr. Shultz said he expected that the three currencies that are now floating — the Canadian dollar, the British pound and the Swiss franc — would continue to float. Floating currencies are allowed to find their own levels in international trading.

The devaluation of the dollar requires the formal approval of Congress. However, as with the devaluation of December, 1971, it will go into effect in currency trading immediately.

Under the rules of the International Monetary Fund, the dollar will be devalued by changing the official price of gold to $42.22 an ounce, compared with $38 an ounce now and $35 up to the end of 1971.

The effect of the devaluation will be some increase to American consumers and businessmen of imported products. But the amount of the increase is uncertain and will depend on pricing decisions by foreign exporters.

The purpose of the dollar devaluation is to improve the nation's international accounts—the trading account, which showed a record deficit last year of $6.4-billion, and the over-all balance of international payments. By the most common definition, the deficit in the balance of payments last year was about $10-billion, though the official figures have not yet been published.

The devaluation of the dollar of 8.57 per cent in December, 1971, which worked out to about 11 per cent after counting upward revaluations of several currencies such as the Japanese yen and the West German mark, has so far not produced the desired results in improving the nation's international accounts.

At the news conference at the Treasury Department, Secretary Shultz issued a formal statement and answered questions briefly.

Seated near Mr. Shultz, though not making any comments, were William P. Rogers, Secretary of State; Peter M. Flanigan, Assistant to the President for International Economic Affairs; Arthur F. Burns, chairman of the Federal Reserve Board, and Herbert Stein, chairman of the Council of Economic Advisers.

Mr. Shultz said that the latest devaluation was designed to "speed improvement of our trade and payments position in a manner that will support our effort to achieve a constructive reform of the monetary system."

Associated Press

George P. Shultz at news conference in the Treasury

Nixon's Decision

Mr. Shultz said the "basic fact" about the dollar was that the United States economy is "healthy" and is showing a slower rate of inflation than nearly all other countries. But he said that the devaluation announced tonight "dramatized" the importance of "getting on with the task" of world monetary reform, in which the United States has made major proposals.

President Nixon, Mr. Schultz said, made his "basic decisions"—presumably meaning the devaluation — last Tuesday and had made his final decision this morning.

Although the United States has always been thoretically able to devalue the dollar by simply notifying the International Monetary Fund, in practice it is not possible without international agreement.

Other countries could nullify the devaluation by changing their own exchange rates by the same amount.

International agreement was achieved in the present case during a hurried trip by Paul A. Volcker, Under Secretary of th Treasury for Monetary Affairs, who visited Tokyo and the main European capitals starting last Wednesday.

The essence of the agreement was that key countries such as Germany and France would not change their exchange rates and that Japan would allow the yen to float.

Mr. Shultz said that he expected the floating of the yen would be upward, meaning a "larger" change than the 10 per cent devaluation of the dollar against the major European currencies.

Mr. Shultz's statement said that the United States has "undertaken no obligations to intervene in foreign exchange markets." This means that the new set of exchange rates will be defended by foreign central banks, not by the Federal Reserve.

This was the case both before and after the Smithsonian agreement of December 1971. Only in a reformed world monetary system might the United States, like other countries, use central-bank intervention in foreign-exchange markets to keep the dollar's exchange rate within its internationally agreed limits.

Mr. Shultz, conceding the "serious deficit" in United States foreign trade, said: "Other nations have been slow in eliminating their excessive surpluses, thereby contributing to uncertainty and instability. In recent days currency disturbances have rocked world exchange markets. Under the pressure of events, some countries have responded with added restrictions, dangerously moving away from the basic objectives we seek."

Tonight's announcment was vague on the contents of the forthcoming trade legislation to be sent to Congress, other than the disclosure that the President had "decided" to propose a bill.

Mr. Shultz said there would be "intensive consultations" with business, labor and other groups, including members of Congress, before the legislation was submitted. He said the legislation would provide for reducing tariffs and other barriers to trade but would also "provide for rasing tariffs when such action would contribute to arrangements assuring that American exports have fair access to foreign markets."

The action in Washington followed intensive meetings in European capitals over the last few days. They involved Paul A. Volcker, Under Secretary of the Treasury, the finance ministers of four European nations — Helmut Schmidt of West Germany, Valéry Giscard d'Estaing of France, Anthony Barber of Britain and Giovanni Malagodi of Italy—and Takashi Hosomi, a special representative of the Japanese Finance Ministry.

Dollar Down in Trading

Special to The New York Times

PARIS, Feb. 12 — The value ofthe dollar eroded further against some European currencies today. There were no official foreign-exchange dealings in most of Western Europe and Japan, but rates were quoted in private transactions between banks.

As part of the Smithsonian agreement negotiated 14 months ago, the dollar was devalued by raising the official price of gold to $38 an ounce from $35 an ounce. Other currencies were revalued upward against the dollar. The object was to help the United States move toward equilibrium in its balance of trade and over-all balance of international payments. A devalued dollar cheapens dollar-priced goods in world markets, thereby helping American exporters to sell abroad.

Yesterday, Japan and the major Western European nations agreed to close their foreign-exchange markets to official dealings, pending a settlement of the crisis.

What happened today then was an unofficial float of several currencies, including the West German mark and the Dutch guilder.

When foreign-exchange markets are officially closed, it simply means that the national bank of the country does not intervene in the market, by buying or selling dollars, to control the rate of its currency. So the currency is left to find its own level, or float.

But closing foreign-exchange markets happens only in periods of crisis. It is an emergency measure. Banks continue to buy and sell currencies, dealing with one another. Without the guidance of the central bank they deal hesitantly and nervously in relatively small amounts for customers who absolutely need a different currency at once.

What happened in the very cautious trading of today was that the West German mark, the target of speculators hoping for an upward revaluation, shot through its upper fixed limit against the dollar and traded at the end of the day at 3.06 marks to the dollar, or 3 per cent above its ceiling.

The Dutch guilder and the Belgian franc also broke through their upper limits. No quotation was available for the Japanese yen, which has also been a target of speculators. One reason for this was that, because of Japan's exceptionally tight exchange controls, it is almost impossible to take delivery of yen in Western Europe.

No Change for Mark

BONN, Feb. 12 (Reuters) The West German marke will retain its present parity against all currencies except the dollar and the floating yen, the state secretary in the ministry, Karl-Otto Pöhl, said tonight.

Britain Reopening Markets

Special to The New York Times

LONDON, Tuesday, Feb. 13—The British Treasury announced that in the light of the statement by United States Treasury Secretary George P. Shultz of the dollar revaluation London foreign exchange markets will reopen today.

February 13, 1973

U.S. AND 13 OTHERS ADOPT MEASURES ON DOLLAR CRISIS

Plans Are Designed to Curb Excessive Outflows and Assure Orderly Trading

SHULTZ'S OPTIONS OPEN

Treasury Chief Commits Nothing, but He Lets It Be Known Nation Will Act

By CLYDE H. FARNSWORTH
Special to The New York Times

PARIS, March 16—The United States and 13 other major trading nations agreed today on a loosely formulated package of measures designed to ease the problem of excess dollars abroad and to assure the reopening of official currency dealings under "orderly conditions" on Monday.

Secretary of the Treasury George P. Shultz kept the American options open in the agreement reached here by finance ministers and central bank governors. He committed the United States to nothing publicly while letting it be known that the United States was prepared to do quite a lot, if necessary, to restore orderly market conditions.

This was in part tactics. The battle is now between governments and the multinational corporations, Arab sheiks and rulers, bankers and others who control vast amounts of money, which they shift from financial center to center, either to protect their assets or to make a profit.

Silence Kept on Weapons

The governments are trying to convince them that they cannot continue to force currencies up or down at will. But the authorities are remaining silent about the precise weapons they will use. As the French Finance Minister Valéry Giscard d'Estaing, put it, "Otherwise we would be organizing the speculation we are trying to avoid."

Nevertheless, a 1,000-word communiqué issued after the six-hour meeting indicated the drift of things—more controls on short-term capital flows; more action to bring dollars back to the United States, and intervention by the United States and other nations, if necessary, to try to hold present exchange rates.

Intervention Is Key

The most important section of the communiqué relates to the pledge by the United States and each of the other countries to "be prepared to intervene at its initiative in its own market, when necessary and desirable, acting in a flexible manner" to support its currency.

This is not exactly a commitment to support the dollar, but it is considered to be close to one. This was the principal aim of the Europeans, and specifically the French, in calling the conference.

The authorities hope that the new defenses, together with action taken early last Monday morning by the Common Market in linking the currencies of six members in a joint float, will buy time for what is now considered to be "urgently" needed reform of the monetary system to curb the magnitude of any future disruptions of the exchange market.

It was announced that Sweden and Norway would join the float of the six Common Market currencies.

"I think we will see reasonable conditions in the market," Mr. Shultz said tonight at a news conference in the United States Embassy. He was flanked by other key members of the American delegation: Dr. Arthur F. Burns, chairman of the Federal Reserve Board; Paul A. Volcker, Under Secretary of the Treasury for Monetary Affairs, and J. Dewey Daane, member of the Federal Reserve Board.

Mr. Giscard d'Estaing said the conference results were "very positive," while the West German Finance Minister, Helmut Schmidt, declared that there had been an "amazing" degree of cooperation displayed by the United States and the nine member countries of the European Economic Community—West Germany, France, Italy, Belgium, Luxembourg, the Netherlands, Britain, Ireland and Denmark.

Others represented at the conference were Japan, Switzerland, Canada and Sweden.

The best assessment of market specialists tonight was that the arrangements might produce a period of calm and reflection and even temporary strength in the dollar, but that inevitably the defense weapons would be tested by the speculators.

Dr. Burns denied rumors in New York today that the Americans as a concession to Europeans had agreed at the conference to raise the Federal Reserve Board's discount rate to bring excess dollars home.

He said, "No immediate action is planned" and that "the rumor is false." He added, "The discount rate was not even mentioned by anyone," and that "whatever happens to the discount rate is decided in Washington, not in Europe."

A statement in the communiqué stresses the need for "success of national efforts to contain inflation" and says the 14 nations are resolved to "pursue fully appropriate policies to this end."

No details on the timetable or magnitude or limitation of any future intervention were given. "Such intervention will be financed, when necessary, through use of mutual credit facilities (otherwise known as 'swaps')," the communiqué said, adding they could be enlarged to "insure fully adequate resources."

Dr. Burns said the United States had $11.5-billion of outstanding short-term swap credit lines, of which $1.6-billion had been activated. In a swap, one country borrows another government's currency for three months, although the term can be extended to a year.

To support the dollar, the United States would borrow, say, marks or guilders, and then sell them in the exchange markets to depress their rates against the dollar. The United States used almost all its hard currency reserves in January support actions.

New Cooperation Shown

There are several reasons behind such swap actions. One is that it becomes an American undertaking to support the dollar. During the so-called policy of benign neglect, the United States offered Europeans the choice of supporting the dollar themselves or letting their currencies appreciate. The Europeans did both up to a point, but this caused a steady deterioration in Atlantic relations, threatening a full-scale monetary and trade war. Today's communiqué shows that the United States wants to call a truce. The meeting showed a new spirit of cooperation.

Moreover, if the Europeans support the dollar by buying it in their exchange markets they tend to stimulate inflationary conditions in their countries.

And there is a good financial reason as well. If the Europeans hold dollars and the dol-

Chronology of Money Crisis

January, 1973—The events that were building toward the biggest monetary crisis since the realignment of international currencies in December, 1971, began during January when Italy, bothered by a weakening lira, decided on a two-tier currency market. The ensuing flight of dollars from Italy to Switzerland caused Swiss authorities to float the franc which in turn sent dollars surging into West Germany.

At about the same time, official figures disclosed that West Germany showed a $6-billion trade surplus for 1972, while the United States suffered a record deficit of $6.5-billion.

Feb. 12—After some $6-billion of unwanted dollars had flooded Europe and Japan within a matter of days, and after some hectic international consultations, the United States announced that it was devaluing the dollar against nearly all of the world's major currencies, with devaluation against the yen being greater and being determined by the floating of the yen.

Feb. 22—The price of gold touched $90 an ounce as new speculation against the dollar developed. Gold was being bought with dollars, which were also sold for other currencies. As a result, the dollar's value on European foreign-exchange markets weakened considerably.

March 1—Still another monetary crisis swept across Europe. It brought heavy selling of the weakened dollar and authorities ordered foreign-exchange markets closed in Europe and Japan. Most of the money, a record amount of $2.7-billion, was acquired by the West German Central Bank.

March 12—West Germany's Finance Minister, Helmut Schmidt, announced that the mark would be revalued by 3 per cent when foreign exchange markets reopened March 19. The announcement came at the end of an 11-hour meeting of the finance ministers of the European Common Market, in which it was decided that West Germany, France, the Netherlands, Belgium, Luxembourg and Denmark would jointly float their currencies to defend against the dollar influx.

March 16—The major western industrial nations and Japan agree on measures designed to solve the monetary crisis and assure the reopening of official currency dealings under "orderly conditions" Monday.

lar is devalued, they lose, but if they have lent funds to the United States, there is no loss in a devaluation.

The communiqué said that American authorities were "reviewing actions" to facilitate the "inflow of capital into the United States." One possible action, Mr. Shultz said, would remove the automatic withholding tax deductions on interest or dividends to foreigners owning American securities.

The United States also agreed to consider encouraging "a flow of Eurocurrency funds to the United States." This could mean, Dr. Burns explained, a reduction in the 20 per cent reserve requirement on Eurodollar deposits of American banks.

If American interest rates went up while this reserve requirement went down, there could be a strong incentive for banks to bring their foreign-held dollars home. The requirement was adopted during the 1970-71 credit crunch when outflows of funds from Europe to the United States were troubling Europe.

In still other important action to reduce speculative funds in the international money markets, the 14 nations decided to reduce the amount of official reserves placed in the Eurodollar market.

The communiqué spoke of studies looking forward to getting all the members of the International Monetary Fund—120 nations in all—to limit their placements in the Eurodollar market.

It also spoke of the possible need for nations to follow the American example and apply reserve requirements to their Eurodollar holdings.

France, Belgium and the Netherlands are already tightening their exchange controls, Mr. Giscard d'Estaing said tonight. France, he said, is following West Germany's example by barring interest payments on non-resident bank accounts and making it so expensive for banks to service such accounts that they would probably have to charge their foreign client for taking his money. Details on the Belgian and Dutsch measures were not available.

A further destabilizing element, in their opinion, is the $80-billion held by foreign central banks. The "consolidation of official currency balances," the communiqué said, "deserved thorough and urgent attention" in the coming monetary reform negotiations. There are a number of plans to turn the dollar debt into a long-term obligation of the United States.

March 17, 1973

I.M.F. Committee Agrees On Money Reform Goals

'Stable but Adjustable' Currency Values and Reliance on 'Paper Gold' Asked —Trade Deficit Grew in February

By EDWIN L. DALE Jr.
Special to The New York Times

WASHINGTON, March 27— The 20 nations negotiating world monetary reform agreed in principle today that the new system should "remain based on stable but adjustable" currency values but that floating exchange rates should be permitted in "particular situations."

The finance ministers and central-bank governors of the International Monetary Fund's Committee of 20 also agreed that Special Drawing Rights, the new "paper gold" issued by the fund, "should become the principal [monetary] reserve asset of the reformed system," with a reduced role for the dollar and one or two other reserve currencies, such as the British pound and the French franc, that are held in other nations' monetary reserves. By implication, there would also be a reduced role for gold.

In a related development, the Commerce Department reported another large United States trade deficit in February, with imports exceeding exports by $476.2-million. This was more than in January but less than in the worst months of 1972.

A major purpose of a reformed world monetary system would be to enable the United States to attain equilibrium in its over-all international trade balance. Both United States and foreign officials expect the two-part devaluation of the dollar against most of the other major currencies, culminating with the 10 per cent devaluation last month, to start to bring substantial improvement in the trade figures late this year and in 1974.

The ministers disclosed their agreement on broad principles in a communiqué issued after a two-day session here. It covered more ground than had been generally expected at their first working meeting. They instructed their deputies to tackle the crucial details, and the deputies will begin their negotiations in a five-day meeting here starting May 21.

The agreements announced today went a considerable way in the direction suggested by George P. Shultz, the United States Secretary of the Treasury, at the annual meeting of the International Monetary Fund last September.

For example, the communiqué emphasized the need in a reformed system for much faster adjustment of deficits and surpluses in each nation's balance of international payments, including an obligation on countries with surpluses as well as countries with deficits to act. A key method of adjustment, although not the only one, is a change up or down in a nation's currency exchange rate.

The communiqué also said that judgment on when to act should include the use of "objective indicators." The United States has proposed movements of monetary reserves as the chief indicator, but this issue was not settled in detail today.

Instead, a special "technical group on indicators" will be established in the negotiations. Paul A. Volcker, Under Secretary of the Treasury for Monetary Affairs, said at a news conference after the meeting that the outcome had been "quite satisfactory."

He said the principles agreed upon were "not inconsistent" with the United States position including the general preference for a par-value system, rather than a floating system. Under a par system central banks intervene in currency markets to support internationally agreed upon parities, while a floating system depends on the free-market forces of supply and demand.

But Mr. Volcker emphasized that "very difficult issues" of detail remained to be "thrashed out" in subsequent negotiations. These include, he noted, the detailed working of the "exchange-rate regime" itself, even though the par-value principle has been accepted.

Mr. Volcker said the United States realized from the start that most nations would want a par, or central, value for their currencies as a "center of gravity" for daily trading in foreign-exchange markets.

But, he said, he thinks the present "interim" system, in which most major currencies are floating in one form or another, will be viable while "more permanent" reform is being negotiated.

Fund Surveillance Advocated

The communiqué of the Committee of 20 said, "There was general agreement on the need for exchange-market stability and on the importance of [Monetary] Fund surveillance of exchange-rate policies."

The ministers also instructed their deputies to make an "intensive study" of the problem of massive capital flows from one country to another, which have been a major element in recent monetary crises.

The ministers sought means of dealing with the problem of capital flows "by a variety of measures, including controls, to influence them, and by arrangements to finance and offset them." A second technical group will be established by the deputies to tackle this difficult issue.

Mr. Volcker said this problem "impressed itself on everyone," but he added that "there is no magic answer."

The communiqué also said, "There should be a strong presumption against use of trade controls for balance-of-payments purposes," and it added that less-developed countries should be "exempt wherever possible" from any controls on trade or capital outflow that might be adopted by the industrial countries. This could mean that any future use by the United States of an import surcharge, as in 1971, would exempt imports from the poorer countries.

On another issue, the communiqué said, "The deputies

were asked to study further the conditions for a resumption of general convertibility, including questions related to consolidation of excess reserve-currency balances and to methods of settlement."

The former system of convertibility, ended by President Nixon in August, 1971, centered on the United States' pledge to pay out gold for foreign-held dollars. The European countries want a reformed system to provide some kind of convertibility of currency balances into primary reserve assets, such as Special Drawing Rights.

This may require some means of eliminating or consolidating the huge overhang of dollars now in foreign central banks, which have grown as a result of the periodic dollar selling waves that characterized the monetary crises.

Jeremy Morse of Britain, the chairman of the deputies, said these issues would be taken up by the executive directors of the I.M.F., working in parallel with the Committee of 20 deputies. The Committee of 20 is made up of representatives from the 10 leading noncommunist financial powers and of representatives from 10 developing nations.

The chairman of the two-day ministerial meeting, Ali Wardhana, Minister of Finance of Indonesia, called the agreed communiqué "definitely a major step toward reform." He said there could have been no such agreement among this broad spectrum of nations a year ago.

March 28, 1973

Market Mood: Anxiety but No Panic

By LEONARD SILK

Gold keeps climbing: It closed at $126 an ounce in London yesterday, almost double the price at which it started the year. The dollar keeps sinking: It has now lost about one-fifth of its value in relation to the West German mark since December, 1971. The United States has been suffering from its worst inflation in half a century—and its most intense Presidential crisis in a century. Is panic nigh? The answer seems to be no.

Economic Analysis

The stock market staged a lusty rally yesterday, suggesting that courage and cool have not deserted the professionals of Wall Street.

Secretary of the Treasury George P. Shultz says he is puzzled by the weakness of the dollar and the stock market, and confidently declares that there are "bargains galore" and he would be buying good common stocks if the funds he manages did not belong to the United States Treasury.

Chairman Arthur F. Burns of the Federal Reserve Board journeys to Kirkaldy, Scotland, to celebrate the 250th anniversary of the christening of Adam Smith, worldly philosopher, and announces that there will be no new credit crunch.

On both the Smithian and no-crunch counts, Dr. Burns establishes his credentials as a non-forgetter of history. The only major historic instance when monetary policy was used drastically to support a weakening dollar was in 1931, after the devaluation of the British pound.

On that occasion, the Fed's shift to tighter money in the face of heavy gold losses drove down the price of bonds and caused the collapse of many banks already weakened by the Depression. It was probably the worst blunder in the Fed's history.

Today the banking system is not in weakened condition, although some stockbrokers are. But Dr. Burns does not intend to take any chances of repeating the Fed's 1931 boo-boo.

He has been trying to bring monetary policy around to restraint more cautiously — and to be ready to switch policy on an instant's notice if the brakes show signs of grabbing.

He is back to his old pitch of urging the Administration to adopt a tougher wage-price policy—a pitch that got him in trouble at the White House in the period just before the President switched to Phase 1 in August, 1971.

Dr. Burns is leaning on commercial bankers to keep interest rates from rising too much. And he is trying to "encourage the others" — such as Mr. Shultz and the Cost of Living Council's director, John Dunlop—to toughen the price and wage restraints for which they are responsible.

The Senate Democratic caucus has called unanimously for a mandatory 90-day wage-price freeze. And Senator Hugh Scott of Pennsylvania, the Republican leader, has indicated the President is thinking about tighter anti-inflation moves.

As Wall Street grows desperate over prospects of ever tighter money and higher interest rates, its spirits rise on hopes of stiffer price and wage restraints.

Private economic forecasters these days are widely dispersed on when the next recession will start and how sharp it will be —with the opening dates staggered from late 1973 to mid-1974 and with the degree of severity ranging from about as sharp as 1957-58 to the mildest sort of "growth recession" in which gross national product will not decline at all but simply slow down for a while.

Some Wall Streeters contend that the best news imaginable would be clear signs that the slowdown has actually begun, since this would mean easier money and credit conditions. They are ready to plunge for stocks on the first downward movement of the prime rate of interest.

Watergate appears to be worrying domestic investors as much as foreign holders of dollars. Fear of protracted crisis, immobilizing national economic policy, is the biggest current cloud hanging over Wall Street.

Investors' second biggest worry is the dollar — and the durability of the present international monetary system. Rumors are flying that gold will be officially revalued upward by about threefold — roughly to the current market price of $126.

Gold Futures Up

Gold futures run still higher. At the Winnepeg Commodity Exchange this week, gold contracts for delivery in July, 1974, went up to $139.40 an ounce.

Some economists begin to suspect that in so chaotic a world monetary situation, with the dollar seemingly floating out to sea, gold may indeed regain its position as the premier world money.

As Prof. Henry C. Wallich of Yale said in his Per Jacobsson Lecture at the International Monetary Fund in Washington last September, "If efforts to negotiate a new international monetary system should fail, if in some crisis national or international credit instruments should cease to be universally acceptable, worldwide belief in the 'intrinsic value' of gold, now buttressed by mounting industrial demand, might again restore gold as the basic world money."

Meanwhile, the Committee of 20 of the I.M.F. limps along, with the major nations still badly divided on how to reform the world monetary system.

The European Parliament in Strasbourg has urged the Common Market to reject Secretary Shultz's plan for world monetary reform and to submit a plan of its own.

Yet, with so many reasons for alarm, the mood of markets at home and abroad is more anxious and uncertain than desperate or panicky.

Reasons for Hope

What one needs to explain are the reasons for persistent hope rather than the causes of immediate gloom.

The hopeful reasons appear to be these:

¶All major countries are enjoying prosperity—or excess demand—and have not been weakened by a severe world slump. Modern fiscal and monetary policies seem capable of warding off or checking such a slump, if it should start.

¶The resort to floating exchange rates has staved off the kind of massive speculation that marked earlier monetary crises.

¶The danger that the Western world would split into hostile, competing trade blocs has been held in check by the rise of multinational corporations—with their significant power and their will to hold world trading and investment opportunities open.

¶There is recognition that beggar-my-neighbor policies could beggar oneself—and this realization brings in its train a considerable degree of patience and a determination to avoid drastic or sudden steps (including an official lurch back to gold) to cure the uncertainties of the moment. The present may be awful, but one can imagine much worse.

June 6, 1973

10 NATIONS AGREE ON A WORLD STUDY OF MONEY SYSTEM

Seek Better Payment Plan in First Major Negotiations Since Bretton Woods

By EDWIN L. DALE Jr.
Special to The New York Times

WASHINGTON, Oct. 2 — The non-Communist world's 10 most powerful industrial nations announced today that they would start the first major negotiation and study of the world's financial system since the Bretton Woods Conference in New Hampshire 20 years ago.

The Bretton Woods Conference led to the establishment of the present system by which international transactions are conducted. The system has worked well to date, but it has recently shown strains.

The purpose of the new study and negotiation is to see whether the system can be improved and reinforced, with the aim of assuring that world prosperity will not be disrupted by a purely international financial factor as it was in the nineteen-thirties.

The 10 nations announced their decision in a communiqué during the annual meeting here of the International Monetary Fund and the International Bank for Reconstruction and Development. The Monetary Fund will conduct an independent study of the problem, but the results of the 10-nation talks will determine the outcome.

Paris Talks Planned

The talks will be conducted in Paris by high-level officials from the 10 governments, under the chairmanship of Robert V. Roosa, United States Under Secretary of the Treasury. The vice chairman will be Emil van Lennep, director general of the Netherlands Finance Ministry.

All ideas for improvement of the present international monetary system and for elimination of its flaws except two will be considered. Those ruled out are any change in the present gold price of $35 an ounce and freely fluctuating exchange rates among currencies.

Douglas Dillon, the Secretary of the Treasury, issued today's communiqué in his capacity as temporary chairman of the "Group of Ten." The chairmanship at the ministerial level will rotate according to rules still to be established, but the United States will have the chairmanship of the actual study.

Spring Report Is Target

The first Paris meeting of the study group will be in early November. Mr. Dillon said the target was a preliminary report by next spring and decisions, if possible, in time for next year's World Fund Meeting in Tokyo in late September.

The 10 nations hold about 80 per cent of the world's reserves of gold and foreign exchange.

Mr. Dillon explained today that their studies would not be limited to changes or improvements in the International Monetary Fund itself, which has 102 members. He said that "sovereign decisions" by governments would also be considered. These would include such matters as how much gold to hold and how to grant credit to nations suffering deficits in their balance of international payments.

The Monetary Fund, one keystone of the present system, was established at the Bretton Woods Conference. The 10 nations in the study group are the United States, Britain, France, West Germany, Italy, Belgium, the Netherlands, Sweden, Canada and Japan. The main exception among the leading financial nations was Switzerland, but Mr. Dillon indicated that the Swiss would be brought into the study in one way or another.

Switzerland is not a member from the outset only because she does not belong to the International Monetary Fund.

Underlying Aim

The underlying aim of all the members of the study is to prevent the kind of financial chaos that prolonged and deepened the depression of the nineteen-thirties.

At that time nations withdrew credits from each other rather than granting them, and nation after nation, virtually devoid of gold, had to impose restrictions on foreign transactins and trade, as well as imposing domestic restraints on economic growth.

No member of the group foresees such a crisis in the near future. But the purpose of the study is to make sure that one could not arise. The members are also agreed, however, that international credit should not be so easy that individual nations could freely pursue inflationary policies at home and disregard their international payments.

Authoritative sources from the various countries involved were unanimous in private conversation in saying that the results of the negotiation were impossible to predict. However, there was also unanimity that any results would be evolutionary rather than revolutionary.

There could be such results as changes in the means of granting international credit and possibly an enlargement of the sources of such credit. There could be more precise rules on the holding of foreign currencies—chiefly the dollar—as part of nations' reserves.

No Basic Change Seen

But the basic international system--by which nations have fixed exchange rates, hold their reserves in gold and foreign exchange and borrow reserves from the International Monetary Fund or from each other if they need to--will not be changed.

The chances of significant results from the negotiations were difficult to predict today. It was clear that the 10 nations would start with views that differ both on problems and on the solutions to be proposed.

For example, the Continental European countries are interested in a more orderly system of granting credit to deficit countries, such as the United States. Britain is urgently concerned with the problem of "international liquidity"—the total of countries' reserves and their access to credit—particularly when the United States deficit ceases.

All are agreed, however, that the first priority of business is for the United States to reduce and then eliminate its deficit, meanwhile to assure that the deficit does not disrupt the international system.

Today's formal proceedings at the meeting here were devoted to the affairs of the World Bank, which is not directly involved in the international monetary system. It makes loans for the economic development of poorer countries.

The speeches today generally welcomed the bank's new policy, announced Monday by its president, George D. Woods, of slightly liberalizing lending terms.

October 3, 1963

Monetary Machinery

Economists Rule Out Extreme View In Considering Reforms for System

By M. J. ROSSANT

The effort now underway to strengthen the international monetary machinery is unlikely to involve any radical or revolutionary redesign. This is the only conclusion to be drawn from the speech made on the subject in Vienna last week by Under Secretary of the Treasury Robert V. Roosa.

Mr. Roosa, who is the nation's chief draftsman of international financial arrangements, emphasized that he was not lifting the curtain on the blueprints under consideration. But both the tone and nature of his observations indicated that any changes would be evolutionary rather than revolutionary.

There was nothing defensive about Mr. Roosa's position. On the contrary, he considers that the present machinery possesses great flexibility and efficiency. He is confident that its potential performance can be improved to surpass anything on the drawing boards, so that he is not in the market for anything brand new.

Radical Moves Rejected

The rejection of radical schemes is hardly a surprise. Last September, when the decision to discuss possible reforms was reached, the negotiators ruled out any consideration of extreme proposals, such as a revaluation of the dollar or a return to the gold standard.

Most central bankers engaged in the highly secret negotiations have little interest in some of the other suggestions made by economists. They are not against change, but they do have an instinctive distrust for automatic devices to increase the amount of international liquidity—the amount of gold and currency credit available for trade and investment. In essence, they want to exercise control over both the accelerator and the brake of the machinery.

Their problem is to insure that a country suffering from a payments deficit with the rest of the world is given enough liquidity to correct its situation without seriously curtailing domestic or international expansion.

Those who argue for radical change think that the present system has serious flaws. They believe that the supply of liquidity available to meet a crisis is left too much to chance, or to the shaky reed of international cooperation among central bankers. They insist that an additional buffer of liquidity is essential to keep a country from drawing in its belt too drastically or precipitating an international monetary crisis.

Most reform proposals involve a form of automatic access to credit by a deficit country. Under such a system, any sudden slamming on of the brakes could be prevented.

But central bankers see just as much of a danger in free wheeling. As Mr. Roosa put it, "the function of international liquidity is not to permit countries to avoid the need to make what may sometimes be painful adjustments in domestic policies and practices." In his view, "we do not need, and cannot successfully use, liquidity to avoid the necessity of a cure."

An automatic system might result in too much liquidity, permitting a deficit country to escape internal adjustments inviting an inflationary explosion in the international monetary machinery. Understandably, central bankers are against any design that does not have adequate brakes.

Some Curbs Favored

In fact, Mr. Roosa seems to favor installing firmer and more sensitive braking power in the machinery. For he states that the best insurance against abrupt or painful readjustments on the part of a deficit country is to establish controls that can prevent the deficit from growing to dangerous dimensions.

In arguing that early and mild disciplinary action is far preferable to abrupt change later, Mr. Roosa is in agreement with France's Finance Minister Valery Giscard d'Estaing, who has taken the position that there is no danger of any lack of liquidity provided that the existing supply is efficiently used.

In pointing to more intensive and imaginative use of the arrangements already in existence, Mr. Roosa is insisting that international monetary cooperation is a much more resourceful and responsive force than its critics accept. He also is making plain his belief that the machinery that has been devised in the last years has considerable potential for bolstering the supply of liquidity while increasing its braking power.

Mr. Roosa's contention that continued adaption can keep the machinery as good as new is difficult to rebut. Its critics have been saying that a complete overhaul is needed, but the men who have been engaged in its operation have managed, admittedly with some stress and strain, to keep it in working order by adding new features.

The prospect is that the plans for its present refurbishing will call for shiny new bumpers, brake linings and shock absorbers. As Mr. Roosa sees it, that is all that is needed.

May 25, 1964

STUDIES SEEK RISE IN MONETARY FUND

Urge Increase in Quotas of Member Nations in Move to Bolster Resources

By EDWIN L. DALE Jr.

Special to The New York Times

WASHINGTON, Aug. 10 — Two major studies of the world monetary system concluded today that the system would be strengthened by a "moderate" increase in the resources of the International Monetary Fund.

The studies, started nearly a year ago, were made by the 10 leading financial nations—the so-called Group of Ten—and by the Monetary Fund itself. Together, the reviews constituted the first basic examination of the world monetary system since the Bretton Woods Conference 20 years ago.

While the two studies differed in emphasis and in the points they covered, they did not conflict. Both found that there is at present sufficient international liquidity and that no sweeping reform of the monetary system is necessary.

International liquidity is the total of nations' reserves of gold and foreign exchange, mainly dollars, and their access to credit. A shortage could force the world into deflation and unemployment.

A move to increase the resources of the Monetary Fund, by increasing the members' quotas, will be undertaken at the annual meeting of the Fund next month in Tokyo. While no figure was mentioned in either report, it is understood the increase in quotas will be in the range of 20 to 30 per cent, with some nations receiving a larger increase. These will include West Germany and several other members of the Group of Ten.

The 10 nations are the United States, Britain, West Germany, France, Italy, the Netherlands, Belgium, Sweden, Japan and Canada. Switzerland recently became the 11th member.

The fund is a pool of currencies that can be lent at short term to members having difficulty with their balance of international payments. Thus the Fund is a keystone of liquidity. Its $8 billion of loans over the years have enabled nations to continue liberal trading policies without imposing restrictions that could hurt world trade and prosperity.

Dual Effect of Increase

At present the Fund is running low on usable currencies mainly European, though it has plenty of dollars and pounds. An increase in quotas will have the dual effect of adding to the Fund's supply of currencies and increasing the amounts by which members in difficulty can draw.

Under the prospective timing, the Fund's permanent executive directors are expected to negotiate the details of the quota increase before the end of the year. Then next year the nations will begin paying additional amounts of their currency, with 25 per cent of each quota increase to be paid, as in the past, in gold.

Various devices will be studied to prevent this gold payment from sharply reducing United States gold reserves, directly or indirectly.

Legislation to provide for the United States quota increase is expected to go to Congress early next year.

The eagerly-awaited report of the Group of Ten, besides endorsing a "moderate" increase in fund quotas, also set in motion three institutional changes in the way the leading nations handle international monetary developments.

Special Surveillance

First, there will be a new system of "multilateral surveillance" of the various bilateral deals, such as currency swaps, that have been used in recent years to cope with short-term difficulties, particularly by the United States.

This surveillance will take place through the Bank for International Settlements at Basel, Switzerland. Nations will report all their bilateral deals and transactions under them, and their balance of payments situation in general, for discussion by the group as a whole. However, there will be no need to get group permission before acting or negotiating new deals.

New 'Reserve Asset'

Second, the task of the monetary committee of the Organization for Economic Cooperation and Development, called Working Party Three, will be expanded. It will now conduct a continuing examination of how nations get into surplus and deficit in their international payments and, even more, how they can and should adjust their payments toward balance.

This is known as the problem of adjustment, which is different from the problem of liquidity. If all nations could adjust rapidly there would be much less need for liquidity.

Third, a committee of high officials of the 10 countries will conduct a continuing study of possible future need to create a new "reserve asset" to supplement gold, dollars and pounds. The idea with the strongest backing so far is to create a composite currency reserve unit made up of all 10 currencies.

The study group, under the chairmanship of Rinaldo Ossola of the Bank of Italy, will not be asked to make recommendations. It will explore the details involved in various methods of creating a new reserve asset and report back to the 10 countries within a year.

The need for a new reserve asset may arise because one source of growth in global reserves in the past is now disappearing. This is the United States balance of payments deficit, which has pumped dollars into the world. Both studies concluded that new gold production would not alone provide sufficient growth in liquidity in the future. However, neither study regarded this problem as urgent now.

Finally, the Group of Ten report discussed a device for solving a particular problem of the system that has become evident over the years. This is the problem of leading countries, above all Britain, that for histroical reasons have reserves that are too low for comfort.

Britain has constantly skated on the edge of trouble in the post-war period.

For these countries, which include Japan and possibly Canada, the report suggested the possibility of long-term loans from members of the group with ample reserves. This would be the first use of long-term loans for monetary purposes.

The report made clear that they would have to be negotiated among the countries concerned. One suggestion was that a lender could count on others taking over the loan if its own balance of payments in the future got into difficulty.

All of this remains to be worked out, but the idea is definitely alive.

Both reports recognized a probable future need for the creation of new reserves beyond the annual growth in the supply of gold. But while the Group of Ten set up its study of possible new reserve assets, the Monetary Fund report suggested specific ways by which the Fund itself could add to the supply of liquidity.

Automatic Loan Rights

One such way would be to give member nations virtually automatic drawing rights to, say, half their quota instead of only 25 per cent, as now. At present a drawing beyond 25 per cent requires permission by the Fund after careful examination of a member's policies.

Another method would be a new technique under which the Fund could make "investments" in national or international securities, with the practical effect of increasing the nation's reserves.

It is understood that attention for the next six months to a year will concentrate on working out the Fund quota increase, with new devices to expand liquidity to be looked at in detail only later.

Representative Henry S. Reuss, Democrat of Wisconsin, chairman of the international finance subcommittee of the House Banking Committee, issued a statement today blasting the report of the Group of Ten. He said "The mountain labored for 10 months and brought forth a very small mouse."

Mr. Reuss said "the United States greatly needs an improved international monetary mechanism." The Group of Ten, he said, did not come to grips with either new means of providing international credit or establishing a new international money.

It is known that the United States, Britain and some other members of the group would have liked a somewhat more "expansionary" outcome, and a larger increse in monetary fund quotas than the prospective 20 to 30 per cent. European countries, led by France, were opposed to this. But on the whole officials are satisfied with the outcome.

Among other things, the two studies strongly endorsed and in effect "consecrated" the new network of voluntary international monetary cooperation that has grown up in the last four years. This has proved to be the bulwark of the monetary system at a time of considerable strain, arising largely from the big United States balance of payments deficits.

The cooperation, in practice, has meant the granting of credit to help nations in difficulty, including the United States. The Group of Ten report indicates that the basis for provision of liquidity in the future, in addition to new gold, will be an extension of devices for providing credit, including the Monetary Fund.

The principle of continued cooperation was strongly endorsed by Valery Giscard d'Estaing, the French Finance Minister, in a statement issued in Paris. Mr. Giscard d'Estaing is ministerial chairman of the Group of Ten.

Today's I.M.F. report said the world system had been "able to meet the challenges to which it has been exposed with a more intimate and effective cooperation in international monetary matters than at any time in history." That cooperation will continue, despite some sharp philosophical differences among the leading countries.

August 11, 1964

SCOPE IS SHIFTING FOR WORLD CREDIT

Tacit Consensus Emerging on Need for Managing Monetary Liquidity

FUND DEBATE ASSESSED

Changes in System Weighed as I.M.F. and Bank End Meetings in Tokyo

By EDWIN L. DALE Jr.
Special to The New York Times

TOKYO.

As delegates to the International Monetary Fund and World Bank annual meeting scattered to the four corners of the earth, there was a widespread awareness that something new had been added to the world financial scene.

While few governors of the bank and the fund expressed it openly and publicly, the something new is a tacit decision that in the future the growth in the world's supply of "international liquidity" must be managed to some degree, and not just result from such haphazard factors as how much gold is mined and how big are the deficits in the United States international payments.

Liquidity is the word used to describe the total of nations' reserves of gold and foreign exchange, mainly dollars, and their access to credit. It is the means of settlement of deficits and surpluses in nations' international transactions.

The meeting here was filled with terms that none but a handful of specialists had ever heard of a few years ago—"owned reserves" vs. "credit facilities," "conditional liquidity" vs. "unconditional liquidity."

Orderly Growth Sought

But the very existence of these terms, and the debate, constituted a tacit decision that the world in the future will endeavor to create an orderly growth in liquidity. The issue is of major importance to prosperity in all nations, because insufficient liquidity could force the world into an economic depression as it was forced in the nineteen-thirties.

In practical terms, the new tacit consensus means that there will almost certainly be international financial innovations in the years ahead, though no one can forecast whether it will be in two years or five.

Because there is obviously still no consensus on the extent of the problem and the ways of solving it—a lack of consensus emphasized by the clash of views here between the United States and France—no one can forecast, either, what exact form the innovations will take.

But men who insisted as recently as two or three years ago that there was nothing wrong with the present world monetary system were saying at the bank and fund meeting that gradual changes were bound to come.

It might be a new system of national deposits in the International Monetary Fund. It might be investments by the fund in individual countries or international agencies as a means of creating new national reserves.

But whatever it is, the nations are agreed that new liquidity must not come from a continuation of deficits in their international payments by the United States and Britain, two nations that have "reserve" currencies.

Given this measure of agreement, the clashes between the United States and Britain on one side, and France with the partial backing of some European countries on the other, are important but not decisive for the future, in the view of many here.

In addition, it became evident that the "conservative" Continental Europeans were not as one-sidedly conservative as they had once appeared.

Stinging Criticism

Italy, for example, allowed it to be known in private that she did not endorse the view backed by France and the Netherlands. Norway came out with some stinging criticism of the position expressed by France, West Germany and the Netherlands that the present world system is menaced mainly by inflation.

For the next year or so, the system will function as always, with the increase in members' quotas in the monetary fund agreed upon at the annual meeting as a means of adding to the nations' access to credit, if needed and warranted, to bolster their reserves.

One of the issues here, still unresolved, is whether future additions to liquidity should be in the form of credit or in "owned" reserves. The United States and Britain suggested credit; the Netherlands suggested new reserves that would be owned by nations. But this difference of view, while it raises a difficult problem, does not mask the general awareness of a need for some more conscious management of the monetary system in the future.

"The cage of orthodoxy has been unlocked," a high American official observed. "We will definitely move on from here. And I think you'll find that the movement will be in the direction of expansion of liquidity—prudent expansion but still expansion."

September 13, 1964

I. M. F. AID ACCORD WILL BE RENEWED

10 Nations Reported Agreed on Extension of Pact to Provide Extra Funds

DUTCH PLAN SUPPORTED

French Back the Proposal Although Some Opposition Had Been Indicated

By RICHARD E. MOONEY
Special to The New York Times

PARIS—The 10-country arrangement to provide special extra funds to the International Monetary Fund when needed will be renwed without change, according to a tacit agreement that has been reached by the 10 countries.

This arrangement, among the so-called Group of 10, has been tapped only twice in its three years of existence, both times for the benefit of Britain, most recently last Wednesday. The original agreement still has more than a year to run, but the question of renewal must be decided by October.

France posed the obvious potential obstacle to renewal. The French feel that the arrangement is not sufficiently strict on its beneficiaries. Some officials had indicated that Paris would demand changes.

Accord Reached

But last week the Finance Ministers of the six Common Market countries—France, Germany, Italy, Belgium, the Netherlands and Luxembourg—agreed with little debate, according to official sources, to support a Dutch proposal for a short-term renewal with no strings. It is expected that the term will be two years.

Washington's concurrence was a foregone conclusion and was confirmed later in the week here in Paris in discussions during meetings that involved all 10 countries.

The formal statement of the renewal, which is not likely before summer, may say—or will surely imply—that the participants expect progress on basic reform of the international monetary system during the renewal period. This was the point of the Dutch proposal.

Discussions of reform are currently confined to a technical 10-country subcommittee and public speeches.

Jacques Rueff, the controversial French monetary expert, told the American Club of Paris that he hoped reform would come "before the crisis" but that he doubted it would. Mr. Rueff believes the present system leads inevitably to crisis.

Change Held Necessary

Recently returned from the United States, Mr. Rueff said that he found "full agreement that the present system is at its end and has to be changed," but no agreement on which way to change.

Mr. Rueff favors returning to a system where governments would keep all of their official reserves in gold, instead of—as they do now—in gold, dollars and pound sterling. To make enough to go around, he would double the price of gold.

The French Finance Minister, Valery Giscard d'Estaing, stirred up the gold price question last weekend on a television program by saying—when asked for the Government's position—that France had never taken a position pro or con.

Inasmuch as France had previously gone along with the rest of the world's financial powers in not even admitting the question to official discussion, the minister's remark was widely interpreted to mean that France has an open mind now. Officials explain privately, though, that France remains opposed, on the ground that it would be inflationary, among other things.

The TV show, incidentally, opened with some film from the motion picture "Goldfinger," then showed a frustrated French TV journalist trying to get to see the vaults at Fort Knox, and included some remarks by Mr. Rueff at the Veau d'Or (Golden Calf) restaurant in New York.

Part of France's power to stir up the financial world these days has been the steady growth of her reserves.

Among non-French authorities there has been some gleeful speculation that France's time is running out in this respect—that her balance of payments will not continue strong for long and that she will thus stop piling up reserves.

May 16, 1965

FOWLER PROPOSES A GLOBAL PARLEY ON MONEY SYSTEM

Says President Authorizes Call for Talks to Improve Bretton Woods Setup

LAG IN LIQUIDITY IS SEEN

Steps Are Held Necessary to Spur Growth of Reserves Used for World Trade

By EDWIN L. DALE Jr.
Special to The New York Times

WASHINGTON, July 10 — The United States, in a major initiative, proposed today a world conference aimed at "substantial improvements" in the 20-year-old international monetary system.

The proposal was made by Secretary of the Treasury Henry H. Fowler, who said President Johnson had authorized it.

The last such world conference was at Bretton Woods, N. H., in 1944. The system then evolved has worked well and has been a major factor in the spectacular prosperity of the industrial world.

Strains Develop

But the system has recently come under strain, first because of the persistent deficits in the United States balance of international payments and now, prospectively, because of the ending of those deficits. The dollar is a keystone of the system.

Mr. Fowler disclosed the United States initiative in a speech to the Virginia State Bar Association in Hot Springs, Va. The text of his remarks was made available here. Mr. Fowler conferred with the President about the speech two days ago.

The Secretary said that a world conference, if it was to succeed, "must be preceded by careful preparation and international consultation."

"Before any conference takes place, there should be reasonable certainty of measurable progress through prior agreement on basic points," he declared.

Time Called Appropriate

"Our suggestion," he continued, "is that the work of preparation be undertaken by a preparatory committee which could be given its terms of reference at the time of the annual meeting of the International Monetary Fund this September."

Mr. Fowler said the "happy concurrence of three crucial facts" made the time appropriate to act on reform of the system. The crucial facts, he said, are these:

¶The United States balance of payments "is approaching an equilibrium."

¶There is a "rising tide of opinion" that the world system "can and should be substantially improved," building on the present system.

¶The necessary technical studies have been completed, chiefly by the leading financial nations known as the Group of Ten.

The balance of payments is the relationship between a nation's total payments to foreigners and total receipts from foreigners.

As Mr. Fowler explained today, world financial reserves, called international liquidity, have grown in the last 15 years, largely because of deficits in the United States balance of payments. These deficits have pumped both dollars and gold into the reserves of other nations. The United States was spending more abroad than it earned abroad, even though exports regularly exceeded imports.

As foreign dollar holdings grew and the United States gold stock declined, it became necessary to end these deficits to keep the dollar "as good as gold" and assure other nations that their dollar holdings could always be converted into gold at $35 an ounce.

After long and frequently frustrating efforts by the Government, the deficits now appear to be ending. In any event, the Government, as Mr. Fowler said, is "determined" to end them.

But this will automatically stop the growth in world reserves that is needed to finance internation transactions, a condition that Mr. Fowler called the "paradox" of the present system. Hence the need for an innovation, which may well take the form of some new kind of reserve asset in addition to gold and dollars.

Nations use their reserves to settle deficits in their international transactions. While reserves do not have to grow exactly in line with world trade, there is agreement that they must grow over a period of time so that nations can handle temporary deficits without clamping restrictions on imports or imposing deflationary domestic policies.

Mr. Fowler quoted today a sentence from President Johnson's balance-of-payments message to Congress last Feb. 10: "Unless we can make timely progress, international monetary difficulties will exercise a stubborn and increasingly frustrating drag on our policies for prosperity and progress at home and throughout the world."

Mr. Fowler gave no hint today of what the United States would advocate at the world conference and in the preparatory stage. But he said the Government was now moving into a stage of "intensive internal preparation" to determine "those proposals which will be acceptable to the United States, those which are entirely unacceptable, and those which may well be appropriate for negotiation."

France Opposes Expansion

In discussions on reform that have been under way for nearly two years among the Group of Ten countries, serious differences of opinion have emerged. Essentially, the continental European countries, above all France, have opposed reforms designed to expand world liquidity, contending there is already too much. Britain, the United States and Japan have been more expansionary.

The end of the United States payments deficit, assuming that the recent improvements continue, could sharply alter the negotiating situation. It would improve the United States bargaining power and might persuade many Europeans that a method of adding to world liquidity was needed.

Mr. Fowler disclosed in his speech that he planned to meet later this year with the "ranking financial officials of other Group of Ten countries, to ascertain first-hand their views on the most practical and promising ways of furthering progress toward improved international monetary arrangements." He has already seen the British Chancellor of the Exchequer, James Callaghan, and will confer next week with the Japanese Finance Minister, Takeo Fukuda.

Other Member Nations

Other members of the Group of Ten are France, West Germany, Italy, Belgium, the Netherlands, Sweden and Canada. Switzerland sits with the group as an observer.

Mr. Fowler made it clear that the United States had no intention of trying to impose its own ideas.

"We must be prepared," he said, "not only to advance our own proposals but to carefully consider and fairly weigh the merits of other proposals."

The idea of a world monetary conference has received strong impetus from Congressional Republicans.

Senator Jacob K. Javits of New York has long advocated it. Senator Bourke B. Hickenlooper of Iowa, speaking for the Senate Republican leadership, endorsed the idea last week.

Ellsworth Speech Cited

Also last week, Representative Robert F. Ellsworth of Kansas, speaking on behalf of an informal group of House Republican liberals and moderates, made the proposal in a major house speech. Mr. Ellsworth has been in touch with leading world financial figures, such as Jean Monnet of France, seeking their advice on how to bring about such a conference.

Mr. Fowler quoted today from the Ellsworth speech.

A plan for improving the monetary system that has considerable backing, though there is much disagreement on detail, calls for creating a new composite or collective reserve unit, labeled CRU for short. The reserve would be made up of the 10 or 11 leading currencies in fixed proportions, held in nations' reserves along with gold and dollars. It could be used to settle international accounts.

The idea is supported in varying degrees in Europe, in Japan and in Canada. Britain is known to be sympathetic, provided the new unit could be firmly linked to the existing International Monetary Fund.

The United States has long resisted the idea, mainly because some versions of it would seek to diminish or abolish the role of the dollar as a world reserve currency and a "working" currency for a host of private international transactions.

But if the plan could be worked out in such a way as to leave the role of the dollar intact, and if it could be linked to the Monetary Fund, the United States is understood to be willing to consider it.

A new version of a CRU type of plan will be published next month by Robert V. Roosa, former Under Secretary of the Treasury, who was the leading United States international monetary official for the first four years of the Kennedy-Johnson Administration. This could indicate a move in the United States position toward more sympathy for the basic idea.

Mr. Roosa is a member of a committee, headed by former Secretary of the Treasury Douglas Dillon, that was named to advise Mr. Fowler on international monetary reform. Mr. Fowler disclosed today that the group would have its first meeting Friday.

July 11, 1965

FRANCE REJECTS MONETARY TALKS PROPOSED BY U.S.

Finance Chief Says Parley Now Would Accentuate Split Among Nations

WARNS OF SHAM REFORM

Calls for Improvements in Present System and Test of Payments Progress

By HENRY TANNER
Special to The New York Times

PARIS, July 19—The Government rejected today as "inopportune" an American proposal for a world conference aimed at improving the international monetary system.

Valery Giscard d'Estaing, France's Finance Minister, said that in the present circumstances such a conference would merely accentuate existing differences among the views of leading financial nations or else lead to sham reforms.

He added that two conditions, which did not now exist, would have to be met before a conference should be called: Lasting improvements in the present monetary system would have to be made, and the principal governments involved would have to reach minimum agreement before going to the conference table.

Mr. Giscard d'Estaing made the French rejection known in a statement to the Government-subsidized French News Agency.

Proposal by Fowler

The American proposal for a conference was made by Secretary of the Treasury Henry H. Fowler on July 10. Mr. Fowler made clear that his proposal had the support of President Johnson.

The French statement came as a jolt to United States officials here.

France herself had originally proposed a similar conference. It had not been expected therefore that her rejection of Mr. Fowler's initiative would come so soon and would be so complete, even though it had been known for several days that Paris's reaction was lukewarm at best.

Monetary specialists thought Mr. Giscard d'Estaing's statement was prompted in part by the recent improvement in the international payments position of the United States. This gain, it was noted, would strengthen the United States position at an international monetary conference.

The French Minister, without naming the United States, said it remained to be seen whether the progress achieved by some of the nations that had had massive payments deficits in the past would be lasting or not.

Unless such lasting results were certain, he asserted, a reform of the world monetary system could not be discussed.

Specialists on the French political scene said the allusion clearly was to President Johnson's campaign to improve the United States balance-of-payments position.

Secondly, these observers said, French officials believed that Britain had not even begun to solve her balance-of-payments problems and that Mr. Fowler's proposal for a world conference therefore might have as one primary objective the organizing of another move to help Britain.

French officials, moreover, are believed to have concluded that negotiations in the near future on President de Gaulle's proposal for a return to the gold standard would lead only to confusion and to the further isolation of the French Government.

Effect of de Gaulle Bid

General de Gaulle made the proposal at a press conference last February. His statement, which was couched in broad nontechnical terms, has found little positive reaction abroad and has divided French financial officials.

Many monetary experts believe Mr. Giscard d'Estaing and other French financial officials are reluctant to meet their foreign counterparts any time soon at a conference at which they might be forced either to spell out General de Gaulle's suggestion or drop it.

Some French observers suggested today that one of Mr. Fowler's objectives in suddenly suggesting a world conference was to jump the gun on General de Gaulle and draw him into negotiations on world monetary reforms in circumstances that were not favorable to him.

This, they said, explained the official French rejection.

July 20, 1965

NATIONS DIVIDED ON MONETARY AID

10-Country Study Indicates Deep Disagreements

By EDWIN L. DALE Jr.
Special to The New York Times

WASHINGTON, Aug. 10 — Deep disagreements among leading financial nations on how to reform the international monetary system were disclosed today in the publication of 10-nation technical study of proposals to increase monetary reserves.

The study is known as the Ossola Report, after the chairman of the group, Rinaldo Ossola of the Bank of Italy. Undertaken by high-level officials of finance ministries and central banks, it was commissioned by the Group of Ten, the 10 industrial nations that dominate world finance. The study took a year to complete.

The group's mandate was to explore "the creation of reserve assets." Nations' reserves now are composed of gold, key currencies — mainly the dollar — and drawing rights on the International Monetary Fund. Reform of the world system involves principally new ways of creating reserves, to allow for needed growth as the world economy grows.

The Ossola Report had two main elements.

First, it described about 10 devices for creating new reserve assets, or changing the composition of present assets. Some involved the I.M.F. and some did not.

Second, it presented the arguments for and against each plan, making clear that the study group itself divided deeply on all of them.

So complete was the disagreement that the report admitted, in its final section: "These differences have meant that our report cannot take the form of an agreed exposition of the elements necessary for an evaluation of the respective proposals." That is, the group could not even agree on wordage to describe and evaluate the various plans.

The basic disagreements, the report said, were on these crucial points:

¶"The question of a link between gold and a new reserve asset, the closeness of that link, and its effects on the existing system."

¶"The width of membership for purposes of management and distribution of the assets."

¶"The role of the I.M.F. as regards deliberate reserve creation."

¶"The rules for decision-making concerning the creation of reserve assets."

Collective Reserve Unit

Among the plans discussed was the creation of a new collective reserve unit, or C.R.U. for short, made up of the leading currencies, a move that has been suggested by France. It, like other proposals, was sharply criticized, particularly because of its close link with gold.

At one point in the report the isolated position of France on at least some issues was strongly hinted at. The arguments against using the International Monetary Fund to create new reserve assets "were supplied mainly by one of our members," the report said. Officials left no doubt that the reference was to France.

The same paragraph continued: "Certain of these arguments were supported by some other members of the study group."

The report then presented the pro-I.M.F. arguments, saying, "some of which were supported by all other members of the study group."

The members of the Group of Ten are the United States, Britain, France, West Germany, Italy, Belgium, the Netherlands, Sweden, Canada and Japan. Switzerland is an observer, but no Swiss was a member of the Ossola group.

Goods Urged as Money

Special to The New York Times

JERUSALEM, (Israeli Sector) Aug. 10—Pierre Mendes France, former Premier of France, called today for an international monetary system that would accept certain primary products for payment as well as gold.

He told the Rehovot conference on fiscal problems in developing states that since new countries were the chief sellers of these basic products they would benefit directly.

The former French Premier, an experienced economist, said that while the prevailing system of gold as the basis of international exchange needed to be reformed, it should not be abolished altogether.

What was needed, he told experts from 44 nations, was "a new element which would establish at least a partial correlation between general economic needs and the sum of international liquid assets."

He recommended "a judiciously selected sample of homogeneous, storable and non-perishable basic products." He did not name any.

August 11, 1965

MONETARY ACTION IS EXPECTED SOON

Fowler Reports to Johnson on Sign of Agreement on Start of Negotiations

REFORM PLAN OUTLINED

10 Leading Countries Seek First Stage During I.M.F. Meeting This Month

By EDWIN L. DALE Jr.
Special to The New York Times

WASHINGTON, Sept. 13 — Secretary of the Treasury Henry H. Fowler reported to President Johnson today that the 10 leading financial nations were agreed that the first stage of negotiations on improving the world monetary system should be started this month.

The start of the negotiations would coincide with the annual meeting here of the International Monetary Fund.

Mr. Fowler, just back from a two-week trip through Europe, also reported "general agreement" among these nations that "ways will have to be developed to expand international liquidity [the amount of gold, reserve currencies, or available credit which nations use to finance international trade and payments] after the balance-of-payments deficits of the United States no longer exist."

Under Control

There was also general agreement, Mr. Fowler said, that "such a time is rapidly approaching" because "the United States deficit is already under control."

The group agreed, he added, that "although there is no need for hasty action, neither is there a great deal of time to waste."

Mr. Fowler's report to the President was made public by the White House. It was made at a meeting of the Cabinet.

Although Mr. Fowler's statement did not imply agreement among the leading nations on the methods of reforming the monetary system, it did suggest a greater degree of agreement than had previously been known to exist on two points: the need for additional liquidity, or world credit, and the importance of acting soon.

Technical Studies

Mr. Fowler said there was agreement that the "first stage" of the negotiations should be conducted by the so-called Group of Ten, which has been discussing the problem and conducting technical studies for two years. The group consists of the United States, Britain, France, West Germany, Italy, Belgium, the Netherlands, Sweden, Canada and Japan, with Switzerland as an observer.

These negotiations, he said, could begin "hopefully next month" after a mandate is agreed upon at the time of the I.M.F. meeting late this month. The mandate would be in the form of instructions to the deputies of the 10 ministers, who are top-level officials of their Governments.

Mr. Fowler continued:

"In all discussions the United States participants made clear their strong conviction that a sound and lasting improvement in the International Monetary System must serve the needs of all member nations of the International Monetary Fund — particularly the developing countries — and therefore a second phase of preparatory discussion and negotiation would be desirable before final intergovernmental agreements making formal structural improvements were entered into, in which there would be appropriate and adequate opportunity for the participation of the International Monetary Fund and of countries other than the Group of Ten.

"I am glad to say that this position found support in many quarters."

Thus, Mr. Fowler indicated that at least some of the European countries favored keeping the entire process in the Group of Ten. This question — the second phase of the negotiations is apparently still open, with no unanimous agreement yet reached.

Mr. Fowler said, "Given a successful course of preparation along these lines, the basis would be firmly fixed for a meaningful international monetary conference in the form of a special meeting of the governors of the International Monetary Fund for some other suitable forum."

It was Mr. Fowler's proposal for a world conference, made early last July, that led to his European trip. Originally, he is understood to have wanted negotiations to begin in a "preparatory "commission," which woud have a somewhat different composition from the Group of Ten, but he did not obtain agreement on this.

Today's statement said there was agreement that "careful preparation is necessary to determine the extent of basic agreement among the major countries which would be the sources of additional agreement or credit—the so-called Group of Ten—and that any agreement on improving the system will require assurances that such improvements will be generally acceptable to those countries."

Thus, Mr. Fower continued, there was agreement that the negotiations should proceed first among the members of the Group of Ten.

Mr. Fowler reported he was "extremely pleased" that a new package of standby support for the British pound had been arranged during his visit. France did not join the group putting together the package, which included the other nine members of the Group of Ten and Austria.

September 14, 1965

U.S. OFFERING PLAN FOR WORLD MONEY

Report to Congress Urges Creation of New Unit for Use Among Nations

Special to The New York Times

WASHINGTON, Jan. 27—The Government disclosed today its basic ideas for improving the world monetary system, focusing on the creation of a new international money.

The new money would never be seen by ordinary citizens or even bankers. But it would be held in nations' official reserves along with gold, dollars and pounds, and could be used to settle accounts among nations.

The disclosure of the basic United states approach to reform of the world money system came in a special section of President Johnson's Economic Report to Congress.

Parley in Paris

The section has been agreed upon among the Government agencies concerned, and the outlines of the United States plan will be presented to nine other industrial nations next week in Paris.

Negotiations for reform are proceeding in the Group of Ten, the leading financial nations participating in a December, 1961, agreement to supplement the International Monetary Fund's reserves to cope with possible threats to the stability of the international payments system.

The President met today with Secretary of the Treasury Henry H. Fowler and other key officials concerned with the negotiations, including Frederick L. Deming, Under Secretary of the Treasury, who will present the United States plan in Paris. Mr. Deming and his counterparts in the Group of Ten have been instructed to report on a plan of monetary reform by late spring providing agreement can be reached.

A plan has also been drawn up jointly by four members of the group — West Germany, Italy, the Netherlands and Belgium—that contains provision for a new international money, though there are known to be important differences between this and the United States plan.

The other members of the Group of Ten are Canada, France, Japan, Sweden and Britain. Switzerland is associated with the group as an "11th member" under a special arrangement.

The new international monetary unit would be made up of, and backed by, the currencies of the participating nations, and it would be distributed only to them.

One question to be settled is how many nations could participate, but it is already clear that the plan would be limited to those with strong currencies.

There is still no formal name for the new international money, assuming its creation can be negotiated. However, the name most widely used by the experts up to now is "cru," standing for composite reserve unit.

The cru would probably never be printed but would stand, like a bank deposit, on the books of the I.M.F. or some other "trustee."

Together with the new unit, the United States plan disclosed today also envisages larger automatic drawing rights for all nations on the Monetary Fund as it now operates. This would give benefits to the poor countries, as well as the rich.

The purpose of the new money and the companion drawing rights is to make sure that total official monetary reserves continue to grow in line with expanding world trade and other global transactions, just as the domestic money supply expands each year.

The growth of global reserves since World War II has been achieved largely by deficits in the international payments of the United States. Washington's chronic balance-of-payments problem has had the effect of pumping dollars into other nations' reserves.

Deficit Slashed in '65

The Government has determined to end these deficits to protect the international value of the dollar and the United States gold reserve. The campaign cut the deficit last year to half the level of the year before, and this year's target is balance, with the total payments to other nations to equal the total inflow from abroad.

Newly mined gold also has been a traditional source of reserve growth. But so much has disappeared into private hoards and industrial use that this has long been only a minor source of growth of monetary reserves—and a highly uncertain one from year to year.

A major innovation in the United States plan is that it would set up a target for the desired annual growth in global monetary reserves. The Economic Report hints at a target of $2-billion a year, the average growth of reserves in recent years before 1965, when there was hardly any growth at all.

If there should be a big flow of gold, either newly mined or from the Soviet Union, into official reserves in a given year, then the amount of new international money units to be created, or the addition to drawing rights on the Monetary Fund, could be correspondingly smaller.

If reserves were extinguished, for example by a United States payments surplus, more new units could be created.

The Economic Report recommended the twin approach—crus and expanded I.M.F. drawing rights—on the ground that each "has distinctive characteristics that can make it particularly useful for certain purposes."

"In either case," the report said, "one basic principle holds: The acceptability of the new reserve asset will fundamentally depend on the willingness of participating countries to view it as a form of international money."

The United States plan contains elements of several of the suggestions for reform that have been circulating here and abroad since the international monetary problem began to be generally recognized.

The originator of the idea of a composite reserve unit was Edward M. Bernstein, former director of research of the International Monetary Fund. The plan outlined today also appeared to accept several aspects of proposals by Robert V. Roosa, former Under Secretary of the Treasury.

The four-country European plan would not link the cru to gold in its distribution, but reportedly would create a link to gold in the use of the unit. That is, a nation with a deficit in its international transactions would pay out to other nations both gold and crus in some agreed proportion.

United States opposition to linking the cru to gold was explicit in today's Economic Report.

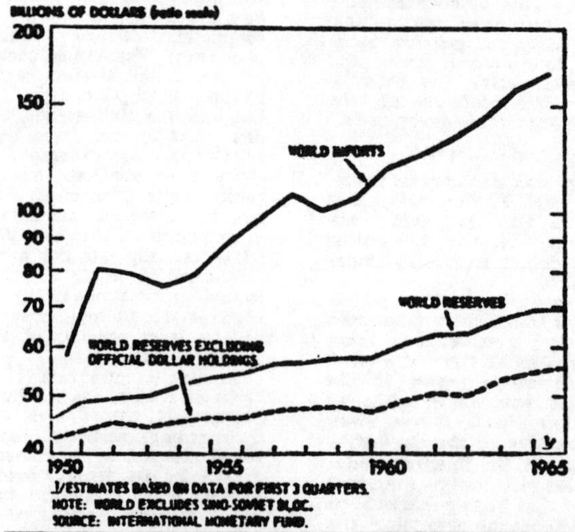

Chart, from the Economic Report, relates world's reserve growth to trade. Same slopes mean equal rates of growth.

January 28, 1966

Parallel Money Studies

Working Party and the Group of 10 Both Weighing Monetary Problems

By RICHARD E. MOONEY
Special to The New York Times

PARIS, March 27—The well-publicized falling out of the countries that have been trying to negotiate a reform of the world monetary system is being duplicated in a second group trying to determine formulas that might make reform less necessary.

The two groups have equally undescriptive titles: the Group of Ten and Working Party III of the Organization for Economic Cooperation and Development.

Their membership, almost identical, is made up of the United States, Canada, Japan and the major powers of Western Europe, give or take one or another of the smaller European countries.

Smooth Expansion

The common denominator of their two studies is world liquidity — how to assure that governments have sufficient monetary reserves to permit a smooth expansion of world commerce, or how to avoid shortages of reserves and crippling protective restraints.

The two groups' assignments are complementary to each other, and both are approaching their deadlines. Both will begin work on their final reports at their April meetings in Paris and Washington in the coming two weeks.

The working party is focusing on the nature of balance-of-payments problems, with an eye to figuring out how deficits and surpluses can be corrected with minimum ill effects on the world, or how they can be avoided in the first place. The Group of Ten is working on schemes to provide additional reserves, should they be needed.

The aim of the working party, considerably less revolutionary than that of the Group of Ten, was to prepare an agreed set of rules — a code of good behavior — to be followed by countries with unbalanced international payments.

Some Continental conservatives, who never put much stock in the grander schemes for monetary reform anyway, felt that this code might be the more significant of the two projects.

Their point was that if the world were spared big swings by the major countries into surplus and deficit, it would be less difficult to assure an overall adequate supply of reserves for the world. In other words, the existing supply of gold and reserve currencies would not be overworked by the big countries.

It appears now, however, that this project is going no smoother than the Group of Ten's work, though for different reasons.

The United States, for one, is said to be reluctant to commit itself to the idea that its economy be controlled by external balance-of-payments factors—that is, that it could be necessary to put a real squeeze on the economy in order to bring the country's payments into balance.

The British, as they are demonstrating currently, feel much the same way. The French have a well known distaste for external control on anything they do these days.

The result of these divergencies is expected to be a code with many loopholes.

As for the Group of Ten, further ruminations on the near-standstill that developed at the last session, earlier this month, indicate little hope among many of the participants for a meaningful outcome.

The fact that France has virtually walked out on the negotiations is only part of the trouble.

The other Continental powers are also unhappy with the United States position, nervous about the much-discussed idea of creating a new monetary reserve unit, and opposed to letting the whole affair pass into the hands of the 103-nation International Monetary Fund.

The nervousness about a new reserve unit leads many participants to feel that this idea is dead, at least for now.

And the distaste for the I.M.F. indicates that this may not be the route for reform either and, thus, that there may be little or none.

March 28, 1966

NATIONS SEEKING WORLD CURRENCY

With France Silent, 9 of 10 Powers Agree New Form of Exchange Is Needed

AT ODDS ON THE DETAILS

Report Cites Disagreement on a Reform Plan—Talks Will Be Expanded

By EDWIN L. DALE Jr.
Special to The New York Times

WASHINGTON, Aug. 25 — With France abstaining, nine of the 10 leading industrial and financial powers disclosed today their agreement in principle that the world will need in the future some kind of international money to supplement gold and dollars in the nations' official reserves.

But the report of high officials of the Group of Ten revealed continuing disagreement on many details of a monetary reform plan. Negotiations will continue, probably including for the first time officials representing the less developed countries.

The report, made public today in 10 capitals, was from the deputies of the Finance Ministers and central bank governors of the 10 countries. They have been negotiating international monetary reform for almost three years, and today's report was the product of the most recent round of talks.

Most Progress to Date

The Group of Ten is made up of the United States, Britain France, West Germany, Italy, Belgium, the Netherlands, Sweden, Canada and Japan. The chairman of the deputies making the report was Otmar Emminger of the German Central Bank.

The report marked the greatest progress so far in that nine of the 10 agreed on "the necessity to set out now a full-scale contingency plan" for adding to world monetary reserves in the future. The nine said:

"We are agreed that, while global reserves are sufficient at present, the existing sources of reserves are unlikely to provide an adequate basis for world trade and payments in the longer run, because a continuance of large United States [balance of payments] deficits must be ruled out as a source of future reserve increases for the rest of the world and because gold alone is not likely to supply sufficient additions to monetary reserves.

"Accordingly, we are agreed that at some point in the future existing types of reserves may have to be supplemented by the deliberate creation of additional reserve assets."

No Accord on Assets

The report made clear at many points, however, that there was still no agreement on the exact nature of these additional "reserve assets." The tw types discussed, the report said, were "issues of a new reserve unit which is directly transferable between monetary authorities and-or special reserve drawing rights in the International Monetary Fund."

"It is essential to distinguish clearly between the working out of a contingency plan and the activation of that plan. Activation should not take place unless it was decided, on the basis of a collective judgment, that a clear need for reserves would arise in the near future."

Frederick L. Deming, Under Secretary of the Treasury for Monetary Affairs, told a news conference that "no particular plan has a lot of support."

At the moment, including the United States plan for creating both a new monetary reserve unit backed by the leading currencies and a special automatic drawing right in the International Monetary Fund to supplement national reserves.

But Mr. Deming said he thought there was "a will to agree" among the negotiating nations and added the target was for a detailed agreement by mid-1967.

The finance ministers of the 10 countries have instructed their deputies to keep talking and to report again by the middle of next year. In addition they have, in effect, invited the participation of other countries. This would take place through joint meetings of the deputies of the 10 with the 20 executive directors of the International Monetary Fund, who represent the fund's 104 members.

France will dontinue to take part in the talks.

In the end any agreement would have to be ratified by Parliaments. The new plan for expanded negotiations may be approved at next month's annual meeting here of the governors of the fund.

Today's report indicated a general agreement among the nine countries that support the principle of creation of new international reserves that "activation" of the plan would be done by some system of weighted voting, rather than by unanimity. Mr. Deming said this principle was 'quite clearly accepted."

However, the report also disclosed a firm determination on

the part of the richer nations to play a special role in any plan for creating new reserves, largely because their moneys would back the new reserve units, or monetary fund drawing rights.

Thus, no simple majority of the Monetary Fund members would be able to vote new international money into existence. The report said:

"The organizational arrangements for decisions on the creation and management of reserve assets should reflect both the interest of all countries in the smoot working of the international monetary ssystem and the particular responsibilities of a limited group of countries."

August 26, 1966

A New Step Toward 'Paper Gold'

By EDWIN L. DALE Jr.
Special to The New York Times

WASHINGTON, Oct. 1 — The world took another step this week toward eventual creation of a new international money to supplement gold. The occasion was the annual meeting of the 105 members of the International Monetary Fund. Ironically, while there was some progress, at least procedural, toward a new international money, a number of important nations at the meeting emphasized their belief that this was not now an urgent problem.

For example, Marius W. Holtrop, governor of the Netherlands Central Bank, said he believed in "contingency planning" for a new reserve money when needed, but that this issue "does not have any relevance to the problems that haunt us today."

These problems, for the rich countries, are inflation, high interest rates and balance of payments deficits in some key countries, and, for the poor, the continued insufficency of the flow of aid of economic development.

Nonetheless, if the clear desire expressed here this week for eventual creation of a new reserve money materializes, even three or more years from now, it will be a tremendous event in the development of the world economy.

The issue arises because of the probable insuffficency in the future of monetary "reserves." These now consist of gold, dollars and British pounds, held by countries to meet deficits in their international transactions. If a nation runs out of reserves, it must devalue its currency or impose severe controls on imports and all sorts of other international transactions, such as tourism and the flow of capital. This slows world trade and other exchanges and eventually disrupts world prosperity.

New Source Needed

It was widely agreed that global reserves are now sufficient, though some individual countries such as Britain have a shortage. But over time, reserves must grow with the growth of international transactions, as they have grown in the past. Where are they to come from?

Newly-mined gold is not enough, especially because most of it is now finding its way into private hoards. In the past 10 years much of the growth of reserves has come from deficits in the United States balance of payments, which have pumped dollars out into the world, many of which were retained by foreign countries in their reserves.

But this process has been accompanied by a loss of U.S. gold, as some of the dollars were turned in for the metal. While the less developed countries are still happy to hold any dollar surplus they may happen to earn, the rich countries of Western Europe are no longer willing to pile up dollar holdings.

Deficit Reduced

For these reasons, the United States has made it a major policy priority to eliminate the balance of payments deficit, and the deficit has already been reduced. While the war in Vietnam will prevent a balance this year, there is little doubt that the U.S. deficit eventually will be wiped out.

Thus dollars will no longer be a source of world reserve growth. Pounds are now a relatively minor factor, and Britain, too, is eliminating her payments deficit.

The answer to the problem of future reserve growth that has emerged is deliberate creation of a new international monetary reserve unit. Nations would pay in their own currencies to the International Monetary Fund, or a new affiliate of the Fund, and get back "reserve units," which have been called "paper gold." The backing for them would be the currencies that have been paid in, primarily the currencies of the rich countries.

France blasted the whole idea this week, and other European countries took a cautious attitude. But except for France, all the members of the Fund were willing to press ahead with negotiations on the crucial details on a "contingency planning" basis. Perhaps the major issue to be resolved in creating a world money for the first time is the issue of control—who would decide when and how much to create, and what sort of voting system should be arranged.

The negotiations will continue, as in the past, among the leading financial nations known as "The Group of Ten." But it was agreed this week that the poorer countries would be brought in, indirectly, in the negotiations. This would occur through joint meetings between the negotiators for the Group of Ten and the 20 executive directors of the Fund, who represent all 105 members.

The aim, which may or may not be achieved, is to have a plan ready for consideration at the Monetary Fund's annual meeting a year from now in September.

While few nations or experts believe new reserves are needed now, the importance of a successful negotiation was put well here by Xenophen Zelotas, governor of the Central Bank of Greece.

"Psychological factors," he said, "are no less important than considerations about the present adequacy or inadequacy of world reserves. . . The simple announcement of international agreement on the eventual course of action would suffice to combat uncertainty and restore confidence."

October 2, 1966

World Monetary Reform Approved by 10 Nations

By EDWARD COWAN
Special to The New York Times

LONDON, Aug. 26—Ministers of 10 nations agreed tonight on a plan for a reform of the international monetary system that is expected to facilitate the growth of world trade.

In the United States' view, the plan is a first step toward gradually ending the role of gold in world finance.

American officials expressed deep satisfaction with the plan, although it is decidedly less liberal than the one they had first sought.

The Secretary of the Treasury, Henry H. Fowler, called it "the most ambitious and significant effort" since a 1944 conference in Bretton Woods, N. H., at which the foundations for the postwar international financial system were laid.

That system has been built around gold the British pound and the dollar. The new plan, agreed upon tonight after 10 hours of hard bargaining, will begin to move the world away from the Bretton Woods system by reducing the importance of gold, the dollar and the pound sterling in world finance.

Although the plan fell perceptibly short of the United States' goals, it was regarded as the first step in a new direction, one from which there would be no turning back. Some American officials believed it was a step that would lead to a transformation of the International Monetary Fund into a world central bank with the power to regulate the flow of international credit in much the same way as the Federal Reserve System regulates the domestic money supply in the United States. Such an evolution would take decades.

James Callaghan, the British Chancellor of the Exchequer, said the new plan would make it easier for countries that spend more than they earn abroad to put their books back into balance without going through a severe deflation. But Mr. Callaghan cautioned that the new plan would not be a license for any country to run a continuing deficit.

To the extent that the drawing rights will allow nations to pursue expansionist economic policies and avoid deflation, they will stimulate world trade by allowing the recipients to buy more from other countries.

The meeting today in Lancaster House, a 19th-century mansion near Buckingham Palace, ended a four-year search by the 10 nations to devise something that would supplement gold, dollars and pounds as the reserves countries hold to meet their international obligations.

They found a device that is somewhat intangible from the average citizen's viewpoint, but nonetheless real. It is a special drawing right in the 106-nation International Monetary Fund.

Neither money nor credit in the usual sense of those terms, the special drawing rights will exist on the books of the fund. Governments will be able to use the rights to settle accounts among themselves.

Accounts now are usually settled in gold, dollars and pounds. A country spending more than it is earning can borrow from the fund's $6.3-billion pool of currencies supplied by the member nations. That is the traditional type of drawing right, which will not be impaired or reduced by the creation of special drawing rights.

The plan agreed upon tonight is to be submitted to the fund's annual meeting in Rio de Janeiro on Sept. 25. Its approval there is virtually certain. Then it will go to national legislatures for approval.

When the plan would come into use and how large the special drawing rights would be will be voted upon by the fund's members.

Special drawing rights will be allocated to each member nation in accordance with its quota in the monetary fund. Britain, for example, which has provided 11.6 per cent of the fund's regular currency pool, would be entitled to 11.6 per cent of the special drawing rights created.

A communiqué issued by the ministers stressed that the special drawing rights would not come into use immediately. They were intended, the ministers said, "to meet the need, as and when it arises, for a supplement to existing reserve assets."

The ministers agreed that the plan could be activated only if member countries with 85 per cent of the fund's votes approved it. That would give a veto to the members of the European Economic Community, or Common Market, if they voted as a bloc because they jointly have 17 per cent of the votes. Voting in the fund is based on contributions to it.

The United States fought the voting proposal for months but finally gave in, recognizing that on this point of political prestige France had the support of her Common Market partners, Belgium, West Germany, Italy and the Netherlands. Luxembourg, the sixth market member, is represented by Belgium in monetary matters.

The other members of the so-called Group of Ten that drew up the plan are Britain, Canada, Sweden and Japan.

August 27, 1967

Debre Ties Monetary Pact To U.S. Payments Action

Insists on Elimination of Deficit Before Creation of Reserve Assets

By EDWIN L. DALE Jr.
Special to The New York Times

RIO DE JANEIRO, Sept. 26 —France said today that new monetary reserve assets, known as special drawing rights, could not be created until the deficit in the United States balance of payments was eliminated, but West Germany said the deficit must only be "diminished."

As national attitudes on the new plan for creation of reserve assets became clearer at the annual meeting of the International Monetary Fund here, several points of difference emerged. It was evident that some difficult negotiations remained in the months ahead, though France and all other countries that spoke supported the plan.

Probably the key difference was over the question of reforms in the voting and other rules of the Monetary Fund itself, in parallel with drawing up the legal text of the new plan. The resolution to be voted on later this week would set both efforts in motion.

France, speaking through Finance Minister Michel Debré, made clear that "parallelism of the two reforms is one of the conditions for the agreement of the French Government." West Germany also said the two "are for us a single entity," in the words of Economics Minister Karl Schiller.

But the United States and Britain, supported by Australia and several of the less-developed countries, argued that complex, and probably controversial, changes in the I.M.F. rules should not be allowed to delay the legal processes for creating the new special drawing rights, or S.D.R.'s.

Noting that some changes could be "complicated and controversial," Secretary of the Treasury Henry H. Fowler said "adequate time should be allowed to permit a mature, broad and certain meeting of minds." He added:

"I believe that specific substantive decisions on all these matters should not be regarded as a precondition to taking action on the special-drawing-rights amendment."

James Callaghan, British Chancellor of the Exchequer, agreed. "We must not allow discussion of these other changes to hold up final agreement on the special drawing rights," he said.

Voting System at Issue

Although not a single speaker specified what reforms of the Fund he had in mind, it has become known that the key proposal of the European Common Market countries is to require an 85 per cent voting majority, instead of the present 80 per cent, on all questions of Monetary Fund policy that would have the effect of adding to the world supply of reserves.

An example is decisions to increase the quotas of members of the Fund, thus giving them larger rights to draw foreign currencies to bolster their reserves.

An 85 per cent voting rule would give the Common Market countries a veto if they voted as a bloc. This voting rule has already been agreed to for the new special drawing rights, and the Common Market countries now want to avoid "circumvention" of their veto power by the use of present methods in the Monetary Fund of adding to world reserves.

In practice, the Fund in the past has always acted unanimously. A key European official declared today the proposed changes were more "psychological and political" than practical in their importance, obtain parliamentary ratifica- but he said they were needed to tion of the new drawing-rights plan in some European countries.

Negotiations Scheduled

Nonetheless, the United States attitude toward the proposed change is one of doubt if not downright hostility, at least at this stage. Several less-developed countries also indicated their suspicion of the plan today, and a tough battle seems to be in store.

The negotiations will be conducted by the executive directors of the Fund, representing the member countries, with a deadline of next March 31.

Despite the emergence of this problem, today's speeches were notable for the unanimity with which the plan for creation of the new special drawing rights was greeted. There were no serious complaints from the poor countries, even though they would get only small amounts of S.D.R.'s when they are created.

Only France and Germany touched today on the sensitive issue of the connection between the future decision to create the new S.D.R.'s and the state of the United States balance of payments, which involves the difference between total foreign expenditures and total receipts from foreigners.

Mr. Debré said "disappearance" of the payments deficit was an absolute condition for creation of the new assets. But this does not necessarily mean that France would stick to that position when the time comes, a minimum of a year and a half from now.

In his speech, he reiterated the traditional French hostility to the system of "reserve currencies"—the dollar and the pound—as "an instrument of instability."

"The more quickly we return to the gold standard, supplemented by a good organization of international credit, the more quickly we shall provide the world economy with the conditions for recovery," he said.

The industrial countries that spoke today all indicated their support of a new, and presumably larger, contribution to the exhausted funds of the International Development Association, the "easy loan" subsidiary of the International Bank for Reconstruction and Development, or World Bank. But no concrete pledges were made.

September 27, 1967

Reforming Monetary Policies

Group of 20 Faces a Need to Revive Keynes's Trigger

By LEONARD SILK

The job of reforming the world monetary system is about to begin. The board of governors of the International Monetary Fund has formally approved a new "Group of 20" to negotiate a new monetary system for the 120-nation body that includes the whole of the non-Communist world. The most difficult and important issue the top financial brains of G-20 will face, when they meet for first time in Washington in late September during the annual World Bank and monetary fund meetings, will be how to devise an orderly procedure for preventing nations from getting into deep deficits or heavy surpluses in their balances of payments.

Economic Analysis

Failure to solve that problem has bred crisis after monetary crisis in recent years, culminating in President Nixon's new economic policy of last Aug. 15. One of the critical elements of that program was ending the convertibility of the dollar into gold.

Cutting the golden knot set the United States dollar free to float in the world exchange markets—until it and other currencies were again fastened to new moorings at the Smithsonian Institution in Washington on Dec. 18.

The world has not increased its faith in paper currencies in the meantime. The price of gold has been driven upward; yesterday it exceeded $70 an ounce in London and Paris. This was the highest gold prices ever.

Some monetary experts—such as Miroslav Kriz, a vice president of the First National City Bank of New York—think the official gold price might be raised to $70 by the monetary agreement that the members of G-20 will soon be negotiating.

Significant to Gold Holders

That is not an insignificant issue to gold holders, whether they are private speculators or national Governments—including the gold-producing states, primarily South Africa and the Soviet Union.

As weighty as the gold issue may be, however, it is less significant—and certainly less complicated — than achieving equilibrium in the nations' balance of payments.

The fatal flaw in the monetary system negotiated at the Mount Washington Hotel in Bretton Woods, N. H., 28 years ago during World War II, was the rigidity of exchange rates. Economists generally regard exchange rates as the primary mechanism for restoring balance to a nation's external payments: devaluation makes its exports cheaper and imports dearer, and shrinks a payments deficit; an upward revaluation does the reverse and shrinks a surplus.

It was no accident that the world monetary system acquired extremely rigid exchange rates at Bretton Woods. The United States—by far the dominant power at that conference—wanted it that way.

The American delegation knew that the dollar would be strong in the postwar years, as the products of its undamaged and expanded economy flowed out to a war-shattered world. The United States preferred to supply foreign aid to cover the payments deficits of other countries than to have continuous devalutions against the dollar.

Thus America's White Plan for international monetary reform of 1944 — named for Harry Dexter White, Assistant Secretary of the Treasury and chief United States negotiator—sought to discourage rate flexibility by proposing that "changes in the exchange value of the currency of a member country shall be considered only when essential to the correction of fundamental disequilibrium in its balance of payments, and shall be made only with approval of three-fourths of the member votes. . . ."

The chief British negotiator at Bretton Woods, the eminent economist John Maynard Keynes—by then Lord Keynes—foresaw the problems to international monetary system that an overly rigid exchange rate system would cause.

He was not only concerned about international balance of payments troubles that might result but also about the possibility of jeopardizing a nation's ability to preserve domestic full employment. The crucial background of Lord Keynes's thinking was undoubtedly Britain's long struggle in the nineteen-twenties to defend an overvalued pound, which had caused mass unemployment, necessitated welfare and weakened the nation in the years preceding the Great Depression and World War II.

Inflation Was a Problem

Lord Keynes did not foresee that the principal long-term postwar problem would be inflation rather than depression, in large part as a result of his own influence. But that postwar economic difficulties resulted more from inflation than depression did not affect Lord Keynes's central point: That nations would have their hands tied in dealing with domestic problems, if exchange rates were rigid.

The Keynes Plan for the new monetary system, therefore, included a proposal for a "trigger" an objective criterion that would touch off action by the governing board of the monetary fund to get a nation's balance of payments back into equilibrium—when the nation was in excess deficit or surplus.

The equal responsibility of nations in surplus to take remedial action with those in deficit has been heavily stressed lately by American monetary officials, most recently by Arthur F. Burns, chairman of the Federal Reserve Board, in his Montreal speech of May 12.

Lord Keynes's trigger would have been kicked off by changes in a country's debit or credit balance with the I.M.F. When a country was running deficits and its debit balance reached half its quota with the fund, the governing board could require it to take one or more of the following actions: 1) devalue its currency by a suitable amount; 2) impose tighter controls on outward capital flows; or 3) pay up a suitable proportion of its gold or other liquid reserves to reduce its debit balance. Step 3 was a form of discipline that might force some domestic deflation, if required.

But when the Keynesian trigger was touched off by a country's mounting surplus, it required that country to restore equilibrium by taking one or more of the following steps: 1) expand domestic credit and demand—to help pull in more imports and reduce its exports; 2) revalue upward its currency in terms of what Lord Keynes called "bancor," a rough equivalent of what we now know as special drawing rights; 3) lower its tariffs or other trade barriers against imports; or 4) increase international development loans.

But the Keynes Plan was largely abandoned in favor of the White Plan.

During the earlier postwar years, the Keynesian trigger was neglected in the archives, as the world economy flourished and expanded within a fixed-rate monetary system made possible by continuous deficits in the United States balance of payments—and by occasional devaluations against the dollar.

The heavy loss of American reserves and the growing weakness of the dollar—and of the United States trade position—finally wrecked that system and has caused monetary reformers to search for a way to correct national deficits or surpluses before they breed more monetary crises.

Some economists—such as Prof. Milton Friedman of the University of Chicago—think the whole adjustment problem can be solved simply by letting all currencies float. The adaptation of exchange rates to the market forces of supply and demand for money would, according to this view, keep nations continuously in equilibrium—and thereby virtually obviate the need for monetary reserves to cover actual or potential deficits.

But other economists—such as Dr. Walter S. Salant of the Brookings Institution—contend that market-induced changes in exchange rates cannot be relied upon alone to handle the entire adjustment problem, especially after the much closer integration of the world economy in the postwar years, the rise of multinational corporations, the growth of the huge Eurodollar market, the speed of electronic communications, and the enormous pool of highly liquid capital—amounting to tens of billions of dollars—that can anticipate and swamp a currency devaluation or upward revaluation, or even force one to happen, whether warranted by market conditions and underlying price and wage trends or not.

Dr. Salant says: "Speculation can be massive even when there is no fundamental disequilibrium. . . . The idea that if there's massive speculation there must be fundamental disequilibrium appears to me groundless superstition of market-worshippers. The growth of internationally mobile capital has been all out of proportion to the growth of reserves plus borrowing facilities, and I think too little attention has been devoted to the implications of that fact."

One implication is that a massive increase in world monetary reserves, together with facilities for financing countries in deficit, is needed, in order to defend currencies—such as the dollar—from speculative raids.

A second implication is that exchange-rate changes must be relatively small, frequent, controllable and objectively justifiable, in order to keep the system in relative balance and remove opportunities for huge speculative gains.

Hence the search is on, among the world's monetary reformers, for new mechanisms for bringing about international exchange adjustments. The effort will be to update and, if possible, improve upon the old Keynesian trigger.

August 2, 1972

Fixed Money Rates Put Off Indefinitely

Officials Opt Instead to Set 'Guidelines' for Floating

By EDWIN L. DALE Jr.
Special to The New York Times

WASHINGTON, March 29 — International officials charged with negotiating world monetary reform formally buried today a return to fixed currency exchange rates for the indefinite future. They agreed on a short list of items that could usefully be negotiated for application in the "interim" system of floating exchange rates.

Included in the list is possible agreement on "guidelines" for floating, meaning mainly a set of principles to govern when central banks can properly intervene in foreign exchange markets to influence the exchange rates of given currencies.

Jeremy Morse, of Britain, disclosed the decisions at a news conference this afternoon following a three-day meeting at the deputy level of the Committee of 20 nations involved in the negotiations. He said "most" of the discussion concerned the "guidelines" for floating.

Resisting Rules

Mr. Morse, chairman of the deputies, said the term "guidelines" has been substituted for "rules" because "most deputies feel we cannot have firm or hard rules."

Essentially, the guidelines, if agreed to, will probably seek to prevent artificial manipulation of exchange rates to further an individual country's export or other interests.

Sources present at this week's meeting said there were no sharp disagreements, at least so far, over a tentative draft of guidelines for floating drawn up by Mr. Morse and his staff. In the end the issue will be settled at a ministerial-level meeting of the Committee of 20 in June, which will be its last.

The chief change in the atmosphere is that all countries now recognize that there is no hope of an early return to fixed exchange rates, officials said. Thus nations that once were not even willing to discuss guidelines for floating, because they were so opposed to it on principle, now recognize that the issue cannot be avoided.

Another issue to be settled by June is a new valuation and interest rate for Special Drawing Rights, the monetary reserve asset sometimes called "paper gold."

This is necessary to make S.D.R.'s "usable" again, Mr. Morse said, and might also be recycling might be based on involved in plans to "recycle" money from the oil-producing countries to the rest of the world. A proposed new "oil facility" of the International Monetary Fund aimed at this S.D.R.'s as a standard of value to protect the oil countries against depreciation of specific currencies.

A basic decision has been made to base the S.D.R. value on a "basket" of currencies, but many technical details remain to be worked out. The issue, for the time being, is mainly in the hands of the executive board of the monetary fund rather than the Committee of 20 deputies, and it was not tackled in detail at this week's meeting.

Mr. Morse said the deputies discussed the role of gold in the "interim" system but that positions on this subject remained about as they were when a more permanent reform was being debated last year—no agreement so far.

March 30, 1974

MONETARY FUND OFFERS BLUEPRINT

Committee of 20 Presents Outline for a Reformed World Money System

DISAGREEMENTS NOTED

'Rules of the Game' Will Be Based on 'Stable but Adjustable Rates'

By EDWIN L. DALE Jr.
Special to The New York Times

WASHINGTON, June 14—The 20 nations that have been negotiating reform of the world monetary system today made public their general conclusions on what a permanently reformed system should look like.

The final report of the Committee of 20 identified general principles on which there is agreement — including that the system should be based on "stable but adjustable" currency exchange rates — and a number of important details on which disagreement remains.

Early this year, in light of the turmoil resulting from general world inflation and the particular effects of quadrupled oil prices, the committee decided to abandon its effort to negotiate a full-fledged reform now. But the outline published today will form the basis of future evolution of the monetary system or "rules of the game."

More Detail Offered

The outline was along the lines of the one published last September at the time of the annual meeting of the International Monetary Fund in Nairobi, Kenya, but contained more detail, including a set of annexes on various specific problems such as methods of intervention in foreign-exchange markets to maintain fixed rates for currencies.

Apart from interim agreements announced yesterday, any further decisions on movement toward a permanently reformed system will be in the hands of the Monetary Fund, and in particular its new Committee of Governors, which will comprise 20 finance ministers representing all of the 126 member countries of the fund.

For the conduct of business in the world, the key fact is that currency exchange rates will continue to "float" for the indefinite future, despite the general agreement that a reformed system must be based on stable rates for most currencies. The floating, however, will be "managed" with central bank intervention in daily trading to be governed by a set of guidelines published yesterday.

The Highlights

These are some highlights of the reformed system that may one day be put into place:

For exchange rates, most countries will maintain a "par value" and intervene in the markets to keep the rate within an agreed margin on either side of that value. But, unlike the old system, there will be specific provision to allow countries to float their exchange rates with approval of the Monetary Fund. For those with par values, changes in exchange rates are supposed to be more frequent than in the past to help cure balance-of-payments surpluses and deficits.

¶The system will impose greater pressure than in the past, particularly from the Monetary Fund, for nations to get their payments into balance, whether they be in surplus or deficit. There will be use of "objective indicators,' particularly movements up or down in monetary reserves, as a test of when a country should act. But there is not yet full agreement about how "automatic" the presumption of action should be nor on the use of international "pressures" to force action.

¶There will again be "convertibility," meaning that holders of dollars, for example, will be able to present them at the United States Treasury and obtain "primary" reserve assets, such as gold or special drawing rights.

¶The main reserve asset will be the special drawing rights, with a reduced but still undefined role for gold. The S.D.R. will also be the "numeraire"—the standard of value in which currency values are expressed—instead of gold as in the old system.

¶There will be new means, still not fully agreed on, to control the growth of total world reserves or "liquidity," and in particular reserves of foreign exchange such as dollars.

A summary of the reform says that it "involves an enlargement of the scope of international surveillance and management in a number of important areas, and a consequently larger role for the fund."

June 15, 1974

6 NATIONS PLEDGE ECONOMIC STEPS TO END THE SLUMP

Meeting in France Closes With Call for Recovery and Steady Growth

AGREEMENTS ARE BROAD

Key Industrial Countries Promise to Work Closely for Their Common Goals

United Press International

President Ford being greeted on return to Andrews Air Force Base by his wife, Betty

By CLYDE H. FARNSWORTH

Special to The New York Times

RAMBOUILLET, France, Nov. 17—Leaders of the United States, Japan and four Western European industrial powers pledged today to work closely together to "assure the recovery" of their economies and put them on a course of "growth that is steady and lasting."

The pledge was announced at the end of a three-day meeting held here by President Ford, President Valéry Giscard d'Estaing of France, Chancellor Helmut Schmidt of West Germany and Prime Ministers Harold Wilson of Britain, Aldo Moro of Italy and Takeo Miki of Japan.

The leaders had sought to coordinate their activities more closely in five main fields—currencies, trade, economic revival, energy and relations with developing countries—and they announced in a joint statement that they had reached broad general agreements.

Details Are Scant

The West German Chancellor said afterward that they did not attempt to go into too many details in their general agreements but instead decided to put into operation the same means to achieve the same ends.

"The most important thing," said Mr. Giscard d'Estaing, whose initiative brought the leaders together, "is that this conference has in fact taken place at a moment when the world is going through a crisis that affects the daily lives of our peoples."

"As the result of the work we have started," President Ford said, "the people of our countries can look forward to more jobs, less inflation and a greater sense of economic security."

Accord on Money

As far as could be gathered from conversations with sources from several delegations, the most important achievement at the conference was an agreement to correct erratic fluctuations in monetary exchange rates through more active buying and selling of currencies by national banks. This had come about through the efforts of finance ministers, meeting separately and under strong orders to compromise to get more stability in currency values.

Treasury Secretary William E. Simon, in a brief conversation just after the conference closed, said the finance ministers had agreed on a set of procedures that would bring about a greater coordination of the activities of central banks, but he stressed that there was "no agreement of any kind on fixed exchange systems or controls."

He declined to reveal what the procedures were, saying they had to be discussed first in Washington. Presumably he meant discussions with Arthur F. Burns, chairman of the Federal Reserve Board, who had not been invited to the meeting.

U. S. and French Views

The agreement on more active intervention by central banks was essentially a compromise between the United States, which feels market forces should continue to guide currency movements, and France, which had sought a return to a fixed-rate system such as existed from 1945 to 1973.

On the issue of monetary rates, the joint declaration affirmed the intention of the six industrial nations to "work for greater stability."

"We welcome the rapprochement, reached at the request of many other countries, between the views of the United States and France on the need for stability that the reform of the international monetary system must promote," the joint statement declared.

The meeting was held in a castle in this village, 35 miles southwest of Paris. When the talks ended after lunch the six leaders, accompanied by foreign and finance ministers and an enormous security force, walked across the road to the city hall to read before assembled reporters jubilant statements about what was described as "the spirit of Rambouillet."

Village Wedding Hall

They sat clustered in front of a green felt table in a ceremonial room where the villagers come to get married.

In discussing economic prospects, the leaders concluded, according to Mr. Giscard d'Estaing, that the United States and Japan were well launched on their recovery cycles, that recovery was about to start in West Germany and France, and that Italy's situation was improving.

For Britain, Mr. Giscard d'Estaing noted, there was no talk of economic recovery but only of improvement in the inflation rate.

Secretary of State Henry A. Kissinger had proposed that there be periodic meetings of the six leaders, joined by Canada, but the other leaders did not accept the idea at this time.

This meeting has already caused bitterness among those countries not invited. Especially sharp criticism came from the Netherlands, which saw it creating deep divisions within the European Common Market between the participants at the meeting and their uninvited neighbors.

November 18, 1975

Text of Statement After 6-Nation Economic Parley

RAMBOUILLET, France, *Nov. 17 [AP]—Following is the text of the statement issued at the end of the meeting here of the leaders of the six principal non-Communist industrialized nations:*

The heads of states and governments of France, Federal Republic of Germany, Italy, Japan, the United Kingdom of Great Britain and Northern Ireland and the United States of America; met in the Chateau de Rambouillet from 15th to 17th of November 1975, and agreed to declare as follows:

[1]

In these three days we held a searching and productive exchange of views on the world economic situation, on economic problems common to our countries, on their human, social and political implications and on plans for resolving them.

[2]

We came together because of shared beliefs and shared responsibilities. We are each responsible for the government of an open, democratic society dedicated to individual liberty and social advancement. Our success will strengthen, indeed is essential to, democratic societies everywhere. We are each responsible for assuring the prosperity of a major industrial economy. The growth and stability of our economies will help the entire industrial world and developing countries to prosper.

[3]

To assure in a world of growing interdependence the success of the objective set out in this declaration, we intend to play our own full part and strengthen our efforts for closer international cooperation and constructive dialogue among all countries, transcending differences in stages of economic development, degrees of resource endowment and political and social systems.

[4]

The industrial democracies are determined to overcome high unemployment, continuing inflation and serious energy problems. The purpose of our meeting was to review our progress, identify more clearly the problems that we must overcome in the future, and to set a course that we will follow in the period ahead.

[5]

The most urgent task is to assure the recovery of our economies and to reduce the waste of human resources involved in unemployment. In consolidating the recovery it is essential to avoid unleashing additional inflationary forces which would threaten its success. The objective must be growth that is steady and lasting. In this way consumer and business confidence will be restored.

[6]

We are confident that our present policies are compatible and complementary and that recovery is under way. Nevertheless, we recognize the need for vigilance and adaptibility in our policies. We will not allow the recovery to falter. We will not accept another outburst of inflation.

[7]

We also concentrated on the need for new efforts in the areas of world trade, monetary matters and raw materials, including energy.

[8]

As domestic recovery and economic expansion proceed, we must seek to restore growth in the volume of world trade. Growth and price stability will be fostered by maintenance of an open trading system. In a period where pressures are developing for a return to protectionism, it is essential for the main trading nations to confirm their commitment to the principles of the O.E.C.D. pledge and to avoid resorting to measures by which they could try to solve their problems at the expense of others, with damaging consequences in the economic, social and political fields. There is a responsibility on all countries, especially those with strong balance of payments positions and on those with current deficits, to pursue policies which will permit the expansion of world trade to their mutual advantage.

[9]

We believe that the multilateral trade negotiations should be accelerated. In accordance with the principles agreed in the Tokyo declaration, they should aim at achieving substantial tariff cuts, even eliminating tariffs in some areas, at significantly expanding agricultural trade and at reducing non-tariff measures. They should seek to achieve the maximum possible level of trade liberalization therefrom. We propose as our goal completion of the negotiations in 1977.

[10]

We look to an orderly and fruitful increase in our economic relations with socialist countries as an important element in progress in détente and in world economic growth.

[11]

We will also intensify our efforts to achieve a prompt conclusion of the negotiations concerning export credits.

[12]

With regard to monetary problems, we affirm our intention to work for greater stability. This involves efforts to restore greater stability in underlying economic and financial conditions in the world economy. At the same time, our monetary authorities will act to counter disorderly market conditions, or erratic fluctuations, in exchange rates. We welcome the rapprochement, reached at the request of many other countries, between the views of the U.S. and France on the need for stability that the reform of the international monetary system must promote. This rapprochement will facilitate agreement through the I.M.F. at the next session of the interim committee in Jamaica on the outstanding issues of international monetary reform.

[13]

A cooperative relationship and improved understanding between the developing nations and the industrial world is fundamental to the prosperity of each. Sustained growth in our economies is necessary to growth in developing countries: And their growth contributes significantly to health in our own economies.

[14]

The present large deficits in the current accounts of the developing countries represent a critical problem for them and also for the rest of the world. This must be dealt with in a number of complementary ways. Recent proposals in several international meetings have already improved the atmosphere of the discussion between developed and developing countries. But early practical action is needed to assist the developing countries. Accordingly, we will play our part, through the I.M.F. and other appropriate international fora, in making urgent improvement in international arrangements for the stabilization of the export earnings of developing countries and in measures to assist them in financing their deficits. In this context, priority should be given to the poorest developing countries.

[15]

World economic growth is clearly linked to the increasing availability of energy sources. We are determined to secure for our economies the energy sources needed for their growth. Our common interests require that we continue to cooperate in order to reduce our dependence on imported energy through conservation and the development of alternative sources. Through these measures as well as international cooperation between producer and consumer countries, responding to the long-term interests of both, we shall spare no effort in order to insure more balanced conditions and a harmonious and steady development in the world energy market.

[16]

We welcome the convening of the conference on international economic cooperation scheduled for Dec. 16. We will conduct this dialogue in a positive spirit to assure that the interests of all concerned are protected and advanced. We believe that industrialized and developing countries alike have a critical stake in the future success of the world economy and in the cooperative political relationship on which it must be based.

[17]

We intend to intensify our cooperation on all these problems in the framework of existing institutions as well as in all the relevant international organizations.

November 18 1975

Associated Press

The Chateau de Rambouillet, near Paris, the site of the recently completed economic conference.

Detente at Rambouillet

U.S.-French Monetary Differences Seemingly Resolved at Conference

By LEONARD SILK

What happened at the Chateau de Rambouillet? For one thing, Rambouillet produced a communiqué—not just an ordinary communiqué, written in bureaucratic language, but one written in resonant and cadenced prose poetry. The heads of state "came together because of shared beliefs and shared responsibilities." Their success "will strengthen, indeed is essential to, democratic societies everywhere."

Economic Analysis

Specifically, the leaders at the meeting agreed to overcome "high unemployment, continuing inflation and serious energy problems." And, far more specifically, with regard to monetary problems they agreed to work together for greater stability, not only of underlying economic and financial conditions but even of exchange rates.

"Our monetary authorities will act," said the leaders—though Arthur F. Burns, chairman of the independent Federal Reserve Board, was not invited to Rambouillet—"to counter disorderly market conditions, or erratic fluctuations, in exchange rates."

Perhaps there was no need in Rambouillet for Dr. Burns, despite his independence, since five days before the meeting in France, President Valéry Giscard d'Estaing had told a reporter from Le Figaro:

"In the present state of affairs, we would wear ourselves out if we were to engage in another argument on this subject [of fixed exchange rates]. It's not the right time to put an over-all reform of the monetary system down on paper."

But why, the reporter wanted to know, was France now ready to accept "stabilized" parities when France used to advocate "fixed parities"?

Because, said the President of France, the idea of completely rigid exchange rates "was conceivable under other circumstances," but today he had to acknowledge that the system "needs some flexibility to cushion it against the blows to which it is and will remain exposed."

Too great a fluctuation in the values of currencies in relation to each other would, on the other hand, upset economies, rational investment programs and "more basically, even the maintenance of a relatively stable flow of trade," he said.

President Giscard d'Estaing said he wants to modify the existing system of floating exchange rates so that it would move from the present fluidity (like water) to one of "viscosity" (like maple syrup.) To achieve this state there would have to be—to use another piece of French economic jargon — "concertation" for viscosity.

Despite the formidable jargon, something significant may have happened at Rambouillet on the exchange-rate front.

For Mr. Giscard doesn't want just the status quo. Former Assistant Treasury Secretary Charles Cooper (who has just left the Treasury) told a Congressional committee a month ago that the "philosophy of our intervention policy is to aid the functioning of the private market and avoid the emergence of disorderly conditions, not to attempt to supersede the market and set a par for the level of the exchange rate."

But Mr. Giscard d'Estaing wants the United States and the rest of the world to go farther than that.

He really wants a return to stabilized parties. Persumably, however, he is willing to settle now for motion toward stabilized values for currencies rather than a sudden leap. Thus he says he wants, first of all, a system that will be viscous—"one where movements take place in a medium that restrains them, and this is what we have achieved with the European snake."

The European snake — the joint float—includes the currencies of France, West Germany, Sweden, Denmark, and the Benelux countries. They oscillate under constraints in relation to one another.

"Over and above the viscosity of this system," says Mr. Giscard d'Estaing, speaking of the world monetary system, "we

Secretary Simon indicated yesterday that the French and the Americans had worked out must aim for a system of stabilized parities.

Secretary of the Treasury William E. Simon, just back from France, said in a telephone interview yesterday that he considers the agreements reached on the exchange-rate mechanism the most important achievement of the Rambouillet meeting.

Mr. Simon said that the other countries left it up to the United States and France to work out an agreement between themselves and that he negotiated it with Finance Minister Jean-Pierre Fourcade of France.

The agreement, Mr. Simon said, has two main sections—one operational and the other having to do with the reform of the monetary system.

The Treasury Secretary puts his major emphasis on agreements to stabilize the "underlying," economic and financial conditions rather than the stabilization of exchange rates as such.

He insists that President Giscard d'Estaing did not raise the issue of a return to par values.

However, French sources are insisting that Mr. Giscard d'Estaing won a great victory at Rambouillet—an agreement to end the more-or-less free floating of the dollar in world money markets.

The French concede that Mr. Giscard d'Estaing before theme-

eting had dropped his demand for fixed exchange rates and said hewould be satisfied with some limits—through a more active and open intervention by central banks—to give the monetary system more stability. President Ford, say the French sources, wearily accepted greater constraints on the dollar's freedom to float.
"formal mechanisms" for intervention to curb "erratic" movements of currencies. But he insisted that there is still freedom for the dollar to move

Just after the meeting in Rambouillet broke up, Mr. Simon stressed that there was "no agreement of any kind on fixed exchange systems or controls."

However, the United States and France did come together, Mr. Simon indicated, on how to amend the articles of agreement of the International Monetary Fund at the January meeting of the I.M.F. in Jamaica, particularly with respect to the exchange-rate adjustment mechanism.

This, he indicated, would clear the way for a more durable reform of the international monetary system, with respect to gold, par values, rate flexibility and other issues.

The Rambouillet communiqué took jubilant account of this, stating, "We welcome the rapprochement, reached at the request of many other countries, between the views of the United States and France on the need for stability that the reform of the international monetary system must promote" (here poetry gave way to bureaucratese) to give the Americans their stress on the interpretation of stability as resulting from reform of the system, rather than reform of the system consisting of stabilization of rates.

But if the French have given up their insistence on fixed exchange rates, and if the Americans insist they are happy with a deal that preserves flexibility and a floating system, what does the agreement of Rambouillet really mean?

"It may create an erogenous zone for currencies," said Prof. Walter W. Heller yesterday. The former chairman of the Council of Economic Advisers under Presidents Kennedy and Johnson suggested that the nations, in the spirit of affectionate interdependence reached at Rambouillet, would be expected to stay within those "erogenous zones."

But this is not so—certainly not according to the agreement reached at Rambouillet, which contains nothing whatsoever on the establishment of zones within which currencies can fluctuate in relation to one another.

The precise meaning of Rambouillet appears to be:

¶Differences between the United States and France have been resolved.

¶Some rules have been added to a floating-rate system and some institutions have been created to deal with erratic or disorderly markets.

¶Some "institutions" — as Treasury officials prefer to call them—have been set up to deal with the underlying instability of economies and the system as a whole. These "institutions" are to include broadened daily contacts among central banks, more frequent meetings and consultations among finance ministers and consultations among their deputies on a weekly basis.

¶There will be I.M.F. surveillance to prohibit manipulative practices by governments on foreign exchange rates.

The American Treasury officials are acting enthusiastic about the deal, and Secretary of State Kissinger has hailed it as a great stride toward economic stability and reform of the monetary system.

Maybe it is.

November 19, 1975

PS
MOVIMIENTO INDIGENA DE CHILE
CASA DEL MAPUCHE
P S

CHAPTER **5**

U.S. Investments Abroad

Salvador Allende Gossens addressing Chileans, 1971.
Courtesy The New York Times

U. S. CAPITAL SEEN GOING ABROAD AGAIN

Commerce Official Predicts Outflow of 8 to 10 Billions of Private Money

OFFERS INVESTING GUIDE

Bilateral Benefits, Effects on Productivity, Economic Bases and Terms All Factors

Private investments abroad during the post-war period will be from $8,000,000,000 to $10,000,000,000, supplementing the Government loans which will amount to about $10,000,000,000, H. B. McCoy, chief of the division of industrial economy, office of international trade, United States Department of Commerce, predicted yesterday.

Speaking at a meeting of the foreign trade committee of the Commerce and Industry Association at 233 Broadway, Mr. McCoy said that many businesses previously unwilling to consider investments abroad, were entering now into negotiations with foreign concerns and groups of potential foreign investors. The department, he disclosed, is considering the formation of a group of bankers and manufacturers to guide it in developing information about foreign conditions and needs that would be of use to prospective investors.

Holds Lending Profitable

Despite the number of "black spots" in our previous foreign investment record, the impression which apparently prevails that such investments represented a loss to us and no gain to foreign countries, is incorrect, Mr. McCoy declared. Over the long term, he said, American investors were able to realize more on their investments than they had put in, and from 1919 to 1940, interest payments from these investments amounted to about 90 per cent of the net capital investments abroad.

"Furthermore," he declared, "our past unsatisfactory experiences could have been eliminated if investments had been directed to purposes which after careful study were deemed to be sound business ventures and made a real contribution to employment and output in the recipient countries.

"If past mistakes are to be avoided it is essential that our foreign investments be beneficial to both lender and borrower, that the loans are made for productive purposes with sound economic justification for the economy of the recipient country, and that the terms are fair and reasonable. It is essential that full information be available upon which the investor can base his decision."

Fears that in certain areas expropriation of foreign investments might be undertaken are generally no longer valid, Mr. McCoy said, provided private foreign investors make every effort to conform with regulations and procedures laid down by foreign countries. The Government, which has been charged with lacking a policy on foreign lending and investment, now has such a policy and program, he asserted, adding that "business must do its part in private foreign lending and investment if we are to achieve full production and employment and by so doing benefit ourselves as well as the rest of the world."

Sees Slowing of Buying Here

Sometime within the next eighteen months to three years accumulated buying power in the domestic market will have run its course, Mr. McCoy declared. During this period the more urgent demands from foreign markets will be satisfied, at least to the extent that dollar exchange is available for purchases, but in two years, more or less, we will be looking for larger markets abroad for our products, he said. Development of industrialization in foreign countries advances their prosperity and consequently their ability to purchase American goods, Mr. McCoy asserted.

"A foreign lending program adequate to meet the minimum needs of foreign countries," he declared, "will provide additional production and employment in many American industries, and any temporary sacrifice involved in other areas of the economy will be small compared to the long-range advantages to the United States of a peaceful, active and growing world economy."

March 8, 1946

Exchange Officers of Hemisphere Meet Here for First Conference

Heads of Stock Markets Come From the U. S., Canada and 9 Latin-American Countries—Action on Peace Treaties Urged

Securities Exchange leaders from the United States, Canada and nine Latin-American countries met yesterday in the first hemispheric stock exchange conference in the Plaza Hotel.

They were told by James S. Kemper, president of the Inter-American Council of Commerce and Production, that "unless the Foreign Ministers' meeting in Moscow in November results in agreement for the right sort of peace treaties with Germany, Japan and Austria, the countries of this hemisphere should act independently."

Mr. Kemper called the plan to reduce Germany to a pastoral state as stupid as it was vindictive.

"A grammar school student with figures on European production, imports and exports for the five years before the war," he said, "could demonstrate to anyone that elimination of Germany as a producing and exporting nation easily could wreck the whole European economy.

"We should announce forthwith **that we no longer will tolerate continuance of the present policy of delay and obstruction. That announcement should carry with it the statement that we intend to proceed at once with the negotiation of separate peace treaties.**

"The right sort of peace with Germany should completely shackle her against any disturbance of world peace, but restore her productive capacity to the great benefit of western Europe and the world."

Emil Schram, president of the New York Stock Exchange, welcomed the delegates at a luncheon yesterday.

"We do not yet know in what form the growth of reciprocal business will develop among the capital markets that are represented here," he said. "I am sure, however, that this will come about.

"It may involve mutual listings of the shares of important and successful companies of one country on the stock exchanges of other countries. This would open **the resources of private investment funds of those countries which have surplus capital available.**

"It might accelerate international arbitrage among members of different exchanges, thus contributing to the stabilization of prices, the further development of natural resources and so forth."

A reversal of the pattern of the eighteenth and nineteenth centuries, when foreign capital aided the United States, was predicted by Francis Adams Truslow, president of the New York Curb Exchange.

"Our capital—our excess productive capacity," he declared, "will move abroad, attracted by the potential of greater profits in areas of new production. As that capital moves abroad, it will leave bonds and stock in the hands of our citizens to represent it here. The corporate form will become as well known and productive in foreign lands as it has become in the United States, to which it was transplanted from England."

Tomas Eduardo Rodriguez, president of the Stock Exchange in Santiago, Chile, was elected chairman of the conference.

"The imperialist enterprise," he said, "is disappearing and is giving way to the enterprise formed by capital and technicians, with which not only a strong economy is being created, but also confraternity and comradeship."

The business men of the world should unite, Frederick E. Hasler, honorary president of the Pan American Society of the United States, declared last night at a dinner for the delegates in the Waldorf-Astoria Hotel.

"One of the major weaknesses of the business world today," Mr. Hasler said, "is the lack of organization and unity which leaves business men at the mercy of politicians and labor leaders. True, we have chambers of commerce and trade associations in all parts of the country, but their scattered efforts are ineffective against the solid front presented by more than 15,000,000 members of organized labor groups.

"If the system of free enterprise is to be preserved and strengthened, business, too, must present a united front."

September 16, 1947

BIG ECA ROLE PLAYED BY PRIVATE ENTERPRISE

Three-fourths of Funds for Europe Flow Through Business Channels

By CABELL PHILLIPS

Special to THE NEW YORK TIMES.

WASHINGTON, Aug. 28— American private enterprise is getting a sizable bite out of the multi-billion-dollar operations of the Economic Cooperation Administration. An even greater degree of participation is expected in the months immediately ahead as the program settles into full stride.

As of a week ago, slightly more than three-fourths of the total expenditures authorized up to that time for the procurement of goods represented direct negotiations between buyers and sellers in "normal channels of trade." Within another fortnight it is contemplated that the first of a long series of private United States investments in foreign enterprises, with returns partly underwritten by the ECA, will be consummated.

Thus, the gigantic relief and rehabilitation program is fulfilling one of the cardinal directives written into its legislation by Congress: "* * * The Administrator shall to the maximum extent * * * utilize private channels of trade."

Such a doctrine is, of course, a reversal of previous Government practice in similar circumstances. Under lend-lease and other foreign procurement programs during the war years, the Government retained full authority as purchasing agent and dispenser. Today, under ECA, the Government encourages buyers and sellers to negotiate face to face in the open market. Its role is that of an aloof and watchful umpire.

Enough Safeguards

This has led to some premonitory fears that the recovery program would become a seed-bed of fraud and scandal, and that unscrupulous business men would endeavor to use it as a means of having their dubious excursions into the export field underwritten at Government expense. So far, these fears have not materialized.

The umpires have not had to call a foul or even to make a close decision. Furthermore, it is said in official circles, there are enough regulations and safeguards to prevent all foreseeable occurrences of the sort in the future.

Business men by the score, sample cases and order books in hand, continue to solicit business directly from the ECA. Administrator Paul G. Hoffman and his aides emphasize repeatedly that theirs is not a purchasing agency, but a financing agency. With the exception of wheat and certain agricultural products in the "relief" category, they negotiate directly for virtually no export goods at all. Even this category is being progressively narrowed.

What does happen is this: The "X" company in Paris, let us say, needs electric motors of a certain type to rehabilitate its plant. It requests its Government to put these on its next requirements list. This list is "screened" by the Office of European Economic Cooperation, which finds the request for motors justified. The request is passed on to ECA in Washington, which concurs. Through channels, the French Government is told that ECA dollars may be used for the transaction. It may stipulate that not more than a certain price shall be paid for them.

Buys in Open Market

At this point manufacturer "X" starts negotiations with American suppliers of the sort of motors he wants. He may come to this country and shop around personally. He may call in the European representatives of American motor manufacturers, or he may ask for sealed bids. In any event, he makes his purchase in the open, competitive market, making the best deal he can on price and quality just as though there were no ECA.

When the motors are delivered, he pays his Government the agreed price in francs. The Government then authorizes, through an intricate banking procedure, the release of an equivalent amount of its stock of ECA dollars to the American supplier. The American supplier, meanwhile, to be eligible for this conversion of francs to dollars, will have executed an agreement with the ECA setting forth the terms and conditions of his contract with the buyer, and evidence of the satisfactory fulfillment of that contract.

Free Enterprise Stressed

This, of course, is a vast oversimplification of what is often an extremely complex operation. It leaves out of account, for example, the functions of a number of foreign purchasing commissions stationed here to act officially on behalf of buyers within their countries. Nor does it take into account the vagaries of commercial practice, such as state monopolies and quasi-monopolies, that exist in many of the ECA countries.

However, it is illustrative of the manner in which ECA endeavors to encourage the use of private trade channels. It looks with open disfavor on the continued existence here of the foreign purchasing missions, and covertly it is not any too happy about the state monopolies and nationalized buying pools abroad. It is felt that they impede the full flowering of the free enterprise system as it is understood in the United States. However, up to now, Administrator Hoffman and his aides have hesitated to insist on the abandonment of such practices hallowed by long usage in the countries of Europe.

The full extent to which private trade of the sort described above has been utilized in carrying out the ECA program can be appreciated from figures released early this week. This tabulation showed that of all procurement authorizations to date, totaling $1,188,321,689, about three-fourths, or $875,449,716, was for purchases through regular trade channels. Both industrial and agricultural products are included. A relatively small sum was spent "off-shore." The remainder went in orders to American suppliers.

Another outlet for American enterprise through ECA is making less headway at the moment, principally because this phase of the program has been operative only since July 1. This concerns the investment of capital in foreign enterprises, with returns partly guaranteed by ECA.

Convertible Into Dollars

The extent of the guarantee is simply this: Investors in approved projects are assured of the convertibility of their dividends or liquidated capital into dollars up to 100 per cent of their investment.

ECA does not assume any business risks on such ventures, but merely assures the American investor that he will not have to be paid off some years hence in francs, lire or other foreign currencies. Nor does it assume any risks as to fluctuating exchange rates. The pay-off is assured at the rate prevailing at the time of payment. A slight variation of this program is applicable specifically to publishers and others in the field of informational media.

While considerable curiosity has been evidenced in financial circles over this provision of ECA, so far only twenty firms have applied for investment guarantees. Several of these applications may be approved in the next two weeks, officials predict, and this is expected to stimulate other potential investors to action.

"BLUNTING IT"

Carmack in The Christian Science Monitor

Congress earmarked a total of $300,000,000 of ECA funds to be used for convertibility guarantees for investors. Of this sum, a maximum of $10,000,000 may be used to convert the proceeds from the sale of informational media abroad —newspapers, books, motion pictures, etc. The guarantees extend to April, 1962.

ECA officials point out that while the guarantee provisions offer attractive opportunities for the profitable employment of American capital overseas, the cardinal purpose of the program is to promote the rehabilitation of Europe's economy. Each application for investment guarantees, therefore, will be examined by this yardstick, and will stand or fall according to the degree to which it promotes recovery. Furthermore, it is pointed out, each such enterprise must have full approval of the country in which it is to be located, and will be subject to such regulations and restrictions as that Government may impose.

The ECA legal staff is still wrestling with the problem of a standard form of document to be used in these guarantee transactions. It is also struggling with formulas on which future "existing" exchange rates will be computed. Both have proved troublesome but most of the hurdles are now out of the way.

August 29, 1948

INDUSTRY SURVEYS ROLE IN RECOVERY

Machinery Institute's Bulletin Cites Need for Leadership in War-Depleted Lands

OPPORTUNITY FOR EXPORTS

Developed Areas Are Termed Better Customers for U. S. Than Undeveloped Ones

WASHINGTON, Feb. 6—An analysis of factors which must be considered in a program of industrialization for war-depleted and undeveloped areas abroad was presented today by the Machinery and Allied Products Institute, speaking for the capital goods industries of the country.

The institute, in a bulletin, said that for more than four years it has been stressing the opportunities for American business and industrial leadership in this field. It hailed President Truman's inaugural address as encouraging because it indicated his Administration recognizes the inadequacy of the industrial plant of this country and of the world, and identifies technological advancement as a way to higher living standards both at home and abroad.

"A plan of economic cooperation with other countries based upon such sound economic principles will be welcomed by the capital goods industries as a far-reaching program to be thoughtfully examined and aggressively pursued," the bulletin said. "We believe that American government and American business together, within the framework of the free enterprise system, will be successful in accomplishing much in the right direction. The degree and rate of progress that is realized will depend heavily upon the interest and enterprise of top business executives in America, especially in the manufacturing industries, capital goods and consumption goods alike."

Chance to Sell "Know-How"

Studies of opportunities for the export of capital goods and industrial "know how" have been conducted by the institute, principally under the leadership of George H. Houston, a member of its executive committee.

"The best customers of countries like the United States are other developed areas, rather than undeveloped areas," the institute said.

"The export of capital goods to undeveloped localities must be accompanied simultaneously by the export of the corresponding techniques involved in the use of such goods and the arts of industrial and commercial organization, management and administration required to apply these techniques effectively.

"Unless a community to be thus industrialized is willing to go through the process of evolution through which the related techniques and managerial arts were evolved in the older industrialized communities, these techniques and arts, of necessity, must be supplied by importation."

Financial problems of industrializing undeveloped areas have been overemphasized, the institute says. Four phases of this subject were discussed: (1) internal savings of the community seeking development, and its ability to expand its internal credit prudently; (2) availability of foreign exchange arising primarily from exports in excess of imports; (3) importation of permanent venture capital, and (4) eventual development of long-term foreign capital.

February 7, 1949

U. S. INVESTMENTS 12 BILLIONS ABROAD

Direct Participation Census, First Since War, Shows 70% in Canada, Latin America

Special to THE NEW YORK TIMES.

WASHINGTON, Dec. 22—A new Government census, the first of its kind since the end of World War II, revealed today that private American direct investments abroad totaled $11,804,100,000 at the end of 1950.

Of these foreign holdings, the study showed that 70 per cent of the sum, or $8,239,100,000, was in Canadian and Latin-American enterprises.

The Office of Business Economics of the Department of Commerce, which conducted the census, viewed this preponderance of investment in the Western Hemisphere as customary.

This trend was taken to mark a desire to participate in the development of near-by sources of raw materials for use in an expanding economy and to assist in building the industrial potential of countries like Canada, Venezuela and Brazil where progress already has been great.

Latin-American investments were $4,675,000,000 of which $1,390,000,000 was in oil, $1,044,100,000 in transportation, communications and public utilities, and $617,400,000 in mining and smelting.

Canadian Industries Popular

Most of the investments in Canada, $3,564,100,000 were in manufacturing enterprises. This category, in all, had more than half of the holdings, or $1,881,400,000. Next in order of importance were these commitments. Petroleum, $418,100,000; mining and smelting, $334,300,000, and finance and insurance, $313,200,000.

Investments in Western Europe, according to the census, were $1,773,900,000 while another $429,800,000 had been put in enterprises in the dependencies of Western European countries.

More than half of the Western European investment total, in excess of $970,500,000, was in manufacturing enterprises, while $292,400,000 of the total for dependencies was in oil ventures. Petroleum investments ranked second in Western Europe with $440,800,000.

Investments in all other countries totaled $1,361,300,000, with $895,600,000 in oil, and $210,700,000 in manufacturing undertakings.

Countries outside the Western Hemisphere in which large investments have been made were these: United Kingdom, $840,000,000; Persian Gulf countries, $726,000,000; France, $285,000,000; Australia, $198,000,000 Union of South Africa, $140,000,000; Philippine Republic, $149,000,000; Indonesia, $58,000,000; Egypt, $40,000,000, and India, $38,000,000.

Data in the census, reported in the December issue of the Department's Survey of Current Business, revealed that, on a world-wide basis, American investment in manufacturing topped that in oil—$3,844,500,000 against $3,436,900,000. Of the investments in petroleum, the Office of Business Economics noted that a great deal was in the refining branch of the industry which might be classed as manufacturing.

The breakdown on other categories of world investment were: Transportation, communication and public utilities, $1,428,200,000; mining and smelting, $1,113,500,000; trade, $758,500,000; agriculture, $544,900,000; finance and insurance, $439,700,000, and miscellaneous, $237,900,000.

December 23, 1952

EUROPEAN MARKET GROWTH SPURS U.S. INVESTMENT

More Firms Are Entering an Area Once Served by Only a Few

By EDWIN L. DALE Jr.

Special to The New York Times.

GENEVA, Feb. 18—One of the half dozen major elements that enters into the United States balance of international payments is investment abroad by American corporations. This investment means both money leaving the United States and money coming back. In addition, it indirectly affects exports and imports.

When the Kennedy Administration set out to tackle the big deficit in the United States balance of payments and the resulting loss of gold, it looked to Government expenses abroad first, tourist spending second, and private corporate investment third. It has reached conclusions on the first two but not yet on the third.

Rise in Europe

Although total corporate investment abroad in the past four years has not risen—1957 was a peak not since approached —it has risen strongly here in Europe. There has been a genuine "invasion" of Europe by American companies. Some four hundred of them, for example, have set up foreign headquarters here in Geneva and elsewhere in Switzerland, for tax and operating reasons.

The situation is much discussed, sometimes with more heat than light. American jobs, the United States balance of payments, the "independence" of the economies of some European countries—all these are part of the controversy.

What follows is an effort to summarize the facts on the situation as far as they are available.

(1) *What are the dimensions of the invasion? Where are the companies going?*

The presence of United States concerns in Europe is nothing new. Several score of the biggest have been here for decades, some since before World War I. Indeed, there is sketchy evidence that, in dollar terms, the bulk of the new investment in Europe that has caused so much interest in the last three or four years has been made by companies that have been here for some time—General Motors and Ford, I. B. M. and Goodyear, International Harvester and Monsanto, Jersey Standard and Socony.

What is distinctly new is the increasing number of concerns that have begun to take an interest in Europe—and put cash in it. Also new is the magnitude of the annual investment.

Britain in the Lead

Britain retains her lead, with more American investment than all the Common Market countries put together, but that may not last much longer.

The unusual and huge "one-shot" purchase by the Ford Motor Company of its minority foreign-held shares in its British subsidiary brought the total outflow of dollars to $800 million last year. Although this transaction was virtually unique, it dramatized the whole issue of foreign investment and balance and payments.

The amount is large, but it must be kept in perspective. Plant and equipment spending by all United States manufacturing concerns in Europe in 1960 is estimated at $580,000,000, which is less than 5 per cent of the amount spent in the United States.

(2) *Why are they coming?*

When an American company announces that it is transferring to Europe manufacture of a product that it has been exporting to Europe, there is often a headline and sometimes an immediate loss of American jobs. But this has gone on for decades—tire, auto, chemical, machinery companies came to Europe long ago. In the case of the British Commonwealth, exports followed by investment has gone on for more than a century. Meanwhile, exports of other British and American companies increase.

A few publicized cases—cars, tractors, typewriters, outboard motors—have given the impression that United States companies take advantage of cheaper European labor to manufacture here and sell in the United States. The figures show how limited this sort of thing is.

Near the Market

By far the most important part of the answer is often overlooked: because this is where the market is growing fastest. Many a company decides to invest in France for precisely the same reason as it decides to invest in California or Texas: to be near the market.

The great bulk of the annual output of American branches and subsidiaries in Europe is sold in Europe. In 1957, the only year for which exact figures are available, sales of United States manufacturing concerns in Europe totaled $11,000,000,000, but only $195,000,000 worth was exported to the United States. Another portion was exported elsewhere, of course, but most is sold here.

In addition, there is a special factor. American companies here import a good deal of material, equipment and spare parts from the United States. In 1957, the only year for which details are available, imports of this kind totaled $440,000,000, compared with $195,000,000 in exports to the United States of products made by the concerns here (of which nearly half was British-made cars).

The formation of the European Common Market undoubtedly has created an additional incentive to invest in Europe. This incentive, according to many American companies which are taking the leap, is not so much because of the need to "get inside" the new tariff wall that will surround the Common Market as because the Common Market is becoming a growing market of 160 million consumers.

American exports to the Common Market nations rose by almost 50 per cent last year at the same time as American investment took a great leap forward.

(3) *What is the effect on Europe?*

The United States, in the form of Ford and General Motors, owns half the British auto industry. However, this situation is very much the exception rather than the rule. Over all, the share of United States concerns in the total output of European countries remains small.

Little in The Nashville Tennessean

U.S. INVESTMENT ABROAD

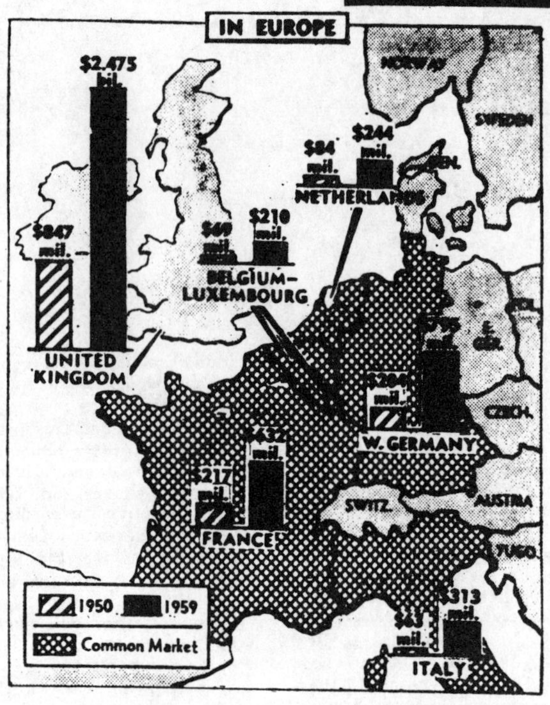

WORLD TOTAL

WHERE INVESTED (Total: $29.7 bil.)

Western Europe $5.3 bil.; Canada $10.2 bil.; Latin America $9.0 bil.; Other $3.2 bil.; Mid-East and Africa $2.0 bil.

HOW INVESTED (Total: $29.7 bil.)

Oil $10.4 bil.; Manufacturing $9.7 bil.; Mining $2.9 bil.; Other $4.3 bil.; Public Utilities $2.4 bil.

Most United States investment in Western Europe has been in manufacturing enterprises, though petroleum investment is also important. Some six hundred American firms have invested funds in Western European enterprises since 1958.

Britain is the country where most agitation occurs on this subject. But nowhere in Europe is American industry even approaching "dominance" except in isolated cases.

(4) ***What is the effect on the United States balance of payments?***

The outflow from the United States for investment in Europe is only a little more than half the total cost of new investment. Almost half of new investment comes from ploughed back earnings, plus funds raised here.

Of the $725,000,000 in new investment in Europe in 1959, $466,000,000 came from the United States and affected the balance of payments. For the Common Market, the whole "invasion" cost the United States $171,000,000 in the balance-of-payments sense. The estimate for 1960 is $500,000,000 for Europe as a whole, of which about half will be in the Common Market.

Dividend Income

On the other side, there is the return of dividends.

For the world as a whole, the inflow of dividends to the United States has been running at about $2,200,000,000 a year in the last four years, or considerably more than the annual outflow of new capital except for the unusual year of 1957.

For Europe, the same was true until last year, but new investment outflow probably exceeded the dividend return then.

(5) ***What about taxes, and should the United States Government try to curb the "incentives" to invest abroad?***

There is only one major "incentive," and it has been in effect for many years: Earnings abroad are not taxed until they are taken home.

The tax issue is complex, and perhaps some "loopholes" exist. The Kennedy Administration has promised to look into the matter. So far, despite some early indications that it was going to move quickly on this front, the issue is still in the study stage. There is no evidence that it has decided to change the basic principle of taxation only after earnings are repatriated.

February 19, 1961

RENAULT ACCEPTS COLOMBIAN TERMS

Contract May Set a Pattern for Developing Nations

Special to The New York Times

MEDELLIN, Colombia, July 19 — A plant for assembling Renault automobiles has been opened here on terms that leading United States automobile makers are said to have scored, but which some observers consider to represent the pattern of future private foreign investment in developing countries.

Key provisions in Renault's obtaining the assembly plant contract included:

¶Agreement to buy and market Colombian exports of a value equivalent to that of the components brought from France for incorporation in the cars assembled here.

¶Acceptance that the Colombian Government should have a half share in the venture. This half share is held by the Government's Institute for Industrial Development.

Renault won the assembly plant contract in competition with at least 15 automobile firms from the United States, Europe and Japan.

A source close to the evaluation of the bids said here that United States bidders — he named General Motors, Ford, Chrysler and American Motors —had looked upon both key provisions listed above as "nonsensical".

Pierre Dreyfus, Renault president in Colombia for the opening of the plant, told a press conference that while Renault had brought in components to a value of only $300,000, it had since the beginning of 1969 bought Colombian coffee, meat, tobacco, cotton and rice to a value of $3-million.

July 20, 1970

WORLDWIDE CODE ON INVESTING SET

International Business Unit to Offer Plan to Nations

By CLYDE H. FARNSWORTH
Special to The New York Times

PARIS, Dec. 18—The International Chamber of Commerce an organization with 10,000 members in 43 countries, has just come out with an international code of investment conduct that is designed to promote confidence between investors and governments.

The code is now to be presented to governments in hopes that eventually it, or something similar to it, can be adopted by the United Nations.

The Chamber's effort, a first for the business community, was completed only after some fierce battles within the business community, authoritative sources reported.

Divisions Noted

Especially accentuated were the divisions between enterprises in the so-called third— or developing — world and Western multinational giants with third-world subsidiaries.

The guidelines, which have just been published in a 16-page booklet by the Chamber, appear at first reading to be simply a catalogue of pious wishes.

For instance, there is a recommendation that investors should not seek undue protection from competition from imports and that host countries should cooperate towards liberalization of international trade.

Enterprises in the developing countries in this case took positions allied to those of their governments, demanding that multinational companies in the West end certain practices that the poorer countries find objectionable.

Two Tendencies Mentioned

Specifically mentioned in the documents were two tendencies: for multinationals to require payments from third-subsidiaries for property rights or technology "of no real value to the [subsidiary] enterprise," and for the multinationals, in the event that a capital market develops in a third-world country, to absorb all the local funds.

It is understood the Western multinational corporation men, while angry at the mention of these points in a public document, finally bowed to the third-world contingent in order to get a united front for the next stage.

What the multinationals would get out of the guidelines is certain protection against nationalization.

December 19, 1972

Multinational Ventures Backed

Study by Economist Says Projects Aid Global Economy

By BRENDAN JONES

Multinational corporations, already shaping a new global economy, are ideally equipped to carry out needed world economic development, according to a report made for the Internatonal Chamber of Commerce.

The 174-page report, by Dr. Sidney E. Rolfe, economist, was released by the chamber's United States Council at a news conference last week.

In a wide-ranging account of the growth, nature and problems of the multinational, or worldwide, business organization, the study stresses that:

¶They are neither a new, nor peculiarly American, phenomenon.

¶With investment, technology and organization of worldwide production, they are creating an international economy that is supplanting trade and providing a means for rapid, large-scale development.

¶National governments, especially in developing countries, should learn to weigh the benefits obtainable from the big international concerns against the "psychological security" of nationally controlled, but limited, economic growth.

Background Paper

The report will serve as the background paper for the biennial congress of the International Chamber, to be held in Istanbul May 31 to June 7.

The New York Times

Dr. Sidney E. Rolfe, right, discussing his report on multinational corporations at a news conference here last week. At rear is Judd Polk, acting president of the U.S. Council, International Chamber of Commerce, which issued report.

The conference will be attended by some 1,500 business leaders from more than 40 countries, including a large group from the United States.

Dr. Rolfe, who is professor of finance at Long Island University, has taught at Princeton and Columbia Universities and has been a consultant to many official and private groups.

His report, entailing about a year of research, contains statistical data and critical comment that make it one of the most comprehensive of recent studies on multinational corporations.

With international oil concerns a prototype, the report notes, modern multinational corporations began developing in the early twentieth century and now number several hundred.

Response to Technology

Dr. Rolfe describes them as "a rational response to modern technology," and as seeking "to produce, finance and market wherever resources can be most efficiently utilized, without respect to national boundaries."

Because American statistics are more detailed and easily obtained, Dr. Rolfe holds, American concerns have appeared to be most promient in the multinational field.

He offers other data, however, that show there are a substantial number of European, Canadian and Japanese multinational concerns.

Dr. Rolfe cites as the most significant fact about multinational corporations the rapid growth of their production.

That growth by American-based companies, he observes, recently has reached $120-billion a year—more than most countries' gross product—and has grown more rapidly than United States production and export-import trade.

The main object of the study, Dr. Rolfe said at the news conference, was to examine the position of the multinational corporation, its effects on integrating international economies and its challenge to the nation state.

"We are in the midst of change," he remarked, "and not sure where we're going, except we know change is toward a new world economy."

In the report, Dr. Rolfe suggests that developing countries would find multinational corporations the most practical medium for gaining investment, production and technology, management and marketing skills that they could learn to use themselves.

Dr. Rolfe maintains that efforts by developing countries at import substitution have failed because of small markets and high costs.

He notes also that developing countries' insistence on joint ventures limits investment benefits and proposes, instead, stock ownership in parent companies by investors in such countries.

Suggestion on Help

The report suggests, in addition, that multinational companies can help developing countries with industries specializing in export and organize production of components for vehicles and other products by groups of countries.

Most of the fears of multinational corporations, that they would dominate national and social institutions, or callously discharge thousands of workers, have not materialized, the report contends. It adds:

"The economic growth which the international corporation has brought is in fact in the best interests of the nation, which must look to the preservation of economic growth and rising standards of living as one of its most important functions."

May 12, 1969

Foreign Subsidiaries Rock Currency Boat

By CLYDE H. FARNSWORTH

Special to The New York Times

PARIS—Sometimes known as the third largest producing unit in the world after the United States and the Soviet Union, the foreign subsidiaries of international companies are complicating problems of the monetary system, and no one really knows what to do about it.

These enterprises — and they are not all American by any means—are behind the massive flows of money that have intensified recent currency crises.

The companies are not out to break the system. In fact, they have perhaps the greatest stake in its stability. But their multinational operations compel them to make "an astute use of their financial sinews," and devise "strategies to offset exchange rate fluctuations," as a background report for the International Chamber of Commerce put it recently.

Corporate treasurers, sensing that all is not well with the British pound or the French franc, draw down their balances in these currencies to absolute minimums. Conversely, they maintain fat accounts in German marks, expecting this currency may be upvalued.

Prudent Management

If they can postpone an order or payment in Britain and France they will do it, and if they can step up purchases in Germany they will do so. This is not speculation as much as it is prudent money management.

"A treasurer would look pretty foolish," one observer said recently, "if he was stuck with a pile of francs on the eve of devaluation."

While the corporate money flows accentuate the problems of central bankers, they may in the long run become an effective device for equalizing wages, rents and interest rates throughout the world.

There are some signs that this may be happening already. The most dramatic example is the upward move in European interest rates reacting through the ratchet effects of the Eurodollar market to the money squeeze in the United States.

Similar Situations Seen

Prof. Charles P. Kindleberger 2d, an American economist, compares the situation today with those national corporations in the United States after 1890 that spurred the economic integration of the country by borrowing in the cheapest markets and investing where it was most productive in terms of costs and markets.

The international company similarly seeks to produce, finance and market wherever its resources can be most efficiently utilized.

This equalizer effect, however does little to help balance-of-payments adjustments, the key to the functioning of the monetary system.

Some economists contend that the multinational companies may be changing the rules of the game.

Big American companies after their tremendous postwar overseas expansion tend naturally to meet exports orders as much as possible from foreign plants nearer the markets. Though some foreign earnings are repatriated to the parent company, a sizable portion is plowed back into the foreign subsidiary. Meanwhile, additional direct investments may be pumped out by the parent.

All this is a sign of American economic strength. But it does not help the United States get a trade or balance-of-payments surplus.

A Paris-based economist on the staff of the Organization for Economic Cooperation and Development said that surpluses and deficits are becoming anachronisms in the world of multinational companies. Perhaps he puts the case too strongly. But his opinion shows the extent to which some traditional attitudes are changing.

Moves Criticized

The reactions of authorities in Washington and London (where balance-of-payments problems are also acute) have been to restrict private overseas investment with measures that have been criticized by the business communities of the two countries.

The action represents "the temptations of expediency," says economist Sidney E. Rolfe in his background paper for the International Chamber of Commerce.

Why hit investments, he argues, "when all other factors which contribute to adjustment—including the gold price, the level of employment, tourist expenditures, fixed exchange rates, military expenditures and others —are left untouched or actually allowed to work against adjustment?"

The overseas assets of American companies are placed in this study at $60-billion. This is about twice the foreign assets of other countries' corporations.

Dr. Rolfe points out, however, that both the Netherlands and Switzerland invest abroad a greater percentage of their gross national product than does the United States. "France, Germany and Japan probably lag," he reports, "but the latter two promise to catch up quickly."

June 15, 1969

International Rules On Business Asked

By CLYDE H. FARNSWORTH

Special to The New York Times

PARIS, Jan. 13—An American and a French authority on multinational companies agreed today on the need for some form of international supervision of the giant enterprises to avoid conflicts with national administrations.

The American expert, Prof. Raymond Vernon of the Harvard Business School, said he could envisage a treaty signed by the advanced countries limiting the capacity of overseas subsidiaries to interfere with national-policy objectives.

While Washington would never initiate such a move, he said, the United States might respond favorably to an initiative from the European states during a period in which, he noted, Americans are becoming increasingly sensitive to the "arrogance of power."

Four-fifths of the multinational companies are American-based. Their subsidiaries dominate many key sectors of European industry.

The French expert, Robert Lattes, joint managing director of an important French consulting group, the Society of Econmics and Applied Mathematics, said that although success should not be penalized, guidelines should be enforced to control the multinational behemoths.

German Issue Cited

He said he favored the establishment of an independent international institution to provide the guidelines and to act as the arbiter in disputes.

The two men spoke at a Paris forum organized by the Atlantic Institute, a body that studies Atlantic-area economic, military and political problems. The forum was held at the headquarters of the 22-nation Organization for Economic Co operation and Development.

In citing the power of multinational companies, Mr. Lattes said they were responsible for 55 per cent of the capital flows out of West Germany after the October upward revaluation of the mark.

On the other hand, he conceded, they have furthered international economic integration and accelerated the transfer of technology.

Professor Vernon and about 40 other academic colleague in the United States have been studying the operations of multinational companies for four and one half years under a $500,000 grant from the Ford Foundation.

For Governments, he said the problem is largely psychological—"not being master of your own house, not being in control."

January 14, 1970

National Opposition To Giant Companies Is Found in Study

By BRENDAN JONES

Opposition encountered by giant international corporations seeking to establish a world economy is compared in a newly published study with the American conflict of the nineteen-thirties between the "mama-and-papa" grocery stores and the chain stores.

Nationalistic resistance to multinational companies, Dr. Sidney E. Rolfe asserts in a critique for the Foreign Policy Association, is proving tougher than the earlier smaller-scale resistance of a more effective form of production and marketing.

The reason is that integration of resources, production and distribution on an international scale, Dr. Rolfe concludes, weakens the control of national economies that has come to be an accepted function of bureaucratic elites.

How the issues of "external control" and "national interest" will be resolved is still uncertain, Dr. Rolfe concedes, but he adds that continuing multinational expansion by major companies seems inevitable.

Development of multinational industry by both American and European corporations is discussed by Dr. Rolfe in the current issue of the policy group's Headline Series. The analysis designed for the layman, attempts to give a non-technical account of the growth of multinational corporations in recent years and how they are influencing the organization of a world economy.

Dr. Rolfe is professor of finance at Long Island University.

Dr. Rolfe offers varying definitions of a multinational corporation as one with six or more plants in other countries, or one with 25 per cent or more of its earnings, assets, employment or sales (excluding exports) in other countries.

On this basis, he estimates that there are about 160 companies in the multinational class, about half of them American, the rest, mainly European with the addition of some Japanese concerns. Complete information on investment and output of multinational companies is lacking, but he notes that estimates put investment at about $90-billion and production at about $240-billion.

In terms of gross production values, the study points out, such figures make multinational corporations, as a whole, a type of world economic power surpassed only by the United States and the Soviet Union.

March 18, 1970

Overseas Earnings Bolster U.S. Companies

Gains Help To Offset Domestic Decline

By BRENDAN JONES

"Foreign business made all the difference." . . . "It pulled us out of the hole. . . ."

Such comments by major companies' officials have become fairly common lately in response to the question of how important foreign sales and earnings have been in offsetting the unfavorable effects of the domestic recession.

That overseas operations have given a more-than-usual lift to over-all performance of many of the country's multinational corporations has been evident in the recent run of annual and first-quarter earnings reports.

In many cases the reports have shown gains in foreign business ranging upwards from 15 to 25 per cent acting as a strong counterbalance to the slacker showing on the domestic side of ledgers. And the regularity of the evidence appears to indicate that it is not merely the experience of a few companies. In some industries, foreign business also has offset strike losses.

Clearly, multinational operation has been proving what it is intended to be—the diversification of markets that evens out the ups and downs of recessions in different parts of the world. But it would seem that it has taken a prolonged domestic recession to give special emphasis to this almost axiomatic, reason-for-being aspect of the multinational corporation.

A canvass last week of more than 15 multinational companies disclosed not only the recent profit contribution of foreign business, but also indicated that the surge of expansion abroad of American business is beginning to pay off handsomely.

The canvass, on a random sampling basis, included companies in a variety of fields—automotive, chemical, electronic, metals and a mix of consumer products. In addition to leaders such as General Motors, International Business Machines, Union Carbide and others, the check-out included some medium-sized multinationals.

Along with the statistics, comment was obtained on how corporate officials view foreign business both now and in the future. Among highlights of the findings were the rising percentage of foreign business in total operations of many companies—approaching a rather magic 50 per cent mark—and in a few instances, the emergence of foreign earnings last year as the chief source of profit.

Some of the other findings follow:

For IBM the steady rise of foreign sales through its World Trade Corporation, produced earnings last year that for the first time were more than 50 per cent of the total. Earnings in the United States for 1970—$505-million—were, in fact, some $31-million less than in 1969. But earnings abroad from 108 countries — $512.5-million—were up nearly $115-million, a seesaw reversal of the previous year's performance.

From a peak of $601-million in 1968, IBM's domestic annual earnings have dropped by almost $100-million, but in the same time, international earnings have risen by nearly $242-million.

Against this background, I.B.M.'s chairman, Thomas J. Watson Jr., had good reason to comment at the company's recent annual meeting on the steady growth of foreign operations.

"During the year just closed," he said, "more of I.B.M.'s profit was derived outside the United States than inside—a very exciting turning point in our history."

For companies such as Union Carbide and Minnesota Mining and Manufacturing, which produce and market in all but the Communist countries, foreign business, as against only slight gains in domestic sales, gave a healthy tone to 1970 annual reports.

The big chemical company, which has the largest international sales of any of the American chemical companies, was slightly under its 1969 total for domestic operations, with sales of $2.16-billion. But international sales, at $869.7-million, were up 13 per cent, accounting for 29 per cent of the total, as against 26 per cent in 1969, and this trend has held through the company's first-quarter report.

Maynard H. Patterson, vice president of 3-M's international group, said, "We have been mighty glad to have our foreign business, and our diversification both in products and in markets has proven just the benefit we sought, a way of washing out the bumps of ups and downs in business and also in currency values."

Last year, 3-M's domestic sales, at $1.08-billion, were just $5-million over the 1969 total. But international sales, at $605-million, were up by $70-million, and were close to twice their volume in 1966.

"We are looking ahead," Mr. Patterson commented, "to seeing our international business become the greater part of the total than domestic business. We still haven't attained the penetration of foreign markets we want, but I think that by the early nineteen-eighties, our international sales will have passed the 50 per cent mark."

Despite the growing share of producing countries in oil revenues, the Standard Oil Company (N. J.) saw foreign earnings again become the major part of its total last year. For Standard, foreign earnings had been showing a declining percentage of the total, but in 1970, with domestic earnings at $647-million, they moved ahead to $681-million, or 52 per cent of the total. The gain on the domestic side was $18-million, as against $85-million on the international side.

Commenting on foreign developments, Emilio G. Collado, Standard's executive vice president and a director, said:

"It is particularly clear today that the results of foreign investment are now paying off. Without foreign income, the earnings of many companies would not have fared so well, and without remittances from abroad, our balance-of-payments situation would be much more critical than it already is.

"Direct foreign investment has produced $31.6-billion in profit remittances over the past five years, or $17-billion more than the net capital outflow of $14.6-billion for new investment during the same period."

Commenting on the National Cash Register Company's 1970 showing, in which foreign sales made a seesaw pattern with domestic, Harry R. Wise, the company's vice president for international marketing, said:

"N.C.R.'s strength as a truly multinational company was never better in evidence than in 1970. While economic conditions in the United States were less than good, the International division was able to maintain a fair head of steam with its 25th consecutive record year."

N.C.R., now strong in computer sales, is among the oldest American companies in foreign business, with production and sales in 100 countries. Its domestic earnings last year were $70-million, down from $95.7-million in 1969. But international earnings of $73-million reduced the loss with a gain of $15-million.

Although hard hit in 1970 by the United Auto Workers strike, General Motors found some compensation in a lesser decline in overseas earnings. G.M.'s total earnings last year of $609-million were down sharply from the $1,711,000,000 total of 1969. Overseas earnings—$118-million—also were down, but to a lesser extent, from $160-million in 1969 and accounted for 19 per cent of total earnings, as against 9 per cent the preceding year.

For General Electric, international sales produced a larger percentage of earnings gain than domestic last year. Net international earnings, at $66-million, were up $18-million, or 37 per cent, while the domestic net of $242-million, was up $32-million, or 14 per cent.

Armco Steel Corporation, the leader in its industry in international operations—30 companies in 20 countries and distributors in 70 others — had a 15 per cent rise in foreign sales last year to $218.8-million, while domestic sales, at $1,365,000,000, fell slightly below their 1969 level.

The Dow Chemical company, another leader in international business, has shown a stronger performance abroad than at home through 1970 and the first quarter of this year. Domestic sales last year, at $1,139,000,000, were off from the preceding year, but earnings held even at $144-million. Foreign sales last year, at $771-million, were up $128-million, while foreign earnings rose $20-million to $115-million.

C. B. Branch, Dow president, said that foreign markets obviously would continue to be of great importance and added that "we expect to achieve the 50-50 ratio between the United States and the rest of the world that we have been working toward within the next few years."

Some other companies for which foreign business has been a substantial plus in total returns were Johnson & Johnson, Gillette, Goodyear Tire & Rubber and Cincinnati Milacron.

Johnson & Johnson did well both at home and abroad with net earnings last year of $83.6-million, of which $30-million came from international sales. For Gillette, foreign income of $36-million last year topped domestic by nearly $3-million, a reversal of the 1969 pattern.

June 6, 1971

Let the Multinationals Help

By JOSE R. BEJARANO

The multinational corporation today is a force that can serve global needs of mankind far better than the medieval concept of nation states.

Such a corporation may be the beginning of a modern supranational form adapted to many worldwide functions. The modern multinational corporation brings together materials, energy, capital and technology, each of which may be concentrated in different parts of this planet, to serve the world market.

Technology transfer, a new area with basic supranational scope, provides an opportunity for pioneer supranational corporate thought and action.

It is impractical, and certainly wasteful, for each country to try to generate its own all-embracing technical knowledge. First, the time spans for developing modern technology of 10, 20 or more years are too long. Second, it would be impossible in many cases. The total cost of technology in such fields as nuclear energy, aerospace and communications far exceeds the gross

"Governments are notoriously poor managers. Few nations have the management experience and capability that we can find in most large corporations."
—José R. Bejarano

national product of most nations.

The first step in solving a problem is to recognize it.

Leaders of backward nations must recognize that solutions of technological problems are beyond their means. It is too costly an experiment to find this out by trial and error.

Officials of emerging countries can best foster technological development by enlisting the aid of the transnational business enterprise.

Resources and experience in the modern world of this enterprise are far greater than those of ethnocentric nation states that have been left behind just because of their lack of capacity.

In the pre-industrial era the needs of a society depended upon materials and energy, mostly in the form of human labor. With the advent of the machine, capital became an equal factor with materials and energy. Invisibly, just as pre-industrial labor included craft, capital included technology — how to use the machine.

Even though the industrial revolution found explosive expression through the new legal concept, the corporation, technology remained an implicit factor, more or less accepted as a part of capital when recognized.

Corporations grew, performing miracles beyond imagination and transcending national boundaries. At the same time the nation state, that archaic political form that has survived from the past through a tax partnership with industry, felt the threat of its partner, not only for its domestic prowess but also because the corporation, unlike the state, was not bound by lines on the map.

After recognizing technology as a partner equal in importance to capital, energy and materials, yesterday's governments sought to purchase or steal it in some insome instances. In others, the creation of technology was stimulated.

Some corporations secreted their technology, some sold it, some traded it. And recognizing its tremendous power, they set about a massive effort to enhance it in a proprietary form.

Some wealthy nations, made rich by industrial enterprise, tried to match or surpass the private corporation through government-sponsored programs. The poorer nations found themselves hopelessly behind, with their sovereignty at risk. For the technology they could buy turned out to be at best today's technology — which tomorrow would be yesterday's technology. Their scant capital driveled into obsolescence. Hopefully, they learned that the problem was greater than they could solve alone.

Before the days of political awakening, developing countries encouraged the multinational corporation to serve national markets and to provide export income. The positive response of multinational corporations in such instances is well known. Many of these same nations, however, under the guise of threatened sovereignty, or to serve political demagoguery, have seriously disrupted the delicate technology transfer network for which they have no alternative.

There are many pressures today to take away from corporations their discretionary practices with regard to technology transfer. There are political pressures that say we are exporting jobs when we are exporting technology. There are nationalists who want to prevent high technology products from being manufactured abroad. And there are pragmatists who want to recoup technological leadership in certain areas where we have been edged out.

Valid arguments can be made for these positions, at least on a short-term basis. Certainly, however, protecting excessive labor costs, declining productivity, obsolescent plant, low product quality or mismanagement are not bases for a valid argument.

The disruptive effects of nationalistic politics are exactly contrary to the alleged concern of some political leaders for the welfare of their people. If the starving and illiterate people of the backward nations are to be fed and educated, they certainly should enlist the aid of those who have learned to do it.

It used to be said that money was a very special thing because it could not be bought with happiness. We are now finding out that technology also is something special, since it cannot be bought with only money.

Many experts believe that the basic cultural patterns of undeveloped nations must change before technology can become a part of their life. Caryl Haskins has pointed out that Asians missed the scientific revolution of the past three centuries because through their history their technology was pragmatic and utilitarian in orientation rather than curious and creative.

Governments are notoriously poor managers. Few nations in the world have the management experience and capability that we can find in most large corporations. Let us remember that people are poor because of antiquated social structures —not because of business.

Logically, therefore, we should reject the artificial dichotomy between government interest and private interest. There is only one interest, the social interest, and all efforts should be reconciled to serve it. Political abuse is just as censurable as business abuse—Big Brother Government is just as bad as Big Stick Business.

Responsible governments in a cooperative effort with enlightened world corporations can serve efficiently the social interest everywhere.

Nationalism must be recognized as an expensive emotion..

The world corporation to be effective must reach across what essentially are imaginary lines on the map to synergize crude natural resources of undeveloped regions with the capital, technology and markets of the rest of the world.

National technology policies usually are related to certain broad national objectives such as environmental protection, enhancement of international economy, competitiveness in external markets, military capability and intellectual expansion.

An analysis of these objectives leads us to a grouping of technologies into various classes whose distinctiveness is self-evident.

First, there is the Basic Social Group, which would include sanitation, medicine, water treatment, power production, pollution, building, transportation, agriculture and food processing. These are indeed important technologies relating to the elementary fabric of society. As such, each should be readily accessible on a transnational basis, possibly under supranational supervision, but providing for adequate compensation of the developers.

The second group is the Cultural Group. This includes software technology of how to educate, how to govern, how to sell, how to manage, and covers an area of broad human application. This group differs from the first, however, in that it is more closely related to the individual character and mores of the social milieu where it is to be applied.

The third group, the Scientific Group, includes a very advanced field of technology devoted to finding new knowledge. Naturally, this is a highly coveted area, accessible only to highly developed nations who have the necessary trained manpower and financial resources. From this knowledge will grow new technologies.

The fourth array, the Military Group, involves such technologies as how to destroy, or how to make instruments of destruction, or how to manage armies, or how to occupy a territory. This has been in the past an area of very large technology flow between allies while at the same time a most secretly guarded area among potential enemies.

Finally, we have the fifth aggregation, the Industrial Group, which is best known, and in many ways resembles the Military Group because of its commercial warfare aspects—easily transferrable among friends, elusive among enemies.

The world business enterprise, sometimes more powerful than nations, has spawned new social structures. Thoughtful persons in all walks of life may well agree with Anthony Jay when he says:

"I find it hard to imagine what harm the international corporation could do that would be comparable to the harm that has been done by nation states."

Remember that the American technological explosion at the beginning of this century was based largely upon European scientific discovery. Charles Kettering wisely put it:

"When you close the door to technology transfer, you close out more than you close in."

Mr. Bejarano is vice president of the Xerox Corporation in charge of its Latin American division. This article is based on remarks he made last month at the National Foreign Trade Convention.

December 5, 1971

Freeman Terms Arguments Not True

By ORVILLE L. FREEMAN

Does foreign investment by American companies threaten the jobs of American workers?

There is an undeniable appeal to the argument that if United States business would only keep its money at home instead of spending it to build factories in other countries, new jobs would be created for American workers and most of our economic problems would be solved.

That was a key argument in Senator Hartke's article (Feb. 27) in support of the bill he has sponsored with Representative Burke to limit United States business investment abroad, control the export of American technology, and place quotas on imports America's world trading partners.

The rallying cry of those supporting the Senator's position is that "foreign investment exports jobs."

The trouble with this argument is that, while it may sound logical, it simply is not true. It is an emotional catch-phrase whose validity has never been established by any serious research or study. Most of the arguments advanced to promote other aspects of the bill are equally lacking in hard facts.

On the contrary, there is a large body of evidence available which clearly indicates that foreign investment actually creates jobs at home and has other strengthening effects on the United States economy.

A number of objective studies to determine the domestic effects of overseas investment have recently been made public. The most exhaustive of these was conducted by Business International, an independent research and business advisory organization, whose study covered detailed interviews with 86 multinational American firms with annual sales of $85-billion. The study proves rather conclusively that the more money a company invests overseas, the greater its domestic rate of growth in exports and employment.

In one aspect of our study, we grouped all the companies into four categories according to their level of foreign investment (related to United States investment) — the first category very high, the last very low. To eliminate bias, a company's size was not a factor in making the groupings. The study shows that companies in the top group had by far the largest increases in exports in the period covered, the 1960-70 decade. Specifically, these

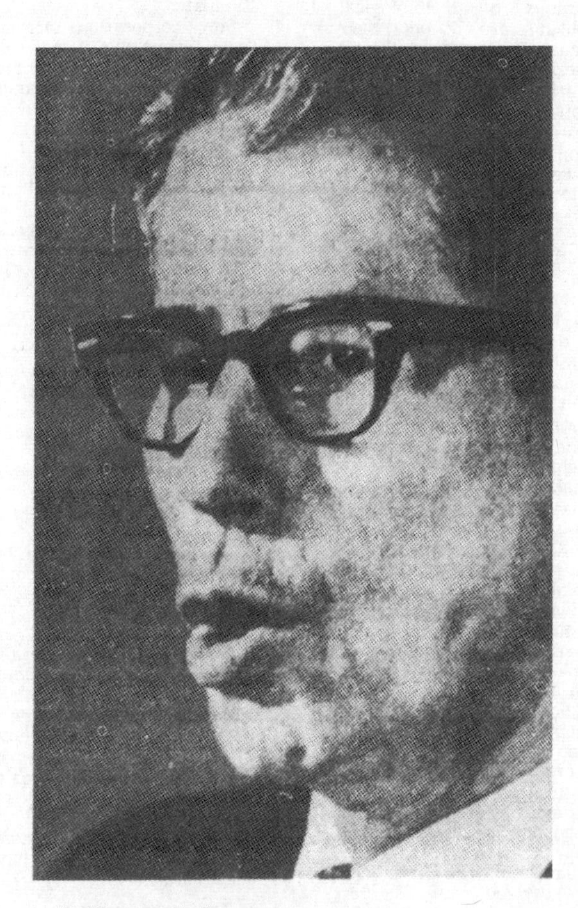

"The rallying cry . . . is that 'foreign investment exports jobs.'"
—Orville L. Freeman

firms had 1960 exports of $777-million, and 1970 exports of $2.84-billion, an increase of 266 per cent. Companies in the lowest group increased their exports by only 161 per cent. The intermediate categories showed intermediate growth percentages.

The study also shows that the rate of employment growth in the United States by large investors in overseas facilities was more than twice as high as the nation as a whole.

To say, as Senator Hartke does, that foreign investment (i.e., foreign manufacturing plants) export jobs is to say that these plants are producing goods that would otherwise have been produced in the United States, either for domestic consumption, or for export overseas.

The facts say otherwise. With the exception of automobiles produced in Canada, imports from United States-owned plants are presently only 2.4 per cent of all imports. And this is limited largely to office equipment and consumer electronics. The reason many American companies established overseas plants in the first place was to enable them to gain new markets or retain markets that otherwise would have been lost to foreign competition.

If we listen only to the critics of foreign investment, we might get the idea that the efforts of American companies to obtain their fair share of the world's markets are detrimental to the United States economy and do not return any benefits. What is overlooked, or perhaps not even known, is that earnings from foreign operations play a substantial role in the balance sheets of many American companies. This is true in just about any industry you can name.

In 1970, for example, 42.8 per cent of Goodyear's net income came from foreign earnings. Comparable figures, taken at random, for other well-known corporate names include Polaroid, 16.3 per cent; Otis elevator, 35 per cent; Gillette, 49.6 per cent; National Cash Register, 50.9 per cent; Kimberly-Clark, 26.2 per cent.

If American companies were deprived of their foreign earnings, the effect on our economy would be devastating. Many companies might not be able to survive. In order to be able to keep operating, many would be forced to increase prices, triggering sales resistance that would start a downward spiral. The effect on the stock market can easily be imagined, not to mention employment and personal income.

Supporters of the Hartke-Burke bill seem to suggest that investment abroad somehow precludes investment at home — that if you invest overseas, you automatically reduce or forgo domestic investment. This is another fallacy, contradicted by Business International's investment and trade study, which, shows that the firms that have been expanding their overseas operations at a rapid rate are generally the same ones expanding most rapidly at home.

Furthermore, policy makers should be aware that American companies get only about one-seventh of their capital for overseas investment from domestic sources. Better than 80 per cent of the financing comes from foreign investors. One thing is certain: the establishment of overseas facilities does not inhibit domestic investment. Neither does it add to our balance-of-payments deficit.

As a matter of fact, quite the reverse is true. The largest single "inflow" item in the United States balance-of-payments picture is our dollar income from foreign investments. To curtail or cut off this income would have a most damaging effect on our economy, which would be felt in as little as two to four years. Such a step just doesn't make sense.

Another aim of the bill is to use taxes as a weapon to punish American investors abroad: foreign earnings would be taxed on a current basis, rather than after they are remitted to the United States.

This would be a crushing blow to American companies by pricing them right out of foreign markets. Since their overseas plants are not replacing American labor, and they are generating earnings in competition with foreign companies, one wonders what the purpose of such a punitive action might be.

Senator Hartke also alleges that American workers are hurt by the export of American technology. No sources or evidence for this claim are offered, and to the best of our knowledge, no study on this subject has ever been undertaken. As a practical matter, it is hard to visualize how any effective way could be developed to prevent the export of technology.

We export technology every time we export a product. American companies seem to have little trouble learning each other's techniques and processes, and foreign companies would have just as little. The world of science is nourished by the excnange of ideas and information through books, periodicals, meetings and other forums.

Finally, we get to the subject of quotas and other import restrictions. And here, it may be helpful to get down to basics and remind ourselves what foreign trade is really all about.

Countries simply wouldn't trade with each other if such trade didn't help both of them. The purpose of international trade is to raise the real income and the standard of living of the people in both countries involved. By erecting barriers against the free flow of goods, quotas undermine this objective. Quotas increase prices and play a basic role in generating inflation, which in turn is a major cause of trade deficits. More quotas are demanded for protection, and the vicious spiral grows.

Mr. Freeman, Secretary of Agriculture in the Kennedy and Johnson Administrations, is president of the Business International Corporation.

March 5, 1972

Multinational Companies Shift Course

Survey Finds They Adopt New Methods to Prosper

By BRENDAN JONES

"There is only one way to keep a business going in a foreign country. It must provide benefits for them and for us. You might be able to buy the government for a while, but that kind of arrangement won't last. You'll be out in the end."

This comment by a British executive appears to reflect the working philosophy of most multinational corporations in meeting the growing force of "economic nationalism" in many parts of the world.

It was made in a survey by correspondents of The New York Times on the changing relationships of governments and the big international companies — mainly American — that have burgeoned with the expansion of world trade.

A main finding of the study was that in much of the developing world—notably, the Latin American and the oil-producing countries—the big international companies now are more on the defensive against the power of government than the other way about.

A Sharp Contrast

This role reversal, which has come in only relatively recent years, is in sharp contrast with a past era of "economic imperialism," when international corporate giants such as United Fruit virtually owned many countries.

Some other highlights of The Times correspondents' survey:

¶Economic nationalism, broadly, a heightened concern of governments and peoples with control of their resources

Robert Strimban

Many corporations have been spreading around globe

and economies, is increasing in many forms. These range from large government ownership of foreign companies to greater regulation of foreign investment.

¶Multinational corporations, however, still retain great political influence in the industrial countries—their "native habitat"—but it is exercised with more circumspection than in the past.

¶A trend toward partnership of government and business, primarily in the international field. This development is typified by the term, "Japan, Inc.," a reference to the close collaboration of government and industry that has been a dynamic force in Japan's economic upsurge. Trade competition and regional blocs seem to foreshadow also a "U.S.A., Inc.," and a "Europe, Inc."

The Times' study, which covered major world regions, was prompted by the controversy that recently has flared over the impact, politically and economically, of the multinational corporation.

The big world companies, more numerous and more diversified than earlier counterparts, have evolved with the reduction of trade barriers.

In geographical "spread" many clearly range far beyond the bounds of any national or multinational authority.

Some are wealthier than the countries in which they operate and their interests in one part of the world may adversely affect operations in individual countries.

A main spark to controversy has been the charge that the International Telephone and Telegraph Corporation, one of the biggest multinationals, tried to protect its holdings in Chile by plotting to overthrow that country's Marxist President, Salvador Allende Gossens.

Debate over whether the multinational, as such, is good or bad for national economic interest, has been sustained by organized labor's demands for curbs on foreign investments by the big companies. The contention is that these investments in plants abroad are "exporting American jobs."

As a result, major unions are backing the Burke-Hartke Bill to provide Presidential authority to restrict such investment and also limit imports.

From being a major supporter of liberal trade, organized labor has swung to a protectionist stance with the multinationals as their chief target.

Critics of the multinationals see them as shadowy private states putting their own interests ahead of those of any single country. Proponents see them as efficient, profitable instruments for world development.

The Times study indicated that there is as yet little precise evidence to show what effects the multinational corporation—as an institution—may have on national economic policies.

It is evident, however, that the rise of economic nationalism represents a confrontation of governments and multinationals that reflects a considerable uneasiness over the power of the big corporations.

The sheer size of multinationals and the fact that they are largely an enigma to the average person seems to be a main basis for the fears they arouse.

Spread of Concerns Traced

This is aptly expressed by Professor Raymond Vernon in his recent book, "Sovereignty at Bay," on the spread of American multinational companies.

Professor Vernon is an economist and professor of international management at Harvard University's Graduate School of Business Administration. Of the multinationals, he writes:

"They sit uncomfortably in the structure of long-established political and social institutions. They sprawl across national boundaries, linking the assets and activities of different national jurisdictions with an intimacy that seems to threaten the concept of the nation as an integral unit.

"Accordingly, they stir uneasy questions in the minds of men. Is the multinational enterprise undermining the capacity of nations to work for the welfare of their own people? Is the muntinational enterprise being used by a dominant power (read 'United States') as a means of penetrating and controlling the economies of other countries?"

Professor Vernon gives no answers to the questions but suggests the creation of a kind of global Justice Department to regulate multinational concerns.

Code Being Drafted

A similar approach has been taken for self-regulation by the International Chamber of Commerce, which presently is drafting what might be called a "code of good behavior" for both governments and multinationals in their treatment of each other.

The sweep of economic nationalism, The Times report indicated, continues in conspicuous forms in the less-developed, ex-colonial countries.

An outstanding example of its effects was the success last year of the 11-nation organization of Petroleum Exporting Countries in winning an increased share of oil countries' earnings from 50 to 75 per cent.

O.P.E.C. members possess about 70 per cent of the world's proven crude oil reserves. And in recent weeks, they have begun, with Iraq's nationalism of the Western-owned Iraq Petroleum Company, a movement for fuller ownership of the big oil companies properties.

The take-over of the once-powerful oil companies has followed also the partial or full nationalization of international copper companies in Zambia, Zaire (the former Congo) and Chile. The trend here is with companies involved with natural resources, a sensitive point with economic nationalists.

Sophistication Grows

There is evidence also that governments of developing countries, apart from whether they favor socialistic policies, have also gained a greater sophistication about the earnings of big multinationals and the extend to which they can tolerate government participation.

There is, in effect, a kind of trade-off in that the governments need the revenue, the technology and the sense of control, while private corporations will continue at a smaller share of profits.

Economic nationalism has shown itself also in moves by the Canadian Government—although considered mild—for restriction on foreign investment for the take-over of existing Canadian companies rather than for starting new enterprises. In Australia, which like Canada has been an active promoter of foreign investment, similar regulations are being prepared.

The kind of counter-trend in the more developed countries, where multinationals appear to be maintining influence, may or may not reflect a deliberate exertion of power by the big companies, the survey indicated.

Rather, the main evidence is that in the industrialized countries, those of Western Europe and also the United States, there is a tendency for governments to be pro-business.

Multinational corporations in countries such as France and Britain are said by observers to have "enormous" political influence, but there is no surface evidence that it is exerted in other than legitimate ways.

As in this country, the survey reports said, big companies practice "conventional lobbying"—a term that takes in all the influence promotion devices—both at home and abroad.

These may include everything from above-board campaigning for or against legislation to the ethically gray areas of lavish entertainment and nepotism.

In a circumspect country such as the Netherlands it is no secret that a company such as Unilever will be assured a sympathetic hearing by government on any matters affecting its prices or earnings.

Top Jobs Assured

Equally, in another circumspect country — Switzerland— the fact that former presidents of the country can be virtually certain of a top job with multinational companies such as

Nestle or Brown Bovari raises few eyebrows.

In this country, multinationals seem to be starting a campaign against their critics. The main attack so far has been against the Burke-Hartke Bill in the contention that multinationals have increased domestic employment more than other companies.

There are assertions also that the multinational is the great hope of developing countries and the key to solution of world problems such as poverty and food production.

The growing overlap of the government and business worlds in many countries seems to foreshadow the kind of partnership expressed by the term "Japan, Inc."

For this country, the Nixon economic program has frankly stressed that increased sale of cars is a key economic need, so that, in effect, what will be good for the country will be good for Detroit.

The Administration, in addition to its moves for reshaping world monetary and trade relations, has also taken a lead in making government the means to attaining textile and steel import quota agreements.

And in Europe, the Common Market is a good way along to closer government-business collaboration.

For the multinational and for government, the old byword seems appropriate: "If you can't lick them, join them."

June 19, 1972

'The New Globalists'

Multinational Corporations Are Held To Create a Basis for World Peace

By LEONARD SILK

Economic Analysis

In 1848 Karl Marx and Friedrich Engels put forth the thesis that world peace and a new world order would ultimately be founded upon the common economic interests of workingmen in all countries. "Workers of the world, unite!" proclaimed the Communist Manifesto.

Now, after a century of global wars, some leading businessmen are offering a counter thesis: that multinational business is creating the basis for peace and a new world order. A spokesman of this doctrine, William I. Spencer, president of the First National City Corporation, recently declared in an address to the American Chamber of Commerce in Frankfurt, West Germany:

"The political boundaries of nation-states are too narrow and constricted to define the scope and sweep of modern business."

Quiet Progress Seen

At a time when politicians have been moving to create regional markets to supersede national markets, he said, businessmen—whom he called "the new globalists" — have been making quiet progress on a much larger scale.

"They see the entire world as a market and as a site for the production of goods and services," said Mr. Spencer. "They understand that ideas can be born anywhere and expressed in any language. They seek profitable opportunity in addressing themselves not to the demands of the privileged few but to the urgent needs of the overwhelming many. Operating with this kind of global vision, they have created that unique economic phenomenon known as the multinational corporation."

Lest this sound like pie in the sky, he noted that his own company had tripled its foreign branches in the last 10 years and now carried on banking operations in 90 countries, with stockholders in 63 countries.

Output Compared

More broadly, he said, multinational corporations now produce an estimated $450-billion in goods and services—15 per cent of the gross world product.

This multinational explosion, said Mr. Spencer, is much more than what Jean-Jacques Servan-Schreiber, the French editor, first named "the American Challenge." The Citicorp president said that, of the $450-billion total, American multinational companies account for only $200-billion, foreign multinationals based abroad and also operating in the United States account for $100-billion, and what he calls "interproduction abroad" accounts for the remaining $150-billion.

But a leading academic authority on the multinational corporation, Prof. Raymond Vernon of the Harvard Graduate School of Business Administration, warns that resistances to the rapid growth of the multinationals are building up.

Observing the upsurge of nationalism and the squeeze being put on the multinationals in oil, copper and other industries in many parts of Latin America, Africa, the Middle East and Asia and the growth of anti-Americanism in Canada and Western Europe, Professor Vernon asks whether the multinationals may not be approaching the end of an era.

Growth and Decay

He observes that multinational business in particular areas has characteristically undergone "life cycles" of growth and decay. At first, the poorer "host" country eagerly invites the multinational companies in because it needs capital, technological knowledge and access to foreign markets.

But, as time passes, the host country grows less dependent on foreign capital and technology. For a time, it may still fear loss of access to foreign markets. But, as its domestic economy grows and its knowledge of other markets abroad widens, the host country expresses its outrage over the inequity of the terms on which the multinational corporation is operating and exploiting its resources and people. It may eventually expel the foreign element altogether.

That is the scenario unfolding in oil. Professor Vernon thinks the multinational oil companies have played into the hands of the oil-producing countries by—as he sees it—exaggerating the world fuel shortage.

Similar life cycles, he says, can be found in the role of multinational companies in high-technology industries. At first the host countries are worried about technological gaps and capital shortages. When their fear of such gaps and shortages diminishes, they take a less hospitable view toward foreign investors.

At the moment the Europeans are inclined to believe that the technological gap in which they lagged behind the United States—and which alarmed them until the mid-nineteen-sixties — has been closed. They are now more concerned about inflation than capital shortage.

But Professor Vernon thinks the Europeans' complacency may be premature. He foresees a renewal of American technological supremacy in several major areas, such as environmental protection and the development of deep ocean resources.

Indeed, he expects American leads to continue in computers, outer space and aircraft. He says that Europe is littered with the "bleached bones" of failed efforts in those areas.

Certain Advantages

The United States, he believes, has certain enduring advantages in high-technology fields: its high proportion of capital to labor; its very large, high-income domestic market; the heavy demands of the Federal Government; the ample resources in science, technology and higher education, and its national attitudes toward change and competition.

In the diverse and turbulent American economy, says Professor Vernon, "businesses cannot easily negotiate with their environment to stand still." That is, American companies cannot control and moderate change as readily as can companies in Europe or Japan.

Even if American businessmen were willing to enter into such anticompetitive deals, the United States Government stands by with an antitrust pitchfork, which it is fully prepared to jab at giants. So European companies, to increase profits, tend to focus on cost-cutting; Americans are more likely to try to reduce business risks and go after bigger profits through product innovation and diversification.

But Professor Vernon finds no basis for American smugness or euphoria in the likelihood that the United States may re-open technological gaps as the nineteen seventies wear on. He fears new gaps may worsen political tensions if the foreigners' sense of dependence on the United States starts to grow again.

Businessmen — Mr. Spencer's "new globalists" — can't cope with such nationalistic tensions and have not the power to offset national governments, even small ones. "The firm cannot govern," says Professor Vernon, "and government is the problem of the human race."

Yet, within the pattern of "minicycles" that in the past

have affected such diverse industries as railroads, life insurance, public utilities, oil, copper and other resources and that may yet arrest the postwar multinational boom in manufacturing and finance, there does appear to be a strong, over-all growth trend.

In 1919 there were only about 180 multinational corporations; today there are some 4,000. The growth trend is likely to slacken, but it still seems far from its limit.

Many factors are working on the side of the business globalists. The speed and availability of communications and transportation are increasing. The international money and capital markets are expanding. There is growing desire in all countries — Communist and capitalist alike — for economic development. And the onrush of new technology promises, on one hand, to satisfy the desire for higher living standards and, on the other hand, intensifies fear of war between the great powers.

Whether the politicians can create the enabling conditions for further progress of the multinational revolution remains the great unknown.

October 25, 1972

Speculators vs. Governments

By EDWARD COWAN

WASHINGTON — The role of banks and other multinational corporations in the tumultuous currency speculation that led to last week's devaluation of the dollar has been outlined in a general way in a Tariff Commission study just published.

The study finds that the balance of financial power has now tilted steeply in favor of the speculators and against governments that try to maintain a specified official value for their currencies.

This tilt portends more frequent changes in posted exchange-rate parities and more frequent use of temporary floats — the withdrawal of official support for a currency at a floor or ceiling price — when the speculative juggernaut gets rolling.

The study, impressive in its detail and clarity of expression, explains why more frequent changes in the posted value of the dollar and other major currencies are to be expected.

In the nineteen-sixties, Britain defended the pound at $2.80 for several years before finally devaluing to $2.40 in November, 1967. As last week's devaluation of the dollar and flotation of the Japanese yen showed, the time span in which governments can resist speculative tidal waves has shortened to weeks.

The reason, the Tariff Commission study makes clear, is the enormous pool of money in the hands of banks, corporations and other sophisticated currency speculators — institutions that individually move not millions of dollars through the currency exchanges but tens of millions.

The study estimates that of a total of $268-billion in the international money market at the end of 1971, United States banks and corporations control $190-billion, or 71 per cent.

"Only small fractions of the potential flow" of this money from one currency to another "are fully capable of producing monetary crisis," the study finds.

In other words, there is an "independent, largely uncontrolled monetary system that has sprung up within the comfortable old world" of national central banks that try to keep money movements and trade patterns from gyrating wildly.

The study reaches the inferential conclusion — one not based on positive evidence, because the data for such analysis are not available — "that destructive, predatory motivations do not characterize the sophisticated international financial activities of most multinational corporations, even though much of the funds which flow internationally during the crisis doubtlessly is of multinational corporation origin."

These findings underscore the importance of the work of the International Committee of 20, which seeks to devise a new set of monetary rules to replace the wreckage of the post-World War II system of fixed parities. One of the committee's assignments is to come up with a way to moderate massive speculative surges of the kind that poured $5-billion into West Germany in a few days prior to last Monday.

The 930-page Tariff Commission report was requested and published by the Senate Finance Committee. The 21-month study is the most ambitious attempt official Washington has made to assess the effect of multinational companies on trade, investment and jobs.

Entitled "Implications of Multinational Firms for World Trade and Investment and for U.S. Trade and Labor," it is available from the Government Printing Office in Washington for $9.25 postpaid.

Written under the direction of Robert A. Cornell, deputy director of the Tariff Commission's Office of Economic Research, the study presumably will figure prominently in the continuing debate in Congress about trade policy and whether corporate investment abroad is more good then bad for the American economy.

The 36-year-old Mr. Cornell is a native New Yorker and an economist who once worked for the old Grace National Bank. Mr. Cornell, assisted by Waldo Abbot, a graduate student at the Wharton School of the University of Pennsylvania, wrote the chapter on international money markets.

That chapter emphasizes the disparity of power between the corporations and governments. In part it arises from the disparity in their financial resources. For example, the $268-billion pool of liquid assets was more than three times the $88.5-billion of official currency reserves of the industrial countries.

"These are the reserves with which central banks fight to defend their exchange rates," the study observes. "The resources of the private sector outclass them."

In part, the study argues, the superior force of the corporations results from superior knowledge. Banks and corporations, having high-speed communications, computers and highly specialized, aggressive managers, are equipped "for independent action rather than mere reaction."

"Contrast these systems with those of governments," the study suggests. "It is unsettling in the extreme to see much of a country's knowledge about what has happened in an international monetary crisis listed under 'errors and omissions' in the balance of payments.

"One has to presume that a handful of central bankers in the world possess some better knowledge about the details—but this 'better knowledge' cannot be very well organized, because the best that central banks can muster for the struggle is a reactive, delayed defense rather than an offense, and they often lose."

February 18, 1973

No U.S. Job Losses Found At Multinational Concerns

By EDWIN L. DALE Jr.
Special to The New York Times

WASHINGTON, Nov. 19—The most exhaustive survey yet made by the Government of the operations of large multinational companies supports a central conclusion of various private surveys—that domestic employment and exports of these companies have continued to grow relatively rapidly despite their foreign investments.

This and other results of the survey were disclosed last week by government analysts who put the study together. It was released earlier in the week by the Commerce Department in the form of nearly 100 pages of tables, without any interpretive comment.

An earlier and less thorough study of multinational companies by a different division of the Commerce Department came under considerable criticism for its statistical methods.

On the key and controversial issues involved, the one released last week by the highly respected Bureau of Economic Analysis appears to lead to the same basic conclusions, however.

The sensitivity of the data arises from the strongly held position of organized labor that the multinational companies are "exporting jobs." In the case of the newest study, policy-making officials of the Commerce Department apparently decided to let the figures speak for themselves.

The survey provides extensive detail on the operations of 298 United States-based multinational companies with about 5200 foreign affiliates. The years covered are 1966 and 1970.

Highlights of Survey

The following were some highlights derived from the figures by Commerce Department analysts:

¶Domestic employment of the 298 companies rose by 2.7 per cent a year during this period, while total private employment in the economy grew by 1.8 per cent a year.

¶The same conclusion on employment growth was reached when comparison was made on an industry-by-industry basis.

¶Exports of the 298 companies rose from $12.7-billion in 1966 to $29-billion in 1970, a faster rate of growth than for the nation's total exports.

¶The companies also showed a growth in imports, but their surplus of exports rose to $7.6-billion in 1970 from $5.3-billion in 1966—a time when the nation's over-all trade surplus was declining from $3.6-billion to $1.9-billion.

¶There was a rise from $3.4-billion to $6.2-billion in sales by foreign affiliates to the parent companies, but the great bulk of this was accounted for by "United States-type" automobiles from Canada under the special auto agreement, and petroleum imports.

The survey showed that sales, assets and employment of the overseas affiliates grew much faster in percentage terms in the 1966-70 period than those of the parent companies.

But the parents remained substantially larger than their offspring. For example, total sales of the parent companies in 1970 were $309.2-billion, compared with sales of $114.7-billion by the foreign affiliates.

What Multinationals Have Done

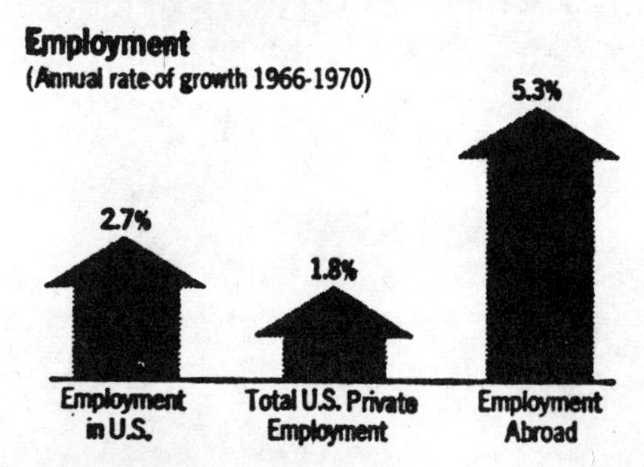

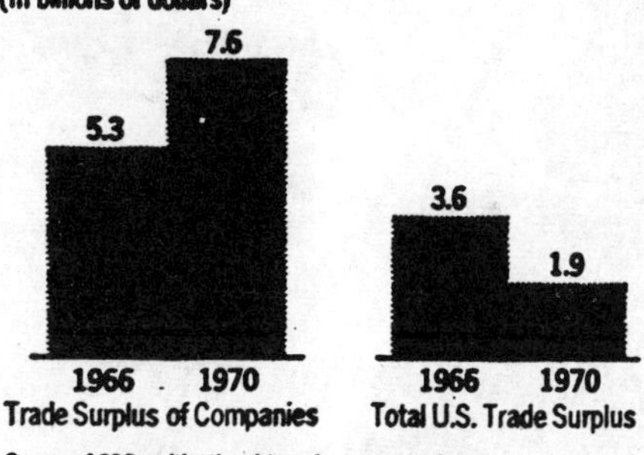

Survey of 298 multinational American companies.
Source: U.S. Department of Commerce

The New York Times/Nov. 20, 1972

November 20, 1972

...A New Form of 'Imperialism'

Should Companies Export Ethics?

By JACK N. BEHRMAN

Many countries have felt their independence threatened by political and economic imperialism, and more recently by the spread of the multinational enterprise.

Added to this is a new penetration — ethical imperialism—a direct descendant of manifest destiny, for it avows that nations with power and the emonstrable success of higher living standards also know what is right.

Now as special interests in the United States — representing both stockholders and consumers—demand social, ethical, even religious, changes in companies operating overseas, it is likely that more host countries will be antagonized.

•

Whether we're tampering with the family structure of French Canadians, the racial laws of South Africa or the leisurely lunch-at-home tradition in Italy, the influence of the company is being extended into new, controversial spheres.

Competitively, the subject is crucial. For the multinational companies based in such countries as West Germany, Japan and Italy, tend not to get into these areas. It's the Americans who tend to try to change things, with their concentration on the almighty dollar gilded with wide-eyed idealism.

Richard C. Gerstenberg, chairman of General Motors, under pressure from some stockholders and black groups, says he wants to see for himself in South Africa "that General Motors is doing everything it can to hasten the day of equality."

The First National City

Assembly line for I.B.M. typewriters in Amsterdam. Should a multinational concern try to impose traditions of its native land on the countries to which it expands?

Bank has declared that the social responsibility of a company will be "a new criterion for investment."

And the emphasis in annual reports on socially responsible activities has increased. Given the international activities of these companies, can social responsibility stop at the water's edge?

Several recent cases have demonstrated that United States shareholders and interest-groups consider that these corporations have a responsibility to apply United States ethical standards wherever they may be operating in the world. Polaroid, International Business Machines, Ford and others have been charged with perpetuating apartheid in South Africa by simply following the country's laws.

They have been urged either to break those patterns by not discriminating or to close their facilities. After some soul-searching and on-the-spot investigation, several of the companies have moved quietly to improve the opportunities and pay scales for blacks, concluding that to pull out would be harmful to the workers.

An overt breaking of the customs and laws would likely result in the companies' expulsion, but covert changes have not yet brought down the wrath of the Government or of white citizens.

•

Yet, the ethical pressures proliferate from other sources. This year the World Council of Churches sold stock worth $1.5-million, representing holdings in 650 companies in the United States, Britain, the Netherlands and Switzerland that have investments in South Africa.

The racial problem is one among the sensitive ethical issues faced by multinational enterprises.

Typically, pressure has arisen in Canada for American-owned affiliates to contribute to educational institutions and community programs in the same way that the parent concern does in the United States. But often the final decisions are made by the parent company, and it is frequently reluctant to establish a pattern of corporate giving that is not accepted by Canadian-owned companies.

Increasing domestic concern over consumer protection has brought pressure for higher ethical standards in product quality and tightened regulations, such as the disclosure on cigarette packs of potential dangers of use. Concerns range from safety in toys and children's clothes to use of radio-active materials in medicine.

American companies, however, seldom give the same warnings or take the same precautions in other countries, where it is not required by local laws or regulations. Many proponents of greater "corporate responsibility in the United States inveigh against this use of situational ethics, and individuals in other countries join in questioning the ethics of a company's selling items that the Food and Drug Administration of the United States has not yet approved.

Attempts to implement the simple prescription "equal pay for equal work" embroils international companies, international unions, host communities and governments in multifaceted negotiations.

For example, the request by Canadian unions in the auto industry, which is predominantly owned by Detroit companies, for equal pay with American workers was resolved by adopting a cost-of-living differential, which permitted a lower rate of pay in Canada.

Application of the principle would have raised costs to differentially high levels in Canada and hurt sales. Salaries and fringe benefits for engineers and scientists in foreign countries commensurate with those received by engineers and scientists in the United States would break the pattern of wages and in the foreign countries and raise tensions with competing companies. But not to make them equal would raise tensions within the international company.

In the same field of employe treatment, is it ethical for an American international company to impede the formation of labor unions in a foreign country, although such action is consistent with the behavior of locally owned concerns.

Alternatively, should it promote the formation of unions oriented toward collective bargaining, where the traditonal objectives of unions are political?

Environmental pollution is another thorny issue. Ford, for example, has been permitted to export to Canada some 1973 autos that have not met environmental specifications domestically.

As Ambassador Charles Malik of Lebanon wrote in 1966:

"The question then becomes: Is the developing

country morally prepared to pay the social and cultural price for the coveted development? Is it prepared to transform the family, free women, revolutionize its concept of the child, do away with class distinctions, liberate serfs, promote a free middle class, reform its religion, dignify labor as the noblest thing in the world?

"Confronted with such a price, especially if the full implications are clear, it may balk and say: To hell with all development? It will then begin talking about the value of its culture, about its not wanting to barter away its soul and its distinctive national imprint. But what if imprint, culture and soul are incompatible with development?"

Finally, there is a much larger problem involving the ethics of consumption patterns. There are, for example, considerable ethical connotations in an automobile-oriented economy. The connotations involve concepts of individual freedom implications of personal power, dispersion of the community, isolation from the crowd and the form of pleasure to be enjoyed.

Similarly, decisions to produce goods for upper or middle classes rather than for the poor are ethical judgments. Does development mean a rise in average incomes, despite the distribution of incomes, or does it mean an increase in the standards of living of the poor?

Such issues cannot be avoided. They must be pondered now by a socially responsible business community.

For it is unlikely that Americans would be successful in exporting their ethics piecemeal to different countries in specific situations. Any such attempt would be seen as a new form of imperialism.

Americans can and should demonstrate to others their belief in ethical concepts of freedom with responsibility, opportunity for all to be creative and useful and of the opportunity to belong to and be a useful part of a group —that is, "liberty, equality and fraternity."

But it is difficult to export what we do not have ourselves. Our first task, then, is to give proof of how an ethically based economic system works. Having done so, it is likely that others will import and adapt it as suitable, thereby removing completely the stigma of imperialism.

Professor Behrman teaches international business at the Graduate School of Business Administration of the University of North Carolina, Chapel Hill, and is a former assistant secretary of commerce for domestic and international business.

September 2, 1973

Multinational Companies Defend Role Before U.N.

By KATHLEEN TELTSCH

Special to The New York Times

UNITED NATIONS, N.Y., Sept. 11 — Leaders of five big corporations went before a United Nations panel today to insist their concerns behave as good guests abroad, contribute to the prosperity of the countries in which they do business and do not meddle in politics.

Almost without exception, they also complained of exaggerated fears that the increasing size and spread of their commercial empires made them an all-powerful group operating beyond the control and regulation of governments.

These were recurrent themes at the opening here of public hearings on the activities of multinational corporations — an inquiry stimulated largely by Chile's charges that the International Telephone and Telegraph Corporation and the Kennecott Copper Corporation tried to subvert the Marxist-oriented regime of Dr. Salvador Allende Gossens. Reports today said the Allende Government had been ousted.

The panel is to take further testimony here and abroad and in the next 12 months make recommendations on the role and activities of some national corporations. One idea already proposed in a United Nations' study is that some form of international monitoring be devised for international corporations.

While the corporation spokesmen today were clearly unwilling to embrace the idea of regulations of their operation, all in varying degrees saw some areas for possible United Nations action, such as in harmonizing tax laws.

There also was sentiment for selective and gradual action that could lead to an agreement covering direct foreign investment.

"No one is in the dark," remarked L. K. Jha, former governor of the Reserve Bank of India and the panel chairman, as the open meetings began in an atmosphere of cordiality. Despite such reassurances, some of the corporation spokesmen tended to sound defensive as they mentioned their concerns' support of such causes as building schools and hospitals or stressed their policies of training foreign nationals for key posts.

Action Areas Discussed

However, some areas for international action did find favor with the corporations:

Irving S. Shapiro, vice chairman of the board of E. I. du Pont de Nemours, Inc., told the panel that serious study should be given to international agreements covering foreign investments that would be similar to those already in existence for trade under the General Agreement on Tariffs and Trade. Du Pont would like to participate in such a study, Mr. Shapiro declared. Like others, he also cautioned against exaggerating the power of multinationals to unduly influence governments and pointed out that even the smaller states possessed enormous power to control foreign enterprises, "ranging from the subtleties of taxation to expropriation."

Jacques G. Maisonrouge, president of the I.B.M. World Trade Corporation, cautioned the panel against devising institutions for devices that would restrict the useful role that such concerns can play in economic development. Among other measures he had in mind, he said, were demands for divided ownership or local control and he warned: "moves such as these would cripple the effectiveness of many high technology companies, most certainly including "I.B.M."

The I.B.M. executive said a proposal for a code of conduct for multinationals—made in the United Nations study—would be difficult but worth pursuing. It should emphasize greater employment of foreign nationals, especially on directors' boards, he said, adding that this was I.B.M. policy. All the Americans working aboard could be flown back in a single aircraft—providing it was a 747 plane, he said, evoking laughter.

John J. Powers Jr., honorary chairman of the board of Pfizer, Inc., was strongly critical of proposals to create international machinery to control or supervise foreign investment.

"In my view this is an attempt to do too much too soon. For that reason I believe it would fail and we would have lost ground." The most that the United Nations could do at this time, he maintained, was provide a forum for discussion.

Thomas A. Murphy, vice chairman of General Motors, expressed skepticism about attempting to make multinationals accountable to the international community. To add still another layer of regulations to world business would be a step backward, he declared.

Emilio G. Collado, executive vice president of the Exxon Corporation, favored the idea of a voluntary code of conduct, saying it would discourage some corporations from activities that create ill-will. However, he suggested the need for international agreement to reduce the investment risks taken by multinational corporations.

September 12, 1973

NADER ACCUSES MULTINATIONALS

Says Concerns Use Secrecy to Perpetrate Abuses

By KATHLEEN TELTSCH
Special to The New York Times

UNITED NATIONS, N.Y., Sept. 12 — Ralph Nader, the consumer advocate, charged today that the abuses committed by the giant corporations were concealed by secrecy. He urged a United Nations panel inquiring into the impact of multinational companies to try to get at the "priceless information" now being withheld.

Mr. Nader, testifying at an open hearing here, declared that the success of the consumer movement in the United States has depended on rooting out information. He cited the pressure on the automotive industry to recall vehicles once the defects in their manufacture were disclosed.

"The test of the mettle of the United Nations' inquiry," he declared, is whether it can get corporations to divulge information about their corporate behavior now kept secret.

Mr. Nader, in a wide-ranging attack on the conduct abroad of "world corps," as he called them, charged some companies with dumping products on overseas markets when they were compelled for reasons of safety to remove them from United States sale.

He accused other concerns of selecting overseas sites for pollutant-creating manufacturing. American-based companies permit mining operations in Asia, Africa and Latin America that are virtually "snake pits" and would not be tolerated at home, he added.

These and other abuses continue, Mr. Nader maintained, because "world corps" operate without any controls or regulations on their conduct.

Mr. Nader's attack on the multinationals followed a day of public hearings in which five of the top companies had testified, emphasizing the contributions their operations were making to the economic development of poorer countries.

Ernest Keller, president of the Adela Investment Company, another speaker, told the panel that multinationals increasingly were becoming the "convenient scapegoat" for every mishap.

They are being blamed, he declared, "for the consequence of unseasonable economic and monetary policies, unviable economic concepts, experiments and legislation, that is, for every conceivable mistake and failure for which no one else wants to accept the blame."

September 12, 1973

Economic Adviser Backs Wage Rise 'Deceleration'

By EDWIN L. DALE Jr.
Special to The New York Times

WASHINGTON, Nov. 8—The Government will have to maintain some degree of restraint on the expansion of the economy to achieve a needed "deceleration" of the present rate of wage increases, a member of President Nixon's Council of Economic Advisers said tonight.

William J. Fellner, the newest member of the council, told the National Economists Club here that it would be "very undesirable" for the Government to aim its fiscal, or budget, and monetary policies solely at the elimination of all risk of recession next year.

While he expressed hope and belief that a recession would be avoided, he said a policy aimed at vigorous expansion next year would "practically assure" a continuation of rapid inflation, "apt to accelerate anew."

Views Differ

Mr. Fellner conceded that from the worker's point of view this year's wage increases, averaging 7.5 per cent including fringes, have not been enough to keep up with the rise in prices. But he said that from the employer's point of view, such a rate of wage increase is far above productivity improvement and would require further price increases.

"Given a reasonably restrained monetary and fiscal policy," he said, "there would be a good chance of money-wage deceleration before long, coupled with the restoration of a healthy and steady rise in real wage rates." Real wages rise when the increase in money wages is larger than the rise in prices.

Mr. Fellner placed great hope in the probable flattening of food prices from now on, with a consequent lessening in the rate of increase in consumer prices as a whole.

"This could be the case during a period of considerable duration," he said, "and I do not believe it to be hopeless at all to try to create an environment in which the money-wage trend will decelerate at that time."

Expansionary Danger

The danger, he said, would be a "climate" in which unions and employers believed that Government expansionary policy would "vindicate" large wage increases and resulting price increases by pumping up total demand.

"If these were the prevalent expectations," he continued, "to put an end to an inflationary spiral, policy makers would after a while be forced to much more severe and costly measures [of restraint] than are now under consideration."

While he did not spell out the needed fiscal and monetary restraint in detail, Mr. Fellner strongly supported the Administration's aim of a balanced budget in the current fiscal year and said he hoped, on the monetary policy side, that "in 1974 the various money and liquidity measures that must be watched will be growing less rapidly than they did from the last quarter of 1972 through the third quarter of 1973."

Describing a recession, an actual decline in output and employment, as a "bumpy" landing from the recent boom in contrast to the desired "soft" landing, Mr. Fellner concluded:

"It is the objective of our policy makers to follow a line not involving any substantial risk of an uncomfortably bumpy landing. . . . What I am suggesting is that an attempt to reduce the risks of some degree of bumpiness to practically zero—an attempt to play safe in one direction only—would involve a very substantial risk of accelerating inflation."

November 9, 1973

U.S. Company Payoffs Way of Life Overseas

Washington Often Sanctions Fees Paid to Other Governments' Officials

By MICHAEL C. JENSEN

American companies doing business abroad are spending hundreds of millions of dollars each year for agents' fees, commissions and outright payoffs to foreign officials.

The payments range from $5 bribes for customs agents and other minor officials to multimillion-dollar rake-offs on defense contracts. Sometimes even heads of state are involved.

The practice of funneling cash into the hands of government officials or their representatives is long-standing and is defended by many businessmen as the only way they can compete effectively abroad. Indeed, some such payments are officially sanctioned by the United States Government.

Nevertheless, the practice is coming under increased scrutiny in the United States, spurred by disclosures that the United Brands Company, based in New York, paid more than $2-million in bribes to officials in Honduras and Europe.

Inquiry Started

The Senate Foreign Relations subcommittee on multinational corporations has begun a full inquiry into the United Brands case.

It is also looking into expenditures by the Northrop Corporation, which paid out more than $30-million in agents' fees and commissions, much of it for overseas sales, from 1971 to 1973.

The Gulf Oil Company's disbursements of more than $4-million overseas, most of it reportedly to a single unidentified country, is also being investigated.

Until now, most of the Government attention to corporate bribery has come from the Securities and Exchange Commission, which is responsible for insuring adequate disclosure of corporate activities to shareholders. The current investigations are an outgrowth of the Watergate prosecutions of illegal campaign contributions.

The Internal Revenue Service, which is concerned with the proper handling of foreign transactions for tax purposes, also is looking into some of the foreign situations.

Question of Law

It is apparently not a violation of United States law for an American corporation to bribe foreign officials. Such action may be illegal in the host country, but bribery laws are seldom enforced in many parts of the world.

Few American businessmen will discuss their companies' payoff practices openly, although some agreed to interviews with news reporters with the understanding that they not be identified.

Some of the most blatant cases of bribery have become public, however, and a few have spawned major scandals overseas.

In the United Brands case, for example, Eli M. Black, the chief executive of the company, committeed suicide shortly before the company's overseas bribes became known publicly. The ensuing scandal also resulted in the overthrow of the chief of state of Honduras, Gen. Oswaldo Lopez Arellano.

Gulf Testimony

In other cases, there is almost certain to be a growing furor as further details become known. For example, the reported testimony of Bob R. Dorsey, chairman of the Gulf Oil Corporation, about cash "contributions" abroad is being studied by the S.E.C.

Mr. Dorsey and other Gulf officials reportedly told the S.E.C. that foreign politicians had forced them to pay large amounts of cash in order to stay in business.

While some commissions and agents' fees are nothing more than thinly disguised bribes, others are said to be legitimate payments to local representatives overseas, designed to cut through red tape.

The Defense Department authorizes defense contractors to pay "reasonable" agents' fees as part of their "cost of sales" and to pass these costs along to the Pentagon when it acts as the middleman in arms contracts.

Pattern of Fees

In an advisory memorandum issued to several defense contractor associations last summer, the Defense Security Assistance Agency said United States arms manufacturers selling major systems usually limited their standard agents' fees to 4 to 6 per cent of the selling price. It added, however, that on less expensive equipment the percentage sometimes exceeded 25 per cent.

Some Middle Easterners have gotten rich on such fees. Persian Gulf sources say that Adnan M. Khashoggi, a Saudi Arabian businessman who has an international string of industrial and financial ventures, including a bank in California, made his initial capital as the Saudi agent for Raytheon Hawk missiles and Lockheed aircraft bought by Saudi Arabia.

Mr. Khashoggi's connection is said to be his friendship with Prince Sultan, the Saudi Defense Minister, and his commissions were said to run to $10-million to $20-million.

A Vexing Region

American executives says the Middle East is one of the world's most vexing regions as far as doing business is concerned. An illustration of the problems they face there was contained in a limited-circulation Defense Department memorandum entitled "Agents' Fees in the Middle East."

There is the classic example," the memo said, "of a new vice president of a United States firm who, after reviewing agents' fees, decided that a local Middle East agent's contract could be canceled. All that the company had in the country at that time was a continuous but lucrative servicing contract that had been negotiated many years ago.

"Within 48 hours after the agent had been canceled all local work permits of the company's employes were withdrawn. Needless to say, the agent was reinstated immediately."

In another case cited by the memorandum, two American companies in a North African country were competing for a contract. As the competition became keener, one of the contractors found it almost impossible to obtain visas for its sales personnel and was thus prevented from making a sales presentation. The reason? The influence of a competitive agent, the memo said.

One agent admitted, the memo said, that three members of his country's national assembly were on retainer fees to provide "inner circle intelligence" and to promote his principal's products.

It also said influence was not always bought with cash. "It can include the rent-free use of a villa in France or a flat in London, along with car and servants. Sometimes the government official is a silent partner in the agency or other business completely divorced from his normal activities."

Although the most dramatic instances of corruption are those involving millions of dollars, a far more widespread type of bribery takes place at a much lower level. It is variously called baksheesh, la mordita or dash, depending on whether it is offered in the Middle East, Latin America or Africa.

One businessman in Africa said in an interview: "In countries like Nigeria and Zaire, you have to pay small bribes, called 'dash,' to get anything done. It's part of the price of visas, getting customs clearance on materials — even getting your suitcase in the instance of Nigeria."

In other parts of the world, the pressures take a different form. For example, one type of harassment for American companies in the Philippines is the stream of requests for donations for charities from government and military officials or members of their families. Such requests, invariably granted, sometimes run to more than $100,000.

Political Requests

In Italy, on the other hand, requests are more likely be for contributions to political parties.

An executive of a United States-controlled multinational electronics group, who insisted on anonymity, said: "To do business in Italy, as in other European countries, you have to render all sorts of favors, including outright bribery.

"It's up to your ingenuity to disguise such practices in reports to your board and in financial statements. You send lavish gifts to key people and their wives. You have your own workers install costly appliances in their seaside villas free of charge. You hire their relatives and protégés if you have staff vacancies. Sometimes cool cash changes hands.

"Don't expect company headquarters to give you any instructions on how to handle such situations," he continued. "You are completely on your own—just keep the sales performance going up."

Although many Americans profess astonishment and sometimes disgust at reports of bribery and under-the-table gratuities offered abroad, such practices are also widespread in this country.

Gifts, some of them lavish, often are pressed on officials with purchasing responsibilities in the United States, and a number of corporate contributions to political campaigns were uncovered during the Watergate investigations.

Furthermore, American companies are quick to point out that overseas competitors also employ such methods, making it more difficult to resist the pressures.

For example, the president of a French-based company in international transport won contracts from a foreign ministry official by seeing that he found his way to one of the exclusive and illegal brothels of Paris. He said he clinched the contract by giving the official's wife a high-speed, electric sewing machine from Switzerland.

Gasoline Coupons

In another case, still in the French courts, Guy Schneider, president of a public works company called Ermest, confessed that he had bribed public officials with gasoline coupons, paid holidays at a winter sports retreat and special funds placed at their disposal to win civic contracts.

Faced with such an atmosphere, some American companies say they have no choice but to compete on equal terms. In India, for example, there are about 40 American companies, and it is widely believed that many of them deal with "liaison officers" who in turn bribe Indian officials.

These companies make donations to political parties, spend money to maintain lobbies inside the Government and in Parliament and provide other inducements such as liquor supplies, entertainment in luxury hotels and hospitality outside India when officials are traveling.

In many countries, corruption in the military is widespread, particularly where officers are poorly paid and have major responsibilities.

Corruption surfaced in the Brazilian Army's quartermaster corps in 1973 when an investigation was ordered into allegations that a dozen high Army officers had received kickbacks from civilian contractors who supplied food and equipment Some sources said the bribes totaled as much as $5-million.

American officials who deal with high military officers abroad confirm such stories.

A former Defense Department official said in an interview that the general in charge of procurement for one Persian Gulf country insisted on siphoning 15 per cent "off the top" of all defense contracts except those negotiated with the United States military.

Little Black Book

"When foreign countries try to sell the general, he has a little black book," the former official said. "If they give a quote on a price, he'll look at the book and say, 'Ah, the U.S. price is such-and-such.' Then, if there's something in it for him, he might consider giving them a contract. Otherwise he insists on going for our military sales."

The importance that American companies attach to employing local representatives was vividly demonstrated by the International Telephone and Telegraph Corporation in mid-1971 after Salvadore Allende Gossens, a Marxist who was opposed by I.T.T., was elected President of Chile.

Confronted with a hostile regime and anxious to protect its telephone properties, I.T.T. moved quickly to foster better relations. In a memo to P. J. Dunleavy, who is now president of I.T.T., J. W. Guilfoyle, another I.T.T. executive, related what had been done to try to improve matters for the company.

Meeting Arranged

He said that two I.T.T. officials were meeting with a Dr. Schaulson, "the consultant I obtained on our last trip," to determine the outcome of Dr. Schaulson's discussions with President Allende.

"Schaulson is a lawyer and a former politician," Mr. Guilfoyle wrote, "and is considered friendly with Allende and, as a Christian Democrat, is not committed to the U.P. [Allende's party]."

Later, despite the hiring of Dr. Schaulson, Chile expropriated the telephone company, and I.T.T. was subsequently compensated by a United States Government agency which insures overseas investments.

I.T.T., in response to a query, confirmed that it had hired a Chilean legal consultant but declined to confirm that it was a Dr. Schaulson. The company said it had hired the consultant on the advice of its Chilean outside counsel.

In the Northrop case, a private report written by the accounting firm of Ernst & Ernst disclosed that Northrop made more than $9-million worth of consultants' payments in 1971, then $7.8-million in 1972 and $12.9-million more in 1973. The report pointed out that the big aircraft manufacturer employed 400 to 500 consultants and agents in the 1971-73 period.

The S.E.C. is looking into these overseas disbursements, which it says were made "without adequate records of controls." The commission also says there was no indication whether services provided in exchange for the $30-million were "commensurate with the amounts paid."

One internal Northrop memorandum included in the Ernst & Ernst report was from James Allen, a former Northrop executive, to Thomas V. Jones, Northrop's chief executive. In the memo, Mr. Allen described attempts by the company to sell its P-530 aircraft to the Netherlands, and he told of his discussions with William Savy, a European consultant.

Contents of Memo

The Allen memo said: "Depending upon developments in the Netherlands and the situation in France, he [Mr. Savy] anticipates that commitments of a substantial nature may have to be made and made soon.

"He said that he did not like to go ahead even preliminarily unless he is covered by adequate funds . . . He suggested we send an advance of $60,000 to him at Euradvice, in Basel, to cover the Netherlands operation and an equivalent amount to him directly to cover the more sensitive French operation."

Another instance of high-level dealings between Americans and foreign officials took place in Kenya. This involved John Saul, United States geologist who attempted to develop a ruby mine in Tsavo National Park.

Mr. Saul and his partner, Elliott Miller, gave a 51 per cent interest in the mine to a group of Kenya politicians, including the country's vice president, Daniel Arap Moi.

However, the two Americans were expelled from Kenya when they resisted pressures to take in more partners. A new claim on the mine was subsequently filed by a Greek entrepreneur who is a business partner of the wife of Kenya's President, Jomo Kenyatta.

One of the most dramatic instances of corruption and bribery abroad involved military clubs and post exchanges in the Far East and Europe.

The Senate Permanent Subcommittee on Investigations reported in late 1971 that military personnel, both uniformed and civilian, stole and received kickbacks and gratuities with the "complicity" of vendors, brokers and salesmen.

"Many American brokers and salesmen representing large American firms were reminiscent of camp followers of former times moving with United States troops from Korea to Vietnam to West Germany," the committee reported.

"They used every corrupting device—gifts, bribes, kickbacks, free housing, entertainment, sex—to persuade PX and club personnel to buy their goods."

One such "camp follower," the committee said, was William J. Crum.

Luxurious Villa

A typical example of Mr. Crum's methods, the committee said, "was his providing a luxurious villa in 1965 to the principal procurement executives of the Army Air Force Exchange System. Not only did he place them in his debt in this fashion, but he bragged about it to officials of James Beam Distillers and Carling Brewery, whom he represented as a broker in Vietnam."

"People have said what can we do," said Irving Pollack, an S.E.C. commissioner. "They say, 'It's overseas, and we can't do business in a country without paying off. If we don't do it, the customer will go to the Japanese, or the Germans or someone else, and they will pay off.'

"The only answer I can see is if the contract goes to the Japanese or the Germans, the Americans should speak up and say, 'You know, we were offered it, but we didn't take it because they wanted us to put $5-million into a Swiss bank account.'"

May 5, 1975

NEW POLICY TO AID INVESTORS ABROAD

Thorp's Statement Regarded as Clarification of Rights and Obligations

By GEORGE A. MOONEY

Long awaited by the investment community, the statement of policy regarding direct American investments abroad was presented last week by Willard L. Thorp, Assistant Secretary of State for Economic Affairs. It was the first such public announcement to be offered by the United States Government, financial observers asserted yesterday. Speaking at a session of the First Hemispheric Conference of Stock Exchanges at the Union Club here, Mr. Thorp presented the State Department's official views of the rights and obligations of private capital in foreign lands.

The action, according to one financial spokesman, provides "the first certainty in a sea of uncertainties." Until now, he explained, direct private investments abroad, although presumably desirable, have received little cooperative consideration by the authorities. Mr. Thorp's statement, according to this view, seems to indicate that the State Department, as a matter of policy, now plans to take cognizance of the needs of the investment community. However, unless and until this policy is detailed further and implemented by the department's insistence that foreign nations observe the tenets outlined, the expansion of American investments will continue to be discouraged, the spokesman added.

Private Actions Handicapped

Since before the war's outbreak, during the war period, and afterward, American investors have felt that the atmosphere for their capital in foreign countries was highly unsuitable. Faced with discriminatory tax and labor laws, inability to withdraw profits, and the constant threat of expropriation, these investors have been inclined to shun such investment "opportunities." As a result, governmental lending agencies have been marshaled to take over a substantial part of the activity which could be handled more effectively by private enterprise.

This process has been accelerated by socialistic and nationalistic trends, especially in Britain, the Balkans, Poland, Czechoslovakia and Western Europe, generally. In some instances, where nationalization has been undertaken, private enterprises, financed by American capital, have experienced a type of discrimination which exempted them from the process, only for the deliberate purpose of causing them to linger and die.

The charter developed at the recently concluded sessions of the International Trade Organization in Geneva, although not yet published, contains portions dealing with safeguards for foreign capital within the boundaries of the participating nations. However, in view of the professed socialistic policies of many of these nations, financial observers here have not been anticipating that these references would be adequate to meet the views of American investors. Instead, it is believed, the charter deals with the problems in terms of the lowest common denominators, and thus will be largely ineffective.

The nations, it is held, should specify clearly, and more or less finally, those areas in which nationalization will not be undertaken, thus serving notice on private capital that it will be free to enter. Then, further, the nations should undertake to provide to foreign capital the same safeguards and privileges, requiring only the same obligations, as are common to foreign investors active in the United States.

"In the process of economic development there should be no invidious distinctions between domestic and foreign capital," Mr. Thorp declared. "Capital has a contribution to make, regardless of its origin, but if it is to expect security and remuneration, it must not seek special privileges.

"The need for United States investment abroad is greater than ever and the opportunities are many. Nevertheless, we all know that the climate for international private investment is not now as favorable as it was in the nineteenth century and in the early years of this century. This is not because foreign capital has no constructive role to play. Our own country, like our good neighbor Canada, was developed with the aid of foreign capital. Nor is it simple xenophobia. As engineers and technicians, we are more than welcome; our skills are eagerly sought; but as businessmen, as entrepreneurs, we are often not so welcome. Sometimes we feel that at the same moment that our capital is sought, every obstacle is being put in the way of its use on a fair and equitable basis.

"It goes without saying that investors must comply in spirit as well as in letter with the domestic laws of the countries in which they operate; that they must refrain scrupulously from any action that might be regarded as interference in the political life of the country or the subversion of public officials. What are malpractices at home are no less malpractices abroad. Foreign capital working in association with local capital promoting local skills, interested in the local needs of the community, and respecting the national integrity of the country of investment, will find that, in the broad as in the narrow sense, it pays big dividends."

These are the objectives, although it is recognized that because of the very nature of European politics and economics under current conditions, they are not likely to be achieved by voluntary agreement among the nations.

September 21, 1947

SUCCESS IN BOGOTA HELD EXAGGERATED

21-Nation Agreement Is Viewed as Clouding Basic Inequality of Hemisphere 'Partners'

By MILTON BRACKER
Special to THE NEW YORK TIMES.

WASHINGTON, May 2—Fellow diplomats are unlikely publicly to challenge former Ambassador William D. Pawley on his assertion that the ninth Conference of the Inter-American States was a "magnificent success."

One of the lessons of Bogotá was that the rhetorical amenities are maintained in Latin America even when fatal rioting breaks out. Those delegations that were privately most eager to leave during the trouble—and were dissuaded largely by the firmness of Secretary of State Marshall—were later among those to praise the results of the conference most fulsomely.

But with the signing of the exchange accord in the Colombian capital today and the arrival here of Dr. Alberto Lleras Camargo of the Pan American Union and most of the United States technical experts last night, the crescendo of praise misfired. That is to say, the shock suffered by the conferees beginning on April 2 shook a lot of basic Pan-American problems into clearer focus than would have been the case had Jorge Eliécere Gaitán not been assassinated.

Here are some of the basic problems, on the basis of collective analysis by many observers, including some of the most qualified delegates:

First, as General Marshall was aware from the start, and as has been the case at every pan-American conference, the economic difference between the United States and the Latin nations assumed a prominence beyond that assigned in the agenda.

In terms of the discussions, the key indication was that Mr. Pawley was forced to warn the Latins that elimination of the guarantee of "prompt, adequate and effective" payment for expropriated property would in effect kill the proposed economic treaty for the United States.

Some observers felt that the United States delegate was bluffing to the extent that he knew such a threat was something that none of the Latins had bargained for; that his gesture was more tactical than strategic. Regardless, it reflected a basic mutual distrust; the distrust of American business men for Latin constitutions and laws, or the lack of them on expropriation—and the distrust of the Latin governments for investors who, they feel, will not hesitate to bring governmental pressure to obtain their stakes and high profits.

The fact is that on the test vote, the United States "victory" was only 10-9—technically not even a majority.

Incidentally, a paradox in the Latin position was revealed by a Mexican who, within minutes of a moving speech on the economic plight in his country, was confiding to a North American the difficulties that he as a business man himself had in ridding his enterprise of inefficiency and graft. The business abuses that many Latins attribute to the United States investor are by no means restricted to the foreigner; some North Americans left Bogotá feeling that the guarantees the United States delegation sought in the chapter on private investment would be of more immediate value to a local business man than to outsiders.

A second point, widely noted, was the continuing general instability of some Latin countries. If Colombia, proud of her peaceful democratic tradition, could reach the verge of a complete overturn in a few hours, how about other countries whose history has been relatively less tranquil? Frequently it was asked, what would happen in Peru if Victor Raúl Haya de la Torre, head of the Aprista party, were slain? The Apristas are outspokenly anti-Communist; and Señor Haya de la Torre's sincerity in his anti-communism has certainly been accepted by the United States diplomatic mission in Lima, which aids his trips to the United States, some honors and the like.

This leads into the third point—the much-discussed anti-Communist resolution. One United States delegate, asked to what extent it had been facilitated and strengthened by the outbreak in Colombia, laughed, "It certainly didn't hurt any."

The more important question is, will the anti-Communist resolution be sincerely applied, or will it serve as an instrument for strengthening the worst regimes in the hemisphere?

The very debate on the controversial measure—ultimately passed unanimously — brought out this possibility in eloquent terms.

Paraguay, Nicaragua, Honduras and the Dominican Republic most fervidly and least qualifiedly endorsed the original version. Paraguay's César Vasconsellos—whose last job was private secretary to Dictator Higinio Moringo—yelled himself hoarse and menaced the delegate at his side as he pounded home his support. But when he placed the blame for the entire Paraguayan civil war of 1947 on "Moscow," every informed diplomat in the place had to look the other way, or figuratively shake his head. What could this approach augur, many of them asked, for a political opposition of any kind that might seek to challenge General Moringo or his successor, J. Natalico Gonzáles?

The Costa Rica-Nicaragua border flare-up, and the fulsome expressions of affection that it evoked from the chief delegates of the countries involved, was another example of the paradox between physical realities and diplomatic amenities at an inter-American meeting.

In the sense that it achieved some solid texts, some agreements in principle and some needed reorganization of the Pan American Union—through a difficult period that tried the stamina and patience of everyone—the conference was indeed a success.

But that success was qualified. It was qualified by the basic realities of the relationship between the most economically powerful nation in history—and twenty less fortunate ones, which include some of the least naturally endowed on the globe.

"The basic trouble is," sadly observed one North American—not a delegate—"that we really have much less in common with these people than we like to pretend."

May 3, 1948

TAX EASING URGED FOR LOANS ABROAD

Truman Sends Congress Data of Advisory Council to Spur Private Investment

Special to THE NEW YORK TIMES.

WASHINGTON, Jan. 20—President Truman sent a report to Congress today urging removal of tax deterrents to a revival of investment of American private capital abroad. Five categories of tax relief were recommended in the report of the National Advisory Council on international financial and monetary problems.

Designed especially to attract private investment capital in support of the Administration's Point Four program of economic improvement of underdeveloped areas, the recommedations are expected to be emphasized in President Truman's message on taxes early next week.

The council said it had recommended that the Secretary of the Treasury propose legislation "to remove tax deterrents to private foreign investment."

"Such legislation," it added, "would liberalize present limitations on the foreign tax credits allowed to American business so that increased tax relief would be accorded where foreign operations result in profits in some countries and losses in others.

"The present laws pertaining to taxation of corporations having foreign subsidiaries would be liberalized so that a majority of stock ownership would no longer be required to be eligible for the tax credit for foreign taxes paid by the foreign subsidiaries.

"Furthermore, it was proposed that the law be liberalized so that an American citizen abroad may receive the exemption from the United States tax on his foreign earned income retroactively to the time he first became a bona fide resident of a foreign country.

"It was recommended that estate taxes imposed by foreign governments be allowed as a credit against United States estate taxes similar to the credit under the income tax.

"Finally, it was proposed that, if practicable, taxes on the profits of foreign branches of domestic corporations should be postponed until the profits are remitted to the United States, similar to the present treatment of foreign subsidiaries."

The top coordinating agency for Federal foreign economic and financial policy, the council includes as members the Secretaries of the Treasury, State and Commerce Departments, the chairmen of the Federal Reserve Board and the Export-Import Bank and the Economic Cooperation Administrator.

Although Secretary of the Treasury John W. Snyder, as chairman of the agency, has not formally proposed legislation to Congress, he is known to concur in the recommendations. Officials explained that the recommendations would not have gone to the White House and been made public today without the Secretary's approval.

January 21, 1950

TAX EASING URGED AS SPUR TO POINT 4

Inducement to Invest Abroad Seen Enhanced by Allowing Credit to Minor Holdings

SNYDER FAVORS PRINCIPLE

Conference Board Business Record Discusses Aspects of Unguaranteed Backing

By GODFREY N. NELSON

Although President Truman's program for Point Four was originally intended to be that of "a cooperative enterprise in which all nations work together through the United Nations," its most important economic phase appears now to be directed toward accomplishing the objective largely through private investment, with a minimum of guarantees by the Government.

The scope and propriety of such guarantees may be questions of government policy. An analysis of such guarantees, with a general discussion of the subject, is contained in an article appearing in the July issue of The Conference Board Business Record, published by the National Industrial Conference Board, under the title, "Bold New Program," prepared by J. Frank Gaston and Lawrence A. Mayer of the division of business economics of that publication.

In this article three major reports upon Point Four are compared: A report to the President by the International Development Advisory Board, entitled "Partners in Progress" by the Rockefeller Committee; a report to the President on Foreign Economic Policies, known as "The Gray Report"; and one by a group of experts appointed by the Secretary General of the United Nations, entitled "Measures for the Economic Development of Under-Developed Countries."

This discussion will be confined to matters of taxation pertaining to the promotion of Point Four objectives, with a specific recommendation by this column for the stimulation of foreign investments by means of more favorable tax laws.

Proposal as to Taxes

The Rockefeller Committee recommends that income from business, located abroad, should be taxed only in the country where the income is earned; that any exemptions permitted should be applied only to new investments in foreign countries; that any "partial exemption" should only be allowed to individuals and not be applicable to investments by corporations and that double taxation should be eliminated by bilateral treaties.

The Gray Report merely recommends that "Further study should be given to the desirability and possibility of promoting private investment through tax incentives." According to the United Nations report, foreign-earned incomes should be exempted from double taxation. While all of these reports favor tax reform to stimulate investments in foreign countries they vary in the matter of favoring foreign investments over domestic investments. This presents the question of possible discrimination against domestic investments.

In this connection, it would seem highly advisable to extend the benefits of the foreign tax credit to minority stockholders in foreign corporations. Under existing law a domestic corporation must own a majority of the voting stock of the foreign corporation. By extending the benefit of the foreign tax credit to minority holdings the inducement to assume the greater risk of making foreign investment would be greatly enhanced.

This principle has already been approved and recommended by the United States Treasury. Secretary John W. Snyder is on record as unqualifiedly favoring the extension of the foreign tax credit in a statement on the 1950 Revenue Bill. Although he made no reference to Point Four, his statement was pertinent.

"There has been an increasing emphasis in foreign countries on the participation of local capital in the ventures of United States business men. Such participation enables the foreign country to benefit to a greater extent from the development of its resources and to educate its business men in the technique of modern enterprise. From the point of view of the United States investor, the participation of local capital may be desirable, because it helps to achieve a more receptive attitude toward the business. It is also a growing practice for American business men to spread the risk (and the profits) from a foreign venture by joining with other United States firms in organizing a corporation to conduct the enterprise."

Illustrating the effect of a divided American ownership under existing law, he said: "If the foreign firm is owned in equal shares by the American corporation, none of them obtains the benefit of the foreign tax credit. If there is a 60-40 distribution of ownership, one of them is eligible for the foreign tax credit and the other is not."

Secretary Snyder concluded his statement with a definite recommendation to the Congress, as follows:

"It is proposed, therefore, that the majority-control test be abandoned so that the credit will be available to all owners of a foreign enterprise. This would encourage potential investors to pool their resources in undertaking new ventures in foreign countries, and it would facilitate greater participation of foreign capital in enterprises that United States business men undertake."

These statements having been made to a legislative body, without regard to Point Four, become the more convincing as an argument for the development of Point Four.

Opinions expressed herein by Mr. Nelson are his own and not necessarily those of THE NEW YORK TIMES.

July 15, 1951

INVESTING ABROAD MEETS OBSTACLES

Exchange Controls, Retarded Development and Absence of Skilled Labor Listed

U. S. TAXES ALSO A FACTOR

Industrial Conference Board Reports on Survey of 54% of Companies Concerned

Obstacles to direct foreign investment have been encountered by about 80 per cent of American companies with overseas interests, according to a survey released for publication today by the National Industrial Conference Board. These hindrances include exchange controls, lack of skilled labor and the retarded economic development of some countries.

The board's report, prepared at the request of President Truman's committee for financing foreign trade, included replies from American companies with 1,097 branches and subsidiaries in ninety-eight foreign countries and holding "at least 54 per cent" of the direct foreign investment of all American companies.

In addition to obstacles emanating from foreign countries, another complicating factor, the report states, are taxes imposed by the United States on income originating abroad. Many of the executives surveyed recommended the elimination or modification of this "double taxation."

Profits Not Commensurate

The absence of profit opportunities "does not appear to limit foreign investment," the survey notes. About 11 per cent of the respondents said profit prospects were not commensurate with risk abroad.

Export or import quotas were the most frequently mentioned obstacles to direct investment. More than 50 per cent of the respondents cited the existence of quotas as a problem arising in the foreign country in which their currently active investment is located. This hindrance was reported more often than any other and is evidently widespread geographically, the board said.

The second most important obstacle, according to the report, is the limitation that many countries have placed primarily upon the remittance of earnings, but also on the remittance of other income and expenses payable in dollars. More than one-third of the respondents encountered this problem. The problem was less severe in Africa than in the more industrialized countries.

Regulations governing the movement of capital into or out of the country was next in importance, the board noted. About 25 per cent of the replies to the questionnaire listed this complaint. In Europe, 34 per cent mentioned this complaint, but only 17 per cent dealing with Africa complained. More than 25 per cent of those in Asia and Latin America listed it.

Social Insurance Impediment

Various types of social insurance also were listed as impediments. About 19 per cent of the replies reported this factor. More than 28 per cent of the responses from those dealing with Latin America mentioned the social insurance regulations. Africa was second with 13.4 per cent and only 11 per cent reported it in the other areas.

The lack of trained native personnel was mentioned by 18 per cent of the respondents. Only 3.6 per cent of the investors in Europe mentioned the labor difficulty, but 42 per cent of those operating in Africa reported the problem.

Among the recommendations for alleviating the situation were encouragement of more favorable "investment climate," guarantees of earning convertibility, assurances against expropriation and nationalization, the elimination of discrimination and general encouragement of world trade.

August 20, 1951

U. N. SETS UP POLICY ON NATIONALIZING

Affirms States' Rights to Take Resources, but Warns Them of Obligation to Investors

By WILL LISSNER
Special to THE NEW YORK TIMES.

UNITED NATIONS, N. Y., Monday, Dec. 22—Taking account of the misgivings of investors in various parts of the world, the United Nations General Assembly amended last night a controversial resolution on nationalization of resources before adopting it by a vote of 36 to 4. There were twenty abstentions.

Both by a new Indian amendment and by statement from the delegations of Uruguay and Bolivia, the resolution, which reaffirms the sovereign right of peoples "freely to use and exploit their natural wealth and resources," now reminds member states of their obligations toward private investors when they feel they must exercise the right to nationalize resources.

However, Dr. Isador Lubin, United States representative on the Economic and Financial Committee, voted against the amended resolution.

Dr. Lubin argued that adoption of the resolution would seriously hinder the economic progress of underdeveloped nations.

"In our opinion, this resolution will be interpreted by private investors as a danger signal—a warning to private investors, everywhere in the world, that they had better think twice before they place their capital in underdeveloped countries," he said. "The fear that this resolution has already stirred up is evident."

Senator Angel Maria Cusano of Uruguay and Dr. Eduardo Arze Quiroga of Bolivia interpreted the first operative paragraph of the resolution as reminding states, in exercising their sovereign right freely to dispose of their resources, of their obligations to respect the rights of private investors—national and foreign.

This paragraph read:

"The General Assembly recommends all member states, in the exercise of their right freely to use and exploit their natural wealth and resources wherever deemed desirable by them for their own progress and economic development, to have due regard, consistently with their sovereignty, to the need for the maintenance of mutual confidence and economic cooperation among nations."

An amendment offered by Nawab Ali Jawar Jung of India was presented, he said, not to change the substance of this recommendation but to clarify it to dispel misconceptions in financial circles and elsewhere. It commended the need for "maintaining the flow of capital in conditions of security, of mutual confidence and economic cooperation among nations." This was adopted by 36 to 4, with twenty abstentions.

Dr. Lubin explained that the United States delegation felt that the "amendment considerably improves the resolution." He abstained on the amendment, he said, because it was felt that it did not go far enough.

The United States did not disagree with the statements of principle in the resolution, he pointed out. The right of eminent domain is a constitutional principle in the United States, and the United States has subscribed to treaties, such as that of the Organization of American States, that bar acts designed to impede the exercise of sovereignty by any state, he continued.

"We voted against this resolution not because of what it does contain, but rather because of what it does not contain," he declared.

The Indian amendment was a "step in the right direction," Dr. Lubin went on, but "did not go far enough." The resolution "is still one-sided," he declared.

In the midst of a discussion that amounted to a renewal of committee debate, the session took up a resolution sponsored by Egypt, India and Indonesia embracing a practical program for advancing land reform, particularly on the basis of regional cooperation in agricultural development. The first part, providing for studies of financial problems, was adopted by 53 to 0, with five abstentions (the Soviet group). The second part, dealing with regional programs, was adopted unanimously by 56 votes.

The Assembly adopted by 52 to 0, with five abstentions, a resolution urging member states to contribute toward a $25,000,000 goal for the fund for the expanded program of technical assistance.

It also adopted by 52 to 1, with five abstentions, a resolution designed to spur action on proposed international funds to make long-term, low-interest loans and grants for economic development of the underdeveloped countries and to provide capital for industrial undertakings.

December 22, 1952

Investors, World Bank Asked To Join 'Trade Not Aid' Drive

By CHARLES E. EGAN

Special to THE NEW YORK TIMES.

WASHINGTON, June 20—The Administration began a drive this week to develop a program for increasing American private investment abroad in line with its "trade not aid" policies.

A score of the nation's top business leaders familiar with international trade and investment problems were entertained at a private dinner at which the Secretary of the Treasury, George M. Humphrey, was host and Sinclair Weeks, the Secretary of Commerce, the chairman. They asked for suggestions and, later, for written briefs on the best means to speed up the development of plans for enticing American "venture capital" to go abroad.

In a free-for-all discussion in which the guests engaged, they voiced a wide variety of views but there was general agreement that the Government should stay out of the foreign investment picture as much as possible.

Among the suggestions put forward were:

¶That earnings from foreign investments be made tax-free by the United States or, alternatively, that Americans investing in plants erected abroad receive a form of accelerated tax amortization benefit similar to that under which those who expand defense production facilities in the United States are permitted to write off a percentage of their investment within five years instead of the normal twenty to twenty-five.

¶That investors look to the International Bank for Reconstruction and Development, rather than to any individual government, to participate in sound foreign enterprises. The World Bank, as it is known, could function in cases in which the sum of American private capital plus capital raised among investors in the country where a project was under way, was insufficient to provide proper financing. By using the World Bank, which has an international reputation for sound operations, political difficulties that might arise if any one foreign government invested in projects in another country could be avoided. Also, it was held, it would also eliminate the onus of charges of "imperialism."

¶That the United States limit participation in foreign investments to guarantees of the convertibility of exchange so that profits earned by American money abroad could readily be transferred to this country.

¶That tourist spending abroad be encouraged by lifting to $1,000, from the present limit of $500, the amount of goods that may be brought into this country duty-free.

¶That Government money advanced by this country be limited to amounts to aid in the improvement of public roads in foreign countries.

Proposals Will Be Assayed

No conclusions were reached at the gathering, but each guest was asked to submit his arguments in written form so that they could be studied by experts of the Treasury, State, and Commerce Departments and by the Mutual Security Administration.

The guests were in agreement that an era of large grants-in-aid by this country was approaching and that normal foreign trade must be stimulated along with a reduction in trade barriers. They said that larger investments by American private capital must be developed to help the free nations of the world.

Those attending the dinner given by Mr. Humphrey included:

Joseph R. Grace, president of W. R. Grace & Co., and director of the Grace Line, Inc.; Nelson A. Rockefeller, now Under Secretary of Health, Education and Welfare, but who has also been president of the American International Association for Economic and Social Development; Frank R. Denton, Vice chairman of the board of the Mellon National Bank & Trust Co., Pittsburgh; Eugene Holman, president of the Standard Oil Co. (New Jersey), and George D. Woods, chairman the First Boston Corporation.

Also Eric Johnston, president of the Motion Picture Association of America, Inc.; Paul Hoffman, formerly head of the Economic Cooperation Administration; John L. Collyer, president of the B. F. Goodrich Company; John Abbink, head of the National Foreign Trade Council and Carl J. Gilbert, of The Gillette Company.

Others were Philip D. Reed, chairman of the board of the General Electric Company; Juan T. Trippe, president of Pan-American World Airways, Inc.; Warren L. Pierson, chairman of the board of Trans World Airlines, and Langbourne M. Williams Jr., president of the Freeport Sulphur Company.

Those present representing the government included, in addition to Messrs. Humphrey and Weeks:

Harold E. Stassen, director of the Mutual Security Agency, successor to the Economic Cooperation Administration; Andrew N. Overby, Assistant Secretary of the Treasury; W. Randolph Burgess, special deputy to the Secretary of the Treasury in charge of management and monetary policies; Samuel W. Anderson, Assistant Secretary of Commerce for international affairs, who is leaving next week for a tour of Latin America, and Samuel Waugh, assistant Secretary of State for economic affairs.

In line with the Administration's interest in speeding up a program for investing American private capital abroad, the Department of Commerce this week was putting the finishing touches on a comprehensive study dealing with impediments to the investment of capital abroad. The survey, which is expected to be released within a few days, is understood to cover a score of countries. It was undertaken by the department with the cooperation of the Mutual Security Agency.

June 21, 1953

U.S. Studies Way to Cushion Effect of Foreign Aid Cuts

More American Private Investment Abroad and World Trade Are Put First—Farm Surpluses Also Are in the Picture

By DANA ADAMS SCHMIDT

Special to THE NEW YORK TIMES.

WASHINGTON, Dec. 20—Officials of the Foreign Operations Administration on the policy-making level are considering means by which private capital can replace diminishing United States foreign economic aid.

It is assumed in these deliberations that direct economic aid to Europe will draw almost to an end in the fiscal year 1954-55, except for France, Spain, Greece and Turkey. These four nations support heavy military programs. Economic aid to the rest of the world also is expected to be on a much reduced scale. Probable exceptions are Korea, Indo-China and Japan.

As the so-called "give-away" programs taper off, the margin of dollar and gold reserves built up by many countries under direct aid may be endangered. The Administration's experts believe movements of private capital and expansion of private trade can offset this menace.

First, the planners are weighing means to increase private United States investments in Europe and, even more so, in the "underdeveloped" regions of the Middle East, the Far East and Southeast Asia.

A signpost probably will be apparent in the interim report of the Commission on Foreign Economic Policy, due at the White House and on Capitol Hill some time before Christmas.

The seventeen - member study group, headed by Clarence B. Randall, chairman of the board of the Inland Steel Company, is looking at all economic aspects of this country's foreign policy, including reciprocal trade.

Its final report, to be submitted in March, most likely will lay down the Administration program in hopeful terms, despite a pessimistic minority report.

Discussing investment prospects one highly placed official said that as a result of the Randall Commission's activities the Turkish Parliament was considering a bill to ease the way for foreign investors. He anticipated similar action in other countries to "create a favorable atmosphere" through providing for easier convertibility of profits, and the offering of guarantees against confiscation.

This official pointed out that in the last few years something like $1,000,000,000 of American capital had been invested in Canada where convertibility or confiscation were not problems.

"Supposing conditions for investment in Brazil were as favorable as they are in Canada," he declared. "You can imagine the possibilities."

The Administration also is planning to simplify procedures by which United States business men can get "investment guarantees" from the United States Treasury. Although Congress has provided $250,000,000 that could be used to guarantee investors against losses by confiscation or through inconvertibility of foreign currencies, only $54,000,000 of the sum has been used.

Farm Surpluses Also in Picture

A second approach under study by Foreign Operation Administration officials is development of the program for sale of surplus United States agricultural commodities to foreign countries for foreign currencies into a kind of economic aid.

The last Congress authorized the agency to use $100,000,000 to $250,000,000 of existing funds for this purpose, but only a $20,000,000 deal for tobacco and a transaction involving $5,000,000 for prunes to be supplied to Great Britain have been worked out to date.

Officials of the F. O. A. are thinking of asking Congress to allocate a special fund for the buying of farm surpluses in the next fiscal year to stimulate multilateral trade as follows:

Japan might need cotton and be capable of supplying a machine tool needed by India. The United States would send the cotton to Japan which would pay in local currency. The local currency would be used to produce the machine tool for India, which would, in turn, pay in local currency that Japan could use to produce goods needed by yet another country, and so on.

A third approach, mentioned in a report of Eric Johnston's International Development Advisory Board to Harold E. Stassen, Foreign Operations chief, last week, may be the setting up of an international finance company to underwrite developmental projects in backward countries. The United States Government, American private capital, foreign governments and foreign private capital might all participate in the organization. One of the special objectives here would be to activate local private capital in such regions as the Middle East.

As an alternative or supplement to an international finance company, some experts are proposing a category of special "nonbankable loans" out of appropriated aid funds. These might be repayable in local currencies. Such advances would finance projects of general importance to the development of countries—such as the proposed Jordan Valley Authority—but which could not be expected to be self-liquidating, let alone profitable.

The fourth approach, also mentioned in Mr. Johnston's report, is to employ voluntary philanthropic and religious organizations and colleges to carry out part of the technical assistance program hitherto performed directly by experts employed by the F. O. A. Several contracts of this nature are almost ready for signature.

December 21, 1953

U.S. FOR NEW BODY ON OVERSEAS HELP

$100,000,000 Agency Would Finance Industrial Projects in Underdeveloped Lands

By JOHN D. MORRIS
Special to The New York Times.

WASHINGTON, Nov. 11—The Eisenhower Administration gave its blessing today to a proposed $100,000,000 international corporation that would help finance private industrial enterprises in underdeveloped countries.

The decision is considered here to rank in importance with the birth in 1949 of the Point Four, or technical cooperation, program under former President Truman.

George M. Humphrey, Secretary of the Treasury, announced the program in his capacity as chairman of the National Advisory Council on International Monetary and Financial Problems. The council, highest Administration authority in the international economic field, approved the new policy at a secret meeting yesterday.

Secretary Humphrey said Congressional approval would be sought for United States participation in the proposed organization, a subsidiary of the International Bank for Reconstruction and Development to be known as the International Finance Corporation.

Many details are still to be worked out with the World Bank, however, and the plan may not be ready for submission to Congress until the 1956 session.

Agency Would Buy Securities

Membership subscriptions in the corporation would range from $35,000,000 for the United States to $5,000 for Panama. All fifty-seven members of the World Bank would be eligible.

The organization, when established, would make repayable loans to industries in underdeveloped countries and also buy securities from such concerns. The securities would pay interest to the extent that profits were realized. Some of them would be convertible into voting stock when sold to private interests by the corporation.

The corporation's initial capital would be augmented as operations got under way by sales of its securities and other obligations to private investors.

It was not expected that the corporation of itself would go very far toward meeting the grave needs of Latin-American and Asian countries for foreign capital in developing their national economies.

Beyond that, however, the idea is to create a favorable "climate" in such nations for the flow of private capital into productive enterprises. The new corporation, besides supplementing private investment funds, would cooperate with business men here and abroad in setting up new enterprises in underdeveloped lands. It would help them find private capital and itself provide a share of the money, if necessary.

The corporation's activities would complement those of the World Bank and the United States Government's Export-Import Bank, according to advocates of the proposal.

The World Bank is barred from making loans to private enterprise unless the recipient's Government guarantees repayment. The Export-Import Bank is limited to loans to encourage foreign purchases of United States products.

Among the results, advocates said, will be to reduce the demand for direct aid from the United States and for loans by the Export-Import Bank.

The proposal, in a slightly different form, was devised in 1951 by a Presidential commission on foreign economic policy headed by Nelson Rockefeller.

It has long been advocated by the World Bank and the United Nations Economic and Social Council. The United States, however, had consistently viewed the plan with much coolness. As recently as last summer, the Eisenhower Administration had turned thumbs down on the plan.

The Export-Import Bank announced today that it had granted two lines of credit aggregating $10,000,000 under a new program designed to promote exports of capital equipment.

One, amounting to $4,000,000, is for use of the Oliver Corporation of Peoria, Ill., in financing the sale abroad of agricultural equipment. The other, for $6,000,000, is available to Combustion Engineering, Inc., of New York, to finance exports of steam boilers and related equipment.

November 12, 1954

2 Roads, One Goal: Latin Progress

Bankers Lead Drives to Recruit Private and State Capital

By PAUL HEFFERNAN

An approach to stimulating the flow of capital to underdeveloped nations is going forward actively on two fronts—those of state capital and private savings.

The private financial enterprise is the Interamerican Capital Corporation, an investment company that is now recruiting its first $10,000,000 of capital from investing institutions and other financial interests in a position to take calculated risks. This company, first proposed at the inter-American conference at New Orleans in March, is the brain child of Rudolf S. Hecht, New Orleans banker and shipper.

The governmental approach is represented by the International Finance Corporation, a proposed $100,000,000 company that would belong to at least thirty member nations of the International Bank for Reconstruction and Development.

Now before Congress, with the backing of the Administration, is legislation that would authorize the United States to participate in the I. F. C. with a subscription of $35,168,000, or slightly more than one-third of the total. The proposed equity-financing affiliate is a prime enthusiasm of Robert L. Garner, vice president of the World Bank.

Their Paths Crossed

Both Mr. Hecht and Mr. Garner have had lifelong backgrounds in banking, but their careers have matured far apart. A native of Germany, Rudolf Hecht came to the United States in 1903, as a youth of 17. Robert Garner, eight years his junior, was then growing up in Mississippi.

The banking call lured young Mr. Hecht south—to Louisiana's bustling port of New Orleans, with its bent to marine finance. But the Mississippi Garner was drawn east, to the Wall Street community of "bankers' banks," where he rose to become a vice president of the Guaranty Trust Company.

If the privately financed and the state-financed companies come into being, as seems likely, these lifelong money men will at last be brought together in partnership on a new investment frontier, the Louisianan still bearing his half-century-old German accent, and the Wall Streeter his Mississippi drawl.

The finishing touches are now being put to the private financial effort, the Inter-American Capital Corporation. The initial capital is to be raised by the sale of income debentures, convertible preferred stock and common stock.

Public Issue Deferred

Subscription of this capital on a private solicitation basis is being directed by Lehman Brothers and other major investment banking houses. It is not likely that the corporation will undertake any public offering of securities until it has gone through a period of trial and error and established a satisfactory earnings experience.

Negotiations are under way to have the company's investments managed by the South American Gold and Platinum Company, which has had success in recent years in investing in Latin areas.

Major policies to be followed by the private investment company are:

¶To harness the company's capital wherever practicable with local capital and local management.

¶To join new or existing industrial enterprises in the Western Hemisphere—especially subsidiaries or potential subsidiaries of United States enterprises—through the purchase of common stock, convertible bonds or other securities offering compensation for risk capital.

¶To keep clear of public utility, mining and oil enterprises where national political interests may fear infringement of sovereignty.

¶To work with the International Finance Corporation, if it is established.

Sparkplug Agency

While serving the same basic purpose—the furnishing of equity capital to enterprises in backward lands where the requisite private financial resources are inadequate—the proposed affiliate of the International Bank

Rudolf S. Hecht, New Orleans shipping leader, is sponsor of move for a private financing agency to serve the Americas.

Interamerican Capital Corp. (I. C. C.)

Incorporation. The I. C. C. is to be incorporated as a Panamanian company. The promoters regard this as most favorable for a corporation whose securities are to be sold privately initially, and it identifies the enterprise with Latin America. Further, Panama has no corporate income tax.

Capitalization. The company will start off with paid-in capital of $10,290,000, consisting mostly of $5,000,000 of 3 per cent income debentures and a like amount of $50 par value preferred stock, both convertible into common stock. Authorized common stock is to total 2,500,000 shares, with 908,000 to be outstanding at the start.

Robert L. Garner, World Bank executive, is the leading advocate of state-financed agency to stimulate private investment.

International Finance Corp. (I. F. C.)

Capitalization. The paid-in capital is to be $100,000,000, in the form of 100,000 shares of stock.

Subscription. Membership is to be restricted to member nations of the International Bank for Reconstruction and Development and capital subscriptions are to be related to the subscriptions of such countries to World Bank capital. The United States would put up $35,168,000. The United Kingdom would be next with $14,400,000. The agreement would not take effect before Oct. 1, 1955. It would become binding when signed by not less than thirty governments whose subscriptions comprise not less than 75 per cent of the total potential capital.

would be more in the nature of a pump-priming device.

Instead of keeping I. F. C. money invested in profitable, proved ventures, it would be the policy of the World Bank affiliate to sell its stake in a going enterprise to private financial interests as soon as practicable and to put the money to work elsewhere.

By this means, the initial $100,000,000 capital could, by frequent turnover, be harnessed over a period of ten years to $1,000,000,000 of investments.

The World Bank officials have come around to this idea because of disappointing experiences it has had in limiting its loans to government or government-guaranteed enterprises. Time and again the Bank has seen worthy investment propositions fold up because private enterprisers refused to participate in a state-guaranteed—and therefore, state-controlled—deal. The proposed I. F. C. would be free to advance equity or debt money without the issue of state direction being raised.

Major policies that the I. F. C. plans to follow are:

¶To have only a minority stake in any enterprise; that is, to require private financial interests proposing deals to put up most of the money themselves.

¶To sell its investments to private investors as speedily as possible, so as to have the capital available for employment elsewhere.

¶To foster the improvement of the investment climate affecting the employment of foreign private capital.

While the capital of the I. F. C. would be available for use anywhere in the world, it is probable that much of it would be put to work in Latin America. The reason is that pools of foreign and local private capital are already being tapped in Latin America, even though they may not be adequate. In the underdeveloped areas of Asia and Africa, the shortage of capital is more acute and hence there is less opportunity for the partnership of private and state finance envisioned by the two budding organizations.

May 22, 1955

5 Banks and Senate Move To Aid Foreign Investment

Participation by U. S. in $100,000,000 World Agency Approved

Special to The New York Times.

WASHINGTON, June 21—United States membership in a $100,000,000 International Finance Corporation was approved by the Senate today without dissent.

The authorization, providing for a United States subscription of $35,168,000, was passed by voice vote and sent to the House after a brief discussion. It is a major feature of President Eisenhower's foreign economic program.

The new agency, an affiliate of the International Bank for Reconstruction and Development (World Bank) is intended to encourage investment in underdeveloped countries, particularly Latin America. Its chief functions would be:

¶Investing in productive enterprises in association with private investors where sufficient private capital is unavailable on reasonable terms.

¶Serving as a clearing house to bring together investment opportunities, private capital and experienced management.

¶Creating conditions conducive to international investment of private capital.

Senator J. William Fulbright, Democrat of Arkansas, told the Senate that the bill was one of the measures offering "the greatest hope for improvement in our international economic relations."

He signed the bill as chairman of the Banking and Currency Committee. Senator Homer E. Capehart of Indiana, the senior Republican on the committee, was co-sponsor. Mr. Capehart had drafted an amendment to give similar authority to the Export-Import Bank, a United States Government agency, but did not offer it.

The new corporation, according to its advocates, will fill a big gap in international finance facilities. The World Bank may not lend to private projects unless repayment is guaranteed by the recipient country's government. The Export-Import Bank is limited to loans contributing to United States trade.

The International Finance Corporation would arrange with private interests to share capital outlays for productive enterprises. For example, it might buy $1,000,000 of debentures in a new company to supplement $2,000,000 of private capital available to establish a cannery in Brazil.

The I. F. C. would have authority to sell the debentures later to private investors and thus replenish its own capital. It could also increase its original capital by selling securities of its own.

Debentures purchased by the corporation could be convertible into voting stock upon their sale to private interests. The corporation, however, could not hold securities that would give it a voice in management of any enterprise.

Membership in the I. F. C. is open to the fifty-six members of the World Bank. The bank's board of governors will serve as directors, with the bank's president, Eugene R. Black, as chairman. The corporation president is to be appointed by Mr. Black with the concurrence of the directors.

The corporation is to start functioning when thirty governments have subscribed $75,000,000. So far, only a few Latin-American countries, with relatively insignificant subscriptions, have authorized participation.

Subscriptions specified by the articles of agreement, as drafted by the World Bank on recommendation of the United Nations General Assembly, range from $35,168,000 for the United States to $2,000 for Panama. The United Kingdom's subscription is fixed at $14,400,000.

June 22, 1955

U. S. MAY SURVEY CAPITAL ABROAD

Study Is Sought to Clear Up Some Misunderstandings

By BRENDAN M. JONES

Proposals for a world-wide study of the role of private United States foreign investments are nearing a decisive stage.

The study would have these major objectives:

¶To show the full benefits of such investments to most countries.

¶To clear up misunderstandings about private foreign investment, particularly a tendency to underestimate its effectiveness in contrast to official foreign aid.

¶In developing these points, together with details on conditions under which private capital can be most effective, to encourage further flow of investment abroad.

As a result of efforts by the United States Council of the International Chamber of Commerce, funds to start the survey have been included in the Department of Commerce budget for the next fiscal year. The initial request is for $50,000, covering about half the total costs. It is expected that hearings on the project will be held this week by a House Appropriations Subcommittee.

The study would be modeled on a pioneering effort in the field reported early last year by the Commerce Department. This survey covered United States private investments in Latin-American countries. It demonstrated that these investments had a beneficial effect much greater than supposed, especially in their contribution to production, wages, tax receipts and economic activity generally.

This study covered 1955. It showed the "book value" of American concerns' investments in Latin-American countries that year as totaling $6,556,000,000. But it showed also the inadequateness of this yardstick—which is based on original cost of investment—by surveying the full economic effects of the companies concerned.

In showed that American companies produced nearly $5,000,000,000 of goods and services in Latin America in just the single year studied. This total was a substantial part of the net production of the area and accounted also for nearly one-third of its total exports for the year. The net direct foreign exchange return to Latin America from these operations was estimated at $1,000,000,000.

Governments in Latin America received a similar amount in income and other taxes from the investing companies. The study showed also that the companies—representing some one thousand enterprises in mining, manufacturing and other industries — paid 600,000 employes nearly $1,000,000,000.

Indirect benefits in stimulating secondary production, introducing new techniques and in contributions to health, education and social services were found to be extensive.

Business leaders were greatly impressed by the Latin-American survey. They regarded it as a highly effective contribution toward better understanding of the continuous and increasing benefits generated by private capital abroad.

The study served to show also that a majority of companies in Latin America expended a major portion of income on new plant and investment. Profits, it was demonstrated, were a subtraction from newly-created wealth and not the drain on financial resources feared by many governmental officials.

The proposed world-wide study would cover 1957. It would be based mainly on a questionnaire directed to every company with foreign investments. The Department of Commerce would make it with the same legal authority as is provided in the census of business. Companies would be assured of privacy but would be legally required to respond to the questionnaire.

Generally it has been indicated that most companies would be glad to participate in the study. Its compilation by the Commerce Department, together with the agency's other sources of data, mainly assures a much more effective coverage than could be achieved by private means.

The "book value" of private United States investments abroad is approximately $35,000,000,000. Since this original-cost standard of measurement has been recognized as drastically inadequate, the global study of the full effect of investment is expected to prove highly significant.

In addition to measuring the benefits generated by private capital, the study also would include much basic economic data on countries and regions. The United States, it has been shown, is often able through its experience in economic surveys to compile a wealth of new data on countries having scant statistical information. Such reports in the past have been welcomed by other countries as being of basic help in better understanding their own economic requirements.

Getting foreign Governments to appreciate the economic benefits of private investment, advocates of the survey believe, can be a decisive step toward encouraging its application.

While most countries do not actively oppose foreign investment, many have not established firm policies for attracting it.

There is a vast supply of potential investment available in this country and in others. But it has been repeatedly demonstrated that the investor in foreign fields is extremely sensitive to what is generally called "a poor investment climate." He must have assurances of fair taxation, guarantees against predatory expropriation and a cooperative attitude by governments on a lasting basis before he is even ready to consider a venture.

April 27, 1958

Multilateral Pacts Termed Premature At Investing Parley

By TAD SZULC

Special to The New York Times.

BELO HORIZONTE, Brazil, June 24—The United States delegation to the International Investments Conference here described today as premature plans for multilateral agreements for the protection of investments in foreign countries.

The German and Brazilian delegations presented proposals for the creation of international organizations that would seek to protect investors against expropriations and other forms of discrimination or harassment. A suggestion submitted on behalf of the Deutsche Bank of Frankfurt called for the establishment of a special international arbitration court for investment disputes.

But Henry W. Balgooyen, executive vice president of the American and Foreign Power Company, speaking for the United States group, said bilateral treaties between governments of investor and recipient countries should be a "prerequisite" for any world-wide pacts.

Groundwork Urged

The conference was organized by the Brazilian National Confederation of Industries to debate investment problems. The United States delegation, like most of the others, is a private group not representing the Government.

Mr. Balgooyen said that, although the ultimate goal should be multilateral agreements, much groundwork was needed that could be accomplished through bilateral treaties. He declared that a factor that was far more important to the investor than any agreement was "the record of performance of a nation seeking the assistance of foreign capital."

Touching on one of the most sensitive investment problems in Latin America, Mr. Balgooyen said every nation had a sovereign right to decide what areas it should open to private capital, but that it was most important that no decision of this type be retroactive.

At the opening conference yesterday, President Juscelino Kubitschek said that in underdeveloped countries like Brazil the Government must make pioneering investments in basic fields where private capital was not attracted, and where there was special political sensitivity.

At yesterday's evening session, Gen. Anapio Gomes, former president of the Bank of Brazil and one of the outstanding theorists of the Brazilian nationalist movement, said the nationalists were not opp[illegible] to the entry of foreign capital here but wanted to guide it toward "pioneer sectors" and away from "basic sources of wealth."

The immense development possibilities of the jungle-bound Amazonas region were sketched for the conference by Gabriel Hermes, president of the Federation of Industries of the northern state of Para. He said the greatest reserve of useful land in the world was there.

With the disappearance of malaria, he continued, prospects in the area were limitless. He said it had the world's highest known yield for rice and vast fields, of which only 10 per cent were under cultivation.

He declared that the area had a great future for cattle and fisheries, while the Amazonas subsoil was rich in iron, manganese and oil.

June 25, 1958

Guaranty Program Backs 206 Million Invested Overseas

By JAMES J. NAGLE

Quietly the International Cooperation Administration has been successfully conducting a program to induce American companies and individuals to invest abroad.

Since 1948 the Administration, for a fee, has been guaranteeing Americans investing in foreign enterprises against loss by expropriation and against non-convertibility of investment earnings or return of capital.

To date 108 American concerns and individuals have received such contracts, which aggregate $206,812,405. Of this, $134,543,841 represents guarantees against inconvertibility and $72,268,609 is in guarantees against expropriation. The cost to the companies is one-half of 1 per cent a year of the amount of protection stated in each contract.

The money received from fees has been paid into the Treasury as part of the fund to be used in the event it becomes necessary to pay claims. Up to April 30 such monies totaled more than $2,500,000. As yet no payments by the I. C. A. have been required and no application for payment is pending.

Under the law, provision has been made for the payment of claims from the fees as long as the latter are available. Thereafter they would be paid from funds resulting from the sale of currency or other assets acquired under previous claims, or from funds received from the sale of up to $200,000,000 in notes by the director of I. C. A. to the Secretary of the Treasury.

The purpose of the program is to stimulate new private investment abroad. Thus, the making of an investment or entering into a contract to make an investment prior to the filing of an application for guarantees are grounds on which an application may be denied.

When an application for guarantees is filed before the investment or commitment to invest is made, the I. C. A. sends a letter to the applicant. This assures him that his application will not later be denied on the grounds that he had made the investment or commitments before a guaranty contract was issued.

However, there might be a considerable lapse of time between the sending of the letter and the issuance of a contract. This could be because of a delay in implementing the investment plan, hesitation on the part of the investor to conclude a guaranty contract until the whole investment had been made, or a delay in obtaining a foreign government's approval of the project.

Ford Meets Delay

The Ford Motor Company experienced such a delay in connection with an investment in the French automobile company, Simca. After making an application to the I. C. A. and receiving the letter of assurance, Ford purchased stock in the French concern in 1956. However, it did not receive final approval by the French Government until last March 21 and a contract with the I. C. A. was not completed until two weeks ago.

Under the contract, Ford received guarantees of $6,987,310 against nonconvertibility and $3,493,655 against expropriation. It had purchased 222,260 shares in the French motor concern, said to be France's largest privately owned auto company.

Ford, incidentally, has the largest guaranty against expropriation, or a total of $17,907,925 under two contracts, covering investments in Germany for the making of trucks and autos.

Other companies and individuals with large guarantees against expropriation are Edwin W. Pauley for oil exploration in Jordan, $6,000,000; Olin Mathieson Chemical Company for the making of industrial chemicals in Italy, $4,275,900; Mobile Overseas Oil Company, Inc., $3,617,000 and $2,800,000 for a cracking unit and oil refinery respectively in Italy; and Godfrey L. Cabot, Inc., with two contracts of $2,215,000 each for making carbon black in France.

The largest guaranty against nonconvertibility ($14,487,500) is held by the Standard Oil Company (New Jersey) on an oil refinery in Italy. Other companies having large guarantees are Olin Mathieson Chemical Company, $11,051,800 on industrial chemicals manufacture in Italy; Godfrey L. Cabot, Inc., $8,830,000 for the manufacture of carbon black in France; the Kellog Credit Corporation, $8,220,468 for providing telephone service in Peru; Mobil Overseas Oil Co., Inc., $5,600,000 for an oil refinery in Italy; and Caltex Oil Products Company, $4,630,000 also for an oil refinery in Italy.

The Department of State says there has been an increase in both the guarantees applied for and issued during the last two years. The department says this is the result of greater knowledge by business emn of the program; a rise in the number of countries eligible for such insurance (now thirty-seven) and an increase in investments abroad by American business.

June 29, 1958

CREDIT IN PESOS STARTS AID PLAN

New Loans of Export-Import Bank Go to Affiliates of U. S. Concerns Abroad

By ALBERT L. KRAUS

Largely unheralded, the Export-Import Bank authorized last week its first credits in a foreign currency—eleven credits totaling 41,034,000 Mexican pesos, the equivalent of $3,282,720, to affiliates of American concerns in Mexico.

Designed to aid the growth of American investment overseas, the new program originates under an amendment enacted last year to the law governing sales of surplus American farm products abroad. The amendment authorizes the bank to lend up to 25 per cent of the proceeds of commodity sales abroad, as agreed with the purchasing nation, to private concerns for expansion there.

The program is limited generally to United States concerns or their affiliates. However, foreign concerns that help in the development of markets for American agricultural products overseas also may qualify as borrowers.

Since initiation of the surplus sales program, purchasing nations have been permitted to reserve a portion of the proceeds for their own concerns.

The new program is unlikely ever to compete in size with the bank's previously established lending programs, loans to governments and private concerns to purchase American equipment for foreign economic development, and loans to American exporters to facilitate overseas sales and shipments.

18 Nations Are Eligible

If the eighteen nations eligible to borrow under the program in its first year of operation make full use of it, which is unlikely, an equivalent of $88,500,000 will be borrowed.

In comparison, in the year ended June 30 the bank authorized 191 credits in thirty countries totaling $856,000,000 under its older programs. In addition, it approved 111 transactions totaling $45,900,000 under credits previously authorized.

But if the size of the new program is not expected to be large, its exponents say, it is expected to be valuable to American concerns that want to expand abroad. Among the eleven credits arranged in Mexico, one, equal to $800,000, will permit the Sears, Roebuck & Co. affiliate in Mexico to expand parking facilities at its stores.

Schering Corp. Gets Loan

Another, for $400,000, will permit John Deere de Mexico, S. A., to build a farm equipment plant to serve the Mexican market. A third, for $45,760, will permit an affiliate of the Schering Corporation, pharmaceutical makers, to build a plant for the manufacture of hormones for export to the United States.

The law prohibits loans for the manufacture of products to be exported to the United States in competition with American-made products. In the case of the hormone plant, however, construction of the Mexican unit will permit an American concern to make and import a product it is unable to produce here.

After enactment of the legislation, commodity sales agreements were completed with twenty-three countries. The agreements with fifteen countries provided that the full 25 per cent of sales proceeds be made available for Export-Import Bank loans. In Greece and Turkey 15 per cent and in Korea 4 per cent of the proceeds were to be made available to the bank.

No provision was made for bank loans under the sales agreements with Burma, Poland, Spain, Great Britain and Yugoslavia.

Agreements Vary

No American concerns or their affiliates operate in Communist Poland and Yugoslavia, so the program there would have had no practical significance. Under the British agreement, the entire proceeds will go to the United States Government. In Burma and Spain it was not possible for the American negotiators to obtain an agreement which reserved funds for the loans.

Demand for loans has proved uneven. Applications for loans in Mexican, Israeli, French and Colombian currencies were far in excess of the potentially available funds. The demand for loans in Italian, Greek and Peruvian currencies, on the other hand, was more moderate.

And Loans in the currencies of Nationalist China, Finland, Iceland, Korea, Turkey and Pakistan have virtually gone begging.

Well over 70 per cent of the applications received in the first year of the new operation were in Mexican and Israeli currencies. The bulk of applications from foreign concerns, restricted to facilities for expanding the sales of American farm products overseas, was for loans in Israeli pounds.

Restricted Use in Mexico

Although the program permits loans both for fixed assets and working capital, in countries like Mexico where the number of applications has been great, the proceeds will be restricted to the purchase of bricks and mortar and productive equipment.

In Pakistan, on the other hand, it seems likely that almost any worthy application would be entertained.

Interest rates, in accordance with standards prevailing in Mexico for similar loans, were established at 10 per cent on the eleven Mexican credits. The loans were written for terms of six to seven years.

Under present plans, funds once loaned will not be returned to the bank for relending. Consequently, applications under the initial program for loans in Mexican pesos were cut off in March, in Israeli pounds in May, and in French francs and Colombian pesos in July.

August 10, 1958

NATIONALISM SEEN AS BAR TO CAPITAL

Chauvinism Must End if U.S. Industry Is to Invest Abroad, Expert Says

An authority on Latin America said yesterday that the trend toward exaggerated nationalism, antagonistic to foreign capital, must be reversed if American enterprise was to continue to venture abroad.

The speaker was Spruille Braden, former United States Ambassador to Argentina and to Cuba, and a former Assistant Secretary of State for Latin American Affairs. He spoke at a luncheon and panel discussion of "United States-Latin-American Relationships in Transition," held at the Astor Hotel. About 300 business men attended the event, part of the regular monthly meeting of the international section of the New York Board of Trade, Inc.

Mr. Braden said there must be no confiscation and expropriation by foreign countries without adequate, prompt and effective compensation. He suggested that there must be equitable treatment of foreign enterprises, and no discrimination in matters such as the use of American managerial and technical employes.

Mr. Braden said that foreign governments should remember that the surest way to paralyze existing industries and frighten away potential investors was by excessive or discriminating imposts, waste and corruption.

Gains Held Exaggerated

He said "* * * a misconception prevails that mining and oil companies make exorbitant gains."

"Actually," he continued, "the investigation, equipment and operation of a large mineral deposit, require millions of dollars, plus other millions which must be expended on unfruitful explorations and dry holes. It is absurd to expect such ventures to accept the low return of a triple A bond. Profits must be commensurate with risk."

Another speaker, James H. Stebbins, executive vice president of W. R. Grace & Co., said that his company had found that it paid to identify its interests with the interests of the country in which it operates.

"We believe in selecting businesses which serve and improve the local economy * * * in the development of local management talent and in working in partnership with local capital * * * in requiring our American employes to identify themselves with the South American community, and in staying out of politics."

Henry F. Holland, a former Assistant Secretary of State for Inter-American Affairs, told the group that never before had the foundation of this country's relations with the other American republics been so sound, realistic and constructive as today.

He listed this country's basic foreign policy objectives in this hemisphere as follows:

¶To guarantee the peace and safety of the community against all attack or violence.

¶To create a policy of nonintervention in the affairs of our neighbors.

¶To contribute effectively to the establishment of strong, self-reliant economies in the other American republics.

October 23, 1958

TAX STUDY TO SIFT INVESTING ABROAD

House Group Will Consider Easing of Laws to Funnel Funds to Poorer Lands

By BRENDAN M. JONES

Tax benefits to encourage expansion of private United States investment abroad will be considered at hearings of a House Ways and Means subcommittee opening in Washington tomorrow.

The importance of such investment has recently been given new emphasis by President Eisenhower in reference to the economic needs of less developed lands. The President has urged that these lands, notably those of Asia and Africa, rely more on private capital for economic assistance.

While laws and policies of other lands vitally affect inflow of investment dollars, Federal tax laws become a decisive factor when all others are favorable. Uncertainties prevalent under these laws as to tax liability of foreign-derived investment profits, however, have become a chief deterrent to capital outflow.

The House subcommittee, which is studying the entire field of foreign trade policy, is expected to hear proposals for eliminating this uncertainty. In addition it is anticipated that it will be asked to consider encouragement of foreign investment through reduced tax rates on earnings.

Boggs Weighs Tax Incentives

Representatives of foreign trade groups as well as executives in the field of international financing and industry are expected to testify. The group's chairman, Representative Hale Boggs, Democrat of Louisiana, has shown that he favors legislation to provide some tax incentives to foreign investment.

Mr. Boggs has warned, however, that measures to stimulate foreign investment with tax benefits face heavy opposition in Congress. Even though they might provide an alternative helping to rationalize cuts in foreign aid, they would be in conflict with moves to increase taxes.

In a talk at the recent National Foreign Trade Convention here, the Louisianan cited still another source of opposition to foreign-investment tax measures. He said:

"Perhaps more important than the facts of Federal fiscal life in appraising the chances for effective implementation of a policy of encouraging private foreign investment is the incomprehensible bias found in many quarters against foreign-source income. I dot not understand this bias. It arises from a lack of public education, from a lack of understanding.

"It is not unusual to pick up a newspaper or magazine and find an article on foreign 'tax-havens.' The gist of such stories often lumps a reputable American business with modern-day Al Capones and implies, if not fraud, at least evasion of United States taxes."

Mr. Boggs recommen[illegible] that foreign trade groups concentrate initially on gaining a "deferral" benefit. Under this proposal, tax on foreign-source income would be deferred until the earnings were remitted to this country. Present law follows the general principle that income is taxable when earned even though it may be kept abroad by a corporate subsidiary for reinvestment or expansion.

The "deferral" proposal is considered to have a favorable chance of enactment, since it would not, theoretically, mean a tax waiver.

Generally, the proposals for tax benefits to increase movement abroad of capital development funds rest on practical considerations. These involve both the question of Government right to tax income earned abroad as well as its desire to assist economic development of other lands.

Under present tax law, reflecting the revisions of 1954, it has been recognized that the "host" country has priority taxing rights on income earned within its jurisdiction even though from foreign capital. In line with this principle, it has now become possible for countries to enter into treaties, defining their mutual taxing rights, particularly when the foreign-earned income is remitted to its home country.

In the latter case, it then clearly becomes taxable for a second time, so that tax treaties have the effect of eliminating "double taxation."

Advocates of special benefits for foreign investment consider that they are warranted by the extra risks and probable extra taxes on foreign-derived income. They also hold that if foreign investment serves national policy, as in aiding economic development abroad, it should merit a lower tax rate.

One basis for this view is the constitutional provision barring tax on exports from this country. Since in many ways establishment of subsidiaries abroad is a replacement of physical exports with local production, it is felt that the same principle should apply in terms of income taxes.

Precedent Has Been Set

As for the question of national policy, precedent already exists in law providing a fourteen-point reduction in corporate tax rate on income of Western Hemisphere corporations. These corporations, 95 per cent or more of whose income must be from sources within the Western Hemisphere but outside the United States, were designed to encourage regional trade and development.

This objective, aiding indirectly economic growth of this country, is similar to that sought in other areas.

The aim of tax proposals is establishment of a recognized trading corporation. It would be legally and physically domiciled in the United States. To qualify for reduced tax rates it would have to meet specific requirements in reporting on its foreign operations.

At present no foreign-based corporation, even though established by United States capital, is legally obliged to report such operations to the Internal Revenue Service. This condition, itself adds to the expense of collecting taxes on profits earned overseas.

November 30, 1958

CAPITAL AVOIDING POOREST NATIONS

Private Investments Scant In Needy Lands, Where Reds Push Cause

HOUSE STUDY BEGUN

Extreme Nationalism and Fear of Expropriation Called Difficulties

By BRENDAN M. JONES

United States foreign investment is at a record level of some $55,000,000,000, more than two-thirds of which is private capital. This figure represents a three-fold increase in the last twelve years.

In light of this growth, present emphasis on increasing private dollar investments in underdeveloped countries seems to entail a relatively simple problem. With such substantial funds already working abroad it might appear that all that was needed would be a little more concentration on the needs of the less developed lands.

That such is not the case may seem obvious to those even slightly acquainted with the trend of private foreign investment. But to those members of Congress, who will be dealing with the sharp issue of foreign aid, it may seem that a shift to private investment aid has been needlessly delayed.

A closer examination of the foreign investment picture, however, reveals that private capital especially has tended to avoid those areas where investment is now considered so essential. Direct, or corporate, dollar investment particularly has been markedly scant in Asian and African lands.

These are the very regions that the Administration has urged to rely more heavily on private capital. They also are the regions in which the Communist "economic challenge" is being most vigorously pursued.

Problem of Direction

The problem, in essence, is to get private capital to go where, so far, it has shown little inclination to go.

Some details of the present distribution of private dollar investments abroad provide basic clues to the over-all problem. In direct, or corporate, investments, which represent the largest portion of private capital abroad, some $25,250,000,000 is at work in foreign lands. This is more than three times the amount of such investments in 1946.

Of the total almost 35 per cent is accounted for by the Latin-American republics. Another 33 per cent is engaged in Canada alone. Western Europe has received nearly 16 per cent and Western European dependencies, more than 3.5 per cent. This leaves a little more than 12 per cent distributed over the rest of the world, chiefly in Africa and the Far East.

Of this balance, some $3,216,000,000, the bulk is invested in such countries as Australia, the Union of South Africa, Japan and the Philippines. None of these nations falls in the class of what may be termed the "least developed" countries that are prime targets of the Communist offensive.

These "least developed" countries are mainly those of Southeast Asia and parts of the Middle East and Africa. Nearly all are newly independent nations and former colonial possessions, where there is generally a strong antipathy for private capital as closely associated with "Western imperialism."

Still there is about $1,400,000,000 of direct dollar investments in these countries. This figure, although only about 5 per cent of world-wide total of such investments, appears to represent a sizable contribution to their economic development.

Most of it, however, is engaged in extractive and trading industries, those that take something out of a country. While these industries generally should have a beneficial economic effect, they are not considered to be as helpful to rapid progress as those that bring something into a country,

Here again, the distribution of direct dollar investment abroad shows a relatively small amount of manufacturing capital working in the "least developed" countries.

After petroleum, manufacturing is the largest category of private direct dollar investment abroad. Of the more than $7,900,000,000 of the manufacturing investment, 92 per cent is accounted for by Canada, Latin America and Western Europe. For the rest of the world, in which some $635,000,000 is invested in manufacturing more than three fourths is employed in the more developed or industrialized countries such as Australia and Japan.

Only about $130,000,000, or less than 2 per cent of the total, is invested in the underdeveloped countries of Southeast Asia, Africa and the Middle East.

Many of these facts were presented last week to a House Ways and Means subcommittee on foreign trade policy. A presentation by Henry Kearns, Assistant Secretary of Commerce for International Affairs, showed that security, profit, as well as this country's need for raw materials, were prime inducements to private capital abroad.

Mr. Kearns detailed such formidable obstacles abroad to dollar investment as extreme nationalism emphasizing state management, political instability, high taxes and the danger of expropriation and lack of currency convertibility for profits. In addition, he noted, the United States Government tended to compete with private enterprise in its aid programs and failed to offer tax benefits or other encouragement to direct it toward under-developed lands.

In sum, the committee hearings showed the problem of encouraging private investment in underdeveloped lands to be extremely complicated.

Philip Cortney, chairman of the United States Council of the International Chamber of Commerce and president of Coty, Inc., viewed the problem last week in these terms:

"It will require more intelligence than dollars, enlightened selfishness and unselfishness of the free nations and people, a great responsibility of their leaders, if we are to stave off the flux of the barbarians. So help us God."

December 7, 1958

PRESIDENT SIGNS TAX LEGISLATION

Law Reduces Rates of Some American Corporations Operating Overseas

COMPUTATION IS EASED

Companies May Consolidate Net of All Units Abroad to Determine Limits

WASHINGTON, Sept. 14 (UPI) — President Eisenhower signed legislation today reducing some income taxes of American corporations operating abroad.

The tax relief starts next year at an estimated loss to the Treasury of $20,000,000 to $40,000,000 a year. It stems from a liberalization of the rules governing foreign tax credits.

American corporations deduct as a credit against their 52 per cent United States income tax any income taxes paid to foreign governments. This credit under the old rules was computed on a country-by-country basis. Under certain circumstances this worked to the disadvantage of companies operating in more than one country.

The new rules will permit companies to consolidate all of their foreign earnings for purposes of determining the limits on their foreign tax credit.

As an example, a corporation subject to a 60 per cent foreign income tax now pays no United States income tax on its earnings in that country. But it cannot apply the excess 8 per cent as a credit against United States taxes on income earned in another foreign country where the levy may be less than 52 per cent. The new law, in effect, would permit it to do this.

The President did not request the legislation and signed it without comment. Congressional sponsors argued that the old law discriminated unfairly against certain concerns by depriving them of the full advantage of foreign tax credit and requiring them to pay a combined United States and foreign tax rate in excess of 52 per cent.

This disadvantage would still be felt by any American corporation operating in only one foreign country and one where the taxes are higher than 52 per cent. However, such companies get credit for the excess tax by setting up operations in other countries with lower tax rates.

September 15, 1960

SAFEGUARD ASKED ON U.S. INVESTMENT

I. T. & T. Head Challenges Nominees to State Policies in Light of Cuban Action

Harold S. Geneen, president of the International Telephone and Telegraph Corporation, challenged both Presidential candidates yesterday on the issue of safeguarding foreign investments of American citizens.

His challenge was contained in an open letter addressed to Vice President Nixon and Senator John F. Kennedy. Disclaiming any desire to determine what matters should be discussed by the candidates in their series of debates, Mr. Geneen said:

"However, as one of the many companies with a healthy stake in business around the world, we are disturbed about the apparent lack of understanding, as evidenced in statements made to date by both candidates, of the need to maintain a healthy climate for United States investments abroad."

"Replica" of Vatican Gift

After suggesting that the candidates might discuss the question in their debate tonight, Mr. Geneen criticized a statement by Senator Kennedy that the Cuban Telephone Company, an I. T. & T. subsidiary, had given a "solid gold telephone" to Fulgencio Batista, the ousted Cuban dictator.

He said the phone "was gold-plated and was not presented to Batista."

"The fact is" he went on, "it was a gold-plated replica of the gold telephone set presented by I. T. & T. in November of 1930 to His Holiness, Pope Pius XI, commemorating installation of telephone service in the Vatican.

"This replica was made available by I. T. & T. in 1957 for an exhibit arranged by the Cuban Telephone Company in the Palace of Fine Arts in Havana, and it was returned in January of this year with the thanks of the current Cuban Government."

Mr. Geneen quoted the Democratic nominee as having described the phone as a symbol of "excessive" rates received by the corporation.

Says Policy Is Needed

"At the same time that we are being exorcised about our investments in Cuba," he continued, "Vice President Nixon talks about the need to double or triple the level of our private investments abroad in underdeveloped areas, and Senator Kennedy, in spite of his comments last week, also urges an increase of private investment overseas."

"A clear understanding" of what is required to achieve the growth of private American investment abroad will not be accomplished "by talking about gold telephones or round sums of money running into the billions," he declared.

"What is required," he said, "is a Government policy that will help the United States citizen feel safe in putting his dollars to work in United States enterprises abroad."

Mr. Geneen said the corporation had operated Cuban Telephone thirty-eight years, and "our average rate of return was approximately 4 per cent."

"This was considerably less than telephone companies are permitted to earn in the United States," he commented.

"In the face of statements by both candidates that we need more investment abroad, it seems clear to us that if our Government pursues short-sighted policies toward overseas investments; if it criticizes and second-guesses, as Senator Kennedy did last week; if it fails to see that our private investments are treated fairly by foreign nations, then the additional billions which both the Vice President and the Senator would like to see poured into such enterprises will have to come completely from United States Government funds supported by taxes."

October 13, 1960

NEW TAX BOUQUET IS CALLED THORNY

Form of Relief to Companies With Units Overseas is Criticized Strongly

By **ROBERT METZ**

Congress presented the business community with roses last year in the form of legislation providing tax relief to corporations with operations overseas. But accountants and business men are complaining that the roses are thorny.

Before the bill was passed an amendment was tacked on that was designed to increase a corporation's responsibilities for reporting on its overseas operations and imposed stiff penalties for failure to live up to the reporting rules.

Senator Albert Gore, Democrat of Tennessee, proposed the amendment originally. He said that some of the "most flagrant abuses being practiced [by business] today center around the creation, collapsing of corporations, transfer of funds and other manipulations of foreign subsidiaries of domestic corporations.

"Through the use of third country tax havens and other devices, the payment of dividends to the parent company in the United States may be delayed for many years, ordinary income may be converted into capital, and funds may be moved about much as the carnival prestidigitator plays the shell game. The Treasury and the Internal Revenue Service never know under which shell, if any, certain transactions may be found.

"In order for the Treasury even to know what is going on—and this does not necessarily mean anything can be done to stop these manipulations as they occur—an improvement in reporting is vital."

Bars to Compliance Seen

Congress left it up to the Internal Revenue Service to spell out the reporting requirements under the new law. The result is a list of requirements tentatively proposed that Leslie Mills, chairman of the Federal taxation committee of the American Institute of Certified Public Accountants says will make compliance "next to impossible, extremely expensive."

"Two sections of the proposed reporting rules, in particular, have been singled out for criticism. One would require a list of transactions between related corporations and the other calls for an analysis of accumulated profits of foreign operations.

Mr. Mills attacked the proposed rules at hearings held before the Commissioner of Internal Revenue held on Nov. 17. He told the Commissioner that he had just returned from Canada and said the Canadian lawyers and accountants had read the proposed rules, considered them "entirely unnecessary and an unwarranted invasion and interference in the manner of operating businesses in Canada."

Mr. Mills was one of a number of business representatives who attacked the proposed rules at the hearing. The outcry is intense, in part, because of the penalties involved.

Under the law, a corporation failing to file a timely information return loses 10 per cent of the foreign taxes otherwise credited against the United States tax impost. After ninety days notice the corporation still in default loses another 5 per cent, with additional 5 per cent penalties for each additional ninety days' default.

At the hearings one corporation estimated that from 50,000 to 100,000 transactions would have to be reported each year. Another reported that its tax department would require the services of two additional men. Most of those testifying expressed doubt that the mass of information would serve any useful purpose.

Rulings Expected

John B. Inglis, senior partner in Price Waterhouse & Co., an accounting firm with clients in forty-four countries, said that the requirement calling for an analysis of accumulated profits would mean maintaining "two sets of records." Or, "at least the reconstruction of a set of records from the date of the formation of the foreign corporation to the present time. * * *"

Now that the hearings have been held, final regulations may be forthcoming within days, weeks or possibly as long as six months. The Internal Revenue Service conceded that any time was possible, but would not comment further.

In a discussion of overseas problems at a meeting sponsored by the New York State Soicety of Certified Public Accountants last week, Julian Phelps, administrator of the International Services Division of Lybrand Ross Bros. & Montgomery, accountants, said he believed the reporting requirements would become final this month. If they should be, the rules could be put into effect in January.

Under the new law, a corporation operating abroad may offset against its United States taxes on foreign earnings, the average foreign taxes paid around the world. Thus, if the world-wide tax rate averages out to 52 per cent or higher, the corporation pays no United States income taxes on its foreign operations. Fifty-two per cent is the top United States Corporate income tax rate.

The corporation can choose to be taxed under this rule beginning next year. Peculiarities of the law may cause some corporations to elect to be taxed under the old rule.

That rule considers each country separately. Thus, taxes higher than those of the United States, paid in one country, cannot be averaged in with taxes lower than those of the United States, paid in another. That is, a company is limited to a tax credit of 45 per cent on earnings in a country with that top limit, and a 52 per cent tax credit in a country with a 65 per cent top limit, for example.

November 27, 1960

CONGRESS ACTING ON EXPROPRIATION

Senate Group Wants Bill on Foreign Aid to Require Adequate Compensation

PROPOSALS ARE STUDIED

Foreign Seizures and Loss on Bond Defaults Hit U.S. Earning Power Abroad

By PAUL HEFFERNAN

The seizures of private United States business investments by nations getting special financial aid from the United States are getting under the skin of Congress.

Washington is sensitive for two reasons. The first is resentment that the tax resources of a private capitalistic system are being used to underwrite the spread of socialistic practices abroad.

The second reason—and this, at the moment, is the more touchy—is the way such expropriations threaten to worsen the imbalance in the international payments of the United States, an imbalance that is seemingly unshakable so long as the United States keeps handing out a sizable fraction of the nation's resources in the form of foreign aid. Unless full compensation for such seizures is forthcoming, the imbalance in international accounts will be aggravated and the maintenance of the standing of the United States dollar will be more difficult.

Johnson Act Dead Letter

Congressional leaders probably have not been so concerned about the treatment of United States private property abroad since the adoption of the Johnson Act in the Nineteen Thirties. As originally drafted, the Johnson Act would have prohibited any nation in default of debt to United States interests from raising money in this country. Amendments in time sapped the force of the Johnson Act and today it is virtually a dead letter.

But the Foreign Relations Committee of the Senate is now directing its staff to draft for inclusion in the pending foreign-aid bill a workable requirement assuring the payment of adequate compensation to United States private-property interests subjected to expropriation by governments abroad. Proposals by Senator Richard B. Russell, Democrat of Georgia, and Senator Homer E. Capehart, Republican of Indiana, are under study.

Big Losses in Cuba

The most notorious leakage of United States assets abroad as a result of foreign expropriation is Cuba, where the losses ran to $1,000,000,000. More recently, Brazilian moves to take over private property owned by United States and other non-Brazilian corporations have raised misgivings as to the adequacy of compensation.

In recent years, moreover, the leakage in United States earning power abroad from uncompensated expropriations has been equaled by the earnings loss from debt investments abroad — defaulted foreign-bond issues that either were settled on a cut-rate interest basis or are still in default.

Over the last seven years, about $1,000,000,000 in foreign earnings leakage are traceable to such private debt investments. Of defaulted bond issues "restored to good standing" on a cut-rate interest basis, the United States loss in interest earnings from the requirements of the original contracts ran to about $370,000,000.

The loss in principal ran to about $550,000,000 because of the workings of privileged sinking funds. The foreign borrowers retired much of the debt at a cut rate by harnessing their foreign exchange resources to sinking funds that would buy up the reduced-interest-coupon bonds at discounts of from thirty to fifty market points ($300 to $500 per $1,000 bond) in the open market.

Further leakage in foreign investment earnings stems from about $300,000,000 of foreign dollar bonds that are still in default. These include not only obligations of the Soviet Union and her satellites, but Costa Rica, the Congo, Bolivia and Greece.

Integrity of Contracts

Even though the persistence of imbalance in the United States international payments is properly a matter for public concern, an issue of more far-reaching importance lies in the continuing integrity of international contract.

In contrast with the recurring talk about the gold outflow from the United States since 1955, little thought is given to the great growth of United States investment assets abroad during the same period and to the need for safeguarding this earnings stake.

On one hand, Uncle Sam since 1955 has seen his gold reserves dwindle from $22,000,000,000 to $16,000,000,000 and he is sensitive about the fact that short-term foreign money claims could drain away $10,000,000,000 more. This would leave the United States gold kitty at about $6,000,000,000, or about $2,000,000,000 more than before the Great Depression of the Thirties, when most of the world's gold fled here for refuge.

On the other side of the international balance sheet are United States foreign investments abroad. Over the past ten years these have increased from about $18,000,000,000 to $46,000,000,000.

This rise in Uncle Sam's foreign earnings assets, of course, dwarfs the scope of even the gold outflow. But the gold outflow represents a drain of liquid assets, while the rise in foreign investments represents an enrichment in the form of assets of nonliquid kind.

The problem that Washington is now at last coming to grips with is to prevent this great foreign investment stake from being eroded.

So far as international payments are concerned, it makes no difference whether the erosion takes the form of uncompensated seizure of equity or official reluctance to honor debt investment contracts.

May 13, 1962

HIGH COURT BARS JUDGING OF CUBA ON EXPROPRIATION

1897 POLICY IS AFFIRMED

8-to-1 Ruling Cites Right of Nation to Act on Its Soil—Puts Task to Diplomats

By ANTHONY LEWIS
Special to The New York Times

WASHINGTON, March 23—The Supreme Court ruled today that United States courts would not question the legality of a foreign government's expropriation of property within its own borders.

The decision, which has major implications for international law, came in a suit by the Government of Cuba. The court upheld the Castro Government's right to sue here and said its seizures must be treated as valid for purposes of litigation.

The United States Government, while denouncing the Castro seizure decrees as violations of international law, had urged the results reached today. Its view, accepted by the Court, was that the whole expropriation issue was one to be settled by diplomats, not judges.

Justice White Dissents

It was an 8-to-1 decision. Associate Justice John Marshall Harlan wrote the opinion of the Court. The dissent, a stinging one, was by Associate Justice Byron R. White.

The ruling reaffirmed a policy known as the "Act of State Doctrine." As phrased by the Supreme Court in 1897, it says:

"The courts of one country will not sit in judgment on the acts of the government of another done within its own territory."

This doctrine, Justice Harlan said, "expresses the strong sense of the judicial branch that its engagement in the task of passing on the validity of foreign acts of state may hinder rather than further this country's pursuit of goals both for itself and for the community of nations as a whole."

The decision leaves it to the State Department, the President and other Federal officials to contest foreign expropriations of United States property.

Many weapons may be used, the Court pointed out. For example, the freeze on Cuban assets here is a form of pressure on the Cuban regime to compensate former property-owners.

The opinion also remarked that judicial noninterference in expropriation conflicts was desirable "however offensive to the public policy of this country" the seizures might be.

The case arose from the sale of sugar that had been taken over by the Government of Fidel Castro. This sale involved $175,000. But much more is understood to have been awaiting the outcome of this case.

The money claimed by the Castro Government cannot,

however, go to Cuba now because the United States has frozen all Cuban assets in this country. The money will presumably be held until relations thaw or Congress directs some other dispotition of it.

Originally the sugar was owned by a Cuban company known as C.A.V. It contracted to sell the lot to Farr, Whitlock & Co. of New York for shipment to Morocco.

The sugar was seized by a Castro decree when it was on a ship in a Cuban harbor. Under the pressure of being unable to move the ship out of the harbor, the New York company signed a new contract promising to pay a Castro agency, rather than C.A.V., for the sugar.

Money Held in Escrow

After the shipment was completed, C.A.V. and the Cuban Government both claimed the $175,000 from Farr, Whitlock. The money has been held in escrow while the suits went on.

The lower Federal courts in New York rejected the claim of the Castro agency. They accepted the Act of State Doctrine in general but said it did not apply because the Cuban expropriation had violated international law. The lower courts said international law had been violated, because among other things, the seizures discriminated against United States property and had not been adequately compensated for.

This view was wholly rejected by Justice Harlan today. He said a charge that an expropriation violated international law did not except the case from the Act of State Doctrine because such a charge would itself be highly disputed.

Views Are Opposite

The opinion noted that Communist and Western nations had wholly different views of the legality of nationalization.

It would be wholly optimistic, Justice Harlan suggested, to suppose that judicial decisions in the United States, a "principal exponent of the free enterprise system" would be accepted as "disinterested expressions of sound legal principle by those adhering to widely different ideologies."

Justice Harlan said that the courts would be freer to act if the issue were one in which there were greater "codification or consensus" in international law.

He thus restricted today's decision to the area of expropriation, summarizing the decision as follows:

"The Judicial Branch will not examine the validity of a taking of property within its own territory by a foreign sovereign government, extant and recognized by this country at the time of suit, in the absence of a treaty or other unambiguous agreement regarding controlling legal principles."

The court declared for the first time that the Act of State Doctrine was a matter of overriding Federal law, arising out of the relationships of all courts to the foreign policy power of the Executive Branch of the Federal Government.

In the past some have thought that each state's courts were free to adopt the Act of State Doctrine or not. Today's opinion said such a course would produce chaos and defeat the purpose of allowing the nation's diplomats a free hand.

Justice White began his dissent by saying he was "dismayed that the Court has, with one broad stroke, declared the ascertainment and application of international law beyond the competence of the courts of the United States in a large and important category of cases."

The dissent called this "a backward-looking doctrine" and said "no other civilized country has found such a rigid rule necessary for the survival of the Executive Branch."

Justice White was also highly critical of the majority's finding that the courts must entertain Cuba's suit at all. This, he said, puts them in the position of having to "render judgment and validate the lawless act."

Reversal of Idea Asked

He said he was especially concerned about the possibility of seizures in situations involving racial or religious discrimination, such as Hitler's seizures of Jewish-owned property. Surely, Justice White argued, American courts should be able to look into the validity of such seizures under international law.

Lower Federal courts in the past have developed an exception to the Act of State Doctrine. This is that they may examine foreign acts' validity if the State Department specifically says that it has no objection.

Justice White urged that this concept be turned around, so that courts could pass on the validity of foreign acts under international law unless the State Department specifically objected.

This position was urged by the committee on international law of the Association of the Bar of the City of New York, in a brief as a friend of the court. It was rejected by the majority today on the ground that it would put too great a burden on the State Department.

The case was argued for Banco Nacional de Cuba, the Cuban agency that brought the suit, by Victor Rabinowitz of New York. The Deputy Attorney General, Nicholas de B. Katzenbach, argued for the Government as a friend of the court.

On the opposing side were C. Dickerman Williams and Whitney North Seymour of New York. They represented, respectively, Farr, Whitlock & Co., and C.A.V., the owner before nationalization.

March 24, 1964

Pact on Investor Dispute Is Set as 20th Nation Acts

Special to The New York Times

WASHINGTON, Sept. 15—The new convention for conciliation and arbitration of disputes between nations and foreign private investors will come into effect Oct. 14, the International Bank for Reconstruction and Development (World Bank) announced today.

The ratification of the convention yesterday by the Netherlands brought total ratifications to 20, the number necessary to make the convention effective.

The United States has both signed and ratified the new convention.

The convention establishes a new international center for settlement of disputes, under the auspices of the World Bank. The most common of the disputes involved are those where a foreign private company is nationalized and there is disagreement over compensation.

September 16, 1966

PRESIDENT PROPOSES TAX ON INVESTMENTS ABROAD TO EASE DRAIN ON DOLLAR

LEVY WOULD VARY

15% Rate on Stocks and 2.75 to 15% on Bonds Asked

By TOM WICKER

Special to The New York Times

WASHINGTON, July 18—President Kennedy asked Congress today to impose a tax on Americans purchasing long-term securities of foreign countries or foreign corporations.

The purpose would be to slow the flow of capital and gold abroad and thus improve the country's balance of payments position—the record of both public and private transactions made through foreign currency exchange, such as trade and investments.

The tax, which would expire in 1965, would, if passed, be made retroactive to today, in most cases. On stocks, the levy would be 15 per cent of their value. On debt securities, the rate would vary from 2.75 to 15 per cent of the value, based on the period of maturity.

1% Interest Rise

The effect would be to increase by about 1 per cent the interest cost to foreigners seeking capital in the United States through the sale of securities maturing in more than three years.

It would have that effect because Americans buying such foreign securities would be expected to demand higher earnings on these securities to absorb the tax they would be required to pay to the Federal Government.

Thus, Mr. Kennedy said, the flow of long-term capital out of the United States could be substantially checked and the nation's balance of payments position improved.

The proposal calls for a number of exemptions from the tax, including direct investments made by American companies in overseas subsidiaries and loans made by commercial banks.

Gold Supply Drops

The nation's monetary gold stock dropped an additional $50,000,000 in the week ended on Wednesday, bringing to $345,000,000 the loss so far this year and cutting the gold stock to $15,633,000,000, its lowest level since April 19, 1939.

The Treasury Department announced late today that purchases of foreign securities traded on any of the major stock exchanges in the United States could be made up to and including Aug. 16 without being subject to the tax.

This change in the plan proposed by the President to Congress, Treasury sources said, was made because of difficulties in setting up stock exchange record-keeping systems that would identify the nationality of the seller of foreign securities.

Such identification would be necessary because Americans buying foreign securities from other Americans would not be liable to the tax at any time.

The tax would be a companion move to the discount rate increase announced by the Federal Reserve Board this week. That increase, the Administration believes, will hold down the outflow of short-term interest rates.

Together, Mr. Kennedy told Congress in a special message sent to the House and Senate at noon, the two steps should reduce the balance of payments deficit by about $900,000,000 annually.

Moreover, a drop in United States Government expenditures abroad of about the same amount in the next 18 months, Mr. Kennedy said, will bring the over-all reduction to nearly $2,000,000,000 a year.

In his message Mr. Kennedy said that "the deficit in our balance of payments has been reduced from $3,900,000,000 in 1960 to $2,400,000,000 in 1961 and $2,200,00,000 in 1962."

Under a somewhat different method of computation, the payments deficit in the first quarter of this year rose again to an annual rate of $3,200,000,000. Informed sources have estimated that second quarter deficit figures, not yet announced, may reach an annual rate of $3,500,000,000 or more.

If the gains he envisioned materialized, the President said, they will "give us the time our basic long term program needs to improve our international competitive position, and increase the attraction for investment in the United States."

"These two objectives," he went on, "must be the basis of any permanent closing of the payments gap."

Mr. Kennedy announced one other major step in today's message. It was an intricate arrangement with the International Monetary Fund. The aim is not to reduce the payments deficit but to help finance it and to assist some other countries with large dollar holdings.

Most of the lengthy message was devoted to a review of the balance of payments situation, steps taken by the Administration to cope with it, and the effect of these steps.

"There is much from which to take heart" the President said, citing an expanding economy, a dollar bulwarked by "nearly 40 per cent of the Free World's monetary gold stock" as well as by bilateral and multilateral arrangements with other nations, and a gold outflow that he said "has been halved."

The President also said he saw "signs of longer-run improvement in our world competitive position, as our prices and costs hold steady while others are rising."

More Action Urged

But, Mr. Kennedy said, "more remains to be done today to eliminate" the payments deficit.

"The single most important step that can be taken to achieve balance abroad as well as growth here at home," he said, is passage of his comprehensive tax reduction and revision program, as a stimulus to the domestic economy.

"A prosperous, high-investment economy," Mr. Kennedy said, "brings with it the rapid gains in productivity and efficiency which are so essential to the improvement of our competitive position abroad."

He also insisted that the maintenance of reasonable price-cost stability, "limiting wage and profit increases to their fair share of our improving productivity," would be "a powerful force working to restore our payments balance over the longer run."

But the President rejected, as he has before, restrictions on trade and capital movements, a slackening of defense and assistance efforts abroad, or any action that would prevent the dollar from being considered "as good as gold."

Under the tax method of restricting long-term outflows of capital, Mr. Kennedy said, "reliance will be placed on price alone to effect an over-all reduction."

That reduction was necessary, he said, because such outflows—the total spent by Americans for investments in foreign securities and Government obligations—had risen from about $850,000,000 in 1960 to about $1,200,000,000 in 1962 and were running at an annual rate so far this year of "well over" $1,500,000,000.

Administration sources said they hoped the tax, which would be effective through 1965, would reduce this outflow to approximately the level of the three-year average of 1959 through 1961. That would be about $600,000,000 annually, or less than half this year's prospective rate.

The tax would work in the following manner, as explained to Congress by the President and in more detail by Administration sources:

Any United States citizen, corporation or resident purchasing here or abroad a stock of debt security issued by a foreign corporation, government or person, whether the issue was new or outstanding, would pay the tax.

The rate of taxation would be graduated to achieve the desired effect of adding about 1 per cent to the borrower's interest costs.

On stocks, it would be 15 per cent of their value. In the case of debt securities, the rate would be graduated from 2.75 per cent to 15 per cent of the value, based on the period of maturity. For instance, a 5½-year bond would be taxed at the rate of 5.10 per cent; a 10½-year bond at the rate of 8.30 per cent; a 21½-year bond at 13.05 per cent; and all those maturing in more than 28½ years at the maximum of 15 per cent.

Debt securities having a maturity other than those cited would be graduated accordingly. Altogether, 17 different rates would be established, Administration sources said.

A number of exceptions, exemptions and exclusions would be permitted. The most important of these are as follows:

¶The tax would not apply to purchases of foreign securities already held by an American.

¶It would not apply to direct investments by Americans in overseas subsidiaries or affiliates, nor to securities maturing in less than three years, nor to loans by commercial banks.

¶Underwriters and dealers would not be taxed on stock or obligations acquired and resold to foreigners as part of the underwriting of a new issue.

¶The tax would not apply to purchases of securities issued by underdeveloped nations, by corporations centering their activities in those nations, or by international organizations of which the United States is a member.

Mr. Kennedy would designate countries considered underdeveloped, as he already does for other purposes. Those presently on the list include all in Central and South America, all in Africa except the Republic of South Africa, all in the Middle East, and all in Asia except Japan and Hong Kong.

Effect Elsewhere

Thus, the main impact of the tax would be absorbed by European borrowers, and those in Australia, New Zealand, Japan and Canada, with Canada the most affected. So far this year, American purchases of Canadian securities have totalled $590,000,000. The 1963 total for all foreign securities is $880,000,000.

A secondary result of the tax plan, if approved by Congress, would be about $100,000,000 in annual revenue for the Federal Government.

Administration sources said Representative Wilbur D. Mills of Arkansas, the Democratic chairman of the House Ways and Means Committee, had promised to give the tax proposal "high priority" once the President's comprehensive tax reform and reduction production had cleared the committee.

They would not offer an estimate of the new tax's chances for passage. Mr. Mills said he had an "open mind" on the proposal. Everett McKinley Dirksen of Illinois, the Senate Republican leader, questioned it sharply, calling it "virtually a capital tax."

Senator Thruston B. Morton, Republican of Kentucky, also expressed opposition. A number of Democrats and Senator Jacob K. Javits, Republican of New York, said they favored the proposal.

The Administration asked that the tax be made retroactive to today, to prevent heavy dealing in foreign securities before passage. Thus, purchases of such securities seemed sure to be slowed while the issue is before Congress, even if the proposal ultimately is rejected.

The last-minute change by the Treasury would permit transactions in foreign securities to be made on major stock exchanges until Aug. 16 without being subject to the tax. That would not apply to debt securities sold elsewhere.

The new International Monetary Fund arrangement announced in the balance of payments message requires no Congressional approval and is already effective to all intents and purposes.

The arrangement was made necessary because the I.M.F. now holds virtually all the United States dollars that its rules allow. Thus, countries holding most of their official reserves in dollars must make repayments to the I.M.F. either in other currencies or in gold.

To ease their problem, and to help finance part of its own payments deficit, the United States has arranged with the I.M.F. to draw up to the equivalent of $500,000,000 in the coming year.

When a country wishes to make a repayment to the I.M.F., and could most conveniently do so in dollars if the I.M.F. could accept dollars, the United States will draw the equivalent of the proposed repayment in some other currency.

The United States then will exchange this currency at par value for dollars from the country concerned. That country then will transfer the other currency to the I.M.F., completing the transaction.

The United States will be left in the position of owing the I.M.F. an amount in dollars equal to the amount of the foreign currency it withdrew to initiate the transaction.

In fact, Administration sources said, this debt—which could rise to a total of $500,000,000—would not have to be repaid. This is so because the United States, under I.M.F. rules, gets a credit in dollars whenever another country withdraws dollars from the fund.

Calling Trade Parley

The credit would be equal to the withdrawal and future withdrawals would be expected to provide enough credits to cover obligations the United States would incur under the new arrangement.

Other important points of Mr. Kennedy's balance of payments message were as follows:

Mr. Kennedy called again for a broad program of export expansion, including approval of a $6,000,000 appropriation for Department of Commerce educational programs, elimination of ocean freight rate differentials now injuring American exporters, and a White House conference on export expansion for Sept. 17 and 18.

He asked greater efforts to bring tourists to the United States, to offset in part the $2,500,000,000 American tourists spent abroad last year.

The President announced that economies and modernization programs would reduce defense expenditures abroad, and that more effective "tying" of foreign aid funds to purchases in the United States would be instituted. Together, he said, by January, 1965, these programs would effect a reduction of $900,000,000 to $1,000,000,000 in the payments deficit.

Mr. Kennedy also promised continued pressure for a greater sharing of the foreign aid burden with other nations and for the elimination of trade barriers on impending United States exports.

He said the rise in the discount rate, resulting in increased short-term interest rates, would "make it considerably more attractive" for foreigners to hold their assets in dollars, including short-term United States Government securities.

July 19, 1963

JOHNSON URGES RESTRAINT IN U. S. INVESTING ABROAD TO CUT PAYMENTS DEFICIT

CURB ON TOURISTS

Would Cut Purchases for Travelers to $50 —Tax Widened

By EDWIN L. DALE Jr.
Special to The New York Times

WASHINGTON, Feb. 10—President Johnson called on American business and banking today for a broad new voluntary effort to cut down their lending and investing abroad to eliminate the deficit in the nation's international payments.

The President's specific measures in a special Balance of Payments Message to Congress were relatively few and relatively mild. But the potential savings from his appeal to private business and banking would be enormous, running into the billions of dollars, if he gets cooperation.

[Leading bankers and businessmen reacted cautiously, though generally favorably, to President Johnson's message. What seemed to impress them most was Mr. Johnson's request that they exercise voluntary restraint in lending money or making investments abroad.]

Would Cut Outflow

Mr. Johnson asked Congress to reduce the duty-free exemption for purchases abroad by tourists from $100 to $50, with the $50 limit applying to the retail instead of the wholesale price. The exemption would be allowed only for goods actually carried by the traveler when he returned to the United States.

This set of changes, it is expected, would cut about $100 million from the nation's net tourist dollar outflow of $1.6 billion a year.

The President also announced, as a second specific measure, that he had extended the new interest-equalization tax to loans made abroad by banks. It now applies only to the purchase of foreign securities.

Congress was asked to extend the tax for two years beyond its scheduled expiration date of next Dec. 30, and to apply it, effective today, to loans by lenders other than banks.

The heart of the President's program was his appeal for a new program of voluntary restraint by banks and business. He asked Congress for an antitrust exemption to permit participation of banks in his program.

The Federal Reserve Board announced some details of the bank program today and the Commerce Department will elaborate on the business aspects of the plan within two weeks. The President will call separate meetings of leaders of both groups at the White House to ask for cooperation.

The program will include such elements as voluntary targets for reducing the outflow of funds by individual companies and banks, but there will be no coercion.

Last year the total outflow of private capital was $6.5 billion, up more than $2 billion from the year before, and these flows were the major reason why the balance of payments, which measures flows of funds into and out of the country, has continued to show a large deficit. The size of the capital outflow indicates the scope for improvement if business and banking heed the President's appeal.

The payments deficit last year, according to the Commerce Department, was $3 billion, only a small improvement from the $3.3 billion deficit in 1963. The President said in his message that improvements over the last four years in such areas as exports, tying foreign aid to purchases of American goods, and reduction of overseas military spending had saved $3.5 billion, but that this was offset by a rise of $2.5 billion in capital outflows, most of it in 1964.

These outflows include direct investment by corporations in foreign plants and other facilities, purchase of foreign stocks and bonds, medium-term loans by banks to foreigners and a variety of short-term lending and investment.

Corporations were asked not only to "limit" their direct investments abroad but also "their deposits in foreign banks and their holding of foreign financial assets, until their efforts—and those of all Americans—have restored balance in the country's international accounts."

Cooperation Urged

This was a reference to the practice of corporations of investing temporarily idle funds in foreign banks to earn a slightly higher rate of interest.

At a press briefing, a high-ranking Government official said, "If voluntary programs don't work, some other means will have to be found and that will probably be less agreeable."

In his message, the President said, "I have no doubt that American bankers and businessmen will respond to the nation's need. With their cooperation, we can block the leakage of funds abroad without blocking the vital flow of credit to American business."

The President said today, "The state of the dollar is strong—far stronger than three or four years ago." Pledging again that its value of $35 to an ounce of gold would be maintained, the President said, "Those who hope for its weakness hope in vain."

But he said progress in eliminating the payments deficit was "too slow." He vowed a "firm determination to bring an end to our balance of payments deficit."

"We cannot and do not assume that the world's willingness to hold dollars is unlimited," the President said.

The message cited four basic

strengths of the dollar:

¶"The world's most productive and efficient economy."

¶"The world's largest supply of gold, fully pledged to honor this country's dollar obligations."

¶Overseas assets of all kinds of $88 billion, $37 billion larger than foreign dollar holdings, including a margin of $15 billion in private assets.

¶"The world's most favorable trade position," with a surplus of exports over imports of $3.6 billion excluding exports financed by foreign aid.

In Congress, Democrats almost unanimously praised the message, though there was a cautious note from Senator A. Willis Robertson, Democrat of Virginia, chairman of the Banking Committee, who said the President should have curbed foreign aid and other overseas Government spending. Republicans were generally critical, saying the President had not proposed measures that were tough enough.

Government officials said the efficacy of the program would depend largely on the degree of cooperation offered by business and banking and said they hoped the cooperation would be forthcoming.

The President announced that Japan would be allowed to float new securities or make bank loans up to a total of $100 million a year exempt from the interest-equalization tax. Canada is already exempt from the tax on securities, but will not be exempt for bank loans.

The President said he had received "firm assurance" that the Canadian Government would pursue policies that would limit the new issues of securities to an amount that would just cover Canada's own international payments deficit on trade and other accounts. Capital from the United States has been used for years by Canada to balance her accounts.

Technical Changes

The President said he would ask Congress for technical tax changes to help induce more foreign investment in United States securities.

He also said the Defense Department and the foreign-aid program would "step up their efforts to cut dollar costs to the bone." With most of such savings already achieved, officials estimated that further savings would be only about $50 million a year. Savings up to now are estimated at $600 million a year and they would have been greater if prices had not risen abroad where troops were stationed.

There was no proposal for an exit tax of $50 or $100 on tourists—an idea that was considered in the Government and rejected.

The President said that if the United States measured its balance of payments the way most foreign countries do, it would have showed a deficit of only $1.3 billion in 1964 instead of $3 billion. The difference is that the United States counts a rise in foreign private holdings of dollars as an outflow, whereas other countries count an increase in foreign private holdings of their currency as an inflow of investment.

The President said that while this way of measuring the deficit gives "in many ways a better measure of our progress," than the traditional accounting, it "does not reduce our need for further action."

Notably Brief

The President was notably brief on the use of monetary policy as a cure for the payments deficit. Many bankers have argued that tighter money would curb the flow of dollars abroad by reducing the availability of funds in the banks and by raising domestic interest rates, and this view has some support in the Federal Reserve System and much support abroad.

The President said only that he was confident the Federal Reserve would "continue its efforts to maintain short-term rates of return in the American money market."

"At the same time," he continued, "in view of the heavy flow of private savings into our capital markets, I expect the continuation of essential stability in interest rates."

The President was emphatic in saying that American wages and prices must be held in check to preserve the present competitive position of the United States in world export markets.

"Unless American business and labor hew to the Government's price-wage guideposts," he said, "we will run grave risks of losing our competitive advantage."

In a discussion of the international financial system, the President firmly rejected the recent call of President de Gaulle of France for a return to a pure gold standard, in which all deficits and surpluses would be settled by a transfer of gold among nations.

The President said, "Rather, we must build on the system we now have, a system which has served the world during the past 20 years."

He noted that when the United States eliminates its payments deficit, the world will no longer have a source of new reserves through accumulations of dollar holdings to supplement gold, and this could create "a shortage of reserves."

"We need to continue our work on the development of supplementary sources of reserves to head off that threat," the President said.

February 11, 1965

COMPANIES IN U.S. HELP TO NARROW GAP IN PAYMENTS

DEFICIT REDUCED

Cut in Investments Abroad Curtails Dollar Outflow

By RICHARD RUTTER

The money comes in, but more goes out.

That is the essence of the nation's balance-of-payments problem. American corporations are doing their part to help solve it.

The result has already showed up. Last week Secretary of Commerce John T. Connor announced that the United States in the second quarter had a surplus in its international payments. Mr. Connor, although pointing out that for the year as a whole there might be a payments deficit—the gap between funds leaving the country and those coming in—did cite a large return of liquid funds from abroad under the voluntary program adopted by business last February.

That program involved a cutback in foreign investment and other spending abroad. Banks were asked to curtail overseas loans and corporations to watch their foreign commitments.

First-Quarter Deficit

In the first quarter of this year there was a deficit in the nation's international payments of $733 million, indicating an annual rate of $2.9 billion. In the second quarter there was a small surplus, estimated at $200 million.

To flash back: the deficit in 1962 was $3.6 billion; in 1963, some $3.3 billion, and last year, $3.1 billion.

Commerce Secretary Connor has said publicly that business cooperation in the problem has been "magnificent" and he means it. He has also said, however, that some elements of the program are likely to "come apart" if it is continued beyond 1966.

The Government is known to be particularly pleased at the efforts of business to raise money abroad for foreign investments, such as a recent big Socony Mobil loan. Those borrowing plans involved $310 million, including $244 million in Europe, almost all of it at higher interest rates than in this country.

Problem Remains

The big problem is exports. Well over half of the planned reduction in the balance of payments of $1.3 billion was to come from export expansion, but developments like the New York dock strike and the slowdown of business in a few foreign countries such as Japan are threatening the target. It is not now clear that the $1.3 billion target can be achieved.

But the problem does remain.

Only last Thursday a member of the Federal Reserve Board noted that a continuing deficit in the nation's international payments would be needed "for some time" to stimulate expanding world trade. The remark was made by J. L. Robertson in testimony before a Senate Banking subcommittee. Mr. Robertson said:

"It seems to me that in the present situation there will be a continuing need for more dollars in the world. These should be supplied either through a deficit in our balance of payments or some other kind of unit."

Meanwhile, a New York Times survey shows that companies with a big stake in foreign business are taking decisive steps to reduce the outward move of funds. For instance:

E. I. du Pont de Nemours & Co. is working out details for

the financing of two new construction projects in Europe. The company has indicated that financing will be done so as not to affect adversely this nation's balance-of-payments situation in accordance with President Johnson's voluntary program for industry.

The construction will include facilities for the manufacture of plastics and fluorocarbons at Dordrecht, the Netherlands. A plant for the manufacture of polyester fiber and nylon for the European market will be constructed near Uentrop, in the province of Unna, Germany.

Olin Cooperating

Gordon Grand, president of the Olin Mathieson Chemical Corporation, last week made the following statement:

"When President Johnson called for the assistance of business early this year to alleviate the imbalance of payments, Olin immediately took steps to cooperate and to improve on its already favorable balance.

"Olin's efforts have borne fruit. With exports ahead of forecasts, because overseas borrowings have been increased, and as a result of the increasing business from existing overseas operations, our company is making a substantial and increasing contribution to the inflow of dollars.

"While cooperating to help to improve the nation's payments balance, Olin is continuing its planned growth overseas. To an important extent such investment in the past is contributing to improved dollar earnings at present. However, each new overseas project will be analyzed carefully to minimize dollar spending. We believe we can continue an aggressive overseas program and comply with the President's wishes.

"We believe also there is a mutuality of responsibility, that the Government in its overseas activities must watch its own expenditures."

Malcolm C. Stewart, vice president of the Gillette Company, said last week: "Gillette is living within the guidelines the President requested and has had no problems in complying with the balance-of-payments program. Neither earnings nor expansion plans have been affected by the program."

Frank L. Linton, vice president and controller of the Allied Chemical Corporation, commented: "Allied Chemical Corporation has a large positive, indeed, very favorable, balance of payments. And we anticipate that the company will make the improvement in 1965 that was requested by President Johnson."

U.S. Rubber's Position

The United States Rubber Company, with large overseas investments, also is con... ...ns of the voluntary program. George R. Vila, chairman and president, said last week:

"For some time it has been our policy when making investments abroad to borrow as much capital as possible in the country of operation and export a minimum of capital from the United States.

"Since 1961, when we set up a company in Switzerland, we have been able to borrow money in the Swiss money market. In 1963 we were able to float debentures in that country. We plan to continue if possible with these arrangements and hence continue to contribute to a favorable balance of payments for the United States, as we have done for several years."

United States Rubber plans to construct a new tire cord fabric plant in Luxembourg, which, it is hoped, will be the start of a European textile center to serve the needs of the Common Market. Initial investment in the tire cord plant will be about $6 million and financing will be obtained through European sources. Construction will begin in the near future and completion is expected by mid-1966.

Then just the other week, United States Rubber announced that its Luxembourg subsidiary, known as United States Rubber UniRoyal Holdings, had completed an arrangement to borrow $14 million by issuing bonds in the European market. The purpose of the borrowing is to finance expansion programs and provide working capital for overseas operations.

The company said, "the borrowing is consistent with the Federal Government's policy of encouraging American companies to limit the flow of dollars for their international operations." The bonds will be quoted on the London and Luxembourg stock exchanges.

A spokesman for the General Motors Corporation, which is one of the largest overseas investors, said last week: "We are continuing to examine every phase of our overseas operations to see if we can improve the situation." But the official also said the company stands on remarks made by Frederic G. Donner, chairman, back in March. A part follows:

"As a matter of fact, we could go back to 1954, when we had a very simple statement in the annual report on the way we operate abroad. We explained at that time the development and expansion programs which were in process at Opel and Vauxhall.

"We explained that those programs would be financed as in the past, principally by retained earnings of the local plants or by local borrowings."

General Motors reported that in the 19 years since 1946, its overseas earnings abroad averaged 9 per cent of all earnings. But, at the same time, dividends remitted from abroad averaged 9 per cent of all dividends paid to the stockholders in this country.

Mr. Donner added: "If we take the last five years, we have been able to contribute to the balance of payments, to achieving the favorable balance of payments, on account of export of product and on account of the remission of dividends, an amount of approximately $2.2 billion."

Jersey Standard

From the Standard Oil Company (New Jersey) came this report:

"The company generated about one-third billion dollars in 1964 to the United States balance of payments." Jersey Standard added that it is cooperating with the recommendations of the Secretary of Commerce and added that its foreign affiliates have been borrowing abroad for many years and that any increase in borrowing would be a continuation of past practices.

William S. Sneath, treasurer of the Union Carbide Corporation, had this report:

"We are acutely aware of the necessity to increase the favorable balance of payments of the United States. As a matter of fact, we have always conducted our overseas operations in line with the principles recently established by the Administration for conducting our current affairs. As a result, Union Carbide had a favorable balance of payments in 1963 of $74 million. This increased to $135 million in 1964, and we expect it to reach $170 million this year.

"The most important factor in our balance - of - payments position is our export sales, which reached $158 million in 1964. Sales so far this year have continued at this high rate, totaling $75 million for the first six months, and we are confident these sales will attain last year's level.

"Our experience has been that these investments stimulate export sales from this country, particularly sales of newer, more sophisticated products."

I.B.M's Comment

The International Business Machines Corporation operates overseas through its I. B. M. World Trade Corporation, a giant of its own. In regard to the balance-of-payments situation, the parent company had this comment:

The I. B. M. World Trade Corporation expects to accomplish an increase in its favorable balance-of-payments position over 1964. It plans to finance its overseas growth primarily from overseas sources.

The Ford Motor Company said last April that it fully shared President Johnson's concern over the balance-of-payments situation of this country and that it was participating actively in steps to restore a favorable balance. Last week Ford said:

"Ford's net contribution for improvement in the transactions required for reporting to the Department of Commerce are being maintained. We are watching the matter closely to ensure that Ford's level of net contribution to reducing the United States' balance of payments deficit will be met."

Henry Ford 2d, chairman of Ford, said: "We intend to finance our spending for expansion in other countries almost entirely from funds obtained outside the United States so that it will not have an adverse effect on the balance of payments. On the contrary, we expect to increase our net positive contribution last year to more than $400 million."

I. T. & T. Arrangements

The International Telephone and Telegraph Corporation does not find itself in a bind as far as the balance - of - payments situation is concerned. The nature of its operating policies has enabled the company to work out financial arrangements with local banks and most expansion funds have come from internally generated funds and from local borrowings.

In addition, there has been a steady flow of distributed income from its foreign affiliates to the United States, which has been used for domestic investment. As a matter of operating procedure, the parent has never held short-term assets abroad.

The head of Pfizer International, a subsidiary of Chas. Pfizer & Co., Inc., told a Senate subcommittee the other day that American investments in manufacturing plants and distribution facilities overseas, particularly in developed countries, make an important and growing positive contribution to the United States balance of payments.

Richard C. Fenton, president and chairman of Pfizer International, urged that government and private programs be undertaken to encourage as many as 10,000 United States companies to establish themselves abroad. This will create jobs at home by stimulating production of materials for export and help the balance of payments.

American Investment Abroad Is an Inviting Target for Critics

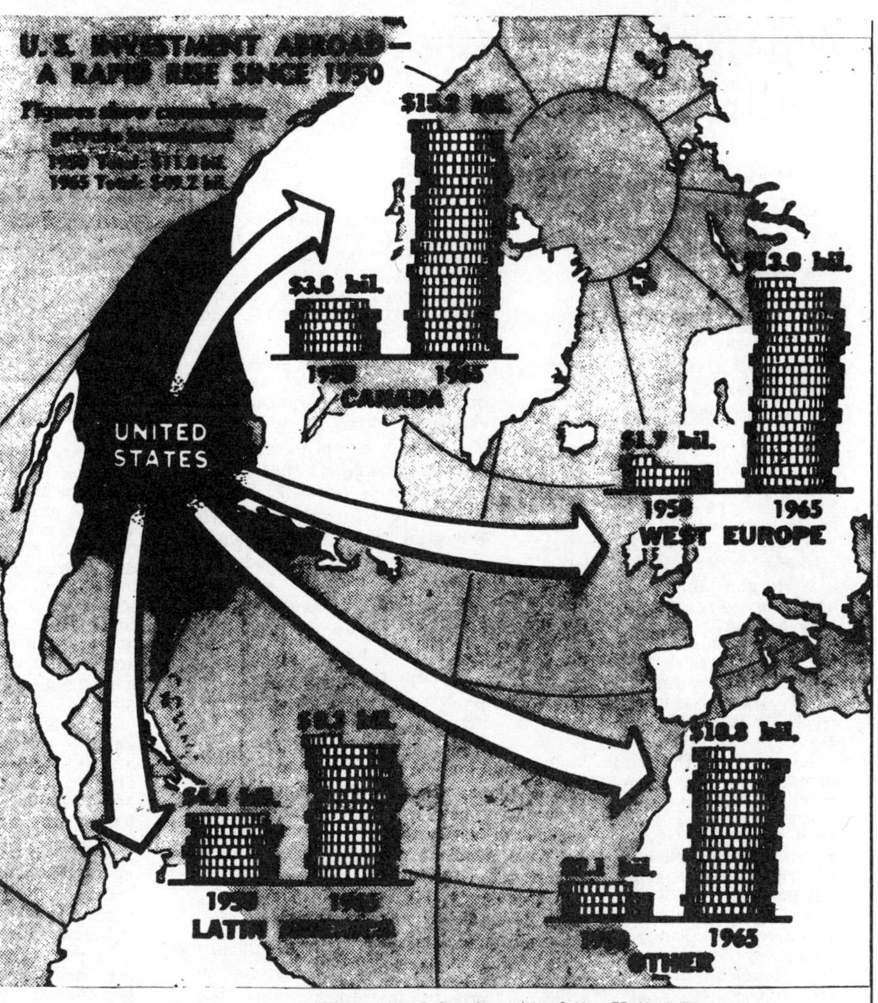

By RICHARD E. MOONEY
Special to The New York Times

PARIS, Dec. 17—"Rather than be judged as a rival, it ought to be considered an auxiliary all the more precious because it alone permits an increased amount of productive labor and useful enterprise to be set to work."

Alexander Hamilton said it, in 1791, about foreign business investment in the United States. Today the issue runs the other way. The statesmen, financiers and business men of the world talk now about the rising tide of U. S. investment abroad, and not all of them are so tolerant as Hamilton.

The most recent case in point is Britain's Prime Minister Harold Wilson, who said in London recently: "Our American friends, because they are friends, will understand when I say that, however much we welcome new American investments here, as in other parts of Europe, there is no one on either side of the Channel who wants to see capital investment in Europe involve domination or, in the last resort, subjugation."

The British, it must be said, are neither so hostile to, nor leery of, U. S. investment as Mr. Wilson implied. The point of his remarks was not to scare Americans away, but to soften up France for Britain's entry to the European Common Market by appealing to the well-known French hostility *and* leeriness about the overseas expansion of American industrial giants.

The United States is, after all, the greatest and most talented industrial power the world has ever known, and it is still growing. Most European big business is small by the American scale. And thus the European tends to be awed if not frightened, respectful if not resentful.

The over-all book value—which greatly understates the actual value—of direct private American investment in business operations overseas at the end of last year was almost $50-billion. It has grown in recent years at an average rate of more than 6 per cent, and last year alone it grew by 11 per cent.

The impact of all this investment is felt in several ways and many places, mostly in the countries where the investment is made but also in the United States. The impact at home is on the balance of international payments, where the strain of this ever increasing wave of outflowing capital caused Washington to tighten controls on it once again this week.

The U. S. business community argues endlessly but futilely that the return on overseas investment eventually brings back into the country much more money than is sent out. The plain fact remains that the Government is concerned with the current outflow and feels it cannot wait for the eventual greater inflow.

This capital flowing out of the United States is, of course, capital flowing into other countries, all of them smaller. It is capable of at least as much impact where it goes as where it comes from. As an inflationary force it can indeed be a problem, but well within the power of the national authorities to dampen. On the other hand, in Hamiltonian terms, the greater effect is the economic benefit of increased "productive labor and useful enterprise."

The big political question, implied by Prime Minister Wilson and asserted by General de Gaulle, is whether this investment leads to "domination" or "subjugation."

To take an extreme but significant example, the United States dominates France's computer industry. To General de Gaulle's distress, this important French industry is almost all American. Moreover, this domination became subjugation when Washington refused to permit the French Atomic Energy Commission to buy some extra-large computers made in the United States. Recently this ban was lifted, but the French will remember it for a long, long time.

In less extreme circumstances, American subsidiaries are repeatedly under attack for laying off workers, or shifting production, or otherwise disrupting things to suit their worldwide plans, without concern for local conditions.

In general terms, American investment overseas is rarely more than a small fraction of any country's total business activity. In specific businesses in specific countries it can be, and is, much more. But in any case, it is foreign—big, rich foreign. It is an inviting target.

December 18, 1966

OUTLAYS ABROAD CALLED PERILOUS

Moratorium Urged as Balm to Economic Nationalism

By M. J. ROSSANT

A moratorium on private American investment in foreign countries has been put forward as the first step in a sweeping new program to combat the rising tide of economic nationalism abroad.

The call for a moratorium is the provocative brainchild of Leo Model, head of the Wall Street concern of Model, Roland & Co., Inc., which does a substantial international securities business.

Writing in the current issue of Foreign Affairs, the prestigious quarterly put out by the Council on Foreign Relations, Mr. Model notes that the American stake abroad makes it "the third largest economy in the world" in terms of gross national product.

He reasons that this huge increase in American investment abroad has generated a resurgence of economic "nationalism" that may have very painful consequences for the United States if something is not done to curb it.

A curbing of investment, particularly in Europe, where American companies have almost doubled their stakes in the last five years, is his remedy for removing the threat of American domination and assuring better treatment of American companies.

He also calls on American companies operating abroad to act as good corporate citizens of their host countries. He thinks they should be guided by foreign rather than American practices and suggests that they make more use of foreign nationals in the managements of their subsidiaries, encourage local investors to buy their shares, and deliberately refrain from seeking to control basic industry.

Mr. Model envisions a full-scale effort that goes beyond "nominal" attempts at foreign participation. He insists that American companies abroad must not be subject to the Government's Trading With the Enemy Act, except in emergency, and he suggests that American companies consider setting up holding companies for their European subsidiaries, selling shares wherever the subsidiaries operate.

It is his contention that American business would be served if it took the initiative in reform rather than reacting to foreign demands or depending on the power of the State Department. He said, "The exercise of diplomatic pressure for the benefit of U. S. companies may create serious resentment and merely worsen the investment climate."

Even though Mr. Model wants less Washington influence, the Administration may be more inclined than American industry to welcome a moratorium on private investment. For one thing, a check on dollar outflows would provide immediate help to the nation's ailing balance of payments. For another, it would blunt anti-American attacks, from General de Gaulle and the Arab states, that have grown in virulence.

The plan may gain some support from established American enterprises abroad because Mr. Model puts limits on a moratorium. He does not want to interfere with investments to retain a market position abroad. But he insists that there should be a period of consolidation to prevent expansion into new fields and to buy up existing companies.

Outlook Not Good

A moratorium on new investment would follow the Administration's policy in setting up its voluntary program of restraints for banks and businesses, which hit hardest at companies that were planning to go abroad but had not yet made investments.

But the Administration's program was adopted primarily for balance of payments reasons. Mr. Model is much more concerned about foreign fears and resentment that have arisen from the so-called American "invasion" of their economies.

Since the outlook for the balance of payments is not good and the Arab-Israeli conflict brought new threats of nationalism against American companies, the need for fresh action may gain ground. And in some quarters, at least, the idea of a moratorium seems as attractive as a capital issues committee or other devices to cut down on investment.

In proposing a new program, Mr. Model drew heavily on his personal experience. A native of Germany and a member of the Council on Foreign Relations, he has participated in many foreign ventures in Europe and South America, particularly in Brazil.

He thinks American investment has played a constructive role and can do a great deal more, but he is impressed by the increasing amount of discrimination against American concerns, which could ultimately provoke wholesale discrimination abroad. In his view, Washington's major responsibility is to see to it that wherever discrimination takes place, it is not aimed solely at American companies, and where nationalization is decreed, fair compensation is provided.

It is evident that Mr. Model does not believe his program will eliminate economic or specific anti-American discrimination. With many American companies having resources greater than the entire economy of Belgium and with total American output abroad ranking behind only the United States and the Soviet Union, there is bound to be fear and suspicion about the American presence.

But Mr. Model does think that excessive discrimination can be avoided, provided American companies recognize their responsibilities in time. He sums up, "If our companies use heir power with consideration for the well-being of other countries, as well as our own, they can be of tremendous help in creating a prosperous world economy . . . Otherwise, their economic power will be a constant irritant in our diplomatic relations with the rest of the world and will ultimately defeat their own interests."

June 25, 1967

Opinions Vary on Capital Flow Abroad

By KATHLEEN McLAUGHLIN

Periodically in recent years a hue and cry has been raised against United States investors abroad, with implications of an imminent take-over of one or another nation's economy by alien capital. Protests have been most resounding and most frequent from Canada, but they come by no means exclusively from there.

At a meeting in Brussels a few months ago, Ambassador at Large W. Averell Harriman was irked by a prediction from a Belgian financial adviser that a "confrontation" between Europe and America would develop over increasing United States participation in industry in that region.

If Europeans complained about American investments in their area, retorted Mr. Harriman, why didn't they invest more in the United States, which stood ready to welcome their capital?

Shortly thereafter an executive of an American multinational corporation commented on the growing warmth of the welcome he and his compatriots were getting in Europe, as present and potential investors. Never before, he declared, had they been so ardently wooed.

Divergent Groups

Such conflicting attitudes characterize the divergent groups in most goegraphical regions, either advocating or opposing entrance of exterior capital. Those opposed to such moves see it as a menace to national sovereignty the advocates hold it to be a boon, essential to maximum development.

Statistically, the record is woefully inadequate, but other evidence is mounting that outward and onward movement of investment funds is increasingly reciprocal, not confined to Americans, and that the tendency to seek profits wherever opportunity offers is common to international-minded business interests at all points of the compass.

Publication in September of the annual report by the Department of Commerce on "International Investments of the United States in 1966" suggests that Americans offer a natural target for attacks by nationalists because of the larger scope of their operations. An equally potent factor undoubtedly is that totals are in the public domain and may be gauged, while those of other countries can only be guessed, for the most part.

Comparable data published over the last 25 years by major industrial nations are no longer available. Those from Britain and Canada, notably, have not been released since 1964.

Sources in this country state that the records are consistently maintained abroad in even more detail, especially by governments exercising close financial controls.

Two reasons are advanced as logical explanations for the cessation of publication elsewhere. One is the complexity of keeping an accurate and up-to-date tally in the face of liquidations in some regions, and delayed notifications of new investments, in others. Another is the risk if unintentional disclosures of identity of some large corporations, through shrewd dededuction from changes in an area or country report.

Details Listed

Figures in the latest Department of Commerce summary show that total assets held abroad by United States residents and the Federal Government amounted to $112-billion at the end of 1966, while those held in the United States alone, by foreign residents, were $60-billion.

The tabulated distribution of United States assets abroad last year puts Western Europe in first place, with $32.2-billion; Canada, second, with $27.5-billion, and Latin America third, with $19.4-billion.

The same sequence held true for foreign investments in the United States. Western Europe was credited with $35.2-billion, Canada with $8-billion, and Latin America with $5.9-billion.

Until and unless disclosure is made by these and other countries of their assets and investments in addition to those in the United States, the picture of global interchange of investments will remain fragmentary.

Minus the financial aspects, however, the proliferation around the world of crosscurrents of investment capital is readily apparent through hundreds of periodicals and newspapers reporting on international business developments. Their coverage links projects with the names of corporations, large and small, in developing as well as developed lands.

Among emerging countries, those with a growing influx of foreign funds to publicize are usually endowed with commercially valuable natural resources, plus progressive regimes alert to offer a receptive climate for what is often "risk" capital from external sources. In their eagerness, some of these governments have even mortgaged their future revenues too far ahead, by going overboard on the incentives conceded.

Some Keep Barriers

Others, clinging to old resentment and suspicions, have sacrificed years of progress by keeping the barriers high and electing to go it alone, on local initiative.

On the middle ground, both capital-exporting and capital-mporting countries at present tend toward the "joint venture" type of partnership, in which technology and backing from abroad are merged with the domestic team's knowledge of their nation's language, traditions and contacts, indispensable in a successful enterprise.

The present tendency of multinational corporations to leapfrog national borders in pursuit f profits could be—and are—mpeded by adverse political shifts, or the repercussions of a wave of protectionism, at east temporarily. On the other hand, an impressive number of qualified executives—to whom frontiers loom as irritating frustrations—visualize as inevitable the gradual evolution of the world as an economic whole.

November 5, 1967

INVESTING CURBS OUTLINED BY U.S.

3 Categories of Countries Affected by Controls

By H. J. MAIDENBERG

Special to The New York Times

WASHINGTON, April 23—The Administration outlined today the three categories of foreign lands that were affected by its controls on foreign investment and repatriation of overseas earnings.

The controls were ordered by President Johnson on New Year's Day to help correct the nation's adverse balance of payments this year.

The lists were presented to a closed session of the Foreign Economic Policy Subcommittee of the House Committee on Foreign Affairs by Joseph W. Bartlett, acting director of the Office of Foreign Direct Investments.

Mr. Bartlett told the subcommittee that "to accomplish the ambitious and important $1-billion savings sought under the program, the regulations are structured with three major provisions." These are:

¶Annual limits have been established for new foreign direct investment capital transactions, comprised both of capital outflows from the United States and the re-investment of earnings abroad.

¶A specific portion of total annual earnings yielded by investments abroad must be repatriated home each year.

¶Bank deposits and other liquid assets held abroad may not exceed the end-of-month average balances held during 1965 and 1966.

To effect these regulations, non-Communist countries and Yugoslavia have been classified according to their economic needs and potential drain on the United States balance of payments. They have been scheduled A, B and C lands.

The C countries are Austria, Belgium, Denmark, France, West Germany, Italy, the Netherlands, Norway, Portugal, South Africa, South-West Africa, Spain, Sweden and Switzerland, as well as the so-called "tax havens" of Andora, Liechtenstein, Luxembourg, Monaco and San Marino.

Although C countries are under a moratorium imposed on new capital outflows overseas, a direct United States investor may reinvest in 1968 up to 35 per cent of his average direct investment transactions during 1965-66.

The B countries were listed as Australia, the Bahamas, Bermuda, Canada, Hong Kong, Iran, Iraq, Ireland, Japan, New Zealand and Britain, along with Abu Dhabi, Bahrain, Kuwait-Saudi Arabia (neutral zone), Libya Qatar and Saudi Arabia, al' oil-rich lands.

Monetary specialists here said that the richer oil lands are traditionally large buyers of gold in London, which they obtain by trading dollar profits. Canada, on the other hand, has been exempted but was listed because legislation toward that end is pending.

B countries other than Canada may not receive capital outflows and reinvested earnings this year in excess of 65 per cent of the average in the base period of 1965 to 1966.

However, the Department of Commerce said that United States investors would not be permitted to utilize the Canadian exemption as "a means of transferring unauthorized funds to a third country."

As for A lands, which include all non-Communist countries and Yugoslavia, the Government authorized new capital transfers and investments as high as 10 per cent above the average for the base period.

"The preferential treatment with respect to Schedule A lands is consistent with United States policy that encourages investment in less developed countries in order to stimulate their economic advancement and stability," Mr. Bartlett testified.

Generally, the controls apply to individuals or companies that own at least 10 per cent of a foreign business that is worth more than $100,000 and has earnings of more than $50,000.

The acting chief of the Office of Foreign Direct Investments of the Department of Commerce said that the mandatory controls were needed because the balance of payments deficit had soared to $3.6-billion last year from $1.4-billion in 1966 and $1.3-billion in 1965.

"The deterioration in our deficit, coming at a time when the world monetary system was already under great strain, added new doubts as to United States financial stability and made decisive action on our part essential," he added.

The first-quarter balance of payments deficit, expected to be issued in mid-May, is expected to be a "shocker," according to one Government official, because "last year's figures were helped by certain special transactions arising from monetary conditions." He did not elaborate.

In addition, he said that the large but as yet unmeasured outflow of money because of the gold crisis in the first quarter had not been tallied. He also said that the deficit would reflect the heavy cost of the copper strike and imports of steel in anticipation of a strike in that industry this summer.

April 24, 1968

U.S. RESTRICTIONS ON FUND OUTFLOW EASED SLIGHTLY

Nixon Bars 'Patchwork Quilt of Controls' to Improve Balance of Payments

URGES CURE FOR CAUSES

Officials See Little Rise in Capital Export Because of Tight Credit at Home

By EDWIN L. DALE Jr.
Special to The New York Times

WASHINGTON, April 4—The Nixon Administration announced today a modest relaxation of the three controls imposed by Presidents Kennedy and Johnson over American lending and investing abroad.

President Nixon, in a statement issued in Florida, said the United States balance-of-payments problem must be solved by dealing "with fundamentals" aimed at correcting "the root causes of our problem" and not by "a patchwork quilt of controls."

In Washington, officials announcing the details of the relaxation said it would probably produce little additional flow of dollars abroad because of tight credit conditions at home. They termed the new and larger allowed outflows under the lending and investing programs largely "theoretical" in today's conditions, but said the more liberal regulations could help in some cases.

Details of Moves Given

These were the measures announced today:

First, Secretary of Commerce Maurice H. Stans announced five changes in the program of controls over direct investment abroad by American business corporations. A major one will exempt from control investments of up to $1-million, instead of $200,000 as at present.

Taken together, the five changes would permit a theoretical increase of $400-million in the dollar outflow for direct investment this year over the target established in December—from $2.95-billion to $3.35-billion.

Second, the Federal Reserve Board announced a second, optional method for each bank to calculate its ceiling under the "voluntary" program governing lending to foreigners. The main purpose is to make sure that all banks have enough room under the ceiling to finance United States exports, the board's statement said. Another major reason is "to resolve some serious equity problems," it added.

$400-Million More

The increase in the ceiling would permit an additional $400-million of lending abroad, again in theory.

The new Federal Reserve optional ceiling would be 1½ per cent of a bank's total assets as of last Dec. 31. For the larger banks, the present ceiling is 103 per cent of their foreign loans outstanding at the end of 1964. For non-bank financial institutions, the ceiling was simply increased, from 95 per cent of an end-of-1967 base to 100 per cent.

Third, the President signed an Executive order reducing the effective rate of the interest-equalization tax, applied to purchases by Americans of foreign stocks and bonds, from 1¼ per cent to ¾ of 1 per cent. The tax, in effect, raises the effective interest rate that a foreign borrower must pay.

With present high United States interest rates, the effect of this change will be "negligible," according to Paul A. Volcker, Under Secretary of the Treasury for Monetary Affairs.

In his statement, President Nixon emphasized that the cure for the balance-of-payments problem was the same as the cure for inflation at home—"a strong budget surplus and monetary restraint."

"Fundamental economics," he said, "call for conditions that make it possible to rebuild our trade surplus and ultimate dismantling of the network of direct controls which may seem useful in the short run but are self-defeating in the long run."

The President listed proposed action or negotiation—largely similar to programs of the previous Administration—in fields such as trade, offsetting the cost of stationing troops abroad and encouraging foreign travel to the United States.

Mr. Nixon repeated that "we seek no restrictions on the American tourist's freedom to travel." He also endorsed publicly for the first time "early activation" of the new plan for "paper gold," known as special drawing rights, in the International Monetary Fund.

The five changes made in the corporate direct foreign investment control program were to:

¶Increase the minimum free from control to $1-million from $200,000.

¶Abolish quarterly reporting requirements for the smaller investors — those investing less than $1-million.

¶Permit companies, in establishing their investment "allowable," to use either the present 1965-66 base period or an alternate amount equal to 30 per cent of their 1968 foreign earnings.

¶Relax regulations governing extractive industries, including oil, affecting mainly exploration and development costs.

¶Relax regulations governing international airlines, aimed in particular at allowing investments abroad needed for accommodating the new jumbo jets.

April 5, 1969

NIXON ANNOUNCES TOUGH U.S. STAND ON EXPROPRIATION

Says Countries That Fail to Give Compensation Can Lose Foreign Aid

EXCEPTIONS PERMITTED

'Major Factors' Affecting American Interests May Prevent Retaliation

By ROBERT B. SEMPLE Jr.
Special to The New York Times

WASHINGTON, Jan. 19—President Nixon announced today that the United States would now follow a tougher attitude toward foreign countries that expropriate private American holdings without adequate and swift compensation.

He said in a statement that foreign countries could assume that the United States would refuse to make any new aid agreements with them unless they were taking "reasonable steps" to provide just compensation, or unless there were other factors that in the judgment of the United States required the continuation of aid.

The statement, issued at the White House, appeared to be directed largely at several Latin-American countries that have nationalized United States investments.

International Law Cited

The key passage declared:

"Under international law, the United States has a right to expect that the taking of American property will be nondiscriminatory; that it will be for a public purpose; and that its citizens will receive prompt, adequate, and effective compensation from the expropriating country.

"Thus when a country expropriates a significant United States interest without making reasonable provision for such compensation to United States citizens, we will presume that the United States will not extend new bilateral economic benefits to the expropriating country unless and until it is determined that the country is taking reasonable steps to provide adequate compensation or that there are major factors affecting United States interests which require continuance of all or part of these benefits."

For the first time Mr. Nixon set forth a systematic Presidential view of expropriations. **Officials said that until now most expropriations had been handled case by case without general guidelines.**

The new policy represents a compromise between the positions taken by John B. Connally, Secretary of the Treasury, and the State Department. Mr. Connally had wanted an automatic cutoff of United States loans to countries that take over private foreign hold-

ings without prior settlements. The State Department had wanted more flexibility.

Economic retaliation will not be automatic, as the Treasury had hoped, but the new policy includes the threat of eventual retaliation if the expropriating country fails to move quickly to provide compensation.

Peter G. Peterson, the President's foreign economic adviser, who briefed newsmen, said that the policy should also "accelerate decisions" on expropriations and presumably those decisions would be to withhold funds.

The State Department got the flexibility it wanted, however, in Mr. Nixon's language permitting aid to continue if other "major factors"—that is, national security— were considered more important than prompt and fair compensation. The State Department had argued that an approach that was too tough would jeopardize American foreign policy interests for the sake of a few investors.

The statement also said that to strengthen its bargaining position with nations that expropriate American-owned companies, the United States could be expected to "withhold its support from loans under consideration in multilateral development banks."

This was a reference to the World Bank, the Inter-American Development Bank and other international lending institutions in which the United States, because of its large contributions, wields great influence. In the case of the Inter-American Bank, its influence permits it to veto long-term, interest-free loans to countries of whose policies it disapproves.

The statement said that the new policy would not apply to "humanitarian assistance"—earthquake and famine relief, for example. And Mr. Peterson emphasized that any cutoff in aid would not apply to funds already obligated, but to "new requests."

The debate within the Administration that finally produced today's statement began after several Latin-American countries, including Chile, Peru, Ecuador and Bolivia, expropriated private foreign holdings of which the United States share is estimated by its owners to be worth between $500-million and $1-billion. A large part of this is accounted for by the holdings of three major copper companies—Kennecott, Anaconda, and Cerro—seized by Chile.

In his statement, Mr. Nixon voiced strong belief in the value of foreign aid, especially to less-developed nations. But he suggested that the chief victim of expropriation was not the United States but the country that stood to lose American investment—both public and private—because of its actions.

Mr. Nixon said that "the wisdom of any expropriation is questionable," but he did not deny the right of a nation to take such action.

Mr. Peterson readily conceded in his briefing that the Administration hoped the new policy statement would head off mounting sentiment in Congress for "mandatory withholding" of aid. And Mr. Nixon, in his statement, made an appeal for more Congressional support for the United States contribution to the Inter-American Development Bank.

"Our contributions to this bank represent our most concrete form of support for regional development in Latin America," he said. "While the Congress did approve partial financing for the bank before the recess, it is urgent that the integrity of this international agreement be preserved through providing the needed payments in full."

January 20, 1972

Company Investment Rule Abroad Eased

Special to The New York Times

WASHINGTON, May 16—The Commerce Department relaxed today its regulations governing direct investment abroad by United States corporations by exempting export credit extended by the parent corporation on shipments from the United States to its affiliates abroad.

Previously such credit counted against each corporation's allowable foreign investment unless it was exempted following an application covering each specific case. Now all credit that is repaid by the foreign affiliate on normal commercial terms is automatically exempt.

The Administration has announced its intention to end the entire direct investment control program by the end of 1974.

May 17, 1973

Canada, a Sleeping Giant, Awakes and Stretches

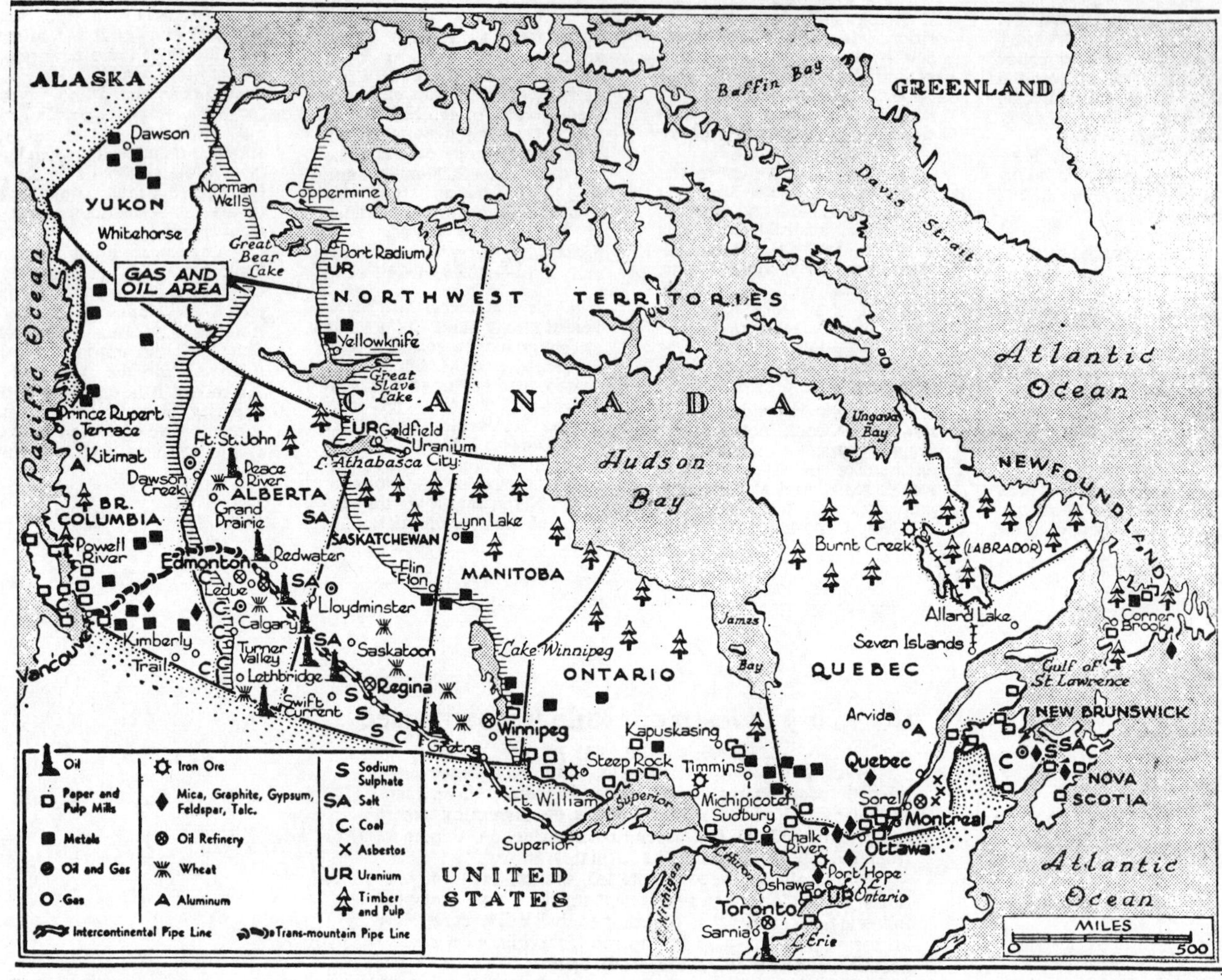

The New York Times July 27, 1952

TAPPING UNTOLD WEALTH: A great economic boom is well under way throughout the length and breadth of the Dominion. Old industries are being expanded and many new ones are being started. The map above locates the principal resources of the country and new facilities for exploiting them, such as the Labrador railroad and pipelines in the south.

Dominion on the Threshold of Expansion Like That in United States Century Ago

By JOHN G. FORREST
Financial and Business Editor

Canada, the third largest country in the world, is rapidly developing her natural storehouse of raw materials and industrializing her economy at the same time.

Within its borders, huge reserves of oil, natural gas, iron ore and other basic materials are providing the foundation for an expansion similar to that experienced by the United States nearly 100 years ago. But in opening up her vast underground wealth, Canada has the advantage of scientific and technological developments of importance since that time, as well as America's mass production know-how. Canada's development program will undoubtedly benefit the "good neighbors" on both sides of the border.

A stable and friendly Government has created a healthy atmosphere for the development of Canada's resources. Her people, too, have the ambition and tenacity that generally is attributed to Americans, necessary to wrest out of the rough terrain the wealth that lies beneath her soil.

Thus, it appears that former Prime Minister Sir Wilfrid Laurier was just about fifty years premature when he prophesied at the beginning of this century: "The Twentieth Century is Canada's."

Like a giant awakening from a long sleep, Canada is beginning to stretch economically—and the rest of the world knows it. Outside capital has been flowing into the country for development. This is one of the reasons the Canadian dollar is selling at a premium. The United States has nearly $8,000,000,000 invested in the Dominion, and this fact is not being overlooked by people living above the border. Of the $4,500,000,000 invested in new businesses last year, about 85 per cent was supplied by Canadians themselves.

American interest in Canada has always been active. The latest outburst of enthusiasm stems from World War II and the post-war scramble for raw materials needed for defense production. A rapid drain on United States raw materials, particularly depletion of iron ore in the Mesabi Range and torpedoing of tankers and ore boats at sea, focused attention on new sources of supply. Two magic words, oil and iron ore, marked Canada as the most logical place with the best potentialities.

Although Canada has been producing oil in Ontario 100 years, as late as 1947 nine barrels had to be bought, paid for with scarce dollars, and transported to meet the needs of Canadian refiners for every barrel of oil produced in Canada. All that changed on Feb. 13, 1947. Imperial Oil Company, Ltd., after spending $22,000,000 to drill 133 wells, with mediocre success, made the first "real" find at Leduc, Alberta, just south of Edmonton. That was the start of the "black gold" rush which is still continuing.

Oil Search Pressed

Since then, every major oil company in the world has been drilling for oil in Alberta, and the search has spread into British Columbia, Saskatchewan and Manitoba. Natural gas, the fellow-traveler of petroleum, has been found in sufficient quantities to warrant building a pipeline from Peace River, Alta., to Vancouver, B. C., thence down to Portland, Ore., if the Federal Power Commission grants permission to enter the United States.

As oil fields developed and production increased, pipelines were needed to take the surplus to dis-

...ent refineries. The largest at the present time, the Interprovincial Pipeline, runs 1.126 miles from Edmonton to Superior, Wis., where a tank farm is located. From here it is relayed by the world's largest fresh-water tankers to Sarnia, Ont., where it is refined. Another line, the Trans Mountain Pipeline, from Edmonton to Vancouver, is under construction. Oil production on the prairies has brought down the price of gasoline and allied products and at the same time natural gas is producing a cheap fuel for heating, cooking and industrial use.

All of this also has meant the development of a large petrochemicals industry in the vicinity of Edmonton, Sarnia and Montreal East, using refinery and natural gases as primary raw materials. Many items that formerly had to be imported will be made in the new plants. Among these will be alcohols, glycols, ammonia for fertilizers and explosives, acetone, formaldehyde, ethylene for the new plastic polyethylene, carbon black for automobile tires and synthetic fibers for the textile industry.

Iron Ore Looms Large

More than 396,000 tons of sulphur worth $8,900,000 were imported from the United States last year, but production from petroleum gases and waste smelter gases from basic metal refining is expected to supply future needs. The one thing lacking is a large and accessible market. High freight rates and United States tariff walls act as barriers and may limit the size of the industry for some time.

High-grade iron ore is being mined in Canada on a large scale for the first time. Located on the bottom of a wilderness lake at Steep Rock, Ont., 140 miles west of the head of Lake Superior, the deposit came into prominence when the outlook for iron ore reserves became so critical in 1942. The United States and Canada helped finance draining the lake and making available the ore, which is 60 per cent iron. The operation is being handled by the Frobisher interests of Canada, with Cyrus S. Eaton, Cleveland industrialist, and Inland Steel Company participating.

A newer and "richer" development is now under way at Burnt Creek on the Labrador-Quebec boundary, 360 miles north of Seven Islands on the Gulf of St. Lawrence. Lying in what is known as the Labrador Trough, more than 500,000,000 tons of ore has been proven, running close to 65 per cent in iron content. The Timmins-Hollinger gold mining interests of Canada, and the M. A. Hanna Company of Cleveland are developing the property. Plans are under way to ship ore when the 360-mile railroad to the property is completed.

Boom Under Way

Using any yardstick, Canada is having a boom. It is developing secondary industries and producing many things for the first time which it formerly had to import and pay for with dollars. Expansion programs under way will provide an even greater output in the future. The four principal sources of Canadian income are forests, farms, minerals and waterpower. And into those divisions of the economy a total of more than $2,000,000,000 will be spent by 1955 for construction, equipment, machinery and modernization.

Tieing the country together are the two great transcontinental railroads, Canadian Pacific and Canadian National, the latter government-owned. Trans-Canada Airlines, also in the latter category, furnishes the faster transportation medium although flights are few compared with the air system in the United States. Spreading out from the main lines of the railroads are the secondary lines which feed the east-west arteries, with Canadian Pacific Airlines handling north-south traffic. The depression of the Thirties canceled branch line construction, but it has started up again to reach the outposts of new resources. Dieselization is under way, with the Rocky Mountains divisions scheduled to be so equipped first.

With the expansion and development of many companies mapped on a five-year basis, there are bound to be some headaches as well as glowing optimism. Basically, the Canadian economy depends on foreign trade. Exports are its life-blood, and its best customer is the United States; conversely, Canada is our best customer. Newsprint, lumber, base metals and wheat are the cornerstones of Canada's foreign trade.

Big Trade Deficit

Last year Canada imported more goods from the United States than she exported, resulting in a deficit of $955,000,000. The net capital inflow of money from the United States amounted to $560,000,000, or $395,000,000 short of being in balance. Funds received by the Dominion from other countries in settlement of foreign trade balances, enabled it not only to finance a deficit in foreign trade but to add $39,000,000 to the official gold and dollar holdings. With sterling area and other countries cutting down on their purchases from Canada to bolster their own hard currency reserves, a weak spot in the Canadian economy is aggravated.

Canada is one of the few nations in the world to write their budgets in black ink. Each year since the end of the war the Dominion has had a surplus, and the current fiscal year should prove no exception. While much has been said regarding the cuts which have been made in individual income taxes, the cut really represents a consolidation of defense taxes into a general higher tax structure. The combined Dominion and provincial taxes on corporations total 54 per cent in Ontario and Quebec, and 52 per cent in other provinces; there are no excess profits or capital gains taxes.

Washington could learn a great deal regarding finances from Canada. Henceforth, all Crown companies—which are owned by the Dominion Government—and which in general compete with private business, will pay a Dominion income tax for the first time. And at standard rates! Since 1946, direct and guaranteed funded debt of the Dominion Government has been reduced $2,000,000,000, or 11½ per cent of the total.

Banking System Ideal

The banking system of the country, modeled after the Scottish system of branch banking, has been found ideal after nearly 140 years of operation. There are ten chartered banks operating under the Canadian Bank Act which limits and controls their activities. Competition is keen, and the discovery of a new mining area usually finds one or more branch banks opening for business as soon as people need the service. The Bank of Canada, or central bank, established in 1934, is comparable to the Federal Reserve System in this country, but there the government owns all the stock.

Holding first position in the Canadian economy is the pulp and paper industry. It is first in employment, wages paid, export value, production value and capital invested. The coniferous forest belt is 600 to 1,000 miles wide. It extends from the Maritimes northward on the prairies, then dips southward to cover a good portion of British Columbia.

Operations of the industry are becoming more integrated with a better utilization of existing products. The objective is to achieve a perpetual crop or "forest everlasting." For every tree cut, a seedling must grow—even if the loggers have to give nature an "assist" by planting it. But it took two Royal Commissions in British Columbia and Ontario to prove it. British Columbia now operates on a forest management plan, and the other provinces are working toward the same objective. With an investment of $1,500,000,000 in equipment and machinery which cannot be moved to a new location as trees are cut, the pulp and paper industry is naturally interested in seeing the plan work.

Lumbering Big Business

Lumbering is big business in Canada, particularly on the west coast of British Columbia. A mild climate and heavy rainfall promote a fast growth on Vancouver Island and operations are carried on throughout the year. The only time operations stop is when the humidity goes below 30 per cent, then the dryness creates a fire hazard. Tractors are replacing horses and heavy trucks haul the logs.

Trees and branches formerly considered waste and left to rot on the ground are now being made into pulp. Last year Canada exported 2,260,000 tons of pulp, more than any other country in the world. There is also a steady trend toward diversification. In 1946, about 61 per cent of Canada's output of pulp and paper was newsprint; last year newsprint accounted for 56 per cent. Today, for every log going into newsprint, another goes into pulp and paper products.

About three out of every five newspaper pages are printed on Canadian newsprint. The three mills with the largest output of newsprint in the world are at Powell River, B. C., Corner Brook, Nfld., and Three Rivers, Que. Wood left over at the big sawmills after cutting lumber is being used by the sulphate mills; sawdust is being made into charcoal briquets, while higher grade hemlock, spruce and balsam are made into viscose and acetate pulps for processing into plastics and rayon yarns.

When it comes to aluminum, Canada is the world's second largest producer. It has no bauxite—the primary ingredient used in making the light metal—but must import it from Jamaica, B. W. I., and British Guiana. Producing aluminum requires cheap power. Fortunately, Canada has tremendous resources for hydro-electric development. There is more than 12,500,000 of developed horsepower at the present time, but this represents only 23 per cent of the known resources.

The building of hydro-electric power plants in Quebec was the principal reason for the Aluminum Company of Canada locating its principal plants at Arvida, Shipshaw and Shawinigan Falls, in that province. A new hydro development at Peribonka, capable of generating 270,000 horsepower, will be dedicated next month. Cheap electric power also has been responsible for the rapid development of industry in the area. Before the war Quebec imported electric refrigerators; now it has three plants producing them. With an area of 597,000 square miles—almost twice the size of Texas—and a population of more than 4,000,000 people, Quebec is a world supplier of asbestos, aluminum and newsprint.

Aluminum to Fore

In British Columbia the Aluminum Company is constructing a plant at Kitimat. Here again, cheap hydro-electric power is the answer; for bauxite carriers will have to make the transit of the Panama Canal, sail up the Pacific to docks which will be built to handle the ore at the new smelter. Power will be generated at a plant in the heart of a mountain through which water will be fed by a 10-mile shaft running up to the Nechako Dam in the Rockies. The first stage, scheduled for completion in 1954, will produce 90,000 tons. The eventual cost will be $500,000,000 and production of 500,000 tons of aluminum a year is expected, making it the largest plant of its kind in the world.

Although interest centers on oil, natural gas and iron ore, agriculture still remains the most important primary industry, and a large factor on the export balance sheet. Enough wheat is produced every year to feed 100,000,000 people, but farming is becoming more diversified. Potatoes and apples are the principal crops in the Maritimes; mixed farming in Quebec and Ontario; grains in Manitoba, Saskatchewan and Alberta, with cattle, hogs and sheep ranching expanding on a large scale.

Irrigation Aids Farmers

An outbreak of hoof-and-mouth disease in Saskatchewan has cut off a $150,000,000 market for Canadian beef in the United States this year. However, large scale irrigation projects are helping the farmers in the southern portion of the western provinces, where sugar beets are the big crop. British Columbia has more intensive farming and greater diversity than any other province. Although the area suitable for farming is limited, it is gradually being extended. All fruits, except those indigent to the

Although interest is turning more and more to oil, natural gas and iron ore, agriculture remains the most important primary industry. Many areas, such as that surrounding Leduc, Alberta, sown with crops for decades, have been found to contain large reserves of oil and natural gas.

tropics, can be grown in the Okanagan and other valleys of the province.

One of the richest agricultural sections in the Dominion is the Peace River country straddling the Alberta and British Columbia border. In this area 70 bushels of wheat per acre are produced, or more than four times the country's average. Although comparatively isolated, completion of the John Hart Highway linking Vancouver at one end with the Alaska Highway at Dawson Creek at the other, will soon open up the territory.

Salmon is the principal money producer in the Dominion's fisheries, but loss of foreign markets and high prices have left the canners holding a good portion of last year's catch. More attention is being paid to freezing and filleting fish for the United States markets. In the Maritime, lobsters still provide the principal sea harvest and dollar producer. Many of the so-called Maine lobsters really come from Nova Scotia. Everything from whales to clams is caught by Canadian fishermen.

One result of the increased industrialization of the country is the drift of people away from the farms. In 1939 the numbers of workers in industry and agriculture were evenly matched. Since then, the ratio is two people in industry for one on the farm. But with some 20 per cent fewer farmers, 30 to 40 per cent more farm items are being produced. Officials attribute the change to greater mechanization on the farm, thereby releasing younger people to industry.

People a Big Need

If there is one thing Canada needs more than money, it is people; its population totals 14,430,000 people, 70 per cent of whom live within 100 miles of the boundary. A total of 190,000 immigrants came into the country last year, but there has been a marked change in the racial character of immigration. In 1948 the British proportion of immigrants was 36.7 per cent, but in 1951 it totaled only 15 per cent. Germany and Italy accounted for 29 per cent, displaced persons 33 per cent, and the rest were from other countries. The bars have recently been put up against all immigration, with certain exceptions, until the country can absorb and place those who have arrived. Canada needs people, but it wants those who can contribute something to its future.

Canada is a large producer of base metals, and mining is now the second largest primary industry, being carried on in every province except Prince Edward Island. The bulk of the mines are located on the great pre-Cambrian Shield, which covers more than two-thirds of Canada's land mass. The mineral wealth underlying the Shield is responsible for more than 90 per cent of the gold production, 56 per cent of the silver, 95 per cent of the copper, and all the nickel, lead, zinc, uranium, radium, cobalt, the platinoids, asbestos and many other metals and minerals.

Source of Minerals

With development of the atomic age more and more dependence will have to be placed on Canada by the United States. Uranium, the raw material of atomic fission and formerly used as a ceramic coloring agent, was originally found at Port Radium in the Northwest Territories. A new and richer deposit has since been discovered at Beaverlodge, Sask., and the Eldorado Mining Company, a Crown-owned corporation, is shipping the ore to its refinery at Port Hope, Ont. Restrictions against anyone other than the Government owning uranium ore mines has been lifted, and prospectors are searching with Geiger counters for new deposits.

Titanium, used chiefly in the manufacture of paint, but with the possibility of becoming a new wonder metal, is being mined at Allard Lake, Que., by Kennco Exploration, Ltd., a subsidiary of Kennecott Copper. In association with New Jersey Zinc Company, ilmenite, the mineral from which titanium is made, is treated at Sorel, fifty miles below Montreal, in electric furnaces which separate the titanium from iron.

Many United States companies have branches or are building plants in Canada as a result of recent developments. Approximately 2,500 plants doing about one-third of all manufacturing in Canada are owned by United States interests. The close relationship which exists through joint development by both countries, will become even closer in years to come. European companies of Swiss, Netherlands, Belgian and German interests are operating or planning to build new industries.

What the future holds is anyone's guess, but there is a growing interdependence between the United States and Canada. Although Canada's growth is rapid, officials are taking measures to hold it within bounds. With the increase in population and a higher standard of living, a broader base is being established which could utilize a substantial portion of the expanded output. Competition will undoubtedly come from other countries that have surpluses of raw materials, but Canada has faith in its own future.

July 27, 1952

U. S. BUSINESS TIES RUFFLING CANADA

Maryland Bar to a Brewery and Financing of Pipeline Stir Anger in Ottawa

By RAYMOND DANIELL

Special to The New York Times.

OTTAWA, March 17—National pride, natural gas and beer have served to ruffle economic relations between Canada and the United States.

A good many Canadians feel that United States capital is getting too firm a grip on the Canadian economy. They complain that some United States corporations operate plants here as branches excluding Canadians from top posts and sometimes freezing out Canadian investment.

The whole issue was brought to a boil when the Government proposed to underwrite the building of the unprofitable part of a pipeline for a corporation in which United States corporations own 51 per cent of the stock.

It was aggravated when on the same day it became known in the House of Commons that the Maryland Legislature had passed a law to bar any brewing company in which less than 51 per cent of the stock was owned by United States citizens from operating in that state.

The Maryland law was aimed at the Carling Brewing Company, Inc., United States subsidiary of Canadian Brewers' Ltd., which was planning to build a $12,000,000 brewery in Maryland.

Pearson Assures House

Lester B. Pearson, Secretary for External Affairs, hastened to assure the House of Commons that, upon learning of the legislative action, he had expressed "concern" to the State Department. He said such action could have "serious consequences."

Since United States investment in Canada amounts to nearly $9,000,000,000, Mr. Pearson's utterance was an example of understatement. Discriminatory action in the United States against Canadian enterprises could result in retaliation against United States corporations in Canada. Mr. Pearson said that he had received assurances from Washington that his concern was shared there.

The row over the Transcanada Pipeline to bring natural gas from Alberta to Ontario and Quebec is another story. The company found itself unable to interest private capital in building the $175,000,000 line through the unsettled parts of northern Ontario, where no markets exist, and so turned to the Government for help. The Federal Government and Ontario agreed to build the "bridge" between the western and eastern markets and sell it back to the company for cost plus 3½ per cent interest when the company could afford to buy it.

U. S. Ownership Cited

Transcanada Pipelines, Ltd., is 51 per cent owned by United States interests. These are the Tennessee Gas Transmission Company, Gulf Oil Company, through Canadian Gulf, and Continental Oil Company, through Hudson's Bay Oil and Gas Company. The Government proposals brought roars of protest from the Conservatives, who want Canadian financial control, and from the Socialists, who want the whole pipeline publicly owned.

George Drew, the Conservative leader, expressed doubt that it was impossible to finance the project with Canadian funds. However, if after further investigation that proved to be true, the Conservatives, traditionally wedded to free enterprise, were prepared to support public ownership for the Transcanada Pipeline. He warned at length of the growing danger of economic dominion by United States capital.

M. J. Coldwell, Socialist leader, went even further, declaring "that domination of our economic life by these foreign corporations is threatening the independence of this country."

Mr. Coldwell and his small group of supporters argued that the whole pipeline, not just the unprofitable part of it, should be publicly owned. He said that if any Canadian corporation was seeking Government assistance for some Canadian enterprise from United States taxpayers it would be laughed out of Congress.

March 18, 1956

U. S. POLICIES HELD TO HARM CANADA

Ottawa Economists' Report Deplores Effect of Farm and Tariff Programs

By RAYMOND DANIELL

Special to The New York Times.

OTTAWA, Jan. 23—Two leading economists reported to an official commission today that United States agricultural and tariff policies and some aspects of private financial operations were harmful to Canada's economy.

The 347-page report was made to the royal commission seeking to forecast the development of Canada in the next twenty-five years by Prof. Irving Brecher of McGill University and S. S. Reisman, Director of International Economic Relations in the Ministry of Finance. It is one of the most exhaustive studies of the economic relations between Canada and the United States yet made.

United States farm policies, especially the surplus disposal program for wheat and wheat flour, the report said, are the greatest causes of "friction" between the two countries. For the next few years, the report added, there is little prospect of an easier time for Canada in the markets of the world or for more liberal tariff policies in the United States.

Shift in Long Run Foreseen

In the long run, however, the economists said, the position of the United States as leader of the non-Communist world and the Soviet industrial expansion may force the United States to treat friendly nations with greater consideration for their economic well-being. The report said that, while in the past the United States had little to gain economically from freer trade, political considerations were becoming more important.

"What is unmistakably clear," the report declared, "is that Soviet industrial expansion has been proceeding at such a remarkable pace as to call into question the traditional assumption of the automatic and indefinite maintenance of Western economic supremacy.

"Indeed the time for bold Western measures on the economic front may be fast approaching and it is difficult to see how the United States—given its overwhelming economic power and an understanding of the political and economic facts of international life—can long avoid taking the lead with strong unilateral easing of the conditions of access to the American market."

Almost all the wheat and wheat flour exported by the United States in 1954-55, the report said, was subsidized in one way or another to the damage of Canadian sales overseas. Half was disposed of by unconventional marketing and half by the Commercial Credit Corporation at prices below the domestic support prices, the report asserted.

The report said it was not unlikely that in the next twenty-five years the United States price support system would be "curtailed if not entirely abandoned," as responsible for economic distortions and misallocation of resources.

"Contributing to this end" the report continued, "may be a growing awareness in the United States that its responsibilities of world leadership entail increasing attention to the impact of its agricultural policies on the economic welfare of other countries.

"Thus it appears reasonable to expect that the long-existent gap between economic analysis and practical expediency will be substantially bridged over the next two or three decades in the development of United States farm policy."

The extent of foreign ownership of Canadian industry and resources was examined by the committee. This long-term foreign investment amounted to $13,500,000,000 at the end of 1955.

The report said that without foreign capital Canada's expansion could not have taken place so rapidly. The non-resident investment went mostly into manufacturing, the petroleum industry and mining and smelting, the report said.

Some wholly owned subsidiaries of United States corporations tend to exclude Canadians from investing in them and offer few opportunities in the managerial field, the report complained, urging closer "integration" in the Canadian economy.

Some corporations with head offices in the United States tend to allocate markets, thus sometimes excluding Canadian subsidiaries from competing in foreign markets, the report said.

However, while the report was critical of some aspects of United States operations in Canada, it saw no cause for alarm.

While the bulk of Canada's 1,200,000 labor union members belong to international unions with headquarters in the United States, the study showed, according to the report, that the Canadian branches enjoyed autonomy in collective bargaining and in strike votes. It estimated that Canadian wages were about 25 per cent lower than in the United States.

January 24, 1958

U.S.-CANADA TIES MAY BE WIDENED

Talk of Economic Union Is Heard—Climate Set by Huge Sales of Grain

By H. J. MAIDENBERG

Probably the most important and controversial subject confronting Canadian-American relations today is slowly being discussed in larger and larger groups—economic union of the two countries.

The climate for the latest private off-the-record talks on this sensitive and politically dangerous topic is set by the windfall that Canada is to realize from the huge sales of grain to Communist nations.

In times of fiscal crisis, talk of economic union takes on more than a defeatist tinge in Canada. It becomes enmeshed in patriotism and other emotions.

Even now, few Canadian politicians, businessmen, bankers or economists dare to speak on the subject publicly. But over and over as one talks with Canadian businessmen and bankers on the problem of integrating the economies of the two largest countries in North America, the word "inevitable" keeps popping up. The subject is still taboo, however, for Americans to broach.

Economic union, which should not be confused with political integration, consists basically of two goals. One is the elimination of tariff barriers; the other is a common currency and treasury for Canada and the United States.

Arguments Stronger

The arguments for these moves are growing stronger, advocates of integration assert. The recent heated exchange between Ottawa and Washington over Canada's export policies is cited as a case in point. Opposition, they claim, seems to come from some Canadian businessmen who fear loss of protected markets, and those "waving the bloody shirt of nationalism for private ends."

At present, Canada is likened to two nations living in one country and dependent on a third for a livelihood.

Central to the arguments for economic union are five concerns. These are Canada's geography and population spread, her tariffs, soundness of money, deficits and culture.

In the case of geography and population, it is held that the artificial trade patterns resulting from about 19,000,000 living in a narrow belt stretching 4,000 miles precludes logical economic development.

This is said to have created uneconomic and unnatural rail, pipeline and other communications systems. Producers have to go far afield to find outlets, when a rich convenient market is only a short distance south of the border.

An example of the confusion may be seen in Canada's latest move to bolster her industry, particularly the big-ticket auto sector. Canada now proposes to rebate the tariff to the Canadian auto industry to the extent that their exports are increased.

In the case of the 25 per cent tariff on automatic transmissions, imposed last year, output of the item has increased in Canada. However, as most auto makers in Canada are American subsidiaries, the producers are caught in the middle.

The same drive to increase Canada's exports, mainly south of the border, has placed more than 1,000 American subsidiaries and affiliates there in a quandry.

Emphasis on the auto industry is caused by the trade figures for last year. Canada imported $642,077,000 in automotive goods in 1962, of which $519,251,000 was for American products. By comparison, Canada exported only $61,740,000 of such goods.

However, in order to sustain and develop Canadian industry, that country spends $2,000,000,000, or 5 per cent of the gross national product a year for tariff protection. This is the figure that A. H. Cameron, Canadian economist, says is only one of the penalties his country pays for economic "independence."

Issue is Tackled

For example, The Financial Post of Toronto reported last week on how the practice of tariffs can feed on itself. The financial weekly showed how Canadian provinces are erecting their own walls of protection. It said:

"Over the years, provincial governments have been quietly pushing more and more business to local firms. Now this practice is reaching such proportions that, in Quebec at least, Government buyers will pay up to 12 per cent more for Quebec-produced goods, if necessary, to give the business to a local manufacturer. If the competition is foreign, the premium may rise to 15 per cent."

The report added that "Quebec was no more insular than any other province."

Canadian businessmen favoring economic union maintain that the competition for markets puts their country at a disadvantage. The resultant frustrations often "lead to political experiments such as nationalization of industry, as in the case of power utility takeovers in Quebec recently."

Tariff Walls Rising

Mr. Cameron, the economist, is one of the more outspoken proponents of economic union. In a speech a few months ago to the American Management Association in New York, he boldly touched all bases in this sensitive area.

He said that tariffs are but a method of subsidizing industry and such overprotected enterprises usually become a drag on the ecenomy.

"I believe economic union would benefit the average man, whose pocket has suffered from the Canadian East-West trade pattern. Nationalistic slogans have less mileage among several million postwar arrivals in Canada, now getting votes, people who care little about bloody shirts from the last century; even native Canadians can get cynical too."

With a free movement of commerce across the border, Canadian industry would have a market of more than 200,000,000 customers. Lower wage costs in Canada—70 per cent of the United States—would provide the cushion during transition, economic unionists say.

Advocates of a single currency for Canada and the United States support this view by reciting what happened at the last devaluation north of the border. They believe that whatever the strength of each dollar, a single unit would be stronger.

The Canadian dollar was devalued in May, 1962, to 92.5 United States cents after being pegged, artificially some thought, at more than an American greenback. To foreign investors in Canadian industry or securities, it meant that holders of $1,000 of property found it worth $925. The Midland Securities Corporation of Toronto summed up one line of thought on this in a recent special letter:

"We do not intend to argue that the domestic economy should be insulated entirely from the structures of the external payments situation—in actual fact, Canada officially accepted those structures [devaluation] only one year ago—but a way out must be found to prevent the development of constant crises."

Austerity Ruled Out

Previously, the Midland letter said: "Belt-tightening and unemployment will not be tolerated at the expense of some vague expression as to the external condition of the economy."

These thoughts are cited by advocates of economic union as reasons for abandoning separate financial systems by two countries that are so closely entwined in all areas of human experience.

Along this path of thinking, the Canadian trading deficits are termed unavoidable. Economic-union advocates believe that the chronic Canadian trade imbalances will continue, "just as California's will because both are importers of capital and are undeveloped areas."

The Canadian banker who said this recently added: "Developing areas such as California need capital, yet if that state were to go it alone the books would show deficit after deficit. The cost of borrowing would jump. State officials would have to come up with all sorts of weird systems to keep it from being thought of as bankrupt or nearly so.

"Now, no one in his right mind would call California bankrupt. The state has one of the most enviable credit ratings in the bond market. And all because Californians use United States money and do not publish separate trade statistics, even if they were obtainable."

With Canada's net international indebtedness at $19,200,000,000 in 1962, the outlook for a balanced external trade picture is dim. For that size debt alone, Canada must raise about $570,000,000 to pay interest and dividends to foreigners.

Economists see no end to the need for foreign capital in Canada unless, as one Canadian businessman said recently, "we build a wall across the border; jam American communications, and force the population to sacrifice a few generations to develop an independent economy as they did in Russia."

Proponents of economic union believe their biggest hurdle, which comes under the heading of culture, will be the toughest one.

While businessmen may quote from Thomas Jefferson thus: "Merchants have no country. The mere spot they stand on does not constitute so strong an attachment as that from which they draw their gains"; nationalism is a more difficult challenge.

However, some signs of the future in this area may be seen in an article that appeared in McLeans, a national magazine in Canada, last April. Written by columnist Pierre Berton, it declared:

"National sovereignty is on the wane. If this election [the last Federal vote that elected the Pearson Government] proves anything it proves that anti-Americanism is finished as a political issue. We have cast our lot with this continent for better or for worse and the people know it. The world is reassembling itself into larger units and I doubt if we could escape the tide even if we wished to.

"But all the evidence suggests that in spite of some high-sounding talk, we don't wish to. We have eagerly accepted the American way of life, lock, stock and bauble, whenever it has been profitable, comfortable or amusing to do so. Thus we find ourselves part of the Western-American social units and if we are to achieve our distinct identity we must do so within the unit and not outside it. This does not mean we need to become the 51st state; it does mean that we have to become a junior partner, perhaps one of several, in a new kind of larger fraternity which finds the United States, for the present at least, in the senior position."

October 13, 1963

WALL ST. GREETS MOVE BY CANADA

Dropping of Plan to Tax Dividends Is Welcomed

By ROBERT METZ

United States investors received the news warmly but calmly yesterday that Canada would not raise by 5 percentage points its tax on dividends sent home by United States-owned companies.

Securities dealers specializing in Canadian securities said Canadian stocks traded here and stocks of American concerns with Canadian affiliates scarcely fluttered following the news.

The calm in the securities market was one reserved for foregone conclusions. One specialist noted that it had been obvious to investors for a long time that the new tax would hurt Canadian concerns with American affiliates more than it would hurt the American counterpart.

Treaty Involved

By raising the withholding rate on dividends sent to America from the present rate of 15 per cent, the Canadians would have abrogated a United States treaty. The effect of this would have been to raise automatically the tax on dividends crossing the Canadian border to 30 per cent.

The Canadian-based Moore Corporation, the continent's largest manufactuer of business forms, indicated recently that it had made headway in attempting to get the Canadian Government to back down on the proposal.

Its annual statement, dated Feb. 28, 1964, said that the Government's unilateral action would cause the tax on dividends from Moore's United States operations to rise to 30 per cent for a "very substantial" income-tax cost increase. The company made "representations to the Government that were sympathetically received," the statement indicated.

About the only aspect left of Finance Minister Walter L. Gordon's original withholding tax plan is a reduction in withholding taxes for some American concerns.

These are concerns whose Canadian affiliates are 25 per cent owned by Canadians. On Jan. 1, 1965, the withholding tax on dividends emanating from such companies will drop from 15 per cent to 10 per cent.

Aluminium, Ltd., is one of these companies. Imperial Oil, Ltd., a Standard Oil Company (New Jersey) affiliate, and the International Nickel Company are two others, according to Kenneth K. G. Murton, vice president of A. E. Ames & Co. Inc. a Canadian securities specialist.

The various changes were designed to increase local ownership of Canadian business after a wave of nationalism swept both political parties. The Canadian Government, according to a United States tax expert, found that there was "no money in Canada to buy the stuff."

At least two American companies recently offered stock to Canadians apparently so that they could take advantage of the lower withholding rates. The Federal Pacific Electric Company of Newark sold enough shares of its Canadian subsidiary F. P. E.-Pioneer Electric, Ltd., to qualify for the lower rate, as did the Harbison-Walker Refractory Company. Its Canadian subsidiary is Canadian Refractories. Harbison Walker is traded on the New York Stock Exchange. The issue closed yesterday at 39¼, up ⅛.

There are a number of considerations in evaluating the consequences of the reduction to 10 per cent in the withholding rate for 25 per cent Canadian-owned United States affiliates.

Earning Power

Relatively few American companies have enough of their income producing assets in Canada for the reduction to rising to $2.7982 from $2.7980 affect significantly their overall earning power. Apparently, the two concerns that sold stock in Canada to qualify for the lower rates are exceptions.

Any American citizen who owns shares in Canadian companies directly will have to pay the normal United States tax on his Canadian dividends after subtracting any tax already paid to the Canadian Government.

Pension funds with investments in Canadian securities are subject to the withholding tax. They are exempt from any tax on their investments in United States securities. Thus, the dropping of the rate to 10 per cent on any of the Canadian securities they already hold is a windfall. The Canadian Government's decision not to raise the tax to 20 per cent on those companies which are not 25 per cent owned by Canadians pleased pension-fund officials.

An overriding consideration for many potential American investors in Canadian shares is the proposed interest-equalization tax which was recently passed by the House of Representatives. It is awaiting action by the Senate. Securities analysts said this, more than Canada's threatened withholding tax, had slowed their markets.

March 18, 1964

MORE TIES URGED FOR U.S. CANADA

Trade Pact for the Auto Makers Raises Question of Economic Union

OTHER AREAS SOUGHT

But Officials in Ottawa Say the Time Is Not Ripe for Outright Unity

By JOHN M. LEE

Special to The New York Times

TORONTO, Jan. 23—The question of economic union between Canada and the United States has been raised again by the agreement for free trade between automobile manufacturers in the two countries.

Canadian politicians, in their public statements, are encouraging the idea that other areas of economic integration might be found. And a number of United States business leaders, in recent speeches in Canada, are advocating stronger economic ties.

Despite this apparent crescendo of interest, both United States and Canadian officials in Ottawa say that although economic agreements will continue to be made and freer trade sought, the time is not politically ripe for outright economic union.

Politicians here are quick to recall the election of 1911 in which the Liberal Government was defeated on the issue of freer trade with the United States. Economic union has such overtones of United States dominance that opposition parties could crucify a Government that advocated such a policy.

'No Over-All Policy'

"We are just not ready to haul down the economic flag and say economic union is great and let's get on with it," a top Canadian trade official said.

Another trade official acknowledged, not entirely facetiously, that "we have had a number of unique situations for free trade and we will continue to have unique situations." A United States official who has participated in Canadian trade talks said, "We have no over-all policy that can be said to be looking toward economic union."

Some persons point to examples of Canadian-United States integration in newsprint and pulp, farm implements, defense production and, to a growing extent, electricity and oil and gas.

With the important addition of autos and original-equipment parts, what will come next? Office machines? Rubber? Aluminum?

C. M. Drury, Canadian Minister of Industry, said of the auto plan that there was "no reason to believe that if appropriate measures are worked out, similar benefits wouldn't flow from other industries."

Prime Minister Lester B. Pearson, upon signing the auto agreement with President Johnson on Jan. 16, said, "We will certainly be anxious to have a look at the other situation to see if we can apply this. Anyway, we have made a start."

Held Inevitable

Stanley Randall, Ontario's economic minister, believes some form of economic integration is inevitable and envisions the day when manufacturers in eastern Canada, aided by freer trade policies, might do a major part of their business in the eastern United States.

Roger M. Blough, chairman of the United States Steel Corporation; George S. Moore, president of the First National City Bank, and Edward Lamb, Toledo, Ohio, industrialist, are among the American businessmen who have spoken out recently for a greater intertwining of the two economies.

The Economic Council of Canada, a quasi-official body, is calling for greater economic interdependence for Canada, without being specific, and the Canadian-American Committee of the National Planning Association, a private Washington group, is drafting a suggested plan for economic union.

The reasons might seem compelling. Trade between Canada and the United States is larger than between any two other nations. The United States absorbs more than half of Canada's exports, with about half the exports already entering the United States duty-free.

The extent of United States investment here means, if not control, than certainly strong influence over the economy. The outflow of Canadian funds to service that investment presents Canada with an almost unsolvable payments deficit.

In addition, Canadian costs are higher and living standards lower than in the United States primarily because this country is only one-tenth as large in population as its southern neighbor.

Increasingly Conscious

Despite these factors, Canadians are increasingly conscious of their national identity. Despite some magazine polls showing that a large minority of Canadians would welcome economic union, there is still fear of United States political dominance.

One of the best known phrases in Canadian history arose from the National Policy of 1879 in which Canadians chose not to be just "hewers of wood and drawers of water" but set out to create, behind protective tariffs, a diversified secondary industry.

Union with the United States, some persons fear, might consign Canadians to being perpetual producers of raw material while the United States enjoyed the benefits of industrial production.

The National Policy has been attacked of late by some political economists, such as Prof. John H. Dales of the University of Toronto, but it still carries weight through modification. Thus, although the auto trade plan gives up hope that Canada might develop a diversified auto industry of its own, it hopes for a specialized, protected Canadian auto industry.

Indeed, it is argued by some persons here that the auto plan is not free trade at all but its antithesis. Under a free movement of goods, production would be allocated by market forces where it is most economic.

But under the plan just agreed upon, only Canadian car makers can import low-cost cars duty-free from the United States, and Canadian car maker have been required to promise in writing that they will not just maintain but rather increase their production in Canada. The program is intended to create more Canadian jobs and more Canadian production.

An Unusual Opportunity

The automobile industry produced an unusual opportunity for this sort of program inasmuch as the Canadian industry is dominated by the Canadian subsidiaries of General Motors, Ford and Chrysler. With large sales organizations in force in both countries, Canadian-made or United States-made cars can be sold freely in the two countries.

Such a program would run into difficulty in the electrical-appliance industry, where small Canadian manufacturers would have to compete in a broader market with Canadian-based subsidiaries of United States companies with the advantages of extensive sales channels in both countries.

Some United States subsidiaries have been organized as branch offices behind Canadian tariff walls and are little interested in, or equipped for, free trade. One key industrial official said he found no strong feeling for free trade in Canadian industry generally.

It is usually the Canadian raw materials producer who calls for free trade, and, indeed, some Ottawa trade officials say free trade in raw materials might well be attainable.

Another question is the economic nationalism of Walter L. Gordon, the Finance Minister, who has agitated for greater Canadian ownership of United States subsidiaries. Mr. Gordon is frequently needling American equity capital and seems to have little use for American equity investment.

Yet an internationalization of business continues. Last year, it was the United States' Jos. Schlitz Brewing Company that bought out John Labatt, Ltd., a major Canadian brewer. This year, Molson Breweries, Ltd., of Montreal, has bought out the Theo. Hamm Brewing Company of St. Paul, Minn.

January 24, 1965

Report of Canadian Economists Urges Curbs on U.S. Concerns

By JAY WALZ

Special to The New York Times

OTTAWA, Feb. 15 — A Government-sponsored committee or economists recommended today radical new controls on United States companies opeating in Canada.

The economists charged that the American hold on Canada's economy encroached on Canadian sovereignty, influencing in particular this country's foreign policy.

According to the economists, the United States prohibits branches of American companies in Canada from selling to Communist countries whenever these sales are banned by Washington. To stop this practice, the Government was urged to create a Canadian trade agency to buy goods from American subsidiaries for resale to Communist states. Parliament should then pass a law making it a crime to refuse to sell to the exporting agency.

The report issued today after a year's study was submitted to Walter L. Gordon, a Cabinet minister, who hailed it as "excellent." The committee's general conclusions and many of its recommendations matched Mr. Gordon's views, expressed many times when he was Minister of Finance, and more recently in his book "A Choice for Canada."

Economist From Toronto

Mr. Gordon, himself an economist from Toronto, has long held that the multibillion dollar American investment in Canadian industry and resources had overwhelmed Canadian independence.

Today's report is not yet Government policy, but Mr. Gordon said it would receive "serious consideration." This means that it would first be forwarded to a standing committee on finance, trade and economic affairs in the House of Commons.

More United States capital is invested here than in any other foreign country. Americans have invested more than $25-billion in Canadian subsidiaries and securities. Americans control nearly two-thirds of Canada's manufacturing, mining and petroleum production.

More than 500 corporations with taxable incomes of $1-million are controlled by foreigners, mostly Americans.

Mr. Gordon became a controversial figure in Ottawa because many Canadians, including some colleagues in the cabinet of Prime Minister Lester B. Pearson, argued that the huge American investment brought Canada many benefits.

Mr. Pearson has contended that the injection of millions of United States dollars into the Canadian economy each year permitted this country to enjoy a standard of living comparable with that of the United States. The investment also enables the Canadian Government to finance a large annual trade deficit with the United States.

However, the task force working under the direction of Melville H. Watkins, economics professor at the University of Toronto, agreed with Mr. Gordon in expressing "concern" over the implications of so large a foreign investment "for Canada's long-run prospects for national independence and economic growth."

Study Began Last Year

The task force began its study early in 1967, shortly after Mr. Gordon returned to Mr. Pearson's Cabinet. The Prime Minister appointed the former Finance Minister President of the Privy Council with the additional assignment of studying the problem of American investment.

The economists noted that the United States balance of payments policy was growing "increasingly stringent." They made reference to Washington's new guidelines limiting American investment in Canada to 65 per cent of the 1965-66 level. This would amount to about $1-billion. Through the early nineteen-sixties Americans were investing increasingly in Canada until a peak of $1.5-billion was reached in 1965-66.

What the American subsidiaries here would probably find most distasteful about the Watkins report was the recommendation that they provide detailed information on their operations to the Canadian Government.

The economists also expressed concern over the "low level" of Canadian participation in American concerns and said there was a need "to insure a Canadian presence in the decision-making of multinational enterprises."

February 16, 1968

CANADA DEBATES U. S. TAKE-OVERS

Recent Acts Spur Protests That Country Is Not an American 'Satellite'

INDEPENDENCE IS CITED

Official Emphasizes Laws That Bar Foreign Hold of Certain Industries

By EDWARD COWAN
Special to The New York Times

TORONTO, June 1—Philip Morris and Merrill Lynch, which are among the best-known names, respectively, in the American tobacco and securities industries, have set Canadians to wondering anew whether their country is destined to become the 51st state.

Recent moves by the two United States concerns to take over Canadian companies have touched off a new round of debate about the advantages and risks of American ownership of Canadian industry, already widespread.

In the House of Commons last Thursday, the Minister of Finance, Edgar J. Benson, was forced by opposition questions to protest that his Government was "not a political satellite of the United States or of any other country, nor do we intend to be. We have an independent foreign policy."

Timely Reference

The reference to "independent foreign policy" was timely. Canada had just outlined in Brussels her unilateral plan for reducing her troop strength in Europe.

She was also pressing ahead with her effort to establish diplomatic relations with Peking. Washington dislikes both developments.

Mr. Benson in effect conceded, however, that those who worry that American ownership of Canadian industry can erode Canadian independence may have some basis for concern.

He ticked off legislation, going back to the 19th century, that restricts foreign ownership of Canada's railroads, airlines, broadcasting stations, newspapers, insurance companies, banks and some other financial institutions.

In their own ways, the Merrill Lynch and Philip Morris actions pointed up two sensitive aspects of the foreign-control issue.

Brokerage House

Merrill Lynch negotiated the acquisition of Royal Securities Corp., Ltd., an old-line brokerage and underwriting house.

Had Merrill Lynch, the biggest brokerage firm in the United States, moved into codfish or most any other Canadian industry, there would have been little or no repercussion.

But banks and underwriters, by the very nature of their work, have a lot of inside information and influence on what happens in many industries.

With Merrill Lynch already closely linked to many big American corporations, it was easy to envisage an unholy trans-border alliance.

Prime Minister Pierre Elliot Trudeau, who is no economic nationalist, seemed to concede the point, telling Parliament "there are certain areas of our economy which are of great importance to us."

Mr. Trudeau hinted broadly that the Government was thinking about extending to brokerage houses the ban on foreign ownership that applies to banks.

Philip Morris, like other tobacco companies eager to diversify because of the cancer scare, reminded Canadians how much money and muscle there is south of the border.

It offered to buy half the stock of Canadian Breweries, Ltd., at $12 a share for a total of $130-million.

A few days later, from the Wall Street offices of Lehman Brothers, Philip Morris president George Weissman upped the ante to $15 a share, throwing another $33-million into the pot.

That kind of market power, and the instinct of shareholders —no less strong north of the border—to make a profit have led even the ardent economic nationalists in Canada to forget about escaping American ownership.

Instead, they seek to stiffen Ottawa's spine in negotiating with Washington such issues as oil exports and the auto trade pact (Ottawa is said to have dealt timidly on both).

Protection Is Sought

They seek also ways to protect or enlarge Canada's political "independence" in the face of what former Finance Minister Walter Gordon calls the naturally strong influence "in our kind of society" of property owners on public policy.

That brings up the question of regulating the multinational corporation, the company that avows its loyalty to the country in which it does business but is controlled elsewhere—in Geneva, Athens, New York or Tokyo, for example.

Canada hasn't solved that question to its satisfaction and may not. What makes nationalistic hearts beat faster is another prospect, formation of a Canada Development Corporation, first promised by the Liberals in May, 1963.

The general idea is for the Government-controlled corporation to invest in industries not yet come of age, industries in which a secure, profitable Canadian presence, if not dominance, can be established.

How much money the economy-minded Trudeau government will scrape up, the mandate it will give the corporation and the speed with which the project, once begun, moves ahead are all question marks.

With the legislation just postponed again, at least until autumn, the timing is uncertain.

Sooner or later, despite the opposition of the financial community, the Canada Development Corporation is likely to come into being.

It would be too good a political achievement for Mr. Trudeau to let go by.

June 2, 1969

CANADA'S BROKERS BACK NATIONALISM

Seek to Block New Foreign Ownership of Firms

By EDWARD COWAN
Special to The New York Times

TORONTO, June 21—A committee of securities industry leaders has embraced the essential arguments of Canada's leftish economic nationalists with respect to the undesirability of foreign ownership.

The committee's reasons, in a report issued last week, for recommending a flat ban on any new foreign investment in Canadian securities firms were not much different from the nationalists' arguments against foreign ownership of Canadian natural resources and manufacturing.

The securities report followed by a few days the release of new Government statistics on foreign ownership and publication of a "trendy" new book that could help to spread the nationalistic viewpoint.

The new figures, for 1967, showed foreign—chiefly United States—ownership of 56.7 per cent of manufacturing assets, 82.6 per cent for oil and gas, 42 per cent for metal mining, 99.9 per cent for oil refining and 84.9 per cent for smelting.

The new book, "Gordon to Watkins to You, a Documentary: The Battle for Control of Our Economy," was published by New Press. It was edited by Dave Godfrey, the intensely anti-American writer and teacher who is a partner in New Press, and Mel Watkins, a University of Toronto economist.

Mr. Watkins, who studied economics at the Massachusetts Institute of Technology, headed a Government task force on foreign ownership and is now a high priest of Canadian economic nationalism and socialism. The task force reported in January, 1968, to Walter Gordon, then Minister of Finance, who is now the high priest emeritus.

The task force report, which stressed that Canada does not benefit enough from foreign investment in relation to the cost, was a seminal document. For example, the cost-benefit approach is used in the securities industry report.

More revealing of the spread of the new nationalism, the seven-man securities committee, with only one quibble, has adopted conclusions in the spirit of the Watkins report. Five years ago that could not have happened.

Concern about Canada's growing sensitivity to foreign ownership was evident in the lavish two-day party given last week by Kaiser Resources, Ltd., to dedicate its new deep-water coal loading terminal near Vancouver, British Columbia. Kaiser, a subsidiary of the Kaiser Steel Corporation of Oakland,

Calif., spent well over $100,000 on the ceremony, luxurious hotel accommodations, a banquet, a platoon of hostesses and a trip by chartered 737 jet to the mine, near the Alberta border — all in the name of public relations.

The study of capital requirements of the securities industry on foreign ownership was prompted by the acquisition a year ago of Royal Securities, Ltd., by Merrill Lynch, Pierce, Fenner & Smith, Inc., an event that shook up the industry and Ottawa.

The study noted that Merrill Lynch, the world's largest securities house, has a net worth of $271-million, more than the $183-million combined total for the 167 Canadian-owned firms covered by the study.

From the disparity, and the Canadian belief that American businessmen are more aggressive, the committee concluded that without restrictions United States companies could quickly achieve a "preponderant position" in the Canadian securities industry.

In such circumstances, the committee feared, Canadian interests, such as raising capital for fledgling companies, would suffer. Underwriting decisions would be made in head offices south of the border and Canadian considerations would carry little weight. Also, the committee suggested, the Canadian Government might have more difficulty in floating its debt issues.

Foreign conrtol of securities firm, the resport said, would diminish Ottawa's power of moral suasion in support of economic and financial policy.

June 22, 1970

CANADIAN GROUP FIGHTS U.S. ROLE

Attracts Interest in Curbing Influence of Neighbor

By EDWARD COWAN
Special to The New York Times

TORONTO, Feb. 6—From a two-room Toronto office, the Committee for an Independent Canada is striving to mobilize public opinion behind a drive to curtail United States influence on Canadian life.

Appealing to what it calls Canada's "surging mood of self awareness," the committee declares: "If we are to insure this country's survival, the Federal Government must adopt legislative policies that will significantly diminish the influence presently exerted by the United States — its citizens, its corporations and its institutions — on Canadian life."

Most United States citizens, only dimly aware of Canada, might find the committee's alarm unfounded or exaggerated. Among Canadians, however, the "independence" viewpoint is well entrenched and spreading.

One reason is that this newest surge of Canadian nationalism has a broad appeal. The committee is concerned not only with business investment but also with education, culture, trade unionism, foreign policy and environment.

Take-over Issue Revived

Hardly a week goes by without controversy in Canada about United States influence. This week, the smoldering issue of take-overs by United States corporations burst into flames anew with a promise by the Government to do "everything possible" to prevent Ashland Oil, Inc. of Kentucky from gaining control over Home Oil Company, Ltd., a Canadian-controlled oil producer.

Also this week, voices were raised to protest the proposed flooding of the Skagit Valley in southern British Columbia as part of a power project for Seattle.

A few months ago, the acquisition by American companies of two Canadian textbook publishers produced a furor. Last summer there was a hue and cry about the thousands of United States citizens who have bought vacation properties in Canada, either for their own use or for land speculation.

The long-held belief that Canada needs foreign capital is being questioned. The Toronto-Dominion Bank commented the other day that Canada's strong export-import surplus was "a healthy sympton of declining Canadian dependence on foreign capital."

Development Unit Started

Last week the Government introduced legislation to create a Canada development corporation to promote Canadian ownership and control of business.

In Ontario, the five candidates for the provincial leadership of the Progressive Conservative party have been stressing economic nationalism, a departure from the policies of the Tory Government.

This week, Flora MacDonald, the executive director of the Committee for an Independent Canada, made an organizing trip to the Western provinces. Later this month she will visit Eastern Canada.

The committee already has a substantial beachhead in the West, where people are usually more eager for United States investment than are Canadians in the East.

"We have three children and somehow in the generations of children that are yet to come there must be an independent Canada for them to live in," a couple wrote from British Columbia.

A letter to the committee from a Vancouver suburb says: "In our community of Surrey, our main street is virtually littered with American chain drive-ins and restaurants."

The independence issue is keenly felt by young people. "Every political science student in the country is doing a paper on it," commented Christina L. Yankou, the committee's office manager.

The committee's long-range strategy is to create a climate of opinion that will cause the Government to restrict but not stop new foreign investment in Canada and to regulate more closely foreign-owned industry.

To achieve the widest possible following, the committee couches its goals in general terms.

It says, for example, that "trade unions in Canada must have the autonomy necessary for them to reflect the aspirations of their Canadian membership." Few Canadian members of United States-based unions would disagree.

On the highly controversial question of limiting university teaching jobs open to United States citizens, the committee says: ". . .without in any way isolating ourselves from the benefits to be obtained abroad, there should be a reasonable degree of information about Canada in the curriculum and a reasonable knowledge about Canada on the part of the members of the teaching personnel."

The committee was conceived a year ago by Peter Newman, editor in chief of The Toronto Daily Star, Walter Gordon, the former Finance Minister, and Abraham Rotstein, an economics professor at the University of Toronto. A founding committee of 13 included members of the three major political parties.

February 7, 1971

Canadian Plan Described As 'Mild' by Businessmen

Faint Praise in Ottawa

By JAY WALZ

Special to The New York Times

OTTAWA, May 3—Most business leaders, including heads of United States-controlled branch establishments, reacted favorably today to the Federal Government's proposals to oversee future foreign take-overs of sizable Canadian business.

However, comments, ranging from "moderately constructive" to "innocuous" were for the most part faint praise for a program "that really doesn't rock the boat."

Canadian managers of American-owned plants, among others, felt they need not be disturbed by the Government's "mild" approach to the challenge of foreign—most United States—domination of Canada's economy. And the comments reflected the feeling of Canadians that there was little in the new policy to "rock" the economy that depends so heavily on United States-owned enterprise.

Spokesmen for the big United States-controlled automotive companies — General Motors, Ford and Chrysler—offered no formal comment. One explained that the effect of Government plans to review future business transactions would be minimal. The legislation, introduced in the House of Commons yesterday by Revenue Minister Herbert E. Gray, has no retroactive provisions.

Normal manufacturing operations of existing plants owned by United States interests are unaffected, just as Canadian businesses are left undisturbed.

The reaction of the Canadian Manufacturers Association, to which many subsidiaries of United States-owned companies belong, was representative of business comments heard today. "The Government appears to take a moderate position and to lay the groundwork for a policy of constructive nationalism," said an association statement.

J. S. Dewar of Toronto, president of Union Carbide Limited, asserted that the Government legislation covered "a moderate, wise scope."

The legislation placed before Parliament would provide a review by the Minister of Industry, Trade and Commerce of all applications for the foreign purchase of Canadian businesses worth more than $250,000 and earning more than $3-million a year.

A prospective buyer would be judged on the basis of Cabinet-level findings that his purchase "will result in significant benefit" to Canada.

James McAvity, president of the Canadian Export Association, praised the Government for taking a "common sense" approach to the problem of foreign ownership.

Robert Scrivener, president of Bell Canada, called the Government's action a "constructive approach" to the problem of foreign ownership.

May 4, 1972

Canada Placing Controls Over Foreign Investors

Commons Passes First Bill to Restrict American Business Take-Overs—Speedy Senate Approval Seen

Special to The New York Times

OTTAWA, Nov. 26 — After years of controversy and months of debate, the House of Commons today passed a bill that will impose strict controls for the first time on a broad range of foreign investments in Canada.

The bill is a response to growing concern among Canadian nationalists about the huge share of this country's economy tthat is controlled by foreigners —mostly Americans.

The legislation provides for Cabinet review of both new investments and take-overs of existing businesses in this country. It now goes to the Senate, Canada's largely ceremonial upper chamber, where its passage is expected to be an easy matter.

"These measures are not against foreign investment in any absolute sense, but seek to help Canadians develop an expanding economy for the benefit of Canada," Trade Minister Alastair W. Gillespie said.

Private United States investment here has soared since World War II and is now estimated at something over $35-billion. Americans control more than half the manufacturing in the country. In some industries, such as automobiles and rubber, foreign control is near 100 per cent.

Critics of this trend concede that the American investment has helped Canada achieve a degree of development and prosperity that might not otherwise have been possible, but they resent and fear the power that is wielded over Canada from south of the border.

A common complaint, as Mr. Gillespie put it, is that "both the structure and the growth of our economy are heavily influenced by corporate decisions taken outside our border, and these business decisions can be affected by the actions of governments which are not answerable to the Canadian electorate."

Under the new legislation, a foreigner or a foreign corporation will need Cabinet approval to establish any new business in Canada regardless of its size or to take over an existing company with a value of more more than $250,000 or annual revenues of more than $3-million.

The Government plans to begin restricting the take-overs soon after the bill becomes law. But application of the section on new businesses—which also covers expansion by an existing company into a new field —will be deferred until "after the Government has gained experience in operating the take-over review process," the Trade Minister said.

Deliberation Is Explained

The reason for the two-stage application, which requires no further legislative action, is that the legislation has so potentially broad an effect on the Canadian economy. Government sources said that the second stage might be put off a year or even more to insure that each move is deliberate.

"The kind of Canada we want to build must be more than a mere appendage of foreign corporate giants south of the border and the resource-hungry multinational firms of other industrialized countries," Mr. Gillespie told the House as its debate neared an end. The bill is a strengthened version of legislation introduced last year but never acted upon.

"Will the board rooms of New York, Detroit, London, Düsseldorf and Tokyo recognize Canada's needs and abilities if we do not insist?" he asked.

In the past, this country has left the door wide open to foreign investors, but now they will be judged by a new basic standard: Will the proposed investment result significant benefit to Canada?

Passed by Acclamation

The bill had been debated for months and it had many opponents. It was passed this afternoon by acclamation with no recorded vote.

It will establish a new body, the Foreign Investment Review Agency, headed by a commissioner of deputy minister's rank, to study business proposals from non-Canadians, using the following criteria: The effect the new investment would have on competition and on economic activity here, including employment; the degree and significance of participation in the venture by Canadians, and the effect it would have in such areas as industrial efficiency and technological development for Canada.

That last point is aimed at dispelling what Canadians call "the branch-plant mentality" that has accompanied much of foreign investment here. Products manufactured here for Canadian consumers unswervingly following patterns for design specifications sent up by a head office in New York, Detroit or Cleveland.

For example, a Canadian can get a job assembling fans at Canadian General Electric, but if he wants to design them he probably has to go to work at the parent company in the United States.

Tired of Second Fiddle

"We have become too accustomed to expecting others to do our research, product innovation and market development and too accustomed to others telling us what we might do," Mr. Gillespie declared. "The degree of foreign control has dulled or inhibited entrepreneurship in Canada by Canadians in Canadian firms.

"Canadians have become too accustomed to playing second fiddle. If we continue to rely so heavily on others, we shall never ourselves become more innovative. If we lose the power to innovate, we turn over the future development of Canada to those who retain that power."

Significantly, a Government paper describing how the law will work noted that a potential investor's willingness "to locate new research and development" in this country could improve his chances.

The legislation envisions a degree of negotiation and bargaining between the Government and the potential investor during which changes might be made in the terms of the investment proposal.

If the Cabinet ultimately rejects a proposal on the ground that it would not significantly benefit Canada, there can be no appeal. But the bill does provide for appeal of proposals rejected on other grounds—for judicial review of what constitutes control, for example, or whether a particular group of investors is really foreign.

November 27, 1973

Canada Ends a Tax Break for U.S. Publications

After years of prodding by Canadian nationalists, the Canadian Government is going to end a tax concession that the nationalists say has allowed Canadian editions of Time and Reader's Digest magazines to flourish at the expense of Canadian periodicals. The action is one of several that seek to lessen United States influence on Canada's cultural and economic life.

In the mid-1960's Canada passed a law making it unprofitable for Canadian advertisers to place ads in non-Canadian publications. They cannot deduct such advertising for income tax purposes. Under pressure from Washington, Time and Reader's Digest were exempted, because, it was said they were printed in Canada. As a result, the Canadian critics say, while the two publications have used only a small amount of Canadian editorial content they have been able to attract 48 per cent of the Canadian magazine industry's advertising revenue.

Hugh Faukner, the Canadian Secretary of State who is responsible for cultural affairs, says ending the tax concession will strengthen Canadian magazines, many of which have faced closure; he expects them to get most of the $16.2-million in advertising revenue Time and Reader's Digest received last year. The Government has also suggested, however, that if the editions become at least 75 per cent Canadian-owned and increase their Canadian editorial content, perhaps to the 55 or 60 per cent that radio and television programs must have, the tax change would not apply.

Canadian nationalists are also upset by what they see as infringment of Canadian sovereignty resulting from curbs imposed on American-owned subsidiaries in Canada who wish to sell products to Cuba, North Korea and other Communist nations. Several recent sales to Cuba, for example, have been at least temporarily shelved because Washington insists that they contravene the Trading with the Enemy Act. Legislation now before the Canadian Parliament is designed to shift the power to make the final decisions on such deals from Washington to Canada.

"The issue," Allen J. MacEachen, the Secretary of State for External Affairs, said last week, "is our economic independence."

January 26, 1975

Most Parties in Chile Find C.I.A. a Useful Target

By MALCOLM W. BROWNE
Special to The New York Times

SANTIAGO, Chile, Dec. 16—The United States Central Intelligence Agency has become nearly as potent a political target in Chile as was the Communist party in the United States during the era of the late Joseph R. McCarthy.

To impute a link between a political rival and the United States Government, especially the C.I.A., has become a tactic used by virtually every political party in Chile.

In past years, allegations of agency penetration into Chilean political affairs were made principally by Chile's Communist party and other major parties of the far left.

High Officials Called

Communists and Socialists charged, for example, that the left-of-center Christian Democratic party came to power in 1964 largely because of financial and political support by the agency. In recent months, however, the hunt for real or imaginary American spies has been joined by the center and right as well as the far left.

Two weeks ago the Chilean Senate was called into closed session for two days to study charges that the C.I.A. had engineered an attempted military coup on Oct. 21. Significantly, the charge was brought not by one of the Marxist Senators but by Renán Fuentealba, former president of the governing Christian Democratic party.

The Ministers of Foreign Relations, Defense and Interior were among the officials called to testify.

Government leaders reportedly told the Senate that there was no evidence to support the contention that the C.I.A. had backed the abortive uprising by the army's garrison here.

The hearings brought little or no substantial evidence to light, according to various participants. Mr. Fuentealba based his charge mainly on the fact that the United States Ambassador to Chile, Edward M. Korry, was absent from the country for several months and was away at the time of the uprising. The Senator suggested that this implied that Mr. Korry had known the uprising was coming and wished to divert suspicion from himself.

The Marxist parties readily accepted the charge as true, but denounced Senator Fuentealba as a "C.I.A. puppet" himself.

"[Senator] Fuentealba is not acting on his own," a Socialist politician said. He added, "after all, he was Frei's campaign manager, and he's still at the center of his party," referring to President Eduardo Frei Montalva. He continued:

"This is a smokescreen. The Christian Democrats want to make it seem that they are tough on the C.I.A., but, in fact, they intend to go on feeding quietly at the C.I.A. trough. They want it both ways—they need leftist support and imperialist money."

A strikingly similar analysis was offered by members of Chile's conservative and rightwing parties.

In a Senate speech, Senator Pedro Ibáñez of the Conservative National party discounted current charges of C.I.A. intervention, but attacked both the Christian Democrats and the United States.

U. S. Ambassador Accused

Mr. Ibáñez charged that Ralph Dungan, former United States Ambassador to Chile, had abused his post by openly supporting the Christian Democratic Party. Referring to all Chilean political parties other than his own, Mr. Ibãnez said:

"Those other parties accept and even stimulate foreign intervention when it favors their own political designs, and only express opposition when it runs counter to their interests."

"The intervention of Ambassador Dungan," Senator Ibáñez continued, "therefore was accorded the complicity of silence on the part of the Government. It was the same when some time thereafter the Soviet armed intervention in Czechoslovakia was accorded the specific support of the Chilean Communist party.

The Senate investigation probably will be dropped because of the lack of tangible evidence. A somewhat similar Senate investigation earlier this year, into charges that the Peace Corps was spying in Chile, also apparently has been dropped. But Chile's presidential election is scheduled next September, and the campaign is already fully under way.

For various reasons, each of Chile's five major parties stands to profit by accusing the others of having clandestine ties to the United States. It seems certain, therefore, that the C.I.A. will remain a lively campaign topic.

December 24, 1969

Allende, Chilean Marxist, Wins Vote for Presidency

By JUAN de ONIS
Special to The New York Times

SANTIAGO, Chile, Sept. 5—Dr. Salvador Allende, a Marxist who says he would like to see Chile follow the road of revolutionary Cuba, won first place in Chile's presidential election yesterday, it was announced today. Since he fell short of a majority, Congress will have to decide who will be the new President.

If Dr. Allende takes office Nov. 4 succeeding President Eduardo Frei Montalva, he will be the first President freely elected in a non-Communist country on a Marxist-Leninist program.

Dr. Allende's victory came in an orderly election yesterday that was a model of democratic voting in the best Chilean tradition.

The official results announced by the Ministry of the Interior gave Dr. Allende, a 62-year-old Socialist Senator, a victory margin of 39,000 votes over Jorge Alessandri Rodriguez, the candidate of the right.

Radomiro Tomic Romero, the candidate of the Christian Democratic party, finished a bad third.

The official totals were:

Allende	1,075,616
Alessandri	1,036,278
Tomic	824,849

Dr. Allende's total represented only 36.3 per cent of the ballots, including blanks, and the Chilean Congress will have to decide between the first and second place finishers in a joint session Oct. 24. The Chilean Constitution requires a majority of the popular vote for the direct election of a President.

The general opinion in political circles here today was that Dr. Allende is very likely to be named by Congress. It is an unbroken tradition in Congress that the first-place finisher in the popular vote is elected.

Moreover, the Popular Unity coalition of left-wing parties that backed Dr. Allende, with the Chilean Communist party as the main organizing force, has 80 members in Congress, which is made up of 200 Senators and Deputies.

In addition, a large number of Christian Democratic Congressmen are expected to vote for Dr. Allende.

Won on Fourth Attempt

Dr. Allende, who was running for President for the fourth time since 1952, promised to carry out the program of the coalition, which called for rebuilding Chilean society on a Marxist-Leninist model.

Among the first measures Dr. Allende has pledged to carry out are re-establishment of diplomatic relations with Cuba and full nationalization of all basic industries, banks and communications systems.

"I come without pride or a spirit of vengeance," said Dr. Allende, but his program means that the wealthy families in this country of nine million will be divested not only of political influence, but of their major holdings.

Dr. Allende has also pledged a more drastic agrarian reform than that begun by the Christian Democrats, who gained control of the Government for the first time in Chile in 1964. Dr. Allende proposes to turn all large farm properties into peasants' cooperatives.

Rate for Dollars Rises

The expectation of a possible victory by Mr. Allende has already driven the black market rate for a dollar to as high as 25 escudos, nearly double the official rate. Many people have been buying dollars so that they can send their savings outside the country.

Airlines reported that international flights were booked up a week ahead in an unusual rush of reservations by people planning to travel abroad.

There are tight exchange controls here, however, and the flight of dollars through the black market has only a minor effect on the large holdings of the central bank, estimated at more than $300-million, which the next Government will inherit.

Among the major companies that would be affected by a nationalization program are the Braden Copper Company and Anaconda Copper Company. Both have entered into joint ownership arrangements of major mining properties with the Chilean Government under Mr. Frei's program of "Chileanization" of this basic export industry.

However, Dr. Allende proposes to take over the companies entirely. The United States investment in Chile in copper, iron mines, nitrates and a variety of industries is estimated at more than $500-million.

Dr. Allende has said he will compensate companies that are nationalized, but the conditions of payments and methods for establishing fair value are not clear.

Congratulated by Tomic

Mr. Tomic, the defeated Christian Democratic candidate, visited Mr. Allende at his home this morning and congratulated him on the victory. A delegation from the Christian Democratic Youths also visited Mr. Allende.

At a news conference later, Mr. Allende said he hoped these visits were an indication that the Christian Democrats would vote for him in Congress.

In reply to a question on his position on foreign investment, particularly by United States companies, Mr. Allende said, "We do not have anything against the people of the United States, but we do have a good deal against the United States capitalists that have deformed our economy."

Mr. Allende said in reply to another question that rumors of a military coup to prevent his taking office "have no foundation."

"To believe that would be to place the Chilean armed forces in a similar role to that of armed forces of other countries that are not professionals, but pretorian guards," he said.

Dr. Allende lost the presidency to Mr. Alessandri by

United Press International

AFTER RESULTS WERE IN: Dr. Salvador Allende acknowledging cheers from well-wishers in Santiago yesterday.

Associated Press

People in Santiago celebrating Dr. Salvador Allende's victory under union flags. At left is Government House.

only 30,000 votes in 1958. Then, as now, his main backing was from his own Socialist party and the strong Chilean Communist party, one of the best-organized in Latin America.

Radicals in Center

In this election, Dr. Allende also had the backing of the Radical party, a non-Marxist party of the center, and of a group of dissidents from the Christian Democratic party led by Jacques Chonchol, former head of the Agrarian Development Institute.

In the last Congressional elections, in 1969, the National party won 20 per cent of the national vote. This and Mr. Alessandri's personal appeal as an austere administrator during his past presidency were supposed to pull in enough votes to defeat Dr. Allende.

The poor showing by Mr. Tomic, and Dr. Allende's apparent success in winning votes among peasants dissatisfied with the agrarian reform, contributed to the victory.

September 6, 1970

U.S. Government and Business Resigned to a Marxist Chile

By TAD SZULC

Special to The New York Times

WASHINGTON, Sept. 20—The Nixon Administration and the United States business community—which has extensive operations in Chile—are facing with resignation the prospect of a Marxist regime in Santiago and the expected nationalization of American property.

As they wait the probable inauguration next Nov. 4 of Dr. Salvador Allende, the Marxist leader who won a plurality in the presidential elections on Sept. 4, both the Administration and the affected corporations — with investments exceeding $1-billion—have adopted a policy of public silence.

In private conversations, the attitude of the big United States corporations is that since the Allende election apparently cannot be reversed, the next best thing is to avoid antagonizing the new regime and hope for fair payment if United States holdings are nationalized. The judgment here is that an Allende government would be able to carry out most of the reforms advocated by the Socialist Senator without fear of United States economic reprisals.

No U. S. Move Expected

Dr. Allende fell short of a majority in the popular vote, and under Chile's Constitution Congress will meet Oct. 24 to choose between him and the runner-up, Jorge Alessandri Rodriguez, a conservative former president. It is generally accepted here, however, that Congress will elect Dr. Allende.

In the view of officials here the United States lacks political, economic or military leverage to change the course of evens in Chile, even if the Administration wished to do so.

"As it is," an Administration official said, "we are going to be blamed anyway for anything that goes wrong in Chile."

Many officials believe that any United States interference could lead to a civil war in Chile and a surge of anti-United States feelings in Latin America as well as to domestic protest comparable to the demonstrations that followed last spring's incursion into Cambodia.

Experts doubt that Mr. Alessandri can muster the votes in Congress to defeat Dr. Allende, who is backed by a leftist coalition of Socialists, Communists and several independent parties. Dr. Allende already commands at least 80 out of the 200 votes in Congress and is virtually certain to win most of the ballots from Christian Democratic senators and deputies whose candidate, Radomiro Tomic Romero, came in third in the popular elections.

Coup Is Doubted

United States analysts discount the likelihood of an anti-Allende coup d'état by the military. They believe it would be possible only if Dr. Allende, as President, violated the Constitution to carry out his pledges to transform Chile into a socialist society.

The Nixon Administration's silence has been made possible by a virtual lack of United States public reaction to the Allende election.

There have been no speeches in Congress against Dr. Allende, the conservative press in the United States has adopted a markedly philosophical stance and the big corporations, which face expropriation, have placed no pressure on either the White House or the State Department.

Dr. Allende, who promised to complete the process of nationalizing the copper industry and the public utilities begun by outgoing President Eduardo Frei Montalva, is committed to compensating the expropriated companies.

A New York business executive said that all the United States companies could do was "to cut our losses and come out the best we can in this catastrophe."

Companies Prepare for Worst

The three big United States copper corporations with interests in Chile — Kennecott, Cerro and Anaconda — have been preparing themselves for the worst for some time. Under President Frei's nationalization program, the Government had already purchased, at least in theory, 51 per cent of control in the foreign-owned copper mines.

In exchange for the shares, the Government issued promissory notes to the companies with the requirement that these funds, in Chilean escudos, would be lent back to Chile while additional dollar investments were made in the country to double copper production by 1971.

Under this program, the companies theoretically lost some of their holdings in Chile, but they have received large profits in recent years as a result of the high world price of copper. In 1967, the earning ratio on capital invested in mining enterprises was 27.3 per cent. In 1968 it was 26 per cent. Some of these profits, however, were reinvested in Chile. The 1968 return on all United States investments in Chile was 17.4 per cent.

The amount of direct United States investment in Chile cannot be calculated because of the shift from equity to promissory notes under the Frei nationalization of the copper industry. The same applies to a United States-owned power company, which was forced to sell 40 per cent of its share interest to the Chilean Government on similar terms.

Besides the mining companies and the utilities, there are nearly 100 corporations in Chile wholly or partly owned by United States companies. The gross revenue of these corporations stood near $700-million in 1968.

Dr. Allende is committed to nationalize foreign banks—two American banks have branches in Chile—but it is not clear how he will treat the other businesses, which range from manufacturers of electronic equipment to automotive assembly plants and oil-product importers and distributors.

Due to high copper prices, the Chilean foreign exchange reserves stand at a record $500-million. Ninety per cent of the Chilean copper is sold in Western Europe and Japan and all the estimates indicate continuing high demand and prices.

As a result of her reserves, Chile does not urgently require United States economic assistance — only $2.5-million in loans were approved this year —and if she seeks aid it will probably be from the World Bank or the Inter-American Development Bank.

It is acknowledged that it is up to Chile to set the tone for her relationship with the United States. The Administration takes it for granted that Dr. Allende will establish diplomatic ties with Cuba and Communist China, but it does not assume that open hostility toward Washington must ensue.

Thus, if invited, the Administration is believed ready to send a delegation to Dr. Allende's inauguration. Officials also believe that the official silence here is a form of positive response to the gestures Dr. Allende has made toward the United States, such as his victory speech in which he went out of his way to cite approving remarks made by some United States figures about the democratic Chilian election.

The United States, however, will wait and see how Dr. Allende acts domestically and internationally before forming a firm policy toward Chile.

September 21, 1970

ROGERS REPROVES CHILE ON SEIZURES

Assails Plan to Nationalize U.S. Copper Interests Without Compensation

By BENJAMIN WELLES
Special to The New York Times

WASHINGTON, Oct. 13—Secretary of State William P. Rogers sharply reproved Chile today for what he termed a "serious departure from accepted standards of international law."

Mr. Rogers cited Chile's announcement Monday that she would pay no compensation for the United States copper interests she is expropriating—except for modest amounts in the case of two smaller properties.

The Secretary warned in a statement that this action might jeopardize the flow of private investment funds to Chile. It might also erode the base of support for foreign aid for Chile and other developing countries, he said.

Meanwhile, Latin-American diplomatic sources said that the Government of Dr. Salvador Allende Gossens, a Marxist, would assume the foreign debts of the United States companies being taken over. These debts are said to amount to $550-million plus $220-million in interest.

The sources, who declined to be identified but who are informed on developments in Chile, said that Chile's foreign debts included $180-million to the Export-Import Bank; $92-million to the Kennecott Corporation and $100-million to five major New York City financial institutions—Chase Manhattan Bank, Manufacturers Hanover Trust, Chemical Trust Company, First National City Bank and the Morgan Guaranty Trust Company.

Other foreign debts that the Chilean Government intends to assume and repay, these sources said, include $50-million to the Banca Commerciale Italiana, $18-million to the Cerro Corporation, $15-million to the Japanese Mitsui group and $17-million to the Sumitomo group of Japan. Including some smaller obligations, they said, the total approaches $550-million.

With accumulated interest, they added, the over-all obligation may exceed $770-million.

These debts, informants here said, are to be repaid in the currencies in which they were made and over the period of the original debt. It is possible but unlikely, they said, that the Allende Government will seek to reschedule debt repayment.

The Rogers statement, read by a State Department spokesman at a news briefing, was more moderate than many persons in high levels of government reportedly had been urging. It was, nonetheless, the most critical so far in a period of deteriorating relations between the United States and Chile.

The Allende Government, elected 11 months ago with a third of the national vote, has pursued a strongly leftist economic policy and has amended the Constitution so as to expropriate United States copper interests and other assets with little more than token compensation.

On Sept. 28, President Allende announced that the "excess profits" of the United States copper companies totaled $774-million.

On Oct. 6, Foreign Minister Clodomiro Almeyda had a long private conversation in the Chilean Embassy here with Henry A. Kissinger, President Nixon's assistant for national security affairs. The next day Mr. Almeyda hinted at a news conference here that Chile might deduct only about $300-million or $400-million in "excess profits" from future compensations because, he said, the United States companies were co-owners of the mines with the Chilean Government and not the sole owners.

Mr. Almeyda's private talk with Mr. Kissinger and the conciliatory tone of his news conference the next day led to hopes here that there might still be a chance of an agreed solution with Chile over fair compensation to the copper companies.

But two days ago, Hector Humeres, Chile's Controller General, dashed such expectations here by virtually ruling out any meaningful compensation.

In his statement, Secretary Rogers noted that the determination of excess profits in the copper company cases was "not obligatory" in Chile's expropriation laws.

He said that "the U.S. companies earned their profits in Chile within Chilean law and under specific contractural arrangements made directly with" preceding Chilean governments. He stressed that Chile was not contending that such profits were based on "violations of Chilean law."

Chile Deplores 'Pressure'

SANTIAGO, Chile, Oct. 13 (UPI)—Foreign Minister Almeyda accused Mr. Rogers today of exercising "veiled pressure" against Chile because of her refusal to pay for the copper properties.

In a nationwide radio address, he criticized the Rogers statement for not mentioning that Chile had assumed $700-million in debts owed by the expropriated companies.

Mr. Almeyda said he was "concerned by the reference to possible negative financial consequences for Chile and similar effects in foreign aid since that constitutes veiled pressure over our country which we can do nothing less than reject."

October 14, 1971

Chile Takes Fight With I.T.T. to U.N. Unit

By JUAN de ONIS
Special to The New York Times

SANTIAGO, Chile, April 13—President Salvador Allende Gossens put before a United Nations economic conference of 141 nations today his quarrel with the International Telephone and Telegraph Company and United States copper corporations.

Addressing the opening session of the third United Nations Conference on Trade and Development, Dr. Allende called for condemnation of American multinational corporations that he said had sought to "upset the normal functioning" of the Government and "its economic relations with the rest of the world."

He accused the American copper companies whose properties here have been nationalized, in most cases without compensation, of exercising pressure on the United States Government to "prevent Chile from obtaining new terms and new time limits for the payment of external debt."

The New York Times/Renato Perez

President Salvador Allende Gossens, right, of Chile and Kurt Waldheim, United Nations Secretary General, during yesterday's U.N. economic conference in Santiago.

Virtual Extortion Seen

The United States is the major creditor among the Western countries from which Chile has been seeking a three-year postponement of payment on debts totaling $1.2-billion. The negotiations, which began in December, resume next week in Paris.

The failure to obtain debt relief from the American, Western European and Japanese creditors would amount to virtual extortion, Dr. Allende said.

The major copper companies, Anaconda and Kennecott, whose properties with a book value of more than $600-million were nationalized last year, regard the take-over without compensation as confiscation. A special five-member tribunal, appointed by Dr. Allende to review the nationalization, is weighing an appeal by the concerns against a ruling by Dr.

Allende charging $724-million in "excess profits" against book value.

Shift on Money Policy Urged

Dr. Allende said the control of international telecommunications by American corporations such as I.T.T. posed "a formidable danger" that developing countries would be "flooded by information and publicity directed from abroad" through satellite transmissions.

I.T.T., whose Chile Telephone Company has been put under state administration, is the major target of a Government campaign designed to point up foreign intervention in Chilean politics.

Among those listening to Dr. Allende were the members of the United States delegation, headed by John D. Irwin 2d, Under Secretary of State.

On international issues, Dr. Allende said that the developed countries could no longer run world monetary policies without giving socialist and developing countries a direct voice.

He called for negotiations in the framework of the United Nations trade group for a more equitable system of international trade through which developing countries would obtain better prices, freer access to developed markets and help on modern technology.

Secretary General Waldheim, the other speaker at the inaugural session, said that "in the two crucial fields of monetary reform and of primary commodities, in particular, the interests of the poorer countries have not yet been duly taken into account."

April 14, 1972

ALLENDE ACCUSES U.S. OF 'BLOCKADE'

Asserts That Washington Impedes Loans to Chile

By JUAN de ONIS
Special to The New York Times

SANTIAGO, Chile, May 1—President Salvador Allende Gossens accused the United States today of imposing an economic blockade on Chile and made a dramatic appeal to labor for more work and sacrifice.

He said this year would be "the most difficult and the most crucial" for the establishment of socialism and the consolidation of "the government of the workers" in this country of 10 million people.

Dr. Allende spoke at an annual May Day labor rally attended by about 25,000 persons carrying banners of the political parties, left-wing movements and labor unions that support his Popular Unity coalition Government.

Although the United States joined other Western creditors last week in refinancing $300-million in official Chilean debts, Dr. Allende lashed out at what he called an "economic blockade" sponsored by Washington.

The United States, he said, blocked the granting of long-term development credits to Chile by international banks, such as the World Bank and the Inter-American Development Bank.

He also charged that Washington had closed off several hundred million dollars in lines of credit that Chile had with private United States banks before Dr. Allende came to office in November, 1970, and had caused problems for copper companies, nationalized by his government, and other concerns in obtaining spare parts and equipment.

Dr. Allende said the debt refinancing obtained by Chile was "no panacea" and forecast a residual foreign payments deficit of $146-million.

He said it was imperative for peasants on nearly 3,000 large farms expropriated under the agrarian reform program and for small farmers to increase production of wheat and milk, which will cost Chile $250-million in imports this year.

Dr. Allende acknowledged that production at the five big nationalized copper mines and at cement and textile plants under state control was below the goals set.

The workers, he said, had to understand that only through greater efforts and the participation by labor in management and planning could the success of Chile's "socialist revolution" be secured.

The opposition majority in Congress, led by the Christian Democratic and National parties, has adopted a constitutional reform that would strip the executive of its power to extend state control over an important group of private industries.

Dr. Allende said that his Government would "not step back one millimeter from the advances" already made in taking control of banks, farms, industries and mines that form the "social area" of the economy.

He warned that if attempts were made to override his vetoes of the reform he might call a national plebiscite to dissolve Congress.

"If we go to a plebiscite, we will scratch the earth for votes and we will win," Dr. Allende said.

May 2, 1972

ALLENDE, AT U.N., CHARGES ASSAULT BY U.S. INTERESTS

Chilean President Declares Pressure Is Intended to Topple Government

By ROBERT ALDEN
Special to The New York Times

UNITED NATIONS, N. Y., Dec. 4—President Salvador Allende Gossens of Chile came before the General Assembly today to charge that his country was the victim of "serious aggression" initiated by United States corporations, United States banking interests and United States governmental agencies.

"From the very day of our election triumph on Sept. 4, 1970," Dr. Allende said, "we have felt the effects of large-scale external pressure against us, which tried to prevent the inauguration of a Government freely elected by the people and which has tried to bring it down ever since.

"It is action that has tried to cut us off from the world, to strangle our economy and to paralyze trade in our principal export, copper, and to deprive us of access to sources of international financing."

Speech Acclaimed

Speaking in Spanish before a packed Assembly hall that erupted into enthusiastic applause and shouts of "Viva Allende!" at the end of his 90-minute speech, the Chilean President said that despite all efforts to counter international economic exploitation, "here we are well into the nineteen-seventies, suffering from yet another manifestation of imperialism, one that is more subtle, more cunning and terrifyingly effective in preventing us from exercising our rights as a sovereign state."

Responding to Dr. Allende at a press conference immediately after the speech, George Bush, the United States representative, said that the investment of American capital abroad was not intended to exploit foreign countries, but rather was of mutual benefit to the investor and to the people of the country in which the investment was made.

"We don't think of ourselves as imperialists," Mr. Bush said. "Foreign trade is not necessarily evil."

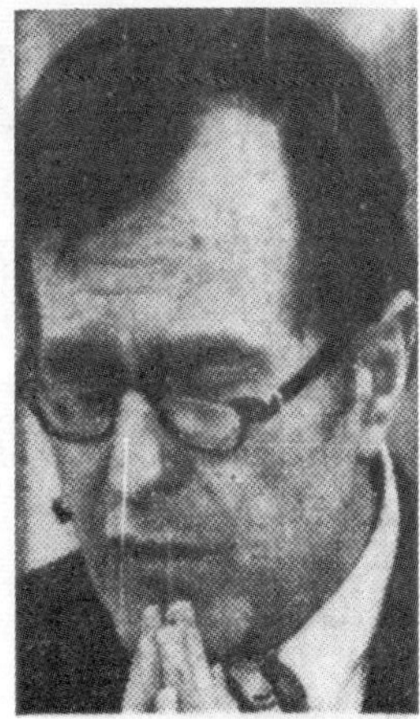

The New York Times

George Bush, U.S. delegate to the U.N., discussing charges by the President of Chile yesterday.

In his speech, Dr. Allende said that, because of the nature of the Chilean economy, the "financial strangulation" of his country had had an immediate and brutal effect and had severely limited the country's ability to secure equipment, spare parts, food and medicine.

"Each and every Chilean is suffering from the consequences of these measures, because they affect the daily life of each citizen and naturally his internal political life," the Chilean President said.

With his slightly graying hair and trimmed mustache, his impeccably tailored blue-gray suit and white shirt, Dr. Allende looked more like an international banker than a Marxist leader. But he was outspoken in his denunciation of the economic aggression of which he said his country was a victim.

He said Chile was being crippled by decisions to cut off lines of credit by such agencies as the Export-Import Bank, the World Bank, the Inter-American Development Bank, private banking interests within the United States and the United States Agency for International Development.

Such actions, Dr. Allende said, were "legally and morally unacceptable." He went on:

"Such misuse represents the exertion of pressure on an economically weak country, the infliction of punishment on a whole nation for its decision to recover its own basic resources, and a form of intervention in the internal affairs of a sovereign state.

"In a word, it is what we call imperialism."

2 Companies Attacked

The Chilean President had still harsher words for two United States companies, the International Telephone & Telegraph Corporation and the Kennecott Copper Corporation, which, he said, had "dug their claws into my country" and which proposed "to manage our political life."

"The I.T.T., a gigantic corporation whose capital is bigger than the national budgets of several Latin-American countries put together, and bigger even than that of some of the industrialized countries, launched a sinister plan to prevent me from acceding to the presidency just as soon as the people's triumph in the September, 1970, election became known," he said.

"Before the conscience of the world I accuse the I.T.T. of attempting to bring about civil war in my country. That is what we call imperialist action."

Dr. Allende said that from 1955 to 1970 the Kennecott Copper Corporation had made an average annual profit of 52.8 per cent on its investment.

He said that huge "transnational" corporations were waging war against sovereign states and that they were "not accountable to or regulated by any parliament or institution representing the collective interest."

Actions Defended

"In a word," Dr. Allende said, "the entire political structure of the world is being undermined."

In a statement issued in reply to Dr. Allende's charges, Frank R. Milliken, president of Kennecott, referred to legal actions now being taken by his company in courts overseas to prevent the Chilean Government from selling copper from the nationalized mines:

"No amount of rhetoric can alter the fact that Kennecott has been a responsible corporate citizen of Chile for more than 50 years and has made substantial contributions to both the economic and social well-being of the Chilean people."

"Chile's expropriation of Kennecott's property without any compensation violates established principles of international law. We will continue to pursue any legal remedies that may protect our shareholders' equity and we have been encouraged by last week's decision of the Paris court that expropriation without equitable compensation is illegal."

A spokesman for I.T.T. said: "I.T.T. never intervened or interfered in the internal affairs of Chile in any way. I.T.T. has been interested only in the safety and well-being of its employes in Chile and in receiving just compensation for those assets which the Chilean Government might acquire.

"The record shows that over a period of years, I.T.T. has always respected a host's country's desire to nationalize an I.T.T. property. This has been true in Argentina, Brazil, Mexico and Peru."

During his day at the United Nations, Dr. Allende met privately with Secretary General Waldheim, who also gave a luncheon for him to which the representatives of all member countries were invited.

December 5, 1972

ALLENDE OUT, REPORTED SUICIDE; MARXIST REGIME IN CHILE FALLS IN ARMED FORCES' VIOLENT COUP

JUNTA IN CHARGE

State of Siege Decreed by Military Chiefs—Curfew Imposed

By The Associated Press

SANTIAGO, Chile, Wednesday, Sept. 12—President Salvador Allende Gossens was deposed yesterday in a violent military coup, and the Santiago police said that he had committed suicide rather than surrender to the attackers.

Dr. Allende, a Marxist who was elected President in 1970, was reportedly found slumped over a blood-stained sofa in the presidential palace, a bullet through his mouth. The palace had been captured after a 20-minute assault in which the military used bombers and heavy artillery.

Proclaiming a mission of liberating Chile "from the Marxist yoke," a four-man military junta took control of the Government and declared a state of siege. Censorship and a curfew were imposed.

Noon Deadline Set

The coup followed weeks of nationwide strikes and economic chaos, with growing groups of workers and professionals joining in demands that Dr. Allende halt his attempts to bring socialism to Chile and resign. Yesterday morning, the chiefs of the army, navy, air force and national police sided with the anti-Marxist opposition and issued an ultimatum for the President to resign by noon.

But the President refused. In his last public statement, made by radio as two air force jets were making runs on the palace, he declared:

"I will not resign. I will not do it. I am ready to resist with whatever means, even at the cost of my life in that this serves as a lesson in the ignominious history of those who have strength but not reason."

Bombs Fell on Palace

Attacking only moments

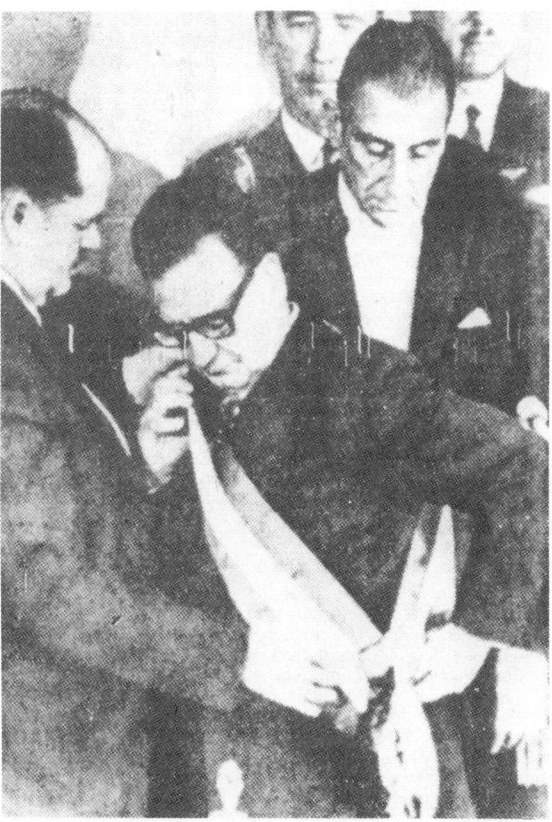

Associated Press

Dr. Allende receiving the presidential sash from Tomás Pablo, Senate leader, as he assumed power in Santiago on Nov. 3, 1970. Behind Dr. Allende were Eduardo Frei Montalva, the outgoing President, and military aides.

United Press International

An anti-Allende demonstration in Santiago last week. One sign says "Mr. Allende, Enough!" "Trucks, No!" is a reference to the trucking industry, which went on strike to oppose Government attempts to control it.

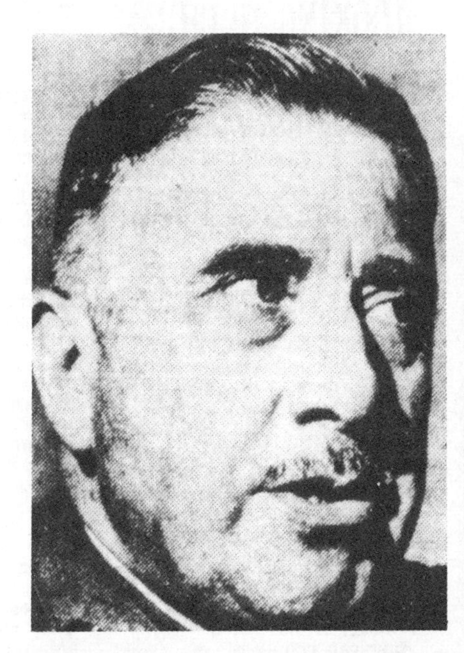

Associated Press

Gen. Augusto Pinochet Ugarte, left, the commander of Chile's Army, is a member of the four-man military junta that overthrew President Salvador Allende Gossens, at right.

after the deadline set by the military had passed, the air force jets dropped bombs and fired rockets, severely damaging the fortress-like presidential palace. The President's official residence, about a mile away, was also bombed, the junta said, after guards there "resisted the armed forces and police."

A statement that the President had committed suicide was issued after the attack by Rene Carrasco, a police prefect. He said Augusto Olivares, a close Presidential adviser, had also killed himself.

Newsmen for the Santiago daily El Mercurio were allowed inside the palace, and the newspaper's chief photographer, Juan Enrique Lira, said he saw the President lying dead on a blood-soaked sofa in the anteroom of the palace's dining hall. He said the President had apparently shot himself once in the mouth.

series of orders was issued immediately after the coup by the junta, composed of Gen. Augusto Pinochet Ugarte, commander of the army; Gen. Delaire Gustavo Leigh Guzman, commander of the air force; Adm. José Toribio Merino Castro, acting commander of the navy, and Gen. Cesar Mendoza Frank, chief of the national police.

A list of 68 prominent Socialist and Communist leaders was broadcast, and they were ordered to appear at the Defense Ministry or face arrest. More than 100 Communist and Socialist party members were reported arrested in Santiago and Valparaiso, a port city where naval units began the coup early yesterday.

Foreigners were ordered to report to the nearest police station to identify themselves.

The junta also broadcast an order freezing all bank accounts.

In a radio broadcast monitored after the coup, the junta said that it would soon name new ministers, including some civilians, but that Congress would remain in recess "until further order."

The new Government said it would maintain diplomatic relations with all nations except for Cuba and a few others.

In several monitored broadcasts the military junta made no mention of Dr. Allende. It said its aim was to "avoid violence and lead the Chilean people along the road to peace."

While the military attacks were under way yesterday, long-distance telephone and telegraph services in this city of three million people were shut down.

They were resumed late in the day, but communications were cut off again after a few hours.

What other casualties there might have been besides those at the presidential palace was not immediately clear.

A spokesman at the United States Embassy said no United States citizens were known to have been wounded.

The coup marked the first time in more than 40 years that the traditionally nonpolitical Chilean military had overturned a civilian Government. In 1931, a dictatorial President, Carlos Ibanez del Campo, was forced out during a general strike and other economic troubles.

Dr. Allende, a physician turned politician, took office nearly three years ago insisting that he would lead Chile to Socialism within a democratic framework, but growing opposition from Chile's large middle class made that impossible.

His leftist coalition, which succeeded the Christian Democratic Government of President Eduardo Frei, encountered political and labor turmoil, economic crises and strong opposition in Congress, which is controlled by anti-Marxist parties.

In October, 1970, Gen. René Schneider, then the army commander, was kiled by right-wing extremists in an unsuccessful plot against the Allende Government. Last June, about 100 soldiers attacked the palace in a coup attempt that was crushed by loyal army units.

Warned of Coup

The 65-year-old President warned repeatedly in recent speeches that "fascists" were planning a coup against him. With unrest against him growing, he named military leaders to his Government in an attempt to keep them with him. The army and air force commanders now in the military junta that deposed him were appointed by Dr. Allende to his Government only two weeks ago.

Last week the military leaders left the Allende coalition, and he appointed lower ranking officers to succeed them.

The junta moved against him yesterday morning as a general strike by merchants went into the fourth day and 50,000 private truckers remained off the job for the 47th day.

In their first communiqué, the junta members said they were demanding Dr. Allende's resignation in the face of "the extremely grave economic, social and moral crisis that is destroying the country." The communiqué added that the armed forces and national police were united in "fighting for the liberation of the country from the Marxist yoke."

The communiqué, described as a "proclamation of the military Government junta," declared that, because the Government was unable to "stop the growth of chaos," the President "must proceed immediately to hand over his high office to the Chilean armed forces and national police."

"The workers of Chile may be certain," the declaration went on, "that the economic and social benefits they have achieved to the present will not suffer fundamental change."

The communiqué also warned that the Government's newspapers and radio and television stations must suspend their activities at once or "they will be assaulted by land and air."

First word of the revolt came from the port city of Valparaiso and Dr. Allende rushed from his residence to the palace. Shortly after 8 A.M. yesterday he made a brief statement over his Socialist party's radio station, saying "a sector of the navy" had rebelled and "I am awaiting now a decision from the army to defend the Government."

Bombs Strike Palace

Ten minutes later he went on the air again, saying "irresponsible elements" were demanding that he quit.

The heavy action centered at noon on the presidential palace, a fortress-like building that once was a mint and covers a block in the heart of the city.

Bombs and rockets smashed into the graceful interior patios and Dr. Allende's office was reported badly damaged. Several tanks opened fire at the front of the building when President Allende's guards refused to surrender.

Fires broke out and a column of black smoke rose from the building. Spectators gathered at intersections but then darted for cover as bullets struck near them.

Guests in the luxurious Carrera Sheraton Hotel fell to the floor as their windows were shot out. They were led to a relatively secure area at the rear of the second story.

The revolt left only four South American countries in the hands of civilians: Argentina, Colombia, Venezuela and Guyana. The other countries are directly ruled by the military, as in Brazil and Peru, or under heavy influence of military men, such as in Uruguay, which came under armed forces domination last May.

September 12, 1973

U.S. COMPANIES LOOKING TO CHILE

Some Would Return if They Received New Welcome

By MICHAEL C. JENSEN

Some of the big United States corporations whose properties were seized by the Chilean Government of President Salvador Allende Gossens indicated yesterday that they might consider resuming manufacturing in Chile if a new government there were receptive to investment.

Most of the companies warned, however, that it was too early to assess the prospects of returning. Some of them said they were monitoring developments in Chile through radio stations transmitting from other Latin-American countries.

Properties of more than a dozen United States companies have been seized or sold under pressure to the Allende Government in the last few years. They include copper, steel, chemical, rubber, automobile, communications nd banking installations.

Estimates of the total value of the property run as high as $1-billion, most of it for the copper mines and processing facilities that provide Chile with her dominant industry.

Officials in the auto, chemical and communications industries indicated either that they might be interested in returning to Chile, or that they did not rule out such a possibility.

One exception was a copper company official who said "there's no way we'd go back in." The domestic copper industry was especially hard hit by seizures of copper mines in Chile in the last few years.

Official comments were mainly of the wait-and-see variety, but behind the scenes there was some talk of returning.

A Ford Motor Company spokesman said that the company already had been holding informal discussions with the Allende Government about resuming its auto assembly ac-

tivities, and that it would have to study the new developments.

An industry source, however, said the company was clearly interested in returning because of the favorable market for automobiles in Latin America. Ford's assembly plant, valued by it at about $7-million, was taken over by the Chilean Government in mid-1971.

E. I. du Pont de Nemours & Co., the big chemical manufacturer, said it sold products in Chile, and would look at the country, as it did other Latin-American countries, for possible investment opportunities.

Chile bought a small explosives plant from du Pont for $1-million in early 1972.

A spokesman for the International Telephone and Telephone and Telegraph Corporation said his company's action would depend upon "what government emerges and what its position is going to be."

I.T.T.'s controversial action in offering the United States Government up to $1-million to prevent the election of Dr. Allende has been highly publicized.

The company still owns two hotels, a telephone parts factory and a telecommunications operation on Chile. Its 70 per cent share of the Chilean telephone company was seized by the Government.

Although some corporate officials did not eliminate the possibility of returning to Chile, many remained skeptical about the outlook for her economy.

"We don't know what condition our old plant is in now," said one chemical company executive, "but more important, we don't know what shape the economy is going to be in."

Some companies still were negotiating with Chile for compensation for their seized properties, and were uncertain what impact the political coup would have.

The Cerro Corporation, a copper producer, said Chile had valued its seized properties at $13.3-million, and that the Government there owed it $18-million more in loans and $6.3-million in uncollected interest. The company said it had received no reimbursement from Chile.

"We just don't know what's happening," one Cerro official said.

A number of companies whose Chilean properties have been seized have claims pending with the Overseas Private Investment Corporation, which insures United States investors against loss from political upheavals.

The largest claim is from the Anaconda Company, which filed last year for $171.4-million. It was awarded $11.9-million and has submitted the rest to binding arbitration.

I.T.T. has a similar claim for $92.5-million with the insurer, which is being arbitrated, and Cerro last December filed for $14.2-million. The Dow Chemical Company submitted a claim for $8.9-million.

Some other companies have already been paid. Kennecott, for example, settled last December for $66.9-million, after asking for $76.7-million.

There was no consistent impact in the stock market on companies with either past or current Chilean involvement. In a market that was down slightly, I.T.T. closed down $1.25 at $29.75. Cerro was unchanged at $15.12½; Kennecott was off 25 cents at $32.37½, and Anaconda was up 87½ cents at $22.87½.

September 12, 1973

I.T.T. Officers Testify on Chile; Senator Church Voices Concern

By JAMES M. NAUGHTON
Special to The New York Times

WASHINGTON, March 16—Senator Frank Church said after hearing closed-door testimony by two officers of the International Telephone and Telegraph Corporation today that he remained "concerned about the implications" of its involvement in the internal politics of Chile.

Senator Church, Democrat of Idaho, declined to be specific, but he said that the cause of his concern would become evident when the Foreign Relations subcommittee he heads resumes its hearings in public next week.

The corporation was accused a year ago of having sought the cooperation of the United States—and the involvement of the Central Intelligence Agency—in preventing Dr. Salvador Allende Gossens from taking office as President of Chile in 1970 and in trying to topple his Government a year later.

Harold S. Geneen, chairman and chief executive officer of I.T.T., and John A. McCone, a director who once headed the Central Intelligence Agency, met with the subcommittee on multinational corporations for two hours. Senator Church said that the meeting had been a courtesy intended to "review the general course of questions we intend to ask in the public hearings."

The investigation will be the **beginning of a two-year inquiry by the subcommittee into the broader issue of how multinational corporations can influence United States foreign policy and have a bearing on the United States economy.**

Senator Church said that the hearings next week would be important not only to get the facts about I.T.T. and its relations with the Marxist Government in Chile but also to help establish guidelines for corporations to follow in foreign countries.

I.T.T. has asked for $92.6-million in compensation from the Overseas Private Investment Corporation, a United States Government agency, because of the seizure of its Chilean telephone company by President Allende's Government.

Senator Church said today that the hearings next week could have some bearing on whether the compensation is granted. At issue is whether I.T.T. involvement in Chilean affairs might have provoked justifiable reaction by the Allende Government.

The Senator said that the corporation officials had been cooperative and that I.T.T. appeared to have complied with a subpoena demanding all corporate documents bearing on the charges.

March 17, 1973

C.I.A.-I.T.T. PLANS ON CHILE REPORTED

Company Aide Says Agency Also Urged Measures to Bar Allende in 1970

By EILEEN SHANAHAN

Special to The New York Times

WASHINGTON, March 20 — A vice president of the International Telephone and Telegraph Corporation said today that a top official of the Central Intelligence Agency had "agreed with the recommendations" the corporation made to try to prevent the election of Salvador Allende Gossens, a Marxist, as President of Chile.

The recommendations in 1970 reportedly included steps to maneuver the departing Chilean President back into power, to foment violence that might bring about a military takeover of the country, to use American governmental agencies to supply anti-Allende propaganda to other Latin American countries, or some combination of these things.

C.I.A. Official Identified

The C.I.A. official who was said to have "agreed with" these proposals was William V. Broe, director of the agency's clandestine activities in Latin America.

The I.T.T. official who testified about this conversation and many others with Mr. Broe and other high officials of the United States Government was William R. Merriam, formerly head of the corporation's Washington office.

Mr. Merriam said he first met Mr. Broe on July 16, 1970, with Harold S. Geneen, the company's president and chairman, who was also meeting Mr. Broe then for the first time. The three men met around 10:30 P.M. in the lobby of the old Carlton Hotel in downtown Washington, Mr. Merriam said.

He said that Mr. Geneen had arranged the meeting by telephone and that Mr. Broe and Mr. Geneen had left him after a few minutes, and gone off together to talk. He said that he did not know what they talked about.

The July date was sometime before the Chilean election, which was on Sept. 4.

He was instructed by Mr. Geneen to "keep in touch" with Mr. Broe, Mr. Merriam said, and he subsequently talked with him on the telephone "many times" and had several luncheons with him.

Mr. Merriam was the first witness to be heard in public session by a special subcommittee of the Senate Foreign Relations Committee that is headed by Senator Frank Church, Democrat of Idaho.

The subcommittee will conduct what is expected to be a two-year inquiry into the behavior of United States corporations that operate around the globe.

Among the main things the subcommittee wants to find out is the extent to which these multinational corporations influence United States foreign policy.

The first two weeks of the hearings will deal exclusively with the reported attempts of International Telephone and Telegraph to enlist the help of various branches of the United States Government to keep Dr. Allende out of office.

What came of the reported agreement on a course of action between the corporation and the agency was not made clear in the opening day's hearings.

Dr. Allende was elected President of Chile and took office on Nov. 3, 1970. He subsequently took over business properties belonging to I.T.T. and some other United States companies.

Disclosed a Year Ago

The outlines of the corporation's attempt to enlist the help of the Government to preserve its interests in Chile were disclosed a year ago when portions of a number of internal I.T.T. documents were published by the columnist Jack Anderson.

Today's testimony, together with additional documents made public by the subcommittee — documents that were voluntarily submitted by the corporation — depicted a much more prolonged and extensive pattern of consultation between the company and various Government officials than had previously been disclosed.

Mr. Merriam spoke, for example, of "25 visits" to the State Department and of having talked with Mr. Kissinger and members of his staff for a "year."

His testimony also indicated that most of the visits by company officers to six high Nixon Administration officials in 1970 and 1971—these were disclosed yesterday by another Congressional committee—had the dual purpose of talking about the company's antitrust problems with the Justice Department and about I.T.T.'s attempts to keep Dr. Allende from being elected and, later on, attempts to oust him.

The ouster plans centered on ideas to bring about "economic collapse" in Chile, according to company documents and testimony.

As part of this plan, according to Mr. Merriam, C.I.A. officials made "repeated calls to firms such as General Motors, Ford Motor Company and banks in California and New York," asking them to stop or reduce their activities in Chile to hurt her economy. These companies refused, according to other I.T.T. documents that were put into the record.

Among other items of economic warfare against the Allende Government that were proposed by the company were a cessation of all United States aid, under the guise of a review, and intercession with the World Bank and the Inter-American Development Bank to get them to stop making loans to Chile. It was not clear whether any of these proposals were accepted.

Mr. Merriam also acknowledged, when asked, that a group of Washington representatives of companies with economic interests in Chile had met several times in his office to discuss how to cope with the Allende Government.

It was not he who initiated the meetings of this ad hoc group, Mr. Merriam said, but rather the Washington representative of the Anaconda Copper Company. Other companies represented included, he said, Kennecott Copper, W. R. Grace, Pfizer, Ralston-Parma and the Bank of America.

Mr. Merriam said that the group had never arrived at any conclusions on what to do.

Senator Edmund S. Muskie, Democrat of Maine, asked why I.T.T. wanted to bring about the collapse of the Chilean economy if its aim was, as Mr. Merriam said, to make sure that Chile gave the corporation "better terms" in payment for Chitelco, the telephone company owned largely by the corporation, after the Allende Government took it over.

Mr. Merriam replied that he thought "the threat of economic collapse" might prove effective with Mr. Allende "if he knew that the banks might stop lending."

March 21, 1973

McCone Defends I.T.T. Chile Fund Idea

Denies Company Sought to Create Chaos to Balk Allende Election

By EILEEN SHANAHAN

Special to The New York Times

WASHINGTON, March 21— John A. McCone, former head of the Central Intelligence Agency and now a director of the International Telephone and Telegraph Corporation, denied repeatedly today that a fund of $1-million or more that the company had offered the United States Government for use in Chile had been intended to finance anything "surreptitious."

The willingness of I.T.T. to commit the money to the cause of preventing the election of Salvador Allende Gossens, a Marxist, as President of Chile was apparently made known both to the C.I.A. and to Henry A. Kissinger, President Nixon's adviser on national security. The person who decided to offer the money was Harold S. Geneen, board chairman of I.T.T.

Mr. McCone no longer headed the C.I.A. at the time of Mr. Geneen's original offer, in mid-1970, though he was still a consultant to the agency. He said that as an I.T.T. director he had not been told of the offer until after the first phase of the Chilean election in September, 1970, in which Dr. Allende won a plurality but not a majority.

Dr. Allende was elected by the Chilean Congress a month later and took office in November, 1970. Subsequently he took over business properties belong-

The New York Times/Mike Lien

John A. McCone, former C.I.A. head, testifying yesterday

ing to I.T.T. and some other United States companies.

Mr. McCone was testifying today before a special subcommittee of the Senate Foreign Relations Committee that is looking into the activities of American corporations that operate all over the world.

Mr. McCone said that at no time had Mr. Geneen contemplated that the proffered fund would be used to create "economic chaos," despite repeated recommendations to that effect from various people within I.T.T. and others wtihin the C.I.A.

"What he had in mind was not chaos," Mr. McCone said, "but what could be done constructively. The money was to be channeled to people who support the principles and programs the United States stands for against the programs of the Allende-Marxists."

These programs, he said, included the building of needed housing and technical assistance to Chilean agriculture.

Both Democratic and Republican members of the subcommittee reacted with considerable skepticism.

Senator Frank Church, Democrat of Idaho, the chairman of the subcommittee on multinational corporations, noted that there was nothing in the scores of internal I.T.T. documents in the committee's possession that indicated the money was for such "constructive uses."

Senator Clifford P. Chase, Republican of New Jersey, asked whether the money might not have been intended to bribe members of the Chilean Congress, who had to decide the election because none of the three candidates had won a majority. Mr. McCone denied this.

Economic Aid Noted

Senator Case noted that the United States had put more than $1-billion in economic aid into Chile in the decade before the election of Dr. Allende and that he was elected anyway.

"How could a man of Mr. Geneen's intelligence possibly think that $1-million for these kinds of purposes in six weeks could make any difference?" he asked, referring to the period remaining before the Chilean Congress decided the election. "I have too much respect for his intelligence to think that."

Senator Charles H. Percy, Republican of Illinois, suggested that another way in which $1-million might have been used to real effect would have been in subsidizing anti-Allende newspapers, which were in financial difficulties.

Other testimony has showed that I.T.T. officials had proposed this, but, according to Hal Hendrix, the company's director of public relations for Latin America, the plan was never approved.

Mr. Hendrix, who was another of today's witnesses, explained that he had proposed doubling the advertising in such newspapers by Chitelco, the Chilean telephone company controlled by I.T.T.

But he said this was vetoed by Chitelco officials "and other executives in New York" because they feared the purpose would be too obvious.

Chilean Source Cited

Mr. Hendrix also disclosed that a well-informed Chilean was the source of one of the most widely discussed assertions contained in the internal I.T.T. memoranda that have come to light—that in September, 1970, the American Ambassador to Chile, Edward M. Korry, had received a "green light" from President Nixon to do all possible short of military action to keep Dr. Allende from taking power.

Mr. Hendrix said that the information had come to him from a highly placed member of the Christian Democratic party, which was opposed to Dr. Allende, a man whom he had known and trusted for years.

Mr. McCone disclosed that as head of the C.I.A. he had received offers of financial help, similar to that made later by I.T.T., from various American corporations.

Such offers were infrequent, he said, and had always been "summarily rejected."

A main point in Mr. McCone's testimony was that none of the plans for interfering in the Chilean election—either by the C.I.A. or by I.T.T.—had been approved by the necessary high officials in either the Government or the company.

Propriety Questioned

Senator Edmund S. Muskie, Democrat of Maine, expressed concern, however, that the plans were ever "seriously considered."

"The instinct for returning to such measures in the future will be very strong and that's what concerns us," he said.

Senator Church questioned the propriety of interference by either the American Government or a company in what appeared to be a free election, no matter how much the United States might dislike the outcome.

Mr. McCone replied that "almost two-thirds of the people of Chile were opposed to Allende."

The popular vote in the election had split fairly evenly among the three candidates, with Dr. Allende receiving a small plurality.

Mr. McCone said that his general philosophy about private corporate involvement in situations such as that in Chile was that any action taken should conform with governmental policy. That is what I.T.T. was proposing, he said.

Senator Church suggested that private financing of such activities abroad was potentially so dangerous—partly because it would put the operations beyond Congressional control—that it might be wise to pass a law forbidding it.

March 22, 1973

I.T.T. Officials in Conflict On Purpose of Chile Fund

By EILEEN SHANAHAN

Special to The New York Times

WASHINGTON, March 22—A clear-cut conflict in the testimony of three officials of the International Telephone and Telegraph Corporation emerged today as a Senate subcommittee continued its inquiry into the company's alleged attempts to prevent the election of Salvador Allende Gossens, a Marxist, as President of Chile.

At issue was the question of what use was supposed to be made of the $1-million or more that the chairman of I.T.T. offered to the Federal Government in 1970—whether it was for "constructive" purposes or for covert means to prevent the election of Dr. Allende.

Today's hearings also disclosed that I.T.T. officials planned to make a deal with Dr. Allende, after he became President, under which they would be paid full value for the telephone company that I.T.T. owned in Chile, even if the properties of other Ameri-

The New York Times/George Tames

Senator Charles H. Percy, left, member of panel conducting inquiry, and Edward J. Gerrity, I.T.T. official who testified on the corporation's offer to the C.I.A.

can businesses were confiscated without payment.

The idea was to persuade President Allende that he could win world opinion to his side by making a "fair deal" with I.T.T. and that he would then be able to confiscate the properties of the Kennecott and Anaconda mining companies with impunity, using the argument that copper was a basic national resource and in a different category from a telephone company.

The company memorandum that disclosed this plan said that I.T.T. had "handled the situation in Peru" in 1968 on the "same basis." The Government of President Juan Velasco Alvarado seized the properties of International Petroleum Company, an Exxon subsidiary, but paid for its take-over of the telephone company owned by I.T.T.

The plan was never put into effect in Chile because the Allende Government broke off negotiations over the purchase of the telephone company after publication of internal I.T.T. documents showing company plans for interference in the 1970 election.

Among other developments, the subcommittee made public internal I.T.T. documents that bore mainly on the company's attempts to bring pressure on the Justice Department to settle three antitrust suits against the company.

They included a leter from Edward J. Gerrity, I.T.T.'s senior vice president for corporate relations and advertising, to Vice President Agnew in which Mr. Gerrity said, "I deeply appreciate your assistance" but did not explain for what.

Mr. Gerrity then asked for further help in getting to the then Attorney General, John N. Mitchell, "the facts" concerning the supposed attitude toward I.T.T. of Richard W. McLaren, then head of the Justice Department's antitrust division. According to Mr. Gerrity, Mr. McLaren was out of step with Administration policies, prosecuting I.T.T. simply because it was big, and more interested in the opinions of Democratic members of Congress than of the Nixon Administration.

The new documents also showed that a summary of them released earlier this week by another Congressional committee may have left a false impression about the involvement of Mr. Mitchell in the I.T.T. antitrust suits.

The summary indicated that Mr. Mitchell had talked directly with President Nixon about the suits, contrary to what he testified last year. The complete documents do not support the implication that Mr. Mitchell discussed the matter with the President.

The newly released documents also contained details about a party that was to be given in 1970 at the farm of Rogers C. B. Morton, now Secretary of the Interior, and that I.T.T. people were instrumental in arranging.

Among those who were to be present were Harold S. Geneen, the chairman of I.T.T.; Attorney General Mitchell; Vice President Agnew and his wife; a White House assistant, Peter M. Flanigan; Postmaster General Winton M. Blount, and other high officials and members of Congress. "You know the reason for this party," John F. Ryan of I.T.T. wrote to his boss, W. R. Merriam, the head of the company's Washington office.

Mr. Morton was a member of the House at the time and chairman of the Republican National Committee.

The newly released memorandum also contained a cryptic notation concerning "Dita and dollars." The reference obviously was to Mrs. Dita Beard, whose internal memorandum indicating that the company was trying to trade financial support for the Republican 1972 convention for settlement of its antitrust suits came to light a year ago. The memo mentioned the necessity "to get some feel from Dita as to what is required" without saying what the money was for.

The conflict in testimony among various I.T.T. officials that became clear today involved John A. McCone, former head of the Central Intelligence Agency and now a director of I.T.T., Mr. Gerrity, the senior vice president, and Jack D. Neal, the company's director of international relations.

Mr. McCone testified yesterday that when $1-million was first offered to the C.I.A. in mid-1970, before the first phase of the Chilean election, it was for "constructive" purposes, such as low-cost housing.

Later, Mr. McCone said, after Dr. Allende had won a plurality but not a majority of the vote in September of that year the money was intended to finance an anti-Allende coalition in the Chilean Congress, which had to make the final choice of a president.

Today Mr. Gerrity insisted the purpose was always "constructive."

He was asked who made the offer to the Government after the September election and he said it had been Mr. Neal, who made it to the Assistant Secretary of State for Latin American Affairs, Charles A. Meyer.

Jerome Levinson, counsel to the special subcommittee on multinational corporations, then read back Tuesday's testimony by Mr. Neal on his meeting with Mr. Meyer in which he said "I didn't elaborate" on what the $1-million would be used for. "We didn't go into it," he said then.

The subcommittee chairman, Senator Frank Church, Democrat of Idaho, suggested that Mr. Neal should be recalled to explain the discrepancy. Mr. Meyer is scheduled to testify next week.

In addition, the subcommittee is trying to obtain from the Government permission to release testimony it took in secret from William V. Broe, director of clandestine activities in Latin America for the C.I.A.

Subcommittee sources said that Mr. Broe's testimony showed that the purpose of the $1-million from the start was to use covert means to prevent the election of Dr. Allende.

The Chilean Embassy here published a three-page statement today complaining about what it said were falsehoods in testimony by I.T.T. officials.

The main point of the statement was that the Allende Government had never intended, or said it intended, to seize control of I.T.T.'s Chilean telephone subsidiary without payment of compensation.

C.I.A. Aide Says He Gave Anti-Allende Plan to I.T.T.

By EILEEN SHANAHAN
Special to The New York Times

WASHINGTON, March 28—An official of the Central Intelligence Agency has testified that in 1970 he proposed to the International Telephone and Telegraph Corporation a series of steps that it and other American companies might take to create enough economic instability in Chile to prevent the election of Dr. Salvador Allende Gossens as President.

The testimony came from William V. Broe, who was in charge of the Central Intelligence Agency's clandestine operations in Latin America in 1970. Mr. Broe, still a C.I.A. official, said that he had acted with the full knowledge of the man who at the time headed the agency, Richard Helms.

'Substantial Fund' Offered

Mr. Broe testified yesterday before a closed session of the subcommittee on multinational corporations of the Senate Foreign Relations Committee. Twenty-six pages of transcript were made public today. The subcommittee and the Central Intelligence Agency are still discussing the release of 18 more pages, but the subcommittee chairman, Senator Frank Church, Democrat of Idaho, said that he thought that the remaining pages were of relatively little importance.

Mr. Broe also said that Harold S. Geneen, chairman of the board of I.T.T., had initiated the first contacts between his company and the Central Intelligence Agency in the summer of 1970.

At that time, according to Mr. Broe, Mr. Geneen offered the C.I.A. "a substantial fund" to support the election of Jorge Alessandri Rodriguez, one of two relatively conservative candidates running against Dr. Allende, a Marxist who was the candidate of a Socialist-Communist coalition.

Mr. Broe said that he had turned down Mr. Geneen's offer, as I.T.T. officials testified earlied had been the case.

Mr. Broe also said that he had told Mr. Geneen that the C.I.A. could not "serve as a funding channel" for I.T.T. and that "the United States Government was not supporting any candidate in the Chilean election."

About three and a half months later, however, Mr. Broe took a different position with his proposal to the company that steps be taken to create such adverse economic conditions in Chile that Dr. Allende might be defeated.

Major Changes in Chile

What took place between the Geneen-Broe conversation in July and Mr. Broe's conversation later with Edward J. Gerrity, senior vice president of I.T.T., was not made completely clear by the transcript.

A major change was that the first phase of the Chilean election had occurred by the time of the meeting with Mr. Gerrity. Dr. Allende in the popular vote on Sept. 4, 1970, had won a plurality but not a majority of the popular vote and the final decision lay with the Chilean Congress—which elected Dr. Allende President on Oct. 24.

The transcript of the testimony here does not show whether it was the increasing likelihood that Dr. Allende would be elected that had changed the apparent position of the C.I.A. or whether other forces had been at work. International Telephone and Telegraph Corporation officials had in the meantime, been talking to the State Department and President Nixon's adviser on national security, Henry A. Kissinger Business properties belonging to I.T.T. were seized after Dr. Allende took office in November, 1970.

'Thesis' About Economy

Mr. Broe said that when he saw Mr. Gerrrity about a month before the Chilean Congress vote, "There was a thesis that additional deterioration in the economic situation could influence a number of Christian-Democratic Congressmen who were planning to vote for Allende" not to do so.

The following exchange then took place in the hearing here:

Senator Church: Did you discuss with Mr. Gerrity the feasibility of banks not renewing credits or delaying in doing so?

Mr. Broe: Yes, sir.

Senator Church: Did you discuss with Mr. Gerrity the feasibility of companies dragging their feet in spending money [in Chile] and in making deliveries and in shipping spare parts?

Mr. Broe: Yes, I did.

Senator Church: Did you discuss with Mr. Gerrity the feasibility of creating pressure on savings and loan institutions in Chile so that they would have to shut their doors, thereby creating stronger pressure?

Mr. Broe: Yes.

Senator Church: Did you discuss with Mr. Gerrity the feasibility of withdrawing all technical help and not promising any technical assistance in the future?

Mr. Broe: Yes, sir.

Suggestions Were Rejected

According to internal I.T.T. memorandums that were read into the subcommittee's record last week, Mr. Geneen rejected Mr. Broe's suggestions because he felt that they would not work.

Mr. Broe also testified, in contradiction to the contents of other I.T.T. documents, that the purpose of attempting to create instability was not to encourage a take-over by the Chilean military.

Nor, he said, had the C.I.A. made any approaches to the Chilean military, contrary to what appeared to have been reported in a memorandum from William R. Merriam, the head of I.T.T.'s Washington office.

The questions and answers on this point were as follows:

Senator Church: Did you advise Mr. Merriam that approaches continue to be made to select members of the armed forces in an attempt to have them lead some sort of uprising?

Mr. Broe: No. On a number of occasions Mr. Merriam questioned me regarding possible action by the military, as this was a subject everyone was interested in. I advised him that our coverage of the military gave no indication they would take action.

Other matters, either contained in I.T.T. documents or testified to earlier by I.T.T. officials, were also contradicted by Mr. Broe and other witnesses today.

Chief among these was the assertion that Central Intelligence Agency officials had directly approached officials of United States banks, suggesting that they cut off credit to Chilean businesses and citizens.

Mr. Broe said that "the only company that I had anything to do with in regard to Chile was I.T.T."

Officials of the First National City Bank, the Chase Manhattan Bank and Manufacturers Hanover Trust, all in New York City, all denied discussing any cutoff of credit with either C.I.A. or I.T.T. personnel.

All said, however, that they had been approached by Chilean politicians for financial help in the presidential campaign.

Mr. Broe's testimony left unanswered the question of whether anyone in a higher position than Mr. Helms, the Director of Central Intelligence at the time, had known of Mr. Broe's proposals to Mr. Gerrity that the International Telephone and Telegraph Corporation and other American companies in Chile attempt to create economic instability there.

He was not asked the question and subcommittee sources said that the reason was that the subcommittee had agreed in advance to limit its questions to the subject of Mr. Broe's contacts with I.T.T. officials.

Since regulations covering the operations of the Central Intelligence Agency are not made public, it is not clear whether Mr. Broe's approach to Mr. Gerrity should have been cleared by the so-called 40 Committee, an inter-agency body with members from the State and Defense Departments, the C.I.A. and the National Security Council. The committee is supposed to approve, in advance, certain C.I.A. operations.

In releasing the transcript, Senator Church said that he thought it improper for either private companies or the United States Government to intervene in a free election—which the election of Dr. Allende was, by all accounts. He commented that at the same time the ideas for intervention in Chile were being discussed, the United States was fighting a war in Vietnam, the stated purpose of which was to assure free elections there.

March 29, 1973

Geneen Concedes I.T.T. Fund Offer To Block Allende

By EILEEN SHANAHAN
Special to The New York Times

WASHINGTON, April 2—Harold S. Geneen, chairman of the International Telephone and Telegraph Corporation, said today that he did not recall having offered a "substantial" sum of money to the Central Intelligence Agency in 1970 to help prevent the election of Salvador Allende Gossens as President of Chile.

But Mr. Geneen told a Senate subcommittee that, since he had "no recollection to the contrary," he would accept the testimony of William V. Broe, a C.I.A. official who

said he had been offered the money in 1970. At the time, Mr. Broe was the head of the intelligence agency's clandestine operations in Latin America.

Mr. Geneen testified about the events of 1970 and 1971 before the subcommittee on multinational corporations of the Senate Foreign Relations Committee. He was the final witness in the first phase of the subcommittee's inquiry into the actions of these large companies, which operate all over the world, and the extent to which they may influence United States foreign policy.

Mr. Geneen said that, assuming he did make the offer of cash to Mr. Broe, it was probably an "emotional reaction" to learning from their conversation that the United States was planning no action to attempt to defeat Dr. Allende, who is a Marxist and who had campaigned on a platform of nationalization of basic industries.

Mr. Geneen said that the hands-off policy of the United States in 1970 represented a reversal of a policy dating back 14 years—"the policy to maintain a democratic government in Chile," through large-scale economic aid and in other ways.

He said he was particularly upset because he, with other American businessmen, had been encouraged to invest in Chile as part of the United States Government's program

The New York Times

Harold S. Geneen, head of I.T.T., before the Senate Foreign Relations subcommittee yesterday.

of helping to develop the country and keep it democratic.

Mr. Geneen defended his action in going to the C.I.A. to discuss the election in Chile and confirmed that it was John A. McCone, a former head of the intelligence agency and now a director of I.T.T., who had first suggested this to him.

Mr. Geneen said he saw nothing improper in an American corporation dealing with the C.I.A. since the agency was part of the Government and any company had the right to "petition the Government" on behalf of its own interests.

Senator Frank Church, Democrat of Idaho, asked why Mr. Geneen went to the intelligence agency if the company was only "petitioning" the Government.

Mr. Geneen replied, "I think of them as suppliers of good information." He said his basic mission had been to find out what the Government thought about the situation in Chile.

Senator Charles H. Percy, Republican of Illinois, asked why Mr. Geneen thought the agency had designated Mr. Broe to talk to I.T.T. officials when he was in charge of covert operations if the purpose of the talks was merely information.

Mr. Geneen replied that he "never knew there was a distinction" between intelligence gathering and clandestine operations until the subcommittee's hearings. "Broe just identified himself as involved in Latin America or something like that," he said.

Mr. Geneen's acknowledgement that he might have made a cash offer to Mr. Broe, along with testimony by other I.T.T. officials today, removed from the hearing record some of the inconsistencies that had caused Senator Church last week to threaten prosecution of someone for perjury.

The question of perjury centered on the persistent claims of I.T.T. officials—continued by Mr. Geneen today—that the money that was offered to the Government was for "constructive" purposes, such as aid for low-cost housing in Chile.

Mr. Geneen today argued that there were two offers. The first, he said, was the one he may have made in an emotional moment to Mr. Broe and promptly forgot this was aimed at financing an anti-Allende candidate. The second and later offer, he said, was intended to be made to the State Department and the White House office of Henry A. Kissinger and was for the "constructive" purposes.

The second offer was never clearly explained to anyone in the Government, according to today's testimony, because officials in the company's Washington office never received the instructions Mr. Geneen intended them to get about the "constructive" purposes of the proffered $1-million.

Edward J. Gerrity, a senior vice president of I.T.T., testified that he thought he had made this intention clear to William R. Merriam, then the head of the company's Washington office, but that he had apparently failed to do so, since Mr. Merriam seemed never to have made it clear to his subordinates who were dealing with the Government.

April 3, 1973

Senate Group Finds I.T.T. And U.S. at Fault on Chile

Allende Target of Proposals

By E. W. KENWORTHY

Special to The New York Times

WASHINGTON, June 21 — A Senate subcommittee said today that the International Telephone and Telegraph Corporation had "overstepped the line of acceptable corporate behavior" by seeking to enlist the help of the Central Intelligence Agency to prevent the election of Salvador Allende Gossens as President of Chile in 1970.

The Senate Foreign Relations subcommittee on multinational corporations also critized the United States Government, charging that it had apparently approved a C.I.A. effort to engage the help of I.T.T. for the same purpose.

As it turned out, the intelligence agency did not accept the I.T.T. proposals, which the subcommittee said, involved an offer to contribute $1-million to finance any plan "to manipulate the outcome" of the election in Chile, where the corporation had large investments.

Nor did I.T.T. agree to what was described as a C.I.A. plan to create economic chaos in Chile to rally anti-Allende sentiment in the Chilean Congress.

At that point in 1970, Dr. Allende, a Marxist, had won a bare plurality in a three-way race for the Presidency, requiring, under the Chilean Constitution, that the choice be made by a joint session of Congress. On Oct. 24 Congress elected him President by a vote of 153 to 42.

The criticism of both the corporation and the United States Government came today in a final report by the Senate subcommittee on its inquiry last March and April into the relations of I.T.T. and the C.I.A. during the Chilean elections.

The subcommittee made two proposals. The first and, according to the subcommittee's staff, the most important, was that clandestine operations of the C.I.A. be subject to responsible and effective review, both within the executive branch and by the United States Congress.

The second proposal was for a bill that would make it a criminal offense for a United States citizen or resident to make, or offer to make, a contribution to a government agency or officer to influence a foreign election. It would likewise be a criminal offense for a government agency or officer to solicit such a contribution.

The penalty for violating the act would be a fine of up to $10,000, or up to five years in prison, or both.

In its report, the subcommittee was particularly critical of the so-called Forty Committee, an interdepartmental group that reviews the C.I.A.'s clandestine operations. It is headed by Henry A. Kissinger, President Nixon's adviser on national security.

Senator Frank Church, Democrat of Idaho, who is the subcommittee's chairman, said at a news conference that it was not clear whether the Forty Committee was informed in advance of the C.I.A.'s proposal to International Telephone and Telegraph to create economic chaos in Chile, or whether it had considered the consequences, either for the United States Government or for American business abroad, of using "companies like I.T.T. for clandestine C.I.A. assignments."

At present, only the Senate Armed Services Committee oversees the Central Intelligence Agency. Mr. Church said today that it "has done very little overseeing."

The subcommittee's inquiry grew out of several columns by Jack Anderson, the syndicated Washington columnist, beginning March 21, 1972, charging that I.T.T. had been involved in "a bizarre plot" to stop Dr. Allende's election and that it had sought the intelligence agency's cooperation. The articles were based on I.T.T. documents obtained by Mr. Anderson.

The company feared Dr. Allende's election, according to its internal documents and testimony by its officials, because of the possibility he might order the expropriation of the Chilean Telephone Company, in which I.T.T. had a 70 per cent interest worth $153-million.

According to testimony before the Church subcommittee by Charles A. Meyer, former Assistant Secretary of State for Inter-American Affairs, United States policy before Dr. Allende won a plurality in the popular election for President on Sept. 4, 1970, was that the Presidential race was an internal Chilean matter to be allowed to run its course without interference.

The subcommittee reported that, according to testimony it had taken, the I.T.T. offered funds to the C.I.A. on two occasions for use against the candidacy of Dr. Allende.

The first was said to have been on July 16, 1970, when Harold S. Geneen, the corporation's chairman, met in Washington with William V. Broe, the intelligence agency's chief of clandestine services for Latin America.

According to Mr. Broe, Mr. Geneen offered a "substantial" election fund to be used to help a conservative opponent of Dr. Allende. Mr. Broe said he refused the offer.

The second offer was reportedly made in September, 1970, after Dr. Allende had eked out a plurality in the three-way race. Mr. Geneen was quoted as having said at an I.T.T. board meeting that he was prepared to put up as much as $1-million "in support of any plan that was adopted by the Government for the purpose of bringing about a coalition" in the Chilean Congress to defeat Dr. Allende.

John A. McCone, a director of the corporation and former head of the C.I.A., testified that he had transmitted the offer to Mr. Kissinger and Richard Helms, then the Director of Central Intelligence. According to Mr. McCone, Mr. Kissinger said he would call back on the matter but never did.

Then on Sept. 29, 1970, about a month before the Chilean Congress confirmed Dr. Allende as President, the United States government took the initiative, according to the report of the Church subcommittee.

It said that Mr. Broe, on Mr. Helm's instructions, met with Edward J. Gerrity, I.T.T.'s vice president for corporate relations, and proposed a plan for creating economic chaos in Chile as a means of defeating Dr. Allende.

The plan was said to have called for American banks to refuse further credits, for companies to "dray their feet in sending money, in making deliveries, in shipping spare parts" and for the United States Government to withdraw all technical aid.

Mr. Gerrity and Mr. McCone both told Mr. Geneen they thought the C.I.A. plan was unworkable, according to the subcommittee's report, and Mr. Geneen decided not to go along with it.

June 22, 1973

SAUDI ARABI

CHAPTER 6

The Oil Crisis

The OPEC meeting in Algiers, 1975.
Courtesy The New York Times

OIL PARLEY SEEKS TO RESTORE PRICE

Caracas Conference Also Is Reported Aiming at Regulating Output

Special to The New York Times.

CARACAS, Venezuela, Jan. 16—Restoration of crude oil prices to the level prevailing before cuts were made last year and machinery to regulate production were cited by President Romulo Betancourt as the principal aims of the second conference of the Organization of Petroleum Exporting Countries, which he officially opened here today.

It is the first meeting held since the formation of the organization in Baghdad on last Sept. 14. The conference will lay the foundation for a permanent organization and also will adopt resolutions concerning the principal reason for its formation: falling prices of oil. The participants are Venezuela, Iraq, Saudi Arabia, Iran, Kuwait and Qatar, the last named to be admitted this week. Together, these countries are said to represent 90 per cent of the international trade in oil.

Restoration of Prices

The oil producing nations, Señor Betancourt said, "cannot sell at bargain prices a wealth which is every day more valuable." The organization, he said, would unify the policies of members and endeavor to restore prices to "levels prevailing before reductions." It will also aim at securing consultations with companies before any price modifications are made, he said.

Señor Betancourt asked for machinery for regulation of production. Such machinery, he said, exists within the United States. The present organization should, therefore, surprise no one, he said.

The conference will last four days starting today. The temporary chairman today was Mohammed Salman of Iraq, who said he hoped "cooperation with companies" would grow out of the conference.

Inspection Trips Set

The Iraqi delegate later turned over the chair to Dr. Juan Pablo Perez Alfonzo of Venezuela. Beginning on Friday, delegates will make inspection trips to oil installations of Venezuela.

The four days of sessions this week are closed to all but delegates. However, it is known that they will establish a budget and work out details of organization; they will decide on permanent headquarters; they will admit the Sheikdom of Qatar; they will consider admission of other countries — although, according to statutes, members must be net exporters; they will discuss the future role of the Soviet Union in international petroleum trade; they will discuss the possibility of prorationing their production; and, above all, they will decide what policies to adopt concerning prices.

Delegation heads are: for Venezuela, Dr. Juan Pablo Perez Alfonzo; Iraq, Mohammed Salman, Minister of Petroleum; Saudi Arabia, Abdulla Tariki, Minister of Petroleum; Kuwait, Ahmad Sayed Omar; Iran, F. Rouhani. Qatar is represented by Hussen Kamel.

January 17, 1961

WORLD OIL GROUP LISTS ITS GOALS

Exporting Countries Will Work Out Proposals on Prices and Profits

SEAT TO BE IN GENEVA

Decisions Made at Caracas Parley Are Reported—'Understanding' Asked

CARACAS, Venezuela, Feb. 14—The organization of Petroleum Exporting Countries has decided to ask each member nation to state its position "in the matter of determination of oil prices" and will then decide on measures to adopt. It has also heard "from most of the members" that oil companies' profits are "in excess of what may be regarded as fair" and will prepare recommendations for the next meeting "in order to correct the position."

However, no specific measures have yet been decided upon.

These were some of the conclusions reached at the recent January conference in Caracas of O. P. E. C. They are being released simultaneously by all of the member countries. The organization said it would refer statements of member countries on prices to its legal advisers and then decide on recommendations "with the object of restoring prices to levels which members consider justified."

The conference also resolved to ask "friendly countries" that had policies of restrictions and quotas—presumably such countries as the United States—for a discussion of these quotas in order to arrive at "satisfactory solutions."

Proposals for Venezuela

Concerning Venezuela, O. P. E. C. said it had been informed "of the curtailment of activities in the development of the Venezuelan petroleum industry" and would examine the situation and propose remedies.

The statement also asked for "a spirit of understanding" in discussions now going on between some of the members and the companies.

The permanent seat of O. P. E. C. will be in Geneva, it was announced.

The organization will consist of a "conference," which will be held twice a year; and a board of governors—each member with one governor—which will meet at least four times a year. The chairman of the board will also be secretary general. The first chairman is Fuad Rouhani of Iran. The secretariat in Geneva will contain the departments of technology, including geology, marketing, production and finance; administration; public relations, and an enforcement section.

Budget Set

The initial budget for the organization will be £150,000.

It is not supposed that the statement on profits applies to Venezuela, which has said it has a satisfactory share, but rather to Middle Eastern countries.

No comment was as yet available concerning the statements made.

It was noted that most of the text had to do with the establishment of the organization and that specific measures on such questions as prices and prorationing were referred to special groups for study and later decisions.

The organization was founded last September in Baghdad with the object of raising oil prices and protecting the interests of member countries. Its members are Venezuela, Kuwait, Iran, Saudi Arabia, Iraq and Qatar—presumably representing more than 90 per cent of the international oil business.

February 15, 1961

OIL CONCERNS FACE FOREIGN DILEMMA

Producing Nations Pressing for a Larger Share of Concession Profits

By J. H. CARMICAL

Oil operations abroad by private companies are becoming increasingly unattractive. To cover growing costs of governmental operations, including ambitious long-term development programs, some of the host countries are demanding a bigger share of the profits.

For a little more than a decade, the practice generally has been to split profits from oil operations equally between the operating company and the government of the producing nation. Since the oil companies had to assume the risk of discovering the oil and also had to provide transportation and markets for it when found, the consensus generally had been that such an arrangement was fair to both parties.

Pattern Broken

Now, however, it seems that this old formula is being discarded. Since the profit-sharing is done through taxation, there is little the companies can do when assigned a higher rate other than to pay it or withdraw from that particular country. With heavy investments at stake, they usually try to work under the new rates.

The first important break in the fifty-fifty profit-sharing pattern came late in 1958, when Venezuela decreed a rise in the income tax that made the Government's take 60 to 65 per cent.

The oil companies in Venezuela were surprised by this action, but had to accept it. Washington took the position that the question of levying taxes in Venezuela was a matter for that Government to determine.

The result was that oil drilling and exploration efforts in the country dropped sharply and Venezuelan oil was placed in a less advantageous competitive position in world oil markets.

The next most important break in the pattern came late last month, when President Sukarno of Indonesia decreed that Government would take 60 per cent of the profits of foreign oil companies there.

This action came in the midst of discussions which had been going on since January between the Government and the foreign oil companies in Indonesia on whether the companies should come under a new petroleum law promulgated late in October, 1960. Under that law, foreign-owned companies would operate under contract to state-owned companies and would be able to obtain further concessions.

Terms Will Vary

Just how the new profit-sharing plan will work out has not yet been determined. However, it is understood that its terms will vary somewhat with the three companies involved, bcause of their different operating positions in Indonesia.

The three foreign companies are the Caltex Pacific Oil Company, owned jointly by Texaco, Inc., and the Standard Oil Company of California; the Standard Oil Company (New Jersey) and the Socony Mobil Oil Company, Inc., and Shell Indonesia Company, Ltd., a member of the Royal Dutch-Shell Group.

The combined production of these companies in Indonesia now is about 420,000 barrels a day, of which Caltex accounts for about 235,000 barrels, Shell Indonesia 115,000 barrels and Standard-Vacuum 70,000.

Indonesia is among the oldest known oil-producing aras in the world. As far back as 971 A. D., when a Chinese emperor claimed sovereignty over the area, jugs of crude oil from oil seepages were sent to the emperor as tribute. Later, the Portuguese mixed oil from the seepages with a type of wild cotton to calk their ships.

The first oil concession was granted in 1883. This was to a person who later merged it into the Royal Dutch Company, which was formed in 1890 to work the oil wells of the East Indies. In 1892, Royal Dutch built its first refinery in Sumatra.

In 1912, when the predecessor company to Standard-Vacuum bought out a small company in Java, Royal Dutch had practically all the production of what is now Indonesia. In 1922, however, the Standard Oil organization opened in Sumatra was then one of the world's most prolific oil field with wells flowing up to 15,000 barrels a day.

Caltex's entrance into Indonesia was through the California Standard Oil, which obtained a concession in 1930. Its first productive discovery was in 1939, after Texaco had become a partner. With the outbreak of World War II, operations soon were suspended and it was not until 1952 that Caltex was making commercial sales of Indonesian oil.

Investments Noted

It is estimated that Caltex has invested about $135,000,000 in Indonesia—$120,000,000 since the end of World War II. Since the end of the war, Standard-Vacuum has spent about $80,000,000 to modernize and expand its installations and develop new fields.

After 1945, Shell Indonesia's expenses were extremely heavy because of extensive damage incurred in the war at its refineries and oil fields. At present, Shell is making vast expenditures involving principally the development of a new field in Borneo and construction of a 160-mile pipeline from that field to its Balikpapan refinery.

In addition to these foreign-owned companies, there are three concerns formed after the war by the Indonesian Government, which have a combined production of about 50,000 barrels a day.

Grants Made by Dutch

The concessions that three foreign oil companies now operate in Indonesia were obtained under the old Dutch regime. Since Dec. 27, 1949, when the Netherlands granted Indonesia independence, the oil companies have continued to operate under the old Dutch laws, with profits shared roughly fifty-fifty between the new Government and the companies.

No new concessions have been granted by the Indonesian Government, because it has been awaiting the promulgation of a new petroleum law. Such a law was difficult to enact because of the conflicting views represented by the large number of political parties that emerged after independence was gained.

In 1959, after several rebellions, President Sukarno declared a state of emergency, dissolved Parliament and declared the Western type of parliamentary government not suited for the country. Another Parliament was appointed, but with limited powers. Under emergency regulations, President Sukarno now rules the Indonesia by decrees.

Tax Outlook Unclear

Since the start of this year, the tax position of foreign oil companies in Indonesia has been unclear, and ultimately it will have to be resolved on a retroactive basis. Generally, the new tax decree is regarded essentially as a detail in the implementation of the 1960 law. However, it is indefinite and the oil companies still do not know exactly where they stand.

The position of the companies is that they will continue to operate, assuming that something can be worked out later in the year, perhaps when President Sukarno returns from a foreign tour.

So far as can be ascertained, none of the companies has agreed to profit-sharing on the basis outlined in the decree. If a rate as high as 60 per cent is put into effect, the companies assert, Indonesian oil would not be competitive with that produced in other areas.

September 10, 1961

OIL GROUP SEEKS CRUDE PRICE RISE

Eight Exporting Nations Call Concerns to Talks

Special to The New York Times.

GENEVA, July 2—The Organization of Petroleum Exporting Countries has called for the opening of negotiations with the oil companies concerning a crude price rise.

The request that each member state open negotiations "forthwith" with the companies was made in a resolution the organization published here today.

The resolution was adopted by the oil-producing nations at their fourth conference, which ended here last month.

With the admission of Libya and Indonesia by another resolution adopted at that session, the organization now comprises eight states representing over 90 per cent of the free world's oil exports, a spokesman said. The other members are Venezuela, Kuwait, Saudi Arabia, Qatar, Iran and Iraq.

Earlier Protest Recalled

The resolution on prices recalled the organization's earlier protests over the August, 1960, reductions in the price of crude by the companies.

Unless the negotiations are assured within a "reasonable period" and prices restored to no lower than those before the 1960 cuts, the resolution said, member countries "shall consult with each other with a view to taking such steps as they deem appropriate" to achieve the desired result.

The resolution complained that the fall in the prices of crude has reduced the revenue the member countries receive from their oil and has "seriously" dislocated their economies.

In the same resolution, the conference decided that member countries would formulate a "rational price structure to guide their long-term policy."

"An important element of the price structure to be devised," it was stated, "will be the linking of crude oil prices to an index of goods, which the member countries need to import."

The conference decided to hold its fifth session at Riyadh, Saudi Arabia, beginning Nov. 17.

July 3, 1962

MIDEAST IS IRKED ON OIL ROYALTIES

Exporting Lands Chide Big Concerns on Payments

Special to The New York Times.

GENEVA, March 21 — The Organization of Petroleum Exporting Countries denounced today the "uncompromising attitude" of the big Western oil groups toward its demand for higher royalty payments for crude oil sold by its members.

The unsatisfactory state of the negotiations of the demand has necessitated the postponement of the conference the organization was to hold at Riyadh, the Saudi Arabian capital, on March 30, the export group said.

Instead, it was explained, "chief representatives of the organization's eight member governments are to meet at the agency's headquarters here on April 2 for a "full discussion of all aspects of the situation."

The member countries are Iran, Iraq, Saudi Arabia, Qatar, Kuwait, Libya, Indonesia and Venezuela, but the dispute concerns primarily the Middle East countries.

Separate negotiations were begun last year by Iran and Saudi Arabia with the oil companies holding concessions from them. Most of the major Western companies were involved.

End of Price Cut Sought

The negotiations were on the so-called "Geneva Resolutions" in which the organization called for the restoration of a 1960 cut in posted prices for Middle East crude oil. The resolutions also aimed at increasing government oil revenues in the producing countries by eliminating company deductions for royalty payments and marketing expenses.

An official of a United States oil company has estimated that the demands would cost the companies more than $500,000,000 a year.

The statement issued today said that "an extraordinary" meeting held here by the exporting organization's board of governors found that the situation resulting from the negotiations "was not satisfactory." Nevertheless, it added, the situation "could not be regarded as a deadlock."

The board said that the companies had shown a "spirit of willingness to discuss matters in a friendly atmosphere," but gave "no indication of intending to comply" with the proposal on royalties.

Fuad Rouhani of Iran, secretary general of the organization, told a press conference that the outlook for an increased return on the oil companies' investment could change the position. Already, he said, company profits have improved.

As the return on investment continues to improve, the companies "will be better able to meet our wishes," Mr. Rouhani remarked.

In response to a question on the possible loss of markets to Soviet oil, Mr. Rouhani said that Soviet shipments had not attained a "serious magnitude." But, he added, it is hoped that the West "will remember that anything done to encourage increased penetration of Western markets by Soviet oil will be considered unfortunate by our countries."

Companies Are Named

GENEVA, March 21 (Reuters) — The eight oil companies criticized by the Organization of Petroleum Exporting Countries were Standard Oil of New Jersey, Gulf, Texaco, Socony and Standard of California, all American, and British Petroleum, Shell and France's Compagnies Francaises de Petrol.

March 22, 1963

MIDEAST OIL PACT IMPROVES PICTURE

Stability Seen in Agreement by Saudi Arabia, Aramco

By J. H. CARMICAL

A recent agreement between the Saudi Arabian Government and the Arabian American Oil Company covers a full range of issues that have plagued the relationship between the company and the Government for many years.

With the settlement of these issues, the agreement may usher in an era of stability not only between Aramco and the Saudi Arabian Government but it may have an important bearing in improving the relationship between the governments of other Middle Eastern countries and the oil companies.

These countries are under constant pressure from within and without, regardless of how they deal with the companies. The fact that differences may be settled without government recourse to drastic action is considered most important.

Another encouraging factor of the agreement is that it was made within the framework of the 50-50 split in profits between the oil company and the Saudi Arabian Government.

Probably the most important part of the agreement concerned the stand of the Saudi Arabian Government that Aramco should have accounted in its income tax returns for sales of crude oil at the Mediterranean port of Sidon, Lebanon, at the posted price there rather than at Ras Tanura, Saudi Arabia. The oil is transported by the Trans-Arabian Pipe Line Company from the vicinity of Ras Tanura to Sidon, but the shareholding interest in the pipeline is the same as in Aramco.

Government's Stand

The question was first raised in 1956 and the Saudi Arabian Government held that it should have shared in the profits from the higher Sidon price, which now is $2.17 a barrel compared with $1.80 at Ras Tanura. The differential over the years has varied from 37 cents a barrel to 72 cents during the Suez Canal crisis late in 1956 and early in 1957.

The Government said that, after deducting the cost of operating Tapline, as the pipeline is called, it should be paid as taxes 50 per cent of the profits resulting from the pipeline operation. In the recent settlement this is provided for back to Oct. 6, 1953.

For the years prior to 1953, the Government reserves its right on this issue, but the agreement provides that claims prior to that date be submitted to arbitration, since Aramco maintains that a 1954 agreement settled all issues prior to Oct. 6, 1953.

The parties to the agreement have not disclosed the cost to Aramco, but various unofficial estimates indicate that it will be in the neighborhood of $100,000,000, excluding any claims that may result from the question to be submitted to arbitration.

For the future, Aramco also has agreed to pay taxes at the rate of 50 per cent of the profits from pipeline operations. This will be based on the difference between the posted prices of crude oil at Sidon and at Ras Tanura after operating costs have been deducted.

In addition, if necessary, Tapline will pay a transit fee sufficient to bring total payments to Saudi Arabia up to a rate equivalent to that provided in the transit agreements concluded in 1962 with Jordan, Syria and Lebanon.

Territory Relinquished

The added payments that Saudi Arabia will receive from Tapline and Aramco will amount to about $12,000,000 a year at the present throughput of 350,000 barrels a day.

The settlement also provided that Aramco relinquish immediately 227,000 square miles of territory on which it had a right to explore for oil and gas. The maximum area over which Aramco had these rights covered some 500,000 square miles, but that previously had been reduced to 352,000. Aramco now has been left 125,000 square miles, which is a territory about one-half the size of Texas.

The New York Times April 14, 1963

Map shows Aramco's maximum and remaining oil areas

Over the next 30 years, the agreement provides that Aramco periodically will make additional relinquishments that will reduce the retained area in which it has exclusive rights to 20,000 square miles at the time of the expiration of the concession in 1999.

The company has selected the areas that will be given up now and also will select any area to be relinquished in the future. The areas that have been released have been fairly well explored and at present have no oil production.

Aramco further agreed to capitalize and amortize all exploration costs at a rate of 5 per cent a year rather than deduct them as a charge against income in the year in which they were incurred. Intangible drilling costs, mostly expenses for labor, will be amortized at the rate of 10 per cent a year rather than charged against current income.

Tapline also has agreed to build an asphalt highway parallel to the pipeline between the Persian Gulf and the Jordanian border. It is estimated that the road will cost about $7,000,000.

After the road is built, $500,000 a year will be given to the Saudi Arabian Government as a contribution to its maintenance. Aramco has an obligation to maintain the present unpaved road, which also parallels the pipeline. After the new road is paved this obligation will cease.

Aramco is owned 30 per cent each by the Standard Oil Company (New Jersey), Texaco, Inc., and the Standard Oil Company of California. The remaining 10 per cent is held by the Socony Mobil Oil Company, Inc.

Production by Aramco in Saudi Arabia last year averaged 1,520,000 barrels a day, a new high. At the year-end known reserves developed by Aramco in the country were about 52,000,000,000 barrels, or enough at last year's rate of production to last nearly 100 years.

In 1962 the Saudi Arabian Governent received actual cash payments of a bit better than $400,000,000 from oil operations nearly all of which came from Aramco.

April 14, 1963

Better Royalties Sought By Oil Exporting Countries

GENVA, Aug. 10 (Comtelburo)—Members of the Organization of Petroleum Exporting Countries (O. P. E. C.) have agreed to bargain collectively for better royalties from the big oil companies, officials of the organization said here. They hoped to obtain a uniform rate of not less than 20 per cent.

The move primarily concerns Iran, Iraq, Kuwait, Saudi Arabia and Qatar, which at present get about 12.5 per cent of crude prices.

The other members of the O. P. E. C. are Libya, Venezuela and Indonesia. The O. P. E. C. has authorized its secretary, Euad Ruhani of Iran, to carry out the bargaining.

August 11, 1963

MIDEAST NATIONS REJECT OIL OFFER

Special to The New York Times

GENEVA, Dec. 6—The organization of Petroleum Exporting Countries announced today that it had rejected an offer concerning royalties made by the major oil companies operating in the Middle East.

It also said it had scheduled for Dec. 24 at Riyadh, Saudi Arabia, a conference to decide the action to be taken in view of the breakdown in the negotiations with the companies.

The royalty issue directly concerns only six of the eight-nation organization's member states and the companies holding concessions from them to extract oil.

The six states are Iran, Iraq, Saudi Arabia, Libya, Kuwait and Qatar. Indonesia and Venezuela are the other two member countries.

The dispute is primarily over the question of the "expensing" of royalties. The countries concerned object to royalty payments made to them by the companies being treated by these as a credit against their income tax liability. In short, the governments are seeking a higher rate of income from their oil.

December 7, 1963

U.A.R. NATIONALIZES TWO OIL COMPANIES

CAIRO, March 24 (Reuters)—President Gamal Abdel Nasser tonight issued a decree nationalizing properties of the Shell International Petroleum Company and the former Anglo-Egyptian Oilfields Company, now called Al Nasr Oilfields Company, the Middle East News Agency announced.

The oil operations affected by the nationalization decree are small by Middle Eastern oil standards but fairly large in terms of the limited production of the United Arab Republic.

Al Nasr Oilfields Company, formerly Anglo-Egyptian Oilfields, produces about 20,000 barrels of crude oil a day, or about one-sixth of the nation's total daily output of 120,000 barrels. It operates a refinery at Suez with a capacity of 60,000 barrels a day. According to a Shell spokesman in London, the Shell company in the U.A.R. is a marketing organization.

The British Petroleum Company, in which the British Government owns a large interest, and the Royal Dutch-Shell Group have a 31 per cent interest in Al Nasr. The Government holds most of the stock.

In recent months, the Government has awarded exploration concessions to two American companies — Phillips Petroleum Company and Standard Oil Company (Indiana) — and the Italian Government's oil company, Ente Nazionale Idrocarburi.

March 25, 1964

SYRIA IS CLAIMING RIGHTS TO HER OIL

Government Will Refuse to Grant Any Concessions

By DANA ADAMS SCHMIDT
Special to The New York Times

BEIRUT, Lebanon, Dec. 24—The Syrian Government has decided to "nationalize" its oil resources in advance, before the problem arises.

The Presidency Council, the highest Government body, has decided all oil and mineral resources will be exploited directly by the state—and that no concessions will be granted to anyone.

A decree issued by the Socialist Government of Syria, whose ruling party is called Baathist, meaning Socialist Renaissance, recalled that according to the interim constitution, all natural wealth belongs to the masses of the people and the state owns public utilities and the means by which the peoples' basic needs are produced.

Therefore, it concluded, "The state must by itself and directly exploit mineral and petroleum wealth in accordance with its Socialist policy and must not grant concessions to any agency outside the administration of the state."

Made at Meeting

The decision was made at a meeting attended by Lieut. Gen. Amin-el-Hafez, the President, and Sheik Abdullah Tariki, former Saudi Minister of Oil, whose activities as oil consultant now include advising the Syrian Government.

The Syrian Government's decision was a big disappointment to the West German company, Concordia, which has discovered oil in Syria's easternmost province at Suwaidiya and has been working hard for exploitation rights. Concordia would have been the first German firm to win exploitation rights in the Arab Middle East. Some diplomats believe the Germans were even tying final action on their promise of a 350 million mark loan for a dam on the Euphrates to approval of Concordia's concession.

Concordia's field at Suwaidiya is Syria's largest, according to official Syrian statistics, which show proven reserves of 450 million tons. The next largest field, discovered by Soviet technicians employed by the Syrian General Petroleum Authority is Karachuk, whose proven reserves are less than half those of Suwaidiya.

Syria is expected to establish her own company to exploit and market oil. She will be the first Middle Eastern country to attempt doing so without a previous partnership with one of the big international oil companies. But almost all Middle Eastern oil producers now have national oil companies in addition to international companies. In Iran, the national oil company has actually undertaken exploitation of areas given up by the international companies. In Iraq and Kuwait, national companies are on paper. In Saudi Arabia, Petromin is building a refinery and talking about exploiting some fields abandoned by the Arabian American Oil Company.

December 25, 1964

Mideast War Still Slows Trade

Canal Closing Is Assessed

By BRENDAN JONES

Nearly six weeks after the closing of the Suez Canal, world trade finds itself a little breathless but far from strangled.

Even before the latest closing of the 103-mile waterway, the old concept of the canal as a vital artery, if not the jugular vein, of international trade had become debatable. But the speed with which the flow of trade has adjusted to alternative routes is raising a basic question: How essential is the Suez to global commerce—now and in the future?

It obviously will be some time before there are clear answers to the question. Much depends on how long the canal remains closed and on the continued flow of oil, particularly by the long route around the Cape of Good Hope, from producers east of Suez.

Adjustments to the closing of the canal, ordered by President Gamel Abdel Nasser of the United Arab Republic on June 6, have been costly. The cost for Western Europe, largely in terms of higher shipping costs for oil, has been estimated roughly at about $1-billion for the balance of this year.

The essential fact, however, is that adjustment on the vital need—oil—has been accomplished, even though it is costly and also inconvenient in terms of longer delivery times. Otherwise, a survey here and in other key trading nations indicates, the effect of the canal shutdown on trade has been more a dislocation than a disruption.

The dislocation has been widespread, but it has been taken with a kind of fatalistic calm that is in sharp contrast with the crisis caused by the shutting down of the waterway under similar circumstances only 10 years ago. The canal then was considered so vital that Britain and France were willing to risk a world war to protect their interests in it.

When the canal was nationalized by President Nasser in July, 1956, the expropriation aroused resentment as well as anxieties about its continued operation.

When Israel invaded the Sinai in November of that year, Britain and France landed troops at the Suez Canal to protect the waterway. The Egyptians retaliated by sinking

Pix

The Suez Canal is blocked not only by sunken ships but also by unresolved political questions. Revenue lost by U.A.R. is in millions.

ships in the canal, an action that blocked it for five months.

This stoppage of shipments in the waterway brought a severe oil shortage in Western Europe and caused other economic dislocations. Clearing the canal became the goal of an international crash salvage operation financed and carried out by the United Nations.

This time, Suez has become a kind of "no man's land," the cease-fire line between Israeli and Egyptian forces. Although officially closed by the Egyptians, it is also blocked by a few minor obstacles. But these could be cleared in a month at most.

Real Obstacle

The real obstacle to reopening the canal, obviously, has been the failure of the United Nations or anyone else to resolve the Arab-Israeli deadlock through peace negotiations or other means.

Significantly, there have been no notable pressures by Western European countries or other nations for a reopening of the canal. If there had been any Egyptian hopes that closing the canal would put pressure on the Israelis to withdraw, they have been a miscalculation.

The rest of the world has not exactly shrugged off the closing of the canal. If exports of oil from east of Suez had stopped for any length of time, or if the canal had been shut in the wintertime when Europe's fuel needs are greater, it might have been a different story.

These and other "if's" have made the decisive difference between the blocking of Suez 10 years ago and now.

Dire Consequences Possible

If Arab unity had held and the boycott on shipments of oil to Britain and the United States had worked — it could not because transhipment is a simple matter — the consequences would have been acute.

Also, if there had not been a tremendous increase in production of oil in the Western Hemisphere and in African areas, the shutting of Suez might have repeated the severe squeeze of 1956-57.

According to the survey of effects of the canal closing so far, Britain has been hardest hit, chiefly because of her heavy dependence on Middle East oil and the need to bring much of it around the costlier Cape route.

Gasoline, or petrol, prices in Britain have risen about 2½ cents an Imperial gallon. The Imperial gallon is equivalent to 1.2 United States gallons. In West Germany and France, less dependent on Middle East oil because of supplies from North Africa, gasoline costs have risen only 1 cent a gallon. In Italy, there has been talk of a rise in gasoline prices, but so far the only change has been to keep a special 1-cent-a-gallon, flood-rehabilitation surcharge in effect beyond the expiration date, possibly until November.

In this country, apart from increased freight and insurance costs on shipments to the Middle East, the closing of Suez has had no adverse economic consequences.

Termed a 'Nuisance'

The general comment by traders has been "it's just a damned nuisance." According to a Commerce Department official: "Nothing of any importance to the United States comes through the canal."

According to Jerome Gilbert, economist of the Port of New York Authority, the closing of Suez has brought dislocations, but not disruptions, for world trade.

"Relatively," he commented, "a strike on New York's subway system would have produced more serious transportation problems than has the closing of the Suez Canal. The myth of its essentiality has been exploded."

Of the total of this country's crude petroleum imports last year, amounting to 66-million long tons, more than 56 per cent came from Latin America. The rest came from the Middle East and Africa. But only a little more than half of these imports might be affected by the closing of the canal to the extent that they would have to be diverted around South Africa.

As noted by economists and other experts, in the 10 years since the last stoppage of Suez, there have been significant technological changes in shipping.

In 1956, ships that averaged only 10 knots an hour have been replaced by ships that average 16 knots. Oil tankers and ore carriers have doubled in size. A tanker of 80,000 tons, for example, cannot pass through Suez loaded, and tankers of 100,000 and 200,000 tons are becoming increasingly popular because of their economies in operation.

For such vessels, obviously, the Suez Canal might as well not exist. But even for smaller tankers, the costs of the longer route around Africa is offset by the savings in Suez Canal tolls. These tolls have been going up and, according to trade sources, they average twice as much as tolls for the Panama Canal.

Although Western Europe's oil consumption has trebled since 1956-57, only about 50 per cent of it has been coming through Suez, compared to 80 per cent 10 years ago.

The effects of the Suez closure on countries such as Britain are still difficult to assess, but it is probable that they may put some strain on efforts to improve the trade balance. With its large merchant fleet and substantial trade with the Far East, Britain stands to lose the most in exports.

Considerably increased oil costs, particularly supplies that will have to be paid for in dollars, will add to the payments deficit. But these may be offset to some extent by higher earnings of British oil companies supplying other markets.

Of all West European countries, France seems least likely to be affected by the closing of the canal. Of her some 63-million tons of crude oil imports a year, almost half comes from Algeria and Libya. About 80 per cent of French trade is in Europe and most of the rest is in the former French West African possessions and North America.

West Germany also gets a large part of her oil from Libya, and a good part of other supplies comes in giant tankers that normally take the Cape route because they cannot negotiate Suez.

Boom in Chartering

For countries such as Norway and Greece, the routing of oil shipments around South Africa has brought a boom in tanker chartering. Since the canal closure, the demand for tankers has soared and idle tonnage of nearly 500,000 was brought back into service in June alone.

The big Norwegian tanker fleet is now fully employed at the highest rates in years. Earnings from tankers and other ships pressed into service because of the canal closing are expected to earn Norway $100-million to $150-million.

The Suez closing has also been a windwall for South Africa in increased earnings from the servicing of ships putting in for refueling and other supplies at Durban and Cape Town.

The other main adverse effects of the closing of Suez in Western Europe are expected to be higher costs of rubber, hides and wool that now must be shipped by longer routes.

India, with her present need for large grain food imports, appears most likely to expeience serious difficulties. It is xpected that delivery time on these shipments which normally would have gone through the canal, will be increased by 50 per cent.

In terms of delivery time, a year of food shipments to India will now take upward of 18 months.

Of all world areas, the Middle East itself appears to be feeling the effects of the Suez stoppage more than any other. The canal still is essential for the area, not only for more speedy oil exports, but also for food imports, especially by the more arid regions east of Suez.

In addition to the canal losure, the consequent lack of hips in the area may seriously urtail vital imports.

Egypt, already in extreme inancial straits, is losing foreign-exchange earnings from uez of some $200-million a year. These earnings, plus nearly $100-million from a tourist trade that has ceased, make up more than a third of the country's income.

Egypt's biggest income producer, cotton exports, also have been curtailed by the closing of the canal and the lack of shipping.

Change Marks Oil Industry

By WILLIAM D. SMITH

Although the dust of fighting and the haze of political maneuvering continue to hover over the Middle East, one fact has already emerged clearly from the confusion: the nature of the world petroleum industry has been changed by the conflict.

The extent of the changes and their exact nature are yet to be determined, but oil men are unanimous in the opinion that the petroleum world will never return to its pre-June condition.

"The consuming nations have been forced to examine their basic positions and far-reaching changes will be made by most of the countries," an oil analyst for a major New York bank commented last week.

John Lichtblau of the Petroleum Industry Research Foundation said "new sources of supply will be sought and exploration will begin in new areas. This is what happened after the Suez conflict in 1957 and it will happen again. Remember that present production in Libya and Nigeria was a direct result of the Suez stoppage."

Japan is the prime example of a country that has had to rethink its oil supply situation. The nation presently receives 90.4 per cent of its oil from the Middle East.

Following the outbreak of the war in the Middle East, Japanese officials met to hasten the activation of a proposed Petroleum Development Public Corporation, a body whose job it would be to seek out new oil sources.

The Japanese Ministry of Trade and Industry has announced that it is seeking to lower its dependence on Middle East oil to 60 per cent by 1985. The Japanese are looking toward Canada, Sumatra, New Guinea and the Soviet Union as suppliers.

In the United States, a country that is not dependent on Arab oil but which is one of the chief objects of Arab hostility, the problems brought on by the conflict could bring the adoption with Canada of a continental policy on petroleum. "There have been many discussions about the need for a continental policy on oil, but the war has given added impetus to the argument of those who are in favor of such a policy," according to Wil-

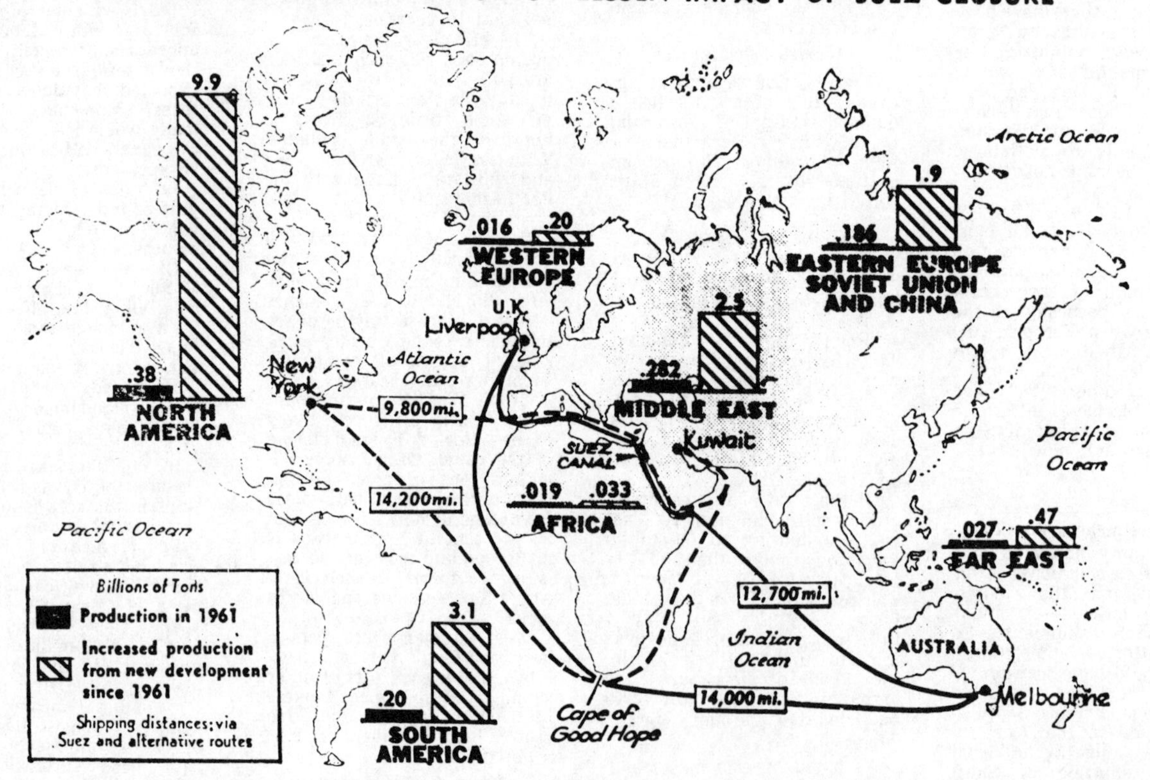

liam Cliadakis, senior oil analyst for E. F. Hutton & Co.

A pipeline connecting the Canadian oil fields in the West with the big population centers of the American Middle West appears to be one likely result if a continental oil policy is adopted.

Efforts to develop economical ways of getting petroleum out of shale and tar sands have increased since the Middle East war, according to a bank analyst. "I am willing to bet that the research budgets of most of the major companies for shale oil retrieval are considerably increased next year," he added.

Britain May Cut Dependents

Britain will undoubtedly step up its activities in the North Sea, according to informed sources. Britain is also likely to decrease her dependence on the Arab bloc just as she did after the 1957 crisis. Britain received about 60 per cent of her oil supplies just prior to the June hostilities, compared with more than 80 per cent in 1957.

In Italy, the crisis has given support to a pending law to allow exploration on the Adriatic shelf. Italy, the Soviet Union's best European customer for oil, is expected to increase its imports from the Soviet Union.

Although in 10 years' time, it is likely that places like the North Sea and the Adriatic shelf will supply part of the world's oil needs, this does not mean that Arab oil can be ignored. "No matter how you slice it, Middle Eastern oil is needed," one analyst observed.

Although there will always be plenty of buyers for Arab oil, it is likely that some of the development and exploration funds that would have gone into the Middle East will now be used elsewhere, according to Arthur Schaffer, senior oil analyst for R. W. Pressprich & Co.

"The Arabs will lose some of their markets in a long-term sense because of the conflict, but the rapidly growing demands for petroleum ensure that the Middle Eastern oil will never lack buyers," the security analysts said.

"The war may even have served a purpose, for some of the have nations in the Middle East such as Saudi Arabia and Kuwait will be far less eager to lose revenues that support their national economies for an ideological cause," he added.

Anther permanent effect of the recent war may be a change in petroleum shipping habits.

At present, the world's oil companies are chartering almost anything that will float in a mass effort to keep world petroleum supplies moving. This near-record activity, only exceeded by the 1957 crisis, has sent tanker rates skyrocketing and increased industry costs.

The second petroleum-shipping crisis in 10 years could lead to a movement to avoid using the canal even after it has been cleared, according to some oil-company transportation officers.

Lord Geddes, vice president of the United Kingdom Chamber of Shipping and head of Trident Tankers, Britain's largest independent tanker fleet, said recently that shipowners would be thinking seriously of avoiding the canal, having been "bumped twice in 10 years."

If the oil companies seriously follow up on an "avoid-the-Suez" campaign, it will accelerate the existing trend to bigger and bigger tankers. At present, the point where it is more economical to ship oil around the tip of Africa instead of through the canal is when the tanker has a deadweight tonnage of slightly more than 100,-nage of slightly more than 100,000. At that point, toll charges, if the tanker lies shallow enough to get through the locks, exceed the cost of the longer trip around the cape.

Time for Experiment

Informed industry sources believe that it would take at least a month to clear the canal channel if equipment and men were there now. They contend that it will therefore take at least three months to reopen the waterway, giving the oil companies a lengthy period to experiment with advantages and disadvantages of shipping around the cape.

Short-term affects of the crisis have been numerous and some could last beyond the present emergency situation.

The most important of these probably is the increased price for petroleum products in Europe. Prices have increased in Switzerland, the Netherlands and Germany, and the other countries are considering price advances.

The price increases were instituted to make up for the increased costs of shipping oil around the cape, but product prices have been low in Western Europe for several years, according to industry sources.

"The question is, how much of the price increases can be retained after the emergency is over?" according to William Stanhope, oil analyst for Paine Webber, Jackson & Curtis. "If some of the price improvement is retained, it will be a constructive force for the industry, in Europe," he added.

The price increases have not gone unnoticed by the European governments. In Germany, the Cartel Authority, which has a somewhat comparable function to the United States Justice Department's antitrust division, has instituted a study of the price increases.

In the United States, warnings of Government action if product prices are raised have been sounded. Gardner Ackley, the chairman of President Johnson's Council of Economic Advisors, for one, has cautioned the oil industry on a price rise as an aftermath of the Middle East crisis.

Crude Oil Price Rise

Product prices in the United States have not risen yet, but the price being paid by the companies for crude oil in the Southwest advanced last week. On Monday, the Phillips Petroleum Company announced that it had increased by 5 to 7 cents a barrel the price it pays for 194,000 barrels of crude oil it purchases in Kansas and the Southwest.

The other major companies failed to follow suit, but on Friday the Humble Oil and Refining Company, chief domestic subsidiary of the Standard Oil Company (New Jersey) announced it had raised the prices it pays for crude oil in a number of western Texas fields by 3 to 5 cents a barrel.

Another major short-term affect that could turn into a long-term situation was the increase of production in Nigeria and Venezuela.

Production has also been raised sharply in the United States. The Texas Railroad Commission, the state oil regulatory agency, announced Wednesday that it was increasing allowable production by 203,000 barrels a day for the rest of July. This would raise production for July to a daily rate of 3,166,000 barrels.

To achieve this production, the rate of regulated wells was increased to 48 per cent, the highest level since the 1957 Suez crisis. Louisiana has also increased its production.

How much the recent fighting has changed the future of the oil business only the passing years will disclose. There is no question, however, that this most volatile of industries has been altered.

July 16, 1967

For the Oil Industry, Future Is Written in Arabic

The oil industry moved into the new year with pride in its 1967 performance, high hopes for its opportunities in 1968—and a premonition that the events of last summer may have signaled the beginning of a new era in petroleum history.

The catalyst was the Arab-Israeli conflict.

It provided the industry with some of its finest hours yet contained the seeds of future troubles.

In the face of war, the closing of the Suez Canal, embargoes and diplomatic embroilment, the industry was able to maintain free-world petroleum supplies without rationing or even a major shortage at the consumer level.

This was no small feat when it is considered that the Arab nations produce one-third of the world's total supply of oil and the Suez Canal is the chief artery for petroleum transport.

When the Arabs turned off the oil taps, Iran (a Moslem but non-Arab nation), Venezuela, Canada and the United States opened their valves wider.

U.S. Production Soars

United States production soared 48 million barrels above normal levels during the summer and early fall to help maintain free-world supplies. During seven of the crisis weeks American refineries broke all records by processing more than 10 million barrels of crude oil a day, compared with an average of 8.3 million barrels a day prior to the conflict.

Of the extra production from June through September, about 22 million barrels went to Europe and 21 million barrels to the east coast of the United States to replace interrupted imports. Exports of crude oil from the United States averaged nearly 8.4 million barrels a month during July and August, a 70-fold increase over the level of exports for the comparable period in the preceding year.

While the United States and other countries were straining to produce more oil the international petroleum companies were busy chartering anything afloat to keep supplies moving. Tanker charter prices soared as the oil vessels were forced to sail around the tip of Africa, a trip 17 days longer than passage through the Suez.

The outcome for the Arabs was a defeat in their economic war against the West just as in their shooting war against Israel. Their embargo of Britain and the United States folded before it even began. Little damage was done to any major oil installation and Arab production was back to normal by the end of the summer.

So for all outward appearances, the international petroleum situation has returned to its prewar status, except for the Suez Canal, which is still closed.

But that is just a surface view. "The war and its aftermath have forced both the producing and consuming nations to examine their basic policies," according to John Lichtblau of the Petroleum Research Institute. Few serious analysts of the industry would disagree.

For the consuming nations it means an attempt to become less dependent on Middle Eastern oil by diversifying their sources of energy.

The search for oil and gas has already intensified in Africa, Indonesia, Australia, Canada, South America, the United States and Europe. Much of the action is offshore, where the play is getting deeper and more expensive.

According to Walter Levy, a noted oil consultant, the complete loss of Arab oil could not be made up by any combination of other sources within a decade, if at all.

The Arabs fully realize the strength of their basic position.

The present courtship between France and Iraq is possibly indicative of an emerging new era in petroleum politics and policy. France is trying to create a "third world" force in petroleum while Iraq is anxious to pay back Britain and the United States for their supposed support of Israel.

Russian Control Seen

A more ominous spector is put forward by a small group of analysts who suggest that Middle East oil will come under Russian control because of the Arab belief that the United States and Britain supported Israel.

On the domestic scene the production push to meet Europe's needs during the crisis moved United States output of crude oil to a record 3.2 billion barrels from the 3,027,700,000 barrels in 1966. In 1968 production is expected to inch forward about 0.5 per cent.

Demand for petroleum in this country is expected to rise 3.4 per cent this year. World petroleum demand is expected to experience an even sharper gain with a 9 per cent increase being the general estimate.

Most companies in the industry reported higher profits last year with the average gain for the major concerns being around 8 per cent. Analysts anticipate a somewhat smaller earnings advance this year.

A few hangover problems from 1967 are expected to enliven the domestic picture this year.

The unused import tickets from the time of the crisis cast a slight shadow over the price situation since many oil men remember the price-depressing glut caused by the flood of imports after the 1956 Suez crisis. Government officials, however, have promised that the timing on the filling of unused tickets will be judiciously decided.

January 8, 1968

U.S. Policies in Mideast Are Under Fire

Industrialists Reported to Warn Nixon on Loss of Influence With Arabs

By TAD SZULC
Special to The New York Times

WASHINGTON, Dec. 21 — President Nixon is reported to have received warnings from a group of top American industry leaders with oil and other interests in the Middle East that the United States is rapidly losing political and economic influence in the Arab states because of its present policies.

The industrialists' concern over the deterioration of the United States position in the Middle East and over the proportional growth of the Soviet importance there — attributed by them in part to Washington's past support for Israel—was expressed at an unpublicized meeting at the White House on Dec. 9.

Bankers Attended

A White House spokesman has confirmed that Mr. Nixon had asked the group to discuss with him the "political situation in the Middle East." The members included David Rockefeller, president of the Chase Manhattan Bank; John J. McCloy, former president of Chase Manhattan, and Robert B. Anderson, former Secretary of the Treasury and a director of Dresser Industries Company, which has oil interests in Kuwait and Libya.

Administration officials said that the President had invited them to hear their views on the eve of the Dec. 10 session of the National Security Council, which was dedicated to a review of the United States policy in the Middle East.

Attending the industrialists' meeting with Mr. Nixon was Henry A. Kissinger, the President's special assistant for national security affairs. White House officials emphasized that those conferring with the President were "people with a political knowledge of the Middle East situation and the oil situation in the Middle East."

Action Was Urged

Administration officials declined, however, to disclose what specific advice the industrialists had offered Mr. Nixon and none of the participants were available today for comment.

According to officials familiar with the discussion, the consensus in the group was that the United States must act immediately to improve its relations with oil-producing and other Arab states. The group was said to feel this was necessary to deflect what the group feared to be an imminent loss of United States standing in the Middle East that might be reflected politically as well as in terms of American petroleum interests in the area.

The group was said to feel that United States weapons deliveries to Israel, including the recent shipment of supersonic Phantom jets, and Washington's alleged support of Israeli policies in the Middle East conflict were turning moderate and conservative Arab leaders as well as radical Arabs against the United States.

That basic evaluation was presented to Mr. Nixon early this year by William W. Scranton, former Governor of Pennsylvania, who toured the Middle East on a presidential mission.

But the increase in Middle East hostilities in the intervening period and the aggravation of the over-all situation had led a group of United States oil executives to submit a private memorandum to Mr. Nixon last September urging the preservation of American interests as a basis for the United States policy in the region.

The September meeting of oil executives was reportedly held in Beirut, Lebanon. Subsequent meetings were held in Beirut in October, informants said, and a session on Oct. 29 was attended by Mr. Rockefeller.

According to authoritative sources, Mr. Rockefeller then met with President Abdel Gamal Nasser of the United Arab Republic in Cairo on Oct. 31, to discuss the Middle East political situation along with some of the Chase Manhattan Bank's projects in Egypt.

Official quarters said that Mr. Rockefeller reported to the Administration at the time that President Nasser hoped the United States, through a change in its policies, could help him to become freer of the growing Soviet influence. The Soviet Union supplies most of the United Arab Republic's military equipment. The United States has had no diplomatic relations with Cairo since the 1967 Middle East war.

Others who conferred with Mr. Nixon on Dec. 9 have had direct communication with Arab leaders as well. Mr. Anderson, for example, talked with President Nasser and King Hussein of Jordon in Cairo last March.

It was this direct experience in the Middle East that, in the judgement of the White House, qualified these industrialists to present their views to Mr. Nixon.

However, officials said that the views expressed by the visiting group to the President were not mentioned directly when the National Security Council met Dec. 10 to debate the Middle East policy.

Authoritative informants said that the United States oil industry is concerned over the danger of Arab terrorist attacks on American petroleum installations and over the possibility that the greater British and French sympathies for the Arab policies may in time result in the erosion of the American oil presence in the Middle East.

December 22, 1969

Oil: A World of Deepening Strife

By WILLIAM D. SMITH

"Double, double toil and trouble; fire burn and cauldron bubble."

The witches in Macbeth could well have been describing the present world oil situation in terms of United States Government and American oil company interests.

In recent weeks several new volatile ingredients have been added to the already boiling concoction of politics, power and money that make up the international oil business.

The center of most of these events is also the center of the oil industry—the Middle East. The reverberations, however, affect the entire globe, both politically and economically.

At worst they present a frightening scenario for the future of American interests. At best they point toward continuing and probably growing difficulties.

"These are terrrible, dangerous and difficult times," Walter J. Levy, dean of American oil economists, said last week. Mr. Levy, it should be noted, is no Cassandra, and until recent weeks was one of the more optimistic among the band of men whose special interest is the study of the politics and economics of international oil.

The outlook of many oil company executives has also changed in recent weeks. The old attitude could be summed up. "Things are tough, but we can live with it."

Last week a senior executive with one of the industry's giant concerns commented, "For the first time in my 20-year involvement in the Arab World, I am afraid for the lives and property of our employes." This was the most extreme opinion voiced by any executive, but all acknowledged that a horrible situation had become much worse.

The oil men, as usual, insisted upon anonymity.

Events of last week indicate the trend of events in the area.

¶The Algerian Government nationalized properties of four foreign oil companies, the Phillips Petroleum Company, a member of the Royal Dutch Shell group of companies, a West German company and an Italian company.

¶The Iraqi Government supported the Algerian move, and urged all Arab oil-producing countries to cooperate to form a front against "international oil cartels."

¶Libya ordered a joint venture of Texaco, Inc., and the Standard Oil Company of California to cut back production. This followed a similar command to the Occidental Petroleum Corporation.

¶Libya blocked the loading of two special tankers built by the Standard Oil Company (New Jersey) to export liquefied natural gas from Libya to Italy and Spain.

These events were just harassments. Far more ominous was the growing power of the Palestinian guerrillas, who now appear to have captured a role in the actual governing of Jordan, where King Hussein had to choose between his closest friend and the Fedayeen and chose the guerrillas.

There are indications that the Fedayeen also appear close to having some say in the affairs of Lebanon. It is likely that their ever-expanding lists of supporters in other Arab countries will also exert influence over those countries, ranging from such conservative monarchies as Saudi Arabia to the "progressive" Arab states, such as the United

Arab Republic. "It is no longer just Arab against Israeli; it is Arab government against Arab government and Arab revolutionaries against Arab governments. The mix has become that that much more complicated, and a settlement that much more difficult," according to David Mizrahi, editor of the Mid-East Report.

Mr. Levy, the oil economist, commented: "Even if the Arab Governments want to play it cool, there is now a very real question of whether they can. A United States Government policy decision such as sending Phantom Jets to Israel could trigger the masses. Whether the governments could keep control of the situation, even if they wanted to, is a very real question, and major destruction of United-States-owned facilities a very real possibility."

Palestinians Scattered

Mr. Levy pointed out that Palestinians in large numbers are scattered throughout the Arab world and that other groups such as the labor unions and religious Muslims would likely join in a crusade of destruction against anything American.

The most frightening aspect of the whole situation is that the world's two major nuclear powers, the Soviet Union and the United States, are coming closer and closer to an eyeball-to-eyeball confrontation.

Fuad W. Itayim, editor of the Middle East Economic Survey of Beirut, commented recently, "Vietnam is a brush fire. Either you (the United States) or the North Vietnamese could walk away from it at any time if one so choose. The Arab-Israeli conflict holds the potential to end the world."

Kohler Sees Danger

Foy D. Kohler, former United States Ambassador to the Soviet Union, commented in a recent issue of the U.S. News and World Report, "I certainly regard the Middle East as the one area in the world in which the potential danger of an ultimate confrontation between the two powers is greater than anywhere else. That anywhere else includes Southeast Asia, which happens to be a very unhandy part of the world for Russia to project its power.

"But I don't think Russia wants a confrontation in the Middle East—at least not in the forseeable future."

But what does the Soviet Union want? One theory holds that the Soviets are in the early stages of practising a subtle form of petroleum blackmail that would isolate the United States from the rest of the world. It holds that the Soviets are outflanking the United States in terms of control of world energy sources.

According to this theory, the Russians are exerting increasing influence in the Middle East, where some 62 per cent of the total world oil reserve and some 70 per cent of the "free world" reserves lie buried beneath the sand. Europe imports about 8.1 million barrels a day from Arab countries, or about 73 per cent of its total imports. Japan receives almost 80 per cent of her oil supplies from Arab nations.

Supplies Could Be Cut Off

These supplies could be withheld, stopping the cars and factories of both the Western and Asian allies of the United States.

But this in not the only front on which the Soviets are active. The Russians, in a very business-like fashion, are selling natural gas to Europe.

The Russians, sitting on top of mammoth reserves of gas in Western Siberia and Central Asia, have so far this year signed agreements to exchange huge quantities of natural gas with Italy and West Germany for the large-diameter pipe necessary to build the pipelines and equipment needed to develop the fields. In September, 1968, the Russians began piping gas into Austria.

The new agreements mean that, in the near future a large part of Western Europe will be linked to the widely spread Soviet gas grid. Russian deliveries to Western Europe will be stabilized at about 11 billion cubic meters annually from the late nineteen seventies onward according to present agreements. These call for the Soviets to supply about 7.5 per cent of the West German gas requirements and possibly as much as 25 per cent of the Italian requirements.

Possible Negotiations

The Russians, however, appear willing to negotiate for even larger deliveries to West Germany and possibly to Italy, and there is the possibility of some future deliveries to France. There have also been proposals for Russian deliveries to Finland and Sweden.

These moves have brought the Russians into direct competition with two of the most powerful capitalist organizations in the world, the Royal Dutch Shell Group and Jersey Standard, which jointly control the vast Groningen Field in Northern Holland. The Soviets so far appear to be beating the capitalists at their own game in giving the customers what they want at a price they are willing to pay. In the process the Russians are setting the energy supply patterns for Europe for the years to come.

The Soviets are also trying to sell natural gas to the Japanese on the same pipe-and-equipment barter basis. The ostensible purpose of the proposed export deal with Japan would be to help develop Russian gas reserves in the remote and underpopulated Eastern part of the U.S.S.R. with a minimum of capital expenditure. The Russians are trying to interest the Japanese in participating in the construction of a 1,000-mile pipeline from the new Yakutsk in Eastern Siberia to the Pacific port of Magadan. An earlier proposal invited the Japanese to get natural gas from the Island of Sakhalin.

Agreements Signed

The Russians at the same time have signed agreements to import gas on the basis of sheer economics from Afganistan and Iran.

Advocates of the petroleum blackmail theory argue that in time the Soviets will be able to wean the NATO allies and the Japanese away from support of United States policy, as these governments and people become more and more aware that the energy that drives their economies is dependent on Soviet good will. "It doesn't have to be crude. No threats. It can be very subtle and still very effective. One day the United States will find itself isolated.

Mr. Levy, the economist, for one, does not buy this theory in toto, although he subscribes to parts of it. He holds that the gas sales are for the very large part strictly commercial deals with only peripheral political mischief involved. He also believes that the Russians have no desire to become the middle men in Arab oil, and doubts the Arabs would allow that.

He contends, however, that a new flare-up in the Middle East over something like the sale of Phantom Jets to Israel could greatly diminish American participation in Middle East oil.

"The Arabs would likely try to do business directly with the national oil companies of the consuming nations. Europe would not be deprived of oil in any case, and it is unlikely that the Arabs would find any need for Russian brokers."

The one bit of good news for American and Western oil interests, was the discovery of a potential giant oil field in the North Sea giving Europe for the first time a major indigenous supply of crude oil. Some estimates have placed the find at 1 billion tons of oil, or more than four times present known total European reserves.

Arabs Hold Trumps

It should be noted, however, that like the North Slope of Alaska, the find, although large, does not change the rules of the international oil game. Those fields are good cards for Western Europe and the United States to have in their hands, but the Arab nations still hold all the trumps.

Western Europe is at present consuming about 560 million tons of oil a year, and thus the 1 billion tons would supply the area for a year and a half. The Alaskan North Slope find would supply only two years of United States demand, if it were the only source.

There have been increasing rumors in recent days that the Russians intend to open the Suez Canal, the closing of which has affected the Russians relatively more than any other country outside Egypt. One version holds that the United States and Russia have come to an agreement to open the canal. The United States is supposed to pressure the Israelis to allow the Soviets to dredge the waterway, and, in return, the Russians would get the North Vietnamese to agree to a peace with honor for the United States in Southeast Asia.

A second version of the rumor says that the Russians intended to open up the canal despite any acquiescence from the United States by just sailing in dredges. If the Israelis fired, the Russians would fire back, all the time protesting that they were serving the world community of nations by opening an international waterway.

Proponents of a Russian "Grand Strategy Theory" contend that the Soviets are eager to get the canal open so that when the British pull out of the Persian Gulf area in 1971, they will be able to step in and control the area, completing the encirclement of the Arab oil wealth.

Supporters of this theory point out that Yemen, South Yemen and Aden are already under considerable Soviet influence, and only a potential alliance between Iran and Saudi Arabia stand in the way of Russian dominance of the area. They add that the Russians are also anxious to prevent the Chinese from increasing their influence in the area.

Despite the horrors and rumors of horrors, some oil and Middle East experts see hope of a settlement through the gloom.

A vice president at a major oil company commented, "Things are so frightening that the moderates on both sides have become increasingly anxious to work out some sort of arrangement before Armageddon."

Mr. Levy commented, "More and more, Israelis are beginning to believe that they can't win every war, and that they can't keep fighting forever."

Mr. Mizrahi, of the Mid-East Report, points out that an increasing number of responsible Arabs feel that their Governments and social structures will fall before Israel falls.

Those hopeful of peace point to the fact that in recent weeks Foreign Minister Aldo Moro of Italy visited with President Nasser, and, at the moment, Foreign Minister Abba Eban of Israel is in Italy. There are reports that the Pope has urged the Italian Government to make every effort to set up some sort of meeting of the minds, if not parties.

June 21, 1970

Mideast Oil

MIDDLE EAST OIL—A STUDY IN POLITICAL AND ECONOMIC CONTROVERSY. By Dr. George W. Stocking 461 pages. Vanderbilt University Press. $15.

•

For the businessman or government official interested in the climate for private venture capital throughout the Middle East and North Africa, this book should be required reading. Dr. Stocking, in what obviously must have been a labor of love, has painstakingly researched and documented the entire, often controversial, history of oil concessions in the major oil-producing nations of the Middle East.

Dr. Stocking starts his narrative with an analysis of the formation of the oil concession arrangements negotiated in Iran and Iraq prior to World War I and in Saudi Arabia and Kuwait in the years between that conflict and World War II. He carefully chronicles the advantageous position secured by the seven major international companies, along with the overt help and assistance given those companies by the British and American Governments. That these oil concessions were one-sided in favor of the companies, there is no doubt. That such one-sidedness sowed the seeds of distrust—indeed, the feeling of helpless exploitation—in the minds of later and better educated Arab and Iranian public officials is also obvious.

Dr. Stocking next turns to the post-World War II period, including the, by now famous, 50-50 tax arrangements negotiated by Aramco (California Standard, Texaco, Esso and Mobil) and the Saudi Arabian Government in 1950. However, even that "new deal" proved heavily weighted in favor of the companies and, in actual practice, yielded far less than a true 50-50 split for the countries. As a result, the suspicions and hostilities of some host countries' officials grew, particularly those who had garnered an education and the beginnings of technical and financial know-how.

In perhaps the best single portion of the book, the author next turns to the more recent negotiations initiated individually and collectively by Iran, Saudi Arabia, Kuwait, Iraq, Syria, Libya and Egypt during the nineteen-sixties. From his lucid description of this long and torturous series of negotiations and settlements, it is easy to gain insight into the troubled path that lies ahead for the oil companies operating in the Middle Eastern and North African countries.

If there is any negative criticism to be made, it is that Dr. Stocking has spent too much time dealing with Iraq and Syria and, conversely, too little with Libya and Egypt. It also is difficult to accept Dr. Stocking's conclusion that the international companies still hold the whip hand by virtue of their control over international markets.

However, the book can be recommended as a unique and worthwhile contribution to understanding the political and economic factors that have operated to undermine American and British influence in the Middle East in recent years. It is immediately clear that Dr. Stocking has brought to his study a fair-minded approach and deep understanding of the conflicting goals, aspirations and objectives of both parties.

If you are looking for heroes or villains, you won't find them here. There is neither an effort to whitewash nor to fix the blame on either the countries or the companies. Rather, this is an honest and scholarly explanation of the roots of differences, which, in turn, makes the course of recent history in these countries far more understandable.

Perhaps the best exposition of the unrest and uncertainty that have permeated oil company concessions throughout the Middle East over the last decade is Dr. Stocking's own statement that the difficulties " . . . originated in the humus of distrust and suspicion laid down by the abrasive impact of Western technology and a business culture on economically underdeveloped countries wholly dissimilar in their political and social institutions and ther history and traditions. Once planted, they [the difficulties] thrived under a blanket of hostility kept warm by the clash of a corporate quest for profits with the interests of underdeveloped countries as conceived by their politicians and their people."

Despite the difficulties and hostilities outlined here, this reviewer found cause for optimism. This stems from the fact that, despite the disparity of interests involved and the highly charged and emotional fervor occasionally displayed by government officials seeking a more equitable deal for their countries, the system has worked reasonably well. There has been give and take. And, in every country except Iraq, new arrangements have been peacefully arrived at. There has been, in most cases, an understanding by both sides of the need for give and take.

Moreover, this book clearly shows that the old-fashioned, power politics under which one party simply imposes its will on the other do not and cannot work any longer. The days when oil companies, backed by their governments, could dictate terms to undeveloped, but sovereign, nations are over. The problems in the Middle East can no more be solved through the rather simplistic methods of the past than can most of the other problems that we in the United States or in other industrial countries face around the globe.

For this reason, this book—in effect, a case study of working out problems over the negotiating table—must be of particular interest to informed citizens everywhere, whether from the "home" countries, of the international oil firms (United States and Britain), from consuming countries (Europe and Japan) that depend on Middle East oil, or from the producing countries themselves.

JAMES G. BUCKLEY

November 8, 1970

Mideast Oil Talks Nearing Crucial Stage

By JOHN M. LEE
Special to The New York Times

LONDON, Jan 15—The price and the supply of much of the Western world's oil are at stake in negotiations moving to a climax with unexpected speed in Tripoli and Teheran.

International oil men in London are alarmed by the pace and the implication of events since Dec. 28, when the 10-nation Organization of Petroleum Exporting Countries published new demands for higher payments.

The Arab producers and Iran imposed $750-million in extra charges on the companies in negotiations last summer and fall. Now, in a sellers' market of strong demand, rising consumer prices and higher profits, the producer countries want more in tax and royalty revenues.

Higher costs would doubtless be passed on by the companies to European motorists, United States electrical generating stations and others. In addition, oil men fear that the producer countries, as a negotiating tactic, might curtail supplies, as Libya already has done.

Heavy Buyers in Mideast

Western Europe draws 75 per cent of its oil supply from the Arab countries and Iran; Japan, 90 per cent. The United States, however, depends on this source for only 3 per cent of its needs.

A possibly crucial meeting is scheduled to be held tomorrow morning in Tripoli. The Libyan military rulers have summoned two relatively small American oil producers—Occidental Petroleum and Bunker Hunt, each almost totally dependent on Libyan supplies—to reply to Libya's latest demands.

It was Libyan militancy that broke the resistance of the big American and British oil companies last year.

A breakthrough Libyan agreement with Occidental on Sept. 1 produced a startling 30-cents-a-barrel increase to $2.53 in the posted price of light crude oil and an increase in the income-tax rate to 55 per cent—or 58 per cent for various companies — from 50 per cent, in settlement of Libyan claims for retroactive price increases.

Companies Yield on Rates

Although the Libyan demands were based primarily on closeness to market, with the Suez Canal still closed and oil tanker rates for the trip around Africa soaring, the oil companies found it politic in November to agree to a 55 per cent tax rate in other countries, such as Iran and Kuwait, as well as to a modest 9-cent-a-barrel increase on heavy crude oil.

The meeting of the Organization of Petroleum Exporting Countries last month included in its manifesto a demand that the 55 per cent rate become standard and a demand that all posted prices be raised to the highest level, allowing for differences in freight costs.

The international oil companies were summoned to a meeting in Teheran last Tuesday to negotiate on the new demands.

But in the meantime, Libya had leapfrogged ahead, arguing that since her tax increases represented retroactive payments, she was entitled to a further 5 per cent, or a total of 63 per cent in Occidental's case. In addition, Libya demanded further increases in the posted price of oil to reflect her transportation advantages.

The posted price for oil is used as the basis for computing the tax and the 12½ per cent royalty payments, even though the market price has been substantially lower than the posted price for years. The computation of, say, a 55 per cent tax rate on a $1.80 posted price when the market price is only $1.30 increases the effective tax rate to some 70 per cent.

Feb. 3 Deadline Set

The Teheran meeting on Tuesday broke off in deadlock after 90 minutes, and the producer countries have set a Feb. 3 deadline to achieve their demands or resort to unspecified "concerted and simultaneous action."

The meeting, which a four-man delegation representing the oil companies insisted was only a preliminary fact-finding session, was significant, since it represented the first confrontation of the international oil industry with the producer countries as an assertedly unified group.

However, oil men believe there is considerable divergence of view among the petroleum exporting countries on the tactics to be used. The principal issue at Teheran is an increase rumored to be anywhere from 30 cents to 60 cents a barrel in the posted price.

The Financial Times of London said today that the eight big international oil companies —five of them American—met in New York on Wednesday and pledged common resistance to the Middle Eastern and North African demands.

The New York meeting followed one last Friday and Saturday in Washington, the paper said, among representatives of the United States, Britain, France and the Netherlands, the home countries of the big oil companies.

The paper quoted French oil sources as having said that Washington had been active in attempts to draw up a common consumers' front.

January 16, 1971

5-YEAR OIL ACCORD IS REACHED IN IRAN BY 23 COMPANIES

SHUTDOWN IS AVERTED

Europeans and Asians Face Higher Fuel Bills—Little Effect in U.S. Is Seen

By JOHN M. LEE
Special to The New York Times

TEHERAN, Iran, Feb. 14—Twenty-three Western oil companies agreed today to additional payments of more than $10-billion to six Persian Gulf states for a five-year oil agreement intended to stabilize the crisis-prone industry.

The settlement increases payments by more than $1.2-billion this year, rising to $3-billion dollars in 1975. Without the new payments, oil income in the Gulf area has been $4.4-billion a year.

The agreement, reached after a month of maneuvers and only under threat of government-dictated terms beginning tomorrow, averts the danger of a halt in oil supplies from the Persian Gulf, the major source for Western Europe and Japan.

However, European and Asian consumers will be presented with a huge bill. The price of gasoline, fuel oil and other petroleum products will almost certainly be raised.

Importers to Pay More

In addition, importing countries will pay more for their oil to the detriment of their balance of payments. Less-developed countries such as India are expected to be hard hit.

The immediate effect on American consumers should be limited since the United States imports only 3 per cent of its oil requirements from the Middle East. However, since these imports are largely fuel oil, these prices could be raised. The world oil picture is so interrelated, however, that other increases could show up in time.

For the Persian Gulf governments, heavily dependent on oil income, the settlement swells their financial resources. Iran, for example, will get about $450-million more.

Iranian Official Happy

The agreement was signed shortly after 3 P.M. at the Iranian Finance Ministry, where the talks have been taking place between the oil companies and the Gulf states—Iran, Iraq, Saudi Arabia, Kuwait, Abu Dhabi and Qatar.

Dr. Jamshid Amouzegar, Iranian Finance Minister and leader of the producer countries' negotiating team, later talked to newsmen and said, "I was so happy I had tears in my eyes."

Lord Strathalmond, a managing director of the British Petroleum Company and co-chairman of the five-man company negotiating team, was asked earlier if he was happy about the agreement. He replied, "We can only be satisfied."

The package includes an immediate increase of 35 cents a barrel in what is called the posted price for crude oil at Persian Gulf terminals, plus an annual increase of 5 cents a barrel, to match company profits from higher product prices, and an annual 2.5 per cent increase in posted price to compensate for Western inflation and the reduced purchasing power of the producer governments' oil revenues.

The annual increases begin June 1, and are to be repeated, at the beginning of 1973, 1974 and 1975.

Various regional differentials and marketing allowances are removed with the effect that, for Iran, the price increase is equivalent to 46 cents a barrel, Dr. Amouezegar said.

Iranian light crude oil, for example, currently carries a posted price of $1.79 a barrel, or 42 American gallons. The posted price of the official export price and constant reference point for taxes and royalties. The market price could be 50 cents less than the posted price.

The oil companies represented in the negotiations, most of them American, gained the assurance of a stable tax rate of 55 per cent and the assurance that the Gulf states would abide by the agreement and forgo "leapfrog" claims if other countries should get a better deal than they did.

However, the agreement left to later negotiations the price increases for oil exported by two Gulf countries, Iraq and Saudi Arabia, by pipeline to the Eastern Mediterranean.

Bigger Demands by Libya

Iraq wants to wait and see what happens in Libya where the Government has demanded even bigger increases and has refused to deal with the companies as a group.

Mediterranean oil commands a premium price since companies buying it avoid the high tanker charges for the long trip around the southern tip of Africa. Dr. Amouzegar said that if the Suez Canal were reopened and freight rates fell, the Gulf states would receive an additional payment.

The companies will begin negotiations with Iraq and Saudi Arabia on the Mediterranean question on Tuesday.

The Gulf states affected by today's agreement are all members of the 10-nation Organization of Petroleum Exporting Countries. The other members are Libya, Algeria, Venezuela and Indonesia.

According to company sources, the Gulf states had demanded $1.4-billion in increased payments in the first year, rising to $11.8-billion in 1975.

The companies' opening offer when formal negotiations began on Jan. 19 was $436-million for this year. Their best offer before negotiations broke down on Feb. 2 was $788-million, rising to $1.6-billion, according to the same sources.

The five-year projections assume an increase in the volume of production of 8 to 10 per cent a year.

To some observers, the importance of the negotiations went beyond the financial details. The meetings, while cordial, took on the air of confrontations between Western industrialists and the developing countries.

For many, the negotiations demonstrated a clear shift of power toward the producing countries acting as a bloc. Even the giant oil companies acting in concert apparently could not prevail against countries asserting sovereign rights to charge whatever they wanted for their natural resources.

The countries' strongest point was that there is no alternate source for vast quantities of cheaply produced oil. Strong demand has produced a seller's market and the oil states have pushed their advantage to compensate for what they saw as sluggish growth in their revenues.

"We received in full whatever we had agreed among ourselves in the Gulf," Dr. Amouzegar said, "and we gave the assurances of a couple of points the companies wanted which were reasonable."

Dr. Amouzegar said the Gulf states had also given assurances they would not retaliate against the oil companies in support of unreasonable demands by any other countries. This was a clear warning that Libya could not count on Gulf support if she persisted in her demands for a 60 per cent tax rate, a 70-cent increase in the posted price and huge retroactive payment.

Signing the agreement for the Gulf states besides Dr. Amouzegar were Ahmad Zaki Yamani, the Saudi Arabian Oil Minister; Abdul Rahman Atiki, Oil and Finance Minister of Kuwait; Dr. Saadun Hamadi, Iraqi Oil Minister, and Hassan Kamel, adviser to the Ruler of Qatar. Abu Dhabi was unrepresented.

Signing for the companies, besides Lord Strathalmond, were George T. Piercy, senior vice president of the Standard Oil Company (New Jersey), cochairman of the negotiating group; William P. Tavoulareas, president of the Mobil Oil Corporation, John E. Kircher, president of the Eastern Hemisphere Petroleum Division of the Continental Oil Company, and Alfred C. DeCrane Jr. of Texaco Incorporated.

Associated Press

OIL PACT SIGNED IN TEHERAN: Dr. Jamshid Amouzegar, center, Iranian Finance Minister and leader of producers' team, affirms agreement after Ahmad Zaki Yamani, left, Oil Minister of Saudi Arabia. Dr. Saadun Hamadi, Iraqi Oil Minister, waits turn.

Some Benefits Expected

Special to The New York Times

PARIS, Feb. 14—The Persian Gulf oil settlement was expected to have far-reaching consequences, not all of them unfavorable, for the West.

While the cost of energy will rise in Western Europe, a large part of the funds obtained by producer governments will be spent in western markets. Some producer countries, such as Iran, will use the money to promote development projects. They will be buying more tractors and trucks and more machinery, from the industrial countries.

The money that is not spent in the West may be banked in London or New York.

The dollar may be strengthened as a result of the accord. This is because it is the chief industrial competitors of the United States that will feel the effects of the higher energy costs most severely.

February 15, 1971

ARAB LANDS WIN OIL PRICE RAISE

Six Nations of Persian Gulf Sign Pact at Geneva

By THOMAS J. HAMILTON
Special to The New York Times

GENEVA, Jan. 20—The major Western oil companies signed an agreement here tonight under which they will pay at least $700-million a year to six producing countries on the Persian Gulf to compensate them for the devaluation of the dollar last December.

The agreement, which goes into effect immediately, provides for an 8.49 per cent increase in the posted price of oil. Before the increase this averaged $2.23 a barrel in the six countries—Abu Dhabi, Iran, Iraq, Kuwait, Qatar and Saudi Arabia.

Although the oil is sold at less, the posted price determines the royalties and taxes to be paid.

The oil companies are now paying the six countries $8.2-billion a year for the eight billion barrels of oil being produced there. The agreement will raise the bill to about $8.9-billion, company sources said.

Company executives declined to predict how much of the increase would be passed on to consumers in Western Europe and Japan, which take almost all of the Persian Gulf oil. They said that it would be a factor in determining the price of crude but that the competitive situation among the 23 countries represented at the negotiations would determine the price of the finished product.

Officials of the Organization of Petroleum Exporting Countries, which had insisted upon compensation for the 8.57 per cent depreciation in the value of the dollar under the Washington agreement last month, estimated the increased payments to the six Persian Gulf producers at more than $800-million. They insisted that the companies would not be justified in raising prices since the currencies of the principal consumer countries had gained more against the dollar than the amount of today's increase.

'A Realistic Settlement'

The increase will be valid for the life of the Teheran agreements, which expire at the end of 1975. However, further adjustments, either up or down, are provided for in the event of any significant changes in the relation of the dollar to other key currencies.

The agreement also provides for increased posted prices for oil produced in Iraq and Saudi Arabia reaching the eastern Mediterranean through pipelines. Only oil exported by ship had been covered by the Teheran agreement.

George T. Piercy of Standard of New Jersey, the chief negotiator for the companies, termed it "a realistic settlement." He said it demonstrated the continuing ability of the two sides to resolve difficult issues "in a matter compatible with the interests of the exporting and consuming countries alike."

The settlement is expected to set a pattern for an increase in the posted price for two other producer countries, Nigeria and Libya. Venezuela had previously obtained an increase of more than 12 per cent.

Negotiations with the two other members of the Organization of Petroleum Exporting countries, Algeria and Indonesia, which compute oil payments by a different method, are also in prospect.

January 21, 1972

Oil Countries Press 'Equity' Demands

By THOMAS J. HAMILTON
Special to The New York Times

GENEVA, Jan. 21—The oil-producing countries started their talks today with a dozen Western oil companies on the new request by the nations for "participation" in company subsidiaries extracting oil from their territories.

The six Persian Gulf producer countries, which signed an agreement last night under which major Western oil companies increased payments by 8.49 per cent, to make up for the devaluation of the dollar, took the lead in explaining how they envisaged this participation.

These nations were expected to try to obtain 20 per cent participation, whereas Nigeria, another champion of the producer-country demand, wants 33 per cent.

Other members of the Organization of Petroleum Exporting Countries — Venezuela, Algeria, Libya, and Indonesiaa —have already nationalized or are about to nationalize a substantial part of the oil operations with which they are concerned. They were mainly interested spectators in the four hours of closed-door discussions, which will be resumed tomorrow.

Although today's discussions were entirely exploratory, it was learned that the producer countries envisage "equity" ownership, with the right to take part, as joint owner, in the operations of the subsidiaries.

Because most of the operating companies are wholly owned subsidiaries and others have complicated relations with parent companies, the producer countries conceded that the problem of dividing ownership would present numerous complications.

Some of them, in fact, are known to favor simplifying the corporate structure by the creation of new subsidiaries for each country, which would have the sole function of getting the oil out of the ground. This, they believe, should make it easier for them to acquire part ownership.

According to reliable sources, the producer countries envisage paying off the cost of participation in stages, by charging off some of the royalties and taxes due from the companies, rather than by paying cash.

Some of them, it is understood, would like to be paid their share of the profits in crude oil. In that case, the company extracting the oil would be the first choice to buy it back for refining and marketing, reliable sources said.

In accordance with a secrecy commitment accepted by both sides, there was no information on what is thought to be the crucial problem — how the value of the operating companies' assets, and hence the cost to the producer countries of buying in, would be determined.

According to one authority, the parent companies have understated the book value of their assets, for tax reasons, and have fixed the total book value of their Middle East operations at about $1.4-billion, thus making little provision for oil reserves.

Before today's discussions began, company sources indicated that they would insist on using book value as at least a partial basis for determining the cost of participation.

Producer-country sources conceded today that the complicated arrangements for partial ownership would have to be worked out in negotiations with individual countries and would take months.

They do not expect the current session to do more than produce acceptance in principle by the oil companies of participation, subject to arrangements safeguarding company interests. This, they believe, would pave the way for individual negotiations later.

January 22, 1972

SOVIET ANNOUNCES PACT TO DEVELOP LIBYA'S OIL FIELDS

Agreement Breaks Western Monopoly — Viewed as a Pressure Tactic

SIZE IS NOT DISCLOSED

Tass Says Accord Provides for Cooperation in Refining and Extracting Deposits

By HEDRICK SMITH

Special to The New York Times

MOSCOW, March 4—The Soviet Union announced tonight that it had signed an agreement with Libya to jointly develop and refine Libyan oil.

The size of the agreement, the first break in the Western monopoly on Libyan oil development, was not disclosed. It was initially seen here as a pressure tactic against Western oil companies more than as an indication that the Russians were about to play a major role in the Libyan oil industry.

The Libyans have been demanding a role in the Western companies' Libyan operations.

Tass, the Soviet press agency, provided few details on the agreement reached with the 25-man Libyan delegation that arrived here Feb. 29.

The delegation is headed by the regime's second-ranking figure, Major Abdul Salam Jallud, the Minister of Industry and Economy as well as a member of the ruling Revolution Command Council. It also includes the Libyan Deputy Chief of Staff, Maj. Mustafa el-Kharubi.

Tass said that the agreement "provides for cooperation in prospecting, extracting and refining oil, in developing power generation and other branches of Libya's economy, as well as prospecting for mineral deposits and gas, and in training Libyan national cadres."

Western diplomats have noted stepped-up Soviet efforts over the last two months to achieve greater legitimacy for Communist parties in the Arab world and closer links with Arab Socialist parties, improved relations with Syria and Libya and a new friendship treaty with Iraq.

The shift in Soviet tactics is generally attributed to Moscow's pessimism over prospects for breaking the Arab-Israeli negotiating impasse as well as to its deep disillusionment with the Egyptian Government of President Anwar el-Sadat.

Despite Moscow's irritation at the persistently outspoken anti-Communist line of Libya's leader, Col. Muammar el-Qaddafi, the Kremlin has been courting the Libyan regime lately.

Two days ago, Leonid I. Brezhnev, the Communist party leader, held a friendly and well-publicized meeting with the Libyan delegation.

The Soviet Union, hedging against continued frictions with the Sadat regime, today took the new step in its campaign to broaden Soviet influence in the Middle East and solidify ties with radical Arab countries.

The Soviet diplomatic campaign, overshadowed by the Israeli four-day military operation in Lebanon, has involved a marked de-emphasis of Moscow's special relationship with Cairo that has figured so prominently as the cornerstone of Soviet policy in the Middle East since the 1967 Arab-Israeli war.

Lately, Soviet media have directed new attention to the "unity of Arab progressive forces" promoted by the congress of the Lebanese Communist party in January. The congress brought together Arab Socialist parties from Syria, Iraq, Egypt, Algeria, Morocco, along with Palestinian groups and the Communist parties of Syria, Iraq, the Sudan and Jordan. The authoritative Soviet party newspaper Pravda a few days ago highlighted a lengthy analysis of the congress.

Until the Libyans' arrival, the Soviet press had been giving the Libyan regime scant attention. An authoritative commentary in Izvestia on Feb. 23 defined the "progressive" Arab countries as Egypt, Syria, Iraq, Algeria and Southern Yemen, pointedly excluding Libya and the Sudan.

It is in Iraq that the Russians are believed to have made the greatest gains lately. The Soviet press had reported Moscow's pleasure that the ruling Baath Arab Socialist party was willing to accept the long-suppressed Communist party in a coalition with the Baath and the Kurdish Democratic parties.

On Feb. 17, at the conclusion of a high-level visit by Iraqis, the two sides agreed to consider raising their relations "to a new, higher level within the framework of a treaty." Western diplomats expect that Moscow and Baghdad will soon sign a treaty along the lines of the Soviet-Egyptian friendship treaty. For the Soviet Union this is seen as a means of stabilizing relations with Iraq, where the Communist party's fortunes and Soviet aid have risen and fallen over the last decade.

The Iraqi talks were quickly followed by a visit to Syria by a Soviet delegation led by Kirill T. Mazurov, a Politburo member and a First Deputy Premier. Soviet pledges of new arms for Syria were matched by promises from Damascus of regular exchanges between the Syrian Baathist party and the Soviet Communist party, something that some Syrian leaders have been wary of.

West European diplomats suspect that the Russians see contacts in Syria and Iraq as an important opening for long-term penetration of domestic politics in those countries. One view is that the campaign among the Arab countries is part of the Kremlin's intensified worldwide rivalry with China. But the prevailing view is that the Russians are hedging their bets against further troubles with Egypt and demonstrating to President Sadat that Soviet aid and influence is welcomed in other radical Arab countries regardless of Soviet-Egyptian troubles.

March 5, 1972

OIL LANDS ACCEPT OFFER BY ARAMCO

6 Persian Gulf Area States Agree to a Stake of 20% in 4 U.S. Companies

Special to The New York Times

BEIRUT, Lebanon, March 12—The world's major oil-producing countries today accepted an offer by four United States petroleum concerns to give six nations a 20 per cent share in the companies, and urged other international oil companies to follow suit.

A communiqué issued at the end of a two-day meeting of the ministerial council of the Organization of Petroleum Exporting Countries, formed of 11 states with two-thirds of the world's known oil reserves, said that the offer represented an "effective" step toward the countries' objective of participation in development of their oil reserves.

The offer had been submitted Friday night by the Arabian American Oil Company, or Aramco, which is owned by Standard Oil of New Jersey, Standard Oil of California, Texaco and Mobil. Aramco develops and markets the rich oil resources of Saudi Arabia.

Confrontation Averted

The American offer averted a confrontation with the six countries, which had been considering drastic legislative action against the companies. In the oil industry, Aramco's new position was regarded as a major concession to the six producing lands of the Persian Gulf area.

On Friday night the companies, in a letter to Sheik Ahmed Zaki al-Yamani, the Saudi Arabian Minister for Oil, had announced their agreement in principle to the demand of the Persian Gulf states for a minimum of 20 per cent participation in the companies' capital and existing concessions.

The six are Saudi Arabia, Kuwait, Iraq, Iran, Abu Dhabi and Qatar, which share membership in their organization with Libya, Algeria, Nigeria, Venezuela and Indonesia.

The organization's communiqué said that the governments concerned were determined "to achieve promptly the effective implementation of participation."

Sheik Ahmed has been conducting negotiations with the American companies toward participation. The organization's ministerial council again delegated him to conduct further negotiations in its behalf with executives of the parent companies of Aramco, and he told reporters that talks would begin in Riyadh, Saudi Arabia, a week from today.

Industry sources here noted that the Organization of Petroleum Exporting Countries has avoided setting a deadline for fulfillment of participation, but pointed out that Sheik Ahmed, by deciding on prompt negotiations, had indicated indirectly that the companies would be pressed for early agreement.

Today's communiqué said that

holding emergency meetings here in Beirut.

The communiqué today said that the positive attitude of the Aramco partners "should be adopted by all companies in member states."

The organization, in what was interpreted here as anticipation of a negative attitude on the part of some of the companies, decided to establish a fund "to assist any member country that may be affected by action taken against it by oil companies."

The organization's secretary general, Dr. Adnan Pachachi of Iraq, was instructed to convene a panel of experts from member-states to prepare a study on establishment of that fund.

Industry quarters believe the minister would report back to his organization at its next meeting, for which no date has been set. Sources close to the organization believe the meeting will be held in June and assert that Sheik Ahmed intends to achieve the agreement by the end of the year.

Emergency Meetings

It was he who, last month, initiated negotiations with the four American companies in Jidda. But those talks failed, and the organization began that the difficulty is not expected so much from the companies operating in the gulf states as from those with concessions in Libya and Nigeria, which are demanding 51 per cent participation.

A crisis could develop if Libya and Nigeria resorted to legislative action in the event of a refusal by the companies. In such circumstances, the companies have usually taken action against the individual governments concerned, such as imposition of embargoes on oil sales from those countries.

In this eventuality, the organization's member states would presumably come to the aid of the governments involved.

March 13, 1972

Oil-Producing Lands Weigh Nationalization

11 OPEC Members Ask Concerns for Equity Share

By CLYDE H. FARNSWORTH

Special to The New York Times

VIENNA, June 5—The head of an organization representing 11 oil-producing countries warned today that if the countries' demands for 20 per cent equity ownership in Western-owned facilities were not met, they might well nationalize the properties, as Iraq did last week. Their eventual aim is for 51 per cent "participation," he said.

Dr. Nadim Pachachi, Secretary General of the Organization of Petroleum Exporting Countries, warned in an interview that the gap is big — too big" between the countries and the producing companies over participation. He said that a crisis could be avoided only if companies "come down from their high horse and negotiate seriously."

Sheik Ahmed Zaki al Yamani, the Oil Minister of Saudi Arabia, is negotiating with major Western companies on behalf of the Gulf states.

Compensation Differences

Essentially the differences are over compensation. Companies are demanding the market value of their assets plus payment for loss of profits until their concessions expire, in some cases at the end of this century. The countries are willing to pay the considerably lower book value, representing what the assets originally cost.

"We are the owners and, therefore, will not compensate for loss of profits," Dr. Pachachi said.

"Participation is the issue of the day," he said. "It overwhelms all other Government-company problems. Failure [by companies] to recognize the force of new trends in public thinking and to take home the lesson of changing circumstances could eventually oblige member countries to take a second look at nationalization.

"Our governments have, so far, acted as 'sleeping partners' and tax collectors," he said. "We wish to have a say on substantial matters and policy decisions."

While 51 per cent is the eventual demand, Dr. Pachachi said, it can be met over "a period" and is "negotiable" with the companies.

He said that had there been participation by Government in the Western-owned Iraq Petroleum Company, "I.P.C. nationalization need never have occurred."

Dr. Pachachi, a dapper, slim Iraqi with slightly stooped shoulders, was interviewed at OPEC's Vienna headquarters in a building shared, by chance, with Texaco, Inc., across the street from Vienna University.

The 12-year-old OPEC is made up of Iran, Iraq, Kuwait, Saudi Arabia, Qatar, Libya, Abu Dhabi, Algeria, Nigeria, Indonesia and Venezuela.

It was not over the controversial participation issue that Iraq nationalized, but over the I.P.C. Consortium's decision to cut crude-oil production in Iraq's northern fields by nearly 50 per cent.

The consortium wanted Iraq to reduce prices by 35 per cent. Iraqi authorities reacted by taking over properties owned for half a century by the consortium, which is owned by British Petroleum, Compagnie Française des Pétroles, the Royal Dutch-Shell Group, the Standard Oil Company (New Jersey), the Mobil Oil Company and the C. S. Gulbenkian Estate.

Dr. Pachachi said, "It was dangerous for the companies to play around with the [Teheran] Agreement," which set a new schedule of oil prices in the Persian Gulf and Mediterranean areas where most of the world's oil is still found.

OPEC issued a formal statement last Tuesday just before the nationalization, applauding the Iraqi authorities for being "right and wise" in rejecting the companies' approach, which, it said, would lead to "disruption of the structure of oil prices."

The Iraq situation will be discussed by OPEC ministers at a special meeting June 9 in Beirut.

Sometime before the next OPEC Congress, which is scheduled for Vienna June 26, Shiek Ahmad Zaki for the Gulf states will resume negotiations with the major oil companies over the deadlocked participation question. That meeting is expected to take place in Riyadh, Saudi Arabia.

"We are headed for a major crisis if the companies persist in their attitudes," Dr. Pachachi said.

Until recently, he said, the companies refused even to consider participation, citing the "sanctity of contracts."

"The basis of a valid contract is the free will of the two parties," he said. "Most of the oil concessions granted in the Middle East before and after World War II were concluded by states under the mandate or influence of a colonial power. The I.P.C. agreement was concluded in 1925."

Dr. Pachachi said that since

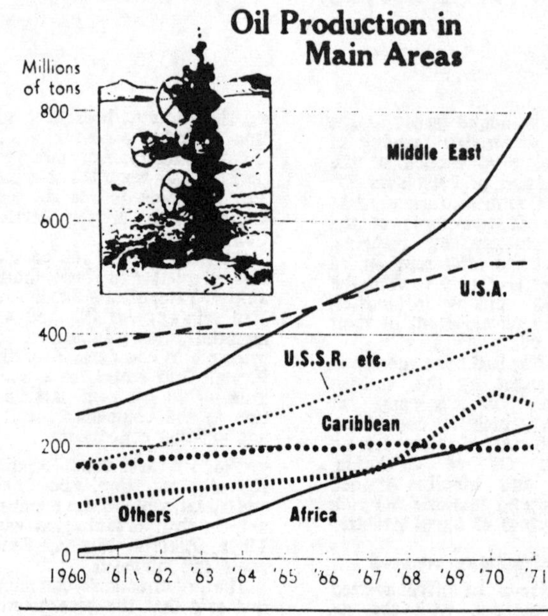

The New York Times/June 6, 1972

1957 all new agreements in the Middle East—with Italian, American, independent and Japanese producers—had included the right of the national oil company to participate in a local venture by up to 50 per cent.

Investment Returns

Discussing the compensation for the 20 per cent equity that the producer governments now demand in the older contracts, Dr. Pachachi said the major oil companies had recovered their investments many times over.

He cited these figures as estimated annual returns on investment: I.P.C., 56.6 per cent between 1952 and 1963, the Arabian-American Oil Company, 61 per cent from 1956 to 1960; the Iran Consortium, 69 per cent from 1959 to 1964 with the average for the Middle East, being 67 per cent from 1948 to 1960.

Dr. Pachachi cited other figures published by the American Commerce Department on direct American investment in 1970. They showed the net assets of the American petroleum industry in the Middle East at $1.47-billion, which yielded $7.16 billion in 1970 in profits. The net assets are book figures, which are substantially undervalued.

This was an annual rate of return of 79.2 per cent.

The rate of return of United States investments in the mining and smelting industries in developing countries, by contrast, was 13.5 per cent in 1970. In manufacturing industries in the developing countries it was 10.2 per cent in the same year.

June 6, 1972

Oil Concerns Set Accord With Five Arab Countries

Details of the Agreement for Eventual Control of Western-Held Concessions by Nations Are Not Disclosed

By WILLIAM D. SMITH

Representatives of five Persian Gulf oil-producing countries and the major Western oil companies reached agreement here yesterday on terms for the five countries eventually to take over control of the companies' concessions in the area.

Details of the historic agreement, reached after nine months of sometimes acerbic negotiations, were not made public, pending final approval by the governments of Saudi Arabia, Qatar, Kuwait, Iraq and Abu Dhabi, a member of the Union of Arab Emirates..

Approval seems almost certain in every case except that of Iraq, whose radical Government may disagree with the extent of the provisions for payment to the companies by the countries for equity in the concessions.

Participation Sought

The producing countries originally demanded an initial 20 per cent participation, growing to a 51 per cent controlling interest, in the concessions on their soil.

The companies accepted the principle of participation in March, and seven negotiating sessions since then have been devoted chiefly to setting the price the countries would pay for their equity interests, the timing of the transfer of control to the producing countries and the price to be paid by the companies for the oil they buy back from the countries.

1980 Date Expected

One of the principal provisions of the agreement meets the demands for eventual rise to a maximum participation level of 51 per cent.

Most informed sources believed that the majority control would be reached by 1980. One usually reliable source contended that the agreement called for control by the countries by the end of five years.

As to payment for participation, sources close to the Arab negotiators contended that it would be considerably higher than book value of existing investments. The producing nations originally offered to make payment on book value only. Book value has traditionally been understated by the companies for tax purposes; more importantly it does not take into consideration the multibillion-dollar value of the oil reserves still under the ground.

Sources say that payments by the Gulf states will be 40 to 100 per cent above book value. On a concession with a book value of $800-million, payment at book value for 20 per cent of the concession would be $160-million. The value of the oil in the ground could be many billions of dollars.

The companies are believed likely to try to pass along the costs of participation to the consumers, and prices could go up in Europe and Asia. The United States, where domestic crude oil prices are considerably higher than world prices, should not be directly or immediately affected.

In the future, however, the United States will become increasingly dependent on foreign oil's moving from the present level of about 23 per cent of consumption to 40 to 60 per cent by 1980. The world oil price then will directly affect the cost of driving a car, heating a house or running a factory in this country.

The agreement was a personal triumph for Sheik Ahmed Zaki Yamani, Saudi Arabia's 42-year-old Minister of Oil and Minerals, who beginning four years ago, developed and championed the concept of participation as an alternative to nationalization.

With this agreement—and the likely prospect that other oil countries will demand and get similar arrangements—there will be a basic transformation in the giant international oil industry. Majority control over production of the reserves, which were developed during the last half century by private American and European companies, will pass to the governments of the oil-producing countries, mostly Arab.

Participation, is an attempt to tie together the interests of the producing nations, the consuming nations and the oil companies in a mutually beneficial arrangement while also allowing the countries to have majority control over their own natural resources.

Nationalization on the other hand would be a unilateral expulsion of Western interests.

A spokesman for the companies said:

"We feel that we have now reached a milestone in the relations between the oil-producing countries and the private oil companies. In this new era we hope we can move forward together to discharge our continuing responsibilities to the producing and consuming countries alike."

Sheik Yamani said in his room in the Delmonico Hotel after the final session:

"I believe that participation will be proven to be the only instrument available in the oil trade that will provide prosperity and stability for posterity."

A statement issued by the industry negotiating team, which was headed by George Piercy of the Standard Oil Company (New Jersey), said that the agreement was comprehensive. It calls for each Gulf country or emirate to negotiate separate agreements with the oil companies operating within its territory to implement the over-all arrangements, it said.

The companies affected by the agreement are Jersey Standard; the Standard Oil Company of California; Texaco, Inc.; the Mobil Oil Corporation; the Royal Dutch Shell Group; the British Petroleum Company, Ltd., and Company, Ltd., and Compagnie Française des Pétroles.

From the very beginning of the negotiations it was obvious that the countries would get what they wanted.

Since the 1967 Arab-Israeli war the balance of power in the oil industry has swung away from the Western companies to the producing countries.

A big question is whether the producing nations will hold to the agreement. In recent years the producers have gathered for themselves a larger and larger share of the revenues from their oil—the split now runs about 79 per cent for the countries and 21 per cent for the companies. On several occasions in the recent past the producers have demanded changes in terms after signin long-range agreements.

Walter J. Levy, one of the world's most respected oil economists, commented: "Considering my natural skepticism with regards to any long-term agreements in the oil business, I am optimistic. I am convinced, however, of the honorable intentions of all parties."

The New York Times/Neal Boenzi

Sheik Ahmed Zaki Yamani, left, of Saudi Arabia, as he conferred during the week with George T. Piercy, center, of Standard Oil of New Jersey and Alfred C. DeCrane Jr. of Texaco. The negotiators reached agreement yesterday.

October 6, 1972

OIL NATIONS BACK PLAN ON SHARING

Participation Agreement by 4 Persian Gulf Exporters With Companies Approved

By JUAN de ONIS
Special to The New York Times

RIYADH, Saudi Arabia, Oct. 27—A conference of the Organization of Petroleum Exporting Countries approved today a plan by four Persian Gulf nations to gradually take over foreign - owned oil - producing companies in their territories.

Saudi Arabia and Kuwait, first and second among world exporters, are the leaders in the participation plan, an alternative to abrupt nationalizations such as those that have hit Western oil companies in Libya, Iraq and Algeria.

Under the plan, the four countries—Saudi Arabia, Kuwait, Qatar and Abu Dhabi—have agreed in principle with major interested Western oil companies to reach 51 per cent ownership by host countries in 1983, starting with an immediate purchase of 25 per cent control of existing foreign concessions.

Historic Turning Point

Sheik Ahmed Zaki Yamani, Saudi Arabia's Minister of Petroleum, said this "historic turning point in the international oil industry" would give countries achieving majority participation "political strength to be taken into account in the world balance of power."

But he said that, in relation to consumer countries, this power should be used "in cooperation and not in confrontation."

This statement before the delegates of the 11-nation Organization of Petroleum Exporting Countries, meeting here to consider the participation accords, was ratified in the closing statement by all participants except Venezuela, which asked more time before expressing an opinion.

"Effective participation is an event marking a turning point in the history of the oil industry and benefiting the interest of the countries concerned and their peoples," said the statement.

Reservations in Private

Libya, Iraq, Iran and Nigeria joined in this endorsement despite reservations in private about applying the same formula to their own relations with foreign companies.

Kuwait will open negotiations next Saturday on details of the agreement, particularly the price at which the foreign partners will buy the oil to be controlled by the host countries. The foreign companies concerned are the British Petroleum Company and the Gulf Oil Company, which own the Kuwait Oil Company concession.

Iran, which is seeking a somewhat different formula, is expected to begin talks next week with the foreign oil company consortium of British, French and United States concerns that have controlled most of Iran's oil since 1953.

Sheik Yamani said that Saudi Arabia hoped to have the participation principle in effect by Jan. 1 when it would begin to pay the Arabian-American Oil Company, a consortium of United States oil companies, the first installment on $500-million, the estimated price for a 25 per cent interest.

The effect of participation will be, not only to increase the revenue per barrel of the oil to the producing countries, but to give them direct control over an increasing part of their output and a managerial voice in marketing of crude and products.

For the consuming countries, it will continue the trend of higher prices for oil products, but is also expected to provide greater stability for foreign countries operating in these countries, which hold major reserves.

Venezuelan Explains

Hugo Perez la Salvia, Venezuela's Minister of Petroleum, said he had not joined in the general endorsement of the participation formula "because it does not aply to our situation."

Under concessions covering 75 per cent of Venezuelan production, the largest source of exports to the United States in the Western Hemisphere, the oil fields and their installations are to revert in full to state ownership in 1984.

Iraq, while endorsing the participation principle, indicated that the compensation formula to be applied did not conform to the law by which the Iraq Petroleum Company's major Kirkuk fields were nationalized this year. The issue of compensation has not been resolved with the British, French and United States owners.

Libya did not attack the participation formula directly, but Izz Al Din Mabruk, Libya's Petroleum Minister, reported in detail on an arrangement with ENI, the Italian state oil company, which gave Libya an immediate 50 per cent share of production from a concession held by ENI.

October 28, 1972

4 Arab Nations Temporarily Halt Flow of Oil in Symbolic Protest

BEIRUT, Lebanon, May 15 (Reuters) — Four Arab countries, staging a symbolic protest against Israel's continued existence as a nation, today temporarily halted the flow of oil to the West.

The demonstration, in response to an appeal issued after a pan-Arab trade-union conference in Cairo earlier this month, was supposedly timed to coincide with Israel's 25th anniversary. Israel celebrated the anniversary May 7.

Though the stoppage was meant to last an hour Libya shut her pumps for 24 hours; the others taking part were Iraq, Kuwait and Algeria. The stoppage had special significance because of world preoccupation with the world's energy supply.

There was no indication that Saudi Arabia, the Middle East's major oil producer, had participated in the demonstration.

At a meeting of the Arab Defense Council, composed of Arab League members, earlier this year in Cairo, Iraq urged the use of oil in the battle against Israel and indicated that she was willing to stop the flow of oil to the West completely as part of such a move.

Kuwaiti Government officials also said in recent public statements that their country was ready to shut the oil pipelines the moment that the battle against Israel began.

Saudi Arabia has opposed stopping the flow of oil as a political weapon. King Faisal was quoted three years ago as having said that the stoppage of pumping was "out of the question."

But a possible change in Saudi Arabian policy was seen in an interview given last month in the United States by the Saudi Arabian Minister of Petroleum Affairs, Sheik Ahmed Zaki al-Yamani.

He said that Saudi Arabia might not increase oil production "unless there was a change in the political climate." This was interpreted to mean a change in United States support for Israel.

Sadat Again Asks Pressure

CAIRO, May 15 (AP)—President Anwar el-Sadat has called on the Arab nations again to use their oil to apply pressure on the United States to abandon support for Israel.

Warning that this generation may not see an end of the Arab-Israeli conflict, Mr. Sadat told the Parliament: "The case is one of a protracted struggle and not only the Suez Canal battle. There is the battle of America's interests, the battle of energy, the battle of the Arabs. These are big battles for which we must plan and coordinate."

Mr. Sadat made the remarks last night and part of a transcript was published today. He stressed that he was continuing talks with leaders of the Arab oil countries, including King Faisal of Saudi Arabia, who was his guest last weekend.

President Sadat said that Saudi Arabia was expected by 1975 to produce 25 per cent of the world's oil needs and that Iraq, the world's eighth-largest oil producer, was participating in talks with him. Libya, the fourth largest oil exporter, is due to merge with Egypt this year.

May 16, 1973

That Arab Oil Wealth

By EDWIN L. DALE Jr.

WASHINGTON — Will the inevitable pile-up of large sums of money in a handful of small oil-producing Arab countries mean "continuous monetary crises" or "a highly advantageous mutual bargain" with the industrial countries?

The first phrase, descriptive of a widespread fear in financial circles here and abroad, comes from a booklet of briefing material prepared for the recent hearings of the subcommittee on international finance and resources of the Senate Finance Committee.

The second phrase comes from a speech in Paris last week by Secretary of the Treasury George P. Shultz on the monetary aspects of the energy problem, which was somewhat overlooked in the flood of other events.

Mr. Shultz spelled out in detail for the first time the Government's case for its view that the "Arab oil money" problem is probably being exaggerated.

The case was also presented, with somewhat less detail, at the Senate subcommittee hearings, by Jack L. Bennett, Deputy Under Secretary of the Treasury for monetary affairs.

Although Mr. Shultz did not put the matter in precisely these terms, a key aspect of the case, surprisingly, is that $100-billion is not really all that much money.

The figure, derived from a recent foreign affairs article by James E. Akins, the State Department's leading expert on Arab oil, is an estimate of the possible maximum of monetary reserves by 1980 of the four Arab oil-producing states whose populations are so small that they cannot possibly spend all their oil earnings on imports: Saudi Arabia, Kuwait, Abu Dhabi and Qatar. It is a figure that has frightened the financial world.

But Mr. Shultz pointed out that by 1980 the "annual capital formation of industrialized countries will probably approximate $700-billion" and, even more startingly, the annual issue of *new* stocks and bonds "will probably be on the order of $250-billion." New issues in the United States alone last year exceeded $100-billion.

And finally, according to Mr. Shultz, "it takes no stretch of the imagination — if one looks beyond the last few months in Wall Street — to suggest that the total market value of outstanding stocks and bonds in the world could exceed $3-trillion by 1980."

What all this means, of course, is that, even if the Arabs have $100-billion, their capacity to "buy up" any significant portion of the assets of the industrial countries would not be large but that, if they invest the money in the industrial countries, they will make a useful contribution in a situation of probable shortage of capital.

But will they invest it? Mr. Bennett suggests that they have no real alternative. He says:

"They will be seeking secure and productive investments to replace their assets from the ground. They know that their reserves of oil will not last forever and that an important part of their income must be invested wisely in order that it may provide income for the time when their production is declining and newly developed alternative sources of energy have reduced the dependence of the industrialized world on their supplies."

In answer to fears that the Arab money could be "sloshing about" and causing violent monetary instability, Mr. Shultz argues that in their own interest they will have to seek "stable, secure and profitable investment opportunities — not for a year or two, but for long periods." Long-term investments do not slosh about, Mr. Shultz continues:

"As they turn to world financial markets, there is no inherent reason to believe their asset preferences will not be subject to the same profit instincts that lead most investors to place a substantial portion of their funds in longer-term form, provided the climate is favorable."

Mr. Bennett told the Senate hearing that information from "a number" of the Arab oil countries showed that they did not speculate against the dollar in the monetary turmoil in February and March, at least not with government reserves.

But what about the United States in particular, and the impact of the oil picture on the exchange rate of the dollar? Here two points are made.

First, Europe and Japan together will actually increase their total oil imports from the Arab countries by more than the United States will increase them, despite the big projected jump in United States imports. Thus there is no inherent reason why the exchange rate that matters—the dollar against the European currencies and the yen—should change.

The issue becomes simply one of whether the United States will get its appropriate share of both exports to some oil countries and investments from others. Mr. Shultz was confident on both counts. He said, without too much fear of contradiction, "I am unabashed in feeling we can compete with any nation in investment opportunities."

All in all, Mr. Shultz argued, "the United States could well be the gainer" in its over-all balance of payments vis-à-vis those of Europe and Japan.

None of this is certain, of course, any more than it is certain that the four Arab countries will pile up as much as $100-billion. Also, the Arabs may be of several minds about long-term investments in the industrial countries, despite what seems to be their self-interest. Such a respected Arab official as Abdel-Rahman Salem al-Atiqi, Kuwait's Minister of Finance and Oil, spoke in April of putting an end to "these unsatisfactory relationships which make us a mere source of finance for economies stronger than ours."

But even if the Arab oil countries "invest" their money in the form of aid to the less-developed countries, including other Arab countries, the money will ultimately be spent on imports from the industrial countries.

In any event, all the rich countries are in roughly the same boat as far as oil, the balance of payments and exchange rates are concerned. There is no a priori reason why the United States should come out worse than the others.

June 10, 1973

LIBYAN TAKE-OVER EXPECTED TO LIFT WORLD OIL PRICES

U.S. and Industry Officials See Growing Pressure to Alter Support of Israel

By EDWARD COWAN

Special to The New York Times

WASHINGTON, Sept. 4—Government and oil industry sources expressed the common view today that Libya's take-over of 51 per cent of several major American oil companies last weekend presaged higher world oil prices generally and intensification of the already growing pressure on Washington to modify its support of Israel.

In addition to proclaiming the take-over on Saturday, a move that had been expected in light of earlier Libyan action, Libya startled the oil industry by announcing on Sunday a price increase of more than $1, to $6, for the standard 42-gallon barrel.

The State Department, reiterating an earlier position, asserted that the take-over "does not comport" with Libya's obligations under her oil-producing agreements with American companies.

Earlier Criticism

The State Department had been similarly critical of nationalization of the Nelson Bunker Hunt Oil Company, one of several smaller, independent companies against which Libya moved earlier this summer before tackling the major companies.

As for the oil industry, it appears ready to make a strong stand against Libya's nationalization action, although the companies seem to have few weapons in their arsenal.

Industry and diplomatic experts unhesitatingly expressed the belief that Libya would find buyers for her oil at $6 a barrel, the price announced by Premier Abdul Salam Jalloud.

Worldwide Demand

"Everybody is crude hungry," explained one executive. He noted that Libyan crude is highly desirable because it is low in sulphur and gives a high gasoline yield, the most valuable refinery product.

Six dollars a barrel is markedly higher than the $4.90 figure Libya announced in August when the Occidental Oil Company, one of the independents, agreed to Tripoli's terms for 51 per cent "participation," a euphemism for ownership and operating control. As recently as Aug. 1, Libya's posted price, a benchmark for tax and royalty purposes which until recently exceeded transaction prices, was $4.59 a barrel.

Most of Libya's production of 2.3 million barrels of crude a day has been refined in Europe. Libyan crude has accounted for 4.2 per cent of United States oil imports, which in turn amount to about one-third of domestic consumption of crude oil and petroleum products.

A State Department spokesman, Paul J. Hare, told reporters that the department had not yet seen the text of Saturday's nationalization decree aimed at Libyan subsidiaries of Exxon, Mobil, Texaco, Standard Oil of California, Atlantic Richfield, W. R. Grace, Royal Dutch Shell and Gelsenberg, A. G. Shell is predominantly British-Dutch, and Gelsenberg is West German.

Other officials suggested that the State Department might announce no specific retaliatory measures for two reasons. The first was that no suitable ones present themselves. One official laughed at reports that a boycott was being considered. "they've got what everybody needs," he said. "There's not much to boycott."

The second reason was avoidance of any action that might cause other Middle East oil producers to feel that Arab solidarity required them to harden their attitudes toward the United States and American companies.

Libya's weekend action, which didn't surprise Middle East oil analysts here, caused one of them to comment that "the questions of price and degree of control of the companies are escalating more rapidly."

Officials are worried that Libya's move, which the oil companies are expected to resist, will put additional pressure on Saudi Arabia to accelerate her timetable for achieving 51 per cent participation in the Arabian-American Oil Company, an American consortium, and to become bolder in her foreign-policy demands on Washington.

The Saudis, under pressure from Cairo and perhaps from radical elements elsewhere in the Middle East, have been threatening to slow their expansion of production unless Washington modifies its support for Israel. Several United States oil companies also have been lobbying for such a change.

The State Department some weeks ago made a discreet effort to nudge Israel toward rethinking her position on the territories occupied in the 1967 six-day war. A number of department officials feel that this effort should be continued and intensified, because of the United States' growing requirements for Saudi oil.

"There is a growing recognition in all circles here that some accommodation has to be reached,'" one official said. "It will be a settlement less attractive than Israel could have had last month."

Officials here seemed to be unconcerned over Premier Jalloud's notice that Libya no longer would accept payments in United States dollars. There was some possibility that this change could add to downward pressure on the dollar, but the extent of such potential pressure was not immediately clear.

Mr. Hare, the State Department spokesman, noted that the United States position on expropriation is that it must be for a public purpose and must provide for "prompt, adequate and effective" compensation. In the case of Bunker Hunt, the department protested in a note to Libya that the take-over appeared to be a "political reprisal."

Mr. Hare also commented that Libya's agreements with the oil companies provided for arbitration of disputes. Libya has rejected that course.

Officials here said they believed that Libya would be able to increase production from the independent companies' fields, as Premier Jalloud suggested, to cover any reduction in output from the majors' fields.

Libya's production has been as high as 4 million barrels a day, it was noted.

A senior official of one of the newly affected companies explained that the company was unwilling to discuss the situatio.. openly because "we're in a negotiation now" and because of fear of reprisal against United States citizens employed by the company in Libya.

"The Libyans are unpredictable," he said, "and now that the Government has taken over there could be penalties for our people."

Permission Required

The company official said that under the decree foreigners had to get permission to leave Libya. That requirement probably was meant to forestall wholesale withdrawal of senior staff members to shut down production.

Industry sources also said they were in the dark about Libya's intentions for selling back to the companies her 51 per cent share of the oil. It is assumed that the Government doesn't expect to market the oil itself. However, in light of the rapid pace of events, some industry sources said that even that assumption didn't look as safe as it once did.

September 5, 1973

A MIDEAST PLEDGE

President Is Seeking a Settlement to End Oil Threats by Arabs

By BERNARD GWERTZMAN

Special to The New York Times

WASHINGTON, Sept. 5—President Nixon said today that he was giving "highest priority" to achieving a Middle East settlement that would put an end to Arab threats to curtail future oil deliveries to Western countries.

Assigning blame to both Israel and the Arab states for the deadlock in the area, Mr. Nixon said the United States planned to use its influence on both sides to get negotiations "off dead center."

At a news conference in the White House, Mr. Nixon expressed considerable concern about recent warnings from Arab states that they might reduce or limit their oil production if the United States did not press Israel to make concessions to the Arab side.

Greater U.S. Output Urged

At the same time, however, Mr. Nixon urged greater efforts to increase American oil production so that the United States would not be "at the mercy of the producers of oil in the Mideast."

The President also warned "radical elements" in the Arab world, such as in the Libyan Government, that they ran the risk of alienating their market—Europe and the United States—if they continued to raise prices, expropriate foreign holdings, and failed to give "fair compensation."

Mr. Nixon's remarks accompanied an appeal to Congress to enact seven legislative measures aimed at increasing the United States' own energy supplies.

The President's comments on the Middle East amounted to a shift in the Administration's public position.

Linkage Is a Shift

Up to now, except for occasional statements by State Department officials such as Joseph J. Sisco, Assistant Secretary for Near Eastern and South Asian Affairs, the Administration had avoided linking Middle East diplomacy with the question of oil supplies.

In his own energy message to Congress last April, for instance, Mr. Nixon did not mention the Middle East.

But today, Mr. Nixon raised the problem of reliance on Middle East oil in his opening statement, which called on Congress to act in the energy field.

In answer to a question, he said that "we presently depend upon [oil] in the Mideast—we depend on it, not, of course, nearly as much as Europe, but we're all in the same bag when you really come down to it."

"The problem that we have here is that as far as the Arab countries are concerned, the ones that are involved here, is that it's tied up with the Arab-Israeli dispute," Mr. Nixon said.

He said that because of this connection, he and Henry A. Kissinger, his nominee as Secretary of State, had given "highest priority" to making some progress toward a settlement of the dispute.

Efforts for a negotiated settlement have been deadlocked for some time.

The Israelis assert that they want "unconditional" negotiations with the Egyptians, Jordanians and Syrians but they also assert the determination to retain some of the territory occupied as the result of the Arab-Israeli war in June, 1967.

The Egyptians have refused negotiations until Israel agrees in principle to withdraw from all occupied territory.

U.S. Position Recalled

The Administration, which has offered various peace plans, has recently taken the position that it is up to the two sides to come up with ideas and compromises, with the United States acting as an honest broker to facilitate talks, if called upon.

Despite Mr. Nixon's assertion that the "highest priority" was being given to the Middle East, there have been no signs lately of any major American diplomatic effort in that area.

In recent months, the Libyan Government has publicly called on other Arab producers to seize American companies to press the United States to end its support for Israel.

Of more concern to the Administration, Saudi Arabia, the largest oil producer in the Arab world, with the greatest potential for expansion, has threatened to hold production at the current level of nine million barrels a day and not raise it to the 20-million-barrels level sought by the West unless the United States brings pressure on Israel.

The wide publicity given the Arab threats has aroused concern in Israel and within American Jewish organizations about the possibility that the United States might slacken its support for Israel, which includes the delivery of modern F-4 Phantom fighter-bombers for the next four years.

Mr. Nixon was given the opportunity by a questioner to affirm American backing for Israel, but he turned it aside and instead stressed American neutrality in the area and the wish for a negotiated settlement.

Asked if it were "possible" that the Arab threat would cause "a moderation" in American support for Israel, Mr. Nixon replied that it would be "highly inappropriate" for an American President "to relate our policy toward Israel" to what happens on Arab oil. He noted, in passing, that the United States was dedicated to Israel's independence.

Mr. Nixon's comments seemed likely to arouse concern in Israel where they may be interpreted as a sign of weakening American resolve in the face of Arab threats.

The President seemed to offer no solution to the problem caused by the recent nationalization by Libya of 51 per cent of several American oil companies, except to suggest the possibility of a Western effort to block the sale of such expropriated oil.

He cited the failure of Dr. Mohammed Mossadegh, the Premier of Iran in the early nineteen-fifties who seized British oil fields in his country.

At the time, because of a world oil surplus, the British—aided by the United States—were able to block the sale of that Iranian oil and ultimately to encourage Dr. Mossadegh's overthrow.

Oil Needs a Market

"Oil without a market, as Mr. Mossadegh learned many, many years ago, doesn't do a country much good," the President said. "We and Europe are the market." Mr. Nixon omitted Japan, which is also a major importer of Middle Eastern oil and which up to now has been reluctant to join in any concerted effort to influence Arab states.

The oil and Middle East diplomacy dominated the foreign policy portions of the news conference. on other topics, Mr. Nixon mentioned that Mr. Kissinger would go to China after his expected Senate confirmation as Secretary of State—something already disclosed by Mr. Kissinger himself.

In the opening statement Mr. Nixon also urged Congress to leave his defense budget alone because of the need to have a strong military posture in the forthcoming negotiations with the Soviet Union on offensive strategic arms, and on mutual reduction of forces in Central Europe.

September 6, 1973

GLOWING REPORTS CARRIED ON RADIOS

Many Surprised by Clash —Iraq Takes 2 U.S. Oil Interests in Reprisal

By JUAN de ONIS
Special to The New York Times

BEIRUT, Lebanon, Oct. 7—The Arabs are in a curious mood, between exhilaration and uncertainty, over the outbreak in the Middle East.

The reports carried on Arab radio stations for an avid public give encouraging, even spectacular, official accounts of victories on the Syrian and Egyptian fronts.

In Damascus, the Syrian capital, clusters of people gathered around radios today and cheered reports of Israel planes shot down and Arab advances on the Suez Canal and the Golan heights.

In five communiqués during the day, the Damascus radio reported that 43 Israeli aircraft had been shot down and that Syrian forces continued to advance in the Golan heights.

The Syrian radio broadcast in Hebrew an appeal to Israeli soldiers and settlers in the Golan heights to surrender, and said that the Syrian troops would be "magnanimous."

But the defeat at Israeli hands in the war of 1967 has not been forgotten, and there is an underlying Arab fear that the news may turn bad. The reports from Israeli radios are also heard in the Arab countries with accounts that conflict sharply with the Arab version.

The fighting clearly took many Arabs by surprise. Until a few days ago, it was assumed that Egypt was following a policy emphasizing diplomacy, not war, as the most effective way to bring international pressure to bear for a Middle East political settlement.

Libya Pledges Funds

But many offers to aid the fighting were received. Algeria announced that she had sent an unspecified number of combat aircraft to Egypt to join in the fighting. Iraq already has some air force unts there.

In Syria, Moroccan troops were reportedly fighting alongside Syrian forces in the Golan heights. A Moroccan brigade went to Syria two months ago.

The Libyan leader, Col. Muammar el-Qadafi, announced in a speech tonight that his country would finance Egypt's and Syria's battle with Israel. The Middle East News Agency said that funds would be transferred immediately.

Earlier in Paris, a spokesman said that Libya would enter the Middle East war if the confict was not stopped by an international decision.

Yemen offered to send troops. Other pledges of support also have come from South Yemen, Lebanon and the Sudan. It was not known if these offers included military involvement.

In Iraq, the Government announced that as a reprisal against United States support of Israel, it was nationalizing the interests of two American oil companies in the Western oil consortium that operates there.

The companies concerned are the Exxon Corporation and Mobil Oil Corporation, which together owned 23.7 per cent of the Basra Petroleum Company.

Iraq broadcast an appeal to all Arab oil-producing countries to cut off supplies to the United States and other supporters of Israel, but there was no indication that Iraq was suspending her own shipments.

Kuwait Reacts

In a sudden diplomatic shift Iraq offered to re-establish diplomatic relations with Iran, with which she has had serious differences on borders and ideological issues. The move was seen as an attempt to free Iraqi troops for support of Syria and Egypt, since the major part of the Iraqi armed forces are along the border with Iran.

After a Cabinet meeting, the Kuwaitis said that "Kuwait views this battle as a battle of all Arab countries and will consider any interference by world powers in the Arab countries as aggression against Kuwait."

In Saudi Arabia, the major Arab oil-producing country, there was no report of any action to interrupt oil production. Yesterday a message from King Faisal, the Saudi ruler, to Secretary of State Kissinger called on the United States to "force Israel to pull out of Arab lands and to restore the rights of the Palestinian people in their land."

King Faisal warned that the fighting in the Middle East "may explode into a global conflict involving the major powers."

In Jordan, which took an active military part in the 1967 war, there was no move to join the fight. King Hussein inspected troops and air force units along the cease-fire line with Israel, according to the Amman radio, but the only shots fired in Jordan were some antiaircraft rounds against a formation of Israeli Phantom jets that flew over the Jordan River.

King Hussein met last month with President Anwar el-Sadat of Egypt and President Hafez al-Assad of Syria to discuss the establishment of an "eastern front" along the Jordan River facing the West Bank, occupied by Israel in 1967.

As a result of the meeting, Egypt and Syria restored diplomatic relations with Jordan, which had been broken after King Hussein's army drove Palestinian guerrillas out of Jordan in 1970 and 1971.

The Jordanian King has said repeatedly in recent months that he would not commit Jordanian forces to combat with Israel unless he felt that the Arabs had at least a 50 per cent chance.

The absence of Jordanian forces from the fighting suggested that King Hussein had not been convinced that a new conflict had a reasonable chance.

Palestinian guerrillas were reportedly fighting with Syrian forces in the battle for the Golan heights, according to the Palestinian press agency. The Palestine Liberation Organization, headed by Yasir Arafat, issued a statement calling for the mobilization of the "army of the Arab masses" and urged all Arab oil producers to cut off exports to supporters of Israel.

October 8, 1973

SIX OIL COUNTRIES RAISE PRICE 17%

Persian Gulf Producers Say Step Is Not Tied to War

KUWAIT, Wednesday, Oct. 17 (AP)—The six largest oil producing countries on the Persian Gulf announced a 17 per cent price increase for their crude oil early today but said the move had nothing to do with the Middle East war.

Officials of a group of Arab oil-exporting nations will meet here later today to decide about using their oil as a weapon in the Arab cause in the war against Israel.

The price increase—from $3.12 to $3.65 a barrel for standard light Arabian crude—is not expected to affect consumers in the United States right away. The most direct immediate affect is likely to be felt in Europe and Japan, which depend mostly on the Middle East for their oil.

The United States gets about 6 per cent of its oil requirements from the Middle East.

The countries that announced the price increase today are Iran, which is non-Arab, and Iraq, Kuwait, Saudi Arabia, Abu Dhabi and Qatar, all Arab. Together they account for about 40 per cent of the oil production in the non-Communist world.

Negotiations Suspended

The announcement said that they had taken their action in direct response to what one envoy called the "intransigence" of the Western countries in negotiating a price increase. Oil price talks that had been going on in Vienna were suspended last Friday after oil companies asked for two weeks to study the situation.

All the major Western oil companies are represented in the Persian Gulf. They are over-ll buyers of crude oil and thus have little choice but to accept the new conditions. However, the oil ministers at the meeting that begins today said that if the companies refused these conditions, the six countries would sell to other buyers at the new price.

The oil countries said that from now on the cost of crude oil to the companies would not be a matter of negotiation but would be set by market prices, which now are rising. The announcement in effect dismembered all curent price agreements negotiated with the companies in recent years.

The 17 percent increase will bring prices in the Persian Gulf into line with those in North Africa and Venezuela when transport differences are calculated. During his reading of the announcement, Finance Minister Jamshid Amouzgar of Iran said in an aside, "You see, we are being entirely reasonable."

Rise Viewed as Moderate

Special to The New York Times

WASHINGTON, Oc. 16—The announcement from Kuwait

was seen provisionally here as an indication that the producers were settling for a relatively moderate price increase but were presenting it to the major international oil companies as a unilateral, nonnegotiable action.

One source very close to price negotiations that took place in Vienna last week has reported that producers' representatives have proposed a price of $26.20 a barrel. Other accounts have said the producers were aiming at $24.50 a barrel.

In recent days, Washington has been more worried about cutbacks in production than about price rises, which are regarded as inevitable.

The Arab countries were believed to be withholding any announcement of reduced production, if that is to come, until after a meeting scheduled for tomorrow morning between President Nixon and the foreign ministers of Algeria, Morocco, Saudi Arabia and Kuwait.

The ministers had hoped to see Mr. Nixon today, and it was for that reason that a meeting of Arab oil ministers in Kuwait to consider what to do about production was deferred from today until tomorrow.

Analysts here said that the higher Persian Gulf prices would have an early, if indirect, effect on wholesale and retail prices in this country. Although most of the Persian Gulf crude goes to the Middle East, the price mark-up is bound to have a firming effect on other crude oil prices generally, if it does not start a new round of price leapfrogging with Libya and Venezuela.

Kuwait to Aid War Effort

KUWAIT, Oct. 16 (Reuters) —Kuwait decided today to contribute about $350 million to the Arab war effort, amid indications that this oil-producing state is advocating a moderate stand on the use of oil as a weapon in the conflict.

The decision came at a private session of the National Assembly, which was believed to be discussing Kuwait's war role in both oil and military matters.

A Government bill called for the $350-million grant "to defend our sacred Islamic places, because the Arabs are engaged in a struggle for their dignity, and because the world powers aid Israel in its continued aggression."

Informed sources said the Government would decide how to allocate the money between Egypt and Syria.

October 17, 1973

ARABS CUT OIL EXPORTS 5% A MONTH

U.S. CHIEF TARGET

Reduction Is Smaller Than Expected—Effect Uncertain

By RICHARD EDER
Special to The New York Times

BEIRUT, Lebanon, Oct. 17— The Arab oil-producing nations proclaimed tonight a monthly cut in exports of oil, with the burden to fall on the United States and other nations considered to be unfriendly to the Arab cause.

The long-awaited formal decision to use oil as a weapon in the Middle East conflict was announced at the end of an eight-hour meeting in Kuwait of ministers from 11 countries.

The monthly export reduction was set at 5 per cent off each previous month's sale, starting with the level of sales in September. The measure was at once more modest, more flexible and vaguer than had generally been predicted.

A Significant Shift

"It was about as mild a step as they could have taken," said one oil expert who had talked to the participants. At the same time, to have finally come to the use of oil as a weapon, as had been threatened for years, marks a significant evolution in Middle Eastern affairs.

The cuts would continue, month by month, until Israel evacuated the territories occupied in the 1967 war, and made provision to respect Arab rights. This deliberately imprecise formulation alludes to the claims of the Palestinian refugees.

France May be Exempt

There was no specific mention of any country on the "unfriendly" list other than the United States. This was one of many flexible aspects of the decision. It allows the Arab states to grade customers in order of their support of the Arab cause. The participants promised to insure that the 5 per cent monthly export cut would not reduce sales to "friendly" countries, but again they did not say which countries these were.

Observers at the meeting assumed that France, for example, would not be subject to reductions. West Germany, presumably, might be. Japan, whose position was described by one participant as that of "odious neutrality," might experience some difficulties. It was hard to say what treatment would be given to Britain, which has also tried to be neutral.

The 5 per cent cutback would be computed against the previous month's exports. The cut is less than it would be if this 5 per cent were computed from some single point. Thus, after six months the actual reduction would be 23 per cent instead of 30, and at the end of a year, 43 per cent instead of 60.

The 11 countries involved in the decision, not all of which are oil-producing countries, were Abu Dhabi, Algeria, Bahrain, Dubai, Egypt, Kuwait, Iraq, Libya, Qatar, Saudi Arabia and Syria.

Egypt and Saudi Arabia, opposing more militant proposals, are reported to have insisted on avoiding measures that would put relations with the United States beyond "the point of no return," a phrase used by the Egyptian President, Anwar el-Sadat, in his speech yesterday.

Reduction Is Modest

Tonight's decision appears to take account of this view. The dimensions of the cut were considerably more modest than the kind of all-out action called for by countries such as Syria and Iraq.

The United States uses some 17 million barrels of crude oil and refined products each day, and some 6.4 million barrels of this are imported. From the Arab countries the United States takes a total of crude and heating oil estimated variously at 1.5 million to 1.9 million barrels a day.

This week the United States released figures purporting to show that Americans would not be seriously affected even by major cuts in Arab oil production.

William E. Simon, chairman of President Nixon's oil policy committee, said that the United States could decrease its consumption of oil by as much as three million barrels a day if it made the necessary effort.

October 18, 1973

4 More Arab Governments Bar Oil Supplies for U.S.

By RICHARD EDER

Special to The New York Times

BEIRUT, Lebanon, Oct. 21—Four Persian Gulf oil producers — Kuwait, Qatar, Bahrain and Dubai -- today announced a total embargo of oil to the United States.

The announcements made the cutoff of Arab oil to the United States theoretically complete. Of the 17 million barrels of crude and heating oil and refinery products used by the United States each day, approximately 6 per cent has been imported from the Arab states.

At the same time, the Netherlands, which has been accused by the Arabs of being pro-Israel, was the object of reprisals today. Iraq announced the nationalization of Dutch oil holdings in the country. Previously Iraq had nationalized American holdings.

Not even the Arab producers themselves believe that the use of the oil weapon against the United States will have much immediate effect, although if maintained for a long period it could present serious problems. There is, for example, no simple way to prevent oil sold to European countries from finding its way to the United States.

Today's moves completed a second phase of Arab governments' decision to use oil to put pressure on the United States to abandon or reduce its support of Israel.

Last Wednesday, meeting in Kuwait, the Arabs announced that each nation would cut oil production by 5 per cent each month. These escalating cuts would continue, it was declared, until Israel evacuated the lands taken in 1967 and made restoration to the Palestinian refugees. This over-all squeeze on oil consumers was to be applied flexibly. Countries that gave "concrete assitance" to the Arab cause, it was announced, would not suffer cuts. Countries considered unfriendly — the United States in particular —would be made to bear the effects of the progressive curtailment.

The formula was purposely unclear and flexible. It was designed not simply to punish countries for supporting the Arabs insufficiently, but also to encourage them to change their policies. Countries that adopted a stiffer line toward Israel could find themselves placed in a more favored category.

At the same time, the use of the over-all reduction in production, especially as it escalated each month, would make it less and less likely that the European countries, for instance, would allow oil sold to them to be sent to the United States.

The Kuwait meeting was followed by announcements of more United States military aid to Israel and President Nixon's request for a $2.2-billion appropriation to pay for it. This seems to have set in motion the second phase of the oil squeeze.

Several states, among them Saudi Arabia and Qatar, announced that the first production cut would be 10 per cent rather than 5 per cent. In the case of Saudi Arabia, whose production dwarfs that of the others, the 10 per cent cut would replace the first two monthly 5 per cent reductions.

The results would be roughly the same, but the initial bite would be much harder.

Then over the last three days, the oil states began successively announcing a total embargo on oil to the United States. By tonight these included Saudi Arabia, Libya, Kuwait, Abu Dhabi, Qatar, Algeria, Bahrain and Dubai.

The total embargo on the United States could mean that the other form of pressure, the production cut, will begin to be felt in Europe and Japan somewhat later than it otherwise would have done. This is because the United States took close to 10 per cent of the Arab output.

October 22, 1973

Nixon Says Some Allies Failed U.S. on Middle East

Oil Is Called a Factor

By DAVID BINDER

Special to The New York Times

WASHINGTON, Oct. 26 — President Nixon chastised this country's Western European allies tonight for withholding the support the United States would have liked for its Middle East policies and actions, suggesting that Europe "would have frozen to death this winter unless there had been a settlement."

The Administration's resentment over the attitude of most of its allies in the North Atlantic Treaty Organization came out into the open at the President's news conference tonight and in statements earlier by Defense and State Department officials.

Mr. Nixon noted with approval statements by the State Department that European allies had not been as cooperative as they might have been in attempting to help the United States work out a Middle East settlement. The neutral stance taken by many allies was widely ascribed by American officials to a concern among Europeans that they might be cut off from Arab oil.

"I can only say on that score that Europe, which gets 80 per cent of its oil from the Mideast, would have frozen to death this winter unless there had been a settlement," the President said.

He went on to point out that the United States "gets only approximately 10 per cent of its oil from the Mideast."

The United States chastisement of its allies, said to be the first direct American criticism of them since NATO was founded in April, 1949, began today with statements by Secretary of Defense James R. Schlesinger and the State Department spokesman, Robert J. McCloskey.

Both men singled out West Germany as one of the allies that had taken a line "separate" from that of the United States on the Middle East.

They alluded to the statement issued yesterday by the West German Foreign Ministry calling on the United States to stop loading American weapons for Israel aboard Israeli freighters at the United States forces port in Bremerhaven.

'Some Lengths' From U.S.

At a State Department briefing, Mr. McCloskey said, in reply to a question, that "we were struck by a number of our allies going to some lengths to separate themselves publicly from us" on the Middle East.

At a Pentagon briefing, Dr. Schlesinger said: "The reaction of the Foreign Ministry in Germany raises some questions about whether they view enhanced readiness in the same way that we view enhanced readiness."

Both men appeared to be reflecting official United States annoyance over what was regarded as a flaccid Western European response to the worldwide alert of American armed forces yesterday.

The disappointment of the Nixon Administration in the response of its allies has been mounting for over two weeks, United States officials said. It began when the nine members of the European Economic Community issued what the Administration regarded as a boneless declaration during the first week of fighting, which erupted Oct. 6.

The annoyance grew when several NATO members issued "neutrality" declarations and went on to advise the United States that it could not use their facilities or airspace for resupply of arms to Israel.

In response to a question, Mr. McCloskey said that "one country in particular" among the allies had been helpful. This was understood to be Portugal, which let American transports and fighters land and refuel in the Azores.

The McCloskey and Schlesinger remarks concerned not only the division of views on the degree of threat posed by the Middle East situation but also on the meaning and future of the 24-year-old Atlantic alliance.

Mr. McCloskey said: "Our view is that maintenance of the military balance and establishment of a durable peace in the Middle East — which in our view and in our actions is what the resupply of Israel is about — is just as much in the vital interest of West Germany and the other NATO allies as it is in our interest. We were and have been in a very critical period which affected in many ways all of us. We found ourselves in a period of tension and we would have appreciated some unified support."

Diplomats Are Puzzled

A telephone check with diplomats from major European allied nations drew expressions of puzzlement over the asperity of the McCloskey and Schlesinger comments.

One remarked that none of the covenants on stationing of American forces in Europe provides for their transfer or transfer of their equipment to other crisis points.

It is understood that the Wes Germans were content to let United States military hardwar go through their country and over it on the way to Israel, as long as it was done quietly. But the loading of the Israeli freighters at Bremerhaven was done, according to German sources, without United States notification to the Bonn Government. So, when the Bremerhaven newspaper Nordseezeitung reported the news last Wednesday, the Bonn Foreign Ministry felt compelled to take a position — especially since a cease-fire had been called in the Middle East.

October 27, 1973

OIL-CURB SPREAD WORRIES EUROPE

Extension of Arab Embargo to Dutch a Threat to Major Transport System

RATIONING IS PREDICTED

U.S. Suppliers in Caribbean Will Also Be Affected by Saudi Arabian Cut

By CLYDE H. FARNSWORTH
Special to The New York Times

PARIS, Oct. 29—The Arab boycott of oil shipments to the Netherlands, which would curb supplies sharply in the continent's northern area, has intensified Europe's anxiety over the availability of petroleum products this winter.

One industry analyst, Dr. Paul Frankel, a London-based consultant, said in a telephone interview: "European governments are whistling in the dark if they feel they can postpone a petroleum allocation system, or even rationing, for long."

The embargo on shipments to the Dutch will also affect the United States, to which the Arabs also have cut off shipments. The Netherlands, through her giant port facilities at Rotterdam, is a transit point for oil throughout Northern Europe. In addition, Dutch colonies in the Caribbean make refined products chiefly for the American market from Middle East crude.

Saudi Action

The embargo question became critical over the weekend when Saudi Arabia, the largest oil exporting nation, joined other Arab states in their boycott of the Netherlands because of that nation's alleged pro-Israeli policies.

For the Netherlands herself, the impact will be cushioned by the fact that 40 per cent of her energy requirements are satisfied with natural gas from the neighboring North Sea. The wider worry is the threat to the small nation's role as a major transport and refining center for Europe and elsewhere.

Caribbean Shortages

In the Caribbean, the Shell refinery at Curaçao and the Exxon refinery at Aruba face a supply shortage now that Saudi Arabia has followed Algeria, Iraq, Kuwait, Qatar, the United Arab Emirates and the Sultanate of Oman in banning shipments to Dutch interests.

The Dutch, including their colonies, import approximately 2.5 million barrels daily, two-thirds of which is supplied by the Arab states. Saudi Arabia, alone, supplies one-third.

The United States also gets refined products from another major center in the Caribbean, Trinidad. The effects of the cutbacks on Texaco's refinery there are not yet known.

European countries have been warned by the oil industry that a quota basis will have to be established for them on supplies. Last weekend, Japanese refiners were told by British Petroleum, Shell and Exxon to expect cuts of 10 per cent.

Europe and Japan are far more dependent on Middle East oil than is the United States. The Arabs say their boycotts are meant to strike at the United States for its support of Israel. But the supply cuts ultimately chiefly affect the biggest customers. Apparently, Arab strategy is to get American allies to put pressure on Washington.

Divisions have already begun to appear in the Atlantic alliance against the background of the Middle East conflict, and oil has probably played a major role in the dissension. West Germany has protested against being used as a staging point for American arms shipments to Israel. The United States in turn has criticized the Europeans for not being, in President Nixon's words, "as cooperative as they might have been in attempting to help us work out the Middle East settlement."

Substantial quantities of crude oil landed in Rotterdam are piped directly to West Germany and Belgium; more is transhipped to Scandinavia. In addition, Dutch refineries sell petroleum products to many European countries.

If Saudi Arabia interprets her embargo as covering even transhipments, Europe will face the loss of another 500,000 to 1 million barrels daily on top of an existing shortfall of some 4.5 million barrels daily, according to industry figures.

Action Postponed

Members of the Organization for Economic Cooperation and Development met last week to assess the oil situation. Shelved for the time being was activation by Europeans of an oil-sharing plan. The Europeans were afraid that any concerted action would give Arabs the impression that the industrial states were "ganging up" against them and would lead to even further cutbacks.

Despite the shaky cease-fire in the Middle East, the prospects for an improvement in the supply picture are not considered good.

The Dutch are considering a ban on Sunday driving. The Times of London reported that some British ministers believed gasoline rationing or restriction of supplies to distributors would be necessary within six weeks.

Like the United States, most European governments have so far simply urged their citizens to husband energy resources more prudently.

The Europeans are counting on their plentiful stocks — two to three months' supplies — to see them through. But if the cutbacks continue the situation could easily become critical.

October 30, 1973

U.S. SAYS OIL CUT WILL NOT ALTER MIDEAST POLICY

Kissinger Says That Retaliation May Have to Be Considered

By BERNARD GWERTZMAN
Special to The New York Times

WASHINGTON, Nov. 21— Secretary of State Kissinger asserted today that the United States would not alter its Middle East policies because of the Arab oil embargo and warned that countermeasures might have to be considered if the embargo continued "unreasonably and indefinitely."

At a news conference devoted almost entirely to the Middle East, Mr. Kissinger also sketched the "elements" of what the United States believed should be included in any Arab-Israeli settlement reached in an Arab-Israeli peace conference, which may begin next month.

Direct Threat Avoided

But he stressed again that the United States would resist offering a specific and detailed peace plan because that would "tempt both parties to start shooting at the American proposal rather than to concentrate on what it is that they should accomplish."

On the American reaction to the oil embargo, Mr. Kissinger sought to avoid making any direct threats against the Arabs at a time when delicate negotiations are going ahead for the start of the peace talks.

He indicated, however, that there were limits to American patience, even though Washington had a "full understanding" of the reasons for the Arab oil embargo that was started during the October war to force the United States to bring pressure on Israel.

"We still hope," he said, "that some of the steps that were taken when certain assumptions were made about the principal American objective in that area will be changed when it became apparent that we are attempting to bring about a just peace.

He stressed that United States policy was determined not by the pressures that this or that nation might attempt to generate, but "by the American conception of the national interest and of the interest of general peace."

"We will not be pushed beyond this point by any pressure," he said.

"However, it is clear that if pressures continue unreasonably and indefinitely, that then the United States will have to consider what countermeasures it may have to take. We would do this with enormous reluctance and we are still hopeful that matters will not reach this point."

Mr. Kissinger refused to give a deadline when such "countermeasures" might be considered, but he seemed to indicate that the United States did not expect much of a change in the Arab position until after the peace talks actually began.

He also declined to specify what steps Washington might take against the embargo, but he noted that "you should remember that 85 per cent of our energy is produced in the United States, so that we are not a total prey to outside pressure."

Some officials in recent days have said that there was little the United States could do by itself to counter the embargo. They said that only a concerted decision by all major Western nations could bring effective pressure on the Arabs, but this seemed unlikely given the reluctance of Western Europe and Japan to antagonize the Arab countries.

Mr. Kissinger referred to this allied attitude when he deplored the other countries' "taking isolated action" instead of working closely with the United States to get a solution to the Middle East crisis.

Last night at a dinner for the Israeli Foreign Minister, Abba Eban, Mr. Kissinger was more explicit, asserting that the position taken by West European nations made the forthcoming Arab-Israeli negotiations "more difficult" because it would encourage the Arabs to take a less conciliatory stance at the talks.

After the news conference, Mr. Kissinger met with Mr. Eban at the State Department to discuss the Middle East diplomatic activity that will probably lead to a peace conference in Geneva around Dec. 17.

Mr. Eban, at his own news conference later, reported his Government's view that since the Israeli elections would not be held until Dec. 31, the Israeli delegation to any peace conference next month could not negotiate seriously on substantive issues, pending the formation of a new post-election government. But he said he was aware of the American desire to get the talks started promptly and would report the American ideas to the Israeli Cabinet.

Mr. Kissinger, in his news conference, said that while there were "no absolutely firm assurances" that the talks would start next month, "we have some rather substantial understandings with all the parties on the time frame."

In answer to questions, Mr. Kissinger sketched the "elements" of the final agreement the United States would seek.

He said that "it is obvious" that Israel will have to give up occupied territory she held as the result of the June, 1967, war, but he refused to be precise on where the final boundaries should be.

The final accord, he said, "will have to have an element of 'security arrangements" between the Arabs and Israelis and "may have to have an element of outside guarantees" —a reference to a possible American security pact with Israel to bolster any treaty.

In addition, he said that the questions of the Palestinians displaced when Israel was formed in 1948 and of Jerusalem "will undoubtedly have to be discussed in some form or another at a peace conference."

It has been widely assumed here and in Israel that the United States was prepared to exert pressure on Israel to make concessions to the Arabs to hasten the peace talks. Mr. Kissinger, when asked about this, said:

"We hope that Israel as well as the Arab countries will recognize that one of the clear consequences of recent events is that a purely military solution to the problems of the Middle East is impossible and that all countries therefore have the problem of the right balance between their security needs and the needs of legitimacy, acceptance or whatever you want to call it.

"We do not consider it axiomatic that this can only be achieved by pressure on Israel by the United States to make concessions. We expect to have full consultations with Israel as we expect to have discussions with the Arab participants. And the positions we will take as the negotiations develop depend on the positions the various parties take during the course of the negotiations and cannot be assumed ahead of time."

This was Mr. Kissinger's first news conference since he returned to Washington Friday from a 12-day round-the-world trip to the Middle East, China and Japan.

Among other points, made by Mr. Kissinger today were the following:

¶He "regretted" having

promised on Oct. 25 to release within a week the justification for the alert in response to signs that the Soviet Union might move forces to Egypt. He said that it would not serve any useful purpose "to recreate an episode of confrontation" at a time when all sides were moving to negotiations.

¶The awaited peace conference should be conducted by Moscow and Washington, but "be generally blessed by the United Nations" and, in addition to Israel, the Arab nations, the Soviet Union, and the United States, should be attended by Secretary General Waldheim.

¶The United States hoped to decide by next week how to help certain countries, such as the Netherlands and Japan, that had special oil problems caused by the Arab embargo.

¶The United States was disappointed with the response of the North Atlantic Treaty allies during the Middle East crisis. Mr. Kissinger said "one cannot avoid the perhaps melancholy conclusion" that some European allies "saw their interests so different from those of the United States that they were prepared to break ranks with the United States on a matter of very grave international consequence." Except for Portugal, the NATO allies dissociated themselves from the American military support of Israel, and several refused landing rights to American supply planes.

In response to a question about his China visit he said that he was encouraged by signs of interest in Peking toward further normalization of relations. But he added that this in no way meant a change in American policy toward Taiwan.

On relations with the Russians, Mr. Kissinger sought to refute a questioner's suggestion that détente had turned out to be illusory because at the time of the alert, the United States had to resort to military means to "signal" the Soviet Union.

He acknowledged that a confrontation had developed over the Middle East, but he said that "one also has to consider how rapidly the confrontation was ended and how quickly the two sides have attempted to move back and are now moving back to a policy of cooperation in settling the Middle East conflict."

November 22, 1973

Saudi Arabia Warns U.S. Against Oil Countermoves

Official Says That Flow Might Be Cut by 80% —Cautions on Force

By Reuters

COPENHAGEN, Denmark, Nov. 22—Saudi Arabian Oil Minister Ahmed Zaki al-Yamani threatened today to cut oil production by 80 per cent if the United States, Europe or Japan took measures to counter current Arab oil embargoes and reductions.

The minister, speaking in a television interview here, also threatened to blow up certain Saudi Arabian oil fields if the United States should take any military action.

Sheik Yamani, here since Tuesday on a private visit, issued the warnings when asked his reaction to Secretary of State Kissinger's remarks at a news conference yesterday that America might have to consider countermeasures if the Arab oil embargo against it continued too long. Mr. Kissinger did not mention military action.

The Arab countries have placed an embargo on oil to the Netherlands and placed the other eight European and Common Market countries and Japan under a 25 per cent oil reduction.

"Obviously, the U.S. and Japan and Europe could take some countermeasures," Sheik Yamani said.

"I think what we have as an oil weapon is far greater," he said. "What we have done is

The New York Times
Ahmed Zaki al-Yamani

nothing at all. I think we can cut down production to, let's say, 20 per cent. Instead of 25 per cent [the cut] would be 80 per cent."

"The United States have their own local supply," he said. "They are in a much better position than Europe and Japan."

But he cautioned against Europe and Japan joining the Americans in any kind of countermeasures, "because your whole economy will definitely collapse all of a sudden."

He said that American military action "is also another possibility," but warned that this would be suicide.

"There are some sensitive areas in the oil fields in Saudi Arabia which will be blown up," depriving Europe and Japan of oil from Saudi Arabia for many years, he said.

When asked if Saudi Arabia could survive economically if it cut production by 80 per cent, he replied: "Yes, sir."

He said the country would get more income from 20 percent production than from current production levels because market forces would drive the price per barrel up from about $3 to $15 or $20 dollars.

Meanwhile, King Faisal of Saudi Arabia said today in an interview with the Cairo Daily, Al Gomhouria, that his country would continue to use oil in the Arab struggle until three objectives had been gained.

The objectives are complete Israeli withdrawal from all occupied Arab territories, granting of the right of self-determination to the Palestinian people and affirmation of the Arabism of Jerusalem.

The king said: "In clearer and more decisive words, Saudi Arabia will not change its attitude of suspending oil exports to some countries and cutting back quantities to other countries except after the fulfilment of these points collectively and in a manner acceptable to all Arabs—no matter how long it takes."

Price Held Unrealistic

Industry sources said here last night that the $3 price per barrel of oil was unrealistic. They pointed out that currently some Saudi Arabian oil was being sold at $4.80 a barrel.

Lifting of Embargo Asked

BEIRUT, Lebanon, Nov. 22 (UPI)—The Shah of Iran, whose country is a major non-Arab oil producer, has urged the Arabs to lift their oil embargo against nations that support Israel.

"Since you have accepted the cease-fire and moves toward a peaceful settlement," Shah Mohammed Riza Pahlev said, in an interview with a Beirut weekly, "why are you continuing to shut off oil supplies and reducing production?"

"Oil is like bread. You cannot cut it off during time of peace. Why do you want to look as if you want the world to starve? Why do you want to punish those in Europe who stood on your side? What did Japan do to deserve a 20 per cent cut in its national production?"

Dutch Cut Supplies 15%

AMSTERDAM, Nov. 22 (Reuters)—The major oil companies in the Netherlands today announced an average cut of 15 per cent in supplies of raw materials to the petrochemical and chemical industry.

The companies, which include Shell, Esso, British Petroleum and Gulf Oil, said the cut also would apply to their own petrochemical activities.

The measure follows the total oil boycott of the Netherlands by the Arab countries because of allegedly "pro-Israel" sentiments by the Dutch in the recent Middle East conflict.

The oil companies said today that the cuts of 15 per cent already had gone into effect for some products, while others would be affected within the next few weeks.

Germans Look to Coal

BONN, Nov. 22 (Reuters)—West Germany today announced a major effort to switch from oil to coal as a source of industrial energy.

At a cabinet discussion of the looming energy crises caused by the Arab oil embargo, Chancellor Willy Brandt warned, that the cuts in oil supplies from the Middle East could have serious social and economic consequences.

In an official statement at a press conference here, the government spokesman said the Chancellor had made it clear that the Government would not hesitate to take all necessary measures to avert the worst effects.

November 23, 1973

President Hafez al-Assad of Syria, left, being welcomed in Algiers by President Houari Boumediene of Algeria

Arab Leaders Open Meeting on Strategy

By ERIC PACE

Special to The New York Times

STAOUELI, Algeria, Nov. 26 —The conference of Arab heads of state opened today with spokesmen talking exultantly of the Arab "oil weapon" and its impact on the outside world, but adding notes of caution about its use.

President Houari Boumediene of Algeria proudly told the assemblage that the reduced flow of Arab oil had made "Europeans and Americans experience hardships in certain areas of their life," but the Secretary General of the Arab League, Mahmoud Riad, spoke circumspectly of using oil "in a judicious manner" to bring pressure in the fight with Israel.

The Arabs in Staouéli listening to Mr. Riad included eight Arab presidents, four ruling sheiks and one sultan, in addition to King Faisal of Saudi Arabia and Yasir Arafat, the bearded guerrilla leader of the Palestine Liberation Organization. Among those absent was Gaafar al-Nimeirey, who was reported not feeling well. Leaders and spokesmen of Arab Governments gathered in the great hall of the Palais des Nations in this farm village west of Algiers.

The meeting opened after renewed wrangling behind the scenes over who should speak for the Palestinians, well-placed Arab informants reported, but Mr. Riad and Mr. Boumediene —addressing the initial, public session of the conference— made the customary appeals for restoration of the Palestinians' rights.

The stress on the oil weapon was a new note at top-level Arab sessions, and the leaders spoke in general terms, not specifying further reductions in oil exports.

King Faisal made no speech, but by some accounts his aides had taken a hard line in preparatory talks here that touched on the oil weapon. They reportedly advocated cuts in exports beyond those already agreed on. But Kuwaiti officials were less militant, by some accounts, and Tunisia's President Habib Bourguiba, when he arrived for the conference, observed that the oil weapon was a double-edged sword that could provoke hostility.

Newspaper Gives Warning

El Moujahid, a Government-owned Algiers newspaper, cautioned in an editorial this morning that "it is necessary to study carefully the use of the oil weapon in a prudent and discerning manner; in particular, a full distinction between friends and enemies is essential."

Egypt's President, Anwar el-Sadat, made no public comment, but a spokesman, Tahsin Bashir, said that among Egypt, Saudi Arabia and other Arab nations, there existed "agreement that our oil policy be elastic enough for our needs."

"We will use it," he continued, "to respond positively to those who help to implement the United Nations resolutions" on the Middle East, notably the one calling for Israeli withdrawal from occupied Arab lands.

Asked whether Arab nations would indeed cut exports of oil further, Mr. Bashir said: "We would rule out any precipitate actions; we want a sustained effort to tell the world in every possible way that we are not going to allow the Palestinians to have a cold winter in their tents while the world and the Israelis bask in warmth."

Asked whether the Arabs might do the opposite and ease their embargo on oil exports to the United States, he said: "If the United States helps to implement the United Nations resolutions, then we'll be forthcoming. We can ease anything as soon as there is real progress."

Mr. Bashir's remarks dovetailed with private statements at the ministerial-level talks ending yesterday that the Arabs wanted to manipulate oil exports to influence the

Associated Press and United Press International

Other leaders, from left: Gaafar al-Nimeiry, Sudan; Anwar el-Sadat, Egypt; King Faisal, Saudi Arabia.

course of the expected peace talks with Israel.

They added that the Arabs were determined to avoid having the talks bog down—as was the case with the Vietnam negotiations in Paris.

But the notes of prudence struck today reflected several considerations, Arab informants said. One was the prospect of damaging the economies of friendly nations. Another was the possibility of reprisals by Western countries, as suggested by Secretary of State Kissinger.

Firm Actions Also Seen

But the conference is also expected to lead to a ban on Arab oil exports to Portugal, Rhodesia and South Africa—whose white rule in Africa the Arabs oppose.

And President Boumediene, who is the conference chairman, said, according to an unofficial translation of his address, that the "hardships" caused by the Arab oil action would make Europeans and Americans "ask themselves questions about the real causes of this ordeal."

Exulting at the Arabs' having made their power manifest, Mr. Boumediene observed, "How long we have been waiting for Europe to reappraise its relationship to the Arab nations"—to think of the Arabs, "a great human community."

Security precautions were evident today as the leaders gathered while local farmers squatted by the road to watch. A small Algerian warship — technically a frigate — was on guard in the Mediterranean a few hundred yards from the seaside conference site, which was dotted with guards and equipped with fire engines.

The atmosphere of preparedness reflected President Boumediene's statement that "we should make real preparations for the coming battle" with Israel, which should "prove decisive." But he did not say when he thought that battle would come. He added, however, "The last word will be with the Arabs."

November 27, 1973

Arab Brinkmanship

Output Pledge May Signal Recognition of Potential Risk

By LEONARD SILK

Economic Analysis

The announcement by the Arab oil nations that they will increase production by 10 per cent in January and supply Britain, France, Japan, Spain and other "friendly countries" with their "full oil needs" suggests that the Arabs have grown wary of causing an economic disaster in the industrial world that could backfire upon them. Speaking in Kuwait, the Saudi Arabian oil minister, Sheikh Ahmed Zaki al-Yamani said, "We do not wish the nations of the world to suffer."

Associated Press

Sheik Ahmed Zaki al-Yamani speaking in Kuwait.

The move suggests that the Arabs see scant immediate prospect that the Europeans or Japanese could bring sufficient pressure on Israel and its principal ally, the United States, to force the Israelis to return to their 1967 borders or yield to other Arab demands. "We only intended to attract world attenion to the injustice that befell the Arabs," said Sheikh Yamani.

Nevertheless, the Arabs are keeping the heat on the United States and other countries, including the Netherlands, Portugal, Rhodesia and South Africa, that it accuses of sympathy or support for the Israelis.

The Arabs' announcement of a 10 per cent increase in output — which by somewhat murky arithmetic is described as reducing the cutback from 30 per cent to 25 per cent—will still leave the world short of normal oil requirements, though it is impossible to know precisely how much, since there have been, apparently, surreptitious deliveries to countries above the quotas. The move suggests the familiar tactics of a cartel threatened with "chiseling"—to ease up somewhat on restrictions.

The timing of the announcement also looks like a shrewd way to follow up — and nail down — the 128 per cent increase in the posted price of crude oil announced Sunday in Tehran, Iran.

Alarm has been growing in the West over what looks like conomic warfare, or blackmail, even against countries that have "tilted" against Israel.

The aggressive price actions **by the Persian Gulf states appeared to be directed, without too much discrimination, against the rich industrial powers that have long dominated the Middle East and North Africa. A British official, hearing the news from Teheran, said, "The last chicken of colonialism is coming home to roost."**

Indeed, it seemed clear that the strongest economic monopoly in history — the Organization of Petroleum Exporting Countries, established in 1960 — has moved to challenge the rich industrial powers to hand over an almost inconceivable sum of money in exchange for the oil on which 20th-century industrial economies have come to depend.

Shah Mohammed Riza Pahlevi of Iran declared, in announcing the price rise, "The industrial world will have to realize that the era of their terrific progress and even more terrific income and wealth based on cheap oil is finished."

Rules of Game

The Shah in effect told the West it had been living high on the hog long enough—and that the oil-producing countries were moving in to take a major share of the loot.

The Persian Gulf oil ministers, OPEC leaders, deliberately warned the Western countries against increasing prices on their exports, on penalty of a continuing soaring in the price of oil.

The OPEC countries have already demonstrated their recognition of the strength of their hand. Last January OPEC raised the posted price of oil from $2.48 to $2.59. On Oct. 1, just before Egypt and Syria attacked Israel, it raised the posted price of oil to $3.01 a barrel. On Oct. 16, in the midst of the war, and three days before the announcement of the Arab oil embargo, OPEC boosted the posted price to $5.11.

This week's rise to $11.65, effective Jan. 1 and expected to become OPEC-wide represented a 470 per cent price increase in just one year. And even the latest increase, described by the Persian Gulf oil ministers as "moderate," may hold only through the first quarter of 1974, according to Abdul-Rahman Salem al-Atiqi the Kuwaiti minister of oil.

Dollar Flows

The implications for the flow of dollars to the oil-producing states is almost inconceivable. Earlier estimates that the Persian Gulf and North African oil producers would reap revenues of over $80-billion annually by 1980, with cumulative revenues from 1973 through 1980 of about $350-billion, were postulated on an average price of only $5 per barrel of oil.

It is possible to write various horror stories based on that flood of wealth to the oil-producing states—the devastation of the balance of payments of the industrial economies, the collapse of the dollar as an international currency, the unleashing of global inflation or the breakup of the Western alliance, with the European countries and Japan so heavily dependent on Arab oil, splitting off from the United States. There are fears of a major interruption in world production and trade.

To continue: with their untold billions of dollars to spend, Saudi Arabia, Iran and other oil-producing giants could not only acquire a huge stake in Western industries but could also greatly increase their military power — for instance, by purchasing a nuclear capability and the personnel to develop and operate it.

Some Complications

To be sure, such scenarios may be exaggerated and far too simple. The money the oil producers earn in the capitalist world must be spent somewhere or it is nothing but printed paper. Indeed, even gold is basically worthless unless it can be used to acquire goods and services.

Too rapid an escalation of oil prices would inevitably bring an escalation of the prices of Western goods and technology.

The oil exporting countries could find themselves in the position of those classic traders who wound up exchanging million-dollar cats for million-dollar dogs.

Nevertheless, the power of the oil producers to extract

monopoly prices and payments can still cause enormous transfers of income and wealth to themselves from the industrial countries, set off shock waves of inflation and recession in the West and Japan, and induce political disorder.

In every Western capital, the question is being asked: How can the power of the oil cartel be curbed?

The history of other international cartels as well as domestic industrial conspiracies may be instructive. All have had a history of instability and ultimately have broken down.

Cartels form and hold together during times of prosperity, when their customers are eager for their goods and prepared to pay higher and higher prices to get them.

But they tend to fall apart when hard times come and the capacity of the cartel members exceeds market demand. Prices then start to drop, chiseling multiplies, and price wars may develop.

If the oil-producing cartel succeeds in causing a serious recession in the West, it would almost certainly create the conditions for its own undoing. This may be the basic explanation of why Sheik Yamani and the other Arab oil ministers are starting to back off from too tough an embargo.

Ununited Front

Even today the oil cartel is anything but rock solid. While Saudi Arabia and most other Arab states have imposed their embargo, Iraq—extremely hostile to Israel—has stayed out, as have such other major OPEC countries as Iran, Nigeria, Indonesia and Venezuela.

Reports from several sources have cast doubt on the actual depth of the cuts in oil shipments. It is conceivable that, with relatively minor cuts in actual deliveries, the Arab states succeeded in panicking the oil importers and users into massive buying and hoarding, in advance of anticipated price increases. This self-fulfilling behavior bred both price hikes and shortages.

The chaotic world oil market was then exploited not only by the Arab states but by all members of the OPEC cartel.

Cartel Weaknesses

Feeding on its triumphs, the cartel now looks stronger than ever. But it is actually a large and diverse assemblage of countries, jealous of one another and with no single producer able to control more than a fraction of total output and exports and thereby enforce discipline, should trouble come in the form of falling sales. As of 1970, the principal oil producers in OPEC, according to the United Nations, were.

Country	Production (millions of metric tons)	Exports (millions of metric tons)
Venezuela	194.4	127.6
Iran	191.7	165.4
Saudi Arabia	176.9	148.8
Libya	161.7	160.2
Kuwait	137.4	121.0
Iraq	76.4	73.3
Nigeria	54.2	51.7
Algeria	48.3	46.0
Indonesia	42.2	30.8

Saudi Arabia is currently regarded as the leader of the assault with the oil weapon. King Faisal has threatened to withhold his country's oil if the West does not cause Israel to withdraw to behind its 1967 borders.

Yet Saudi Arabian oil exports constitute only about 15 per cent of the OPEC total—and only 13 per cent of all world oil exports. And not all oil producers would be willing to see their oil exports slump.

Monopoly-Busting

The best way to break the cartel would be for the United States and other oil importers to cut their oil consumption and convert to other technologies.

But cutbacks in oil usage would meet strong resistance from producers, consumers and workers in all countries. Converting to other energy uses would involve massive new investments, research and development outlays and construction that will take years.

However, the enormous increases in the price of oil are giving great impetus to the search for new energy sources and ultimately should lead to the conversion of Western economies to technologies far less dependent on oil.

This is a necessity that would have come within the next half century, even without the squeeze of the OPEC cartel.

Meanwhile, however, the oil cartel is gambling with an economic disaster to the industrial world—which could produce a political explosion that would wreak havoc in the oil-producing countries as well. It remains to be seen whether the Arab oil producers and the other oil states have decided to back off before it is too late.

December 26, 1973

Corporate Profits Surge

The impact of the energy crisis on corporate profits is dramatized by the displacement of the General Motors Corporation as the American manufacturer with the highest annual profits. The new champion is the Exxon Corporation, However, the all-time leader is still the American Telephone & Telegraph Company. It hasn't reported full 1973 results yet, but it has reported profits of $2.9-billion for the 12 months ended last November.

Following are profits for the 1973 fourth quarter and for the full year, along with percentage changes over the 1972 periods, as reported by the major oil companies and other large corporations.

Figures are in millions of dollars.	1973 4th qtr.	per cent change from 1972 4th qtr.	1973 year	per cent change from 1972 year
Exxon	$784.0	+59.6	$2,440.0	+59.5
Texaco	453.5	+70.1	1,290.0	+45.1
Standard Oil (Cal.)	283.1	+94.2	843.6	+54.2
Mobil	271.6	+68.2	842.8	+46.8
Standard Oil (Ind.)	121.5	+52.8	511.3	+36.4
Shell	79.4	−1.5	332.7	+27.7
General Motors	517.0	−22.5	2,398.0	+10.9
I.B.M.	468.7	+37.7	1,580.0	+23.4
duPont	143.0	+26.2	586.0	+41.5
General Electric	191.0	+7.8	585.0	+67.1
U.S.Steel	104.5	+81.0	325.8	+107.5

February 3, 1974

Energy Talks: Why U.S. Position Won

By LEONARD SILK

Economic Analysis

The Washington energy conference did not live up to its advance billing as a probable bomb for the Western alliance or at best a meaningless dud. Instead, it has resulted in startling progress toward the cooperative international programs on energy sharing and development favored by the United States—and a jarring rejection of the everyone-for-himself line championed by France.

The French had not sought to disguise their advocacy of the principle of looking out for No. 1 when the going gets rough. "Of course, when everything is going well, approaches are friendly and completely elegant," said the French Foreign Minister, Michel Jobert.

"But when everything is going badly, everyone tries to save his own hide," Mr. Jobert added. "I see nothing against this. Except that we don't all have the same hide. Some of us have tight, shiny hides; others are skinny and worry about food for tomorrow. Let's remember this before making ethical condemnations."

Three Major Factors

Why did the Europeans and the Japanese not rally to this realistic French position? In a sense, before the conference began, they already had. Mr. Jobert, trying to smite emergent multilateralism before it got on its feet, cited a news dispatch from Japan that said that seven countries were seeking bilateral agreements and reaching them.

"I will not be so cruel as to name them," Mr. Jobert said. "Moreover, this list does not seem complete to me."

Nevertheless, Secretary of State Kissinger, with Treasury Secretary George P. Shultz and William E. Simon, head of the Federal Energy Office, in important supporting roles, managed to snatch multilateralism from the jaws of bilateralism in the 11th hour.

The Americans achieved this result with the help of three major factors.

The first was that the United States set goals that were jointly acceptable—and that genuinely served the interests of the joint community. The Americans scarcely could be scolded for proposing to conserve their own glutenous appetite for oil while encouraging others to restrain their demands.

The second factor that brought all the Europeans except the French into line was an implicit but strong American warning that, if the others would not cooperate on energy, the United States would have to rethink its military plans and posture.

Here Secretary Kissinger received a major assist from President Nixon, who told the representatives of this nation's major allies that "security and economic considerations are inevitably linked and energy cannot be separated from either."

This message got through with particular force to the West Germans, ever-fearful of an American weakening of its commitment to the North Atlantic Treaty Organization. It was the West German Finance Minister, Helmut Schmidt, who nettled his French colleague, Mr. Jobert, by openly declaring that "everybody did not have to try to save his own hide."

Thirdly—and perhaps most importantly—support for the American position was mustered by the powerful appeal of the United States economy itself. After a period in which the fall of the dollar was regarded as a symbol of the sinking of American economic dominance, the dollar has strengthened—and the weight of the United States in the world economy has grown more impressive.

Paradoxically, this awareness has resulted in part from the energy crisis itself.

American economic weight extends well beyond its energy resources. France is, after all, the birthplace of the concept of "the American challenge"—this nation's strength in technology, capital and managerial resources.

And, for other European countries and Japan even more than for France, the United States remains an enormous market—and one that appears to be increasingly essential to their economic and financial interests at a time when the world seems to be sliding into more serious "stagflation"—stagnation combined with inflation.

During the conference, the American spokesmen drove home the point that man does not live by oil alone, with the warning that cooperation from and access to the huge American economy should not be taken for granted.

This is not to say that the course of international cooperation among the United States, Canada, Western Europe and Japan on energy and other matters will run smoothly from here on in.

Individual nations, as Mr. Jobert correctly said, have their own bilateral deals for oil going with the Arabs and Iran. France has taken a beating and lost face—and may create more serious problems for its Common Market partners as well as the United States.

But for now, the major oil-consuming countries have taken an important step toward unity, and it is unlikely that this progress will be brushed off likely in the capitals of the oil-producing countries.

February 15, 1974

The Petrodollar Flow

If the Panglossian Economic Theory Is Right—and It's Not—All Is Well

By LEONARD SILK

Economic Analysis

There is a school of economics whose fundamental tenet is that everything happens for the best. Among the historic claims for this principle are the following:

¶If the taxes of the rich are cut, the benefits will trickle down to the poor. Similarly, if the rich or the middle class build more new houses, this will benefit the poor, because the standing stock of existing houses will trickle down to the poor. (The trickle-down theory is one of the major contributions of this school of Panglossian economics.)

¶A fall in output, income and employment is good because it will restore the economy to a sound basis.

¶For every seller of stock, there is a buyer. Strong hands will take over the assets once held by the weak.

¶Equilibrium is the law of economic life. If people spend more money for food, they will have less to spend for other things, so inflation will not result. If one nation loses monetary reserves, another nation will gain them, so the world monetary system will not suffer from either inflation or deflation.

To those principles of symmetry, balance and divine automaticity, the contemporary followers of Dr. Pangloss (Voltaire named him "Professor of Metaphysico-Theologo Cosmolonigology") have added the following doctrines:

¶It doesn't matter how much money the oil-consuming countries pay out to the oil-producing countries, because the money will flow back to the oil-consuming countries as investments or to pay for goods.

¶It doesn't matter if the outflow of money to pay for oil causes a temporary cut in consumption in the oil-consuming countries, because this will constitute a form of saving, and the "petrodollars" will then increase the world's stock of capital, furthering growth and damping down inflation.

Volume to Be Great

However, the volume of petrodollars may be too great for the world monetary system to handle. The whole system could break down.

J. Carlin Englert of New York University has made fresh estimates of the money flows from 11 major industrialized nations to defray the costs of higher-priced petroleum and petroleum products this year. He found that the United States, Canada, Japan, West Germany, France, Britain and five other European countries would see their oil bills increase from $42.6-billion in 1973 to $108.7-billion in 1974.

What will the Arab oil states do with their money? Much of it will indeed flow west.

Ibrahim M. Oweiss, a native of Egypt who is an associate professor at Georgetown University in Washington, notes that the Arabs have already set up four major financial consortia in collaboration with American and European interests.

One is the Union des Banques Arabes et Française (U.B.A.F.), established in Paris in 1970 with more than $700-million in assets. This is 40 per cent owned by Crédit Lyonnais the big French bank, but it is controlled by 14 Arab banks. U.B.A.F. has subsidiaries in London, Rome, Frankfurt, Luxembourg and Tokyo; partners of these subsidiaries include several big European banks and the Bank of Tokyo.

The three other consortia are:

¶The Banque Franc-Arabe d'Investissement Internationaux (E.R.A.B.), chartered in Paris in 1969 by the Kuwait Investment Company in partnership with the French Société Générale and the Société de Banque Suisse;

¶The European Arab Bank, started in 1972, with headquarters in Luxembourg, which is made up of 16 Arab financial institutions (including E.R.A.B.) and seven European banks;

¶And la Compagnie Arabe et Internationale d'Investissement, incorporated in Luxembourg in January, 1973, which is owned by 24 Arab and other banks, including the Bank of America, West German, Italian, Japanese and French institutions.

Arab Business Sought

In addition to these major Arab combines, many Western banks and brokers are competing for Arab business, led by the First National City Bank of New York, with branches in Beirut, Saudi Arabia, Bahrain and Dubai, and the Chase Manhattan Bank, with branches in Beirut and Bahrain. Chase Manhattan and the Morgan Guaranty Trust Company of New York are the largest holders of Saudi Arabian Government deposits.

But the flow of capital from the oil-consuming to the oil-producing countries is so huge as to threaten hyperinflation in the Western economies.

The more moderate Arab countries, such as Saudi Arabia, Kuwait and Abu Dhabi, appear to recognize this.

Professor Oweiss noted that Saudi Arabia has proposed to reduce the current price of Persian Gulf oil "once justifiable political and economic demands of Arab countries are met and once rich oil-consuming countries pursue a policy of genuine cooperation with the developing countries."

He added that "it is not in the economic interest of oil-exporting countries to push the price of oil beyond the interval in which demand is inelastic."

The sharp increases in oil

prices will mean a huge transfer of real income and wealth from the West—a real lowering of living standards.

As economists of the First National City Bank put it, "The discomfort of facing up to this harsh truth has engendered illusions—notably that, for consuming countries, the adjustment can be eased by more rapid inflation or by government intervention in the marketplace."

But the real transfers of income and the potential disruption of the world economy threaten to exacerbate both global inflation and recession.

Hopes for Price Cuts

It is the belated recognition of the gravity of these dangers—not only to the industrialized nations but to the oil-producing states as well—that has given rise to hopes that the Arab states meeting in Tripoli today may be ready to lift the oil embargo and expand production. The Western nations and Japan are also hoping for some price cuts.

The United States has pressed hard for such concessions to the Western nations, while France has been following a go-it-alone line, seeking to make her own deals with the Arabs.

Even if the Arabs end the embargo, however, the threat to the world economy will not evaporate over night. Inflation is raging, and the Western political and economic alliance is severely strained — possibly shattered.

The deciples of Dr. Pangloss should remember that their master barely missed losing his head in the Inquisition and wound up living humbly on the farm of Candide.

March 13, 1974

What Arabs Taught the Industrial Giants

By LEONARD SILK

Like a small bomb triggering a larger one, the October war in the Middle East triggered a larger war: the economic attack by the Arab oil-producing states against the industrialized nations. The oil embargo has largely been lifted, but the consequences of that display of economic power are likely to be long-lasting for the world's economy. Western statesmen and money managers are struggling to find the technical answers to questions raised by the "oil war."

What is the key to the problem?

It is the price of oil. Before October, the price of crude in the Persian Gulf was about $2. Today it's about $8.

That sounds prosaic enough: What will it do to the world economy?

First of all, it will mean a vast transfer of resources from oil-importing nations to the Saudis, Kuwaitis, Iranians and the other oil producers. By the end of this year they will have piled up about $100-billion in investible funds. Of course, oil prices could decline, but if the present price holds—and the oil nations are likely to restrict supply to keep it up—the members of the Organization of Petroleum Exporting Countries could have, according to one estimate, investible funds of half a trillion dollars by 1980.

Will that be inflationary, or will it cause a contraction in the world economy?

It could be both.

First, for contraction. King Faisal, the Shah of Iran and others have transferred money earned in the West to their own accounts. This money has been taken, in the final analysis, from Western consumers paying more for gasoline, electricity, heating oil, food grown on petrochemical fertilizers, synthetic clothing and so on. The more of their real resources Westerners commit to paying for imported oil, the less they will have to spend on other goods. That means a real drain on Western living standards.

The inflationary effect is more obvious. Given current technology, oil is the premier raw material and higher-priced oil raises the production costs of many other goods. That raises the cost of living. But individuals will struggle to maintain their incomes and nations to maintain full employment in the face of those higher oil bills. Governments and central banks will seek to spur employment by putting enough money into the system to offset the contractionary effect of the oil debts paid to foreigners. This will be inflationary and it will only disguise but not reverse the real loss of income.

But will the oil producers not put the bulk of the money they get back into the industrial countries?

Yes. Literally speaking, most of it will never leave the West. Deposits at Western banks will be shifted from American, European and Japanese ownership to Arab and Iranian accounts. Some minor fraction will buy goods or real estate—an island off South Carolina, gold, Cadillacs (if they are still being made) and so on. But most of it will be invested in securities of one kind or another.

Much of it now seems to be going into short-term loans in the Eurodollar market. The Arabs, wary of the possibility that their funds could be blocked or investments nationalized, prefer high liquidity and anonymity to long-term direct industrial investment. Some of the money will be invested in the poor lands of Africa and Asia. Arab money, for example, is expected to finance reopening of the Suez Canal and the Arab League last week was told that a development bank for Africa has now reached $231-million in capitalization. But, compared to the billions the Arabs will gain, these funds are small.

If all the petrodollars are used in the world economic system one way or another, what is the danger?

One is that the big shift of funds from buying goods and services to the purchase of highly liquid investments could imbalance the industrialized economies. Money used to buy financial instruments has a different effect from money used to buy plants, machinery, housing or consumer goods.

Another danger is that the recycling of petrodollars may feed money back to big capital markets, such as the United States, West Germany or Switzerland, but leave other countries in heavy over-all

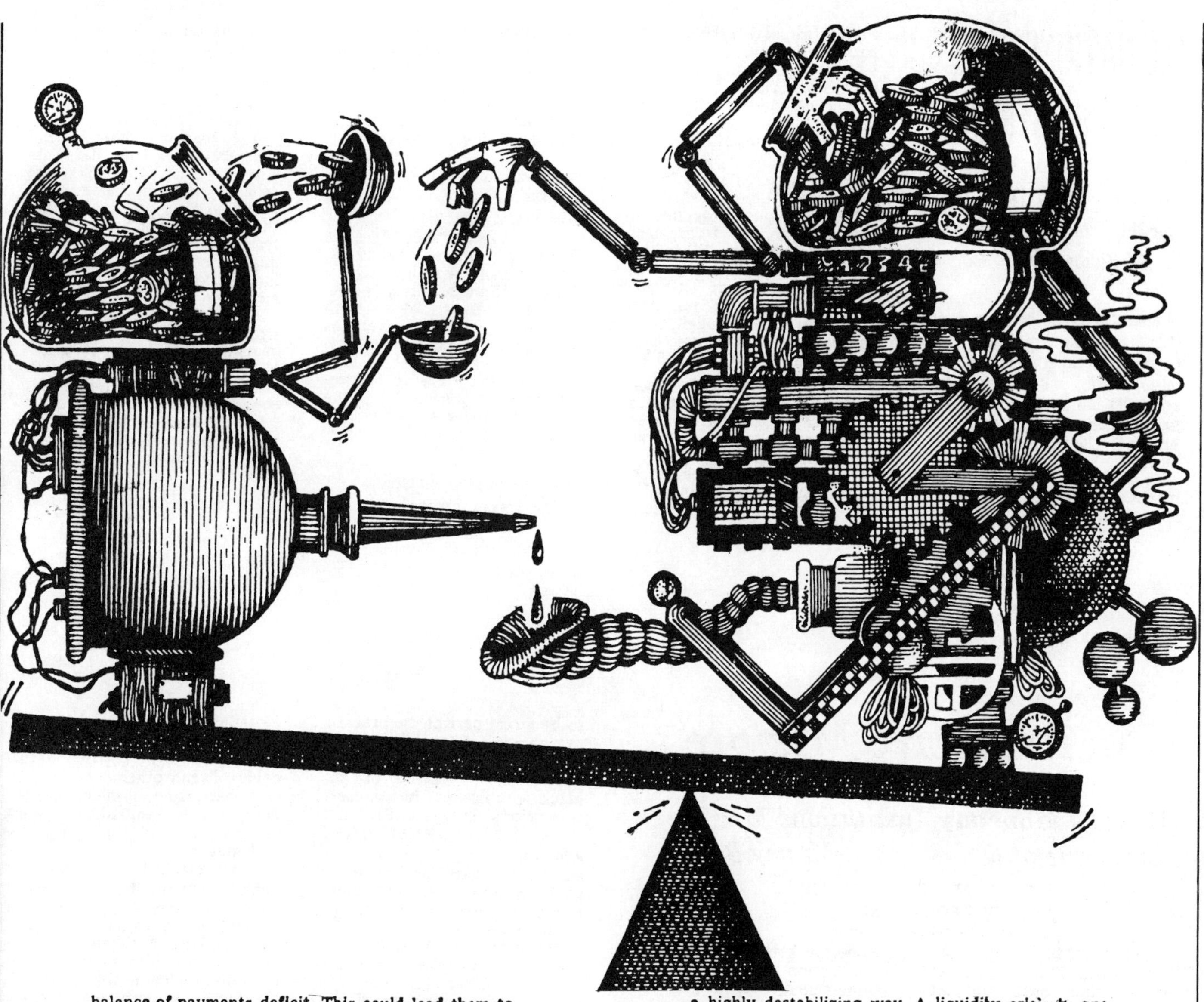

balance-of-payments deficit. This could lead them to try to protect themselves by blocking imports. Even without protectionism, their import demand could fall and cause world trade to contract.

A third danger, and in some ways the most serious one, is to the Third World, which literally faces starvation and can be thrown into political upheaval. Poor nations will try to raise the price of their exports—bauxite, copper or whatever—in imitation of the oil cartel. The bauxite producers, for example, met recently in Guinea to try exactly that. Although the effort was less than successful, Jamaica, the second largest bauxite producer, in the past few days has told the United States and Canadian Governments the taxes and royalties on bauxite are going up. Moreover, Jamaica wants a share in ownership of the mines.

Finally, there is the threat to the entire monetary system. Floating exchange rates have taken the shock reasonably well so far, but the highly liquid funds are building up. Chase Manhattan, First National City and Morgan Guaranty are large holders of Arab deposits and the Arabs have also joined four major international banking consortia with billions in assets.

Without intending harm, nervous holders of those billions could shift them from country to country in a highly destabilizing way. A liquidity crisis in one country could run through the world like wildfire. No present international agency could cope. And no single nation, including the United States, could either.

Is there no alternative to oil?

Prof. William D. Nordhaus, a Yale economist, expects the United States virtually to exhaust domestic petroleum resources by 1980. From then on, until 2000, the nation will have to rely on imported oil and gas. But as this runs out, too, the price will rise and coal and shale will become more economically attractive. For the United States, with enormous reserves of both coal and shale, this will be a buoyant period. Then about 2120, the fossil fuels will be exhausted and the nuclear age, in the form of the breeder reactor, will take over.

But the immediate threat to the world economy is pressing and the need for international cooperation on energy and raw material sources has grown correspondingly. At the Third World's insistence, the United Nations will begin a special session on the subject next week but its effect is not expected to be great. Producing a workable solution is the key challenge facing the world economy in the seventies. A failure to do so would be devastating.

OIL NATIONS SPUR U.S. INVESTMENTS

Treasury Estimates Figure for the Producing Lands at $7-Billion This Year

WASHINGTON, Sept. 19 (Reuters)—The Treasury Department estimated today that oil-producing nations invested about $7-billion in the United States and about $3-billion in Britain in the first eight months of 1974.

In a report to the Senate permanent Subcommittee on Investigations, the Treasury said that it estimated the member nations of the Organization of Petroleum Exporting Countries may have had a surplus "of somewhere between 25 billion and 28 billion dollars" in the first eight months of this year.

In the report, however, the Treasury stressed it could not be certain of its figures. It said: "We have pieced together information derived from many different sources. What we have is fragmentary. Many of the reports cannot be confirmed. We can do no more than offer a very rough guess as to where funds may have been invested thus far in 1974."

Of the estimated $7-billion invested in the United States, the Treasury said that some $4-billion was invested in various types of marketable United States Government securities with most of the remainder being placed with commercial banks and a few hundred million dollars invested in corporate securities and real estate.

"At least 3 billion dollars may have been invested in the United Kingdom in sterling, some of which no doubt involved purchases of British Government securities and some sterling deposits in British banks," the treasury said.

The report continued that the Treasury "suspects" that $2-billion or more was invested in Europe through direct placement loans to official or quasi-official agencies as well as through direct purchases of private securities and real estate.

It said the Treasury had received commitments by the OPEC countries to developing nations and international lending institutions.

Receipts Estimated

The Treasury report estimates that the oil producing nations would have receipts of about $80-billion in calendar 1974, of which they would have to invest outside their own countries some $55-billion.

The report notes that some of the OPEC countries have apparently placed "a high value on anonymity" in making their investments in such a way that the owner cannot be traced for fear that the host countries might freeze those assets "to induce modification of governmental policy."

United States imports of petroleum for the first half of the year were estimated at $11.8-billion and this is expected to rise to !14-billion during the second half.

United States exports to producers have more than doubled to $2.4-billion in the first half from $1.1-billion a year ago.

September 20, 1974

An Explosive Mixture

World's Monetary Institutions May Be Incapable of Defusing Oil-Money Bomb

By LEONARD SILK

Special to The New York Times

Economic Analysis

WASHINGTON, Oct. 1—Damon Runyon, the great sports writer, once said that where the human race is concerned, the odds are 9 to 5 against. An observer at the current annual meeting of the World Bank and International Monetary Fund would see no reason to quarrel with that conclusion.

In private conversations here, finance ministers and central bankers, normally given to the softest of euphemisms and the most Pollyannish of prognoses, are expressing grave concern about the dangers facing the world monetary system. Many officials agree that never in the history of these two institutions has anxiety run so high.

The explosive mixture of oil and money is what they are worrying about.

Although inflation, in part aggravated by soaring oil prices, is rampant, many officials are concerned that efforts to stop it by clamping down on monetary growth would result in deflation and bring mass unemployment.

Individual nations facing mounting balance-of-payments deficits are being driven to try to increase exports and cut other imports, to conserve disappearing foreign-exchange reserves. But the battle to increase exports could lead to international price wars, with falling rather than rising prices. And the drive to curb imports could lead to breakdowns in trade and further damage to national economies.

In these alarming circumstances, the most hopeful thing to be said about the present conference is that the finance ministers and central bankers are facing up to reality and refusing to panic. Constructive programs are receiving the most intensive consideration, although action appears unlikely before the meetings adjourn the end of this week.

Prophecies that once would have been dismissed as lunatic or vulturish are now perceived to be a real part of the problem overhanging financial markets and banking institutions.

The most extreme of the black prophecies heard here was offered by Franz Pick, the international currency expert and champion of gold, whose reputation, like that of other gold bugs, has been greatly enhanced by soaring bullion prices in recent years.

Asked fo: his current prediction, Dr. Pick replied: "Banking holiday. Moratorium on all debts except mortgage debts. Closing Wall street for good including the bond market. Exchanging dollar bank notes for new dollars at a rate of 10 for 1 or 20 for 1."

In the face of such forecasts, and the near panic they have excited in stock and money markets, what can Government officials say that will not sound flatulent or like soft soap?

William E. Simon, Secretary of the Treasury, in his statement to the monetary conference today said he did not believe the world was in imminent danger of a drift into cumulative recession or depression. But, he added, "We must be alert and ready to act quickly" should the situation change unexpectedly.

Borrowings to Mount

Mr. Simon said he did not believe the international financial market was about to collapse, although he did believe individual countries might face serious problems in borrowing to cover oil and other costs. Food is a particular problem, especially as it is being added to the already explosive mix of oil and money.

The question is no longer recognition of the depth and gravity of the danger, but the adequacy of governmental response. Thus far this conference has provided only moderate reassurance on that ground. Mr. Simon, for instance, is still urging nations to give highest priority to the attack on "devastating inflation."

On measures to bring down the price levels set by the Organization of Petroleum Exporting Countries, Mr. Simon was vague. The United States is being accused by others here of, in effect, doing the opposite of what President Theodore Roosevelt prescribed for the conduct of foreign policy: talking loudly and carrying a small stick.

Focus on Recycling

In the general mood of pessimism on prices, the conference is focusing on the issue of how to "recycle" oil dollars—transfer them to nations with the deepest deficits and little or no ability to attract money directly from the oil exporters.

H. Johannes Witteveen, managing director of the monetary fund, has proposed increasing the existing oil facility—christened by the British as the

Witteveen Mark I—of $3.4-billion by a few hundred million dollars to get through the current year. Presumably a larger sum will be sought for the future.

Denis Healey, Chancellor of the Exchequer in Britain, wants to build a Witteveen Mark II with a much bigger supply of funds.

The American response to such proposals, as voiced by Mr. Simon, is thus far low key almost to the point of being lackadaisical. Thus far, he suggested, the recycling problem had been handed "quite adequately" in private financial markets.

However, private bankers here—especially those representing British and European institutions—are far less sanguine. Several talk about reaching the limits of their ability to take and recycle petrodollars in the near future.

Quota Alternative

The International Monetary Fund could also provide more money to help governments in trouble by increasing the $34-billion of quotas loaned to the Fund by member governments. Mr. Simon said in an interview that the United States might be willing to see a 25 per cent rise to about $42-billion total.

But he insists the United States should keep its present share of the total—about 23 per cent—although he realizes oil producers want a bigger share, with which would go greater voting power in the fund.

At present Iran's share of the quota total is two-thirds of 1 per cent; Saudi Arabia's is one-half of 1 per cent; Venezuela's is a little more than 1 per cent and Kuait's is two-tenths of 1 per cent. The cummulative total share for all OPEC members is less than 3 per cent.

Speaking Softly

The leaders of the fund and the World Bank are themselves speaking softly to and about the oil producers. Few Arabs are actually in evidence here, this being the period of the religious holiday of Ramadan.

But the address of Robert S. McNamara, president of the World Bank, was printed in Arabic this year; his plans for keeping the World Bank going and growing depend heavily on a continuing inflow of petrodollars.

Likewise, Dr. Witteveen of the I.M.F. refused to comment on the price of oil in response to press questions, saying in effect that it was none of the fund's business.

The bank and fund, with the political cross tugs of oil-producing and oil-consuming, industrial and developing countries may be simply incapable of coming to grips with the grim problems besetting the world economy.

Search for Action

It may be necessary for real action to come from some other grouping.

The so-called Big Five non-Communist financial powers—the United States, France, West Germany, Britain and France—have been exploring new approaches. But, as one West German put it, their discussions thus far have been more in the nature of brain-storming than decision-making.

Some American observers believe that the old Group of Ten—which includes all the Western European democracies, and Canada as well as the United States and Japan—is a better theater for action. However, the Canadians, on all issues, seemed to be behaving like OPEC fellow travelers these days.

No Neat Solution

There appears to be general agreement that there is no neat solution to the problem of how to conduct national economic policy in the midst of this world crisis. Each nation is bound to pursue some unique mixture of unilateral, bilateral and multilateral strategies.

The French, for example, have already announced a $10-billion limit on the amount of oil she will import—unilateral. At the same time they appear determined to continue to pursue bilateral arms and other economic deals with the Iranians and other oil producers.

Yet they appear to be moving closer to multilateral approaches with the United States and other Western nations to problems that might get out of hand.

For balance-of-payments deficits this year will generally be huge. The Italians are apparently headed for a deficit of close to $9-billion. France is expected to run one of about $7-billion. Japan is likely to be in the hole by $7-billion to $8-billion. And Britain's red ink may run to $10-billion.

The cumulative deficit of the oil importers is likely to grow to perhaps $650-billion by 1980, according to estimates of the World Bank itself.

The clock, then, is ticking. A realistic appraisal of the current conference is that nations have begun to respond in a serious and constructive way, and that the situation is not yet hopeless. But too timid or belated a response might make it so.

October 2, 1974

SHAH EXPANDING IRAN'S INFLUENCE

5-Country Tour Underlined His Objective of Gaining Political Role in Asia

By JAMES F. CLARITY
Special to The New York Times

TEHERAN, Iran, Oct. 8—Shah Mohammed Riza Pahlevi, on his recently concluded 17-day trip to five Asian countries placed new emphasis on two of Iran's major foreign policy objectives.

One objective, the maintenance of oil prices at a level acceptable to the Shah, was stated more clearly and firmly than ever in his response to declarations by President Ford and Secretary of State Kissinger that high oil prices were threatening world stability.

The other objective, the Shah's intent to increase Iran's influence in Asia, was also elaborated in his remarks in the countries he visited — Singapore, Australia, New Zealand, Indonesia and India.

In the matter of oil prices, the Shah said in Australia that "nobody could wave a finger at us because we could wave back." In India, he said, "Nobody could dictate to us. It is impossible to get anywhere on dictation terms."

The Shah also said, however: "We have very close relations with the United States." He added: "So we have got, as I said before, to sit down and find ways to save the world economy, provided that it is based on justice."

The Shah's statements, in the view of diplomats here, made it evident that he will respond to rhetoric with rhetoric, but that he is also ready for serious discussion.

Camera Press
The Shah of Iran

For, in addition to his remarks about finger-waving, the Shah proposed that an index be compiled linking oil prices to the prices of 20 or 30 items that the Iranians import from the developed countries at what Iranians consider inflated prices.

Some diplomats here feel that the Shah's indexing proposal, as it is called, would provide a focus for the talks he is to have in Teheran early next month with Mr. Kissinger. Other diplomats, however, contend that agreeing to an index would amount to institutionalizing inflation. According to this viewpoint, the Shah would insist on keeping oil prices more than high enough to compensate for fluctuations of prices in imports from the West.

Arms Obtainable Elsewhere

The Shah, according to diplomats who have studied his policies and have tried to perceive his motives, cannot be moved by implied threats, such as those from Washington, that the sale of American weapons to Iran might be curtailed to gain leverage toward lower oil prices. The Shah would buy the planes or other equipment he wants from Sweden or France if he had to, the diplomats say.

More effective in softening the Shah's position on oil prices, the diplomats feel, would be a carefully reasoned and economically documented argument by Mr. Kissinger to demonstrate that reduced prices would be in Iran's own long-term interest. In any event, there seems little doubt that the Shah, judging from his remarks and his index proposal, wants to sit down with Mr. Kissinger to discuss the crisis with a view toward a new agreement.

The other major policy objective, Iran's campaign to extend her influence in Asia, was considered the main purpose of the trip. Although the Shah concluded trade agreements in the countries he visited, his major interest seemed to be political.

He repeated some of his familiar proposals — a Middle East free of nuclear weapons, a "zone of peace" in the Indian Ocean—but he also intensified calls for a common-market arrangement embracing Iran, Indian Ocean countries and Australia and New Zealand. Whether or not such a vast market is practical, the proposal was thought to have given the Shah the image of a leader with vision.

The Shah also advanced a proposal for eventual achievement of a "military understanding" by countries of the Indian Ocean area, including Australia and Iran. The aim of the collective security proposal would be to persuade the United States and the Soviet Union to remove their naval forces from the Indian Ocean. It is a concept presumed to have great appeal to the peoples of the area.

October 9, 1974

Western Nations Doing Little to Conserve Energy

Only the French Seem to Heed Kissinger

By WILLIAM D. SMITH

Secretary of State Kissinger's suggestions that Western nations cut back their oil consumption by 10 to 14 per cent appears to be falling on deaf ears—even here at home.

Since the end of the Arab oil embargo last March, the major industrial countries, including the United States, appear to be talking more about energy conservation than doing anything about it.

There have been declines in oil consumption in most nations, but it appears that consumer reaction to higher prices, rather than to government restrictions on usage, is the major factor. Of the major industrialized nations, only France appears so far to have taken serious, official steps to curb oil usage.

Conservation Slipping

In the United States, the Federal Energy Administration estimates that there was a 5 per cent drop in oil demand in the first eight months of 1974 compared with the same period of 1973. Conservation efforts are slipping, however, according to most informed sources.

Apathy, the lack of a crisis atmosphere, surplus oil supplies and perhaps concern over international and domestic political repercussions have kept many nations from more decisive action on energy. The chief reason in most industrialized nations other than the United States appears to be fear of alienating the oil-exporting nations.

In the United States, domestic political considerations seem to be the dominating factor. In speeches at the United Nations and at a World Energy Conference officials of the Ford Administration appeared to be throwing down the gauntlet to the oil-producing nations.

The energy program presented by President Ford earlier last week, however, had few teeth, in the view of most analysts.

A leading energy expert described the program as one "fired not by long-range fear of the oil producing states but by short-term fear of the American voter."

The difference in attitude can be attributed to a difference in basic position on energy supplies. The European nations and Japan are overwhelmingly dependent on the oil-exporting states for their energy, while the United States, although growing increasingly dependent on imports, still produces domestically almost two-thirds of its oil.

Whatever the reasons, however, the industrialized world at the moment remains not only without any common conservation position but also without any great impetus behind individual national efforts.

Following are the situations in major industrial countries:

JAPAN

Japan is the world's second largest oil importer after the United States. The massive industrial complex built by the Japanese since World War II is 99 per cent dependent on foreign oil.

The Arab oil restrictions last year threatened Japan's "economic miracle," and the nation has since suffered from the soaring price of oil.

Japan's increase in oil consumption was 5.2 per cent in 1971; 7.3 per cent in 1972, and 11.3 per cent in 1973.

The Government has projected a 2 per cent drop in oil imports this year, however, with a recent Government study showing that 85 per cent of the Japanese people have undertaken one form or another of conservation, however minor.

No major, permanent conservation moves have been taken yet, but most analysts believe that a decisive program will soon appear.

BRITAIN

Britain has reduced oil consumption over last year by about 10 per cent, more because of higher prices than Government conservation actions.

Denis Healey, Chancellor of the Exchequer, has made it clear that he is little inclined to cut back British consumption by much more even as part of a united consumer front to force back oil prices. He said it would be "totally illogical and irrational" to curtail oil imports if such a move threatened industrial production in any way.

The nation is more worried about a major recession than the cost of oil. Indeed, the government has done little to emphasize even voluntary energy conservation.

Of course Britain will begin reaping the benefits of the North Sea oil and gas fields towards the end of the decade but as one observer commented:

"We've always had a tendency to spend a penny before it is actually in our hand. Now some people in Britain think they can use the oil before it's out of the ground."

WEST GERMANY

West Germany is the largest oil consumer in Western Europe and the world's third-largest oil importer.

Yet the effect of the oil situation on the average West German citizen is scarcely perceptible. Gasoline, heating oil and other petroleum products are plentiful. Gasoline prices have declined from the peaks reached during the carless weekends during the Arab oil production cutback in 1973 and heating oil prices are down from their highs.

The last vestige of Government-sponsored conservation measures is a recommended speed limit of 87 miles an hour on major highways—often ignored by drivers.

An Economics Ministry official said "we are now relying on voluntary measures and the effect of market forces to hold consumption down."

West Germany's oil consumption in 1974 is indeed expected to drop, by about 5 per cent to 2.6 million barrels a day, with about 95 per cent of it imported.

FRANCE

With oil production of 25,000

barrels a day and consumption of 2.5 million barrels a day in 1973, France has taken by far the most dramatic steps to reduce consumption. The Government has set a $10.1 billion ceiling on spending for oil imports for 1975 and ordered cutbacks in industrial and home heating oil consumption.

Even before the announcement of the proposed measures, France had cut its consumption of oil products by 6 per cent from 1973 levels.

The $10.1 billion ceiling means, because of a fourfold increase in oil prices, that France will be buying 10 per cent less oil by volume, than in 1973, at current prices.

The rationing of heavy fuel oils used by industry is to be implemented through contracts agreed on by the Industry Ministry and various industrial sectors. Gasoline is not to be rationed.

The government is hoping to maintain the average 10 per cent decrease in demand for heating oil registered so far this year by reducing supplies to customers to 80 per cent of deliveries in the 12 months up to May 31, 1974.

It is also seeking powers to limit temperatures in homes and plans to create incentives for fuel saving measures.

France is looking to alternate indigenous sources of energy, including increased coal production, nuclear supplies and offshore drilling for oil.

THE NETHERLANDS

The nation, the last taken off the Arab embargo list, produces next to no oil itself, but its port of Rotterdam is Europe's main transfer center for Middle Eastern crude oil.

In addition, the Netherlands is a major natural gas producer supplying her own needs as well as exporting.

Natural gas provides 50 per cent of the country's energy needs and oil, 45 per cent. The Government plans to actually increase the use of oil while it is available, believing it is better to keep gas in the ground as a reserve against a real emergency.

Despite the embargo days, Dutch oil consumption is only running about 5 per cent below the 1973 level, and the rate of conservation has been slipping considerably in recent months.

The Government is beginning to put into motion a long-term conservation program involving tax advantages for diesel-powered automobiles, improvements in house insulation and electric machinery, increased use of coal and nuclear energy and regulation of house-heating levels.

ITALY

Although Italy appears to be in the worst condition economically of any nation in Western Europe, largely because of the oil situation, she seems to be doing the least on energy conservation.

Consumption this year is down about 1.5 to 2 per cent from last year, compared with an average annual increase of 7 or 8 per cent in recent years.

Italy imports about 99 per cent of her oil, with more than two-thirds coming from Arab sources.

There have been reports that the government may impose a Sunday driving ban, as it did last winter. A gasoline rationing system has been proposed, but it has met with very little support. Only about 15 per cent of Italy's oil consumption goes toward gasoline, compared with 46 per cent in the United States.

President Giovanni Leone has let it be known that it is Italy's policy to cooperate with the oil-producing nations in every reasonable way and that the nation would do nothing that might jeopardize its relations with the Arab countries.

CANADA

The country is the only industrialized one in the West that produces more oil than it consumes. It is both a major importer and exporter, with production in the Western half of the country, while the bulk of consumers are in the East with no connecting pipeline between.

Traditionally Canada has exported its Western oil to the United States while importing cheaper foreign oil from Venezuela and the Middle East for use in Eastern population centers. In view of the fourfold increase in foreign oil prices, the Canadians are planning a West-East pipeline.

Canada consumes 1.8 million barrels of oil a day, just about the same amount as a year ago. She produces about 1.9 million barrels a day and exports about 900,000, while importing 800,000 barrels a day. Increased costs of imported oil are balanced by higher prices charged for exports to the United States.

Last fall the Government made an effort to encourage Canadians to save fuel, but nobody took it too seriously. No consumption cutbacks are planned. Even if necessary, they would be politically difficult as long as large exports of oil and gas still go to the United States.

October 14, 1974

Big International Banks, Under Strain, Reject Petrodollar Deposits

By TERRY ROBARDS
Special to The New York Times

LONDON, Oct. 28—With the commercial banking system's capacity to cope with the massive flow of money from the oil-producing nations under intense strain, possibly approaching the saturation point, major international banks operating in the London financial center are turning down "petrodollar" deposits.

The banks involved, some of the world's largest, are doing this either by quoting uncompetitive interest rates or by declining to quote rates at all.

In general, they continue to deal with the oil-producing countries. But instances in which they find they are unable to accept deposits are becoming more and more frequent as the multi-billion-dollar influx gathers momentum.

Seeming Conflict

Their increasing refusal to continue absorbing petrodollars reflects their inability to lend out the same money on terms that they consider favorable or prudent. In other words, the flow of oil money has become so large that the banks can no longer handle it safely or efficiently in all cases.

The emerging situation appears to conflict with the assurances offered on several occasions in recent months by William E. Simon, the United States Treasury Secretary, who has maintained that the commercial banking system is fully capable of handling the flow.

Bankers trying to cope with the buildup of oil funds here contend that the producing countries must be more willing to channel their money into investments other than deposits in major banks and must learn to rely less on their traditional banking outlets.

Many bankers have been expressing doubts for months that the system's capacity would be adequate in light of the quadrupling of oil prices in the last year. The revenues of the 13 members of the Organization of Petroleum Exporting Countries will approach $100-billion this year alone.

Their current-account surpluses, roughly reflecting the difference between what they take in and what they spend abroad, are expected to reach $65-billion in 1974—an average of more than $1-billion a week.

Short-Term Deposits

Because most of the producing countries are relatively undeveloped, their economies do not have the capacity to absorb the funds themselves. So most of the money must be invested elsewhere. The funds have been moving mostly into major commercial banks as short-term deposits.

But the banks must lend the funds out to earn the money they need to pay interest to the depositors and presumably to earn a profit. A major part of the present problem is finding creditworthy borrowers in need of such large amounts of short-term funds.

A separate but equally difficult problem is the impact

The New York Times/Bill Raffery

The Bank of England in the heart of the City, London's financial district. Major international banks are straining to handle the massive flow of "petrodollars."

that the deposits have on each bank's capital ratio. Large increases in deposits theoretically should be matched by expanded capital, but the depressed state of the capital markets has made it almost impossible for banks to expand their capital bases.

Technically, there is no difference between petrodollars and other deposits—except for the quantities. The big New York-based international banks that have attracted much of the flow receive the funds in batches of $100-million or more.

"We've actually seen half a billion dollars at one time," a top banker reported with exasperation. "Do you realize how much money that is and that it's subject to call? Maybe we can handle it when it comes in, but what do we do when half a billion suddenly wants to go out?"

Because the oil money is rarely invested on a long-term basis, it tends to earn the prevailing day-to-day interest rates, now around 9.5 per cent. But some of the big banks already are tending to quote under this rate, while smaller banks may quote above it.

Rate Has Fallen

As a further indication of the growing imbalance of supply over demand, the rate has fallen sharply. In January, it was 12 per cent. At the end of May, it was 11.75 per cent. The decline reflects the flood of money moving into the system.

Bankers interviewed here in recent days expressed hope that the system ultimately would find ways to cope with the situation. But most foresaw major difficulties for the next three to six months at least, when the system will be subject to strains never before experienced.

In calling for new methods of coping with the money flow, Gordon Richardson, governor of the Bank of England, said the other day: "The flow of oil money is still accelerating. It is expected to grow by as much in the last three months of this year as it did in the first nine—and may go on at a high rate for some years."

The upsurge under way at present is due partly to seasonal factors and partly to the catching up of price increases announced some time ago. Although the higher prices have been in effect for months, the actual receipt of the payments customarily lags. Now the payments are catching up with the higher prices.

Much Leeway Used Up

"I think I have felt for some time that the test period for the system is just about to begin," David Bodner, senior vice president of the Chemical Bank of New York, said here today. "The flow is just reaching peak levels in the fourth quarter.

"A lot of the early leeway in the banking system to absorb these flows has been used up. The problems are going to get considerably more difficult from here on out. The banks getting the biggest flow are reaching the saturation point."

Mr. Bodner, who supervised foreign-exchange operations for the Federal Reserve Bank of New York before joining Chemical in April, said the commercial banking system had capacity left to accept additional deposits, but he added that this capacity was diminishing rapidly.

It was his view that the oil-producing countries must begin to deal directly with borrowers, to expand the range of banks they deal with and to become willing to make longer-term deposits. Even then, he said, the private system would be unable to handle the entire flow.

Some Capacities Reached

An official of First National City Bank of New York said here today that it was his bank's view that the saturation point for petrodollars was not yet being reached for the banking system as a whole, but he conceded that some large institutions had reached their capacities.

"The situation varies from bank to bank," he said. "Some have reached their self-imposed ceilings; others have not. It is important to examine the reasons.

"I feel it is the concentration that most banks are afraid of, rather than the

Camera Press

Gordon Richardson, governor of the Bank of England, predicted acceleration in the growth of Arab oil dollars.

amount. If you find half your liabilities are with four or five customers, you are exposed and you may be willing to pay more for funds from somebody else."

Implicit in this statement was that some banks have found it expedient to quote interest rates below the market to some depositors, thereby discouraging them. The fact that these depositors are able to find other banks willing to accept their funds may indicate that the system is not yet saturated, but it also shows the strain it is under.

Self-Imposed Limits Apparent

Senior officials of the Chase Manhattan Bank and the Morgan Guaranty Trust Company of New York expressed an awarness of the situation and acknowledged that some banks apparently had reached self-imposed limits in accepting deposits.

"I think everybody sees it," a Morgan officer said. "People are talking about it. The amounts are so enormous that it's hard to see where it will all end."

He and most other bank officers here foresee greater involvement by Governments in recycling the oil money. "I rather think that the oil-producing as well as the oil-importing countries will come to the same conclusion: Government - to - Government deals are the answer," a Citibank officer said.

Agreements Set to Deal With Flow of Oil Money

By EDWIN L. DALE Jr.

Special to The New York Times

WASHINGTON, Jan. 16—Finance ministers representing both rich and poor countries announced tonight agreements intended to help the international economy cope with the vast flow of money to oil-producing countries and to deal with several other monetary problems.

Under the agreements announced today, many countries that might otherwise be pressed to pay for their oil imports will be able to borrow money to do so for at least another year.

Some important details were not settled at this week's meetings of the Group of 10 leading industrial countries and the new 20-nation "interim committee" of the international monetary fund, which includes representatives of the poorer countries. Nevertheless, a substantial package was put together, part of which had become known prior to tonight's formal disclosure in two communiqués.

John N. Turner, Canadian Finance Minister and chairman of the interim committee, said of the agreements, "I think it can be said we have made significant progress in assuring world economic stability . . . The agreements will reinforce business confidence around the world and the confidence of governments."

Jack F. Bennett, the United States Under Secretary of the Treasury for Monetary Affairs, said "The United States is extremely pleased by the breadth and depth of the agreements."

The principal elements of the agreement were the following:

¶The I.M.F. will establish a $6-billion special "oil facility" for 1975, larger than last year's. As before, it will borrow money mainly from the oil-producing countries and lend it to the consuming countries, mainly the less developed ones. The way was opened for subsidized interest rates on loans to about 30 of the world's poorest countries, but the funds for this—from both oil producers and some industralized countries—will have to be raised later.

¶The group of 10 announced agreement on all the main essentials of the United States's plan for a $25-billion financial "safety net," or insurance fund, open to participation by the 24 countries of the Organization for Economic Cooperation and Development—that is, the major industrial countries. Formal approval is expected by the end of February, followed by submission to Congress and other national parliaments.

The interim committee approved an increase of 32.5 per cent in members' quotas—and hence access to loans—in the monetary fund, with some reshuffling of shares to increase the weight of the oil-producing nations.

¶The committee made progress, but did not reach final agreement, on a series of important amendments to the fund's charter, including one settling the future monetary role of gold. These will be taken up again at a meeting in Paris in June, with the air of submitting them, together with the increase in quotas, to national parliaments late this year.

The key to the package was the part involving oil. The problem has arisen because the sharp rise in oil prices has created huge balance-of-payments surpluses for the oil producers and deficits for most of the rest of the world. A major part of the problem is "recycling" these funds — by loans, deposits and investments —to the consuming countries.

The enlarged I.M.F. oil facility will handle part of the problem. The $25-billion United States plan, in which the United States share will be about $7-billion, is not designed to recycle petrodollars but to make loans available, if needed, to members of the group that are hard-pressed.

The one important issue left to be decided in the coming weeks was what share of any help proferred would be from national treasuries and what would be in the form of guarantees of loans on world capital markets. These other parts of the plan were agreed upon:

The key to the package was the part involving oil. The problem has arisen because the rise in oil prices has created huge balance-of-payments surpluses for the oil producers and deficits for most of the rest of the world. A major part of the problem is "recycling" these funds—by loans, deposits and investments—to the consuming countries.

The enlarged I.M.F. oil facility will handle part of the problem. The $25-billion plan, in which the United States share will be about $7-billion, is not designed to recycle "petrodollars" but to make loans available, if needed, to members of the group that are hard pressed.

The oil-producing countries were represented at the meeting of the interim committee and concurred in the extension and enlargement of the oil facility for 1975, though amounts for individual countries were not negotiated this week.

The one important issue left to be decided in the plan in the coming weeks was what share of any help proferred would be from national treasuries and what would be in the form of guarantees of loans on world capital markets. These other parts of the plan were agreed upon:

¶The standby fund will be $25-billion for a period of two years once all the parliaments concerned, including the United States Congress, have approved it.

¶Every member country will have a quota, which will establish its initial borrowing right—though this can be exceeded by a vote of the other members —and will set the upper limit on how much money it must put up for loans to others.

¶Loans from the facility will be made only "as a last resort" and borrowing countries "will be required to show that they are encountering serious balance-of-payments difficulties and are making the fullest possible use of their own reserves and of resources available to them through other channels."

¶A weighted voting system will be used, based on countries' quotas, and a two-thirds vote will be needed to approve any loan. For a loan larger than a nation's quota, higher voting percentages will be needed until, for a loan of double the quota or more, the vote of lending members must be unanimous.

The exact quotas were not disclosed, but United States officials said this country's share would be about $7-billion.

Mr. Bennett said he hoped the plan could be submitted to Congress as early as March. But activation is not likely—even assuming Congressional approval—until late in the year.

January 17, 1975

OIL STATES OFFER TO DISCUSS PRICES

But OPEC Leaders Demand Stabilization Be Linked to World Economic Situation

By JUAN de ONIS

Special to The New York Times

ALGIERS, March 6—The oil-exporting countries offered today to negotiate with industrial nations on the "stabilization" of oil prices. But they stressed that the agenda of a conference could not be limited to discussion of prices.

They said the international conference they envisioned would have to deal with issues of raw materials, monetary relations and the development of poorer nations.

This announcement was made here at the close of the first meeting of the sovereigns and chiefs of state of the 13-nation Organization of Petroleum Exporting Countries.

The declaration said that future oil prices, which have been frozen by the organization until September to facilitate negotiations, would have to be based on factors of conservation, the "availability and cost of alternative sources of energy" and the uses of petroleum for such nonenergy purposes as chemical products.

But at the same time, the leaders of the OPEC countries said, the value of petroleum must be protected against inflation and monetary depreciation. They said this should be done by linking oil prices to the prices of manufactured goods and services.

The declaration issued by the leaders contained an outline of the organization's negotiating position in preparation for a conference with the industrial consumers. A preliminary meeting for such a conference is to open in Paris on April 7.

The members of the Organization of Petroleum Exporting Countries are Algeria, Ecuador, Indonesia, Iran, Iraq, Kuwait, Libya, Nigeria, Qatar, Saudi Arabia, United Arab Emirates, Venezuela and Gabon.

The oil-producing countries declared readiness to assure oil supplies to the industrialized countries to meet their "essential requirements." They also said they were prepared to negotiate with the consumer countries on "the provision of financial facilities."

But the leaders warned against any grouping of consumer countries that would have the "aim of confrontation." They vowed "immediate and effective measures" to counter "any plan or strategy designed for aggression, economic or military, by such grouping or otherwise against" any member country of their organization.

The 13 oil-producing countries declared themselves the vanguard of the commodity exporting countries of the third world and said they would support negotiations with the consumers "if equal attention is paid to the problems facing both the developed and developing countries."

President Houari Boumediene of Algeria said in a closing statement that the industrial countries were prepared to negotiate now with producers because the oil countries had gained control over their resources and could regulate prices.

In the past, Mr. Boumediene said, the commodity-exporting countries had no "real bargaining power" and their views on international economic cooperation were not taken into account.

This has changed with the creation of the Organization of Petroleum Exporting Countries, he said.

President Carlos Andrés Pérez of Venezuela said:

"Our oil is at the disposal of the third world as an instrument of negotiation with the industrial countries."

Shah Mohammed Riza Pahlevi of Iran also spoke at the closing meeting, held at the Palais des Naciones.

"We are more united than ever," he said, "strong in our rights, and supported by the third world, which will be the main beneficiaries if there is stability of prices."

The declaration that concluded the meeting reflected the moderating influence of Saudi Arabia on key issues, rather than the more radical socialist line of Algeria.

Saudi Arabia, the world's major oil exporter, has been in close contact with the United States on the preparatory producer-consumer conference to be held next month in Paris.

Of the 10 countries invited to the Paris meeting, four are from the oil producers' organization — Saudi Arabia, Iran, Venezuela and Algeria. Representing the developing countries that are not major oil producers will be Brazil, Zaire and India. France, as the host has also invited the United States, Japan and the European Economic Community to represent the industrial consumers.

Essential Supplies Assured

In a key section of the declaration here today, the oil countries' chiefs of state said they would "insure supplies that will meet the essential requirements of the economies of the developed countries, provided that the consuming countries do not use artificial barriers to distort the normal operation of the laws of demand and supply."

In addition, the declaration said the OPEC members were "prepared to negotiate the conditions for the stabilization of oil prices which will enable the consuming countries to make necessary adjustments in their economies" to higher energy costs.

The meeting did not endorse Algeria's call for a special OPEC fund of $10-billion to $15-billion, to assist developing countries. Instead, it called for coordination of grants and loans by funds under the control of individual countries or by regional funds.

The declaration also avoided any explicit commitment to finance stabilization funds for other commodities, as was urged by a meeting of nonaligned countries last month.

The OPEC members, which now hold reserves and foreign financial assets totaling more than $50-billion, also insisted on reform of the international monetary system providing a "substantial increase in the share of developing countries in decision-making, management and participation in the spirit of partnership for international development and on the basis of equality."

Venezuela to Act on Oil

ALGIERS, March 6 (AP) — President Carlos Andrés Pérez of Venezuela said at the oil-producers' conference here that he would make a formal announcement next Wednesday of the nationalization some time "this year" of foreign oil holdings in his country.

The draft nationalization bill was submitted to the President in December, and at the time it was expected he would submit it to the Congress in March for debate and approval. He said in January that the Government would take over the oil industry within the "next few months."

March 7, 1975

Frustrations of Oil Conference

By LEONARD SILK

Economic Analysis

The first conference in Paris of oil-exporting and oil-importing countries, which was supposed to have set the agenda and improved the atmosphere for a world energy conference next summer, has got nowhere. Instead, by over running its intended time limits — it was well into its second week when it adjourned yesterday—and by polarizing the differences among participants, it has served to dramatize the radical conflicts that exist within the non-Communist world over two critical issues:

¶Whether the world economy will be run essentially according to liberal principles of trade and payments, which have existed through most of the period since World War II, or whether an open economy will give way to one of bloc trading and price fixing.

¶And, closely tied to that issue, how to divide the world's product and its wealth among industrial countries, oil-producing countries and oil-poor developing countries.

The Paris talks have demonstrated how far from resolution these issues remain.

The United States—whose energy and foreign economic policies are now dominated by Secretary of State Kissinger—remains the chief proponent of a tough line of resistance to the oil-exporting countries. Although there are ambiguities in the American position, it still is pointed at reducing the dependency of the West on insecure Middle Eastern oil and, if possible, at breaking the oil cartel, the Organization of ePtroleum Exporting Countries.

Algeria, led by President Houari Boumediene, has emerged as the outstanding champion of both the oil-exporting countries and their third-world allies. Ageria—herself oil-rich, per-capita income poor, anti-colonialist in its revolutionary origins and leftist leaning—is a natural bridge between the rich OPEC states and the poor third world.

Seeking to play the role of mediator between the antagonistic views of the United States and Algeria is President Valéry Giscard d'Estaing of France. He pushed hardest to get discussions going between the oil producers and oil consumers; he is still striving to prevent the conference from failing.

Mr. Giscard d'Estaing is well cast in the role of mediator: He has much to offer not only his European partners but also the United States, which is not eager to be cut off from its traditional Western allies over the oil issue. And he has much to offer the oil-producing countries and nonoil-producing third-world countries, especially in Africa, by way of trade and markets.

Nor is the French President isolated from other European leaders in their desire to maintain close economic relations with both the oil-rich and oil-poor third world, even if this involves giving some ground to their demand for "a new economic order."

The OPEC nations issued that deman dlast month in President Boumediene's capital, Algiers, at a meeting called by "the President of the Revolutionary Council and of the Council of Ministers of the Democratic People's Republic of Algeria."

At the Algiers meeting, the OPEC nations denounced the "short-sighted" economic policies of the industrialized world and rejected "any allegation attributing to the price of petroleum the responsibility for the present instability of the world economy."

They denounced "any grouping of consumer nations with the aim of confrontation," and they condemned any plan or strategy "designed for aggression—economic or military."

They declared their solidarity with nonoil developing countries and declared their support for "exporters of raw materials and other basic commodities in their efforts to obtain an equitable and remunerative price level for their exports."

As a modest olive branch, the OPEC nations said they were prepared to negotiate the conditions for stabilizing oil prices that would "enable the consuming countries to make necessary adjustments to their economies."

But, in echange, the developed countries would have to support "measures taken by developing countries" directed toward price stabilization of their exports of raw materials and other basic commodities.

What OPEC Wants

The developed countries, OPEC said in the Algiers "solemn declaration," would also have to give financial aid and food to the developing countries, accelerate the transfer of modern technology to them, build "a major portion" of planned or new petrochemical complexes, oil refineries and fertilizer plants in OPEC nations and provide protection against the depreciation of the value of OPEC nations' external financial holdings as well as "assurance of the security of their investments in the developed countries."

The Paris meeting has made plain that OPEC members and third-world countries mean to continue and broaden an attack on the system of liberal international trade, which they believe worked in the past only to the benefit of the rich industrialized countries.

While they recognize that too brutal an attack would backfire, the resource-exporting countries have demonstrated that they are capable of inflicting severe economic damage on the West and the entire world economy.

European leaders recognize only too clearly that the massive increase in oil prices by OPEC has shaken to its foundations the present world economic system. However, they are moving to the position that, if they can only come to satisfactory terms with the oil producers, they can turn the crisis to their advantage by tapping capital flows from the oil states and expanding their markets in those countries.

Camerapix

Houari Boumediene, Algeria's President, has emerged as a champion of oil-exporting and third-world countries.

At the same time they see the diversion of vast flows of funds to the oil-producing states as providing a means of funneling more money to the poor, developing countries and solving one of the most vexatious and dangerous of global problems.

There is recognition in Europe that foreign aid from the industrial states has been inadequate to the task—and is likely to remain inadequate, given the domestic political constraints on aid. Those constraints have been intensified now by huge oil bills and the consequent weakened balance-of-payments positions of virtually all the industrialized countries except West Germany.

But the United States is unwilling to go along with the implied validation of the power of OPEC—and the possibility that it could lead to similar monopolistic extortion from other groups of raw-material producers.

Secretary of State Kissinger's energy policy, emphasizing a high floor price that would cut domestic oil consumption and stimulate production, is designed to break the cartel.

But Mr. Kissinger has been unable to gain support for a high floor price either from the other industrial countries or even from the United States Congress.

Congress wants to make a more direct assault on both OPEC and any OPEC imitators. Congress inserted into the Trade Act of 1974 a clause denying trade preferences to any country that is a member of OPEC or "a party to any other arrangement of foreign countries . . . the effect of which is to withhold supplies of vital commodity resources from international trade or to raise the price of such commodities to an unreasonable level and cause serious disruption of the world economy."

Request From Ford

In his foreign policy address last week, President Ford asked Congress to reconsider this clause. He said it punished two South American "friends" of the United States, Ecuador and Venezuela, as well as other OPEC nations, such as Nigeria and Indonesia, which had not participated in the oil embargo against this country.

Such exclusions, said the President, "seriously complicated our new dalogue with our friends."

However, many European economists feel that both the United States Administration and Congress are barking up the wrong tree if they think that the solution to the threat to world economic stability is a break-up of OPEC and a sharp decline in the external price of oil.

They think the strain on the price now is due almost entirely to the widespread economic slump in Western Europe, the United States and Japan and that recovery—and perhaps a coming boom—will force oil prices higher, unless some progress can be made on price-stabilization agreements.

Many American economists, however, question whether such price-stabilization deals would hold and would prefer the United States and its allies to act now to put maximum pressure on OPEC. Some would do this by fixing quotas against foreign oil, requiring would-be suppliers to compete for "tickets" to sell here. Others, who think they will not work, favor high, discriminatory tariffs that would encourage those nations willing to supply oil on a fair and stable basis.

United Press International

Valéry Giscard d'Estaing, the President of France, is seeking the role of mediator between opposing oil views.

As the West wrangles indecisively, the OPEC nations bide their time—waiting and hoping for economic recovery that will strengthen the market for oil and their bargaining position.

And the poor, developing countries—despite the damage to their own economies of high-priced oil and shrunken markets in the West, partly due to the impact of the oil crisis—continue to back OPEC.

Ideology may play a part in the poor countries' position, but it also seems to represent a judgment about where power now resides and can be used to fulfill their hopes for extracting more money and resources from the rich, industrial nations.

April 16, 1975

U.S. AFFIRMS SHIFT ON WORLD PRICES

Kissinger Tells Users of Oil He Also Favors Stability for Other Raw Materials

By CLYDE H. FARNSWORTH

Special to The New York Times

PARIS, May 27—The United States, calling for a new preparatory meeting for an international energy conference, affirmed today that it was willing to consider arrangements for greater price stability for raw materials exported by developing countries.

It said also that it hoped new efforts to deal "seriously" with the problems of the developing world would break a deadlock between oil-producing and oil-consuming countries and help the world avoid another energy confrontation.

These statements, which entailed a change in American foreign economic policy, were made by Secretary of State Kissinger at a ministerial meeting of the International Energy Agency, a grouping of 18 major oil-consuming countries.

Kansas City Proposal

He had made similar statements two weeks ago, in a speech in Kansas City where he announced a United States readiness to consider international arrangements covering the prices of raw materials, a stand that contrasted with the long-standing American reluctance to enter into international commodity agreements.

The first preparatory meeting for an international energy conference, held here last month, broke down over whether the agenda should include the wider problems of all raw materials. Oil-producing and developing countries insisted on a broad agenda; the United States, the European Common Market and Japan were opposed.

Today Mr. Kissinger suggested that a similar impasse could be avoided at a new preparatory meeting through the establishment of a series of commissions, with the principal one dealing substantially with energy. Development issues and raw materials would be discussed in others.

The foreign ministers of the consumer countries meeting here issued a communiqué tonight offering to resume "discussions at any time and in any manner found mutually convenient." But it did not pick up proposals made by Mr. Kissinger for taking up raw materials as well, saying only that the governing board of the International Emergency Agency would "examine the manner in which the dialogue should be continued."

This was the first ministerial meeting of the agency since it was formed 6 months ago, largely at Mr. Kissinger's initiative, to unify Western Energy positions and prepare for a dialogue with the major oil-exporting states.

Third-world countries have been pressing for a new international economic order to restructure financial systems in a way that would increase their wealth and power and reduce the gap with the rich industrial countries.

High on List of Demands

The stabilization of fluctuating commodity prices has been high in the catalogue of third-world demands, which the oil producing states supported in last month's preparatory meeting.

Countries that depend on export earnings of a few primary products, such as copper, tin or coffee, are hurt when prices for these products fall in world markets.

American officials said today that Washington now felt this question of excessive price volatility must be addressed not only because it hurts producers but also because it causes costly dislocations in the production process that inevitably affect consumers.

Mr. Kissinger remains in Paris tomorrow for a ministerial meeting of the Organization for Economic Cooperation and Development, an economic strategy body of the Western nations. He said today that he intended to present more detailed proposals tomorrow on the way the United States will tackle the issue of third-world demands.

"It has become clear —as a result of the April preparatory meeting —that the dialogue between the producers and consumers will not progress unless it is broadened to include the general issue of the relationship between developing and developed countries," Mr. Kissinger said today.

He added that there was "no reason to recoil from a discussion of all the issues of concern to developing countries."

The Secretary of State then went on to disclose American thinking about the way in which the conference with oil-producer countries could be resumed.

He said commissions should be created to deal with critical areas such as energy, problems of the most seriously affected nations and raw materials.

Speech Is Revised

"Membership in these commissions should be limited if they are to be effective," he said. "We suggest that this be decided by objective criteria. In energy, for example, countries exporting or importing more than a certain volume of energy in the world market should be members."

A first version of Mr. Kissinger's speech, distributed to the press this morning, gave the commissions equal importance. But a later version, which was actually read to the other ministers said that only the energy commission would do substantive work, while commissions on development issues and raw materials would be limited to monitoring and reviewing work already done within international bodies such as the United Nations.

Foreign Minister Garret FitzGerald of Ireland told newsmen this evening that the Kissinger plan was a "good starting point," but that Ireland felt the status of the commissions would have to be modified to satisfy the developing countries.

Mr. Kissinger told newsmen tonight that the United States had already conducted bilateral conversations with several oil-producing countries and that his impression was that "we have some support."

After a breakfast meeting with President Valery Giscard d'Estaing, who convened the preparatory conference last month and remains ready to call another one, Mr. Kissinger said he thought the dialogue could be resumed in the coming months.

At the breakfast, Mr. Kissinger was served along with coffee and croissants a birthday cake with red, white and blue candles. He was 52 today. The French President also gave Mr. Kissinger a present, the works of Metternich in eight volumes. The Secretary of State is an acknowledged expert on the 19th-century Austrian statesman.

In his speech on May 13, delivered before the Kansas City International Relations Council, Mr. Kissinger said that the United States was ready to attend a new preparatory meeting for an international energy conference and to consider international arrangements covering the prices of raw materials "on a case-by-case basis."

"Our thinking on the issue of raw materials and the manner in which it can be addressed internationally has moved forward," he added in that speech.

At his news conference here tonight, Mr. Kissinger noted that there had been "rather firm opposition" in the United States Government to discussing the issue of raw materials. He termed his address today "a step to tell the developing nations we are listening to their concerns."

But he said that the United States remained opposed to an indexation system linking raw material prices to the prices of manufactured goods imported by the developing countries.

Zaki Cites U.S. Pledge

ZURICH, May 27 (Reuters)—Saudi Arabia's Petroleum Minister, Sheik Ahmed Zaki al-Yamani, said here today that his country had received assurances from the United States that it had ruled out military confrontation over the oil issue.

Italy Asks U.S. Atom Aid

Special to The New York Times

ROME, May 27—Italy has asked the United States for assistance in a nuclear power program aimed at reducing her dependence on imported oil, a Foreign Ministry spokesman said today.

In return for the requested financial and technological help and for guaranteed supplies of atomic fuel, Italy has reportedly promised to back United States proposals for a floor price for crude oil.

May 28, 1975

France Invites 27 Lands To Meet on Economic Ills

By CLYDE H. FARNSWORTH
Special to The New York Times

PARIS, Sept. 15—France has invited major developed and developing countries to reconvene a preparatory meeting on energy and other problems of the world's rich and poor nations in Paris on Oct. 13.

An announcement by the Elysée Palace, said that conditions were now favorable for resumption of the dialogue, which had broken down last April.

Foreign Minister Jean Sauvagnargues told his Common Market colleagues in Brussels today of France's decision to call the preliminary conference, and all market members accepted the idea.

In Washington the State Department issued a statement tonight saying it, too, would accept the French invitation. A conflict erupted at an April meeting in Paris over the agenda for a full-scale conference. Industrialized nations wanted principal emphasis on the problems of oil. Developing countries, including oil producers, insisted that additional primary products be brought into the discussion.

Forming a bloc, third world countries wanted to relate the prospective conference to broad issues, involving besides overall problems of commodity income, the transfers of technology and capital from rich to poor.

Through diplomatic channels, efforts have continued over the spring and summer to work out compromises.

The principal accord was an agreement, qualified sources said, in which the full-scale conference would be divided into four separate commissions — one on energy, another on commodities other than oil, a third on problems of development and the fourth on the financial questions relating to the other three.

The same group that attended the April meeting will reconvene in October, the sources said.

Noncommunist industrialized nations were represented by the United States, Japan and the nine members of the European Common Market, which worked as a single bloc.

Iran, Venezuela and Saudi Arabia sat for the oil producers, and Zaïre, India and Brazil for the developing countries that do not produce oil.

Twenty-seven countries are to participate in the full-scale conference, which, sources said, will now probably take place before the end of the year.

Timing Significant

Of the 27, eight would come from the industrialized consumer group (the Common Market counting as one), and 19 from the third world group, both oil producers and nonproducers.

The agreement to set up the four commissions, with membership yet to be decided, represents a concession by the developed industrialized countries. There was also agreement that progress in all the commissions should be "parallel," although what this means has still to be tested.

The timing of tonight's announcement was seen as significant. It was viewed as an effort to demonstrate that the rich and poor countries are making some headway in dealing with their problems.

The announcement came as a United Nations Special Economic Session on Development Issues was nearing its end in New York.

Delegates there have been trying to devise a program to narrow the gap between rich and poor.

French sources said tonight that the invitations should now help produce a favorable conclusion of the General Assembly meeting.

In nine days oil-producing nations are due to gather in Vienna to set new prices. Prices have quadrupled over the last two years.

The industrial consumer countries, qualified sources said, wanted the invitations to be sent out well before the beginning of the oil-price conference. They hoped this would induce the oil producers to go slow on any price increase.

OPEC Set Condition

French sources pointed out tonight that the Organization of Petroleum Exporting Countries (OPEC), had made resumption of the dialogue a condition for moderation on prices.

American officials have warned that another large oil-price increase would jeopardize global economic recovery from a severe recession and, as Secretary of State Kissinger put it, "erode both the will and the capacity in the industrial world for assistance to developing countries."

Despite such warnings, some oil producers, such as Iraq, Venezuela, Algeria and Libya, have been pressing for a major increase—in the area of 35 to 40 per cent. Counseling moderation, however, is the biggest OPEC producer, Saudi Arabia, whose Oil Minister, Sheik Ahmed Zaki al Yamani, has said his country will do its best to hold the line against a stiff price rise.

Qualified sources also said tonight that the participants at the October preparatory meeting had agreed that it should not last more than two or three days. The April meeting lasted more than a week.

Belgian officials said numerous procedural questions were still open about the preliminary meeting. Among these is the issue of the presidency. France has suggested that the presidency alternate between developed and developing countries.

Another important question is the membership of the four commissions. But objective criteria are expected to be used, and experienced diplomats said they did not expect problems in settling the matter.

September 16, 1975

Suggested Reading

General

Banke, Harvey C. *A Primer on American Economic History*. New York, Random House, 1967.

Colm, Gerhard, and Theodore Geiger. *The Economy of the American People*. Washington, D.C., National Planning Institute, 1967.

Faulkner, Harold Underwood. *American Economic History*. 8th ed. New York, Harper and Row, 1960.

Galbraith, John Kenneth. *The Affluent Society*. Boston, Houghton-Mifflin, 1958.

Hillsman, Roger. *The Crouching Future: International Policy and U.S. Foreign Policy—A Forecast*. Garden City, N.Y., Doubleday, 1975.

Huff, Darrell, and Irving Geis. *How to Lie with Statistics*. New York, W. W. Norton, 1954.

Janeway, Eliot. *The Economics of Crisis*. New York, Weybright and Tally, 1968.

Meadows, Donella, H., *et al. The Limits to Growth: A Report for The Club of Rome's Project on the Predicament of Mankind*. A Potomac Associates Book. New York, Universe Books, 1972.

Walett, Francis G. *Economic History of the United States*. 2nd ed. New York, Barnes and Noble, 1963.

Wilcox, Clair, Willis D. Weatherford, and Holland Hunter. *Economies of the World Today*. New York, Harcourt, Brace & World, Inc., 1962.

Business Cycles

Burns, Arthur F. *The Business Cycle in a Changing World*. New York, National Bureau of Economic Research, 1969.

Morgenstern, Oskar. *International Financial Transactions and Business Cycles*. Princeton, Princeton University Press, 1959.

Okun, Arthur M., ed. *The Battle Against Unemployment*. New York, W. W. Norton, 1968.

——————*The Political Economy of Prosperity*. Washington, D.C., Brookings Institute, 1970.

Silk, Leonard. *Nixonomics*. 2nd ed. New York, Praeger, 1974.

Foreign Trade

Cooper, Richard N. *The Economics of Interdependence: Economic Policy in the Atlantic Community*. New York, McGraw-Hill, 1968.

Johnson, Harry G. *The World Economy at the Crossroads*. Oxford, Clarendon Press, 1965.

Kenen, Peter B. *Giant Among Nations: Problems of United States Foreign Economic Policy*. Chicago, Rand, McNally & Company, 1963.

Peterson, Peter G. *The United States in the Changing World Economy*. Washington, D.C., Government Printing Office, 1971.

Preeg, Ernest H. *Traders and Diplomats: An Analysis of the Kennedy Round of Negotiations Under the General Agreement on Tariffs and Trade*. Washington, Brookings Institute, 1970.

Sevran-Schreiber, J. J. *The American Challenge*. New York, Atheneum, 1968.

Foreign Aid

Baldwin, David Allen. *Foreign Aid and American Foreign Policy*. New York, Praeger, 1966.

Clark, Paul Gordon. *American Aid for Development*. Council on Foreign Relations. New York, Praeger, 1972.

Friedmann, Wolfgang, G., *et al. International Financial Aid*. New York, Columbia University Press, 1966.

Galbraith, John Kenneth. *Economic Development in Perspective*. Cambridge, Mass., Harvard Univ. Press, 1962.

Myrdal, Gunnar. *The Challenge of World Poverty*. New York, Pantheon, 1970.

Ward, Barbara. *The Rich Nations and the Poor Nations*. New York, W. W. Norton, 1962.

Monetary Policy

Bernstein, Peter L. *A Primer on Money, Banking, and Gold*. New York, Random House, 1965.

Board of Governors of the Federal Reserve System. *The Federal Reserve System: Purposes and Functions*. Washington, D.C., Government Printing Office, 1963.

Friedman, Milton, and Anna Jacobson Schwartz. *A Monetary History of the United States*. Princeton, Princeton Univ. Press, 1963.

Mason, Edward S., and Robert E. Asher. *The World Bank since Bretton Woods*. Washington, D.C., Brookings Institute, 1973.

Rolfe, Sidney E. *Gold and World Power*. New York, Harper & Row, 1966.

——————, and James L. Burtle. *The Great Wheel: The World Monetary System*. New York, Quadrangle/The New York Times Book Co., 1973.

Schultze, Charles L. *National Income Analysis*. 3rd ed. Englewood Cliffs, New Jersey, Prentice-Hall, 1971.

U.S. Investments Abroad

Blake, David H. *The Multinational Corporation*. Annals of the American Academy of Political and Social Science. Vol. 403. September, 1972. Philadelphia, 1972.

Kindleberger, Charles P. *American Business Abroad: Six Lectures on Direct Investment*. New Haven, Conn. Yale Univ. Press, 1969.
——————. *The International Corporation*. Cambridge, Mass., M.I.T. Press, 1970.
Safarian, A. E. *Foreign Ownership of Canadian Industry*. Toronto, McGraw-Hill, Canada, 1966.
Tugendhat, Christopher. *The Multinationals*. London, Eyre & Spottiswoode, 1971.
United Nations, Department of Social and Economic Affairs. *Multinational Corporations in World Development*. New York, United Nations, 1973.
Vernon, Raymond. *Sovereignty at Bay: The Multinational Spread of U.S. Enterprises*. New York, Basic Books, 1971.

The Oil Crisis

Diamond, Robert A., ed. *The Middle East: U.S. Policy, Israel, Oil and the Arabs*. 2nd ed. Washington, Congressional Quarterly, Praeger, 1967.
Hartshorn, J.E. *Politics and World Oil Economics*. New York, Praeger, 1967.
Sampson, Anthony. *The Seven Sisters: The Great Oil Companies and the World They Made*. New York, Viking Press, 1975.
Shwadran, Benjamin. *The Middle East, Oil and the Great Powers*. Rev. ed. New York, Council for Middle Eastern Affairs Press, 1973.

Index